DERIVATIVES AND RISK MANAGEMENT

SECOND EDITION

Rajiv Srivastava
Consultant

OXFORD
UNIVERSITY PRESS

Oxford University Press is a department of the University of Oxford.
It furthers the University's objective of excellence in research, scholarship,
and education by publishing worldwide. Oxford is a registered trade mark of
Oxford University Press in the UK and in certain other countries.

Published in India by
Oxford University Press
22 Workspace, 2nd Floor, 1/22 Asaf Ali Road, New Delhi 110 002

© Oxford University Press 2010, 2014

The moral rights of the author/s have been asserted.

First Edition published in 2010
Second Edition published in 2014
Seventh impression 2022

Digitally Printed in 2024

All rights reserved. No part of this publication may be reproduced, stored in
a retrieval system, or transmitted, in any form or by any means, without the
prior permission in writing of Oxford University Press, or as expressly permitted
by law, by licence, or under terms agreed with the appropriate reprographics
rights organization. Enquiries concerning reproduction outside the scope of the
above should be sent to the Rights Department, Oxford University Press, at the
address above.

You must not circulate this work in any other form
and you must impose this same condition on any acquirer.

ISBN-13: 978-0-19-808915-5
ISBN-10: 0-19-808915-5

For product information and current price, please visit www.india.oup.com

Typeset in Times New Roman
by Time Digitech Private Limited, Noida
Printed in India by Manipal Technologies Limited, Manipal

Third-party website addresses mentioned in this book are provided
by Oxford University Press in good faith and for information only.
Oxford University Press disclaims any responsibility for the material contained therein.

*Dedicated to my parents
Jai Behari Lal and Kailash*

Foreword

Globalization has helped the world become more competitive than ever. Where businesses have expanded astronomically during the past two decades, financial markets have also grown alongside. This has encouraged people to invest in various financial instruments with underlying in the form of stocks, indices, currencies, commodities, etc. With increased financial integration of the world, the stock market in India and in various allied sectors such as financial services, mutual funds, and investment consultancies has offered a wider menu of investments to investors. However, all of these are subject to a variety of risks, and thus investors need to be aware of how to measure as well as minimize risks. The subject of derivatives is concerned with these financial markets, risk measurement, and risk minimization.

In the light of the fact that more and more people are taking positions in derivatives like futures and options and are trading in both capital and commodity markets, there is an imperative need for practitioners, academicians, and students alike to learn about these markets, mechanisms, instruments, processes, phenomena, and strategies to minimize risks associated with derivatives of various kinds.

Increased interest in derivatives has prompted most management institutions across the world to include courses on derivatives and risk management that go beyond the traditional domain of corporate finance. Derivatives and risk management has become the foremost subject for management students and has found popularity among them. The demand for management graduates with knowledge and insight into derivatives, capital and commodity markets, and techniques of risk management has steadily risen over the years. The trend is likely to continue in future, with increased emphasis.

Unlike most courses in finance and management, derivatives and risk management is a rather highly technical subject demanding considerable mathematical insight. This volume starts with an introduction to the world of derivatives, and graduates to advanced topics such as credit risk, securitization and credit derivatives, accounting for derivatives, weather and energy derivatives, and real options. The book also dwells on complicated areas of option pricing, option-trading strategies, and exotic options very widely used in the corporate world. The theoretical construct is well supported by real-life examples and solved problems besides tables, figures, screenshots, and schematic diagrams, and also throws light on cases referred as 'derivative disasters' that focusses on the dangerous side of derivatives, the study of which provides critical learning outcomes. Various pedagogical features such as sideboxes and business snippets in the form of 'derivatives in practice' highlight real-world applications of derivatives. All these features make the book easy to read and comprehend, and apply concepts in practice.

It is indeed a great pleasure reading this book and I am confident it will fill any gap in the literature on this subject. I would like to place my appreciation for the author for having put in quality time and sincere effort to come out with such an excellent and comprehensive book, which I consider to be a must read for anyone associated with derivatives.

Pratip Chaudhuri
Chairman
State Bank of India

Preface to the Second Edition

Derivatives and risk management is a subject that has always eluded the grasp of most people. With the growth and proliferation of financial and commodity markets, the importance of derivatives as a tool of risk management has increased manifold. The importance of the knowledge of this subject is alike for both practitioners and students. The dynamics of stock, commodity, currency, and other markets has grown at an astronomical pace because of more and more investments being made in mutual funds and other financial instruments. This has necessitated the world to find ways of managing increased risk and, hence, the need to study the subject and develop a keen understanding of the various markets. With increased investments, the natural propensity to manage risks is also the need of the hour.

India's inclusion among the top economies of the world in recent years has helped the stock market to soar higher than ever. People are therefore taking keen interest in investing in stocks and other financial markets as well as various derivatives. Stock market enthusiasts are no longer restricted to buying and selling stocks and shares but have broadened their purview of dealings to various derivatives such as futures, options, and commodities.

Financial instruments are subject to market risks and volatility. The causes of volatility in the markets are numerous and sometimes it becomes difficult to establish a cause–effect relationship. India losing a game of cricket can be a reason assigned to fall in the financial markets. Even the rumour of Lord Ganesha drinking milk had the stock market soaring by a few hundred points! In the light of these characteristics as well as the fact that investing involves high risks, it is imperative that one develops a keen understanding of the various concepts of derivatives and risk management. Thus, the mainstream management courses with finance specialization have included derivatives and risk management as one of their primary electives.

About the book

Derivatives and *Risk Management, Second Edition,* is a book that caters to the syllabi requirements of postgraduate students specializing in finance. Since the publication of the first edition of this text, I have been receiving encouraging feedback about the book from students as well as faculty members. This second edition further improves the coverage of the original edition, making the text much more comprehensive and better structured. I hope that it will further aid students in understanding the basic principles of this subject. The following are the key features and additions in the second edition:

Key Features

- Explores new issues in derivatives and risk management such as volatility and value at risk, options on bonds, options on swaps—swaptions, and structured credit derivatives,
- Examines corporate securities such as debt and equity as options,
- Provides examples and boxed exhibits for illustrating the key applications of derivatives.
- Includes case studies from various organizations on derivatives that led to disasters, to provide some learnings.

New to the Second Edition

- Four new chapters on corporate securities and derivatives, real options, volatility and value at risk, and derivatives disasters
- New sections on topics such as futures contract on T-bills in India, Monte Carlo simulation, various exotic options such as lookback option, gap options, pay-later options, and so on
- Fresh discussions on recovery rates, default rates, credit value at risk, and valuation of CDS—Merton model
- A new feature called *derivatives in practice* to acquaint students with real-life situations
- Five new real-life cases on derivatives disasters in the last chapter along with lessons learnt from them

Online Resources

The following resources are available to support the faculty using the text:

- Instructor's Manual
- PowerPoint Slides

The following resources are available to support the students using the text:

- Multiple Choice Questions

Extended Chapter Material

- Forward rate agreements (FRAs) (Chapter 6)
- Future contracts on T-bills in India (Chapter 7)
- Monte Carlo simulation (Chapter 11)
- Volatility and value at risk is a completely new chapter (Chapter 14)
- Naked call (Chapter 16)
- Recovery rates, default rates, credit value at risk, valuation of CDS—Merton model, securitization, and structured credit derivatives (Chapter 20)
- Corporate securities and derivatives is a completely new chapter (Chapter 21)
- Real options is a completely new chapter (Chapter 22)
- Derivatives disasters is a completely new chapter (Chapter 25)

Coverage and Structure

With its expanded coverage, the book now contains 25 chapters. Chapter 1 introduces readers to the world of derivatives and the risks involved.

Chapter 2 discusses the concepts of forwards and futures in detail; thereby, touching upon topics such as futures contract, pricing and value of futures and forward contracts, and convergence.

Chapter 3 deals with commodity futures and delves deep into developing an understanding of topics such as long and short positions, long and short hedges, hedge ratio, and spread strategies.

Chapter 4 deals with stock and index futures, while Chapter 5 describes currency forward and futures, thereby discussing concepts such as foreign exchange preliminaries, non-deliverable forwards, and arbitrage with currency futures.

Concepts such as interest rate markets and forward rate agreements are described in Chapter 6. This chapter includes sections on repo and reverse repo transactions, term structures of interest rates, bootstrapping method, and continuous compounding.

Chapter 7 explains interest rate futures on T-bills, Euro Dollar futures, treasury bond futures. The key concepts of interest rate swaps, currency swaps, valuation of swaps, and other swaps are discussed in Chapter 8.

Chapter 9 introduces readers to the fundamentals of options. Chapter 10 delves deeper into the various concepts of option pricing. Chapter 11 delves further into the concepts of options pricing and discusses the Binomial model in detail.

Chapter 12 describes the Black Scholes model in options pricing. The chapter discusses concepts such as factors affecting options prices, Logarithmic distribution, mean and standard distributions, and Merton model for valuing options on dividend paying stock. Options Greeks—sensitivities are discussed in chapter 13. Concepts such as Delta and Delta hedging, Theta, Gamma and Gamma neutrality, and other Greeks such as Vega are discussed in this chapter at length.

Chapter 14 is a completely new chapter that discusses volatility and value at risk. Concepts such as measures of risk, exponential weighted moving average method, GARCH (1, 1) model, historical simulation, and stress testing. Concepts on hedging with options are discussed in chapter 15. Topics such as hedging with stock options, hedging portfolios with index options, hedging with currency options, and range forward-zero cost structures are discussed in detail in this chapter.

Chapter 16 explains options trading strategies and concepts such as income generation with options, straddle, strangle, straps and strips, and synthetic positions are discussed at length with real life data. Chapter 17 describes exotic options within which concepts such as path dependent options like barrier and Asian options, lookback options, and other exotic options are explained.

Chapter 18 covers concepts on interest rate options and discussed topics such as cap, floor, collar, and options on bonds. Chapter 19 discusses options on futures and swaps, and Chapter 20 explains credit risk, securitization, and credit derivatives. New sections on recovery and default rates, credit value at risk, value of CDS – Merton model, and structured credit derivatives have been included.

Chapter 21 is a completely new chapter that delves deep into the concepts of corporate securities and derivatives. Chapter 22, also a new inclusion in this edition, explains options on real assets such as option to delay, expand, and abandon.

Chapter 23 takes us through the concepts of weather and energy derivatives. Chapter 24 is about accounting for derivatives and discusses concepts such as types of financial instruments, fair value, hedge accounting, types of hedges, fair value and cash flow hedges. Chapter 25, the concluding chapter, throws light on derivatives disasters and mentions five organizations whose investments in derivatives have gone awry.

Acknowledgements

As in the first edition, the motivation to undertake the much-improved second edition came from my students of this subject who constantly demanded more and more coverage and depth to the topics. This resulted in reorganization of the book and addition of new topics and extended the number of chapters from 16 to 25. Indeed, I am thankful to my students for enlarging the content and scope of the book, thus making it more comprehensive than before.

I am also thankful to the management and faculty of the Indian Institute of Foreign Trade, New Delhi, which has continued to provide an extremely conducive atmosphere and the encouragement to undertake the endeavour in this rather relatively new field, especially for India where books on the subject and those that deal with the Indian environment are lacking. The literature and the books available in the library of the Indian Institute of Foreign Trade have been an immense source of knowledge and information. I have enriched greatly from these books and literature and the academic interactions that I have had with my faculty colleagues.

I continue to be particularly thankful to Dr Anil Misra, Associate Professor at Management Development Institute, Gurgaon, for having graciously agreed to allow me to use some part of the contents of my earlier book titled *Financial Management* in which he is the co-author.

I sincerely appreciate the reviewers for their constructive criticism and useful inputs. I would like to thank the editorial team at Oxford University Press, India, for enabling several improvements in the contents and presentation of this book.

I am also grateful to my wife, Anita Srivastava, for her endurance, encouragement, and support throughout the preparation of this work.

While extensive use of the information from a large number of books, research papers, and other publications has been made, I remain solely responsible for the errors and omissions in the book. Any feedback or correction could be sent either directly to rajiv1234@hotmail.com or through Oxford University Press and would be highly appreciated.

Rajiv Srivastava

Preface to the First Edition

Derivatives have been in use for a long time but they still remain mystical for a vast majority. While commodity derivatives solely occupied the spectrum for a long time, its proliferation commenced in the 1970s when derivatives were introduced gradually on a large number of underlying assets. These were instruments used by corporations to reduce their exposure to a variety of risks.

Derivatives in the Indian markets, whether over-the-counter or exchange-traded, are gaining momentum day by day by involving popular products such as options and futures on stocks and indices. Specific over-the-counter products for the corporate world such as barrier options on currencies and derivatives on interest rates are also available today. Beginning June 2000, the financial markets in India have witnessed a rising interest in advanced financial products such as derivatives, index and stock futures and options. Thus, we have witnessed an introduction of a new line of derivatives on a regular basis.

Exchange-traded derivatives on commodities, currencies, interest rates, etc. all have evolved over a short period of time. The pace of development and the increased level of interest in derivatives in Indian markets make one believe that India would soon be one of the major markets in the world, both in terms of volume and product range. The popularity of exchange-traded derivatives can be measured from the fact that the turnover in derivatives has surpassed the turnover in capital markets in less than five years of its commencement.

About the Book

There are numerous complexities attached with the conceptual comprehension of pricing and the working of derivatives. A better understanding of the applications of derivatives to provide a desired risk return profile to match individual needs would further widen its usage and increase its popularity. Clarifying such doubts and apprehensions was the major motivating factor while developing the contents of this book. The aim of this book is to present the subject in a simple language while minimizing the use of complex mathematics. This not only makes the subject interesting, but also enables a better understanding of the subject. Further, by providing adequate knowledge regarding the purpose of derivatives, i.e. risk management, and fair price discovery, all the other topics covered would dispel the common belief that derivatives are pure speculative products.

Apart from the theoretical concepts, the book discusses some important issues such as the increased volatility in the prices of commodities, stocks, and financial products. Such volatility is enhanced due to the increased integration of the economies all over the world, which has also increased the need for understanding and use of the various techniques of risk management. The number of variables that impact the prices of commodities and financial assets has expanded and so the need for understanding the inter-linkages of these variables have also increased.

Pedagogical Features

Each chapter lists the learning objectives followed by an introduction and discussion of the relevant topics. To facilitate understanding and learning, the following has been included in the book.

- A large number of numerical examples to illustrate usage of derivatives and applications
- A section of solved problems at the end of each chapter to elaborate on the different concepts and applications discussed within
- A number of side bars that highlight the crux of key concepts discussed in each section
- A comprehensive summary and a list of key terms at the end of each chapter

Some of the key features of the book are as follows:
- Commodity derivatives along with financial derivatives
- Non-deliverable forward (NDF) market
- Complete coverage of Accounting for Derivatives in the Indian perspective by incorporating the essence of Accounting Standard AS 30 which is applicable in India
- Detailed discussion on currency futures and interest rate futures

Acknowledgements

The motivation to undertake this project has been provided by the students whom I have tried to train in the area of derivatives and risk management. Their thoughtprovoking questions have prompted me to answer some of them in the form of this book. I am indeed thankful to these students.

I am also thankful to the management and faculty of Indian Institute of Foreign Trade, New Delhi which has provided an extremely conducive atmosphere and the encouragement to undertake the endeavour in this rather relatively new field, especially for India which lacks books on the subject that deals with the Indian environment.

The literature and the books available in the library of Indian Institute of Foreign Trade have been an immense source of knowledge and information. I have been enriched greatly from these books and literature.

I am particularly thankful to Dr Anil Misra, Associate Professor at Management Development Institute, Gurgaon for having graciously agreed to allow me to use some part of the contents of my earlier book titled *Financial Management* in which he is the co-author.

I sincerely appreciate reviewers for their constructive criticism and useful inputs. I would like to thank the editorial team at Oxford University Press, India for enabling several improvements in the contents and presentation of this book.

I am also thankful to my wife, Anita Srivastava, for her endurance, encouragement, and support during the preparation of this work.

While extensive use of the information contained in large number of books and research papers and other publications has been made, I remain solely responsible for the errors and omissions in the book.

Rajiv Srivastava
rajiv1234@hotmail.com

Brief Contents

Foreword iv
Preface to the Second Edition v
Preface to the First Edition ix
Detailed Contents xii

1. Introduction — 1
2. Forwards and Futures — 24
3. Commodity Futures — 55
4. Stock and Index Futures — 85
5. Currency Forwards and Futures — 116
6. Interest Rate and Forwards — 155
7. Interest Rate Futures — 176
8. Swaps, Interest Rate, and Currency — 215
9. Options—Basics — 258
10. Option Pricing—Basics — 277
11. Option Pricing—Binomial Model — 298
12. Option Pricing—Black–Scholes Model — 336
13. Option Greeks—The Sensitivities — 366
14. Volatility and Value at Risk — 392
15. Hedging with Options — 420
16. Options Trading Strategies — 445
17. Exotic Options — 479
18. Interest Rate Options — 517
19. Options on Futures and Swaps — 533
20. Credit Risk, Securitization, and Credit Derivatives — 550
21. Corporate Securities and Derivatives — 586
22. Real Options — 597
23. Weather and Energy Derivatives — 618
24. Accounting for Derivatives — 628
25. Derivatives Disasters — 645

Index 671

Detailed Contents

Foreword iv
Preface to the Second Edition v
Preface to the First Edition ix
Brief Contents xi

1. Introduction — 1
Introduction—Risk Management — 1
Managing Risk — 2
Types of Business Risk — 3
   Price Risk — 3
   Exchange Rate Risk — 4
   Interest Rate Risk — 4
Derivatives — 4
Distinguishing Features of Hedging
   with Derivatives — 5
   Derivative's Hedge and Diversification — 6
   Derivative's Hedge and Insurance — 7
   Derivative's Hedge and Strategic
     Risk Management — 8
Derivative Products — 9
Types of Derivatives — 9
   Classification Based on Product — 9
   Classification Based on Underlying Asset — 10
   Classification Based on Trading — 11
Participants in Derivative Markets — 13
   Hedgers — 13
   Speculators — 14
   Arbitrageurs — 14
Evolution of Derivatives — 15
   Commodities — 15
   Financial Derivatives — 16
   Currency — 17
Functions of Derivative Markets — 19
   Price Discovery — 19
   Transfer of Risk — 20
   Leveraging — 20
Consequences of Derivative Markets — 20
Misuses and Criticism of Derivatives — 21
   Increased Volatility — 21
   Increased Bankruptcies — 22
   Burden of Increased Regulation — 22

2. Forwards and Futures — 24
Introduction — 24
Forward Contract — 25
   Motive for Forward Contract — 25
   Features of Forward Contract — 26
   Settlement of Forward Contracts — 27
Futures Contract — 28
   Counterparty Risk — 28
   Futures Exchange, An Intermediary — 29
   Standardized Contract/Product — 29
   Specification of a Futures Contract — 30
   Settlement and Delivery — 32
   Delivery Logic — 34
   Open Interest — 35
Cash Flows Under Forward and
   Futures Contracts — 36
   Margin Requirements — 36
   Minimum Margin and Margin Call — 37
Pricing a Forward/Futures Contract — 38
   Cash-and-Carry Arbitrage — 41
   Reverse Cash-and-Carry Arbitrage — 42
   Pricing Investment Assets — 43
   Pricing Consumption Assets — 43
Value of a Forward Contract — 44
Convergence — 46
   Normal Market and Inverted Market — 46
Relationship Between Futures
   and Forward Prices — 47
Relationship of Futures Price and
   Expected Spot Price — 47
   Normal Backwardation Hypothesis — 48
   Contango — 48
   Expectation Hypothesis — 49
Expectancy Theory of Futures Pricing — 49
   Types of Futures — 49

3. Commodity Futures — 55
Introduction — 55
Benefits of Commodity Futures — 56
   On Price and Volatility — 56
   On Market Structure — 56
   On National Economy — 58
Commodity Futures and Financial Futures — 59
Pricing Commodity Futures — 61
Hedging with Commodity Futures — 62
   Long and Short Positions — 62
   Short Hedge — 63
   Long Hedge — 64
Perfect and Imperfect Hedge — 66
   Mismatch of Asset and Quality — 66
   Mismatch of Quantities — 67
   Mismatch of Maturities — 67
Basis and Basis Risk — 68
Basis Risk and Hedging — 70
Hedge Ratio — 71
Hedging for Changes in Volume — 73
Hedging for Gross Profit Margin — 76
Strategic Implications of Futures — 78
Speculation with Commodity Futures — 78

Spread Strategies with Futures	79

4. Stock and Index Futures — 85
Introduction	85
Index Futures	86
Forward Contracts on Stocks	86
Futures Contract on Indices and Individual Stocks	88
Features and Specifications of Stock/Index Futures	90
Margining System	92
Pricing Stock and Index Futures	92
Applications of Index Futures	95
Hedging Through Index Futures	95
Hedging Existing Portfolio	*95*
Hedge Ratio	*97*
Hedging Short Position of Portfolio	*97*
Insulating Against Market Risk	*98*
Controlling Risk of Stock Portfolio	*99*
Speculation with Stock Index Futures	104
Arbitrage with Stock Index Futures	105
Calendar Spreads	*107*
Other Applications of Index Futures	108

5. Currency Forwards and Futures — 116
Introduction	116

Foreign Exchange Preliminaries
Foreign Exchange Risk	117
Foreign Exchange Markets	118
Foreign Exchange Rates	118
Bid Rate vs Ask Rate	*118*
Spot Rate vs Forward Rate	*119*
Forward Premium/Discount	119
Arbitrage and Foreign Exchange Rates	121

Currency Forwards
Foreign Exchange Transactions	123
Spot and Forward Transaction	*123*
Swap Transaction	*124*
Outright Forward vs Swap	*125*
Option Forwards	*127*
Hedging Through Forward Contracts	128
Hedging Receivables (by Exporter) with Forward Contract	*128*
Hedging Payable (by Importers) with Forward Contract	*129*
Cost of Forward Hedge	*132*
Speculation with Forward Contracts	133
Arbitrage with Forward Contract	133
Determining Forward Rates	134

Non-deliverable Forwards
Non-deliverable Forward Contracts	135
Evolution and Growth of NDF	136
Features of NDFs	136
How NDFs works?	137
NDF and Interest Rate Parity	137
Are NDFs Desirable?	138

Currency Futures
Pricing Currency Futures and Forwards	143
Hedging Through Currency Futures	146
Hedge for Importer—Long Hedge	*146*
Hedging for Exporter—Short Hedge	*147*
Speculation with Currency Futures	148
Arbitrage with Currency Futures	148

6. Interest Rate and Forwards — 155
Introduction	155
Interest Rate	156
Desirable Features of Interest Rates	*156*
Repo and Reverse Repo Rates	*156*
Treasury Rates	*157*
Interbank Transactions	*158*
Term Structure of Interest Rates/Yield Curve	160
Bootstrapping: Obtaining Zero Rates from YTMs of Bonds	*162*
Forward Contracts on Interest Rates—FRAs	165
Forward Rate Agreement—The Product	166
Borrower's FRA	*167*
Investor's FRA	*168*
Settlement of FRAs	*169*
Pricing an FRA	*169*
Hedging with FRAs	172
Hedging Against Rising Interest Rates	*173*
Hedging Against Falling Interest Rates	*174*
Speculation with FRAs	175
Arbitrage with FRAs	175

7. Interest Rate Futures — 176
Introduction	178

Interest Rate Futures on T-Bills
Treasury Bills	180
Futures Contract on T-bills	181
Pricing of T-bills	*181*
Price Quotation on T-bill Futures	*182*
Futures Contract on T-bills in India	183
Hedging with T-Bill Futures	185
Hedging Against Falling Yields (Long Hedge)	*185*
Hedging Against Rising Interest (Short Hedge)	*188*
Speculation with T-bill Futures	189
Arbitrage with T-Bill Futures	190
Implied Repo Rate	*190*

Eurodollar Futures
Eurodollars	195
Futures Contracts on Eurodollars	195
Pricing of and Hedging with Eurodollars Futures	196

Treasury Bond Futures
Treasury Bonds	198
Pricing T-bonds	198
Futures Contract on T-bonds	199
Pricing of T-bond Futures	200
Conversion Factor	*201*

xiv   Detailed Contents

Finding Conversion Factors	*203*
Cheapest-to-deliver Bond	204
Interest Rate Futures in India	205
Hedging with Interest Rate Futures	206
Hedge Ratio	*207*
Duration and Modified Duration	*207*
Optimal Hedge Ratio:	
Duration-based Hedging	*209*

8. Swaps, Interest Rate, and Currency — 215
Introduction — 215

Interest Rate Swaps
Features of Interest Rate Swap	217
Need for Swap Intermediary:	
Swap Dealer/Bank	218
Applications of Interest Rate Swaps	220
Transforming Nature of Liabilities	*220*
Transforming Nature of Assets	*221*
Hedging with Swaps	*222*
Reducing Cost of Funds	*223*
Rationale for Swap—Comparative Advantage	225
Types of Interest Rate Swaps	227

Currency Swaps
World Bank–IBM Currency Swap	*228*
Hedging Against Exchange Rate Risk with Currency Swap	*231*
Reducing Cost of Funds with Currency Swaps	*232*
Distinguishing Features of Currency Swaps	236

Valuation of Swaps
Valuing Interest Rate Swaps	*238*
Swap Quotes and Initial Pricing	242
Counterparty Risk and Swaps	244
Valuing Currency Swaps	246

Other Swaps
Commodity Swaps	*250*
Equity Swaps	*251*
Conclusion	253

9. Options—Basics — 258
Introduction	258
Terminology of Options	259
Call Option	259
Put Option	261
Who Benefits?	*262*
Moneyness of Options	263
In-the-money, At-the-money, and Out-of-the-money Options	*263*
Types of Options	264
Nature of Exercise: American vs European	*264*
Nature of Markets: Over-the-counter vs Exchange-traded	*264*
Nature of Underlying Assets	*265*
Understanding Options Quotations	266
Trading and Settlement	267
Assignment	*268*

Margins in Options	269
Adjusting for Corporate Actions on Stock Options	270
Options Other than Stocks/Indices	271
Differences Between Options and Forwards/Futures	271

10. Option Pricing—Basics — 277
Introduction	277
Intrinsic Value and Time Value	277
Boundary Conditions for Option Pricing	279
Call Option	*279*
Put Option	*281*
Effects of Dividend on Lower Bounds	*283*
Lower Bounds for Currency Options	*284*
Lower Bounds for Options on Stock Indices	*285*
Arbitrage-based Relationship of Option Pricing	285
Put–Call Parity	288
Put–Call Parity for American Options	*292*
Put–Call Parity for Dividend Paying Stock	*293*
Put–Call Relationship for Currency Options	*293*

11. Option Pricing—Binomial Model — 298
Introduction — 298

Binomial Option Pricing Model
Resolving the Dilemma	*302*
Risk-neutral Valuation	303
Finding Risk-free Portfolio	*305*
Equivalent Portfolio Approach for Option Valuation	*306*
Binomial Model for Put Pricing	307
Multi-period Binomial Model	309
Valuing American Options	312
Valuing European Call	*312*
Valuing American Call	*314*
Valuing European Put	*315*
Valuing American Put	*316*
Valuing Options on Dividend Paying Stock	319
European and American Calls on Dividend Paying Stock	*320*
European and American Puts on Dividend Paying Stock	*323*
Binomial Solution for Multi-periods	324
Binomial Model for Index Options	325
Valuing Currency Options	326
Binomial Model in Practice: Constructing Binomial Tree	327
Monte Carlo Simulation	328
Conclusion	331

12. Option Pricing—Black–Scholes Model — 336
Introduction	336
Factors Affecting Option Price	337
Black–Scholes Option Pricing Model	339
Stock Returns have Log-normal Distribution	*340*

Detailed Contents **xv**

    Mean and Standard Deviation
        of Ln R are Proportional to Time   341
    Ln R has Normal Distribution:
        Central Limit Theorem   342
    Time Value of At-the-money Option is Highest   346
    Applying BSM   346
  Assumptions of BSM   348
  Interpreting the BSM   348
    Put Pricing using BSM   349
  Merton Model for Valuing
    Options on Dividend Paying Stock   349
  Valuing Options on Indices   351
  Valuing Options on Currencies   351
  Valuing American Options   353
    American Call vs European Call
        on Non-dividend Paying Asset   353
    American Call on Dividend paying Asset   353
    Pseudo-pricing of American Call   354
  Exact Pricing of American Option   356
  Volatilty   357
  Measuring Historical Volatility   358
  Implied Volatility   361
  Estimating Implied Volatility   362

13. Option Greeks— The Sensitivities   366
  Introduction   366

Delta and Delta Hedging
    Computing Delta   367
    Meaning of and Limits on Value of Delta   368
    Assumption of Linearity   368
    Behaviour of Delta   369
    Delta and Time to Maturity   370
    Additivity of Delta: Portfolio Delta   371
    Deltas of Other Derivatives   373
  Delta Hedging   374
    Delta Neutrality   375

Theta
    Computing Theta   377
    Meaning of Theta   377
    Theta and Time   377
    Theta for Put Option   378
    Portfolio Theta   378

Gamma and Gamma Neutrality
    Computing Gamma   380
    Behaviour of Gamma with
        Spot Price and Time   380
    Meaning of Gamma   381
    Portfolio Gamma   382
    Gamma Neutrality   383

Other Greeks
    Vega   385
    Rho   387

14. Volatility and Value at Risk   392
  Introduction   392

  Measures of Risk   393
  Volatility   393
  Exponential Weighted Moving Average   394
  Correlation and Covariance   396
  Garch (1, 1) Model   397
  Volatility Index   399

Computation of India VIX
    Forward Price, F   401
    Finding ATM Option, X_0 401
    Time to Expiry, T   401
    Risk-free Rate, r   401
    Option Values, Q_i 401
    Option Interval, Δx 401

Value at Risk
    Features and Concerns of the Financial Sector   405
  Definition and Meaning of VaR   405
    VaR with Normal Distribution   405
    Portfolio Effect on VaR   408
  Decisions in VaR   408
    Selection of Confidence Level   409
    Selection of Time Horizon   409
  Methods of Calculating VaR   409
    Valuation   410
    Estimation of Volatility   410
  Historical Simulation   411
  Monte Carlo Simulation   416
  Limitations   416
  Stress Testing   416

15. Hedging with Options   420
  Introduction   420
  Hedging with Stock Options   422
    Hedging Long Position in Stock
        with Put Option   422
    Hedging Short Position in Stock
        with Call Option   423
  Hedging Portfolios with Index Options   426
    Hedging Long Portfolio with
        Put on Index   427
    Hedging Short Portfolio with
        Call on Index   429
  Hedging with Currency Options   431
    Hedging Foreign Currency
        Receivable with Put Option   432
    Hedging Foreign Currency
        Payable with Call Option   433
    Range Forward—Zero Cost Collar   434

16. Options Trading Strategies   445
  Introduction   445

Income Generation with Options
  Naked Call and Covered Call   446
  Writing Put   448
    Speculation with Single Option   449
    Arbitrage with Options   449

Option Trading Strategies

Long and Short Straddle 451
Strangle 453
Straps and Strips 455
Bull Spread 456
Bear Spread 458
   Debit and Credit Spreads 458
   Risk–Reward Ratio 460
Butterfly Spread 460
Condor Spread 462
Calendar Spreads 465
Diagonal Spreads 466
   Spreads on Different Assets 466
Box Spread 467
Factors Affecting Spreads 468

Synthesizing Instruments and Positions

Synthetic Long Position in Stock 469
Synthetic Short Position in Stock 470
Other Synthetic Positions 471

17. Exotic Options 479
Introduction 479
Forward Start Option 480
   Valuation 480
   Applications 481
Binary or Digital Option 482
   Applications 482
   Valuation 483
Chooser Option 484
   Valuation 485
Shout Option 486
   Valuation 487
Exchange Option 487
   Applications 488
   Valuation 488
Gap Option 489
   Applications 490
   Valuation 490
Pay-later Option 492
   Applications 493
   Valuation 493
Compound Options 496
   Applications 496
   Valuation 497
Barrier Options 499
   Valuation 500
Asian Options 504
   Applications 504
   Valuation 505
Lookback Options 508
   Applications 509
   Valuation 509

18. Interest Rate Options 517
Introduction 517

Interest Rate Options
Cap 518
   Hedging with Cap 518
   Valuation of Cap 521
Floor 524
   Valuation of Floor 525
Collar 526

Options on Bonds
   Valuation of Options on Bonds 529

19. Options on Futures and Swaps 533
Introduction 533
Futures Options 533
   Payoff 534
   Need for Options on Futures 535
   Put–Call Parity for Options on Futures 536
   Binomial Model for Pricing Futures Options 537
   Valuation of Futures Options—Black's Model 539
Option on Swaps—Swaptions 540
   Payoff for Swaption 541
   Swaptions and Options on Bond 542
   Valuation of Swaptions 543

20. Credit Risk, Securitization, and Credit Derivatives 550
Introduction 550

Credit Risk
Probability of Default 551
   Recovery Rates 554
   Default Rates 555
   Transition Rates 556
Credit VaR 556

Credit Derivatives
Credit Derivative 560
   Types of Credit Risks 561
Credit Default Swaps 562
   Cash Flows of CDS 563
   Settlement of CDS 564
   Variants of CDS 566
   Applications of CDS 567
Valuation of CDS—Merton Model 568
Total Return Swap 573
   Features of TRSs 574
   Total Return Swaps vs Swaps and CDS 575

Securitization
   Risk in Securitization 578

Structured Credit Derivatives
Credit-linked Notes 579
Collateralized Debt Obligations 581

21. Corporate Securities and Derivatives 586
Introduction 586

Equity Shares—Common Stock	587		Electricity	626
Agency Cost of Debt	*588*		Natural Gas	627
Debt as Options	590			
Subordinated Debt	*591*	**24.**	**Accounting for Derivatives**	**628**
Callable and Puttable Bonds	592		Introduction	628
Convertible Bonds	593		Accounting Definition of Derivatives	629
Warrants	594		Types of Financial Instruments	630
			Fair Value	631

22. Real Options — 597

Introduction — 597
Kinds of Real Options — 598
   Option to Delay — *598*
   Option to Expand — *598*
   Option to Abandon — *599*
Differences Between Financial
   and Real Options — 599
   Real Assets are Not Traded — *600*
   Variance of Real Options is
     Difficult to Estimate — *600*
   Exercise of Real Options is
     Time Consuming — *600*
   Terms of Exercise of Real
     Options are Not Clearly Defined — *600*
Option to Delay—Timing Decision — 601
   Evaluating Timing Decision with DCF — *601*
   Valuing Option to Delay
     with Binomial Model — *603*
   Discounted Cash Flow and
     Binomial Option Valuation — *604*
   Using Black Scholes Model
     for Investment Timing — *605*
Option to Expand — 607
   DCF Valuation — *608*
   Valuing Option to Expand
     with Binomial Method — *609*
   Valuing Option to Expand
     using BSM — *611*
Option to Abandon — 612
   DCF Valuation — *612*
   DCF Valuation without the Put Option — *613*
   DCF Valuation with Option to Abandon — *614*
   Valuing Put Option with Binomial Method — *614*
   Value of Put with BSM — *615*

23. Weather and Energy Derivatives — 618

Introduction — 618

▰ Weather Derivatives ▰
   Temperature — *619*
   Derivative Products on Temperature — *620*
   Pricing Weather Derivatives — *620*
Emission Trading — 621
   Distinctive Features of Weather Derivatives — *623*

▰ Energy Derivatives ▰
   Crude Oil — *625*

24. Accounting for Derivatives — 628

Introduction — 628
Accounting Definition of Derivatives — 629
Types of Financial Instruments — 630
Fair Value — 631
   Measurement of Fair Value — *632*
Hedge Accounting — 633
Types of Hedges — 634
Steps for Hedge Accounting — 635
   Hedged Item — *635*
   Hedging Instrument — *636*
   Hedging Relationship — *637*
Accounting for Derivatives — 638
   Derivative Held for Trading — *638*
   Derivative as Fair Value Hedge — *639*
   Derivative as Cash Flow Hedge — *641*
Conclusion — 643

25. Derivatives Disasters — 645

Introduction — 645

▰ Metallgesellschaft AG: ▰
An Intelligent Programme That Went Awry

The Contract — 646
Hedging Programme — 647
Problems — 647
   Size of the Exposure — *647*
   Hedge Ratio and Mismatch
     of Positions and Timings — *648*
   Marked-to-market and Cash
     Flow Mismatch — *648*
   From Backwardation to Contango — *649*
   US and German Accounting Methodologies — *650*
The outcome — 651

▰ Barings Plc: ▰
The Earthquake That Crumbled the Old Strong Edifice

   Dual Role — *652*
   Switching — *653*
   Unauthorised Trading and
     Misrepresenting Accounts — *653*
   The Trap of Losses — *654*
   The Straddle — *654*
   Kobe Earthquake — *655*
   The Exposure — *655*
   Funding MTM Losses — *655*
   The Outcome — *656*
   Analysis — *656*

▰ LTCM: ▰
The Risk Management Models That Crashed

Hedge Funds — 657
Growth of LTCM — 658

xviii   Detailed Contents

The Strategy 658
   Digression from Practice
      and Beyond Frontiers 659
   From Bonds to Equity 659
   Directional Trade and Derivatives 659
   Speculation of Corporate Activities 660
   Volatility Trades 660
Events 660
   Asian Financial Crisis 660
   Russian Default and Brazil's Devaluation 661
   Salomon Brothers' Withdrawal 661
Failure of Risk Models 661
   Volatility 661
   Correlations 661
   Normal Distribution 662
   Value at Risk 662
   Liquidity 662
   Leverage 662
   Convergence 663

Index   671

The Outcome 663

■ Sumitomo: ■
The Perils of Price Manipulation
   Overconfidence of Leader 664
   Concentration of Authority 664
The Outcome 665

■ Procter and Gamble: ■
The Gamble That Didn't Pay Off
   Markets are Supreme 666
   Models Do Not Work Always 666
   Complacency and Lack of Supervision 667
   Star Status 667
   Concentration of Power and Responsibilities 668
   Complexity of Long Term and Short Term 668
   Systemic Risk 668
   Need vs Greed 669
   Absence of Legal Framework 669

Introduction

INTRODUCTION—RISK MANAGEMENT

Risk is inherent in all the activities we undertake in our day-to-day lives, and is a constant concern for all of us. *Risk* can be defined as deviation of the actual results from the expected. While we would prefer to eliminate this risk altogether and live in a world of certainty, complete elimination of risk is not possible. However, steps can be taken to mitigate the risk to a considerable extent. In our personal lives, when we buy an insurance policy against theft in the house or for a vehicle, we are trying to minimize the potential loss that we may incur upon occurrence of the rather unlikely event of theft.

The impact or magnitude of risk is normally estimated from the following two factors:

- the probability of an adverse event happening, and
- in case the event occurs, the magnitude of the loss it may cause

> Risk can be classified in two ways: (a) risk of small losses with frequent occurrence and (b) risk of large losses with infrequent occurrence.

The measurement of risk is determined by the combined impact of the probability and magnitude of loss, that is, the product of the two. From the perspective of its management, risk can be viewed in two ways: (a) risk of small losses with high probability and (b) risk of large losses with low probability.

The first category of small losses with high probability includes events such as changes in the stock prices, commodity prices, exchange rates, etc., where the changes are small but occur frequently and almost continuously. In the second category, we have events such as earthquakes, tsunami, thefts, road accidents, etc., which cause large losses but the probability of their occurrence remains low. Even though the expected loss in

Learning Objectives

After going through this chapter, readers should be familiar with

- different kinds of risks and ways of managing them
- diversification and transfer of risk
- types of business risk—price, exchange rate, and interest rate
- derivatives and derivative products
- functions, uses, and misuses of derivatives
- classification of derivatives
- roles of hedgers, speculators, and arbitrageurs as participants in the markets

the two categories may be the same, the strategies for managing the two different types of risk differ significantly.

In business enterprises, the management of risk is mainly confined to the events of small losses with high probability. Firms are exposed to changes in prices of commodities, exchange rates, interest rates, etc. The management of the second type of risk, involving large losses with low probability, is more strategic in nature such as from domains of capital budgeting, capital structure, etc. The tools for handling such risks form a different subject altogether. With derivatives, we focus on the management of the risks that emanate from the conduct of normal operations of the business, that is, risk of small losses with a rather high probability of change.

MANAGING RISK

There are various ways in which people manage different kinds of risk. Insurance policies are a classic example of a method of managing risk. All the tools of risk management focus on control of the damage the changes can cause and insulate the operations of a business enterprise from adversities. Those who are able to manage the risk better are likely to outperform competitors.

One may choose to avoid risk by *not undertaking an activity* at all. There are people who abstain from air travel because they foresee too great a risk in travelling by air. Likewise, some people do not invest in the stocks because of the risk associated with the stock market; they prefer to invest in safer avenues. While certain activities can be avoided purely on grounds of high risk (e.g., one can do without investing in the stock market), it may not be possible to abstain from some mandatory activities. Not entering a business in order to avoid business risk is not a solution to the problem. Rather, it is a problem in itself. One has to find better solutions to manage risk rather than avoiding the activity altogether.

The other option is to manage risk—to *control the potential damage*. For example, once we decide to own a vehicle as a means of transport, we observe speed control and traffic rules to avoid loss of life and property. Furthermore, we buy an accident insurance policy. Similarly, firms can protect themselves against potential loss by buying suitable 'loss of profit' insurance.

Another way of managing risk is by *diffusing the risk* across sources. Many call centres prefer to have multi-location operations to protect against natural disasters. This is referred to as *disaster management*. Similarly, most network operators maintain redundancy by having alternative routes available in case one of the communication channels breaks down.

We are familiar with *diversification of risk* through portfolio management. Investors prefer to invest in different types of securities in order to protect themselves against fall in expected return from a single investment. The risk of failure of all investments simultaneously is lower than the risk of failure of a single investment. Likewise, firms do not prefer to have a single supplier or single customer to manage the business well. They prefer to have many suppliers/customers as all the suppliers are less likely to fail to deliver simultaneously and all customers cannot be wooed away by competitors at the same time.

> Different ways to manage risk include controlling potential damage and diffusing, diversifying, and transferring risk to those who are willing to accept it.

One can also manage risk by *transferring* to another party who is willing to assume it. Insurance companies do not help to reduce the risk per se; they merely assume risk on your behalf. They have no means of controlling the thefts, floods, earthquakes, riots, etc., but offer insurance against these risks. It is the business of the insurance company to assume such risks, as it earns an income by offering such products. Similarly, there are people who are willing to assume risks of other kinds in return for compensation. Risk as such does not and cannot vanish from the environment but gets transferred from those who want to avoid it to those who are willing to bear that risk for a price.

Here, we are concerned with various kinds of risks that a business enterprise is likely to face and ways of managing the same. There exist a wide array of financial markets and instruments that enable business enterprises to contain risks inherent in their day-to-day operations. Here, we focus on the risks of small losses with high probability and ignore the other type of risk. Non-financial risks (such as financial loss due to a key employee leaving an organization, failure of the research and development department to develop a product, breakdown of production machinery, losses due to the vagaries of nature, etc.) are not within the scope of the subject of derivatives. Although there could be some mechanism to control or mitigate such risks, there does not exist a free market where the instruments providing protection from risk can be freely traded amongst the market participants, and hence the free determination of price of risk.

Management of risk through derivatives is commonly referred to as *hedging*. It helps in offsetting *substantial losses likely to be suffered by an individual or an organization*. Hedging is fundamentally the transfer of risk from those who prefer to avoid risk to those who are willing to take it. Risk per se has negative connotations. It is perceived as something undesirable. However, if risk is perceived as an opportunity, it can convert potential pitfalls into gains. Some people perceive risk as an opportunity that provides higher returns. Derivatives help to develop a better perspective or understanding of risk, although there is also a huge scope of misunderstanding them purely as an opportunity to reap profits quickly.

> Hedging refers to the management of risk through transfer from those who prefer to avoid it to those who are willing to bear it.

TYPES OF BUSINESS RISK

With a focus on the day-to-day risks that have high probabilities of producing small losses, some risks that business enterprises face and for which suitable financial instruments and deep markets exist are as follows:

> Business risks are characterized by small losses and high probability and are concerned with changes in prices, exchange rates, and interest rates.

- Price risk
- Exchange rate risk
- Interest rate risk

These risks are described briefly as follows:

Price Risk

All markets, whether commodities, stocks, or materials, are dynamic in nature. From the well-established economic principle, the price is determined by quantity demanded and quantity supplied. The forces affecting demand and supply vary continuously. Though striving for equilibrium, the prices are never stable. The prices of commodities, shares, industrial products, etc., are subject to continuous change. These changes in the price render instability to revenue, cost, and profit of a business enterprise, which is a cause for concern for managers of the firm. The investors also face the same situation when they invest in financial securities, the prices of which vary continuously, causing uncertainty of returns. The risk of change in the prices can be mitigated or kept within acceptable limits with the help of financial instruments specifically devised for the purpose.

Exchange Rate Risk

Exchange rate risk emanates from the transactions denominated in foreign currency, where a firm or individual faces uncertainty regarding the exchange rate at which the foreign currency will be converted in the domestic currency or vice-versa. As an example, consider a firm selling goods on credit and realizing the sales proceeds in foreign currency. Even though the price in foreign currency is fixed today, the firm faces an uncertainty regarding the amount that will be realized in domestic currency, which depends upon the rate prevailing at the time of realization of sales and its conversion to domestic currency. Similarly, an importer who has to make payment in foreign currency at a later date would be uncertain about the actual amount to be paid in domestic currency. The risks of variation in the exchange rates are managed through specific financial instruments such as futures, options, and swaps on foreign currency.

Interest Rate Risk

Interest rates change similar to prices and exchange rates, depending upon various national and international macro-economic factors.

All the firms that need capital resort to borrowing, while those with surplus invest funds. Both the borrowers and lenders face the risk of changes in the interest rates subsequent to the transaction. In fact, interest rate risk is far broader than pricerisk and exchange rate risk. In fact origin of exchange rate risk can be traced to changes in interest rates. Certain industries such as infrastructure and banking are extremely sensitive to changes in interest rates while some others are not as sensitive. The risks emanating from changes in the interest rates can be hedged through standard products or tailor-made instruments.

DERIVATIVES

Three kinds of risks described in the preceding section can be managed through specially designed products. These products are called *derivatives*. They are best suited to manage the risk of small losses with high probability. Derivatives are instruments that derive their value on the basis of prices of some other asset, called the *underlying asset*. These underlying assets can be physical commodities or financial securities or may be notional that are devoid of physical substance but have financial implications. The following example illustrates the meaning of a derivative product.

> Derivatives are products that derive their value from some other asset called the underlying asset.

Consider that an Indian exporter is expecting to realize $1000 in six months' time from now. The exporter had priced his product with a profit target of ₹2000 based on the current market price of dollar at ₹45. The actual amount that will be realized by him in Indian rupees will depend upon the exchange rate prevailing six months later. This rate is not known today. The exporter expects ₹45,000 but he might end up getting ₹44,000 if the exchange rate falls to ₹44/$ after six months, or if fortunate enough, he might realize ₹46,000 if the exchange rate rises to ₹46/$. If the rate falls to ₹44, his profit will stand reduced by ₹1000. Although he cannot control the price of dollar in the currency market or his profit, he can take protective measures to reduce the uncertainty of the exchange rate and consequential profit.

One of the ways he can reduce the uncertainty is to sell dollars to a party who needs them six months later and negotiate the exchange rate today. By doing so, he would be assuring himself of definite cash flow in Indian rupees and profit. Such a contract will be called a *forward contract*, where the actual exchange of currency will take place later but at a price that is determined today. Of course, the price at which this forward contract will be negotiated depends upon the current exchange rate of the dollar, known as the *spot price*. Since the price of the forward contract is determined by or *derived from* the spot price in the foreign currency markets, such a contract is classified as a derivative. Here, the spot price of foreign exchange, on the basis of which the forward contract price will be negotiated, is called the underlying asset. Besides the price of the underlying asset, there will be other factors too that can influence the price of the forward contract. In the case of a foreign exchange forward contract, the other factors influencing the price would be the interest rates of the currencies involved in the transaction.

Similarly, a forward contract can be negotiated for any commodity, subject to legal constraints and feasibility. For example, a wheat farmer can sell his crop before harvesting, at a predetermined price to a buyer. The price is negotiated today but the physical delivery of the crop and exchange of cash will take place on the due date of the contract. Selling the crop in advance at a price known today will help the farmer concentrate on his work rather than worrying about the price that would prevail when he harvests the crop. Here, the underlying asset is the crop of wheat, whose current price will govern the price of the forward contract. Other factors determining the price of the crop will be the expected demand and supply scenario at the time of harvest, interest rates prevailing now and expected in the near future, etc.

DISTINGUISHING FEATURES OF HEDGING WITH DERIVATIVES

A *derivative* is a contract whose value is derived from the price of the underlying asset but in all other respects remains distinctly independent from the underlying asset. This underlying asset is traded in the spot market or the physical market. Hence, there exist two markets for the same commodity—the spot market and the derivative market. The price in the derivative market is derived from the spot market as shown in Fig. 1.1. Normally, if the price in the spot market goes up, it will lead to an increase in price in the derivative market as well. The spot market and the derivative market are strongly correlated with each other.

> A derivative is a contract whose value is derived from the price of the underlying asset, but in all other respects remains distinctly independent from the underlying asset.

6 Derivatives and Risk Management

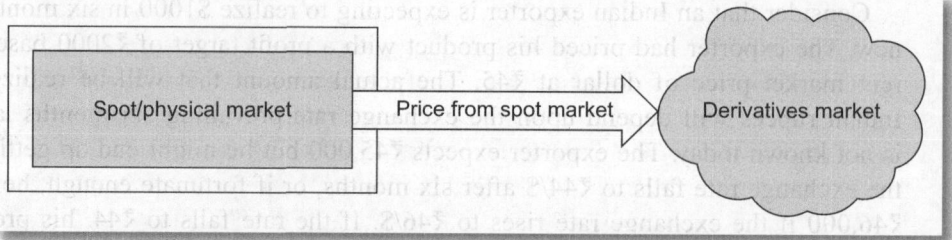

Fig. 1.1 Spot market and derivative market—the relationship

If the prices in the two markets follow the same or a similar pattern, then why have two different markets for the same commodity, as one can always fulfil commodity needs from the spot market? This is because there are two important differences between the two concepts—the independent nature of the two markets, and the timeline. It must be stated that with the exception of linkage in the prices, the mechanisms of the two markets are independent of each other. The commitments made in the spot market are to be fulfilled independently from those in the derivative market and vice versa. The commitments in the two markets are also different in terms of timeline. While the commitments in the spot are fulfilled on 'here-and-now' basis, the derivative market is a promise for future delivery. The commitments in derivatives are fulfilled at a later date.

The independent nature of the two markets results in an interesting possibility—it makes hedging feasible. Since the commitments made in the two markets are independent and have to be satisfied separately, one can take opposite positions in the two markets, that is, be a buyer in one market and seller in the other. The opposite positions in the two markets would have compensating effect on the price. For example, one can buy wheat in the spot market and sell the same quantity in the derivative market for future delivery. Between now and the future date, the price would change. If the price decreases, there is a loss in the spot position while there would be gain in the derivative position. If the price increases, the outcome is reverse. In either case, the loss in one market would be compensated by an equal gain in the other. Since losses are offset by profits, the net price paid/realized would remain unaffected. The objective of hedging—stability of price—would thus be met.

> The independent nature of spot and derivatives market enables one to take offsetting positions in the two, thus rendering stability to the price.

Derivative's Hedge and Diversification

As stated, derivatives are apt instruments for hedging against the business risk emanating from the environment. Under portfolio management, risk is managed using the popular strategy of diversification. In order to ensure stable portfolio returns, the investors are advised to diversify their portfolio. Diversification eliminates the risk arising from returns of a single security assuming that the other securities in the portfolio would make up for the potential loss, rendering consistent performance of the portfolio under a wide range of economic conditions.

Though the principle of offsetting the losses of one with the profit of another in the strategy of diversification seems to be same as that of derivatives, there is a fundamental difference in the risk management between the two. While diversification eliminates the company-specific risk, that is, *unsystematic risk,* the market risk called the *systematic risk* remains. A diversified portfolio carries the systematic risk, measured by the beta of the portfolio, as professed under the capital asset pricing model.

Since risk management with derivatives involves opposite positions in the two markets that bear the same characteristics and are subjected to the same risks, both systematic as well as unsystematic, besides loss/gain, all the risks too would be offset by opposite positions. However, if the positions in the spot markets and derivative markets are not on the identical assets (e.g., owning a stock while selling a future on it) but on similar assets (e.g., a portfolio of stock with derivative position on index), the derivatives hedge would nullify the systematic risk that is common to both spot markets and derivatives markets. The unsystematic risk would continue to remain in the hedged position to the same level as it was under the unhedged position. It is evident that strategies of diversification and hedging with derivatives do not substitute each other but are complementary. While diversification reduces or smoothens the unsystematic risk, derivatives can eliminate the systematic risk.

> Risk management with derivatives and that by diversification are complementary and not substitutes for each other.

In the context of portfolio returns, deploying simultaneous strategies of risk management by diversification followed by derivatives makes the portfolio risk-free. While the unsystematic risk is eliminated by diversification, the systematic risk vanishes by an opposite position in derivatives. Such a portfolio would become entirely risk free.

According to the capital asset pricing model, the investor must get a reward on the portfolio commensurate with risk. Then, the question arises as to whether one must deploy a derivatives hedge for a well-diversified portfolio. The natural response would be negative, because if one were to use diversification followed by a derivatives hedge, ending up in the risk-free portfolio, the need for creating a portfolio in the first place is not justified. One creates a diversified portfolio to earn more than the risk-free rate of return commensurate with the market risk. The extent and nature of diversification by selecting securities would be governed by the risk appetite of the investor. Taking a hedged position in derivatives subsequent to diversification would erode the desired returns to the level of risk-free rate. Should the strategy of diversification be followed by derivatives hedge? Clearly the answer is no as the investors are not aiming for risk-free rate of return. A better option of investing directly in risk-free assets such as government securities, fixed deposits with banks, etc., is always available to them.

> A derivatives hedge for a well-diversified portfolio can be used only for the short term and not for extended periods of time. Such a combination would give only risk-free returns.

Thus, it is apparent that strategies of diversification and hedging with derivatives cannot run concurrently for all time. Risk management with derivatives for a well-diversified portfolio makes sense only for a short period of time where the investors feel threatened in the short term with the risk exceeding their risk appetite. To control the level of risk and manage it within the bounds of the risk appetite, one can resort to derivatives hedge for a well-diversified portfolio only for temporary periods of extreme uncertainties and not perennially.

Derivative's Hedge and Insurance

Risk management with derivatives ensures a fixed price for the underlying asset. Hence, it can be said that derivatives in a way provide an insurance against the declining value of an asset. Is risk management with derivatives different from risk management with insurance? The following are the differences in risk management with derivatives and with insurance:

- Insurance requires payment of some premium upfront, which is not necessary for hedging with derivatives. In some hedges with derivatives (options hedge), an upfront payment is required, which is akin to insurance premium, but not all derivatives need to be paid for.
- Insurance protects the value of the asset only in case of occurrence of certain events, such as earthquake, flood, accident, theft, etc. These events are rare and the premium is determined by actuarial science. Under the derivatives hedge, the actual happening of the event leading to deterioration in value need not take place. The probability of occurrence of an adverse situation is extremely high. In cases where the upfront premium is involved, its calculation is based on past and likely future behaviour of asset prices.
- Under insurance, in order to get compensated for the loss, two things are mandatory: (a) the event (theft or accident) must have occurred, and (b) the loss due to occurrence of the event must be proved. One cannot get a claim that results into profit. Under the derivatives hedge, the payoff is neither dependent upon occurrence of the event nor is the actual loss required to be proved. The payoff under the derivatives hedge is automatic, without ascertaining the happening of the event or the occurrence of the loss. The market bears the payoff.

> While insurance manages event risk, depending on occurrence of event and the losses caused by it, derivatives protect against the price risk and provide automatic payoff.

As such, insurance covers event risk, while derivatives cover the market risk due to inherent volatility in the prices of the assets.

Derivative's Hedge and Strategic Risk Management

There are several ways in which the risk can be managed, for example, diversification and insurance. Yet another distinction one can make in the management of risk is its strategic nature. We know that marketing managers are fond of product diversification/differentiation and market segmentation. Attempts to develop different brands for different markets can be viewed as efforts to reduce the risk a single product or a single market poses to the cash flows of the firm. By having several brands of the same product, a firm renders stability to the cash flows of the firm just as an investor makes a portfolio of several stocks to stabilize returns.

Similarly, the production function prefers to produce at several locations to avoid the risk of disasters. Besides saving in the transportation cost, the firm, by having several plants at different locations, manages several risks such as natural disasters, riots, strikes, etc. Similarly, the purchase function prefers to develop multiple vendors for supply of inputs to eliminate or reduce risks from the supply side.

All these measures are strategic in nature and require substantial investment, time, and effort. Further, they are mostly irreversible.

> A derivatives hedge is a method of tactical risk management. It is economical, quick, reversible, and provides protection in the short term.

How is risk management with derivatives different from strategic risk management? The fundamental difference is that management of risk through derivatives can be regarded as tactical, at best. Strategic risk management, such as a decision to launch a new product or set up another plant, involves considerable deliberation, data input, and time. Besides, these decisions involve substantial cost outlay and are often irreversible. Most deliberations regarding risk are subjective rather than quantitative and are focused on the long-term survival of the firm. In contrast to strategic risk management, the decision to use derivatives for risk management is quick, economical, reversible, and a short-term measure providing protection from temporary uncertainties. Hedging with derivatives can be done at very nominal costs and can be lifted when the risk scenario seems to be within the acceptable levels. The time horizon of managing risk through derivatives, in most cases, is confined to a few days, weeks, or months.

DERIVATIVE PRODUCTS

Forwards are the oldest form of derivative contracts. Several financial innovations have taken place, especially during and after the 1970s, and a host of derivative products have come into existence since then. Innovations continue unabated, making products more and more complex and difficult to comprehend. The growth, both in terms of innovations and the volume of trading in derivatives, has been enormous. Innovations in the derivatives markets have made financial instruments so complex that understanding them requires special aptitude and knowledge. Without a reasonable background in mathematics and statistics, it is difficult to interpret some of the instruments and their pricing mechanisms, although the applications remain simple enough to attract a large number of investors of all kinds.

> The field of derivatives is full of innovations with a vast range of standard as well as tailor-made products, which serve a variety of needs.

The prolific growth in derivatives trading has also occurred due to the vast number of business applications that the investors and academicians have devised. These applications cover a wide array of situations, ranging from speculation and hedging to profiting from mispricing. Due to a wide variety of applications, the interest of investors is ever increasing.

Forwards, futures, options, and swaps are some basic derivative products. There are some complex variants of these as well, such as options on futures, swaptions, and so on. Each of these products has been discussed in chapters specifically devoted to them. Besides, we also have some strange derivatives on underlying assets such as temperature, rainfall, etc.

TYPES OF DERIVATIVES

There is a wide range of instruments available as derivatives. Each of the instruments is different in some respect or the other, conceptually, operationally, or application-wise. Derivative products are continuously evolving and can be categorized in various ways. We describe three ways of classifying derivatives based on product features, underlying assets, and manner of trading. These classifications are briefly discussed here.

> Four broad types of derivatives are forwards, futures, options, and swaps.

Classification Based on Product

There are mainly four basic products—forwards, futures, options, and swaps.

Forwards Forwards are contracts where the buyer and the seller agree to exchange the asset and its price, at a future date, but at a price fixed in advance. The underlying asset could be a stock, a foreign currency, a commodity, an interest rate, or any other. The buyer of the forward contract is called the 'long' and the seller of forward contract is called the 'short'.

Both the parties mutually decide the forward contract's terms and conditions, such as when and where the delivery will take place, and the quantity and quality of the underlying asset. Due to these features, forward contacts are known as customized private contracts. In forward contracts, each party is subject to default risk, that is, the party with a loss on the contract can possibly default as there is no guarantee against loss.

Futures A futures contract is an extension of the forward contract. It has the same concept and pricing mechanism, but some additional characteristics clearly differentiate it from a forward contract. Unlike forward contracts, futures are traded on an exchange. A futures contract can also be defined as an exchange-traded forward contract. The features of futures contracts are standardized in terms of quantity, delivery dates, delivery places, quality of the product, etc., which facilitate exchange-based trading, unlike forward contracts. These features and differences will be discussed in later chapters.

Options Options are contracts for delivery in future, like forwards and futures, except that one of the two parties involved holds the option to withdraw from the contract, while the other party is obligated to perform at the behest of the first party. An option is a right without an obligation to buy or sell an asset at a predetermined price within a specified time interval. The option that gives the right to buy is known as a *call option*; an option that gives right to sell is known as a *put option*.

Swaps Swaps are agreements between two parties to exchange a set of future cash flows according to a predetermined method. For example, one party may pay a fixed rate of interest in exchange for receiving a variable rate of interest on a notional principal amount for specified intervals of time.

More complex derivatives involve combination of these products such as forward swap, swap options, options on futures, etc.

Classification Based on Underlying Asset

Derivatives can be classified on the basis of the vast range of underlying assets on which they are traded. One can have derivative contracts on any asset, financial or non-financial. These assets can be physical or hypothetical. It is the compulsion of delivery of the underlying assets that makes the price of derivatives linked to the spot price of the asset. However, in some cases, the underlying asset can be hypothetical such as index futures where the delivery of the underlying asset is not possible, yet one can trade in them for beneficial outcome.

> Derivatives can be classified on the basis of definitions, underlying assets, and trading mechanism.

Derivatives can be classified on the basis of the underlying asset, as follows:

Commodities The commodities on which derivative contracts exist are the following:

- Agricultural products such as rice, wheat, cotton, oils, soya, tea, coffee, rubber, and pulses, etc.
- Metals such as copper, tin, gold, silver, and aluminium, etc.
- Energy derivatives such as crude oil, natural gas, and heating oil, etc.

Currencies Derivatives can be based on the exchange rates of various currencies, such as US dollar, Canadian dollar, euro, yen, and Mexican peso. All the basic derivatives of forwards, futures, options, and swaps based on exchange rates are actively traded. Currency derivatives are extensively used by banks and corporations to mitigate foreign exchange risk. US dollar dominates currency derivatives trade for historical reasons.

Interest Rates Derivatives can also have interest rates as the underlying asset. Internationally LIBOR (London Inter Bank Offer Rate) is the most common interest rate used in derivative contracts. LIBOR is the interest rate at which one London bank lends dollars to another London bank. Interest rate derivatives can also be based on instruments whose value is dependent upon yields on treasury bills (T-bills) and treasury bonds. In India, interest rate derivatives are best represented by MIBOR (Mumbai Inter Bank Offer Rate) which is akin to LIBOR.

Equity Shares The most popular underlying assets of derivatives are stocks. In spite of the forward contracts' popularity in the past, futures and options on stocks are traded more actively in India these days.

Indices Derivatives on various indices in the stock markets are possibly the most sought-after products because of their ability to provide protection against market risk. Futures and options on stock indices exist all over the world in all major stock exchanges.

Credit Credit derivative is the most stimulating innovation in the derivatives market. These contracts are based on the credit rating or credit risk of cash flows such as instalment on loans and other forms of receivables. Credit default swaps are the most common derivatives in this category, where the value of the derivative is a function of default risk. Credit derivatives are actively used by banks and financial institutions subject to default risk.

Weather Weather derivatives are the latest type of derivatives. The objective of weather derivatives is to make natural phenomena as underlying assets, so that the vagaries of weather can be evened out. Derivatives based on the temperature of specific locations are already being traded abroad, while those based on rain are in the offing in India. Industries such as agriculture, utilities, and so on, can use weather derivatives as a hedging tool, as the earnings of such industries are subject to weather conditions.

While derivatives on commodities and weather form a separate class, the other derivatives discussed so far are often collectively referred to as financial derivatives because the underlying assets are financial instruments or products.

Classification Based on Trading

Derivatives can also be classified based on the way they are traded. In this sense, the derivatives can be of the following two types:

- Over-the-counter contracts
- Exchange-traded contracts

> Exchange-traded derivatives are standardized contracts with low transaction costs, no counter-party risk, and easy entry and exit mechanisms.

Over-the-Counter Contracts The contracts that are directly entered into between two mutually consenting parties known to each other with matching needs are called over–the-counter (OTC) products/contracts. These contracts are specific to the parties involved and are not traded in the market. These contracts are customized to the requirements of counterparties and are often settled by delivery of underlying assets, though there is a possibility of exiting the obligations by entering into a subsequent contract opposite to the initial contract. The price of these contracts is settled between the parties concerned and may remain confidential.

Forward contracts are OTC products that dominate the foreign exchange markets. Swaps are also OTC products. The OTC products give rise to another risk called counterparty risk concerned with the failure of one of the parties to the contract to honour the obligations undertaken. These products also suffer from the disadvantages of finding matching parties and skewed pricing, as the two parties may not be equally strong. This disparity will make the exit difficult for the weaker party.

Exchange-traded Contracts The second category of derivatives, namely the exchange-traded products, is traded on the organized exchanges where the buyer and seller need not know each other. The exchange serves as counterparty for both the buyer and the seller. Exchange-traded derivatives are standard products whose specifications are designed by the exchange authorities, taking into consideration the characteristics of the underlying assets.

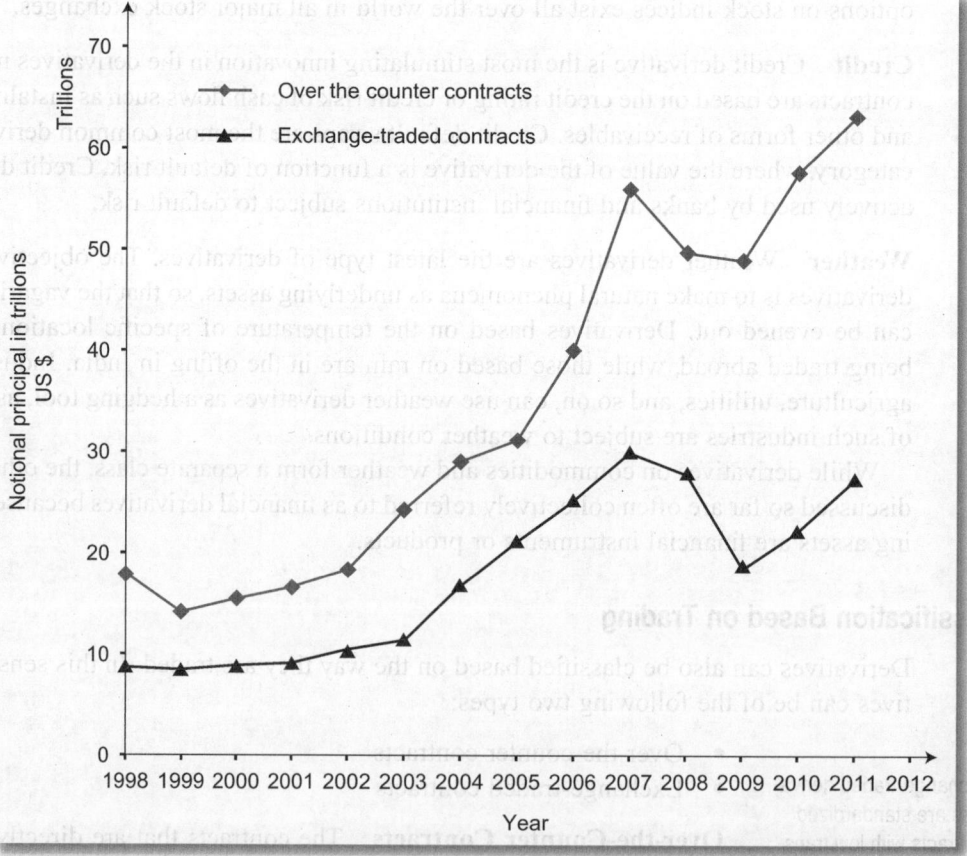

Source: BIS Quarterly Review, June 2012, www.bis.org.

Fig. 1.2 Total notional amounts outstanding of underlying assets in OTC and exchange-traded markets from end-June 1998 to June 2011

Exchange-traded derivatives are practically free from counterparty risk. The transaction cost in exchange-traded products is transparent and nominal, while in the case of OTC products, the transaction costs are included in pricing.

Exchange-traded products are traded continuously with prices in the public domain; this enables investors to conveniently enter or exit derivative positions.

Futures are traded only on exchange, while options can be traded on both exchange as well as OTC. Options on stocks and indices are mostly exchange-traded while options on foreign exchange rates are mostly traded OTC. Swap is also an OTC product.

Size of OTC and Exchange-traded Product Markets Over-the-counter and exchange-traded contract markets have grown immensely over the past decade. The OTC market is bigger than that for exchange-traded contracts. The size of both the markets is best measured by the notional principal. The notional principal represents the total amount of underlying assets covered by a derivative contract. The OTC contract is difficult to measure as the transactions are private and unregulated. Bank of International Settlements conducts surveys semi-annually to provide a measure of size of derivatives market. All the data is published in its semi-annual report. The total size of the market can also be measured by the market value of the contracts, but market value is subject to estimation errors. Therefore, the notional amount is considered as a more reliable measure in comparison to market value. Figure 1.2 depicts the total notional amounts outstanding of underlying assets in OTC and exchange-traded markets from end-June 1998 to June 2011.

PARTICIPANTS IN DERIVATIVE MARKETS

> Participants in the derivatives markets have three different motives: hedging, speculation, and arbitrage. Each activity has a role in efficient functioning of the market.

The participants in the derivative markets can be broadly classified into three categories, depending upon their motives, as follows:

- Hedgers
- Speculators
- Arbitrageurs

We discuss their roles and functions here.

Hedgers

Hedgers are those who enter into a derivative contract with the objective of covering risk. A farmer growing wheat faces uncertainty about the price of his produce at the time of the harvest. Similarly, a flour mill that requires wheat also faces uncertainty of price of input. The farmer and the flour mill can enter into a forward contract, where the farmer agrees to sell harvested wheat at a predetermined price to the flour mill. The farmer is apprehensive of a price fall while the flour mill fears price rise. Both the parties face price risk. A forward contract would eliminate price risk for both the parties. A forward contract is entered with the objective of hedging against the price risk that is faced by the farmer as well as the flour mill. Such participants in the derivatives markets are called *hedgers*. Hedgers would like to conclude the contract with the delivery of the underlying asset. In the example, the contract would be settled when the farmer delivers wheat to the flour mill on the agreed date at a predetermined price. Both the farmer and the flour mill have avoided price risk.

Speculators

Speculators are those who enter into a derivative contract to make profit by assuming risk. The derivative price reflects the expected price of the asset in future. Speculators have an independent view of the future price of the underlying asset and take appropriate position in derivatives with the intention of making profit later. For example, assume the forward price in US dollars for a contract maturing in three months is ₹48.00. If the speculator believes that the price of the US dollar would be ₹50 three months later, he/she would buy a US dollar forward today and sell later in the spot market. On the contrary, if the speculator believes that the US dollar would depreciate to ₹46.00 in three months, he/she would sell now and buy later. Note that the intention here is not to take delivery of the underlying asset but instead gain from the differential in price. Speculators have a different view on the price of the asset than the one reflected in the price of the derivative.

If only hedgers were to operate in the derivatives market, the number of participants in the market would have been extremely limited. A farmer would find it difficult to locate a flour mill with perfectly matched and complementary requirements in terms of quantity, quality, and timing of the delivery of the asset (wheat in this case). Similarly, a flour mill will also find it difficult to locate a suitable farmer to supply the exact requirements. If speculators are permitted to operate, the hedgers need not look for an exact match, and instead they can deal with the middlemen who would buy the produce from the farmer in advance, anticipating a hike in wheat price in future at the time of harvest. Such middlemen speculate on the future price and bid on the current price in a manner that is likely to result in a profitable position for them. By entering into a contract on the derivatives, the speculators are assuming the risk of price in future.

Speculators perform an extremely important function. They render liquidity to the market. Without speculators in the market, not only will the hedgers face difficulties in finding suitable parties but also the hedge is likely to be far from being efficient. The presence of speculators makes the markets competitive, reduces the transaction costs, and expands the market size. More importantly, speculators are the ones who assume risk and serve the needs of hedgers who wish to avoid risk. Because of speculators, hedgers find counterparties conveniently.

> Speculators facilitate smoother and easier hedging through increased liquidity and reduced transaction costs.

Arbitrageurs

It would seem that hedgers and speculators would complete the market. But this is just a fallacy because we assume that markets are efficient by themselves and they operate in tandem. We describe derivatives as contracts that derive their value from the underlying asset. Structurally, the markets for derivatives and the underlying asset are separate. For example, agricultural products would be bought and sold in the *mandis*, while futures on the same products are traded at the commodity exchanges. Ideally, there should be complete harmony between the prices in *mandis* and at the commodity exchanges. There cannot be any disparity in the prices in the physical market (*mandis*) and the commodity exchange. The existence of disparity in prices may give rise to arbitrage opportunities.

Arbitrageurs is the third category of participants in the derivatives market. An arbitrageur performs the function of making the prices in different markets converge and be in tandem with each other. While hedgers and speculators want to eliminate and assume risk, respectively, the

> Arbitrageurs perform the economic functions of making markets efficient by taking riskless positions in different markets.

arbitrageurs take riskless positions and yet earn profit. Arbitrageurs constantly monitor the prices of different assets in different markets and identify opportunities to make profits that emanate from mispriced assets in two markets. The most common example of arbitrage is the price difference that may be prevailing in different stock markets. For example, if the share price of Hindustan Unilever is ₹175 at the National Stock Exchange (NSE) and ₹177 at the Mumbai Stock Exchange (BSE), an arbitrageur would buy at NSE and sell at BSE simultaneously and pocket the difference of ₹2 per share.

An arbitrageur takes a riskless position and makes profits because markets are imperfect. Naturally, these imperfections are extremely short lived. An arbitrageur cashes upon these short-lived opportunities. Such actions restore the balance in prices and remove distortions in the pricing of assets.

Fundamentally, the speculators and arbitrageurs fall in the same category as long as they are not looking at owning or disowning the underlying asset by delivery (like hedgers). Both speculators and arbitrageurs also try to render competitiveness to the market, thereby helping the price discovery process. The difference between the two participants lies in the amount of risk they assume. While speculators have their opinion about the future price of the underlying asset by making investment, the arbitrageur concentrates on the mispricing in different markets by taking riskless positions with no investment of his/her own. By his/her actions, an arbitrageur restores the balance and consistency among different markets, while speculators only hope for a desirable movement in prices. Arbitrageurs also help in prohibiting speculators from overbidding or underbidding in the derivatives as compared to the physical markets.

EVOLUTION OF DERIVATIVES

The markets for derivatives have been growing at a phenomenal pace. The variety of derivatives in terms of nature of products as well as underlying asset has expanded greatly. The developments relating to commodity and financial derivatives including those on currency are briefly discussed here.

Commodities

Derivatives emerged as hedging products out of the need to control price risk. Forward contracts have been in vogue for several centuries. Earlier, commodity prices were almost the sole concern of the business community, and, therefore, it was natural that derivatives on commodities were the first ones to emerge. Traders were entering into firm price contracts for future delivery to eliminate price uncertainty. Naturally, derivatives on commodities were the first amongst all classes of derivatives.

Possibly the first organized attempt was undertaken by the Chicago Board of Trade (CBOT). It provided the initial platform for buyers and sellers to enter into forward contracts in 1864 and overcome the credit risk in the forward contracts. These exchange-traded forward contracts later came to be known as futures. Started with trading in pits, today CBOT operates round-the-clock and is present virtually across the globe. With the advent of information technology and fast computers, CBOT has moved from an open outcry pit-based system to an all pervasive electronic trading system since 1992.

The CBOT has been a pioneer in the development of most derivative products—both on derivatives such as futures, options, and swaps and on vastly different asset classes such as commodities, energy, weather, exchange rates, indices, and interest rates. Now merged with the Chicago Mercantile Exchange (CME), it handles more than 1 billion contracts per year, valued at around US $1000 trillion[1].

Contrary to general notions and the fact that India is a less developed economy, the development of derivatives in India started several decades ago. Bombay Cotton Trade Association Ltd was set up in 1875 for futures trading in cotton. Later, in 1893, Bombay Cotton Exchange Ltd was established for the same purpose. Several regional associations came into existence for commodity-specific trading in futures contracts. In 1900, with the establishment of the Gujarati Vyapari Mandali, futures trading in groundnut, castor seed, and cotton commenced. Futures trading in wheat was also done at several places in Punjab and Uttar Pradesh. But the most notable futures exchange for wheat was the Chamber of Commerce at Hapur, set up in 1913. Futures trading in bullion began in Mumbai in 1920. Calcutta Hessian Exchange Ltd was established in 1919 for futures trading in raw jute and jute goods. But organized futures trading in raw jute began only in 1927 with the establishment of East Indian Jute Association Ltd. These two associations amalgamated in 1945 to form East India Jute & Hessian Ltd to conduct organized trade in both raw jute and jute goods[2].

Forward Contracts (Regulation) Act was enacted in 1952 and the Forwards Markets Commission (FMC) was established in 1953. In due course, several other exchanges were created in the country to trade in diverse commodities such as coffee and rubber.

A major change in the commodities derivatives environment resulted after the recommendations of the Kabra Committee report, preceded by three other committees, namely, Shroff, Dantewalla, and Khusro. Since 2003, trading in futures on commodities is permitted, while options contracts on commodities still remain out of bounds. Today, four major national level commodity exchanges, namely, Multi-commodity Exchange (MCX), National Commodities and Derivatives Exchange (NCDEX), National Multi-commodity Exchange (NMCE), and National Board of Trade (NBOT), trade futures contracts on a large number of commodities. Besides, several regional exchanges for specific commodities also continue to exist. The trading has also moved from localized centres to the national level, through electronic means.

Financial Derivatives

Financial derivatives became popular only after 1970s when there was an increasing integration of the world economy. Increased globalization caused firms to expand business beyond their national boundaries. Besides, the competitive environment too became global, increasing complexities for business and resultant uncertainties. Further, increasing deregulation of economies and freer movement of capital across geographies caused stock prices and interest rates to become increasingly important for investment and financing decisions. Today, financial derivatives constitute the largest segment in derivatives.

---

[1] www.cmegroup.com, accessed on 12 July 2009.
[2] *Commodity Derivatives* by NSE, pp. 24, 25.

The CBOT, now merged with CME, remains the largest exchange in the world for financial derivatives, both in terms of volume and value of derivatives contracts. In India, derivatives trading is mostly performed at the NSE, which is among the top 10 exchanges in the world in terms of number of contracts traded.

Forward trading in stocks was extremely popular in India at the BSE, which was established in 1875 and is one of the oldest stock exchanges in the world. These forward contracts were exchange-traded but lacked the financial discipline of marking-to-market and other risk-containment measures. Due to several reasons such as difficulties in settlements, lack of financial discipline, dominance of a few in the trade, and lack of control and regulatory measures, these forward transactions in shares had to be discontinued and were ultimately replaced by other derivatives on stocks and indices (such as futures and options) in the year 2000.

The Securities Contracts (Regulation) Act (SCRA) was amended in 1999 to include derivatives as securities, thus paving the way for their trading. In 1996, the Securities and Exchange Board of India (SEBI) appointed a committee with Dr L.C. Gupta as chairman to develop a regulatory framework for derivatives trading. It submitted the report in March 1998. Soon after, trading in derivatives commenced in futures and options on index and individual securities. Index futures took off in June 2000, while options on index began a year later in June 2001. Futures and options on individual stocks followed in July and November 2001, respectively.

The growth of trading in derivatives in India has been quite phenomenal. In a short span of time, the turnover at NSE increased from a mere ₹2365 crore (US $207 million) in 2000–2001 to a mammoth ₹1,57,58,592 crore (US $3.50 trillion) in 2011–2012[3]. It signifies a tremendous interest in stock and index derivatives at the retail level and is reflective of the potential that derivatives have, both as hedging and speculative instruments. It would not be wrong to say that within a short span of time, derivatives have achieved the completeness of a market and made significant contributions in making the financial markets more efficient.

In September 2010, NSE was rated among the top two Asia-Pacific derivatives exchanges *for recording the highest volumes of trading in financial derivatives*. Figure 1.3 shows clearly that the trading in derivatives has grown exponentially since inception.

Currency

Currency derivatives came into existence only after 1972 when the fixed exchange rate regime under the Bretton Woods system came to an end. Post Bretton Woods, most currencies were floating and the volatility in the exchange rate markets started resembling that of stocks. One of the major developments of the abandonment of Bretton Woods system of exchange rate was the migration of the world economy from fixed to flexible exchange rates. As firms started doing more and more business globally, the concerns for exchange rate fluctuations increased and, hence, the need for hedging against foreign exchange rates became a necessity.

The CBOT commenced derivative trading in currencies in 1972 and today it trades in all major currencies that are fully or partially convertible. As of 2011, it had products on 19 such currencies.

---

[3] *Indian Securities Market—A Review*, Vol. XIV 2011, National Stock Exchange.

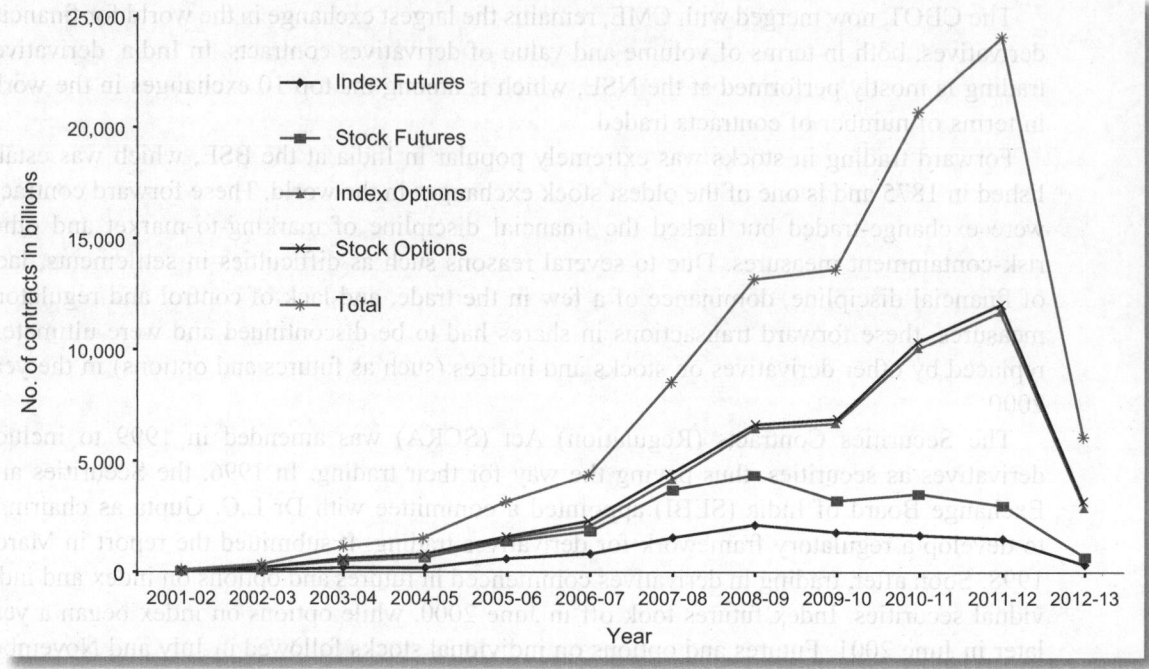

Fig. 1.3 Growth in derivatives trading at NSE

There are two distinguishing features of foreign exchange derivatives markets: (a) dominance of US dollar in foreign exchange transactions and (b) dominance of OTC products rather than exchange-traded products. Foreign exchange trading in spot as well as derivatives remains dominated by the US dollar because of its legacy (it was the anchor currency in the fixed exchange rate system under Bretton Woods). Prior to 1973, all currencies were allowed to denominate their values in terms of the US dollar, and hence it served as a vehicle currency in determining most cross-currency rates even when the Bretton Woods era came to an end. Today, free and market-based exchange rates prevail, making the forecast of exchange rates a challenge as they are determined by local as well as global factors.

However, most foreign exchange transactions in the spot and derivatives segments remain OTC and proportions of exchange-traded products remain negligible in comparison to the total foreign exchange markets. Dominance of OTC products in foreign exchange is evident from the data[4] shown as follows:

Average daily turnover in April 2010, in billions of US dollars

Year	2004	2007	2010
Total foreign exchange instruments	1,934	3,324	3,981
Spot transactions	631	1,005	1,490
Exchange-traded derivatives	26	80	168

Source: http://www.bis.org/publ/rpfxf10t.htm.

---

[4] Adapted from *Triennial Central Bank Survey of Foreign Exchange and Derivatives Market Activity in 2010—Final Results*, Bank for International Settlements.

Foreign exchange derivatives showed 72% growth from 2004 to 2007 and a mere 20% growth from 2007 to 2010.

Despite a three-fold increase in the foreign exchange derivatives from 2004 to 2007, the futures contracts comprise less than 2% of the total foreign exchange turnover. Another interesting feature of currency futures has been that futures on currencies are settled by deliveries (99.77% during January–September 2007 at CBOT). While futures in most other underlying assets are normally cash-settled by entering into an opposite contract, the participants seem to overwhelmingly favour physical settlement in case of futures on currencies. Most contracts on currencies that are not fully convertible are cash-settled due to non-convertibility of the currencies for fear of increased volatility if settlement by delivery is permitted. However, the proportion of futures contracts on the currencies that are not fully convertible also remains extremely small.

Realizing the dominance of the US dollar and partial convertibility of the Indian rupee, India commenced cash-settled futures trading in August 2008 with monthly contracts of the rather small size of US $1000, with the aim of providing a convenient platform for trading to retail and small exporters and importers. The objectives of such trading in currency futures include alternative avenues for hedging currency exposures and a gradual move towards full convertibility. After USD–INR, other currency pairs in British pound, euro, and Japanese yen were introduced.

Following the trends in other parts of the world, the Indian market in currency derivatives also remains dominated by OTC products rather than exchange-traded ones. The daily turnover in foreign exchange has increased from US $23.7 billion in March 2006 to US $33.0 in March 2007.

In India, trading in derivatives outside the exchange is classified as illegal as per the SCRA 1956. However, the Reserve Bank of India (Amendment) Act, 2006, overrides the SCRA and makes derivative transactions legal if one of the parties to such derivative trade transactions happens to be a bank.

FUNCTIONS OF DERIVATIVE MARKETS

> Derivatives perform the important functions of efficient price discovery, transfer of risk, and leveraging.

Derivatives were invented to fulfil the need for hedging against price risk. They enable the transfer of risk from those wanting to avoid it to those willing to assume it. Besides hedging, derivatives perform three other important functions. These have led to many advantages at broader level making market more competitive, informative, deeper, and more efficient.

Price Discovery

First, derivatives markets increase the competitiveness of the spot market as they encourage more participants with varying objectives of hedging, speculation, and arbitraging. With broadening of the market, the changes in the price of the product are observed by many, regardless of any significant reason. Even a minor variation in price prompts action on the part of the speculators. Active participation by a large number of buyers and sellers ensures fair price. The derivative markets therefore facilitate price discovery of assets due to increased participants, high volumes, and increased sensitivity of participants to react to the smallest of price changes. Increased depth in the derivatives market and fast and smooth dissemination of information among participants have made the process of price discovery more efficient.

Transfer of Risk

Hedgers could eliminate risk amongst themselves if two parties face risk from the opposite movement of price. A wheat farmer who wants to sell his produce faces a risk from the fall in price while the flour mill trying to buy wheat is worried about the rise in price. Since risk arises from opposite directions of price movement, the convergence of the needs of the two parties is possible. If both the farmer and the flour mill want to hedge against price rise, the needs of two would not meet. When speculators enter the market, they discharge an important function and help transfer of risk from those wanting to eliminate to those willing to assume risk.

Leveraging

Taking a position in derivatives involves only a fractional outlay of capital when compared with the position in the underlying asset in the spot market. Suppose a speculator is convinced that the price of wheat will be ₹16 per kg in six months and a farmer agrees to sell at ₹15.50 per kg. To take advantage, the speculator will have to pay the full price of ₹15.50 now and realize ₹16.00 six months later. Instead, if a mechanism is available by which he/she can absolve himself of making the full payment, he/she will be glad to enter into a contract and perhaps take a much larger position. Derivatives provide such an exit route by letting the speculator first enter into a contract and then permitting him/her to neutralize his/her position by booking an opposite contract at a later date. This magnifies the profit manifold with the same resource base. This also helps build volumes of trade, thus helping the price discovery process further.

CONSEQUENCES OF DERIVATIVE MARKETS

Efficient price discovery, ability to transfer risk and property of leverage have rendered many benefits. Some of them are descended as follows.

Efficient Portfolio Management The functions of leveraging and transfer of risk help in efficient portfolio management. With smaller funds at one's disposal, better diversification can be achieved with allocation of part of the fund to derivative assets. Derivatives provide a much wider menu to portfolio managers who constantly seek better risk–return trade-off. The range of choices would be far more restricted in the absence of derivatives.

Lower Transaction Costs and Prompt Information Dissemination Since a very large number of participants become active in the market (due to leveraging), the transaction costs become relatively low in derivatives markets. Derivatives provide various tools of managing risk; they are used as a form of insurance. No one will be interested in buying insurance if the costs are too high relative to the value of the asset. In this sense, derivatives may become a better substitute as they have low transaction costs. Shrinking transaction cost, reflected in the spread of sell and buy prices, is a sure sign of free market economy and, therefore, efficient allocation of resources. Faster and efficient dissemination of information also helps in removing price disparities across geographies.

Smoothening Seasonal Variations Derivatives can be extremely useful in smoothening out the seasonal variations in the prices of the underlying assets. Hoarding is viewed as social stigma. Hoarding used for speculative purposes requires scanty trading with large price variation among financially powerful persons acting in concert. Derivatives can help curb hoarding by continuous trading and increasing participation as it requires little capital outlay, leaving the field open to large number of participants, thus reducing the financial muscle power of the few engaged in hoarding.

MISUSES AND CRITICISM OF DERIVATIVES

Derivatives act like a double-edged sword. When used properly and conservatively, they are highly effective but when used with indiscretion, they are capable of causing miseries of unimaginable proportions. Some of the disasters due to derivatives are discussed in the last chapter. Unfortunately, there is no pragmatic way to distinguish discretion and indiscretion. Derivatives are misunderstood as a form of legalized gambling. There is a very fine line that separates calculated risk and gambling. Derivatives often extend benefits across the society by making financial markets function in a more organized way. However, gambling involves social costs. The following are often cited as demerits of derivatives:

> Derivatives are often said to be causing increased volatility in the prices, leading to numerous bankruptcies; hence, the need for close regulation and monitoring.

Increased Volatility

Since derivatives offer extremely leveraged positions, a large number of participants are attracted towards the market with the nominal capital available to them. Giving rise to speculative tendencies, derivative markets are often blamed for causing extreme volatilities in the prices, which are also seen in the spot markets. However, it remains to be seen whether such volatility in the prices would be absent in the spot markets if derivatives did not exist.

There are several instances in India, especially in commodities, where the trading in derivatives has been banned. The reason cited for the ban is often the wide and unexplainable divergence between the prices in the spot market (for the underlying asset) and derivatives market. In such circumstances, it is often propagated that it is the derivatives markets that influence the prices in the spot market. The notion that the derivatives markets can influence the price in the physical markets is at best misplaced and lacks conviction. In fact, trading in derivatives should be seen as a precursor to what may happen in the spot market. With a highly leveraged position, it is natural that the volatility in prices would be more than in the spot market, but it would be wrong to state that volatility in derivatives will get transferred to the physical markets due to provisions for delivery-based settlements. In fact, volatility in markets is inherently caused by the mismatch of more fundamental factors governing demand and supply. Derivatives serve a social cause to provide an advance indication about the events that are likely to unfold in the future.

Increased Bankruptcies

Inherent leverage in derivatives may easily cause bankruptcies when one assumes a position in derivatives that is totally out of sync with the financial position. Since positions in the financial markets are taken sequentially, one default may trigger a chain of defaults and can cause market failure. Such risk is termed as systemic risk and very often has been cited as the reason for bail-out involving huge public funds to rescue some organizations who engaged in misadventure.

Burden of Increased Regulation

With increasing derivative activity, it is opined that there in an increasing need for regulation to check misuses. Since derivatives allow accumulation of large positions with little capital, the disclosure of identities and positions taken is imperative. Most derivative transactions escape accounting and make audit difficult. In addition, there is a need to discourage overly speculative positions to prevent bankruptcies and a chain of defaults. Disclosure requirements and the need to control has placed onerous responsibilities on the monitoring and regulating agencies. Such requirements and control mechanisms are often disliked by some of the participants in the market because they are seen as impediments in the development of free markets.

The failure of some financial leaders in the United States of America in 2008 and 2009 and several other disasters (discussed in Chapter 25), due to excessive and innovative derivative positions by some investment and commercial banks, has emphasized the need for government intervention. It may be noted that the positions of these financial institutions was in OTC derivatives that did not warrant any disclosures in financial statements. These positions surfaced only when they assumed disastrous proportions. The actions of governments to bail-out these institutions are criticized for extreme burden on society as they are essentially seen as 'privatizing profit and socializing losses'.

SUMMARY

Risk is all pervasive; no one can escape it. However, risk can be managed. From the perspective of management, risk can be classified as (a) small losses with high probability of occurrence and (b) large losses with low probability of occurrence. Business risk predominantly emanates from changes in price, exchange rates, and interest rates.

Derivatives are defined as instruments that derive their value from some other asset called the underlying asset. They serve the purpose of managing the risks involving small losses with high probability rather than risks having potentially large losses with small probability. The business environment is full of risks involving small losses with relatively large probabilities.

The basic principle of hedging with derivatives involves taking opposite positions in the spot and derivatives markets. Since the prices in the derivatives market are dependent upon those in the spot market, opposite positions in the two would result in the offsetting of gains and losses. This renders stability to price and achieves the objective of hedging.

Hedging with derivatives is different from managing risk through diversification. While diversification eliminates unsystematic risk, derivatives would deal with systematic risk. Price protection with derivatives is also different from insurance. Insurance covers event risk while derivatives hedge against changes in the price of the assets.

Hedging with derivatives is a tactical decision that is economical, reversible, and quick in contrast to strategic risk management, which is focused on long-term survival and growth, involving large outlays, substantial time, and irreversible changes.

Basic derivatives are forward contracts, futures, options, and swap, though there can be large number of variants and combinations available. They are available on various assets called underlying assets. They include commodities, currencies, stocks, interest rates, indices, and weather. Some of these assets are physical and deliverable but some are hypothetical and are not deliverable (such as indices, interest rates, and weather). Derivatives can be traded on an exchange like shares (called exchange-traded derivatives) or negotiated across the table between the parties (called OTC derivatives).

There are three different participants in the derivatives market—hedgers, speculators, and arbitrageurs. Hedgers are those who would like to eliminate risk while speculators are those who like to assume risk for earning a reward. Speculators facilitate hedging. Arbitrageurs perform the balancing function by ensuring that the prices in different markets and for different instruments are not out of line. They take positions that enable them to make profit. This causes the imbalance in the markets, if any, to vanish.

Derivatives perform several economic functions such as enabling price discovery, facilitating transfer of risk, and providing leverage. These further enable efficient portfolio management, asset allocation, and faster and efficient dissemination of information, removing imperfections in the markets.

One of the criticisms of derivatives is that they encourage excessive speculation leading to excessive volatility. Further, this volatility causes volatility in the prices of the underlying asset in the physical markets. Leveraging also leads to increased bankruptcies, warranting increased need for monitoring and regulation.

KEY TERMS

Arbitrageurs Arbitrageurs assume riskless positions with no net investment in different markets and instruments, so as to make a profit due to mispricing in different markets.
Exchange rate risk Risk emanating from changes in the foreign exchange markets.
Forwards Forwards are contracts where both buyer and seller agree to exchange the asset and its price at a future date, but at a price fixed in advance.
Futures Forward contracts traded on exchanges.
Hedgers Those who enter into a derivatives contract with the objective of covering risk.
Interest rate risk Risk emanating from changes in the interest rate.
Options It is a right without an obligation to buy or sell an asset at a predetermined price within a specified time interval.

Over-the-counter product When a contract is directly entered into between two mutually consenting parties known to each other with matching needs, it is called an OTC product.
Price risk Business loss resulting from change in the prices of inputs and outputs.
Risk It is a variance of the actual result from the expected.
Risk diversification It is a risk reduction strategy by taking positions in several alternative markets and instruments.
Risk transfer Risk transfer refers to the passing of risk from those unwilling to take it to those willing to assume it.
Speculators Those who enter into a derivatives contract to make profit by assuming risk.
Swaps These are agreements between two parties to exchange a set of cash flows according to a predetermined method.

QUESTIONS

1.1 What do you understand by risk and what are the different ways of classifying and managing them?
1.2 What are the various kinds of business risks?
1.3 What is a derivative? Define.
1.4 How is risk managed with diversification and derivatives?
1.5 What are the advantages of risk management with derivatives in contrast to strategic risk management?
1.6 Define four different types of derivative products.
1.7 What are the differences between exchange-traded and OTC derivatives?
1.8 What are the different underlying assets on which derivatives exist?
1.9 What are the functions of derivatives? What are their disadvantages?

2

Forwards and Futures

INTRODUCTION

As described in Chapter 1, derivatives are contracts that derive their value from the price of an underlying asset. The underlying asset can be commodities (wheat, rice, silver, tin, etc.), financial products (stocks, currencies, etc.), or hypothetical assets (interest rates, indices, etc.)

For example, one may agree to sell foreign currency (say US $1000) three months later with the price decided today (say at ₹48/$). Clearly, the other party would agree to buy US $1000 at ₹48/$ three months later. Such a contract between the buyer and the seller of US dollars would be a forward contract. Under a forward contract, the price of the underlying asset, foreign currency in this case, is fixed beforehand.

Forwards and futures are the most common forms of derivatives. These are contracts that specify the price of an asset today, but are settled at a later date. The extinguishment of obligations undertaken at the time of initiating the contract is referred to as settlement. How do we determine the price of an asset that is to be delivered at a later date? Naturally, this price would be dependent upon the price of the asset that is prevailing today, called the *spot price* for the underlying asset. Hence, a forward or a futures contract derives its price inter alia from the price of the underlying asset prevailing today (spot price). The value of a derivative fluctuates, as does the value of the underlying asset in the spot market. The underlying asset can be a commodity, metal, stock, currency, bond, index, T-bills, a reference interest rate, or any other real or hypothetical asset.

We shall now discuss the concept and distinguishing features of a forward contract and a futures contract.

Learning Objectives

After going through this chapter, readers should be familiar with

- forward contracts and their operational mechanism
- features of forward contracts and their settlement
- futures contracts and their benefits over forward contracts
- the concept of counterparty risk
- the specifications of a futures contract
- the difference between open interest and volume
- margins and marking-to-market
- the pricing of forward or futures contracts
- the principle of convergence
- cash-and-carry and reverse cash-and-carry arbitrage
- the relationship of the futures price with the interest rate and the future spot rate

FORWARD CONTRACT

> A forward contract is an agreement to buy or sell an asset at a price determined today, with settlement scheduled for a later, predetermined date.

Forward contracts are all pervasive. Knowingly or unknowingly, we all enter into forward contracts. In most cases, we acquire assets and pay the consideration for the same simultaneously. All transactions of cash are made on the spot. However, in some cases, we book a purchase in advance and execute the delivery and payment of its consideration at a later point of time. Booking a movie ticket over the phone is an example. It is a sort of forward contract, because we buy the ticket now (though there is no formal written contract) and pay its price only after reaching the cinema hall. Similarly, most automobiles are booked with a token advance, and the full price is paid only upon physical delivery of the vehicles. This, too, is like a forward contract, where an asset and its purchase consideration are exchanged at a later date.

A typical forward contract that extends for a considerable time is a rental agreement for a house/flat, where a fixed amount of rent is determined for a specific period of time, usually a year. The fixed amount of rent the tenant pays the landlord every month is determined today. The essence of the forward contract lies in the fixing of the price in advance, while the asset and its consideration are settled at a later date.

Besides unconscious agreements that resemble forward contracts, here are a few examples of forward contracts that are consciously entered into by firms and individuals in business situations:

- An exporter expecting to receive €10,000 after six months may agree to sell the same to a bank at the exchange rate of ₹66/€ that is decided today, with the foreign exchange to be delivered only after six months.
- In November, a farmer may agree to sell 20 tons of wheat at a price of ₹20 per kg to a rolling mill. The wheat is to be delivered at ₹20/kg in April.
- A stock market investor may want to sell 10,000 shares of Reliance Industries Ltd today, to be delivered two weeks later at a price of ₹2500 per share that is negotiated today.

Here, the forward prices of the assets, i.e., ₹66/€, ₹20/kg of wheat, or ₹2500 per share of Reliance, respectively, in the three examples, are fixed now and derived on the basis of the prices prevailing for these assets in the spot foreign exchange (euro), commodity (wheat), and stock (Reliance) markets.

Motive for Forward Contract

One might reasonably ask what the need is for entering into a contract that decides the price in advance. The necessity for entering into a forward contract for both buyer and seller arises from both parties' need to eliminate price risks. For example, PepsiCo, producer of potato chips, may enter into a contract with potato-growing farmers to deliver their harvests later, at a price determined today. By entering into a forward contract, both PepsiCo and the farmers are assured of the transaction prices, i.e., the farmers know what price their crop would fetch, and PepsiCo knows what it would have to pay to get the required potatoes. Therefore, PepsiCo is able to plan profits better. Without the forward contract, both PepsiCo and the farmers would have to wait till the harvest time to know the price that would prevail then, which exposes both the parties to price risk. Forward contract would eliminate such price risk.

Features of Forward Contract

The forward contracts mentioned earlier have the distinguishing features described as follows:

(a) **Two parties** Like any contract, a forward contract too involves a minimum of two parties, a buyer and a seller of the asset. In the nomenclature of derivatives, the buyer of the contract is referred to as having taken a *long position*, while the seller is referred to as having taken a *short position*.

(b) **Over-the-counter product** In an over-the-counter (OTC) product, all the relevant aspects of the contract such as the asset, its quantity and quality, the price, and the delivery date and venue are fixed on a one-to-one basis, customized to the needs of the parties involved. The buyer and the seller are in direct touch with each other, although the existence of brokers is not ruled out.

(c) **Price is determined today** The price at which the exchange of the asset will be done is negotiated in advance and is called the *forward price*. Both the buyer and the seller attempt to avoid price risk by locking-in a price today, thus rendering irrelevant the price that will prevail at the time of maturity of the contract.

(d) **Mutual obligation to perform** On the due date of the contract, the seller makes the delivery of the asset and the buyer pays the price. There is a mutual obligation to perform on both buyer and seller. The seller is committed to make delivery, and the buyer is obligated to pay the consideration, on the due date.

(e) **Counterparty risk** Both the buyer and the seller who are parties to the contract assume risk, referred to as counterparty risk. The seller may fail to deliver the asset, and the buyer may fail to make the payment on the agreed date. When entering into a forward contract, both the contracting parties are aware of the possibility of default by the other party, and take adequate precautions to prevent such default. It is worthwhile to mention here that upon maturity of the forward contract, only one party would be in an advantageous position. The party in the losing situation is more likely to default.

(f) **Mutual consent for cancellation** Once a forward contract is booked, both parties are obliged to perform. Cancellation can only be done through mutual consent at any time prior to the maturity of the contract. The feasibility and the terms and conditions of cancellation too may be decided in advance.

(g) **No upfront payment** No exchange of money is made at the time of execution of the forward contract, though either party can insist on an initial deposit, adjustable against price or delivery, to mitigate counterparty risk.

It may be noted that these features of the forward contract are neither essential nor exhaustive. As a forward contract is an OTC product, the buyer and seller are free to modify it to suit their specific needs. Some of the features described here may be missing from the contract, while some features not described here may be included. However, the essence of a forward contract lies in fixing the price today for settlement at a later date.

Settlement of Forward Contracts

Settlement refers to the extinguishment of the obligations created under a forward contract. On the due date of the forward contract, i.e., upon maturity, there are two possible ways of settling these obligations:

> A forward contract is normally settled by delivery of the asset, though it is possible to annul the contract by entering into a contract opposite to the original.

By Delivery of the Asset and the Consideration For example, if an exporter had sold €10,000 to a bank 6-m forward at, say, ₹66/€, then at maturity, the contract would be settled by delivery of €10,000 by the exporter to the bank, who would pay the exporter ₹6,60,000.

By Entering into an Offsetting Contract Opposite to the Original Contract at Maturity or Earlier, at a Price Prevailing then For example, the exporter, having sold €10,000 6-m forward at a price of ₹66 per euro, may, after three months, decide to buy €10,000 3-m forward at ₹67 per euro. Of course, this is subject to acceptance by the bank.

Settlement by delivery is depicted in Fig. 2.1, where upon maturity of the contract period, the buyer and the seller discharge their mutual obligations.

Settlement by cancellation is done by entering into a new contract that reverses the initial contract. The buyer in the initial contract can sell the asset at a new price P' at any time prior to maturity, or upon maturity, to another party or the original seller. Similarly, the seller in the initial contract can buy the asset from any party prior to, or upon maturity, at a new price. However, the obligations entered into in the first contract would still have to be discharged upon maturity. By mutual adjustment, the exchange then reduces to the differential of the prices in the original and the offsetting contracts. This is depicted in Fig. 2.2.

Settlement by cancellation may not be feasible for several reasons. Applicable law may make delivery essential, or in case the underlying asset is not tradable, cancellation may become almost impossible.

Forward contracts are very common in foreign exchange markets. Exporters expecting to receive money in foreign currency can sell it forward, while importers can buy foreign currency forward to meet future liabilities. Banks offer forward contracts on various currencies to importers and exporters. Banks also offer facilities for cancellation prior to maturity.

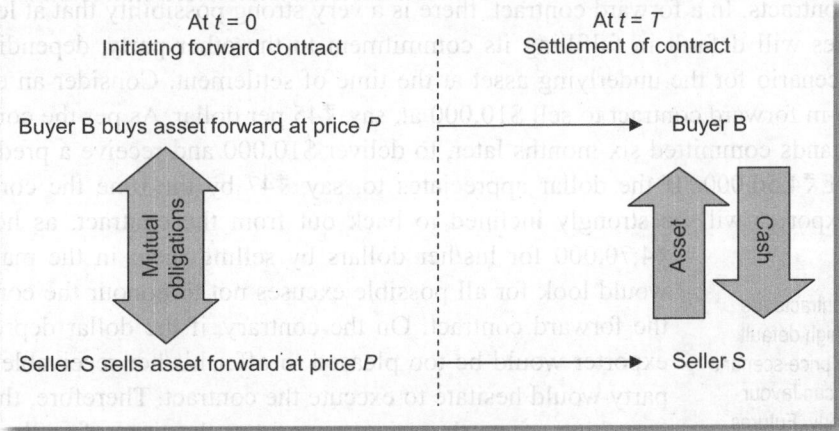

Fig. 2.1 Settlement of forward contract by delivery

28 Derivatives and Risk Management

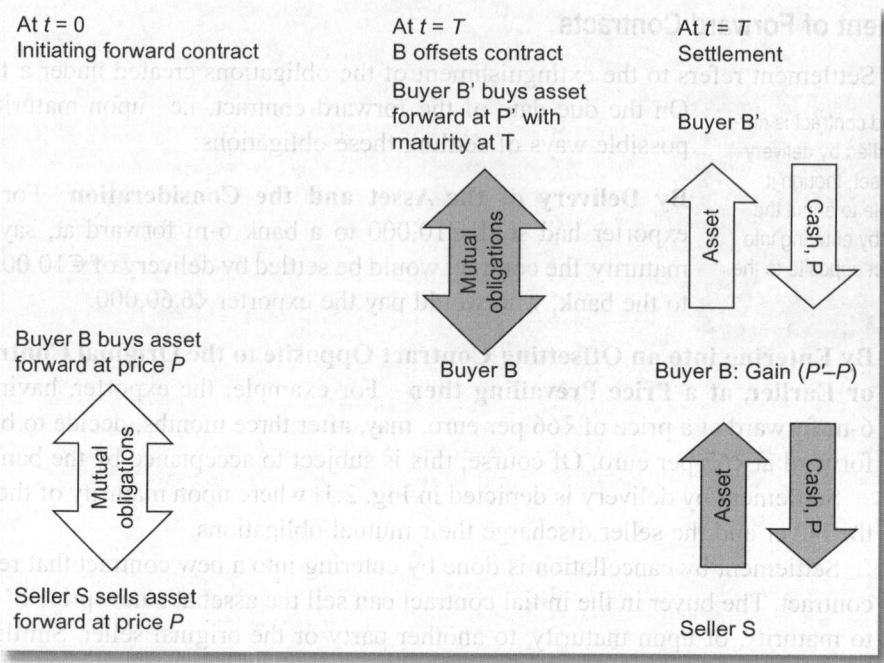

Fig. 2.2 Settlement of forward contract by cancellation

FUTURES CONTRACT

The futures contract is a relatively newer instrument than the forward contract, and is the next generation of derivatives. A futures contract is a modified version of a forward contract with the same fundamentals, i.e., promising settlement on expiry at a price fixed now. Operationally, however, there are substantial differences between forward and futures contracts.

Counterparty Risk

Futures contracts came into existence to overcome the problems associated with forward contracts. In a forward contract, there is a very strong possibility that at least one of the parties will default in fulfilling its commitment to the other party, depending upon the price scenario for the underlying asset at the time of settlement. Consider an exporter booking a 6-m forward contract to sell $10,000 at, say, ₹45 per dollar. As per the contract, the exporter stands committed six months later, to deliver $10,000 and receive a predetermined amount of ₹4,50,000. If the dollar appreciates to, say, ₹47 by the time the contract matures, the exporter will be strongly inclined to back out from the contract, as he/she can now get ₹4,70,000 for his/her dollars by selling them in the market. The exporter would look for all possible excuses not to honour the commitment made in the forward contract. On the contrary, if the dollar depreciates to ₹43, the exporter would be too pleased to offer his/her receivable, while the buying party would hesitate to execute the contract. Therefore, the risk of default is very high, since the price scenario at the time of settlement would favour only one party to the contract. Only when the spot price at maturity happens to be identical to the forward price would the two parties stay indifferent. The

> Forward contracts are subject to high default risk, as the price scenario at maturity can favour only one party. Futures, being exchange-traded, nullify default risk.

chances that the spot rate would turn out to be identical to the forward contract price are remote.

One way of eliminating counterparty risk is to involve another party in the transaction as the intervening party to guarantee settlement. The forward contract is executed on a one-to-one basis and the two parties assume the counterparty risk. It is not hard to realize that one default may trigger a chain reaction, resulting in the collapse of the whole market.

This raises the issue of credibility of the parties involved in a forward contract. Unless both the parties are convinced of each other's credibility, the forward contract will not fructify. This kind of failure will seriously limit the volumes of trade in the forward markets. When volumes are inadequate, prices cannot be said to be driven competitively. As a solution, the two parties in a forward contract could involve a third party to assure performance of the contract. However, locating a third party acceptable to both buyer and seller is another onerous task.

Futures Exchange, an Intermediary

The issue of counterparty risk can be solved if the transaction is done at an exchange that serves as counterparty to both buyer and seller. Rather than conducting business on a one-to-one basis, they route their business through the exchange. Both buyer and seller become liable to the exchange, which in turn makes and meets commitments to both parties. In case of default by one party, the exchange meets its commitment from alternate sources. To protect itself, the exchange can develop suitable risk containment measures. With the exchange serving as guarantor to both buyer and seller, contract performance is assured, as depicted in Fig. 2.3. This also eliminates the need for the parties to establish credibility with each other before undertaking a forward deal.

> Futures contracts have to be standardized if they are to be exchange-traded.

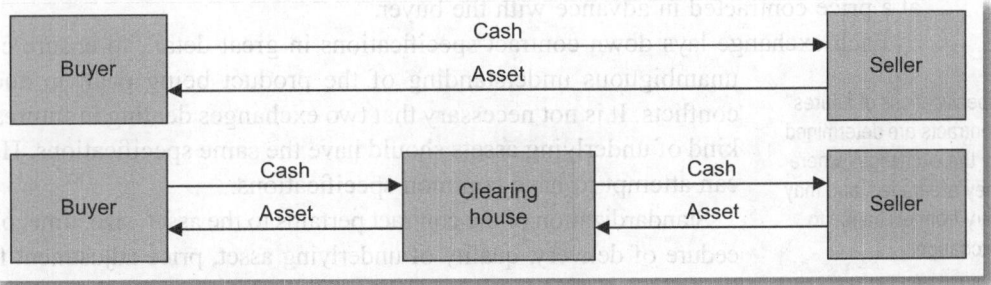

Fig. 2.3 Role of clearing house

The role of the guarantor, to ensure a default-free execution, can be performed by an organized body, i.e., an exchange. Rather than settling the transaction, both the buyer and seller can make good on their promises to an exchange, obviating the need for the buyer and seller to know each other. Futures exchange is similar to stock exchanges where shares are traded.

Standardized Contract/Product

However, if the trade has to take place on an exchange, the product cannot be tailor-made to the specific needs of the two parties, and, instead, would have to be standardized. The exchange cannot commit itself to any quantity, quality, and timing of the asset as per the specific requirements of individual buyers and sellers. If the exchange has to serve as counterparty, it has to deal in standardized products in terms of asset quantity, quality, and delivery timing and centres. For example, the exchange may find it difficult to comply with contracts involving an exporter selling $10,254 forward for delivery on 26 December and another selling $11,999 for delivery on 29 December. Instead, it will be easier for the exchange to deal in standard contracts of, say, $10,000 for one particular delivery date in the month of December. Therefore, individual buyers and sellers would have to adjust their own requirements and decide on the best possible course of action offered by the menu of standard products available on an exchange.

> The standardization of futures is in terms of size, quality, delivery time, delivery centres, and price quotation.

The introduction of exchanges to facilitate transactions has other advantages, too. While most forward contracts are settled with delivery, forward markets would limit participation to actual users. Speculators and arbitrageurs not interested in actual delivery of the underlying assets may desist from participation in forward markets. Since exchanges would provide an alternative route for exiting contracts through an offsetting contract, futures would invite participation by speculators and arbitrageurs, thereby increasing size and liquidity in the market. This, in turn, would enable better price discovery.

> The major advantages of futures contracts vis-a-vis forward contracts are (a) the elimination of counterparty risk, (b) flexibility of entry and exit anytime, and (c) cash settlement.

Specification of a Futures Contract

Thus, the need to eliminate counterparty risk causes intervention by an exchange, which in turn forces standardization of the contracts that can be traded. A futures contract may be defined as a standardized forward contract that is traded on an exchange, where a seller agrees to deliver a specified quantity of an asset of defined quality at a predetermined date at a price contracted in advance with the buyer.

Each exchange lays down contract specifications in great detail, to ensure complete and unambiguous understanding of the product being dealt in and to prevent conflicts. It is not necessary that two exchanges dealing in futures in the same kind of underlying assets should have the same specifications. However, they can attempt to have common specifications.

> Specifications of futures contracts are determined by the exchanges where they are traded, and may vary from exchange to exchange.

Standardization of the contract pertains to the asset, size, time, place and procedure of delivery, quality of underlying asset, price adjustment for variations in quality of the asset being delivered, etc. It is the prerogative of the exchange to determine the specifications of the futures contract. Details of futures contracts on gold, as traded on the National Multi-commodity Exchange of India (NMCE), are presented in Table 2.1.

Explained here are a few of the terms used in futures contracts:

(a) **Underlying asset** Futures, being derivatives, are priced according to the assets on which they are written. Contracts are normally specified by the name of the underlying asset, and the month and year of the expiry of the contract. For example, a futures contract in rice at Multi-commodity Exchange (MCX) will be denoted as RICE DEC12, implying that the underlying asset is rice and the contract is due for delivery in December 2012.

(b) **Contract expiry** Contract expiry refers to the time at which the contract comes to an end. Mutual obligations must be settled on or before the expiry of the contract. The

Table 2.1 Futures contract on gold at NMCE

Asset code	GOLD
Unit of trading	100 g of fineness 0.999
Delivery unit	Gold bars of 100 g serially numbered and of fineness 0.999
Quotation/base value	10 g of fineness 0.999
Tick size	₹1
Quality specification	The gold delivered under the contract must be bars weighing 100 g each and assaying not less than 0.999 fineness, bearing a serial number, and identifying the origin of the refiner/brander.
No. of delivery contracts in a year	Maximum 12 monthly or minimum 2 monthly contracts running concurrently
Delivery centres	Central Warehousing Corporation, Cochin
Opening of contracts	Trading in any contract month will open on the 16th day of the month, 12 months prior to the contract month
Due date	The 15th day of the delivery months; if the 15th happens to be a holiday, then the previous working day
Closing of contract	Squaring up of positions will be permitted between the 12th and 15th of the delivery month. No fresh position building will be allowed. From the 12th to the 15th of the delivery month, the seller can tender warehouse receipt for settlement, which will be accepted at the closing price of the previous day.
Delivery Logic	Compulsory delivery

Source: www.nmce.com; last accessed on 18 May 2012.

exchange specifies when the contracts for delivery in a particular month will come into force and when they will close for trading. For example, gold contracts will open for trading 12 months prior to the delivery month. The opening date and last day of trading will be specified by the exchange. Unlike a forward contract, where delivery is in accordance with the contract between two parties, the delivery date is fixed by the exchange in a futures contract.

This has important implications in terms of the period for which hedging can be done or a speculative position can be taken. For example, in the case of gold, at any point of time there are 12 contracts available corresponding to the next 12 months, implying that hedging is possible for the next 12 months.

(c) **Contract size** Contract size or trading unit refers to the standard contract size that will be traded on the exchange. Each futures contract for gold on the NMCE is for 100 g.

Price quotation The quotation is the basis on which the contract price, i.e., the value of the futures contract, is set. The price quotation for the product generally follows the convention of price quotations in the spot/physical markets. For example, the price quotation for a futures contract on rice is in terms of rupees per quintal. Hence, a quotation for ₹550 would mean ₹550 per quintal, and the contract value would be ₹55,000 (the value of 10 MT). Similarly, for contracts in gold, the price is quoted for 10 g (as in the spot market), while the contract size is 100 g at the NMCE. Similarly, futures on oil would be quoted on a per barrel basis, a practice followed in the spot market for oil.

Tick size Tick size is the minimum change that will be recognized in the price quotation. For rice contracts, it is ₹1. Hence, a price quotation of ₹551.50 is not possible. The tick size for the contract (the minimum by which the value of the contract changes) will be ₹100 (₹1 per quintal over 10 MT).

Figure 2.4 depicts the futures prices of select commodities at National Commodities and Derivatives Exchange (NCDEX) in India, with expiry dates of contracts on commodities, opens, highs/lows, and last traded prices, and compares them with spot prices. It also provides open interest figures.

Product Name	Exp DT	Open	High	Low	Close	LTP	Chg	(%)Chg	Spot P.	OI
Barley	18 May 2012	1370	1433	1370	1387	1418 ▲	31	2.24	1420.55	8990
Barley	20 Jun 2012	1413	1464	1403	1417.5	1444 ▲	26.5	1.87	1420.55	30200
Barley	20 Jul 2012	1446	1490	1435	1449	1473.5 ▲	24.5	1.69	1420.55	5400
Barley	17 Aug 2012	1476	1525.5	1474	1495.5	1494 ▼	-1.5	-0.1	1420.55	780
Barley	20 Sep 2012	1518	1548.5	1518	1518	1520 ▲	2	0.13	1420.55	40
Castor Seed	18 May 2012	3099	3155	3075	3088	3145 ▲	57	1.85	3016.8	2630
Castor Seed	20 Jun 2012	3140	3194	3126	3138	3183 ▲	45	1.43	3016.8	28790
Castor Seed	20 Jul 2012	3206	3256	3186	3194	3244 ▲	50	1.57	3016.8	16480
Castor Seed	17 Aug 2012	3265	3285	3225	3219	3277 ▲	58	1.8	3016.8	2000
Chana	18 May 2012	4185	4300	4135	4193	4269 ▲	76	1.81	4154.15	5110
Chana	20 Jun 2012	4211	4365	4184	4241	4329 ▲	88	2.07	4154.15	99950
Chana	20 Jul 2012	4320	4456	4277	4342	4420 ▲	78	1.8	4154.15	27860

Source: www.ncdex.com; last accessed on 18 May 2012.

Fig. 2.4 Futures prices

Settlement and Delivery

Forward contracts are either settled by delivery or by closing out of the position at the expiry with an opposite contract (with the consent of the counterparty). Settlement of futures contracts can be done in three possible ways:

- **Offsetting** By entering into an offsetting contract prior to the expiry of the futures contract
- **Delivery based** By opting for delivery of the underlying asset
- **Close-out** By close-out at expiry of the futures contract at a price determined by the exchange

The first option of settlement, by entering into an offsetting contract, is an effective way of hedging, due to convergence of the futures price with the spot price. Entering into an offsetting contract (sell if bought earlier, or buy if sold earlier) nullifies the delivery requirements of the underlying asset. What remains to be settled is the price difference between the initial and offsetting contracts. Offsetting is also called *squaring up* of the position. This is by far the most preferred option for speculators and hedgers alike.

The second option to reach settlement is by making delivery. At the NMCE, contracts are delivered during the last three days prior to the expiry date. No one is allowed to enter any

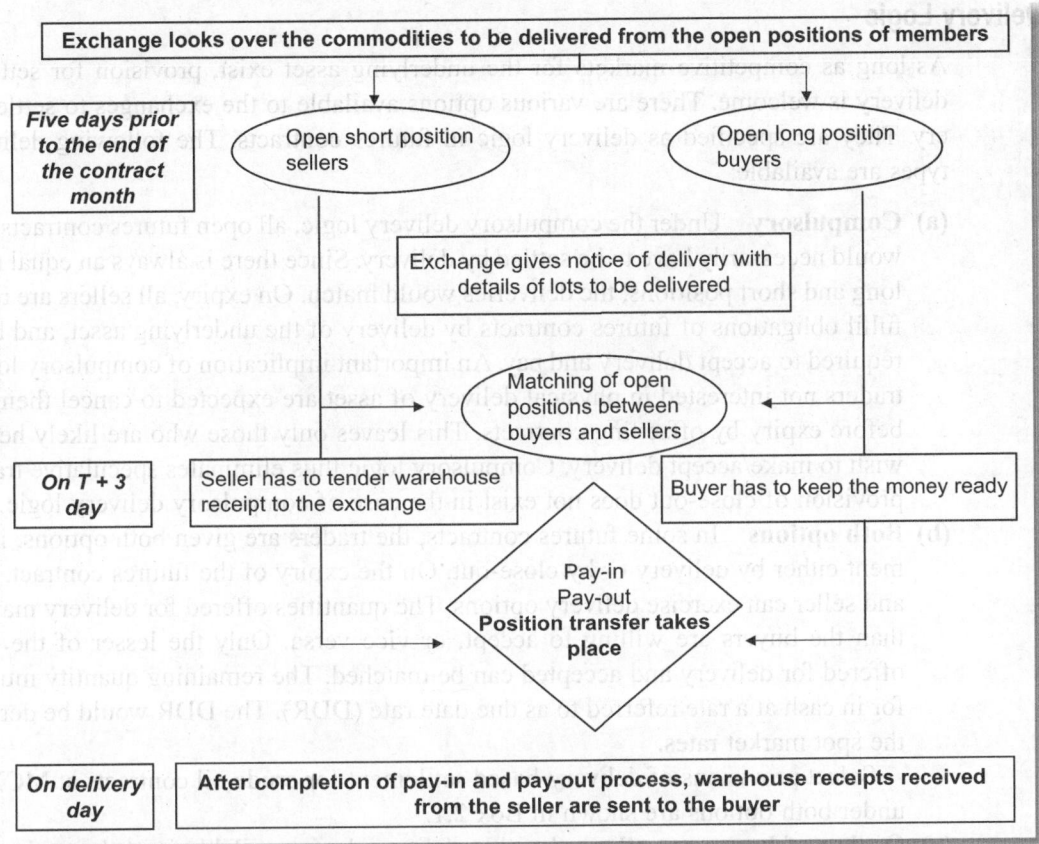

Fig. 2.5 Settlement by delivery

Source: www.ncdex.com; last accessed on 18 May 2012.

fresh position in contracts that is about to expire in three days. Figure 2.5 shows the various steps involved in settlement of contracts by delivery.

The third option is settlement by close-out. This option is resorted to by the exchange upon expiry of open futures contracts that are not squared up by the investor, if the exchange rules clearly state that futures contracts are necessarily cash-settled. The necessity for cash settlements arises in the case of futures contracts based on (a) hypothetical assets such as those on indices or (b) assets that are not permitted to be delivered due to laws of the land, such as futures on foreign currency in India. The contract specifies whether an exchange would resort to a close-out or not.

Settlement mechanisms in the futures markets essentially must provide for delivery, to maintain efficient price discovery and strong linkages between the spot and futures markets.

Absence of settlement by delivery may give rise to a doubt that futures prices are not driven by spot market. A healthy and vibrant spot market for the underlying asset is a prerequisite for futures trade. Delivery becomes crucial in case the underlying asset is an essential commodity such as wheat, rice, or sugar, with great political appeal and economic significance. Various types of delivery systems are referred to as 'delivery logic' discussed next.

> There are three ways to settle a futures contract—offsetting before maturity, physical delivery, or close-out on maturity.

Delivery Logic

As long as competitive markets for the underlying asset exist, provision for settlement by delivery is welcome. There are various options available to the exchanges to settle by delivery. They are specified as delivery logic in futures contracts. The following delivery logic types are available:

(a) **Compulsory** Under the compulsory delivery logic, all open futures contracts on expiry would necessarily have to be settled by delivery. Since there is always an equal number of long and short positions, the deliveries would match. On expiry, all sellers are required to fulfil obligations of futures contracts by delivery of the underlying asset, and buyers are required to accept delivery and pay. An important implication of compulsory logic is that traders not interested in physical delivery of asset are expected to cancel their positions before expiry by offsetting contracts. This leaves only those who are likely hedgers and wish to make/accept delivery. Compulsory logic thus eliminates speculative traders. The provision of close-out does not exist in the case of compulsory delivery logic.

(b) **Both options** In some futures contracts, the traders are given both options, i.e., settlement either by delivery or by close-out. On the expiry of the futures contract, the buyer and seller can exercise delivery options. The quantities offered for delivery may be more than the buyers are willing to accept, or vice versa. Only the lesser of the quantities offered for delivery and accepted can be matched. The remaining quantity must be paid for in cash at a rate referred to as due date rate (DDR). The DDR would be derived from the spot market rates.

Select provisions of delivery-based settlement for crude oil contracts at MCX in India under both options are shown in Box 2.1.

(c) **Option of buyer or seller** Another delivery logic available is at the option of either the seller or the buyer. If the seller exercises the delivery option, then buyers would have to be identified from those still having open long positions. Similarly, if the delivery option is with the buyer, sellers would be identified for making deliveries. The intentions to deliver the underlying asset are notified in advance, and before the expiry of the relevant futures contracts. Under such delivery logic, the party that opts for delivery has voluntarily surrendered the right to square up the position, but the party that is allocated the delivery is forced to have delivery-based settlement, and loses the chance to square up the contract. The assigned buyer/seller would have to settle by physical delivery.

(d) **Assignment** Where the option of delivery-based settlement is restricted to one party, the counterparty for settlement would have to be identified. The procedure for allocating the delivery is called assignment. The exchange decides the rule of assignment. It may be random, willing party, or longest outstanding contract. Under compulsory delivery, there is no assignment. Under the delivery logic of 'both options' and 'option of the buyer/seller', the exchange would have to frame rules of assignment of delivery.

> Assignment refers to the method of finding the counterparty for delivery when either the buyer or the seller of futures has opted for settlement by delivery.

Provisions for compulsory delivery are necessary to some extent, otherwise futures markets become purely speculative. Lack of delivery may influence the prices in the markets for the underlying asset.

The objectives of hedgers and speculators trading in the futures market differ substantially from each other. However, exchanges in India do not

> **Box 2.1 Select delivery provisions for crude oil at MCX India**
>
> | | |
> |---|---|
> | **Delivery logic** | **Both options** |
> | Both buyers and sellers can express intention to take and make delivery of crude oil. In a way, traders have the option to have either delivery-based settlement or cash settlement. Contracts not declaring intentions for delivery would be settled in cash. | |
> | **Delivery period** | **Up to two working days after expiry of futures contract (T + 2)** |
> | Delivery has to be made good within two days of the expiry of the futures contract. | |
> | **Intentions for delivery** | **On the day of expiry of contract** |
> | Buyers and sellers must notify the exchange of delivery-based settlement to enable the exchange to take appropriate steps to allocate delivery. | |
> | **Matching delivery** | **Assigning delivery to buyers and sellers** |
> | The exchange matches the delivery quantities for buyers and sellers. As the quantities notified by the sellers and buyers in most cases would not match, the exchange would allocate buyers and sellers, and surplus quantities would be settled in cash at the DDR. | |
> | **Delivery period margin** | **25%** |
> | Against the usual initial margin of 5%, both buyers and sellers with intentions of delivery have to deposit the enhanced margin to ensure that commitment of delivery is met. Sellers exercising the delivery option are exempt from delivery margin upon submission of documentary proof of delivery (warehouse receipt). | |
> | **Due date rate** | **For cash settlement** |
> | This is the ex-Mumbai price exclusive of all taxes in US dollars, converted into Indian rupees at the exchange rate prevailing on the day. | |

distinguish between a hedger and speculator, as they apply a uniform margin for both. Contrarily, some markets in the world do waive or reduce margins for hedgers who provide evidence of delivery or underlying trade transaction.

Selection of delivery logic is dependent upon several factors. The availability of goods of similar nature in the spot market, desire to prevent over-speculation, competitiveness in the spot markets, warehousing infrastructure, availability of quality assayers, a reasonable formula for price adjustment of different grades of the same commodity, etc., are some of the factors that would dictate the selection of delivery logic.

Open Interest

An important parameter in the futures markets is *open interest*. The number of contracts outstanding (not squared up) at any point of time is called open interest. As a new contract is introduced, investors start taking a view on the market of the underlying asset and assume an exposure on the futures contract. For every buyer of a contract, there is a seller. Under normal circumstances, the open interest rises with time as more and more investors start evincing interest in the new contract. They either buy or sell a contract depending upon their respective opinions. But as the maturity of the contract approaches, investors tend to reduce their exposures

> Open interest is the number of futures contracts outstanding. It reduces to zero upon maturity of the contracts.

and unwind the initial position. Those who went long initially would unwind by selling their contracts, and those who took short positions initially would cover themselves by buying contracts. Hence, the open interest starts declining as maturity approaches. It signifies reduced investor interest in the contracts that have a short time left to expire.

Ultimately, on the expiry of the contract, all positions would be squared up. The positions that are left open by investors are compulsorily settled by the exchange either by delivery or close-out. Where positions are settled by close-out, the difference between the closing price and the price of initial contract would be paid or received by the exchange.

Open Interest and Volume Open interest and volumes are often thought to be the same. However, they are different. 'Volume' refers to the number of contracts traded in a day. Cumulatively, it would always increase. 'Open interest' is the number of new contracts opened in the day. Contracts that offset initial positions do not add to the open interest, but they do add to the volume. Table 2.2 highlights the differences between open interest and volume.

Table 2.2 Open interest and volume

Day	Actions		Open interest	Volume for day
1	A goes long; B goes short	50	150	150
	C goes long; D goes short	100		
2	E goes long; F goes short (Two new parties add to open interest)	100	250	100
3	B goes long; H goes short (One party offsetting and second party opening keeps open interest unchanged)	50	250	50
4	C goes short; D goes long (Both parties closing initial position reduces open interest)	100	150	100

CASH FLOWS UNDER FORWARD AND FUTURES CONTRACTS

As we have seen, the principle and purpose of the forward contract and the futures contract are the same. However, there are key differences with cash flow implications that must be understood.

Besides standardization, and as exchange-traded products, the cash flow of futures differs in two substantial ways from that of forward contracts, as follows:

- Initial and variation margin
- Marking-to-market margin

Margin Requirements

The exchange serves as counterparty to both buyers and sellers of futures contracts. Delivery of the underlying assets and cash flow are the two essential ingredients of futures contracts. Despite the fact that most contracts are neutralized prior to delivery, the link between delivery and the resultant cash flow cannot be broken. The exchange works to eliminate counterparty risk, and, therefore, it has to assure itself of the financial standing of the participating members. Further, the exchange needs to curb members' overtrading tendencies.

To assure itself of the financial credibility of participants and to check speculative tendencies, the exchange prescribes the margin to be deposited with it. The margin is a percentage of the contract value and is prescribed by the exchange depending on the volatility in price of the underlying asset. An initial margin is required to be deposited to open a short or long position in the futures, and is normally set equivalent to the maximum loss that the position can suffer in a day. Both buyer and seller are liable to pay margins.

> To cover the default risk, futures require an initial margin, and are marked to market on a daily basis.

Minimum Margin and Margin Call

If an initial margin of 4% is stipulated by the exchange, it implies that the loss would not normally exceed 4% in a day. Suppose a trader buys one contract for 10 MT of rice valued at ₹55,000, i.e., ₹550 per quintal. He will be required to deposit 4%, i.e., ₹2200 as initial deposit. While the position remains open, the trader can incur loss or profit as the price changes. If the price falls to ₹535 the next day, the trader has incurred a loss of ₹1500 and his margin now stands reduced to ₹700 (₹2200 – ₹1500). This may make the exchange uncomfortable and insecure, as any further decline in price will wipe out the entire margin. The exchange, therefore, prescribes a minimum level below which the margin should not fall. If it does, the exchange asks the trader to immediately replenish the margin to the original level of 4% (known as margin call).

The initial margin is intended to cover potential loss in an open position for the next day. However, the loss that is already incurred during the day has to be compensated for at the end of the day. It is the practice of exchanges to settle price differences on a daily basis. This daily settlement is referred to as *marking to market*. The difference of initial and final margin represents profit or loss. Example 2.2 illustrates the mechanism of marking to market.

EXAMPLE 2.1 Margin and margin call

An investor buys five futures contracts on gold at the MCX of India. Each contract is for 100 g. The price quotation is ₹15,550 per 10 g. The tick size is ₹1. Initial margin is set at 4%, while the minimum margin is 90% of the initial margin. Find out the following:

(a) What is the minimum change in value of a contract?
(b) What is the amount of initial margin the investor has to deposit with the exchange?
(c) At what price level would the investor get a margin call?
(d) If the investor sold the contract, what price level would trigger a margin call?

Solution

(a) The minimum change in the price quotation is ₹1 per 10 g. The contract size is 100 g. Therefore, the minimum change in the value of the contract would be 1 × 100/10 = ₹10.
(b) Initial margin = Value of contract × margin% × no. of contracts = 100/10 × 15,550 × 4% × 5 = ₹31,100
(c) The minimum margin is 90% of the initial margin. Therefore, till the loss reaches ₹3110 (₹622 per contract), the investor would not get a margin call. When the price falls by more than ₹62.20 per 10 g, the margin would fall below the minimum required. Any price below ₹15,487.80 would warrant a margin call.
(d) For initial short position, the price rise would erode the margin. Price rise by more than ₹62.20 to ₹15,612.20 (15,550 + 62.20) would trigger margin call.

Assume an investor has bought a futures contract on the stock of Maruti Udyog at the National Stock Exchange (NSE) at a price of ₹410. As each contract consists of 400 shares, the exposure is worth ₹1,64,000. There is no cash flow from the buyer to the seller at the time of entering the contract. The initial margin payable by both the buyer and the seller to the exchange is ignored for the purpose of this illustration. If the investor holds this position till day 4 and closes out by selling the contract when the price is ₹440, the ultimate profit is ₹12,000 from the transaction (a gain of ₹30 per share for 400 shares).

However, what happens to the price during the intervening period is to be accounted for in the futures contract. At the end of each day, the profit or loss on the position is calculated, and the loss, if any, is made good to the exchange by the investor. Likewise, any profit at the end of each day is credited to the account of the investor. Profit or loss is settled at the end of each day as if the investor were closing out the position. If at the end of day 1 the closing price increased to ₹420, the investor's account will be credited with the profit of ₹4000. Similarly, if at the end of day 2 the price fell to ₹400, the investor will have to a loss of ₹8000 with the exchange. This way, the position is marked daily to the end-of-the-day price. The net impact on profit or loss remains the same as the difference between buying and selling price, as would be the case under a forward contract. But with futures, the net profit/loss is represented as a series of cash flows on a daily basis, as can be seen from Table 2.3.

Table 2.3 Marking to market

Day	Price (₹)	Cash flow (₹)	Remarks
Day 1: Opening a contract	410	None	A long position opened for one contract (400 shares) valued at ₹1,64,000
Close of Day 1	420	(420 − 410) × 400 = +4,000	Investor receives ₹4,000
Close of Day 2	400	(400 − 420) × 400 = −8,000	Investor pays ₹8,000
Close of Day 3	390	(390 − 400) × 400 = −4,000	Investor pays ₹4,000
Day 4: Closing the contract	440	(440 − 390) × 400 = +20,000	Position closed out with contract value of ₹1,76,000. Investor gets ₹20,000
Net profit		(440 − 410) × 400 = 12,000	

The final profit given by the difference between the selling and the buying prices of ₹12,000 is a series of cash flows of +4000, −8000, −4000, and +20,000.

Besides the margin and marking to market, there are other differences between forward and futures contracts. For convenience, these differences are summarized in Table 2.4.

PRICING A FORWARD/FUTURES CONTRACT

We now attempt to understand how the price of a forward/futures contract is decided. As defined, the value of derivative contracts depends upon the spot price of the underlying asset. The price of forward contract or futures contract is determined using the same principle, as fundamentally it is the same contract that specifies the price today for future delivery of the asset.

EXAMPLE 2.2 Marking to Market

For the contract specified in Example 2.1, find out the gain or loss on a daily basis for short and long positions in five contracts of gold if the clearing prices for the next 10 days are as given:

Day	1	2	3	4	5
Price (₹)	15,520	15,305	15,410	15,220	15,440
Day	6	7	8	9	10
Price (₹)	15,340	15,600	15,630	15,670	15,870

Indicate the position of the margin account and margins calls, if any, on a daily basis when the contracts are marked to market. Assuming that investors square off their positions at a price of ₹15,870 on the 10th day, find out the gains and losses of the long and short positions in futures. Confirm the same from the margin account cash flows.

Solution
The investors have opened their positions at a price of ₹15,550 by depositing a margin of ₹31,100, calculated at 4% of the initial outlay. The minimum margin requirement at 90% works out to ₹27,990 (0.90 × 31,100). The margin accounts of investors would be credited with any profit and debited with any loss. For long and short positions, the amount of profit and loss would be equal with a changed sign. On the basis of daily clearing prices, the daily profit and loss position, the margin account position, and margin call would be as follows:

Day	Clearing price (₹)	Profit/loss for day (₹)		Margin account (₹)		Margin call (₹)	
		Long position	Short position	Long position	Short position	Long position	Short position
0	15,550						
1	15,520	−1,500	1,500	29,600	32,600		
2	15,305	−10,750	10,750	18,850	43,350	12,250	
3	15,410	5,250	−5,250	36,350	38,100		
4	15,220	−9,500	9,500	26,850	47,600	4,250	
5	15,440	11,000	−11,000	42,100	36,600		
6	15,340	−5,000	5,000	37,100	41,600		
7	15,600	13,000	−13,000	50,100	28,600		
8	15,630	1,500	−1,500	51,600	27,100		4,000
9	15,670	2,000	−2,000	53,600	29,100		
10	15,870	10,000	−10,000	63,600	19,100		12,000
Closing position of margin account				63,600	31,100		
Margin calls paid						16,500	16,000

Profit and loss is calculated from the clearing price of the previous day. The aggregate profit and loss can be found by the difference between the closing and opening prices as follows:

Opening price = ₹15,550   Closing price = ₹15,870
Profit for long position = (15,870 − 15,550) × 100/10 × 5 = ₹16,000
Profit for short position = (15,550 − 15,870) × 100/10 × 5 = −₹16,000

The aggregate profit or loss would be the sum of the daily profits and losses over 10 days. It can also be obtained from the cash flow in the margin account. The profit or loss from the margin account position is given by

Profit/loss = Final margin position − initial margin position − margin call paid
For long position: Profit = 63,600 − 31,100 − 16,500 = ₹16,000
For short position: Profit = 31,100 − 31,100 − 16,000 = −₹16,000

This confirms the profit and loss calculated directly from the opening and closing prices.

Table 2.4 Comparison between forward and futures contracts

Features	Futures	Forwards
Location	Exchange	Over the counter
Counterparty	Unknown to each other, exchange serves as counterparty	Counterparties are known to each other
Counterparty risk	Minimal	Considerable
Initial cash flow	Initial and variation margins required	None
Explicit cost	Brokerage to be paid	No intermediary and no cost
Settlement	Implicitly daily by marking to the market	No marking to the market
Final settlement	By delivery or cash	By delivery
Exit prior to maturity	Possible by entering an opposite contract to square up the position	Generally not possible unless both the parties agree
Quantity specification	Fixed standard size/lot	Any quantity
Time of delivery	On fixed dates	Any time mutually decided by the parties concerned
Cost of hedging	Very nominal	High
Period of hedging	Contracts available for a limited period	Unlimited

> The futures price is based on spot price and the cost of carry for the period less benefits of ownership.

As a simplest case, let us consider an asset that provides no income to the owner of the asset during the period of the forward contract. Let the asset be 100 g of gold. Let the current price of gold, S_0, be ₹7000 per 10 g in the physical market. The owner of the asset sells the asset 12-m forward at price F_1. Once the contract period is over, ownership will get transferred to the buyer upon payment of the contracted price F_1. Purely from a financial perspective, the buyer of the contract has owned the asset on deferred payment basis, while the seller of the asset will receive payment only after the end of the contract period. The seller is deemed to hold the asset till the end of the forward period on behalf of the buyer.

The new buyer has saved the cost of interest. Since there is a certainty of delivery and cash payment, we can safely assume that the buyer saved the interest cost r, applicable for risk-free investment. Let us assume $r = 10\%$. If the contracted price was F_1 he must have $F_1/(1 + r)$ today so as to mature to F_1 at the expiry of the contract period. Hence, the current price of the asset, S_0, must be less than or equal to $F_1/(1 + r)$, or else he or she would not enter into a forward contract. Mathematically,

$$S_0 \leq F_1/(1 + r) \text{ or } F_1 \geq S_0 \times (1 + r) \tag{2.1}$$

From the viewpoint of the current owner of the gold, if he had sold the asset on the spot at the current price and invested the proceeds at a risk-free rate, his wealth would have grown to a minimum of $S_0 \times (1 + r)$. Therefore, the forward contract price F_1 must exceed or equal $S_0 \times (1 + r)$ to motivate him to enter a forward deal. Mathematically,

$$F_1 \geq S_0 \times (1 + r) \tag{2.2}$$

The only way the two inequalities of Eqs 2.1 and 2.2 can be satisfied is by equating both equations. The forward deal will take place only when the buyer and the seller of the asset feel indifferent to the price. Therefore, the forward contract will take place if and only if both inequalities (Eqs 2.1 and 2.2) are satisfied, that is,

$$F_1 = S_0 \times (1 + r) \qquad (2.3)$$

Here, we have assumed annual compounding of interest. If the compounding period is made infinitesimally small (continuous compounding), Eq. 2.3 can be represented as follows:

$$F_1 = S_0 \times e^{rt} \qquad (2.4a)$$

For compounding at periodic intervals (n times p.a.) and time t expressed in years, the forward price is given by

$$F_1 = S_0 \times (1 + r/n)^{nt} \qquad (2.4b)$$

where, r is referred to as the cost of carry.

Arbitrage Argument Equations 2.1 and 2.2 are necessary conditions for the forward price. Any other price will give rise to arbitrage opportunity. Let us see how arbitrage as a process will derive the price of the asset as given by Eq. 2.4(a) and (b). Assume the current spot price of 10 g gold to be ₹7000, the risk-free rate to be 10% p.a., and the forward contract period of one year. Using simple compounding, the 12-m forward price of gold should be ₹7700 (₹7000 + 10% interest).

Any other price gives rise to arbitrage. Let us examine how arbitrage works for the assumed forward prices of (a) ₹8000 and (b) ₹7300.

Cash-and-carry Arbitrage

When forward is overpriced at ₹8000

If the forward price of gold is ₹8000 (i.e., more than the spot price plus cost of carry), an arbitrageur can take the following actions simultaneously today at $t = 0$:

> When a futures contract is overpriced, cash-and-carry arbitrage can be executed by selling the futures now and buying the underlying asset to derive a riskless profit.

- Borrow ₹7000
- Buy gold spot
- Sell forward contract at ₹8000

Note that this is a riskless and investment-free position created because no owned funds are involved and no risk is assumed. The arbitrageur has borrowed funds at a definite rate and the forward contract is covered by having the underlying asset now. The arbitrageur would own and therefore be able to deliver the underlying asset one year later, realize the forward price, and pay back the loan along with interest thereon. The following cash flow would result after one year:

Realize cash from forward contract by delivery of gold	+₹8,000
Pay back the borrowed money and interest thereon	−₹7,700
Profit	**₹300**

Since all the cash flows are known at $t = 0$ with no uncertainty about them at maturity, the profit of ₹300 represents arbitrage. This is referred to as *cash-and-carry arbitrage*.

Reverse Cash-and-carry Arbitrage

When forward is underpriced at ₹7300

On the contrary, if the price is ₹7300 (i.e., less than the spot price plus cost of carry) an arbitrageur can take the following actions today:

- Borrow gold
- Sell gold spot at ₹7000
- Lend at a risk-free rate of 10%
- Buy a forward contract at ₹7300

> When a futures contract is underpriced, reverse cash-and-carry arbitrage can be executed by buying the futures now and selling short in spot to derive riskless profit.

Note that this is again a riskless position created with no investment, because it is set up with borrowed gold, and its future delivery is covered through a forward buy contract. One year later, the following cash flow will result:

Realize cash from lending activity	+₹7,700
Pay for the forward contract and return borrowed gold	−₹7,300
Profit	**₹400**

This is known as *reverse cash-and-carry arbitrage*.

To arrive at a price that does not allow arbitrage either by cash and carry or reverse cash and carry, the profit must vanish in both the cases. It is not difficult to see that if the price of the forward contract is ₹7700, it will ensure no profit from arbitrage.

EXAMPLE 2.3 Cash-and-carry arbitrage

The price of Suzlon shares at the NSE is ₹85, while a three-month futures contract on Suzlon is being traded at ₹90. If one can borrow at 12% and Suzlon is not paying any dividend in the next three months, is there an arbitrage opportunity available in the prices ruling in the spot market and futures market? If so, how can a profit be made? Assume the size of the futures contract to be 1000 shares.

Solution

The cost of carry is 1% per month. For three months, the cost of carry is 3% of the spot price of ₹85.00. Accordingly, the 3-m forward price should be $1.03 \times 85 = ₹87.55$. Futures contract trading at ₹90.00 is overpriced and, hence, cash-and-carry arbitrage can be executed. An investor can take the following actions simultaneously today at $t = 0$:

- Borrow ₹85,000.
- Buy 1000 shares of Suzlon at a spot price of ₹85.
- Sell one futures contract at ₹90 with exposure of ₹90,000.

Three months later, the investor would deliver the underlying asset against the futures contract, realize the contracted price of ₹90,000, and pay back the borrowing along with interest with the following cash flow:

Realize cash from futures contract	+₹90,000
Pay back the borrowed money and interest thereon	−₹87,550
Profit	**₹2,450**

Since all the cash flows are known at $t = 0$ with no uncertainty of the cash flows at maturity, the profit of ₹2450 represents arbitrage profit obtained through cash-and-carry.

Pricing Investment Assets

For pricing a forward contract, we used the principle of arbitrage. For pricing futures, the same principle of arbitrage applies as in Eq. 2.4, albeit with some caution. For pricing a futures contract, we need to consider the characteristics of the underlying asset. The underlying asset can be differentiated as (a) carry type or investment asset and (b) non-carry type or consumption asset.

Investment assets such as gold, silver, stocks, and currencies need adjustment of the following two factors:

- Benefits that accrue to the owner of the asset till it is delivered
- Cost of storage and carry to be incurred by the owner till the delivery is made

The benefits of ownership do not accrue to the buyer of a futures contract. Instead, they go to the seller, who is physically holding the asset during the intervening period. For example, if the underlying asset involved was a stock, the dividend on it will accrue to the owner of the physical asset and not to the owner of the futures contract. Ideally, this benefit must be passed on to the buyer of the futures contract. This benefit must, therefore, be deducted from the futures price. If the present value of the benefit is D, then the futures price will be as per Eq. 2.5.

$$F = (S_0 - D) \times e^{rt} \qquad (2.5)$$

Note that the spot price is decreased to the extent of the present value of the benefit.

Similarly, till the asset is delivered, the owner of the physical asset will have to incur storage cost, which the buyer of the futures contract avoids. This has an impact opposite to that of the benefits. Since the seller of the contract is holding the asset on behalf of the buyer, he is entitled to recover the cost from the buyer. The spot price needs to be revised upwards by the present value of the storage cost s. Therefore, the futures price is calculated as given in Eq. 2.6.

$$F = (S_0 - D + s) \times e^{rt} \qquad (2.6)$$

If the benefits and costs are proportional to the futures price, then they can be adjusted against the cost of carry, not in the spot price of the asset. Therefore, the future price now is expressed by Eq. 2.7.

$$F = S_0 \times e^{(r - D + s)t} \qquad (2.7)$$

Pricing Consumption Assets

While pricing futures on consumption assets, the principle of arbitrage may not be applicable because of the utility of consumption, referred to as convenience yield. Deriving profit from the asset no longer remains the motive when an item is required for consumption. Consumable assets incur no income, but they normally have carrying cost, which is treated as negative income. Hence, with carrying costs, the arbitrage profit can be computed as follows:

If $F \geq (S_0 + s)e^{rt}$ then

- borrow $(S + s)$ at r to buy commodity and fund storage cost;
- sell the futures contract; and
- at maturity, derive profit $= F - (S_0 + s)e^{rt}$.

> **EXAMPLE 2.4** Upper bound on the futures price of consumption asset
>
> A jute processing unit requires raw jute as input to its operations. The spot price of jute is ₹1900 per quintal and the 6-m futures for raw jute at MCX is traded at ₹2080. If the cost of funds for the jute processing unit is 10% p.a. and storage costs are 2% p.a., find out the upper limit on the futures price. If the actual price exceeds the upper bound, how can the firm profit from such a situation?
>
> **Solution**
> The upper limit on futures price is given by Eq. 2.8.
>
> $$F \leq S_0 e^{(r+s)t} \quad \text{or} \quad F \leq 1900 \times e^{0.12/12 \times 6} \quad \text{or} \quad F \leq 2017.49$$
>
> At a price greater than ₹2017.50, cash-and-carry arbitrage can be executed by (a) borrowing (b) buying jute in the spot market, and (c) selling the futures now. At the expiry of the futures contract, the commitment of delivery of jute may be made good on receiving the futures price.

If $F \leq (S_0 + s)e^{rt}$ then

- sell the commodity, save storage cost, and invest at r;
- buy the futures contract; and
- at maturity, derive profit = $(S_0 + s)e^{rt} - F$.

The consumption value associated with commodities tests arbitrage arguments. For a consumption asset, only the strategy of cash-and-carry can be implemented, but the strategy of reverse cash-and-carry is not possible. One cannot sell a commodity that is required for consumption purposes and buy a futures contract instead. Physical holding of the asset and futures on the same are not equivalent due to the consumption value attached to the commodity. For an oil producer, buying oil futures and selling in the physical market leaves no stock of oil required for production. Due to the consumption value of the asset, we only have an upper bound to the futures price (refer to solved problem SP 2.2). Hence,

$$F \leq (S_0 + s)e^{rt} \tag{2.8}$$

The owner of the assets may feel that holding the asset in a physical form will provide benefits that cannot be obtained by investing in future contracts.

Convenience yield refers to the benefits enjoyed by the owner of the asset due to its possession and consumption. It is extremely difficult to objectively measure convenience yield, as it is specific to individuals. In rare situations where an estimate of convenience yield can be made, the futures price can be given by:

$$F = (S_0 + s)e^{(r-c)t}$$

where c is convenience yield measured as a proportion of the price in annual terms.

VALUE OF A FORWARD CONTRACT

When one enters a forward contract, its value must be zero. Assume that an investor holds 10 g of gold and enters a 6-m forward contract to sell the gold at ₹15,000. It implies that he would receive ₹15,000 after six months and deliver the gold. Since there is no cash flow at the time of the forward contract and the delivery price is fixed, the seller of the forward contract is indifferent to selling the gold today at the spot price or 6-m later at the forward price. Following the same logic, we may say that the buyer of the forward contract is indifferent to buying gold now at the spot price or paying the delivery price under the forward contract six months later. Hence, the present value of the forward price must be equal to the spot price. The value of the forward contract at inception is zero.

If F_1 is the forward price, S_0 is the spot price, and T is the maturity of the forward contract, then at inception,

$$\text{Value of the forward contract}, f = (S_0 - F_1)e^{-rT} = 0$$

At any other time, t, a long forward contract f plus present value of the forward price in cash must be equal to the spot price of the asset, or

$$f + F_1 \times e^{-rt} = S_0 \qquad (2.9)$$

After having entered the forward contract at ₹15,000 for 10 g of gold, the value of the forward contract would not be zero because the forward price would change. If the price changes to F_2 immediately after the long position in the forward contract, what is the value of the initial forward contract? The best way to find this out is to enter the opposite contract maturing at $t = T$. If the initial contract is long, the subsequent contract is short and vice versa. For an initial long contract and a subsequent short contract, both maturing at the same time, T, the cash flow at maturity would be

	Cash flow at $t = T$
Pay under initial long contract	$-F_1$
Receive under subsequent short contract	$+F_2$
Net cash flow	$F_2 - F_1$

$$\text{Value of the forward contract}, f = (F_2 - F_1) \times e^{-rT} \qquad (2.10)$$

Therefore, the value of the forward contract already entered at F_1 at any time subsequently is the present value of the difference between the current forward price F_2 and F_1.

EXAMPLE 2.5 Value of forward contract

The current price of Bharti's share is ₹ 800. An investor A is ready to buy one share of Bharti at ₹ 900 for future delivery after six months. A goes long with the contract. After one month, another investor, B, offers to buy Bharti's share at ₹ 925 for delivery after five months. If the risk-free interest rate is 9% p.a., what is the value of the forward contract that investor A is holding?

Solution
As of now, five months are left for the expiry of the forward contract that investor A is holding. He is committed to paying a price of ₹ 900 to get delivery of one share of Bharti.

If investor A goes short with a five-month forward contract, he/she would receive ₹ 925 from investor B for delivery of one share of Bharti, which he would receive under the initial contract. Therefore the value of the forward contract, f, using Eq. 2.10 is

f = present value of the difference of current price and original contract price
$\quad = (925 - 900) \times e^{-0.09 \times 5/12} = ₹ 24.08$

CONVERGENCE

As per the cost of carry model discussed, the difference between the futures price and the spot price represents the cost of carry for the remaining period before the expiry of the contract. Accordingly, a futures contract with longer maturity will be priced higher than a contract with shorter maturity because of the time value of money. As maturity nears, the difference between the futures price and spot price shrinks and on the day of maturity, the two prices must necessarily be identical, as shown in Fig. 2.6.

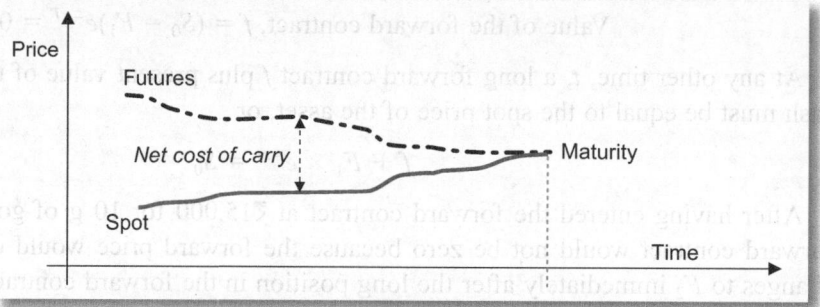

Fig. 2.6 Convergence of spot and futures price

This happens due to compulsion of delivery attached with the futures contract. Note that delivery is not obligatory in the futures contract, and one nullifies the open position by entering into a contract with terms opposite to those of the original one and exchanging the price difference. This is the most common method followed by investors to square up their positions in futures contracts.

Even though settlement of a futures contract is rarely done through delivery, the futures price cannot be different from the one prevailing in the physical market. The mere possibility of either buyer or seller forcing the delivery is a sufficient reason for prices in the physical and the financial markets to converge with time. The difference between the futures price and the spot price represents the cost of carry for the remaining period of the futures contract. As time elapses, the cost of carry would reduce, being directly proportional to the time remaining; on the day of the maturity, the cost of carry would be zero.

> The difference between futures price and spot price is called basis. As time progresses, basis declines and becomes zero on maturity, i.e., spot and futures prices converge.

If the provision for delivery is withdrawn, a futures contract will be reduced to a purely speculative instrument, and the very purpose for which futures contracts were conceived would be defeated. On the date of delivery, the prices in the physical and financial markets must essentially converge; if they do not, arbitrage will drive them to a single common value.

Normal Market and Inverted Market

A market where the futures price exceeds the spot price is referred to as a normal market, as the cost of carry is positive. The difference is the cost of carry. However, there are instances where the futures price is less than the spot price. This can happen due to changing demand and supply positions of the underlying asset. For example, spot prices of wheat may be high due to short supply of wheat now but when the crop matures in future, supplies will be abundant and hence the price of futures contract may fall. Markets where the futures price is lower than the spot price are known as *inverted markets*.

In both cases (normal and inverted markets), the principle of convergence of price applies. In either case, the futures price must converge to the spot price as maturity approaches, as all cost of carry, benefits of ownership, storage costs, convenience yields, etc., tend to become zero on the day of the delivery of the futures contract.

RELATIONSHIP BETWEEN FUTURES AND FORWARD PRICES

In efficient and perfect markets, the forward price and the futures price must be identical, both contracts being the same fundamentally. However, from the point of view of cash flow, there are two major differences between forward and futures contracts, as discussed earlier: forward contracts are not subject to (a) *initial margin* requirement and (b) *marking to the market*. The cash flows from a forward contract and a futures contract may be different, though the net position at the end would be the same. Both forward and futures prices should yield the same profit at the end of the contract period, except for the interest on resettlement payments. A gain of ₹100 in the forwards market may mean a gain of ₹300 on day 1 and a loss of ₹200 on day 2 in the futures market.

> The prices of futures and forward are identical in perfect markets, where the interest rates are constant; otherwise, they would be marginally different depending upon the correlation of the prices with interest rates.

The relationship of spot prices with interest rates determines the difference in pricing of futures and forwards. If there were no correlation between the spot price and the interest rate, the cash inflows and outflows arising out of the process of marking to market would tend to cancel out each other. In such a case, there is no reason to believe that futures and forward prices would be different.

When spot prices are positively correlated with interest rates, a long position in futures will be better than in the forward, as it will provide interim cash inflows that may be invested. Hence, the futures price will exceed the forward price. With a negative correlation between spot prices and interest rates, the forward prices will be higher than the futures prices, as there would be cash outflows in futures contract. The relationship is summarized as follows:

Correlation of spot and interest	Relationship of futures and forward price
Positive correlation	Futures price > forward price
Negative correlation	Futures price < forward price
No correlation	Futures price = forward price

RELATIONSHIP OF FUTURES PRICE AND EXPECTED SPOT PRICE

We have seen that on the maturity date, irrespective of whether the market is normal or inverted, the futures price and the spot price must converge. Does this mean that we can take today's futures price to be the expected spot price, S_1, on the date of maturity? There are three theories that attempt to establish the relationship between the futures price and expected spot price.

Normal Backwardation Hypothesis

Propounded by the famous economist Lord Keynes, the normal backwardation hypothesis states that the current future price is a downward biased indicator of the future spot price. Consider the following paragraph:

'A wheat farmer doing plantation today does not know what wheat price will prevail at the time of harvest. However, he can lock-in a price by selling a future contract for delivery around harvest time at a rate determined today. If farmers are taking the short position (sell futures) to hedge, some group (speculators) must take the long position (buy futures). If the price at the time of harvest happens to be the same at which the futures contract was made, then the speculator has provided an assurance of the same price much in advance, without any compensation. To provide compensation for the risk assumed by the speculators, the spot price at the time of maturity of futures contract must be higher than the price of the futures contract. Therefore, the futures price must underestimate the future spot price'.

The premise of Keynes is based on the assumption that hedgers are net short and speculators are net long and if this is true, the backwardation hypothesis holds.

Contango

Contango assumes the opposite of the Keynes' hypothesis. If hedgers are net long and speculators are net short, then the future price must overestimate the spot price. This is known as *contango*. This can happen because it is assumed that speculators are better informed about the conditions and inefficiencies of the market and, therefore, they become enthusiastic about buying and pulling up the prices. Hence, the futures price is an overestimate of the expected spot price. Though lacking rationale, contango can result due to inefficient market conditions.

When the futures price is less than the expected future spot price, it is referred to as normal backwardation, while the situation when the futures price is more than the expected future spot price is referred to as contango. However, in common usage, contango and normal backwardation are used in the context of the current spot price, S_0. When the futures price exceeds the current spot price, it is called contango; when it is less than the current spot price, it is called backwardation. Figure 2.7 shows the futures price behaviour.

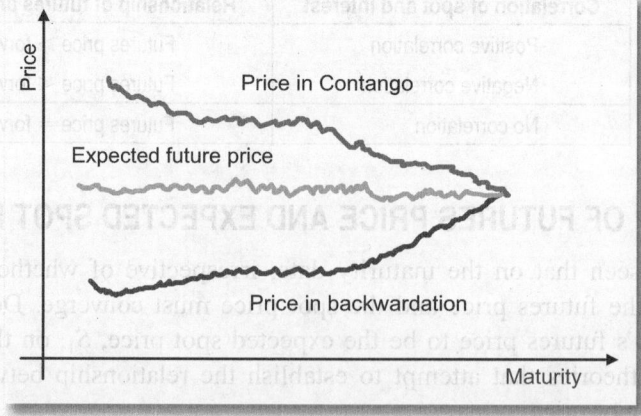

Fig. 2.7 Futures price behaviour

Expectation Hypothesis

Expectation hypothesis assumes that the futures price is an unbiased indicator of the expected spot price. This would be the case when markets are efficient and hedgers and speculators correctly read the minds of each other. One group cannot outsmart the other group. Under efficient market conditions, all the factors determining the futures price, such as the cost of storage, insurance, carrying costs, and convenience yield are well known. Since there is no element of surprise, the futures price must genuinely reflect the future spot price.

The normal backwardation hypothesis seems to be strong because irrespective of the level of efficiency of the market, hedgers must be willing to accept a lower than expected future spot price for their peace of mind. This is like paying insurance premium for a firm price in the future, even though it may be slightly lower than the price the hedgers could obtain if they were unhedged.

EXPECTANCY THEORY OF FUTURES PRICING

In case of consumption assets or non-carry type assets, the cost of carry model cannot work properly. According to the cost of carry model, the futures price must exceed the spot price by the cost of carry for the period remaining before maturity of the futures contract. This is referred to as *full cost of carry*. In case the futures contract is not at full cost of carry to the spot, then the process of arbitrage sets in. In some cases, we often find that the futures price is not only at full cost of carry but at a discount to the spot price or at a partial cost of carry.

Clearly, the process of arbitrage appears to be failing here. In such cases, either arbitrage cannot be executed or the gains are too little to offset the transaction and delivery costs. The expectancy theory of futures pricing states that the futures price is a reflection of the future spot price. It represents a view of what the spot price is likely to be at the maturity of the futures period, considering the demand and supply situation expected to prevail then. The expectancy model suggests that the relationship is between the futures price and the future spot price and not between the futures price and the current spot price. If that be the case, futures contracts would defy the basic definition of derivative.

However, we cannot ignore the fact that sometimes, even for the carry type of financial assets, we find futures at a discount to the spot price. The expectancy model relates to the expected direction of the price in the futures. If the futures trades lower than the spot, it suggests that the price is expected to be lower in future. It can be easily justified in case of agricultural commodities. For example, at the time of harvest, the supply of wheat would be large and while the current prices may be high, in the future wheat may be available at a much lower price. Naturally, the futures price in this case would be lower than the current spot price. For agricultural commodities, reverse cash-and-carry arbitrage is constrained as they have consumption value (convenience yield).

Types of Futures

Futures can be classified on the basis of the underlying asset. As stated earlier, there can be a host of assets on which a futures contract can be created. It is a matter of standardization of the contract. Broadly, futures fall into either of the two categories—commodity futures and financial futures.

> **Derivatives in Practice** Futures and Price Discovery
>
> **Futures trade points to stable prices**
>
> The futures price is expected to reflect the future spot price. After taking into account the large number of factors that govern price determination, the futures trade is expected to reflect the potential price in the spot market. It is the best estimate of the market. No amount of economic modelling perhaps can match and replace the collective wisdom of millions of traders speculating on the futures price of the underlying commodity.
>
> The price data in this table for September futures expiring 20 Sept 2011 reflect the possibility that in case of wheat, sugar, and soya oil, the prices are likely to decline in about 25 days' time. In case of the gram, the price is expected to go up in September. That seems alright. But what about prices in December? The market seems to ignore the fact that a fresh crop would be available between September and December. Higher price for December indicates a further rise in price. Is this pure speculation or a grim reminder to policy makers that despite a fresh crop hitting the market, the supply would be far less than the expected demand? Should the government be proactive in taking corrective measures right now to import gram or remain reactive, only to act when the prices actually increase (as the futures forewarned), much to the discomfort of the people?
>
> In the past, futures trading was blamed for rise in prices; this was considered a good enough reason to ban futures trades in several commodities, taking away the vital market information that such markets provide.
>
> *Source*: Based on *The Times of India*, 2 September 2011.
>
> | Commodity | Spot price on 24 August 2011 (₹) | Futures price | |
> |---|---|---|---|
> | | | September contract—20 September (₹) | December contract—20 December (₹) |
> | Gram | 3,150 | 3,256 | 3,480 |
> | Wheat | 1,173 | 1,137 | 1,192 |
> | Potato | 418 | NA | 588 |
> | Sugar | 2,750 | 2,711 | 2,811 |
> | Soya Oil | 667 | 661 | 637 |
>
> *Source*: NCDEX data as published in *The Times of India*, 2 September 2011.

Commodity Futures Commodity futures are those where the underlying asset is a commodity. Contracts are available in India on agricultural commodities such as wheat, rice, soya, coffee, sugar, tea, *jeera*, pepper, edible oils, cotton, and coconut. Contracts on metals (gold and silver) are also available. Futures contracts on copper, aluminium, etc., also fall under the commodity category.

> Futures are broadly of two types: commodity futures and financial futures, depending upon the underlying asset.

Financial Futures Financial futures are those futures where the underlying asset is a financial product. They can be further divided into four sub-categories:

- *Currency futures* have underlying assets as currencies. Futures contracts on various currencies are available in major centres such as Chicago, London, and Singapore. They are also available in India at several exchanges.
- *Stock futures* have stocks as underlying assets. Stock futures were introduced in 1982 by the Kansas City Board of Trade. Stock futures were introduced in India on 12 June 2000 for indices and on 9 November 2001 on select individual securities at NSE.
- *Interest rate futures* have interest rate as the underlying asset. In India, interest rate futures were launched on 24 June 2003 at NSE. This attempt was not successful, and they were relaunched on 31 August 2009 with modifications in the underlying assets and other contract features.

- *Index futures* are those futures where the underlying assets are stock indices, such as the BSE SENSEX or Nifty.

Another system of classification can be based on the deliverability of the underlying assets. Certain futures contracts are made on hypothetical assets, which do not exist in the physical form. Futures contracts on indices and freight are non-deliverable. Futures on foreign currencies are also non-deliverable in India due to the partial convertibility of the Indian Rupee.

Having discussed the common features of futures and forwards on all underlying assets, we shall discuss each type of forward and futures contracts in detail with respect to their applications in the subsequent chapters.

SOLVED PROBLEMS

SP 2.1 REVERSE CASH-AND-CARRY ARBITRAGE

The price of the Suzlon share at the NSE is ₹85 while a 3-m futures contract on Suzlon is being traded at ₹86. If one can borrow at 12%, and Suzlon is not paying any dividend in the next three months, is there an arbitrage opportunity available in the prices ruling in the spot market and futures market? If so, how can profit be made? Assume the size of the futures contract to be 1000 shares.

Solution
The cost of carry is 1% per month. For three months, the cost of carry is 3% of the spot price of ₹85.00. Accordingly, the 3-m forward price should be $1.03 \times 85 = ₹87.55$. The 3-m futures contract trading at ₹86 is clearly underpriced, and reverse cash-and-carry arbitrage can be executed as follows.

The investor can take the following actions simultaneously today at $t = 0$:
(a) Short 1000 shares of Suzlon at ₹85 and realize ₹85,000.
(b) Invest ₹85,000 for three months at 12%.
(c) Buy one futures contract at ₹86 with exposure of ₹86,000.

Three months later, the investor would obtain the underlying asset against the futures contract, i.e., shares of Suzlon to be delivered back to the lender of the shares, realize the lent amount with interest, aggregating to ₹87,550, and make good the payment liability of ₹86,000 towards the futures contract. The following cash flow would result after three months:

Realize cash from lending activity	+₹87,550
Pay against the futures contract	−₹86,000
Profit	₹1550

Since all the cash flows have no uncertainty about them at maturity, the profit of ₹1550 represents arbitrage profit obtained through reverse cash-and-carry.

SP 2.2 FUTURES ON A CONSUMPTION ASSET

A refinery uses crude oil as a major input. The current price of crude oil is ₹3000 per barrel. Futures contracts on crude oil for 100 barrels each are being traded at ₹3100 per barrel with three months to delivery. The cost of capital for the refinery is 12%, while for storage of the oil, it incurs an annual cost of 3%.

(a) Do you find the futures market and the spot market prices to be consistent so as to offer no arbitrage profit possibility?
(b) Is there any arbitrage opportunity? If yes, how can the arbitrage be executed?
(c) Up to what price is this arbitrage feasible?
(d) What might constrain the refinery from executing the arbitrage?
(e) How would you interpret the inability of the refinery to execute the arbitrage?

Assume annual compounding for your analysis.

Solution
(a) The cost of carry, including storage, is 15% p.a. For a 3-m futures contract, the price should be $3000 \times (1 + 0.15 \times 3/12) =$ ₹3112.50. The futures of crude oil is underpriced by ₹12.50 at ₹3100. Therefore, an arbitrage possibility by the reverse cash-and-carry process exists.

(b) The arbitrage can be executed by selling crude oil from stock, investing the proceeds, saving the storage costs, and simultaneously buying a 3-m futures contract. The stock of oil can be regained after three months on maturity of the futures contract, as shown here:

Reverse cash-and-carry arbitrage
The refinery could do the following now:

	₹
Sell 100 barrels of crude oil in the spot market (₹3000 × 100)	= 3,00,000
Invest proceeds for three months and save storage cost	= −3,00,000
Buy one 3-m futures contract at ₹3100	−

After three months

Pay for the futures and take delivery of 100 barrels of crude oil	= −3,10,000
Receive invested cash = ₹3,00,000 × 1.03	= +3,09,000
Save storage cost = ₹3,00,000 × 0.0075	= +2250
Saved amount	= 1250

(c) Saved amount per barrel   12.50
The upper bound on the futures price = 3100 + 12.50 = 3112.50

(d) The constraining factor for the refinery is the inability to execute reverse cash-and-carry arbitrage. It would have to go without the level of stock of crude oil required for production purposes. Selling crude oil implies closure of the refinery.

(e) If the refinery is unable to execute the arbitrage, this implies that it is in no position to sell the crude oil and be out of stock. The implied convenience yield for the refinery for holding oil in inventory can be taken as a minimum of ₹12.50 per barrel.

SP 2.3 PRICING FORWARD CONTRACT

The price of a Reliance share at the NSE is ₹1980. The risk-free borrowing rate in the market is 10% p.a.

(a) If a 6-m forward contract for delivery of 100 shares is available at ₹2100, can you take advantage of the situation?
(b) If a 6-m forward contract for delivery of 100 shares is available at ₹2000, can you take advantage of the situation?
(c) Assume that you have gone long on 6-m forward contract for Reliance at ₹2000. After three months, a 3-m contract is available at ₹2050. What is the value of the contract in hand?

Assume no dividend by Reliance in the next six months and annual compounding of interest.

Solution

(a) The cost of carry is 5% for a period of six months. Therefore, a forward contract for delivery after six months must be priced at 1.05 × ₹1980 = ₹2079. The forward contract at ₹2100 is overpriced by ₹21, and as such, a profit of ₹2100 can be made for 100 shares as follows:

	₹
Buy spot 100 shares at ₹1980	−1,98,000
Borrow at 10%	+1,98,000
Sell 100 shares forward at ₹2100	−
Net Investment	0
After six months	
Deliver 100 shares and receive forward price	+2,10,000
Pay borrowing with interest (₹1,98,000 × 1.05)	−2,07,900
Profit	2100

(b) If 6-m forward is ₹2000, the process can be reversed to make arbitrage gains. One can borrow 100 shares of Reliance and sell them at spot price to realize ₹1,98,000, invest the money at 10% for six months, and buy 100 shares six months' forward. At the end of six months, the amount received for the invested money would be ₹2,07,900 and the forward price payable would be ₹2,00,000, providing a gain of ₹7900.

c) The value of the forward buy contract after three months would be the present value of the difference between the price of the original buy contract, i.e., ₹2000 and the price prevailing, i.e., ₹2050. The value of the forward contract for 100 shares (assuming simple compounding) is

(₹2050 − ₹2000) × 100/1.025 = ₹4878

SUMMARY

Forwards and futures are two very similar derivative products that can exist on a variety of underlying assets. The underlying asset could be commodities, stocks, indices, currencies, interest rates, etc. Forward contracts are so pervasive that one does not realize that they are being entered into. They are part and parcel of our day-to-day life. In business situations, most forward contracts are executed in the foreign currency markets. The motive for entering into a forward contract is to remove price uncertainties.

Forward contracts are executed between at least two parties, directly negotiating the terms of the contract, including fixing price today. Settlement is done at a future date. The drawback of such a contract would be that the counterparties assume risk on each other, and consent of the other party would be necessary if one party wants to cancel the contract. The advantages of a forward contract include the ability to tailor it as per specific needs, with no upfront payment. Most forward contracts are settled by delivery, though one can enter an offsetting contract at any time prior to or on maturity.

Futures contracts are the same as forward contracts, but are exchange-traded. Due to the involvement of exchanges, (a) the product is standardized, (b) entry and exit are extremely convenient, and (c) counterparty risk is virtually eliminated. Elaborate specifications are required for futures contract to make them tradable on exchanges. Exchange authorities decide on these specifications. The settlement of futures contracts can be done in three ways: physical, offsetting, and close-out. Settlement is mostly done by entering into an offsetting contract, unlike forwards, where the popular mode is physical settlement. There are various types of settlement delivery options, decided by the exchange authorities. The problem of assignment refers to situations where a counterparty has to be found when either the buyer or the seller opts for physical settlement with no matching counterparty. One of the observed parameters of futures trading is open interest, which refers to the number of open contracts at any point of time.

From the perspective of cash flow, futures are different from forwards on two counts—margins and marking to market. Margins are required to be deposited with the exchange as guarantee of settlement. Marking to market implies that profit or loss on all open positions is settled on a daily basis.

The pricing principle for forwards and futures is the same. The cost of carry model is used to price a forward or a futures contract. It essentially uses arbitrage arguments to state that the fair price of a forward or a futures contract would be spot price plus cost of carry for the forward period. If futures are not fairly priced, cash-and-carry arbitrage or reverse cash-and-carry arbitrage would make the price fair. Cash-and-carry arbitrage can be executed with relative ease but it may be difficult to execute reverse cash-and-carry arbitrage, as it requires short selling of the asset. In case of assets that have convenience yield, such as commodities, reverse cash-and-carry arbitrage is not executable. This places an upper bound on the price of the futures contracts for assets that are of the non-carry type. For carry-type assets, arbitrage is executable either way.

One of the most important concepts in pricing of futures is the convergence of the futures price and the spot price at the maturity of the futures contract. The requirement of delivery would force the futures price to be the same as the spot price on maturity. Further, since the cost of carry is proportional to time to maturity, the gap between the spot price and the futures price must reduce. With no time to maturity, the cost of carry tends to be zero, and, hence, the futures price would be the same as the spot price on maturity.

There would be no difference in futures prices and forward prices if interest rates remain constant. Since there are intermittent cash flows in a futures position in the margin account, any surplus would be invested, and the shortfall would be borrowed. Hence, there would be a marginal difference between the prices of futures and forward contracts.

A futures price for an asset is assumed to be an unbiased indicator of the futures spot price for that asset. The normal backwardation hypothesis states that the futures price would be underestimating the future spot price so as to build the cost of hedging.

Futures can be broadly classified into two categories—commodity and financial. Financial futures can further be divided into four sub-categories—currency, stock interest rates, and index futures, each of which is discussed in the following chapters.

KEY TERMS

Backwardation A situation where the futures price is less than the expected future spot price. In common use, it refers to a situation where the futures price is less than the current spot price.

Cash-and-carry arbitrage A risk-free profit-making situation where one could buy an asset by borrowing and then selling a future contract.

Commodity futures Futures that have commodities as underlying assets.

Contango A situation where the futures price is more than the expected future spot price. In common use, it refers to a situation where the futures price is more than the current spot price.

Convergence Convergence refers to the fact that on the day of maturity of the futures contract, its price must converge with the spot price.

Cost of carry The cost that one would incur if a physical asset is possessed and carried for a period of time, i.e., till the time of maturity of the futures/forward contract.

Counterparty risk The risk for one party to a contract that the other party would not perform its commitments on the due date of the forward contract.

Financial futures Futures that have financial assets as underlying assets.

Forward contract An agreement to buy or sell an asset at a price determined today, though the contract is settled later at a predetermined date.

Futures contract A forward contract that is traded on an exchange.

Margin The amount of money required to be deposited with the exchange for taking a long, short, or combination of futures contracts for covering potential loss.

Margin call The replenishment of margins in case of mark-to-market losses exceeding the prescribed minimum level of margin.

Mark to market The daily settlement of profit or loss incurred on the position of derivatives, as if the position in derivatives is closed out.

Open interest The number of futures contracts still outstanding, awaiting settlement either by delivery or by an offsetting contract.

Over-the-counter A direct contract between two parties, addressing their specific needs and getting settled between them at maturity.

Reverse cash-and-carry arbitrage A risk-free profit-making situation where one could sell an asset and lend the proceeds, and then buy a future contract.

Settlement It is the fulfilment of obligations under a forward contract (derivative) of delivery of the asset and cash consideration (or cash differential), or extinguishing of the claims of the counterparties on the agreed date.

Tick size The minimum change in the price that would be recognized in the price quotation of the futures contract.

Underlying asset The asset on which the price of the derivative (forward or futures) is based.

QUESTIONS

2.1 What do you understand by a forward contract? Illustrate with an example.
2.2 What are the merits and demerits of forward contracts?
2.3 How are forward contracts settled? Illustrate.
2.4 What are the advantages of futures contracts over forward contracts?
2.5 What are possible modes of settlement of futures contracts?
2.6 What are the key specification parameters of a futures contract?
2.7 What is the difference between open interest and volume?
2.8 Describe marking to market using a suitable example.
2.9 Explain cash-and-carry and reverse cash-and-carry arbitrage.
2.10 How would you value a forward contract once it is entered?
2.11 What is convergence?
2.12 Explain backwardation and contango.

PROBLEMS

P 2.1 Understanding a forward contract
A conductor manufacturing company has entered into a forward contract to buy 2000 kg of aluminium after six months at ₹100 per kg. What is the gain/loss for the manufacturing company if at the end of six months the price of aluminium turns out to be (a) ₹105 per kg and (b) ₹98 per kg?

P 2.2 Pricing a forward contract
Assume that the current spot price of aluminium is ₹94 per kg. What should be the price of a 6-m forward contract on aluminium if risk-free interest rate in the market is 12% p.a., with quarterly compounding, and cost of insurance is 4% p.a., with annual compounding?

P 2.3 Cash-and-carry arbitrage with futures
Refer to Problem 2.2. Assume that a futures contract on aluminium is selling for ₹103.20. How can you take advantage of the situation in the futures market scenario?

P 2.4 Reverse cash-and-carry arbitrage with futures
A stockbroker is holding 1000 shares of Reliance Industries Ltd, each selling currently at ₹1800. A futures contract expiring in one month is trading at ₹1808. Each futures contract is for 100 shares. If the stockbroker can borrow/invest at 12% p.a., can he or she take advantage of the situation? Assume annual compounding of interest rates.

Commodity Futures

INTRODUCTION

Commodity futures are standardized contracts to buy or sell a commodity at a specified price at a predetermined date in the future. Commodity futures derive their value from the spot price of the commodity that is the underlying asset. There are a large number of commodities on which futures contracts are available. Underlying assets for futures contracts can range from agricultural/cereal products (wheat, rice, sugar, etc.) to metals (gold, silver, etc.) to plantation products (rubber, coffee, etc.) to energy products (oil, furnace oil, etc.).

Trading in forwards and futures on commodities is not new. It has been in vogue for more than 100 years. Trading in agricultural commodities started at the Chicago Board of Trade in 1865. During the late 1800s, the Buenos Aires exchange-traded futures in grain. The Bombay Cotton Exchange came into existence as early as 1921.

> Commodity futures have commodities as underlying assets.

With increased globalization and removal of international trade barriers, futures markets on commodities have gained prominence as tools of risk management. The cost of managing the risk and volatility in the prices of commodities, when controlled by a government using subsidies, is normally borne by the public in the form of increased taxation. Market-based activity on futures exchanges induces willingness in participants to perform the role of price discovery, relieving the government of this onus.

Futures on given commodities help mitigate price risks on those commodities. Futures exchanges facilitate easy entry and exit into and from futures contracts at all points of time, providing an opportunity to maximize benefits such as efficient price discovery and faster dissemination of relevant information.

Functioning of futures exchange is governed by the rules framed by the exchange, and supervised by national regulator.

Learning Objectives

After going through this chapter, readers should be familiar with

- commodity futures and their relevance for the economy
- differences between commodity and financial futures
- pricing of commodity futures
- using commodity futures for hedging
  - a long position against fall in commodity prices and
  - a short position against rise in commodity prices
- basis and basis risk
- perfect and imperfect hedge
- cross-hedge and hedge ratio
- how to speculate and arbitrage with commodity futures
- hedging for gross profit margin using futures
- hedging for quantity variations

The functioning of commodity exchanges in India is regulated by the Forward Markets Commission.

BENEFITS OF COMMODITY FUTURES

Commodities offer great utility value to the society; the government always endeavours to provide commodities at reasonable prices. The usual tools for assuring supplies, such as adequate buffer stocks, controlled and phased release of commodities, and minimum support prices have either failed or proved too expensive for the economy to control volatility in commodity prices. No method can replace the market-based control mechanism of price negotiation. Stability in commodity prices can be achieved by futures and forward trading in commodities, in such a way that the market bears the cost, reducing the burden on the public exchequer.

There has been considerable debate on the need for futures contracts on commodities. Futures contracts on commodities of basic nature are often considered as unwarranted and a disservice to the nation, due to their speculative potential. However, some important benefits of futures on commodities, which may help dispel these notions, are discussed here under broad heads of price and volatility, market structure, and national economy.

On Price and Volatility

Price Discovery The availability of various futures contracts enables farmers, industries, and all other users of these commodities to hedge against price risk as well as to help discover the right price by providing increased transparency. This facilitates managerial decision making for scheduling production, adequate inventory, and marketing.

Seasonal Volatility Uneven supply of commodities coinciding with even consumption results in demand–supply mismatch, thereby necessitating storage of commodities. It is believed that with efficient futures markets, the risk premium associated with storage costs tends to reduce. A futures market would help reduce seasonal volatility in the prices of commodities. Speculators would be ready to take positions in volatile markets and even out seasonal variations to a great extent. In the absence of a futures market, hoarders would have an increased and arbitrary premium on the storage function due to financial muscle power. Excessive control over the supply chain can be damaging. Commodity futures help prevent monopolistic control over supply chains.

> Commodity futures result in price discovery, reduced seasonal variations, efficient dissemination of information, reduced cost of credit, and more efficient physical markets.

On Market Structure

Faster Dissemination of Information Further, an efficient futures market helps faster disseminate information to the public. Increased participation makes pricing information available on a continuous basis to a wider geographical area. In the absence of futures markets on commodities, producers and farmers, who remain geographically apart, would have little information. A futures market creates greater awareness and helps informed decision making due to the ready availability of prices on the exchanges as futures prices are available in public domain on continuous basis.

Derivatives in Practice

Rubber Futures

Price discovery, seasonal variations, and futures

In January 2005, after two years of trading in rubber futures, the volumes of trading in three commodity exchanges that trade in rubber futures started falling. Experts were of the opinion that this is a normal trend when prices in the spot market stabilize. Daily volumes in the first fortnight of January 2005 never crossed the 1500 tonne mark in any of the three exchanges. During the period 1–15 January 2005, the largest volume on a particular day at the National Multi-commodity Exchange (NMCE) was 1327 tonnes, while at Multi-commodity Exchange (MCX) and National Commodity and Derivatives Exchange (NCDEX), it was 645 tonnes and 702 tonnes, respectively. The daily volume during this period was in the range of 600–1000 tonnes at NMCE. As against this, the daily volume averaged about 2000 tonnes in March 2004.

The reason attributed to the declining interest in futures is the stability of rubber prices in the spot markets. Since the introduction of futures, the tendency of rubber prices to fluctuate wildly came down, dampening the enthusiasm of speculators. Speculators moved to other commodities where the price volatility is high. Natural rubber prices had skyrocketed during June–July 2004, boosting the interest of speculators in the futures markets. Subsequently, prices fell, and stabilized at around ₹52 per kg. The volatility in January was 2005 confined to ₹2 per kg, leaving no room for speculation in futures. In case the volatility increases, activity in the futures market should pick up.

Even though the volumes thinned in rubber futures, the participation of retail traders increased, as evidenced by the fact that delivery-based transactions were around 7–8%, as against the global average of 0.5%.

Source: Based on an article by Mr Vipin V. Nair in Business Line, 20 January 2005.

More Efficient Physical Markets Futures markets should have a positive impact on the functioning of physical markets and make them more efficient—a desirable characteristic for a growing and maturing economy. Continuous quotations of prices at various centres would make the prices converge in different locations in the physical markets. They can only differ in terms of delivery costs. The prerequisite of delivery in futures contracts has improved warehousing facilities in India without the involvement of public funds.

Abhijit Sen's Committee Report of 2008[1], in examining the impact of futures trading on the prices of agricultural products, has specified the following conditions for efficient and effective functioning of the futures markets.

- *Vibrant spot market* The commodity should have suitable demand and supply conditions, i.e., volume and marketable surplus should be large.
- *Volatility in prices* Prices should be volatile to necessitate hedging through futures trading. Entities with a spot market commitment face price risks. As a result, there would be a demand for hedging facilities.
- *Absence of regulation* The commodity should be free from substantial control arising from government (or other authority) regulations that impose restrictions on supply, distribution, and prices of the commodity.
- *Homogeneity* The commodity should be homogenous or, alternately, it must be possible to specify a standard grade and to measure deviations from that grade. This condition is necessary for futures exchanges to deal in standardized contracts.
- *Storability* The commodity should be storable. In the absence of this condition, arbitrage would not be possible, and there would be no relationship between spot and futures markets.

---

[1] Report of the expert committee to study the impact of futures trading on agricultural commodity prices, Ministry of Consumer Affairs, Food and Public Distribution, Government of India, 2008.

There is a school of thought that holds that trading in futures in essential commodities encourages speculation. Here, it is pertinent to mention that without speculators, there would be no one to assume the risk from those who want to eliminate it. The presence of speculators should be seen as a necessity rather than as an evil, as without them, the market would be extremely shallow and the process of price discovery would be severely constrained. However, due to the sensitivity of the general population towards the prices of essential commodities, the commodity futures markets should be more regulated than derivatives markets for financial instruments.

On National Economy

Commodity futures trading in a developing country can contribute a lot to the stability of fiscal management, increasing the effectiveness of price protection at a national level, and improving the efficiency of social programmes and pricing of credit.

Stability to Government's Revenue At a macro level, in the case of developing economies such as India, commodity futures offer great potential to cover price risks. Many developing countries in Africa, Asia, and Latin America depend heavily on exports of commodities. Government budgets, developmental expenditure, and balance of payment positions crucially depend upon prices of commodities. Volatility in commodity prices causes volatility in budgetary provisions and government's developmental expenditure. Therefore, at a macro level, volatility in commodity prices needs to be reduced. Containing the volatility of commodity prices should thereby contain the volatility of the fiscal imbalances.

> Commodity futures trading helps smooth out the variability in government revenue, transfers, and price risk management from the government to private participants.

Due to government ownership of natural resources like oil, the revenues of governments in developing nations are highly dependent upon the prices of these commodities, especially oil. For instance, in Mexico, oil contributed to 10% of exports, but constituted 40% of government revenue[2] in 1998. A fall of $1 per barrel would have caused a reduction in government revenue of $800 million. Targeting a price of $21 per barrel, the market saw a price decline of $4.40 per barrel, adversely affecting the expenditure programme. Commodity futures and derivatives provide great opportunities for developing nations to make the government revenue stable and bring about smooth development as government would be able to hedge through commodity futures market.

Eliminating Minimum Price Support and Subsidies A common policy in developing nations is to provide assurance of prices of sensitive commodities to farmers; the underprivileged. By implementing a minimum support price (MSP), governments try to stabilize prices by making the MSP a floor price. Another mechanism to protect the prices of commodities is by resorting to various types of subsidies. The MSP and subsidies are a topic of hot debate because they are politically motivated but economically imprudent, and thus these programmes cause a heavy drain on government resources and place the burden on the public, willing or unwilling. These programmes are supported by direct and indirect taxes imposed by the government. Such MSP programmes not only encourage inefficiency in the form of

---

[2]*Commodity Risk Management and Development,* Donald F. Larson, Panos Varangis, Nanae Yabuki: Paper for roundtable discussion on New Approaches to Commodity Price Risk Management in Developing Countries, Washington DC, 28 April 1998.

low yields, but also burden the users of these products. The MSP of sugarcane, where sugar producers and consumers directly bear the cost of the minimum price of sugarcane offered to farmers is one illustration. Similarly, minimum procurement price programmes in many commodities, aimed at helping a select category of people, create a burden on taxpayers.

Without doubting the noble intentions of governments to provide support to a section of the society, there is the additional aspect of inefficiency in the administration of such programmes. These inefficiencies limit the quantum of benefits actually reaching the segments of societies at whom such programmes are aimed. Trading in commodity futures would help remove or reduce subsidies, and also dismantle inefficient administration, saving funds for implementing newer developmental plans.

With commodity derivatives, price risk can easily be managed through market-determined forces, with risk mitigation provided by those willing to assume risk. Due to commodity futures, price risk can be managed without government intervention. There is no need for a government to provide price protection when people in the market are willing to absorb such risks. Healthy and competitive commodity exchanges, therefore, serve the economy better, and help reduce taxes. In fact, futures in commodities are highly efficient mechanisms for providing the much-needed price protection and shift responsibility from the state to private parties.

Reducing Cost of Credit Since commodity futures make hedging possible, they also serve the extremely useful purpose of making credit available at a lower cost. Because of the relative certainty of the price of the commodity, financial institutions and banks can confidently offer loan on reasonable interest rates to farmers and producers. This enables even credit flow across the various sectors of the economy. In this sense, a futures market reduces the need for selective credit control on the part of regulatory bodies. A futures market must also help in preventing misuse of credit for purposes of hoarding.

COMMODITY FUTURES AND FINANCIAL FUTURES

Apart from the difference in the underlying assets, financial futures and commodity futures are substantially different from each other in the following respects:

> Commodities futures differ significantly from financial futures in terms of quality specifications and delivery mechanisms.

Valuation Financial futures are easier to understand as the *cost of carry model* applies for their valuation. The argument of arbitrage also holds because of the absence of convenience yield in financial futures. Financial futures involve financial instruments that have an investment value but no consumption value. Consumption value makes the valuation of futures contracts on commodities difficult. Due to the non-feasibility of reverse cash-and-carry arbitrage, the lower bound of the futures price would be hazy.

Delivery and Settlement The provisions of delivery are equally applicable to both commodity futures and financial futures. In case of financial futures, delivery of the underlying assets is prompt and hassle-free, and so is the settlement. Further, there are very nominal costs of transportation, storage, or insurance, etc., involved in financial futures. For futures on financial assets, price adjustment on account of discrepancy in quality between what was contracted and what is being delivered is not required. The quality of the underlying asset is immaterial in the case of financial products, whereas there is ample scope for controversy over quality in the case of commodity futures. In the case of futures on indices or intangibles, the underlying asset is non-deliverable, and futures contracts on them are necessarily settled in cash.

Contract Features and Life Commodity futures are governed by seasons and the possible perishable nature of the underlying assets. Delivery is linked to availability and therefore contract specifications have to consider the physical characteristics of the underlying asset. The maturity period for futures contracts on commodities normally does not exceed 90 days, while there is no such limitation on financial futures. Financial futures can have a much longer life, though generally the maturity of many financial futures is kept at 90 days.

Supply and Consumption Patterns In the case of financial products such as stocks, indices, and foreign exchange, supply can be considered as unlimited and independent of weather and seasons. It also does not suffer from the vagaries of nature. The supply of commodities depends upon factors over which people have no control. The total supply is dependent upon weather, storage capacity, shelf life, etc. Further, the supply of most commodities (agricultural products) is confined to the harvesting period, while consumption is uniform throughout the year. Deterioration in the value of commodities with time is another phenomenon that does not affect futures on financial products.

Quality Constraints Futures contracts on commodities have some features similar to those of any other futures contracts on financial assets. A contract on gold is presented in Table 2.1 in Chapter 2. Significant differences arise in commodity futures in two areas, i.e., (a) the extremely elaborate descriptions of the quality attributes of the commodity and (b) the procedure for settlement by delivery, deliverable quality, place of delivery, etc. Such complexities do not arise in the case of futures contracts on financial assets.

Futures contracts on commodities have specific quality requirements. The price may need to be adjusted to account for any difference in the quality specified in the contract and the quality delivered. For example, there is a significant difference in the prices of basmati rice and ordinary rice. What is deliverable against a futures contract needs to be specified.

Delivery Notice Period Besides, the exchange also has to provide for a reasonable time for both the buyer and the seller to arrange for giving/taking delivery of the underlying asset. Usually, futures contracts on commodities provide for a delivery notice period, when the parties are required to disclose the intentions of settlement by delivery.

Modes of Settlement and Assignment Futures contracts on commodities can be settled in any of the three ways described in Chapter 2, i.e., by physical delivery, cash settlement, or closing out. Settlement by closing out or by cash has the same form in commodities as is in financial assets. However, unlike futures contracts on financial assets, the settlement of futures contracts on commodities by delivery requires special treatment. Settlement of commodity futures by delivery is cumbersome. Financial assets are either non-deliverable (such as an index) or do not have very elaborate quality/time limitations.

In the case of settlement by delivery, the exchange has to provide for ascertainment of the quality and price adjustment, location of the delivery, adjustment of taxes and freight, the option for the delivery logic (seller/buyer/both), and assignment. All these issues are dealt with extensively in the specifications of futures contracts. This makes the task of designing futures contracts on commodities more onerous and complex.

> The pricing of commodity futures cannot use the 'no arbitrage' argument" due to the convenience yield attached with commodities.

Assignment refers to the matching of short and long positions. For example, if the delivery is at the option of the seller, the exchange has to find a willing buyer and devise rules for assigning the delivery to a specific buyer. If the delivery logic is compulsory (all open positions at the expiry of futures contracts are to be settled by delivery), the problem of assignment does not arise, as there is a matching long position for each short position.

PRICING COMMODITY FUTURES

We discussed pricing of forwards and futures in Chapter 2 using the argument of arbitrage with the cost of carry model. It must be reiterated here that we can categorize commodities as investment commodities or consumption commodities. It is hard to find a commodity that has only investment value and not consumption value; but commodities such as gold and silver are regarded more as investment assets rather than as consumption assets.

From the perspective of pricing, it is essential to have such categorization because consumption assets have a consumption value called *convenience yield*. People hold such assets to satisfy consumption needs. Wheat, rice, pulses, and edible oils are consumed by one and all. Similarly, crude oil, tin, copper, jute, etc., form raw material for many manufacturing concerns. Therefore, the motive of holding or trading in such assets is essentially attributable to the consumption value, rather than to the possibility of obtaining returns by trading in them.

Under the cost of carry model, the futures price is given by the spot price plus the cost of carry till the expiry of the futures contract. This price would satisfy the 'no arbitrage' condition for cash-and-carry as well as reverse cash-and-carry arbitrage. This should apply to investment assets. For discrete (compounding n-times per year) and continuous compounding, the fair price of futures is given by Eqs 3.1 and 3.2, respectively.

> If the upper bound is violated, then cash-and-carry arbitrage can be executed to correct the futures price.

$$F_1 = S_0 \times (1 + r/n)^{nt} \tag{3.1}$$

$$F_1 = S_0 \times e^{rt} \tag{3.2}$$

For cash-and-carry arbitrage, the following must hold good:

$$F \geq (S_0 + s)e^{rt} \tag{3.3}$$

For no cash-and-carry arbitrage, we must have

$$F \leq (S_0 + s)e^{rt} \tag{3.4}$$

where S is storage cost.

EXAMPLE 3.1 Pricing futures on investment asset

Assume that the spot price of gold is ₹14,000 per *tola* (1 *tola* = 10 g). If the financing cost is 12% p.a. with continuous compounding, warehousing and insurance costs with continuous compounding are placed at 3%. What would be the value of 2-m futures contract on gold with and without warehousing and insurance cost?

Solution
The fair value of a futures contract with financing cost only is given by Eq. 3.2.

$$F_1 = S_0 \times e^{rt} = 14{,}000 \times e^{0.12 \times 2/12} = ₹14{,}282.82 \text{ per 10 g}$$

Warehousing and insurance cost would be added to the financing cost for determining the fair value of the futures, as given by Eq. 3.6.

$$F_1 = S_0 \times e^{rt} = 14{,}000 \times e^{0.15 \times 2/12} = ₹14{,}354.41 \text{ per 10 g}$$

Due to the consumption value of the asset, reverse cash-and-carry arbitrage (implying short sale of the asset and buying futures) may not be executable. Since futures contracts cannot substitute the consumption value of the commodity, the contract can remain underpriced. Therefore, we only have an upper bound to the futures price, as specified in Eq. 3.4.

In case storage cost and benefits are associated with possession of the commodity, with s and D being present values, respectively, the futures price is

$$F = (S_0 - D + s) \times e^{rt} \quad (3.5)$$

> Since reverse cash-and-carry arbitrage is not executable in case of commodity futures due to convenience yield, futures can remain underpriced.

If both storage and benefits are continuous, the fair price of the futures would be

$$F = S_0 \times e^{(r - D + s)t} \quad (3.6)$$

EXAMPLE 3.2 Pricing futures on consumption asset

Assume that the spot price of cardamom is ₹714 per kg. If the financing cost is 10% p.a., with continuous compounding, what should be the price of a 3-m futures contract on cardamom? If warehousing and insurance costs are placed at 1%, what would be the fair value of the 3-m futures contract inclusive of warehousing and insurance cost?

Solution
Only an upper bound is given to the fair value of a futures contract, as per Eq. 3.4 with $S = 0$.

$$F_1 \leq S_0 \times e^{rt} \leq 714 \times e^{0.10 \times 3/12} \leq ₹732.07 \text{ per kg}$$

Warehousing and insurance cost would be added to the financing cost for determining the upper bound of the fair value of the futures, as given by Eq. 3.4 with $S > 0$.

$$F_1 \leq S_0 \times e^{rt} \leq 714 \times e^{0.11 \times 3/12} \leq ₹733.91 \text{ per kg}$$

HEDGING WITH COMMODITY FUTURES

> Like all futures, commodity futures too have three major applications: hedging, speculation, and arbitrage.

Hedging strategies with futures revolve around compensating anticipated losses in the spot market with equivalent gains in the futures market. This is done by taking a position on the futures market that is opposite of the position in the spot market.

Long and Short Positions

When a party holds the underlying asset, it is said to be long on the spot market. For example, a jeweller holding gold or silver is long on the underlying asset. A wheat farmer is long on wheat when he sows the crop. A long position gains with price rise and loses with price fall.

Similarly, a party that requires the underlying asset in the future is said to be short on the underlying asset. For example, a tea exporter who needs a stock of tea to execute a pending order is short on tea, the underlying commodity/asset. A wheat flour mill needing wheat in the future is short on wheat. A short position gains with a fall in price and loses with a rise in price.

Similarly, in the futures market, one who buys a futures contract is said to be long, and one who sells a futures contract is said to be short on futures. Here, too, the long position would gain while the short position would lose with a rise in price.

To execute a hedge, the following steps are taken:

- One who is long on the underlying asset, goes short on the futures market, and one who is short on the underlying asset, goes long in the futures market.

- At an appropriate time, one can neutralize the position in the futures market, i.e., go long on futures if one was originally short and go short on futures if one was originally long, and receive/pay the difference in prices of futures.
- One can access the physical market for meeting the needs of the underlying asset.

Short Hedge

A short hedge means a short position in futures. It is used by those who are long on the underlying asset that faces the risk of a fall in price. To hedge the long position on an asset, it is necessary to take a short position in the futures market. When one takes a short position in futures, the hedge is referred to as a *short hedge*.

Consider, for example, a sugar mill in Uttar Pradesh. It is expected to produce 100 MT of sugar in the month of April. The price in the month of February is ₹22 per kg. An April futures contract in sugar, due on 20th April, is trading at ₹25 per kg. The sugar mill apprehends that a price less than ₹25 per kg will prevail in April due to excessive supply. How can the sugar mill hedge its position against the anticipated decline in sugar prices in April?

To execute the hedging strategy, the sugar mill has to take a position in futures opposite to that of physical position in spot. The sugar mill is long on sugar because it gains with price rise. Therefore, it needs to sell the futures contract today. The number of contracts that needs to be sold is dependent upon the extent of exposure in the physical asset and the value to be covered. Assuming that a 100% cover is desired, we can find the number of contracts to be sold.

> When one takes a short position in futures hedges, it is referred to as a short hedge.

Assuming each contract for sugar is for 10 MT, the number of futures contracts to be sold is 10 for a physical position of 100 MT.

Number of contracts to be sold
= Quantity to be hedged/quantity in each futures contract
= 100 MT/10 MT = 10

The sugar mill goes short on futures in February. Prior to April, before the future contract expires, the sugar mill buys the futures contract to nullify its position in the futures market. The underlying asset, i.e., sugar, is sold in the spot market. The price realized by the sugar mill in two different scenarios—decline or rise in sugar prices—using the principle of convergence of price on the due date of the contract, is worked out as follows:

When the price falls to ₹22 per kg			When the price rises to ₹26 per kg	
Situation A			Situation B	
In the futures market			In the futures market	
	Cash flow, ₹/kg			Cash flow, ₹/kg
Sold futures contract in February	+25.00		Sold futures contract in February	+25.00
Bought futures contract in April	−22.00		Bought futures contract in April	−26.00
Gain in the futures market	+3.00		Gain in the futures market	−1.00
Price realized in the spot market	+22.00		Price realized in the spot market	+26.00
Effective price realized	₹25.00 per kg		Effective price realized	₹25.00 per kg
Here, the loss of ₹3 (₹25−₹22) in the spot market is made up by an equal gain in the futures market.			Here, the gain of ₹1 (₹26−₹25) in the spot market is offset by the equal loss in the futures market.	

The fact that the prices of sugar in the spot market and futures market must converge, a fixed price of ₹25 per kg is realized by the sugar mill. The loss/gain in the spot market is fully compensated by a gain/loss in the futures market.

Long Hedge

A long hedge implies taking a long position in futures. It is used by those who are short on the asset and need protection against a rise in price.

For example, consider a petrochemical plant that needs to process 10,000 barrels of oil in three months' time. To hedge against the possibility of a price rise, the plant needs to go long on a futures contract for crude oil. The spot price of crude oil is ₹1950 per barrel, while a futures contract expiring three months from now is selling for ₹2200 per barrel. By going long on the futures, the petrochemical plant can lock-in procurement at ₹2200 per barrel. Assuming a size

---

EXAMPLE 3.3 Long hedge

Today is 24 March. A refinery needs 1075 barrels of crude oil in the month of September. The current price of crude oil is ₹3000 per barrel. September futures contracts at MCX are trading at ₹3200. The firm expects the price to go up further, and even beyond ₹3200 in September. It has the option of buying the stock now. Alternatively, it can hedge through a futures contract. The size of futures contract is 100 barrels.

(a) If the cost of capital, insurance, and storage is 15% p.a., examine whether it is beneficial for the firm to buy now.
(b) Instead, if the upper limit to buying price is ₹3200, what strategy can the firm adopt?
(c) If the firm decides to hedge through futures, find out the effective price it would pay for crude oil if at the time of lifting the hedge the spot and futures prices are (i) ₹2900 and ₹2910, respectively, (ii) ₹3300 and ₹3315, respectively.

Solution

(a) If the cost of carry (including interest, insurance, and storage) is 15%, the fair price of the futures contract is
$S_0 e^{rt} = 3000 \, e^{6/12 \times 0.15} = ₹3233.65$. It implies that if the firm buys crude oil today to be used after six months, it would effectively cost ₹3233.65 per barrel.
(b) Since futures are trading at ₹3200, it can lock-in the price of around ₹3200 through a long hedge. Under a long hedge, the firm would buy the futures on crude oil today and sell it six months later, while simultaneously meeting the physical requirements from the market at the price prevailing at that time. Irrespective of the price six months later, the firm would end up paying a price of around ₹3200.
(c) If the firm adopts the strategy mentioned in (b), the effective price to be paid by the firm in the two cases of rise and fall in spot values is calculated as follows:

Quantity of crude oil to be hedged	= 1,075 barrels	
Size of one futures contract	= 100 barrels	
Number of futures contracts bought = 1,075/100	= 11 contracts	
Futures price	= ₹3,200	
Value of futures bought = 3,200 × 11 × 100	= ₹35,20,000	

Six months later, the firm would unwind its futures position and buy its requirement from the spot market.

	₹	₹
Futures sold at price	2,910	3,315
Value of futures sold	32,01,000	36,46,500
Gain/Loss on futures	−3,19,000	1,26,500
Spot price	2,900	3,300
Actual cost of buying 1,075 barrels	31,17,500	35,47,500
Effective cost of buying	34,36,500	34,21,000
Effective price	3,197	3,182

> Being short on the asset means that one needs to take a long position in futures to hedge. This is referred to as a long hedge.

of 100 barrels for a futures contract, the firm buys 100 futures to cover its exposure of 10,000 barrels.

Let us examine the price that would be payable under two scenarios—rise in price to ₹2400 or fall in price to ₹1800 per barrel after three months.

(Figures in ₹/barrel)

	Situation	
	Price fall	Price rise
Price after three months	1,800	2,400
Actual purchase price	1,800	2,400
Gain/loss on futures		
Bought futures at	2,200	2,200
Sold futures at	1,800	2,400
Profit/loss on futures	−400	+200
Effective price	2,200	2,200

Here again, we observe that the loss in the physical position is offset by the gain in the futures position, and vice versa. This results in an effective price that is equal to the price of the futures at the time of setting up the hedge.

The strategies of short hedge and long hedge are depicted in Fig. 3.1. By adopting a short or long hedge, the price locked in would be equal to the futures price of the initial contract, and is shown in Fig. 3.2.

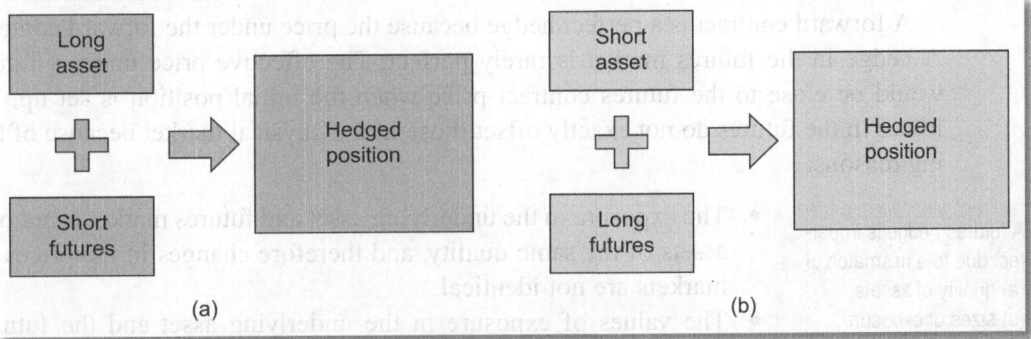

Fig. 3.1 Hedging with futures (a) short hedge (b) long hedge

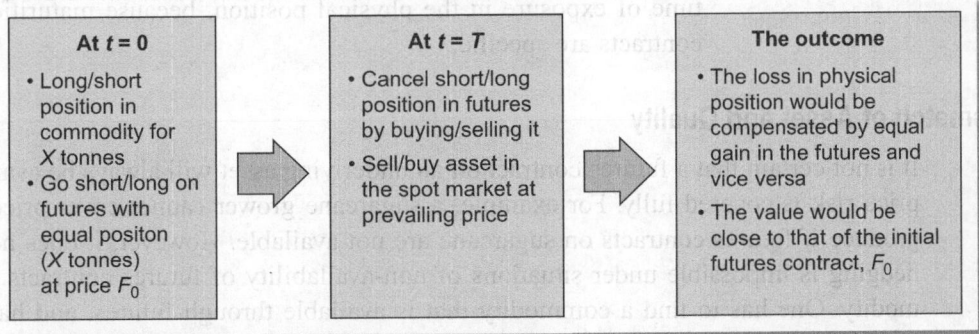

Fig. 3.2 Hedging with futures: process and outcome

PERFECT AND IMPERFECT HEDGE

In the earlier examples of short and long hedges by a sugar mill and a petrochemical plant, respectively, the hedging strategy of the sugar mill resulted in an exact offsetting of gains and losses in the futures and the physical market. Such a hedge is called a *perfect hedge*. In a hedge, the positions in the physical market and the futures market are opposite, and therefore the gains or losses with changing prices would also be opposite. The hedge where a loss in the physical market is exactly offset by a gain in the position in the futures market (or vice versa) is known as a perfect hedge, as depicted in Fig. 3.3.

> A forward contract offers a perfect hedge, whereas a futures contract is rarely a perfect hedge.

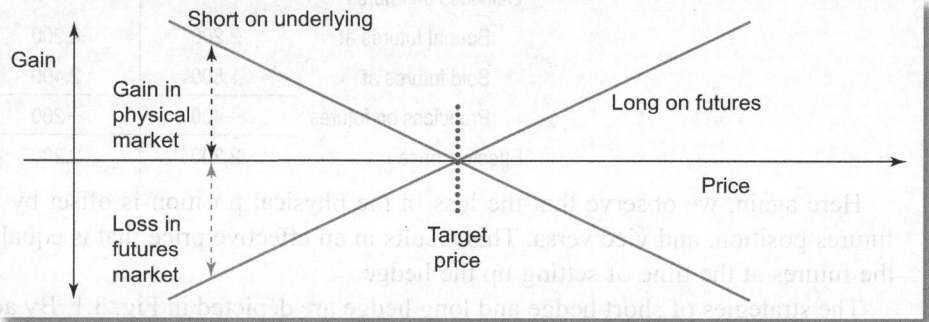

Fig. 3.3 Perfect hedge

A forward contract is a perfect hedge because the price under the forward contract is firm. A hedge in the futures market is rarely perfect. The effective price under a futures hedge would be close to the futures contract price when the initial position is set up. The gains/losses in the futures do not exactly offset those in the physical market because of the following reasons:

> A futures hedge is imperfect due to a mismatch of (a) quality of assets, (b) sizes of exposure, and (c) maturities of exposure in the physical and futures positions.

- The exposure in the underlying asset and futures market is not on identical assets of the same quality, and therefore changes in the prices in the two markets are not identical,
- The values of exposure in the underlying asset and the futures do not match exactly, because the size of the futures contract is standardized.
- The time of maturity of the futures contract may not coincide with the time of exposure in the physical position, because maturities of futures contracts are specific.

Mismatch of Asset and Quality

It is not certain that a futures contract on an underlying asset will always be available so that price risk is covered fully. For example, a sugarcane grower cannot cover price risk on his produce if futures contracts on sugarcane are not available. However, it does not mean that hedging is impossible under situations of non-availability of futures contracts on the commodity. One has to find a commodity that is available through futures, and has a positive/negative correlation with the prices of the commodity to be hedged. The effectiveness of the hedge will depend upon the degree of correlation in the prices of the commodity and the futures contracts. If the correlation between the two commodities is perfect, the hedge could be as effective as the one carried with a futures contract on the same underlying asset.

In the case of the sugarcane grower, a hedge is possible through futures contracts available on sugar, as prices of sugarcane and sugar go hand-in-hand. A hedge executed through a futures contract on an asset different from, but related to, the underlying asset is referred to as a *cross hedge*.

The mismatch in the assets scenario also covers variances in the quality of a commodity. Different qualities of sugar are sold at different prices, and futures contracts on all these qualities may not be available. However, an effective hedge can still be set up as long as there is a correlation of prices and there is nothing else to worry about.

Mismatch of Quantities

Another reason for deviations from a perfect hedge is the inability to cover the exact quantity of the asset in the hedge with futures contracts as they are standardized in terms of quantity. For example, one standard contract of sugar futures is of 10 MT. A quantity that is not a multiple of 10 MT cannot be hedged exactly. If a sugar mill wanted to hedge 95 MT, it would have a choice of booking either 9 (90 MT) or 10 (100 MT) contracts for hedging. It would either be under-hedged or over-hedged. Even if the price changes are identical, the hedge may be sub-optimal because the exposures in the two markets do not match. The gain or loss in physical position would be on 95 MT while futures position would offset either 90 MT or 100 MT, as the case may be.

Mismatch of Maturities

Since futures contracts are standardized with respect to delivery dates, the exact matching of the period to a hedge cannot be achieved except by coincidence. For example, if a sugar mill wanted to hedge against price risk till 30th April, it would not be able to do so because April contracts expire on 20th April. The sugar mill may have the choice of booking a futures contract for April or May, which would expire on 20th May. If it books an April contract, the position is covered till 20th April, and is exposed from then onwards till 30th April. Alternatively, by booking a May contract, the period of exposure in the assets is covered, but while exiting the May contract on 30th April, convergence of prices in the physical and financial markets would not happen, leaving unequal losses and gains in the two markets. Further, if one keeps the futures position open beyond the date of liquidation of asset, 30th April, it would amount to speculation for a period of 20 days.

Despite imperfect hedges in futures and perfect hedges in forwards, it is not necessary that a forward hedge is preferred over a futures hedge. The evaluation needs to be based on the costs and benefits offered by each of the contracts. The transaction cost in futures is extremely nominal and transparent in comparison to forward contracts. A future contract offers easy flexibility of entry and exit at any time. On the contrary, a forward contract incurs a larger transaction cost in the form of bid–ask spread. Further, the contract price is not transparent, as it changes from customer to customer. Besides, forward contracts do not offer convenient entry and exit from the hedge, as do the exchange-traded futures.

BASIS AND BASIS RISK

> Basis is the difference between the futures price and the spot price, and declines as time to maturity approaches.

The principle of convergence of price states that the futures price and the spot price must converge on the date of maturity. If this happens at the time of maturity of the underlying asset, a perfect hedge is possible. However, the efficiency of the hedge depends on convergence and the correlation between the futures price and the spot price. This aspect can be understood through *basis*, which is defined as the difference between the futures price and the spot price. If today the futures price and the spot price are F_0, and S_0, respectively, the basis is

$$B_0 = F_0 - S_0 \tag{3.7}$$

Note that in a normal market, the basis will be positive, while in an inverted market, it will be negative. The principle of convergence assumes that basis shall become zero on the maturity date, with futures and spot prices being equal. At the time of setting up a hedge by going long/short on futures, the basis is known.

During the period of the hedge, spot prices as well as futures prices change with time and are unknown. At the end of the period of the hedge (when one squares up the position in the futures market, or the underlying position is liquidated), if the futures and spot prices are F_1 and S_1, respectively, then the basis at the end of hedge period is

$$B_1 = F_1 - S_1 \tag{3.8}$$

Let us look at the gain or loss of the hedger in the spot market and the futures market separately. If the hedger went long on the underlying asset valued at S_0 today, then at the end of the period of hedge his payoff in the spot market will be:

$$\text{Gain/loss in the spot market} = S_1 - S_0$$

Derivatives in Practice

Commodity Derivatives

The basis risk: physical settlement and delivery

In August 2010, in the futures trading of pepper contracts traded on the National Commodity and Derivatives Exchange Ltd. (NCDEX), a controversy broke out over the quality of pepper delivered, with buyers complaining of inferior quality of pepper resulting in increased processing cost for buyers. This happened on 20 August 2010, when delivery of about 1400 tonnes of pepper was due.

It was alleged that the exchange-approved warehouse at Kozhikode stored pepper inferior in quality to the one specified in the futures contract. The same was the case with another approved warehouse at Kochi. The warehouse at Kozhikode was opened for delivery of pepper coming from nearby locations. The pepper cultivated in the area was considered to be of inferior quality to the pepper from the areas around Kochi. As on 5 August, 2011 there were 4279 tonnes of pepper deposited at the two accredited warehouses in Kochi and Kozhikode.

NCDEX claimed that goods deposited in the accredited warehouses were accepted only after quality certification by assayers appointed to do the sampling and testing. Besides certification, the assayers also conducted periodic audits and ascertained if the quality of goods was in conformity with contract specifications. Besides, the exchange authorities also conducted random quality audits. NCDEX also claimed that in case the buyers suspected inferior quality, they were free to ask for resampling and testing in the presence of their representatives.

The problem arose when the goods were stored for a long time. Material once deposited upon certification cannot be rejected upon revaluation after three months unless justified. The traders alleged that when the certification is done by the same person on both occasions, the deposited inferior material becomes valid for delivery.

Source: Based on an article by G.K. Nair in *Business Line*, 24 August 2011.

Commodity Futures **69**

> Hedging price risk with futures is not perfect. Price risks can get replaced by much smaller risk, called basis risk.

The hedger went short on the futures market at F_0 and bought back at F_1 at the end of the period of hedge. His payoff on the futures market is:

$$\text{Gain/loss in the futures market} = F_0 - F_1$$

The total gain/loss on the combined position in the spot and futures markets is

$$\begin{aligned} \text{Net gain/loss} &= S_1 - S_0 + F_0 - F_1 = (F_0 - S_0) - (F_1 - S_1) \\ &= B_0 - B_1 \\ &= \text{Difference between basis at the start and at the end of the hedge} \end{aligned} \tag{3.9}$$

For a perfect hedge, the net gain/loss must be zero, and, hence, the hedge will be perfect if the difference in basis is zero. The hedger will achieve his/her objective if he/she minimizes the differential of the basis. If he/she remains unhedged, then the price risk will be

$$\text{Price risk} = S_1 - S_0 \tag{3.10}$$

With hedging, the hedger's risk is limited to the difference in basis, which is expected to be much smaller than the price risk. The difference in the basis is referred to as *basis risk*, being the risk borne by the hedger. By hedging, the larger price risk is replaced by a much smaller basis risk. Basis risk arises due to mismatch of positions in the physical and futures markets, as discussed earlier.

Besides quantity and quality of the asset, basis risk may also arise due to difference in the time of maturity of the futures contract and the period for which the underlying asset is to be hedged. As an example, consider a sugarcane trader who would like to get rid of his stock on a particular date in April, whereas future contracts expire on, say, 25 April. Since the exposure on the asset owned and the time of square-up of the futures contract will not be the same, the sugarcane trader would either be over-hedged (when the futures position is open and the position in the physical asset is closed) or under-hedged (when the futures position

---

EXAMPLE 3.4 Basis risk

From the data of Example 3.3, the effective price worked out to ₹3197 and ₹3182 as against the target price of ₹3200. What are the reasons for variation in the actual price paid and the target price, and how much variation would you attribute to each reason?

Solution
The difference between the target price and the price actually paid is due to basis, which is attributable to (a) mismatch of assets, (b) mismatch of timing, and (c) mismatch of quantity in the futures market and the spot market.

Mismatch of asset quality There is no mismatch of assets, as a futures contract on crude oil was available and the same was required in the spot market. Therefore, there is no mismatch of quality of the asset in the spot market and the futures market.

Mismatch of timing If the futures contract was maturing and the asset was to be bought in the physical market at the same time, then the prices in the spot and the futures would have been identical, i.e., basis would then have been zero. Due to mismatch of timing, the prices would differ by the amount of basis at the end of the hedge. The price differential due to mismatch of timing is:

$$\begin{aligned} \text{Effective price paid} &= S_1 + F_0 - F_1 = F_0 - (F_1 - S_0) = F_0 - \text{basis when hedge is lifted} \\ \text{When price declined} &= 3{,}200 - (2{,}910 - 2{,}900) = ₹3{,}190 \text{ per barrel} \\ \text{When price increased} &= 3{,}200 - (3{,}315 - 3{,}300) = ₹3{,}185 \text{ per barrel} \end{aligned}$$

Mismatch of quantity The remaining difference between the spot and forwards prices is attributable to mismatch of quantity. The actual requirement of quantity was 1075 barrels, whereas the position taken in the futures was 1100 barrels, i.e., 11 contracts of 100 barrels each.

is closed prior to closure of the position in the asset) with respect to time. This implies that the convergence of futures price to spot would not take place. Some element of the basis risk will remain, although the basis reduces as contract approaches maturity.

Basis Risk and Hedging

As we know, hedging with futures replaces price risk (difference in the spot prices, i.e., $S_1 - S_0$) with basis risk (the basis at the end, i.e., $F_1 - S_1$). Due to convergence of the futures price with futures, the basis risk is expected to be much smaller than the price risk. Therefore, it makes sense to hedge the commodity price risk with commodity futures. In case of convergence of futures and spot prices, the basis risk would be zero. The lesser the basis risk, the more attractive is hedging through futures. Whether or not convergence of futures and spot prices is achieved is dependent upon the efficiency of the futures markets and the spot markets. Prices in the spot markets are governed by more fundamental factors affecting demand and supply, while futures prices are greatly dependent upon how well and quickly the information is absorbed by the futures markets. If the futures market is efficient in discounting the price information, the impact on spot prices would be smoother, reducing volatility in spot prices.

In a study conducted 2–3 years after the introduction of futures in July 2004, it was revealed that the basis risk was larger than the price risk on 14 out of 26 occasions in the case of wheat and 13 out of 26 occasions in the case of sugar[3]. Far from being negligible, the basis risk was in fact greater than the price risk. This clearly indicates several shortcomings. It reflects that either the futures market was poorly informed, did not transfer information to the spot markets, or was dominated purely by speculative activity. Probably the process of arbitrage (*cash-and-carry* and *reverse cash-and-carry*) that establishes the link between futures and spot markets and achieves convergence was constrained. If the basis risk is larger than the price risk, hedging with futures becomes redundant. However, it may be appreciated that markets cannot become efficient immediately after coming into existence. The participants in the market need time to go through the learning curve and understand intricacies of the process.

There is a strong perception in the minds of politicians and economists that large players are capable of manipulating prices in the futures market and causing spot prices to rise to the detriment of users and the general public. On that pretext, trading in futures for essential commodities, which is perceived to cause unwarranted inflation, is banned repeatedly.

Rather than banning the trade and making hedging avenues unavailable, there are many intermediate options available. Unduly large basis risks may be indicative of structural deficiencies rather than the influence and dominance of a select few in the market. Unavailability of adequate and suitable warehousing facilities, lack of education and knowledge on the part of hedgers, unavailability of credit for physical delivery, regulation of prices in physical markets by governments, etc., are some of the reasons that do not allow integration of futures markets with spot markets. Integrating markets to make them more attractive for hedgers should be one side of the coin; introduction of a separate regulatory framework to contain speculative activity should be the other side. Speculative activity could be contained

---

[3]Report of the expert committee to study the impact of futures trading on agricultural commodity prices, Ministry of Consumer Affairs, Food and Public Distribution, Government of India, 2008.

by devising futures contracts with reduced daily price movement limits, compulsory delivery logic, smaller exposure limits, etc. Though it may be hard to explain the benefits of futures markets to comparatively illiterate farmers, intermediaries who are educated enough, especially those in regulatory and government bodies involved in procurement and distribution of essential agricultural commodities, must be encouraged to use futures markets. As these agencies generally deal in large volumes, their participation should substantially increase hedging and strengthen the linkage between physical and futures markets.

Hedge Ratio

With the presence of basis risk, a hedge is likely to be imperfect. This imperfection results due to mismatches of assets, maturity dates, and quantities. Though the larger price risk is replaced by a much smaller basis risk, it cannot be eliminated altogether. The objective is then to minimize the risk if it cannot be eliminated.

> The hedge ratio is the number of futures contracts having the minimum risk possible. It depends upon the risks in the spot prices and in the futures prices, as well as the coefficient of correlation between the two.

The hedge ratio is defined as the ratio of the value of a futures contract to the value of the underlying asset. The *optimum hedge ratio* is the ratio that eliminates or minimizes the price risk. While hedging through an identical asset underlying the number of contracts that are booked to cover long/short positions, the hedge ratio is equal to the exposure in the underlying asset. In such a case, we implicitly set the hedge ratio as being equal to one, which is regarded as optimum.

By definition, the hedge ratio is given by

$$h = \frac{N_H}{N_A}$$

where N_A is the value of the underlying assets and N_H is the value of the hedged contracts.

The optimum hedge ratio (value of a futures contract to the value of the underlying asset) is dependent upon the degree of correlation between the spot and futures prices. If a change of 1% in the spot prices causes an equal change in the futures price in the same direction, the coefficient of correlation is +1. For a hedge through futures, the optimum hedge ratio is the ratio that minimizes the risk of the combined portfolio of the underlying and futures.

If h is the number of futures contracts booked, then the risk of the combined portfolio of underlying assets and the futures is given by the variance of the return from the portfolio so constructed.

$$\text{Return from the portfolio} = h(F_1 - F_0) - (S_1 - S_0) = h\Delta F - \Delta S \quad (3.11)$$
$$\text{Variance of the portfolio } V = \text{Var}(h\Delta F - \Delta S)$$
$$V = h^2 \sigma_f^2 + \sigma_s^2 - 2h\rho\sigma_f\sigma_s$$

In order to find out the optimal hedge ratio, we need to minimize the variance of the portfolio, by setting the first partial derivative equal to zero.

$$V = h^2 \sigma_f^2 + \sigma_s^2 - 2h\rho\sigma_f\sigma_s$$
$$\frac{dV}{dh} = 2(h^*)\sigma_f^2 - 2\rho\sigma_f\sigma_s$$

By setting $\frac{dV}{dh} = 0$, we get the following equation:

$$2(h^*)\sigma_f^2 - 2\rho\,\sigma_f\sigma_s = 0$$
$$2(h^*)\sigma_f^2 = 2\rho\,\sigma_f\sigma_s$$
$$h^* = \rho\frac{\sigma_s}{\sigma_f}L \qquad (3.12)$$

where h^* = optimum hedge ratio

ρ = correlation coefficient of spot and futures prices

σ_s, σ_f = standard deviations of spot price and futures price, respectively.

The hedge ratio given by Eq. 3.12 minimizes the total risk of the combined portfolio of the underlying asset and the futures contacts. Any deviation from this ratio will be sub-optimal, as can be seen from Fig. 3.4.

Correlation of spot prices and futures prices can be obtained through a regression. If $\rho = 1$ and $\sigma_s = \sigma_f$, then $h^* = 1$. This is likely to be the case where hedging is done through

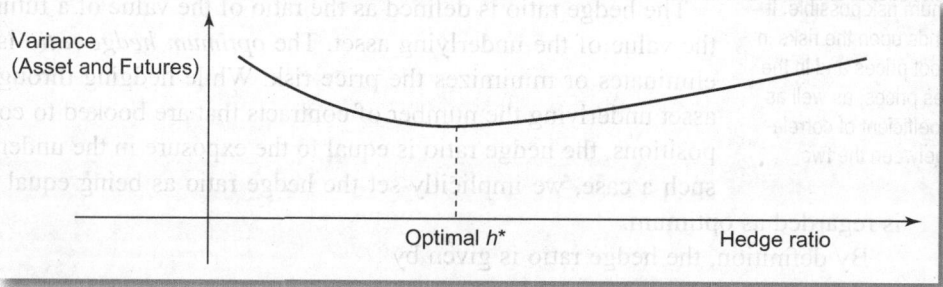

Fig. 3.4 Risk and hedge ratio

> The hedge ratio is generally 1 for commodities where futures contracts are easily available. For a cross-hedge, the hedge assumes special significance.

the same asset. If a 1% change causes a 2% change in the futures price, the most efficient hedge will be obtained from the futures contracts of half the value of the underlying asset. If the future prices move by only 0.5% with a 1% change in the spot price, the optimal hedge required for exposure in the futures contracts should be twice the value of the underlying asset for minimization of risk. The hedge ratio becomes an extremely important variable while using a cross hedge. This is illustrated in Example 3.5 and Example 3.6.

Forward Rolling of the Hedge Another problem faced by hedgers arises when futures contracts are not available for the period of hedge. For example, when a hedge is required for 12 months and futures contracts are available for a maximum period of six months, the hedger faces the problem of remaining exposed for the period that the futures contracts do not cover. Under such circumstances, the hedger has to roll futures contracts covering the entire period of the hedge. If a hedger is long on an asset for 12 months and futures are available for a maximum of six months, he/she can take the following actions:

- Initially execute a short hedge for six months
- Six months later, unwind the position of the original contract by going long, and take a fresh short position in a new contract for the next six months
- After 12 months, unwind the position in the second futures contract

EXAMPLE 3.5 Cross hedge and hedge ratio

A sugarcane trader is expecting a stock of 200 MT from various farmers to be available to him after three months, next April. In the normal course, the prices of sugarcane in the month of April remain at ₹80 per quintal (₹800/MT). As a bumper sugarcane crop is anticipated, he is worried about a fall in prices. Futures contracts in sugarcane are not available. However, futures in sugar are available, and 3-m contracts of 10 MT each are selling for ₹800 per quintal (₹8000/MT). How can the trader hedge his position using futures contracts in sugar, assuming the prices of sugar and sugarcane are perfectly and positively correlated?

Solution
Hedging strategy
Futures contracts in sugarcane are not available. Hence, the trader has to hedge his position by using a cross hedge. He can hedge by taking an opposite position in futures. Since the trader is long on the asset, he has to go short on futures. Therefore, the trader sells the 3-m futures contracts on sugar now and buys the same contracts back after three months, just prior to maturity. The number of contracts to be traded will depend upon the hedge ratio or the sensitivity of prices of the asset to be hedged to the prices of the futures contract.

When the prices of sugarcane and sugar change equally, then

$$\text{Number of contracts to be sold} = \frac{\text{Value to be hedged}}{\text{Value of future contract}} \text{ or } \frac{200 \times 800}{10 \times 8{,}000} = 2$$

The prices of sugarcane and sugar are perfectly positively correlated. Changes in sugarcane prices will be just as much as changes in sugar prices. The price of sugarcane, therefore, must be $\frac{1}{10}$ of sugar, i.e., ₹88 per quintal (₹880 per tonne)/ ₹72 per quintal (₹720 per tonne) for a 10% change in the price of sugar. The hedging outcome for 10% increase/decrease in prices is as below:

	Prices rise by 10%, ₹	Prices fall by 10%, ₹
Value of futures contracts sold	1,60,000	1,60,000
Value of futures contracts bought	1,76,000	1,44,000
Profit/loss on the futures market	−16,000	+16,000
Spot sale of sugarcane (quantity × price) = 200 × 880 = 200 × 720	1,76,000	1,44,000
Total value realized	1,60,000	1,60,000

Even if futures are available for extended time periods, the rolling over of the hedge is considered a better option because near futures have greater liquidity and are more fairly priced than distant futures, which suffer from poor liquidity.

HEDGING FOR CHANGES IN VOLUME[4]

So far, we have considered situations relating to uncertainty about the price and how it could be hedged through futures. Sometimes, uncertainties can prevail over the quantity of future contracts. Most of the time, farmers face uncertainty about the quantity of the crop that they would be reaping at the end of the season. Under such circumstances, this interesting question pops up: can such a situation be hedged with a position in futures?

Futures can also be used for hedging against quantity uncertainties, as price and quantity have an inverse relationship.

Since price and quantity are inversely related, one may believe that there is a negative correlation between price and quantity. Ideally, in order to hedge against quantity risk, we must adopt a strategy that is the opposite of the strategy used to protect against price risks.

---
[4]For a detailed discussion, refer to *The Futures Market—Arbitrage, Risk Management and Portfolio Strategies* by Daniel R. Siegel and Diane F. Siegel, Probus Publishing Company, Chicago.

EXAMPLE 3.6 Cross hedge and hedge ratio

Refer to Example 3.5. How would the hedging strategy change if (a) the price of sugarcane changes by half as much as that of sugar, and (b) the price of sugarcane changes by twice as much as that of sugar?

How can the trader immunize himself from the changes in price?

Solution

(a) *Hedging strategy:*

When the price of sugarcane changes by half of that of sugar

$$\text{No. of contracts to be sold} = \frac{0.5 \times \text{value to be hedged}}{\text{Value of future contract}}, \text{ or,}$$

$$\frac{0.5 \times 200 \times 800}{10 \times 8{,}000} = 1$$

The prices of sugarcane and sugar are positively correlated. The change in the sugarcane price will be half as much as the change in the sugar price. The price of sugarcane, therefore, must be 5% more/less than expected, i.e., ₹84 per quintal (₹840 per tonne)/ ₹76 per quintal (₹760 per tonne) for a 10% change in the price of sugar. The hedging out come is as below:

	Prices rise by 10%, ₹	Prices fall by 10%, ₹
Value of futures contracts sold	80,000	80,000
Value of futures contracts bought	88,000	72,000
Profit/loss on the futures market	**−8,000**	**+8,000**
Spot sale of sugarcane (quantity × price) = 200 × 840	1,68,000	
= 200 × 760		1,52,000
Total value realized	**1,60,000**	**1,60,000**

(b) When the price of sugarcane is twice that of sugar

$$\text{No. of contracts to be sold} = \frac{2 \times \text{value to be hedged}}{\text{Value of future contract}}, \text{ or,}$$

$$\frac{2 \times 200 \times 800}{10 \times 8{,}000} = 4$$

The prices of sugarcane and sugar are positively correlated. The change in the sugarcane price will be twice as much as the change in the sugar price. The price of sugarcane, therefore, must be 20% more/less than expected, i.e., ₹96 per quintal (₹960 per tonne)/ ₹64 per quintal (₹640 per tonne) for a 10% change in the price of sugar. The hedging out com is as below:

	Prices rise by 10%, ₹	Prices fall by 10%, ₹
Value of futures contracts sold	3,20,000	3,20,000
Value of futures contracts bought	3,52,000	2,88,000
Profit/loss on the futures market	**−32,000**	**+32,000**
Spot sale of sugarcane (quantity × price) = 200 × 960	1,92,000	
= 200 × 640		1,28,000
Total value realized	**1,60,000**	**1,60,000**

Note that when sugarcane price change only half as much as that of sugar the hedge ratio dropped to half from two contracts to one contract. When sugarcane price changed twice as much, the hedge ratio doubled from two to four.

Practically speaking, though, this is not exactly true. When the quantity is known for certain, the revenue/cost is proportional to the price. Hedging actions are aimed at protecting against falling revenue or rising cost. When price and quantity become related, the focus must change to revenue and cost, i.e. the product of quantity and price.

Uncertainty about quantities primarily arises due to poor weather conditions that affect the aggregate output. If production is more, the price is lower and if production is less, the price is higher. Let us assume that a farmer faces uncertainty about the quantity and price of his wheat crop under the following possible scenarios:

Probability	Price of wheat, ₹/kg	Quantity, kg	Revenue, ₹
0.6	20.00	40,000	8,00,000
0.4	30.00	30,000	9,00,000

The expected price of wheat is 0.6 × 20 + 0.4 × 30 = ₹24 per kg.

Since futures prices are supposed to be unbiased indicators of the expected prices, it is fair to assume that wheat futures would be selling for ₹24.00. Further, in order to hedge, the farmer would go short on wheat futures for the expected quantity of 36,000 kg (0.6 × 40,000 + 0.4 × 30,000). If the farmer does so, the resultant position under two possible scenarios of price would be as under:

Price, ₹/kg	Gain/loss on futures, ₹	Revenue from crop, ₹	Total revenue, ₹
20.00	(24 − 20) × 36,000 = 1,44,000	8,00,000	9,44,000
30.00	(24 − 30) × 36,000 = −2,16,000	9,00,000	6,84,000

It may be seen that contrary to the expectation of reducing the variability of revenue, the position in futures has resulted in increased volatility. In fact, the position taken in futures is inappropriate. One need not hedge for the expected quantity of 36,000 kg, because the impact of reduced quantity is partially offset by increased price (and vice versa), due to the negative relationship between price and quantity. The quantity that would render stability to the revenue would be dependent upon the covariance of revenue with the price, and is given by Eq. 3.13.

$$\text{Quantity for hedging} = \frac{\text{Covariance of revenue with price}}{\text{Variance of price}} \quad (3.13)$$

> The hedge ratio for quantity hedging depends upon the ratio of covariance of revenue and variance of price.

Using Eq. 3.13, we find out the optimum position that needs to be taken in futures to hedge against the risk of changing revenue due to combined volume and price changes. The expected revenue is 0.6 × 8 + 0.4 × 9 = ₹8.4 lakh and the expected price is 0.6 × 20 + 0.4 × 30 = ₹24/kg. The variance of price and its covariance with revenue are shown below:

Probability	Price, ₹/kg	Revenue, ₹'000	Variance of price	Covariance of revenue and price, ₹'000
0.6	20	800	−4 × −4 × 0.6 = 9.60	−40 × −4 × 0.6 = 96
0.4	30	900	6 × 6 × 0.4 = 14.40	60 × 6 × 0.4 = 144
		Total	24.00	240

$$\text{Quantity for hedging} = \frac{\text{Covariance of revenue with price}}{\text{Variance of price}} = \frac{2,40,000}{24} = 10,000 \text{ kg}$$

Since protection is required for declining revenue, we go short on futures (for rising costs we would go long on futures) to the extent of 10,000 kg of wheat and not 36,000 kg, as stated earlier. The hedging outcome with shorting futures worth 10,000 kg results in stable total revenue at ₹8,40,000 and is evaluated below:

Price, ₹/kg	Gain/loss on futures, ₹	Revenue from crop, ₹	Total revenue, ₹
20.00	(24 − 20) × 10,000 = 40,000	8,00,000	8,40,000
30.00	(24 − 30) × 10,000 = −60,000	9,00,000	8,40,000

HEDGING FOR GROSS PROFIT MARGIN

> Spread strategies can be used for protecting the gross profit margin where futures are available on inputs and outputs of an enterprise.

Most business situations involve related inputs and outputs. The prices of finished products are dependent upon the prices of raw materials. For example, sugar prices depend heavily on the price of sugarcane. Similarly, rolling mills price their products depending upon the prices of ingots. The prices of petroleum products are heavily dependent upon the prices of crude oil. For most agricultural products, the prices are linked to the prices of inputs.

Firms normally tend to pass on any increase in raw material prices to the finished product to maintain gross profit margins, and finally the risk of price is borne by consumers. However, despite strong correlation between the prices of inputs and outputs, it may not always be feasible, for strategic reasons, for firms to adopt the strategy of passing on changes in prices of inputs to consumers, even at the risk of a fluctuating gross profit margin. Further, this philosophy of passing on the entire changes in prices to consumers would become impractical when changes in prices are temporary and too frequent. Firms have to offer fixed prices, generally valid for some time. As a marketing strategy to preserve reputation and credibility, the prices of end-products cannot be changed too frequently. At the same time, firms cannot afford to put their profit margins at risk.

Futures markets can serve the useful purpose of protecting the gross profit margin in the short run against small and frequent changes in the prices of inputs and outputs. Let us consider an example to highlight the utility of futures in preserving gross profit margin.

Sugar mills use sugarcane as a major input for producing sugar. For simplicity of exposition, assume that 100 kg of sugarcane yields 9 kg of sugar besides many by-products, and it takes about one month for converting sugarcane into sugar. Therefore, the gross profit of the sugar mill is given by:

Gross profit = (Quantity of sugar × price of sugar × 0.09)
− (quantity of sugarcane × price of sugarcane)

The sugar mill needs to sell sugar and buy sugarcane. It is long on sugar (the finished product) and short on sugarcane (the raw material). Exposure in sugar can be hedged by going short on futures contracts on sugar, while the prices of input can be hedged by going long on future contracts on sugarcane. Therefore, in order to hedge the gross profit margin, the sugar mill would take simultaneous positions of (a) long on futures contract on sugarcane, and (b) short on futures contracts on sugar. The time and quantities, too, need to be matched. If the sugar mill needs to plan two months in advance, it has to take actions, as depicted in Fig. 3.5.

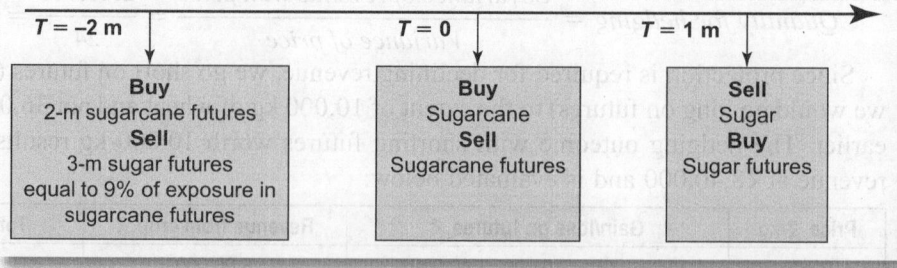

Fig. 3.5 Hedging for gross profit: Sugar mill

Commodity Futures

> Going long on futures of raw material and short on futures on finished goods provides a tactical way of protecting gross profit margin, making strategic policies more stable.

We consider a simple example of how gross profit margin can be protected by a sugar mill[5], as depicted in Fig. 3.5. We know that the sugar mill has a yield of 9%. One quintal (1 quintal = 100 kg) of sugarcane yields 9 kg of sugar, with a processing time of one month. The mill needs to plan two months in advance, and, hence, would need to buy a 2-m futures contract on sugarcane and sell a 3-m futures contract on sugar equal to 9% of the quantity of sugarcane. Consider the following scenario relating to the futures price today:

2-m futures on sugarcane   :   ₹180/quintal
3-m futures contract on sugar :   ₹25/kg

With a futures contract, the price realized/paid is equal to the futures price now less the basis at the end. Assuming the basis for sugarcane is zero at the end of two months and zero at the end of three months for sugarcane to keep the exposition simple, the gross profit margin per quintal of sugarcane is proportional to ₹45, as can be seen here:

Gross profit = Price of 9 kg sugar − cost of 1 quintal of sugarcane
             = 9 × 25 − 180 = ₹45

It may be realized that the protection of gross profit margin is a combination of inter-commodity spread using futures on sugarcane and sugar, and calendar spread using 2-m and 3-m futures (discussed in the next section).

Having taken a long position in futures of sugarcane and short position in futures of sugar, the sugar mill would hedge against fluctuating gross profit margin. Table 3.1 demonstrates

Table 3.1 Hedging for gross profit: Sugar mill

Price scenario		
Sugarcane	₹190/quintal	₹170/quintal
Sugar	₹22/kg	₹27/kg
Sugarcane futures		
Bought at	₹180	₹180
Sold at	₹190	₹170
(a) Profit/loss on sugarcane futures	₹10	−₹10
Sugar futures		
Sold at	₹25	₹25
Bought at	₹22	₹27
(b) Profit/loss on sugar futures	9 × 3 = ₹27	9 × −2 = −₹18
(c) Profit on futures contracts (a + b)	₹37	−₹28
Spot position		
Price realized for suger	9 × 22 = ₹198	9 × 27 = ₹243
Price paid for sugarcane	₹190	₹170
(d) Gross profit on spot position	₹8	₹73
Aggregate profit (c + d)	₹45	₹45

---

[5]Based on Crack Spread at NYMEX for futures on crude oil for input and futures on gasoline and heating oil for output.

hedging for profit for two different sugarcane and sugar price scenarios. Profit and loss in the spot position would be compensated by loss and profit in the futures position. We have assumed the convergence of prices at the end of the hedge, matching with actual buying of sugarcane and selling of sugar. Barring basis risk, the actual profit margin would differ marginally from the targeted figure of ₹45 per quintal of sugarcane.

We can clearly see that futures can protect day-to-day fluctuations in the gross profit margin, obviating the need for frequent adjustment of prices of finished goods in accordance with changes in the raw material prices.

STRATEGIC IMPLICATIONS OF FUTURES

The preceding examples of hedging against quantity risk and hedging to protect gross profit demonstrate the capability of futures as a tool for handling a variety of situations. Despite the limitations of imperfect hedges with futures, there are other benefits that are possibly difficult to evaluate in financial terms. Futures should not be seen merely as financial products capable of providing an effective hedge against price changes. The futures market in commodities throws up many more managerial options, and can be used as strategic tool rather than a tactical tool for hedging transactions.

> Futures can be viewed as a strategic product rather than a mere tactical product capable of providing hedging of routine day-to-day transactions.

- With regard to pricing, consider, for example, a wheat grower expecting to reap a harvest in six months' time. He can continuously monitor the price of futures for the next six months and trade at the most favourable price that he finds. A range of prices prevailing over an extended period of time is not available to him in the absence of a futures exchange. Futures markets thus compliment marketing strategies.
- On a similar note, we can say that purchasing strategies also have much wider choices with access to a vibrant futures market.
- With respect to inventory management, futures are of tremendous use in protecting the value of closing stock. At an appropriate target price, futures can be traded to have the values of inventory protected.
- From a strategic viewpoint, steady cash flows enable the investor to command a better valuation of stock prices when borrowing from lenders, etc., and can help to bring down the cost of capital.

SPECULATION WITH COMMODITY FUTURES

Just as with forward contracts, commodity futures can be used for purely speculative gains. As smaller payments (initial margins) are required to book futures contracts than to take an equivalent position in the cash/spot market, futures provide highly leveraged positions. This magnifies the potential profit as well as the potential loss.

> Futures can be used for speculation if the estimate of future spot price is different than the futures price.

To speculate on the prices of the commodity in the physical market, one requires huge resources to first buy and store goods till the desired price is reached, and then sell at higher prices at a later date. Note that that no short sale is possible in the commodities market. Speculating on the commodities markets is tantamount to hoarding, which is generally regarded as a social evil.

Rather than using cash or the physical market, one can speculate on futures to achieve the same objective, with the advantage of a much smaller capital outlay. Speculation in the commodities markets through futures also saves the speculator from the social stigma attached with speculation (hoarding) in the physical markets. To speculate on the prices of commodities, one has to do one of the following:

- *If a trader expects a price fall, he/she simply has to sell a futures contract today and buy it later.* For example, in September 2010, futures contracts of silver for delivery in December 2010 are quoted at ₹10,921 per kg. A trader in silver believes that the price in December will not be more than ₹10,000 per kg. The trader can take a speculative position in futures by selling them today and square up later by buying the same any time prior to December 2010, presumably at a price lower than the selling price; thus, the trader makes a speculative profit.
- *If a trader anticipates a rise in prices, he/she simply has to buy futures today and sell later.* For example, in September 2010, futures contracts of pepper for delivery in January 2011 are quoted at ₹6627 per quintal. A trader in pepper believes that the price in January will be not less than ₹7300 per quintal. The trader can take a speculative position in futures by buying them today and square up by selling the same any time prior to January 2011, presumably at a price higher than the buying price; thus, the trader makes a speculative profit.

SPREAD STRATEGIES WITH FUTURES

The use of single futures contracts with speculative motive is referred to as *open position trading*, where one speculates on favourable price movement. Many traders perceive this to be too risky a proposition and prefer to monitor basis (the difference between futures and spot prices) rather than price. The speculation on basis is referred to as *spread trading*. Spread trading is speculation on the price differential between two contracts, and involves buying one futures contract while selling another. Spreads can be categorized into three types:

- Inter-commodity spread
- Inter-market spread
- Intra-commodity spread (also known as time/calendar spread)

Inter-commodity Spreads These are derived from buying a futures contract in one commodity and selling another in a related commodity. For example, a trader may buy gold futures and sell silver futures of the same maturity if he/she feels that gold is underpriced as compared to silver today, and that by the time the futures contracts mature, the markets will have restored the balance between gold and silver prices. Similarly, a trader may buy tea futures and sell coffee futures if he/she believes that coffee futures are overpriced as compared to tea, and that the aberration in the prices of these related commodities will not last long. He/she expects either tea prices to go up, coffee prices to fall, or both. Speculation with spreads is in fact equivalent to two open positions: a long position in one commodity and a short position in another related commodity. However, a spread position may involve a smaller outlay in terms of initial margin than the sum of two independent

> Spread strategies in futures are concerned with the mispricing of futures contracts (a) in two assets, (b) in two markets, or (c) of two different maturities.

open positions, if the commodities are on the same exchange, subject to its bye-laws. In case the expectations of the trader fall apart, the losses of the trader will be proportionately large. Here, the relative valuation is of significance rather than speculation on the absolute price of one commodity, considered riskier than bets on relative prices. Refer solved problems SP3.2 for comprising spot and futures position for speculative gain.

Inter-market Spreads These involve opposite positions in the same commodity, but at different markets/exchanges. The price differential in two exchanges for the same commodity may exist because of transportation costs involved, or two exchanges may specify different delivery locations/centres. For example on 28 September 2005, *jeera* futures for December delivery at NCDEX and MCX were quoted at ₹6698 and ₹6783 per kg, respectively[6]. One may buy *jeera* futures at the cheaper location, NCDEX, and sell at the more expensive location, MCX, to book a profit. This implies two independent positions in two different locations in the same commodity, with the intentions of pure arbitrage. This arbitrage is, of course, subject to transportation costs and any other differences in the contract features. The apparent disparity in prices may not actually be there, because the two locations may specify different delivery centres.

Time Spreads These involve opposite positions in the same commodity on the same exchange, but with different maturity dates. Consider the prices of *jeera* futures at NCDEX as on 28 September 2005 for October, November, and December deliveries as ₹6345, ₹6528, and ₹6698[7], respectively. The price differential between November and October is ₹183 (6698−6528) while the differential between the December and November contracts is ₹170 (6698−6528) only. If cost of carry is assumed to be proportional to the time, a trader may believe that an equivalent differential is appropriate. However, at a differential of ₹183 per month, the December futures seem underpriced as compared to the November futures. Hence, the trader may go long on the December futures and short on the November futures. Subsequently, if the differential of ₹183 becomes a reality, the trader gains on the spread created earlier. Solved problem SP3.2 illustrates application of calender spread.

SOLVED PROBLEMS

SP 3.1: Short hedge with commodity futures

A jute packaging unit has planned production of 4300 kg of jute to be sold six months later. The spot price of jute is ₹1900 per kg and a 6-m futures on the same is trading at ₹1850 per kg. The prices are expected to fall as low as ₹1700/kg six months later. What can the jute packaging unit do to mitigate its risk of reduced profit? If it decides to make use of the futures market, what would the effective realized price for the sale of jute be when the spot and futures prices were ₹1750 and ₹1755, respectively? Assume size of futures contract as 200 kgs.

Solution

In order to hedge, the firm would go short on futures at the current futures price of ₹1850. By doing so the firm ensures a price realization of around ₹1850 per kg irrespective of the spot price prevailing at the end of six months.

Quantity of jute to be hedged		4300 kg
Size of one futures contract		200 kg
No. of futures contracts sold	4300/200	≈ 22 contracts
Futures price		= ₹1850
Value of futures sold	1850 × 22 × 200	= ₹81,40,000

[6 & 7] *Source: Business Line*, 29 September 2005.

Six months later, the firm would unwind its futures position by buying the futures contract back and selling the goods in the spot market.

	₹
Futures bought at price	1755
Amount bought for 22 contracts	77,22,000
Gain/loss on futures	4,18,000
Spot price	1750
Actual cost of selling 4300 kg	75,25,000
Total value realised after hedge	79,43,000
Effective price realised	1847

SP 3.2: Speculation with commodity futures

A trader in sugar is extremely bullish with the current price at ₹25 per kg. A futures contract on sugar with three months to maturity is trading at ₹28 per kg. One contract in sugar is for 1000 kg, with a 10% margin.

(a) With funds of ₹1,00,000 available, what could the strategy of the trader be if the price is expected to rise by 20% in three months?
(b) At what minimum expected price after three months of taking a position in futures would the strategy be more profitable?
(c) What happens if the price of sugar actually fell to ₹24 per kg?

Solution
Since the prices of sugar are likely to go up, the trader has two options—(a) buy sugar in the spot market, store, and sell after three months at a higher price, (b) buy sugar futures now and sell them three months later.

(a) Price now: Spot = ₹25.00   Futures = ₹28.00
    Price three months later   Spot = ₹30.00   Futures = spot = ₹30.00

    Dealing in the spot market:
    Amount of stock of sugar that can be bought   = 1,00,000/25   = 4000 kg
    Profit at the end of three months   = 20% × 1,00,000   = ₹20,000

    Dealing with futures market:
    Value of one contract   = 28 × 1000   = ₹28,000
    Margin required   = 0.10 × 28,000   = ₹2800
    No. of contracts that can be bought   = 1,00,000/2800   = 35 (rounded off)
    Exposure in sugar   = 35,000 kg
    Profit on 35 contracts with price rise of 20%   = (30 − 28) × 35 × 1000   = ₹70,000

(b) With the same amount of funds, the cash position is 4000 kg at ₹25 while a futures position is 35,000 kg at ₹28. With cash and futures price equal at the end of three months at X, for the profit in futures position to exceed the cash position, the following must hold:

$$(X - 28) \times 35,000 \geq (X - 25) \times 4000$$
$$X \geq ₹28.39$$

For a speculative position to be more profitable, the expected price must exceed ₹28.39/kg.

(c) If the price actually fell to ₹24
    Loss in cash position   = 1 × 4000   = ₹4000
    Loss in futures position   = 4 × 35,000   = ₹1,40,000

SP 3.3: Calendar spread with commodity futures

The spot price of crude oil is ₹3000 per barrel. In the futures market, 3-m and 6-m contracts are trading at ₹3125 and ₹3200, respectively. The cost of carry, inclusive of storage and insurance, is 15% p.a. If the cost of carry model applies, find the following:

(a) Fair price of the futures contracts for three months and six months. What action can an arbitrageur take in this situation?
(b) If at the end of three months the spot price were ₹3500 and the futures market stood corrected, what would the profit to the arbitrageur be?
(c) If at the end of three months the spot price were ₹2700 and the futures market stood corrected, what would the profit to the arbitrageur be?

Solution

(a) The fair price of 3-m and 6-m futures with cost of carry of 15% and spot value of ₹3000 is

$F_3 = S_0 \times e^{rt} = 3000 \times e^{0.15 \times 3/12} = ₹3114.64$ Actual price = ₹3125
$F_6 = S_0 \times e^{rt} = 3000 \times e^{0.15 \times 6/12} = ₹3233.65$ Actual price = ₹3200

An arbitrageur would act as follows:
  (i) The 3-m futures are overvalued and must be sold.
  (ii) The 6-m futures are undervalued and must be bought.

(b) If at the end of three months the spot price increased to ₹3500 and the future prices stand corrected, then the fair values of futures would be ₹3500 and ₹3634, at which the arbitrageur squares off. His position would be

Original 3-m futures
Sold at   ₹3125   Bought at   ₹3500   Profit/loss   −₹375
Original 6-m futures
Bought at   ₹3200   Sold at   ₹3634   Profit/loss   +₹434
Net profit on the calendar spread   ₹59

(c) If at the end of three months the spot price decreased to ₹2700 and the future prices stand corrected, then the fair values of futures would be ₹2700 and ₹2803, at which the investor squares off. The position of the investor would be:

Original 3-m futures
Sold at   ₹3125   Bought at   ₹2700   Profit/loss   +₹425
Original 6-m futures
Bought at   ₹3200   Sold at   ₹2803   Profit/loss   −₹397
Net profit on the calendar spread ₹28

SUMMARY

Commodity futures are perhaps the oldest futures with commodities as underlying assets. With increased globalization and integration, volatility in prices of commodities such as crude oil is governed not only by local factors but also by international economic and political conditions. Hence, there is a greater need for protecting prices in a competitive atmosphere, for efficient dissemination of information, and for constant monitoring. Commodity futures help in price discovery, reduction of seasonal volatilities, faster flow of information, reduced cost of credit due to certainty of price, and creation of more efficient physical markets.

At the macro-level, a commodity futures market serves the extremely useful purpose of making fiscal management pragmatic and independent of volatility in the prices of commodities. It helps to reduce budgetary burdens involving MSP programmes and subsidies by transferring the function of price management to private bodies and individuals ready to provide risk reduction. In aggregate, it makes the whole structure most efficient.

There are major differences between commodity and financial futures. The specifications of contracts on commodities face several constraints that contracts on financials do not. Commodities are characterized by limited shelf life, seasonal variations, elaborate delivery requirements and quality differentials, etc. None of these constraints are present in financial futures.

The pricing of commodity futures is not as simple as the pricing of financial futures. The argument of no arbitrage, which forms a fundamentally sound basis for futures pricing for financial assets, cannot be used as very effective logic while pricing commodity futures. While a one-way arbitrage of cash-and-carry is possible, the arbitrage of reverse cash-and-carry is not executable, as most commodities have consumption value, and are not held as investment assets. This places an upper bound to the prices of futures on commodities.

Hedging with commodity futures can be classified as (a) short hedge and (b) long hedge. Hedging with futures is done by taking a position in futures that is opposite to the position in the physical asset. If one is long on the asset, protection is required against any fall in price. To hedge, one takes a short position (sells) in futures. This called a short hedge. A short position in commodities needs to be protected against price rise. Here, the hedger buys a futures contract (goes long on futures). This is called a long hedge.

A hedge with futures is rarely perfect, unlike a forward hedge, which is perfect. Since futures are cash-settled with the hope of offsetting the gains/losses in the physical market, the offsetting is rarely complete. This happens because of mismatch of quality, mismatch of quantities, and mismatch of timing between the futures and physical positions.

Any difference between the futures price and the spot price is called basis. The imperfect hedge results because of varying basis. If the basis were constant, offsetting would be complete. However, any change in the basis is far smaller than any change in price due to the correlation between futures and spot prices and opposite positions. Therefore, in futures, hedge price risk gets replaced by a much smaller basis risk.

More often than not, only price risks of commodities are hedged with futures. However, hedging can also be to cover risk against uncertain quantities. Fluctuations in revenue due to uncertainties in quantity are hedged by fixing the hedge ratio based on the covariance of revenue and variance of price.

Effectiveness of the hedge as measured from the degree of offsetting is dependent upon the correlation of prices of futures with those of the spot/physical market. The optimum hedge ratio is defined as the number of futures contracts that are required for minimum risk in the combined portfolio of asset and futures. It depends upon the volatilities of the spot and futures prices and the coefficient of correlation between the two.

Apart from hedging, futures can also be used for speculation and arbitrage. When one expects prices to increase, one has to buy futures now and sell later. In case prices are expected to decline, the strategy would be to go short now and square up later. Arbitrage is executed in case one finds prices in the physical market and the futures market are out of sync. One would buy in the cheaper market, sell in the more expensive market, and nullify positions in both when the price disparity disappears. Arbitrage can also be executed in the futures market alone when the prices of futures maturing at different times are not consistent. Arbitrage is executed by taking simultaneous and opposite positions in two futures contracts and exiting when the prices of the two contracts become consistent.

The same philosophy of taking simultaneous opposite positions of long on futures contracts for input and short on futures contracts for output with different maturities would protect the gross profit margin, without frequent adjustment to the prices of output or input.

KEY TERMS

Basis The difference between the futures price and the spot price.
Basis risk The possibility that the basis would not be equal at the inception and termination of the hedge, resulting in an imperfect hedge.
Commodity futures Futures whose underlying assets are commodities.
Consumption assets Assets primarily held for consumption and not for investment purposes
Cross hedge When an exposure in an asset is covered by a position in futures not in the same asset but in another strongly correlated asset for hedging. It is referred as cross hedge.
Hedge ratio The ratio of positions taken in the futures and spot markets in the hedge.
Imperfect hedge In an imperfect hedge, gain/losses in the cash market are only partially offset by losses/gains in the derivative market.

Investment assets Assets primarily held for investment purposes.
Long hedge A long position in futures in order to hedge the short position in the cash market.
Optimum hedge ratio The ratio of positions in the futures and spot markets that minimizes risk is optimum hedge ratio.
Perfect hedge In a perfect hedge, gain/losses in the cash market are fully offset by losses/gains in the derivative market.
Rollover hedge Under rollover hedge, position in near month contracts is squared up at maturity and new position opened to cover the entire hedging period.
Short hedge A short position in futures in order to hedge the long position in the cash market.
Spread The difference in the prices of futures for different assets, different markets, or different maturities.

QUESTIONS

3.1 What do you understand by commodity futures?
3.2 What are the benefits of commodity futures at national level?
3.3 What are the differences between commodity and financial futures?
3.4 What do you understand by (a) long hedge and (b) short hedge? Illustrate.
3.5 What are the possible modes of speculation with commodity futures?
3.6 How is pricing of commodity futures different from that of financial futures?
3.7 What is a calendar spread? Explain with an example.

PROBLEMS

P 3.1 Basis and price—short hedge
A trader in gold holds stock of 1 kg valued at ₹15 lakh at the spot price of ₹15,000 per 10 g. A 3-m futures contract with a size of 100 g on gold is ₹15,400 per 10 g. In order to protect against any fall in value of the gold, the trader decides to sell 10 contracts in gold for 3-m delivery. However, after one month, the trader is

required to sell the stock of gold at ₹14,500, and therefore also cancels his position in futures at ₹14,700. Find out the price the trader realized.

P 3.2 Basis and price—long hedge

Assume in P 3.1 that the trader had planned to buy gold and thus went short on the futures on gold. After one month, the trader bought gold and lifted the hedge. What price did the trader end up paying?

P 3.3 Hedge ratio

The risk of spot prices on gold as measured from its standard deviation is placed at ₹120. Similarly, the price risk of a 3-m futures contract on gold is estimated to be ₹150. The coefficient of correlation between the two is placed at 0.85. In order to hedge a spot position on gold, what ratio of futures contract would be optimal?

P 3.4 Cross hedge

An industrial firm uses tin as raw material and has a requirement for 400 kg of tin to be procured six months from now. The prices of tin are expected to rise substantially. The firm needs to hedge against price rise. There are no derivative contracts available on tin, but futures contracts on aluminium are popular.

The prices of aluminium and tin are strongly correlated. A study has revealed that standard deviations of prices of tin and aluminium are 21% and 20% of their current prices of ₹720 per kg and ₹90 per kg, respectively. The coefficient of correlation is placed at 0.95. One futures contract on aluminium is for 1000 kg. How can the firm hedge?

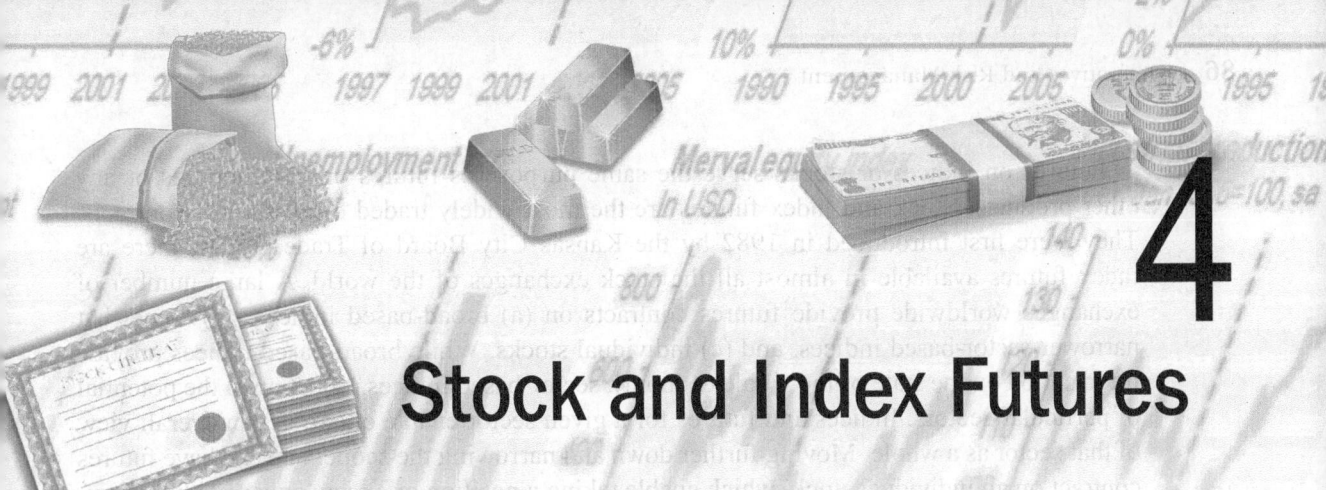

Stock and Index Futures

INTRODUCTION

All of us have heard about the terms SENSEX and NIFTY. Besides other applications and indications of indices, they are devised by stock exchanges to measure the day-to-day movement of stock prices. Indices were developed to enable a bird's eye view of the state of the financial markets. For example, changes in the consumer price index or the wholesale price index reflect the rate of inflation; similarly, changes in the stock indices measure the state of the financial markets at any given point of time, and will reflect growth in the value of stocks. In general, stock indices are regarded as barometers of the state of the economy.

> An index is a representative sample used for examining the state of the stock markets and the economy.

There is a huge number of shares listed on each stock exchange, and changes in the price of each of the stocks will indicate the state of the market. It would be a difficult task indeed to monitor the changes in value of all the stocks listed on an exchange. In order to make qualitative and quantitative judgements of the activities going on in the market, one has to develop a representative sample, just as we develop a basket of goods that are included in the consumer price index to measure inflation. Since indices are developed to include all sectors of the economy and all prominent stocks in each sector, the changes in the value of the index are regarded as a fair indicator of market risk.

A stock index is supposed to reflect the state of the financial markets and provide a bird's eye view. Inflation rates and interest rates are indicators of the economic state of a nation, and, similarly, the index is an aggregate single measure that reflects the mood and sentiments of the stock market, and serves as a proxy for the state of the economy.

Learning Objectives

After going through this chapter, readers should be familiar with

- various terms associated with futures contracts on indices and individual stocks
- the margining system used in futures contracts
- use of futures contracts for hedging
  - a long position in a portfolio against fall in price
  - a short position in a portfolio against rise in price
- applications of index futures to
  - eliminate market risk in a portfolio, and
  - control the beta of a portfolio
- speculation and identification of arbitrage opportunities in the futures market
- other applications of index futures

Futures on indices or stocks serve the same purpose as futures on commodities or any other products. Stock and index futures are the most widely traded of all futures contracts. They were first introduced in 1982 by the Kansas City Board of Trade. Today, there are index futures available in almost all the stock exchanges of the world. A large number of exchanges worldwide provide futures contracts on (a) broad-based indices, (b) somewhat narrower sector-based indices, and (c) individual stocks. While broad-based indices provide information on the state of the whole economy, sector-based indices reflect upon the potential of particular sectors. Indices and futures for a given sector enable one to get an overall view of that sector as a whole. Moving further down and narrowing the scope, one can have futures contract on an individual stock, which enable taking a position or a view on a particular firm. Futures on broad-based indices, sector-based indices, and individual stocks present a vast choice of instruments to a large number of investors to hedge, speculate, or arbitrage. Futures on indices and on individual stocks make financial markets complete.

INDEX FUTURES

Stock index futures can be defined as a commitment to buy or sell at a future date a portfolio of stocks comprising the index. Construction of a stock index involves select shares, their prices, and the number of outstanding shares. As the prices of the stocks change, the value of the index also changes. To attach value to index futures, each point is assigned a monetary value. If each index point is equal to ₹1, as is the case with the National Stock Exchange (NSE)'s NIFTY or the Bombay Stock Exchange (BSE)'s SENSEX, then an index of 4400 would be equal to a monetary value of ₹4400.

> Stock/index futures are derivatives with stocks/indices as underlying assets.

A stock index is a hypothetical product and does not have a physical form, which makes it a non-deliverable asset in practice; theoretically, though, it is possible to have an index as a portfolio of stocks comprising the index in the same proportions that make up the index construction. Unlike commodities and currency futures, where delivery can be enforced, stock indices cannot be delivered. In theory, an index may be deliverable, and the delivery will consist of shares included in the stock index in their relative proportions. However, for all practical purposes, we can deem the stock index to be a non-deliverable asset.

As we have learnt before, the delivery of an underlying asset is essential in derivative transactions for them to be true indicators of future spot prices, and to serve as effective instruments of hedging. However, index futures are cash-settled by an offsetting contract that is opposite to the original contract. Since the delivery of an index is impractical, contracts in stock index futures are necessarily cash-settled. Cash settlement implies the exchange of differences in the prices upon cancellation of the original contract. Stock exchanges deem all outstanding open positions as squared up at the prices prevailing of the day of closing of the relevant futures contracts.

FORWARD CONTRACTS ON STOCKS

Stock index futures were introduced in India in mid-2000 after some legal hurdles were overcome. The act governing securities, i.e., the Securities Contracts Regulation Act (SCRA) had prohibited dealing in futures and options. With the passing of the derivative bill by the parliament, stock index trading began at the BSE on 9 June 2000 and at the NSE on 12 June 2000, with trading on SENSEX futures and NIFTY futures, respectively. Though several other indices and futures on them have come into existence since then, futures on the NSE NIFTY-50 remains the most popular.

Prior to the introduction of futures on the Indian financial markets, a somewhat similar product called *badla* had been in vogue in the market for a long time. *Badla* enabled forward trading in stocks and provided a tool for speculation in stock prices. In the olden days, when suitable technology was not available, the stock market had settlements on a fortnightly basis and, later, on a weekly basis. Netting of positions was allowed over the settlement period. For example, if one bought 100 shares of Reliance Industries Ltd (RIL) on Monday and sold them the next Wednesday, the net delivery position would be zero. Today, this settlement period stands reduced to one day, where the netting is allowed over a single day rather than a week or a fortnight. The term *day traders* has become associated with investors who believe in zero outstanding positions at the end of the day.

> Forward contracts in stocks have been allowed in India for a long time, even prior to the introduction of futures. The system of *badla*, perhaps unique to India, enabled speculation in Indian stock exchanges.

Besides netting over the settlement period, trading in stocks on Indian stock exchanges also allowed *carry forward* of the trade to the next settlement period. Assume that an investor bought 100 shares of RIL at a cost of ₹500 per share on Monday with weekly settlement; the investor faced the following three options on Friday, the settlement day:

- *Settle by delivery*   Pay ₹50,000 and take delivery of 100 shares of RIL.
- *Square up*   Sell the shares at the clearing price of Friday, say ₹600, and receive ₹100 × 100 = ₹10,000. If the price was ₹450, then the investor would pay ₹5000 (₹50 × 100). One could do so prior to the settlement also.
- *Carry forward the transaction*   Neither settle by delivery nor square up, but defer the commitment to pay the contract value of ₹50,000 and carry forward the transaction involving cash and delivery of shares to the next settlement period, due the next Friday. This carry forward is referred to as *badla*.

While the first two options are straightforward, the *badla* transaction may need some elaboration. To carry forward to the next settlement period, one has to pay a carry forward charge. In essence, a carry forward defers payment, and the buyer must pay the equivalent interest for this deferment. Charges for carrying forward transactions are fixed by the exchange and reflect the interest rates prevailing, as also the technical position of demand and supply of the security in question. The difference between the contracted price and the settlement price is paid/received by another party called a *badla* financier, who takes delivery of the shares at the settlement price in one settlement period and passes them on to the original investor in the next settlement.

For speculative investors, *badla* enables deferment of delivery. One could repeat the position on the next settlement, and, therefore, while the price of the share remains fixed at ₹500 as originally contracted, delivery is deferred by paying the carry forward charges, a feature that a forward contract or a futures contract offers today. *Badla* charges were proportional to the interest rates prevailing then and reflected cost of carry. While *badla* meant payment of cost of carry, the differential between settlement and contracted prices was paid or received by the *badla* financier and can be termed analogous to marking to market (MTM).

When sellers instead of buyers sought deferment of delivery, they had to pay the buyers to agree to defer delivery; this payment was called *ulta badla*. The system depended on whether those who were willing to accept delivery on settlement day were more in number than those who were interested in giving delivery. It is analogous to backwardation, or negative cost of carry.

In today's market, two alternatives for taking delivery and squaring up are still available, with the settlement period reduced to a single day. As mentioned earlier in this chapter, those who square up on the same day are referred to as *day traders*. However, the third option of carrying forward a trade is not available in stock markets today. If one does not intend to deliver or square up on the scheduled day, one has to conduct operations in the futures market, different from the spot market.

In earlier days, the intention of delivery or carry forward was not required to be disclosed on the day of opening of trade. Spot deals and forward deals could be conducted in the same market, except that the carry forward facility was limited to a few active stocks. A decision with regard to delivery or carry forward could be taken on the settlement day, as the markets for spot and forward were integrated then. Today, separate markets exist for spot and future deliveries. The markets or segments meant for future delivery are referred to as *derivatives market*.

For several reasons, such as a number of payment crises, operational difficulties, misuse of the system by a select few, etc., the system of forward trading or *badla* was banned, reintroduced, and then banned again from the market. An alternative to speculators was made available in the form of another product called futures, which inter alia served the objective of speculation, but was better regulated, with systems for initial margins, MTM and settlement procedures. An added advantage with futures was that the product could be applied to the index, while *badla* was confined to select individual stocks. *Badla* was a relatively simple and conceptually strong product that did not suffer from major fundamental deficiencies. It was banned because it had operational and implementation problems. The system of *badla* stands abolished today, and has been superseded by futures and options on stocks and indices, with elaborate margining and control mechanisms. We now discuss futures on indices and stocks.

FUTURES CONTRACT ON INDICES AND INDIVIDUAL STOCKS

As we already know, a futures contract means delivery of the underlying asset at a future date at a price fixed today. While the forward contract could be tailor-made to the requirements of the buyer and the seller, the futures contract needs standardization with the intervention of an exchange between the buyer and the seller. Note that *badla*, too, required intervention of an exchange, yet we call it a forward contract, as it lacked the level of standardization that is conventional with futures.

Stock exchanges define the characteristics of futures contracts, such as the underlying indices, market lots, and the maturity dates of the contracts. Futures contracts are available for trading from introduction to expiry date. The NSE and BSE in India offer futures contracts on several indices such as NIFTY and NIFTY Junior, and indices for sectors such as information

> Besides futures on indices, we also have futures on individual stocks in India.

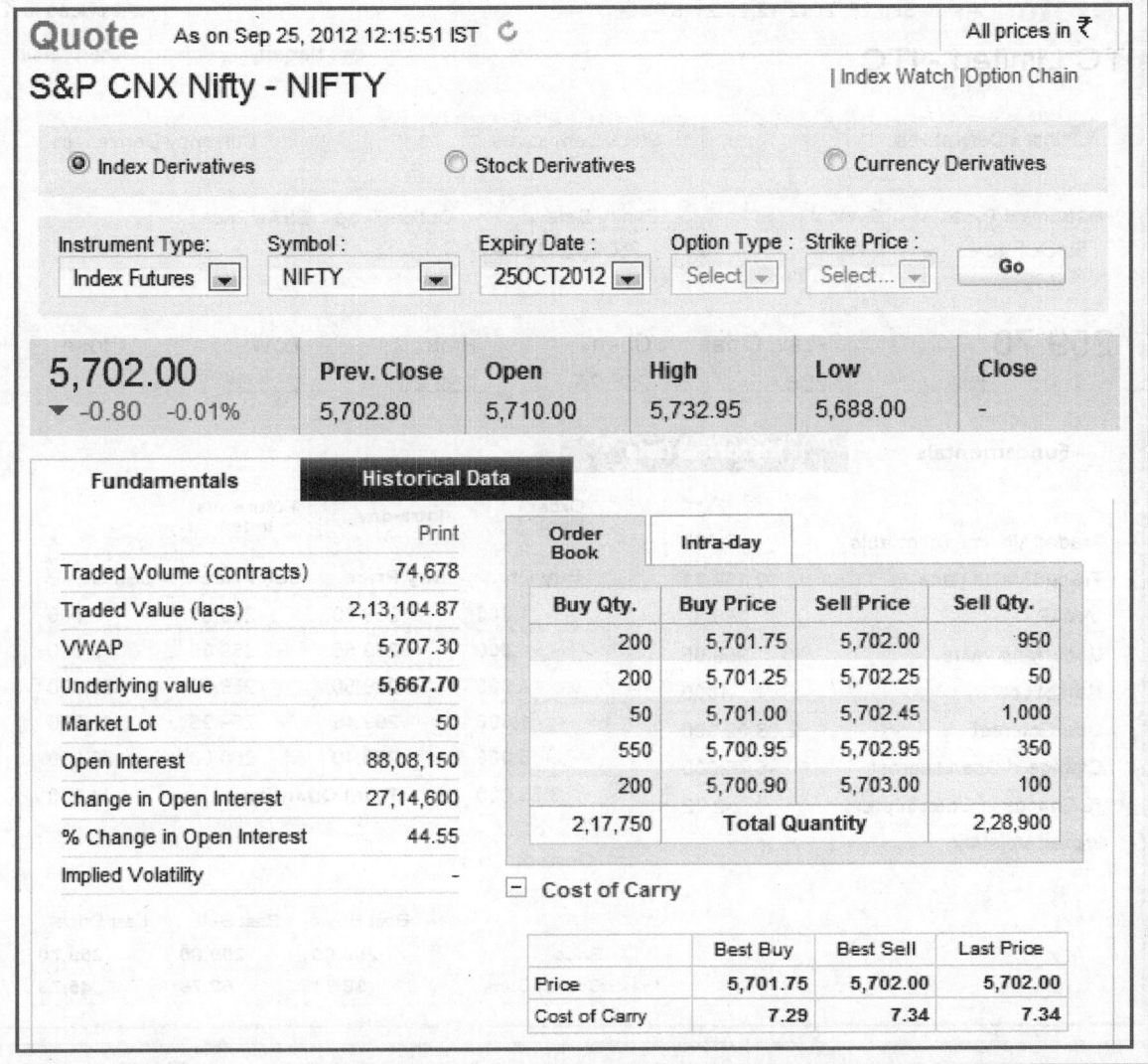

Fig. 4.1 Price information of futures contracts on index (NIFTY) at NSE

Source: www.nseindia.com, accessed on 25 September 2012.

technology (IT) and banking, besides on many individual stocks. Figure 4.1 depicts the price information on futures contracts on the popular NIFTY index. Figure 4.2 depicts the price information for futures contracts on the stock of ITC Ltd.

A stock exchange acts as a market maker by offering two-way quotes. It also functions as a clearing house, and each member signs a separate agreement with it. Though futures contracts can be offered for long-term maturities by stock exchanges, exchanges in India have introduced monthly contracts maturing on each of the next three months. For example, in the month of January, three contracts, referred to as January, February, and March contracts, would be available. The day of settlement has been fixed as the last Thursday of each month. The next month's contract would be introduced on the following Friday.

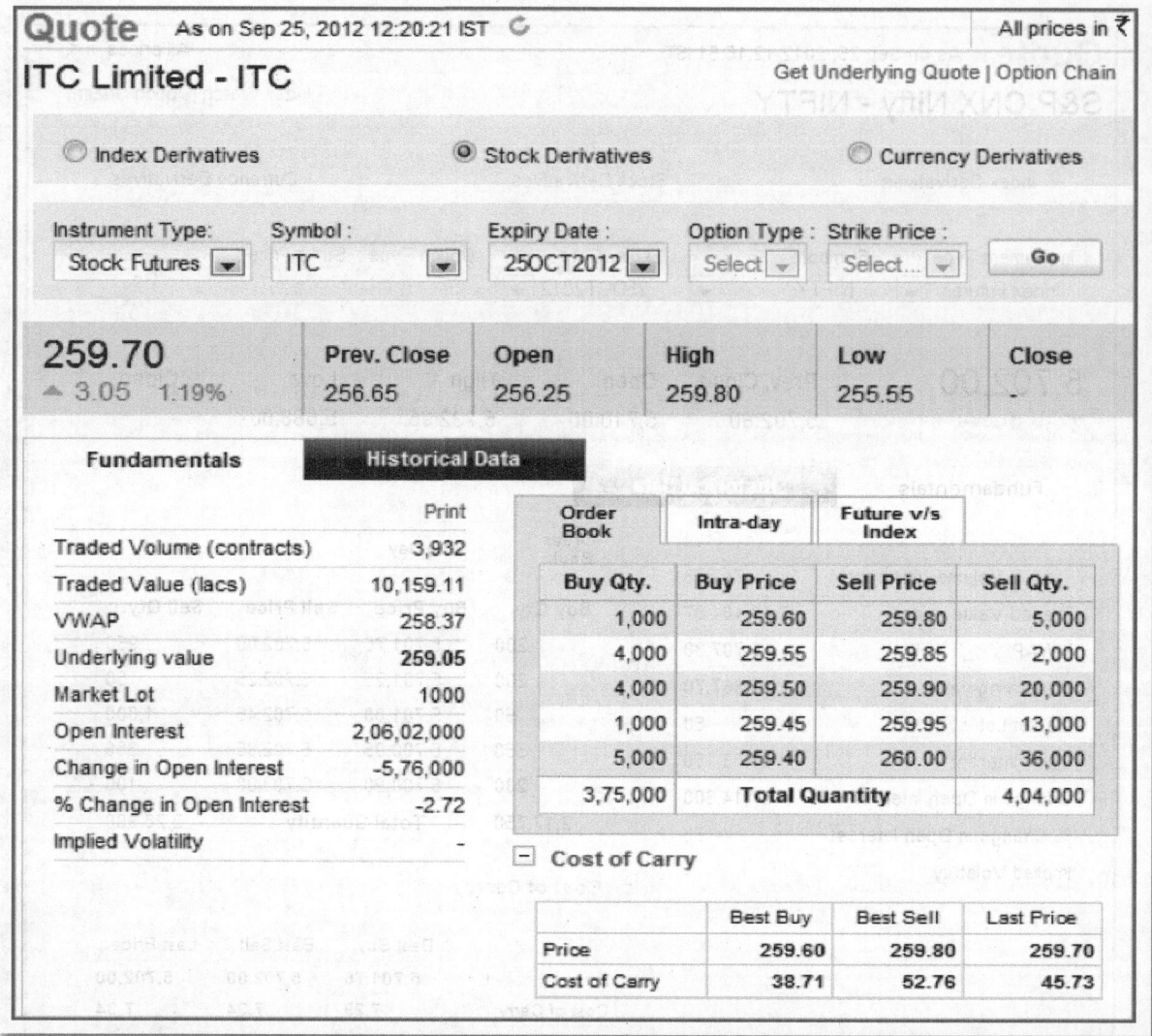

Fig. 4.2 Price information of futures contracts on ITC Ltd at NSE

Source: www.nseindia.com, accessed on 25 September 2012.

FEATURES AND SPECIFICATIONS OF STOCK/INDEX FUTURES

Standardization aspects of futures contracts currently available in Indian stock exchanges, with indices as underlying, relate to lot size, tick size, price quotation, settlement date, etc. Explanations of the details of futures contracts on indices and individual stocks are as follows:

Contract Size The minimum contract value is set to be close to ₹2 lakh at the time of introduction. The minimum lot for the BSE SENSEX was fixed at 50, while for NIFTY it was 200, initially. Today, the size of lots in NIFTY futures contracts is also set at 50.

Contract Value Each point is considered to be equivalent to ₹1. If NIFTY has a value of 5050, the contract size would be 5050 × 50 × 1 = ₹2,52,500.

Tick Size Tick size indicates the minimum change that is allowed in the price quotation. It is fixed at 0.05 points for both SENSEX and NIFTY. Hence, the minimum change in value of a NIFTY contract will be 50 × 0.05 = ₹2.50.

Margins Futures have an elaborate margining system. Whether for a buy or a sell transaction, the margin (percentage of contract value) determined by the exchange needs to be compulsorily deposited with the exchange before executing the trade. It is called the *initial margin*.

Besides the initial margin, profit/loss adjustments on a daily basis (MTM) are also required.

Number of Contracts At any point of time, three monthly contracts are available. Therefore, the period of hedge or speculation is confined to the next three months. The contract expiring first is referred to as the *near-month* contract, and the contract expiring last is called the *far-month* contract.

Maturity/expiry Each contract expires on the last Thursday of the delivery month. A new series comes into existence on the following Friday.

Settlement As indices are non-deliverable, a futures contract is cash-settled. However, obligations under futures contracts can be liquidated by entering into a contract opposite to the original contract before expiry. If not closed by the last day of trading, the open position is automatically closed on that day at a price determined by the exchange, called the *final settlement price*.

Besides index futures, we have futures contracts on individual stocks in India. One such contract is depicted in Fig. 4.2. Stock futures are financial contracts, where the underlying assets are individual stocks. These contracts have standardized specifications too. In India, the amount of each futures contract is determined by the respective stock exchange and was fixed initially at around ₹2 lakh. Thus, the number of shares in each stock futures contract depends upon the prevailing value of the stock.

Unlike index futures, the delivery of stock futures is possible, as the stock in question can be delivered. However, for the sake of uniformity, stock futures are only cash-settled at present, and there is no requirement for delivery. The final settlement is done at the final settlement price on the last day of the contract.

All over the world, futures contracts on indices are preferred, as they are used for hedging diversified portfolios held by financial institutions. Futures on individual stocks do not exist in all countries. However, they are gaining acceptance with time, as futures on individual stocks are being introduced in several countries. Futures on individual stocks are not encouraged for the following reasons:

- Institutional investors and large equity holders use futures for hedging fairly diversified portfolios supposed to carry only market risk. Index futures serve that objective well.
- Price volatility in individual stocks is much higher than in the index comprising them.
- Due to higher volatility, futures on individual stocks carry more risk of clearing, and for investors, they require higher margins.
- The prices of stock indices are more difficult to manipulate as compared to those of individual stocks.

> Index futures are of greater utility than stock futures because they are used for hedging diversified portfolios.

MARGINING SYSTEM

As stated in the features of the futures contracts, trading is facilitated by exchanges that face the onus of settlement of all contracts on their due dates. In order to contain the risk of default, exchanges stipulate margins, which are held as an assurance of honouring of contracts. Both buyers and sellers are required to deposit margins with the exchange while initiating their positions. These margins are specified in terms of percentages of values of the contracts, and represent the magnitude of potential loss that a position in futures can incur on any given day. The margins are linked with volatility of the price of the underlying asset. Since prices of individual securities are considered more volatile than the index, the margin requirement for futures on individual stocks is higher.

With the initial margin covering the potential loss on any given day, the loss for the day that has just gone by must be made good to the exchange if the position is carried forward to the next day. Similarly, profit, if any, on the outstanding position would be paid by the exchange to the investor. The exchange deems all positions closed at the end of the day. The amount of profit or loss that would have accrued if the investors were to close out their positions at the end of the day is called the MTM margin. All outstanding positions are brought to a common value called *clearing* or *settlement price*.

For example, an investor buys one contract of futures on NIFTY at 3170. With a contract size of 50 and an initial margin of 12%, the investor needs to deposit ₹19,020 (3170 × 50 × 12%). At the end of the day, assume that NIFTY closes at 3180, with a clearing price of 3185 (*clearing price* is normally a weighted average price of the last 30 minutes of trade, and, hence, may differ from the last traded price). MTM would result in a gain of ₹750 (15 × 50), resulting in cash inflow to the investor. Similarly, on the next day, if the clearing price was 3150, the loss would be ₹1750 (35 × 50), and the investor would pay this amount to the exchange. The MTM process would continue till such time the investor closes out by offsetting his contract. If the investor does not close out till the last trading day, then the exchange clears all the positions on the clearing price of the last trading day, called the final settlement price. The process of MTM does not alter the overall profit, but splits the profit/loss on a daily basis. The overall profit/loss of the investor remains the same, that is, the difference of his buying and selling prices.

PRICING STOCK AND INDEX FUTURES

Pricing of futures on a stock or an index follows the cost of carry model. The cost of carry is rather easy to determine in case of financial assets. The absence of convenience yield in financial assets further simplifies the determination of price. In case of financial futures, the cost of carry comprises only the interest cost adjusted for dividend yield on the index. It represents the cost of funds that would be incurred if a similar position were taken in the cash market and carried till maturity of the futures contract, less any income, typically dividends accruing on the stocks comprising the index. Therefore,

> Index futures are based on non-deliverable assets, yet we can use the cost of carry model for pricing Index futures.

Futures price = spot price + cost of carry r − benefits of ownership d
Cost of carry = financing cost in case of stock index futures/financial asset.

For discrete compounding:
$$F = S(1 + r/m)^{mt}$$
For continous compounding:
$$F = Se^{(r-d)t}$$
(4.1)

where r is the annual interest rate, m is the number of compounding intervals in a year, d is dividend yield, and t is time to maturity in years.

The theoretical value or the fair value of the index future, F, as given by Eq. 4.1, depends upon the cost of carry and the benefits of dividend accruing during the period. The cost of the carry model is based on the arbitrage argument. Example 4.1 illustrates the application of the cost of the carry model for pricing index futures.

EXAMPLE 4.1 Fair price of index futures

The following data as on 29 December 2008 are available:
NSE NIFTY = 2500, 1-m futures on NIFTY, maturing 29 January 2009 = 2,568.

(a) Find the value of one contract on NIFTY assuming a size of 50 indices.
(b) Find the fair value of the futures contract, assuming the interest rate to be 12% p.a.
(c) Is there an opportunity to profit from the above calculation? If yes, how can this opportunity be realized?

Solution

(a) Value of 50 futures contracts on NIFTY = 50 × 2568 = ₹1,28,400
(b) Fair value of the futures contract
    = current price of underlying + cost of carry (taken for 1 month)
    = 2500 + 25 = 2525 (assuming a financing cost of 12% p.a., i.e., the cost of carry is 1% of 2500)
(c) Yes, there is an opportunity to make profit, since the actual price 2568 is above the fair value. Hence, the futures contract is overpriced. One must sell futures in the hope that it would correct to fair value and converge to the spot for the underlying NIFTY on the day of delivery. When that happens, the investor would buy back futures contract to make a profit.

Consider the present value of NIFTY index to be 3150. The 3-m interest rate is 12% p.a., while the dividend yield on the index is estimated to be 6%. Based on the data given, the fair value of the index futures with 90 days remaining for maturity is,

Fair value of the index future
= value of index + cost of carry for 90 days − dividend benefit for 90 days
= 3150 + 3150 × 12% × 90/365 − 3150 × 6% × 90/365
= 3150 + 93.20 − 46.60 = 3196.60

If a futures contract sells for anything other than the fair price, it offers an arbitrage opportunity. Consider a futures contract on index that is selling for 3210. Clearly, the index futures contract is overpriced and cash-and-carry arbitrage is possible. An investor can execute the arbitrage by taking the simultaneous steps of:

Stock index futures offer arbitrage opportunities if the actual price is different from the theoretical price.

- selling the futures at 3210;
- buying the underlying assets (this may be done through basket buying/programme trading) at the current value of the index of 3150; and
- borrow the required amount at 12%.

This will ensure profit to the investor upon closing out of the position just prior to the maturity of the futures contract, irrespective of the value of the index at that point of time. Because of the convergence, the index and the futures contracts would be at the same price on the closing day. Upon maturity of the futures contract, the investor would do the following:

- Buy back the futures
- Sell the underlying stocks
- Pay the borrowing along with interest

Table 4.1 gives the profit for the investor at two different closing levels of the index: 3100 and 3300. In both cases, the profit is ₹13.40; the difference between the actual price and the fair price at $t = 0$ (3210.00 − 3196.60). If the index goes down, the profit from the index futures exceeds the loss on the underlying stocks; and if the index goes up, the loss in the futures is lesser than the gain on the underlying asset.

Table 4.1 Fair price of futures and arbitrage

Cash flow in ₹

Index closing		3,100.00	3,300.00
Initial position			
Sell futures at 3,210			
Borrow funds		3,150.00	−3,150.00
Buy underlying stocks		−3,150.00	+3,150.00
Initial net cash flow		**0.00**	**0.00**
Closing position:			
Buy futures		3,100.00	3,300.00
(a)	**Profit/loss on futures**	**+110.00**	**−90.00**
Sell underlying stocks		+3,100.00	+3,300.00
Interest payment		−93.20	−93.20
Dividend received		+46.60	+46.60
Pay borrowings		−3,150.00	−3,150.00
(b)	**Net cash flow on borrowing and underlying stocks**	**−96.60**	**+103.40**
Profit of portfolio of futures and underlying stocks (a + b)		**13.40**	**13.40**

When the futures is underpriced, reverse cash-and-carry arbitrage is executed by buying the futures, selling the underlying asset, and lending the funds realized till the maturity date of the futures contract. These actions would not imply any initial cash flow. On the date of maturity, when the futures price converges to the spot value of the underlying asset, the initial actions are reversed. One would offset the long position in futures, buy the underlying asset back, and realize the funds lent along with interest. This would result in a positive cash flow, irrespective of whether the spot price moved up or down.

The actual value may vary from the theoretical value depending on demand and supply of the underlying at present and expectations about the future. Under normal market conditions, futures contracts are priced above the spot price due to positive cost of carry. Sometimes, the futures price may possibly be below the spot price. Such a situation is known as *backwardation*.

The fair value as per the cost of carry model states the value of the futures under ideal conditions, but in reality, the price may deviate from the fair value. If this be the case, the divergence from fair value represents an opportunity for arbitrage, as explained here.

APPLICATIONS OF INDEX FUTURES

Stock/index futures are used in the same way as any other futures contract is used: for (a) hedging, (b) speculation, and (c) arbitrage. A few other applications of convenience are also discussed. We illustrate each one of them.

EXAMPLE 4.2   Fair price of stock futures with dividend

A stock is trading at ₹600 today. What would be the fair value of a futures contract on the stock maturing after 90 days if risk-free interest rate is 12%, and after 45 days, the stock is expected to give a dividend of ₹30? What would the fair value of the futures contract be if there were no dividend? Assume annual compounding.

$$D_0 = \frac{D}{\left(1 + \frac{r}{365} \times 45\right)} = \frac{30}{\left(1 + \frac{0.12}{365} \times 45\right)} = ₹29.56$$

Solution
The present value of the dividend is,
Therefore, the ex-dividend price at today's value = 600.00 − 29.56 = ₹570.44
The fair value of the futures contract
  = current price of the underlying + cost of carry (taken for 90 days)
  = 570.44 + 570.44 × 0.12 × 90/365 = ₹587.32
If there were no dividend, then the fair value of the futures with 90 days to expiry would be,
  = current price of the underlying + cost of carry (taken for 90 days)
  = 600 + 600 × 0.12 × 90/365 = ₹617.75

HEDGING THROUGH INDEX FUTURES

Portfolio can be hedged using index futures. We discuss hedging long and short portfolios with respect to fall and rise in prices.

Hedging Existing Portfolio

Investors long on their portfolios or their stocks fear a decline in the value of the assets in case the price declines. They need to protect the value of their existing portfolios against fall in price. They can do so by going short on the index futures. This is known as a *short hedge*.

> Stock index futures can be used for hedging a long position in a portfolio by going short on futures.

For example, consider a mutual fund that fears a fall in the value of the portfolio in the near future. While owning the portfolio and expecting the market to fall, it has the following three options:

Do Nothing With faith in the long-term fundamentals, the mutual fund may decide to remain invested and do nothing about the temporary fall in value expected. In such a case, the portfolio faces the risk of a temporary fall becoming permanent and losing value over the long-term. Here, the fund decides to carry the risk of fall in the market.

Sell and Buy Back Alternatively, the fund can sell the portfolio now and buy back later when the prices have fallen. Such a strategy suffers from the following drawbacks:

Transaction costs First selling and then buying back the portfolio would result in transaction costs, reducing the returns.

Impact cost If it is a large mutual fund, the action of selling may trigger panic selling by others, causing prices to fall more than normal. Similarly, while repurchasing the stock, prices may go up. Besides transactions costs, the mere action of first selling and then buying back the stocks may cause prices to change unfavourably, bringing down the returns. The effect on price due to the size of the order in the actions of selling and buying and vice versa is known as *impact cost*. This cost accrues over and above the transactions costs of brokerage, taxes, etc.

Risk proves illusory If the threat of decline in prices actually does not materialize, and if the markets were to rise instead, it would cost more to reacquire the portfolio. Besides, the fund will unnecessarily incur transactions cost and impact cost.

Hedge with Futures Hedging with futures would involve taking a short position in futures hoping to compensate any fall in the value of the portfolio with gain in the position of the futures when unwound. Such a strategy would provide protection of the value of the portfolio, while avoiding repurchase cost, transaction costs, and impact cost.

Let us consider the mechanics of the third alternative of hedging with futures. The fund is long on the asset and in order to protect the value against a fall in the price, it must go short on futures. The fund must sell futures now and buy later, keeping the portfolio intact. As stated earlier in this chapter, such a strategy will save transaction cost as well as impact cost, and, besides, will keep the intention confidential.

Assume that the fund holds a portfolio worth ₹1 crore at current spot prices. A fall in price is expected, and therefore, a protection of the value is imperative. Assume that a futures contract on NIFTY maturing three months from now is trading at 2650. With each point valued at ₹1 and a contract size of 50, the value of one contract on NIFTY futures is ₹1,32,500 (2650 × 50 × 1). The number of contracts required to be sold to cover the exposure of ₹1 crore is 75.47 (rounded to 75). At the end of the hedging period of three months, 75 contracts have to be bought back. Let us now consider the position after three months under two contrasting scenarios of fall and rise in the prices.

If the market falls as expected, the value of the portfolio would decline, but the position in futures would result in a profit, compensating for the loss in the value of the portfolio. However, if the markets appreciated instead, the value of the portfolio would increase, but this would be offset by the loss in the futures position. Table 4.2 presents the position in two cases: a 10% decline and a 10% rise.

We note that the value of a portfolio comprising long positions on stocks and futures contracts remains almost the same irrespective of what happens to the market. If the market falls by 10%, the physical portfolio would decline by ₹10 lakh, but the loss would be marginal at ₹6250. Instead, if the market gains 10%, the value of the aggregate portfolio would have a marginally improved position at ₹6250. Note that the hedge through futures is not a perfect one, because the position taken in futures of ₹99,37,500 did not exactly match the value of the portfolio of ₹1 crore.

> Hedging with index futures is the most efficient way of handling risk as it saves transaction costs and impact costs.

Table 4.2 Hedging with futures

Cash flow in ₹

Index value	2,385 (10% decline)	2,915 (10% rise)
Futures position		
Sold 75 futures contracts at 2,650	+99,37,500	+99,37,500
Bought 75 futures contracts	−89,43,750	−1,09,31,250
Profit/loss on futures	+9,93,750	−9,93,750
Portfolio position		
Initial value	1,00,00,000	1,00,00,000
Final value	90,00,000	1,10,00,000
Profit/loss on portfolio	−10,00,000	+10,00,000
Aggregate position of portfolio and futures at the end of 3 months	−6,250	+6,250

Hedge Ratio

In the preceding analysis, it was assumed that the portfolio would decline in the same proportion as the market, i.e., a 10% change in the index would also mean a 10% change in the portfolio. What if the proportionate change in value of the portfolio is not the same as the proportionate change in the market index on which the futures position was taken? In such a case, the number of contracts would have to be adjusted such that the profit/loss on futures equals the loss/profit on the portfolio.

We know that the sensitivity of the portfolio to changes in the market is given by the beta of the portfolio. In the preceding analysis, the beta of the portfolio was assumed as 1.00, and, hence, the exposure of the short position in futures was equal to the value of the long position in stocks. If the beta of the portfolio were 1.1, the decline in value would be 11% as a consequence of a 10% fall in the market. Therefore, one would need to short 83 (1.1 × 75.47 = 83.02) contracts to compensate for the extra fall. Similarly, if the beta of the portfolio were 0.85, 64 contracts need to be sold (0.85 × 75.47 = 64.14).

The hedge ratio (the number of futures contracts to be traded) in the case of index futures is equal to the beta of the stock/portfolio. Recall that the optimum hedge ratio is given by:

> Any change in value of a portfolio is determined by its beta. The position in futures should be equal to beta times the portfolio value.

$$h^* = \rho \frac{\sigma_s}{\sigma_f} = \beta \text{ by definition}$$

Hedging Short Position of Portfolio

It is difficult to conceive of a short position in stocks. However, consider the position of an individual who will be superannuated soon, and who intends to invest his/her retirement funds in stocks, or an investment fund awaiting research findings before deployment of the proceeds of the new public offer. These instances of proposed or planned acquisition of a portfolio are regarded as short positions in stocks/portfolio. These positions would lose if prices rise in the interim period between contemplated and actual purchase of stocks.

A short position in the portfolio can be hedged against any likely rise in the value of stocks by assuming a long position in futures. Such a hedge is called a *long hedge*. The mechanics of the long hedge would be similar to the one explained for the short hedge.

With a long position in futures, the rise in the market would result in a profit, which could be used to fund the extra cost of acquisition of stocks. In case the market fell, the cost of the acquisition of the portfolio would be less but at the same time, there would be a loss in the futures. In any case, the investor would lock in the cost of acquisition of the contemplated portfolio at current prices.

While ensuring a fixed price for acquiring the portfolio, one forgoes the benefit of any price decline in the future.

The hedge ratio for a long hedge remains the same as explained for the short hedge.

Insulating Against Market Risk

We highlighted the aspect of hedging the value of a portfolio using futures. This was under the assumption that the portfolio was well diversified and did not contain any risk other than market risk. The risk for a small non-diversified portfolio or a single stock is somewhat different from the risk for a well-diversified portfolio. Changes in the price of a given stock may not only be

---

EXAMPLE 4.3   Short hedge—hedging long position of portfolio of stocks

Consider a mutual fund having a huge portfolio of ₹100 crore. Today is 2 February, and the expectation of a general budget this 28 February is not very realistic. The current value of the BSE SENSEX is 6500. February and March futures maturing on 25th February and 25th March, consisting of 50 SENSEX, are selling at 6525 and 6600 respectively. How can the fund be protected against the uncertainty of the budget? Analyse position of portfolio with 5% fall and 5% rise in SENSEX.

Solution

The hedging strategy:

The fund is long on the asset and must go short on futures. It must sell futures contracts for March, as uncertainty over the budget will last till February 28, and cannot be covered by selling February contracts expiring prior to that date. To cover the risk fully, the fund must sell March futures contracts. Alternatively, it can be protected by selling February futures contracts, which would leave the fund exposed for the period between the dates of expiration of the futures and the date of the budget.

No. of contracts to be traded
Value of one BSE SENSEX contract = 50 × 6600 = ₹3.30 lakh
Value of the portfolio to be hedged = ₹10,000 lakh
No. of contracts to be sold = 10,000/3.30 ≅ 3030 contracts.

(assuming the fund is diversified enough, and that a 1% change in the market causes the same degree of change in portfolio value) The fund buys back the index at an appropriate time after 28 February.

If the market goes down by 5% as anticipated:

The value of the portfolio stands reduced by ₹5 crore to ₹95 crore. The March futures falls from 6600 to 6270 when the fund squares up its position.

Gain on futures = (6600 − 6270) × 50 × 3030 = ₹499.95 lakh

Therefore, the fund more or less compensates itself for the loss incurred on the portfolio value. Remember that futures cannot provide permanent protection, and if market sentiments become bearish, the fund will have to resort to other methods, including rolling over of the hedge. A longer period of uncertainty can be covered by closing out the position in March futures and opening a new position by going short on, say, June futures.

If the market goes up by 5% against expectations:

The value of the portfolio stands increased by ₹5 crore to ₹105 crore. The price of March futures rises from 6600 to 6900 when the fund squares up its position.

Loss on futures = (6600 − 6930) × 50 × 3030 = ₹499.95 lakh

Therefore, the increase in portfolio value is offset more or less by the loss incurred on the futures contracts, keeping the value of the portfolio almost constant. Note that hedging through futures does not mean protecting against loss while preserving gain. It only ensures a constant value of the portfolio.

> Index futures can only be used to insulate against the market risk of individual stocks.

due to changes in the market but may also be due to internal factors in the organization that floated the stock. According to the portfolio theory, the risk of a non-diversified portfolio consists of

- unsystematic risk (stock-specific risk); and
- systematic risk (market risk).

An exposure to a single stock (or a non-diversified portfolio) means a risk exposure of both types. For example, an investor buys stock of Infosys worth ₹10 lakh on the expectation of good news. By doing so the investor is assuming the following:

- *Unsystematic risk* The risk that his assessment of the potential of the company may prove to be wrong.
- *Systematic risk* The risk that his assessment of the potential of the stock may be correct, and, yet, his investment provides poor returns because the market, in general, falls.

The total risk as measured by the variance of returns is the sum of the two components, i.e., systematic risk (market risk) and unsystematic risk (stock-specific risk). This is expressed as

$$\sigma^2 = \beta^2 \sigma_m^2 + \sigma_i^2 \tag{4.2}$$

where σ = standard deviation of the security/portfolio
β = beta of the portfolio/stock
σ_m = standard deviation of the market
σ_i = standard deviation of the security/portfolio due to itself

Futures can help to eliminate the market risk of the portfolio/security by taking a position in futures opposite to that of the underlying market, and the value of the index futures changes according to the overall market. The risk in the index futures is σ_m^2. Since the position of the index futures is beta times the position in the physical market, its risk would be $\beta^2 \sigma_m^2$. The aggregate risk of the portfolio of physical and futures positions would, therefore, only be the unsystematic risk of the stock, σ_i^2. Therefore, hedging with index futures can cancel out market risks while stock-specific risks still remain.

The stock-specific risk is assumed to be a small component of the total risk. As we enlarge the portfolio, the amount of unsystematic risk diminishes, and can be deemed negligible for a portfolio consisting of a large number of stocks. A large portfolio would face only market risk, called systematic risk, and index futures become an effective tool for managing this risk. While unsystematic risk is taken care of by diversification, the systematic risk is offset by a position in index futures.

Example 4.4 demonstrates the use of futures as tool for reduction of market risk.

Controlling Risk of Stock Portfolio

With a diversified portfolio of stocks, unsystematic risk is eliminated, while the risk that cannot be eliminated is systematic risk. With changing market conditions, the portfolio returns become sensitive to the market risk alone. A portfolio manager or any intelligent investor would like to beat the market. The strategy that is often employed by investors to outperform

EXAMPLE 4.4 Hedge against market risk

An investor wants to buy stock in Hindustan Lever Ltd (HLL) worth ₹20 lakh due to its very strong fundamentals. However, the market in general is considered to remain weak for about three more months. The beta of HLL is 1.2, and the current value of NIFTY is 2250. A 3-m index futures contract is selling at 2310. Answer the following:

(a) How can the investor hedge himself against the expected fall in the market?
(b) Analyse his position (i) if the market falls by 10% in three months and HLL drops to ₹178 from ₹200, and (ii) if the market registers a rise of 6% and HLL rises to ₹215 from ₹200.
(c) Given the standard deviations of the market and HLL as 12% and 18%, respectively, what is the risk faced by the unhedged and hedged portfolios

Solution

(a) One option for the investor was to wait for three months and then buy. He runs the risk of a rise in the price of the HLL share after three months. With stock index futures available, he does not need to defer the purchase and take the risk of a rise in prices. A better strategy would be to buy the shares now and protect against the risk of a falling market by taking a short position in 3-m futures. Since the beta of HLL is 1.2, the futures position must be 1.2 times the position in the physical market. Therefore, the investor

- buys stock worth ₹20 lakh due to strong fundamentals; and
- sells 3-m futures worth ₹24 lakh (1.2 × 20 lakh) to insulate oneself against market risk

No. of shares of HLL = 20,00,000/200 = 10,000
No. of futures contract sold = value to be hedged/value of one futures contract
= 24,00,000/(200 × 2310) ≈ 5.19 (say 5 contracts)

(b) (i) The market falls by 10% to 2025 from 2250 and HLL share falls to ₹178:

Selling price of futures = 2310
Purchase price of futures = 2025
Gain in futures market = 285
Gain on position of futures = 5 × 200 × 285 = ₹2,85,000
Loss on 10,000 HLL shares = (200 − 178) × 10,000 = ₹2,20,000
Net gain = ₹65,000

If the investor was unhedged, his/her loss would have been ₹2,20,000

(ii) The market rises falls by 6% to 2385 from 2250 and HLL share rises to ₹215:

Selling price of futures = 2310
Purchase price of futures = 2385
Loss in futures market = 75
Loss on position of futures = 5 × 200 × 75 = ₹75,000
Gain on HLL 10,000 shares = (215 − 200) × 10,000 = ₹1,50,000
Net gain = ₹75,000

If the investor was unhedged, his/her gain would have been ₹1,50,000

(c) If the investor remained unhedged, he/she would carry the entire risk of HLL shares of 18%. With a hedged position in futures, the amount of variance reduction is

$\beta^2 \sigma_m^2 = 1.2^2 \times 12^2 = 207.36$ of standard deviation of 14.4%
Residual variance = $18^2 - \beta^2 \sigma_m^2 = 18^2 - 1.2^2 \times 12^2 = 116.64$ equivalent to 10.8%

A hedged portfolio will reduce the risk of the asset from 18% to 10.8%

the market is (a) to increase the beta of the portfolio to more than 1 when a price rise is expected, to ensure greater portfolio returns than the market, and (b) to reduce the beta of the portfolio to less than 1 if a fall in prices is expected, to ensure a smaller decline in the value of the portfolio than the market. Therefore, a need to change the beta of the portfolio arises whenever a change in the trend of the market is anticipated. There are many ways to alter the beta of the portfolio, as discussed here.

Portfolio Balancing Portfolio balancing is done to achieve the desired level of beta by constantly adjusting the portfolio. If the beta needs to be increased, the portfolio manager may replace some low-beta securities with high-beta ones. Similarly when the beta is to be reduced, securities with higher betas are replaced by securities with lower betas. Portfolio balancing requires frequent buying and selling of stocks, with increased costs of transactions as well as equity research. This also sends unwarranted and avoidable signals about the changing perception of the fund manager. If the size of the portfolio is large, impact costs would also reduce the returns.

Resort to Lending and Borrowing Another way to adjust the beta is to switch the portfolio between capital markets and debt markets. For reduction of beta, the portfolio manager can divest a suitable proportion from equity markets for reinvestment in debt markets. Remember that the beta of the bonds/fixed income instruments portfolio would be close to zero. The portfolio's beta would fall if some funds are invested in bonds. To increase the beta of the portfolio, one may resort to borrowing and investing the borrowed funds in stocks.

This change in beta is achieved by making use of the additive properties of beta, i.e., the beta of the portfolio is the weighted average of the betas of the individual assets comprising the portfolio. Refer to Example 4.5. Like portfolio balancing, the strategy of switching of portfolio between capital and debt markets will involve transaction costs. The amount to be invested in the debt markets requires liquidation of the same proportion of existing investments in the portfolio, to leave the beta of the portfolio untouched.

The beta of the portfolio of two assets, 1 and 2, is given by Eq. 4.3.

$$\beta_p = f_1 \times \beta_1 + f_2 \times \beta_2 \tag{4.3}$$

where f_1 and f_2, respectively, are the proportions of money invested in assets 1 and 2, with betas of β_1 and β_2.

For example, consider an aggressive investor with ₹25 lakh invested in a portfolio having a beta of 1.50. He fears a decline in the market. The investor wants to reduce the beta of the portfolio to a conservative figure of 0.75. To do so, the investor can retain fraction f_1 in the portfolio and sell $(1 - f_1)$ to invest in T-bills (beta = 0). Using Eq. 4.3, we can find the proportion of wealth that must continue to remain in the portfolio, or the wealth that must be divested from the portfolio and invested in T-bills.

Desired beta, $0.75 = f_1 \times 1.5 + (1 - f_1) \times 0$
Or f_1 = desired beta/portfolio beta = 0.75/1.5 = 0.5

This implies that the investor must sell, $(1 - f_1) = 50\%$ of his portfolio and invest the proceeds in T-bills.

Similarly, if the investor wants to increase the beta to 2.0, the proportion that must be invested in the portfolio will be

or f_1 = new beta/portfolio beta = 2.0/1.5 = 1.33

This implies that the investor must borrow 33% of the amount already in the portfolio and make further investments in the same portfolio. Note that while selling or buying, all the portfolio stocks that are bought/sold must be in the same proportion so as have the beta of the portfolio unchanged.

> Stock index futures provide a cost-effective way of controlling the beta of the portfolio by eliminating the transaction costs and impact costs associated with other methods.

Using Futures to Adjust the Beta of the Portfolio Yet another way of adjusting the risk of the portfolio is to switch the exposures between the equity markets and derivatives markets. The beta of the portfolio can readily be adjusted by using index futures. Any index has a beta equal to 1.

EXAMPLE 4.5   Finding the beta of the portfolio

An aggressive fund 'A' has a portfolio aggregating to ₹202.75 lakh, comprising the following 10 stocks.

Scrip	No. of shares	Price (₹)	Value (₹)	Beta
State Bank of India	2,500	930	23,25,000	1.10
HLL	6,000	180	10,80,000	1.25
ITC	8,000	140	11,20,000	1.40
Reliance	2,000	530	10,60,000	1.30
Bharti	7,000	350	24,50,000	1.70
Larsen & Toubro	2,000	1,500	30,00,000	1.25
Tata Steel	6,000	340	20,40,000	1.05
Maruti	4,000	550	22,00,000	1.25
Infosys	1,000	2,500	25,00,000	1.40
Ranbaxy	5,000	500	25,00,000	0.80
Total value of the portfolio			2,02,75,000	

Find out the beta of the portfolio.

Solution
The beta of the portfolio using additive property is computed as follows:

SCRIP	No. of shares	Price ₹	Value ₹	Beta	Weighted beta
State Bank of India	2,500	930	23,25,000	1.10	0.13
HLL	6,000	180	10,80,000	1.25	0.07
ITC	8,000	140	11,20,000	1.40	0.08
Reliance	2,000	530	10,60,000	1.30	0.07
Bharti	7,000	350	24,50,000	1.70	0.21
L & T	2,000	1,500	30,00,000	1.25	0.18
Tata Steel	6,000	340	20,40,000	1.05	0.11
Maruti	4,000	550	22,00,000	1.25	0.14
Infosys	1,000	2,500	25,00,000	1.40	0.17
Ranbaxy	5,000	500	25,00,000	0.80	0.10
Total value of the portfolio			2,02,75,000		
Beta of the portfolio					1.24

EXAMPLE 4.6 Portfolio balancing

Refer to Example 4.5. How much reduction in beta can be achieved by divesting in stock of beta higher than 1.40, and investing the proceeds in low-beta Ranbaxy stock?

Solution

Portfolio balancing:
If the investor wants to reduce the beta, he/she can divest the high-beta stocks of ITC, Bharti, and Infosys and reinvest the proceeds in the low-beta Ranbaxy stock. We can achieve a beta of around 1, as shown here

SCRIP	No. of shares	Price ₹	Value ₹	Beta	Weighted beta
State Bank of India	2,500	930	23,25,000	1.10	0.13
HLL	6,000	180	10,80,000	1.25	0.07
ITC	–	140	–	1.40	–
Reliance	2,000	530	10,60,000	1.30	0.07
Bharti	–	350	–	1.70	–
L & T	2,000	1,500	30,00,000	1.25	0.18
Tata Steel	6,000	340	20,40,000	1.05	0.11
Maruti	4,000	550	22,00,000	1.25	0.14
Infosys	–	2,500	–	1.40	–
Ranbaxy	17,140	500	85,70,000	0.80	0.34
Total value of the portfolio			2,02,75,000		
Beta of the portfolio					**1.03**

Due to the leveraging offered by futures, the desired beta can be achieved by trading in futures by using the following strategy:

- Sell futures to reduce beta
- Buy futures to increase beta

If the value of the portfolio is P, having a beta of β_p, and the investor goes short on futures of the value of F, then the beta of his/her combined position β_n is

$$P \times \beta_n = P \times \beta_p - F \times 1$$

The value of futures to be sold $(+)$/bought $(-)$ = $\pm P \times (\beta_p - \beta_n)$

Example 4.7 illustrates the strategies of adjusting beta using debt markets and futures markets.

The advantages of the strategy of adjusting beta through futures over the strategies of portfolio balancing and switching to and from the debt markets are easy to see:

- Avoids frequent buying or selling of equities from the portfolio
- Saves transaction costs, and yet adjusts the beta on a regular basis to the desired level of risk
- Avoids sending unnecessary signals to the market by avoiding constant buy and sell orders
- Avoids impact costs if the volumes of trade are large

EXAMPLE 4.7 Adjusting the risk of the portfolio

Refer to Examples 4.5 and 4.6. What would you do to achieve a beta of 0.8 using (a) debt markets and (b) using index futures? 3-m index future is selling at 2675.

Solution

(a) *Using debt market:*
The investor can divest the portfolio and invest in T-bills to achieve the desired beta of 0.8. If f_1 is the fraction retained in the portfolio, then

$$0.8 = f_1 \times 1.24 + (1 - f_1) \times 0$$

or $f_1 = 0.8/1.24 = 64.5\%$ to be retained in the portfolio. The fund must sell portfolio stocks worth 35.5% (₹69.95 lakh) and invest in T-bills. After three months, when the uncertainty is over, the fund can be divested of the T-bills and reinvested in the same portfolio.

(b) *Using futures:*
The investor can sell futures to lower the beta to 0.8. Exposure in the futures market must be equal to F, given by:

$$F = P \times (\text{old beta} - \text{new beta}) = P \times (1.24 - 0.8) = 202.75 \times 0.44 = ₹89.21 \text{ lakh}$$

Price of 3-m futures = 2675
Value of one contract = 200 × 2675 = ₹5.35 lakh
No. of contracts to be sold = 89.21/5.35 = 16.67 (say 17 contracts).

The fund can buy back the contracts to nullify its position any time prior to the expiry of the futures. In this strategy, the fund leaves the portfolio untouched. The fund needs neither to sell nor buy back any securities. Yet it achieves the desired beta.

SPECULATION WITH STOCK INDEX FUTURES

Hitherto, we looked at the hedging applications of index futures. It will not be wrong to say that derivatives markets were designed for the purpose of hedging against risk. Ironically, the same derivative markets can serve the opposite purpose, and may be used to create or magnify risk. The risk is increased when a participant in the market does not have any position in the underlying cash/physical asset. The risk arising from absence of position in the physical market can be compounded by the fact that a financial outlay is not required in the derivatives markets. A position in futures requires only the deposit of the initial margin with the exchange, and MTM provision as long as the position remains open.

A futures position provides an opportunity to take a view on the market. It is a leveraging mechanism that enables increased returns. As a simple strategy to benefit from an expected move in the market, one can buy or sell futures, rather than take a position in the cash market that would involve a large cash outlay. The following are the leveraging strategies:

- If the markets are expected to go up, buy futures now and sell later; and
- If the markets are expected to go down, sell futures now and buy later.

> Stock index futures are used to take speculative positions and make way for magnified returns, with equally magnified risk.

Using futures involves an outlay only in the form of initial margins. If the margin requirement is 10%, the investor can take a position 10 times larger than a corresponding position in the cash market. Accordingly the returns, positive or negative, will be magnified 10 times, even if the margin, which actually takes the form of a security deposit, is considered to be an investment.

Assume that an investor has ₹10 lakh to invest. He/she is currently bullish about the market. The current level of the index he/she is considering is

6500, and a 3-m futures contract of 50 indices is trading at 6650. The margin requirement is 20%. The investor has the option of buying a balanced portfolio from a mutual fund. However, he/she is highly optimistic about the rise of the market, and expects the level of the index, at a minimum, to be 10% higher in three months' time. How can he/she benefit from his/her optimistic forecast?

As one alternative, the investor can buy a balanced portfolio in the cash market. If the market goes up by 10%, the profit will be 10% of the investment in the cash market, i.e., ₹1,00,000. In case the market falls by 5%, the loss will be ₹50,000.

Alternatively, if the investor is extremely confident of his/her forecast, he/she can take a larger risky position in futures by buying 15 contracts on index futures needing margin of ₹9,97,500, leaving a cash balance of ₹2500, which is ignored.

Value of 3-m futures	= 50 × 6650 = 3,32,500
Margin required per contract	= ₹66,500
No. of contracts that can be bought	= ₹10,00,000/66,500 = 15

The investor subsequently sells these contracts at a higher price.

If the market goes up by 10%

The selling price of the contract	= 7150
Purchase price	= 6650
Profit per contract	= 500
Total profit	= 15 × 50 × 500 = ₹3,75,000

If the market falls by 5%

The selling price of the contract	= 6175
Purchase price	= 6650
Loss per contract	= 475
Total loss	= 15 × 50 × 475 = ₹3,56,250

Hence, with futures, the gains as well as the losses are magnified, as compared to a position in cash. While the gain on investment can be as high as 37.50% with only a 10% rise in the market, the loss would be equally high, at more than 35% with a 5% fall in the market. Here we are considering margin as investment which indeed is not correct because margin is required by exchange to cover settlement risk.

Futures can also be used in falling markets. An investor can benefit from a predicted fall in the prices of stocks by selling futures. As the prices of the futures fall in line with the underlying stocks in the index, the investor will make a greater positive return.

ARBITRAGE WITH STOCK INDEX FUTURES

When there is mispricing of futures, arbitrage with stock index futures is an excellent tool for enhancing yields on the portfolio.

We explained arbitrage with futures if the price of a futures contract is not same as its fair value. This may be used as a tool for enhancing the yield of the portfolio.

A portfolio consisting of stock index futures and T-bills produces the same returns as a stock portfolio replicating the index, if there is no mispricing of futures. If the theoretical price and actual price differ suffi-

EXAMPLE 4.8 Arbitrage with futures: Yield enhancement

An investor has ₹10 lakh available for investment. The spot value of the index he/she is considering is 6650, while a futures contract on the index maturing after 60 days is trading at 6670. The risk-free rate is 8%, while the dividend yield on the index is 4%. The investor is considering investment in a market portfolio to capitalize on the potential of an increase in the value of the securities and earn some dividend yield.

(a) Find out the true value of a 2-m futures contract.
(b) Is there a strategy you can suggest to make the investor earn more than what he/she can through investment in a portfolio of index stocks?

Solution

(a) Fair value of the 2-m futures contract:
$$F = S_0 e^{(r-d)T/365} = 6670 e^{(8\% - 4\%)(60/365)} = 6693.87$$
The actual price of the futures is 6670, which is lower than its fair value. Hence, futures are underpriced.

(b) Rather than buying a portfolio in the physical market, the investor can replicate a portfolio by buying futures contracts and investing in T-bills. The strategy will have the same risk as that of a portfolio in the physical market. A comparison of the payoffs under the two strategies is presented as follows:

Strategy I: invest in a portfolio of index stocks	
Amount invested in securities	10,00,000
Strategy II: Invest in T-bills and go long on futures	
Amount invested in T-bills	10,00,000
No. of futures bought	
Current value of a 2-m futures	6,670
No. of indices in a futures contract	50
Value of one futures contract	3,33,500
No. of contracts bought	3

The payoffs of the strategies are analysed for three different scenarios: a 10% increase, no change, and a 10% decrease in the market from the current level of 6650.

	Increase by 10%	No change	Decrease by 10%
Strategy I Have a portfolio of ₹10 lakh			
Value of the portfolio	11,00,000	10,00,000	9,00,000
Dividend yield at 4% on ₹10 lakh for two months	6,667	6,667	6,667
Total value of investment	**11,06,667**	**10,06,667**	**9,06,667**
Strategy II Invest in T-bills & buy 3-m futures			
Value of T-bills	10,00,000	10,00,000	10,00,000
Interest on T-bills	13,333	13,333	13,333
Position on futures			
Selling price of futures	7,315	6,650	5,985
Purchase price of futures	6,670	6,670	6,670
Profit/loss on index points	645	−20	−685
Profit/loss on futures	96,750	−3,000	−1,02,750
Total value of investment	**11,10,083**	**10,10,333**	**9,10,583**

As can be noticed Strategy II is always superior to Strategy I and hence in case of mispricing of futures the yields can be improved by investing in futures and T-bills.

ciently, then arbitrage opportunities that result in increased yield are created. One can adopt the following strategies in case there is mispricing of futures:

- If the actual price is less than the theoretical price, buy futures.
- If the actual price is more than the theoretical price, sell futures.

Example 4.8 illustrates an arbitrage opportunity that enhances the yield of a portfolio. When futures are overpriced, a reverse strategy can be used as follows:

- Sell futures
- Borrow at a risk-free rate
- Invest in the cash market, buying securities consisting of index stocks

Calendar Spreads

A calendar spread is created by simultaneous opposite positions in the same contract expiring at different times. For example, a long position in futures expiring in the month of May, when combined with a short position in the contract expiring in the month of June, will be termed calendar spread. There are two legs to a spread. A spread position is closed by reversal of both the legs simultaneously. The reversal of the long position in May futures would be selling May futures, while simultaneously buying June futures. In India, for index and stock futures, contracts for each of the next three months are available at any time. Hence calender spread can be created for next three months.

The risk profile of the calendar spread is substantially different from that of a single position. One leg of the spread is opposite to the other leg. If one leg is bearish, the other leg is bullish, and vice versa. Therefore, the risk in a spread position is much smaller, attracting lesser margins compared to the margins applicable for two independent stand-alone contracts.

The margin on calendar spread is calculated on the basis of the delta of a portfolio consisting of futures contracts for each month. The delta represents the rate of change of the value of the derivative with respect to change in the price of the underlying asset. Delta of futures is given by e^{rT}. For long position on 1-m future, the delta would be 1.0084 at 10% risk-free rate. For short position on 2-m future delta would be -1.0168. Thus, a portfolio consisting of a near-month contract with a delta of 100.84 and a far-month contract with a delta of -101.68 will attract a margin equal to the spread charge for a portfolio that has long 100 near-month futures and short 100 far-month futures. The spread charge is specified as 0.50% per month for the difference between the two legs of the spread, subject to a minimum of 1% and a maximum of 3%, as specified in the J.R. Varma committee report.[1]

> A calendar spread is used for taking advantage of mispricing of two futures expiring at different times by simultaneous and opposite positions.

Investors engaging in spread transactions are basically taking a position on the interest rate scenario. Futures prices are based on interest rates and are subject to change as perceptions of future interest rates change. A spread trader is essentially looking at the differential in prices of two futures contracts as compared with interest rates. As the interest rate goes up, the far-month futures will rise more than the near-month futures. Further, far-month futures are more volatile than near-month futures, as the delivery time is farther away, adding to

[1] As per BSE rules

> Calendar spreads have much lower margins because of two contrasting positions and are used to bet against future interest rates.

uncertainty. This gives rise to arbitrage opportunities, as mispricing between the futures of near months and far months is likely.

If an investor believes that interest rates are expected to rise, he/she might buy far-month futures and sell near-month futures. If interest rates do rise as expected, then the far-month futures would appreciate more, and the investor makes a profit. Similarly, if he believes that interest rates are expected to fall, he/she will buy near-month futures and sell far-month futures.

OTHER APPLICATIONS OF INDEX FUTURES

Apart from the three universal applications of derivatives, i.e., hedging, speculation, and arbitrage, there are a few more uses of futures that investors can adopt. These are discussed in the following paragraphs.

Opportunity for Naïve Investors Investment in the stock markets is often considered to be a strategy meant for sophisticated, learned, and financially savvy investors who are expected to understand the nuances of the capital markets. An investment in futures provides a convenient way for naïve investors to capture market-based returns, rather than remaining confined to safer investments like bank deposits offering moderate returns. The myth that investing in stocks requires considerable expertise and thorough understanding of the vagaries of the stock markets stands somewhat demolished with the avenue of investment provided by futures contracts. The prerequisite for investing in the stock market is not knowledge but orientation towards risk.

> Besides hedging, speculation, and arbitrage, index futures have benefits for naïve investors, such as elimination of research and tracking of errors.

The only possible shortcoming with investments in futures is the inflexibility of the investment horizon. Investment in index futures is constrained by the limited life of such contracts. At present, we find that the life of futures contracts is limited to three months, which could be a deterrent to investors with long-term commitments. The limited maturity of futures contracts leads to a belief that futures are appropriate only for investors with short-term speculative motives. However, this belief seems to be unfounded, as investors with longer time horizons of investment can adopt the strategy of rolling over from one futures contract to another, once the earlier futures contract matures.

Avoiding Equity Research Apart from the opportunities given to naïve investors, futures also provide considerable benefits to more sophisticated investors. Futures impart the ability to capitalize on bearish or bullish markets without undertaking equity research, which is time consuming and costly. Making an investment choice requires time, effort, and cost. Sophisticated and learned investors like mutual funds can simply take an appropriate position in futures without having to identify specific securities and save much cost, effort, and time. This is one reason that index funds have gained tremendous popularity.

Eliminating Tracking Errors Index mutual funds are mandated to provide market returns by replication of index by investing funds in the spot market in the same securities and the same proportions as that of the index. Therefore, the physical portfolio is supposed to track the index and thereby provide index returns to subscribers. Due to the continuous movement of prices, impact costs, and transaction costs involved, it is indeed difficult to provide returns equal to the index. They often fall short of the index returns due to the compulsion to hold back some liquidity to meet redemption pressures, administrative overheads, transaction costs, periodic changes in index construction, and the inability to reinvest dividends immediately on receipt. Any deviation of portfolio returns from index returns is referred to as a tracking error. The lesser the tracking error, the better managed is the fund. Every fund likes to keep tracking error to the minimum. Futures can reduce such tracking errors due to the absence of impact costs and to lower transaction costs, as well as the enhancing of returns due to leveraging features. If funds invest some part of the corpus in futures, shortfall in returns can be compensated for. Tracking errors would be minimised.

Facilitating Asset Allocation Portfolio managers often need to switch among debt, equity, and derivative markets to match the risk profile of their clientele. Changing the mix of stocks and bonds in a portfolio involves significant costs as well as discontinuity in operations.

Derivatives in Practice **Integrating Financial Markets**

India launches derivatives on DJIA and S&P 500

With effect from 29 August 2011, the NSE introduced derivatives contracts on indices of US stock markets, i.e., the Dow Jones Industrial Average (DJIA) and S&P 500, the most popular indices the world over. It is supposed to be the first instance across the world that a listing is granted for US indices outside the USA. It was perhaps a reciprocal arrangement to the listing of an Indian index, i.e., NIFTY, on the Chicago Mercantile Exchange (CME), after NIFTY was denominated in US dollars in July 2011. Besides CME, NIFTY has also been traded in the Singapore Stock Exchange since September 2000, while BSE SENSEX is also listed on the Eurex exchange, enabling traders to take a view on the Indian economy through its indices.

While S&P 500 offers futures and options through NSE, DJIA offers only futures contracts. The contract specifications are as given in the table below.

Select contract specifications on US indices

Underlying index	DJIA	S&P 500
Contract size	250	25
Contracts available	3 monthly contracts followed by 3 quarterly contracts for January, March, September, and December	
Expiry	The third Friday of the expiry month; in case that day is a holiday, the preceding day	
Mode of settlement	Cash settlement in Indian rupee	
Quantity freeze	15,000	

Such contracts are aimed at providing an opportunity to resident Indians to participate in US stocks and indices. Trading in these contracts is not allowed for non-resident Indians and foreign institutional investors, as they have other avenues available.

As per current guidelines, Indians are allowed to participate in the US spot markets to the extent of US $2,00,000 every year, but are allowed no positions in derivatives deemed inherently speculative in nature. Rupee-based cash settlement opens up the avenues for Indian investors who hitherto were not allowed to participate in exchanges abroad by the Reserve Bank of India. With cash settlement in Indian rupees, Indian investors can take a view on US stocks and trade accordingly. All of this is possible without their being exposed to any kind of currency risk.

This has important implications for hedging too, as now Indians can have a global portfolio, thereby reducing systematic risk, measured by beta of the portfolio. According to the portfolio theory, a portfolio with global stocks poses a smaller systematic risk than a portfolio comprising stocks from one nation alone. Though this move is not expected to draw strong interest from investors and traders, it is without any doubt a very promising beginning and attempt to integrate Indian capital markets with the world.

Rather than liquidating one asset in one market and then investing funds in another market, portfolio managers can trade in futures to achieve the risk profiles desired by clients. They can sell stock futures to decrease risk in stocks, and buy interest rate futures to increase exposure in bonds, and vice versa, with much lower transaction costs.

Assuming Only Company-specific Risk Owning stock and selling futures eliminates market risk and leaves the investor with company-specific risk. With futures available on individual securities, investors can leverage positions. Investors do not need a position in the cash market. Instead, they can go long on the futures of individual stock and, simultaneously, sell index futures to have company-specific risk in the portfolio with the effect of leverage. For example, if bullish on Wipro stock, an investor may like to buy futures on Wipro and short index futures. This eliminates systematic risk but retains the unsystematic risk of Wipro.

Integrating Financial Markets Across the World Investment in financial assets by non-residents is regulated by the government. From the viewpoint of economic efficiencies, such denial or restriction is undesirable as it handicaps the determination of true value of the stocks. The wider and larger the investor base, the truer would be the value of the firm. Though restrictions on direct participation in equities by non-residents may still have some merit due to foreign currency and reserve implications or capital flight considerations, their investments in futures or derivative should be viewed positively. Since futures can always be settled in cash in local currency, they are safer bets. Trading in the futures of stock indices of a foreign country would provide an opportunity to investors abroad to take a view on other economies, increasing market efficiency—something that must be beneficial.

SOLVED PROBLEMS

SP 4.1: Understanding stock/index futures quotations

From Fig. SP 4.1, answer the following:

(a) Name of the underlying asset and its current value
(b) Market lot and expiry
(c) Value of the contract traded during the day
(d) Latest value of the underlying asset
(e) Open interest at the end of today and the previous day
(f) Cost of carry
(g) Number of contracts squared up today
(h) Volatility of the index for one day and one year.

Solution

(a) Name of the underlying asset and its current value: NIFTY index futures, 4905.00
(b) Market lot and expiry: 50, 31 May 2012
(c) Value of the contract traded during the day ₹9,83,785.10 lakh
(d) Latest value of the underlying asset, i.e., NIFTY, 4891.45
(e) Open interest on 17 and 18 May
No. of contracts open as at the end of 18 May = 2,07,61,850
Change in the open interest during the day = −7,19,200
Open interest the previous day, i.e., 17 May 2012 = 2,14,81,050
(f) Cost of carry: 7.77% calculated as follows:

$$\text{Cost of carry (\%)} = \frac{\text{Futures price} - \text{Spot value}}{\text{Spot value}} \times \frac{365}{\text{days to maturity}} \times 100 = \frac{4905.00 - 4891.45}{4{,}891.45} \times \frac{365}{13} \times 100 = 7.77\%$$

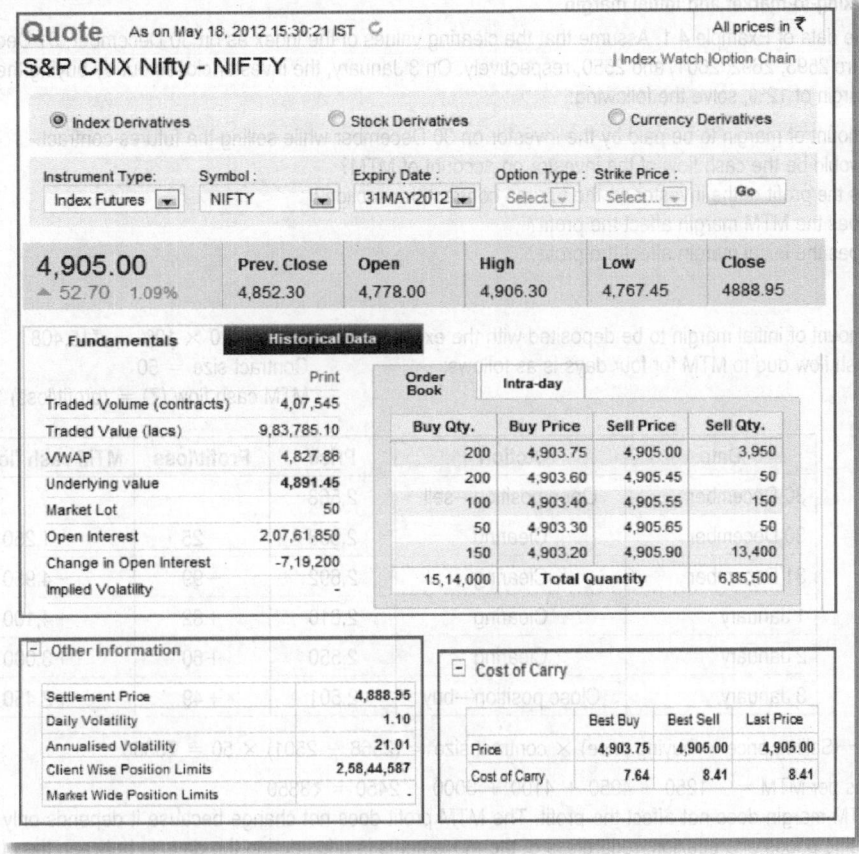

Source: www.nseindia.com, accessed on 19 May 2012.

Fig. SP 4.1 Snapshot of index futures quote as on 18 May 2012

(g) Number of contracts not squared up till the previous day: 7,19,200/50 = 14,384
(h) One-day volatility of futures is 1.10% and annual volatility is $\sqrt{365} \times 1.10 = 21.01\%$

SP 4.2: Understanding stock/index futures quotations

From Fig. 4.2 in the text, answer the following questions:

(a) Name of the underlying asset and its current value
(b) Market lot and expiry
(c) Latest price and value of the contract
(d) Cost of carry
(e) Number of contracts not squared up till the previous day
(f) Number of contracts squared up on the day

Solution

(a) Name of the underlying asset and its current value: I. T. C Ltd, ₹259.05
(b) Market lot and expiry: 1000; 25 Oct 2012.
(c) Latest price and value of the contract: ₹259.70; ₹2,59,700
(d) Cost of carry:

$$\text{Cost of carry (\%)} = \frac{\text{Futures price} - \text{Spot value}}{\text{Spot value}} \times \frac{365}{\text{days to maturity}} \times 100 = \frac{259.70 - 259.05}{259.05} \times \frac{365}{30} \times 100 = 3.05\%$$

(e) Number of contracts not squared up till the previous day: (2,06,02,0000 + 5,76,000)/1000 = 21,178
(f) Number of contracts squared today: 5,76,000/1000 = 576

SP 4.3: Marking-to-market and initial margin

Consider the data of Example 4.1. Assume that the clearing values of the index as on 30 December, 31 December, 1 January, and 2 January are 2593, 2692, 2601, and 2550, respectively. On 3 January, the investor closes out by buying the contract at 2501. With an initial margin of 12%, solve the following:

(a) The amount of margin to be paid by the investor on 30 December while selling the futures contract.
(b) What would be the cash flow of the investor on account of MTM?
(c) What is the profit of the investor on the futures contract transaction?
(d) How does the MTM margin affect the profit?
(e) How does the initial margin affect the profit?

Solution:

(a) The amount of initial margin to be deposited with the exchange is $2568 \times 20 \times 12\% = ₹15,408$
(b) The cash flow due to MTM for four days is as follows:

Contract size = 50
MTM cash flow (₹) = (profit/loss) × contract size

Date	Action	Price	Profit/loss	MTM cash flow (₹)
30 December	Open position—sell	2,568		
30 December	Clearing	2,593	−25	−1,250
31 December	Clearing	2,692	−99	−4,950
1 January	Clearing	2,610	+82	+4,100
2 January	Clearing	2,550	+60	+3,000
3 January	Close position—buy	2,501	+49	+2,450

(c) Profit = (Selling price − buying price) × contract size = $(2568 − 2501) \times 50 = ₹3350$
(d) Profit as per MTM = $−1250 − 4950 + 4100 + 3000 + 2450 = ₹3350$

The MTM margin does not affect the profit. The MTM profit does not change because it depends only upon the opening and the closing prices of a position, regardless of the movements in price during the days in between the opening position and the closing position. In fact, the profit is the sum of all MTM cash flows.

(e) The initial margin is only a security provided by the client through the clearing member to the exchange. It can be withdrawn in full after the position is closed. Therefore, it does not affect the calculation of profit or loss.

SP 4.4: Hedging short portfolio—long hedge

A bureaucrat retiring in three months' time is planning to invest ₹20 lakh from his superannuation benefits in an equity portfolio. He has identified the portfolio at current market prices as given in table below:

Stock	No.	Price (₹)	Value (₹)	Beta
Hind Unilever	1,000	230	2,30,000	1.10
Infosys	100	1,700	1,70,000	1.25
Indian Hotels	5,000	60	3,00,000	0.90
DLF Ltd	2,000	175	3,50,000	1.40
RIL	500	1,900	9,50,000	1.15
Total			20,00,000	

The market as measured by the index is 4060. The market is expected to rise, as reflected in the 3-m futures trading at 55 points' premium over spot at 4115. The index is likely to go up by 10% by the end of three months. Having chosen an aggressive portfolio, the bureaucrat is worried that he/she would have to spend more than 110% to acquire the same portfolio or else reduce the number of shares accordingly. What strategy can be suggested to the bureaucrat to hedge? Demonstrate that hedging would enable him to acquire the same number of shares by staying within his/her target investment amount of ₹20 lakh even at increased prices.

Solution

The market, currently trading at 4060, is expected to rise by 10% to 4466 (1.1 × 4060). However, the value of the proposed portfolio would rise by beta times the market rise. The beta of the portfolio is 1.159, computed as below table.

Stock	No.	Price (₹)	Value (₹)	Beta	Wt beta*
Hind Unilever	1,000	230	2,30,000	1.10	0.127
Infosys	100	1,700	1,70,000	1.25	0.106
Indian Hotels	5,000	60	3,00,000	0.90	0.135
DLF Ltd	2,000	175	3,50,000	1.40	0.245
RIL	500	1,900	9,50,000	1.15	0.546
Total			20,00,000		1.159

$$\text{Wt Beta*} = \frac{\text{Value of particular stock}}{\text{Total value of portfolio}} \times \text{Beta of stock}$$

Hedging can be achieved by going long on the index futures, currently trading at 4115. The number of futures to be bought is computed as follows:

Current value of the portfolio		= ₹20,00,000
Beta of the portfolio		= 1.159
Exposure to be covered by index futures	= 1.159 × 20,00,000	= ₹23,18,000
Current market price of index futures		= 4115
Value of one futures contract	= 50 × 4060	= ₹2,03,000
No. of contracts bought and adjusted for basis:	= 23,18,000/2,03,000 × 4115/4060	= 12 (rounded)

At the end of three months, if the markets indeed went up by 10%, the long position in futures may be squared up by selling the futures, registering a gain that can be utilized for acquisition of the portfolio. If the market index is at 4466, then the position of the futures and the proposed portfolio would be:

Gain in the position of the index futures	= (4466 − 4115) × 12 × 50	= ₹2,10,600
Increase in the value of the portfolio	= 10% × 1.159 × 20,00,000	= ₹2,31,800

The increased cost of acquiring the portfolio, ₹2,31,800, is compensated considerably by the gain of ₹2,10,600. The bureaucrat would need an extra ₹21,200 only. In the absence of any hedge with the futures, the increased cost of the proposed portfolio at ₹2,31,800 would have to be funded fully, or it can be reduced by reducing the number of shares of each stock.

SP 4.5: Arbitrage when futures are overpriced

The current value of NIFTY is 1990, with a dividend yield of 4%. A 3-m futures contract is selling at 2030 and the risk-free interest rate is 10%. Half of the stocks in the index will pay dividend in the next three months.

(a) Spell out a strategy that yields risk-less profit
(b) Evaluate gains if the index, after three months, is at (a) 1900, and (b) 2080.

Solution

(a) The fair value of a 3-m index futures = Spot value + cost of carry − dividend
= 1990 + 1990 × 0.10/4 − 1990 × .04/2
= 1990 + 49.75 − 39.80 = 1999.95 ≈ 2000

The futures at 2030 are overpriced. The strategy that yields profit would be to:

- sell the futures, borrow funds at 10%, and invest in index securities; and
- after an appropriate time, buy back futures, sell the securities, and refund the loan with interest.

(b) The payoff under two different scenarios will be given as follows:

	Index at 1,900	Index at 2,080
Position in futures		
Selling price	2,030	2,030
Buying price	1,900	2,080
Gain/loss	130	−50
Position on index		
Buying price	1,990	1,990
Selling price	1,900	2,080
Gain/loss	−90	90
Dividend received	39.80	39.80
Interest paid	−49.75	−49.75
Profit	**30.05**	**30.05**

SUMMARY

Index futures and stock futures are perhaps the simplest, most talked-about, and popular instruments of investment, speculation, and hedging. Stock exchanges all over the world have huge numbers of stocks listed with them and have developed an index to provide a comprehensive and realistic view of the ongoing activity. An index is a representative sample of activity in the market and is also supposed to be a barometer of the economic situation.

There are contracts for future delivery based on index values. An index, comprising of proportions of select stocks, is a non-deliverable product. A futures contract on an index necessarily has to be cash-settled, i.e., by offsetting the initial contract and exchanging the price difference. Similarly, there are futures on specific stocks, called stock futures. They, too, can be cash-settled. India is amongst the few countries that have futures on individual stocks, possibly because of the long-standing practice of forward trading in stocks prevalent in India prior to the introduction of futures. Index and stock futures too are standardized contracts, like any other futures.

Index and stock futures are subject to cash-and-carry and reverse cash-and-carry arbitrage, and, therefore, the cost of carry model is used in determining the fair prices of futures. Index and stock futures do not have storage costs, but have dividends attached to them, which may be accounted for in the cost of carry model when pricing them.

Index futures, besides having the basic applications of hedging, speculation, and arbitrage, are useful in many other ways. Hedgers can use index futures to cover the exposures of long and short positions in their portfolios. Index futures can also be used for controlling the sensitivity of the portfolio, which may require frequent adjustments in changing scenarios. They are also useful in eliminating the systematic risk of an individual stock. Like any other futures, index and stock futures also provide tremendous leverage to speculators to take an advantageous view of forthcoming situations.

Besides, they can be used by naïve investors for investment on a broad-based portfolio. Index futures can also be used for minimizing the systematic risk of portfolios. They are very useful in providing a cost-effective solution to equity research, which is a costly proposition indeed, with no certainty of outcome.

KEY TERMS

Beta A measure of systematic risk, and specifies the change in the value of the stock or portfolio with a 1% change in the market.
Clearing price The weighted average price for the last trading slab at which all outstanding contracts at the end of the day are marked to market.
Impact cost The difference in price caused by a change in size of the buy/sell order.
Index A representative sample of the stocks/assets that fairly represents the whole and is used for gauging the state of the market and the economy.

Index futures Futures whose underlying assets are indices.
Stock futures Futures whose underlying assets are stocks.
Systematic risk The change in price of a stock or portfolio attributable to market factors.
Tracking error The difference between the actual returns of an index-based portfolio or fund attempting to replicate the returns of the index and the actual returns of the index.
Unsystematic risk The change in price of a stock or portfolio attributable to factors specific to the stock or portfolio.

QUESTIONS

4.1 What do you understand by index and index futures?

4.2 What are the benefits of index futures overstock futures?

4.3 How would you hedge a long position in a portfolio of stocks with index futures? Explain with an example.

4.4 How would you control the beta of a portfolio with futures? What are the other ways of doing so and what is the advantage of adjusting beta with index futures?

4.5 What risk can be reduced with index futures if used in conjunction with an individual stock?

4.6 Explain calendar spread in index futures with an example.

PROBLEMS

P 4.1 Pricing a forward contract
Suppose a 6-m forward contract on shares of ITC Ltd is available. The current market price of ITC is ₹180. If the risk-free interest is 6% per annum, what should the price of the 6-m forward contract be?

P 4.2 Pricing a forward contract with dividend
In P 4.1, what would be the value of the forward contract if (a) the interest rate was continuously compounded, and (b) ITC declared a dividend of ₹2 payable after two months.

P 4.3 Pricing a futures contract on an index
The spot value of NIFTY is 4800. With the risk-free interest rate at 8% and dividend yield on the 50 shares comprising NIFTY at 4%, what should be the fair value of futures on NIFTY with (a) one month, (b) two months, and (c) three months to maturity?

P 4.4 Arbitrage with index futures
Refer to P 4.3. NIFTY futures with 1-m, 2-m, and 3-m maturity are trading at 4820, 4825, and 4855, respectively. What strategies can you adopt with each of the futures contract to profit?

P 4.5 Hedging market risk with index futures
An investor holds shares of Suzlon worth ₹20 lakh, which have a standard deviation of returns at 25%, with a beta of 1.5. The standard deviation of market returns is 16%. Index futures on NIFTY are priced at 4000, with a contract size of 50. If an investor hedges with the NIFTY futures, find out what position he/she must take. Also find what risk the investor would face with a hedged portfolio.

P 4.6 Hedging a long position in stock
An investor is holding 2000 shares of RIL, currently trading at ₹1800. The beta of RIL is 1.2. Though there is no adverse news regarding RIL, market sentiments are expected to turn weak for the next three months. The investor decides to hedge his position through 3-m futures on NIFTY, a broad-based index of 50 shares currently at 4200. One contract on NIFTY futures is worth ₹50 times the index value. How can the investor hedge against risk?

P 4.7 Hedging a short position in stock
Upon his retirement in three months' time, Gyan Prakash would receive ₹24 lakh as superannuation benefits, 50% of which he intends to invest in shares of State Bank of India (SBI). The current market price of the SBI share is ₹1200, with a beta of 1.05. The market is currently rising and is expected to remain upbeat. The current level of the market is 4200, while a 3-m futures contract on NIFTY sells for 4260, with a lot size of 50. Gyan Prakash is worried that he would only be able to buy a much smaller number of shares when he actually gets the funds, compared to what he can hope to buy now. What strategy can you suggest to Gyan Prakash? Examine your recommended strategy if the market rises by 10% in three months' time.

P 4.8 Price and basis
Examine P 4.7. Do you find that after hedging through futures, Gyan Prakash would be in a position to buy the contemplated 1000 SBI shares after a rise in the price of SBI stock? What could be the reason for the shortfall be?

P 4.9 Decreasing the beta of the portfolio
Dynamic Funds Limited (DFL) owns a well-diversified portfolio valued at ₹10 crore with an aggressive beta of 1.2. The market scenario in the coming few months is expected to remain bearish, and, therefore, the fund needs to reduce the beta of the portfolio to a defensive 0.9. Find out what the managers of DFL should do if they want to (a) divest part of the portfolio to treasury bills, and (b) control the beta through a position in index futures.

P 4.10 Increasing the beta of a portfolio
Refer to P 4.9. Assume that the market scenario is changed and sentiments have turned bullish. DFL now want to be more aggressive and wishes to increase the beta from the existing 1.20 to 1.50. Examine how this can be achieved (a) through the government securities market, and (b) in the derivatives market. Assume that DFL does not want to change the composition of the existing portfolio.

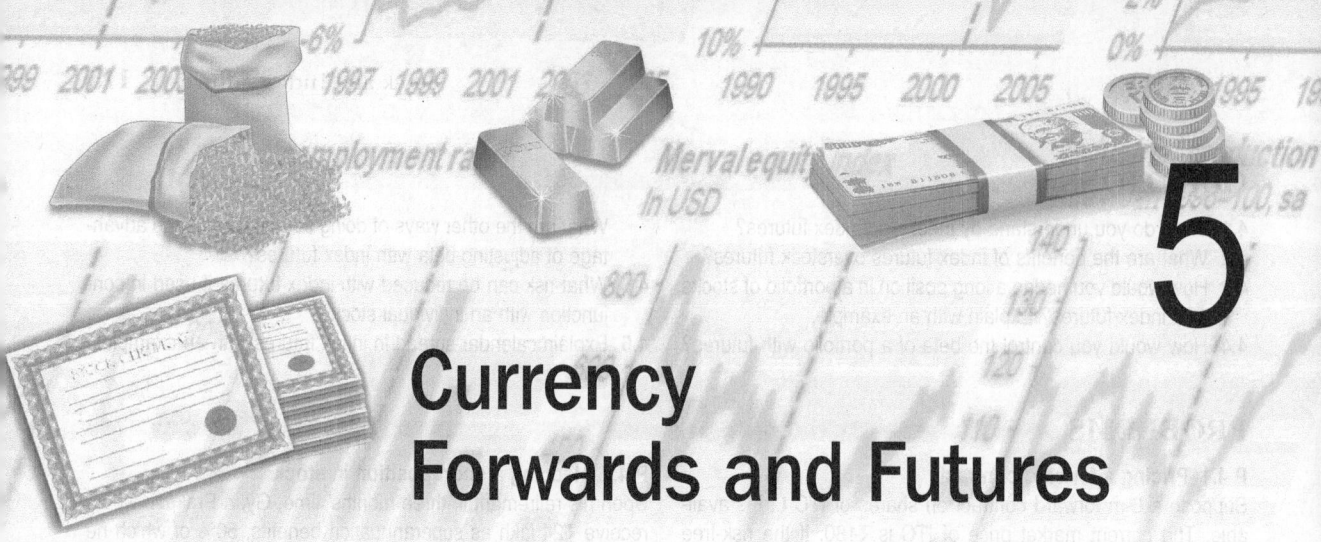

5
Currency Forwards and Futures

INTRODUCTION

Globalization of business is the theme of almost all firms in the world. As economies grow and become more and more open by relaxation of regulations concerning international trade, firms are expanding businesses from local markets in domestic currencies to global markets in multiple currencies. International markets present several different challenges in finance in terms of the additional understanding required, due to the added dimension of choosing the currency of trade and for finance. As the world economy becomes more and more integrated, a finance manager is required to make additional decisions with respect to strategic issues such as the currency of borrowing, impact of globalization on capital structure, and tactical issues (such as the currency of invoicing). These new dimensions have added complexities to trade. The dynamics of derivatives markets, too, has witnessed major changes ever since the onset of globalization.

Apart from the selection of currency for finance and trade, another important dimension that figures prominently on the agenda of finance managers is the exposure to additional risk arising from deals in currencies other than the domestic currency. Apart from broadening the conceptual scope of understanding the interest rate structures followed in various countries and financial assets denominated in foreign currency, the finance manager has the onerous task of gathering, assimilating, and analysing the vast information that is generated all over the world. In this way, an international firm, referred to as a multinational corporation (MNC), becomes different from a purely domestic firm dealing in a single currency.

> When multi-currency options are available, the evaluation of all finance avenues is not as simple as it is with a single currency.

Learning Objectives
After going through this chapter, readers should be familiar with

- foreign exchange rates, markets, and transactions
- how forward contracts on currencies work
- hedging foreign currency exposures of importers and exporters through forward contracts
- speculation and arbitrage with forward contracts
- non-deliverable forward contracts; their evolution, need, and relevance
- currency futures
- hedging with currency futures for importers and exporters
- speculation and arbitrage with currency futures

One may argue that the concepts of corporate finance must remain the same irrespective of the currency being evaluated. All the three major decisions in finance—the investment decision, the financing decision, and the dividend decision—should be independent of the currency being considered. The argument is valid, but the presence of multiple currencies makes each of these decisions more complicated, as the number of options available increases significantly. Numerically, it is simple multiplication involving exchange rates to convert one currency into another, but the decision-making framework changes drastically with regard to international business, as managerial inputs are significantly larger, more complex, and different.

FOREIGN EXCHANGE PRELIMINARIES

From the perspective of risk, dealing in foreign currencies adds a new type of risk, called exchange rate risk. To understand exchange rate risk, it is essential to understand the basic structure of foreign exchange markets, their terminologies, and their practices. This section is aimed at providing the necessary background for all of this.

FOREIGN EXCHANGE RISK

An additional dimension for transactions denominated in currencies other than the domestic one is exposure to the risk of conversion of currency. Since foreign exchange rates change in the same way as stock prices change in the stock markets, all transactions denominated in a foreign currency face exchange rate risk. The MNCs deal in and possess assets and liabilities denominated in various currencies. They need to bring down all these transactions, assets, and liabilities to a common single currency—the domestic currency of the country where the MNC's headquarter is located.

Basically, all firms that have transactions, assets, or liabilities denominated in foreign currency face the risk of changes in the position of assets or liabilities and/or cash flows. The amount of foreign currency outstanding either as payables or receivables is referred to as currency exposure. If the rate of exchange moves in an unfavourable direction, the impact on the balance sheet or the income statement is termed exchange rate risk. For example, if an export firm has sold goods worth US $1000 on credit of 60 days, the transaction would be completed only after 60 days, upon receipt of the payment of US $1000. If from the date of invoicing to the date of realization, the US dollar depreciates, the exporter realizes a lesser sum in Indian rupees than what he/she envisaged at the time of invoicing. However, an appreciation in the US dollar would be favourable to the exporter, as he/she will realize more than expected. Similarly, an importer needing to pay an outstanding in some foreign currency is worried about its appreciation during the intervening period between creation of liability and its actual liquidation. In contradiction to an exporter, an importer would welcome depreciation of the foreign currency to which he/she is exposed.

> MNCs and firms dealing in foreign currencies face the additional risk of exchange rates, and need to understand the nuances of foreign exchange markets.

FOREIGN EXCHANGE MARKETS

Foreign exchange markets mainly consist of banks, called authorized dealers in India, These markets are of the over-the-counter (OTC) type, where individuals and corporate traders come with their requirements for either buying or selling specific currencies. There is no organized exchange where foreign exchange can be traded, in the manner of the various stock exchanges where customers can place their orders for buying and/or selling stocks in the physical or electronic market. Despite the fact that foreign exchange markets are OTC in nature, the price behaviour of currencies is akin to that of stocks. This implies that different rates of exchange would prevail in the market for different currencies. The OTC nature of foreign currency markets places an additional burden on corporate finance managers exploring various avenues and possibilities to determine the most cost-effective solutions to their problems. These analyses not only are time consuming but also require deep understanding and good negotiation skills.

> Despite foreign exchange markets being OTC, prices behave much in the same way as stocks. Information gathering and negotiation skills become predominant.

Further, foreign exchange markets are operative round the clock. There is no specific time for opening or closing. Foreign exchange rates fluctuate all the time. Banks and foreign exchange dealers quote foreign exchange rates depending upon the demand and supply position they are facing. Normally, banking hours govern trading in foreign exchange.

FOREIGN EXCHANGE RATES

Trading in foreign currency, unlike trading in shares and other financial assets, is not done in any organized exchange. For exchange-traded assets, a single price in the public domain is available. The buyer and seller both pay brokerage. With a brokerage of 1% on a share priced at ₹200, a buyer would pay ₹202, and the seller would receive ₹198, with ₹4 being the total transaction cost for buyer and seller and the income for the brokers. There are many foreign exchange rates, briefly described in the following paragraphs.

Bid Rate vs Ask Rate

Foreign exchange markets are OTC markets, with various banks quoting rates in bid and ask pairs—one for buying and the other for selling foreign currency. Bid and ask rates are defined as follows:

Bid rate: The rate at which a bank buys foreign currency.
Ask rate: The rate at which a bank sells foreign currency.

To make a profit in foreign exchange transactions, banks must buy currencies at a lower rate and sell them at a higher rate. Therefore, the ask rate is always higher than the bid rate.

> Foreign exchange rates are always two-way quotes, one for buying foreign currency—the bid rate, and other for selling—the ask rate.

While quoting rates, the convention is to specify the bid rate first. The difference between the ask rate and the bid rate is the profit for the bank from a round transaction involving the buying and selling of one unit of foreign currency; this difference is known as the spread. Percentage spread is defined as follows:

$$\% \text{ Spread} = \frac{\text{Ask rate} - \text{Bid rate}}{\text{Mid rate}} \times 100 \quad (5.1)$$

Spot Rate vs Forward Rate

Transactions in foreign exchange may be carried out for settlement either now or at a later date. Spot transactions in foreign exchange require settlement of contracts within two business days. Transactions in foreign exchange involve at least two countries, which hinders the immediate settlement of contracts. Therefore, a provision of two business days is made to facilitate movement of currencies (by debits and credits) for settlement of spot transactions.

Forward contracts in foreign exchange, like any other forward contract, fix the exchange rate today for settlement at some future date. Settlement refers to the actual exchange of currencies.

Since various economic and political factors impact exchange rates on a continuous basis, spot rates change with time, as do stock prices. The exchange rate, therefore, is dependent upon the time of delivery of the currencies. This makes for different spot and forward rates. What is valid today cannot be valid tomorrow. Except by coincidence, the spot and forward rate would not be identical. Essentially, the exchange rates are dependent upon the timing of the settlement of the transaction.

Some people may believe that the forward rate would always be higher than the spot rate at any point of time. However, it is not true. Forward rates, though dependent upon the spot rate, can be lower than, equal to, or higher than the spot rate. We shall address this issue in the section on pricing of forward contracts in foreign exchange in this chapter.

FORWARD PREMIUM/DISCOUNT

There are two ways of quoting exchange rates, *direct* and *indirect*. Under the direct rate convention, the value of foreign currency is stated in terms of number of units of domestic currency per unit of foreign currency, e.g., ₹47 per US dollar in India. The system of direct rate prevails across the world, except for a few countries. Under the direct rate convention, a forward rate that is higher than the spot rate means that the foreign currency will be more expensive in the future than it is today, when it is said to be at premium. Similarly, a forward rate that is lower than the spot rate implies that the foreign currency will be cheaper in the future than it is today, when it is said to be at a discount.

> Foreign currency at a premium/ discount means that the forward rate is higher/ lower than the spot rate.

How expensive or cheap the foreign currency will be, is stated conventionally on an annual basis. Forward rates are available for varying contract periods ranging from one to six months and sometimes up to 12 months. As the foreign exchange market is an OTC market, one can get foreign exchange rates for any forward period on demand, but it is more common to find forward rates available at monthly intervals. The annual premium or discount on the foreign currency can be computed by using the forward rate, as follows:

Annualized forward premium/discount (%)

$$= \frac{\text{Forward rate}_{mid} - \text{Spot rate}_{mid}}{\text{Spot rate}_{mid}} \times \frac{12}{\text{Forward period (in months)}} \times 100$$

Here *mid* refers to the average of the bid and ask rates. Since foreign exchange rates are quoted in pairs of bid and ask rates, the premium or discount is calculated using the average of the two, called the *mid rate*.

> **EXAMPLE 5.1 Calculating forward premium/discount**
>
> Consider the following rates of foreign exchange for euro:
>   Spot (rupees per euro)   57.90   58.10
>   1-m forward (rupees per euro)   57.50   57.80
>
> (a) Find whether the euro is at a premium or discount.
> (b) Calculate the annualized premium or discount for euro.
> (c) What interpretation do you give to the figure arrived at in (b)?
> (d) What do you think would be the average (mid) rate for 3-m, 6-m, and 12-m forward contracts, assuming bid–ask spreads of ₹0.50, ₹0.80, and ₹1.00, respectively?
>
> **Solution**
>
> (a) Since 1-m forward rates are lower than the spot rates, the foreign currency, i.e., the euro, is at a discount to rupee.
> (b) The amount of discount is:
>
> Annualized Forward Premium/Discount (%)
>
> $$= \frac{\text{Forward rate}_{mid} - \text{Spot rate}_{mid}}{\text{Spot rate}_{mid}} \times \frac{12}{\text{Forward period (in months)}} \times 100 = \frac{57.65 - 58.00}{58.00} \times 12 \times 100 = -7.24\%$$
>
> (c) A discount of 7.24% means that the euro is likely to depreciate by 7.24% in a year with respect to the rupee.
> (d) Assuming that the premium/discount calculated using the 1-m forward rate is a fair representative of forward rates for the whole year, the likely forward rates for 3, 6, and 12 months are as follows:
>
>   3-m forward rate (mid) = 58.00 × (1 − 0.0724/4) = ₹56.95/euro
>   6-m forward rate (mid) = 58.00 × (1 − 0.0724/2) = ₹55.90/euro
>   12-m forward rate (mid) = 58.00 × (1 − 0.0724)   = ₹53.80/euro
>
> Assuming even distribution of spread from the mid-rates, the forward bid and ask rates are:
>
>   3-m forward rate (rupees per euro)   :   56.70   57.20
>   6-m forward rate (rupees per euro)   :   55.50   56.30
>   12-m forward rate (rupees per euro) :   53.30   54.30

Since forward rates are available for different maturities, one faces a dilemma as to which of the forward periods is most appropriate for calculating the annualized premium/discount. Purely on consideration that trading thins down as the forward period extends in time, it is most appropriate to estimate the annualized premium or discount on the foreign currency on the basis of the nearest forward contract, i.e., the 1-m forward rate rather than the forward rate for any other forward contract period. This approach is based on the presumption that contracts with near maturity are traded the most. Greater liquidity implies truer representation of fair prices.

Another important feature of forward rates is that the spread in forward rates is larger than the spread in spot rates. Since forward transactions have a greater risk, dealers demand a greater spread. Given the increased risk, banks would expect a greater reward, which is derived from the spread (the difference between the ask and bid rates). By the same logic, the spread increases as the maturity of the forward contract extends, i.e., the spread in a 6-m forward contract is likely to be higher than the spreads in 3-m and 1-m forward rates.

ARBITRAGE AND FOREIGN EXCHANGE RATES

Having discussed the various rates, the question of whether different dealers in foreign exchange would quote the same rates for a currency remains. Basically, the main question is: what is the process involved in determining and quoting rates?

The process of determination of rates is analogous to the process behind stock market quotations. Without concern for the fair value of a financial asset like stocks or bonds, we all appreciate the fact that an asset cannot have two prices. Having two prices provides an opportunity to investors to make immediate profits without investing or assuming risk. The costs of shares of Reliance Industries Ltd in various stock exchanges across India at any given point of time necessarily have to be identical. In case the prices are not the same, the situation gives rise to arbitrage opportunities; traders may earn profits by buying the stock in a market where the price is low and simultaneously selling the stock in a market where the price is high, pocketing the difference between the two prices. This profit is earned without making any investment and without taking any risk.

> Arbitrage is a process that makes prices converge in different markets. It is not concerned with whether the prices are fair or not.

The process of arbitrage would make the prices converge and helps to eliminate such profit opportunities very quickly. The visibility of an arbitrage opportunity is extremely high in cases where trading in financial assets takes place on exchanges that display prices all the time. The same process of arbitrage makes foreign exchange rates converge across different traders and banks.

However, arbitrage opportunities in the foreign exchange markets are not as visible as with stocks and bonds. The primary reasons for this difference are: first, foreign exchange markets are OTC markets where the rates are not displayed for viewing, and, therefore, fewer investors are aware of the rates and the existence of discrepancies, if any. Second, foreign exchange quotations are two-way quotes, with one price for buying and the other for selling. Identification of arbitrage opportunities is relatively difficult in foreign exchange markets, compared to products that are exchange-traded. Apart from these reasons, foreign exchange markets may place restrictions on trading and prohibit taking of speculative positions, unlike stock markets, where such restrictions are almost non-existent.

Let us consider a simple example where two banks, Bank A and Bank B, (assuming both are American banks and follow the convention of direct rates) have offered the following rates:

Amount of US dollars per euro	Bid	Ask
Bank A	1.3160	1.3260
Bank B	1.3280	1.3380

> For arbitrage-free foreign exchange rates, the bid price of one trader must be less than the ask price of another, with both the quotes expressed in a similar fashion.

The rates of Bank A mean that it would buy euro at $1.3160 and sell euro at $1.3260. This means that customers can sell one euro and get $1.3160 (the bid rate) and if they wish to buy one euro, they will have to pay $1.3260 (the ask rate). Similarly, at Bank B customers can sell one euro to get $1.3280 and pay $1.3380 to get one euro. A customer sells the foreign currency at the bid rate and buys foreign currency at the ask rate.

To derive profit, one needs to 'sell high and buy low'. In the foreign exchange markets, if the ask rate of one bank is higher than the bid rate of another, it would offer an arbitrage opportunity, such that the difference between the ask of one and the bid of the other can be earned as profit. The condition for arbitrage is exhibited in Fig. 5.1, and can be simply expressed as,

For arbitrage: $Bid_2 > Ask_1$

With the given rates, traders would buy euros from Bank A at the ask rate of $1.3260 and sell the same amount of euros to Bank B to receive the bid rate of $1.3280, making a profit of $0.0020 per euro without making any investment or carrying any risk.

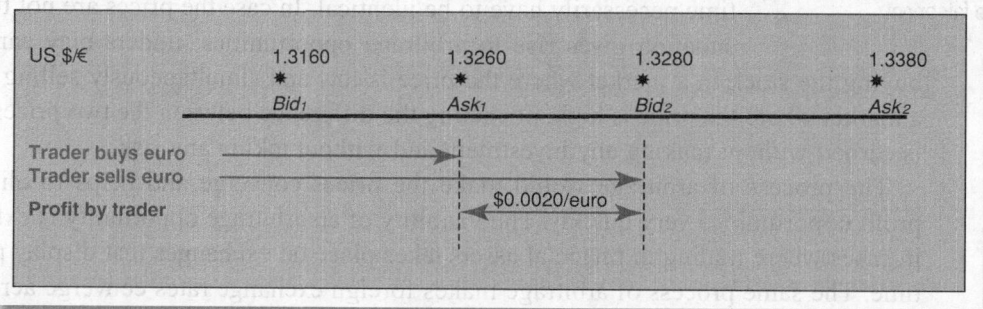

Fig. 5.1 Condition for arbitrage

Obviously, the rates that offer arbitrage cannot exist for long in the market. Arbitrage opportunities have to vanish very quickly. Bank A would face a great demand for euro, indicating that it can increase the ask rate. Continuing with the same rate would also result in the fast depletion of its stock of euro. Similarly, Bank B would face a situation where everybody would be selling euro at $1.3280. This indicates that it can revise its quote downwards, and also prevents unnecessary build-up of euro. Arbitrageurs would signal an upward revision of ask rate of Bank A and a downward revision of bid rate of Bank B. The inventory of foreign currency at hand would tell the bank which rate to revise as well as its direction.

If the quotes of Bank A and Bank B overlap (the ask of one is greater than the bid of another), the arbitrage opportunity would vanish. For example, the banks could revise the rates in the following way:

Amount of US dollars per euro	Bid	Ask
Bank A	1.3160	1.3275
Bank B	1.3270	1.3380

The condition for no arbitrage to exist is depicted in Fig. 5.2, where the rates of the two banks overlap. This may also be stated as

For no arbitrage: $Bid_2 < Ask_1$

In competitive and well-informed markets, such arbitrage opportunities do not exist at all, and if they do, then they vanish as quickly as they are spotted.

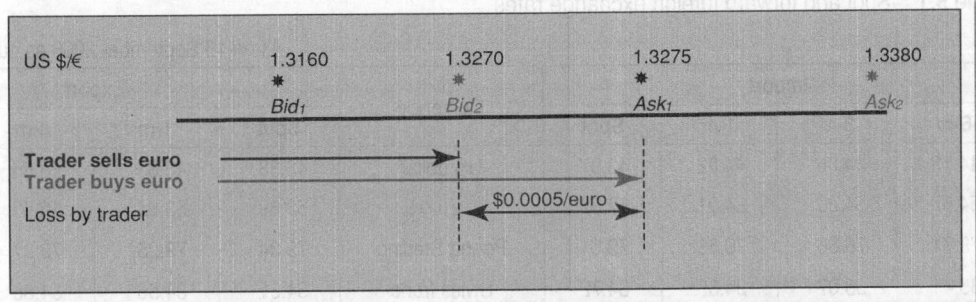

Fig. 5.2 Condition for no arbitrage

CURRENCY FORWARDS

FOREIGN EXCHANGE TRANSACTIONS

Having understood the various rates quoted in foreign exchange markets, we now turn to an understanding of the nature of transactions. For better understanding of the applications of hedging, speculation, and arbitrage, a brief background of various transactions in the foreign currency markets is discussed in this section.

Spot and Forward Transaction

Transactions in foreign exchange can either be spot or forward, depending upon the time of settlement. For all buy or sell currency transactions, the actual exchange of cash (debit or credit to the respective accounts) in the two currencies takes place later, and is referred to as *settlement*. If a transaction is to be settled immediately, it is termed a spot transaction, and the rates applicable for such a transaction are known as *spot rates*. In foreign exchange trade, spot transactions are to be settled within two business days of the transaction to allow for clearance and confirmation on the communication network.

Transactions in foreign currency can also be made for settlement at a later date. Such transactions, where the rate is fixed now but the delivery of currencies is delayed, are known as *forward contracts*. For example a 1-m forward contract for buying dollars executed by an Indian importer at ₹45.00 per dollar implies that physical exchange of dollars and rupees would take place one month after the date of transaction, but the rate of ₹45 per dollar has been fixed today. It further provides for two business days for settlement. It does not matter what exchange rate prevails one month later, on the day of settlement.

Banks usually quote rates for delivery in months, and standard contracts for one, two, three, six, and nine months are generally available. However, banks can also quote rates for forward periods that are not exact multiples of a month. Traders can book contracts for any number of days forward. Such contracts are called *broken date* or *odd date* contracts.

Spot and forward rates, as quoted by the State Bank of India (SBI), are shown in Table 5.1. Note that the forward rates are quoted in unbroken months.

> Forward contracts are settled at a later date, but at rates negotiated in advance. These rates are usually available in advance for time periods comprising months as units.

Table 5.1 Spot and forward foreign exchange rates

As on 16 September 2005 as quoted by the SBI

Import				Currency	Export			
6-m	3-m	1-m	Spot		Spot	1-m	3-m	6-m
44.13	44.06	44.02	43.97	US dollar	43.83	43.83	43.85	43.92
54.57	54.22	54.01	53.87	Euro	53.69	53.63	53.73	53.98
79.71	76.56	79.65	79.61	Pound Sterling	79.34	79.28	79.27	79.32
35.41	35.07	34.85	34.72	Swiss franc	34.61	34.56	34.66	34.90
7.32	7.27	7.24	7.22	Danish kroner	7.20	7.19	7.21	7.24
33.68	33.74	33.83	33.81	Australian dollar	33.69	33.80	33.76	33.72
37.46	37.31	37.21	37.14	Canadian dollar	37.01	36.95	37.00	37.12

₹ per unit of foreign currency

Source: Business Line, 17 September 2005.

Swap Transaction

A *swap transaction* is a combination of spot and forward transactions. The spot and forward legs of the swap are opposite and equal in value. On a given day, for example, a bank may buy $10,000 spot from another bank and simultaneously enter into a 1-m forward contract to sell $10,000 to the same bank. The rates for buying spot and selling forward would be different, but are known on that day itself. This called a swap transaction. With both buying and selling rates known, the bank is not exposed to any risk of fluctuation in exchange rates. Buying foreign currency today and selling later, or selling today and buying later, is a composite contract in the swap deal. However, the same position is obtainable with two independent but opposite and equal contracts—one spot and the other forward. An independent forward contract is called *outright forward contract*. Two independent contracts—one spot and the other outright forward—are more expensive than a single swap contract.

Composite swap contracts are of great utility to banks, as they enable avoidance of risk and the problem of finding an exact matching counterparty. A swap can do this by having offsetting positions in a single contract. Banks usually do trading on behalf of customers who are exporters and importers. The transactions of a bank with its customers are normally on an outright basis, while with other banks, the deals are on a swap basis.

Assume a bank buys a 1-m forward contract of $10,000 at ₹46 per dollar on an outright basis from an exporter. The contract means that after one month, the exporter would deliver $10,000 to the bank and receive ₹4,60,000 from it. After paying ₹4,60,000 to the exporter, the bank would end up with $10,000. While the rupee amount payable by the bank is known today, it does not know what amount of local currency $10,000 would fetch later. Depending upon the rate prevailing at that point of time, the bank may realize an amount more than, equal to, or less than the ₹4,60,000 it paid. Thus by buying dollars from an exporter, the risk of exchange rate fluctuations passed from the exporter to the bank. The bank must find a buyer (an importer-customer) who needs exactly the same amount at exactly the same time. Though a transaction like this is theoretically possible, in practice it is a difficult proposition to fulfil.

> A swap is a composite contract consisting of two legs, with the second leg being opposite and equal to the first leg, but settled only after the first leg is settled.

> Most inter-bank deals are swap deals, which help eliminate the exchange rate risk.

Bankers would not accept such a position since it is not a bank's business to assume risk on behalf of its customers, and, hence, the bank in this position would in turn book a contract with another bank to sell $10,000 1-m forward. Such a step would mean that the bank, after receiving dollars from its customer, would sell them to another bank at a rate known today. While buying dollars forward, the second bank would sell an equal amount of dollars on spot basis to the first bank. The dollars so received can be sold in the market at the prevailing spot price. By doing so, the timings of the cash flows in foreign currency are matched with spot buying and selling and forward buying and selling. Further, all the exchange rate risk is eliminated.

Figure 5.3 depicts the flow of foreign currency (dollars) for Bank A under a swap deal. Note that cash flows on a spot basis as well as a forward basis in the foreign currency are matched with all the rates known today, eliminating any uncertainty about the foreign exchange rates.

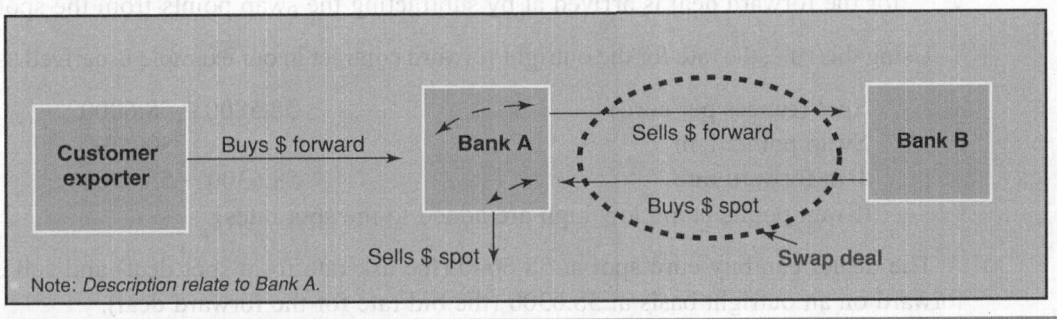

Fig. 5.3 A swap transaction for bank A

Outright Forward vs Swap

We described a swap transaction as either of the following:

- Buy foreign currency spot and sell forward
- Sell foreign currency spot and buy forward

A swap is a composite deal that has two equal legs, one the spot and the other the forward, which is equal and opposite to the spot[1]. The exposure to foreign currency is nullified at the end of the swap period. As both legs are equal and opposite, the net flow of foreign exchange is zero. A swap contract merely changes the timings of the inflow of cash and the outflow of foreign currency. Since the rate for the forward leg is predetermined, the risk of changes in the foreign currency rates is eliminated. As the deal is composite, the foreign exchange rates in the spot and the forward transactions are linked with each other.

Swap deals are quoted in a different fashion. Two rates are required for a swap deal: one for the spot leg and another for the forward leg. While spot rates are readily available, the rates for the forward leg are quoted in terms of swap points, instead of explicit rates. The spot rates, together with the swap points, are used to arrive at the rate applicable for the forward leg. This system can best be explained with an example. Assume a dealer wants to buy euro

---

[1] It is not necessary to have the first leg as a spot under the swap. One can buy (sell) a 1-m forward contract and sell (buy) a 2-m forward contract of equal amount. Such a swap is called a forward–forward swap.

> Forward rates under swap are arrived at by adding or subtracting the swap points. When the swap points are low/high, they are added to the spot rate, and when they are high/low, they are subtracted from the spot rate.

now and sell euro one month later. This is a swap transaction, where the spot leg is a buy and the forward leg is a sell for the dealer. Further, assume that a bank quotes the following rates:

Spot (rupees per euro)	58.5800 – 58.6000
Swap points[2] 1-m	500/700

The dealer can achieve the same outcome as that of a swap by entering into two independent contracts; buy euros spot and sell the same quantity 1-m forward. The rates for the 1-m forward deal on an outright basis are derived from the swap points using the following rules:

- *When the swap points are low/high* The foreign currency is at a premium, and the rate for the forward deal is arrived at by adding the swap points to the spot rates.
- *When the swap points are high/low* The foreign currency is at a discount, and the rate for the forward deal is arrived at by subtracting the swap points from the spot rates.

Using this rule, the rate for the outright forward contract in our example is derived as follows:

Spot (rupees per euro)	58.5800 – 58.6000
Swap points 1-m	500/700
1-m forward rate	58.6300 – 58.6700

(Swap points being low/high are added to the spot rates)

The dealer can buy euro spot at 58.6000 (the ask rate for a spot deal) and sell euro 1-m forward on an outright basis at 58.6300 (the bid rate for the forward deal).

Instead of booking two independent contracts, the dealer can book a composite swap contract. Here, the spot transaction would be executed at the same rate (the ask rate at which the dealer buys and the bank sells euro) of ₹58.6000 per euro. However, the rate for the forward leg would differ and is calculated as follows:

- The rate for the spot leg becomes the reference rate to/from which the relevant swap points are either added or subtracted.
- If the swap points are low/high, they would be added to the spot rate and if they are high/low, they would be subtracted from the spot rate.
- If the forward leg is 'buy' for the bank, the bid points are relevant, and if it is 'sell', then the ask points are relevant.

Here, the reference rate is ₹58.6000 and the forward leg is 'sell' for the dealer and 'buy' for the bank; therefore, the bid points become relevant. Further, since the swap points are low/high, they would be added to the reference rate for the forward leg. The forward rate would therefore be 58.6000 + 0.0500 = ₹58.6500, yielding a profit of ₹0.05 per euro for the dealer. Note that the profit for the dealer was lower at ₹0.03 per euro if he had booked two independent contracts for spot buy and 1-m outright forward sell.

> A swap deal is always cheaper than two equivalent independent contracts.

---

[2] In inter-bank quotations, rates are quoted up to four decimal places. The first two decimal places are called *basis points*, abbreviated as 'bp' and the last two decimal places are referred to as *points-in-points* abbreviated as 'PIPs'. Swap points are quoted in PIPs.

A composite swap contract is always cheaper than the combination of two independent contracts consisting of a spot deal followed by an outright forward contract.

Option Forwards

Parties to forward contracts are committed to settling their individual obligations on the due date. A forward contract is a firm contract that has to be settled on a specific date. While banks are in a better position to meet these commitments exactly on the specific date, it is a rather difficult proposition for merchants dealing in exports and imports. For example, an exporter expecting a payment in one month's time from his customer may decide to sell the foreign currency 1-m forward to his bank. Though the commitment has been made to sell the foreign currency to the bank, the exporter may not realize his payment as expected. In such a case, the exporter would default, as he is not ready with the foreign currency to be delivered to the bank on the scheduled date. A similar instance may happen with an importer who may not be in a position to buy foreign currency on the date fixed in a forward contract booked by him. These circumstances certainly do not imply that the merchants defaulted on their contracted commitments intentionally. Prevailing business circumstances might be a reason for not honouring commitments on the dates decided.

Some flexibility in the timing of maturity of forward contracts is desired by merchants, as they can predict their cash flows only in an approximate basis due to the nature of their businesses. When the exact timing of the cash inflow/outflow is uncertain, a forward contract can be booked for delivery within a given time period, called the *option period*, rather than on a specific date. For example, an exporter expecting payment anytime between two to three months would like the kind of flexibility where he can deliver the foreign exchange any time between two and three months of booking a forward contract. Such a contract is called an *option forward contract*, and is depicted in Fig. 5.4.

> Option forward contracts are not fixed-date contracts, but instead provide flexibility to deliver foreign exchange over a period, called the option period.

Under the option forward contract, a merchant who has booked a forward contract at $t = 0$, has an option period for delivery between two dates: the earliest date and the last date, rather than one fixed date.

The rates offered by banks in option forward contracts are based on the principle of least risk and maximum gain. These rates would depend upon (a) whether the bank is buying or selling the foreign currency forward, and (b) whether the currency is at a premium or discount. For example, if the bank is dealing with an exporter who wants to tender foreign currency anytime between two and three months forward, and the currency is at a premium, the bank would use the 2-m forward rate rather than the 3-m alternative for quoting rates to the customer. Since the foreign currency is at a premium, it is advantageous for the bank to

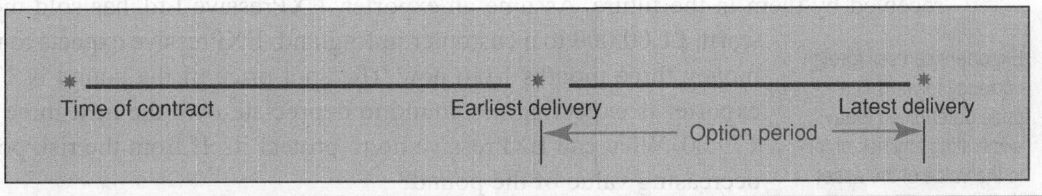

Fig. 5.4 Option forward contract

buy it earlier, as it becomes more expensive at a later date. The advantage to the bank can be maximized if the bank adopts the following strategy for quoting the option forward rates:

Foreign currency state	Buy	Sell
Premium	Earliest	Latest
Discount	Latest	Earliest

Though rates based on this strategy would be expensive for the customer, the customer must be prepared to pay an extra price for having the flexibility of timing when buying or selling, and, therefore, must not feel too aggrieved.

HEDGING THROUGH FORWARD CONTRACTS

A forward contract in foreign exchange can be used to remove uncertainty over exchange rates in the future by buying and selling forward at rates fixed now.

Exporters who expect to realize sales in a given foreign currency face the risk of a fall in the price of that foreign currency. They need protection against any reduction in the value of the asset, the account receivable. If the foreign currency appreciates, the exporters welcome this rise, because it will increase the value of the asset. As it is an unfavourable movement, deprecation of foreign currency is a cause for concern here. This concern may be mitigated by selling the anticipated receipts in foreign currency by entering into a forward contract with a bank, whereby the exporter promises to deliver the foreign currency in exchange for the domestic currency at a rate fixed now.

Similarly, importers who have to make a definite payment in foreign currency at a future date are apprehensive about any increase in the price of that foreign currency. They consider that any increase in the value of the payable must be confined to an acceptable level. In order to eliminate the risks changes in exchange rates, an exporter can freeze the exchange rate prevailing now, by entering into a forward contract to sell foreign currency, whereas an importer would obtain the requisite foreign currency later in exchange for domestic currency at an exchange rate known and accepted today.

> A currency forward is an agreement to give or take delivery of foreign currency in exchange for domestic currency at a future date, at an exchange rate determined today.

Two examples demonstrating how hedging for receivables and payables can be done are presented here.

Hedging Receivables (by Exporter) with Forward Contract

Exporters need to guard against the effects of appreciation of their local currencies, as they realize lesser amounts of the domestic currency against foreign currency payments to be received by them in the future. Assume an exporter, EXPressive Ltd, has sold merchandise worth £1,00,000 to a customer in England. EXPressive expects to receive the money three months from now. The spot price of the pound is ₹79.34. The exporter is expecting the pound to depreciate over the next three months to ₹79.00. What can EXPressive do to protect itself from the risk posed by the decreasing value of the pound?

> Exporters can sell foreign currency forward at a price determined today, eliminating any risk of fall in the value of the asset due to a decline in the exchange rate.

A 3-m forward contract from a bank for buying pounds is available at ₹79.27. If the firm thinks that in three months' time the rupee would not depreciate as much as the forward rate indicates, then it can sell receivable 3-m forward. A forward contract for selling £100,000 may be booked with the bank.

At maturity of the forward contract three months later, settlement will be done as follows:

EXPressive will deliver to the bank: £1,00,000
The bank will pay to EXPressive: ₹79,27,000

By booking the forward contract, EXPressive has mitigated any anticipated loss and has assured itself of a firm level of cash flow in local currency. If the forward contract was not booked, EXPressive would have to sell its pounds at the spot price prevailing three months later. If the rate falls to ₹79.00 as anticipated, EXPressive would have realized only ₹79,00,000. Through the forward sale of pounds, EXPressive ensured it would not lose profits to the extent of ₹27,000. On the other hand, if the pound appreciates to ₹79.50, the local currency collection would be more ₹79,50,000. Here, the spot market would give ₹23,000 more than what could be realized from a forward contract. Note that a forward contract fixes cash flow in the domestic currency. Forward contracts are used to protect future cash flows, not to maximize the value of those cash flows.

Actions and decisions for hedging receivables in foreign currency are shown in Fig. 5.5.

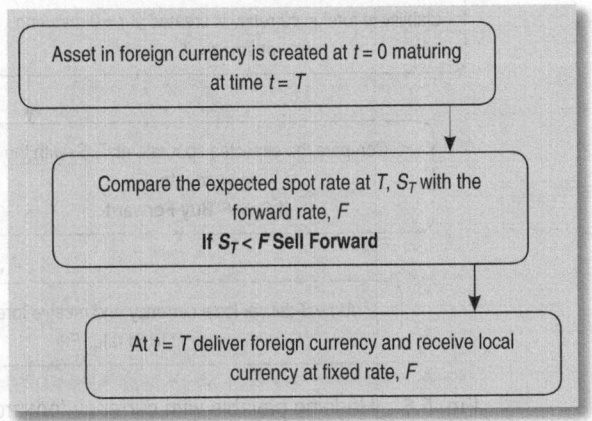

Fig. 5.5 Hedging receivables with currency forward

Hedging Payable (by Importers) with Forward Contract

While exporters do not face any risk from appreciating foreign currency, importers do. In fact, exporters welcome appreciation of foreign currency, as their receivables appreciate in value, and importers welcome depreciation of foreign currency, as their payables fall in value.

> An importer books a forward contract to buy foreign currency at a price determined today, eliminating risk associated with a rise in the value of the liability due to an increase in the exchange rate.

Let us consider how importers can hedge payables against any rise in the price of the foreign currency required. Assume an importer, IMPressive Ltd, has purchased a machine from a supplier in Germany for €10,000, with the payment due in six months. The spot price of the euro is ₹53.84. The importer is expecting the euro to appreciate to a level of ₹55.00 in six months' time, and is worried about the rising value of the euro. What can the importer do to safeguard its interests?

The importer is expecting a cash outflow of ₹5,50,000 based on its forecast for the exchange rate six months later. A forward contract for the euro is available at ₹54.57. To safeguard its position, IMPressive may buy €10,000 from the bank six months forward. At the time of maturity of the forward contract, coinciding with the payment in euro after six months,

> Forward contracts on currency are OTC, settled with delivery, independent of underlying contracts, and have counterparty risk.

The bank will provide IMPressive with: €10,000
IMPressive will pay to the bank: ₹5,45,700

By booking a forward contract to buy the foreign currency at a predetermined price, IMPressive has ensured that it pays exactly ₹54.57 per euro. Whether or not the importer benefits economically from such a deal will be known only at the expiry of the forward contract, i.e., from the spot rate at the time of settlement of the forward contract. If the euro appreciates to a level higher than ₹54.57, then IMPressive benefits from the forward contract. On the other hand, if the price of the euro remains below ₹54.57 IMPressive would have been better off without a forward contract.

Actions and decisions for hedging payables in foreign currency are shown in Fig. 5.6.

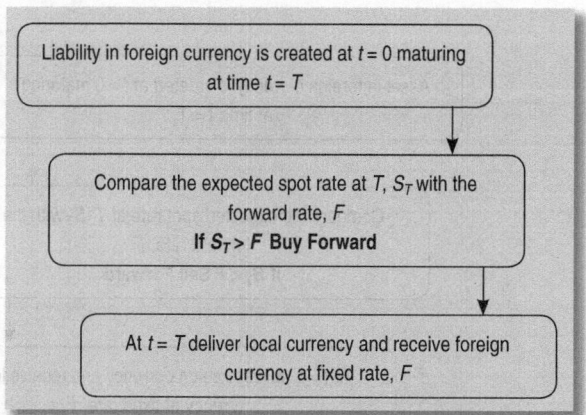

Fig. 5.6 Hedging payable with currency forward

The following points need to be reinforced about forward contracts as hedge tools for exporters and importers:

- A forward contract is a derivative product, which derives its price from the spot price of the foreign exchange that is the underlying asset. All forward prices mentioned in Table 5.1 were derived from the spot price of the concerned currency. If the spot price changes, the forward price will also change.
- The contracts were OTC, as they were tailor-made to the requirements of customers in terms of quantity of the underlying asset and time of delivery. If required, banks could quote prices for any forward period depending upon the requirements of their customers.
- A forward contract is settled with delivery on the due date, when both the bank and the customer honour their commitments to each other for delivery of foreign currency and local currency.

- The obligations undertaken within a forward contract are independent of the underlying contract. Whether or not the exporter actually receives money from its customer or whether the importer actually made the required payment to its supplier is immaterial. Irrespective of this situation, the commitment made to the bank under the forward contract must be honoured. The underlying receivable or payable and the forward contract thereon are independent of each other.
- There is no front-end payment involved at the time of booking a forward contract. There are no interim cash flows either. Only at maturity is the actual exchange of currencies done.
- Default by customers is possible (we do not expect a bank to fail in its commitment), and thus, counterparty risk is present to that extent.

One common misconception about hedging is that it improves profitability/cash flow and can compensate for the losses anticipated. It needs to be clarified that a forward hedge cannot provide the desired price. In fact, the spot price, S_0, of an asset is market determined, and no one can alter it.

Forward contracts ensure a price for the hedger irrespective of the future spot price of the currency, S_1. The forward price, F_1, is also market-determined and also cannot be changed.

> A forward contract is a firm-price contract, providing protection from any downsides in return for forgoing potential from any upsides.

An exporter, while booking a forward contract, realizes the forward price F_1 that is fixed in advance for his receivables, irrespective of the price prevailing at the time of realization. When he/she is unhedged, the amount realized will depend upon the spot price S_1 prevailing at the time of receiving the foreign currency, as shown in Fig. 5.7. The case would be similar as of an importer buying a forward contract for foreign currency.

EXAMPLE 5.2 Hedging payables with forward contracts

Ultra Films Ltd (UFL) has imported raw materials worth US $2 million for which the payment is due after three months. The following rates are quoted by a bank:

Spot (rupees per US dollar)	47.00	47.45
3-m forward	47.50	48.00

The firm is expecting appreciation of the US dollar by more than 5% in three months' time.

(a) Should UFL hedge its payable?
(b) What rate would be paid by UFL if it decides to hedge?
(c) What would be the gain or loss if the actual spot rates after three months turn out to be (a) ₹46.50–₹47.00, and (b) ₹49.30–₹49.85?

Solution

(a) The forward rates indicate an appreciation of the dollar of about 1% in three months' time, while the firm expects a 5% appreciation. It should go for hedging in order to save about 4% by buying US dollars forward.
(b) The forward ask rate is ₹48.00, at which rate UFL can buy US $2 million.
(c) If the spot rates at the end of three months were ₹46.50–₹47.00, UFL would have fulfilled its requirement at ₹47.00. As compared to the forward, the firm loses ₹1 per US dollar. Hence, the loss is ₹2 million.
If the spot rates at the end of three months were ₹49.30–₹49.85, UFL could fulfil its requirement at ₹49.85. As compared to the forward, the firm gained ₹1.85 per US dollar. Hence, the gain would be ₹1.85 × 2 million = ₹3.70 million.

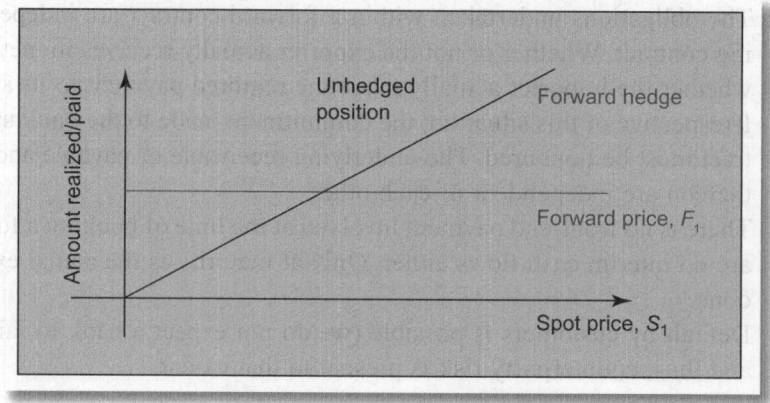

Fig. 5.7 Payoff of a forward hedge

An important feature of the forward contract is that it provides an assured rate of exchange, protecting against downside risk. However, while the rate of exchange is assured, one also forgoes the potential upside gain that one could get if the exchange rates were to move in a favourable direction.

Further, it should be noted that by hedging through a forward contract, the risk was completely eliminated for the exporter and the importer, though it did not vanish from the environment. It merely got transferred from the customers to the bank. Banks cover the risk in many other ways, including a swap transaction with another bank, as described earlier.

Cost of Forward Hedge

Through a forward contract the exporter and the importer have assured themselves of fixed prices, thus removing uncertainties. This price guarantee cannot come free of cost. We need to know what cost is borne by hedgers while booking a forward contract.

Traditionally, the cost of a forward hedge is measured in terms of premium or discount over the spot price. When a foreign currency futures is more expensive in than the spot, i.e., $F_1 > S_0$, it is said to be at a premium and when it is cheaper than the spot, i.e., $F_1 < S_0$, it is at a discount. The cost of a forward hedge is measured as a percentage premium or discount over the current spot price, as shown here:

$$\text{Cost of hedging} = \text{premium or discount} (\pm) = (F_1 - S_0)/S_0 \quad (5.2)$$

In fact, the efficacy of the forward hedge can be measured only after the forward contract period is over. The real cost or benefit of the forward hedge must be measured not when it was set up but when it ended. The cost of the forward at the time of setup only reflects what premium or discount is available. The real measure of effectiveness of a forward hedge comes from the spot price, S_1, at the end of the period of hedge, which tells the story about whether the hedger actually benefited from the forward hedge or not. The real cost of hedging is as follows:

The cost of a forward hedge is judged by the premium/discount of the forward rates over the spot rates.

$$\text{Real cost of forward hedge} = (F_1 - S_1)/S_0 \quad (5.3)$$

SPECULATION WITH FORWARD CONTRACTS

> Forward contracts can also be used for speculation in the currency exchange rate markets by holding a view contrary to the market and taking a position.

While hedging, exporters and importers cover their risks on assets/liabilities owned. The exporter holds a foreign currency receivable and the importer holds a fixed amount of domestic currency for a foreign currency denominated payable. Hence, they book forward contracts with the purpose of hedging their receivable and payable, respectively, and have all intentions of honouring their commitments.

In contrast to the actions of EXPressive and IMPressive, consider a financial firm, BETTERS Ltd, which does not need to buy or sell foreign currency. BETTERS researches foreign exchange movements and forecast rates, and whenever it finds forward rates attractive, bets on them with the sole objective of making a profit.

As per Table 5.1, the spot price of the US dollar is ₹43.83 and a 6-m forward price is ₹43.92 at an annualized premium of a mere 0.41%. BETTERS feels that the US dollar is undervalued and should command a better premium than that indicated by the forward rate. Therefore, BETTERS buys a US dollars 6-m forward at ₹43.92. It keeps a continuous watch on exchange rate movements, specifically of the US dollar. It is convinced that in six months' time, the US dollar will command a higher price. It can do either of the following:

- Whenever the forward price of the US dollar crosses ₹43.92, it can neutralize its position by booking a sell contract such that the maturity of the new sell contract coincides with the maturity of the original buy contract. Suppose that three months later, a 3-m forward contract is available at ₹44.00. BETTERS can book a 3-m forward contract to sell dollars at ₹44.00 and earn a profit of ₹0.08 for each dollar. Note that the delivery dates of both the first and the second contracts coincide, although it is not at all necessary to match maturity dates to take a speculative position.
- Alternatively, BETTERS can wait till the contract matures, when it will be required to take delivery of the dollars by paying at the equivalent rate of ₹43.92, the contracted rate. Rather than taking delivery, BETTERS sells the dollars at spot price, booking either a profit or a loss depending upon the spot price prevailing then.

The actions of BETTERS Ltd are termed speculative, since the firm held a view contrary to the one indicated by forward rates, and was prepared to assume a position on its own regarding the future movement of the prices of US dollars. In fact, BETTERS was not attempting to cover any risk, as it did not have the foreign currency, nor needed it in future; instead, it was taking a risk by opening the first forward contract in the hope of neutralizing the exposure subsequently. In case the likely movement was not in its favour, it would lose some value.

ARBITRAGE WITH FORWARD CONTRACT

As defined earlier, the process of arbitrage requires setting up of a riskless position, in contrast to speculative actions, which set up an initial position and wait for an opportune time to square up the initial position. It is not possible to find an opportunity to make arbitrage profit from the same source, as the rates offered by the same bank will be such that they

> Different banks may quote differing exchange rates for the same currency, which may also provide arbitrage opportunities.

result in profit for the bank, and, hence, loss for the customer. However, it is possible to find another bank that offers rates such that a smart and aware investor can buy from one source at a cheaper rate and sell to the other at a higher rate simultaneously.

In Table 5.1, we note that the State Bank of India (SBI) offers the following rates for the Swiss franc (CHF):

Exchange rates of SBI (₹ per CHF)								
Import				Currency	Export			
6-m	3-m	1-m	Spot		Spot	1-m	3-m	6-m
35.41	35.07	34.85	34.72	CHF	34.61	34.56	34.66	34.90

Hypothetically, let us assume that Citibank offers the following exchange rates at the same time for the Swiss franc:

Exchange rates of Citibank (₹ per CHF)								
Import				Currency	Export			
6-m	3-m	1-m	Spot		Spot	1-m	3-m	6-m
34.41	34.07	33.85	33.72	CHF	33.61	33.56	33.66	33.90

An arbitrageur spots an opportunity to make a profit from the rates available from the banks. The arbitrageur can sell Swiss francs 6-m forward at ₹34.90 to the SBI, and simultaneously buy Swiss francs 6-m forward from Citibank at ₹34.41.

Note that by buying from one and selling to the other, the arbitrageur has assured himself of a profit of ₹0.49 for each Swiss franc transacted, without involving any capital or entering into a promise to perform that cannot be fulfilled. His position stands nullified, as he buys the Swiss francs from Citibank and simultaneously sells the same amount to the SBI, with identical maturities.

Execution of arbitrage in the foreign currency markets through forwards is an extremely unlikely situation. This is because the bid–ask spreads of different banks are not in the public domain. The rates are obtained on demand only.

DETERMINING FORWARD RATES

Determination of forward rates that do not permit arbitrage is linked to the spot rates and the interest rates prevailing for two currencies. Arbitrage in two different markets is dependent upon the rates prevailing in the two markets. Arbitrage in the spot and the forward market for the same underlying asset is governed by borrowing and investing. We borrow in one currency and invest in another, depending upon the interest rates, spot rates, and the forward rates. Because of the bid–ask spread and the borrowing–lending spread, there is a range of forward rates that are feasible without any arbitrage opportunities.

No arbitrage condition places between (a) the lower bound for the ask rate and (b) the upper bound for the bid rate. Within these bounds, any forward rates could be quoted. In Example 5.3, it can be noticed from the upper and lower bounds that many different sets of rates are possible with no arbitrage condition satisfied. Different banks can offer different rates because of the vast range of feasible forward rates that are available. Transaction costs would prohibit arbitrage.

EXAMPLE 5.3 Bounds to forward rates

The following spot and interest rates prevail in the market:

Spot rate (rupees per euro)	60.00	61.00
Interest rate rupee:	8.00%	8.50%
euro:	5.00%	5.50%

Find out (a) the lower bound to the 6-m forward ask rate
(b) the upper bound to the 6-m forward bid rate

Solution

(a) To find the lower bound to the ask rate, we do as follows:
  (i) Borrow foreign currency (euros) at the borrowing rate
  (ii) Convert spot into local currency (rupees) at the bid rate
  (iii) Invest the local currency at the lending rate for the period of the forward
  (iv) Sell the matured amount at the forward ask rate to reconvert into foreign currency

For no arbitrage, the matured amount through the forward must be less than the borrowing.

Borrow €1.00 at 5.50% for six months: Amount to repay   = €1.0275
Convert to rupees at the spot bid rate and get   = ₹60.00
Invest for six months at 8% and get ₹1.04 × 60   = ₹62.40
Sell at the forward ask rate F_a to get   = 62.40/F_a
For no arbitrage, we must have: 62.40/F_a ≤ 1.0275 or, F_a ≥ ₹60.7299

(b) To find the upper bound on the bid rate, we do as follows:
  (i) Borrow local currency (rupees) at the borrowing rate
  (ii) Convert spot into local currency (euros) at the ask rate
  (iii) Invest the foreign currency at the lending rate for the period of the forward
  (iv) Sell the matured amount at the forward bid rate to reconvert to local currency

For no arbitrage, the matured amount through the forward must be less than the borrowing

Borrow ₹1.00 at 8.50% for six months: Amount to repay   = ₹1.0425
Convert to euro at the spot ask rate and get €1/61.00   = 0.0164
Invest for six months at 5% and get €1.025 × 1/61   = 0.0168
Sell at the forward bid rate F_b to get   = F_b × 0.0168
For no arbitrage, we must have: F_b × 0.0168 ≤ 1.0425 or, F_b ≤ ₹62.0415

NON-DELIVERABLE FORWARDS

NON-DELIVERABLE FORWARD CONTRACTS

There exists a product, typical to the foreign exchange markets, which is neither a forward contract nor a future contact. This product is known as the non-deliverable forward (NDF) contract. An NDF contract, as the name suggests, is a forward contract where the delivery of the underlying asset, mostly a currency or a commodity, is not required. The need for such a contract arises from the impossibility of delivery of the underlying asset. It is most prevalent in the foreign exchange markets in respect of currencies that are not freely convertible. The governments of some nations exercise capital control in order to prevent volatility in the exchange rates of their currencies, or for any other political or economic reason.

EVOLUTION AND GROWTH OF NDF

> The NDFs are forward contracts normally entered off-shore and cash-settled for currencies that have capital control.

The NDFs evolved in the 70s, when the Australian currency was subjected to capital restrictions. The NDFs began trading, obviating the requirement of delivery and yet providing an effective means of hedging. They came into existence because of the increased volatility in interest rates, which made hedging difficult with the on-shore banking system through deliverable forward markets. Transactions for hedging were conducted in the NDF market, and, hence, they are also called the *hedge markets*. In the case of Australia, the development of the NDF market was on-shore, with settlement in the local currency, the Australian dollar.

Today, the NDF market primarily consists of six Asian currencies, namely, the Chinese renminbi (RMB), the Indian rupee, the Korean won, the Indonesian rupiah, the Philippine peso, and the Taiwanese dollar, all of which are subject to governmental capital control in varying degrees. One of the popular measures to exercise such control is to ban forward trading in the currency markets. Due to regulations and legal and practical constraints in the free conversion and movement of a currency, an NDF in any currency is normally traded off-shore, i.e., outside the bounds of the home country of that currency. For example, if the Indian rupee is subject to non-delivery outside India, an NDF contract could be traded outside India, say at Dubai or Singapore.

The banking system in a nation may prohibit booking of forward contracts in the absence of exposure in the underlying currency. Such controls make hedging feasible, but other speculative and arbitrage activities are denied, restricting the depth of the forward markets.

> NDFs provide much needed liquidity and depth to non-convertible currencies. The rates in NDF are considered better, as they are market determined and free from controls and regulations.

The NDFs provide alternative hedging avenues for non-residents who cannot participate in the on-shore deliverable market. Further, an on-shore deliverable market may be illiquid too. Capital controls are aimed at restricting short-term capital flows that are not trade related. The growth in NDFs in the 1990s is believed to be related to the Asian currency crisis that led to further tightening of the currency controls. The participation by foreign nationals in the on-shore forward markets is regarded as speculative enough to destabilize the currency's value by making the exchange rate extremely volatile.[3]

FEATURES OF NDFS

Unlike the Australian dollar, today's NDF markets are off-shore. The NDFs are generally quoted and settled in US dollars, though cross rates can be used for NDFs in other currencies too. Since delivery is not possible due to restrictions on convertibility of the currency dealt in, the settlement of a forward contract in the currency has to be on the basis of the difference between the contracted price and the spot price. Further, settlement has to be done in a currency that is freely acceptable. Most NDFs are cash-settled in US dollars. Such contracts have a notional principal amount.

NDFs are foreign exchange derivative products traded OTC. On maturity, the parties to an NDF contract settle the transaction not by delivering the underlying pair of currencies but by

---

[3]Higgins P., and Humpage, O.M. (2005), Non-Deliverable Forwards: Can We Tell Where Renminbi Is Headed, Federal Reserve Bank of Cleveland, September.

making a net payment equal to the difference between the agreed foreign exchange rate and the spot fixing rate[4]. The NDF enables hedging by foreign participants who are not allowed access to on-shore markets for these currencies.

HOW NDF WORKS

An NDF works in the same manner as a deliverable forward contract from the perspective of hedging. However, the mechanism is somewhat different. The settlement of an NDF is done in foreign currency in cash, with the difference between the forward price and the settlement price over a notional principal, as per Eq. 5.4, which follows:

Settlement amount = (1 − forward rate/settlement rate) × notional principal (5.4)

As an example, consider an exporter in Thailand who has supplied goods to India worth ₹4,80,000 and has agreed to accept payment in Indian rupees after six months. However, the Indian rupee is expected to depreciate from the current spot rate of ₹48 per dollar. Assume that a 6-m NDF is quoted at US $0.02 per rupee (equivalent to ₹50 per dollar). The Thai exporter decides to hedge by selling a 6-m NDF at 0.02. By doing so, the Thai exporter locks in his receivable in US dollars at US $9600 (₹4,80,000 × US $0.02 per rupee), based on the NDF rate of US $0.02 per rupee. The position of the Thai exporter for depreciation and appreciation of Indian rupee is demonstrated in the following paragraphs.

If the rupee depreciates excessively to spot at US $ 0.0192 per rupee:
Settlement amount receivable under the NDF
 = (0.02 − 0.0192) × 4,80,000 = US $384
Realized US dollars from the receivable
 = 4,80,000 × 0.0192 = US $9216
Total realization = US $9600

If the rupee appreciates to spot at US $ 0.0217 per rupee:
Settlement amount payable under the NDF
 = (0.02 − 0.0217) × 4,80,000 = −US $816
Realized US dollars from the receivable
 = 4,80,000 × 0.0217 = US $10,416
Total realization = US $9600

NDF AND INTEREST RATE PARITY

We know that when the capital markets are freely accessible, the forward markets and the spot markets are linked with interest rate parity (IRP) as follows:

$$F_n = S_0 \frac{(1 + r_h)^n}{(1 + r_f)^n} \quad (5.5)$$

where F_n is the forward rate for n periods, S_0 is the spot rate, and r_h and r_f are the interest rates in the home and foreign countries, respectively.

---

[4]Guonon Ma, Corrinne Ho, and Robert McCaulay (2004), 'Markets for Non Deliverable Forwards in Asian Currencies', *Bank for International Settlement Quarterly Review* June.

However, when capital account controls exist, lending and borrowing on-shore is restricted for foreigners, distorting the IRP. This gives rise to the off-shore market. The rate of NDF, therefore, would imply an interest rate differential that is not the same as the differential reflected in the deliverable forward markets on-shore. Since NDF is not subject to capital controls, the validity of the IRP tends to be greater.

Assuming a 12-m NDF contract in Indian rupees is quoted at ₹42.60 per dollar as against the spot rate of ₹42.00, with a 6% interest rate in US dollars, the implied interest rate for the Indian rupee would be 7.51%:

$$(1 + r_{NDF}) = 1.06 \times \frac{42.60}{42.00} = 1.0751 \text{ or } r_{NDF} = 7.51\%$$

This may be compared with the interest rate prevailing (one measure could be T-bills yields) that becomes the benchmark for an on-shore forward market. The differential between the off-shore and the on-shore rates as implied in the NDF rate and the forward rate may be taken as the measure of effectiveness of capital controls. The larger the differential, the more effective is the capital control.

An active NDF market and a lower differential between the off-shore and the on-shore interest rates would be an indicator or precursor of the likely exchange rate markets scenario if the capital flow controls were to vanish. The NDF would be regarded as a truer reflector of free market conditions than the conditions prevailing in the on-shore markets for currencies where controls exist on capital flows.

Where local residents operating in on-shore markets also have access to off-shore markets, the differential between the off-shore and the on-shore forward rates (or the differential between the yields) would give rise to arbitrage opportunities. This would make off-shore and on-shore yields and forward rates stay in close proximity with each other, with a nominal differential that probably will not exceed the transaction costs in the two markets.

The differential is likely to be greater where interventions by governments in foreign exchange markets are frequent and large. In situations of fixed exchange rates and restrictions on local residents that prevent access to off-shore markets, the NDF may suggest the likely revaluation/devaluation of a given currency.

ARE NDFs DESIRABLE

The NDF markets are often viewed with suspicion, as they circumvent the local exchange control rules and provide easy alternatives to those who cannot access the on-shore deliverable forward markets. However, they must be viewed from a different perspective. The on-shore deliverable markets in regulated environments provide hedging applications but they inhibit speculative and arbitrage activities. In contrast, those who need to hedge through NDF would be few, but an off-shore NDF market would present opportunities for speculators. Both stand-alone markets would lack depth and only when combined can present a truer and competitive picture regarding the status of a currency.

Further, it is believed that an NDF market[5] (a) facilitates smoother transition of an economy from a controlled regime to full convertibility, as they serve as an intermediate bridge

---

[5] Debelle, G., J. Gyntelberg, and M. Plumb (2006), 'Forward Currency Markets in Asia; Lesson from Australian Experience', *BIS Quarterly Review*, September.

for the interim period, and (b) provide skills and expertise developed in the NDF markets to be adapted to the deliverable forward market as and when capital controls are lifted or full convertibility of the currency is achieved.

CURRENCY FUTURES

Currency futures serve the same purpose as currency forward contracts, i.e., by providing importers/exporters with a way to cover exchange rate risks with respect to their receivables/payables.

Though forward markets have been in existence for long, currency futures markets are relatively a new development. Internationally, futures contracts on foreign currencies developed in the early 70s, when the International Monetary Market at the Chicago Mercantile Exchange (CME) commenced trading on currency futures. Forward and futures markets have co-existed in foreign currencies.

The cost of hedging through futures, being exchange-traded, is expected to be much smaller than that of forward contracts. However, forward contracts offer a perfect hedge, as the exchange rate realized or paid is known with certainty at the time of booking the contracts. The limitations of futures that make a hedge imperfect, i.e., mismatches of quality, quantity, and timing of the hedge, do not occur in forward contracts, which are OTC products matching the specific needs of exporters and importers.

In India, there were no futures exchanges until 2008. The National Stock Exchange (NSE) introduced futures contracts on the US dollar on 28 August 2008, and the Multi-commodity Exchange-Stock Exchange (MCX-SX) did so on 7 October 2008. The features of the futures contract on US dollar available in India are as follows.

Derivatives in Practice — Different Forex Markets

One country, two systems, three currencies

HSBC points out that trading in the Chinese currency, RMB, is hardly simple. There are multiple markets—all of which trade differently—and only a few that foreigners can truly position in, To start with, although the RMB, which is traded both on-shore in China and off-shore (primarily in Hong Kong), is the same currency, it is traded at different rates. This is by design: as regulation has explicitly kept on-shore and off-shore separated, the respective supply and demand conditions lead to separate market clearing exchange rates.

Hence came about the emergence of a new currency code, CNH, to represent the exchange rate of RMB that trades off-shore in Hong Kong. However, it does not end here. There is the traditional off-shore RMB market, the dollar-settled NDF, which itself trades independently of either on-shore CNY or off-shore CNH, as well as a trade-settlement exchange rate (sometimes called CNT) to which off-shore corporates have access, just adding to the complexity.

The CNH is effectively a separate currency altogether, a perfect proxy neither for the domestic RMB (on-shore CNY) nor for the NDF (forward) curve market. The latter is otherwise known as the off-shore dollar-settled NDF market, which is the traditional domain of off-shore participants. And to add to all of that, in July 2010, the RMB itself became officially deliverable in Hong Kong—leading to its own rate, sometimes known as CNT. However, this is only available to off-shore corporate entities.

A diagram from HSBC highlights the different markets for RMB (Fig. I) and Fig. II shows how the three main markets (CNY, CNH, and NDF) have diverged in the recent past.

(Contd)

(Contd)

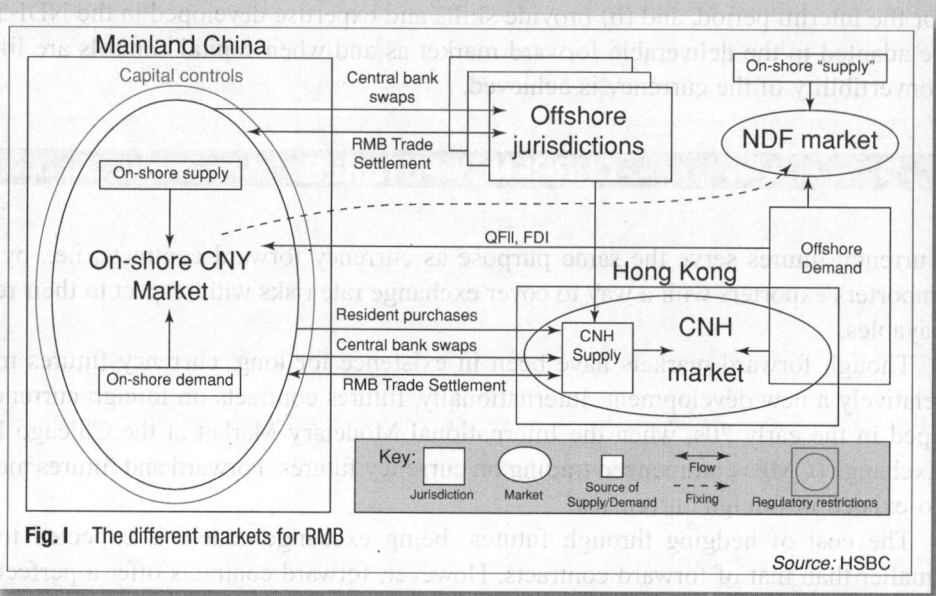

Fig. I The different markets for RMB
Source: HSBC

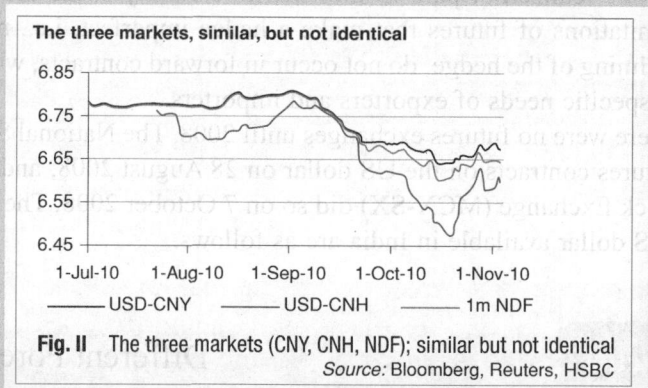

Fig. II The three markets (CNY, CNH, NDF); similar but not identical
Source: Bloomberg, Reuters, HSBC

What about arbitrage? That is the whole point: there is no arbitrage. However, the off-shore RMB market was created explicitly to allow the RMB to start developing internationalization characteristics, while at the same time keeping domestic markets sequestered from global markets. By deliberately separating on-shore from off-shore liquidity, the CNY and CNH are designed not to be arbitraged and, hence, will naturally have distinct market equilibriums.

Source: http://ftalphaville.ft.com/ posted by Izabella Kaminska on 12 December 2010.

Contract Specifications The contract on US dollar futures at MCX-SX is specified in Table 5.2. Specifications are identical with the contract introduced by NSE. Standard contracts with a size of US $1000 are available for the next 12 months, providing hedging period of a maximum of one year. Each contract expires on the last working day of the month on which spot transaction would be settled. For example, the January 2012 contract expired on 27 January 2012, which was the last day of settlement for spot transactions (two business days prior to the last working day of the month).

> Currency futures are derivatives based on exchange rates that are exchange-traded and are a substitute for forward contracts.

Table 5.2 Details of contract specification of dollar/rupee futures at MCX-SX

Unit of trading	1 (1 unit denotes US $1000)
Underlying	The exchange rate is in units of Indian rupees for a unit of the US dollar
Tick size	25 paise or ₹0.0025
Last trading day	Two working days prior to the last business day of the expiry month at 12 noon.
Final settlement day	The last working day (excluding Saturdays) of the expiry month. The last working day will be the same as that for interbank settlements in Mumbai.
Quantity Freeze	Above 10,000
Base price	Theoretical price on the first day of the contract. On all other days, DSP of the contract
Price operating range	*Tenure up to six months* ±3 % of base price *Tenure greater than six months* ±5% of base price
Minimum initial margin	1.75% on day 1, 1% thereafter
Extreme loss margin	1% of the MTM value of the open position
Calendar spreads	₹400/- for a spread of 1 month, ₹500/- for a spread of 2 months, ₹800/- for a spread of 3 months, and ₹1000/- for a spread of 4 months or more
Settlement	*Daily settlement:* T + 1 *Final settlement:* T + 2
Mode of settlement	Cash settled in Indian rupees
DSP	Calculated on the basis of the last half an hour's weighted average price.
FSP	The RBI reference rate

Source: www.mcx-sx.com, accessed on 25 September 2012.

Trading One can start trading in currency futures by initiating a long/short position in foreign currency through the members of the exchange dealing in currency futures. An initial margin is payable as prescribed by the exchange (1.75% in case of MCX-SX), and is released when the position closes. The initial margin is a performance bond used by the exchange as a risk-containment measure in order to cover potential loss over a time period. As such, no cash flow on account of the contract is involved while initiating a buy/sell futures contract.

Daily marking to the market (MTM) is done with daily settlement prices (DSPs) worked out on the basis of the average of the last 30 minutes' trades. The final settlement is done with the RBI reference rate on the last working day of the expiry month.

The price quotation is rupees per unit of foreign currency (per 100 units in the case of Japanese yen), with a tick size of ₹0.0025 (25 paise). The minimum price change for a contract would be ₹2.50 (₹0.0025 × 1000).

Settlement Participants in futures contracts are expected to nullify their positions before the last day of trading for the contract. However, if any position is outstanding, it is treated as closed at the final settlement price (FSP), with any difference between the prices of the opening and the closing contracts paid or received, as the case may be. All futures contracts are cash-settled, and no delivery is asked for. As is true with any futures contract, settlement by delivery is rarely chosen, even on underlying assets where allowed.

In contrast with the currency futures at NSE or MCX-SX, CME deals in various currencies with different lot sizes. Contract sizes are much larger than US $1000, and only four quarterly contracts are available. At CME, different currencies are quoted in terms of the number of US dollars per unit of any other currency, with

- tick size of $0.01;
- delivery standardized in March, June, September, and December; and
- *standard lots* of Australian $10,000; Canadian $100,000; Sterling pounds 62,500; Yen 12,500,000; and CHF 125,000.

Figure 5.8 depicts trading information for US dollar futures in terms of Indian rupees on the MCX-SX. It provides information for 12 monthly futures contracts. The product is specified as USDINR with maturity date. Price information for best buy quantity and price as well as best sell quantity and price is displayed. It also gives information about the *last traded price (LTP), volume,* and *open interest* in terms of the number of contracts (each contract is for US $1000), and the *value* of the contracts is in crores of rupees.

The differences between forward and futures contracts are many, and have already been discussed in Chapter 2. Forward markets in foreign currency are available worldwide, with

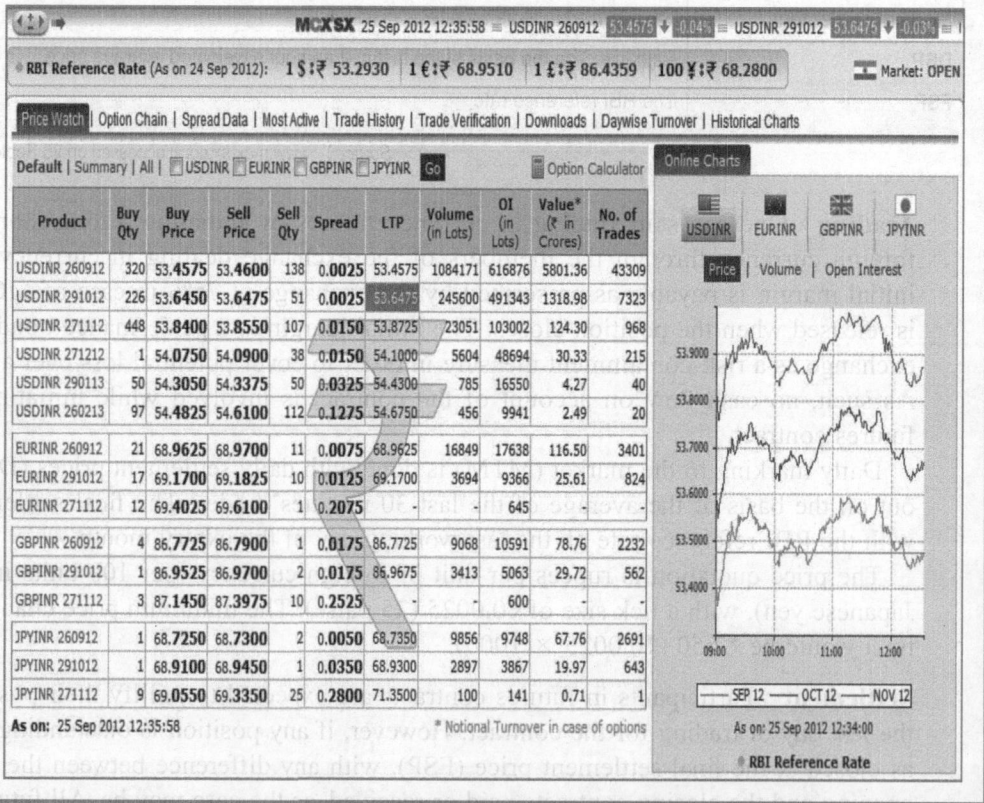

Fig. 5.8 Trading information of currency futures on MCX-SX

Source: www.mcx-sx.com, accessed on 25 September 2012.

no specified time of operation. In contrast, futures markets operate for specified hours. Delivery in forward markets is tailor-made, while futures have a specified maturity date. Despite the emergence of futures market in currencies, the forward market continues to dominate trading in foreign exchange, possibly because of the comfort level banks provide to traders and users.

PRICING CURRENCY FUTURES AND FORWARDS

The pricing of foreign currency futures will depend upon the interest rates of the currencies involved in the contract. The concepts of IRP and covered interest arbitrage are central to the determination of forward rates of various currencies. Under conditions of free trade policies and free flow of capital across international borders, interest rates in the two currencies must determine future exchange rates.

As a standard concept of economics, the price of any commodity is determined by the factors that affect the demand and supply of the commodity. Foreign currency is no different from any commodity. The demand for foreign currency emanates from importers, and supply sources predominantly comprise exporters who enter transactions involving goods and services abroad in currencies other than the domestic one. Apart from the usual risks of trade, importers and exporters face the additional risk of currency exchange rate fluctuations. Importers and exporters have a genuine need to hedge the foreign currency transactions they enter into.

Besides hedgers (importers and exporters), who constitute the demand and supply components of foreign exchange, there are speculators and arbitrageurs operating in the foreign exchange markets, subject to the exchange control regulations in place in any economy. All over the world, speculators and arbitrageurs constitute a majority of transactions. In fact, transactions that are being hedged actually form a miniscule 3–4% of the volumes in foreign exchange markets. Irrespective of speculation or hedging, the pricing of forward contracts is based on conditions that satisfy a no-arbitrage condition.

To examine how arbitrage works in determining forward exchange rates, let us consider an example. Assume that a trader has ₹10 lakh today, available for one year. He/she has a choice of either (a) investing in rupees, or (b) converting these rupees into US dollars at today's spot rate, investing the US dollars and reconverting the US dollars back into rupees one year later. In an efficient market, the two strategies of investment must yield the same reward. Further, the outcome of both the strategies must be certain. Therefore, we assume that the investment must be made in risk-free securities in either market.

If the spot price is ₹50.00 per dollar and the risk-free interest rates for rupees and US dollars are 5% and 3%, respectively, then the two strategies that can be followed are as follows:

> The price of a currency forward contract depends upon the spot price and the differential between interest rates in two different currencies.

- *Invest in domestic markets:*
  - Invest ₹10,00,000 at 5% for a year and get ₹10,50,000 after a year. Here, 5% is the return from risk-free investments such as T-bills.
- *Invest in markets abroad:*
  - Convert rupees into US dollars at the current spot rate of US $1 = ₹50.00 and get US $20,000.

- Invest for one year at 3% to yield US $20,600 at maturity after one year. Again, the investment is in risk-free securities such as T-bills in the USA.
- Obtain Indian rupees back by selling the dollars at the spot rate prevailing after a year, S_1.

Here, the final amount of Indian rupees that the investor would get is dependent upon the exchange rate prevailing at the end of the investment window. Both the investment strategies are depicted in Fig. 5.9.

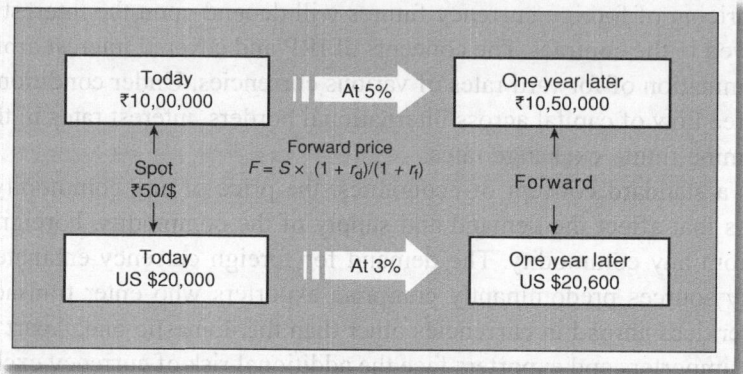

Fig. 5.9 Determination of forward exchange rate

For either strategy, the investor must be indifferent in terms of value in both the markets, i.e., the Indian and the US financial markets. If this has to happen, the spot exchange rate one year later, S_1, must be such that US $20,600 is equal to ₹10,50,000. This implies a spot exchange rate of ₹50.97 per US dollar one year later.

In symbolic terms, if the spot rates today and one year later are S_0 and S_1, and domestic and foreign interest rates are r_d and r_f, respectively, the relationship of the two spot rates is given by Eq. 5.6 as follows:

$$S_1 = S_0 \times \frac{(1 + r_d)}{(1 + r_f)} \tag{5.6}$$

In this argument, we ignored the aspect of risk. There are two sources of risk:

- Rates of interest for making investment
- Spot exchange rate one year later

To be at equal levels of risk in both the markets, we may assume investment at risk-free rates in both rupee and dollar markets. However, the second source of risk remains as it is. While converting the matured amount to rupees, the investor is not aware of the future spot rate S_1. If the investor knew today exactly what rate he would get after a year for the US dollars invested today, the risk of exchange rate fluctuation too would have been covered. Cover for risk relating to the future spot rate can be easily achieved using the forward markets. If the investor sells US dollars forward, the risk is covered. The actions would now be as follows:

- *Step 1* *Invest in domestic markets*:
  - Invest ₹10,00,000 at 5% for a year and get ₹10,50,000 after a year; for one unit of home currency we get $(1 + r_d)$.

- **Step 2** *Invest abroad*:
  - Convert rupees into US dollars at the spot rate of ₹50.00 per dollar and get US $20,000.
  - Invest for one year at 3% to yield US $20,600 after one year at maturity; for one unit of home currency, we get $(1/S_0) \times (1 + r_f)$.
  - Book a forward contract for selling the maturity value at F_1 to get back rupees; for one unit of home currency, we get $(F_1/S_0) \times (1 + r_f)$.

For no arbitrage, the maturity value in step 1 and the sum under the third action under step 2 must be equal. This gives the following relationship between the forward rate and the spot rate:

$$F_1 = S_0 \times \frac{(1 + r_d)}{(1 + r_f)} \tag{5.7}$$

With continuous compounding, Eq. 5.7 gets modified to

$$F_1 = S_0 \times e^{(r_d - r_f)t} \tag{5.8}$$

The relationship expressed by Eqs 5.7 and 5.8 is known as the IRP, which relates the forward markets with the money markets and the spot markets. The price of a forward contract is governed by the interest rates for the two currencies in the transaction and the spot rates prevailing.

Therefore, forward/futures price F (direct) $= S \times (1 + r_d)/(1 + r_f)$

Reconciling IRP and Cost of Carry Models The price of a futures/forward contract arrived at through IRP and the no-arbitrage argument in fact is the same as the price calculated using the cost of carry model.

Under the cost of carry model, spot and futures prices are related by the cost of carry for the period of contract. In the case of a currency, this happens to be the risk-free rate of interest. The future value of an asset is given by $S_0 \times e^{r_d t}$. However, the exchanged asset would have earned risk-free interest in the foreign currency, which is like the value of benefits of owning the asset. Therefore, the net cost of carry is the differential of interest rates between

---

EXAMPLE 5.4 Fair value of currency futures

At MCX-SX, currency futures in US dollar are traded. Today is 12 December and January futures would expire on 28 January. Spot rate in the exchange market for dollar is ₹45.45. The yields in the T-bills markets of India and USA are 5.90% and 2.40%, respectively.

(a) At what price January futures would be traded?
(b) What would be the price of February futures if its expiry is on 24 February?

Solution

(a) The fair value of futures is given by Eq. 5.8.
Here $S_0 = 45.45$, $r_d = 5.90\%$, $r_f = 2.40\%$, and $t = 57$ days (From 12 December to 28 January)

$$F_1 = S_0 \times e^{(r_d - r_f)t} = 45.45 \times e^{(0.059 - 0.024)57/365} = ₹45.6991$$

(b) For February futures, the time to expiry would be $57 + 27 = 84$ days. The price of February futures would be:

$$F_1 = S_0 \times e^{(r_d - r_f)t} = 45.45 \times e^{(0.059 - 0.024)84/365} = ₹45.8176$$

the two currencies. If r_d is less than r_f, it becomes a case of negative cost of carry, as the dividends on the asset are higher than the cost of carrying in local currency.

HEDGING THROUGH CURRENCY FUTURES

Hedging currency exchange rate fluctuations with currency futures is no different than hedging price risks through commodity futures or currency forwards. We use the same principle of taking a position in the futures market opposite to that of the physical market. Subsequently, we enter into another futures contract that offsets the initial contract. In the case of commodities, we strive to nullify gain/loss in the physical market with loss/gain in the futures market in order to achieve a target price as close as possible to the initial futures contract price, with as much certainty as possible.

One must remember that the target price should not be construed as a profitable price. The target price in case of a forward contract is fixed, and is governed by the forward rates available. One cannot desire an exchange rate that is out of line with market conditions. The ultimate price realized in a hedge through futures is dependent upon the prices of futures at the times of initiating the contract and cancelling the contracts, and on the ultimate price prevailing in the spot market.

The following two examples illustrate the mechanics of hedging through futures for the importer and the exporter, they known as long hedge and short hedge, respectively.

Hedge for Importer—Long Hedge

A hedge that involves taking a long position on futures contract is known as a *long hedge*. It is appropriate when one has to purchase certain assets in the future and needs to lock-in the price now. Consider the following situation:

> An importer is short on foreign currency. To hedge against appreciating foreign currency, he goes long on a futures contract.

In June 2008, an Indian importer buys a machine at US $50,000. Payment is due after six months in December 2008. The spot exchange rate is ₹45.5625, while December futures are trading at ₹46.6500, indicating an appreciation of the dollar by about 2.4% over six months. The importer feels that the dollar will appreciate much more. What should he do? Assume that the size of the futures contract available is US $1000.

Hedging strategy As a hedging strategy, the importer buys a futures contract now, trading at ₹46.6500, and sells the same close to the delivery date before December. The importer knows the exact amount of dollars to be covered, and, therefore, he/she buys 50 contracts on MCX-SX.

$$\text{Number of contracts bought by importer} = \frac{\text{Exposure amount}}{\text{Value of one contract}} = \frac{50000}{1000} = 50$$

Having bought 50 futures, the importer would cancel his/her position in the futures by selling the futures at a date close to the actual date of payment in December.

Let us examine two different exchange rates scenarios when the payment falls due in December.

When the US dollar appreciates to ₹47.5600 and a futures contract sells for ₹47.5700

The importer exits the futures contract at ₹47.5700 and buys foreign currency in the spot market at the prevailing spot rate.

Figures in ₹

Buy $50,000 at spot rate;	
Cost = 50,000 × 47.5600	= 23,78,000
Sell 50 future contracts booked earlier at ₹47.5700;	
Net gain on futures (47.5700 − 46.6500) × 50,000	= 46,000
Net rupee amount paid	= 23,32,000
Effective exchange rate (23,32,000/50,000)	= 46.6400

As against the spot price of ₹47.5600, the importer ends up buying dollars at ₹46.6400.

When the US dollar depreciates to ₹44.5625 and a futures contract sells for ₹44.5700

Figures in ₹

Buy $50,000 at the spot rate;	
Cost = 50,000 × 44.5625	= 22,28,125
Sell 50 future contracts at ₹44.5700;	
Net loss on futures (46.6500 − 44.5700) × 50,000	= 1,04,000
Net rupee amount paid	= 23,32,125
Effective exchange rate (23,32,125/50,000)	= 46.6425

As against the spot price of ₹44.5625, the importer ends up buying dollars at ₹46.6425.

It may be observed that irrespective of appreciation or depreciation of the US dollar, the effective cost of buying dollars remains close to the opening futures price, i.e., ₹46.6500. The difference between the actual cost and the futures price is on account of the differential between the spot price and the futures price when the hedge was lifted, referred to as basis risk (discussed in Chapter 3).

Hedging for Exporter—Short Hedge

Exporters are long on the asset, and to cover risk through the future, they have to take an opposite position in futures, i.e., go short on the futures. This strategy is appropriate when one has to sell a certain asset in the future and needs to lock-in the price.

> An exporter is long on foreign currency. To hedge against depreciating foreign currency, he goes short on a futures contract.

Assume that it is December now. A British exporter is expecting to receive US $5 million in six months' time, in June. He is expecting the dollar to depreciate and the pound to appreciate, as is reflected in the following spot and futures rates at CME:

Spot: $1.5530 per pound, and June futures: $1.5600 per pound

Hedging strategy The hedging strategy would involve selling the futures now and covering later. The exporter is facing a loss on his receivable, and he/she is long on US dollars in the physical market. Therefore, he must go short in the futures market, i.e., buy pounds and sell dollars. A standard contract at CME is for £62,500. The number of contracts to be purchased = $5 million/1.5530/62,500 = 51.51. The actual number of contracts purchased = 52 (rounded off).

Say that in June, prior to the settlement date, the following rates are prevailing ($/£)

Spot: 1.6250, and June futures: 1.6275

The exporter squares up and sells the futures contract.

Gain on the futures market = (1.6275 − 1.5600) × 52 × 62,500 = $2,19,375
This is equivalent to £1,35,000 (using the spot price of $1.6250 per pound)
Loss on the receivable = (1/1.5530 − 1/1.6250) × 5 million = £1,42,652
Net loss = £1,42,652 − £1,35,000 = £7652

If the exporter had not hedged, he/she would have received £30,72,196 (50,00,000/1.6275). With hedging, he/she receives £1,35,000 extra from the futures contract, at a realization rate of $1.5590/£.

SPECULATION WITH CURRENCY FUTURES

Like forwards in currencies and futures in stocks, indices, and commodities, foreign currency futures too can be used for taking speculative positions on exchange rate movements. This is also referred to as open position trading. When speculation is made on the movement of price of a futures contract that is not consistent with the opinion held by the speculator on the future spot exchange rates, one may take a position in futures and hope that the opinion held proves correct. Consider the following prices of US dollar:

US $/SGD	Spot	Mar futures	Jun futures	Sep futures
	0.5070	0.5100	0.5150	0.5220

These rates imply that the Singapore dollar (SG $) will appreciate against the US dollar. A speculator does not agree and believes that the Singapore dollar would depreciate or will not appreciate much. Therefore, he/she sells the September futures contract at 0.5220.

However, the Singapore dollar does appreciate to a small extent. The rates (US$/SGD) on 1 September are as follows:

Spot: 0.5150 and futures
September: 0.5158

The speculator squares up his/her position by buying a September contract and gains (0.5220 − 0.5158) = $0.0062 per Singapore dollar or $775 per contract (SG $1,25,000), ignoring the transaction cost and marking-to-market. If the Singapore dollar had depreciated instead, the gain of the speculator would have been even larger.

ARBITRAGE WITH CURRENCY FUTURES

Arbitrage with futures can be executed in case the futures trade at a value other than fair value. If the futures are overpriced, then one can sell them and if they are underpriced, one can buy them. An equivalent position can be created from borrowing/lending and the spot market. The following steps ensure arbitrage:

EXAMPLE 5.5 Arbitrage with currency futures

The following data from the financial markets is available

Spot exchange rate (rupees per dollar)	49.5000
180-day futures	50.4000
Rupee interest rate (T-bill yield)	10%
Dollar interest rate (T-bill yield)	5%

Based on the above data, find out the fair price of a futures contract. Is there any arbitrage opportunity? If yes, how can the arbitrage be executed?

Solution

The fair price of the futures, using simple interest rates, is given by;

$$\text{Fair Price of Futures} = \text{Spot} \times \frac{\left(1 + \text{Rupee interest rate} \frac{\text{days}}{365}\right)}{\left(1 + \text{Dollar interest rate} \frac{\text{days}}{365}\right)} = 49.50 \times \frac{\left(1 + 0.10 \frac{180}{365}\right)}{\left(1 + 0.05 \frac{180}{365}\right)} = ₹50.6912$$

The actual futures trading, at ₹50.40 as against the fair price of ₹50.69, is underpriced. Therefore, we need to buy dollar futures. Hence, we borrow dollars now and do as follows:

	Cash flows	
	$	₹
Now		
Borrow US dollar	1,000.00	—
Convert to rupee using spot market	−1,000.00	49,500.00
Invest rupee at 10% for 180 days		−49,500.00
Buy dollar in futures maturing after 180 days		
Worth ₹51,941		
Total	0.00	0.00
At maturity		
Receive invested rupee		51,941.00
Deliver rupee against futures		−51,941.00
Receive dollars against futures (51,941/50.40)	1,030.58	
Pay dollar borrowed at 5%	−1,024.66	
Total	5.92	—

At the maturity of the futures contract, the arbitrageur can make a profit of $5.92 for every 1000 dollars borrowed.

When futures are overpriced

Now	At maturity of futures
Borrow local currency for the period till the futures mature	Deliver foreign currency against the futures sold
Convert to foreign currency using the spot market	Receive local currency against the futures sold
Invest in foreign currency for the period of the futures	Pay for the borrowed local currency
Sell futures equal to the matured foreign currency investment	

Since the futures are overpriced, the amount of local currency received would exceed the liability of the borrowing.

When future is underpriced

Now	At maturity of futures
Borrow foreign currency till the futures mature	Deliver local currency against the futures sold
Convert to local currency using the spot market	Receive foreign currency against the futures bought
Invest in local currency for the period of the futures	Pay for the borrowed foreign currency
Buy futures equal to the matured local currency investment	

Since the futures are underpriced, the amount of foreign currency received would exceed the liability of the borrowing.

SOLVED PROBLEMS

SP 5.1: Forward premium/discount and forward rates

The following spot rates for the US dollar prevail in the foreign exchange markets:

Spot (rupee per dollar)	47.90	48.10

(a) If the US dollar is at an annualized premium of 5%, find the forward bid rates and the ask rates for 3, 6, and 12 months.
(b) If the US dollar is at an annualized discount of 8%, find the forward bid rates and ask rates for 3, 6, and 12 months.

Assume that in each quarter, the bid–ask spread increases by 20 basis points (bps) for the forward period.

Solution
The spot mid rate is ₹48.00. We can find the forward mid rates for 3, 6, and 12 months using the following equation:

(a) When the US dollar is at 5% premium

$$\text{Forward Mid rate} = \text{Spot mid rate} \times \left(1 + \frac{\text{Annualized \% Premium} \times \text{Forward months}}{100 \times 12}\right)$$

3-m Forward Mid rate = $48.00 \times \left(1 + 0.05 \times \frac{3}{12}\right) = 48.60$

6-m Forward Mid rate = $48.00 \times \left(1 + 0.05 \times \frac{6}{12}\right) = 49.20$

12-m Forward Mid rate = $48.00 \times \left(1 + 0.05 \times \frac{12}{12}\right) = 50.40$

With the bid–ask spread increasing at 20 bps for each quarter, the following would be the forward rates:

	Bid	Ask
3-m forward	48.40	48.80
6-m forward	48.90	49.50
12-m forward	50.00	50.80

(b) When the US dollar is at a discount of 8%

3-m Forward Mid rate = $48.00 \times \left(1 - 0.08 \times \frac{3}{12}\right) = 47.04$

6-m Forward Mid rate = $48.00 \times \left(1 - 0.08 \times \frac{6}{12}\right) = 46.08$

12-m Forward Mid rate = $48.00 \times \left(1 - 0.08 \times \frac{12}{12}\right) = 44.16$

With the bid–ask spread increasing at 20 bps for each quarter, the following would be the forward rates:

	Bid	Ask
3-m forward	46.84	47.24
6-m forward	45.78	46.38
12-m forward	43.76	44.56

SP 5.2: Hedging receivables with forwards

Multiplex Ltd has exported copper castings worth US $1 million for which payment is due after six months. The firm has projected profits assuming the current spot rate of ₹45 per dollar. Though the US dollar has been steady for the last year; the firm anticipates a decline in its value in the coming days. The following rates are quoted by the bank:

Spot (rupee/dollar)	45.00	45.35
6-m Forward	45.50	46.00

(a) Should Multiplex Ltd hedge its receivable?
(b) What realization could be made in Indian rupees it if it decides to hedge?

Solution:
(a) Since the market is expecting a decline in the value of the US dollar, it would be better if Multiplex Ltd books a forward contract for selling its receivable, especially when the firm has projected its profit at ₹45.00. Hedging receivable with forward contracts may help reap high profits.
(b) The forward bid rate is ₹45.50, at which the firm can sell US $1 million, ensuring a rupee cash inflow of ₹455.00 lakh.

SP 5.3: Bounds to forward rates

In the inter-bank markets of New York, the prevailing spot rates and interest with respect to the euro are:

Spot rate (dollar per euro)		1.1200	1.1250
Interest rate	dollar	5.00%	5.30%
	euro	4.00%	4.20%

Find out (a) the lower bound to the 3-m forward ask rate
(b) the upper bound to the 3-m forward bid rate

Solution

(a) To find the lower bound on the ask rate, we (a) borrow €1.00 at 4.20% for three months (to repay €1.0105 after three months) (b) convert spot into US dollars at the bid rate to get $1.1200, (c) invest at 5% for three months to get $1.1340 after three months, and (d) the sell matured dollars forward to get euro to pay for the borrowing.
The matured amount of US dollar is sold to get euros at the forward ask rate. For no arbitrage, the matured amount through forwards must be less than €1.0105.

Alternatively, for no arbitrage, we must have $1.1340/F_a \leq 1.0105$ or $F_a \geq \$1.1222$

(b) To find out the upper bound on the bid rate we (a) borrow $1.00 at 5.30% for three months (to repay $1.01325 after three months), (b) convert spot into euro at the ask rate to get €0.8889, (c) invest at 4% for three months to get €0.8978 after three months, and (d) sell matured euro forward to get dollar to pay for the borrowing.
The matured amount of euro is sold to get dollar at the forward bid rate. For no arbitrage, the matured amount through the forward must be less than $1.01325.

Alternatively, for no arbitrage, we must have $0.8978 \times F_b \leq 1.01325$ or $F_b \leq \$1.1286$

SP 5.4: Settlement of NDF

In Singapore, foreign exchange NDFs are quoted in RMB for settlement in US dollar. An exporter based in Hong Kong has RMB 1 million receivable after three months. The RMB is likely to depreciate. The NDF is being offered at RMB 8.20 per dollar, which the exporter books. What amount would the exporter pay/receive if on the settlement date, the fixing rate is RMB 8.30 per dollar?

Solution
The exporter sells RMB (buys US dollars) at an exchange rate of RMB 8.20 per dollar. Therefore, the notional principal is US $10,00,000/8.20 = $1,21,991.20.

On settlement, the fixing rate is 8.30. The exporter would receive from the bank what is necessary to cover the shortfall he would have on RMB receivables when converted to US dollars at spot rate.

$$\text{Settlement amount} = \text{Notional principal} \times \left(1 - \frac{\text{NDF rate}}{\text{Fixing rate}}\right)$$

$$\text{Settlement amount} = 1{,}21{,}91.20 \times \left(1 - \frac{8.20}{8.30}\right) = \$1469.29$$

SP 5.5: Speculation with currency futures

Dollar futures with expiry in 60 days from now at MCX-SX are trading at ₹48.65. In the spot market, the rate is ₹47.75. Risk-free rates in the USA are estimated to be 9% and 5%. If the estimates are assumed correct, what action would you take to earn profit?

Solution
The fair value of the futures is

$$F = S_0 \times e^{(r_d - r_f)t} = 47.75 \times e^{(0.09 - 0.05)60/365} = ₹48.0650$$

The future is overpriced. Therefore, it must be sold.

SP 5.6: Arbitrage with currency futures

The following data is available from the financial markets:

Spot exchange rate (rupee per dollar)	49.7500
90-day futures	51.4000
Rupee interest rate (T-bill yield)	12%
Dollar interest rate (T-bill yield)	8%

Based on these data, find out the fair price of the futures contract. Is there any arbitrage opportunity? If yes, how can the arbitrage be executed?

Solution
The fair price of the futures using simple interest rates is given by

$$\text{Fair price of futures} = \text{Spot} \times \frac{\left(1 + \text{Rupee interest rate} \frac{\text{days}}{365}\right)}{\left(1 + \text{Dollar interest rate} \frac{\text{days}}{365}\right)} = 49.75 \times \frac{\left(1 + 0.12 \frac{90}{365}\right)}{\left(1 + 0.08 \frac{90}{365}\right)} = ₹50.2312$$

The actual future trading at ₹51.40, as against the fair price of ₹50.23, is overpriced. Therefore, we need to sell dollar futures. Hence, we borrow rupees now and make arbitrage profit as demonstrated below.

	Cash flows	
	$	₹
Now		
Borrow rupees	—	1,000.00
Convert to dollars using the spot market	20.1005	−1,000.00
Invest the dollars at 8% for 90 days	−20.1005	—
Sell the dollars in futures maturing after 90 days worth ₹1,053.55		
Total	0.00	0.00
At maturity		
Receive invested dollars	20.4970	—
Deliver dollars against futures	−20.4970	—
Receive rupees against futures (20.1005 × 51.40)	—	1,053.55
Pay rupee borrowed at 12%	—	−1,029.59
Total	—	23.96

At the maturity of the futures contract, the arbitrageur can make a profit of ₹23.96 for every ₹1000 borrowed.

Currency Forwards and Futures

SUMMARY

With increased globalization and liberalization of trade, an additional dimension of risk is added to the menu of finance managers. Beside business risks, firms that trade internationally face the risk of fluctuating exchange rates for exports and imports. A risks related to foreign exchange is somewhat different, as it involves consideration of global factors that are not only hard to comprehend, but are time consuming and too divergent. They require more managerial time than would be needed to handle other kind of risks.

Foreign exchange markets are intricate and function quite differently in terms of rates. Foreign exchange rates for buying and selling are different, and are known as the bid rate and the ask rate, respectively. Further, foreign exchange markets are OTC. Transactions in spot are settled within two business days, time given to allow for the logistics of exchange of one currency into another, which involves a chain of banks and nations.

Forward contracts are more popular as hedging, speculative instruments, and futures contracts. There also exist NDF contracts, which are mostly handled off-shore and are cash-settled. They are popular instruments in currencies that have capital flow controls. Forward contracts, being OTC, offer flexibility with respect to delivery of foreign exchange, by allowing a period rather than a specific date. Such contracts are called option forwards.

The rates offered in various locations by various banks are different and yet competitive, and it is difficult to capture arbitrage opportunities in foreign exchange markets, because these varying rates are not in the public domain.

Hedging in foreign exchange rates can be done on the same principle of taking a position in forwards and/or futures opposite to that of the physical markets. An exporter is long on foreign currency, and, therefore, he/she sells a futures contract. It is a short hedge. On the contrary, an importer, who needs foreign currency, has to go long in the futures market to hedge. This also remains the position in case of hedging with forward contracts. While speculation on a forward contract is possible, arbitrage is a near impossibility, as forward rates are OTC. Arbitrage and speculation in futures do not suffer from such disadvantages.

KEY TERMS

Ask rate The rate at which a bank sells foreign currency.
Bid rate The rate at which a bank buys foreign currency.
Currency futures A forward contract in foreign exchange that is traded on an exchange.
Forward premium or discount The annualized percentage variation of the forward rate with respect to the spot rate. A forward rate higher than the spot rate means the foreign currency is at a premium.
Forward transaction A transaction that needs to be settled at a future date, at a rate specified now.
Interest rate parity The condition that implies that the forward rate is determined by the equality of returns in different currencies.

Non-deliverable forward An off-shore forward contract in foreign currency where no delivery is required, and the contract is necessarily cash-settled on maturity.
Option forward A contract that allows flexibility of settlement date by specifying a period rather than a specific date.
Spot transaction The transactions in foreign exchange that are settled in two business days.
Swap transaction A transaction consisting of two equal and opposite legs, to be completed at two different points of time.

QUESTIONS

5.1 What are the typical features of foreign exchange markets as compared to markets for other financial assets?
5.2 Differentiate between (a) bid rate and ask rate, and (b) spot rates and forward rates.
5.3 What do you understand by premium or discount in foreign exchange? How it is calculated? Show with an example.
5.4 What is a swap transaction and why is it popular in inter-bank markets?
5.5 What are option forwards and how are they beneficial?
5.6 Explain hedging of payables and receivables with a forward contract.
5.7 What is an NDF? Explain its utility and operation.
5.8 How are currency futures different from currency forwards?
5.9 How are currency futures and forwards priced?
5.10 Describe the hedging strategy for payables and receivables using currency futures.
5.11 Explain with an example the operation of arbitrage when futures are not correctly priced.

PROBLEMS

P 5.1 Triangular arbitrage
Assume that a bank in India has offered exchange rates for the US dollar and the euro at ₹48.00 and ₹78.00 for a 2-m forward contract, respectively. An American bank has quoted a 2-m forward rate of US $1.70 per euro. If you are allowed to book any contract, can you take advantage of the rates offered by the bank in India and the bank in America?

P 5.2 Arbitrage in futures and forward market
A futures contract expiring on 28 October in US dollars at the NSE is selling for ₹48.6800. Your bank has offered a forward contract for delivery on 28 October at ₹48.9000. How can you take advantage of the disparity in the futures and the forward markets? How do you think the position would correct itself?

P 5.3 Pricing futures contracts
The risk-free continuously compounded interest rates in the USA and Japan are estimated at 8% and 3% respectively for 3-m maturity. If the spot rate in Japan is Japanese yen 102 per dollar, what is the likely price for a 3-m futures contract?

P 5.4 Fair price of futures and interest rates
The spot exchange rate in Germany is €1.25 per pound. A 6-m futures contract in Sterling pounds is quoted at €1.27 per pound. With returns of 6% in German government securities for maturities of six months and assuming that the futures are correctly priced, what risk-free rate would you expect in England?

P 5.5 Hedging strategy for receivables with currency futures
As an exporter, you expect to receive US $20,000 three months from now. The spot price of the US dollar is ₹50.00 while a 3-m futures contract at the NSE is trading at ₹49.30, indicating depreciation of the US dollar. Under what circumstances would you like to hedge? What would be the hedging strategy?

P 5.6 Hedging a long position with futures and effective exchange rates
Refer to P 5.5. Assume that the exporter hedges with the futures contract. One futures contract at NSE is for US $1000, and it is cash-settled. Find out the exchange rate realized by the exporter when prior to maturity (a) the spot rate is ₹50.50 and the futures is selling for ₹50.42 and (b) the spot rate is ₹48.40 and the futures is selling for ₹48.48.

P 5.7 Hedging a short position with futures and effective exchange rates
Impex Ltd has to make a payment of US $25,000 after three months. The spot exchange rate is ₹46, and it has been increasing in the recent past. The appreciation of the dollar is expected to continue, as reflected in the 3-m futures quotation of ₹47.50. The management of Impex Ltd believes that the US dollar is expected to go beyond ₹47.50 in three months' time.

(a) How can Impex Ltd hedge its foreign currency exposure?
(b) Assume that Impex Ltd takes position in futures and after 3 months, at the time of making payment, it unwinds position in futures. Find out the effective exchange rate paid by Impex Ltd when (i) spot rate is ₹49.10 and futures price is ₹49.20, and (ii) spot rate is ₹46.75 and futures price is ₹46.80.

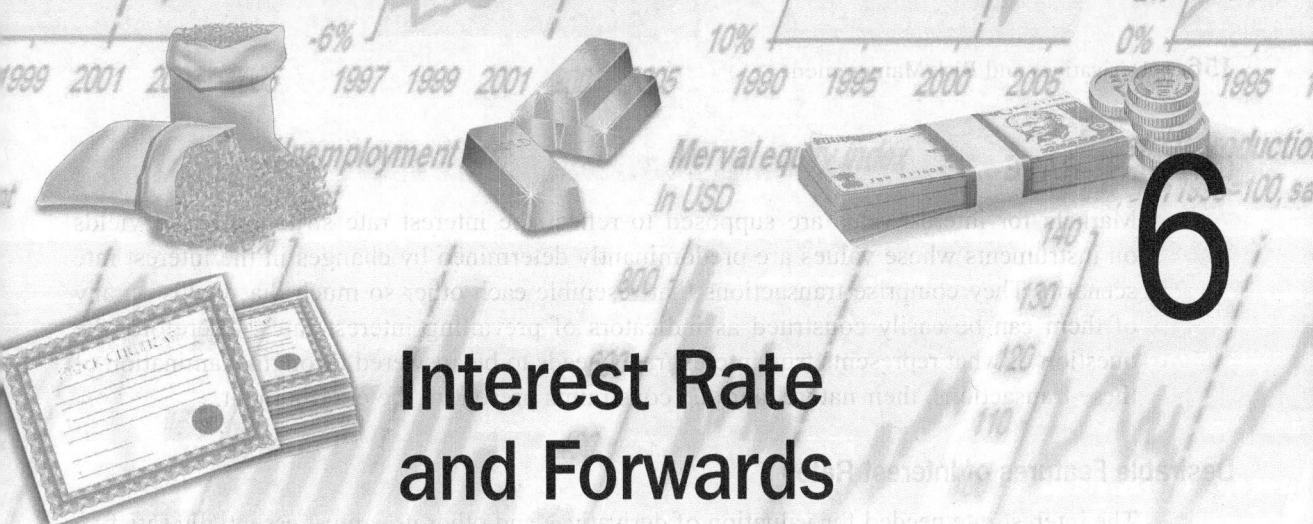

Interest Rate and Forwards

INTRODUCTION

Interest rates in an economy occupy a central position because they are regarded as one consolidated parameter that displays the progress and condition of an economy. In derivatives, the use of interest rates is of special significance because most valuations in derivatives require interest rates as one of the critical inputs. Valuation of futures contracts with any underlying asset such as commodity, stock, index, or foreign exchange is not possible without knowing the relevant interest rates.

In real world situations, many types of interest rates prevail in an economy. In India, like in most other nations of the world, interest rates are a function of the nature of transaction being funded, counterparties to the transactions, currency, place, duration of funding, etc. For example, the central bank of a country would lend/borrow money from banks in its country at certain rates; the banks would lend to borrowers at other different rates; public debt in the economy would be mobilized at different rates, and so on. As such, different measures of interest rates, such as repo (repurchase) rates, reverse repo rates, yields on T-bills, Prime Lending Rate (PLR), etc., prevail at the same time. Even though these rates are all interlinked in some way or the other, the exact relationship is hard to find.

> Different rates prevail for different transactions. They can be direct, such as bank loans, or indirect, implied in the market prices of securities.

For the purpose of valuation and the risks emanating from the changes, interest rates occupy a special place in the study of derivatives and also for devising derivative products to manage interest rate risks. We take a look at the desirable features of interest rates that are used in the study of derivatives.

Learning Objectives
After going through this chapter, readers should be familiar with

- various kinds of interest rates
- desirable features of interest rates to be used
- distinction between yield to maturity (YTM) and zero rates
- arriving at zeros from YTMs through bootstrapping
- interest rate risk
- forward rate agreements (FRAs) as a hedging product
- borrower's FRA and investor's FRA
- settlement of FRA
- pricing FRA
- hedging with FRAs
  - against rising interest rates
  - against falling interest rates
- speculation with FRAs

INTEREST RATE

Markets for interest rates are supposed to reflect the interest rate structure-based yields on instruments whose values are predominantly determined by changes in the interest rate scenario. They comprise transactions that resemble each other so much that yields on any of them can be easily construed as indicators of prevailing interest rates. Therefore, the question of what represents true interest rates needs to be answered through examination of these transactions, their nature, and the constraints present in the environment.

Desirable Features of Interest Rates

The interest rate needed for valuation of derivatives and other uses must essentially satisfy a few features that seem to be unavailable in any single transaction. The most useful and commonly desired features of interest rates must have certain characteristics that are discussed in this section.

> The interest rate desired for derivatives must be free from default risk and market determined.

First, the interest rate should be devoid of credit risk. Normally, when two parties engage in a borrowing/lending transaction, the interest rate decided between them incorporates the counterparty risk or default risk. Ideally, no lending transaction can be said to be completely free from default risk. Second, the interest rates must demonstrate that they are determined by free market forces and are not constrained by legal, environmental, and economic/financial factors, or by compulsions influencing the demand and supply of such instruments. Third, the measurement of interest rates must be done in such a manner that changes in values of the underlying assets may be attributed exclusively or substantially to changes in the interest rate structure and to no other factor. Thus, in a nutshell, any interest rates to be used for valuation of derivatives and for the purpose of designing a suitable instrument for hedging against interest rate risk should be (a) free from default risk, (b) market determined and free from legal compulsions influencing commercial needs, and (c) truly reflective of the changes in the value of the securities dependent on those interest rates alone.

Repo and Reverse Repo Rates

The repo rate applies to borrowing and lending transactions between the central bank of a country and other banks, where the banks borrow/lend on the strength of extremely safe and liquid securities. The difference between the selling rate of the securities and their repurchase price after a predetermined time represents the effective interest rate prevailing at the time of entering a repurchase agreement. It is a pure lending transaction involving extremely safe instruments between two highly creditworthy parties, and, therefore, can be said to be devoid of default risk. In case the repurchase is not honoured, the lending bank keeps/sells the securities.

Valuation, as reflected in the differential between the selling price and the repurchase price, is a pure function of the borrowing rate prevailing in the country. However, there are some important dimensions concerning its appropriateness to serve as a benchmark for risk-free rates. The repo rate is regulated by the central bank, and is also used as an important tool of monetary policy to alter the money supply in the country and achieve wider policy objectives. The repo rate is also influenced by economic conditions and desired growth rates and complements fiscal policy. It is used to alter the interest rate structure rather than represent it. However, it cannot be said to be a true representative of market-determined risk-free interest because only a limited number of participants comprise the market. Though the volumes could be high, the market lacks depth.

Further, changes in the repo rate are not continuous but intermittent. We expect the rates to change as the expectations of return for investors keep changing almost continuously. The change is effected only when the central bank deems it necessary to achieve some monetary and fiscal objectives upon periodic review of its policies. At best, repo rate can be one determinant of risk-free interest rates but cannot be said to be freely market determined.

Treasury Rates

Another set of instruments that invites wider and deeper participation than repo transactions is treasury bills (T-bills) and bonds. Treasury bills and bonds are issued by the central bank for a variety of reasons, among which the need to fund government expenditure is predominant. Repayment is virtually assured because of the unique position of the issuer providing the central bank the authority to print money as a last resort. This virtually eliminates default risk. The issuer would always redeem the securities or pay interest on due dates, though defaults have taken place in history, such as those by Argentina, Mexico, and Russia.

The securities issued by a central bank are normally auctioned and, hence, their pricing is governed by market forces prevailing at the time of the issue. Further after issuance, being transferable and negotiable, these securities are also traded in the secondary markets, where the current prices would reflect the yields expected by the investors. These yields would change on a continuous basis and reflect the current economic conditions and the investors' expectations of return. Note that under a repo transaction, the same securities form the basis of borrowing and lending. However, yields in the secondary market would be different from the repo rate because of wider participation and lesser constraints placed on participants.

However, neither the primary markets (despite processes of auction determining prices/yields) nor the secondary markets can be said to be free markets. Hence, such prices cannot be assumed to be freely market-determined interest rates. In the primary markets, auctions are constrained by the compulsions of banks, the major participants, to subscribe to these securities to meet statutory liquidity ratio (SLR) requirements, whereby they must maintain certain proportions of their total deposits with the central bank. Subscription to these securities cannot be deemed voluntary subscriptions purely guided by financial and economic considerations. These compulsions of SLR are also carried forward to secondary market transactions, casting doubts on whether the yield would be the same if secondary market transactions were to be undertaken out of the free will of participants to buy and sell securities guided purely by the commercial motive of earning higher returns. Besides legal compulsions, initial subscription and subsequent trading in secondary markets are also influenced by some tax rebates, reduced provisioning, and escaping marking-to-the-market requirements for held-to-maturity securities, etc.

> Repo, reverse repo, and treasure rates are considered to free from default risk but are subject to legal considerations that may influence their values.

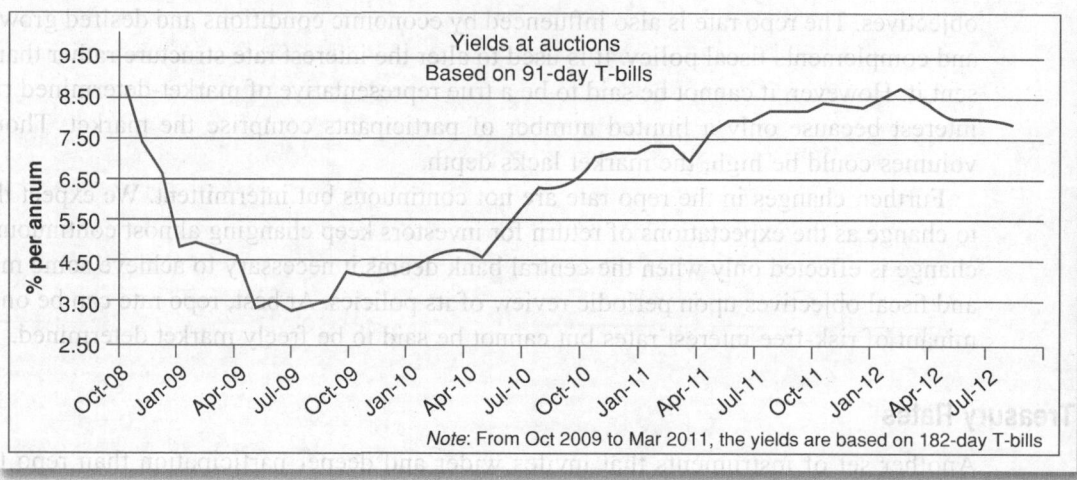

Fig. 6.1 91-day T-bill yields on auction

Figure 6.1 depicts monthly T-bill yields on auctions from January 2008 to December 2011, based on the first auction of each month. Note that these auctions take place every Wednesday, with payment on Fridays, according to a pre-announced calendar notifying the amount of each auction.

Interbank Transactions

Interbank trades constitute a large proportion of trade in financial claims. These trades are done on the basis of bid and ask rates offered by competing banks to each other for accepting deposits and lending funds. Internationally, these rates are determined in London in major currencies for terms up to 12 months. Bid rates are rates to accept deposit while offer rates are rates for lending. These are known as LIBID (London interbank bid rate) and LIBOR (London interbank offer rate), respectively.

On similar lines, the National Stock Exchange (NSE) along with Fixed Income Money Market and Derivative Association of India (FIMMDA), in an effort to develop debt markets, launched MIBID (Mumbai interbank bid rates) and MIBOR (Mumbai interbank offer rates) for overnight rates in June 1998. Later, they expanded the list to 14-day rates and then for 1-m and 3-m deposits and lending. These rates have gained wide acceptance for benchmarking various banking and derivative products.

The MIBID/MIBOR rates are used as benchmark rates for a majority of deals struck for interest rate swaps, forward rate agreements (FRAs), floating rate debentures, and term deposits. These rates are considered the best for these market-oriented products because they are (a) unbiased, as they are determined by professionals with no vested interest, (b) transparent and market-oriented, because these are based on polling by 32 large banks, (c) reliable, since actual deals do take place on these rates, and (d) scientifically determined on the basis of polling and bootstrapping, eliminating cartelization, noise, and extreme values. Further, the default risk is minimal, since banks are not expected to default on the principal and interest repayment of obligations.

Interbank rates satisfy the requirements of being (a) free from default risk and (b) market determined.

These rates are deemed as market determined because they are quoted out of free will by the participants who engage in lending and borrowing transactions. Further, despite the fact that there remains an element of counter-party risk, it is considered negligible due to the high credibility of the banks involved in the process of determining these rates. Unlike repo transactions or trading in treasury securities, where the trading is governed by factors other than complete willingness, the transactions on interbank rates are governed by pure commercial and business considerations. Hence, interbank rates are considered a better proxy for risk-free interest rates, as compared to repo rates or yield on treasury instruments.

Figure 6.2 depicts the trend in 3-m MIBOR rates from January 2008 to December 2011. Though these rates are announced every day, the rates on the first working day of the month are used in the graphical depiction. The similarities and dissimilarities in the trends and values between 3-m MIBOR and yields on 91-day T-bills (in Fig. 6.1) may be seen in this figure. Trends in 3-m MIBOR since 1998 are depicted in Fig. 6.3.

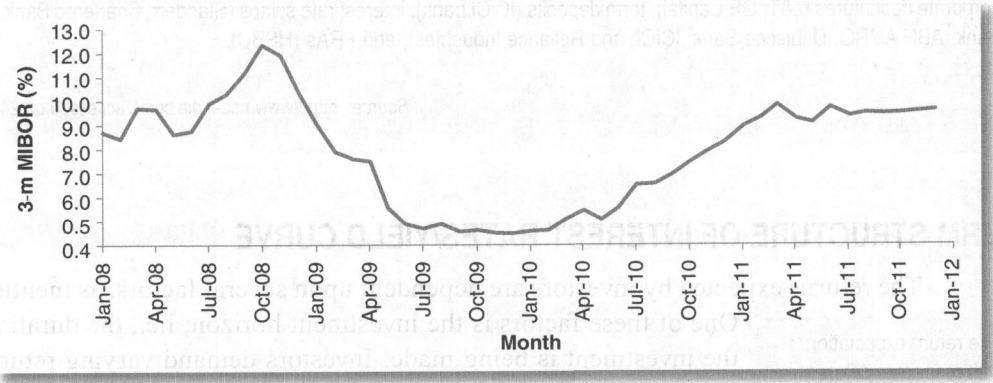

Source: www.nseindia.com, accessed on 30 August 2012

Fig. 6.2 3-m MIBOR from January 2008 to December 2011

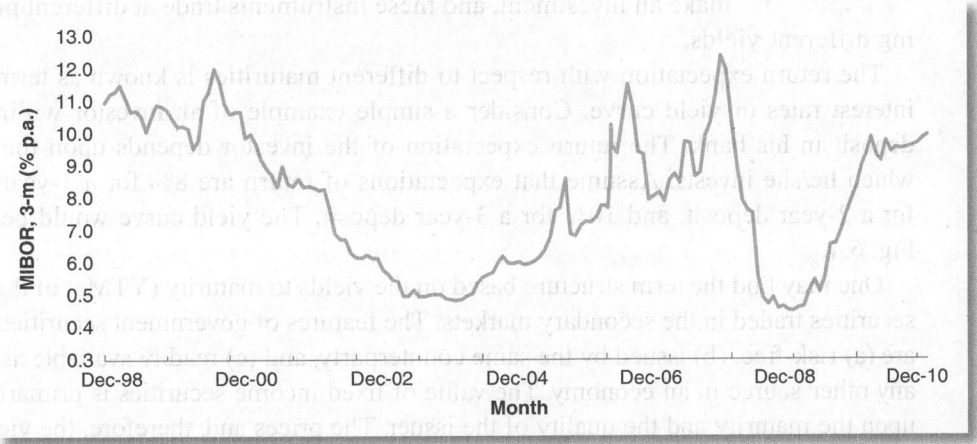

Source: www.nseindia.com, accessed on 30 August 2012

Fig. 6.3 3-m MIBOR since 1998

> **Derivatives in Practice**
>
> ## Interest Rates MIBID and MIBOR
>
> **Determining market-oriented benchmark risk-free rates MIBID and MIBOR**
>
> The determination of interbank rates to serve as benchmarks set by the NSE and the FIMMDA includes large banks and dealers from the public sector such as Bank of Baroda, Canara Bank, Central Bank of India, Punjab National Bank, and State Bank of India, as well as private sector banks including Axis Bank, HDFC Bank, Kotak Mahindra, and, ICICI Bank. Foreign banks include Bank of America, CitiBank, Deutsche Bank, HSBC, and Standard Chartered Bank. Amongst primary dealers, participants include State Bank of India, DFHI, ICICI Securities, PNB Gilts, etc.
>
> FIMMDA–NSE MIBID MIBOR rates are broadcast immediately on release through the NEAT–WDM trading system. The NSE website carries the daily rates as well as historical data on the FIMMDA–NSE MIBID MIBOR. The FIMMDA also disseminates the FIMMDA–NSE MIBID MIBOR rates through its website and through other means.
>
> In addition, leading information vendors such as Reuters, Knight Ridder, and Bloomberg carry these rates on a daily basis. FIMMDA–NSE MIBID MIBOR rates are also carried by all leading financial dailies, including *Economic Times, Financial Express, Business Standard,* and *Business Line*. In addition, FIMMDA–NSE MIBID MIBOR rates are released to contributors and users through e-mail.
>
> Since MIBOR rates exhibit features such as transparency, reliability, and quick and wide dissemination, several products are designed on this benchmark rate. The products that are linked to MIBID and/or MIBOR include floating rate notes (GE Capital), corporate debentures (L&T, GE Capital), term deposits (ICICI bank), interest rate swaps (Standard Chartered Bank, HSBC, HDFC Bank, ABN AMRO, Deutsche Bank, ICICI, and Reliance Industries), and FRAs (HSBC).
>
> *Source*: http://www.nse-india.com/, accessed on 24 February 2012.

TERM STRUCTURE OF INTEREST RATES/YIELD CURVE

The returns expected by investors are dependent upon several factors, as mentioned earlier. One of these factors is the investment horizon, i.e., the duration for which the investment is being made. Investors demand varying returns for varying maturities. A bond maturing after three years is not the same as a bond with a maturity period of 1 year or 15 years. Their yields would differ. Investors do have a variety of instruments available to choose from to make an investment, and these instruments trade at different prices, reflecting different yields.

> The return expectation with respect to different maturities is known as term structure of interest rates or yield curve.

The return expectation with respect to different maturities is known as term structure of interest rates or yield curve. Consider a simple example of an investor willing to make a deposit in his bank. The return expectation of the investor depends upon the duration for which he/she invests. Assume that expectations of return are 8% for a 1-year deposit, 9% for a 2-year deposit, and 10% for a 3-year deposit. The yield curve would be as shown in Fig. 6.4.

One may find the term structure based on the yields to maturity (YTMs) of the government securities traded in the secondary markets. The features of government securities are that they are (a) risk-free, (b) issued by the same counterparty, and (c) readily available as compared to any other source in an economy. The value of fixed income securities is primarily dependent upon the maturity and the quality of the issuer. The prices and, therefore, the yields include a premium towards default risk. Prices of government securities would not include any premium for default, and, hence, differences in the yields can be assumed only to be exclusively on account of differing maturities. Though considered safe, interbank rates are normally available

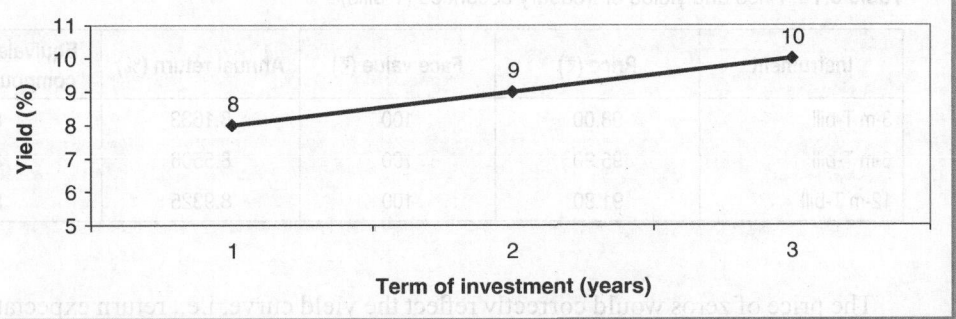

Fig. 6.4 Term structure of interest rates

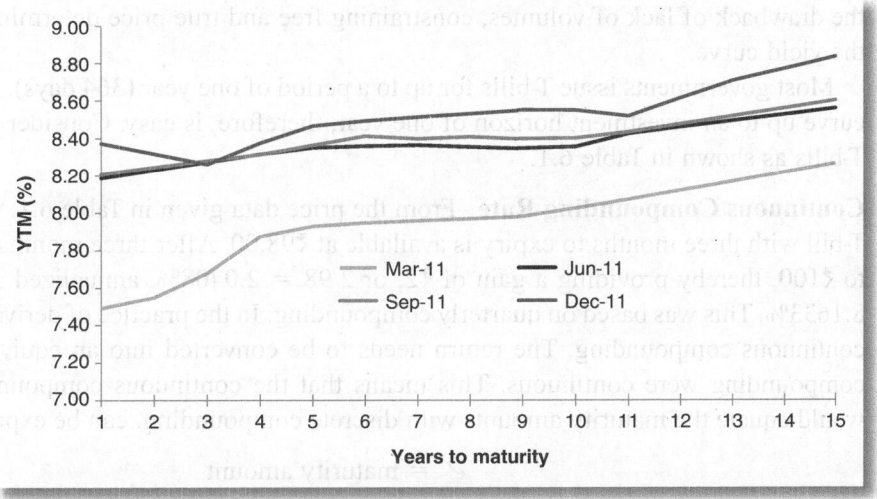

Source: Based on YTMs for Dated Securities Transactions as per *RBI Bulletin* 13 February 2012

Fig. 6.5 YTMs for different maturities

for maturity terms only up to 12 months. Hence, they cannot be used for yield curves that stretch beyond 12 months.

Figure 6.5 depicts a yield curve up to 15 years in March, June, September, and December 2011, based on secondary market trades in government securities. The curve is based on YTMs of securities traded for different maturities.

Treasury Zero Rates Understanding the term structure of interest rates is easy but calculating them poses many practical difficulties. The price of a bond implies a YTM, which is regarded as the average rate of return over the life of the bond. It is erroneous to regard YTMs of bonds with different maturities as term structure of interest rates, because usually bonds are composite instruments representing cash flows spread over their lives that occur at different points of time but are treated as one security. To arrive at the correct yield curve reflecting investor preferences for yields only on account of differing maturities, we need to have securities that pay a single cash flow at different maturities. As such, these securities have no interim coupon payments till maturity and, therefore, are referred to as *zeros*.

Table 6.1 Price and yields of treasury securities (T-bills)

Instrument	Price (₹)	Face value (₹)	Annual return (%)	Equivalent continuous compounding rate (%)
3-m T-bill	98.00	100	8.1633	8.0811
6-m T-bill	95.90	100	8.5506	8.3728
12-m T-bill	91.80	100	8.9325	8.5558

The price of zeros would correctly reflect the yield curve, i.e., return expectations of investors for different maturities. Generally, zero rates are not available for extended maturities because zero coupon bonds for longer maturities are generally not issued; if they are available, they are not liquid enough. Even if such securities are available, they may suffer from the drawback of lack of volumes, constraining free and true price determination and, hence, the yield curve.

Most governments issue T-bills for up to a period of one year (364 days). Obtaining a yield curve up to an investment horizon of one year, therefore, is easy. Consider the price data for T-bills as shown in Table 6.1.

Continuous Compounding Rate From the price data given in Table 6.1, we observe that a T-bill with three months to expiry is available at ₹98.00. After three months, it would mature to ₹100, thereby providing a gain of ₹2, or 2/98 = 2.0408%, annualized as 4 × 2.0408 = 8.1633%. This was based on quarterly compounding. In the practice of derivatives, we assume continuous compounding. The return needs to be converted into an equivalent return as if compounding were continuous. This means that the continuous compounding rate, which would equate the maturity amounts with discrete compounding, can be expressed as follows:

$$e^{rt} = \text{maturity amount}$$

where r is the continuously compounded return for the maturity period of t years.

Therefore, for the compounding rate R with the compounding number of periods in a year n, the maturity amount can be given as follows:

$$e^{rt} = (1 + R/n)^{nt}$$

For quarterly compounding, the continuous compounding rate for the given data for T-bills maturing in three months in Table 6.1 is given by

$$r = 4 \ln(1 + 0.020408) = 0.080811, \text{ or } 8.0811\%$$

On similar lines, the equivalent continuous compounding rates for T-bills are

6 months $\quad r = 2 \ln(1 + 0.085506/2) = 0.083728$, or 8.3728%
12 months $\quad r = 1 \ln(1 + 0.089325) = 0.085558$, or 8.5558%

Bootstrapping: Obtaining Zero Rates from YTMs of Bonds

The compounding rates in the aforementioned calculations are zero rates, as the instruments used have no interim coupons. For maturities beyond one year, there normally would

Table 6.2 YTMs for different maturities

Figures in ₹

Maturity	1½-year bond	2-year bond	2½-year bond	3-year bond
Coupon rate, %	10	12	12	12
Time (months from now)	Cash flows			
Current market price	101.00	104.00	104.00	104.00
6	5.00	6.00	6.00	6.00
12	5.00	6.00	6.00	6.00
18	105.00	6.00	6.00	6.00
24		106.00	6.00	6.00
30			106.00	6.00
36				106.00
YTM (semi-annual), %	4.6353	4.8752	5.0742	5.2067
YTM (annual), %	9.4855	9.9881	10.4059	10.6845

be interim coupon payments, and the prices of these securities include the values of these interim coupon payments. Assuming that an investor would hold the security till its maturity, yields on these instruments are quoted on the basis of YTM. The valuation assumes that YTM is the single discount rate that equates the futures cash flow of the instrument with its current price.

Therefore, while finding the YTMs of the bond, we discount each coupon payment and principal payment at the same rate, irrespective of the timing, rather than the rate as per the term structure applicable for various timings in the cash flow.

> When zeroes are not available, YTMs of bonds can be used to arrive at a yield curve by the bootstrapping method.

The YTMs of coupon paying bonds with maturities from 1½ to 3 years with semi-annual cash flows are shown in Table 6.2.

Do these YTMs truly reflect the return expectations with different terms to maturities of investment? Yes, they do, but these YTMs are approximate values only. To find the true yield curve, we use the bootstrapping approach, where we successively find appropriate yields for progressively increasing maturities.

We already know the true yield curve for maturities of 3, 6, and 12 months. These yields would help us find the appropriate yield for 18 months, through the market price of the bond maturing at that time. Assume that a 1½-year bond that pays a 10% coupon semi-annually sells for ₹101. This bond has three cash flows: (a) ₹5.00 at the end of six months, (b) ₹5.00 at the end of 12 months, and (c) ₹105.00 at the end of 18 months. The market price must be equal to the present values of these cash flows discounted at a rate appropriate to the timing of each cash flow. The rates for 6 and 12 months are already known to us. With the current price already known, we can arrive at the appropriate discount rate for 18 months as follows:

$$5 \times e^{-0.083728 \times 0.5} + 5 \times e^{-0.085558 \times 1.0} + 105 \times e^{-r \times 1.5} = 101$$

$$\text{For 18 months} \quad r = -\frac{\ln \frac{91.6150}{105}}{1.5} = 0.090910 \equiv 9.0910\%$$

EXAMPLE 6.1 Finding the yield curve by bootstrapping

Based on the zero rates given in Table 6.3, find out the zero rates applicable for 42 and 48 months if the following prices prevail for government securities:

Maturity	Coupon	Periodicity	Market price (₹)
42 months	14%	Semi-annual	109.00
48 months	16%	Semi-annual	116.00

Solution

Zero rates up to 36 months are given in Table 6.3. From the price of a bond maturing after 42 months, we can find the zero rate applicable for the term of 42 months. The price of the bond would be calculated as follows:

$$7 \times e^{-0.083729 \times 0.5} + 7 \times e^{-0.085558 \times 1.0} + 7 \times e^{-0.090910 \times 1.5} + 7 \times e^{-0.095884 \times 2.0} + 7 \times e^{-0.100015 \times 2.5} + 7 \times e^{-0.102768 \times 3.0} + 107 \times e^{-r \times 3.5} = 109$$

For 42 months, $r = -\dfrac{\ln\dfrac{73.3806}{107}}{3.50} = 0.107763 \equiv 10.7763\%$

Similarly, after obtaining the zeros' rate for 42 months, we can find the zeros' rate for 48 months using the price of bond maturing after 48 months. The price of this bond is given by

$$8 \times e^{-0.083729 \times 0.5} + 8 \times e^{-0.085558 \times 1.0} + 8 \times e^{-0.090910 \times 1.5} + 8 \times e^{-0.095884 \times 2.0} + 8 \times e^{-0.100015 \times 2.5} + 8 \times e^{-0.102768 \times 3.0} + 8 \times e^{-0.107763 \times 3.5} + 108 \times e^{-r \times 4.0} = 116$$

For 48 months, $r = -\dfrac{\ln\dfrac{69.8057}{108}}{4.0} = 0.109104 \equiv 10.9104\%$

Using the yield investment horizon of 18 months, we can now find out the appropriate rate for a term of two years on similar lines. Therefore, calculation of the appropriate discount rate for 24 months is as follows:

$$6 \times e^{-0.083728 \times 0.5} + 6 \times e^{-0.085558 \times 1.0} + 6 \times e^{-0.090910 \times 1.5} + 106 \times e^{-r \times 2.0} = -104$$

For 24 months $r = -\dfrac{\ln\dfrac{87.5029}{106}}{2} = 0.095884 \equiv 9.5884\%$

Similarly, for 2½ and 3 years, we find the discount rates using the prices of the bond maturing at 2½ and 3 years.

$$6 \times e^{-0.083728 \times 0.5} + 6 \times e^{-0.085558 \times 1.0} + 6 \times e^{-0.090910 \times 1.5} + 6 \times e^{-0.095884 \times 2.0} + 106 \times e^{-r \times 2.5} = 104$$

For 30 months, $r = -\dfrac{\ln\dfrac{84.5499}{106}}{2.5} = 0.100015 \equiv 10.0015\%$

$$6 \times e^{-0.083728 \times 0.5} + 6 \times e^{-0.085558 \times 1.0} + 6 \times e^{-0.090910 \times 1.5} + 6 \times e^{-0.095884 \times 2.0} + 6 \times e^{-0.100015 \times 2.5} + 106 \times e^{-r \times 3.0} = 104$$

For 36 months, $r = -\dfrac{\ln\dfrac{77.8777}{106}}{3.0} = 0.102768 \equiv 10.2768\%$

Now we can have yield curves for periods up to three years at 6-month intervals. The YTM and zero rates based on continuous compounding computed by using the bootstrapping method are consolidated in Table 6.3, and the yield curve based on YTMs and zeros is presented in Fig. 6.6. Note that there is almost a parallel shift in the yields beyond a term of one year.

Table 6.3 Term structure

% p.a.

Years	YTM-based	Zero-based
0.5	8.3729	8.3729
1.0	8.5558	8.5558
1.5	9.4855	9.0910
2.0	9.9881	9.5884
2.5	10.4059	10.0015
3.0	10.6845	10.2768

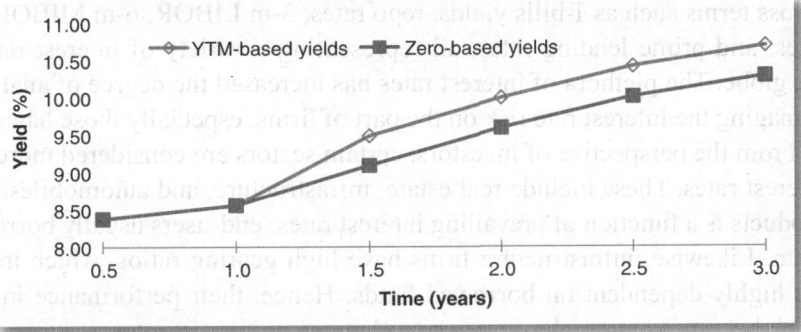

Fig. 6.6 Yield curve

While finding zero rates, we assume that bonds with exact maturities are available, which in general is not true in practice. One may use linear interpolation to arrive at the prices of two bonds to find an approximate yield for the desired term.

FORWARD CONTRACTS ON INTEREST RATES—FRAs

We know that the price risk for various assets can be covered by using forward or futures contracts. When the risk is related to commodities, we use futures on commodities; when the risk is related to currency, we use currency forwards and futures; and when it is related to stocks, stock futures are appropriate to cover the risk of changes in the prices of stocks. Similarly, in order to cover risk on interest rates, we use derivatives on interest rates. A Forward Rate Agreement (FRA) is the forward contract on interest rates and is the basic instrument that covers risk associated with fluctuations in interest rates.

Interest Rate Risk Most organizations borrow funds from banks and other financial institutions to meet their capital requirements. For firms with borrowed funds, the interest rate constitutes a cost, whereas for banks and investing firms, the interest rate provides income.

In either case, the risk of changing interest rates is assumed by the firms, as it impacts profitability, just like the changing prices of commodities, foreign exchange, and stocks pose a risk. Interest is nothing but the price of capital, a critical resource every firm uses, and, therefore, it is equally important to manage this price risk for capital just as it is done for other assets.

> Derivatives on interest rates are used for covering the risk of changing interest rates.

Though for manufacturing enterprises, the proportion of interest in the overall cost may be relatively small, in the case of financial enterprises such as banks, investment companies, and financial institutions, the value is primarily dependent upon the interest rate scenario. The survival and growth of the firms in financial sector are critically dependent upon the level of interest rates, just as the survival of manufacturing firms depends upon the prices of inputs and outputs being produced by them. For banks, capital is the feedstock and the interest rate risk is akin to price risk, interest being the price of capital. This makes management of risk emanating from changing interest rates vital for firms in the financial sector. The value of firms in financial sector is more sensitive to interest rates changes than that for firms in the manufacturing sector.

Volatility in the interest rates is a matter of considerable concern to all enterprises. The expanding range of interest rates in terms of their nature of fixed and floating, their benchmarks, currencies, time horizon of exposure, etc., has added to the confusion. We often come across terms such as T-bills yields, repo rates, 3-m LIBOR, 6-m MIBOR, Eurodollar deposit rates, and prime lending rates, all representing a variety of interest rates prevailing across the globe. The plethora of interest rates has increased the degree of analysis and the need for managing the interest rate risk on the part of firms, especially those having a global presence.

From the perspective of investors, certain sectors are considered more prone to changes in interest rates. These include real estate, infrastructure, and automobiles, as demand for these products is a function of prevailing interest rates: end-users usually borrow funds to purchase them. Likewise, infrastructure firms have high gearing ratios, which imply that these firms are highly dependent on borrowed funds. Hence, their performance in terms of returns on stock becomes extremely sensitive to changes in interest rates.

FORWARD RATE AGREEMENT—THE PRODUCT

Uncertainty about the prices of inputs can be effectively managed by forward contracts, in which the prices of inputs can be fixed in advance. For managing changes in interest rates, the FRA performs the same function as a forward contract on commodities, currency exchange rates, etc. The prices of commodities and exchange rates can be settled in advance through a forward contract and, similarly, the rates for borrowing and deposits can be fixed in advance before actually availing of the loan or making a deposit.

> FRA is a contract to deposit or borrow a notional sum in future for a specified maturity at an interest rate fixed now.

An FRA can be defined as a forward contract for agreeing to advance a loan or accept a deposit at an interest rate fixed now for a notional amount of principal. A typical FRA is quoted as depicted in Fig. 6.7.

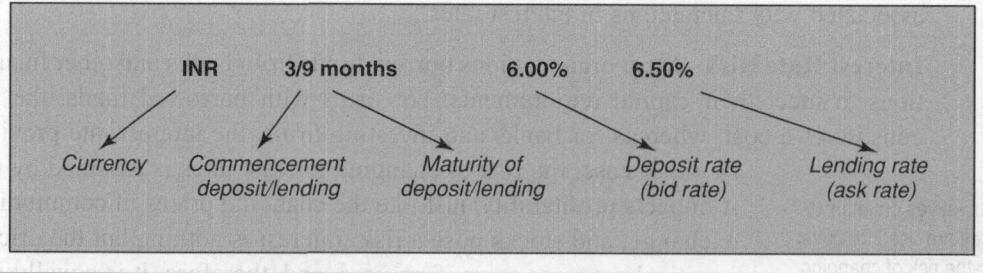

Fig. 6.7 Quotation for FRA

This quotation for an FRA means that the bank is prepared to accept a deposit or extend lending in Indian rupees starting three months from now and ending nine months from now, paying 6.00% on deposit or charging 6.50% on lending. In a way, this is a 3-m forward quote of interest rates for deposit/lending for a tenure of six months. Like any other forward quote, the FRA has two rates—the bid rate and the ask rate, and the difference between the two represents the spread for the bank.

Borrower's FRA

> A borrower's FRA protects against rising cost of borrowing.

A buyer of an FRA (a borrowing company) agrees to take a loan in Indian rupees at 6.50%, commencing three months from now for the next six months, while the seller of the FRA (a bank) agrees to provide such a loan at 6.50%. Such an FRA would enable the borrower to lock-in the borrowing rate three months in advance for a 6-m loan. The amount of the principal agreed upon need not be exchanged either at the commencement or at the termination, and, instead, only the difference between the actual rate and the settlement rate on the notional amount is exchanged between the buyer and the seller of the FRA. The following illustration helps to understand the concept better.

EXAMPLE 6.2 Borrower's FRA

Capital Constructions is expecting to receive an order to build a bridge, for which it would require working capital of ₹15 crore for the next six months. The current rate of borrowing for the firm is PLR + 3%, with PLR currently at 10%. The liquidity situation in the banking circle indicates that PLR would rise in the next three months. Another bank has offered a 3/9 FRA at 9.00%, based on the 6-m MIBOR, which is closely linked with the PLR of banks. How can Capital Constructions hedge against rising interest cost? Find out the effective cost of borrowing if (a) MIBOR rises to 11%, and (b) MIBOR falls to 8%. Assume equal changes in MIBOR and PLR, and also assume 180 days in six months and 360 days a year.

Solution
For a notional principal of ₹15 crore, Capital Constructions buys an FRA at 9.00%. It would lock-in the rate of borrowing prevailing now at 13%. The differential between the actual MIBOR and 9% discounted at MIBOR would be paid/received by Capital Constructions after three months.

(a) *If the 6-m MIBOR rises to 11% and PLR rises to 12%*
After three months, Capital Constructions would receive 2% (actual rate − FRA rate) for six months discounted at MIBOR

$$\text{Cash flow (₹ crore)} = \frac{1}{(1 + 0.11 \times 180/360)} \times (0.11 - 0.09) \times \frac{180}{360} \times 15 \text{ crore} = ₹14.218 \text{ lakh}$$

The firm borrows at 15% (PLR + 3%). The net cost of interest would be:

Interest paid	= 1500 × 0.15/2	= ₹112.50 lakh
Interest earned from FRA	= 14.218 × (1 + 0.11/2)	= ₹15.00 lakh
Net interest paid	= ₹97.50 lakh	
Effective cost of borrowing	= 97.50/1500 × 360/180	= 0.13 = 13.00%

(b) *If the 6-m MIBOR falls to 8% and PLR falls to 9%*
After three months, Capital construction would pay 1% (actual rate − FRA rate) for six months discounted at MIBOR

$$\text{Cash flow (₹ crore)} = \frac{1}{(1 + 0.08 \times 180/360)} \times (0.08 - 0.09) \times \frac{180}{360} \times 15 \text{ crore} = -₹7.21 \text{ lakh}$$

The firm borrows at 15% (PLR + 3%). The net cost of interest would be:

Interest paid	= 1500 × 0.12/2	= ₹90.00 lakh
Interest earned from FRA	= 7.21 × (1 + 0.08/2)	= ₹7.50 lakh
Net interest paid	= ₹97.50 lakh	
Effective cost of borrowing	= 97.50/1500 × 360/180	= 0.13 = 13.00%

Assume that an exporting firm, EXPO Ltd, has bagged an export order. To execute the order, it needs a working capital of ₹1 crore three months from now for the next six months. The need for borrowing is limited to six months, by the end of which period the firm would have realized its dues from its customer. The current borrowing rate for EXPO Ltd is 6.25%, and is likely to go up sharply in the coming days. Consider Fig. 6.7 as a quotation from EXIM Bank. In order to lock-in the borrowing rate, the firm buys a 3/9-m FRA at 6.50% from EXIM Bank. On the settlement of the FRA i.e. three months later, the following cash flow could take place.

If the settlement rate is, say, 7% against the FRA's contracted rate of 6.50%

The bank would pay the differential between the actual rate and the contracted rate (7.00 − 6.50 = 0.50%) to EXPO Ltd on the notional principal of ₹1 crore for six months. EXPO Ltd would borrow at 7%, but would get 0.5% back from EXIM Bank, making the effective cost of borrowing as 6.50%.

If the settlemet rate is, say, 6% against the FRA's contracted rate of 6.50%

The bank would demand the differential between the contracted rate and settlement rate (6.50 − 6.00 = 0.50%) from EXPO Ltd on the notional principal of ₹1 crore for six months. EXPO Ltd would borrow at 6%, but would pay 0.5% more to EXIM Bank, making the effective cost of borrowing as 6.50%.

Investor's FRA

> Investor's FRA provides protection against falling interest rates.

Like in a borrower's FRA where the rate of borrowing is locked in at times of rising interest rates, an investor's FRA enables locking in of the deposit rate when future interest rates are expected to fall.

Assume that an exporting firm EXPO Ltd would have a temporary surplus of ₹1 crore three months from now for the next six months. They need to invest the surplus. The current investing rate for EXPO Ltd is 6.25%, and is likely to fall sharply in the coming days. In order to lock-in the investing rate, the firm buys a 3/9-m FRA at 6.00% from EXIM Bank. On the settlement of the FRA i.e. three months later, the following cash flow could take place.

If the settlement rate is, say, 5.50% against the FRA's contracted rate of 6.00%

The bank would pay the differential between the contracted rate and settlement rate (6.00 − 5.50 = 0.50%) to EXPO Ltd on the notional principal of ₹1 crore for six months. EXPO Ltd would place its deposit at 5.50%, but would get 0.5% more from EXIM Bank, making its effective income from the investment as 6.00%.

If the settlement rate is, say, 6.50% against the FRA's contracted rate of 6.00%

The bank would demand the differential between the settlement rate and contracted rate (6.50 − 6.00 = 0.50%) from EXPO Ltd on the notional principal of ₹1 crore for six months. EXPO Ltd would invest at 6.50%, but would pay 0.5% more to EXIM Bank, again making its effective return on the investment as 6.00%.

It may be noted that the FRA is a product by itself, independent of the actual borrowing or lending. The principal amount remains notional, and the actual borrowing or deposit need not be made; if made, it may not be with the same bank with which the FRA is executed. The actual rate of deposit or borrowing needs to be ascertained for determination of the cash flow. Delinking of the actual deposit or borrowing makes the FRA a hedging as well as a speculative product, as the underlying transaction is not mandatory.

Settlement of FRAs

> Settlement of FRA is done by exchanging the differential cash flow of contracted interest rate and the actual benchmark on the notional principal.

Obligations under an FRA become known at the commencement time for borrowing or lending, when the actual interest rate becomes known. In our example, the FRA would come to an end after three months, when EXPO Ltd and EXIM Bank would know the actual interest rate. The commitment made in the FRA can be satisfied after three months, as all determinants of the cash flow are known. One need not wait for the conclusion of the borrowing/deposit period. Therefore, in the context of our example, the cash flow between the two parties to the FRA could be exchanged at the end of three months, rather than at the end of nine months.

Settlement of an FRA at the start of the contract period requires adjustment to the cash flow. Since interest on a loan or deposit is payable on maturity, the cash flow should be payable at the end of the contract period. Alternatively, if settled now, the cash flow needs to be discounted at the current rate of interest. The amount of cash flow (for the buyer) in a borrower's FRA and an investor's FRA are, respectively, calculated in Eqs 6.1 and 6.2.

$$\text{Cash flow (Borrower's FRA)} = \frac{1}{(1 + r \times d/365)} \times (r - f) \times \frac{d}{365} \times P \quad (6.1)$$

$$\text{Cash flow (Investor's FRA)} = \frac{1}{(1 + r \times d/365)} \times (f - r) \times \frac{d}{365} \times P \quad (6.2)$$

where r = settlement rate; the observed actual rate
 f = FRA rate; the contracted rate
 d = No. of days in the FRA contract
 P = notional principal amount

The amount to be received by EXPO Ltd in the borrower's FRA for national principal of ₹1 crore when the interest rate happens to be 7% would be ₹2,40,907, as follows:

$$\text{Amount to be received} = \frac{1}{(1 + 0.07 \times 182/365)} \times (0.07 - 0.065) \times \frac{182}{365} \times 1,00,00,000$$

$$= \frac{2,49,315}{1.0349} = ₹2,40,907$$

Pricing an FRA

Once forward interest rates are known through an FRA, the buyers of that FRA can lock-in the rate expressed in it. But how does the FRA seller offer an interest rate in advance? The rates quoted in the forward contract are considered to be unbiased predictors of future prices.

In the context of an FRA, the interest rate mentioned is most likely to prevail at the time when the FRA is settled. In our example, the 6-m interest rates after three months are likely to be between 6.00% and 6.50%. How do we estimate this figure?

> The term structure of interest rate implies forward interest rates and forms the basis of pricing of an FRA.

One way of finding the forward interest rate is based on the term structure of interest rates. The term structure of interest rates provides the rate of

Derivatives in Practice

FRA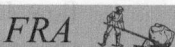

FRA—Indian practices

An FRA is a financial contract between two parties to exchange interest payments for a 'notional principal' amount on the settlement date, for a specified period from the start date to maturity date. Accordingly, cash payments based on the contract (fixed) and the settlement rate are made by the parties to one another on the settlement date. The settlement rate is the agreed bench-mark/reference rate prevailing on the settlement date.

An over-the-counter (OTC) product does not have inflexible specifications; however, market practices in India include the following aspects:

- The minimum notional principal amount for which market makers stand committed to their two-way quote is ₹25 crore.
- Interest rate computation in FRAs will follow the same day count convention as that applicable to the underlying benchmark (floating) rate.
- The benchmark for the FRA can be any Indian rupee interest rate benchmark. However, it should be clearly defined, widely disseminated, and acceptable to the market.
- Unless otherwise stated, the modified following business day convention will be followed for settlement.
- No fixing of rates and compounding of interest will be done on a Saturday.
- It is recommended that regardless of the centre where the deal is transacted, the benchmark and the holiday calendar for the purposes of computation of interest streams be the same as those in Mumbai.
- The computation of interest on the fixed leg would be done assuming that the fixed rate quoted is a nominal rate. Interest computation on the floating rate would be as per the convention used by the underlying benchmark.
- The settlement of an FRA will be on the date the FRA comes into effect.

For example, consider a case where Bank A and X Ltd enter into a 3/6 FRA. X Ltd pays an FRA rate of 9.00%. Bank A pays a benchmark rate based on the FIMMDA Moneyline Telerate 90 Day CP Benchmark.

Additional details are:
Notional principal amount	₹1 crore
FRA trade date	3 January 2002
FRA start/settlement date	3 April 2002
FRA maturity date	3 July 2002
FRA fixing date	2 April 2002

Assume that the FIMMDA Moneyline Telerate 90 Day CP Benchmark on the fixing date (2 April 2002) is 8.50%. If so, interest payable by X Ltd would be:

Interest payable by X	Interest payable by bank
₹1,00,00,000 × 0.09 × 91/365 = ₹224,384	₹1,00,00,000 × 0.085 × 91/365 = ₹211,918

Therefore, a net interest amount of ₹12466 is receivable by Bank A on the maturity date, i.e., 3 July 2002. However, the settlement of the amount is to be done on 3 April 2002 on the discounted value, i.e.,

$$\frac{12466}{\left[1 + \frac{0.085 \times 91}{365}\right]} = 12{,}207$$

X Ltd will pay Bank A ₹12207 on 3 April 2002.

FIMMDA guidelines are intended to bring uniformity and standardization to the market. They are not intended to restrict the freedom of parties to bilaterally decide terms and conditions different from those suggested at the beginning of this text box.

Source: FIMMDA Handbook of Market Practices

return based on the maturity of investment. It reflects the investors' expectations of returns with the maturity of investment. For example, consider the following term structure of interest rates from 3 to 12 months in 3-m steps, given below:

Investment horizon (months)	3	6	9	12
Yields (% annualized)	5.00	5.30	5.60	6.00

The yield for a 3-m investment is 5%, while for a 6-m investment the desired return is 5.30%. It is derived from the prices of different financial securities at any given point of time. Here, the term structure, also known as yield curve, is a rising one, indicating rising yields (annualized) with increasing maturities. This pattern is depicted in Fig. 6.8.

The yield curve contains the expectations of future interest rates. From the data in the table, we can find the expectations of interest rates three months from now for an investment horizon lasting 12 months. From the data, we can find the expected interest rate after three months for a 3-m investment, i.e., $_3r_6$. By equivalency, (a) a direct investment for six months at a rate of 5.30%, $_0r_6$, with (b) initial investment for three months at $_0r_3$, and then a rollover for another three months at $_3r_6$, helps us to find the 3-m interest rate expected to prevail after three months. Such a rate could be used as a guide to quote 3/6 FRA. Mathematically,

$$(1 + {}_0r_3)(1 + {}_3r_6) = (1 + {}_0r_6) \tag{6.3}$$

or
$$(1 + {}_3r_6) = (1 + {}_0r_6)/(1 + {}_0r_3)$$

In terms of the given yield curve, substituting the values[1] in Eq. 6.3, we have:

$$(1 + {}_3r_6) = \frac{1 + 0.053 \times \frac{180}{360}}{1 + 0.050 \times \frac{90}{360}} = \frac{1.0265}{1.0125} = 1.01383;$$

gives $_3r_6 = 0.01383$, or equivalent to annualized $_3r_6 = 5.53\%$

The rate of 5.53% can serve as a guide for the mid-rate of a 3/6 FRA. Assuming a spread of 50 bps[2], we can quote a 3/6 FRA at 5.28–5.78%. The rate arrived here is implied in the current term structure of interest rates, and is assumed to remain constant. Any bank may

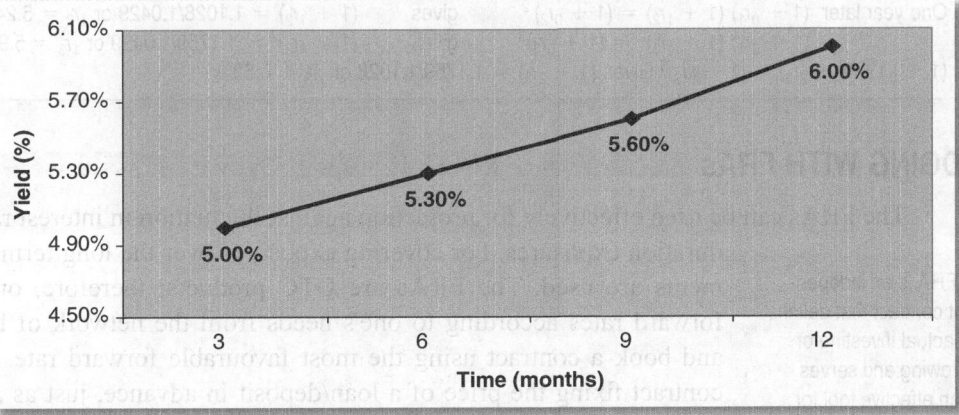

Fig. 6.8 Term structure of interest rates

---

[1]30-day months and 360-day years are used for ease of computation. For accuracy, the exact number of days may be used.
[2]bps refers to basic points. 100 bps = 1%

modulate the same with its own forecast of expected yields and the likely demand and supply scenario, or use any other model, to quote forward interest rates.

Continuing with the same process of equivalency of direct investment with rollover strategies, we can find 3-m forward rates for investments maturing 9 months and 12 months later. From the given yield, we may also find 6-m and 9-m forward interest rates for an investment horizon of up to 12 months. These are shown in Table 6.4.

Table 6.4 Forward rates as implied in term structure

Maturity from today (months)	6	9	12
Forward rate (% annualized)			
3 months from now	5.531	5.827	6.255
6 months from now	—	6.040	6.527
9 months from now	—	—	6.910

EXAMPLE 6.3   Determining forward interest rates

Three zero-coupon bonds A, B, and C, each having a face value of ₹100 maturing after one, two, and three years, respectively, are trading at ₹95.43, ₹90.68, and ₹85.04, respectively.

1. Find out the yield offered by each of the bonds.
2. What forward rates of interest would you expect for (a) a 1-year and a 2-year investment after one year, and (b) a 1-year investment after two years?

Solution

1. The yields offered by bonds A, B, and C for 1, 2, and 3-year investments can be found as follows:

   $95.43 \times (1 + {_0r_1}) = 100$ gives ${_0r_1} = 4.79\%$
   $90.68 \times (1 + {_0r_2})^2 = 100$ gives ${_0r_2} = 5.01\%$
   $85.04 \times (1 + {_0r_3})^3 = 100$ gives ${_0r_3} = 5.55\%$

2. Implied forward rates are calculated as follows:

   a) One year later $(1 + {_0r_1})(1 + {_1r_2}) = (1 + {_0r_2})^2$ gives $(1 + {_1r_2}) = 1.1028/1.0429$ or ${_1r_2} = 5.24\%$
   $(1 + {_0r_1})(1 + {_1r_3})^2 = (1 + {_0r_3})^3$ gives $(1 + {_1r_3})^2 = 1.1759/1.0429$ or ${_1r_3} = 5.93\%$
   b) $(1 + {_0r_2})^2 (1 + {_2r_3}) = (1 + {_0r_3})^3$ Gives $(1 + {_2r_3}) = 1.1759/1.1028$ or ${_2r_3} = 6.63\%$

HEDGING WITH FRAs

> An FRA is an independent contract that delinks the actual investing or borrowing and serves as an effective tool for hedging.

The FRAs can be used effectively for protection against fluctuation in interest rates for short-duration exposures. For covering exposures over the long term, other instruments are used. The FRAs are OTC products; therefore, one can obtain forward rates according to one's needs from the network of banks at hand and book a contract using the most favourable forward rate. An FRA is a contract fixing the price of a loan/deposit in advance, just as any other forward contract, for example on exchange rates.

It would be wrong to believe that FRAs are offered at fixed rates. They can be obtained in terms of floating rates too. Firms that need protection against fluctuation in interest rates and have floating rate exposures can also get FRAs quoted in terms of a floating rate.

Hedging Against Rising Interest Rates

Firms that borrow are always concerned about any rise in the interest rates, as it would increase the borrowing cost adversely, affecting profitability. Further, those who intend to borrow in the future also fear a rise in interest rates. They either avail of the loan today and incur an additional interest burden for the period when the loan is not required, or leave themselves exposed to the vagaries of financial markets. An FRA is a cost-effective and convenient way for them to freeze the borrowing rate in advance. We already demonstrated this while describing the product. The following example helps to understand the concept better.

Assume that Excel Industries Ltd (EIL), while forecasting their annual cash flow, found that they would have a shortfall of ₹500 lakh after six months. The shortfall is expected to last for six months, when internal accruals would suffice to overcome the financial constraints. Assume that the bankers to the firm, Commerce Bank (CB), have been extending loans at MIBOR. With current MIBOR at 9%, the borrowing cost is 9%. The interest rates are expected to go up in the next six months. EIL buys a MIBOR-based 6/12 FRA from another bank, Forward Bank (FB), at 9.25% for a notional principal of ₹500 lakh. We present the position of EIL under two alternative situations after six months: the MIBOR being more than the FRA contract rate and the MIBOR being less than the FRA contract rate.

When MIBOR increases to 10%, against the FRA contract rate of 9.25%

FB would pay EIL the differential between the current MIBOR and the agreed rate of 9.25% on a notional principal of ₹500 lakh for 180 days, discounted at 10%. Using Eq. 6.1, the amount to be paid by FB is

$$\text{Cash flow to firm} = \frac{1}{(1 + 0.10 \times 180/360)} \times (0.10 - 0.0925) \times \frac{180}{360} \times 5,00,00,000$$

$$= \frac{1,87,500}{1.05} = ₹1,78,571$$

With the cash inflow of the FRA and by availing a loan at the current rate, the effective cost of borrowing can be calculated as follows:

		₹
Interest cost for loan from CB	= 5,00,00,000 × 0.10/2	= 25,00,000
Maturity amount of FRA at 10%	= 1,78,571 × 1.05	= 1,87,500
Effective interest amount paid		= 23,12,500
Effective borrowing cost	= 23,12,500/5,00,00,000	= 0.04625
	equivalent to 9.25% p.a.	

When MIBOR falls to 8.60%, below the FRA contract rate of 9.25%

In case the benchmark rate falls to 8.60%, EIL would have to pay FB the differential between the actual and the contracted rate as follows:

$$\text{Cash flow to firm} = \frac{1}{(1 + 0.086 \times 180/360)} \times (0.0860 - 0.0925) \times \frac{180}{360} \times 5,00,00,000$$

$$= -\frac{1,62,500}{1.043} = -₹1,55,800$$

With cash outflow from the FRA and by availing of a loan at the current rate, the effective cost of borrowing can be calculated as follows:

Interest cost for loan from CB	= 5,00,00,000 × 0.086/2	=	21,50,000
Maturity amount of FRA at 10%	= 1,55,800 × 1.043	=	1,62,500
Effective interest amount paid		=	23,12,500
Effective borrowing cost	= 23,12,500/5,00,00,000	=	0.04625
		equivalent to	9.25% p.a.

We may conclude that irrespective of the interest rate prevailing at the time of borrowing, the effective cost of interest would be fixed at the rate contracted under the borrower's FRA., i.e., 9.25% here. Note that EIL borrows from CB while settling the FRA with FB.

Hedging Against Falling Interest Rates

> A borrower's FRA is a contract that covers risk of rising interest rates, while an investor's FRA protects against falling interest rates.

Like firms that borrow are always concerned about any rise in interest rates, investing firms are concerned about falling interest rates, which decrease income by reducing profitability. An investor's FRA is a cost-effective and convenient way to freeze the investment rate in advance. We again consider an example to illustrate this application.

Assume that Investment Management Ltd (IML) will have a surplus of ₹500 lakh after six months, to be invested for six months thereafter. The bankers to the firm, CB, have been accepting deposits at MIBOR. With the current MIBOR at 9%, the return on investment is 9%. Interest rates are expected to fall in the next six months, threatening IML's income. This causes IML to buy a MIBOR-based 6/12 FRA from another bank FB for placing a deposit at 8.75% for a notional principal of ₹500 lakh. We now present the position of IML under two alternative situations after six months: MIBOR being more than the FRA contract rate and MIBOR being less than the FRA contract rate.

When MIBOR goes up to 10% against the FRA's contract rate of 8.75%

IML would pay FB the differential between the current MIBOR and the agreed rate of 8.75% on a notional principal of ₹500 lakh for 180 days, discounted at 10%. Using Eq. 6.2, the amount to be paid by FB is

$$\text{Cash flow to firm} = \frac{1}{(1 + 0.10 \times 180/360)} \times (0.0875 - 0.10) \times \frac{180}{360} \times 5,00,00,000$$

$$= -\frac{3,12,500}{1.05} = -₹2,97,619$$

With cash outflow from the FRA and investment at the current rate, the effective return can be calculated as follows:

			₹
Interest earnings from CB	= 5,00,00,000 × 0.10/2	=	25,00,000
Maturity amount of FRA at 10%	= 2,97,619 × 1.05	=	3,12,500
Effective interest earned		=	21,87,500
Effective return	= 21,87,500/5,00,00,000	=	0.04375
		equivalent to	8.75% p.a.

When MIBOR falls to 8.10% against the FRA contract rate of 8.75%

In case the benchmark rate falls to 8.10%, IML would receive from FB the differential between the contracted rate and the actual rate as follows:

Amount to be paid $= \dfrac{1}{(1 + 0.081 \times 180/360)} \times (0.0875 - 0.0810) \times \dfrac{180}{360} \times 5,00,00,000$

$= \dfrac{1,62,500}{1.0405} = ₹1,56,175$

With cash outflow from the FRA and by availing of a loan at the current rate, the effective cost of borrowing can be calculated as follows:

₹

Interest earnings from CB	$= 5,00,00,000 \times 0.081/2 =$	20,25,000
Maturity amount of FRA at 10%	$= 1,56,175 \times 1.0405 =$	1,62,500
Effective interest amount paid	$=$	21,87,500
Effective borrowing cost	$= 21,87,500/5,00,00,000 =$	0.04375

equivalent to 8.75% p.a.

Thus, with an investor's FRA, a firm can be assured of effective return of 8.75%—the contracted rate—in the FRA, irrespective of the prevalent rate at the time of investment. Here again, IML makes a deposit with bank different from the one with which it books and settles the FRA.

SPECULATION WITH FRAs

When there is no underlying exposure, i.e., need for borrowing or investing, and yet one books an FRA, it reflects a view that opposes the scenario reflected in the FRA. Anyone who buys an FRA without any underlying exposure is speculating on the interest rate behaving against the FRA, thus hoping to make some gains.

If the current interest rate is 8% and an FRA is being offered at 8.80%, it indicates that interest rates in the future are expected to go up. If, on the contrary, one believes that future interest rates would fall, or would not rise to the extent of 0.80%, a speculator may book an investor's FRA to place a deposit. If the rates fall down or do not rise to 8.80%, the speculator would gain the differential between 8.80% and the actual rate. Similarly, if another speculator believes that interest rates are expected to move beyond 8.80%, he may book a borrower's FRA for availing of a loan. If the rates go beyond 8.80%, the speculator would benefit from the differential between the actual borrowing rate and the FRA rate.

Speculation is possible due to delinking of the underlying transaction of lending or borrowing from the FRA, provided laws of the land allow speculation. The presence of an underlying transaction is not of concern to the bank selling the FRA as a product. The FRA seller does not commit itself to either accepting the deposit or advancing the loan. It merely pays or receives the differential between the settlement rate and the contracted rate on the notional principal for the contracted period.

ARBITRAGE WITH FRAs

Arbitrage with FRA seems to be a remote possibility. Arbitrage would be possible if two different banks offer different rates in their FRAs, prompting people to sell FRA to one bank and buy from another. Since the FRA is an OTC product, where rates are not made publicly, arbitrage would be extremely difficult to execute even if such an opportunity arises.

SOLVED PROBLEMS

SP 6.1: Investor's FRA

Pro Investment Ltd is expecting a receipt of ₹10 crore for three months' investment after three months. The yield for the contemplated investment is currently at 7%, but is likely to fall. A bank has offered a 3/6 FRA at 7.00%, based on the 3-m MIBOR as a benchmark. How can Pro Investment Ltd hedge against falling interest rates? Find out the effective return if (a) MIBOR rises to 9%, and (b) MIBOR falls to 6%. Assume equal changes in MIBOR and investment yields, 90 days in three months and 360 days in a year.

Solution

For a notional principal of ₹10 crore Pro Investment Ltd can buy an investor FRA at 7.00%. It would lock-in the yield at 7%. The differential of the actual MIBOR and 7% discounted at MIBOR would be paid/received by Pro Investment after three months, which is presumed to carry interest at MIBOR.

(a) *If the 3-m MIBOR rises to 9%*

After three months, Pro Investment would pay 2% (FRA rate − actual rate) for three months discounted at MIBOR.

$$\text{Cash flow (₹ crore)} = \frac{1}{(1 + .09 \times 90/360)} \times (0.07 - 0.09) \times \frac{90}{360} \times 10 \text{ crore} = ₹4.891 \text{ lakh}$$

The firm borrows at 9%. The return would be:

Interest earned	= 1000 × 0.09/4	= ₹22.50 lakh
Interest paid for FRA	= −4.89 × (1 + 0.09/4)	= ₹5.00 lakh
Net interest paid		= ₹17.50 lakh
Effective return	= 17.50/1000 × 360/90	= 0.07 = 7.00%

(b) *If 3-m MIBOR falls to 6%*

After three months, Capital construction would pay 1% (actual rate − FRA rate) for six months discounted at MIBOR.

$$\text{Cash flow (₹ crore)} = \frac{1}{(1 + .06 \times 90/360)} \times (0.07 - 0.06) \times \frac{90}{360} \times 10 \text{ crore} = ₹2.461 \text{ lakh}$$

The firm invests at 6%. The net return would be:

Interest paid	= 1000 × 0.06/4	= ₹15.00 lakh
Interest received from FRA	= 2.46 × (1 + 0.06/4)	= ₹2.50 lakh
Net interest earned		= ₹17.50 lakh
Effective cost of borrowing	= 17.50/1000 × 360/90	= 0.07 = 7.00%

SP 6.2: Determining forward interest rates

A one-year investment with no interim cash flows yields 5.02%, while 2-year zeros are providing a return of 5.52%. What can you tell about the interest rate after one year for one year investment?

Solution

The yields offered for one-year and one-year investments are 5.02% and 5.52%, respectively. They imply an investment rate for a one-year horizon after one year. This may be found by the equivalence of (a) direct investment for two years, and (b) investing for one year and then rolling over the proceeds for another year at a rate prevailing then. Mathematically, the implied forward rate would be given by:

$$(1 + {_0}r_1)(1 + {_1}r_2) = (1 + {_0}r_2)^2 \quad \text{which gives } (1 + {_1}r_2) = 1.05522/1.0502 \text{ or } {_1}r_2 = 6.02\%$$

SUMMARY

Interest rate is often viewed as a macro-economic variable that reflects upon the state of the economy. For derivatives, the interest rate is also of great significance because it is needed for their valuation. Different rates prevail for different transactions. Sometimes, interest rates are direct, such as those on bank loans but sometimes interest rates are implied in the market prices of securities. The interest rate desired for derivatives must be free from default risk and market determined. Repo and reverse repo transactions between banks are free from default risk but are camouflaged by legal considerations. That is also the case for treasury rates. Interbank transactions governed by commercial considerations alone are true indicators of interest rates.

The term structure of interest rates, also called the yield curve, indicates return expectation for a given term of maturity. It can be arrived at from treasury zero rates. Treasury zeros are securities that pay no interest but are redeemed with face value and are issued at discounts. The discount is determined by the market and represents the yield desired. When zeroes are not available, the YTMs of bonds can be used to arrive at the yield curve by using the bootstrapping method.

Interest rate risks are faced by almost all firms whether they are borrowing or investing. More predominantly, banks and financial institutions are subject to greater interest rates risk as all their assets and liabilities are dependent upon the interest rate scenario.

The FRAs are forward contracts on interest rates that pay or receive the differential between the actual rate and the contracted rate. Tailored to specific needs, an FRA is an OTC product that enables fixing of the investing or borrowing rate in advance for a specific time. Banks offer investing and borrowing rates in advance for deposits and lending for specific periods of time. A borrower firm locks-in the borrowing rate, while an investing firm can fix the investing rate in advance. The product is independent of actual borrowing and lending and, therefore, can serve as a hedging tool as well as a speculative product. The risk of rising interest rates can be covered with a borrower's FRA, while that of falling interest rates can be covered through an investor's FRA.

The pricing of FRAs is dependent upon forward interest rates implied in the term structure of the interest rates. It can be found by using the prices of zeros in the process of bootstrapping.

KEY TERM

Forward interest rate The expected interest rate that is likely to prevail in the future.
Forward rate agreement A forward agreement to make a deposit or borrow a sum commencing at a future date for a specific period.
T-bills Discount instruments issued by governments for a variety of reasons for a fixed maturity, and are virtually free from default risk.
Term structure of interest rate Depicts the expected yields to investors depending upon the terms to maturity of their investments.

PROBLEMS

P 6.1 Finding the yield curve by bootstrapping
Continuing with the zero rates worked out in Example 6.1 and those given in Table 6.3, find out the zero rates applicable for 54 and 60 months if the following prices prevail for government securities:

Maturity	Coupon	Periodicity	Market Price (₹)
54 months	8%	Semi-annual	89.00
60 months	10%	Semi-annual	94.00

P 6.2 Pricing FRA
The following is the term structure of interest rates today:

Term to maturity (months)	3	6	9	12
Yield (% p.a.)	3.40	3.55	3.65	3.95

Assuming 360 days in a year, annual compounding, and a bid–ask spread of 20 basis points, find quotations for (a) 3/6 FRA, (b) 9/12 FRA, and (c) 6/12 FRA.

P 6.3 Payoff for FRA
A borrowing firm books a **6/9 FRA at 7%** for notional amount of ₹10 crore. At the end of 6 months the benchmark rate turns out to be **8%**. Calculate the amount the firm would pay/receive under the FRA. Assume 360 days p.a.

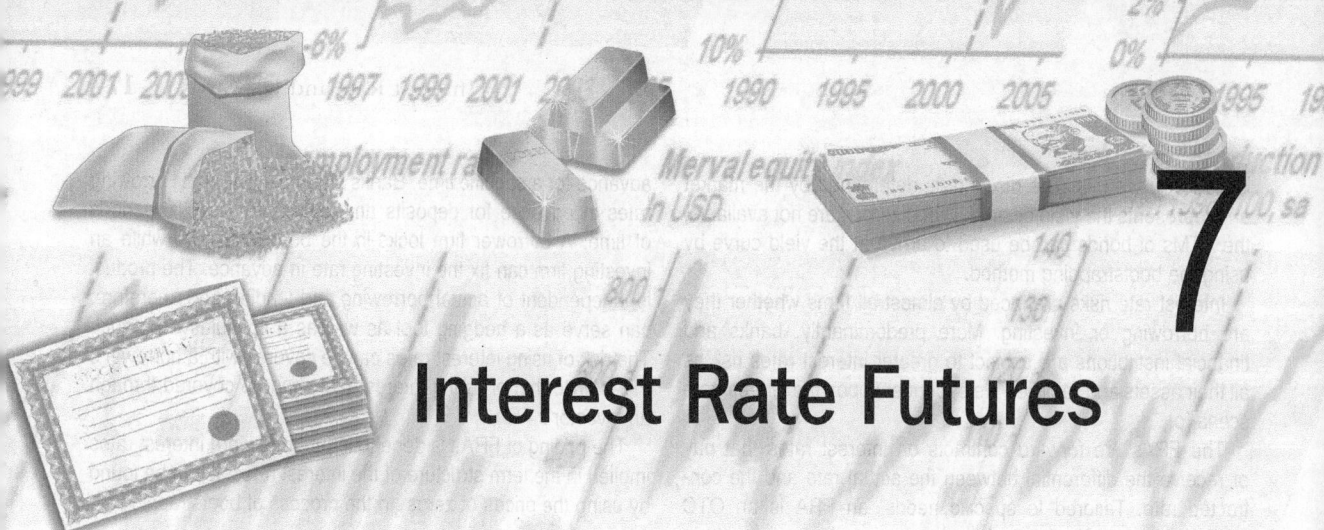

Interest Rate Futures

INTRODUCTION

In Chapter 6, we discussed the characteristics of forward contracts on interest rates, widely known as forward rate agreements (FRAs). Here, we discuss another derivative product with interest rates as the underlying asset, i.e., interest rate futures. As explained in the previous chapters on futures on stocks, indices, and currencies, futures contracts and forward contracts are based on the same concept. Operationally, however, these contracts are significantly different from each other. Due to these operational differences between forwards and futures, market structures of the two are also significantly different.

Like any other futures contract, interest rate futures can also be called exchange-traded FRAs. The underlying asset would be a financial instrument whose value would be almost solely determined by prevailing interest rates. Such instruments include corporate bonds, treasury bills (T-bills), and treasury bonds (T-bonds). Predominantly, these instruments are investment assets because investors target financial gain by investing in these instruments. Financial gain has always been the most alluring objective for investment in stocks, indices, currencies, commodities, etc. However, returns on such assets depend more on factors other than fluctuations in interest rates.

Exchange-traded interest rate contracts are expected to provide many benefits in comparison to over-the-counter (OTC) products such as FRAs. The benefits are as follows:

- Exchange-traded interest rate contracts protect against counterparty risk, whereas FRAs are always subject to counterparty risk. For each exchange-traded interest rate contract, an exchange becomes the counterparty, assuming the risk of settlement, thus encouraging more participation and providing depth to the market.

> **Learning Objectives**
> *After going through this chapter, readers should be familiar with*
> - treasury bills (T-bills), their pricing, and T-bill futures contracts
> - hedging, speculation, and arbitrage with T-bill futures
> - futures on Eurodollar deposits and hedging with them
> - treasury bond (T-bond) futures
> - hedging and speculation with T-bond futures
> - pricing of T-bond futures
> - implied repo rates
> - the calculation and meaning of conversion factor
> - identification of cheapest-to-deliver bonds

> Derivatives on interest rates are used for covering risk arising from changing interest rates.

- Prices quoted on the exchange are all pervasive and, hence, there is greater transparency in futures contracts than in forward contracts negotiated between two parties, with no obligations to disclose the terms of the contract.
- Futures contracts provide ease of entry and exit at any time, while forward contracts would most likely be settled by the delivery of the underlying asset or cancellation of the original contract, necessarily with the consent of the counter-party.
- Futures contracts on interest rates do not pose the problem of physical settlement that exchanges dealing in commodities face. These settlement difficulties relate to grading, price differentials, warehousing, etc., requiring infrastructure and personnel. These difficulties are absent in financial instruments, and hence, both modes of settlements, i.e., physical and cash, can easily be carried out by the exchange.

Interest rate futures can be divided into categories on the basis of the underlying assets. While discussing the term structure of interest rates, we discussed the fact that investors have varying expectations of return, depending upon the term of maturity. Instruments that serve short-term needs are not suitable for long-term needs. These needs range from speculation to arbitrage to hedging.

Instruments that usually form underlying assets for interest rate futures are as follows:

- treasury-bills with maturity period of less than one year, referred to as short-term instruments;
- treasury notes with maturity period between three and seven years, referred to as medium- or intermediate-term instruments; and
- treasury bonds with maturity period over 10 years, referred to as long-term instruments.

Besides, interest rate futures have also been developed based on a reference rate, such as LIBOR (London interbank offer rate) and Eurodollar deposits. We now discuss each of them.

INTEREST RATE FUTURES ON T-BILLS

The value of an interest rate futures contract, just like any other derivative contract, changes when interest rates change. When the underlying instrument matures over a short period of time, futures on such an underlying asset would be used for short-term protection or speculation. When the underlying matures at a distant time, then futures on such an underlying would cover the risk of interest rate changes over the long term.

The FRA, discussed in Chapter 6, is an interest rate derivative that offers a perfect hedge over a short period of time, and is like any other forward contract on a stock, an index, or a commodity. Hedging with interest rate futures would rarely be perfect, like many other futures hedges are.

> T-bills are instruments issued at a discount by governments. They carry no default risk, and hence, serve as ideal underlying assets for futures contracts.

The most commonly used short-term futures contracts in an economy are based on T-bills, while internationally, futures on Eurodollar deposits are most common. To understand futures on T-bills, we need to become familiar with T-bills and their pricing, and quoting conventions, as discussed in the following sections.

TREASURY BILLS

Treasury bills are one of the most important debt instruments issued by the government. A T-bill is a discount instrument, which implies that its price will be equal to the face value minus a discount that represents return or interest. The T-bill rate is acknowledged as a policy measure for managing short-term liquidity, sterilizing foreign exchange interventions and financing to bridge temporary fiscal deficits. The scope for discussion of why T-bills are issued falls under the subject of economics. Here, we are concerned with the pricing and valuation of T-bills.

Risks and returns are inseparable, like the two sides of a coin. The T-bills are borrowing instruments for the issuer, i.e., the government, and subscribers lend money in anticipation of returns. Any return is governed by the risk associated with it. There are usually two kinds of risks inherent in lending and borrowing transactions, namely:

- **Default risk** The risk of default on the repayment of principal and/or interest by the issuer, and
- **Interest rate risk** Any change in the interest rate scenarios between the time of making the investment and divesting it, fetching a return different from what was expected

In the case of T-bills, the default risk can be presumed to be non-existent because of the unique position of the issuer, i.e., the government and the nation's central bank, who control the money supply in an economy and have the sole authority to print money. This unique characteristic of T-bills makes them risk-free assets. A subscription to a T-bill and its price would be based purely on the interest rate risk. The value of such instruments should be purely determined by the risk premium, commensurate with the interest rate risk. T-bills would serve as an ideal proxy for interest rates.

Fixed-income securities issued by the corporate sector do not conform to valuation that is purely governed by changes in interest rates. Unlike T-bills, which carry no default risk, most debt instruments issued by firms are subject to default risk. As such, their valuation is determined not purely by interest rates but includes premium for default risk too. Further, the various corporate bodies that issue fixed income securities vary greatly in their features, causing valuations to differ substantially. Since futures require standardization of the underlying asset, corporate debt securities are not suitable, because debt instruments issued by different firms carry different risk premiums, and their valuations are not comparable. Further, their levels of liquidity are not large enough to justify design of exchange-traded products.

The uniqueness of government securities is that they are frequently issued in large numbers, providing adequate liquidity and continuity, which is required for fair pricing, and making delivery process easy. Though default risk premiums too have a role to play in the determination of pricing of these instruments, the default risk can be assumed to be the same for different securities issued by the same issuer, i.e., a government. In any case, the default risk is minimal. Further, frequent trading of government securities in the secondary markets provides enough liquidity for fair pricing. Liquidity and fair prices are essential pre-requisites for meaningful derivative markets.

The value of T-bills reflects the yields in the money market that can be considered as benchmarks and makes them an appropriate underlying asset for futures contracts. The T-bills with maturities of 91, 180, and 364 days are the most common. T-bills of 91 days are mostly used as the basis for futures contracts.

FUTURES CONTRACT ON T-BILLS

> On expiry, a futures contract on T-bills calls for the delivery of T-bills maturing 91 days thereafter.

Just as futures contracts on commodities require delivery of the underlying commodity on maturity of the contracts, futures contracts on financial instruments, say T-bills, would require delivery of the T-bills. Figure 7.1 depicts transactions of futures contracts on 91-day T-bills. Note that at the end of the futures contract, the contractor is required to deliver a T-bill maturing 91 days thereafter. However, such a T-bill may or may not actually exist when the futures contract matures.

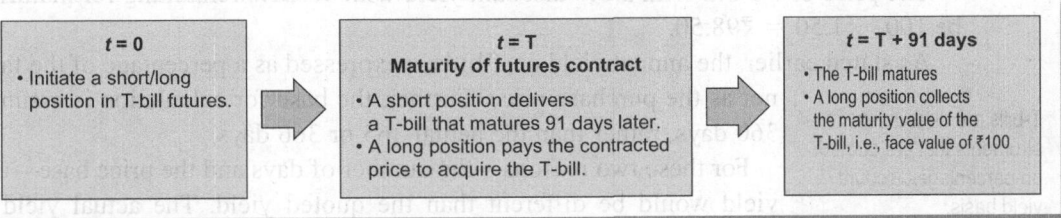

Fig. 7.1 Futures contract on T-bills

T-bills are auctioned frequently as per a pre-announced calendar, when market participants bid for subscriptions. These bids reflect investors' expectations at the time of issue of T-bills. Since T-bills are transferable, there is an active secondary market. The price of a T-bill in the secondary market would change continuously, reflecting changing interest rates. Hence, the price of a T-bill forms the basis of the value of a futures contract on it.

Future contracts with T-bills issued by the US government as underlying assets are traded on the Chicago Mercantile Exchange (CME). However, T-bills future contracts today have lost their sheen because of the competition from Eurodollar futures contracts (described in the section on Eurodollars in this chapter) available at the CME. T-bill rates are highly influenced by government policies, budget deficits, and politics. In spite of this relative inactivity, understanding T-bill futures is essential because the concept of interest rate futures is derived from futures contracts on T-bills.

In India, the National Stock Exchange (NSE) introduced on 4 July 2011 interest rate futures contracts with 91-day T-bills as underlying asset.

Pricing of T-bills

Treasury bills are issued at a discount to the face value, and are redeemed at face value. There is no interim payment between issuance and redemption. The return to the investor in T-bills is provided entirely by the difference between the redemption value (face value of ₹100) and the purchase price. Price quotations for T-bills are mentioned in terms of discount on the face value, as per the market convention. The market specifies the discount yield d, based on the actual/360-day convention. The discount yield, d, and the amount of discount, D, are related, as given by Eq. 7.1.

$$\text{Discount on T-bills, } D = \text{Face value, } V \times \frac{\text{Yield, } d \times \text{No. of days to maturity, } T}{360}$$

or
$$D = V \times \frac{d \times T}{360} \quad (7.1)$$

For a discount yield of 6%, the amount of discount, D, on a T-bill that has 90 days remaining to maturity would be as follows:

$$D = V \times \frac{d \times T}{360} = 100 \times \frac{0.06 \times 90}{360} = ₹1.50$$

The purchase price of a T-bill, P, would therefore be as per Eq. 7.2

$$P = V - D \quad (7.2)$$

The price of a T-bill with a 6% discount yield with 90 days remaining for maturity would be $100 - 1.50 = ₹98.50$.

As stated earlier, the annual yield on T-bills is expressed as a percentage of the face value, not as the purchase price. Further, the base for calculation is assumed to be 360 days, rather than the actual 365 or 366 days.

> T-bills are discount instruments that are quoted on percentage discount yield basis.

For these two reasons—the number of days and the price base—the actual yield would be different than the quoted yield. The actual yield realized would be calculated on the basis of the purchase value using 365 days in a year, as per Eq. 7.3. It is also referred to as bond equivalent yield, y^1.

$$\text{Actual yield, } y = \frac{\text{Face value, } V - \text{Purchase price, } P}{\text{Purchase price, } P} \times \frac{365}{\text{No. of days to maturity, } T}$$

$$\text{Actual yield, } y = \frac{V - P}{P} \times \frac{365}{T} \quad (7.3)$$

For a T-bill with a 6% quoted yield, the purchase price is ₹98.50, and with 90 days remaining for maturity, the actual yield would be 6.176%, shown as follows:

$$\text{Actual yield, } y = \frac{V - P}{P} \times \frac{365}{T} = \frac{100 - 98.50}{98.50} \times \frac{365}{90} = 0.06176 \equiv 6.176\%$$

Price Quotation on T-bill Futures

For futures on T-bills traded on CME, the underlying assets are 13-week T-bills; they require delivery of these T-bills of a face value of $1 million on any of the three successive days following the last day of trading, specified as the last business day. Because of this flexibility, sellers of these bills can deliver on any of the three days. Therefore, a deliverable T-bill can have a maturity of between 90 and 92 days.

Rather than quoting interest rate futures directly on the basis of interest rates, they are specified in terms of index, I. A T-bill's futures price, F, is quoted in terms of the T-bill's yield, I, annualized on the basis of 360 days a year (as is the case with the underlying asset), as per Eq. 7.4.

$$\text{Futures price, } F = 100 - I \quad (7.4)$$

Index-based pricing is the key difference between the way prices are quoted in interest rate futures markets and in other futures markets. This is done in order to be consistent with all other futures markets. In all futures markets, a long position gains with price rise and loses

---
[1] For instruments that have more than 182 days to maturity, the calculation of bond equivalent yield, y, is different.

with price fall. The opposite holds good for short positions. For example, if the price of gold rises from ₹26,000 per 10 g to ₹27,000 on expiry of a contract, the initial long position would gain ₹1000 and the initial short position would lose equivalently. Similarly, if the prices were to fall, the long position would lose and the short position would gain.

This would not hold good if interest rate futures were quoted directly in terms of prevailing interest rates due to the inverse relationship between prices and interest rates, defying the normal convention of making a long position gain with a price rise and lose with a price fall. The most convenient way to become consistent with other futures markets (to make long/short positions gain/lose with rising prices of futures contracts and vice versa) is to introduce a negative sign in the pricing of futures contract. This led to the devising of an appropriate index, as given by Eq. 7.4. With index-based pricing, interest rate futures markets become consistent with other futures markets.

> Futures on T-bills are priced on an index basis because of inverse relationship of their price with interest rates and the convention of a long position gaining with price rise in other futures markets.

What the futures price imply A quoted price of a futures contract on T-bills of ₹92 implies a discount yield of 8%. If in September a December futures contract is being quoted at ₹92, it simply implies that the best estimate of the market for a 3-m discount yield that is likely to prevail in December is 8%. Similarly, if a March futures contract is quoted at ₹91.50, it implies that the market estimates the discount yield on T-bills in the forthcoming March to be 8.50%. Futures prices should not be construed as the prices at which T-bills are traded. They are simply the way futures on T-bills are quoted.

FUTURES CONTRACT ON T-BILLS IN INDIA

In India, the underlying instrument for interest rate futures is the 91-day T-bill. It was introduced at the NSE on 4 July 2011, with contract specifications given in Table 7.1.

The price of futures on T-bills is quoted on the basis of the discount yield, and for convenience, the actual yield is also displayed. Exhibit 7.2 is a snapshot of the trading and pricing patterns of futures on T-bills. For example, 91DTB270711 in Exhibit 7.2 indicates that the underlying asset is a 91-day T-bill, and the expiry of the futures contract is 27 July 2011. It implies that on 27 July 2011, the seller of the futures contract is required to deliver a T-bill that matures 91 days thereafter.

The futures price is index based. The price of ₹92.0800 on 4 July 2011 for 91DTB270711 implies a discount yield of 7.9200%. The contract is for an underlying asset of a 91-day T-bill, expiring on 27 July 2011. The discount yield and purchase price of the T-bill are calculated as follows:

$$\text{Discount yield, } d = 100 - F = 100 - 92.0800 = 7.9200\%.$$

Therefore, the purchase price of the bill would be,

$$\text{Price of T-bill} = 100 - 7.9200/4 = 100 - 1.98 = ₹98.0200$$

The contract size is ₹2 lakh in face value (2000 bills of ₹100 each). The contract value, also known as invoice price, is $2000 \times 98.0200 = ₹1,96,040$. The buyer of the contract on its expiry on 27 July 2011 would pay ₹1,96,040 and receive T-bills worth ₹2,00,000 in face value.

Table 7.1 Contract specifications of futures contract on T-bills

Underlying	91-day Government of India T-bill
Contract size	2,000 units (face value ₹2 lakh)
Quotation	100 − discount yield, d
Tick size	₹0.0025
No. of contracts	Three monthly contracts followed by three quarterly contracts, e.g., in July 2011 the contracts are for July, August, and September 2011, followed by three quarterly contracts maturing in December 2011, March 2012, and June 2012
Contract value	2,000 × (100 − 0.25d)
Daily settlement	Cash on $T+1$ basis
Margins	• *Initial margin*: SPAN[2]-based, subject to a minimum • *MTM*[3]: Based on weighted average yield as long as the contract is open • *Extreme loss margin*: 0.03%
Final settlement price	*Spot value*: Weighted average of discount yield from weekly auction of T-bills by RBI
Mode of Settlement	Only *cash-settled*; there is no delivery-based settlement

Source: http://www.nse-india.com accessed on 20 September 2012

The actual yield corresponding to a futures price of 92.08 and a discount yield of 7.92% is 8.1022%. It is calculated as follows and as shown in Fig. 7.2.

$$\text{Actual yield}, y = \frac{V-P}{P} \times \frac{365}{T} = \frac{100-98.02}{98.02} \times \frac{365}{91} = 0.081022 \equiv 8.1022\%$$

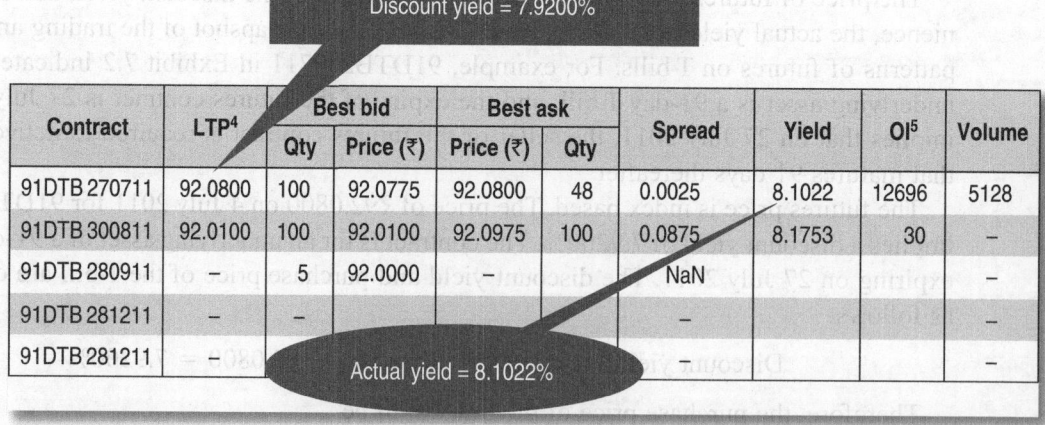

Contract	LTP[4]	Best bid Qty	Best bid Price (₹)	Best ask Price (₹)	Best ask Qty	Spread	Yield	OI[5]	Volume
91DTB 270711	92.0800	100	92.0775	92.0800	48	0.0025	8.1022	12696	5128
91DTB 300811	92.0100	100	92.0100	92.0975	100	0.0875	8.1753	30	–
91DTB 280911	–	5	92.0000	–	–	NaN	–	–	–
91DTB 281211	–	–	–	–	–	–	–	–	–
91DTB 281211	–	–	–	–	–	–	–	–	–

Source: www.nseindia.com, accessed on 19 July 2011.

Fig. 7.2 Futures contracts on T-bills in India

---

[2]Standardized portfolio analysis of risk
[3]Mark to market
[4]Last traded price
[5]Open interest

EXAMPLE 7.1 Yield on T-bills

The discount yield on a T-bill with 90 days to maturity is quoted at 6.25%. What is the purchase price of the T-bill? What actual yield would be realized by one who buys such a T-bill?

Solution
The purchase price of the T-bill is found by calculating the discount and subtracting it from the face value of the T-bill. The discount is calculated as follows:

$$D = V \times \frac{d \times T}{360} = 100 \times \frac{0.0625 \times 90}{360} = ₹1.5625$$

Hence, the purchase price = 100 − 1.5625 = ₹98.4375. The bill has 90 days remaining for maturity. The actual yield, therefore, will be calculated as

$$\text{Actual Yield}, y = \frac{V - P}{P} \times \frac{365}{T} = \frac{100 - 98.4375}{98.4375} \times \frac{365}{90} = 6.4374\%$$

EXAMPLE 7.2 T-bill futures in India

An interest rate futures contract on Government of India T-bills maturing after 29 days on 30 August 2011 is quoted at ₹91.8800.

Contract	LTP *	Best bid Qty	Best bid Price *	Best ask Price *	Best ask Qty	Spread	Yield	OI	Volume
91DTB 300811	91.8800	500	91.8750	91.8900	250	0.0150	8.3110	4769	200
91DTB 280911	—	500	91.7900	91.9800	500	0.1900	—	—	—
91DTB 251011	—	—	—	—	—	—	—	—	—
91DTB 281211	—	—	—	—	—	—	—	—	—

Source: www.nseindia.com, accessed on 23 August 2011.

(a) What is the discount yield based on LTP?
(b) If the contract size on the interest rate futures is 2,000 T-bills with face value of ₹100 each, what is the invoice value of one contract?
(c) What would be the actual yield realized by an investor who buys the futures contract today?

Solution
(a) Discount yield, y is 100 − price quotation. Hence, $y = 100 - 91.8800 = 8.1200\%$
(b) Invoice price for one contract = $2,000 \times (100 - 0.25y) = 2,000 \times (100 - 2.03) = ₹1,95,940$
(c) Actual yield, y_a is worked out for a T-bill with face value of ₹100 based on the actual number of days and 365 days in a year. The invoice value for the T-bill would be $100 - 0.25 \times 8.12 = ₹97.9700$.

$$y_a = \frac{100 - 97.97}{97.97} \times \frac{365}{91} = 0.083110 \equiv 8.3110\%$$

HEDGING WITH T-BILL FUTURES

T-bill futures are used to hedge short-term interest rate risk. Depending upon the prevailing situation, one may need protection against rising or falling interest rates. We discuss hedging with T-bills futures now.

Hedging against Falling Yields (Long Hedge)

As a prospective investor, you are subject to the risk of falling interest rates. You have no cash now, but expect it to come later, when the yields would have fallen, resulting in a rise in the price of the instrument. Hence, you need to invest more funds to buy the same number of T-bills. To protect against falling yields, you can buy futures on T-bills. Let us consider an example.

> Protection against falling interest rates is covered by buying interest rate futures.

It is 12 January today. Assume you have to invest a temporary surplus of ₹10 crore that you expect to receive from a customer three months from now. It would be a temporary surplus that would be available for three months thereafter. The current yield on T-bills is an attractive 7.80%, and you would have bought them now if only funds had been available. The yields are likely to fall in the coming days, and therefore, you are facing the risk of a reduced return on the prospective investment.

Buying T-bills now is ruled out, as you do not have the funds to invest. However, you can buy a futures contract on them and lock-in the yield of 7.80% that is offered today in T-bill futures.

The current T-bill futures price for a March contract is ₹92.20, implying a yield of 7.80%. Assuming a futures contract is based on 91 day T-bills, 360 days count, and that the contract size is ₹2 lakh, you buy 500 futures contracts. The value[6] you have committed to pay is calculated as follows:

$$\text{Price of futures contract} = \text{Face value} \times \left[\left(1 - \frac{\text{discount yield} \times 90}{360}\right)\right]$$

$$\text{Price of futures contract} = 2{,}00{,}000 \times \left[\left(1 - \frac{0.078 \times 90}{360}\right)\right] = ₹1{,}96{,}100$$

Number of contracts bought = 1000 lakh/2 lakh = 500

Amount committed to pay = 500 × 1,96,100 = ₹9,80,50,000

By buying 500 futures contracts on T-bills, you have undertaken to pay ₹9,80,50,000 and receive T-bills with a total face value of ₹10 crore (500 contracts × ₹2 lakh each) at the expiry of the March contract[7].

Table 7.2 Hedging investment return with interest rate futures

Scenario in March	Yield falls to 7.00%	Yield rises to 8.50%
T-bill futures price	₹93.00	₹91.50
Futures contract sold at	₹93.00	₹91.50
Implied yield	7.00%	8.50%
Price of contract sold	$2{,}00{,}000 \times \left[1 - \frac{0.070 \times 90}{360}\right]$ = ₹1,96,500	$2{,}00{,}000 \times \left[1 - \frac{0.085 \times 90}{360}\right]$ = ₹1,95,750
Value to be received on 500 futures contracts sold	₹9,82,50,000	₹9,78,75,000
Value to be paid on 500 futures contracts bought	₹9,80,50,000	₹9,80,50,000
Profit (+)/loss (−) on futures contracts	₹2,00,000	−₹1,75,000
Interest earned on actual deployment of ₹10 crore in T-bills	0.07 × 90/360 × 10,00,00,000 = ₹17,50,000	0.085 × 90/360 × 10,00,00,000 = ₹21,25,000
Actual earnings after adjusting profit/loss on T-bill futures (ignoring time value)	₹19,50,000	₹19,50,000
Effective yield	**7.80%**	**7.80%**

---

[6]Called the invoice price.
[7]If one settles by delivery, the yield would still be 78% calculated on face value of T-bills.

EXAMPLE 7.3 Hedging with T-bills (Long hedge)

Based on his cash flow estimates, a corporate treasurer finds that he will have an investible surplus of ₹20 crore after two months. This surplus is expected to remain with him for three months, after which it would be needed for working capital. The ideal instrument for investment would be T-bills, which are currently yielding an extremely attractive 8.20%. However, T-bills futures with expiry of two months are trading at ₹92.40, (discount yield of 7.60%) indicating falling yields in the times to come.

(a) Describe the ideal hedging strategy for the treasurer.
(b) What rate of return can the treasurer be assured of by the hedging strategy?
(c) Compute the investment return if after two months the discount yield on T-bills is (a) 6.20%, and (b) 8.20%.

Solution

(a) As a hedging strategy, the treasurer must go long on interest rate futures on T-bills expiring two months later at the prevailing rate of ₹92.40. The value of the futures contract would be equal to an exposure of ₹20 crore. With a contract size of ₹2 lakh, the number of contracts bought is 1000 (20 crore/2 lakh). When funds are actually available after two months, the treasurer must sell the futures and invest at the yield offered at that time.

(b) By doing so, the treasure would lock-in an investment return of 7.60%, as reflected in the price of T-bills futures.

(c) *If Discount Yield on T-bills Falls to 6.20%*
The futures price rises to ₹93.80, and T-bills quote at a discount yield of 6.20%.

	₹ per ₹100 of face value of T-bills
Futures on T-bills (bought)	92.40
Futures on T-bills (sold)	93.80
Gain of futures	1.40
Amount to be received on futures contracts = $(93.80 - 92.40) \times \frac{90}{360}$	0.35
Price of T-bills = $1 - \frac{\text{discount yield} \times 90}{360} = 1 - \frac{6.20\% \times 90}{360}$	98.45
Net amount invested = 98.45 − 0.35	98.10
Annualized discount yield on maturity = $\frac{100.00 - 98.10}{100.00} \times \frac{360}{90} =$	**7.60%**

If Discount Yield on T-bills Rises to 8.20%
The futures price falls to ₹91.80 and T-bills quote at a discount yield of 8.20%.

Futures on T-bills (bought)	92.40
Futures on T-bills (sold)	91.80
Loss of futures	0.60
Amount to be received on futures contracts = $(93.80 - 92.40) \times \frac{90}{360}$	0.15
Price of T-bills = $1 - \frac{\text{discount yield} \times 90}{360} = 1 - \frac{8.20\% \times 90}{360}$	97.95
Net amount invested = 97.95 + 0.15	98.10
Annualized discount yield on maturity = $\frac{100.00 - 98.10}{100.00} \times \frac{360}{90} =$	**7.60%**

Just before the maturity of the March contract, you would sell 500 contracts at the yield prevailing at that point of time (You may also choose to make physical delivery of the underlying T-bills). If the yield falls as expected, the futures would be selling at a higher price, and you would receive a higher price than you paid for the initial contract. This would compensate for the loss you would incur by investing in T-bills at reduced yields.

Table 7.2 depicts the position of investment returns when interest rates fall and increase contrary to expectation. In either case, you lock-in a return of 7.80%—the yield in the initial futures contract.

Hedging against Rising Interest (Short Hedge)

As a prospective borrower, you are subject to the risk of rising interest rates. If yields rise in the future, you would end up paying a higher cost than you would today. One alternative is to borrow now, but that would imply keeping resources idle, yet paying for them. Let us again consider an example of how futures on T-bills can hedge against rising interest rate.

Suppose it is 12 January today and that you need to borrow ₹10 crore for three months in March for execution of an order from your customer. The current yield on T-bills is attractively low, and your borrowing would be linked to the yields in T-bills that prevail at the time of borrowing. The yields are likely to rise, and so would the borrowing cost. Therefore, you are exposed to the risk of increased cost of borrowing.

> Protection against rising interest rates is hedged by selling interest rate futures.

In order to hedge against rising interest rates, you would sell a futures contract on T-bills now, and buy the same futures contract back later, locking in the cost of borrowing that is implied today in T-bill futures.

The current T-bill futures price for a March contract is ₹92.20, implying a yield of 7.80%. Assuming the futures contract is based on a 90-day T-bill, 360 days count, and a contract size of ₹2 lakh, you sell 500 futures contracts. The value that you receive is calculated as follows:

$$\text{Price of contract} = \text{Face value} \times 1 - \frac{\text{discount yield} \times 90}{360}$$

$$\text{Price of contract} = 2,00,000 \times \left[\left(1 - \frac{0.078 \times 90}{360}\right)\right] = ₹1,96,100$$

Number of contracts sold = 1000 lakh/2 lakh = 500
Amount to be received = 200 × 1,96,100 = ₹9,80,50,000

Table 7.3 Hedging borrowing cost with interest rate futures

Scenario in March	Yield rises to 8.50%	Yield falls to 7.00%
T-bill futures price	₹91.50	₹93.00
Futures contract sold at	₹91.50	₹93.00
Implied yield	8.50%	7.00%
Price of contract bought	$2,00,000 \times \left[1 - \frac{0.085 \times 90}{360}\right]$ = ₹1,95,750	$2,00,000 \times \left[1 - \frac{0.070 \times 90}{360}\right]$ = ₹1,96,500
Value to be paid on 500 futures contracts bought	₹9,78,75,000	₹9,82,50,000
Value to be received on 500 futures contracts sold	₹9,80,50,000	₹9,80,50,000
Profit (+)/loss (−) on futures contracts	₹1,75,0000	−₹2,00,000
Interest paid on actual borrowing of ₹10 crore* for 90 days	0.085 × 90/360 × 10,00,00,000 = ₹21,25,000	0.07 × 90/360 × 10,00,00,000 = ₹17,50,000
Actual cost after adjusting for profit/loss on T-bill futures (ignoring time value of the gain/loss on futures)	₹19,50,000	₹19,50,000
Effective cost	**7.80%**	**7.80%**

* The amount of actual interest payable would be more than the yield on the T-bills, as the borrowing would be done at higher rates than the yield on the T-bills.

By selling 500 futures contracts on T-bills, you have undertaken to deliver T-bills with a face value of ₹10 crore (500 contracts × ₹2 lakh per contract) at the expiry of the March futures contract.

Before maturity of the March contract, you would buy 500 contracts at a yield prevailing at that point of time. If the yield had indeed risen, as expected, the futures would be selling at a lower price, and you would buy at a price lower than that of the initial contracts you sold. This would compensate for any loss you incur by borrowing at a higher interest rate.

Table 7.3 depicts the position relating to the borrowing cost when interest rates have indeed increased, and also when they have decreased, contrary to expectation. Here, too, your borrowing cost would be at 7.80% of the yield implied in futures now.

Hedging strategies with interest rate futures are summarized as follows:

Situation	Hedging strategy
Investors expecting falling interest rates	Buy interest rate futures now and sell later, and invest at the market interest rate.
Borrowers expecting rising interest rates	Sell interest rate futures now and buy later, and borrow at the market interest rate

SPECULATION WITH T-BILLS FUTURES

Taking a position in futures without exposing the underlying asset to risk is called speculation on future interest rates. When an individual whose views do not match with the present scenario in terms of futures prices takes a position in futures, he/she is said to be speculating. In contrast, the hedger takes a position on the underlying asset.

For example, consider that the prevailing yield in the market is 8%. A futures contract on T-bills maturing after a month is trading at ₹93.00, implying a yield of 7% next month in anticipation of a fall in interest rates. You believe that the yield would rise to 9% rather than fall to 7% from the current level, as the price of futures now is not correctly reflecting the future interest rate. In your opinion, futures are overpriced (they should be at ₹91.00 rather than ₹93.00), and hence, you decide to sell a futures contract (say for ₹10 lakh) at ₹93.00. Therefore, on maturity, you are entitled to receive ₹9,82,500 for delivering a T-bill with a face value of ₹10 lakh. The value of the contract is computed as follows:

$$\text{Price of contract sold} = 10,00,000 \times \left[1 - \frac{0.07 \times 90}{360}\right] = ₹9,82,500$$

If your expectations come true, the futures price over the period of time before maturity would correct to ₹91.00. You would buy a futures contract to nullify the original short position. As a buyer, you would be required to pay the price of ₹9,77,500, as shown here:

$$\text{Price of contract bought} = 10,00,000 \times \left[1 - \frac{0.09 \times 90}{360}\right] = ₹9,77,500$$

> Expectations of a greater rise in the interest rate than is reflected by the futures price can be speculated upon by selling futures now and buying later.

Thus, the total gain will be ₹5000, which is equivalent to 2% (the difference between the expected interest rate and the yield implied in the futures contract).

If one believes that in the future the interest rate would fall (and the price of the underlying asset, T-bills, would rise) one would initiate a long position in futures. With the futures price at ₹93.00, the speculator would buy the futures contract undertaking to pay the price equivalent to futures price. If the interest rates actually fall, the futures would go up in value when you square off your initial position, thus registering a gain.

The strategies of speculators can be summarized thus:

Situation	Strategy
When interest rates are expected to go up by more than what the futures market suggests, the price of the underlying assets as well as futures on them would fall.	Sell futures now and buy later
When interest rates are expected to go down by more than what the futures market suggests, the price of the underlying assets as well as futures on them would go up.	Buy futures now and sell later

ARBITRAGE WITH T-BILL FUTURES

If futures are overpriced in the commodities market, arbitrage can be implemented using the cash-and-carry strategy, implying the selling of a futures contract and the borrowing of cash to buy the underlying asset, carry it till maturity, and deliver it against the futures contract sold, as condensed here:

Cash-and-carry arbitrage	
Today	On maturity
• Sell the future. • Buy the underlying asset. • Borrow equivalent sum.	• Deliver asset against the futures contract sold. • Receive value equal to futures price. • Repay borrowing along with cost of borrowing.

The gain would be equal to the difference between the futures price and the cost of carry. Similarly, if futures were underpriced, reverse cash-and-carry arbitrage may be executed by buying the futures, selling the underlying asset and lending the sale proceeds. On expiry of the futures, receive delivery of the asset by paying for it from the matured value of the funds lent. These reverse cash-and-carry steps are summarized here:

Reverse cash-and-carry arbitrage	
Today	On maturity
• Buy the future. • Sell the underlying asset. • Lend equivalent sum.	• Acquire asset against the futures contract bought. • Receive the funds lent with interest. • Pay for the asset as agreed in futures contract.

> Futures contracts on interest rates are like repo transactions, and therefore, a futures price implies a repo rate.

We may consider arbitrage actions for futures on gold as examples of cash-and-carry and reverse cash-and-carry arbitrage actions. Assuming the spot (cash) price of gold is ₹12,000 per 10 g, and the cost of carry is 1% per month, the theoretical price of a 3-m futures contract must be ₹12,360. If the futures sells at more than theoretical price, say, at ₹12,460, cash-and-carry arbitrage is executed, resulting in a profit of ₹100; on the other hand, if the futures sells for less than the theoretical price, say, at ₹12,210, reverse cash-and-carry arbitrage results in a profit of ₹150. Both these situations are highlighted in Table 7.4.

Implied Repo Rate

Arbitrage opportunities with interest rate futures are not as apparent as they are with other futures markets. In order to examine if arbitrages opportunities exist, we need to compare the

Table 7.4 Arbitrage with commodity futures

Cash-and-carry arbitrage When futures price Is > spot + cost of carry		Reverse cash-and-carry arbitrage When futures price Is < spot + cost of carry	
Action	Cash flow (₹)	Action	Cash flow (₹)
Today		Today	
Sell the futures on gold	—	Buy the futures on gold	—
Buy gold in cash	−12,000	Sell gold in cash	+12,000
Borrow equivalent sum	+12,000	Lend equivalent sum	−12,000
Cash flow today	—	**Cash flow today**	—
On maturity		On maturity	
Deliver gold and realize futures contract value	+12,460	Acquire gold and pay futures contract value	−12,210
Repay borrowing with interest	−12,360	Receive funds lent with interest	+12,360
Cash flow on maturity	+100	**Cash flow on maturity**	+150

market price of the futures contract with the theoretical/fair price, which effectively means estimation of the cost of carry. The T-bills are pure financing instruments; the yields on them represent risk-free rates and are used to determine the cost of carry for futures contracts.

Arbitrageurs can opt for either of the following two strategies:

- *Cash-and-carry* Buy a deliverable T-bill spot, borrow the equivalent sum, and sell a futures contract. On maturity of the futures contract, deliver the T-bill already in hand in exchange for the futures price, and pay back the borrowed funds with interest. Examine if there is any surplus.
- *Reverse cash-and-carry* Sell a T-bill that matures 91 days after expiry of the futures contract spot, invest the proceeds, and buy a futures contract. On maturity of the futures, receive the T-bill by paying for it from the funds you had lent out earlier. Examine if there is any surplus.

Arbitrage would exist if the difference between the futures and the spot prices is not equal to the lending or borrowing rate—the actual repo rate. Selling securities today and agreeing to buy them back the next day is a 1-day *(overnight)* repo transaction. The difference between the repurchase price and the initial price is the actual repo rate. The repo rate is the difference between the selling price and the repurchase price of government securities in the physical market, expressed on an annualized basis. Cash-and-carry or reverse-cash-and-carry transactions are financed at the repo rate, which represents the actual cost of carry.

> If the repo rate implied by a futures price is different from the actual repo rate, it presents an arbitrage opportunity either way.

The difference between futures prices and spot prices represents the implied cost of carry. The difference between the price of a futures contract and the spot price of the deliverable security, referred to as *implied repo rate*, is calculated as per Eq. 7.5.

$$\text{Implied repo rate} = \frac{\text{Futures price} - \text{Spot price}}{\text{Spot price}} \times \frac{360}{\text{No. of days remaining for futures}} \quad (7.5)$$

For example, consider a simple situation where T-bill futures sell for ₹90.00 (indicating an interest rate of 10%) and the contract has exactly 90 days to mature. Assume that a futures

Table 7.5 Arbitrage with interest rate futures

Cash-and-carry arbitrage When implied repo rate > financing cost, say 4%		Reverse cash-and-carry arbitrage When implied repo rate < financing cost, say 8%	
Action	Cash flow (₹)	Action	Cash flow (₹)
Today		Today	
Sell the Interest rate futures	—	Buy the interest rate futures	—
Buy a 180-day T-bill in cash	−96.00	Sell a 180-day T-bill in cash	+96.00
Borrow the equivalent sum	+96.00	Lend the equivalent sum	−96.00
Cash flow today	—	**Cash flow today**	—
On maturity after 90 days		On maturity after 90 days	
Deliver T-bill and realize futures contract value	+97.50	Acquire T-bill and pay futures contract value	−97.50
Repay borrowing with interest	−96.96	Receive funds lent with interest	+97.92
Cash flow on maturity	**+0.54**	**Cash flow on maturity**	**+0.42**

contract on T-bills warrants delivery of T-bills that have 90 days to mature from the expiry of the futures contract. Therefore, a 180-day T-bill is the deliverable asset and its yield is relevant for determination of the cost of carry. Assume that the 180-day T-bill is quoted at a yield of 8%. The prices of the 180-day T-bill and the futures contract would be ₹96.00 and ₹97.50, respectively.

$$\text{Price of 180-day T-bill} = 100 - 0.08 \times 180/360 = ₹96.00$$
$$\text{Invoice price of futures contract} = 100 - 0.10 \times 90/360 = ₹97.50$$

The implied repo rate for the remaining period before the expiry of the futures contract is 6.25%, using Eq. 7.5 (assuming 360 days a year for computational ease):

$$\text{Implied repo rate} = \frac{97.50 - 96.00}{96.00} \times \frac{360}{90} = 0.0625 \equiv 6.25\%$$

The implied repo rate of 6.25% represents the cost of carry for futures pricing. If lending/borrowing is done at a rate different than the implied repo rate, arbitrage can be executed in the manner shown in Table 7.5.

Pricing of T-bill Futures We just discussed a situation where the financing rate (actual repo rate) is different from the implied repo rate; this discrepancy in prices may give rise to an arbitrage opportunity. For better appreciation of this situation, assume that the spot price of a deliverable security is ₹92.00 and futures sell for ₹93.00. By buying today and selling the futures, you expect to gain ₹1.00 on maturity of the futures contract. If the financing cost for the period for ₹92.00 is less than ₹1.00, then your actual gain would be the difference between the profit and the financing cost. Alternatively, if you sell the security and buy futures contract today, you stand to lose ₹1.00. However, if you could invest the amount of ₹92.00 realized from the spot sale and get more than ₹1 when the futures contract matures, you would have an arbitrage opportunity.

> A 'no arbitrage' condition forces the implied repo rate to converge to the actual repo rate, and therefore, determines the pricing of futures contracts on T-bills.

EXAMPLE 7.4 Arbitrage with T-Bill futures

Interest rate futures on GoI 91-day T-bill with 29 days to maturity is selling at 91.88 indicating a discount yield of 8.12%. In the spot market, the following rates are prevailing:

Instrument	Discount yield, %	Indexed quotation
T-bill maturing after 29 days	8.30%	91.7000
T-bill maturing after 91 days	8.50%	91.5000
T-bill maturing after 120 days	9.00%	91.0000

(a) What is the implied repo rate?
(b) How would an investor execute arbitrage?
(c) Calculate the profit on one contract of T-bills futures if the actual borrowing rate is 9% p.a.

Solution

(a) The implied repo rate is given by the difference between the futures price and the spot price. Here, the underlying asset is the 120-day T-bill. The price of the 120-day T-bill would be

Invoice value of 120-day (just as in T-bill) T-bill $= 100 - \dfrac{9 \times 120}{360} = ₹97.00$

The implied repo rate is given by

Implied Repo Rate $= \dfrac{\text{Futures Price} - \text{Spot Price}}{\text{Spot Price}} = \dfrac{97.9700 - 97.0000}{97.0000} = 0.0100 \equiv 1.00\%$

(b) The implied repo rate is 1% for 29 days, corresponding to an annual rate of 12.59%. The actual borrowing rate of 9% is less than the implied repo rate, and, therefore, cash-and-carry arbitrage can be executed by selling the futures and buying the underlying 120-day T-bill by borrowing the required sum for 29 days at 9%. On maturity of the futures contract after 29 days, the underlying asset, already in hand, would have exactly 91 days to mature, and, hence, can be delivered. The invoice value for a 120-day T-bill with a discount yield of 9% would be 2,000 × 97.00 = ₹1,94,000.

The invoice value received would exceed the amount of borrowing and the interest thereon.

(c) An amount of ₹553 per futures contract is derived as profit, as shown in Table E 7.4:

Table E 7.4 Cash-and-carry arbitrage with interest rate futures

	Actions now	Cash flow, ₹
1	Sell one contract of interest rate futures on T-bills maturing 29 days later at the prevailing price of 91.88. With a discount yield of 8.12%, the invoice value is ₹1,95,940	—
2	Buy the underlying asset, i.e., the 120-day T-bill at a discount yield of 9%. For one contract of 2,000 T-bills, the invoice value is ₹2,000 × 97.00 = ₹1,94,000	−1,94,000
3	Borrow for 29 days at 9% as against 8.30%. As reflected in the discount yield of 8.30%, which has an invoice value of ₹99.3314 and an actual yield of 8.4718%.	+1,94,000
Net cash flow, net investment		—
	Actions on maturity of futures contract, i.e., after 29 days	
1	Receive contract value under the futures contract sold	+1,95,940
2	Deliver T-bill already in possession, with 91 days to mature	—
3	Pay borrowing	−1,94,000
4	Pay interest on borrowing at 9% for 29 days	−1,387
Net cash flow, arbitrage profit		**+ 553**

EXAMPLE 7.5 Theoretical price of T-bills futures, implied repo rate, and arbitrage

Assume that today is 12 January and a March futures contract on T-bill expires on 26 March. This futures contract requires delivery of T-bills with a face value of ₹100, maturing 91 days thereafter. Assume that such T-bills are available in the market, and are quoted with a discount yield of 9%. The futures contract is valued at ₹91.75. The repo rate prevailing in the market is 10% for a period up to 75 days. Assume a 360 days in a year in all calculations. Find the following:

(a) The price of the T-bills
(b) The theoretical value of the futures contract
(c) The invoice price of the futures contract on the settlement day
(d) The implied repo rate in the futures market
(e) Examine the feasibility of arbitrage.

Solution

Theoretical price of T-bills futures, implied repo rate & arbitrage

Today	12 Jan
Expiry of interest rate futures on T-bills	25 Mar
No. of days remaining for futures to expire, t	73 days
(a) *Finding purchase price of the underlying asset*	
Face value of the T-bills, V	₹100.00
T-bills deliverable must mature after	91 days
Time remaining for deliverable T-bill, T	164 days
Quoted percentage yield on T-bills with 164 days to maturity, d	9.00%
Discount on deliverable bill, $D = d \times T/360$	₹4.1000
Buying price of the deliverable T-bill, $P = V - D$	₹95.9000
(b) *Finding theoretical price of futures*	
Actual repo rate, r	10.00%
Financing cost for time till expiry of futures, $r \times P \times t/360$	₹1.9446
Theoretical futures price	₹97.8446
Finding implied repo rate	
Futures price, F	₹91.7500
(c) Invoice price of futures, $I = 100 - (100 - F) \times 91/360$	₹97.9146
(d) **Implied repo rate, $(I - P)/P \times 360/t$**	**10.36%**
(e) The future is overpriced. Therefore we sell it.	

In order to eliminate arbitrage either way, futures must be priced at the spot rate plus the actual repo rate. This can be expressed mathematically as follows:

$$\text{Theoretical futures price} = \text{spot price of deliverable security} \\ + \text{actual repo rate for time remaining of futures contract} \quad (7.6)$$

EURODOLLAR FUTURES

> Eurodollars are not subject to controls by the US government, and hence, Eurodollar deposit and end rates are competitively determined by free markets.

Futures contracts on Eurodollar started trading on the CME in December 1981. They are also traded on the London International Financial Futures and Options Exchange (LIFFE). Volumes of futures on Eurodollar deposits are constantly growing, because the returns on Eurodollar are determined by free market forces without any legal or operative constraints. Futures on Eurodollar deposits have become more popular than futures on T-bills.

EURODOLLARS

> Eurodollars are US dollars held outside the USA, and constitute a large supply source.

Another short term interest rate futures contract has underlying asset of Eurodollar deposit. Eurodollar deposit is the US dollar deposit held by banks that are held outside USA or by non USA banks or foreign branches of US banks. Eurodollar deposits came into existence during the 1950s and 1960s, when the erstwhile USSR and East European countries parked their US dollar deposits with banks in London, Paris, and other locations outside the USA for fear of their cold war with the USA turning hot, and the possible consequence of the USA confiscating these deposits. Since non-US banks held dollar deposits, they started lending in US dollars to earn the spread.

Further, in the era of the Bretton Woods exchange rate system, the flow of dollars kept increasing phenomenally because all nations needed to export to the USA to enable them to accumulate the maximum possible US dollars. During the Bretton Woods era, the US dollar was virtually the only currency accepted worldwide.

US dollars outside USA became a very large market over a period of time. Because these deposits and lending by banks in US dollars were not subject to any kind of regulation and control by the US government, they became truer representatives of interest rates. Thus, Eurodollar deposits and lending rates were purely determined by market forces—a perfect market condition conducive for the development of futures markets.

These Eurodollar deposits bear interest on the basis of LIBOR (London interbank offer rate), determined in London. The underlying asset in the case of futures on T-bills is the T-bills. Similarly, LIBOR is the underlying interest rate for the Eurodollar. For the purpose of settlement of futures contracts on the Eurodollar, LIBOR is determined by polling of rates by prominent banks in London on daily basis. Of these rates few highest and lowest are rejected and a mean of the remaining is taken as LIBOR rate. This becomes the LIBOR for settlement purposes.

FUTURES CONTRACTS ON EURODOLLARS

Like futures contracts on T-bills require delivery of T-bills with a face value of US $1 million, maturing 91 days thereafter, a futures contract on Eurodollars requires delivery of a deposit of US $1 million that matures three months thereafter. Delivery of Eurodollar deposits is not possible, as they are non-transferable. They cannot serve as collateral for loans. However, this does not hamper conceptually the process of hedging, speculation, and arbitrage. Eurodollar futures for each of these applications would be used just in the same way as futures on T-bills.

There are two key differences between futures contracts on T-bills and on Eurodollar deposits:

- *Cash settlement*: Eurodollar deposits are non-transferable, and hence, cannot be delivered like T-bills. Therefore, futures on Eurodollar deposits necessarily have to be settled in cash, i.e., by exchanging the difference between the buying and selling prices. T-bills futures can be settled by delivery, as an alternative to cash settlement.
- *Add-on yield*: T-bills are discount instruments that reach face value on maturity, while the yield on Eurodollar deposit is on an add-on basis. Interest is added to the face value

to arrive at the maturity value. The add-on yield is related to the discount yield, as given by Eq. 7.7:

$$\text{Add-on yield} = \frac{\text{Discount}}{\text{Price}} \times \frac{360}{T} \quad (7.7)$$

With a discount yield of 10%, the current price of a T-bill maturing after 90 days would be

$$\text{Price of T-bill} = 100 \times \frac{0.10 \times 90}{360} = ₹97.50$$

The actual yield would be:

$$\text{Actual Yield} = \frac{100 - 97.50}{97.50} \times \frac{360}{90} = 10.256\%$$

A discount yield of 10% means an investment of ₹97.50 grows to ₹100, while an add-on yield of 10% simply means that an investment of ₹100, after 90 days, becomes ₹102.50.

Like all futures, Eurodollar futures are subject to marking-to-market on a daily basis. It is done on the basis of trades in the Eurodollar futures market. Final settlement is done on the basis of the 3-m deposit rates offered by reputed banks in London.

PRICING OF AND HEDGING WITH EURODOLLARS FUTURES

Like futures on T-bills, futures on Eurodollar deposits too are quoted on an index basis. The price of Eurodollar futures is given by Eq. 7.8

$$\text{Eurodollar futures price, } F = 100 - 3\text{-m LIBOR rate} \quad (7.8)$$

With price based on LIBOR, Eurodollar futures contracts are extremely useful for hedging exposures that are LIBOR based. Further, pricing in terms of add-on yield rather than discount yield does not create much difference, because Eurodollar futures are settled in cash. Therefore, the difference between prices at the entry point and the exit point becomes material.

> Because of market-based free pricing, futures contracts on Eurodollars are extremely popular in international markets.

Since LIBOR-based exposures are managed by entering swap arrangements, which extend for protracted periods of time, Eurodollar futures are available for longer terms, extending to 10 years. Eurodollar futures are available for expiry every quarter, ending in March, June, September, and December, for 10 years. Therefore, there are 40 contracts available, corresponding to the next 40 quarters. Each Eurodollar contract is for delivery of a deposit of US $1 million.

A hedging application of Eurodollar futures is illustrated in Example 7.6.

The profit/loss on Eurodollar futures for one who goes long on futures is the difference between the initial buying price, F_0, and the exit/settlement price on cash settlement. F_1 is given by Eq. 7.9:

Profit/loss on Eurodollar Futures

$$\text{For initial long position} = \$1{,}000{,}000 \times \frac{F_1 - F_0}{100} \times \frac{90}{360} \quad (7.9)$$

$$\text{For initial short position} = \$1{,}000{,}000 \times \frac{F_0 - F_1}{100} \times \frac{90}{360} \quad (7.10)$$

Interest Rate Futures **197**

> ### EXAMPLE 7.6 Borrower's hedge with Eurodollar futures
>
> Three months from now, Dynamic Forging Limited (DFL) needs to raise a short-term loan of US $2 million for six months. The current LIBOR rate is 6.50%, and a Eurodollar futures contract with three months' expiry is quoted at $93.00 (implying an interest rate of 7%). DFL expects the interest rate to rise to 8%. How can DFL hedge against rising interest rates? What would be the effective cost if the interest rate actually rises to 8%? Further, analyse the interest cost if LIBOR actually falls to 6%.
>
> **Solution**
> DFL faces the risk of a rising interest rate for its contemplated borrowing of three months. Since a futures contract provides cash flow based on three months and the loan required is for six months, compensation would be equal if the exposure in futures is for twice the actual borrowing. DFL can, therefore, sell four futures contracts equivalent to $4 million.
> If LIBOR rises to 8%, the Eurodollar price would fall to $92.00. The profit on each futures contract would be
>
> Profit/loss on Eurodollar Futures (For Short Position) = $1,000,000 × $\frac{F_0 - F_1}{100}$ × $\frac{90}{360}$
>
> = $1,000,000 × $\frac{93.00 - 92.00}{100}$ × $\frac{90}{360}$ = $2,500
>
> The borrowing cost for a 6-m loan of $2 million = 2,000,000 × 0.08 × 180/360 = $80,000
> Less: Profit earned from 4 Eurodollar futures contracts = 2500 × 4 = $10,000
> Effective interest paid = $70,000
>
> Effective Interest Rate = $\frac{70,000}{2,000,000}$ × $\frac{360}{180}$ = 7.00%
>
> This is the rate implicit in the futures contract that can be locked-in now.
> If LIBOR falls to 6%, the Eurodollar price would rise to $94.00. The loss on each futures contract would be
>
> Profit/loss on Eurodollar Futures (For Short Position) = $1,000,000 × $\frac{F_0 - F_1}{100}$ × $\frac{90}{360}$
>
> = $1,000,000 × $\frac{93.00 - 94.00}{100}$ × $\frac{90}{360}$ = $2,500
>
> The borrowing cost for a 6-m loan of $2 million = 2,000,000 × 0.06 × 180/360 = $60,000
> Loss from 4 Eurodollar futures contracts = 2500 × 4 = $10,000
> Effective interest paid = $70,000
>
> Effective Interest Rate = $\frac{70,000}{2,000,000}$ × $\frac{360}{180}$ = 7.00%
>
> With a fall in the interest rate, the firm would not benefit. It still has to pay the same cost of 7%—the rate implicit in the futures contract now.

If $F_1 < F_0$, then an initial long position would incur a loss, while an initial short position would make a profit. A prospective borrower is subject to the risk of rising interest rates. In order to compensate for any loss in the amount of loan, the prospective borrower must go short on Eurodollar futures.

Similarly, a prospective lender who fears a fall in the interest rates must go long on Eurodollar futures.

Other applications of Eurodollar futures for speculation and arbitrage would be done in the same manner as for futures on T-bills.

TREASURY BOND FUTURES

T-bills futures and Eurodollar futures cover short-term exposures to interest rate risk. However, to cover long-term exposures to interest rate risk, the underlying instruments must have a long-term maturity. Futures on T-bonds are used to protect against long-term exposure to interest rate risk. Treasury bonds futures are more complex than T-bills futures or Eurodollar futures, due to peculiarities such as the delivery process, delivery of the underlying, and the invoice price. Various features of T-bonds are as follows.

TREASURY BONDS

As the name suggests, the underlying instruments for the T-bond futures are the long-term securities issued by the central bank of a country. The central bank issues long-term securities for a variety of purposes; one of them is to use long-term securities as measures of fiscal and monetary policies. These securities are known as *dated securities* or *gilts* in India and in several other countries.

Unlike T-bills, T-bonds are issued by central governments with maturity extending for as long as 50 years. Treasury bonds carry a coupon that is usually payable semi-annually. Like T-bills, these bonds are also regarded as free from default risk. The face value is paid on maturity. The coupon rate reflects the interest rate prevailing at the time of issue. The coupon rate is decided by an auction process, where investors quote a yield. Investors can quote their yields at par, at a discount, or at a premium. *Par-yield* refers to the coupon rate for which the price of a bond is equal to its par value. The coupon rate and the maturity date are specified at the time of issue. The pricing of these instruments is expressed in relation to their face value.

On maturity, a futures contract on government bonds would require delivery of an equivalent government security by the seller during the delivery period specified by the exchange dealing with such futures. However, settlement by delivery would not arise if the initial contract is negated by an offsetting contract prior to maturity. Instead, the settlement would be affected by the payment to be made, on the basis of the prices of the futures contract at the time of initial booking and at the time of offsetting the opposite contract.

> Futures contracts on T-bonds are used for hedging long-term interest rate risk.

PRICING T-BONDS

The pricing of T-bonds is similar to the pricing mechanism of a fixed income security. The price of a fixed income security is determined by discounting the future cash flows of the security at a rate given by the term structure of interest rates. The term structure of interest rates specifies the desired returns for different investment horizons. For example, the term structure of interest rate could be as follows:

Investment horizon (m)	6	12	18	24	30	36	42	48
Yields, %	5.70	6.00	6.40	6.70	6.90	7.20	7.50	7.70

Government securities (gilts or dated securities) have a fixed coupon rate expressed as a percentage of the face value, and normally make semi-annual coupon payments. For example, a Government of India (GoI) bond with an 8% coupon that has three years remaining for maturity would be priced[8] at the discounted cash flow of the coupons denoted by C_t and the principal at the end, denoted by R, as given by Eq. 7.11:

---

[8]It is known as clean price, as computed on the coupon date. It changes only with change in yields, and does not take into account the interest that accrues in the intervening period between two coupons. The quoted price of a bond is a clean price.

$$P_0 = \sum_{t/2}^{6} \frac{C_t}{(1+r_{t/2})^{t/2}} + \frac{R}{(1+r_3)^3} \quad (7.11)$$

$$P_0 = \frac{4.00}{(1.057)^{0.5}} + \frac{4.00}{(1.060)^{1.0}} + \frac{4.00}{(1.064)^{1.5}} + \frac{4.00}{(1.067)^{2.0}} + \frac{4.00}{(1.069)^{2.5}} + \frac{4.00}{(1.072)^{3.0}} = ₹102.63$$

The price of the bond can also be equated to its cash flow discounted at the uniform rate, rather than the rates given by the term structure of interest rates. This uniform discount rate, at which the price equals the projected cash flow of the bond, is called yield to maturity (YTM), signifying the yield that would be realized by the investor if he/she buys the bond at the prevailing price and holds it till maturity. The YTM, denoted by the r of the bond, shall be given by the following equation:

$$P_0 = \frac{4.00}{(1+r)^{0.5}} + \frac{4.00}{(1+r)^{1.0}} + \frac{4.00}{(1+r)^{1.5}} + \frac{4.00}{(1+r)^{2.0}} + \frac{4.00}{(1+r)^{2.5}} + \frac{4.00}{(1+r)^{3.0}} = ₹102.63$$

By solving this equation, we get $r = 3.51\%$ for a semi-annual period, or 7.02% p.a. It implies that if an investor buys the bond at ₹102.63 and holds it till its maturity, the realized yield would be 7.02%. The value of the bond at any time in terms of YTM is expressed as shown in Eq. 7.12, with r as YTM for n coupon payments, each denoted by C_n

$$P_0 = \sum_{n=1}^{N} \frac{C_n}{(1+r)^n} + \frac{R}{(1+r)^N} \quad (7.12)$$

For semi-annual compounding of YTM, a convention that is followed in T-bond futures markets, the value of the bond would be given by Eq. 7.13:

$$P_0 = \sum_{n=1}^{2N} \frac{C_n}{(1+r/2)^n} + \frac{R}{(1+r)^{2N}} \quad (7.13)$$

FUTURES CONTRACT ON T-BONDS

A futures contract on T-bonds requires delivery of a long-term bond with minimum specifications decided by the relevant exchange.

A long-term futures contract would have as underlying asset a T-bond whose price would govern the futures' price.

We illustrate the T-bond futures instrument, its pricing, applications, procedure for settlement, etc., based on the contracts traded on the Chicago Board of Trade (CBOT). The principles applicable to the futures of US treasury bonds/notes[9] remain valid for any other similar futures contract having as underlying asset a long-term debt instrument issued by any other central bank.

The fundamental differences between futures on T-bills and futures on T-bonds are (a) a longer term to maturity, and (b) the presence of coupons (normally payable semi-annually), which makes them complex.

A futures contract on T-bills requires delivery of T-bills that have 91 days to maturity as on the date of expiry of the futures contract. This provision of delivery means that certain other instruments, such as 182-day T-bills or 364-day T-bills that have 90–92 days remaining for maturity are also eligible for delivery. On maturity, a futures contract on US T-bonds requires

---

[9]The features of US Treasury bonds and notes are same, except that they differ in their terms to maturity at the time of issue. In the USA, instruments with maturities of less than 10 years at the time of issue are T-notes, while those with maturities longer than 10 years are referred to as T-bonds.

delivery of bonds, with a face value of US $100,000, with more than 15 years remaining for maturity. Contracts on various T-notes also have a similar range of instruments that can be delivered. Similarly, LIFFE deals in futures contracts on British T-bonds (called gilts), which require delivery of gilts maturing between 8.75 years to 13 years later on the first day of the delivery month.

Futures contracts on CBOT have maturities in March, June, September, and December.

PRICING OF T-BOND FUTURES

Similar to the pricing mechanism for other futures contracts, the prices for T-bond futures are also based on the concept of cost of carry. However, in the case of T-bonds, we also earn an income in the form of accrued interest. Note that the price quoted is a *clean price*. The accrued interest is the interest amount from the date of the last coupon payment to the date of delivery. To arrive at the price payable, accrued interest is added to the clean price. Money receivable on coupons for the period from the date of the last coupon payment to the date of delivery would have to be paid by the buyer to the seller of the bond, because the seller is entitled to interest for the period of his holding.

Cash-and-carry transactions in the futures market would involve (a) buying a T-bond at the current market price, S, (b) borrowing the equivalent sum at r, and (c) selling the futures contract on the T-bond at price F. The bond bought today is available for delivery against a futures contract, and the sum realized in the futures contract is used to repay the borrowed sum, together with borrowing cost. Buying the bond would entitle one to the accrued interest on the bond. There would be arbitrage if the sum receivable against the futures contract exceeds the net cost of borrowing (financing cost less accrued interest).

Consider this underlying asset for a futures contract: a GoI 10-year security with an 8% coupon and 45 days to maturity, priced at ₹96.50. With 10% financing cost, cash-and-carry arbitrage can be executed as follows to yield a profit of ₹0.2760:

		₹
Spot price of the bond (at YTM of 8.60%)		= 96.0291
Accrued interest for 45 days	= 4 × 45/182	= 0.9890
Cost of financing for 45 days	= 96.0291 × 0.10 × 45/365	= 1.1839
Net amount to be paid	= 96.0291 + 1.1839 − 0.9890	= 96.2240
Amount receivable against the futures contract sold		= 96.5000
Arbitrage profit		= 0.2760

For no arbitrage:

$$\text{Futures price} = \text{spot price} + \text{cost of financing} - \text{accrued interest} \qquad (7.14)$$

The futures contract price represents a repo transaction—selling a security and buying it back after some time at a price determined today. The futures price, therefore, implies a repo rate that may be compared with the financing rate to know if the futures contract is correctly priced. Remember that we have to account for accrued interest in the case of bonds, which is not the case with futures on T-bills, which do not incorporate coupon discounts. Modifying Eq. 7.14, the implied repo rate in the spot and futures prices is 12.33%, as computed here:

$$\text{Implied Repo Rate} = \frac{\text{Futures price} - \text{Spot price} + \text{Accrued interest}}{\text{Spot price}} \times \frac{365}{\text{No. of days remaining for futures}}$$

$$= \frac{96.50 - 96.03 + 0.9890}{96.03} \times \frac{365}{45} = 0.1233 = 12.33\% \qquad (7.14)$$

Reverse cash-and-carry transactions would involve (a) selling the T-bond for cash, (b) investing the cash so realized, and (c) buying futures on T-bond.

Conversion Factor

We know that in any financial futures market, a requirement for delivery forces the convergence of the futures price and the spot price. A futures contract on any long-term securities would warrant a delivery of the underlying asset. However, government securities issued at various points of time have different coupon rates and maturities, in consideration of prevailing economic conditions and the requirements of the issuer. For futures markets, the underlying product needs to be standardized, and therefore, futures exchanges would need to identify some government security(ies) on which futures contracts may be traded. This standardized futures contract on a specific security would not be available for delivery.

Recognizing the need for delivery of the underlying asset, the exchange would have to provide for some flexibility in delivery of the asset, subject to the fulfilment of some minimum conditions. The CBOT prescribes the delivery of any T-bond that has more than 15 years to maturity at the time of delivery, thereby making several government securities eligible for delivery. Similarly, there has to be a specified time/duration when the asset can be delivered. The CBOT provides flexibility by allowing delivery on any day in the month of closing of the contract.

Despite having the same face/nominal value, the price of all the securities would not be the same, as securities issued at different points of times have varying coupon rates and maturities. We know that the spot price of bonds is dependent upon, inter alia, the coupon rate and the time remaining for maturity. A bond with a higher coupon is worth more than a bond with a lower coupon, given that all other features of the two bonds remain the same. For example, if a futures contract requires delivery of a bond with a 6% coupon, a seller who chooses to deliver a bond with an 8% coupon would need adjustments to the price for making the contract good. The seller who delivers a high coupon rate bond needs to be compensated more than the seller who chooses to deliver the bond with a lower coupon.

The compensation that the seller must get for delivery of the asset is weighed in terms of the standard contract. Each exchange specifies government securities that are eligible for delivery against a futures contract and the relative value of each in terms of the standardized asset underlying the futures contract. For example, Table 7.6 provides a list of British government bonds and their price factor adjustments that could have been delivered against LIFFE futures contracts maturing in June 2009.

> Many deliverable bonds may be available in the market, and are adjusted for price using conversion factors decided periodically by the relevant exchanges.

To simplify the pricing of futures contracts, the price factor is computed on the basis of a 6% coupon rate. If bonds were perpetuities, the price factor would simply be the ratio of the coupon rate for the bond that is being delivered and 6%. If the coupon rate were 8%, the price factor would be 1.25, as a perpetual bond with an 8% coupon would trade at 1.25 times the value of a 6% bond. Since government securities have definite maturities, any upward or downward adjustment for the price paid is made by the conversion factors.

Table 7.7 presents a list of US T-bonds and the applicable conversion factors that are deliverable on T-bond futures contracts of CBOT for contracts maturing from March 08 to June 09.

Table 7.6 Price factors and accrued interest at LIFFE

Long Gilt Contract (6% Coupon) - Price Factors and Accrued Interest Delivery Month: June 2009				
Coupon	Redemption	Price factor	Daily accrued	Initial accrued
5.00	7 Mar 2018	0.9325024	13.586957	1154.891304
4.50	7 Mar 2019	0.8902618	12.228261	1039.402174
4.75	7 Mar 2020	0.9018195	12.907609	1097.146739

Source: www.liffe.com, last accessed on 22 December 2008.

Table 7.7 6% Conversion factors for T-bond futures at CBOT

Coupon	Issue date	Maturity	Contracts maturing in					
			Mar-08	Jun-08	Sep-08	Dec-08	Mar-09	Jun-09
$4\frac{3}{8}$	02-15-08	02-15-38	0.7757	0.7765	0.7771	0.7779	0.7786	0.7794
$4\frac{1}{2}$	02-15-06	02-15-36	0.7984	0.7992	0.7998	0.8007	0.8013	0.8022
$4\frac{3}{4}$	02-15-07	02-15-37	0.8297	0.8303	0.8308	0.8315	0.8320	0.8327
5	08-15-07	05-15-37	0.8633	0.8637	0.8642	0.8646	0.8652	0.8656
$5\frac{1}{4}$	11-16-98	11-15-28	0.9122	0.9127	0.9133	0.9138	0.9145	0.9150
$5\frac{1}{4}$	02-16-99	02-15-29	0.9116	0.9122	0.9127	0.9133	0.9138	0.9145
$5\frac{3}{8}$	02-15-01	02-15-31	0.9229	0.9234	0.9237	0.9242	0.9245	0.9251
$5\frac{1}{2}$	08-17-98	08-15-28	0.9417	0.9422	0.9425	0.9430	0.9433	0.9438
6	02-15-96	02-15-26	0.9999	1.0000	0.9999	1.0000	0.9999	1.0000
$6\frac{1}{8}$	11-17-97	11-15-27	1.0143	1.0140	1.0141	1.0138	1.0139	1.0136
$6\frac{1}{8}$	08-16-99	08-15-29	1.0148	1.0148	1.0146	1.0146	1.0144	1.0144
$6\frac{1}{4}$	08-16-93	08-15-23	1.0246	1.0245				
$6\frac{1}{4}$	02-15-00	05-15-30	1.0303	1.0300	1.0300	1.0297	1.0296	1.0293
$6\frac{3}{8}$	08-15-97	08-15-27	1.0424	1.0422	1.0418	1.0416	1.0411	1.0409
$6\frac{1}{2}$	11-15-96	11-15-26	1.0554	1.0549	1.0546	1.0540	1.0537	1.0532
$6\frac{5}{8}$	02-18-97	02-15-27	1.0697	1.0693	1.0686	1.0682	1.0676	1.0671
$6\frac{3}{4}$	08-15-96	08-15-26	1.0824	1.0819	1.0811	1.0806	1.0798	1.0792
$6\frac{7}{8}$	08-15-95	08-15-25	1.0931	1.0925	1.0915	1.0909	1.0899	1.0892
$7\frac{1}{2}$	08-15-94	11-15-24	1.1557	1.1542	1.1529	1.1513	1.1500	1.1484
$7\frac{5}{8}$	02-15-95	02-15-25	1.1701	1.1687	1.1671	1.1657	1.1640	1.1625

Source: www.cbot.com, last accessed on 22 December 2008.

The conversion factors for deliverable bonds are determined against standard bonds with a 6% coupon rate; they are greater than 1.00 when the coupon is greater than 6% and less than 1.00 when the coupon is less than 6%.

The invoice amount is dependent upon the conversion factor and the accrued interest on the bond till the date of actual delivery. Exchanges normally allow the whole of the named month for delivery. For example, a June 2009 futures contract may be delivered on any business day of June 2009.

Finding Conversion Factors

The conversion factor system exists to enable a level playing field for all bonds.

As stated earlier, the conversion factor for a deliverable bond is its relative value with respect to the value of the underlying asset of the futures contract. An interest rate futures contract on T-bonds assumes a coupon of 6%, and, therefore, the conversion factor reflects the value of the bond at a YTM of 6%. The CBOT provides conversion factors for deliverable bonds for unit face value as follows:

- For the bonds being delivered, find the completed number of semi-annual periods, N, and the remaining number of months, m, till maturity from the first day of the delivery month of the contract.
- If the remaining number of months, m, is less than a quarter (three months), the conversion factor is equal to the value of the bond immediately after the coupon date, which is equal to:

    Conversion factor = price of the bond immediately after coupon, C
    $= C/2 \times \text{PVIFA}(3\%, N) + \text{PVIF}(3\%, N)$

- If the remaining number of months, m, is more than a quarter (three months), then the price of the bond is increased by one coupon payment and discounted for one quarter at 6% (3% semi-annual), less accrued interest for one quarter, AI. Mathematically,

$$\text{Conversion Factor} = \frac{1}{1.06^{0.5}} \times (C/2 + P) - \text{Accrued Interest}$$

Calculations for the conversion factors for futures contracts expiring in June, September, and December 2008 for a deliverable bond 6-1/4 maturing in November 2026 are demonstrated in Table 7.8.

Table 7.8 Conversion factor for the same bond for three futures contracts at CBOT

Contract	Whole number of periods left, N	Months left, M	Price, P	Coupon, $C/2$	Present value	Accrued interest	Conversion factor
June 2008 contract	36	5 1/2	1.0546	0.0325	1.0711	0.0163	1.0549
Sept 2008 contract	36	2 1/2	1.0546	—	—	—	1.0546
Dec 2008 contract	36	3 1/2	1.0537	0.0325	1.0703	0.0163	1.0540
The following values are used to arrive at the price, P							
			36 periods			35 periods	
PVIFA (3%, N)			21.8323			21.4872	
PVIF (3%, N)			0.3450			0.3554	

The values may be verified from Table 7.7.

CHEAPEST-TO-DELIVER BOND

> The prices of bonds and conversion factors normally imply that not all bonds would be equal. A seller of futures would have to decide which among the deliverable bonds is cheapest to deliver.

The price factor (as it is referred to at LIFFE) or conversion factor (as it is referred to at CBOT) for a specific deliverable bond is an attempt to adjust the price difference between the asset being delivered and the asset underlying the futures contract. However, the actual price of the asset in the market may not conform to the adjustment of the price or conversion factor as prescribed by the exchange. Given the menu of bonds and their conversion factors, the seller of a futures contract would have the option of choosing amongst the bonds eligible for delivery. The seller would deliver the bond that is cheapest-to-deliver (CTD), depending upon the actual price prevailing in the market.

The invoice price for a nominal value of 100 that the seller of a futures contract would receive is determined such that,

Invoice price = settlement price × conversion factor + accrued interest

The bond the seller chooses to deliver would be acquired in the market at the prevailing market price, and the cost would be,

Cost of acquiring the bond = current market price of the bond + accrued interest

Derivatives in Practice

Interest Rate Futures

India: No interest in interest rates

Interest rate derivatives are perhaps the largest segment of traded derivatives the world over. According to an estimate of the Bank of International Settlement in March 2011, interest rate derivatives comprised about 85% of total derivatives turnover on organized exchanges, based on notional principal.

For the first time in India, interest-based derivatives, i.e., interest rate futures were launched in 2003 by the NSE. The pricing of the futures was based on the zero coupon yield curve, a practice unique to India. Though more scientific, it was considered too complex and non-transparent, and there were apprehensions about modelling errors. The major users of interest rate derivatives, i.e., the banks under the control of the Reserve Bank of India, were not allowed to trade in interest rate futures. Interest rate futures provide hedging against the varying yields on debt securities mostly held by banks. Since banks classified such securities under held-to-maturity (HTM) to avoid capital adequacy problems, they did not face interest rate risk on such securities.

A second attempt was made in 2009 to introduce interest rate futures with a 10-year 7% notional with coupon payable semi-annually. Consistent with global practice, delivery-based settlement was provided for. Despite the removal of product deficiency and opening up of the market by allowing financial institutions to participate, trading did not pick up. It was apprehended that illiquid securities that fulfilled the requirements for deliverability were not really liquid enough. There apparently was a 'short squeeze', a phenomenon where deliverable grades of securities are in short supply. Under physical settlement, there are several instruments that can be delivered, and the seller has the option to choose the security, based on what is cheapest to deliver. Though the provision for physical settlement integrates the spot and derivative markets better, success is dependent upon how vibrant the spot markets for interest rate products are.

After long deliberation, the third and latest attempt has been made recently to provide a suitable platform for managing interest rate risk. On 4 July 2011, interest rate futures were introduced with 91-day T-bills as underlying. Settlement price would be based on auction in the spot market, conducted by the Reserve Bank of India, and positions would be settled in cash. It was hoped that this time, participants would show more interest. Unfortunately, it has met the same fate as that of two previous attempts.

We need to create much more awareness on the efficacy of interest rate futures as a hedging tool against interest rate volatility. More money from retail investors must be canalized to institutions such as mutual funds, insurance companies, and pension funds, so that they become much bigger in size.

If the invoice price to be received by the seller exceeds the cost of acquisition, the seller of the futures contract stands to gain. Where the profit in doing so is greatest, the seller would have the choice of selecting one amongst the bonds eligible for delivery. The profit/loss for the seller choosing to deliver would be

$$\text{Profit/loss} = \text{invoice amount} - \text{cost of acquisition}$$
$$= \text{settlement price} \times \text{conversion factor} - \text{current market price}$$

Though profit is the unfailing guide for determining the CTD bond, there are certain rules of thumb that help to quickly determine the bond that is CTD. Some of these rules of thumbs are as follows:

- When the market yield < 6%, deliver short maturity—high coupon
  > 6%, deliver high maturity—low coupon
- If the yield > 6%, deliver bond with highest duration
  < 6%, deliver bond with lowest duration
- Deliver the bond with least theoretical price
- Deliver the bond with highest implied repo rate

INTEREST RATE FUTURES IN INDIA

Futures contracts on interest rates were introduced in India at the NSE and the Bombay Stock Exchange in June 2003. The NSE had three contracts with the following underlying assets:

- 3-m T-bills
- 10-year zero coupon
- 10-year government security, 7% semi-annual

Exchange-traded interest rate derivatives are supposed to provide the much-needed depth in the market, eliminating counterparty risk. Trading in these instruments has left much to be desired and has not attracted active participation for several reasons, including the methodology for the settlement price of futures. Some of the major reasons that trading in interest rate derivatives has not taken off to the desired level include (a) insufficient volume of the instruments available in the government securities debt markets and (b) concentrated holding amongst a few financial institutions, banks, etc. Further, a significant proportion of these government securities may be classified as held-to-maturity (HTM) category investment and as such do not face any interest rate risk, obviating the need for hedging. Contracts on long term did not find markets deep enough.

On as 31 August 2009, the NSE in India re-introduced interest rate futures on GoI security with a notional bond of maturity of 10 years, with a 7% coupon payable semi-annually. If the price of the bond is equal to ₹100, it would denote a market yield of 7%. Given the inverse relationship of bond prices with yield, a price greater than ₹100 indicates a yield lesser than 7% and a price of the notional bond of less than ₹100 signifies market yields in excess of 7%. As of now, there are only two products for interest rate in the exchanges in India—T-bills futures meant for covering short-term risk (discussed earlier) and T-bond futures for covering long-term interest rate risk. Yet another class of futures are on reference rates such as LIBOR, JIBOR (Jakarta interbank offer rate), etc. They have not yet been introduced in India.

> Interest rate futures in India are based on notional GoI securities with 10 years to maturity, bearing coupons of 7% payable semi-annually.

Table 7.9 Interest rate futures—contract specifications

Symbol	10YGS7
Unit of trading	1 lot, equal to notional bonds of face value of ₹2 lakh
Underlying	10-year notional coupon bearing GoI security (notional coupon 7% with semi-annual compounding)
Tick size	₹0.0025
Contract trading cycle	Four fixed quarterly contracts for the entire year, ending in March, June, September, and December
Last trading day	Seventh business day preceding the last business day of the delivery month
Quantity freeze	501 lots or greater
Base price	Theoretical price of the 1st day of the contract On all other days, DSP of the contract
Price operating range	±2% of the base price
Initial margin	SPAN-based margin
Extreme loss margin	0.3% of the value of the gross open positions of the futures contract
Settlement	*Daily settlement marking to market*: $T + 1$ in cash *Delivery settlement*: In the delivery month, i.e., the contract expiry month
Daily settlement price	Closing price or theoretical price
Mode of settlement	Daily settlement in cash
Deliverable grade securities	GoI securities
Conversion factor	The conversion factor would be equal to the price of the deliverable security (per rupee of principal) on the first calendar day of the delivery month, to yield 7% with semi-annual compounding
Invoice price	Daily settlement price times a conversion factor + accrued interest
Last delivery day	Last business day of the delivery month
Intent to deliver	Two business days prior to actual delivery day

Source: www.nseindia.com, last accessed on 28 August 2009

The contract specifications for interest rate futures at NSE are given in Table 7.9.

HEDGING WITH INTEREST RATE FUTURES

Treasury bond futures are mainly used by institutional investors. The hedging principle with futures on T-bonds remains the same, i.e., taking an opposite position in the futures to that of the spot market.

Assume that a portfolio manager is long on a portfolio of bonds. With a rise in the interest rates, the value of the portfolio would reduce, posing the risk of a loss in market value of the portfolio. He/she could hedge the risk of losing the value of the portfolio by taking a short position on futures on government bonds. When the interest rates do indeed go up, the value of the portfolio would fall, and so would the value of the futures contracts. The second leg

> Rising yields erode portfolio values; this risk of diminishing value can be covered by going short on interest rate futures.

of the transaction, i.e., buying the futures contract, would result in a gain, partially or fully offsetting the likely loss in the value of the portfolio of bonds.

Hedge Ratio

To what extent the loss in the value of the portfolio would be offset by the gains in the futures position depends upon the position taken in the futures contracts and the value of the portfolio; this is best represented by the hedge ratio. The hedge ratio in turn would depend upon the sensitivities of the portfolio value and the futures contracts to changes in interest rates. Since portfolios consist of long-term bonds and bear periodic coupons, the risk of interest rate change effects on the value of a long-term portfolio needs to be matched with futures contracts based on similar instruments. Futures on T-bills, which are zero coupon instruments, do not suit the requirements of hedging of a portfolio consisting of coupon-bearing long-term instruments. Where the asset underlying the futures contract and the cash position is the same, the optimal hedge ratio is one. In the case of a portfolio of bonds, the optimal hedge ratio would not be equal to 1, due to the different sensitivities of the values of the assets underlying the futures contract and of those in the cash position.

Duration and Modified Duration

A futures contract, being based on a notional bond, implies that it cannot be satisfied with the delivery of the underlying asset. Instead, the futures contracts could be satisfied with the delivery of any permissible bond that meets the requirement of the exchange. The seller of the futures contract has the option of choosing the bond to be delivered. Logic dictates that the seller would choose the CTD bond. Therefore, a position in futures can at best be regarded as a position in CTD bonds, rather than as a position in a notional bond that is traded.

> The duration of a bond is the measure of sensitivity of its value with respect to changes in interest rates.

By what amount does the value of a portfolio of bonds change with changes in the interest rates? The question is answered by a commonly known statistic of bonds called *duration*. The duration of a bond is obtained by dividing the time-weighted discounted cash flow at the current YTM by the price of the bond. It is given by Eq. 7.15.

$$\text{Duration of the bond, } D = \frac{\Sigma t \times \text{DCF}_t}{P_0} \qquad (7.15)$$

where t = time of the cash flow of the bond
DCF_t = cash flow at t discounted at YTM of the bond
P_0 = current price of the bond, signifying its YTM

The duration of the bond represents the approximate change in the value of the bond for a 1% change in the YTM. A better approximation is obtained by modified duration (MD), given by Eq. 7.16.

$$\text{Modified Duration, } MD = -\frac{D}{1 + r/m}$$

$$\text{For semi - annual payment } m = 2 \text{ and } MD = -\frac{D}{1 + r/2} \qquad (7.16)$$

where D = duration of the bond
r = YTM of the bond
m = number of coupon payments in a year (2 for semi-annual payments)

The negative sign indicates the inverse relationship of the value of the bond with the YTM, i.e., value of the bond decreases when the YTM rises.

Table 7.10 demonstrates the computation of the bond value, its duration, and the MD for a bond with a 7% semi-annual coupon and 10 years to maturity at a YTM of 8%.

Table 7.10 Bond price and duration

Period, t	Cash flow of periodic coupons and principal (₹)	Present value at YTM of 8%	Duration of the bond (Time × DCF)	New YTM = YTM ± 0.1%	
				8.10%	7.90%
1	3.50	3.3654	1.6827	3.3638	3.3670
2	3.50	3.2359	3.2359	3.2328	3.2391
3	3.50	3.1115	4.6672	3.1070	3.1160
4	3.50	2.9918	5.9836	2.9861	2.9976
5	3.50	2.8767	7.1919	2.8698	2.8837
6	3.50	2.7661	8.2983	2.7581	2.7741
7	3.50	2.6597	9.3090	2.6508	2.6687
8	3.50	2.5574	10.2297	2.5476	2.5673
9	3.50	2.4591	11.0657	2.4484	2.4697
10	3.50	2.3645	11.8224	2.3531	2.3759
11	3.50	2.2735	12.5044	2.2615	2.2856
12	3.50	2.1861	13.1165	2.1735	2.1987
13	3.50	2.1020	13.6631	2.0889	2.1152
14	3.50	2.0212	14.1481	2.0076	2.0348
15	3.50	1.9434	14.5757	1.9295	1.9575
16	3.50	1.8687	14.9494	1.8544	1.8831
17	3.50	1.7968	15.2729	1.7822	1.8116
18	3.50	1.7277	15.5493	1.7128	1.7427
19	3.50	1.6612	15.7819	1.6461	1.6765
20	103.50	47.2360	472.3605	46.7841	47.6925
Value of the bond		**93.2048**		**92.5583**	**93.8572**
Time × PV of cash flow			675.4082		
Duration of the bond			**7.2465**		
MD of the bond			**6.9678**		
New price of the bond based on duration					
With 0.1% increase in YTM			92.5554		
With 0.1% decrease in YTM			93.8543		

> **EXAMPLE 7.7** Bond price, duration, and modified duration
>
> AA bond with three years remaining for maturity, bearing a semi-annual coupon of 10%, is trading at a YTM of 12%. Find out the value of the bond, its duration, and its modified duration (MD).
>
> **Solution**
> With cash flows of the bond for the remaining six coupons, a principal of ₹100 at semi-annual intervals, and a discount factor of 12% (6% semi-annual), the value, duration, and MD are worked out as follows:
>
> | Period, t | 1 | 2 | 3 | 4 | 5 | 6 | Total |
> |---|---|---|---|---|---|---|---|
> | Cash flow (₹) | 5.00 | 5.00 | 5.00 | 5.00 | 5.00 | 105.00 | |
> | Present value at 12%, DCF (₹) | 4.7170 | 4.4500 | 4.1981 | 3.9605 | 3.7363 | 74.0209 | 95.0827 |
> | $t/2 \times$ DCF | 2.3585 | 4.4500 | 6.2971 | 7.9209 | 9.3407 | 222.0626 | 252.4299 |
>
> | | |
> |---|---|
> | Value of the bond (₹) | 95.0827 |
> | Duration (years) | 2.6548 |
> | MD (years) | 2.5046 |
>
> The sum of the present values of the cash flows of the bond, i.e., ₹95.08, represents the current value of the bond. The product of time and the present values divided by the value of the bond is its duration, which is 2.65 years. The MD is 2.50 years.

> The duration of a bond is computed by dividing the time weighted cash flows of the bond by its current value.

The last two columns of Table 7.10 also compute the price with a change in the YTM of ±0.1%, i.e., at 7.9% and 8.1%. The value of the bond could also be obtained by MD with a great degree of accuracy for small changes in the YTM. The duration of the bond is 7.2465 years. The MD is 6.9678 years (7.2465/1.04). The value 6.9678 signifies that if the YTM changes by 1%, the value of the bond changes in the opposite direction by approximately 6.9678%. The smaller the change, the better is the approximation. For a 0.1% change in the YTM, the value would change by 0.69%. The value of the bond at a new YTM, which changes by ΔYTM expressed as a decimal, is given as follows:

$$\text{New value} = \text{value at old YTM} \times (1 - \text{MD} \times \Delta\text{YTM})$$

The values of the bond at the new YTMs of 8.1% and 7.9% work out to ₹92.56 and ₹93.85, respectively, when computed using MD; these values are fairly close to the actual values worked out on the basis of new YTM the last 2 columns of Table 7.10.

Optimal Hedge Ratio: Duration-based Hedging

While hedging with futures on bonds, the consideration of changes in value has to be viewed in terms of changes in the value of the bond likely to be delivered against the futures contract. Therefore, one has to make a fair judgement right at the time of the inception of the hedge as to which bond is likely to be delivered when the hedge gets lifted. Since there are many deliverable bonds, there exists the additional dimension of the risk of the actual bond delivered being different from the one perceived at the inception of the hedge. Since this risk is nominal, it may be ignored in determination of the optimal hedge ratio.

The optimal hedge ratio, i.e., the position in futures on T-bonds, would be one that offsets the changes in the value of the portfolio of bonds. It is expressed as

$$\text{Change in value of bond portfolio} = h \times \text{change in value of T-bond futures}$$

The change in the value of the bond portfolio is a function of its duration. The property of additivity of duration comes in handy while computing the duration of a portfolio of bonds. The duration of a portfolio of bonds is the weighted average of the durations of the bonds comprising the portfolio. With this, we may treat the portfolio of bonds as a single bond, with duration equal to the weighted average. If B is the value of the bond at a YTM of r_B and MD_B is the MD, then any change in the value of the portfolio is worked out as follows:

> The optimal hedge ratio for a position in long-term futures depends upon the durations of the bonds in cash position and the perceived CTD bond in the futures contract.

$$\text{Change in value of bond portfolio, } \Delta B = \text{Value} \times \Delta r_B \times MD$$
$$= B \times \Delta r_B \times MD_B$$
$$= B \times \Delta r_B \times D_B/(1 + r_B/m_B)$$

We analyse the changes in the value of the futures in terms of changes in the values of the CTD bond that would be delivered in fulfilment of the futures contract. If G is the value of the CTD bond at a YTM of r_G and MD_G is the MD, then the change in the value of the CTD bond is

$$\text{Change in the value of CTD bond (government security), } \Delta G$$
$$= \text{value} \times \Delta r_G \times MD$$
$$= G \times \Delta r_G \times MD_G$$
$$= G \times \Delta r_G \times D_G/(1 + r_G/m_G)$$

In terms of futures contracts on T-bonds, the value of CTD is expressed as

$$G = \text{futures price, } F \times \text{conversion factor}$$

Therefore, the change in value of the CTD bond, $\Delta G = \Delta F \times \text{conversion factor}$

$$\text{Hedge ratio} = \frac{\text{Change in the value of bond portfolio}}{\text{Change in value of futures on treasury bonds}} = \frac{\Delta B}{\Delta F}$$

$$= \frac{\Delta B}{\Delta G} \times \text{Conversion factor}$$

$$= \frac{B \times \Delta r_B \times D_B}{G \times \Delta r_G \times D_G} \times \frac{(1 + r_G/m_G)}{(1 + r_B/m_B)} \times \text{Conversion factor}$$

Assuming that the change in YTMs of the bonds in the portfolio and the CTD bonds are equal, i.e., $\Delta r_B = \Delta r_G$, and ignoring the differences in frequency of coupon payments, i.e., $m_B = m_G = 1$, we get a hedge ratio as in Eq. 7.18.

EXAMPLE 7.8 Hedging with T-bond futures

A mutual fund is holding bonds worth ₹5.00 crore. The YTMs in the next three months are expected to rise. The portfolio of bonds has a duration of 6.63 years. Futures contract on notional 10-year, 7% semi-annual GoI security is trading at ₹104.3425. The CTD GoI security is expected to have a duration of 7.72 years. How many contracts should the mutual fund trade to hedge against the risk of rising yields? Assume that the YTMs of the CTD bond and the bonds in the portfolio are the same.

Solution
Price in the futures market for a bond with a face value of ₹100 = ₹104.3425
Value of one futures contract (bonds with total face value of ₹2,00,000) = 104.3425 × 2000 = ₹2,08,685
Therefore, the number of interest rate futures contracts that must be booked as per Eq. 7.18 are:

$$\text{Hedge Ratio} = \frac{B \times D_B}{F \times D_G} \times \frac{(1 + r_G)}{(1 + r_B)} = \frac{5,00,00,000 \times 6.63}{2,08,685 \times 7.72} = 205.766 \text{ say 206 contracts}$$

Interest Rate Futures   **211**

$$\text{Hedge Ratio} = \frac{B \times D_B}{G \times D_G} \times \frac{(1 + r_G)}{(1 + r_B)} \times \text{Conversion factor} \tag{7.17}$$

In terms of the futures price, the hedge ratio becomes

$$\text{Hedge Ratio} = \frac{B \times D_B}{F \times D_G} \times \frac{(1 + r_G)}{(1 + r_B)} \tag{7.18}$$

SOLVED PROBLEMS

SP 7.1: Hedging with T-bills futures

Wood Craft Ltd requires funds of ₹1 crore for execution of an order. This amount may need to be borrowed after two months. The requirement of funds will be for a period of three months. The bankers of Wood Craft Ltd would provide the funds at twice the yield of T-bills prevailing at the time of availing of the loan. The current discount yield in T-bills is 6.70%, but 2-m futures on T-bills are suggesting a yield of 7.30%. Wood Craft Ltd is concerned about the increasing cost of borrowing. What action can Wood Craft Ltd initiate to safeguard itself? Evaluate the position if after two months the discount yield on the T-bills is (a) 7.00% and (b) 8.00%.

Solution

As a hedging strategy, Wood Craft Ltd must sell interest rate futures on T-bills today, expiring two months later at the prevailing rate of ₹92.70 (100 − 7.30). The value of the futures contract would be double the amount required to be borrowed. They must sell futures worth ₹2.00 crore. When funds are actually required after two months, the firm must buy the futures back and borrow from a bank. By doing so, the firm would lock-in a borrowing rate of 14.60% (2 × 7.60%).

If Discount Yield on T-bills are at 7.00%

The futures would be priced at ₹93.00, and T-bills would quote a discount yield of 7.00%, which would govern the actual borrowing rate.

Futures on T-bills—sold		₹92.70
Futures on T-bills—bought		₹93.00
Loss of futures		₹0.30
Amount to be paid on 2 futures contracts	$= (92.70 - 93.00) \times \frac{90}{360} \times 2$	₹0.15
Annualized cost paid on futures	$= 360/90 \times 0.15$	₹0.60
Borrowing cost	$= 2 \times 7.00\%$	14.00%
Effective cost of borrowing		14.60%

If Discount Yield on T-bills Rises to 8.00%

The futures would sell for ₹92.00, and T-bills would quote a discount yield of 8.00%, causing a borrowing cost that is equal to 16%. A position in futures helps to bring down the cost to 14.60%.

Futures on T-bills—sold		₹92.70
Futures on T-bills—bought		₹92.00
Gain of futures		₹0.70
Amount to be paid on 2 futures contracts	$= (92.70 - 92.00) \times \frac{90}{360} \times 2$	₹0.35
Annualized benefit on futures	$= 360/90 \times 0.35$	₹1.40
Borrowing cost	$= 2 \times 8.00\%$	16.00%
Effective cost of borrowing		14.60%

SP 7.2: Investor's hedge with Eurodollar futures

Three months from now, American Investors Fund (AIF) needs to invest US $5 million for three months. Currently, the LIBOR is 6.50%, and a Eurodollar futures contract with three months to expire is quoted at $94.00 (implying an interest rate of 6%). The AIF expects the interest rate to fall to 5.50%. How can AIF hedge against falling interest rates? What would be the effective cost if the interest rate actually fell to 5%? Further, analyse the interest cost if LIBOR actually rose to 7%.

Solution

The AIF faces the risk of falling yields. It can therefore buy five Eurodollar futures contracts of US $1 million each at $94.00 to cover the exposure of US $5 million and lock-in a return of 6%.

If the LIBOR fell to 5%, the Eurodollar price would rise to $95.00. The profit on each futures contract would be:

$$\text{Profit/loss on Eurodollar Futures (For long position)} = \$1,000,000 \times \frac{F_1 - F_0}{100} \times \frac{90}{360}$$

$$= \$1,000,000 \times \frac{95.00 - 94.00}{100} \times \frac{90}{360} = \$2500$$

The return on $5 million	$= 5,000,000 \times 0.05 \times 90/360$	$= \$62,500$
Add: Profit earned from five Eurodollar futures contracts	$= 2500 \times 5$	$= \$12,500$
Effective interest earned	$= \$75,000$	

$$\text{Effective interest rate} = \frac{75,000}{5,000,000} \times \frac{360}{90} = 6.00\%$$

This is the rate implicit in the futures contract that can be locked in now.

If LIBOR rose to 7%, the Eurodollar would sell for $93.00. The loss on each futures contract would be

$$\text{Profit/loss on Euro dollar Futures (For long position)} = \$1,000,000 \times \frac{F_1 - F_0}{100} \times \frac{90}{360}$$

$$= \$1,000,000 \times \frac{93.00 - 94.00}{100} \times \frac{90}{360} = \$2500$$

The return on $5 million	$= 5,000,000 \times 0.07 \times 90/360$	$= \$87,500$
Less: Loss from five Eurodollar futures contracts	$= -2500 \times 5$	$= \$12,500$
Effective interest earned	$= \$75,000$	

$$\text{Effective interest rate} = \frac{75,000}{5,000,000} \times \frac{360}{90} = 6.00\%$$

SP 7.3: Conversion factor and invoice price

Assume that the seller of an interest rate futures contract decides to deliver a 6.25% GoI security maturing in 2026 against the futures contract, expiring in December 2009. He/she notifies his/her intentions to deliver on 10 December with the last settlement price of the futures at ₹92.5575. The conversion factor for the bond for December 2009 delivery is 0.9230. Each futures contract at NSE is for ₹2,00,000 (face value of bonds). He would deliver the bonds on 12 December 2009. The coupons for the GoI security chosen for delivery are paid on 20 November and 20 May each year. What is the invoice price of the bonds?

Solution
The invoice price is given by

$$\text{Last settlement price of futures} \times \text{conversion factor} + \text{accrued interest}$$

Contract size = bonds with face value of ₹2,00,000, i.e., 2000 bonds
Accrued interest is computed as follows:

Last coupon payment made		= 20 November 2009
Next coupon payment due		= 20 May 2010
Number of days between successive coupons		= 181
Delivery date for the bond		= 12 December 2009
Number of days since last coupon		= 22
Amount of coupon per futures contract	$= 3.125 \times 2000$	= ₹6250
Accrued interest	$= 6250 \times 22/181$	= ₹759.67
Invoice price per contract	$= 92.5575 \times 0.9230 \times 2000 + 759.67$	
	$= 1,70,861.15 + 759.67$	= ₹1,71,620.82

SP 7.4: Hedging with T-bond futures

A mutual fund is holding a 15-year 12% bond trading at ₹107.2675 at a YTM of 11%, with a duration of 7.54 years. To meet its redemption requirements, three months later, it needs to sell the bonds worth ₹50 lakh. The yields in the market are expected to rise, causing a decline in the market value of the bonds. If this happens, the fund would have to sell more bonds. A 3-m interest rate futures contract at NSE is trading at ₹77.6150 (equivalent to a YTM of 10.70%). The bond likely to be delivered at the end of the futures contract is a 12-year 14% bond selling at a YTM of 13%, with a duration of 6.62 years. How can the mutual fund hedge its position through interest rate futures at NSE? Examine the scenario if the yields go up by 1.50% flat for all maturities.

Solution

The mutual fund is facing the risk of loss due to rising yields. If the yields indeed go up, the price of the futures contracts would fall. Therefore, in order to achieve a gain from the futures to offset the likely loss in the portfolio value, the mutual fund must sell the futures contracts now. The number of futures contracts that needs to be sold is calculated as follows:

Price of futures contract = ₹77.6150

Value of one futures contract (bonds with face value of ₹2 lakh) = 2000 × 77.6150 = ₹1,55,230

The number of futures contracts to be sold

$$\text{Hedge Ratio} = \frac{B \times D_B}{F \times D_G} \times \frac{(1 + r_G)}{(1 + r_B)} = \frac{50,00,000 \times 7.54}{1,55,230 \times 6.62} \times \frac{1.13}{1.11} = 37.34 \text{ say 37 contracts}$$

If the YTM increases by 1.50% flat across all maturities, the futures price would be ₹69.9725 (for a YTM of 12.30%) and the bond price would be ₹96.6500 (for a YTM of 12.50%).

At the end of the hedging period of three months the mutual fund would buy back the futures. The gain from 37 contracts would be,

$$(77.6150 - 69.9725) \times 2000 \times 37 = ₹5,65,545$$

For funds of ₹50 lakh the value to be obtained from selling the bond would now be,

$$50,00,000 - 5,65,545 = ₹44,34,455$$

The number of bonds that need to be sold = 44,34,455/96.65 = 45,882

The mutual fund is hedged in terms of the number of bonds that it needs to sell, as can be seen from the following:

Number of bonds that need to be sold if the YTM stays the same = 50,00,000/107.2675 = 46,613

Number of bond that need to be sold if it remains unhedged = 50,00,000/96.6500 = 51,733

SUMMARY

Interest rate risk is faced by almost all firms, whether they are borrowing or investing. More predominantly, banks and financial institutions are subject to greater interest rate risk, as all their assets and liabilities are dependent upon the interest rate scenario.

Besides the forward rate agreement, another instrument to cover short-term interest rate risk is the futures contract on T-bills. While the FRA is over the counter, futures on T-bills are exchange-traded, eliminating the counterparty risk and making entry and exit easier for users. Futures contracts are prevalent on T-bills and not on any other corporate debt instruments, because they are available in plenty, are issued from the same source, and contain no default risk. Though not very popular in India, they are very widely traded internationally.

On maturity, a futures contract on T-bills calls for delivery of T-bills maturing 91 days thereafter. The T-bills are discount instruments specified by the discount yield. The actual yield is higher than the discount yields. T-bills on futures are quoted on the basis of an index where the price of the futures becomes inversely proportional to the interest rate, as is the price of the underlying instrument. This is primarily set up to be consistent with all other futures markets, where long positions gain with price rise.

Hedging against falling interest rates is achieved by taking a long position on futures on T-bills. For protection against rising interest rates, the hedger has to take a short position in futures. The gains in the futures position are likely to offset the losses in the physical position of borrowing and investing. Speculation with futures is carried out if one differs with the view of future interest rates reflected in the prices of futures. Arbitrage with T-bills futures is based on the implied repo rate, the reflected price of T-bills in the spot market and futures on them. A repo transaction is selling and buying back of securities at prices fixed now. If the actual repo rate is lower than the implied repo rate, then cash-and-carry arbitrage by selling interest rate futures and later buying them back would yield certain profits. For an actual repo rate higher than the implied repo rate, reverse cash-and-carry arbitrage can be executed.

The futures contract on Eurodollars is another short-term instrument priced in terms of the LIBOR rate. Eurodollars are deposits of US dollars held outside USA, are free from all kinds of regulatory controls, and, thereby, are supposed to reflect free market yields. Unlike T-bills, the yield on Eurodollars is add-on. A futures contract on Eurodollar calls for delivery of a Eurodollar deposit of $1 million maturing three months thereafter. Hedging, speculation, and arbitrage are executed in the same manner as that of futures on T-bills.

For covering long-term interest rate risk, futures on T-bonds are available. The exchange specifies the deliverable instrument against the futures on T-bonds. The short position in T-bond futures normally has a choice of delivering one amongst the many bonds available in the market. All available bonds have price conversion factors attached with them and the seller delivers the bond that is the cheapest. Conversion factors are worked out by the exchange concerned.

Hedge ratio for futures on interest rate depends upon the sensitivity of bond prices with changing yields. Since the sensitivities of the bonds in the portfolio would be different than the bond underlying the futures contract, the optimal hedge ratio becomes dependent upon durations of the bonds.

The market for interest rate futures in India remains in the nascent stage despite their introduction in 2003. Lack of enough liquidity, instruments, and number of participants are some of the reasons that explain the lack of interest in interest rate futures. Of late, interest rate futures are introduced in India with a notional GoI security, with 10 years maturity and 7% coupon payable semi-annually as well as on GoI T-bills.

KEY TERMS

Conversion factor Adjustment of prices of all deliverable bonds against the price of the specified bond in the futures contract is done using the conversion factor.

CTD bond The bond that is the cheapest to deliver, amongst the many bonds that satisfy the delivery requirement under the futures contract.

Discount yield The annualized yield on T-bills, in terms of percentage of the face value of the T-bills.

Eurodollars The US dollars held outside the USA.

Eurodollar futures A futures contract with a Eurodollar deposit as the underlying asset.

Implied repo rate The rate implied by the spot price and the futures price on T-bills.

T-bills These are discount instruments issued by governments for a variety of reasons; they have fixed maturity and are virtually free from default risk.

T-bill futures These are exchange-traded contracts with T-bills as underlying asset, calling for delivery of the T-bills on maturity.

Treasury bond futures A futures contract with T-bonds as underlying asset.

QUESTIONS

7.1 What are T-bills and why are they appropriate instruments as underlying assets for futures contracts?

7.2 How does a futures contract on T-bills help in hedging against fluctuating interest rates?

7.3 What is implied repo rate? How do we compute it?

7.4 How can you arbitrage with T-bill futures if the implied repo rate is greater than the actual repo rate?

7.5 What is the Eurodollar and what is a futures contract on the Eurodollar?

7.6 What are T-bonds and how are T-bond futures specified?

PROBLEMS

P 7.1 Invoice price of T-bills futures
If the price of futures on T-bills is quoted at ₹91.45, what would be the invoice price, assuming a contract size of ₹10 lakh worth of T-bills in face value?

P 7.2 Hedging strategy with T-bills futures
A treasurer is expecting to receive funds of ₹1.25 crore in the next three months; this amount would be in surplus for three months thereafter. A 3-m futures contract on T-bills expiring in 90 days is quoted at ₹89.50, indicating a yield of 10.50%. The treasurer is apprehensive about the yield falling in the days to come. What can the treasurer do to hedge against falling yields?

P 7.3 Yields and T-bills futures
Refer to Problem 7.2. Assume the treasurer books the desired number of futures contracts. What yield would the treasurer realize on the investment if after three months the yield (a) falls to 9.25%, and (b) rises to 11.00%?

P 7.4 Value of a bond
Interest rate futures contracts in India are based on notional 10-year GoI security with a 7% coupon payable semi-annually with face value of ₹100. Find out the value of these futures contracts at YTMs of 6%, 7%, and 8%.

P 7.5 Bond value and duration
You are holding a bond with four years to maturity, bearing a semi-annual coupon of 10%. What is the value of the bond if the YTM is 6%? Find its duration also.

P 7.6 Hedging a long position with interest rate futures
Assume that you are holding 10,000 bonds of the type mentioned in Problem 7.5. The yields in the market are expected to rise uniformly for all maturities. If you wish to hedge against the anticipated decline in value of the bond, what would you do if after three months it is expected that the CTD bond would be a 9-year maturity bond that has a YTM of 7% and duration of 6.4068 years? The futures contract is trading at ₹93.2048, implying a YTM of 6%.

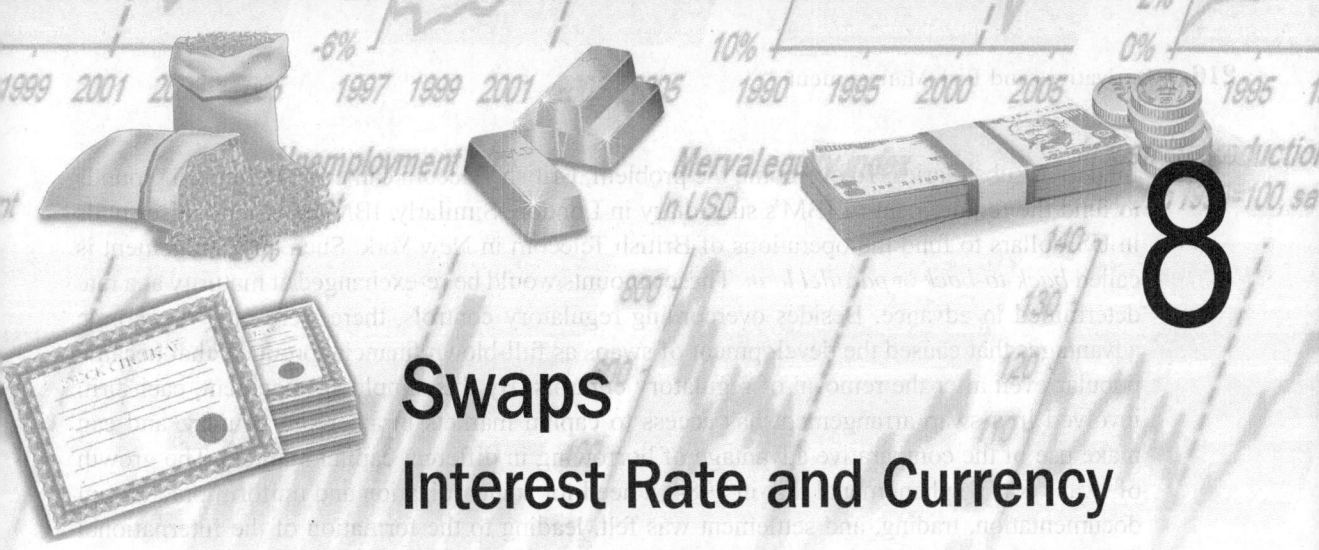

Swaps
Interest Rate and Currency

8

INTRODUCTION

'Necessity is the mother of invention' is a popular saying, and the recent evolution of swaps as financial instruments is a classical example of its validity. There is near unanimity among financial experts that swaps developed out of the constraints and regulatory controls exercised over cross-border capital flow, faced by large corporations in the 1970s. When multinational corporations (MNCs) operating in various countries could not freely remit funds back and forth among their subsidiaries due to exchange controls exercised by various governments on capital flows, they came out with the innovation of back-to-back or parallel loans among themselves. Upon removal of restrictions on capital flows, these loans developed into a full-fledged financial product called swaps. Since then, the market has grown to volumes as big as US $30.5 trillion in foreign exchange swaps and US $22.8 trillion in currency swaps[1] in December 2011—in terms of notional principal involved in swap transactions—and continues to grow at a rapid rate.

> The swap as a financial instrument came into existence due to the presence of exchange controls that restricted the movement of capital from one country to another.

Learning Objectives
After going through this chapter, readers should be familiar with
- the basic concept of swaps, why and how swaps evolved, and the terminology of swaps
- the different types of interest rates and currency swaps
- how to hedge interest rate risk
- how to hedge exchange rate risk through financial swaps
- swap as a tool for reducing financing cost and also as a hedging tool
- how to value a swap
  - as a pair of bonds and
  - as a series of forward contracts
- other swaps such as commodities and equity

Parallel loans involve four parties that agree to re-exchange currencies at a predetermined exchange rate on a pre-decided future date. The four parties usually involve two MNCs and a subsidiary each, in two different countries. Imagine IBM as a USA-based company with a subsidiary in London and British Telecom as another company with operations in New York. The subsidiary of British Telecom needs money in US dollars, while the subsidiary of IBM in London requires funds in pound sterling. Due to regulatory controls, neither IBM USA nor British Telecom can

---
[1] As per Bank of International Settlement's data available for the second half of 2011.

fund their subsidiaries. To overcome the problem, British Telecom can arrange funds in pounds to fund the requirement of IBM's subsidiary in London. Similarly, IBM USA may raise funds in US dollars to fund the operations of British Telecom in New York. Such an arrangement is called *back-to-back* or *parallel loan*. These amounts would be re-exchanged at maturity at a rate determined in advance. Besides overcoming regulatory controls, there were other economic advantages that caused the development of swaps as full-blown financial products that became popular even after the removal of regulatory controls. By this simple arrangement, each firm involved in a swap arrangement has access to capital markets in a foreign country, and can make use of the comparative advantage of borrowing in different capital markets. The growth of swaps was so phenomenal that in 1984, a need for standardization and uniform practices in documentation, trading, and settlement was felt, leading to the formation of the International Swap and Derivatives Association (ISDA).

Back-to-back/parallel loans pose several difficulties: finding matching parties with identical needs in terms of amount of principal, timing, duration of loan, periodicity, and nature (fixed or variable) of interest payments, etc., all of which must match to conclude a successful deal. Solutions to these problems were found by intermediary banks, which later progressed to become dealers in swaps from being mere arrangers of swaps between two parties. Back-to-back loans were an example of financial swaps, which had their origin in the 1970s. By the early 1980s, the same principle was adopted to develop another swap arrangement based on interest rates, known as *interest rate swaps*.

> Swaps overcame the operational difficulties faced in parallel loans, and developed into an instrument independent of the underlying loan transaction.

INTEREST RATE SWAPS

Swap, in the simplest form, may be defined as an exchange of a series of future cash flows between two parties as agreed upon in the terms of a mutual contract. The basis of future cash flows can be the exchange rate for currency/ financial swaps and the interest rate for interest rate swaps. Apart from interest rates and currency rates, the formula for determination of periodic cash flows can include equity returns, commodity prices, etc. In essence, one of the cash flows, called the fixed leg, would be fixed, while the other cash flow, called the floating leg, would be the variable, depending upon the value of the variable identified for the swap.

If the exchange of cash flows is done on the basis of interest rates prevalent at the relevant times, it is known as an interest rate swap. The simplest example of an interest rate swap is a forward contract where only one payment is involved. In a forward transaction of any commodity, the buyer acquires the commodity and incurs an outflow of cash equal to the forward price, F. If the buyer, after acquiring the commodity, were to sell it for the spot price, S, then there would be a cash inflow of S. From the cash flow perspective, a forward contract for a buyer is a swap transaction with inflow of S and outflow of F. The seller would have equivalent cash flows in opposite directions. Therefore, a forward contract can be regarded as a swap with a single exchange of cash flow or, alternatively, a swap can be viewed as a series of several forward transactions taking place at different points of time.

> A swap is a series of exchange of cash flows between two parties, based on terms and conditions agreed upon by them. It is a tailor-made product.

FEATURES OF INTEREST RATE SWAP

Mostly interest rate swaps involve payment of a fixed rate of interest for receiving a floating rate of interest. The basis of exchange of cash flows under an interest rate swap is the interest rate. This fixed-for-floating swap is commonly known as the *plain vanilla swap*, depicted in Fig. 8.1, where company A agrees to pay company B a fixed interest rate of 8.50% in exchange for receiving from company B interest at 30 bps (100 bps = 1%) above the floating interest rate MIBOR (Mumbai InterBank Offer Rate), at predetermined intervals of time.

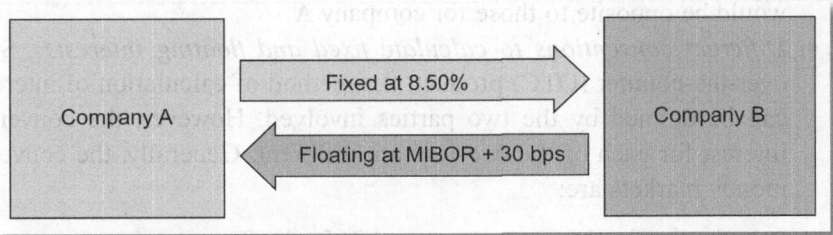

Fig. 8.1 Plain vanilla interest rate swap

Assume that the swap contract between company A and company B is (a) for a period of three years, (b) with semi-annual exchange of interest, and (c) on a notional principal of ₹50 crore. The cash flows for company A for six semi-annual periods for an assumed MIBOR would as per Table 8.1. The amount received/paid by company A is paid/received by company B.

> Cash flows under interest rate swaps are based on a notional principal and are netted, making them independent of the original loan amounts.

Within the context of this example, the salient features of the swap contract may be noted as follows:

- *Effective date* All the cash flows pertaining to the fixed leg are known at the time of entering the swap at $T = 0$, referred to as the *effective date*.
- *Resetting of floating leg cash flow* The cash flow for the floating leg of the swap is determined one period in advance, when the floating rate is known. Thus, at the time of entering the swap, the first set of cash flows of interest is known. The first receipt of cash flow at $T = 6$ months is known at $T = 0$, and is done at the MIBOR of 8% plus

Table 8.1 Cash flow under swap for company A

Time, months	MIBOR, %	Cash flow, ₹lakh		
		Fixed leg	Floating leg	Net
0	8.00			
6	8.15	−212.50	207.50	−5.00
12	8.20	−212.50	211.25	−1.25
18	8.45	−212.50	212.50	0.00
24	8.30	−212.50	218.75	6.25
30	8.50	−212.50	215.00	2.50
36	8.75	−212.50	220.00	7.50

Note: Cash flow for floating leg is decided one period in advance.

30 bps. The date on which the next floating rate payment is decided is called the *reset date*. It will come up every six months in swaps with semi-annual payments.
- *Notional principal* No principal amount is exchanged either at the initiation or at the conclusion of the swap. It remains a notional figure for determination of the amount of interest applicable to both the legs.
- *Exchange differential cash flow* The exchange of interest is done on a net basis, as depicted in the last column of Table 8.1, with positive signs indicating cash inflows and negative signs indicating cash outflows for company A. The cash flows for company B would be opposite to those for company A.
- *Different conventions to calculate fixed and floating interests* Since a swap is an over-the-counter (OTC) product, the method of calculation of interest on the two legs can be defined by the two parties involved. However, the conventions to calculate interest for each of the two legs are different. Generally, the conventions followed in money markets are:

    for the fixed leg   : actual/365
    for the floating leg : actual/360

If the actual number of days in a 6-m period are 182, the amount of interest on both the legs for the first cash flow would be different from the interest rates shown in Table 8-1 and the exact amount is calculated as follows:

For Fixed Leg: Principal × Interest rate × $\dfrac{\text{Nos. of days}}{365}$

$$= 50{,}00{,}000 \times 0.085 \times \dfrac{182}{365} = ₹2{,}11{,}918$$

For Floating Leg: Principal × Interest rate × $\dfrac{\text{Nos. of days}}{360}$

$$= 50{,}00{,}000 \times 0.083 \times \dfrac{182}{360} = ₹2{,}09{,}805$$

For simplicity of exposition in the example we assumed 180 days in each semi-annual period, with a 360-day year for both the legs.

NEED FOR SWAP INTERMEDIARY: SWAP DEALER/BANK

The illustration in the previous section assumed perfect matching of the needs of company A and company B. That brings up this interesting question: how do company A and company B find each other in this big world? Normally, firms prefer not to disclose their specific needs in terms of loans, borrowings, and interest rates. Even the importers and exporters are rarely involved in direct transactions of buying and selling foreign currency in the forward markets. All of them resort to banks for this purpose.

Apart from difficulties in locating each other, if company A and company B were to set up a swap arrangement directly, they would most likely face the following problems.

- Both of them would assume default risk (also known as counterparty risk) associated with the swap on each other, as either party may fail to honour its commitments under the swap.

> Swap intermediaries promote market development by filling the gaps in terms of matching of needs, warehousing, and assuming of counterparty risk.

- Matching mutual needs in terms of principal amount of borrowing, the timing, the periodicity of payment of interest, and the final redemption of the borrowing could indeed be a difficult task.

The existence of intermediaries came into play in order to overcome this sort of problem in swap agreements. Without intermediaries, the swap market would remain extremely small. In fact, the growth in swaps is primarily attributed to the roles banks have played as swap intermediaries. We now proceed to write about the functions of a swap intermediary.

Facilitating the Swap Deal Difficulties in finding a matching counterparty can be mitigated if an intermediary is involved. The intermediary or the swap dealer is normally a bank with a widespread network. Due to their deep knowledge of financial markets, huge networks of customers, and exact understanding of client needs, banks are better placed to locate matching counterparties. Many banks offer forward rates to facilitate foreign exchange transactions. Similarly, a few banks act as market makers in swaps and offer a ready market with opportunities for firms to enter into and exit from swap deals.

Warehousing Banks perform the role of market maker in swaps. One can obtain a quote on demand for a swap deal from a bank without waiting for a matching counterparty. There are several requirements that have to be matched. For example, one party may look for an interest rate swap for ₹100 crore on semi-annual basis for three years, while another party may want a swap for ₹80 crore on a quarterly basis for 2½ years only. Here, the bank may take up exposure of ₹20 crore in the hope of finding another suitable party for that amount in the near future. This is called *warehousing*, where the bank may enter swaps on its own. The bank carries the risk of interest rate fluctuations till a matching counterparty is found. The risk of interest rate in the interim is normally covered through interest rate futures. Hedging through interest rate futures has to be done only for net exposure in swaps, as banks are likely to have a portfolio of swaps that can nullify the interest rate risk for a major part of the exposure.

Assuming Counterparty Risk Most important of all, banks mitigate counterparty risk for both the parties to the swap by becoming the counterparty to each of them. In the example depicted in Fig. 8.1, company A would be far more comfortable if the counterparty was a bank, rather than company B. The same would be true for company B. When a bank becomes a counterparty, the overall risk attached to the swap transaction, which normally is large due to its long-term nature, stands reduced substantially.

Of course, for providing a facilitating role and assuming the counterparty risk, the swap dealer needs to earn some remuneration. This has to be borne by the two parties to the swap transaction. However, each of the party stands to gain in terms of having an exact deal, achieving the desired timing, and reducing the counterparty risk. The benefits are worth the cost.

Figure 8.2 depicts a swap transaction with a bank as an intermediary, charging 5 bps from each party, as each of them receives 5 bps less than what they would receive without the intermediary (see Fig. 8.1). Company A pays a fixed interest rate, 8.50%, to the bank, which pays only 8.45% to company B. In exchange, the bank receives a floating interest from company B at M + 30 bps, but pays 5 bps less to company A at M + 25 bps. The bank hence earns 10 bps.

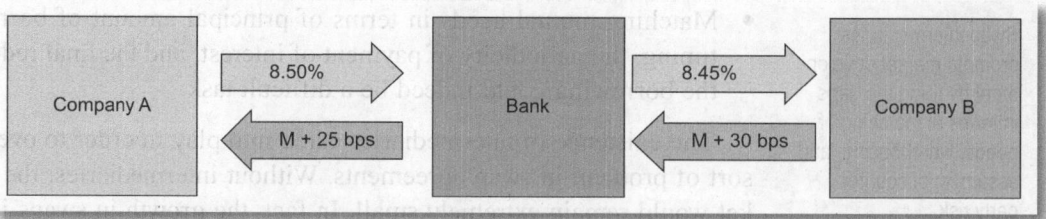

Fig. 8.2 Plain vanilla interest rate swap with intermediary

APPLICATIONS OF INTEREST RATE SWAPS

Having explained the mechanism of the swap transaction, let us focus on what swaps can achieve. Swaps can be used to (a) transform a floating rate liability to a fixed rate liability and vice versa, (b) transform a floating rate asset to a fixed rate asset and vice versa, (c) hedge against fluctuating interest rates, and most importantly, (d) reduce the cost of funds. We now examine each of these factors.

Transforming Nature of Liabilities

Interest rate swaps are generally used for creating synthetic fixed or floating rate liabilities with a view to hedge against adverse movement of interest rates. Let us consider company A, which has borrowed from the market on a floating rate basis at MIBOR + 25 bps. It pays to its lenders at floating rate. Further, it considers that interest rates would rise in the future. In view of the possibility of rising interest rates, company A would like to have a liability that is fixed, rather than variable, in nature. Therefore, it decides to enter into a swap with a bank by paying a fixed 8.50% and receiving MIBOR + 30 bps, as depicted in Fig. 8.3.

Company A pays a fixed interest rate, 8.50%, to the bank. The bank pays M + 30 bps in return. Company A continues to pay M + 25 bps to its lenders, as originally agreed. What is the result of this swap? It simply transforms the liability to a fixed rate at 8.45% p.a., as shown in Fig 8.3.

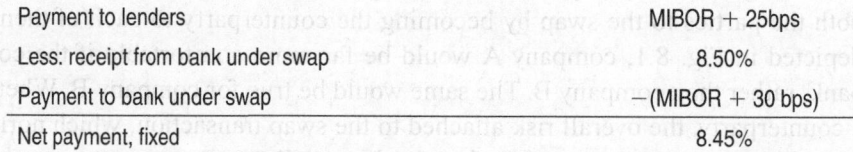

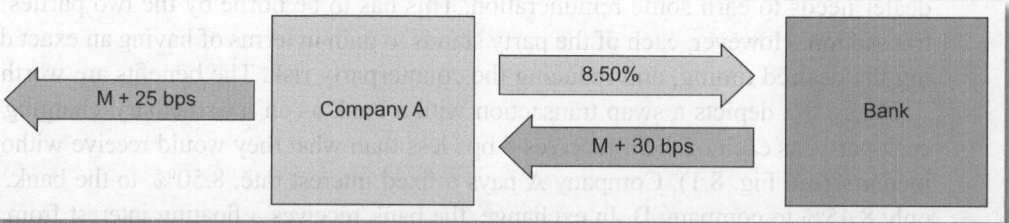

Fig. 8.3 Swap to transform floating rate liability to fixed rate

Similarly, company B can transform its fixed rate liability to a floating rate liability by entering a swap with a bank paying a floating interest rate and receiving a fixed one. Naturally, company B would use such a swap when it believes that interest rates are likely to fall in the future, and locking-in a lower floating rate would prove advantageous. Refer to Example 8.1 for an illustration.

EXAMPLE 8.1   Changing nature of liability from fixed to floating

Five years ago, Fasteners Ltd had raised loans through a 10-year debenture issue worth ₹100 crore with a fixed interest rate of 12%. After the issue, the interest rates remained constant for some time, but have since come down to around 10%, and are likely to come down further. Fasteners Ltd wishes to contain the cost of funding for the remaining five years. A bank has offered a swap rate of 9.50–9.60% against MIBOR for a period of five years. Depict the swap arrangement and find out the new nature of liabilities the firm can have.

Solution
Fasteners Ltd has a liability with a fixed interest rate of 12%. By entering into a swap with the bank, it may transform interest on the liability from a fixed rate to a floating rate based on MIBOR. Under the swap arrangement, Fasteners Ltd can receive a fixed rate and pay MIBOR. The bid rate of the swap (9.50%) would be applicable. The swap arrangement is shown as below:

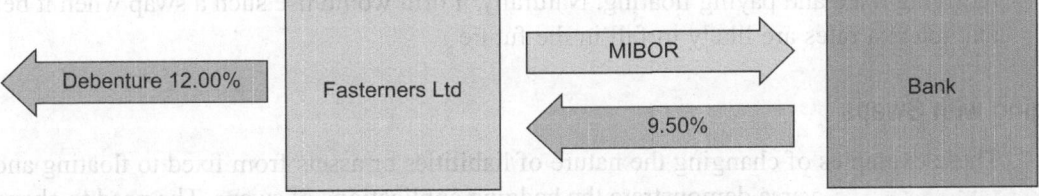

The cost of funds for Fasteners Ltd would be 12.00% − 9.50% + MIBOR = MIBOR + 2.50%.
In case the interest rates fall below 9.50%, which is expected, the firm would end up paying less interest than what it is paying now. The interest rate payable would be market based.

Transforming Nature of Assets

Assets provide income to investing firms based on the interest rates. If the interest rates fall, the income too falls. In circumstance of falling interest rates, firms would like to change the complexion of assets that are on floating rates to fixed rates. Similarly, in times of rising interest rates, firms earning fixed rates of interest would like to remain with the market trend.

Now assume that company A has made an investment by subscribing to bonds carrying a 9% fixed coupon. The bonds have still some years to mature but the interest rates are showing a rising trend, which is expected to continue. Company A faces a potential loss of income.

What should company A do to mitigate the risk associated with the rising interest rates? Changing its portfolio of bonds by selling fixed rate bonds and buying floating rate bonds is one solution. An easier way is to enter the swap depicted in Fig. 8.4, where it receives a floating, MIBOR + 30 bps and pays a fixed rate, 8.50%.

By doing so, the nature of income is transformed from a fixed 9.00% to a floating MIBOR + 80 bps:

> Swaps alter the characteristics of an asset or liability from fixed to floating or floating to fixed, without disturbing the original contract.

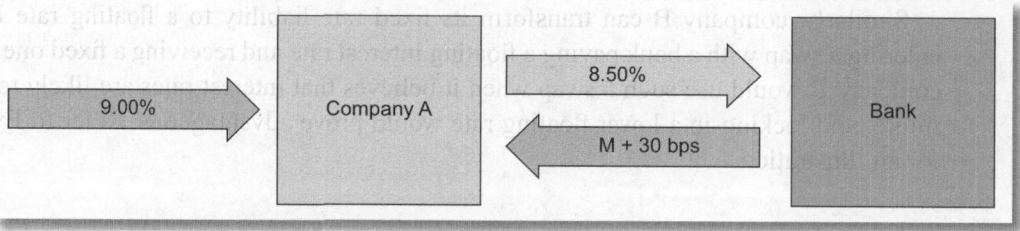

Fig. 8.4 Swap to transform fixed rate asset into floating rate

Receipt from investments	9.00%
Less: Payment to bank under swap	−8.50%
Receipt from bank under swap	MIBOR + 30 bps
Net receipts, floating	MIBOR + 80 bps

If MIBOR moves beyond 8.20% in the future, company A would benefit from the situation. Similarly, one can transform a floating rate income to fixed rate income by entering a swap receiving fixed and paying floating. Naturally, a firm would use such a swap when it believes that interest rates are likely to fall in the future.

Hedging with Swaps

These examples of changing the nature of liabilities or assets from fixed to floating and vice versa demonstrate the hedging applications of swaps. The need to change the complexion of assets and liabilities arises only when the firms stand to gain from such an exercise. Swaps can be fruitfully used to hedge against an adverse interest rate situation, as condensed in Table 8.2.

> The transformable nature of assets and liabilities (from fixed rate to floating rate, or vice versa) helps hedge against the adverse movement of interest rates.

There are many ways to hedge against adverse situations but sometimes a swap agreement hedges the anticipated risk more efficiently. For example, a firm may have borrowed for 10 years on a fixed rate basis. After a few years, if the interest rates start a downward movement, one possible recourse for the firm is to approach the lender to change the nature of loan from fixed to floating. The lender might resist switching to a floating rate of interest. A better course of action is to set up a swap arrangement with another party. The firm achieves its objective without involving the original lender and any of its additional terms and conditions.

Table 8.2 Hedging strategies with swaps

Assets		
Nature	Risk	Hedging action
Fixed rate	Rising interest rates	Swap to transform the nature of asset from fixed rate to floating rate
Floating rate	Falling interest rates	Swap to transform the nature of asset from floating rate to fixed rate
Liabilities		
Fixed rate	Falling interest rates	Swap to transform the liability from fixed rate to floating rate
Floating rate	Rising interest rates	Swap to transform the liability form floating rate to fixed rate.

Derivatives in Practice

Interest Rate Swaps

Interest rate swaps in India—Overnight swap

With the view of deepening the money market and enabling banks, primary dealers, and all-India financial institutions to hedge interest rate risks, the Reserve Bank of India has allowed scheduled commercial banks, primary dealers, and all-India financial institutions to make markets in interest rate swaps from July 1999. However, the market that has taken off most seriously so far is the one based on overnight index swaps. The benchmarks for tenor beyond overnight have not become popular due to the absence of a vibrant interbank term money market.

The National Stock Exchange (NSE) in India publishes MIBOR rates for three other terms, that is, 14 days, one month, and three months. The other longer-tenor benchmark that is available is the yield based on forex forward premiums. This is called MIFOR (Mumbai interbank forward offered rate). Reuters' published 1-m, 3-m, 6-m, and 1-year MIFORs are the market standard for this benchmark.

The overnight index swap is a rupee interest rate swap where the floating rate is linked to an overnight interbank call money index. The swap will be flexible in tenor, i.e., there is no restriction on the tenor of the swap. Interest would be computed on a notional principal amount and settled on a net basis at maturity. On the floating rate side, the interest amounts are compounded on a daily basis, based on the index. At the moment, the NSE overnight MIBOR is the most widely used floating rate index, the Reuters' overnight MIBOR being the other reference rate used.

For example, consider that bank A is a fixed rate receiver for ₹5 crore for a period of one week at 10%, and bank B is a receiver of floating rate linked to the overnight index. The NSE MIBOR rates for seven days are taken and settled at the end of the swap period. At the end of the period of one week, i.e., the eighth day, bank B will have to pay to bank A ₹95,890 (which is the interest on ₹5 crore for seven days at 10%), and has to receive ₹97,508 from A. The payments are netted and the only payment that takes place is a payment by A of ₹1608 (97,508 − 95,890) to B.

Based on 365 days p.a.

Day	NSE MIBOR index, %	Notional principal amount (₹)	Interest for one day (₹)
1	10.25	5,00,00,000	14,041
2	10.00	5,00,14,041	13,702
3	9.75	5,00,27,743	13,363
4	10.125	5,00,41,107	13,881
5 and 6	10.25	5,00,54,988	28,113
7	10.50	5,00,83,101	14,407
TOTAL		5,00,97,508	

Similarly, a fund may have subscribed to a portfolio of fixed rate bonds to generate a desired level of income. If interest rates rise subsequent to the subscription, the fund loses the opportunity to raise its income. One of the alternatives available is to change the portfolio from fixed rate to floating rate bonds. This may face serious limitations, such as lack of availability of such bonds and transaction costs associated with change of the portfolio. An attractive alternative is to enter a swap to transform the nature of assets from fixed to floating, where the fund receives a cash flow based on floating rates in exchange for paying a fixed rate. More importantly, the swap transaction remains off the balance sheet, thereby keeping the much-desired confidentiality.

Reducing Cost of Funds

Perhaps the most important application of swaps, which also seems to be the primary reason for its popularity and growth, is its potential of saving the cost of financing.

An example will illustrate how swaps can be used to reduce financing cost. Assume that a highly rated firm, rated AAA, can raise funds in the fixed rate market at 10% and in the

> One of the major applications of swaps is to reduce the cost of financing.

floating rate market at MIBOR + 100 bps. The current rate of MIBOR is 8%. Another firm, comparatively rated lower, at 'A', can mobilize capital at 12% and MIBOR + 200 bps in the fixed rate and floating rate markets, respectively.

Clearly, firm rated AAA has an advantage over firm rated A, both in the fixed market as well as in the floating market. This advantage can be tabulated as follows:

	Firm rated AAA	Firm rated A	Advantage AAA
Fixed rate	10%	12%	200 bps
Floating rate	MIBOR + 100 bps	MIBOR + 200 bps	100 bps

We further assume that firm rated AAA is interested in borrowing at a floating rate (at MIBOR + 100 bps) and firm rated A wants to borrow in the fixed rate market (at 12%). Notice that for the lower-rated firm, the spread in the fixed rate market is more than for the higher-rated firm. The two firms can set up a swap as follows:

- Firm rated AAA goes to the fixed rate market and borrows at 10%, rather than tapping the floating rate market at MIBOR + 100 bps.
- Firm rated A mobilizes funds from the floating rate market at MIBOR + 200 bps, rather than mobilizing from the fixed rate market at 12%.
- Having accessed different markets by going against their original choice, now the firms enter a swap where,
  - firm rated AAA pays the firm rated A floating at MIBOR + 200 bps
  - firm rated A pays firm AAA fixed at 11.5%

These actions and the resultant impact on the cost of funds for firm rated AAA and firm rated A are shown in Fig. 8.5.

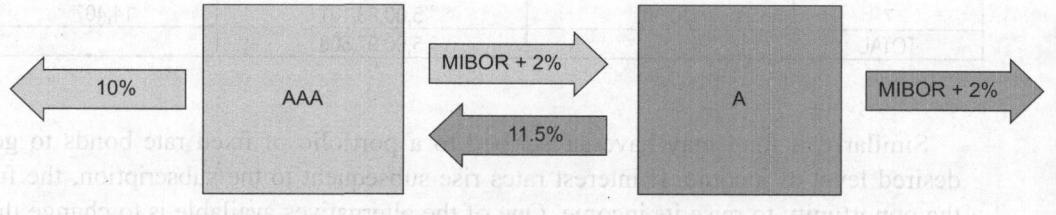

Cost of funds for firms

	AAA	A
1. Payment to investors	10%	MIBOR + 2%
2. Payment to counterparty	MIBOR + 2%	11.5%
3. Receipt from counterparty	11.5%	MIBOR + 2%
Cost of borrowing (1 + 2 − 3)	**MIBOR + 0.5%**	**11.5%**
IMPACT	Firm can raise funds at MIBOR+0.50%, as against MIBOR+1% without the swap, gaining 0.50%	Firm can raise funds at 11.5% as against 12% without the swap, gaining 0.50%

Fig. 8.5 Interest rate swap—reducing cost of funds

As against a fixed payment of 10% to its original lenders, firm rated AAA pays a floating rate of MIBOR + 200 bps and receives a fixed rate of 11.5%. This not only transforms the liability from fixed to floating rate, as the firm wanted in the first place, but also reduces the cost to MIBOR + 50 bps, as against MIBOR + 100 bps that it would have incurred without the swap, thereby gaining an advantage of 50 bps. Similarly, firm rated A too can transform its liability to a fixed rate as it initially desired, and can also reduce the cost of funds to 11.50%, as against the 12.00%, which it would have incurred if it were to go to the market directly. The swap again gives an advantage of 50 bps.

RATIONALE FOR SWAP—COMPARATIVE ADVANTAGE

The remarkable characteristic of the swap agreement was its ability to reduce the cost of funds for both the firms, as shown in Fig. 8.5. Normally, one expects to gain at the expense of the other, as it is reasonable to assume that derivatives are a zero-sum game. The explanation behind why both the parties in a swap agreement gain lies in the theory of comparative advantage.

Regardless of the fact that the firm rated AAA held an edge over the firm rated A in both types of borrowing, comparative advantage played a significant role in the successful completion of the swap transaction between the two firms. Firm rated AAA had an absolute advantage of 200 bps in the fixed rate market and 100 bps in the floating rate market. Alternatively, we can say that firm rated AAA had a comparative advantage of 100 (difference between the two absolute advantages) in the fixed rate market. Put another way, firm rated A had a relative advantage in the floating rate market. The comparative advantage of 100 bps was available for exploitation by both the firms, at the expense of distortions in the financial market.

Therefore, it makes sense for the firm rated AAA to access the fixed rate market, where it had a greater absolute advantage, and then enter into the swap to transform its fixed rate liability into a floating rate one. Similarly, firm rated A must access the floating rate market and then enter into the swap to transform its floating rate liability into a fixed rate one. The total benefit for both the firms would remain fixed at 100 bps, and the amounts of fixed and floating rates would determine who gets how much of the benefit. Of course, sharing of benefit would depend upon the negotiating powers of the two firms involved.

The aggregate advantage remains fixed at a comparative advantage of 100 bps. In case of a direct deal between the firm rated AAA and the firm rated A as depicted in Fig. 8.5, the benefit was shared equally by both the firms. In case such a deal were to be structured by an intermediary, such as a bank, serving as counterparty to each, some part of the benefit would be sacrificed by each of the party. This benefit goes to the bank. One such deal, where the bank gets 20 bps (10 bps each) is depicted in Fig. 8.6 and Table 8.3.

> Reduction in cost of funding through swaps is based on the principle of comparative advantage, and is a classical application of credit arbitrage.

The exploitation of the comparative advantage by the firms is a clear case of arbitrage on the credit rating. The fixed rate market demanded a greater premium from the lower rated firm than did the floating rate market, forcing the firm to access the floating rate market. The premium demanded by the higher rated firm for a fixed rate was lower than the market, making the swap deal attractive. The question that arises is: how can a competitive market

EXAMPLE 8.2 Interest rate swap to reduce funding cost

Two Indian firms, IndoPlas and IndoCar, are contemplating raising finance of ₹100 crore each. They have been offered the following loans by a bank.

	Fixed rate	Floating rate
IndoPlas	12.00%	MIBOR + 70 bps
IndoCar	11.00%	MIBOR + 30 bps

Another bank, acting as a swap intermediary, is willing to work out a swap arrangement for a fee of 5 bps from each firm. IndoCar believes that the interest rate would fall and, hence, wants to raise funds on a floating rate basis. IndoPlas feels otherwise, and wants to raise funds on a fixed interest rate basis. What swap can be arranged between the two parties? What would be the saving in financing cost for each firm if benefits of swap are shared equally?

Solution

The absolute advantage for IndoCar is 100 bps in the fixed rate market, while it is 40 bps in the floating rate market. Although IndoCar wants to raise finance at a floating rate, the firm must access the fixed rate market and then enter into a swap deal with IndoPlas to convert the liability from fixed rate to floating rate. The total benefit to be availed of is 60 bps, the differential of absolute advantage for IndoCar in the two markets. The bank would charge 10 bps as a fee. The remaining 50 bps may be shared equally by both the parties through a swap. One such structure is presented as follows:

Interest rate swap: A schematic view with an intermediary

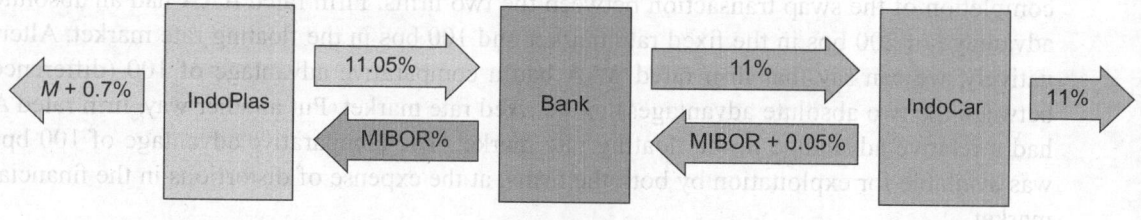

Cost of borrowing

	Indocar	IndoPlas
Payment to investors	11%	MIBOR + 0.7%
Payment to bank	MIBOR + 0.05%	11.05%
Receipt from bank	11%	MIBOR
Cost of borrowing (1 + 2 − 3)	**MIBOR + 0.05%**	**11.75%**

The aggregate cost of funds for IndoCar would be MIBOR + 5 bps, a saving of 25 bps if it accesses the floating rate market. Similarly, IndoPlas obtains funds at 11.75% against 12% without the swap deal, resulting in an advantage of 25 bps.

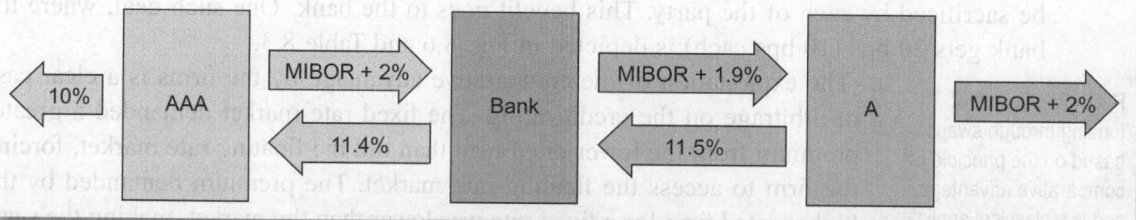

Fig. 8.6 Interest rate swap: A schematic view with intermediary

Table 8.3 Sharing benefits of swap

	AAA	A
Payment to investors	10.00%	MIBOR + 2.00%
Payment to bank	MIBOR + 2.00%	11.50%
Receipt from bank	11.40%	MIBOR + 1.90%
Cost of borrowing (1 + 2 − 3)	MIBOR + 0.60%	11.60%
Cost with direct access to the market	MIBOR + 1.00%	12.00%
Savings	40 bps	40 bps
Earning for the bank	11.50% − 11.40% + (M + 2.00%) − (M + 1.90%) = **0.20% or 20 bps**	

allow this aberration to take place? The answer seems to lie in the gap in the information the market has on firm rated AAA and the firm rated A. Lenders, while lending on a floating rate basis, have the opportunity to review rates every six months, and for the firm rated higher, the spread would usually be a smaller one. In the fixed rate market, the spread would be larger for lower-rated firms. Lenders could rely more on firm rated AAA than they could on firm rated A. The spread in the two markets are unequal due to unequal rating of the firms. The differential of spread reflects the differential of likely default by firm rated A relative to firm rated AAA.

The theory of comparative advantage has been used to structure swap transactions in a manner that both parties in the swaps are able to reduce their costs of funds. Generally, a firm with higher credit rating is able to procure funds at lower rates of interest than a firm with lower credit rating, irrespective of whether the borrowing is on a fixed or a floating rate basis. The firm with higher credit rating is said to enjoy an absolute advantage over the firm with lower credit rating in both the fixed rate and the floating rate markets. The advantage of the higher-rated firm over the lower-rated firm is called the *credit quality spread*.

Despite a credit quality spread in both the fixed rate and the floating rate markets, it may be beneficial for the higher-rated firm to engage in a swap deal with the lower-rated firm due to the likelihood that the credit spreads in both the markets would not be equal. The differential of the two absolute advantages measures the comparative advantage, which in turn forms the basis of the swap deal. This comparative advantage is the aggregate benefit that both parties to the swap deal can share, in proportion to the bargaining powers of each.

> Swaps serve as a tool for reducing financing cost, because of the credit quality spreads prevailing in the different kinds of markets.

Swaps are, therefore, a product resulting from arbitrage on credit rating. The question is, will this credit arbitrage continue? Most likely, the answer is 'yes', as long as gaps in information and credibility remain.

TYPES OF INTEREST RATE SWAPS

Interest rate swaps can be categorized as follows:

Fixed-to-floating In fixed-to-floating rate swaps, the party pays a fixed rate of interest to the bank or swap dealer and in exchange, receives a floating rate of interest determined on the basis of a reference/benchmark rate at predetermined intervals of time. Such a swap is used by a firm that has a floating rate liability and anticipates a rise in the interest rates. Through the swap, the firm will cancel out the receipts and payments of the floating rate and have a cash outflow based on the fixed rate of interest.

> The IRS has two legs of payment of interest, both of which may be based on different parameters, with one leg fixed and the other floating, or with both floating, but on different benchmarks.

Floating-to-fixed In this kind of swap, the party pays a floating rate of interest to the bank or swap dealer and in exchange, receives a fixed rate of interest at predetermined intervals of time. Such a swap is used by a firm that has a fixed rate liability and anticipates a fall in the interest rates. Through the swap, the firm will cancel out the receipts and payments of the fixed rate liability and have a cash outflow based on the floating rate of interest.

Basis Swap In contrast to the fixed-to-floating or floating-to-fixed swaps, where one leg is based on the fixed rate of interest, the basis swap involves cash flows of both the legs based on a floating rate. However, the reference rates for determining the two legs of payment are different. Basis swaps are used where the parties to the contract are tied to one asset or liability based on one reference rate, and want to convert to another reference rate. For example, if a firm having liabilities based on the T-bills rate wants to convert them to a MIBOR-based rate, then the firm can enter a basis swap where it pays a MIBOR-based interest to the swap dealer in exchange for receiving interest based on the T-bills rate.

CURRENCY SWAPS

In a currency swap, the exchange of cash flows between counterparties takes place in two different currencies on the basis of a predetermined formula of exchange rates. Since two currencies are involved, currency swaps are different from interest rate swaps in their uses, functionality, and administration. The first recorded currency swap was initiated in 1981 between IBM and the World Bank.

> Currency swaps, also called financial swaps, are exchanges of cash flows in two different currencies, based on exchange rates.

More complex swaps involve two currencies with fixed and floating rates of interest in two currencies. Such swaps are called *cocktail swaps*—an example is a swap where one party pays 4% in US dollar and receives in LIBOR-based Swiss franc.

World Bank–IBM Currency Swap

The idea of swap was provided by a historical deal in August 1981 when the World Bank entered a swap deal with IBM through Salomon Brothers. The World Bank and IBM entered into a deal to exchange, whereby the two exchanged liabilities in US dollars, Swiss francs, and Deutsche marks. It was the first ever currency swap that recognized the cost-saving potential of the instrument for borrowing by the two parties involved.

The World Bank was looking for funds at a minimum cost for onward lending to developing countries for various projects. The cost consideration was paramount for them because of their inability to charge higher rates of interest from developing countries. In August 1981, the prevailing interest rates for US dollars were around 17%. In contrast, the interest rates in Switzerland and Germany were 8% and 11%, respectively. This interest rate scenario suggested depreciation of the dollar by about 9% against the Swiss franc and 6% against the Deutsche mark. The World Bank believed that depreciation of the dollar would not be as much as suggested by the interest rate differentials, and, hence, it would be inexpensive to borrow in Swiss francs and Deutsche marks.

The World Bank had borrowed its permissible limit in Switzerland and the same was true of the then West Germany. The World Bank, with a credit rating of AAA and backing by several nations such as the USA, Germany, and Japan, was well placed to get a lower financing rate in US dollars at the treasury rate plus 40 bps in the bond market. Another worldwide corporation, IBM, could mobilize funds in US dollar at treasury plus 55 bps. In the Swiss market, the World Bank could raise funds at the Swiss treasury rate plus 20 bps. The problem for the World Bank was that it had exhausted its borrowing capacity in the Swiss and German markets. Constantly searching for low cost funds, the World Bank had approached Swiss and German bond markets frequently in the past. Having already borrowed heavily in both the markets, it had reached saturation levels. Further borrowing was discouraged by lenders. The discouragement to borrow further was manifested in raised interest rates, as is the practice in all markets to contain excessive exposures.

In contrast to this, IBM could raise funds in the Swiss market at the best rate. It could borrow at the Swiss treasury rate and held an advantage of 20 bps over the World Bank, but had a poor rate if it were to borrow in US dollars. At the same time, IBM believed that the US dollar would depreciate much beyond the interest rate differentials of the US dollar vis-a-vis the Swiss franc and the Deutsche mark. It already had loans outstanding in Swiss francs and Deutsche marks, as given in Table 8.4.

The desire of the World Bank to raise money in Swiss francs and Deutsche marks and the existing obligations of IBM in these currencies along with its willingness to raise funds in US dollars created a common meeting ground for the two. The contrasting views of IBM and the World Bank regarding the expected depreciation of the US dollar (the World Bank anticipated a lesser depreciation and IBM expected a higher depreciation of the dollar than reflected by the interest rate differentials) was the main motivation for fruitful engagement in a swap deal.

Table 8.4 Details of loans of IBM for swap with the World Bank

	Swiss franc (CHF) loan	Deutsche mark (DM) loan
Principal, *in millions*	200.00	300.00
Due date for bullet repayment of the principal	30 March 1986	30 March 1986
Annual interest outflow due March 30 each year, *in millions*	12.375	30.000
Effective interest rate	6.187%	10.000%
Interest rate prevailing in August 1981	8.00%	11.00%
Present value of loans in August 1981, in millions	191.37	301.32
Exchange rate prevailing in August 1981, units/dollar	2.18	2.56
Equivalent dollar of present value of loans, in millions	87.78	117.70

The loan liabilities of IBM in Swiss franc and Deutsche mark added up to US $205.48 million in present value terms, as shown in Table 8.4. IBM was willing to pay 16% on a US dollar loan. After adjusting for the issue expenses, the World Bank issued a debt aggregating to US $210 million with maturity on 31 March 1986, coinciding with IBM's loans. Subsequent to the debt raised by the World Bank, cash flows were exchanged whereby IBM paid US dollar obligations at 16% for a principal of US $210 million and the World Bank paid the Swiss franc and Deutsche mark obligations of IBM. A schematic diagram of the swap is presented in Fig. 8.7. Flows of principal amount from World Bank to IBM and vice versa and its repayment at the end of the swap were not required. These flows are shown in Fig. 8.7 to enable an understanding of the mechanism of a swap transaction.

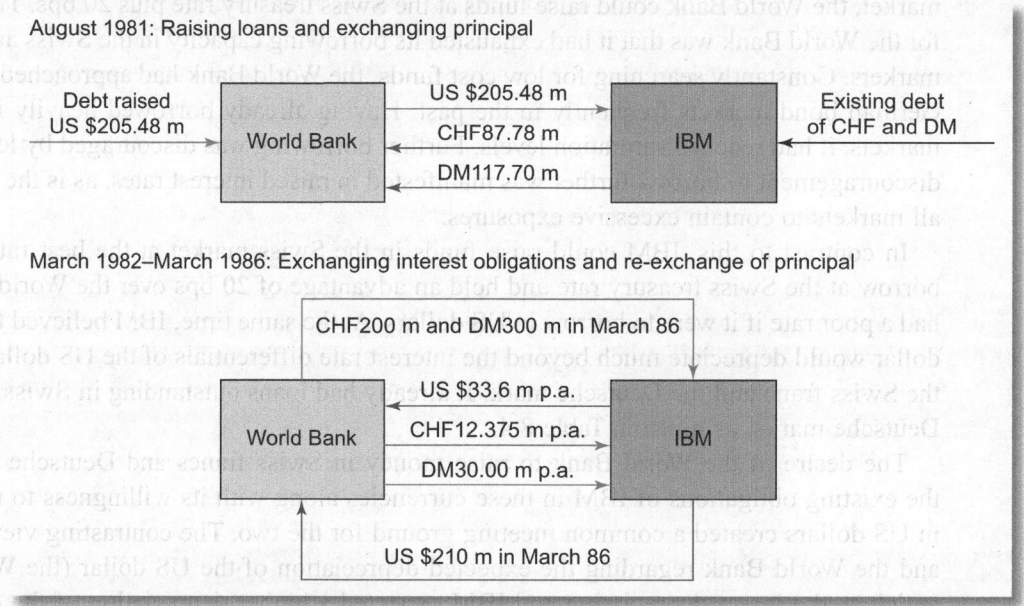

Fig. 8.7 Swap transaction of IBM and the World Bank

The advantage of the swap arrangement was that IBM got US dollars at a lower rate and at the same time the World Bank also received Swiss franc and Deutsche mark loans at lower rates, capitalizing on the strength of each other in the respective currencies. Both IBM and the World Bank got what they wanted. If the World Bank borrowed US dollars and lent them to IBM at US Treasury + 40 bps, it would not incur any loss, and IBM would get a better rate. If IBM borrowed Swiss francs and lent them to the World Bank at Swiss Treasury + 10 bps, IBM would make 10 bps, and so would the World Bank. If both the loans were raised, it would have resulted in a profit of 15 bps to IBM and a profit of 10 bps to the World Bank.

Since IBM and World Bank both borrowed the same amount of money, there is no need to exchange the principal since they cancel each other. On each due date, IBM would pay interest on the US dollar loan of the World Bank and receive interest on the Swiss franc and Deutsche mark loans from the World Bank. However, as the principals were not exchanged in the first place, it was not necessary to re-exchange the principal subsequently. Counterparty risk, i.e., risk of default, was almost non-existent, as both the parties had a sound AAA credit rating.

Banks and financial intermediaries were quick to seize upon the idea, and soon started broking swap deals for a fee. The swap had greater appeal in saving borrowing cost rather than in managing risk. The development of the swaps market has been rapid since the IBM–World Bank swap. It has grown tremendously. Today, swaps are possibly the largest derivative in the market. According to the Bank of International Settlement (BIS), there is over 60 trillion dollars of notional value of transactions in the year 2001, out of a market total of 180 trillion dollars. According to the triennial survey of BIS in 2010, the daily average in foreign currency swaps amounted to US $1745 million out of a total daily turnover of US $3370 million. This is estimated to be more than 15 *times* the size of the US public equities market. In 1987, according to the ISDA, swaps had a total notional value of $865.6 billion. By mid-2006, this figure exceeded $250 trillion, and in the first half of 2010, it stood at $434 *trillion.*

Back-to-back/parallel loans posed several difficulties: finding parties with identical needs in terms of amount of principal, timing and duration of loans, periodicity, and nature (fixed or variable) of interest payments. All of these parameters must match to conclude a successful deal. Solutions to these problems were found by intermediary banks, which progressed later to becoming dealers in swaps, from mere arrangers of swaps between two parties. Back-to-back loans, which originated in the 1970s, are examples of financial swap agreements. Problems associated with back-to-back loans were overcome by banks, and the intermediary role played by banks made these loans a very popular financial product.

The underlying principle that underlines the swap is the exploitation of the comparative advantage of two counterparties, as was done in the World Bank–IBM swap. Although the first swap was a currency swap between the World Bank and IBM, the swap market has been mainly driven by the fixed-for-floating interest rate swaps market.

Hedging Against Exchange Rate Risk with Currency Swap

Currency swaps cover different kind of risk. They are one way of converting liabilities or assets from one currency to another. While in the case of interest rate swaps, assets or liabilities are transformed from fixed interest rates to floating rates or vice versa, providing a hedge against fluctuating interest rates, currency swaps provide a hedge against exchange rate risks, as they transform liabilities/assets from one currency to another.

Let us consider an example to see how MNCs face currency risks and how these could be overcome through a swap deal.

Assume that an Indian firm needs funds for its US operations. The firm raises funds in Indian rupees and commits itself to serve its interest obligations and the final repayment in Indian rupees. The funds raised in rupees are converted to US dollars to acquire assets in the USA. These assets provide income in US dollars. The Indian firm is subject to the risk of appreciation of the rupee (depreciation of the dollar) value in the currency markets, as it would then receive lower rupee amounts for fixed returns earned in US dollars.

Similarly, a US firm, which needs to acquire assets in India while it raises dollar funds in the USA, faces the same risk. Its earnings would be in Indian rupees, and the liabilities need to be serviced in US dollars. Like the Indian firm, the US firm also faces a risk of shortfall in the US dollar if it appreciates (and the rupee depreciates).

232 Derivatives and Risk Management

> Currency swaps are useful in (a) hedging against exchange rate risk, (b) transforming an asset or a liability from one currency to another, and (c) reducing the financing cost.

The vulnerability of both the Indian firm and the US firm is due to the uncertainty of exchange rate movement, which may take place in either direction. Depreciation of the dollar harms the Indian firm, while it benefits the US firm. Risks for both the firms arise because the future movement of exchange rates cannot be predicted accurately. However, an estimate of the likely direction of exchange rates is made based on many theories, such as purchasing power parity and interest rate parity. In this sub-section, we focus on the unexpected and adverse movement of exchange rates, as parties factor in likely movements while making estimates.

The element of risk can be removed if the Indian firm and the US firm enter into a swap agreement, as depicted in Fig. 8.8. A cursory look would reveal that the Indian firm has financed its US operations by creating a rupee liability. This liability, to be serviced by the income generation in US dollars, faces a currency exchange rate risk. Likewise, the US firm, having funded its Indian operations through a US dollar loan, would be serviced by income in rupees, and needs to be converted to US dollars for payment of interest and principal in the future, whenever they fall due.

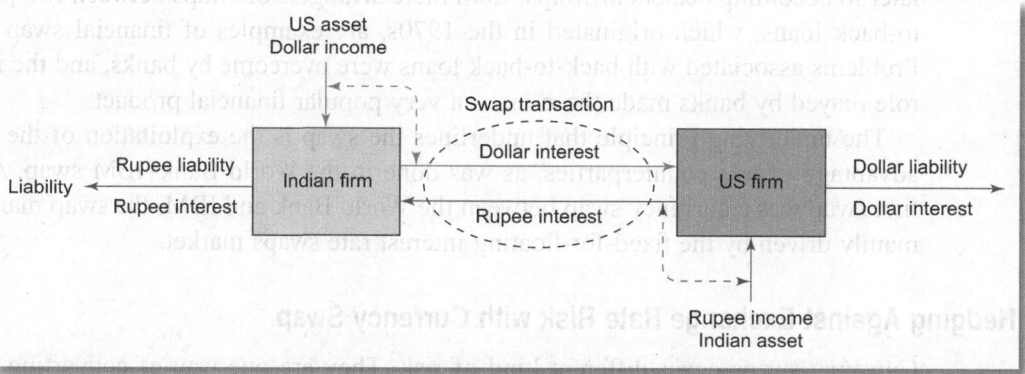

Fig. 8.8 Currency swap: Converting asset/liability from one currency to another

Under the swap transaction, the mismatch of cash inflow and cash outflow in different currencies for both the firms can be eliminated by (a) the US firm agreeing to pay the rupees generated out of its Indian operations to the Indian firm, and (b) in exchange, the Indian firm agreeing to pay US dollars generated out of its US operations. Thus, the rupee asset income flows to the Indian firm, facilitating service of its rupee liability. In exchange, US dollar asset income flows to the US firm to meet its US dollar obligations. Both the firms avoid any conversion of currencies from one to another and thus eliminate exchange rate risks. Through the swap, both the firms will have assets and liabilities maintained in the same currency, eliminating currency risk.

Reducing Cost of Funds with Currency Swaps

Like interest rate swaps, currency swaps can also be used to reduce funding cost for MNCs needing funds in different currencies. Again, the guiding principle is the theory of comparative advantage. In an interest rate swap, the comparative advantage emanates from the

Swaps—Interest Rate and Currency

EXAMPLE 8.3 Currency swap to hedge against exchange rate risk

Assume that an Indian software firm, Inso Ltd, wants to acquire a US firm at a cost of $2.00 crore. For this purpose, it raises the required capital of ₹90 crore (current exchange rate of ₹45/dollar) at 12%. The US acquisition is expected to yield a 15% return. At the same time, a US engineering firm, USENG Inc., is negotiating a joint venture to contribute US $2.00 crore, which promises to yield a 15% return in India. USENG Inc. raises the dollars required at a cost of 8%. Assume that all liabilities need annual payments.

(a) Examine the risk faced by Inso Ltd and USENG Inc. if the
   (i) rupee appreciates to 44, 42, 40, 38, and 36 per dollar for the next five years
   (ii) rupee depreciates to 46, 48, 50, 52, and 54 per dollar for the next five years
(b) Show how a swap arrangement between the two can help eliminate the risk of exchange rate fluctuations.

Solution

(a) Inso Ltd is targeting an annual profit of ₹270 lakh as follows:

Income in US $	= 15% of $200 lakh	= $30 lakh p.a.
Equivalent value in rupees		= ₹1350 lakh p.a.
Interest payment	= 12% of ₹9,000 lakh	= ₹1080 lakh p.a.
Anticipated profit	= 1,350 − 1,080	= ₹270 lakh p.a.

If the Indian rupee appreciates, Inso Ltd, would receive a lesser income than expected, and, hence, carries the risk of reduction in profit due to appreciation of the rupee, as its liability is fixed in rupees.

Similarly, USENG Inc. is targeting an annual profit of $14 lakh as follows:

Income in rupees	= 15% of ₹9,000 lakh	= ₹1,350 lakh p.a.
Equivalent value in US dollars		= $30 lakh p.a.
Interest payment	= 8% of $200 lakh	= $16 lakh p.a.
Anticipated profit	= 30 − 16	= $14 lakh p.a.

If the Indian rupee depreciates, the firm will receive a lesser annual income than expected, and, hence, faces the risk of reduction in profit to the extent of depreciation in the rupee, as its liability is fixed in US dollars.

While appreciation of the rupee is good for the US firm and detrimental to the Indian firm, the position reverses if the rupee depreciates. The impact on the spreads of both the firms for the exchange rate scenario is presented as follows:

Year	Exchange rate (₹/$)	Indian firm			US firm			Scenario
		Income US $	Equivalent ₹	₹ Spread	Income ₹	Equivalent $	$ Spread	
5	54.00	30.00	1,620.00	540.00	1,350.00	25.00	9.00	Favourable to the Indian firm and unfavourable to the US firm
4	52.00	30.00	1,560.00	480.00	1,350.00	25.96	9.96	
3	50.00	30.00	1,500.00	420.00	1,350.00	27.00	11.00	
2	48.00	30.00	1,440.00	360.00	1,350.00	28.13	12.13	
1	46.00	30.00	1,380.00	300.00	1,350.00	29.35	13.35	
Now	45.00	30.00	1,350.00	270.00	1,350.00	30.00	14.00	
1	44.00	30.00	1,320.00	240.00	1,350.00	30.68	14.68	Favourable to the US firm and unfavourable to the Indian firm
2	42.00	30.00	1,260.00	180.00	1,350.00	32.14	16.14	
3	40.00	30.00	1,200.00	120.00	1,350.00	33.75	17.75	
4	38.00	30.00	1,140.00	60.00	1,350.00	35.53	19.53	
5	36.00	30.00	1,080.00	0.00	1,350.00	37.50	21.50	

(b) By entering into a swap arrangement, both the firms eliminate volatility in the spread. Under the swap arrangement, at the current rate of ₹45 per dollar:
   i) The US firm will pay the Indian firm ₹1,350 lakh annually, earned out of its joint venture in India.

(Contd)

EXAMPLE 8.3 contd

Currency swap: converting asset/liability from one currency to another

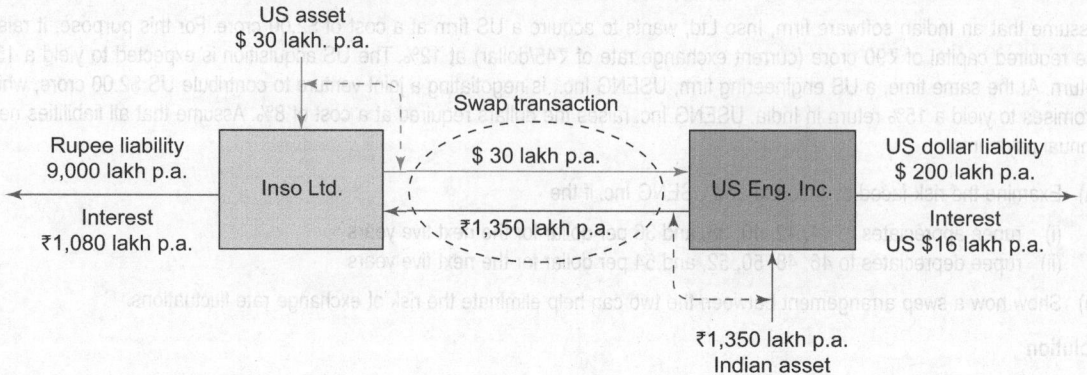

A schematic diagram of the swap arrangement is shown here. The spread after the swap arrangement becomes fixed for both the firms, irrespective of the exchange rate. The US firm will lock-in a return of $16 lakh and the Indian firm will be assured of a profit of ₹270 lakh after the swap arrangement.

Cash flows after swap	Figure in lakh p.a.	
	Inso Ltd	**USENG Inc.**
Income earned abroad	+ $30	+ ₹1,350
Paid to counterparty	− $30	− ₹1,350
Received from counterparty	+ ₹1,350	+ $30
Interest obligation	− ₹1,080	− $14
Spread	+ ₹270	+ $16

Without the swap agreement, income for both the firms in the USA and India was subject to fluctuations due to currency exchange rate changes.

> Currency swaps enable financing in a currency with the lowest interest rate. However, a cheaper source of finance converts the interest rate advantage into exchange rate risk, transforming the asset or liability from one currency to another, while reducing the financing cost.

differential in pricing in the floating rate and the fixed rate markets. Here, the comparative advantage results from two distinct and separate markets in different currencies that are governed by altogether different sets of rules and operate in vastly different economic conditions. Although the exchange rate mechanism provides a link among these markets and economies, the link is a frail one compared to the strong linkages the capital and debt markets have in a single economy. The quality spread in domestic markets is based on the credit rating of the parties. In the international markets, the credit rating for a given firm may vary substantially across nations, as firms are generally better known in their home country than in foreign countries. Further, exchange control regulations of a given land may discourage borrowing by non-residents by stipulating a higher rate. Therefore, the comparative advantage is likely to be more pronounced in two markets in two different economies, as compared to similar markets of the same economy for one currency. As such, the credit quality spread is expected to be larger in the markets for different currencies than the credit quality spread in the markets for fixed and floating rates.

A greater spread in credit quality increases comparative advantage. Increased comparative advantage opens up more avenues for currency swaps. However, the size of the market may be limited, as only MNCs will be the beneficiaries of such currency swap transactions.

As a simple example, consider two MNCs, one Indian and one British. Both the firms enjoy excellent and equivalent credit rating in their countries. However, their funding requirements are confined to their own countries. Now they need to raise funds across boundaries for their ever-increasing expansion needs. In doing so, they can capitalize on any interest rate differentials that may exist in two currencies.

The costs of capital for the two firms in India and Britain in their respective currencies are as follows:

	Indian Rupee market	British Pound market
Indian firm	10%	6%
British firm	14%	4%
Advantage to the British firm	– 4%	2%

Clearly, the Indian firm enjoys an advantage over the British firm in India, and the British firm commands more credibility in Britain as compared to the Indian firm. Notice that the absolute advantage may not be in favour of the same firm as in the interest rate swap case. The comparative advantage here is 6%. If the two firms borrow in the required currencies, the total cost of funds will be 20%, i.e., the Indian firm borrows pound at 6% and the British firm borrows rupees at 14%. However, if they borrow as per the comparative advantage theory and exchange each other's commitment, the total cost of funds can be reduced to 14%, with the British firm borrowing pounds at 4% and the Indian firm borrowing rupees at 10%. Both the firms can benefit by 6% in aggregate if they enter into a swap arrangement wherein the following sequence is followed:

- The Indian firm mobilizes funds in rupees in the Indian market at 10%.
- It lends the rupee funds to the British firm at 11%.
- The British firm raises funds in the British market in pounds at 4%.
- It lends the same funds to the Indian firm at 5%.
- The two firms exchange interest payments periodically.
- Finally, they exchange the principal amounts upon redemption.

The schematic diagram of the swap arrangement and cost of funds for both the firms is shown in Fig. 8.9.

We assumed in the example that the Indian firm and the British firm exchanged the principal amounts of borrowing, and as a natural outcome, would have to exchange the repayment amounts at the time of redemption. However, it is not essential to do so, as both the firms can use the spot market for buying and selling the currencies required independent of each other, both at the time of raising funds and at the time of redemption.

Through the swap the Indian firm is now able to obtain pound funds at 4% as against 6% in the absence of swaps; a benefit of 2%. Similarly British firm has access to rupee funds at 10% as against 14%; a benefit of 4%. The aggregate benefit is equal to the comparative advantage of 6% which may be shared by the two firms depending upon negotiating skills and strength of the two firms involved.

236　Derivatives and Risk Management

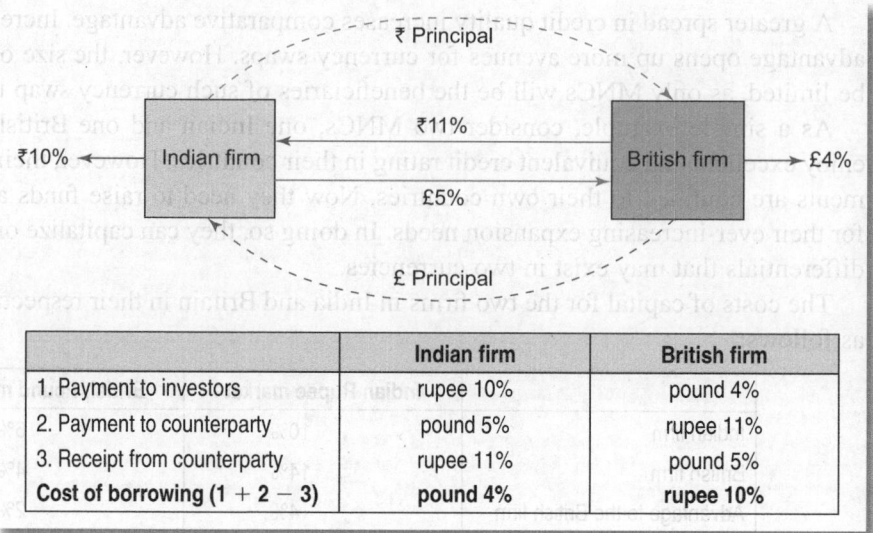

	Indian firm	British firm
1. Payment to investors	rupee 10%	pound 4%
2. Payment to counterparty	pound 5%	rupee 11%
3. Receipt from counterparty	rupee 11%	pound 5%
Cost of borrowing (1 + 2 − 3)	**pound 4%**	**rupee 10%**

Fig. 8.9 Currency swap to reduce cost of funds

DISTINGUISHING FEATURES OF CURRENCY SWAPS

It may be noticed that the mechanism of a currency swap is similar to that of a parallel loan. The existence of an intermediary in a swap contract helps to minimize counterparty risk by locating a suitable counterparty; it makes swaps better than parallel loans.

However, working on the same principle of comparative advantage, currency swaps differ operationally from interest rate swaps. Under a currency swap, the cash flows are as follows:

- exchange of principal amounts at the time of setting the swap deal at the current spot rate
- exchange of periodic interest payments
- reverse exchange of the principal amounts upon maturity at exchange rates prevailing then

Under an interest rate swap, there is no exchange of principal at the beginning of the swap or at its conclusion.

> Operationally, currency swaps are different from interest rate swaps, as the loan principal amounts, which are in different currencies, are exchanged both at the initiation and the conclusion of the swap.

Currency swaps may be classified as follows.

Fixed-to-fixed In a fixed-to-fixed currency swap, the interest rates in the two currencies involved are fixed. For example, a British firm may raise a loan in pounds and exchange it for US dollars with a US firm. Interest payments may be made by the British firm in dollars, while it receives interest in pounds from the US firm. The US firm would do the reverse, making interest payments in pounds and receiving US dollar interest payments. The interest rates in both the US dollar and the pound are fixed.

Fixed-to-floating In a fixed-to-floating currency swap, the interest rate on one of the currencies is fixed, while it is floating on the other. In the earlier example in this chapter of the British and US firms, if the British firm paid interest in US dollars at a fixed rate while receiving interest in pounds, based on LIBOR, from the US firm, such a swap would be a fixed-to-floating swap. Such swaps not only transform the nature of the asset/liability from one currency to another but also change it from a fixed rate to a floating rate. They become complex tools suitable for hedging against currency risks as well as interest rate risks.

Floating-to-floating In a floating-to-floating currency swap, both interest rates are floating, but in different currencies. In the British firm–US firm example, if the British firm makes interest payment in US dollars based on the prime rate in the USA while receiving interest in pounds, based on LIBOR, from the US firms such a swap would be of the floating-to-floating type.

VALUATION OF SWAPS

Swap pricing is important for two reasons. First, as stated earlier in this chapter, banks function as warehouses of swaps, and are ready to offer swaps to desiring customers. For this purpose, they are required to quote swap rates for paying or receiving a fixed rate of interest for receiving or paying the benchmark floating rate. The second reason for valuing a swap is for the purpose of terminating an existing swap. For reasons of economy, a firm may like to cancel its obligations under a swap after some time by abandoning the remaining part of obligations undertaken by it, by paying or receiving the value of the swap at that point of time.

Derivatives in Practice

Currency Swaps

India and Japan agree to $15 billion currency swap

On 28 December 2011, India and Japan agreed to a dollar swap agreement of US $15 billion. An earlier US $3 billion arrangement that came into force in 2008 had expired in June 2011. Currency swaps involve an exchange of cash flows in two different currencies. By their special nature, these instruments are used for hedging risk arising out of volatility in the foreign exchange markets.

The agreement will enable the two countries to swap currencies for US dollars and tap into each other's foreign exchange reserves to ease any liquidity problems. Under the deal, the two central banks will supply each other with up to $5 billion from their foreign currency reserves for possible market intervention in the event of financial turmoil.

The genesis of the deal lies in the need to remove volatility in the foreign currency markets. The Indian rupee had fallen more than 15% in a year. The Japanese yen has also been volatile in the wake of an uncertain global outlook.

There were growing concerns about foreign institutional investors (FIIs) pulling out of the Indian capital markets due to fears of a slowdown in the Indian economy. The FIIs withdrew almost $600 million from the Indian securities market in November 2011. This huge capital outflow has hurt the Indian currency, which hit an all-time low against the US dollar. There have also been fears over the performance of the overall Indian economy due to the protracted sovereign-debt crisis in the global financial markets. A weakening currency adds to the cost of imported goods. The two nations agreed to support each other in the event of a run on their currencies. Under the plan, Japan would lend dollars and other currencies, should India find its foreign-exchange reserves declining disproportionately.

The agreement effectively meant that Japan would accept rupees and give dollars to India up to a stipulated limit, and, similarly, India will take yen and send dollars to Japan if speculators seek to trash the respective currencies.

Besides containing volatility in the currencies, the swap would help to boost trade between the two countries. The move would strengthen the Indian central bank's armoury to tackle any liquidity crisis or volatility in the currency market. For India, the swap arrangement is all the more important, and it might actually draw from the facility, given the situation of net capital outflows, an exacerbating current account deficit (which climbed to a troublesome 4.9% of GDP for the October–December quarter) and the weak composition of reserves. India was struggling to meet the projected level of $72 billion in capital inflows till March 2012, and even the most optimistic forecasts did not put the figure at above $60 billion to $65 billion.

Valuing Interest Rate Swaps

As stated earlier in this chapter, an interest rate swap consists of a fixed rate cash flow and a floating rate cash flow in the opposite direction. At the time of inception of the swap, the present value of these payments must be equal in the opinions of both the parties to the swap, or else they would not agree to it. Therefore, at inception, the value of a swap is zero, implying that the present values of cash inflows and outflows are equal and its aggregate flow is zero.

However, the circumstances would change after the swap is initiated. The value of an interest rate swap at any time is the net difference between the present values of the payments to be received and payments to be made. It becomes positive for one party and is equivalently negative for the other. This tells how much cash the two parties must exchange to nullify the remaining obligations in the swap.

From the valuation perspective, a swap transaction may be interpreted in at least two ways. It can be considered either as a *pair of bonds* or as *series of forward agreements*. Either interpretation of a swap helps in its initial pricing as well as its valuation if and when either or both parties want a premature closure. We take the pricing of swaps by both methods: by treating the swap as a pair of bonds and as a series of forward agreements.

Swap as Pair of Bonds The most common interpretation of interest rate swaps is to consider the inflows and outflows of interest at periodical intervals, equivalent to that of bonds. In an interest rate swap, one leg of the transaction is on a fixed rate and the other leg is on a floating rate of interest. We know that the owner of a bond receives interest and the issuer of bond pays interest. Therefore, a swap is a composite of these two cash flows:

> An interest rate swap can be seen as a pair of bonds: one a floating rate bond and the other a fixed rate bond representing the two cash flows, floating and fixed, of the swap.

1. Cash inflow equivalent to the interest on the bond owned
2. Cash outflow equivalent to payment of the interest on the bond issued

Therefore, a swap is a pair of bonds, one issued and one owned. A swap where one pays a fixed rate and receives a floating rate can be viewed as a combination of (a) having issued a fixed rate bond paying the fixed coupon rate, and simultaneously (b) owning a floating rate bond receiving a floating rate as per market conditions, as depicted in Fig. 8.10.

While setting up the swap, the coupon rate (the fixed leg receipts/payments) is fixed in such a manner that the values of cash inflows and cash outflows are equal and both the parties to the swap arrangement are in equilibrium; the net present value of the cash flows is zero. This forms the basis for fixing the initial price of the swap, determined in terms of a fixed rate of interest payable or receivable upon exchange of a floating benchmark rate. For

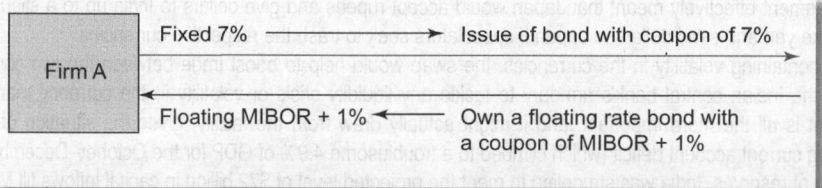

Fig. 8.10 Swap as pair of bonds

firm A in Fig. 8.10, the equivalent of MIBOR may be taken as 6%, at the time of initiating the swap.

However, interest rates are dynamic, and the value of cash flows as determined at the start of a swap will not remain the same as time elapses. The value of the swap will depend upon the behaviour of bond prices with respect to changes in the interest rates. The following rules about bond prices may be kept in mind while valuing swaps:

- The value of a fixed rate bond will increase with a fall in the interest rates.
- The value of a fixed rate bond will decrease with an increase in the interest rates.
- The value of a floating rate bond remains equal to its par value, as the coupon rate is aligned with market rates on each periodic payment of interest.
- The value of a floating rate bond changes subsequent to each interest payment, if the interest rate structure has changed since then.
- The value of a floating rate bond gets aligned again to the par value on the next (and each) date of payment of interest.

> A swap when seen as a pair of bond helps in finding the value of the swap subsequent to its initiation. The value of the swap is zero when it is set up.

Since any change in the value of a floating rate bond will only be nominal and temporary (it changes only during the two interest payment dates), the value of a swap is determined on the basis of the difference between the present values of the fixed leg and that of the floating leg, and thus is predominantly dependent upon the value of the fixed rate bond.

The value of the bond with fixed rate payments will be equal to the sum of coupon payments and the notional principal amount discounted at an appropriate rate. The discount rate to be used for each coupon payment is known from the term structure of interest rates. The value of the fixed leg, V_c, is given by:

$$V_c = \sum_{1}^{n} \frac{C_i}{(1 + r_i)^n} + \frac{P}{(1 + r_n)^n} \tag{8.1}$$

where C_i = coupon payment at time i
r_i = discount rate for period i
n = number of periods remaining
P = notional principal amount

Similarly, we can find the value of the floating rate bond, V_f, which is equal to the present value of the next interest payment and the principal. As we know that the value of a floating rate bond converges to its par value on each payment date, the value of the floating leg can be expressed as:

$$V_f = \frac{F_1}{(1 + r_1)} + \frac{P}{(1 + r_1)} \tag{8.2}$$

where F_1 = next payment of interest
r_1 = discount rate for period 1
P = notional principal amount

The value of the swap at any time for the party receiving a fixed rate and paying a floating rate will be equal to the differential between the fixed leg and floating rate cash flows, given by Eq. 8.3.

Value of swap = PV of fixed coupon bond − PV of floating rate bond or

$V_s = V_c - V_f$

$$V_s = \sum_{1}^{n} \frac{C_i}{(1+r_i)^n} + \frac{P_i}{(1+r_n)^n} - \frac{F_1}{(1+r_1)} - \frac{P}{(1+r_1)} \quad (8.3)$$

Let us consider a simple example of valuation of a swap, assuming it to be a pair of bonds. Assume that two years ago, firm A entered a 5-year interest rate swap where it received a fixed 8% and paid MIBOR + 1%. For simplicity of exposition, we assume annual payments. There are three remaining annual payments.

Since the time of the swap, interest rates have moved causing the value of the swap to change. Note that the value of the swap was zero two years ago when it was set up. Assume that the payment of the floating rate determined one period in advance is at the rate of 9.5% (MIBOR was at 8.50% then). The term structure of interest rates as on today is:

1 year : 10.0%;
2 years : 10.5%; and
3 years : 11.0%

We find the value of the floating rate bond for an assumed principal payment of ₹100 by discounting the interest (₹9.50) and the principal (₹100) at 10%.

The value of the floating rate bond = 109.50/1.10 = ₹99.545

The value of a fixed rate bond can be found by discounting the three cash flows at the appropriate discount rate given by the term structure, which would be

$$V_c = \frac{8}{(1+0.10)} + \frac{8}{(1+0.105)^2} + \frac{8}{(1+0.11)^3} + \frac{100}{(1+0.11)^3}$$

= 7.273 + 6.552 + 5.849 + 73.119 = ₹92.793

The value of the swap = PV of inflow − PV of outflow
= 92.793 − 99.545 = −₹6.752

The present value of inflow of the fixed leg for firm A is ₹92.793 and that of the floating rate outflow is ₹99.545. The swap can be cancelled if firm A pays ₹6.752 now to the counterparty.

Swaps as Series of Forward Contracts In a swap, regular payments of interest are made and received by the counterparties. The next cash flow of interest can be considered as a forward transaction. Similarly, all subsequent cash flows are regarded as future-dated delivery commitments. The timing of each cash flow is known in advance, and hence, a swap can be regarded as a series of forward contracts maturing on specified dates, with the amounts of respective interest payments as shown in Fig. 8.11.

A swap is a single contract encompassing several forward contracts. Hence, the objective achieved by a swap can also be achieved by booking several forward contracts of interests (known as FRAs, covered in Chapter 8). However, forward contracts are normally not available for far extended dates in future. Even if they are, they suffer from poor liquidity and more expensive

> An interest rate swap may also be viewed as a series of forward contracts where the floating rate cash flows are equivalent to the expected interest rates implied by the term structure of the interest rates.

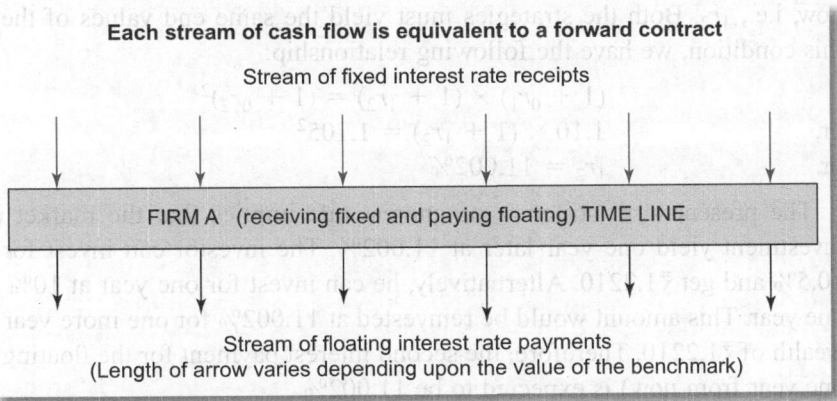

Fig. 8.11 Swap as a series of forward contracts

pricing. Swap quotes and contracts are available for much longer periods as a bundle of several forward contracts, and may be cheaper than a series of independent forward contracts.

The valuation of a swap requires computation of the present values of the fixed rate leg and the floating rate leg. While the interest payments of the fixed rate leg are known for the entire remaining duration of the swap, the cash flows of the floating rate leg is known for only the next immediate payment. For all subsequent periods, the cash flows for the floating rate leg will be determined only one period in advance. Hence, all the payments cannot be known today. This poses a problem in valuation of a swap when we assume it to be a series of forward rate agreements.

Treating a swap as a series of forward rate agreements, the arrangement of the example in the previous section can be viewed as follows:

Period 't'	Year 'y'	Firm receives %	Firm pays %
1	3	8.00	9.50% fixed at $t = 0$
2	4	8.00	Rate to be determined at $t = 1$; $y = 3$ say $_1r_2$
3	5	8.00	Rate to be determined at $t = 2$; $y = 4$ say $_2r_3$

With the given term structure of interest rates, floating rate payments are implied. The term structure of the interest rate is given here:

One-year yield investment starting today, $_0r_1$ = 10.00%
Two-year yield investment starting today, $_0r_2$ = 10.50%
Three-year yield investment starting today, $_0r_3$ = 11.00%

where $_0r_n$ implies the interest rate for the investment period starting at 0 and ending at the nth period.

Forward rates of interests are built according to the term structure of interest rates. The implied forward rate can be calculated on the argument of equivalence of investment under two strategies of (a) making direct investment for the planned horizon, and (b) making an investment now and rolling it over from period to period to cover the entire planned horizon. From the term structure of interest rates given in the previous paragraph, we may have either direct investment for 2 years at 10.5%, i.e., $_0r_2$, or investment for one year at 10%, i.e., at $_0r_1$, and then roll over the matured amount for another year at the 1-year rate one year from now, i.e., $_1r_2$. Both the strategies must yield the same end values of the investment. Given this condition, we have the following relationship:

$$(1 + {_0r_1}) \times (1 + {_1r_2}) = (1 + {_0r_2})^2$$
or, $\quad 1.10 \times (1 + {_1r_2}) = 1.105^2$
or, $\quad {_1r_2} = 11.002\%$

The present term structure of interest rate implies that the market expects a one-year investment yield one year later at 11.002%. The investor can invest for a 2-year period at 10.5% and get ₹1.2210. Alternatively, he can invest for one year at 10% and get ₹1.10 after one year. This amount would be reinvested at 11.002% for one more year to give an ultimate wealth of ₹1.2210. Therefore, the second interest payment for the floating rate (to be decided one year from now) is expected to be 11.002%.

Using the same logic, a 3-year investment should be equivalent to a 2-year investment rolled over for another year at the rate prevailing for a 1-year investment after two years, i.e., $_2r_3$, and thus, we have

$$(1 + {_0r_2})^2 \times (1 + {_2r_3}) = (1 + {_0r_3})^3$$
or, $\quad 1.105^2 \times (1 + {_2r_3}) = 1.11^3$
or, $\quad {_2r_3} = 12.007\%$

With estimated floating rate, payments as derived from term structure of interest rates, we would estimate the value of the swap as under;

Present value of forward cash payment $= \dfrac{\text{Amount of fixed leg} - \text{Amount of floating leg}}{(1 + \text{Discount rate})^n}$

Present value of first swap payment $= \dfrac{(8.00 - 9.50)}{1.10} = -1.364$

Present value of second swap payment $= \dfrac{(8.00 - 11.002)}{(1.105)^2} = -2.458$

Present value of third swap payment $= \dfrac{(8.00 - 12.007)}{(1.11)^3} = -2.930$

The value of the swap comes to $-$ ₹6.752 as computed with the assumption of the swap as a pair of bonds.

SWAP QUOTES AND INITIAL PRICING

Many banks in the international markets play the role of market maker for swaps. These banks quote two-way swap rates in terms of a fixed rate of interest for receiving and paying a floating rate of interest. The bid rate is the fixed rate of interest the bank will pay to receive a floating rate; and the ask or offer rate is the fixed rate of interest the bank will receive for paying a floating rate. The average of the two rates is known as the swap rate. At the swap rate, the value of the swap is zero, i.e., the values of the fixed and floating rates are equal.

> Banks play the role of market makers in swaps by offering two-way quotes for paying and receiving a fixed rate of interest in exchange for a floating benchmark interest rate.

In order to determine the initial swap rate, we equate the present values of the cash flows of the fixed rate leg and floating rate leg. The cash flows of the fixed leg are known for the entire duration of the swap. The cash flows pertaining to the floating leg cannot be determined in straightforward manner.

As Series of Forward Contracts How do we price a swap? We again use the term structure of interest rates to derive the cash flows of the floating rate leg, as they are the best estimates available for interest rates in future.

Let us consider an example for quoting a 5-year swap with annual exchange of cash flows. The pricing will be done in the form of percentage interest of the fixed leg to be received/paid for paying/receiving a benchmarked floating rate of interest. Internationally, the benchmark is LIBOR. However, here we assume an exchange of MIBOR for the fixed coupon for five years in terms of Indian rupee.

To equate the present values of the two legs, we need to estimate the cash flows pertaining to the floating rate bond. The cash flows of the floating rate bonds are normally decided one period in advance, implying that the next payment is equal to the prevailing MIBOR. The remaining payments will have to be estimated. The term structure of interest rates provides the best estimates of the likely payout for the floating leg payments, using equivalence of direct investment for the planned horizon or rolling over periodically. Therefore, the present value (PV) of the floating rate leg is given by:

PV of the floating rate leg

$$= \frac{_0r_1}{(1 + {_0r_1})} + \frac{_1r_2}{(1 + {_0r_2})^2} + \frac{_2r_3}{(1 + {_0r_3})^3} + \frac{_3r_4}{(1 + {_0r_4})^4} + \frac{_4r_5}{(1 + {_0r_5})^5} \quad (8.4)$$

Assuming that X is the fixed payment of interest, the present value of the fixed rate leg is given by:

PV of the fixed rate leg

$$= \frac{X}{(1 + {_0r_1})} + \frac{X}{(1 + {_0r_2})^2} + \frac{X}{(1 + {_0r_3})^3} + \frac{X}{(1 + {_0r_4})^4} + \frac{X}{(1 + {_0r_5})^5} \quad (8.5)$$

For the initial pricing, we equate the cash flows of the fixed and floating rates and solve for the unknown variable, X.

With the term structure of interest rates, we can arrive at the discount factors and floating rate payments as implied forward rates, as shown in Table 8.5.

Table 8.5 Finding floating rate payments

Year	Interest rate	Implied forward rate given by	Implied forward rate	Discount factor
1	$_0r_1 = 6.5\%$	$(1 + {_0r_1}) = (1 + {_0r_1})$	$_0r_1 = 6.500\%$	0.9390
2	$_0r_2 = 7.0\%$	$(1 + {_0r_1}) \times (1 + {_1r_2}) = (1 + {_0r_2})^2$	$_1r_2 = 7.502\%$	0.8734
3	$_0r_3 = 7.5\%$	$(1 + {_0r_2})^2 \times (1 + {_2r_3}) = (1 + {_0r_3})^3$	$_2r_3 = 8.507\%$	0.8050
4	$_0r_4 = 8.0\%$	$(1 + {_0r_3})^3 \times (1 + {_3r_4}) = (1 + {_0r_4})^4$	$_3r_4 = 9.514\%$	0.7350
5	$_0r_5 = 8.5\%$	$(1 + {_0r_4})^4 \times (1 + {_4r_5}) = (1 + {_0r_5})^5$	$_4r_5 = 10.523\%$	0.6650

Substituting the values in Eqs 8.4 and 8.5, we get the following value of X:

$$X(0.9390 + 0.8734 + 0.8050 + 0.7350 + 0.6650)$$
$$= 6.500 \times 0.9390 + 7.502 \times 0.8734 + 8.507 \times 0.8050 + 9.514 \times 0.7350 + 10.523 \times 0.6650$$

Or
$$4.0174\, X = 0.3349$$
$$X = 0.08338 \text{ equivalent to } 8.338\% \cong 8.34\%$$

The swap rate will be 8.34% for paying or receiving MIBOR. To this equilibrium swap rate, the dealer/bank will add its spread to cover its administrative cost and counterparty risk. Assume that the bank wants to add 40 bps for the bid and ask spread; the swap quote of the bank would be 8.14% − 8.54%. This means the bank will pay 8.14% fixed for receiving MIBOR, and receive 8.54% fixed for paying MIBOR. As the tenor of the swap becomes longer, the spread increases.

As a Pair of Bonds The same result would be obtained if we treat the swap as a pair involving one fixed rate and one floating rate bond. The values of the two bonds must be equal at the inception of the swap, making net present value equal to zero, the cash flows of the two bonds being opposite to each other.

The value of the fixed rate bond with a coupon of X would be equal to $4.0174\,X$ for the term structure used. The value of the principal would, however, be $0.6650 \times R$ if R is the principal. Since the floating rate bond adjusts to the par value at each coupon date, the value of the floating rate bond would be equal to its par at the inception of the swap. Equating the two, we get the following expression:

$$1.00 \times 0.6650 + 4.0174 \times X = R$$

If R is taken as ₹1.00, the value of X, the coupon of the fixed rate bond, would be computed as follows:

$$X = (1 - 0.6650)/4.0174 = 0.0834, \text{ equivalent to } 8.34\%$$

The swap rate then can be written thus:

$$\text{Swap Rate} = \frac{1 - \text{Last discount factor}}{\text{Sum of all discount factors}} \tag{8.6}$$

COUNTERPARTY RISK AND SWAPS

The swap rate can be interpreted as a weighted average of the floating rate payments over the period of the swap. It is similar to the yield-to-maturity (YTM) of a bond, which equates all cash flows of the bond to its price with a single discount rate. The floating rate payments are based on the implied forward rates. The two fixed and floating payment legs are not equal, but the aggregates of these payments become equal at the termination of the swap deal.

The floating rate payments will be either more or less than the fixed rate payments, depending upon the direction of the term structure of interest rates.

If the term structure of interest rates is upward sloping, then the floating rate payments will keep increasing with time. Initially, the floating leg will be smaller than the fixed leg and as time passes, the floating rate payments start increasing and exceed the fixed leg payments. For the rising term structure shown in Table 8.5, the expected payments are drawn in Fig. 8.12. Similarly, if the term structure of interest rates is downward sloping, the floating rate payments will be higher than the fixed leg during the initial years of the swap and will reduce subsequently. Assume that from the initial rate of 6.5% now the term

> The counterparty risk in a swap is dependent upon who pays the fixed rate and who pays the floating rate, and changes with the age of the swap.

structure of 6.5%, 6.0%, 5.5%, 5.0%, and 4.5% from years 1–5, the implied forward rates and discount factor would be as follows:

Year	Interest rate	Implied forward rate given by	Implied forward rate	Discount factor
1	$_0r_1 = 6.5\%$	$(1 + {_0r_1}) = (1 + {_0r_1})$	$_0r_1 = 6.500\%$	0.9390
2	$_0r_2 = 6.0\%$	$(1 + {_0r_1}) \times (1 + {_1r_2}) = (1 + {_0r_2})^2$	$_1r_2 = 5.502\%$	0.8900
3	$_0r_3 = 5.5\%$	$(1 + {_0r_2})^2 \times (1 + {_2r_3}) = (1 + {_0r_3})^3$	$_2r_3 = 4.507\%$	0.8516
4	$_0r_4 = 5.0\%$	$(1 + {_0r_3})^3 \times (1 + {_3r_4}) = (1 + {_0r_4})^4$	$_3r_4 = 3.514\%$	0.8227
5	$_0r_5 = 4.5\%$	$(1 + {_0r_4})^4 \times (1 + {_4r_5}) = (1 + {_0r_5})^5$	$_4r_5 = 2.524\%$	0.8025

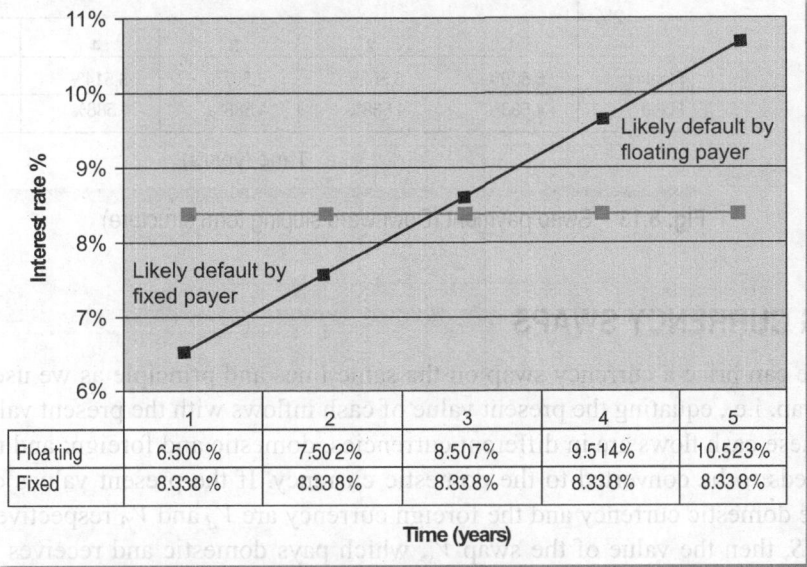

Fig. 8.12 Swap payment (Upward sloping term structure)

Note that initially floating payments are higher than fixed and reduce gradually as shown in Fig. 8.13. In either case of rising or falling term structure the cash payments of two legs are expected to be equal over the life of the swap. This has important implications for the counterparty risk in a swap deal.

In case of an upward sloping term structure of interest rates, the fixed rate payer pays more than what he/she receives in the early part of the swap. There is net cash outflow during the initial years of the swap deal, and, hence, the fixed rate payer is the only party likely to default in the initial years. In the later stages of the swap, the floating rate payments exceed the fixed rate payments, and, hence, the floating rate payer is more likely to be the default party.

The situation reverses if the term structure of interest rates is downward sloping. The intermediary faces default risk from the floating rate payer in the initial part of the swap, while the fixed rate payer is more likely to default in the later stages of the swap deal. The intermediary must take appropriate steps to contain this risk, as it serves as counterparty to both the parties to the swap deal.

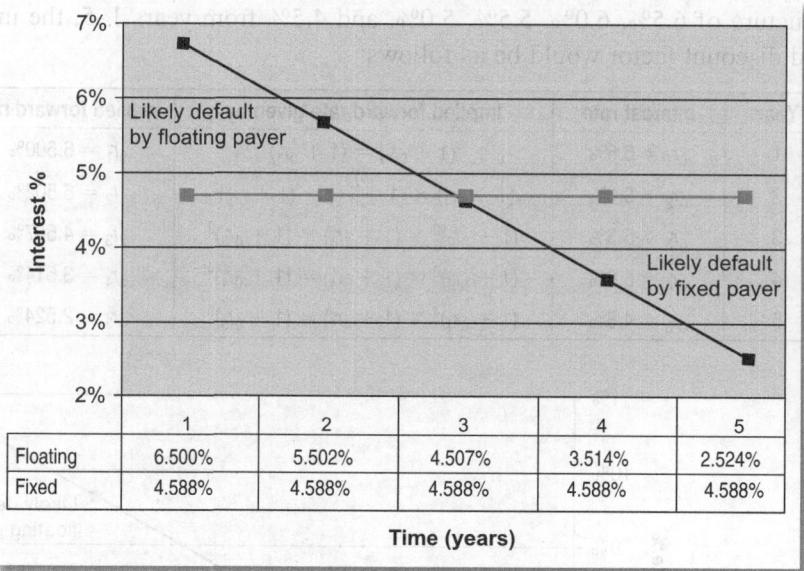

Fig. 8.13 Swap payment (Downward sloping term structure)

VALUING CURRENCY SWAPS

We can price a currency swap on the same lines and principle as we use for an interest rate swap, i.e., equating the present value of cash inflows with the present value of cash outflows. These cash flows are in different currencies, domestic and foreign; and the foreign currency needs to be converted to the domestic currency. If the present values of the cash flows of the domestic currency and the foreign currency are V_d and V_f, respectively, and the spot rate is S, then the value of the swap V_s, which pays domestic and receives foreign currency, is given by:

$$V_s = S \times V_f - V_d$$

The initial pricing of the swap is set such that the present values of the foreign and domestic currency cash flows are equal and the value of the swap is zero. The most common currency swaps involve an exchange of principal in the beginning, periodic payments of interest at predetermined interest rates and intervals, and re-exchange of principal at the end of the swap contract. We have to value these cash flows to know the worth of the swap deal at any time subsequent to the contract, as spot rates as well as risk-free rates of return change.

Any change in the term structure of interest rates in either of the currencies involved or in the exchange rates causes disequilibrium in the cash flows and imparts value to the swap.

The valuation of a currency swap can be understood through a simple example. Let us assume that firm A has entered into a 5-year swap where it receives Indian rupees at 8% and pays US dollars at 4% annually on the exchange of a principal amount of US $100 lakh when the exchange rate was ₹45 per dollar. Assuming a flat-term structure of interest, the value of the swap at its initiation is zero, as can be seen from Table 8.6.

EXAMPLE 8.4 Value of interest rate swap

A firm had entered into a swap arrangement for a notional principal of ₹1 crore with a bank, whereby the bank paid a fixed 9% and received MIBOR semi-annually. It has three more years to go, and has just exchanged the cash flow. The 6-m MIBOR for the next payment of interest was reset at 8%. The next day, the markets exhibited a fall and the 6-m MIBOR fell to 7%, leading the firm to believe that it is overpaying. It wants to cancel the swap arrangement. How much should the firm ask the bank to pay to cancel the swap deal? Assume a flat term structure.

Solution

The value of the swap for the firm is determined on the basis of discounted cash flows (DCFs). Since the rates have changed, the discount rate used would be 7% of the prevalent market rate. The value of the cash outflows on a fixed basis discounted at 7% is ₹115.63, as shown here:

Present value of cash flow of the fixed leg	
Fixed leg payment — cash outflow	9.00%
Present 12-month MIBOR	7.00%
Next interest payment on floating rate	8.00%

Time (months)	Years	Cash flow (₹)	DCF (₹ at 7.00%)
—	—	4.50	
6	0.50	4.50	4.42
12	1.00	4.50	4.35
18	1.50	4.50	4.27
24	2.00	4.50	4.20
30	2.50	4.50	4.13
36	3.00	104.50	94.25
Present value of fixed leg			115.63

The PV of the inflow at a floating rate would be the next interest payment, decided a period in advance, plus the face value of ₹100 discounted at 7%. This amount works out to ₹100.48.

Value of floating leg	
Interest to be received after 6 months	4.00
Principal to be received after 6 months	100.00
Total	104.00
Present value at 7%	100.48

The present value of the cash outflow is more by ₹15.15 for a principal of ₹100. If the bank pays ₹15.15 lakh for the principal amount of ₹1 crore, the firm may exit the swap.

The initial value of the swap is zero, as one would expect, because no deal would take place if either of the party believes it is receiving less and paying more in the given interest rate and exchange rate scenario. Firms receiving and paying rupees per US dollars must feel equivalence in both the currencies at the current interest rates and exchange rates before they enter a swap deal.

The valuation of a swap can also be done on the basis of treatment of the payments as a series of forward contracts (Table 8.7). The forward rates can be worked out from the interest rate structure using interest rate parity. The cash flow of interest of $4 lakh in years 1 to 5 and a principal of $100 lakh in

The valuation of a swap is based on the discounted cash flow technique; the problem arises with projection of cost flows of the unknown floating leg.

Table 8.6 Initial value of swap

(Figures in lakh)

Year	Interest and principal (₹)	Interest and principal (US $)	PV (₹ discounted at 8%)	PV (US $ discounted at 4%)
1	360.00	4.00	333.33	3.85
2	360.00	4.00	308.64	3.70
3	360.00	4.00	285.78	3.56
4	360.00	4.00	264.61	3.42
5	360.00	4.00	245.01	3.29
6	4500.00	100.00	3062.62	82.19
Total			4500.00	100.00
Equivalent domestic currency @ ₹45/$				4500.00
Swap value				—

year 5 are equivalent to forward contracts of the amounts for each year. Given interest rates of 8% and 4% for the rupee and the dollar, respectively, a 1-year forward rate using interest rate parity is,

$$F_1 = S_0 \frac{1 + r_d}{1 + r_f} = 45 \frac{1.08}{1.04} = 45 \times 1.0385 = ₹46.73/\$$$

Likewise, one can find out the implied forward rates for all subsequent periods when the dollar cash flows can be converted into local currency. The differential between the equivalent of dollar cash flows and the local currency will be the net cash flows of the firm under the swap. The differential is discounted at the interest rate applicable to the rupee.

Assuming the swap as a series of forward contracts, the value comes to zero in conformity with calculations based on the assumption of the swap as a pair of bonds.

Let us calculate the value of the swap assuming that the exchange rate has changed from ₹45 to ₹50/$ and the domestic interest rate has gone up from 8% to 10%, while the dollar interest rate remains same at 4%. Note that the absolute values of the cash flows pertaining to

Table 8.7 Currency swap as series of forward contracts

(Figures in lakh)

Year	₹ Interest and principal	$ Interest and principal	Implied forward rate (₹/$)	Equivalent ₹	Value of forward contract	PV of forward contract
1	360.00	4.00	46.73	186.92	173.08	160.26
2	360.00	4.00	48.53	194.11	165.89	142.22
3	360.00	4.00	50.39	201.58	158.42	125.76
4	360.00	4.00	52.33	209.33	150.67	110.75
5	360.00	4.00	54.35	217.38	142.62	97.06
6	4500.00	100.00	54.35	5434.56	−934.56	−636.05
Total						0.00

EXAMPLE 8.5 Value of currency swap

A swap was entered into by an Indian firm with a bank converting its rupee liability into pounds sterling, where the firm received 10% on the rupee and paid 6% on the pound. The amounts of principal involved are ₹120 million and £1.5 million, fixed at the then exchange rate of ₹80/£. The swap has four semi-annual payments to follow. Assume the next payment is due after six months from now and the term structures in Indian rupee and pound sterling are flat at 9.00% and 5.50%, respectively, for the next two years. If the current exchange rate is ₹82.00/£, what is the value of the swap for the Indian firm and the bank?

Solution
The semi-annual payment of interest is 0.05 × 120 = ₹6 million. The final payment would be ₹126.00 million, including the principal amount. With a 9% flat term structure on continuous compounding, the PV of the receivable by the firm from the bank would be:

PV of rupee cash flow = $6.0 \times e^{-0.09 \times 0.5} + 6.0 \times e^{-0.09 \times 1.0} + 6.0 \times e^{-0.09 \times 1.5} + 126.0 \times e^{-0.09 \times 2.0}$

$\quad = 5.7360 + 5.4836 + 5.2423 + 105.2440$ $\qquad = ₹121.7059$ million

PV of rupee cash flow in pound terms = 121.7059/82.00 $\qquad = £1.4848$ million

Similarly, pound cash flow is 0.03 × 1.5 = 0.045 million for interest. Fluid cash flow is £1.545 million. The present value is:

PV of pound cash flow = $0.045 \times e^{-0.055 \times 0.5} + 0.045 \times e^{-0.055 \times 1.0} + 0.045 \times e^{-0.055 \times 1.5} + 1.545 \times e^{-0.055 \times 2.0}$

$\quad = 0.0438 + 0.0426 + 0.0414 + 1.3841$ $\qquad = £1.5119$ million

PV of pound cast flow in rupee terms = 82.00 × 1.5119 $\qquad = ₹123.9735$

Value of the swap for (in millions)	Firm ₹	Firm £	Bank ₹	Bank £
Rupee leg	−121.71	−1.4842	+121.71	+1.4842
Pound leg	+123.97	+1.5119	−123.97	−1.5119

OTHER SWAPS

A swap implies an interchange. It need not be on interest rates or currencies alone. The basic idea of a swap is to have the interchange based on different parameters so that the complexion of asset or liability changes from fixed to variable or vice versa, as may be required.

Commodity Swaps

The prices of commodities change continuously. If the prices of the output were fixed, the profit would be variable. By entering into futures contracts, traders can render stable profits. However, a futures contract as a hedging tool remains a short-term measure, as the hedging period is limited to the maximum maturity of the futures contracts available at any point of time. Swaps, being OTC products, can ensure hedging of profits for longer periods.

Consider the case of a jeweller who makes ornaments using gold. Gold prices change almost continuously, but the prices of the finished product cannot change that often causing the profit margin of the jeweller to fluctuate. By entering into a swap where the jeweller pays a fixed rate for gold, but receives cash flow determined on the basis of the current price of gold, the cost can be fixed. A plain vanilla swap with monthly cash flows where the jeweller pays a fixed rate (₹23,000 per 10 g), but receives on the basis of a monthly average price, is depicted in Fig. 8.14. This swap would provide a hedge against the fluctuating price of gold.

the interest and principal, as fixed at the time of setting up of the swap deal, do not change. With the change in the domestic interest rates, the discounted value of the rupee cash flow changes, as shown in Table 8.8.

Table 8.8 Value of the swap with change in interest rate

(Figures in lakh)

Year	Interest and principal (₹)	Interest and principal (US $)	PV (₹ discounted at 10%)	PV (US $ discounted at 4%)
1	360.00	4.00	327.27	3.85
2	360.00	4.00	297.52	3.70
3	360.00	4.00	270.47	3.56
4	360.00	4.00	245.88	3.42
5	360.00	4.00	223.53	3.29
6	5000.00	100.00	3104.61	82.19
Total			4469.29	100.00
Present value in equivalent rupees				5000.00
Value of swap				−530.71

It is evident from Table 8.8 that with the rise in the interest rates for the rupee, the discounted value of the rupee cash flow falls, and if the firm pays in rupees, the value of the swap would become ₹531 lakh. For a firm that receives rupees and pays dollars, the value of the swap is positive, at ₹531 lakh. These values can be used to reverse the positions in the swaps taken earlier. Therefore, the value of the swap is ₹531 lakh.

The value of the swap is obtained if transactions under the swap are regarded as a series of forward contracts as shown in Table 8.9. One can summaries actions as follows:

- Calculate the implied forward rates as per interest rate parity
- Convert the foreign currency cash flows to domestic currency at the implied forward
- Discount the payment differential at the domestic interest rate

Table 8.9 Value of currency swap as series of forward contracts

(Figures

Year	₹ Interest and principal	$ Interest and principal	Implied forward rate (₹/$)	Equivalent ₹	Value of forward	PV o
1	360.00	4.00	52.88	211.54	148.46	
2	360.00	4.00	55.94	223.74	136.26	
3	360.00	4.00	59.16	236.65	123.35	
4	360.00	4.00	62.58	250.30	109.70	
5	360.00	4.00	66.19	264.74	95.26	
6	5000.00	100.00	66.19	6618.61	−1618.61	
Value of the swap						

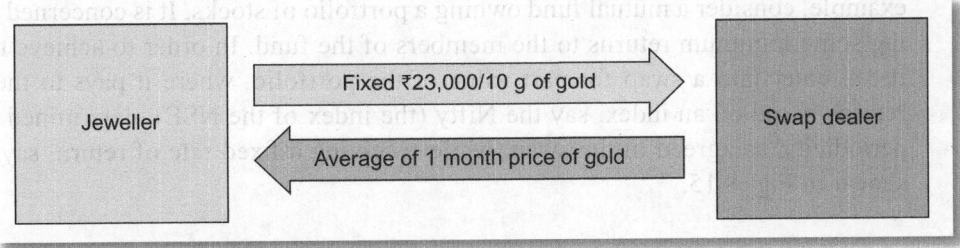

Fig. 8.14 Plain vanilla commodity swap

Like other swaps, the swap can be done for a notional quantity of gold that need not be exchanged. The life of the swap contract can also be fixed. More complex swaps can be executed where the two legs are based on different commodities and different currencies.

Valuation of Commodity Swap Just like any other swap, the value of a commodity swap at the time of its initiation must equal zero, i.e., the likely receipts must cancel out the likely payments in present value terms. The present value of the fixed leg is easy to obtain, as we know the amount of the fixed price and the risk-free rate. The risk-free rate may be obtained from the term structure of interest rates based on 'zeros'. The floating leg would be based on forecasts of the price of the commodity. If one can know the forward price, the present value can be computed using zero rates.

Consider this example. A jeweller wants to receive an average of 6-m prices for gold for a period of three years every six months. The forecast average price and the term structure of interest rate are as given in the first two rows of Table 8.10.

Table 8.10 Valuation of commodity swap

Months	0–6	6–12	12–18	18–24	24–30	30–36	Total
Forward price of gold, average over a period of 6 months (₹/10 g)	23,850	24,300	24,630	25,150	26,470	27,000	
Yield at the end of period (% p.a.)	8.00	8.35	8.60	9.00	9.30	9.50	
Discount factor	0.9623	0.9229	0.8836	0.8417	0.8007	0.7617	5.1728
PV of forward price, ₹	22,950	22,427	21,763	21,168	21,194	20,565	130,066
Value of fixed leg, ₹							25,144

To arrive at the fixed payment, we need to find the present values of the floating rate payments. The initial value of the swap must be zero. Therefore, the present value of fixed leg payments is equal to the present value of floating leg receipts

Equating the two cash flows, the jeweller must pay a fixed sum of ₹25,144 (₹130,066/5.1728) at the end of every six months for the next three years to receive an average gold price.

Equity Swaps

Under an equity swap, one party pays a fixed rate of return and receives a return based on stock index returns for the preceding period. Stock market returns are variable. For example, consider a mutual fund owning a portfolio of stocks. It is concerned about providing some minimum returns to the members of the fund. In order to achieve this objective, it can enter into a swap for part value of the portfolio, where it pays to the swap dealer returns based on an index, say the Nifty (the index of the NSE), determined at a specified periodicity, as agreed in the swap, while receiving a fixed rate of return, say 10%. This is shown in Fig. 8.15.

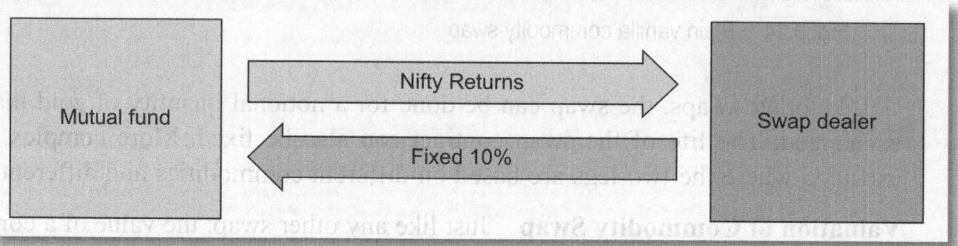

Fig. 8.15 Plain vanilla equity swap

With such a swap, the mutual fund locks in a return of 10% on the value of the swap. The mutual fund pays returns equal to the percentage gains/losses on the index in exchange for receiving a fixed 10%, locking-in a 10% return. Part of the portfolio would then be transformed from equity to bonds. Again, we do not exchange the principal, which remains only notional and serves a purpose in the computation of cash flows. In the event of negative returns in a period, the mutual fund would in fact receive on both the legs of the swap.

There are two important differences between an interest rate swap and an equity/index swap. The payments of fixed and floating rates are decided at the beginning of the period in the interest rate swap. In case of the equity swap, the variable leg is determined at the end of the period only after knowing the value of the stock/index. Further, in case of negative returns on the index, the payer of the variable rate must pay the index returns as well as the fixed payment to the receiver.

To hedge against variability of return, the fund can receive variable and pay fixed. Such a swap would be useful in bearish market conditions with rising interest rates. In case of bearish conditions with falling interest rates, the fund can enter a swap receiving variable and paying floating.

A variant to the equity swap can be the exchange of cash flows that are variable, based on index returns. However, the indices for the two legs would be different. For example, a fund in India, having invested in the Indian equity market, is desirous of taking an exposure in the US markets. Similarly, a fund in the USA is willing to invest in the Indian capital markets. The two funds can enter a swap whereby the Indian fund receives returns based on the Dow Jones Industrial Average and the US fund receives returns based on the Nifty index. The advantage to both the parties is that they are enabled to earn returns from the other market without making an additional investment.

Valuation The valuation of an equity/index swap is surprisingly simple. For valuation of an equity/index swap at any point of time or at the beginning for determination of fixed coupon payments, we may use the expectation hypothesis and futures pricing. The forward price of an index is given by the prevailing price of futures contracts. The fair price of a futures contract is given as its spot price plus the cost of carry computed at a risk-free rate. Hence, the present value of the index return when discounted at the risk-free rate would be the index value now. The coupon rate (equivalent to the swap rate) can be found using Eq. 8.6.

CONCLUSION

Innovations in swaps are taking place at a fast pace. Swaptions (options on swaps) are also becoming popular. A *call* swaption gives one the right to receive a fixed payment of interest and a *put* swaption gives the holder the right to pay a fixed rate of interest. In each case, the holder pays a nominal front-end premium to cover the risk of rising or falling interest rates.

With regard to comparison with other derivatives such as options and futures, a swap is an OTC product taking into account the specific needs of counterparties, with financial institutions and banks serving as intermediaries.

The advantages and popularity of swaps rest on the validity of the theory of comparative advantage of international trade. The theory of comparative advantage would predict the disappearance of swaps as an instrument of reduced financing cost, as with time opportunities for credit arbitrage should vanish. However, the increasing volumes of swap transactions are defying this logic. As long as imperfections in the capital markets persist, swaps would continue to grow. These imperfections have their roots in controls, incentives, and protection measures exercised by various governments, making access to capital markets discriminatory. Governments may prohibit non-resident firms from accessing capital markets or may offer subsidized loans to promote development. Such aberrations based on the domicile of firms are likely to continue, and would offer scope for swaps, as a tool for reducing financing cost, to take place.

SOLVED PROBLEMS

SP 8.1: Changing nature of asset from floating to fixed income

Cash Rich Ltd (CRL) have invested ₹50 crore in market-linked securities, providing them with a current return of 8%, with current MIBOR at 7.50%. Of late, yields in the market have started falling, adversely affecting CRL's income. They need to protect their income. Professional Bank Ltd, their banker, has offered a 3-year MIBOR-based swap with rates at 7.30%–7.40%. Should CRL accept the swap, what income can they lock-in for the next three years? What would be the advantage of the swap? Depict the swap arrangement.

Solution:

Cash Rich Ltd has a current income at 50 bps above the MIBOR, currently at 7.50%. Since the MIBOR is likely to fall, it is advisable for CRL to accept the swap with the bank. The swap arrangement is depicted as follows:

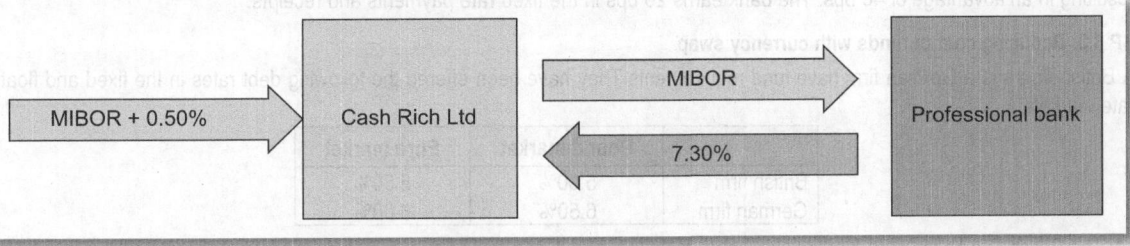

The income for Cash Rich Ltd would be MIBOR + 0.50% + 7.30% − MIBOR = 7.80%

By entering a swap with the bank, CRL may transform its asset from a floating rate to a fixed rate. In case MIBOR falls to less than 7.30%, CRL would have the benefit of the swap.

By entering the swap, CRL does not need to alter its investment portfolio.

SP 8.2: Reducing cost of funds with interest rate swap

Company P and Company Q have equal requirement for funds of ₹50 crore each. They have been offered the following debt rates in the fixed and floating rate markets for debt:

	Fixed rate	Floating rate
Company P	10.00%	MIBOR + 50 bps
Company Q	12.00%	MIBOR + 150 bps

P wants funds at a floating rate, while Q is happy to raise funds on a fixed rate basis. A bank is willing to act as intermediary, with 20 bps as its remuneration. Depict a swap sharing the gains equally and find out the cost of funds for P and Q. What would the saving in financing cost for each firm be?

Solution

The absolute advantage for company P is 200 bps in the fixed rate market, while it is 100 bps in the floating rate market. Therefore, the comparative advantage is 100 bps, which needs to be shared among the bank, P and Q. With the bank wanting 20 bps, the remaining 80 bps are shared equally: 40 bps each for P and Q.

Though company P wants to raise finance at a floating rate, the firm must access the fixed rate market and then enter into a swap deal with the bank to convert the fixed rate liability into a floating rate liability. Similarly, Q can access the floating rate market and enter into a swap with the bank to convert its floating rate liability into a fixed rate liability.

One such structure is presented here:

Interest rate swap: A schematic view with intermediary

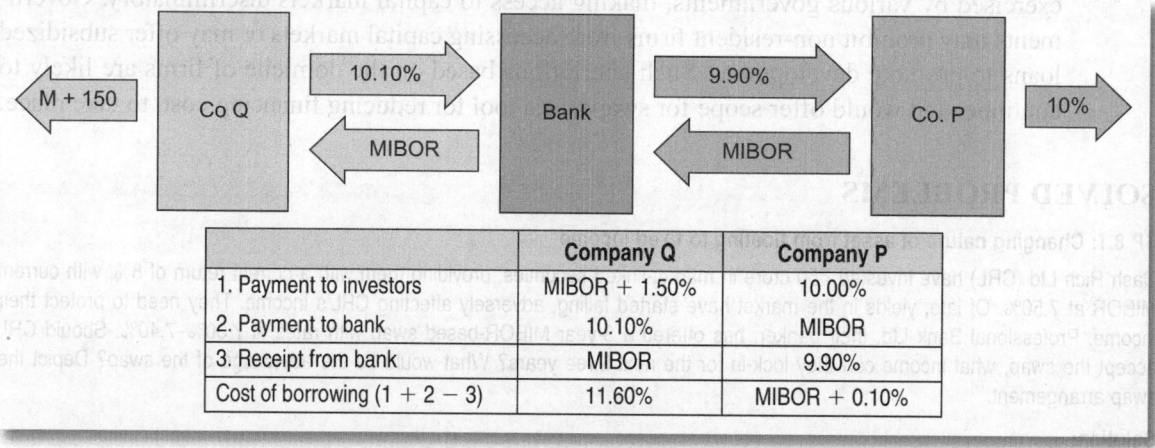

	Company Q	Company P
1. Payment to investors	MIBOR + 1.50%	10.00%
2. Payment to bank	10.10%	MIBOR
3. Receipt from bank	MIBOR	9.90%
Cost of borrowing (1 + 2 − 3)	11.60%	MIBOR + 0.10%

The aggregate cost of funds for P would be MIBOR + 10 bps, a saving of 40 bps on the cost it would have borne if it had accessed the floating rate market. Similarly, Q obtains funds at 11.60% against 12% that it would have otherwise paid without the swap deal, resulting in an advantage of 40 bps. The bank earns 20 bps in the fixed rate payments and receipts.

SP 8.3: Reducing cost of funds with currency swap

A British firm and a German firm have fund requirements They have been offered the following debt rates in the fixed and floating rate markets:

	Pound market	Euro market
British firm	5.00%	5.50%
German firm	6.50%	6.00%

The British firm needs euro funding obtainable at 5.50%, and the German firm requires pounds, available at 6.50%. Demonstrate how both the firms can reduce their cost of funds by having a swap of cash flows. Assume equal requirement of funds.

Solution

The absolute advantage for the British firm is 150 bps in the pound market, while it is at an advantage of 50 bps in the Euro market. Therefore, the comparative advantage is 100 bps, which needs to be shared between the German and British firms. With equal sharing, the advantage to each would be 50 bps.

The British firm must access the pound market and the German firm must borrow in euros; the two firms can then exchange cash flows in pounds and euros, with each paying interest in the currency of loan of the other and re-exchange the principal cash flows on maturity. The swap arrangement is shown here:

The cost of funds after the swap deal would be:

For the British firm: £5.00% − £5.00% + €5.00% = €5.00%; a saving of 0.50%
For the German firm: €6.00% − €5.00% + £5.00% = €1.00% + £5.00%, 6%; a saving of 0.50%

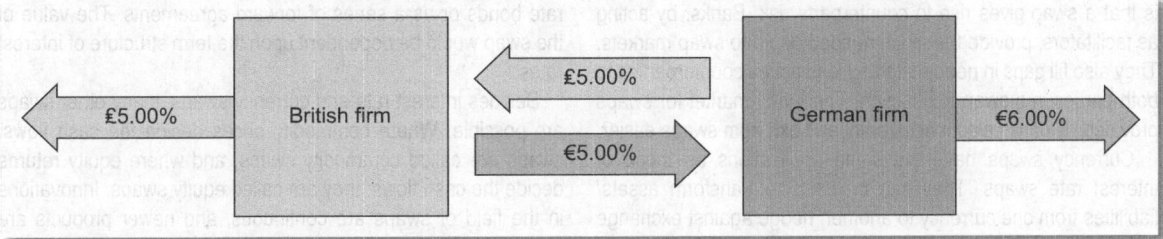

SP 8.4: Value of interest rate swap

A firm has a swap under which it pays a fixed interest of 9% and receives floating interest on a semi-annual basis. The swap has 14 months to go, with the next payment falling due after two months. The rate for the floating payment was fixed four months ago at 10.10%. If the term structure for the next 15 months is flat at 10.10%, what is the value of the swap for the firm?

Solution

The value of the fixed leg of the swap would consist of interest payments at 9% (₹4.50% semi-annual) after 2, 8, and 14 months. If considered as a bond, the final payment would also involve repayment of principal of ₹100.00. The present value discounted at 10.10% (term structure is flat) for all the payments is ₹101.5161, as shown here:

PV of fixed cash flow = $4.50 \times e^{-0.101 \times 2/12} + 4.50 \times e^{-0.101 \times 8/12} + 104.50 \times e^{-0.101 \times 14/12}$
= 4.4249 + 4.2070 + 92.8842 = ₹101.5161

Similarly, payment for the floating leg, determined four months ago at 10.10%, would be ₹5.50, to be made after two months. The next payment would be decided then. It implies that the floating rate payment marks itself to par then. Therefore, the value of the floating leg would be

PV of floating cash flow = $105.50 \times e^{-0.101 \times 2/12}$ = ₹103.2965

Therefore the firm paying fixed and receiving floating would have a value of ₹2.78 (103.30 − 101.52) per ₹100 of the notional amount, or 2.78%.

SUMMARY

Swaps came into being to overcome the limitations posed by regulatory controls over capital flows across borders when MNCs resorted to mutual parallel loans to fund their operations overseas. Later, when capital controls were removed, they developed into full-blown financial products.

A swap may be defined as an exchange of a series of cash flows, based on a parameter, at periodic intervals for a fixed period. Where the cash flows are based on interest rates, the swap is called an interest rate swap. When the exchange of cash flow is based on currency exchange rates, it is called a currency swap. In an interest rate swap, one leg of the cash flow is based on a fixed interest rate on a notional principal, while the other leg of the cash flow, called the floating leg, is based on a market-based floating rate. No principal is exchanged either at the initiation or at the conclusion of the swap. Only the differential of the cash flow is exchanged.

An interest rate swap can alter the complexion of the nature of a liability or an asset from a fixed rate to a floating rate or vice versa, without disturbing the original contract. Interest rate swaps serve as hedging tools against interest rate risks. Faced with rising interest rates, a firm can alter the liability of a loan from a floating rate to a fixed rate with a swap entered into with a bank, without disturbing the original loan contract. Other than working as a tool to hedge against interest rate risk, a swap has the potential to save funding cost. This is due to the fact that different firms have unequal credit spreads in the fixed and floating markets for borrowing. The differential in the spread, referred to as comparative advantage, can be utilized for the benefit of two firms to reduce borrowing costs for either one or both.

A swap normally requires exact matching of needs of the two counterparties in terms of amount, maturity, timing, and periodicity of interest payments—a requirement that is difficult to fulfil and can constrain the development of the market. Another drawback is that a swap gives rise to counterparty risk. Banks, by acting as facilitators, provide the much needed depth to swap markets. They also fill gaps in need matching, and act as counterparties to both parties in a swap transaction. The ready market for swaps provided by banks also makes entry and exit from swaps easier.

Currency swaps have the same applications as those of interest rate swaps. They can be used to transform assets/liabilities from one currency to another, hedge against exchange rate risk, and reduce funding cost for MNCs raising funds in different currencies. Unlike interest rate swaps, where no principal is exchanged, in currency swaps the principal amount is exchanged at the initiation of the swap and re-exchanged upon its termination. During the swap, the interest rates either fixed or floating, are exchanged in two different currencies.

At the initiation of the swap, the value of the swap is always zero, as the PVs of the two opposite legs are equal. The value of the swap is determined on the basis of the interest rate scenario in interest rate swaps. While the cash flow of the fixed leg is known in advance, the payments on the floating leg are decided only one period in advance, and are reset at periodic intervals. A changing interest rate scenario creates value. For valuation, a swap may be treated either as a pair of fixed rate and floating rate bonds or as a series of forward agreements. The value of the swap would be dependent upon the term structure of interest rates.

Besides interest rate and currency swaps, many other swaps are possible. Where commodity prices decide the cash flows, swaps are called commodity swaps, and where equity returns decide the cash flows, they are called equity swaps. Innovations in the field of swaps are continuous, and newer products are being developed from time to time. Being an OTC product, modifications in the terms and conditions of swaps are aplenty.

KEY TERMS

Basis swap A swap in which both the legs are floating, but with different benchmarks.
Commodity swap The exchange of cash flows based on the prices of commodities, with one payment fixed and the other variable.
Counterparty risk The risk that a counterparty to a contract would default on the promised commitment.
Equity swap A swap under which one fixed cash flow is exchanged for another cash flow dependent upon an index.
Financial/currency swap A series of cash inflows and outflows between two parties based on currency exchange rates on a notional principal.

Interest rate swap A series of cash inflows and outflows between two parties based on interest rates on a notional principal.
MIBOR Mumbai interbank offer rate, akin to LIBOR
Parallel loans The loans made by two parties to each other to meet requirements that otherwise could not be met by either party by itself.
Reset date The prior date at which the next payment for the floating leg is decided under a swap.
Swap dealer An intermediary—usually a bank—that facilitates a swap deal by becoming a counterparty to each of the parties to the swap, and fills in any gaps in the transaction.

QUESTIONS

8.1 What do you understand by parallel loans? Explain with an example.
8.2 Describe the features of an interest rate swap.
8.3 How would you convert a floating rate liability into a fixed rate liability using a swap? Draw a schematic diagram to explain your answer.
8.4 If an enterprise has invested funds in securities providing a floating rate of income, what risk does it faces? How would you hedge such a risk using an interest rate swap?
8.5 What are the problems in arranging a swap, and how are they overcome by a swap intermediary/bank?
8.6 Explain hedging of fixed rate and floating rate loans using swaps.
8.7 What is a currency swap, and how is it different operationally from an interest rate swap?
8.8 Currency swaps can be used to convert assets/liabilities from one currency to another. Explain with a suitable example.
8.9 How are currency swaps and interest rate swaps used for reducing cost?
8.10 What do you understand by swap rate? What inputs are required in computing the swap rate?
8.11 In what ways can the value of a swap be found? How is the value of a swap important?

PROBLEMS

P 8.1 Pricing swap: finding the swap rate
The following is the term structure of interest rates prevailing today;

Term (months)	Yield % p.a.
6	4.00
12	4.20
18	4.40
24	4.50
30	4.60
36	4.80
42	5.00
48	5.20
54	5.40
60	5.50

Assuming 360 days in a year, a simple interest rate, 180 days in each semi-annual period, and a spread of 20 basis points, find the swap rate for a 5-year swap with semi-annual payments.

P 8.2 Pricing a forward swap
Refer to Problem 8-1. What rate would be quoted for a 3-year swap commencing two years from now?

P 8.3 Hedge against falling yield
A firm had issued 10-year bonds worth ₹10 crore at a fixed coupon of 12%, payable semi-annually. The coupon was consistent with the yield prevailing at the time of the issue. Since then, the yield has fallen, and the bond has 5 years remaining for maturity.

The swap rate offered by a bank is 9.00–9.20% against a floating rate based on MIBOR. Depict the swap arrangement of the firm with the bank, and find out the cost of the bond after the swap is entered.

P 8.4 Reducing cost of funds with swaps
Firm A and Firm B have identical requirement of funds, and both are exploring raising of funds either at a fixed rate or at a floating rate. The following rates are offered by the market to both:

	Fixed rate market	Floating rate market
Firm A	10%	MIBOR + 1%
Firm B	11%	MIBOR + 3.50%

Firm A is more interested in raising a fixed rate loan, perceiving that rates will increase in the future, while firm B believes to the contrary, and wants to issue floating rate debt instruments. Show how the cost of funds may be decreased for both the firms if benefits of swap are to be shared equally.

P 8.5 Value of an interest rate swap
An interest rate swap entered into sometime back had a fixed rate of 8.50% payable semi-annually on a notional principal of ₹100 crore. The last payment was made exactly three months back, when the next floating payment was decided at 10%. The yield curve has undergone a change since then, and is currently as follows for the remaining 45 months and the next eight payments:

Time (months)	Term structure
3	8.00%
9	8.10%
15	8.20%
21	8.20%
28	8.30%
33	8.50%
39	8.50%
45	8.70%

If the parties are willing to cancel the swap, find out the cash flow involved in cancellation of the swap. Assume simple interest and equal semi-annual periods.

P 8.6 Value of a currency swap
An Indian firm, in order to convert its US dollar loan into a rupee loan, had entered a swap with a bank, receiving US dollars and paying Indian rupees. The swap was fixed for a principal of ₹100 lakh with rupee interest of 6% p.a. payable semi-annually. At the exchange rate prevailing then of ₹40.00 per dollar, the equivalent dollar amount was 2.50 lakh and the interest rate fixed was 3% p.a., payable semi-annually.

The yields in the Indian as well as US markets have changed since then. The yields for the remaining four years in rupee and in dollar are as follows:

Time (months)	Yield—rupee	Yield—dollar
6	5.00%	3.60%
12	5.50%	3.70%
18	5.60%	3.80%
24	5.80%	4.00%
30	6.00%	4.40%
36	6.10%	4.50%
42	6.20%	4.80%
48	6.30%	5.00%

Assuming a simple interest rate and all semi-annual periods equal, with the next payment due exactly after six months, find what value must be paid/received by the Indian firm if it wants to cancel the swap.

Options
Basics

INTRODUCTION

An option is a unique instrument that confers a right without an obligation to buy or sell another asset, called the underlying asset. Like forwards and futures, it is a derivative instrument because the value of the right so conferred would depend on the price of the underlying asset at that time. As such, options derive their values inter alia from the price of the underlying asset. For easier comprehension of the concept of an option, an example using stocks as the underlying asset is most apt.

> Options are unique instruments that confer a right but create no obligation to perform.

Consider an option on the share of a firm, say ITC Ltd. It would confer a right to the holder to either buy or sell a share of ITC. Naturally, this right would be available at a price, which is in turn derived from the price of the shares of ITC. Hence, an option on ITC would be priced according to the price of ITC shares prevailing in the market. Of course, this right can be made available at a specific predetermined price and remains valid for a certain limited period of time.

The unique feature of the option is that while it confers the right to buy or sell the underlying asset, the holder is not obligated to perform. The holder, at his/her option, can force the counterparty to honour the commitment made. Obligations of the holder would arise only when he/she decides to exercise his/her right. Therefore, an option may be defined as a contract that gives the owner the right but not the obligation, to buy or sell an asset at a predetermined price within a given time frame. It is the absence of obligation to perform by one of the parties that makes the option contract a substantially different derivative product from forwards and futures, which are characterized by equal and binding obligations on both parties to the contract. This unique feature of an option makes several applications possible, which may not be feasible with other derivative products.

Learning Objectives

After going through this chapter, readers should be familiar with

- the basic concept of options
- the terminology used in describing options
- the basics of call and put options and their payoffs
- types of options
- the moneyness of options
- how to read options quotations
- how options are traded and settled
- how options are different from forward and futures contracts

TERMINOLOGY OF OPTIONS

Before we discuss how an option contract works, it would be handy to familiarize ourselves with the basic terms that are often used in describing and using options. These basic terms are described as follows:

Call Option   A right, but no obligation, to *buy* the underlying asset at a predetermined price within a specified interval of time is called a *call* option.

Put Option   A right, but no obligation, to *sell* the underlying asset at a predetermined price within a specified interval of time is called a *put* option.

Buyer or Holder   The person who has the right but not an obligation to buy or sell is called the owner or holder of the option. The holder of an option has to pay a premium to obtain the right.

Writer or Seller   The person who confers the right and undertakes the obligation to the holder is called the seller or writer of an option.

Premium   While conferring a right on the holder, who is under no obligation to perform, the writer is entitled to charge a fee upfront. This upfront amount is called the premium. This is paid by the holder to the writer, and is also called the price of the option.

Strike Price   The price predetermined at the time of buying/writing of an option, at which the option can be exercised, is called the strike price. It is the price at which the holder of an option buys/sells the asset.

Strike Date/maturity Date   The right to exercise an option is valid for a limited period of time. The time by when the option must be exercised is called the time to maturity. It is also referred to as expiry/maturity date.

These terms would become more clear when the two basic options, call and put, are described in more detail, which we will do now.

CALL OPTION

Assume that the share of ITC is currently trading at ₹180. An investor, John, believes that the share is going to rise to at least ₹220 in the next three months. John does not have adequate funds to buy the share now but is expecting to receive substantial money in the next three months. He cannot afford to miss an opportunity to own this share. Waiting for three months implies not only a greater outlay at a later point of time, but also means foregoing of substantial potential gains. Another investor, Mohammad, holds contrary views and believes that John's optimism is exaggerated. He is willing to sell the share.

What can John do under the present circumstances where he cannot buy the shares on an outright basis? He could possibly borrow to acquire stock in ITC. Amongst the many alternatives that may be available to John is an instrument called the call option. Instead of buying the share outright from Mohammad, he can instead buy a call option (assuming Mohammad is willing to confer such an option) stating that John has a right to buy ITC shares from Mohammad at a price of, say, ₹190 at any time during the next three months. This would be

> A call option is a right, but not an obligation, to buy an asset at a predetermined price within a specified time.

a call option (the option to buy). John is the holder of the option, while Mohammad is the writer/seller of the option. In case John decides to buy the share (exercise the option) he would pay ₹190, the strike/exercise price. The period during which John can exercise this option is three months. Note that John has an option that he may or may not exercise, but Mohammad has no such choice, and he stands committed to deliver the share by claiming ₹190 from John, irrespective of the price of ITC share at that time. Naturally, Mohammad would not provide such a right for free, as he is obligated to perform at the option of another person. Therefore, Mohammad would charge some fee, called the option premium, to grant this right to John. This premium is determined inter alia by the price of the underlying asset, the ITC share. We shall discuss later how this premium is decided.

> To obtain a right without an obligation, the option holder has to pay a premium price, called option price, to the entity conferring the right.

We now discuss the circumstances if John exercises his option. He would use this right only when the actual price of the ITC share has gone beyond ₹190 (the exercise price). Imagine it has moved to ₹200. By exercising the option, he stands to gain ₹10 immediately, as he gets one share from Mohammad by paying ₹190 and sells it immediately in the market at ₹200. Logically, John would not exercise the option if the price remained below ₹190. In that case, his maximum loss is the premium paid. If the price remains below ₹190, Mohammad would not be asked to deliver, and the upfront premium he received would be his profit.

We may generalize the outcome of a call option in the following manner:

As long as the price of the underlying asset, S, remains below the strike price, X, the buyer of the call option will not exercise it, and the loss to the buyer would be limited to the premium paid on the call option, c; if the price goes higher than the exercise price, the holder exercises the option and generates a profit equal to the difference between the two prices, adjusted for the premium paid. Alternatively, this can be expressed as follows:

> The holder of a call option exercises the option when the price of the underlying asset is more than the strike price.

When $S < X$ buyer lets the call expire   loss = premium c
When $S = X$ buyer is indifferent   loss = premium c
When $S > X$ buyer exercises the call option   gain = $S - X - c$

Mathematically, the value of the call is given by Eq. 9.1.

$$\text{Value of the call option} = \text{Max}(0, S - X) - c \qquad (9.1)$$

A graphical depiction of the payoff of the holder and writer of the call option is easier to comprehend, and is presented in Fig. 9.1 (a) and (b).

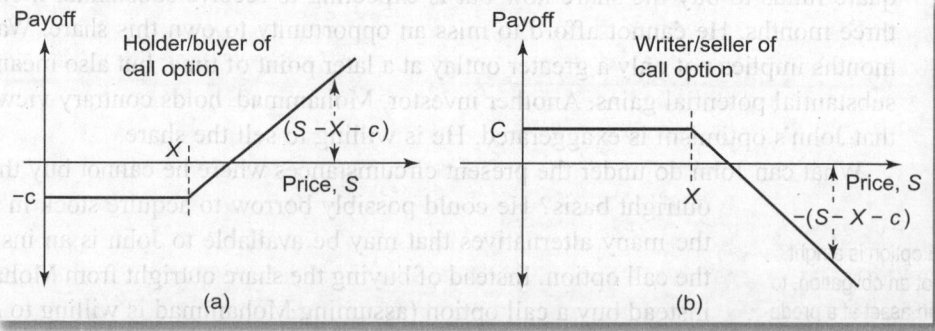

Fig. 9.1 Graphical view of payoff of call option (a) for buyer (b) for seller

PUT OPTION

> A put option is a right, but not an obligation, to sell an asset at a predetermined price within a specified time.

A put option is similar to a call option, except for the fact that it is an option to sell. We again take a small example from the stock markets to clarify how a put option works.

Again, assume that the share of ITC is currently trading at ₹180. An investor, John, who is in possession of the share (it is not necessary to have the share to enter into an options contract) believes that it is likely to fall to ₹150 in the next three months. John is not absolutely sure of a fall, but would still like to exit from his investment at ₹175. He is seeking protection against a heavier fall in the price. Another investor, Mohammad, holds a contrary view and believes that John's pessimism is exaggerated. He is willing to buy the share at ₹175, since he feels that is the lowest it can go.

John believes that ITC is a good long-term buy but is unsure about when the scrip would realize its potential. He does not want to exit unnecessarily. Under these circumstances, John can buy a put option (the right to sell) from Mohammad, stating that he has the right to sell a share of ITC to Mohammad at a price of ₹175 at any time during the next three months. In case John decides to sell the share (exercise the option) he would receive ₹175, the strike/exercise price for the next three months. John has the option, which he may or may not exercise, but Mohammad has no such choice, and he stands committed to pay the agreed price and buy the share from John. Like in the call option, Mohammad would not grant such a right for free, and charges some fee upfront, the option premium. This premium is determined inter alia by the price of the underlying asset, the ITC share.

> The holder of a put option exercises the option when the price of the underlying asset is less than the strike price.

John would exercise his option only when it is profitable to do so. The option would become profitable when the actual price of the ITC share falls below ₹175 (the exercise price). Imagine that it has moved to ₹160. By exercising the option, John stands to gain ₹15 immediately by selling the share to Mohammad and realizing ₹175 from him, and using the proceeds to acquire a share of ITC from the market at ₹160. This keeps his earlier position intact and yet gives him ₹15 as profit. Logically, John would not exercise the option if the price remains above ₹175. However, under all circumstances, he loses the premium paid.

We may generalize the outcome of a put option in the following manner:

As long as the price of the security remains below the strike price, the buyer of the option will exercise it because he stands to gain; otherwise, his loss would be limited to the premium paid on the put option, p. This can be summarized as follows:

When $S < X$ buyer exercises the option   gain = $X - S - p$
When $S = X$ buyer is indifferent   loss = premium p
When $S > X$ buyer lets the contract expire loss = premium p

Mathematically, the value of the put is given by Eq. 9.2.

$$\text{Value of the put option} = \text{Max}(0, X - S) - p \qquad (9.2)$$

The graphical view of the payoff for the put option holder and the writer is shown in Figs 9.2(a) and (b).

262 Derivatives and Risk Management

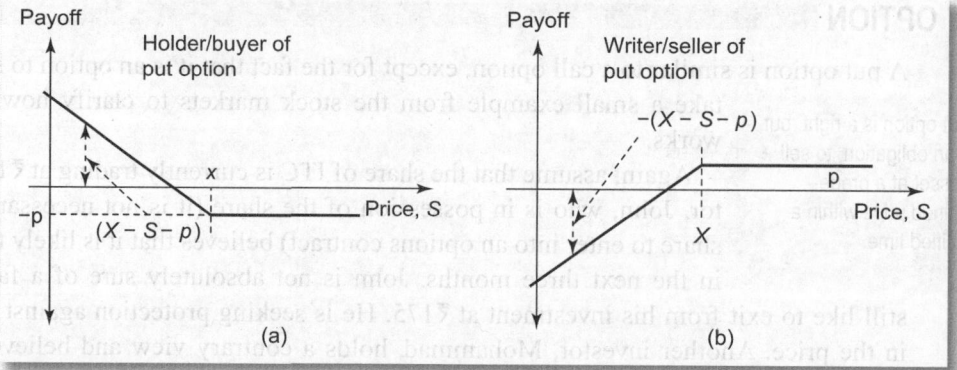

Fig. 9.2 Graphical view of payoff of put option (a) for buyer (b) for seller

> Options have unsymmetrical, non-linear payoff, unlike forwards and futures, because they do not create an obligation.

The payoff diagrams for call and put options as depicted in Figs 9.1 and 9.2 reveal that the payoff on the options is not linear. While it may be unbounded at one end, the other end is limited to a loss/gain equal to the premium on the option. This unsymmetrical, non-linear payoff results from the feature of 'right but no obligation', and makes options different from other derivative products.

Who Benefits?

> Options are a zero-sum game; the gain of the holder is the loss of the writer, and vice versa.

All options are a zero-sum game; what is gained by the holder of an option exactly the same amount is lost by the writer. Similarly, the gain of the writer is exactly the loss of the holder. Table 9.1(a) shows the payoff to the holder and writer of the call option at an exercise price of ₹190 and asset prices ranging from ₹125 to ₹225. The payoff is governed by the actions of the option buyer. If the price of the asset increases beyond the exercise price, the call option holder would buy the asset at the exercise price and sell the same asset in the market to derive a profit. The call option writer would have to obtain the asset from the market, but realizes only the exercise price. The market price being higher, he/she would incur a loss. If the price remains below the exercise price, the holder does not exercise the option, and the writer pockets the premium as a profit.

Table 9.1(a) Payoff of call option $X = ₹190$

Price of the asset (₹)	Payoff—call holder			Payoff—call writer		
	Buy from writer (₹)	Sell in the market (₹)	Profit/loss (₹)	Sell to holder (₹)	Buy from market (₹)	Profit (+) /loss (−)
125	Holder does not exercise the call option; loses premium paid at the time of buying the call option			Obligation of writer does not arise; gains premium received at the time of writing the call option		
150						
175						
200	190	200	10	190	200	−10
225	190	225	35	190	225	−35

Table 9.1(b) Payoff of put option $X = ₹160$

Price of the asset (₹)	Payoff—put holder			Payoff—put writer		
	Sell to writer (₹)	Buy from the market (₹)	Profit/loss (₹)	Pay to holder (₹)	Sell in the market (₹)	Profit/loss (₹)
125	160	125	35	160	125	−35
150	160	150	10	160	150	−10
175	Holder does not exercise the put option; loses premium paid at the time of buying the put option			Obligation of writer does not arise; gains premium received at the time of writing the put option		
200						
225						

Table 9.1(b) shows the payoff of the put option for the holder and the writer. Here, the option becomes profitable if the price remains below the exercise price, and, therefore, the holder exercises his/her option. Here, the holder would sell at the exercise price and buy back the asset from the market. The writer would have to buy from the holder and sell in the market.

MONEYNESS OF OPTIONS

Moneyness of options refers to the relationship between the price of the underlying asset and the exercise price. Generally, we use the terms *in-the-money* (ITM), *at-the-money* (ATM), and *out-of-the-money* (OTM) to explain the relationship between the cash flow of options upon exercise at any instant of time.

In-the-money, At-the-money, and Out-of-the-money Options

Depending upon their nature, payoffs from options are often referred to as ITM, ATM, or OTM. At any time, ITM options are those that, if exercised, would result in a positive cash flow to the holder. Similarly, OTM options would result in cash outflow if exercised and ATM options would have no cash flows.

> Moneyness of the option describes the benefit the holder gets if he/she exercises the option now.

A call option becomes profitable when the price of the underlying asset exceeds the exercise price. Similarly, a put option is worth exercising only when the price of the asset is less than the exercise price. A call option is called ITM when the asset price exceeds the exercise price. A put option would be ITM when asset price is lower than the exercise price.

When the asset price is equal to the exercise price, the option is called an ATM option. It applies to both call and put options.

Similarly, when the asset price is lower than the exercise price, a call option is OTM, while a put option would be OTM when the asset price exceeds the exercise price. This table captures the state of call and put options:

Underlying value, S	$S < X$	$S = X$	$S > X$
Call option	OTM	ATM	ITM
Put option	ITM	ATM	OTM

> **EXAMPLE 9.1 Moneyness of the call options**
>
> Three call options A, B, and C, with exercise prices of ₹100, ₹105, and ₹110 are trading at ₹2, ₹8, and ₹14, respectively, while the underlying stock is trading at ₹105. What is the moneyness of each of the options? What would be the moneyness of each option if the call prices increased by ₹2 each?
>
> **Solution**
> The moneyness of the call option is computed from the difference of the spot price, S, and the exercise price, X. It is the money the holder of the option would get if he/she exercises the option at the spot price prevailing. The moneyness of each option is as follows:
>
> Option A: $S - X = 105 - 100 =$ positive; in-the-money by ₹5
> Option B: $S - X = 105 - 105 =$ zero; at-the-money
> Option C: $S - X = 105 - 110 =$ negative; out-of-the-money by ₹5
>
> If the call prices increased by ₹2 each, there would be no impact on the moneyness of the options because the call price is the sunk cost.

TYPES OF OPTIONS

Options have several features, certainly more than forwards and futures, thus making several differentiations possible in the basic products of calls and puts. Based on several considerations, options can be categorized in the following manner:

- Based on the nature of exercise of options
- Based on how they are generated, traded, and settled
- Based on the underlying assets on which the options are created

Nature of Exercise: American vs European

Based on the timing of the exercise, options can be either American or European. American options can be exercised at any point of time on or before the expiry date of the option, while European options are exercisable only upon maturity.

Nature of Markets: Over-the-counter vs Exchange-traded

Options can also be categorized as over-the-counter (OTC) or exchange-traded, depending upon where and how they are created, traded, and settled. Options may be like forward contracts, which are specific, and are negotiated by two contracting parties through direct mutual negotiations, known as OTC. Alternatively, they can be like futures, which may be bought and sold at a specific exchange where the two contracting parties may not be known to each other, but instead enter into a contract through that exchange. Such contracts are called exchange-traded contracts. In exchange-traded options, the contracts need to be standardized, while an OTC product is tailor-made to the requirements of the parties involved.

> Options can be either tailor-made to requirements or exchange-traded in standardized forms.

The standardization of an option contract would be at the discretion of the exchange and is done in terms of the following:

- *Quantity of underlying asset* Only a specific quantity of the underlying asset, which needs to be predetermined, can be traded on the exchange.
- *Strike prices* Only specific strike prices can be handled in a standardized product traded on the exchanges. The OTC products can have any strike price agreed upon by the two contracting parties.
- *Expiration dates* Like strike prices, expiration dates too, must be known before trading can take place in options at the exchanges. Maturity dates too are standardized in exchange-traded options.
- *Nature of exercise of option* Traders must also know whether the options they are entering into are American or European in nature.
- *Ways of settlement* The mode of settlement can be either cash or physical. Cash settlement at expiry means the exchange of the difference between the exercise price and the price of the underlying asset, or by facilitating the cancellation of the original contract by entering into a new contract that is equal and opposite contract to it. Physical settlement would be executed by the delivery of the asset by one party and payment of the exercise price by the other.

Nature of Underlying Assets

Like forwards and futures, options too can have several assets as underlying. Options on stocks, indices, commodities, currencies, and interest rates are available either OTC or at exchanges. Though not available in India as of now, options on commodities are traded internationally on agricultural products, livestock, food products, energy, and metals.

Options are also available on various currencies, such as US dollar, euro, yen, and pound in major exchanges in the USA and Europe, as also other parts of the world including India. The OTC markets dominate options on currencies.

Besides, options are also traded on exchanges on futures contract rates. Options on futures have a futures contract as the underlying asset, giving the holder a right to buy (call) or sell (put) the specified futures contract within or at a specified time. Naturally, the expiry of the futures contract must extend beyond or match the expiry of the option contract.

Similarly, options can also be traded on interest rates, either on cash assets such as treasury bonds and notes, or on interest rate futures contracts. These options serve the same purposes as options on stocks and indices. Options on stocks and stock indices are most common. Several exchanges across the world offer options on indices and stock. The National Stock Exchange (NSE) in India offers options on several indices such as the Nifty, a broad-based index of 50 stocks from banking, information technology, infrastructure, etc. Options on other indices, including foreign indices, are also available.

Presently, these options cover a limited number of exercise prices and periods up to three months. However, internationally, options for longer periods of up to two or three years are also available. The NSE attempts to provide two strike prices that are in-the-money, one strike price that is at-the-money, and two strikes that are out-of-the-money options at any point of time. Hence, at any point of time, there would be a minimum of 15 call options and 15 put options (five strike prices with three maturities of one, two, and three months) available for trading.

UNDERSTANDING OPTIONS QUOTATIONS

Options prices are read in the same manner as the prices of any stock. Figure 9.3 presents a quotation for a call option at the NSE. The last traded price of the call option was ₹34.90, as on 8 October 2012. This is the price for a call option with a Nifty index as the underlying asset expiring on 25 October 2012, with the exercise price at 5,800, while the current value of the index is 5,671.80. One contract comprises 50 Nifty indices with the settlement date 25 October 2012. It is a European option that could be exercised only on maturity. The investor, who was bullish and assumed the position that the index would close above 5,800 on 25 October 2012, had paid ₹34.90 to the writer of the call.

Apart from stating the last traded price, the template also displays the day's opening, high, and low prices, as well as the previous day's closing price. Other information pertaining to the current value and volume of the underlying asset and the open interest is also given. Information on current investors' interests in terms of the order book is also available during trading hours.

Options quotations appear in business newspapers daily, giving the prices of the previous day. Figure 9.4, which depicts how *The Economic Times*, a business newspaper, displays the prices of options on a given day, is self-explicit. Options have to be specified in terms of their nature, expiry date, and strike price. Besides opening, high, low, and closing prices,

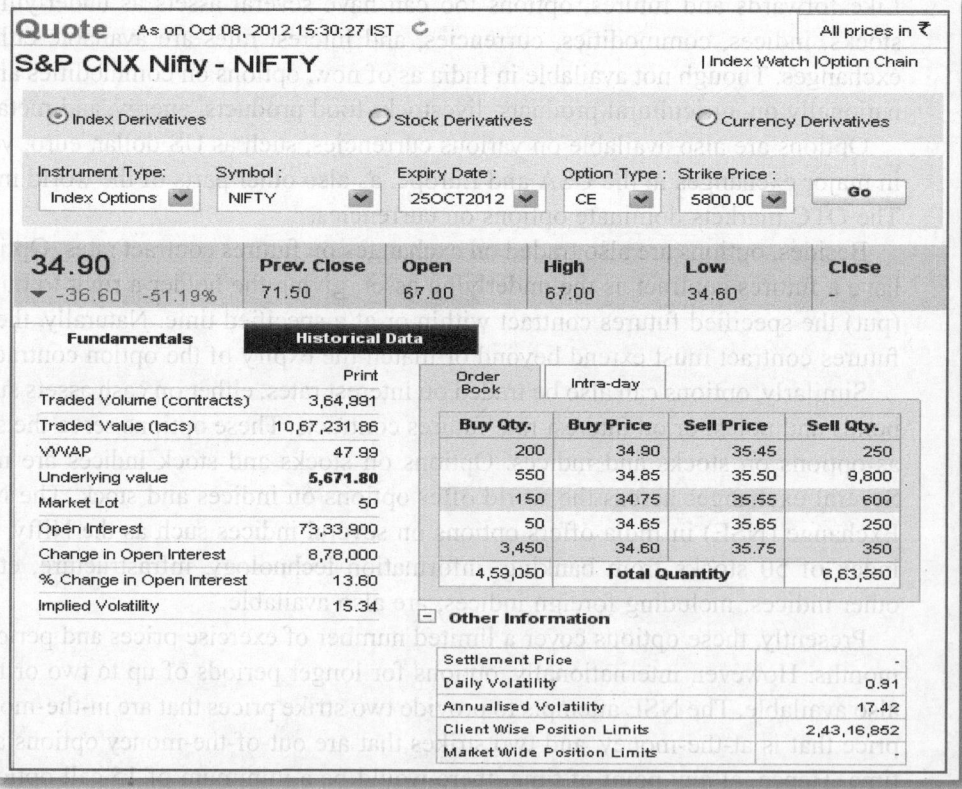

Source: www.nseindia.com, F&O quote, accessed on 8 October 2012.

Fig. 9.3 Price information of call option on NIFTY

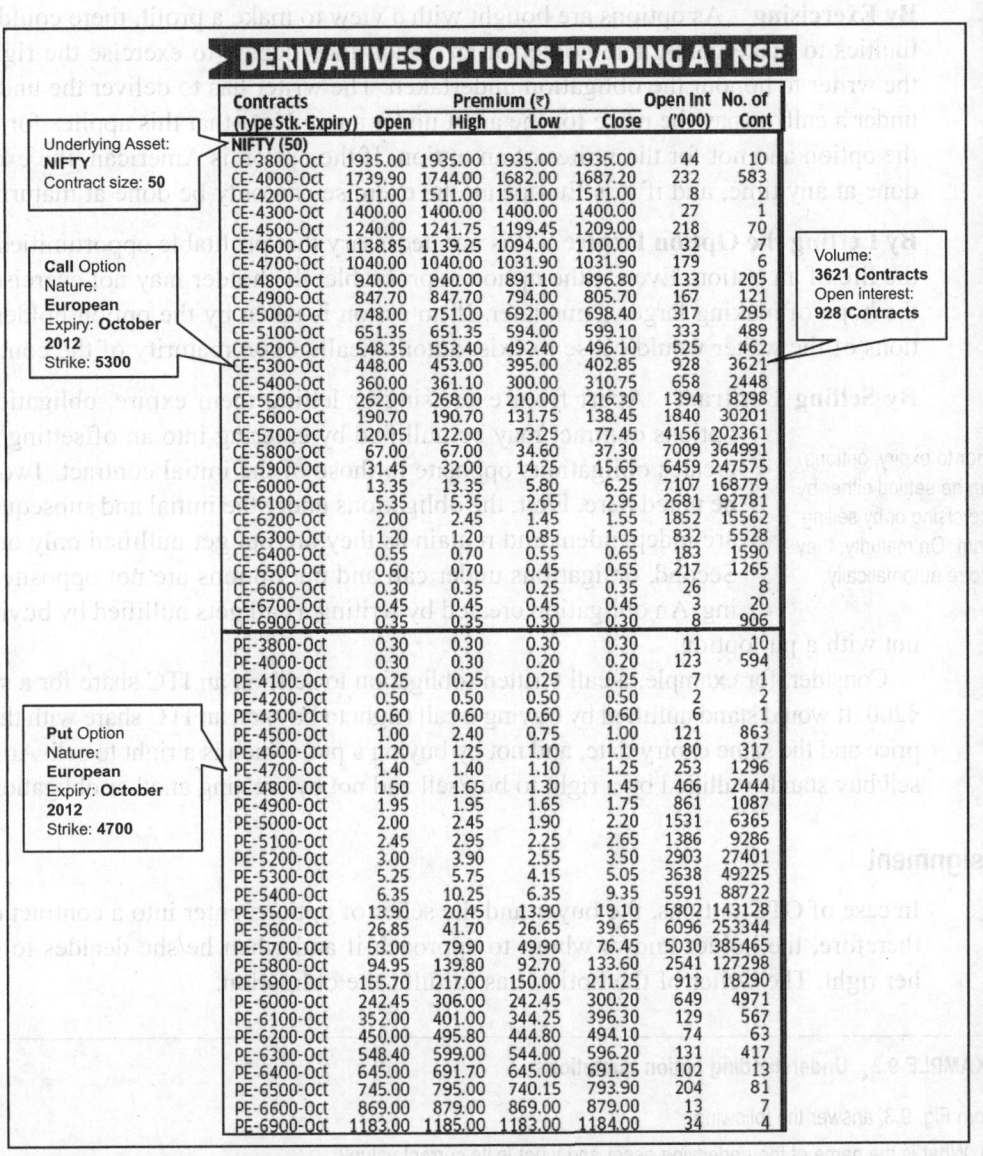

Fig. 9.4 Options quotations *The Economic Times*, Tuesday, 9 October 2012

information regarding volumes for the day and open interest (number of contracts that are yet to be settled) at the close of the day is also published.

TRADING AND SETTLEMENT

When an options contract is executed, the life of the contract is specified. No right can be given forever. The number of contracts that are not yet settled is known as the open interest. All option contracts must come to a close using any one of the three modes: *by exercising, by letting the option expire,* or *by selling.*

By Exercising As options are bought with a view to make a profit, there could exist opportunities to make gains. The holder of an option may decide to exercise the right, and force the writer to honour the obligation undertaken. The writer has to deliver the underlying asset under a call, or pay the price for the asset under a put. Note that this applies for the holder of the option and not for the writer of an option. If the option is American, the exercise can be done at any time, and if it is European, the exercise can only be done at maturity.

By Letting the Option Expire It is not necessary that profitable opportunities arise during the life of an option. Even if the option is profitable, the holder may not exercise the right in the hope of making larger gains later. If no action is taken by the option holder, the obligations of the writer would cease to exist automatically upon maturity of the contract.

By Selling Contract Apart from exercising or letting them expire, obligations under an options contract may be nullified by entering into an offsetting contract that creates obligations opposite to those of the initial contract. Two points must be noted here. First, the obligations under the initial and subsequent contracts are independent and remain as they are but get nullified only on a net basis. Second, obligations under call and put options are not opposite and nullifying. An obligation created by writing a call gets nullified by buying a call and not with a put option.

> Prior to expiry, options can be settled either by exercising or by selling them. On maturity, they expire automatically.

Consider, for example, a call written (obligation to sell) on an ITC share for a strike price of ₹200. It would stand nullified by buying a call (right to buy) on an ITC share with the same strike price and the same expiry date, and not by buying a put, which is a right to sell. An obligation to sell/buy stands nullified by a right to buy/sell and not by creating another obligation to buy/sell.

Assignment

In case of OTC options, the buyer and the seller of options enter into a contract directly, and, therefore, the holder knows whom to approach if and when he/she decides to exercise his/her right. The writer of the option has to fulfil the obligation.

EXAMPLE 9.2   Understanding option quotations

From Fig. 9.3, answer the following:
(a) What is the name of the underlying asset and what is its current value?
(b) Describe the nature of the option, its strike price, and its expiry.
(c) What is the premium paid by the buyer of one contract?
(d) What is the latest price of the option?
(e) What is the number of contracts that were not added up till the previous day?
(f) What is the number of contracts that were added today?

Solution
(a) Name of the underlying asset and its current value: Nifty, 5,671.80
(b) Nature of the option, its strike price, and its expiry: Call European, 5,800, 25 October, 2012
(c) Premium paid by the buyer of one contract: ₹34.90 × 50 = ₹1,745
(d) Latest price of the option: ₹34.90
(e) Number of contracts not added up up till the previous day: (73,33,900 − 8,78,000)/50 = 64,65,900/50 = 1,29,318
(f) Number of contracts added today: 8,78,000/50 = 17,560

In an exchange-traded option, the buyer and the seller are unknown to each other, and enter into a contract through an exchange. To each of them, the counterparty is the exchange. If the buyer needs to exercise the option, he/she has to advise his/her decision to the exchange only. In such a case, the exchange has the task of making good the claim made by the holder of the option. A suitable writer needs to be identified amongst several option sellers.

Suppose you have bought a call option at a strike price of ₹120. You do not know who exactly has written the call. If the asset price has moved up to ₹125, you stand to gain ₹5 by exercising the call. Not all the investors decide to exercise their calls. If you decide to exercise, someone must pay you ₹5 or deliver the asset. The exchange, therefore, assigns the liability to one of the several writers of options. The selection of who will be assigned the liability arising out of your option exercise is normally done on a random basis. The writer who is assigned the liability makes the payment and, therefore, loses the opportunity of cancelling his/her obligation by entering into an opposite contract (buying the call). If the short position in the option was taken as a hedge, the seller now stands exposed to the same risk that he/she had presumably covered through the initial position.

In the case of European options, the issue of assignment does not arise, as on the day of maturity there is an equality of long and short positions. However, American options are exercised at any time before or on maturity. The exchange has the responsibility to assign an exercised option to some option seller. This exercise of assignment is carried out during non-trading hours. Normally, exchanges allow only cash settlement of options, and, therefore, only ITM options are allowed to be exercised.

MARGINS IN OPTIONS

Options are one-sided contracts where the buyer has no obligations to perform except upon exercise, and only the writer has obligations. The holder has to deliver either cash equal to the exercise price, in case of a call option, or the underlying asset, in case of a put option. On initiating a position, the buyer of the option satisfies his/her obligations by paying a premium. On the contrary, the writer of the options assumes unlimited risk in case the price of the asset moves unfavourably. Since an exchange has the responsibility for settlement, it faces the risk of option sellers failing to meet their obligations. Since positions in options are cash-settled, it is assumed that the writer of the option would nullify his/her liability by buying the option back. Thus, his/her obligations would be limited to the premium payable on buying less the premium received from selling the option.

The credit risk of the exchange can be eliminated if positions of sellers are marked to market and losses collected, as is done in the case of futures. In the case of futures, marking-to-market (MTM) losses collected are passed on as MTM profits. This system could also be followed in the case of options, where MTM losses collected from sellers/losers are passed on to option buyers/gainers. If such a practice is adopted, the positions of option buyers too would need to be marked to market and they, too, would be subject to margin calls. Such a practice is referred to as *futures style options*, where both buyers and sellers are marked to market.

As an alternative, the exchange may decide to keep all MTM losses collected from writers with itself and not pass them on to the gainers. This is known as *premium style options*. Most exchanges follow premium-style options for margining, obviating the need for marking to market for option buyers. Only writers of options have to make good any MTM losses.

ADJUSTING FOR CORPORATE ACTIONS ON STOCK OPTIONS

Options are contracts that are settled by delivery or in cash with the implicit assumption that the basic characteristics of the underlying asset do not change during the tenure of the options. However, stocks issued by firms are subject to corporate actions at any point of time. Corporate actions such as declaration of dividend, bonus shares, and stock splits change the value of the stock, and, as such, options on these stocks, too, would change in value. As such, actions are not a part of the normal process of price determination of an option; they call for changes in the characteristics of an option.

Adjustment of Dividend Options traded on stock exchanges do not provide for adjustment of dividend. The price of a stock falls by the amount of dividend on the ex-dividend date. Therefore, the intrinsic value of the ITM call, too, falls by the amount of dividend on the ex-dividend date. The option premium, dependent upon the value of the underlying stock, would change on the ex-dividend date. The difference in the option premium must be equal to the present value of the dividend. Since stock prices are supposed to be the present value of all expected dividends, there seems to be little logic in adjusting for the payment of cash dividend. No adjustment to the option features is made with respect to cash dividend on the stock.

However, extraordinary dividends are not anticipated by investors in pricing underlying assets, or by traders in derivatives. In such cases, adjustments to the option contract can be made by reducing the strike price appropriately. In the Indian stock markets, a dividend in excess of 10% (subject to change) of the value of the stock prompts adjustment to the strike price.

Adjustment for Bonus Shares Instead of cash dividends; firms sometimes make bonus offers by capitalizing their reserves. Though it does not change the aggregate value of the shares in the hands of the investor, it affects the price of shares substantially, as a larger number of shares become available for the same value. For example, consider a 3:5 bonus issue by a firm with a share price of ₹160. The value of five shares is ₹800. After the bonus issue, the same five shares become eight shares, and in order to keep the value same, the share must now trade at ₹100 (800/8). Since aggregate value of the underlying asset has not changed apart from its composition, the value of options contract should also not undergo any change. For parity of cum-bonus and ex-bonus, the following two adjustments must be made to option contracts:

- The number of shares in the contract must increase by (1 + bonus ratio).
- The strike price must reduce to 1/(1 + bonus ratio).

If there is an ATM call option at ₹160 for 100 shares, the contract now must stand modified as an option to buy 100 × 1.6 = 160 shares, i.e., the original contract size × (1 + bonus ratio), at a strike price of 160/1.6 = ₹100, i.e., the original strike price/(1 + bonus ratio). These two adjustments would keep the commitment under the option unchanged.

Adjustment for Stock Splits Under stock splits, the number of shares increases, with the price reduced proportionately. For example, a 2:1 split doubles the supply of shares, and that must reduce the price of the shares by half. Adjustment, as in the case of a bonus issue, with respect to the contract size and the exercise price, are made so that the value of the option contract, pre-split and post-split, remains the same. Therefore, the number of shares in the option contract must double, with the exercise price reduced by half.

Options—Basics 271

> **EXAMPLE 9.3 Corporate actions and option contracts**
>
> An exchange-traded option contract on a stock has 500 shares with a strike price of ₹140. How would the option contract change if before maturity of the contract, the following actions are taken by the company?
>
> (a) A cash dividend of ₹5 per share is declared.
> (b) Bonus shares in the ratio of 2 for every 5 are announced.
> (c) A stock split in the ratio of 4:1 is announced.
>
> **Solution**
>
> (a) For a cash dividend, no adjustment to the option contract is made.
> (b) For a bonus issue, the number of shares in the option contract would become 500 × 1.4 = 700, and the exercise price is reduced to 140/1.4 = ₹100.
> (c) For a stock split, the number of shares in the contract would increase to 500 × 4 = 2000, with the strike price reduced to 140/4 = ₹35.

OPTIONS OTHER THAN STOCKS/INDICES

The process of trading and settlement of options on other underlying assets that are exchange-traded essentially remains the same as that for stocks and indices, as explained earlier in the chapter. In case of OTC options, the issues of closure of contract, margins, and daily settlements do not arise. They essentially remain contracts between two known parties. Most options on currencies are OTC contracts. Some exchanges abroad offer options contracts on several prominent currencies such as US dollar, euro, and pound sterling.

Options are also available with futures contracts as underlying assets, where a buyer of the option has the right to buy/sell a futures contract. These futures contracts are normally based on currencies.

Options on interest rates known as caps, floors, and collars are also available, where the holder of the option has a right to have interest payments, based on the interest rate achieving a certain level.

DIFFERENCES BETWEEN OPTIONS AND FORWARDS/FUTURES

The basic concept behind forwards/futures and options is distinctly different. Forwards/futures and options present distinct risk–return profiles. Consider, for example, futures and options positions on a stock trading at ₹100. You are bullish on the stock, and consider a long position in the stock as beneficial. You have two choices: (a) buy a futures contract now and sell it at maturity or earlier or (b) buy a call option at a strike price of ₹100, selling at a premium of ₹5, and exercise it on maturity or earlier. What would be the risk–return profile under each of these two situations?

> Options have uneven payoff because they do not create equal obligations on counterparties, while forwards or futures have even payoff.

With two opposite scenarios, increased and decreased prices, the payoffs on a forward strategy and an option strategy would be different. Under a futures contract, you stand to gain or lose equally, depending upon the price of the stock. If the price goes up, you gain the difference in price, and if it moves down, you lose the difference in price. However, under an option contract, while you gain proportionately from an upward movement in the price

EXAMPLE 9.4 Option on currency

A call option expiring six months from now on euro has an exercise price of ₹62, and is priced at ₹1.25. Depict a long position on the call. What is the payoff if on expiry, the exchange rate is (a) ₹61.00, (b) ₹63.00, and (c) ₹65.00?

Solution
The payoff on the long position of the call on the euro is depicted as follows:

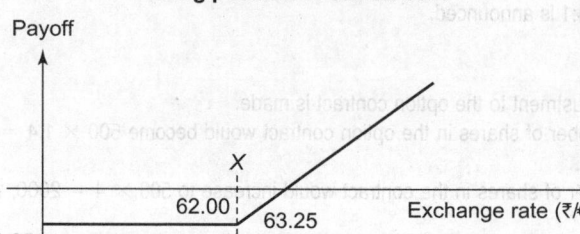

Payoff of the call at expiration is given by Max$(S - X - c, -c)$.

(a) For a price of ₹61.00, the call expires worthless. The payoff is the lost premium of ₹1.25.
(b) For a price of ₹63.00, the call would be exercised, gaining ₹1.00. The payoff would be −₹0.25, recovering most of the premium paid.
(c) For a price of ₹65.00 the gain from the exercise is ₹3.00. Net of premium paid, the payoff is ₹1.75.

of the asset, you contain your losses when prices move down to the extent of the premium paid for buying the call option. The payoff under both situations is presented here and is also depicted in Figs 9.5(a) and (b).

Asset price	Long futures position	Long call option
₹80.00	−₹20.00	−₹5.00
₹120.00	₹20.00	₹15.00

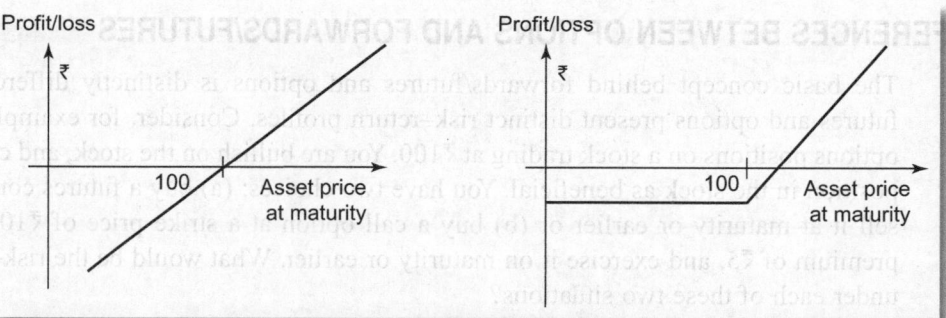

Fig. 9.5 Payoffs (a) Long futures/forward position   (b) Long call

As can be seen, the payoffs under a long position in a forward/futures contract are equal under situations of favourable and unfavourable movements in the price. It is uneven in the case of an option. While it permits full gains, a position in options limits losses.

Similarly, one can realize that a short position in futures loses when the price rises and gains when the price falls. If an investor is bearish, he/she would go short on futures. This may be compared with the payoff on the put option. A put option permits gains with a decline in price, while it contains losses due to a rise in price. Comparing a short position in stock at ₹100 with a long put with a strike of ₹100 and a premium of ₹5, the following would be the payoffs when the price at maturity is (a) lesser at ₹80 and (b) higher at ₹120:

Asset price	Short futures position	Long put option
₹80.00	₹20.00	₹15.00
₹120.00	−₹20.00	−₹5.00

The payoffs for a short position in forwards/futures and a long put are shown in Figs 9.6 (a) and (b).

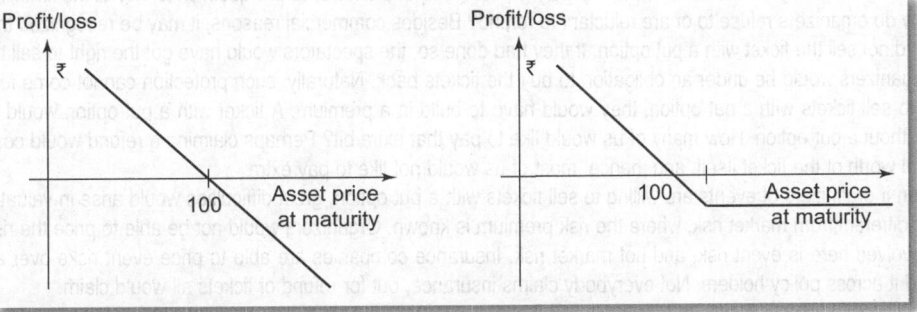

Fig. 9.6 Payoffs: (a) Short futures/forward position (b) Long put

A short position in options, i.e., a short call or a short put, is non-descript in terms of forward/futures positions. A short call in terms of futures appears like a short position in futures with the gain-making area curtailed substantially and all the loss-making positions retained. Similarly, a short put is like a long position in futures with almost the entire profit-making region removed and the whole of the loss-making range retained. Short positions in options do not have a parallel in futures due to the uneven payoff of options and the even payoff of futures.

Table 9.2 Differences between forwards/futures and options

	Forwards/Futures	Options
Payoff	Linear	Non-linear
Obligation to perform	Both buyer and seller	Only on seller of option with a right to the buyer
Trading	OTC for forwards; exchange-traded for futures	Both OTC and exchange-traded
Margin	None for forwards, which are OTC, and as required by exchanges in the case of futures	None if OTC and as per exchange requirement if exchange-traded
Initial payment	None	Buyer pays premium to seller
Settlement	Once on maturity for forwards, and daily for futures	Daily if exchange-traded; once on maturity if OTC

Other differences between options and futures are that under an options contract, only one party (the writer) is obligated to perform, while in a futures/forward contract, the obligations are mutual. There is no upfront payment involved in a futures or forward contract, while a premium is paid by the buyer of an option to the seller. For easier comprehension, the differences between forward/futures and options are condensed in Table 9.2.

Derivatives in Practice

Options Hedge and Insurance

Options and Insurance

Match abandoned due to rain! Opera show cancelled as artists do not turn up! Conference deferred due to non-availability of venue! These are some of the headlines that we often see in newspapers. What happens to the spectators and participants who have paid for such events, only to learn at the last minute that the scheduled event is not taking place? The public goes on a rampage, demanding its money back. Do ticket holders truly get refunds? The answer to this question is, not all the time. That means seldom.

Why do organizers refuse to or are reluctant to refund? Besides commercial reasons, it may be recognized that in the first place, they did not sell the ticket with a put option. If they had done so, the spectators would have got the right to sell the tickets back and the organizers would be under an obligation to buy the tickets back. Naturally, such protection cannot come for free. If organizers were to sell tickets with a put option, they would have to build in a premium. A ticket with a put option would cost more than the one without a put option. How many of us would like to pay that extra bit? Perhaps claiming a refund would cost us more than the original worth of the ticket itself, and, hence, most of us would not like to pay extra.

Even if organizers of events are willing to sell tickets with a put option, great difficulties would arise in valuation of the risk. This risk is different from market risk, where the risk premium is known. Organizers would not be able to price the risk themselves. The risk involved here is event risk, and not market risk. Insurance companies are able to price event risks over a large volume and spread it across policy holders. Not everybody claims insurance, but for refund of tickets all would claim.

The second obstacle to issuing tickets with a put option is that the right to sell must come without any riders with regard to reasons for claiming refunds—rain or no rain, show or no show. This is in contrast to insurance, where an event must take place before a claim can be made.

SOLVED PROBLEMS

SP 9.1: Moneyness of put options

Consider the price data of Example 9.1. Three put options D, E, and F, with strike prices of ₹100, ₹105, and ₹110, are selling at ₹2, ₹5, and ₹13, respectively.

(a) Find out which of the put options are in-the-money, at-the-money, and out-of-the-money.
(b) If the price of each of the put options increases by ₹1, would your answer to the moneyness of options change?
(c) If the price of each of the options decreases by ₹1, what would be the change in the moneyness of each of the options?

Solution

(a) Moneyness of put options is as follows:

Option D: $X - S = 100 - 105 =$ negative; out-of-the-money by ₹5
Option E: $X - S = 105 - 105 =$ zero; at-the-money
Option F: $X - S = 110 - 105 =$ positive; in-the-money by ₹5

(b) and (c) If the price increases or decreases, there would be no change in the moneyness of the options.

SP 9.2: Long position and call option

At NSE, a share of Reliance is trading at ₹2100, a call option with a strike of ₹2200 with three months to expiry is trading at ₹26, while a put option with the same strike is valued at ₹110. Draw a payoff diagram for a long position in the stock, a short position in the stock, a call option, and a put option.

Solution

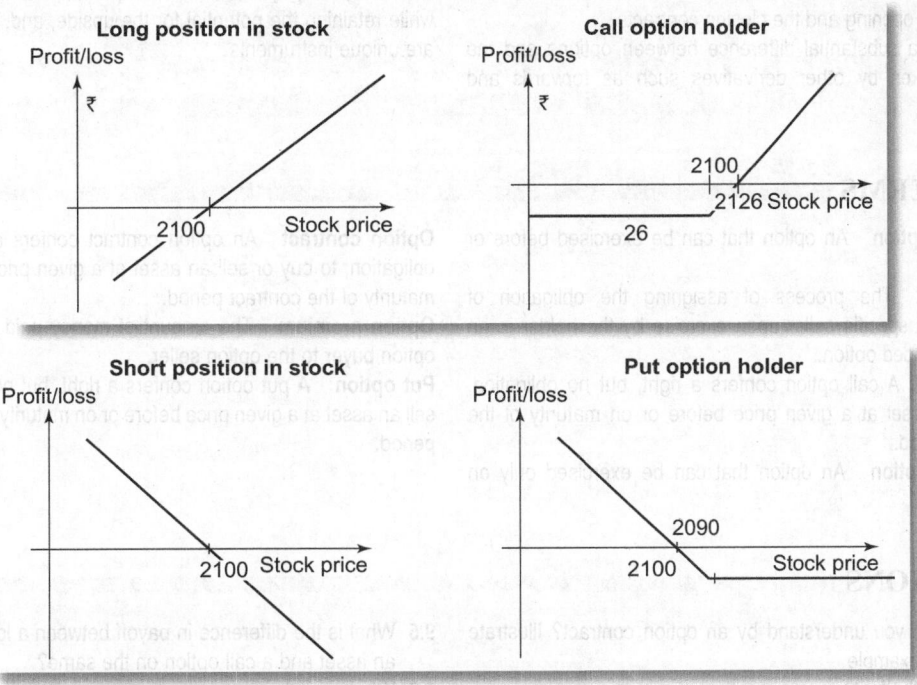

SP 9.3: Long position and put option

A put option on shares of ITC with a strike price of ₹180 sells for ₹10. Draw the payoff of the long position in the put options at maturity. Under what circumstances would the holder of the option make a profit? At what price would the investor break even, and what would be the payoff if the stock price at maturity is ₹160?

Solution

The payoff of the put option is given by Max$(X - S - p, - p)$ where X and S are the strike and spot prices, respectively, and p is the premium on the put option. The payoff diagram is as shown.

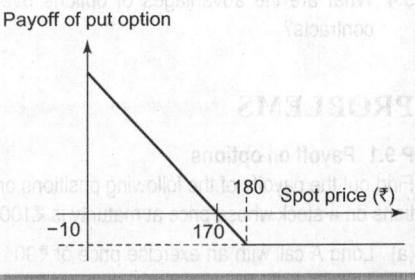

The option would be exercised if at maturity the spot price is less than ₹180. The holder of the put option would be making a profit if the stock price is less than ₹170. At a spot price of ₹160, the profit to the investor would be ₹10, after adjusting the premium paid for buying the option.

SUMMARY

Options are somewhat unique instruments that confer a right to one of the parties to buy/sell an asset, while the other party is obligated to perform at the instance of the former. An option to buy is known as a call option and an option to sell is a put option. The holder of the option pays a premium to the counterparty, called writer or seller, to induce him/her to confer the right. The price at which the asset is sold or bought is called the strike price, and the time during which the right can be exercised is called the time to expiry. If the option is exercisable only on maturity, it is a European option; otherwise, it is an American option.

A call option is bought when the expectation is for a rise in the asset price, and it is beneficial to exercise when the asset price exceeds the exercise price. A put option is used when one expects the price to fall; it is exercised when the price falls below the exercise price. An option is a zero-sum game, where the gain of the holder is equal to the loss of the writer.

Options can either be exchange-traded or customized between two parties. Options on stocks are mostly exchange-traded, while those on currency—the most popular form—are OTC. They automatically become null on expiry. Before or on expiry, they can either be exercised or closed out with an opposite contract with cash settlement of the difference in prices between the opening and the closing contracts.

There is a substantial difference between options and the positions taken by other derivatives such as forwards and futures. Since options do not have equal obligations on counterparties, the payoff is uneven. Options protect the downside, while retaining the potential for the upside, and, therefore, they are unique instruments.

KEY TERMS

American option An option that can be exercised before or on maturity.
Assignment The process of assigning the obligation of delivery to a specific seller upon exercise by the holder in an exchange-traded option.
Call option A call option confers a right, but no obligation, to buy an asset at a given price before or on maturity of the contract period.
European option An option that can be exercised only on maturity.

Option contract An option contract confers a right, but no obligation, to buy or sell an asset at a given price before or on maturity of the contract period.
Option premium The amount of money paid upfront by the option buyer to the option seller.
Put option A put option confers a right, but no obligation, to sell an asset at a given price before or on maturity of the contract period.

QUESTIONS

9.1 What do you understand by an option contract? Illustrate with an example.
9.2 Explain the features of an option.
9.3 How are option contracts settled? Illustrate.
9.4 What are the advantages of options over forward/futures contracts?

9.5 What is the difference in payoff between a long position on an asset and a call option on the same?
9.6 What are the key specifications and parameters of an options contract?

PROBLEMS

P 9.1 Payoff on options
Find out the payoffs of the following positions on European options on a stock whose price at maturity is ₹100:

(a) Long A call with an exercise price of ₹90
(b) Short A call with an exercise price of ₹80
(c) Long A put with an exercise price of ₹110
(d) Short A put with an exercise price of ₹110
(e) Long A call with an exercise price of ₹100
(f) Short A put with an exercise price of ₹100

P 9.2 Payoff on short calls in foreign exchange
You have written a call on the US dollar to rupee exchange rate with a strike price of ₹50/$, charging a premium of ₹1.00. Find the payoff for various exchange rates ranging from ₹45 to 55. At what level of exchange rate would you turn from profit to loss?

P 9.3 Payoff on long put
As an exporter, you are expecting to receive €10,000. You have bought a put option with a strike exchange rate of ₹60 per euro, and have paid a premium of ₹1.50. Depict the payoff of a put option, the receivable, and receivable combined with the put, for exchange rates between ₹55 and ₹65 per euro. Further, determine and depict the value of receivable for the range.

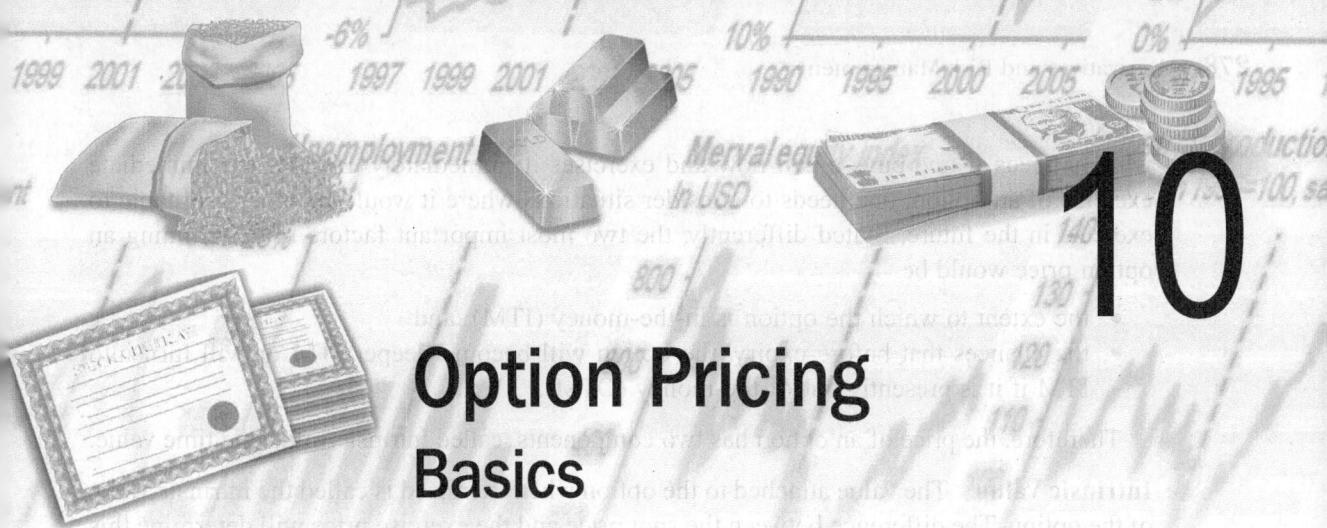

Option Pricing Basics

INTRODUCTION

An option is an uneven contract that gives a right to one party, i.e., the holder or the buyer, while it binds the other party, i.e., the writer or the seller, to an obligation. Naturally, the buyer can not enjoy the right free of cost, since that would make it a lop-sided contract. The buyer of the right has to induce the writer to confer such a right on him and undertake an obligation. The amount paid by the buyer of the option to the writer of the option is called the premium. Calculation of the premium is also known as valuation of the option.

The determination of the option premium has been an area of widely researched complexities. Fortunately, there exist some arbitrage-based relationships that explain a lot about option price behaviour. We shall initially examine and achieve a basic understanding of some broad conditions and rules that govern option premiums. Later chapters will cover some conceptual mathematical models that provide a greater understanding of the complex ways an option price is determined. A broader understanding based on the rules of arbitrage is extremely handy for exploring the various applications of options. Moreover, arbitrage is easier to comprehend. Some simple rules about pricing are presented here. Unless otherwise stated, we shall discuss the pricing of European options only.

> Determination of option premiums has been a major area of research. However, there also exist simple arbitrage-based rules that explain a lot about option price behaviour.

Learning Objectives

After going through this chapter, readers should be familiar with:

- the intrinsic value and time value of an option
- the boundary conditions of option pricing
- the determinants of an option price and its application
- arbitrage arguments regarding option pricing
- relationships of option prices based on arbitrage
- relationship between call and put prices—put–call parity

INTRINSIC VALUE AND TIME VALUE

The valuation of an option, i.e., the premium payable by the holder, is dependent upon several factors that can be viewed in different ways. One way to examine the situation is to understand what happens if one buys a call now and exercises it immediately. Besides the immediate exercise of an option, one needs to consider situations where it would be more profitable to exercise in the future. Stated differently, the two most important factors in determining an option price would be

- the extent to which the option is in-the-money (ITM); and
- the chances that before expiry, the option will become deeper ITM or will turn into ITM if it is presently out-of-the-money (OTM).

Therefore, the price of an option has two components, called intrinsic value and time value.

Intrinsic Value The value attached to the option when exercised is called the intrinsic value of the option. The difference between the spot price and the exercise price will determine this value. The intrinsic value is as follows:

For a call option: Max $\{(S - X), 0\}$
For a put option: Max $\{(X - S), 0\}$

The value of an option can never fall below its intrinsic value. For example, a call option with an exercise price of ₹80 on an underlying stock currently trading at ₹100 would have an intrinsic value of ₹20. This would be the minimum price at which the call would sell. Any price less than ₹20 presents an opportunity to make immediate profit without taking any risk. If one buys a call at ₹19 (less than ₹20) and exercises it immediately, the cash outflow would be ₹99. Then the holder can sell the acquired stock at ₹100, gaining ₹1 immediately.

> The option premium consists of two components: intrinsic value and time value.

The difference between the spot and strike prices would determine the intrinsic value. For an ITM option, exercising would lead to positive cash inflow to the holder. An at-the-money (ATM) option does not lead to a cash inflow to the holder if exercised. An OTM option would cause a negative cash inflow to the holder if exercised. The conditions for ITM, ATM, and OTM options are listed as follows:

	Call	Put
In-the-money	$S > X$	$S < X$
At-the-money	$S = X$	$S = X$
Out-of-the-money	$S < X$	$S > X$

Time Value The value attached to the chances that the spot price would pierce the strike price before expiry is called the time value of an option. The time value of an option can be derived from the observed/actual price and the intrinsic value. It is the difference between the actual price and the intrinsic value. The time value is paid by the buyer for the probability that the option will turn ITM or achieve greater ITM value before expiration. Time value may be written as shown in Eq. 10.1.

> Intrinsic value is the money the holder of an option would get upon exercise. The time value is the excess of the actual value over the intrinsic value.

$$\text{Time value of an option} = \text{actual price} - \text{intrinsic value} \qquad (10.1)$$

Similar to intrinsic value, time value too cannot be negative. At best or worst, it can be zero.
Among options, time value is greatest for ATM options. The entire premium paid for ATM options is attributable to their time values, as their intrinsic values are zero. As the spot price moves away from the exercise price, the time value starts falling. For deep OTM options, the

EXAMPLE 10.1 Call option prices and payoffs

A 2-month call option on Infosys shares with a strike price of ₹2100 is selling for ₹140 when the share is trading at ₹2200. Find out the following:

(a) What is the intrinsic worth of the call option?
(b) Why should one buy the call for a price in excess of the intrinsic worth?
(c) Under what circumstances would the option holder exercise his call?
(d) At what price of the asset would the call option holder break even?
(e) If the price of the Infosys share becomes ₹2150 (lower than the break-even price) should the option holder exercise the call option?
(f) What is the payoff to the holder and the writer if the price of the Infosys share is ₹2000, ₹2250, and ₹2500 on the date of expiry of the option?

Solution

(a) The intrinsic worth of the option is $(S - X) = 2200 - 2100 = ₹100$.
(b) The price of the option is ₹140, i.e., ₹40 more than the intrinsic worth. This is the time value of the option, and is paid because there are chances that in the next two months, the price of the Infosys share may rise further, and the holder would stand to gain more than ₹100.
(c) The option holder would exercise his call if the price of the asset, S exceeds X, the exercise price, i.e., when $S > 2100$.
(d) The call option holder would break even when the payoff on the call $S - X - c = 0$, which happens at $S = ₹2240$.
(e) If the price of the asset is above the exercise price, the call option must be exercised, irrespective of whether it breaks even or not. The premium paid is a sunk cost. If the price of the stock is ₹2150, the option holder stands to gain ₹50 upon exercise of the option, which would partly refund the premium paid and contain the losses to ₹90. If he does not exercise the option, the loss would be ₹140.
(f) The payoff to the call holder and the writer at various prices is

Stock price	Call option holder Max($S - X - c, - c$)	Call option writer $-$Max($S - X - c, - c$)
$S = 2,000$	-140	$+140$
$S = 2,250$	$+10$	-10
$S = 2,500$	$+260$	-260

time value approaches zero. Further, for deep ITM options, the time value approaches zero, and most of the premium paid is attributable to the intrinsic value of the option. It signifies that for deep ITM or deep OTM options, the chances that the spot price would pierce the exercise price are remote.

BOUNDARY CONDITIONS FOR OPTION PRICING

Before any attempt is made to find the cost of buying an option, we should examine the boundary conditions and gain some insight into the maximum and minimum values an option can take, based on simple logic rather than on any mathematical model. The pricing of European options is discussed in the following section.

Call Option

A call option is a right to buy an asset at the exercise price. The maximum value of the call option, c, cannot exceed the price of the asset itself, as no one would pay more money to buy a right to have an asset than what it actually costs. Therefore, the price of a call option is given as follows:

$$\text{Maximum price of a call option, } c_{max} = S \text{ or } c \leq S \quad (10.2)$$

Similarly, the minimum price that a call option would sell for is dependent upon its intrinsic value. If the option is maturing just at the time of buying, the time value of the option can be assumed to be zero and it must sell for its intrinsic worth. However, if there is some time remaining for maturity, the exercise price would be payable only then. Therefore the minimum value of the option shall be the difference between the spot price and the present value (PV) of the exercise price, or

> The maximum value of a call option cannot exceed the value of the asset on which the option is based.

$$c_{min} = S - Xe^{-rt} \text{ or } c \geq S - Xe^{-rt} \quad (10.3)$$

where Xe^{-rt} represents the present value of the exercise price.

Arbitrage Argument A call option with an exercise price of ₹80 and a spot value of ₹100 for the underlying asset must sell for more than ₹20 (spot value − exercise price). Any price less than the intrinsic value presents an arbitrage opportunity. Consider the following strategy, assuming the call option sells for ₹10.

- Buy a call for ₹10
- Short the stock for ₹100
- Generate a cash flow of ₹90

At expiry, the payoff would be:

Stock price	Value of stock	Value of call	Total
If $S < 80$	$-S$	—	$-S$
If $S > 80$	$-S$	$S - 80$	-80

The cash outflow at maturity is always less than ₹80, irrespective of the price of the asset, as against ₹90 already generated.

Therefore, a call option's value will always exceed the difference between the spot price and the Present value of the exercise price.

In case of an American option, the boundary conditions for pricing of a call will apply. The condition for the maximum price needs no elaboration. For the minimum value, the call holder will pay X at the time of exercise of the option, and the condition will hold, since $S - Xe^{-rt}$ will always be higher than $S - X$. Further, it can be proved that it is sub-optimal to exercise an American option before maturity for a stock that pays no dividend.

> The minimum value of a call is given by the spot price less the PV of the exercise price.

The composition of the price of a call option is shown in Fig. 10.1.

As an example, consider a call on the stock of Wipro, with an exercise price of ₹1400 and a spot price of ₹1450, which may be selling at ₹75. It is easy to see that the intrinsic value of the call is ₹50, and the balance is ₹25; the time value is attributed to the fact that the price of Wipro can go further beyond, say, ₹1500 before the option expires. Naturally, the time value of the option cannot be negative.

It may be observed that for a call option, time value is at a maximum when the spot price is around the exercise price. The further away the spot price is from the exercise price, the lesser would be the time value. For a spot price that is far in excess of the exercise price, the value of a call option will mainly comprise its intrinsic value. Similarly when the spot price is far less than the exercise

> Time values of options are the greatest for ATM options.

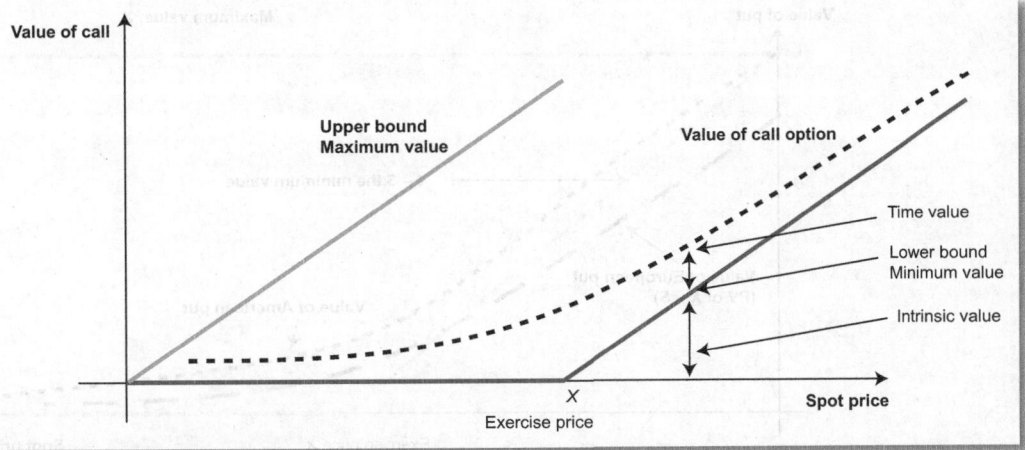

Fig. 10.1 Value of call option

EXAMPLE 10.2 Lower bound to call premium

A stock is selling for ₹500. If the risk-free rate of interest is 10% p.a. continuously compounded, then at what minimum price would the following call options on the stock sell for?

(a) A call with a strike price of ₹450 maturing one month later
(b) A call with a strike price of ₹500 maturing two months later
(c) A call with a strike price of ₹550 maturing three months later

Solution
The lower bound to the call price is given by zero or $S - X \cdot e^{-rT}$
Therefore, the minimum value of the calls would be

(a) Call with $X = 450$ and $T = 1$ month: $500 - 450 \cdot e^{-0.1 \times 1/12} = 500.00 - 446.23 = ₹53.73$
(b) Call with $X = 500$ and $T = 2$ months: $500 - 500 \cdot e^{-0.1 \times 2/12} = 500.00 - 491.74 = ₹8.26$
(c) Call with $X = 550$ and $T = 3$ months: $500 - 550 \cdot e^{-0.1 \times 3/12} = 500.00 - 536.42 = -₹36.42 = 0.00$

---

price, the intrinsic value will be zero, and the entire price of the call option is attributable to its time value. Since the exercise price is high the chances of the spot price exceeding it are lower as compared to ATM option. Therefore, the time value associated with the probability of the spot exceeding the exercise would be less.

Put Option

A put option is a right to sell the underlying asset at an exercise price, X. Therefore, the maximum value that one would pay to get that right is X if it is to be exercised immediately. If there is still time remaining for exercise, the value of the put cannot exceed the present value of the exercise price. Hence, irrespective of the price of the asset, the put option cannot sell for more than the present value of the exercise price, or

> The maximum value of a put option cannot exceed the exercise price.

$$p_{max} = Xe^{-rt} \quad \text{or} \quad p \leq Xe^{-rt} \quad (10.4)$$

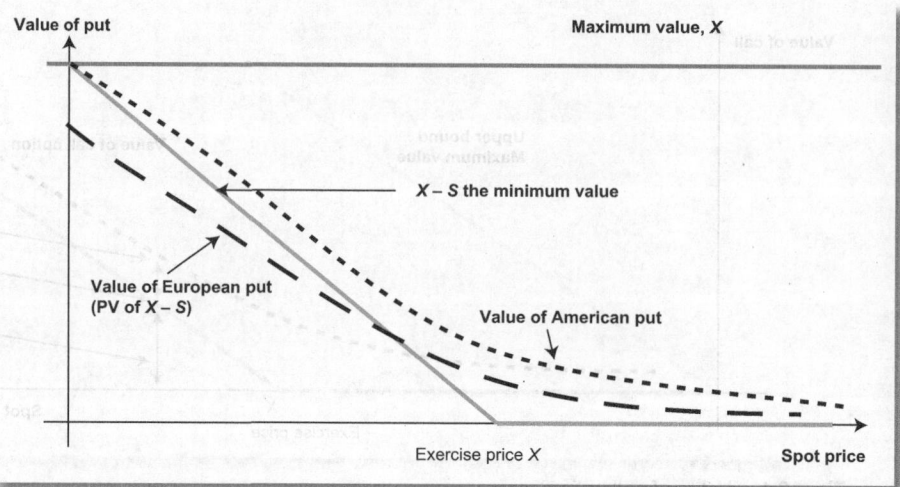

Fig. 10.2 Value of the put option

> The minimum value of a put is given by the PV of the exercise price less the spot price.

The intrinsic value is the amount of profit one would derive if the option is exercised immediately. If it is to be paid at maturity, the difference between the present value of the exercise price and the spot price provides the lower bound. Therefore, the minimum price that a put option would sell for is its intrinsic value, i.e.,

$$p_{min} = Xe^{-rt} - S \quad \text{or} \quad p \geq Xe^{-rt} - S \qquad (10.5)$$

The bounds on the prices of a put are depicted in Fig. 10.2.

Like a call option, a put option too will reach its maximum value when it is close to its ATM condition. Deep ITM and deep OTM put options would have lesser and lesser time values, and the option prices would mainly consist of their intrinsic worth.

Arbitrage Argument A violation of the conditions expressed by Eqs 10.4 and 10.5 presents an arbitrage opportunity. For example, if an asset sells for ₹100, and the risk-free rate is 1% per month, a 6-month put option for an exercise price of ₹120 must be priced at more than ₹13.21 (120/1.06 − 100).

To illustrate the arbitrage, consider the following portfolio if the put price is ₹10, i.e., lesser than the lower bound of the put price.

"A put at ₹10, the stock at ₹100, funded by a borrowing of ₹110 for six months at 12%, with an obligation to pay back ₹110 × 1.06 = ₹116.60."

After six months, the payoff from the portfolio would be as follows:

Stock price	Value of stock	Value of put	Total
If $S < 120$	S	$120 - S$	120
If $S > 120$	S	—	S

With an obligation to pay only ₹116.60, the arbitrageur always ends up with a profit, as the value of the portfolio is always greater than ₹120. The minimum profit is ₹3.40.

In contrast with the call option where an early exercise cannot be more beneficial than waiting till maturity, a put option at times can be more profitable if exercised early. Since the value of the underlying cannot be negative, it may be optimal to exercise the put in order to derive maximum gain. Therefore, an American put, which allows for early exercise, may be more valuable than a European put.

For an American put, early exercise of the option may be preferred. For an ITM option, the investor realizes a larger amount, $(X - S)$, as against $(Xe^{-rt} - S)$. Consider for example an investor A, holding a 6-m put option at $X = 100$ and the underlying share, as against investor B, holding cash of ₹94.34 (present value of the exercise price at a 1% risk-free rate, 100/1.06). At any time before maturity, investor A is worth at least ₹100 $(X - S + S)$ if he/she exercises his/her put option and sells the stock, as can be seen here:

Stock price	Value of stock	Value of put	Total
If $S < 100$	S	$100 - S$	100
If $S > 100$	S	—	S

As against this, investor B attains ₹100 only after six months. Though the put option, together with a long position in the stock, provides insurance against any fall in price of the stock, an earlier exercise of the put option may be desirable to realize the exercise price and forego the insurance, if the prices are falling.

Since an American put option may be beneficially exercised prior to maturity, the value of an American put option will be more than the value of a corresponding European put. The intrinsic value for a deep ITM American put is $X - S$, representing the minimum bound. The European put option may sometimes be valued less than its intrinsic value to the extent of the differentials of the present value of X and X. This differential would be at a maximum when the price of the underlying asset is zero.

EXAMPLE 10.3 Lower bound to put premium

A stock is selling for ₹500. If the risk-free rate of interest is 10% p.a. continuously compounded, then at what minimum price would the following put options on the stock sell for?

(a) A put with a strike price of ₹450 maturing one month later
(b) A put with a strike price of ₹500 maturing two months later
(c) A put with a strike price of ₹550 maturing three months later

Solution
The lower bound to put price is given by zero or $X \cdot e^{-rT} - S_0$
Therefore, the minimum value of the puts would be

Put with $X = 450$ and $T = 1$ month: $450 \cdot e^{-0.10 \times 1/12} - 500.00 = 446.23 - 500.00 = -₹53.73$; ₹0.00
Put with $X = 500$ and $T = 2$ months: $500 \cdot e^{-0.10 \times 2/12} - 500.00 = 491.74 - 500.00 = -₹8.26$; ₹0.00
Put with $X = 550$ and $T = 3$ months: $550 \cdot e^{-0.10 \times 3/12} - 500.00 = 536.42 - 500.00 = ₹36.42$

Effects of Dividend on Lower Bounds

Normally, options on stock are for short maturities. In India, exchange-traded options are available for a period of three months. The effect of dividend on the prices of options can easily be incorporated by adjusting the spot price for the dividend. In case the dividend is payable within the expiry of the option, the spot price S of the asset must be replaced by S less the present value of the dividend. Consider, for example, a stock selling for ₹200. A call with an exercise price of ₹180 and three months to expiry at a risk-free rate of 10% would have a minimum value of ₹4.94. In case the stock is to pay a dividend of ₹2 after two months, the present value of the dividend would be ₹1.97. This must be subtracted from the lower bound of a call on an asset with no dividend. A call with a dividend paying stock would have the lower bound of ₹2.97 (4.94 − 1.97).

Similar adjustments may be made for the lower bounds of put prices, where the present values would be added to the lower bounds.

Equations 10.3 and 10.5 for the lower bounds of call and put prices maturing at time T, respectively, would stand modified for a dividend, D, payable at t, as follows:

Lower bound for call on dividend paying stock

$$c \geq S - Xe^{-rT} - De^{-rt} \quad (10.6)$$

Lower bound for put on dividend paying stock

$$p \geq Xe^{-rT} - S + De^{-rt} \quad (10.7)$$

EXAMPLE 10.4 Lower bound and dividend

Assume that in Example 10.3, the stock would pay a dividend of ₹10 after two months. Recalculate the lower bound of the put price.

Solution
The present value of the dividend is

$$D.e^{-rt} = 10.e^{-0.10 \times 2/12} = ₹9.83$$

This would get added to the lower bound found in Example 9.3:

(a) Put with $X = 450$ and $T = 1$ month: It would remain unaffected, as dividend is paid after the expiry of the option
(b) Put with $X = 500$ and $T = 2$ months: The lower bound would become positive
$500 . e^{-0.1 \times 2/12} − 500.00 + 10 . e^{-0.10 \times 2/12} = 491.74 − 500.00 + 9.83 = ₹1.57$
(c) Put with $X = 550$ and $T = 3$ months:
$550 . e^{-0.1 \times 3/12} − 500.00 + 10 . e^{-0.10 \times 2/12} = 536.42 − 500.00 + 9.83 = ₹46.25$

Lower Bounds for Currency Options

In case of options on currencies, the underlying asset is a foreign currency. The foreign currency is like a dividend paying asset, as it can be invested to yield a risk-free return in foreign currency. As we adjust the spot price with the present value of dividend, the lower bound for an option on a foreign currency can be adjusted for the risk-free interest rate in the foreign currency, r_f.

The lower bounds for call and put on foreign currencies would be

$$c \geq S e^{-r_f T} - Xe^{-rT} \quad (10.8)$$

$$p \geq Xe^{-rT} - S . e^{-r_f T} \quad (10.9)$$

Consider, for example, a call option and a put option on the US dollar, with a strike price of ₹50 and maturity in three months, with a spot exchange rate of ₹48. The risk-free interest rates in the rupee and the US dollar are 6% and 3%, respectively. The lower bounds for calls and puts, as given by Eqs 10.8 and 10.9, are as follows:

Lower bound for call:

$$c \geq S e^{-r_f T} - X e^{-rT} = 48 \times e^{-0.03 \times 3/12} - 50 \times e^{-0.06 \times 3/12} = 47.64 - 49.26 = ₹0.00$$

Similarly, the lower bound for the put option would be:

$$p \geq X e^{-rT} - S \cdot e^{-r_f T} = 50 \times e^{-0.06 \times 3/12} - 48 \times e^{-0.03 \times 3/12} = 49.26 - 47.64 = ₹1.62$$

Lower Bounds for Options on Stock Indices

In case of options on indices, the situation is the same as for an underlying asset paying dividend. In case of indices, the dividend, referred to as dividend yield, d, is deemed to be paid continuously, rather that at discrete intervals of time. The lower bounds for call and put options would be the same as in the case of currency options, as given in Eqs 10.8 and 10.9, with r_f getting replaced by the dividend yield, d.

The lower bounds for call and put on indices are as follows:

$$c_{min} \geq S e^{-dT} - X e^{-rT}$$
$$p_{min} \geq X e^{-rT} - S e^{-dT}$$

ARBITRAGE-BASED RELATIONSHIP OF OPTION PRICING

We just saw how arbitrage places lower and/or upper bounds to option pricing. Though we cannot use the same concept for determination of an exact price, we can use such concepts for the relative prices of different financial assets, such as two calls, two puts, a call and a put, etc. An exposition of arbitrage-based arguments is expected to improve the understanding of the principles of finance.

The concept of arbitrage is central to price determination in economics and finance, as it

- makes the prices of different assets consistent with each other;
- establishes relationships between the prices of different assets;
- causes prices of the same asset to converge in different markets; and
- helps explain the differential in prices in different markets and for different assets.

Of course, application of arbitrage-free pricing is crucially dependent upon its feasibility. Sometimes, restrictive legal frameworks in different markets, other restrictive operational constraints, the presence of differentials in taxes, etc., inhibit execution of arbitrage, causing sustained price differentials in different markets and for different assets.

Though there is a large number of arbitrage-based price relationships, we examine a few of them to illustrate the mechanism of arbitrage as applicable for option price determination.

Call option with higher strike price would be priced lower than call option with lower strike price.

Consider the following price information, which contradicts this statement:
Spot price = ₹100

Strike price	Call price	Strike price	Call price
$X_1 = ₹80$	$c_1 = ₹25$	$X_2 = ₹85$	$c_2 = ₹26$

An initial portfolio may be set up as follows:

Action	Cash flow (₹)
Write call with $X = 85$	26
Buy call with $X = 80$	−25
Net cash flow	+1

The final position at maturity would be:

Price condition	Portfolio status	Profit (₹)
Spot < 80	Both calls, bought and written, are worthless	1
80 < spot < 85	Call bought is in-the-money by $S − 80$. Call written is worthless.	$(S − 80 + 1)$; always positive because $S > 80$
Spot > 85	Both calls, bought and written, are exercised, resulting in cash flow of $(S − 80) − (S − 85)$	6

The portfolio always has a positive value, and, therefore, provides an opportunity to make a profit without risk and investment.

Difference in call or put prices cannot exceed difference in strike prices.

Again, consider the following price information, which contradicts this statement:
Spot price = ₹100

Strike price	Call price	Strike price	Call price
$X_1 = ₹80$	$c_1 = ₹25$	$X_2 = ₹85$	$c_2 = ₹19$

Initial portfolio may be set up as to yield ₹6:

Action	Cash flow (₹)
Write call with $X = 80$	25
Buy call with $X = 85$	−19
Net cash flow	+6

The final position would always result in a profit, as follows:

Price condition	Portfolio status	Profit (₹)
Spot < 80	Both calls bought and written are worthless	6
80 < Spot < 85	Call written is in-the-money by $S − 80$. Call bought is worthless	$(6 − S + 80)$; always positive because $S < 85$
Spot > 85	Both calls bought and written are exercised, resulting in cash flow of $(S − 80) − (S − 85)$	11

On similar arguments, we can prove that the differences between various put prices cannot exceed the differences between the corresponding strike prices.

EXAMPLE 10.5 Arbitrage with options

A stock is selling for ₹450. A call with a strike price of ₹460 is selling for ₹5, while a call with a strike price of ₹475 is selling for ₹6. Both the calls have the same maturity. Do you find the prices of the two calls appropriate? Can you benefit from the situation? If yes, how would you do so?

Solution
The prices of the call represent an anomaly, in that the call with a higher strike price is selling for more than the call with a lower strike price. By writing a call with a higher strike price, one can earn a premium that is lower than what would be required for buying a call with a lower strike price. The liability on account of the call written would always be matched by the asset one has with the call bought with a lower strike. If the call with a higher strike is exercised, the call with a lower strike too would be exercised.

One stands to gain the difference of the call premiums, i.e., ₹1 (6 − 5) by writing a call with a strike price of ₹475 and buying a call for ₹5 for a strike price of ₹460. The payoff at maturity would be always positive, as shown here:

All figures in ₹

	+Call X = 460	−Call X = 475	Initial cash flow	Total
Spot price < 460	—	—	1	1
460 < Spot < 475	S − 460	—	1	S − 459
Spot > 475	S − 460	−(S − 475)	1	16

Call with longer time to maturity must be priced higher than call with shorter time to maturity.

The following price information is not consistent with this statement:

Strike price	Call T = 3 months	Call T = 6 months
X_1 = ₹80	c_1 = ₹25	c_2 = ₹24

If so, we set up the initial portfolio at $t = 0$, as follows:

Action	Cash flow (₹)
Write call with X = 80, T = 3 months	25
Buy call with X = 80, T = 6 months	−24
Net cash flow	+1

During the first three months, if the price remains below ₹80, the call written expires. The call bought still has three months to maturity and can be sold to get an extra profit.

If the price goes above 80 in the next three months and the call written is exercised, then the liability can be met by exercising the call bought. No cash flow occurs then.

Higher the exercise price, more valuable the put is.

Assume the following price information that contradicts this statement:
  Spot price = ₹100

Strike price	Put price	Strike price	Put price
X_1 = ₹80	p_1 = ₹3	X_2 = ₹85	p_2 = ₹2

We may set up the initial portfolio to yield ₹1:

Action	Cash flow (₹)
Write put with $X = 80$	3
Buy put with $X = 80$	−2
Net cash flow	+1

The final position would always result in a profit, as follows:

Price condition	Portfolio status	Profit (₹)
Spot < 80	Both puts are in-the-money, and, hence, are exercised; Cash flow would be $(85 − S) − (80 − S)$	6 (5 + 1)
80 < Spot < 85	Put bought is in-the-money by $85 − S$, put written is worthless	$(85 − S + 1)$; always positive because $S < 85$
Spot > 85	Both puts, bought and written, are worthless	1

PUT–CALL PARITY

There exists a relationship between the prices of calls and puts known by the name of put–call parity, which is derived from the principle of no arbitrage. For this, we examine a special combination that is of significance. The combination uses four instruments, i.e., a stock, a European call option, a European put option, and a debt/bond. The call and the put have the same underlying asset, maturity, and strike prices.

> For the same underlying asset, the same exercise price and the same time to expiry, the call price would exceed the put price by the amount of differential between the spot price and the PV of the exercise price.

Let us consider an example where an investor creates a portfolio of the following securities:

- He/she goes long on a share selling of ₹100.
- He/she writes a call for $X = 100$, maturing at time 'T' and commanding a premium of 'c'.
- He/she buys a put, also for $X = 100$, maturing at time 'T' and selling at a premium of 'p'.

After having formed the portfolio, let us examine the position of this portfolio under various prices for the underlying asset at the time of expiration. Table 10.1 depicts the position of the portfolio for a price range of ₹0 to ₹200.

Table 10.1 Value of the portfolio of stock, short call, and long put at expiration

Figures in ₹

Stock price	0	50	75	100	125	150	200
Long stock	0	50	75	100	125	150	200
Short call at $X = 100$	—	—	—	—	−25	−50	−100
Long put at $X = 100$	100	50	25	—	—	—	—
Total value of the portfolio	100	100	100	100	100	100	100

From the last row of Table 10.1, it is evident that the value of the portfolio remains constant at exercise price X = 100, irrespective of the price of the underlying asset. When the price falls below ₹100, the put becomes valuable, and protects against loss on the asset. When the price goes beyond ₹100, the call holder exercises the option and the asset in hand gets delivered in exchange for the exercise price of ₹100, foregoing any gain from the rise in price.

Payoffs of the individual securities and the combined payoff of the portfolio are depicted in Fig. 10.3.

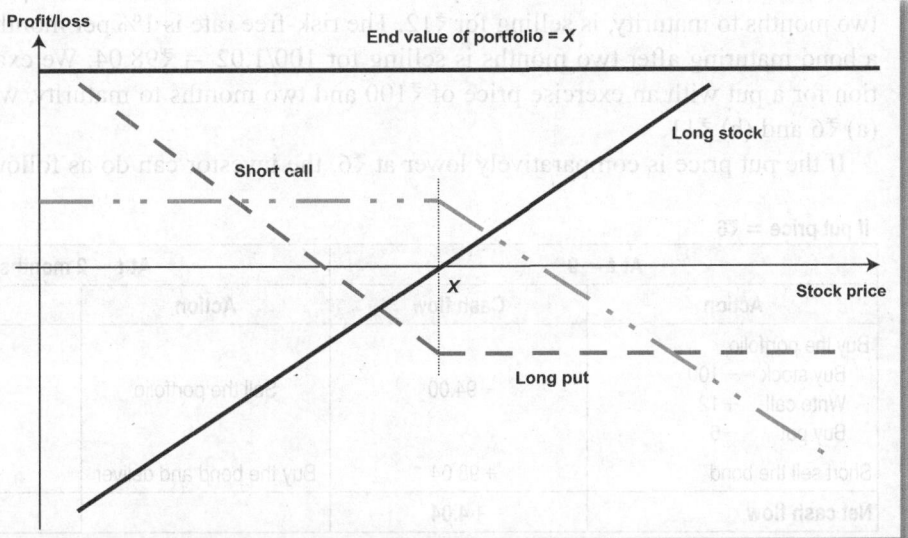

Fig. 10.3 Put–call parity—A riskless portfolio

With no uncertainty in the value of the portfolio at expiration, we can state the following:

- An investor can borrow an amount equivalent to the present value of the exercise price to create a portfolio.
- Since the value of the portfolio is certain at the expiration date, lenders would lend money at risk-free rates.
- This portfolio can be said to be equivalent to a bond that matures to value s, equal to that of the exercise price, and whose maturity coincides with the expiry of the options.

Since the maturity values of the portfolio and the bond are equal, the law of one price demands that the initial cost of the portfolio must be equal to the present value of the bond.

Initial cost of the portfolio of long stock, short call, and long put

= amount that can be borrowed at a risk-free rate
= present value of the bond maturing to the exercise price

If S is the current price of the share, c is the call premium, and p is the put premium, then

$$S - c + p = \text{Present value of } X = X/(1 + r) = Xe^{-rT} \text{ (for continuous compounding)}$$

(10.10)

Equation 10.10 is known as put–call parity, establishing a relationship between the call and put prices of European options. An alternative form of put–call parity is that the difference between the call and put prices must be equal to the difference between the spot price and the Present value of the exercise price. This can be obtained by rearranging Eq. 10.10.

$$c - p = S - Xe^{-rT} \qquad (10.11)$$

> If put–call parity does not hold, it presents an arbitrage opportunity by forming portfolios of call, put, bond, and stock.

If put–call parity is not true, the situation will offer arbitrage opportunities. A numerical example will highlight the arbitrage opportunity available.

Assume that a stock has a current price of ₹100. A call with an exercise price of ₹100, with two months to maturity, is selling for ₹12. The risk-free rate is 1% per month, and, therefore, a bond maturing after two months is selling for 100/1.02 = ₹98.04. We examine this situation for a put with an exercise price of ₹100 and two months to maturity, with put prices of (a) ₹6 and (b) ₹11.

If the put price is comparatively lower at ₹6, the investor can do as follows:

If put price = ₹6 *Figures in ₹*

At t = 0		At t = 2 months	
Action	Cash flow	Action	Cash flow

Buy the portfolio
  Buy stock   −100
  Write call +12
  Buy put   −6
	−94.00	Sell the portfolio	+100.00

Short sell the bond	+98.04	Buy the bond and deliver	−100.00
Net cash flow	**+4.04**		**0.00**

Since the value of the portfolio is riskless at maturity, an investor buys the portfolio at ₹94 and short sells the bond to realize ₹98.04, having a net cash inflow of ₹4.04 now. After two months, the investor can sell the portfolio at ₹100, buy the bond, and meet the short sale commitment. Alternatively, he/she could borrow ₹98.04 at 1% per month now and after two months, pay the maturity value of the loan of ₹100 by liquidating the portfolio. Hence, the initial cash flow of ₹4.04 is the profit from the riskless position.

In case the put price is higher at ₹11, the investor can take a reverse position, i.e., sell the portfolio and buy the bond, and yet profit from arbitrage, as may be seen from the following:

If put price = ₹11 *Figures in ₹*

At t = 0		At t = 2 months	
Action	Cash flow	Action	Cash flow

Sell the portfolio
  Sell stock   +100
  Buy call   −12
  Write put   +11
	+99.00	Buy the portfolio	−100.00

Buy the bond	−98.04	Sell the bond	+100.00
Net cash flow	**+0.96**		**0.00**

> Put–call parity also links the equity, bonds, and derivatives markets for any inconsistent returns in any of them, restoring balance among the three.

Here again, the maturity value of ₹100 is fixed. The investor can sell the bond and utilize the proceeds to buy the portfolio back, resulting in no cash flow. However, he/she generates a profit of ₹0.96 at the time of setting up the risk-less position. As an alternative to the bond, the investor could lend ₹98.04 at a risk-free rate.

The put price that will eliminate arbitrage profit is arrived at by using Eq. 10.10. Accordingly, the equilibrium put price will be

$$p = c - S + \text{Present value of } X = 12 - 100 + 98.04 = ₹10.04$$

In the first case, the put price of ₹6 was too low, and, therefore, the investor bought the put, while in the second case, the put was overpriced at ₹11, inducing the investor to write the put. Rearranging Eq. 10.10, we can restate the call price as follows:

$$c = S - X e^{-rT} + p$$

Call price = lower bound of call price + time value

As the intrinsic value of the call, without the exercise of call, is equal to the spot price less the present value of the exercise price, we may say that the put price reflects the time value of the call. Since a put cannot sell for less than zero, a call will always have some time value. For an OTM put, the put premium reflects the time value of the call, as well as the put.

Put–call parity also establishes a link between capital markets, derivative markets, and debt markets. While we all know that derivatives are driven by capital markets dealing in the underlying assets of shares, the link between the derivatives markets and debt markets was not very apparent. Through put–call parity, we now know that the returns on the bonds also affect the prices of the derivatives. Therefore, all three markets in an economy must be maintained efficiently in balance.

EXAMPLE 10.6 Put–call parity

A stock is prevailing at ₹80.00. A call with a strike of ₹85 and maturing after two months is selling for ₹2.00. Find out the price of a put with an exercise price of ₹85 and expiry of two months, assuming a risk-free interest rate of 6% and no dividend on the stock for the next two months.

Solution
Using Eq. 10.10, we can find the value of the European put option as ₹6.16.

$$p = c + X \cdot e^{-rT} - S = 2.00 + 85 \cdot e^{-0.06 \times 2/12} - 80.00 = ₹6.16$$

The other implication of put–call parity relates to the synthetic creation of an asset. Put–call parity relates the prices of call, put, stock, and bonds. A bond can be replicated using stock, call, and put. Likewise, the payoff of stock can be obtained using bonds, call, and put. In fact, amongst the four assets of call, put, bond, and stock, the profile of one asset can be replicated using the other three. Rearranging Eq. 10.10 will provide a combination for synthesising the asset. A synthetic put can be obtained by buying a bond, buying a call, and short-selling a stock. Synthetic creations can help to establish a position in an asset at a lower cost if there is a temporary imbalance in the capital markets, derivative markets, and debt markets.

> Put–call parity also helps synthesize any one of these four: stock, call, put, and bond, with the help of the other three.

Similarly, a call with a bond that matures to the exercise price must equal the put and stock, as can be seen by rearranging Eq. 10.10.

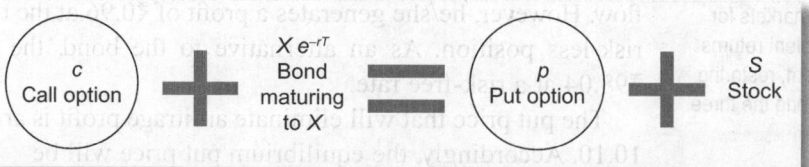

Put–Call Parity for American Options

Put–call parity for European options can help to establish relationships for American puts and calls. American options provide for early exercise of the option. Is this flexibility to exercise early of some value? Let us examine it.

> It is never optimal to exercise an American call prior to maturity because you lose the time value of the call.

Consider an American call as compared to a European call on a non-dividend paying stock. If the call is exercised early, one gets the intrinsic value and no more. Instead, if one sells an American call, one gets the intrinsic value as well as the time value. By exercising at any point of time prior to maturity, one foregoes the time value attached with the remaining life of the

---

EXAMPLE 10.7 Arbitrage with options

Assume that the put option in Example 10.6 is actually selling for ₹8. How can you benefit from the situation? How much profit can you make from the prices prevailing in the market?

Solution
Put–call parity equates the portfolio of call and bond with one each of put and stock. Since the put is overpriced, it must be sold. As per put–call parity, (a) the put is sold, (b) the stock is sold, and (c) the call is bought. By doing so, the following cash flow would result:

Action	Cash flow (₹)
Sold put	8.00
Sold stock	80.00
Bought call	−2.00
Net cash flow	86.00

The cash can be invested at a risk-free rate at 6% for two months, the time left for expiry of the options. It assures a cash flow of ₹86.86 (86 × $e^{0.06 \times 2/12}$). At the end of two months, the portfolio would be in profit of ₹1.86, regardless of the situation, by reversing the initial position. Consider the following three positions of stock price: (a) rising to ₹100, (b) remaining the same at ₹80, and (c) falling to ₹60.

Stock price	₹100.00	₹80.00	₹60.00
Payoff of put written	—	−5.00	−25.00
Bought stock	−100.00	−80.00	−60.00
Payoff of call bought	15.00	—	—
Cash realised	86.86	86.86	86.86
Net cash flow	1.86	1.86	1.86

Option Pricing—Basics **293**

> There are circumstances when it is more beneficial to exercise a put before maturity.

option. Therefore, it is never optimal to exercise the call prior to maturity. With this argument, it can be stated that the American call too would be exercised only on maturity and it is equal to the European call. Therefore, the value of an American call can be written as $c_a = c$, where c_a is the value of the American call.

Can we say the same for an American put? It may be true in most, but not in all, cases. The minimum value of a European put is given by $Xe^{-rT} - S$. The intrinsic value of a put is $X - S$. With a positive rate of interest, the minimum value of the put would be less than its intrinsic worth. For an extreme case of a stock price of zero, the exercise of the put would result in the payoff of X. One cannot get a higher payoff than this. If one waits further, one only stands to lose. Therefore, it may be said that for a sufficiently low price of the stock, it may be optimal to exercise the put option early. Since it is so, there would be a greater value to the American put than the European put. Hence, the value of the American put can be written as:

$p_a \geq p$, where p_a is the value of the American put.

Using Eq. 10.10, we may say

$$p_a \geq p = c + X \cdot e^{-rT} - S$$

Since $c_a = c$, we arrive at the put–call parity for American options in this way:

$$p_a \geq c_a + X \cdot e^{-rT} - S \qquad (10.12)$$

Put–Call Parity for Dividend Paying Stock

In case a stock pays a dividend of q, then the put–call parity would stand modified, with the spot price of the stock adjusted for the present value of the dividend. Since the stock price falls by the value of dividend in ex-dividend dates, it is analogous to saying that the current price of the stock must be adjusted for the present value of the dividend. The put–call parity for a dividend paying stock would, therefore, be:

Put–call parity for a dividend paying stock with a dividend of D at time t would be given by:

$$c + Xe^{-rT} = p + S - De^{-rT} \qquad (10.13)$$

The put–call parity for a dividend paying stock with a continuous dividend of q would be given by:

$$c + Xe^{-rT} = p + Se^{-qT} \qquad (10.14)$$

Put–Call Relationship for Currency Options

A put–call relationship rests on the equivalency of the portfolio: (a) a call option and a bond that matures to X, with (b) a put option and the underlying asset. In case an option is based on currencies, the underlying asset would be a foreign currency. The underlying asset, the foreign currency in question, is like a dividend paying asset that yields a risk-free interest rate in foreign currency, r_f. Therefore, today's equivalent would be $S^{-r_f T}$. Therefore, the put–call parity for currency options would be

$$c + Xe^{-rT} = p + Se^{-r_f T} \qquad (10.15)$$

SOLVED PROBLEMS

SP 10.1: Put option prices and payoff

A 3-m put option on Tata Steel with a strike price of ₹550 is selling for ₹60, while the share is trading at ₹500. Find out the following:

(a) What is the intrinsic worth of the put option?
(b) What is the time value of the put option?
(c) What interpretation do you attach to the time value?
(d) At what price of the asset would the put option holder break even?

Solution
(a) The intrinsic worth of the option is $(X - S) = 550 - 500 = ₹50.00$
(b) The time value of the put is the option price less its intrinsic worth $= 60 - 50 = ₹10.00$
(c) The time value is paid by the buyer of the option since the intrinsic value of the option may rise with a fall in prices. As the price of the underlying falls, the put option becomes more in-the-money, and, therefore, the holder stands to gain a greater amount.
(d) If the value of Tata Steel shares falls to ₹490, the put option holder would get back the entire premium paid by way of the intrinsic worth of the option. However, instead of exercising the option, he/she may like to sell the same, as it would fetch a greater value—the time value over and above the intrinsic value.

SP 10.2: Lower bound to option premium

The price of a State Bank of India share is ₹1800. If the risk-free rate of interest is 6.00% p.a. continuously compounded, then at what minimum prices would the following options on the stock of the State Bank of India, each maturing after one month, sell for?

(a) A call and a put with a strike price of ₹1700
(b) A call and a put with a strike price of ₹1800
(c) A call and a put with a strike price of ₹1900

Solution
The lower bound to the call price is given by zero or $S_0 - X \cdot e^{-rT}$
The lower bound to the put price is given by zero or $X \cdot e^{-rT} - S_0$
Therefore, the minimum values of the options calls will be given by:

	Call	Put
X = 1700	1800.00 − 1691.52 = ₹108.48	1691.52 − 1800.00 = −₹108.48; 0
X = 1800	1800.00 − 1791.02 = ₹8.98	1791.02 − 1800.00 = −₹8.98; 0
X = 1900	1800.00 − 1890.52 = −₹90.52; 0	1890.52 − 1800.00 = ₹90.52

SP 10.3: Arbitrage with options

The put on a stock with a strike price of ₹460 is selling for ₹15, while another put on the same stock with a strike price of ₹475 is selling for ₹32. Both the puts have the same maturity. Do you find the prices of the two puts to be appropriate? Can you benefit from the situation? If yes, how?

Solution
The prices of the puts are inconsistent, as the difference in premiums of the two puts of ₹17 (32 − 15) is larger than the difference between the strike prices of ₹15 (475 − 460). One can set up arbitrage by selling a put with a higher strike and buying one with a lower strike. When the price is lower than the lower strike, both puts are ITM, and the liability would not exceed the premium earned. The same would be the case when the spot value is between the two exercise prices. With a price higher than the higher strike, both the puts are OTM, and the premium earned is pocketed. This is shown here:

Stock price	Put X = 460	Put X = 475	Initial	Total
Spot price < 460	460 − S	−(475 − S)	17	2
460 < Spot < 475	—	−(475 − S)	17	S − 458
Spot > 475	—	—	17	17

SP 10.4: Put–call parity

A stock is trading at ₹500. A call option on the same with three months to maturity and an exercise price of ₹550 is selling for ₹12. What should the price of a put option on the stock with three months to expiry and an exercise price of ₹550 be? Assume a risk-free interest rate at 8%.

Solution
Using Eq. 10.10, we can find the value of a European put option as ₹51.11.

$$p = c + X \cdot e^{-rT} - S = 12.00 + 550 \cdot e^{-0.08 \times 3/12} - 500.00 = ₹51.11$$

SP 10.5: Arbitrage with options

Assume that the put option in SP 10.4 is actually selling for ₹45.00. How can you benefit from the situation? How much profit can you make from the prices prevailing in the market?

Solution
Put–call parity equates a portfolio of call and bond with put and stock. Since the put is underpriced; it must be bought. Therefore, we (a) buy the put, (b) buy the stock, (c) write a call and (d) borrow the shortfall. This transaction would result in the following cash flow:

Action	Cash flow (₹)
Bought put	−45.00
Bought stock	−500.00
Sold call	12.00
Borrowed	533.00
Net cash flow	0.00

The cash borrowed would have to be paid back together with risk-free interest at 8% for three months at the time of expiry of options. The matured amount of borrowing is ₹543.77 (533 × $e^{0.08 \times 3/12}$). At the end of three months, the portfolio would result in a profit of ₹11.64, regardless of the situation, by reversing the initial position. Consider the following three positions, where the stock price rises to ₹600, remains the same at ₹500, and falls to ₹400.

Stock price	₹600.00	₹500.00	₹400.00
Payoff of put bought	—	50.00	150.00
Sold stock	600.00	500.00	400.00
Payoff of call sold	−50.00	—	—
Borrowing paid	−543.77	−543.77	−543.77
Net cash flow	6.23	6.23	6.23

SUMMARY

Option premium, i.e., the amount of money that an option buyer must pay to the option writer to induce him/her to confer the right, is an area that has attracted a lot of attention and involved a lot of effort. Though there are mathematically complex models, a lot of inference about the option premium may be made by understanding simple arbitrage-based relationships.

An option premium consists of two parts—the intrinsic value and the time value. The intrinsic value is the money the holder of the option gets if the option is exercised immediately. The intrinsic value cannot be negative. The time value of an option is the value attached due to the time remaining for maturity, during which the option may become more in-the-money or the intrinsic value may rise (of course, it may decline too). The difference between the actual price and the intrinsic value is the time value of the option. This, too, cannot be negative.

The maximum value of a call option is the price of the underlying asset. One would not pay more than the price of the asset to buy a right to buy the same. The cost of buying a right to buy an asset cannot exceed the price of the asset itself. Since the exercise price is payable only on maturity, the minimum value of the call must be the difference between the asset price and the present value of the exercise price. For deep OTM calls, the entire option premium is made up of time value, while for deep ITM calls, almost all the premium is intrinsic value. The time value of an option is greatest for ATM calls.

Similarly, the maximum value of a put is the exercise price itself. The minimum value is given by the difference between the present value of the exercise price and the spot price. Again, the time value is largest for ATM put options.

For dividend paying assets, the spot price needs to be adjusted for the present value of the dividend.

There also exist some relationships in option prices that are based on the principle of no arbitrage. Some of these relationships are: (a) a call option with a higher X would cost less than one with a lower X, (b) the difference in option premium between calls and puts cannot exceed the difference in exercise prices, (c) options with a longer maturity would cost more than options with a shorter maturity.

There also exists an arbitrage-based relationship between the prices of call and put options, called the put–call parity. A portfolio running long on assets, with a short call and a long put would result in a riskless position at maturity of the options, with assured payoff equal to the exercise price. A long position in a put coupled with a long position in the stock provides insurance to the value of the portfolio. Therefore, it may be equated with a call and a position on a fixed amount of cash.

Put–call parity only holds for European options. For American options, it remains a relationship of inequality in the minimum price of a put. For American calls, the notion that the flexibility to exercise a call at any point of time must cause its value to be more that a European call is wrong. Since by exercising a call option one gets only the intrinsic value and loses the time value, selling the call option is more attractive than exercising it. Therefore, an American call would not be exercised before maturity and hence, its value is the same as that of a European call. However, the same cannot be true for an American put, as there are circumstances when exercising a put is more beneficial. Therefore, an American put option is valued higher than a European put option.

Put–call parity provides a link between call and put prices, thus linking the spot equity markets and the debt markets. Therefore, there needs to be consistency in the equity, debt, and derivatives markets. Put–call parity also helps in creating synthetic positions of equity, call, put, and bond. Given any three, the fourth may be synthesized, and therefore, the pricing of a synthetic product and the actual product needs to be the same.

KEY TERMS

Intrinsic value The money the holder gets upon immediate exercise.
Put–Call parity The relationship between the call price and the put price of the same underlying asset, with the same exercise price and the same time to maturity.

Time value of option The excess of the actual price of the option over its intrinsic value.

QUESTIONS

10.1 What do you understand by the intrinsic value and the time value of an option contract?
10.2 Why do you think time value is the maximum for ATM options?
10.3 What are the minimum and maximum bounds on the prices of call options? Explain.
10.4 What are the minimum and maximum bounds on the prices of put options? Explain.
10.5 Why cannot the difference between two call prices exceed the difference between their strike prices? If this happens, how would you benefit? Explain with the help of an example.
10.6 What do you understand by put–call parity? Provide some information on the relationship between the call and put prices for European options.
10.7 Why is it not a good idea to exercise an American call prior to its maturity?
10.8 What can you say about the relationship between the call and put prices of American options?

PROBLEMS

P 10.1 Lower bound on currency options
The spot rate for the US dollar in India is ₹48.00. If risk-free interest rates in India and the USA are 8% and 5%, respectively, what would the minimum prices for 3-m ATM call and put options be?

P 10.2 Lower bound of option values and dividend
A stock is selling for ₹75. A call option and a put option with a strike of ₹80 and a maturity of three months are available on the stock.

(a) What should the minimum price of these options be if the risk-free rate of interest is 12% p.a. with monthly compounding?

(b) If the stock will be returning a dividend of ₹2.00 in one month's time, how would it affect the minimum price derived in a)?

P 10.3 Minimum bound of call and arbitrage

Hindalco stock is trading at ₹100. A 6-m European call with a strike of ₹80 is available.

(a) What would the minimum price of the call be if the risk-free rate is 10% p.a.?

(b) If the call is actually selling for ₹12.00, what minimum profit can you make? Demonstrate how you would derive such profit.

P 10.4 Put–call parity and arbitrage

Refer to P 10.3. If a call option on the stock sells for ₹15, then

(a) What would be the price of a put option on the same stock, with the same strike and maturity?

(b) If the put actually sells for ₹1, how much profit can you make, and how would you make it?

(c) If the put sells for ₹2.00, how much profit can you make, and how would you make it?

P 10.5 Put option and dividend

Refer to P 10.2. What would the minimum price of the put option be if another dividend of ₹3.00 is proposed at the end of two months?

P 10.6 Minimum value of put and arbitrage

If the put option in P 10.5 is actually selling for ₹6.00, is there an arbitrage opportunity? How would you exploit this opportunity?

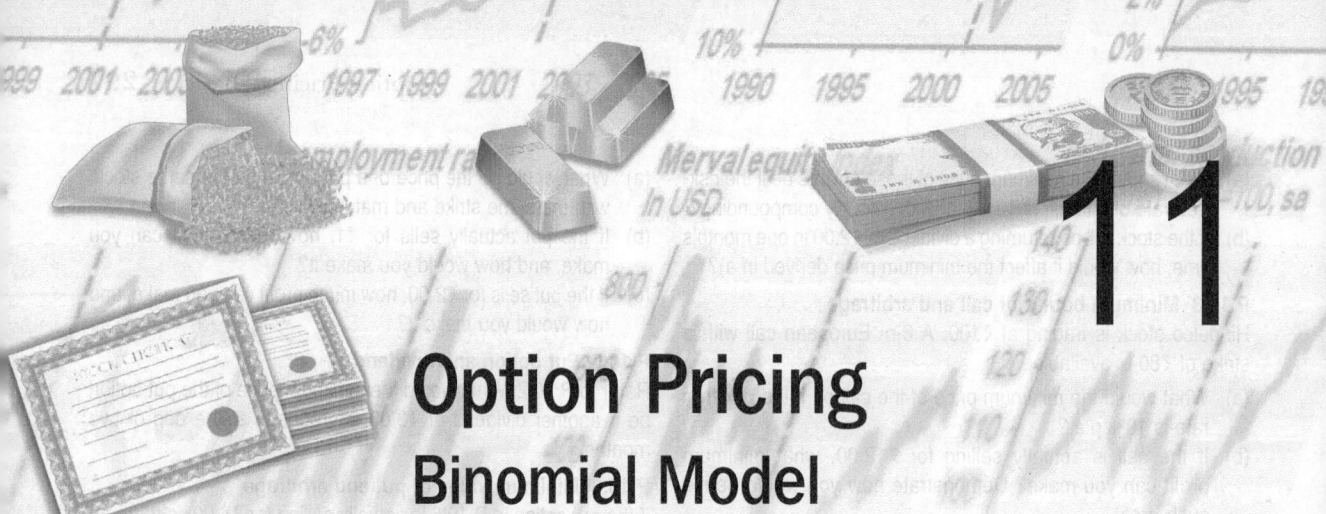

Option Pricing
Binomial Model

INTRODUCTION

In Chapter 10, we discussed some arbitrage-based arguments that placed upper and lower bounds on the prices of options. We also discussed boundary conditions for option premiums, as also the relationship between the prices of call and put options by way of put–call parity. Here, we concentrate on the exact valuation of option premium. Determination of the fair price is important for researchers, practitioners, and traders alike. Investors must know the actual worth of the asset being acquired. For traders, it is important for speculation and identifying arbitrage opportunities.

In this chapter and the next, we shall cover two methods of determination of option premium in detail—the binomial model and the Black-Scholes model. The binomial option pricing method is a numerical method that estimates the value of options. It is a very flexible model for valuing options that are not regularly traded or are specifically negotiated between contracting parties. The Black-Scholes model is a standard model that values conventional options that are regularly traded, though the principle can be extended to value certain exotic options. It may be noted that the two models are not contradictory but they use somewhat different approaches for valuation. It is necessary to understand the conceptual frameworks of both the models to grasp the pricing principles on a wide variety of options that have evolved over time, and would continue to do so.

We discuss the binomial option pricing model now. The binomial model is an extremely simple yet very powerful model that provides deep insights into option dynamics. Like with all other models, it is assumed that there are no market distortions such as transaction costs and unexploited arbitrage opportunities.

Learning Objectives

After going through this chapter, readers should be familiar with

- The behaviour of the prices of assets
- using the binomial model for option pricing
- what risk-neutral valuation means
- the equivalent portfolio approach to value options
- the binomial process to value American options
- incorporating changes in the binomial approach for
  - dividend payments
  - valuing options on indices
  - valuing options on currencies
- making a binomial model more realistic by effecting changes in its parameters
- valuation of American options using the binomial approach
- the Monte carlo simulation for valuing options

BINOMIAL OPTION PRICING MODEL

One way of valuing an option on a stock is to construct a tree of possible values of the stock price and find the worth of the option at each of the values on all branches of the tree. For simplification, we can assume only two possible values and a single period at which the option matures at time $t = 1$. This is known as the binomial model, where the future price of an asset can assume only two possible values: an upside move or a downside move.

> The binomial option pricing model makes a simplified assumption of only two possible values of an underlying asset, one up and the other down from the current price.

To illustrate how the binomial model works, let us assume a stock sells for a price of $S_0 = ₹100$. We assume an investment horizon of one year at the end of which the price S_1 can either be 25% up, i.e., ₹125 or 20% down, i.e., ₹80. Note that it is not essential to have equal movement on both sides. However, we cannot assume movement of the price in same directions because if it were so the price of the stock would rise or fall instantly; it has to be either up or down. It would be injudicious to use both movements in the same direction, though there is no such compulsion while using the binomial model for option pricing. We further assume that the option is European and that the stock pays no dividend during the option period. All returns are arrived at through capital gains. The end values of the stock for up and down movements are depicted in Fig. 11.1.

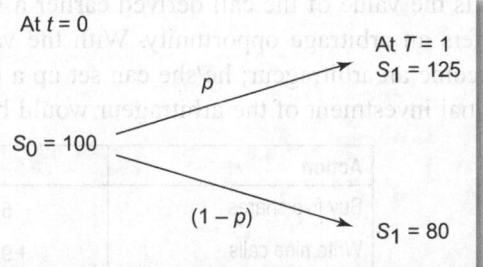

Fig. 11.1 Value of asset under binomial option pricing model

Having assumed this simplistic scenario, let us now attempt to value an at-the-money (ATM) European call with a strike price, X, of ₹100 and time to expiry of one year. We know that the value of the call is Max$(S - X, 0)$. A call with a strike price at $X = 100$ means that if the price of the stock moves up to ₹125, the payoff on the call option would be $125 - 100 = ₹25$, and in case the price moves down to ₹80, the call option expires without any worth.

We also assume that the yield on risk-free instruments in the capital market is 6% p.a.

One naïve way of finding the value of the call is to find the expected value of the stock and then the expected value of the call at $t = 1$. Finally, we discount the value of the call at $t = 0$. To find the expected value of the underlying stock, we need probabilities for both the branches of the binomial model. Assume that the probability of an upward movement is p. The probability of a downward movement then automatically becomes $(1 - p)$. By using this method, we shall analyse three different scenarios for three different investors, A, B, and C—an optimist, a realist, and a pessimist, respectively.

Situation I for Investor A Investor A, an optimist, supposes the probability of an upside movement, p, as 0.90 and the probability of a downside movement, $(1 - p)$ as 0.10. Therefore, the expected value of the stock can be given as follows:

Expected value of stock (at $T = 1$) = $0.90 \times 125 + 0.10 \times 80 = ₹120.80$

Calculation of the expected value of the call is as follows:

Expected value of the call (at $T = 1$)
= Max (expected value of the stock − exercise price, 0)
= Max(120.80 − 100, 0)
= Max(20.80, 0)
= 120.80 − 100.00 = ₹20.80

To find the value of the call today, we need to discount it by an appropriate rate consistent with risk-associated discount on the returns on the stock. Any arbitrary selection of a rate would lead to arbitrary pricing of the call option. Let us assume that investor A is fairly certain of his/her assessment of the probabilities of up and down movements, and, therefore, considers the appropriate rate of discount as a risk-free rate of 6%. Therefore, according to him/her, the present value of the call will be ₹19.62, as shown here.

Value of the call today = 20.80/1.06 = ₹19.62

Is the value of the call derived earlier a valid one? The seemingly valid value of the call offers an arbitrage opportunity. With the value of the call at ₹19.62, another investor can become an arbitrageur; he/she can set up a portfolio of five shares and write nine calls. The initial investment of the arbitrageur would be as follows:

Action		Cash flow (₹)
Buy five shares	−5 × 100	−500.00
Write nine calls	+9 × 19.62	+176.58
Cash outflow at $t = 0$		323.42

The portfolio can be set up by borrowing at 6%. The liability of arbitrageur would be 1.06 × 323.42 = ₹342.83 after a year.

The end position of the portfolio would be as depicted in Fig. 11.2. With the price at ₹125, the value of the holding would be 5 × 125 = ₹625. The call holder would exercise his/her option and the liability would be ₹25 on each call written. Therefore, the arbitrageur would have to pay 9 × 25 = ₹225. The net cash inflow for him/her would be ₹400.

When the stock moves down to ₹80, the value of the stockholding would be ₹400, while there would be no liability for the arbitrageur on the calls written by him/her, which would be worthless for the holder.

> It is fallacious to try to estimate the probability and find the expected value of an option, because we do not know the appropriate discount rate.

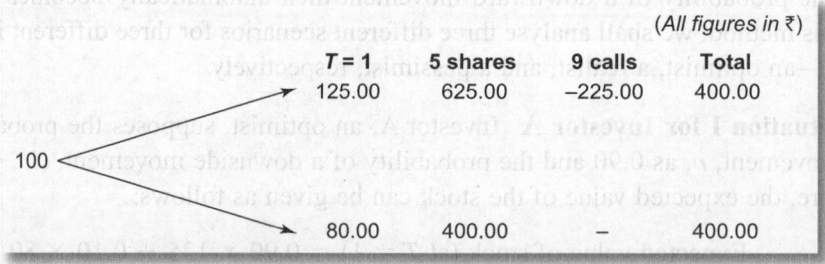

Fig. 11.2 Portfolio value at $T = 1$

Irrespective of which way the stock moves, the end value of the portfolio remains fixed at ₹400. This yields a certain profit for the arbitrageur at ₹57.17, after providing for interest on the borrowing, as shown here:

Value of the portfolio at $T = 1$ = ₹400.00
Gain = 400.00 − 342.83 = ₹57.17

Hence, the value of the call at ₹19.62 is not valid.

Situation II for Investor B Assume another person, investor B, who is a realist. He/she views the expected scenario differently from investor A. For investor B, the probability of an upside movement, p, is 0.5, and the probability of a down movement, $(1 − p)$, is also 0.5. Therefore, he/she expects the price of the stock at $T = 1$ to be ₹102.50.

Expected value of stock at $T = 1$ = $0.5 \times 125 + 0.5 \times 80$ = ₹102.50
Expected value of the call at $T = 1$
= Max(expected value of the stock − exercise price, 0)
= Max(102.50 − 100, 0) = ₹2.50

For investor B, who too is confident of his/her forecast, the discount rate is 6%. The present value of the call would be ₹2.36 as shown here:

Value of the call today = 2.50/1.06 = ₹2.36

Let us assume that investor B is correct in his/her perception of the probabilities assigned to the two branches, the future prices of the stock, and, therefore, the call value. If so, this position, too, would offer an arbitrage opportunity. Another investor can become an arbitrageur and can set up a portfolio, selling five shares and buying nine calls. If one call sells for ₹2.36, he/she can set up the following portfolio:

Action		Cash flow (₹)
Short sell five shares	+5 × 100	+500.00
Buy nine calls	−9 × 2.36	−21.24
Cash flow at $t = 0$		+478.76

The initial portfolio yields a cash flow of ₹478.76, which may be invested at 6%.
The value of the asset at the end of the investment period of one year against the portfolio created would be:

Invest at 6% and earn interest = ₹28.72
Maturity value = ₹507.48

The liability at maturity of the option would depend upon what happens to the portfolio. If the stock rises to ₹125, the arbitrageur would have to buy the stock at ₹125, requiring a cash outflow of ₹625 for five shares. However, he/she also owns nine call options, each of which would be worth ₹25, providing a cash inflow of ₹225. His/her net liability would be ₹400. If the stock moves to ₹80, the arbitrageur would buy five shares for ₹400. Of course, his/her calls are worthless. In either case, his/her outflow would be ₹400 only, giving a certain profit of ₹107.48.

Hence, the price of the call at ₹2.36 is not valid either.

Situation III for Investor C We considered two investors with different perceptions of the expected values of the stock and the call option. Yet, there were arbitrage opportunities for both of them. At the expense of redundancy, let us consider another position, involving investor C, a pessimist who rates the probability of an upside movement, p, at 0.1, and the probability of a downside movement, $(1 - p)$, at 0.9.

> Assuming a probability for upside and downside movement of prices leads to arbitrage opportunities.

Expected value of stock (at $T = 1$) = $0.1 \times 125 + 0.9 \times 80$ = ₹84.50
Expected value of the call (at $T = 1$)
  = Max(expected value of the stock − exercise price, 0)
  = Max(84.50 − 100, 0) = ₹0.00

According to investor C, the value of the call is zero, and, therefore, he/she would gladly write a call if someone offers him/her an amount as little as ₹1. Let us assume he/she is persuaded by an arbitrageur to write nine such calls, to earn ₹9. The arbitrageur promptly sells five shares short to set up the following portfolio and have an immediate cash inflow of ₹491.

Action		Cash flow (₹)
Short sell five shares	$+5 \times 100$	+500.00
Buy nine calls	-9×1.00	−9.00
Cash outflow at $t = 0$		+491.00

The arbitrageur invests the sum at a risk-free rate to realize ₹520.46 at the end of one year.

Invest at 6% and earn interest = ₹29.46
Maturity value = ₹520.46

What would his/her liability at the end of the investment horizon be? His/her liability would again be ₹400, irrespective of which of the two possible scenarios exists. If the stock moves up to ₹125, he/she exercises the nine call options and buys five shares to have a net outflow of ₹400. If the price is ₹80, he/she buys five shares by paying ₹400, letting his/her call options lapse. In any case, he/she stands to gain a whopping ₹120.46. Hence, the price of the call cannot be zero either.

Resolving the Dilemma

The positions of investors A, B, and C, assuming different scenarios depending upon their risk perceptions (attaching higher/lower chances to price moving upwards/downwards) of the stock price in the future would provide different values to the call options, each of which does not seem to be valid, as it offers arbitrage. In a competitive world, an asset cannot command two prices at the same time, and, if so, the process of arbitrage itself must lead to an arbitrage-free single price. The possible ways by which all the investors agree to single price of the call option are as follows:
- They use different discount rates (rather than a common 6%), in such a way that it leads to the same value of the call option.
- They agree on the same future expected value of the stock, implying that they abandon their individual estimates of the probabilities of upside and downside movements of the stock price.

We address these issues in the following section.

RISK-NEUTRAL VALUATION

We saw that each investor, A, B, and C, made an assessment of the expected value of the asset and therefore, different values of the call opening opportunities for arbitrage. There are numerous investors such as A, B, and C in the free and competitive market, who would be forced to review their pricing of the call by arbitrageurs, so that it results in the same value of the call for all. Arbitrage-free valuation, therefore, would combine the risk preferences of the entire market, making the risk estimates of the individuals redundant.

If we assume that the binary state of prices is correct, the market as a whole must agree to the same expected price, $E(S_1)$, of the stock. To know $E(S_1)$, we must know either the growth rate of the stock price or the probabilities of upside/downside movements. To have a universally acceptable $E(S_1)$, the expected returns offered by the stock $[E(S_1) - S_0]$ can be no greater than the risk-free rate of return, r. Such a proposition is referred to as risk neutrality, i.e., in aggregate, the world is indifferent to risk. A risk-free return would imply probabilities to the upside and downside movement. Under a risk-neutral valuation, we presume that the underlying asset earns a risk-free rate of return, i.e., $E(S_1) = (1 + r) \times S_0$, or with continuous compounding $E(S_1) = e^{rt} \times S_0$.

> Under the risk-neutral method, we assume that the expected value of a stock would provide a return equal to the risk-free rate.

Alternatively stated, we can value the derivative by finding the risk-neutral probabilities with which the current market price is nothing, but the expected value of the underlying asset discounted at a risk-free rate of return. The valuation of the derivative on the asset too can follow the same method.

Under the binomial approach, if the risk-neutral probability of an upward movement is p with a gain of $u\%$ and the probability of a downward movement is $(1 - p)$ with a loss of $d\%$, then the expected return must equal the risk-free rate of return. Therefore, we can determine the value of p using the following equation:

$$p \times u + (1 - p) \times d = r$$

$$p = \frac{r - d}{u - d} \quad (11.1)$$

In our case, the risk-free rate is given as 6%, with $u = 25\%$ and $d = -20\%$. Using Eq. 11.1 implies that the probability of the upside movement, p, is

$$p = \frac{r - d}{u - d} = \frac{6 - (-20)}{25 - (-20)} = 0.5778 = 57.78\%$$

This implies that the market as a whole assigns a probability of 57.78% to an up move, so as to have a single value of the call option and thus eliminate any arbitrage opportunity. This is independent of what we may feel about changes in asset price in our individual capacities. Therefore, the market can be regarded as risk neutral when we agree that the expected end value would provide returns no greater than the risk-free rate.

> With a risk-free rate of return, the two branches of a binomial tree would have implied probabilities for a given change in the spot price.

With the implied probabilities known, we may value a call option as the expected value of its payoff. Hence, the value of a call at the end of the option period would be:

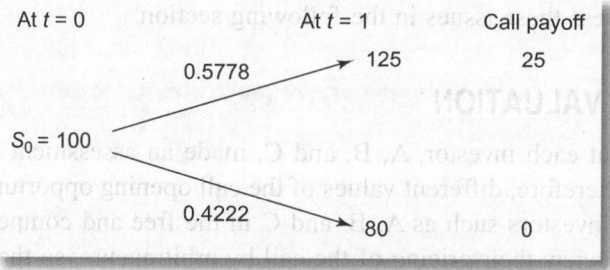

Fig. 11.3 Payoff of call under binomial pricing model

Value of the call
= Probability of upward movement × payoff
+ probability of downward movement × payoff
= $p \times \text{Max}(S_1 - X, 0) + (1 - p) \times \text{Max}(S_1 - X, 0)$

With the payoff as indicated in Fig. 11.3, the value of the call at the end of one year would be

$$0.5778 \times 25 + 0.4222 \times 0 = ₹14.44$$

The present value of the call discounted at the risk-free rate is 14.44/1.06 = ₹13.63.

We may demonstrate that at this price of the call, arbitrage is eliminated. We take the same actions as for Investors A, B, and C.

Action		Cash flow (₹)
Short sell five shares	+5 × 100	+500.00
Buy nine calls	−9 × 13.63	−122.67
Cash flow at $t = 0$		+377.33

The arbitrageur invests the sum at a risk-free rate of 6% to realize ₹400.00 at the end of one year. This would be exactly equal to the value of the portfolio at the end of one year.

Risk-neutral valuation means that while the call option is independent of the probabilities of price changes, the call premium implies a probability of the stock rising to $(1 + u)$. A large number of investors, such as A, B, and C, would make the market risk neutral on an aggregate basis for the purpose of determination of the option price.

The value of the call as determined earlier in this section provides some very strange results. The price of the call option derived is independent of the probabilities of the future price, or of the expected value of the stock. This seemingly strange conclusion is difficult to comprehend. Most of us would believe that the greater the likelihood of the price of the share going up, the larger should be the value of the call option. This belief is misplaced, as we have seen in the three cases involving investors A, B, and C each of whom estimated a call value that created arbitrage opportunities. As such we do not need any estimate of probabilities of movement of stock price. The reason is that the current price of a stock already discounts the future. The higher the chances of an up move, the greater would be the price today. Assuming efficient markets, the expected value and the volatility estimates are already captured in the current price of the stock. Hence, there is no need to make separate individualistic estimates of the future direction of movement or of the probabilities. They are already contained in the current price.

> We do not need individual estimates of probabilities of price changes; instead, we use risk-neutral probabilities to find the value of an option.

To summarize, under the risk-neutral approach, we
- found the risk-neutral implied probabilities of up and down moves;
- calculated the expected payoff of the option at maturity with implied probabilities; and
- discounted the expected payoff at the risk-free rate to arrive at the current value of the option.

Using Up and Down Move as Ratio of Current Price

Sometimes, it is easier to represent the up and down move as a ratio of the current price. In the case of a 25% up move, u can be equal to 1.25, and for a 20% down move, d is equal to 0.80. In that case, the implied probability of an up move, p, would be given by Eqs 11.2 and 11.3, respectively, for discrete and continuous compounding.

$$p = \frac{(1+r) - d}{u - d} \qquad (11.2)$$

$$p = \frac{e^r - d}{u - d} \qquad (11.3)$$

Finding Risk-free Portfolio

We demonstrated that with five shares and nine calls, we end up with a fixed value of the portfolio, irrespective of the asset price. It is interesting to note that despite the extreme volatility associated with options, we were able to combine them with the asset to replicate a risk-free portfolio. The ability to replicate a risk-free portfolio enabled us to price the option.

How did we find a combination of five shares and nine calls to get a risk-free end value of ₹400? We can do this with a little mathematics. Assume that for each share, we write N call options. We choose the value of N such that the portfolio of one long share and N calls short is equal for the two possible price scenarios assumed in the binomial model. We can construct a portfolio that, irrespective of the price scenario at the expiry of the option, yields the same end value, making it independent of the risk appetite of individual investors.

> With derivatives, we can construct a portfolio that provides a fixed value, regardless of the prices of the asset in the future.

When the price of the stock is ₹125, the loss on each call written is ₹25, and the portfolio is worth $125 - 25 N$. When the value of stock is ₹80, the option written does not incur any liability, and the value of the portfolio is ₹80. Setting them equally would give the desired value of the number of calls that can be written for each stock bought. Solving the equation gives this value at 1.80 calls for each share, or nine calls written for five shares bought.

$$125 - 25 \times N = 80$$
$$N = 1.80$$

The value of the portfolio consisting of one share and N calls is depicted in Fig. 11.4.

Value of Call Option

A portfolio of one share and 1.80 calls would have a future value of ₹80 that is certain. Since it is certain to have a value of ₹80 after one year, investment in such a portfolio must yield a return commensurate with the risk-free rate, i.e., 6% in our case. Therefore, the call price must be governed by Eq. 11.4.[1]

---

[1] For continuous compounding, the equation becomes $(100 - 1.80\, c) \times e^{0.06T} = 80$

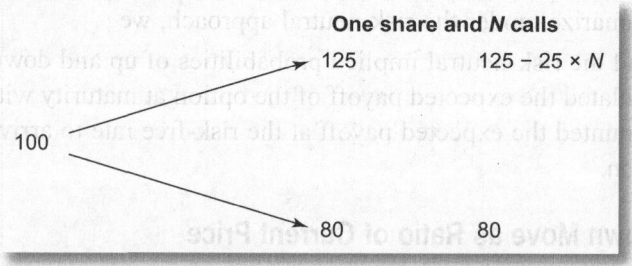

Fig. 11.4 Value of portfolio of one share and N calls

$$(100 - 1.80 \times c) \times 1.06 = 80 \qquad (11.4)$$

This gives $c = ₹13.63$

The value of the call, as determined by Eq. 11.4, does not allow any arbitrage.

Just as the current price of the share does not tell which way the price is going to move in the future, the call price also does not forecast the expected return on the stock. The expected return remains equal to the risk-free rate. Alternatively put, the call price does not say anything about the expected return from the underlying asset. Merely because a call on one asset sells for ₹10 and on another at ₹5, this does not imply a greater return. Instead, the higher price of the call on the same asset, with the same exercise and the same time to maturity, signifies increased volatility.

> Value of call is no reflection on the return on the asset. Instead option prices signify volatility.

Equivalent Portfolio Approach for Option Valuation

An alternative way of presenting the arguments made in the risk-neutral valuation is to construct a portfolio of some shares bought by borrowing, so as to have the same payoff as that of a call option. Replication of the payoff of an option with a risk-free portfolio by borrowing would lead to pricing of the option today. The portfolio of the share and borrowing can be valued easily with the interest rate and the spot prices known. Two portfolios with identical end values must have the same price today. Setting the values equal, we can price the call option today, as demonstrated below.

The payoff of the call option with an exercise price of ₹100 is as follows:

	Share price = ₹125	Share price = ₹80
Payoff of call option (₹)	25.00	0

Now consider a portfolio of 5/9 shares and a borrowing that matures to ₹44.44 after a year. The payoff of this portfolio is identical to the payoff of the call option, as shown here:

	Share price = ₹125	Share price = ₹80
Value of 5/9 shares (₹)	69.44	44.44
Maturity value of loan (₹)	−44.44	−44.44
Value of the portfolio at maturity	25.00	0.00

Since the payoff the portfolio of 5/9 shares and borrowing is the same as that of the call option on maturity, they essentially must have identical present value, i.e.,

> An option delta is the change in value of an option resulting from a change in the value of the underlying asset.

Value of the call option today
= value of the 5/9 share today − value of the loan today
= 5/9 × 100 − 44.44/1.06
= 55.55 − 41.92 = ₹13.63

For the construction of an equivalent portfolio, we need to find the quantity of the shares that are to be purchased for each call, and the amount of borrowing to fund the shares. In order to compute the number of shares to be bought or sold, we use a very important parameter called the option delta. Option delta is the change in value of an option for a change in value of the underlying asset. It is denoted by Δ, and is expressed as

$$\text{Option delta, } \Delta = \frac{\text{Change in the value of option}}{\text{Change in the value of underlying asset}}$$

In our case, the stock is the underlying asset; therefore, we calculate the *option delta* as a ratio of the spread on the call payoffs to that on the share prices.

$$\text{Option delta, } \Delta = \frac{\text{Spread of call option}}{\text{Spread of share price}} \qquad (11.5)$$

For our case the option delta is 5/9, computed as follows:

	Share price	Call value (X = 100)
Up movement	125.00	25.00
Down movement	80.00	—
Spread	45.00	25.00

$$\text{Option delta, } \Delta = \frac{\text{Spread of call option}}{\text{Spread of share price}} = \frac{25 - 0}{125 - 80} = \frac{25}{45} = \frac{5}{9}$$

The traded option must sell for ₹13.63, or else we can profit from mispricing. Suppose the call sells for ₹15, then we can construct a portfolio of long five shares and short nine calls. It would cost us ₹365 (5 × 100 − 15 × 9), which can be borrowed at 6%. The maturity value of the borrowing is ₹386.90 (1.06 × 365), while at maturity of the option, we have ₹400 as the risk-free value of the portfolio. This gives us a profit of ₹13.10 without taking any risk or making an investment.

BINOMIAL MODEL FOR PUT PRICING

The binomial model works equally well for put pricing either by using implied probabilities or by creating a portfolio with identical payoffs.[2]

Using the risk-neutral method, we find the implied probability of an up move and a down move. They would remain same as that of the call option. The payoff is shown in Fig. 11.5.

The value of the put at the end of the option period would be

---
[2] An alternate way of finding the put price, p is to use put–call parity.
$c - p = S - \text{PV of } X$
$p = c - S + \text{PV of } X = 13.63 - 100 + 100/1.06 = ₹7.97$

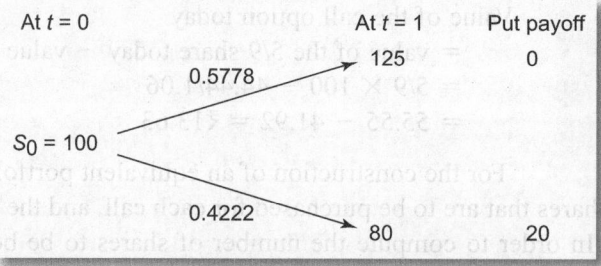

Fig. 11.5 Payoff of put under binomial pricing model

Value of the put
= probability of upward movement × payoff
+ probability of downward movement × payoff
= $p \times \text{Max}(X - S_1, 0) + (1 - p) \times \text{Max}(X - S_1, 0)$

In our case, the value of the put at the end of one year would be:

Value of the put = $0.5778 \times \text{Max}(100 - 125, 0) + 0.4222 \times \text{Max}(100 - 80, 0)$
= $0.5778 \times 0 + 0.4222 \times 20$
= ₹8.44

The present value of the put would be 8.44/1.06 = ₹7.97 (rounded off)

Under the second approach, we set up a portfolio of long on one share and M puts with $X = 100$, and set the value of the end portfolio to be equal under the two stages of the binomial model. When the price moves to ₹125, the put is worthless, with the value of the portfolio equal to the value of the stock at ₹125, and when the price is ₹80, the value of the portfolio would be ₹80 plus the value of M puts. This is shown in Fig. 11.6.

Equating the final values, we get $125 = 80 + 20M$ (11.6)

which gives $M = 2.25$

Setting this portfolio of one share and 2.25 puts to yield a risk-free return must give the value of the put, p' (deviating from the usual notation of p being used for the probability of an upside movement)

$(100 + 2.25 \times p') \times 1.06 = 125$
$p' = ₹7.97$

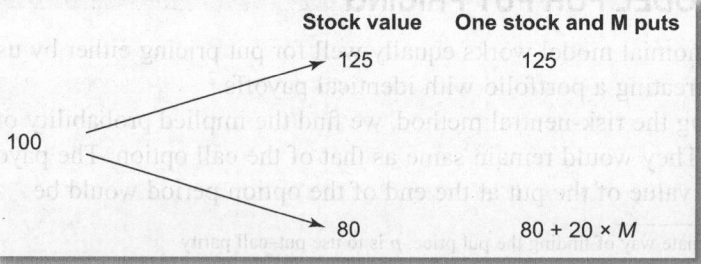

Fig. 11.6 Binomial put pricing

Under the equivalent portfolio approach, we have proceeded as follows:

> The option delta helps in construction of a riskless portfolio, and therefore, is used in the valuation of options.

- We have calculated the option delta, Δ.
- We have set up a portfolio of Δ share and one short call or Δ share and one long put,
- We have found the value of the portfolio at the end of the option period and its present value.
- We have equated it with the cost of the portfolio to find the value of the option.

MULTI-PERIOD BINOMIAL MODEL

The model discussed in the 'Binomial Model for Put Pricing' section had only one period. We may extend the logic for a one-year (a single period; the period need not be a full year) binomial model to find the price of a call expiring two years from now, with two periods, each lasting for one year. Further, we may adopt the multi-period approach by shortening the period too. By doing so intuitively, we expect the valuation to become more accurate, since a higher number of possible scenarios is evaluated. The valuation procedure would now start from the last set of nodes, from the end values therein, and traverse back in time to reach the first node. This is referred to as *backward induction*.

Let us now extend the single period model to two binomial periods. Assuming the same size of up and down moves of 25% and 20%, respectively, in each period of one year, we get a tree for valuing a two-year call, as depicted in Fig. 11.7. Now we would have three end values of the asset at the end of two years, rather than two.

From the values of the stock at $T = 2$, we work out the payoff of the call option at each preceding node to arrive at the value of the call option using risk-neutral probabilities and a

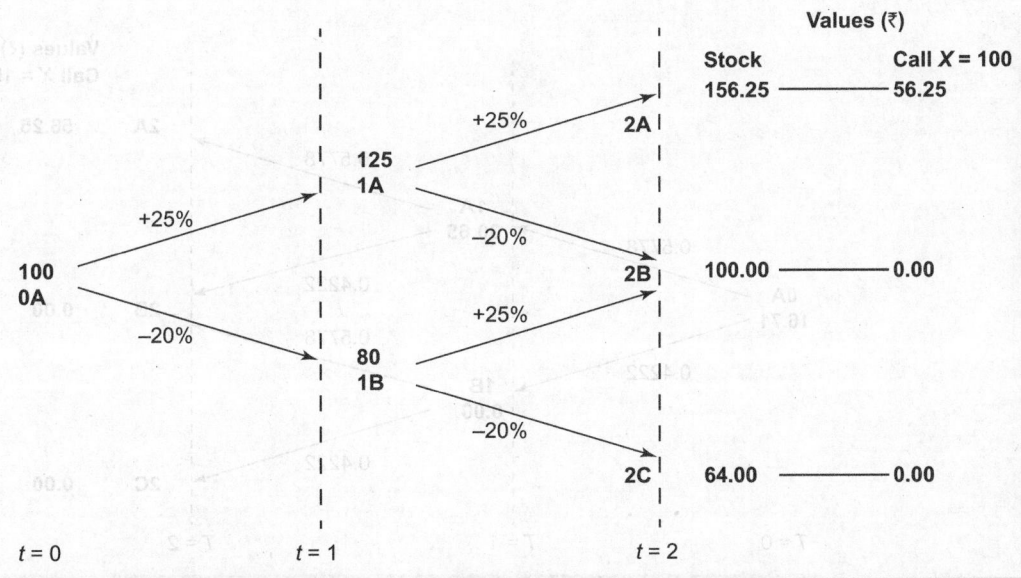

Fig. 11.7 Two-period binomial tree

> The binomial model can be extended to multiple periods, and to finding the value of an option going backwards from maturity.

risk-free rate of return. Assuming the interest rate remains constant over the life of the option with a risk-free rate of return of 6%, a 25% up movement and a 20% down movement, the risk-neutral probabilities remain the same as worked out in Fig. 11.3 at 0.5778 and 0.4222 for up and down movements, respectively. The implied probabilities would change if the risk-free rate changes during the life of the option.

Starting backwards from nodes 2A, 2B, and 2C, we go to nodes 1A and 1B and then to 0A, and calculate the values of the call option at each node, as depicted in Fig. 11.8.

Value of call option for node 1A

Expected value of call option at node 1A

$$= 0.5778 \times 56.25 + 0.4222 \times 0 = ₹32.48$$

Since the return on the position is 6%, the value at $T = 1$ (at node 1A)

$$= 32.48/1.06 = ₹30.65$$

Value of call option for node 1B

The expected value of the call at $t = 1$

$$= 0.5778 \times 0 + 0.4222 \times 0 = 0$$

Hence value for node 1B would be zero

Value of call option for node 0A

From the values at nodes 1A and 1B at $t = 1$, we trace back to node 0A and get the value of the call as

$$= \frac{(0.5778 \times 30.65 + 0.4222 \times 0)}{1.06} = \frac{17.71}{1.06} = ₹16.71$$

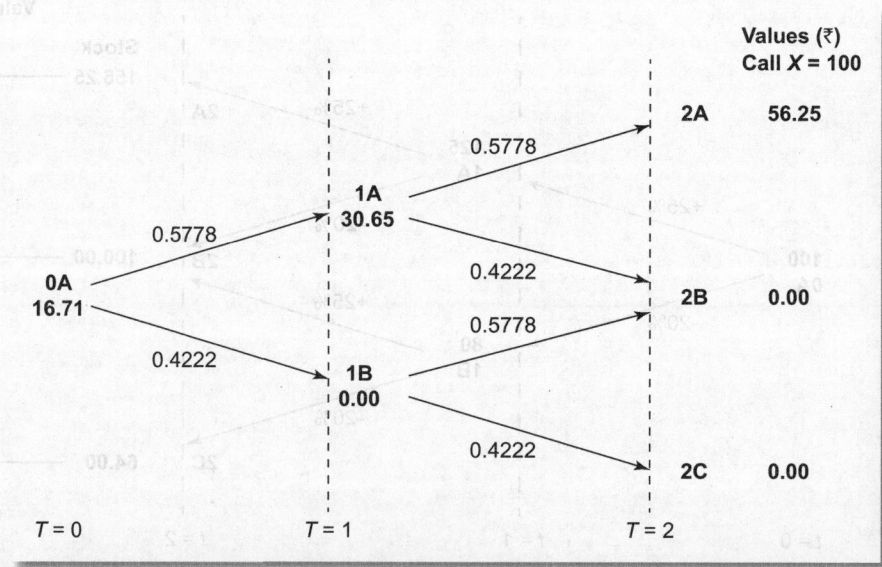

Fig. 11.8 Valuing call option: two-period binomial tree

> **EXAMPLE 11.1 Valuing call using binomial model**
>
> Use the data given in Fig. 11.8 for an asset selling at ₹100, with a 25% up and 20% down movement in price and a risk-free return of 12%. Find out the value of a European call with an exercise price of ₹80 using two periods of six months each.
>
> **Solution**
> Referring to Fig. 11.8, the value of a call with an exercise price of ₹80 would stand modified as follows:
>
> Node 2A: ₹76.25
> Node 2B: ₹20.00
> Node 2C: ₹0.00
>
> The value at Node 1A = 0.5778 × 76.25 + 0.4222 × 20.00 = ₹52.50
> And the value of the call at t = 1 = 52.50/1.06 = ₹49.53
>
> The value at Node 1B = 0.5778 × 20.00 + 0.4222 × 0 = ₹11.56
> And the value of the call at t = 1 = 11.56/1.06 = ₹10.90
>
> Using the values at Nodes 1A and 1B, we may go to Node 0A.
>
> Value at Node 0A = 0.5778 × 49.53 + 0.4222 × 10.90 = ₹33.22
> Value of call at t = 0 = 33.22/1.06 = ₹31.34

Using the multi-period binomial option pricing model, we can value the option by adding a higher number of branches in the binomial tree.

Improving Accuracy The accuracy of the binomial option pricing model can be challenged because of its rather impractical assumption that a price can take only two possible values. This seems far from reality. We assumed only two possible values at the end of one year, whereas in real life, numerous values are possible. However, the option for one year could also be valued using two sets of branches of six months each, or four sets of branches of three months each, or even 365 sets of branches of one day each. We can have an infinite number of small periods to be closer to the reality. Such a process, of increasing the branches by shortening the time interval for each branch, would provide numerous end values of the underlying at the end of one year, moving closer to reality. Such a process, of shortening the period and increasing the number of binary states, would make the constraint becoming less restrictive in fair determination of the option value. However, if we increase the number of nodes, we also increase the computation time. As we reduce the time interval and examine more end values, the value of the option would move closer to the one obtained by using the Black-Scholes model of option pricing[3]; a pricing mode universally accepted as one determining true value.

> The binomial model can be extended to multiple periods to broaden the range of price changes in a given period of time.

Why Unequal Up and Down Moves? In Example 11.1, we used the 25% rise and the 20% fall as the binary states of value of the underlying asset. This caused the price to be equal to the original price after two periods, with a rise in one period followed by a fall in the other, or vice versa. For the prices to converge to the original value, the return relatives for the rise and the fall have to be reciprocal, i.e., 1/1.25 = 0.80 (25% rise and 20% fall). This kind of rise and fall selection would lead to *recombining symmetrical* trees.

> As we increase the number of trees by shortening the time interval, an option price under the binomial model moves closer and closer to the analytical model of Black Scholes.

---

[3] For a detailed discussion on the subject, one may refer to Chapter 21 of *Principles of Corporate Finance*, 6th Edition, Tata McGraw Hill, by Brealey & Myers.

Use of recombining symmetrical trees facilitates development of a model for reiterative calculations, but, theoretically, any change can be handled for determination of option value by the binomial method.

Continuous Compounding In our analysis of option pricing using the binomial method, we used an annual risk-free return of 6% and found the risk-neutral probabilities of 0.5778 and 0.4222 for a 25% upward and a 20% downward movement, respectively, using Eq. 11.1 as shown here:

$$p = \frac{r - d}{u - d} = \frac{6 - (-20)}{25 - (-20)} = 0.5778 = 57.78\%$$

If the return were to be continuously compounded, the risk-neutral probabilities would be given by Eq. 11.3, using the size of the up and down movements in the decimal form. If 6% return were continuously compounded, the risk-neutral probability of an upside movement would be 0.5819, as calculated here

$$p = \frac{e^{rt} - d}{u - d} = \frac{1.0618 - 0.80}{1.25 - 0.80} = 0.5819 = 58.19\%$$

VALUING AMERICAN OPTIONS

We may also use binomial trees for valuing American options, which provide for early exercise rather than exercise at maturity only. With no change in the risk-free rate and the upside and downside movement, the risk-neutral probabilities remain unchanged. However, the value of the option may change, depending upon whether it is more profitable to exercise the option before maturity.

Figure 11.9 shows a binomial tree for three periods of four months each for an asset selling at ₹100, which can move 25% up or 20% down in each period. We shall use the same tree for valuing a European call, a European put, and an American put. We shall also demonstrate that an American call would be valued equal to a European call, and early exercise of the call on a non-dividend paying stock has no value.

> The binomial model is a potent tool to value American options, as it allows for early exercise at each node.

Using the backward induction procedure, we now calculate the value of a call option with expiry period of one year, with a strike price of ₹75, using the binomial method with three periods of four months each. First, we find the risk-neutral probability of an up movement with Eq. 11.3.

$$p = \frac{e^{rt} - d}{u - d} = \frac{e^{0.06/3} - 0.80}{1.25 - 0.80}$$
$$= \frac{1.0202 - 0.80}{0.45} = 0.4893 = 48.93\%$$

Therefore, the probability of a down movement is $1 - 0.4893 = 0.5107$.

Valuing European Call

The value of a European call option at the end of 12, 8, and 4 months are indicated in the tree depicted in Fig. 11.10.

At $T = 12$ months, the call would be exercised, and, therefore, the values of the call at various nodes would be equal to the price of the asset less the exercise price, i.e., $S - 75$.

Option Pricing—Binomial Model

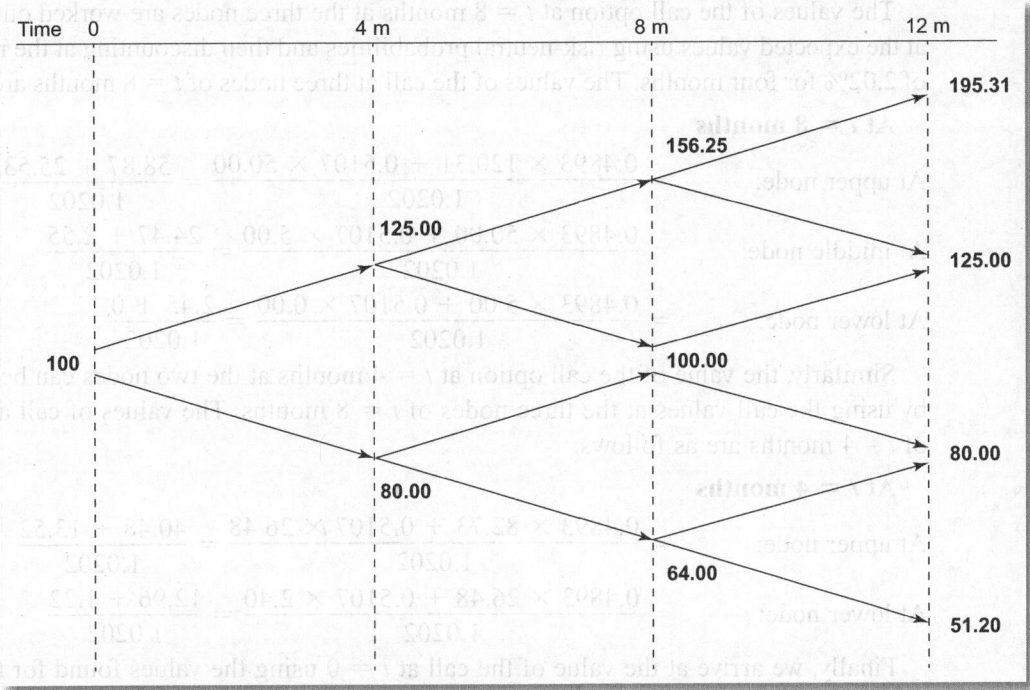

Fig. 11.9 Binary tree for option pricing—asset value
Value of underlying asset with 25% up and 20% down movement

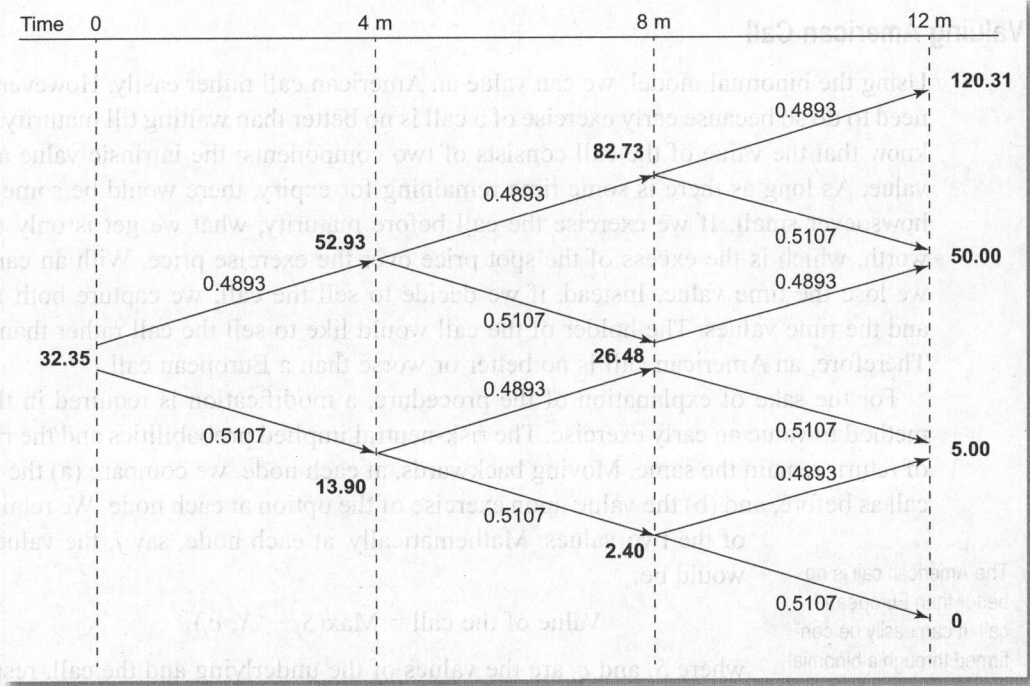

Fig. 11.10 Binary tree for call option pricing—payoffs
Value of call ($X = 75$) on asset with 25% up and 20% down movement

The values of the call option at $t = 8$ months at the three nodes are worked out by arriving at the expected values using risk-neutral probabilities and then discounting at the risk-free rate of 2.02% for four months. The values of the call at three nodes of $t = 8$ months are as follows:

At $t = 8$ months

At upper node: $= \dfrac{0.4893 \times 120.31 + 0.5107 \times 50.00}{1.0202} = \dfrac{58.87 + 25.53}{1.0202} = ₹82.73$

At middle node: $= \dfrac{0.4893 \times 50.00 + 0.5107 \times 5.00}{1.0202} = \dfrac{24.47 + 2.55}{1.0202} = ₹26.48$

At lower node: $= \dfrac{0.4893 \times 5.00 + 0.5107 \times 0.00}{1.0202} = \dfrac{2.45 + 0}{1.0202} = ₹2.40$

Similarly, the value of the call option at $t = 4$ months at the two nodes can be worked out by using the call values at the three nodes of $t = 8$ months. The values of call at two nodes of $t = 4$ months are as follows:

At $t = 4$ months

At upper node: $= \dfrac{0.4893 \times 82.73 + 0.5107 \times 26.48}{1.0202} = \dfrac{40.48 + 13.52}{1.0202} = ₹52.93$

At lower node: $= \dfrac{0.4893 \times 26.48 + 0.5107 \times 2.40}{1.0202} = \dfrac{12.96 + 1.22}{1.0202} = ₹13.90$

Finally, we arrive at the value of the call at $t = 0$ using the values found for the nodes at $t = 4$ months.

Value of call: $= \dfrac{0.4893 \times 52.93 + 0.5107 \times 13.90}{1.0202} = \dfrac{25.90 + 7.10}{1.0202} = ₹32.35$

Valuing American Call

Using the binomial model, we can value an American call rather easily. However, there is no need to do so because early exercise of a call is no better than waiting till maturity. We already know that the value of the call consists of two components: the intrinsic value and the time value. As long as there is some time remaining for expiry, there would be some time value, howsoever small. If we exercise the call before maturity, what we get is only the intrinsic worth, which is the excess of the spot price over the exercise price. With an early exercise, we lose the time value. Instead, if we decide to sell the call, we capture both the intrinsic and the time values. The holder of the call would like to sell the call rather than exercise it. Therefore, an American call is no better or worse than a European call.

For the sake of explanation of the procedure, a modification is required in the binomial method to value an early exercise. The risk-neutral implied probabilities and the risk-free rate of return remain the same. Moving backwards, at each node, we compare (a) the value of the call as before, and (b) the value upon exercise of the option at each node. We retain the higher of the two values. Mathematically, at each node, say j, the value of the call would be:

$$\text{Value of the call} = \text{Max}(S_j - X, c_j)$$

where S_j and c_j are the values of the underlying and the call, respectively, at node j.

> The American call is no better than European call. It can easily be confirmed through a binomial model.

Table 11.1 Values of American call with and without exercise at nodes

Time	Node	Asset value (₹)	Value of call X = 75	
			If not exercised	If exercised
At t = 8 m	Upper node	156.25	82.73	81.25
	Middle node	100.00	26.48	25.00
	Lower node	64.00	2.40	0.00
At t = 4 m	Upper node	125.00	52.93	50.00
	Lower node	80.00	13.90	5.00
At t = 0 m	Start node	100.00	32.35	25.00

While moving backwards to the preceding node, we use the value retained at the succeeding node. For the European call, same value continues, as no early exercise is done because the value without exercise is always higher.

Table 11.1 compares the value of an American call with $X = 75$, with and without exercise at each node.

It is easily observed that the value of the call, if not exercised, c_j, is always greater than the value if exercised, i.e., $(S_j - X)$. Hence, we retain the value of the call and not the value upon exercise at each node, making early exercise redundant. Therefore, the value of an American call would be the same as that of a European call.

Valuing European Put

For the same asset values as in Fig. 11.9, we now demonstrate the valuing of a European put with an exercise price of ₹150. The binomial tree for the payoff of the put at various nodes is depicted in Fig. 11.11. At $T = 12$ months, the put would be exercised, and, therefore, the values of the put at various nodes would equal Max (0, the exercise price less the value of the asset, i.e., $150 - S$).

The values of the put option at $t = 8$ months at the three nodes are worked out by backward induction in a similar manner as that used for the call, by arriving at expected values using risk-neutral probabilities and then discounting at the risk-free rates. The values of put at three nodes of $t = 8$ months are as follows:

At $t = 8$ months

At upper node: $= \dfrac{0.4893 \times 0.00 + 0.5107 \times 25.00}{1.0202} = \dfrac{0.00 + 12.77}{1.0202} = ₹12.51$

At middle node: $= \dfrac{0.4893 \times 25.00 + 0.5107 \times 70.00}{1.0202} = \dfrac{12.23 + 35.75}{1.0202} = ₹47.03$

At lower node: $= \dfrac{0.4893 \times 70.00 + 0.5107 \times 98.80}{1.0202} = \dfrac{34.25 + 50.46}{1.0202} = ₹83.03$

Similarly, the value of the put at $t = 4$ months at the two nodes can be worked out by using the put values at the three nodes of $t = 8$ months. The values of put at two nodes of $t = 4$ months are as follows:

At $t = 4$ months

At upper node: $= \dfrac{0.4893 \times 12.51 + 0.5107 \times 47.03}{1.0202} = \dfrac{6.12 + 24.02}{1.0202} = ₹29.54$

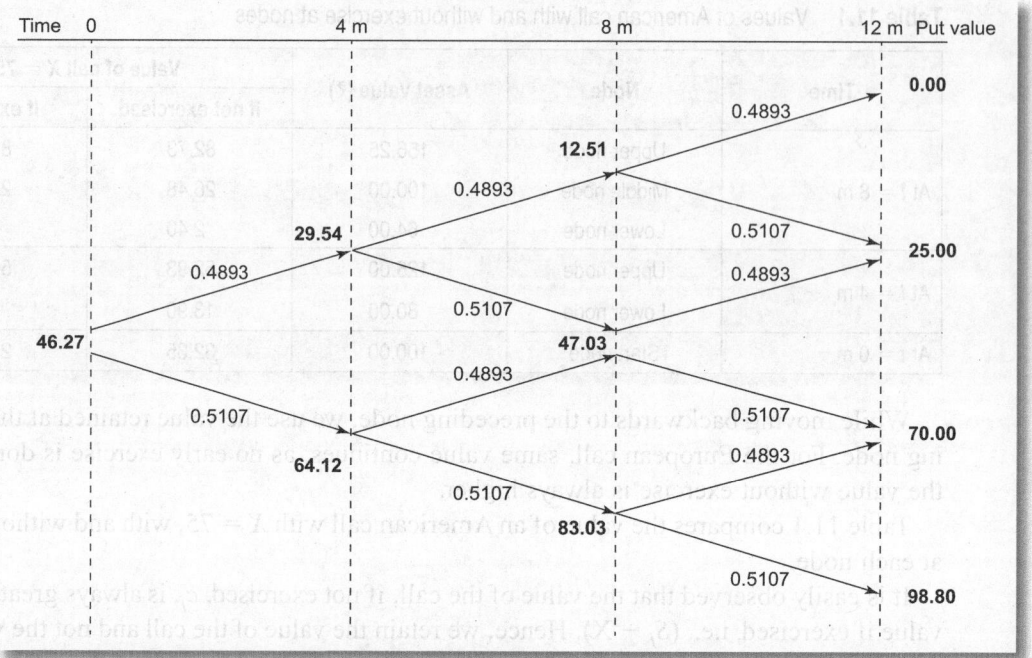

Fig. 11.11 Binary tree for put option pricing—payoffs
Value of put X = 150 on an asset with 25% up and 20% down movement.

At lower node: $= \dfrac{0.4893 \times 47.03 + 0.5107 \times 83.03}{1.0202} = \dfrac{23.01 + 42.40}{1.0202} = ₹64.12$

Finally, we arrive at the value of the put at $t = 0$ using the values found for the nodes at $t = 4$ months.

Value of put: $= \dfrac{0.4893 \times 29.54 + 0.5107 \times 64.12}{1.0202} = \dfrac{14.45 + 32.75}{1.0202} = ₹46.27$

Valuing American Put

What was stated for the equivalency of the values of American and European call is not true for put options. Unlike the call option, it may be more beneficial to exercise the put early rather than wait for maturity or sell it. The procedure for the binomial method remains the same, except that with each node we find whether exercising the put results in a greater pay-off. Examine the three nodes at $t = 8$ months. At the middle and lower nodes, the put has a greater value when exercised. The values of the put when not exercised and when exercised are shown in Table 11.2. The retained values at the nodes are highlighted; they become appropriate for valuation of the preceding nodes.

For an American put, each node, j, is evaluated for payoff in terms of intrinsic value and total value as follows:

$$\text{Max}(X - S_j, p_j)$$

where S_j and p_j are the values of the underlying and the put, respectively, at node j.

The values at the three nodes at $t = 8$ months for the European and American puts are shown in Figs 11.12(a) and (b), respectively.

Table 11.2 Values of put at $t = 8$ months when exercised and not exercised

Time	Node	Asset value (₹)	Value of call $X = 150$	
			If not exercised	If exercised
At $t = 8$ m	Upper node	156.25	12.51	0.00
	Middle node	100.00	47.03	50.00
	Lower node	64.00	83.03	86.00

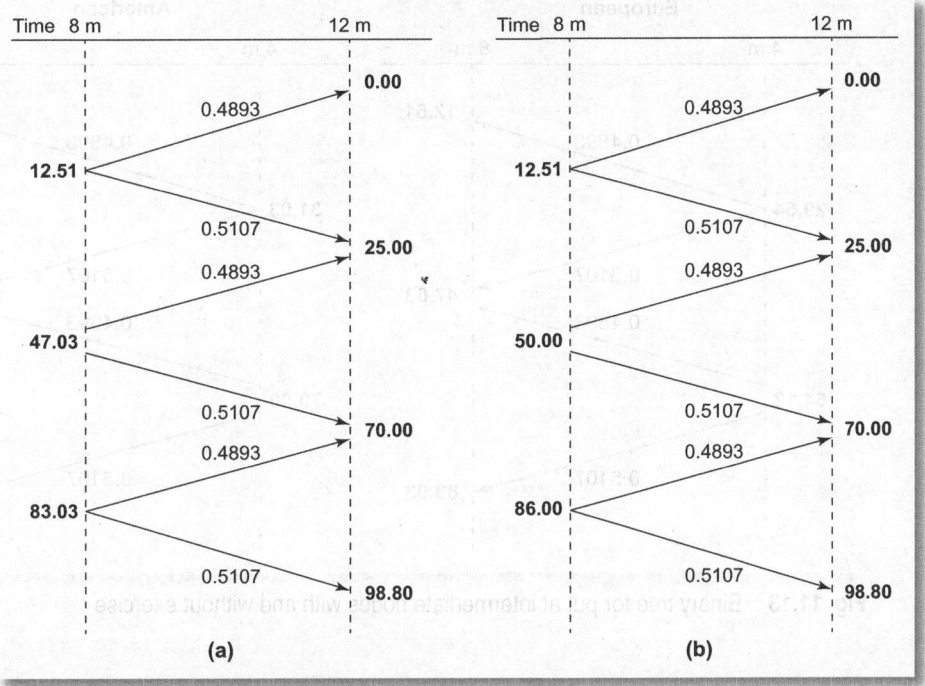

Fig. 11.12 Binary tree for put option payoff
$X = 150$ (a) European put, without exercise (b) American put, with exercise

For the American put, the values at the two nodes for $t = 4$ months are worked out on the basis of the retained values at the nodes shown in Fig. 11.12(b). These are as follows:

At upper node: $= \dfrac{0.4893 \times 12.51 + 0.5107 \times 50.00}{1.0202} = \dfrac{6.12 + 25.54}{1.0202} = ₹31.03$

At lower node: $= \dfrac{0.4893 \times 50.00 + 0.5107 \times 86.00}{1.0202} = \dfrac{24.47 + 43.92}{1.0202} = ₹67.04$

Again, these values, derived using the risk-neutral method, are replaced by the values that can be realized by exercising the put if it is greater. For $t = 4$ months, the values are shown in the Table 11.3.

A comparison of nodal values at time $t = 4$ months under the binomial method for a European put and an American put is made in Fig. 11.13.

Now we value the American put option at time $t = 0$. Again using the risk-neutral probabilities, the price of an American put with an exercise price of ₹150 comes to ₹49.92, as compared to the European put being valued at ₹46.27, as worked out here:

Table 11.3 Values of put at t = 4 months when exercised and not exercised

Time	Node	Asset value	Value of put X = 150	
			If not exercised	If exercised
At T = 4 m	Upper node	125.00	31.03	25.00
	Middle node	80.00	67.04	70.00

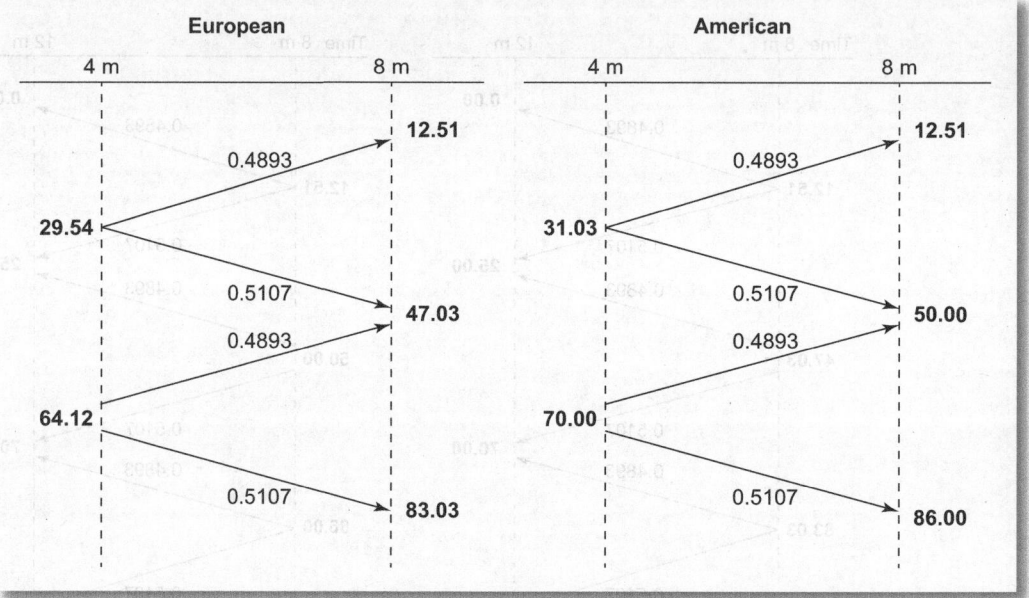

Fig. 11.13 Binary tree for put at intermediate nodes with and without exercise

Value of put: $= \dfrac{0.4893 \times 31.03 + 0.5107 \times 70.00}{1.0202} = \dfrac{15.18 + 35.75}{1.0202} = ₹49.92$

A binomial tree with the value of the European and American puts at $t = 4$ months and now ($t = 0$) are shown in Fig. 11.14. The complete tree for the American put is shown in Fig. 11.15.

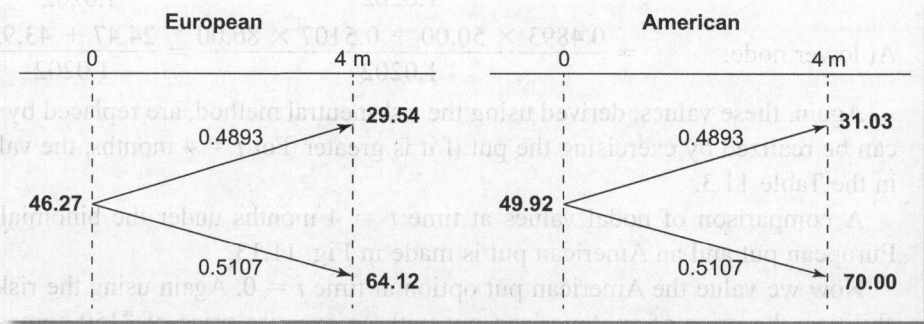

Fig. 11.14 Binary tree for put option pricing at $t = 0$

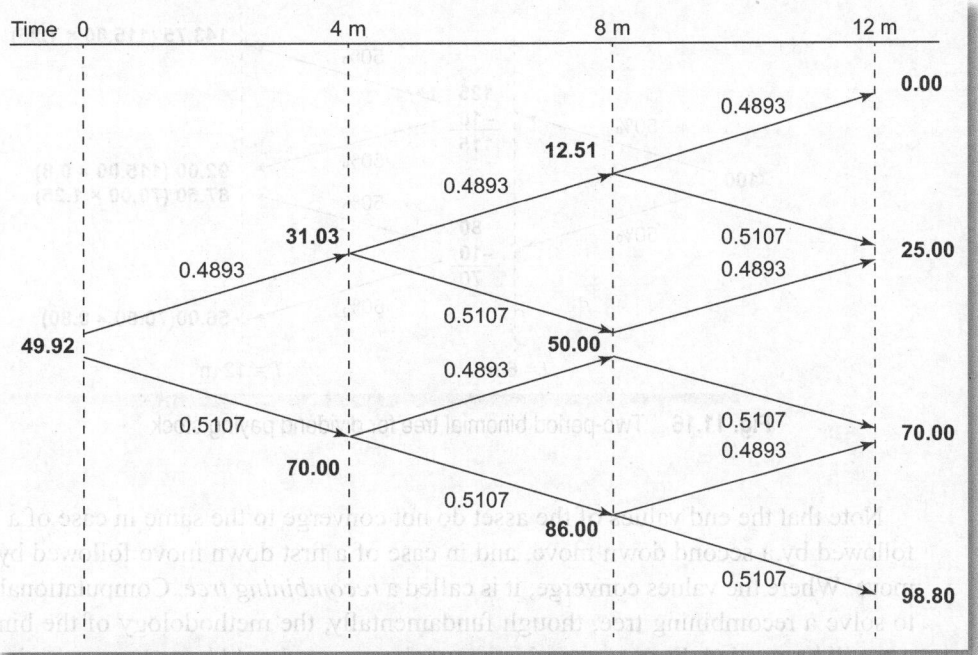

Fig. 11.15 Binary tree for American put option pricing
Value of put ($X = 150$) on asset with 25% up and 20% down movement

VALUING OPTIONS ON DIVIDEND PAYING STOCK

Under the binomial model, we have valued both American and European calls and puts. For valuing American options, we examined the question of whether an early exercise is more beneficial at the decision points called nodes. We chose the higher of the two values for the holder of the option. On similar lines, we can value options on dividend paying assets. We shall value all four options—European call and put as well as American call and put on an asset that pays dividend.

Assume the current value of a stock as ₹100; it may go up 25% or fall 20% in a period of six months. The risk-free rate is 5% p.a. (2.5% semi-annual). Assume that six months from now the stock pays dividend of ₹10. We need to value an option with time to expiry of one year using the two-stage binomial tree. Under our usual practice, the tree would appear like the one shown in Fig. 11.16.

The probability of an up move, p, using Eq. 11.2 is 50%, and a down move, $1 - p$, is 50%, as calculated here:

$$p = \frac{(1 + r) - d}{u - d} = \frac{1.025 - 0.80}{1.25 - 0.80} = 0.50 \equiv 50\%$$

Starting at ₹100 at $t = 0$, the stock can take values of ₹125 or ₹80 on the up or down move, respectively. However, a dividend of ₹10 is paid. On the ex-dividend date, the price would fall by ₹10, either to ₹115 or to ₹70, as the case may be. Using the ex-dividend price, we construct the second branch of the tree. From the upper node at $t = 6$ months, we can either go to ₹143.75 (for an up move) or to ₹92.00 (for a down move). Similarly from a lower node at $t = 6$ months, we can go up at ₹87.50 or down at ₹56.00.

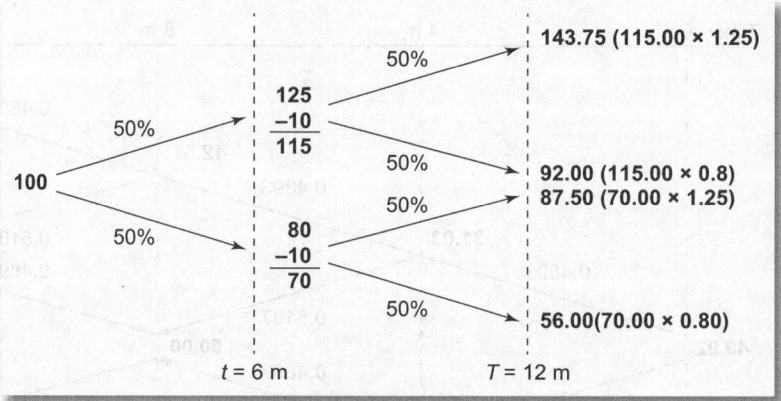

Fig. 11.16 Two-period binomial tree for dividend paying stock

Note that the end values of the asset do not converge to the same in case of a first up move followed by a second down move, and in case of a first down move followed by a second up move. Where the values converge, it is called a *recombining tree*. Computationally, it is easier to solve a recombining tree, though fundamentally, the methodology of the binomial model can still be applied. For computation convenience, we should have a recombining tree. So far, we have been considering unequal up and down moves of 25% and 20%, respectively. These up and down moves made the tree of the recombining type. A recombining tree is obtained if we choose up and down moves as reciprocals of each other. To have a recombining tree and an up move of 25%, we must have a down move at 20%, given by 1/1.25 = 0.80.

We overcome the problem of a non-recombining tree arising due to dividend payment by making a simple modification in the construction of the tree. It does not distort the outcome in any way. We know that the stock would pay a dividend of ₹10 after six months, thereby reducing the price by the same amount at the end of the six months. Rather than adjusting the price on the date of dividend, we construct the tree by deducing the present value of the dividend from the current price. After adjusting the current price for dividend, constructing the tree in the usual way would make the tree recombining.

The present value of the dividend is 10/1.025 = ₹9.76. The current stock price of ₹100 now becomes ₹90.24. At the end of six months, the stock can have a price of ₹112.80 or ₹72.19. Note that this would be ex-dividend price. The cum-dividend price would be greater by the amount of dividend of ₹10. The three possible end prices now would be ₹141.00, ₹90.24, and ₹57.75, respectively. The middle price of ₹90.24 would be identical for (a) an up move followed by a down move and (b) a down move followed by an up move. Based on these values of the asset, a two-stage binomial tree is shown in Fig. 11.17. Using the tree of Fig. 11.17, we now value American and European calls and puts.

European and American Calls on Dividend Paying Stock

Using the binomial tree of Fig. 11.17, the payoffs for both European and American calls with an exercise price of ₹100 would be ₹41.00, ₹0.00, and ₹0.00, respectively, for the three possible values of the asset, as shown in Table 11.4.

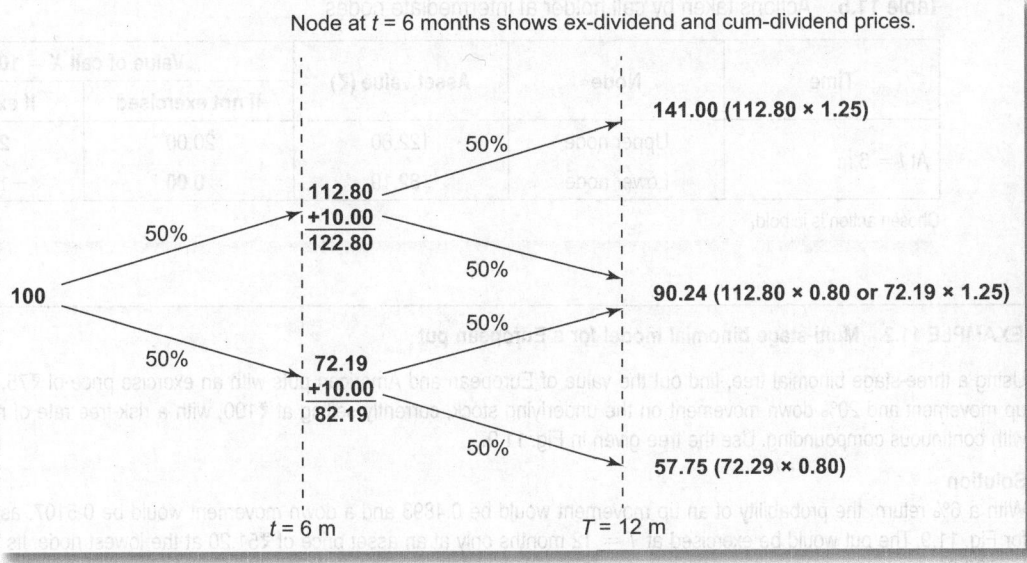

Fig. 11.17 Two-period binomial recombining tree for dividend paying stock

Table 11.4 Payoffs against different possible asset values

Time	Node	Asset value (₹)	Payoff of European and American calls (₹)
At $T = 12$ m	Upper node	141.00	41.00
	Middle node	90.24	0.00
	Lower node	57.75	0.00

For the European call, the expected value of the call would be the discounted value of the sum of the payoffs of the call multiplied by the respective probabilities. For upper and lower nodes at $t = 6$ months, the values are worked out as follows:

At upper node: $= \dfrac{0.50 \times 41.00 + 0.50 \times 0.00}{1.025} = ₹20.00$

At lower node: $= \dfrac{0.50 \times 0.00 + 0.50 \times 0.00}{1.025} = ₹0.00$

Extending the same procedure, we can find the value of the European call to be ₹9.76.

Value of European call: $= \dfrac{0.50 \times 20.00 + 0.50 \times 0.00}{1.025} = ₹9.76$

American Call For the American call, the holder may like to own the underlying asset to capture the dividend if it is more profitable. At $t = 6$ months, the ex-dividend price would be ₹112.80, and the intrinsic value would be ₹12.80. The call value is worth ₹20. However if the call holder exercises just before the stock becomes ex-dividend, the payoff would be ₹22.80 (12.80 + 10.00), which is greater than the value of the call. Hence it would be exercised. At the lower node at $t = 6$ months, the call is out-of-the-money (OTM), and an exercise would result in a loss of ₹17.81. Hence, the investor holds, as shown in Table 11.5.

Table 11.5 Actions taken by call holder at intermediate nodes

Time	Node	Asset value (₹)	Value of call X = 100	
			If not exercised	If exercised
At t = 6 m	Upper node	122.80	20.00	**22.80**
	Lower node	82.19	**0.00**	−17.81

Chosen action is in bold.

EXAMPLE 11.2 Multi-stage binomial model for a European put

Using a three-stage binomial tree, find out the value of European and American puts with an exercise price of ₹75, with a 25% up movement and 20% down movement on the underlying stock, currently selling at ₹100, with a risk-free rate of return at 6% with continuous compounding. Use the tree given in Fig. 11.9.

Solution
With a 6% return, the probability of an up movement would be 0.4893 and a down movement would be 0.5107, as worked out for Fig. 11.9. The put would be exercised at $T = 12$ months only at an asset price of ₹51.20 at the lowest node. Its value would be ₹23.80.

With the rest of the nodes having zero values, the price of the put would be

$$\frac{0.5107 \times 0.5107 \times 0.5107 \times 23.80}{1.0202^3} = ₹2.99$$

The complete binomial tree is depicted here:

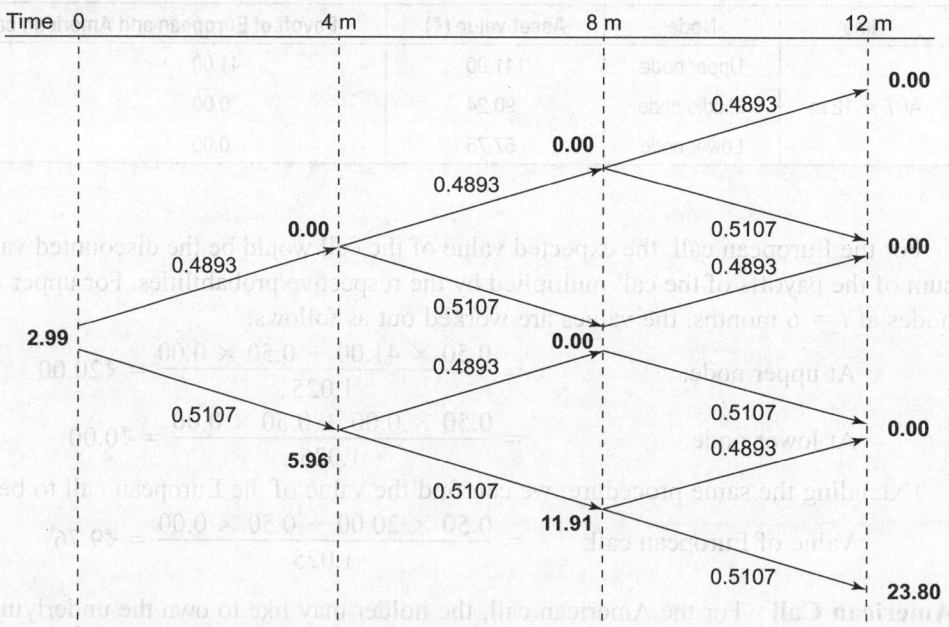

Fig. Binary tree for European put option pricing
Value of put (X = 75) on an asset with a 25% up and 20% down movement

The value of an American put would be same as that of a European put because by comparing the values of the exercise at each node, we find that they are lesser than those of the European put. The value of an American put at a lower node at $t = 8$ would be ₹11.00, and at a lower node at $t = 4$ is ₹5.00; both figures are lesser than those for the European put.

The value of the American call would therefore be ₹11.12 as compared to the value of the European call at ₹9.75.

Value of American call: $= \dfrac{0.50 \times 22.80 + 0.50 \times 0.00}{1.025} = ₹11.12$

European and American Puts on Dividend Paying Stock

Let us now value a 12-m ATM put for the same asset. At maturity, the payoffs on the European and American puts are as shown in Table 11.6:

Table 11.6 Payoffs on European and American puts at maturity

Time	Node	Asset value (₹)	Payoff of European and American puts (₹)
	Upper node	141.00	0.00
At $T = 12$ m	Middle node	90.24	9.76
	Lower node	57.75	42.25

Proceeding exactly in the same manner as is followed for valuing a call, we get the value of the European put at $t = 6$ at two nodes.

At upper node: $= \dfrac{0.50 \times 0.00 + 0.50 \times 9.76}{1.025} = ₹4.76$

At lower node: $= \dfrac{0.50 \times 9.76 + 0.50 \times 42.25}{1.025} = ₹25.37$

With the values at $t = 6$ months known, we value the European put at $t = 0$ at ₹14.70 as below.

Value of European put: $= \dfrac{0.50 \times 4.76 + 0.50 \times 25.37}{1.025} = ₹14.70$

American Put At $t = 6$ months for the upper node when the stock price is ₹122.80, an exercise results into a loss of ₹22.80. Hence, the holder would not exercise. At the lower node, when the ex-dividend price is ₹72.19, exercising the put gives a payoff of ₹27.81, which is more than the worth of the put at ₹25.37. Hence, the holder exercises the put, as shown in Table 11.7.

Table 11.7 Actions taken by put holder at intermediate nodes

Time	Node	Asset value (₹)	Value of American put $X = 100$	
			If not exercised	If exercised
At $t = 6$ m	Upper node	122.80	**4.76**	−22.80
	Lower node	82.19	25.37	**27.81**

Chosen action is in bold.

Using the right values at the node of $t = 6$ months, we get the value of the American put at $t = 0$ as ₹15.89.

Value of American put: $= \dfrac{0.50 \times 4.76 + 0.50 \times 27.81}{1.025} = ₹15.89$

BINOMIAL SOLUTION FOR MULTI-PERIODS

For an n-stage binomial tree, the value of a call on a non-dividend paying asset is given by Eq. 11.7.

$$c_0 = \frac{\sum_{1}^{n} \frac{n!}{(n-j)!\,j!} p^j (1-p)^{n-j} \text{Max}(0, u^j d^{n-j} S - X)}{(1+r)^n} \qquad (11.7)$$

Equation 11.7 is not as complex as it appears to be. It is extremely logical, and can be explained in a rather straightforward manner.

For an n-stage model, there would be a total of n price movements. Each node is reached by certain up moves and down moves. For j up moves, the remaining, $n - j$, must be down moves. The value of the asset at each end-node is given by the number of up and down moves needed to reach that node. For the topmost node, all n price movements must be up. The probability of all n moves up, which is p^n, and asset value would be $u^n \times S$. For the second highest end-value, there needs to be $n - 1$ up moves and 1 down move. The end-value would be $u^{(n-1)} d^1 \times S$. Similarly, for the jth end-value from the top, there have to be j up moves and $n - j$ down moves, and the end-value would be $u^j d^{n-j} \times S$.

With the exercise price of the call as X, the payoff at any node that requires j up moves and $(n - j)$ down moves is $\text{Max}(0, u^j d^{n-j} S - X)$. The probability of such a payoff is the product of the number of paths for reaching the node multiplied by the probability of each such path. The probability of each path with j up moves and the remaining $(n - j)$ down moves is $p(1-p)^{n-j}$. The number of paths available with j up moves and $(n - j)$ down moves is ^nC_j. Therefore, the total value of the call at maturity would be the sum of all payoffs at the end-nodes. To arrive at the value today, the maturity value must be discounted by r for n periods.

EXAMPLE 11.3 Valuing a call with the binomial model

An asset sells for ₹100 today. Value a call assuming an up move of 25% and a down move of 20% value, an ATM call for 12 months using Eq. 11.7, with three periods of four months each, and a risk-free rate of 7% per period.

Solution
With the given parameters, the implied probability of an up move is $(1.07 - 0.8)/(1.25 - 0.8) = 60\%$ and the probability of a down move is $1 - 0.60 = 0.4 \equiv 40\%$. For a three-stage binomial model, $n = 3$. For values of j from 0 to 3, the payoffs are

For $j = 0$ $\quad \frac{3!}{3!\,0!} 0.6^0 \times 0.4^3 \times \text{Max}(0, 1.25^0 \times 0.8^3 \times 100 - 100) = 0$

For $j = 1$ $\quad \frac{3!}{2!\,1!} 0.6^1 \times 0.4^2 \times \text{Max}(0, 1.25^1 \times 0.8^2 \times 100 - 100) = 0$

For $j = 2$ $\quad \frac{3!}{1!\,2!} 0.6^2 \times 0.4^1 \times \text{Max}(0, 1.25^2 \times 0.8^1 \times 100 - 100) = 10.80$

For $j = 3$ $\quad \frac{3!}{0!\,3!} 0.6^3 \times 0.4^0 \times \text{Max}(0, 1.25^3 \times 0.8^0 \times 100 - 100) = 20.59$

Hence, the value of the call today is calculated as under:

$$\text{Value of Call} = \frac{0 + 0 + 10.80 + 20.59}{1.07^3} = ₹25.62$$

BINOMIAL MODEL FOR INDEX OPTIONS

> With a small modification in the risk-free rate, a binomial model can easily be adapted for valuing options on indices.

The binomial approach for valuing options on indices is no different than that for valuation of options on dividend paying stock. In the case of indices, the dividend is continuously adjusted, and, hence, under a risk-neutral approach, the risk-free rate of return must be reduced by the dividend yield on the index. The risk-neutral implied probability of an up move for indices is computed by modifying Eq. 11.3 for the dividend yield, q, on the index.

$$p = \frac{e^{(r-q)} - d}{u - d} \quad (11.8)$$

For working details, refer to Example 11.4 for valuing a European call and a European put on an index.

EXAMPLE 11.4 Binomial model of index options

The current value of Nifty is 4500. In a period of three months, it can go up or down by 10%. If the risk-free interest rate is 8% and the dividend yield on the index is 2%, find the value of a call and a put with strikes of 4600, expiring in three months. Use the single-stage binomial model and assume one index point as ₹1.

Solution
A European call and a European put with a strike price of 4600 and a maturity of three months can be valued with risk-neutral valuation, using a net interest rate of 6%. The risk-neutral probabilities using Eq. 11.5 are

$$p = \frac{e^{(r-q)t} - d}{u - d} = \frac{e^{0.06 \times 3/12} - 0.90}{1.10 - 0.90}$$

$$= \frac{1.0151 - 0.90}{0.20} = 0.5756 = 57.56\%$$

$$1 - p = 1 - 0.5756 = 0.4244$$

Risk-neutral valuation of index options

(Figures in ₹)

	T = 3 m Spot	Call X = 4600	Put
p = 0.5756	4950	350	—
4500			
1 − p = 0.4244	4050	—	550

The payoffs of the call option and the put option with a strike of 4600 at the maturity of the options are depicted above. With payoffs of the call of 350 and 0 with up and down moves, respectively, we may derive the risk-neutral valuation of the call.

Value of the call at the end of three months = 350 × 0.5756 + 0 × 0.4244 = 201.45
Value of the call today = 201.45 × $e^{-0.06 \times 3/12}$ = 201.45 × 0.9851 = ₹198.45

With the payoffs of the put of 0 and 550 with up and down moves, respectively, we may derive the risk-neutral valuation of the put.

Value of the put at the end of 3 months = 0 × 0.5756 + 550 × 0.4244 = 233.42
Value of the put today = 233.42 × $e^{-0.06 \times 3/12}$ = 233.42 × 0.9851 = ₹229.94

VALUING CURRENCY OPTIONS

> The binomial model can be extended to currency options with small modifications in the risk-free rates.

The binomial model can be easily adapted for valuation of currency options. Just as we modified the risk-neutral return by dividend yield in the valuation of index options, we modify the return by foreign interest rates in the case of options on foreign currencies. While calculating the implied probabilities under risk-neutral valuation, the interest rate must be considered net of any foreign interest rate. For example, if the domestic interest rate is 10% p.a. and the risk-free interest rate in foreign currency is 4% p.a., then while computing the risk-neutral probabilities, the interest rate that must be used is 6% (10% − 4%). Equation 11.3, for finding the probabilities of an up move, would stand modified by the interest rate on foreign currency, r_f, as follows:

$$p = \frac{e^{(r - r_f)} - d}{u - d} \qquad (11.9)$$

For example, consider the current exchange rate to be ₹70.00 per euro. Under a binomial situation, the rupee can depreciate or appreciate by 4% over the period of the next two months. Further risk-free interest rates in the rupee market and the euro market are 6 and 2%, respectively. For a European call and put with a strike price of ₹70 per euro and a maturity of two months, risk-neutral valuation is done with the net interest rate of 4%. The risk-neutral probabilities using Eq. 11.9 are as follows:

$$p = \frac{e^{(r - r_f)} - d}{u - d} = \frac{e^{0.04 \times 2/12} - 0.96}{1.04 - 0.96}$$

$$= \frac{1.0067 - 0.96}{0.08} = 0.5836 = 58.36\%$$

$$1 - p = 1 - 0.5836 = 0.4164$$

A single-stage binomial tree for payoffs of 2-m call and 2-m put options with a strike price of ₹70 per euro is depicted in Fig. 11.18.

With the payoffs of the call with up and down moves of ₹2.80 and ₹0.00, respectively, we may have the risk-neutral valuation of the call, shown as follows:

Value of the call at the end of two months = 2.80 × 0.5836 + 0.00 × 0.4164 = ₹1.6341

Value of the call today = 1.6341 × $e^{-0.04 \times 2/12}$ = 1.6341 × 0.9934 = ₹1.6233 ≈ ₹1.62

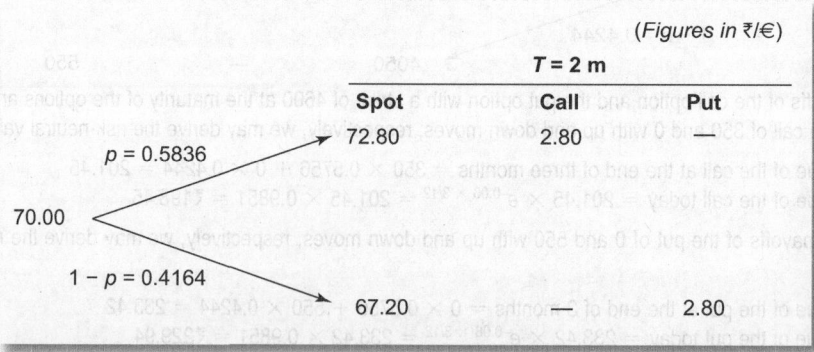

Figure 11.18 Risk-neutral valuation of currency options

Similarly, with the payoff of the put with up and down moves of ₹0.00 and ₹2.80, respectively, we may have the risk-neutral valuation of the put.

Value of the put at the end of two months = $0.00 \times 0.5836 + 2.80 \times 0.4164 = ₹1.1659$

Value of the put today = $1.1659 \times e^{-0.04 \times 2/12} = 1.1659 \times 0.9934 = ₹1.1582 \approx ₹1.16$

BINOMIAL MODEL IN PRACTICE: CONSTRUCTING BINOMIAL TREE

> By increasing the number of branches in a tree and adjusting the up and down move according to volatility, the binomial model can be used with increased accuracy to arrive at the value of options.

The extremely simplified assumption that only two prices of an underlying asset are possible raises doubts about the applicability of the binomial model as an accurate method of calculating option price. The assumption of only two prices seems to be too unrealistic for determination of fair value. Further, it seems that by assuming only two prices, the probability distribution of stock prices would be far from reality. Further, the primary determinant of option value, i.e., the volatility of stock prices, does not figure in the implied probabilities of up and down moves of the binary states.

However, in actual practice, both the objections can be handled very conveniently. The first objection that binomial stages are far from reality and the general acceptance that stock returns have normal distribution can be overcome by increasing the number of stages in the binomial method. As we increase the number of stages, the possible outcomes for asset values increase by a multiplication of 2 in each stage. While valuing options, the binomial approach can be used if the option period is divided into 30 small intervals; with recombining trees, 31 different terminal prices at the end of the option period can be evaluated. There would be 2^{30} different paths to achieve these 31 terminal prices. The two extreme prices could be achieved only in one possible way, i.e., if all 30 are up or down moves. The probability of the maximum price and the minimum price is $1/2^{30}$. The next level of prices (one below the maximum or one above the minimum) would consist of 29 up moves and 1 down move. Out of 30 binary states, this is possible to achieve in 30 different ways, i.e., $^{30}C_1$ combinations. The probability would be $^{30}C_1/2^{30}$. Similarly, we may find the probability of each of the 31 possible terminal prices. Thus, probability distribution would be far closer to reality than what one imagines in the binary state.

The way to overcome the second objection, that the binary system ignores volatility in valuation, is to replace arbitrary selection of up and down moves with selection based on stock volatility. It is possible to equate an up or a down move based on stock volatility, σ. The up move, u, in each binomial period of length Δt is set equal to $e^{\sigma\sqrt{\Delta t}}$ as per the Cox, Ross, and Rubinstein method. For example, to value an option of 3 months on an asset with a volatility of 30% and a 30-stage binomial tree, the parameters under the binomial approach would be determined as follows:

Option period	3 months
Number of binomial steps	30
Duration of each binomial step, Δt	3 days or 0.008333 years
Stock volatility, σ	30%
Up price $u = e^{\sigma\sqrt{\Delta t}} = e^{0.3\sqrt{3/360}}$	1.02776
Down price $d = 1/u$	0.97299

Risk-free rate, r	8%
Probability of up move, p	0.5053

$$p = (e^{r\Delta t} - d)/(u - d)$$
$$= (1.00067 - 0.97299)/(1.02776 - 0.97229)$$
$$p = 0.505329$$

Probability of down move = $1 - p$ 0.4947

MONTE CARLO SIMULATION

> Under the Monte Carlo method, we simulate the values of uncertain variables by picking random numbers for a known probability distribution.

We all live under uncertain conditions. Each day is a new day, with some new events happening and some old events repeating. For each event, we behave differently. So do the asset prices. The events are independent and drive the values of the assets. Is there a way to replicate these independent events and conclude the behaviour of prices of assets for the future? In case there exists a relationship of prices with different variables, then it is possible to assume some values of independent variables, and based on the relationship, the price of a dependent variable can be forecasted.

We can only simulate the conditions that derive the values of the assets. Simulation means creating conditions artificially and observing the outcome under each condition. If we repeat this exercise, a sufficiently large number of times, we can make a reasonable estimate of asset prices. Under simulation, we generate random numbers that follow the likely probability distribution associated with the variable. For example, assume that the US dollar exchange rate for 300 observations was found to vary as shown in Table 11.8.

If we know the relationship of foreign institutional investors (FII) inflows for portfolio investments with exchange rates, then, based on the above distribution in Table 11.8, we can simulate the US dollar exchange rate for tomorrow and forecast the value of FII inflows. The changes in the exchange rate are assumed to occur randomly, but would follow the probability distribution pattern assumed in Table 11.8. We can pick a random number that would be associated with a particular change in the exchange rate. We would repeat the exercise many times by picking one number each time, which would correspond to a specific change in the exchange rates. The number would be picked randomly, i.e., we do not know what the next

Table 11.8 Probability distribution—300 US dollar exchange rate observations

% Increase	No. of times	% Decrease	No. of times
> 5%	3	Between 0 and 1%	39
Between 4 and 5%	11	Between 0 and 1%	42
Between 3 and 4%	19	Between 2 and 3%	33
Between 2 and 3%	27	Between 3 and 4%	12
Between 1 and 2%	46	Between 4 and 5%	10
Between 0 and 1%	51	> 5%	5
No change	2	Total	300

number would be, based on the numbers for the previous periods. Such an exercise is called the Monte Carlo simulation, named after the city of Monte Carlo, famous for its casinos.

The Monte Carlo simulation is another numerical method that can help in valuation of options. In this simulation, values are sampled at random from the input probability distributions. Each sample is called an iteration. The outcome from each iteration is recorded. The Monte Carlo simulation does this hundreds or thousands of times, and the result is a probability distribution of possible outcomes. In this way, this simulation provides a much more comprehensive view of what may happen. It tells you not only what could happen but also how likely it is to happen.

In finance, Monte Carlo methods are used by financial analysts who wish to construct 'stochastic' or probabilistic financial models, as opposed to the traditional static and deterministic models. In valuing an option on equity, the simulation generates several thousand possible (but random) price paths for the underlying share, with the associated payoff of the option for each path. These payoffs are then averaged and discounted to find the value of the option. Similarly, we can value fixed income instruments and interest rate derivatives by simulating the source of uncertainty, i.e., the interest rate. A similar approach can be used in valuing swaps and swaptions.

We demonstrate with a small example the application of the Monte Carlo simulation for pricing a call option. We know the price of European options through the Black–Scholes formula (discussed in Chapter 12). We can test if the Monte Carlo simulation matches with the Black–Scholes model.

Table 11.9 presents 20 iterations under the Monte Carlo simulation for determining the value of an ATM call on a stock with a current price, S, of ₹100. The expiration period is 90 days, and the risk-free return is 5% p.a. The stock is assumed to have volatility, σ, of 30%. The change in value of stock, ΔS, is governed by the following equation:

$$\Delta S = S \cdot r \cdot \Delta t + S \cdot \sigma \cdot (RN) \cdot \sqrt{\Delta t} \qquad (11.10)$$

where S = current value of stock = ₹100, Δt = time remaining for expiry of option = 90 days ≡ 0.2466 years, r = risk-free rate of return = 5%, σ = volatility of stock price = 30%, and RN is the random number generated.

A random number has been generated in MS Excel using the RAND function. The RAND function generates a random number between 0 and 1 that is uniformly distributed. The principle behind the Monte Carlo simulation is to generate another type of distribution based on the uniform distribution random number. It requires a transformation from uniform distribution into other distributions. A reasonable way of generating approximate normal distribution would be to add 12 RAND() functions and subtract six.[4]

> After generating several thousand possible values for uncertain variables, we can determine the values of dependent variables, find an average, and discount back to the present.

The first random number is 0.4954, which gives the change in stock price; as per Eq. 11.10, the change in stock price is as follows:

$$\Delta S = 100 \times 0.05 \times 0.2466 + 100 \times 0.30 \times (0.4954) \times \sqrt{0.2466} = ₹1.8392$$

---

[4]Refer to *An Introduction to Derivatives and Risk Management* by Don M. Chance and Robert Brookes; 8th ed. p519; South Western Cengage Learning. The sum of 12 random numbers has been found to have a mean of 6 and a standard deviation of 1.00. Hence, subtracting 6 from the sum of 12 random numbers would have a mean of zero and a standard deviation of 1, the two properties of normal distribution.

Table 11.9 Monte Carlo simulation—example

S. No.	Random number	Change in spot ΔS	End-value of spot $S_T = S + \Delta S$	Value of call Max(0, $S_T - X$)
1	0.0407	1.8392	101.8392	1.8392
2	0.3468	6.3991	106.3991	6.3991
3	1.1354	18.1468	118.1468	18.1468
4	−1.5498	−21.8543	78.1457	–
5	−0.2814	−2.9591	97.0409	–
6	−0.3259	−3.6220	96.3780	–
7	1.6372	25.6221	125.6221	25.6221
8	−0.2018	−1.7733	98.2267	–
9	1.1743	18.7263	118.7263	18.7263
10	0.1235	3.0726	103.0726	3.0726
11	−0.1322	−0.7365	99.2635	–
12	0.5216	9.0031	109.0031	9.0031
13	0.6977	11.6264	111.6264	11.6264
14	−0.3585	−4.1077	95.8923	–
15	0.9811	15.8482	115.8482	15.8482
16	1.5443	24.2382	124.2382	24.2382
17	0.9812	15.8497	115.8497	15.8497
18	0.0961	2.6645	102.6645	2.6645
19	−0.1918	−1.6243	98.3757	–
20	−1.2106	−16.8013	83.1987	–
Sum of 20 observations				153.0362
Call value based on 20 observations				7.6518

Therefore, the end-value of the asset would be 100.00 + 1.8392 = ₹101.8392, and the payoff on the ATM call is ₹1.8392, as shown in the last column of Table 11.9.

Similarly, the 11th number is −0.1322, which gives the change in the spot price as follows:

$$\Delta S = 100 \times 0.05 \times 0.2466 + 100 \times 0.30 \times (-0.1322) \times \sqrt{0.2466} = -₹0.7365$$

The final asset value is given as 100 − 0.7365 = ₹99.2635 and the resultant payoff of the call is given as zero.

Repeating the exercise for 20 random numbers, we get 20 different values of the call. The average comes to ₹7.6518, which is the call price under the Monte Carlo simulation at maturity of the option. Under risk neutrality, the value of the option should be $e^{(-0.05 \times 0.2466)}$ × 7.6518 = ₹7.4259. Of course, the sample of 20 random numbers is extremely inadequate to arrive at a reasonably accurate value for the call. Normally, one has to pick about 10,000 to 20,000 random numbers to have a reasonably accurate value.

The requirement for a large number of observations adds to computation time. The complex relationship between input and output would further constrain the computation. The computational complexity and the requirement for large drawings of random numbers are, therefore, considered disadvantages of the Monte Carlo simulation.

The advantages of Monte Carlo simulation include giving approximate solutions to many mathematical problems. The method can be used for both stochastic (involving probability) and deterministic (without probability) solutions.

CONCLUSION

The binomial approach to valuation of an option is indeed revealing. It demonstrates how simple representations can solve seemingly complex issues. The risk-neutral valuation highlights how probabilities of up and down moves do not play any role in determining option value—a proposition difficult to digest. This is because of the fact that when a risky asset is combined with an option, another extremely volatile asset can result into a hedged portfolio, providing an assured return. Indeed, this is the cornerstone of the risk-neutral approach. With fast computing devices available, the re-iterative process of valuation can easily be executed. As the number of iterations increases, option pricing by the binomial model would converge to the one given by analytical models.

Another extremely powerful feature of the binomial model is its ability to incorporate managerial flexibilities. As the number of branches in a tree increases, the time interval at each stage shortens. At each stage, nodes can be regarded as decision points. We applied decisions such as early exercise and dividend payments in the valuation of options. This kind of flexibility—incorporating human intervention and managerial discretion in decision-making—is not possible in analytical models, which work as black boxes to provide outputs once the inputs are fed in.

Options are both exchange-traded as well as over-the-counter products. The variety available in over-the-counter options is tremendous, as features of the options are modified by the parties involved. These are referred to as exotic options, and they constitute a major proportion of the commercial world. Therefore, the need to incorporate this kind of flexibility is of paramount importance. It is here that the binomial approach becomes very handy, in contrast to black-box solutions.

SOLVED PROBLEMS

SP 11.1: Binomial model for call pricing

A stock is currently trading at ₹50. It can either go up by 20% or fall by 20% in a period of three months. If the risk-free interest rate is 8% p.a., find the value of a call and a put with an exercise price of ₹50 and maturity of three months using the risk-neutral method under the binomial model for a single period. Verify the put–call parity also.

Solution

The implied probability of an up movement with a risk-free rate of 8%, an up move of 20%, and a down move of 20% is 0.5505. The probability of a down move is 0.4495, as shown here:

$$p = \frac{e^{rt} - (1 - d)}{u + d} = \frac{1.02020 - (1 - 0.20)}{0.20 + 0.20} = 0.5505 = 55.05\%$$

$$1 - p = 1 - 0.505 = 0.4495$$

The payoffs of a call and a put with a strike of ₹50 at the end of the maturity period of three months are as shown here:

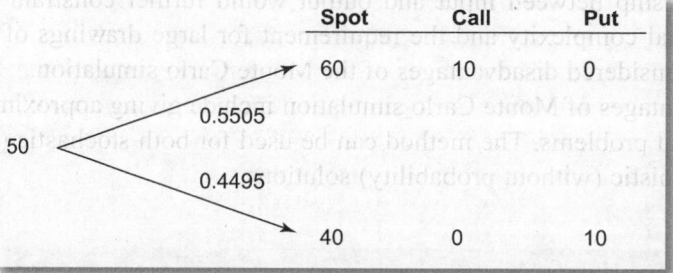

The risk-neutral valuations of the call and the put are

Value of the call at maturity = $10 \times 0.5505 + 0 \times 0.4495$ = ₹5.505
Value of the call today   = Present value of the call at maturity
                              = $5.505 \times e^{-0.08 \times 3/12}$ = ₹5.3960 ≈ ₹5.40
Value of the put at maturity = $0 \times 0.5505 + 10 \times 0.4495$ = ₹4.495
Value of the put today   = Present value of the put at maturity
                              = $4.495 \times e^{-0.08 \times 3/12}$ = ₹4.4060 ≈ ₹4.41
Using put–call parity, $p = c - S + X \times e^{-rt}$ = 5.50 − 50 + 50 × $e^{-0.08 \times 3/12}$ = ₹4.41

SP 11.2: Binomial method with equivalent portfolio approach
Refer to the data in SP 11.1 and re-calculate the values of the call and put using the equivalent portfolio approach.
Solution
Option delta of the call

$$\text{Option Delta} = \frac{\text{Spread of call option}}{\text{Spread of share price}} = \frac{10 - 0}{60 - 40} = \frac{10}{20} = 0.5$$

The value of a portfolio of one long share and two short calls at maturity

Stock price = 60 : $60 - 2 \times 10 = 40$
Stock price = 40 : $40 - 2 \times 0 = 40$

Present value = $40 \times e^{-0.08 \times 3/12}$ = 39.21
Cost of portfolio = $50 - 2 \times c$ = 39.21
$c = (50.00 - 39.21)/2 \approx$ ₹5.40

Option delta for the put

$$\text{Option Delta} = \frac{\text{Spread of put option}}{\text{Spread of share price}} = \frac{0 - 10}{60 - 40} = \frac{-10}{20} = -0.5$$

Value of a portfolio of one long share and two long puts at maturity

Stock price = 60 : $60 + 2 \times 0 = 60$
Stock price = 40 : $40 + 2 \times 10 = 60$

Present value = $60 \times e^{-0.08 \times 3/12}$ = 58.81
Cost of portfolio = $50 + 2 \times p$ = 58.81
$p = (58.81 - 50.00)/2 \approx$ ₹4.41

SP 11.3: Binomial model for call pricing
A stock is currently trading at ₹50. It can either go up by 20% or fall by 20% in a period of three months. If the risk-free interest rate is 8% p.a., find the value of a call and a put with an exercise price of ₹45 and maturity of six months using the risk-neutral method under the binomial model for two periods.

Option Pricing—Binomial Model 333

Solution
The implied probability of an up movement with a risk-free rate of 8%, an up move of 20% and a down move of 20% is 0.5505, as calculated in SP 11.1. A two-stage binomial tree for 6-m call and put options with an exercise price of ₹45, three months in each period, and asset price and payoffs of call and put at expiry is shown here:

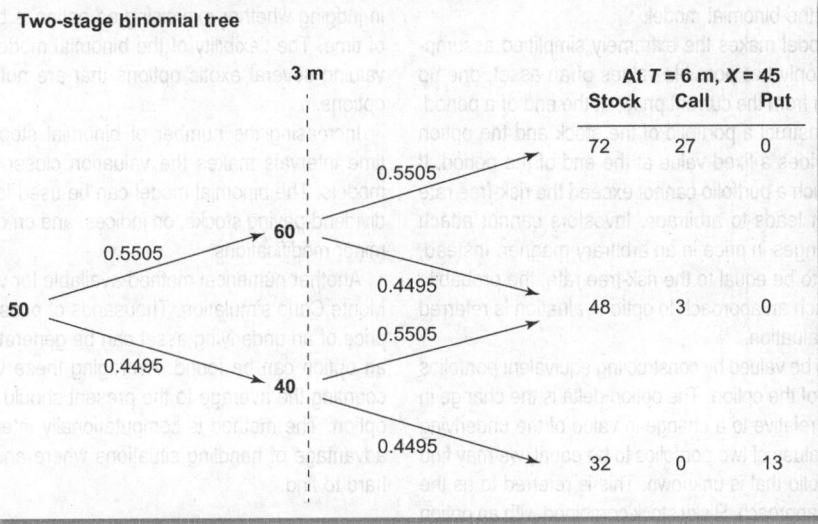

The risk-neutral valuations of the call
At the node with a spot price of ₹60 at t = 3 m
    Value of the call at maturity   = 27 × 0.5505 + 3 × 0.4495 = ₹16.2120
    Value of the call at t = 3 m   = Present value of the call at maturity
        = $16.2120 \times e^{-0.08 \times 3/12}$
        = 16.2120 × 0.9802 = ₹15.8910

At the node with a spot price of ₹40 at t = 3 m
    Value of the call at maturity   = 3 × 0.5505 + 0 × 0.4495 = ₹1.6515
    Value of the call at t = 3 m   = Present value of the call at maturity
        = $1.6515 \times e^{-0.08 \times 3/12}$
        = 1.6515 × 0.9802 = ₹1.6188

At the node with a spot price of ₹50 at t = 0
    Value of the call at t = 3 m   = 15.8910 × 0.5505 + 1.6188 × 0.4495 = ₹9.4756
    Value of the call at t = 0   = Present value of the call at t = 3 m
        = $9.4756 \times e^{-0.08 \times 3/12}$
        = 9.4756 × 0.9802 = ₹9.2880 ≈ ₹9.29

The risk-neutral valuations of the put
At the node with a spot price of ₹60 at t = 3 m
    Value of the put at maturity   = 0 × 0.5505 + 0 × 0.4495 = ₹0
    Value of the put at t = 3 m   = ₹0.00

At the node with a spot price of ₹40 at t = 3 m
    Value of the put at maturity   = 0 × 0.5505 + 13 × 0.4495 = ₹5.5435
    Value of the put at t = 3 m   = Present value of the put at maturity
        = $5.5435 \times e^{-0.08 \times 3/12}$
        = 5.5435 × 0.9802 = ₹5.7278

At the node with a spot price of ₹50 at t = 0
    Value of the put at t = 3 m   = 0 × 0.5505 + 5.7278 × 0.4495 = ₹2.5746
    Value of the put at t = 0   = Present value of the put at t = 3 m
        = $2.5746 \times e^{-0.08 \times 3/12}$
        = 2.5746 × 0.9802 = ₹2.5256 ≈ ₹2.53

SUMMARY

Determination of option premiums has been one of the most challenging areas of derivatives. Various methodologies exist to value options. One of the most powerful, yet simple, approaches to value options is the binomial model.

The binomial model makes the extremely simplified assumption that there are only two possible values of an asset, one up and the other down from the current price, at the end of a period. It is possible to construct a portfolio of the stock and the option on it so that it provides a fixed value at the end of the period. If so, the return on such a portfolio cannot exceed the risk-free rate of return, or else it leads to arbitrage. Investors cannot attach probabilities to changes in price in an arbitrary manner. Instead, if the returns have to be equal to the risk-free rate, the probabilities are implied. Such an approach to option valuation is referred to as risk-neutral valuation.

Options can also be valued by constructing equivalent portfolios based on the delta of the option. The option delta is the change in value of the option relative to a change in value of the underlying asset. Setting the values of two portfolios to be equal, we may find the value of a portfolio that is unknown. This is referred to as the equivalent portfolio approach. Risky stock combined with an option on it can result in a portfolio that is risk free.

The binomial option pricing model is an extremely potent tool, and has the capacity to value American options that can be exercised at any time. The binomial method renders flexibility in judging whether exercising an option is beneficial at intervals of time. The flexibility of the binomial model makes it useful for valuing several exotic options that are not standard European options.

Increasing the number of binomial steps by shortening the time intervals makes the valuation closer to that of analytical models. The binomial model can be used for valuing options on dividend-paying stocks, on indices, and on currencies by making minor modifications.

Another numerical method available for valuing options is the Monte Carlo simulation. Thousands of possible scenarios of the price of an underlying asset can be generated, and the value of an option can be found. Averaging these values and then discounting the average to the present should give the value of an option. The method is computationally intensive, but offers the advantage of handling situations where analytical solutions are hard to find.

KEY TERMS

Binomial option pricing model An option pricing model that assumes that there can be only two possible states of value of the underlying asset.
Equivalent portfolio approach An approach that assumes that two portfolios that have the same value would be equivalent—including the pricing of such portfolios—would fetch the same value, and command the same price.
Monte Carlo simulation The method of simulating the uncertainties for a given probability distribution by generating thousands of random numbers and analysing the outcomes for understanding behaviour and pricing.
Option delta The option delta is the rate of change of an option value with respect to a change in the value of the underlying asset.
Risk-neutral probability The probability that equates the return of a portfolio/asset with the risk-free rate of interest.
Risk-neutral valuation Risk-neutral valuation assumes that a portfolio that provides a definite value cannot grow by more than the risk-free rate.

QUESTIONS

11.1 Describe the binomial model of valuation of options.
11.2 What do you understand by risk-neutral valuation?
11.3 What is the equivalent portfolio approach to value options and how is it different from risk-neutral valuation? Explain.
11.4 What changes would you make in the binomial method while valuing American options? Explain with the help of an example.
11.5 What factors would you consider while constructing a binomial tree? How would you achieve accuracy of results and incorporation of volatility?

PROBLEMS

P 11.1 Understanding the binomial tree
You are required to value a 12-m option on an asset currently trading at ₹100 using a four-stage binomial tree. The risk-free rate is 8% p.a., with quarterly compounding. The stock can take only two values at the end of each quarter, with either a 10% up or a 10% down. Answer the following:

(a) How many end values can the asset have?
(b) Find out all the end-values.
(c) What is the probability of each end-value?

P 11.2 Risk neutrality and binomial tree
Refer to P 11.1. Under risk-neutral valuation with a binomial tree, what would the probabilities of an up move and a down move be?

P 11.3 Option value with the binomial model
For the parameters of P 11.1 and P 11.2, find the value of a European call and a European put with 12 months to maturity and a strike price of ₹120.

P 11.4 Valuing a European put with the binomial tree
For the parameters of P 11.1, depict the 4-stage binomial tree for a European put option with a strike price of ₹120.

P 11.5 Valuing an American put with the binomial tree
What would the value of the put in P 11.4 be if it were an American option?

P 11.6 Risk neutrality and binomial tree
A stock is currently trading at ₹50. Over a period of one month, it can either go up by 10% or fall by 10%. Using the single-period binomial tree, what is the value of a 1-m call and a 1-m put option with a strike price of ₹50? Assume a European option and a 12% risk-free interest rate with monthly compounding. Draw the binomial tree, indicating the values of the stock and the call and put at expiry. Further, verify the put–call parity using the call price found.

P 11.7 Risk-neutral valuation
Value the call and put options of P 11.6 by making a risk free portfolio.

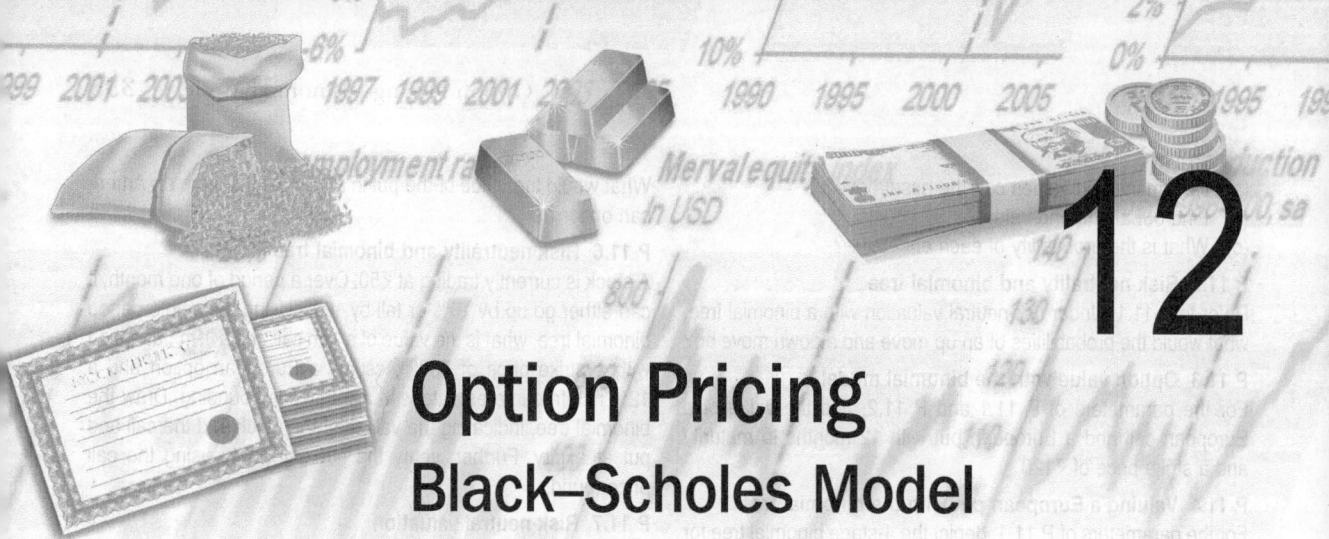

12

Option Pricing
Black–Scholes Model

INTRODUCTION

In Chapter 11, we discussed the binomial model and the Monte Carlo simulation, which used a reiterative approach to value options. In this chapter, we discuss an analytical approach to get solution to option pricing, known as the Black–Scholes–Merton model—more popularly known by its first two discoverers, i.e., Fischer Black and Myron Scholes. They discovered the model in 1973 for European options with no dividend till maturity. Robert Merton later incorporated the dividend payment into the Black–Scholes model (BSM).

The BSM was a landmark in financial literature, as it opened up an entirely new field of research. The understanding of BSM is extremely important for those concerned with option valuation. It is said that Black and Scholes developed option pricing in two different ways—one based on the capital asset pricing model and the risk-neutral approach, and the other based on a mathematical solution to a differential equation. Only when a solution derived by both the methods matched was it accepted. The approach in the mathematical solution to option pricing involved use of much research and results, worked out by many physicists and mathematicians.

In contrast, the binomial approach avoided all complex mathematics. It may be evident that as the number of branches increases in a binomial tree, the accuracy of the option price found increases. Further, as we increase the number of trees in a binomial model by shortening the time interval, the value of the option not only stabilizes but also oscillates around some value—now referred to as the BSM value. It is found that by suitably increasing the number of iterations in the binomial model, the option price converges to the one obtained by the BSM formula.

Learning Objectives

After going through this chapter, readers should be familiar with

- how various factors affect option prices
- valuation of options by the Black–Scholes model
- assumptions of option pricing in the Black–Scholes model
- adapting the Black–Scholes formula to value
  - options on dividend paying stocks
  - options on indices
  - options on currencies
- valuing an American option
- the meaning of volatility and its measurement
- implied volatility

The basic difference between the binomial formula and the BSM formula is that while the former uses discrete steps for price movements, the latter model works for continuous changes in the asset price to arrive at a black-box solution to the option price. While the major strength of the binomial model is its ability to incorporate flexibility, the advantage of black-box solutions such as the BSM formula is to substantially reduce computation time.

FACTORS AFFECTING OPTION PRICE

The BSM requires five inputs (six for options on dividend paying stock) to value European options. Before we dwell on the mathematical model for determination of the exact option price, here are some intuitive explanations on the behaviour of determinants and the effect each of them has on the option premium.

The following are six identifiable factors that affect option premium:

- The price of the underlying asset, S
- the exercise price, X
- the time left for expiration, T
- variability (volatility) in the price of the underlying, σ
- the risk-free interest rate, r
- the benefit that would accrue for holding the asset rather than an option over it, D

Price of the Underlying Asset, S As the price of the asset increases, the value of the call also increases. The value of the call is driven by the differential of S and X for $S > X$. The higher the asset price, the higher the differential, and, hence, the higher is the value of the call. Most investors buy a call option to benefit from price rise, and, therefore, must pay a higher premium if the asset price increases. If the call is out-of-the-money (OTM) and the spot price increases, the probability that it will touch or cross the strike price also increases. If the call is already in-the-money (ITM), its intrinsic value increases even further with an increase in the spot price. A call option becomes more expensive as the writer of the call assumes a greater risk with rising spot prices.

> With any increase in the price of the underlying asset, a call option increases in value while a put option decreases in value.

Similarly with an increase in price of the asset, the payoff to the put holder declines, as the intrinsic value of the put is the difference between its exercise price and the spot price, i.e., $X - S$. As the spot price increases, the differential $X - S$ also decreases, and, therefore, the value of a put must fall with an increase in the price of the asset. Investors buy put options to protect themselves against fall in the price. As the price goes up, the put holder is less likely to exercise his/her option. It is a favourable situation for the writer of the put, and, therefore, he/she can be induced to write the put option with a smaller premium.

Exercise Price, X The impact of the exercise price on the value of options is opposite to that of spot prices. The higher the exercise price, the lower is the value of the call option. As the exercise price goes up, the chances that the share price will exceed it become lesser and lesser. With an increase in the exercise price, the call option becomes more and more out-of-the-money. As stated earlier, the value of a call is driven by the differential between the spot price and the exercise price. With any increase in the exercise price, the intrinsic value of the call falls.

> With an increasing exercise price, the value of a call option decreases and of a put option increases.

Just as the value of the call decreases with an increase in the exercise price, the value of the put increases as exercising the put option by the holder becomes more and more lucrative. Accordingly, the value of a put option must increase with any increase in the exercise price.

Time Left for Expiration, T Intuition would tell us that with more time available, there would be a greater probability of achieving the exercise price from either direction. This general statement must hold true for both call and put options. The farther the expiration date, the more valuable is the option, irrespective of whether it is a call or a put. There are equally greater chances of the price going above X (for a call option) or falling below X (for a put option). Conversely, lesser time available will make the options less valuable. Whether it is an option to buy (call) or to sell (put), the chances that an option will turn in-the-money increase with increased availability of the time before expiry.

> With more time to maturity, the values of calls and puts increase.

Therefore, a call or a put of three months must cost more than a call or a put with expiry in one month. The value of a call as well as a put decreases as the time to maturity approaches; this phenomenon is called time decay.

Variability of Price (risk) of Stock, σ Volatility of the underlying stock is measured using the standard deviation of returns. The larger the standard deviation, the larger is the volatility. In terms of the shape of the normal distribution curve, it will become flatter and wider as the standard deviation increases. The expected profit from the option, either a call or a put, would increase with an increase in the standard deviation. Volatility is not unidirectional, but applies equally to any rise or fall in price. As risk is higher, the price of the asset varies in a wider range. Hence, it has a greater chance of becoming in-the-money. It will not be wrong to say that it is the volatility of the price of the asset that imparts value to an option. Call and put options become more valuable as the volatility of the underlying asset increases.

> With increasing volatility of the price of the underlying asset, both call and put options increase in value.

Interest Rate, r Interest rates also affect the option premium. Their effect is not as apparent as it may be with other determinants of the option premium. To understand the impact of interest rates on option premiums, one has to look into the timing of the cash flows that are attached to owning or writing an option. Assuming an intention to exercise the option at or prior to expiry, we can also assume that the cash flow for the underlying transaction, i.e., the exercise price, is deferred in the options contract.

In case of a call option, the holder is liable to pay to the call writer the exercise price and take over the ownership of the asset at the time of exercise. Essentially, the buyer has deferred the cash flow for owning the asset, and, therefore, can earn interest on the money set aside for the exercise price over the option period. Payment is made only when the call is exercised. It is a liability that arises upon exercise. If the interest rate increases, the earnings for the holder of the option would be more, and, hence, he/she would be willing to pay an additional premium. The other way of ascertaining the direction of change in value of a call option is to view the call premium as being dependent upon the difference between the spot price and the present value (PV) of the exercise price, i.e.,

> With an increasing rate of interest, the value of a call increases and the value of a put decreases.

$$c \geq S - PV \text{ of } X \quad \text{or} \quad c \geq S - Xe^{-rT} \tag{12.1}$$

An increase in the interest rate means that the present value of X decreases, thereby making the call more expensive.

Similarly, holding a put is a deferred potential asset that results in inflow of money only at the time of exercise. The holder of a put foregoes interest for the option period. The quantum of this sacrifice of income would be more if interest rates increase. To compensate for the loss of interest, the holder will be willing to pay a lesser premium if interest rates are higher. With an increased rate of interest, the present value of the potential asset is less. Therefore, the value of the put is less when the interest rate is high. Alternatively, with increased interest rates, the difference between the present value of the exercise price and the spot price decreases, as can be seen from the value of the put:

$$p \geq Xe^{-rT} - S \qquad (12.2)$$

Expected Dividend During Life of Option, D The benefits of ownership (typically dividend) accrue only to the holder of the asset, and not to the person having a derivative exposure. Further, when the dividends are paid, the value of the asset in the market declines by an equivalent amount. With an expected decline in the spot price, the value of the call must decrease and that of the put must increase. It would be more beneficial to hold the stock than to hold the call.

Just as the value of the call decreases with increased dividend, the value of the put increases, as the holder of the put option retains the ownership of the asset, and all benefits accruing on it, till its exercise.

Table 12.1 summarizes the impact on option prices of the various factors that determine these prices:

Table 12.1 Impact of various factors on option prices

Variable (increasing)	Call	Put
Share price	↑	↓
Strike price	↓	↑
Time for expiration	↑	↑
Volatility	↑	↑
Risk-free rate	↑	↓
Dividends	↓	↑

BLACK–SCHOLES OPTION PRICING MODEL

> The Black–Scholes model is an analytical model for valuing European options on non-dividend paying stocks.

The basic valuation model, developed by Myron Scholes and Fisher Black in 1973 using complex mathematics, is the single most important development among the theories of finance. This work, for which its inventors received the Nobel Prize, forms the backbone of modern option pricing theory. It is in the analytical form, providing a formula into which the determinants of option prices are fed and the final outcomes on the values of options are derived. The numerical method of binomial option pricing has already been discussed.

The BSM can be implemented using complex calculus and differential equations. Alternatively, the BSM can also be derived with the risk-neutral valuation approach, which has already been discussed under the binomial method in Chapter 11. With some background in mathematics and risk-neutral valuation, the BSM for valuation of call options on non-dividend paying stock is described in this section.

We know that an option price consists of intrinsic value and time value. For a call option, the intrinsic value is the difference between the spot price and the exercise price if the spot price is more than the exercise price; otherwise, it is worthless. Similarly, for a put option it is the difference between the exercise price and the spot price. The minimum value of either option is zero. Options always have values in excess of their intrinsic values. The excess of the actual value over the intrinsic value is the time value of an option, the value associated with the chances of an increase in the intrinsic value before the option's expiry.

While pricing an option, the intrinsic value is always apparent but estimating the time value of the option poses a problem. The time value attached to an option reflects (a) the possibility of it becoming more in-the-money and (b) the extent to which it can become in-the-money before the maturity date. Therefore, it must be dependent upon the chance that the spot price would exceed the exercise price for a call option, and the chance that the spot price would be less than the exercise price for a put option.

Alternatively, the BSM can also be derived with the risk-neutral valuation approach, which has already been discussed under the binomial method in Chapter 11. The basic assumptions made under the BSM include absence of transaction costs, arbitrage-free perfect market conditions, and continuous trading. The BSM for a call option on non-dividend paying stock further makes the following propositions.

Stock Returns Have Log-normal Distribution

For a European call option maturing at time T with an exercise price of X, we need to compare the price of the stock at maturity, S_T, with the exercise price. If S_T exceeds X, the call would be exercised; otherwise, it expires worthless.

Let us first examine the behaviour of stock prices. For closer and better understanding of this behaviour, we need to examine how the price changes over an infinitesimal time period rather than at the end of the period. This is a deviation from the binomial approach. Stock prices follow a random walk, implying that the next movement of a stock's price is completely independent of its past prices. A rise in price is as equally likely as a fall in price. The present price contains all this information. Though there can be an upwards or downwards bias in stock prices that may be the subject of pragmatic forecasting over longer time horizons, this would not hold good if the time intervals were infinitesimally small. For very small periods, such as daily or hourly periods, the returns are purely random and unpredictable.

Returns are measured by the price relative. We concentrate more on the price relative, i.e., the ratio of the prices at two successive time intervals rather than their absolute values. The price relative, R_1, defined as S_1/S_0 over an extremely short interval of time between 0 and 1, is observed to be identically and independently distributed, where S_1 and S_0 are prices at time $t = 0$ and $t = 1$, respectively. The

> The distribution of stock prices is assumed to be log-normal in the BSM.

final price at the end of the option period at time T can be broken in terms of very small intervals of time 1, 2, 3, ...T, etc., and the return can be stated as in Eq. 12.3.

$$\frac{S_T}{S_0} = \frac{S_1}{S_0} \times \frac{S_2}{S_1} \times \frac{S_3}{S_2} \cdots\cdots\cdots\cdots\cdots \times \frac{S_T}{S_{T-1}} \quad (12.3)$$
$$= R_1 \times R_2 \times R_3 \cdots\cdots\cdots\cdots\cdots \times R_T$$

The relative return at time T is defined as $R_T = S_T/S_{T-1}$. Here, it is assumed that there is no dividend during the period under consideration, and that returns consist purely of the capital gains arising from price changes.

To measure returns over very small intervals of time, we need to assume continuous compounding. If we take the natural logarithm of the returns and define $r_i = \ln R_i$, Eq. 12.3 can be written as follows:

$$\ln\frac{S_T}{S_0} = Y_T = \ln R_1 + \ln R_2 + \ln R_3 \cdots\cdots\cdots\cdots\cdots + \ln R_T \quad (12.4)$$
$$= r_1 + r_2 + r_3 \cdots\cdots\cdots\cdots\cdots r_T$$

If the price relatives, R_i, are identically and independently distributed, their logarithms too would be identical and independent random variables. It implies that if many samples of relative returns are taken, then the values and probabilities would be the same in each case. This also implies that the expected values and standard deviations too would be identical.

A word about why we consider the distribution of the logarithm of the return relative rather than the distribution of the stock prices. We know for sure that stock prices cannot be negative. The minimum value of a stock can only be zero, and loss cannot exceed 100%. Stock prices, if normally distributed, would imply negative prices and loss exceeding 100%, which cannot be true. Assuming normal distribution for stock prices would then be simply erroneous, a log-normal distribution fits the description, as it does not permit negative values, by limiting losses to 100%. As an alternative, we may examine the distribution of log returns. If log returns, Y_T, are normally distributed, then the distribution of the stock price, S_T, is log-normal.

Mean and Standard Deviation of Ln R are Proportional to Time

If log returns are identical and independent, then the different samples taken must have the same expected values and variances. For a definite time period of T, if one sample taken at interval Δt_1 provides a mean and standard deviation of m_1 and σ_1, respectively, and another sample taken at time interval Δt_2 with a mean and standard deviation of m_2 and σ_2, respectively, then

$$m_1 \times T/\Delta t_1 = m_2 \times T/\Delta t_2$$

Similarly, variances too would have the same relationship. This implies that over a given period of time, the expected value, m, and the variance, σ^2, would be proportional to the time. If the sample mean and variance were m and σ^2, respectively, then

> The mean and standard deviation of returns on a stock are proportional to time.

The expected value, $E(Y_T)$ $= m \times T$ and
Variance, $Var\ Y_T$ $= \sigma^2 \times T$

Ln R has Normal Distribution: Central Limit Theorem

> The natural log of returns relative has a normal distribution.

According to the central limit theorem, a sample taken from a population would have normal distribution as the sample size approaches infinity. For a sufficiently large sample size, the *ln* of returns, Y_T, would have a normal distribution, with a mean of mT and a variance of $\sigma^2 T$.

Normal distribution is given by Eq. 12.5.

$$n(x) = \frac{1}{sd\sqrt{2\pi}} e^{-\frac{1}{2}\left(\frac{x-\text{mean}}{sd}\right)^2} \quad (12.5)$$

where *sd* is standard deviation.

The general shape of the normal distribution, applicable to the log of return relative and log-normal distribution as relevant to stock prices is shown in Figs. 12.1 and 12.2, respectively.

With a mean of mT and a standard deviation of $\sigma\sqrt{T}$, the distribution of Y_T, $n(Y)$ as a normal distribution (dropping the subscript T for convenience of expression) is represented as Eq. 12.6.

$$n(Y) = \frac{1}{\sigma\sqrt{T}\sqrt{2\pi}} e^{-\frac{1}{2}\left(\frac{Y-mT}{\sigma\sqrt{T}}\right)^2} \quad (12.6)$$

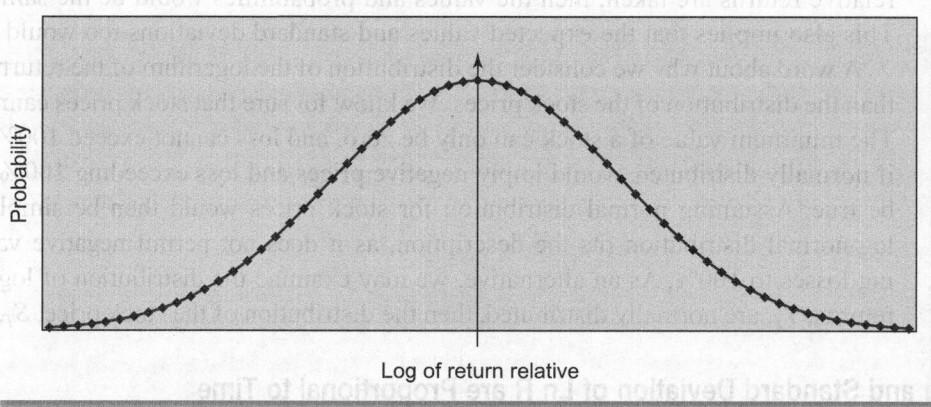

Fig. 12.1 Normal distribution

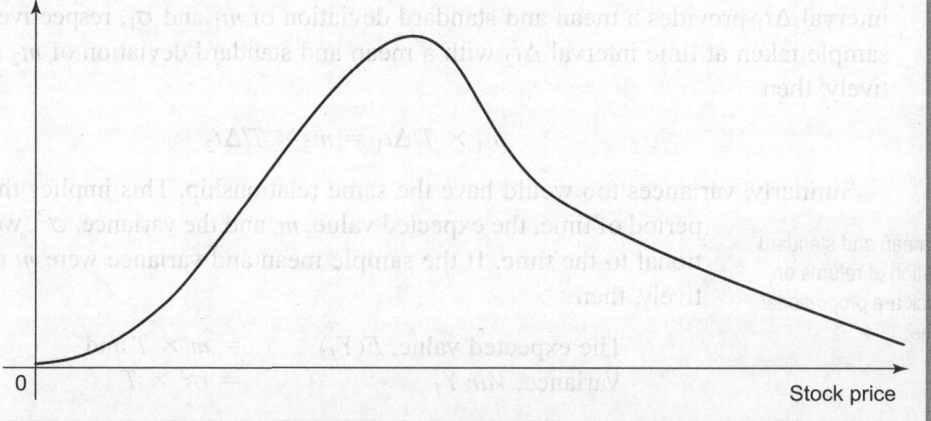

Fig. 12.2 Log-normal distribution

> The expected value of a stock grows at some constant rate and variance. The variance in a stock price or its log would be almost the same.

If Y_T is normally distributed, then S_T is log-normally distributed. In terms of Y_T, the stock price S_T is represented as follows:

$$\ln \frac{S_T}{S_0} = Y_T \quad \text{or} \quad S_T = S_0 e^{Y_T}$$

If Y_T is normally distributed with mean of mT and variance of $\sigma^2 T$, then expected value of Y_T is $e^{(m + \sigma^2/2)T}$

$$S_T = S_0 e^{Y_T} = S_0 e^{(m + \frac{1}{2}\sigma^2)T} = S_0 e^{\mu T} \tag{12.7}$$

The expected value of S_T^1 would be given by

$$E(S_T) = \int_{-\infty}^{\infty} S_0 e^Y n(Y) dY \tag{12.8}$$

Therefore, the expected value of the stock at time T, S_T would rise by μ where

$$\mu = m + \tfrac{1}{2}\sigma^2 \tag{12.9}$$

The stock price is interpreted to grow with time at μ, a constant rate m, and the variance σ^2 of the sample.

What is the standard deviation of stock prices? We have assumed that the standard deviation of returns relative is σ. With extremely small intervals of time, we can take the standard deviation of log returns to be the same as the standard deviation of stock prices.[2] The variance of Y is the same as the variance of S_T/S_0.

Under risk-neutral valuation of the option, we may state that the value of the call option now c_0, would be equal to the value of the option at time T, c_T discounted at the risk-free rate, r.

$$c_0 = e^{-rt} \times c_T \tag{12.10}$$

The value of a call option at maturity T is given by the expected value of $S_T - X$ conditional on the stock price exceeds the exercise price, X, i.e.,

$$E(S_T - X; S_T \geq X) = E(S_T; S_T \geq X) - E(X; S_T \geq X) \tag{12.11}$$

If S_T is assumed to have the distribution $f(S_T)$, then the expected values of S_T and X, as required under Eq. 12.11 to value the call option for $S_T \geq X$, are given by:

$$E(S_T; S_T \geq X) = \int_X^{\infty} S_T f(S_T) ds_T \quad \text{and} \quad E(X; S_T \geq X) = X \int_X^{\infty} f(S_T) ds_T \tag{12.12}$$

Since we know the distribution in terms of Y_T and the values of the standard normal distribution are well tabulated, we need to convert the expression in Eq. 12.11 in terms of the standard normal variable z.

The log of the stock price relative, Y_T, has a mean of mT and a standard deviation of $\sigma\sqrt{T}$. In terms of the standard normal distribution, z is defined as shown in Eq. 12.13.

---

[1] In general, the expected value of any continuous function, x the mean, and variance are given by following expression:

$$\text{Expected value } E(x) = \int_{-\infty}^{\infty} x \cdot n(x) dx \quad \text{and} \quad \text{variance} = \int_{-\infty}^{\infty} x^2 \cdot n(x) dx$$

[2] The Taylor expansion is given by $\ln(1 + a) = 1 - \tfrac{1}{2}a^2 + 1/3 a^3 \ldots$ and for small a Var $(1 + a) = $ Var a

$$z = \frac{Y_T - mT}{\sigma \sqrt{T}} \quad \text{where} \quad Y_T = \ln\left(\frac{S_T}{S_0}\right) \tag{12.13}$$

S_T in terms of the standard normal distribution function, z, is

$$z = \frac{\ln\frac{S_T}{S_0} - mT}{\sigma \sqrt{T}}$$

or
$$\ln\frac{S_T}{S_0} = \sigma \sqrt{T} z + mT \tag{12.14}$$

or
$$\ln S_T = \ln S_0 + \sigma \sqrt{T} z + mT$$

$S_T \geq X$ means $\ln S_T \geq \ln X$, and is equivalent to $z \geq -d_2$ in terms of the standard normal distribution z, as shown in Eq. 12.15.

$$\ln S_T = \ln S_0 + \sigma \sqrt{T} z + mT \geq \ln X$$

or
$$z \geq -\frac{\ln S_0 + mT - \ln X}{\sigma \sqrt{T}}$$

$$z \geq -\frac{\ln\frac{S_0}{X} + mT}{\sigma \sqrt{T}} = -\frac{\ln\frac{S_0}{X} + mT}{\sigma \sqrt{T}} = -d_2 \tag{12.15}$$

where $d_2 = \dfrac{\ln\frac{S_0}{X} + mT}{\sigma \sqrt{T}}$

Similarly, for $S_T \leq X$ means $\ln S_T \leq \ln X$

$$z \leq -\frac{\ln\frac{S_0}{X} + mT}{\sigma \sqrt{T}} = -d_2 \tag{12.16}$$

Expected value of S_T when $S_T \geq X$ is equivalent to $z \geq -d_2$ or

$$E(S_T; S_T \geq X) = E(S_T; z \geq -d_2) \tag{12.17}$$

Substituting the value of S_T in Eq. 12.17 from Eq. 12.12, we get

$$E(S_T; z \geq -d_2) = \int_{-d_2}^{\infty} S_T n(z) dz = \int_{-d_2}^{\infty} S_0 e^{mT} \times e^{\sigma \sqrt{T} z} n(z) dz$$

or
$$E(S_T; z \geq -d_2) = \frac{1}{\sqrt{2\pi}} S_0 e^{mT} \int_{-d_2}^{\infty} e^{\sigma \sqrt{T} z} \times e^{-\frac{z^2}{2}} dz$$

or
$$E(S_T; z \geq -d_2) = \frac{1}{\sqrt{2\pi}} S_0 e^{mT} \cdot e^{\sigma^2 T/2} \int_{-d_2}^{\infty} e^{-\frac{1}{2}(z - \sigma \sqrt{T})^2} dz$$

Making another substitution of $z - \sigma T = a$ gives $dz = da$, and boundary conditions change to:

For $z = -d_2$; $a = -(d_2 + \sigma T) = -d_1$.

This gives the expected value of S_T when $S_T \geq X$ as follows:

$$E(S_T; z \geq -d_2) = \frac{1}{\sqrt{2\pi}} S_0 e^{mT + \sigma^2 T/2} \int_{-d_1}^{\infty} e^{-\frac{1}{2} a^2} da$$

Making use of the symmetrical property of normal distribution as described in Fig. 12.3 we get the expected value of S_T when $S_T \geq X$, as shown in Eq. 12.18.

$$= S_0 e^T \frac{1}{\sqrt{2\pi}} \int_{-\infty}^{d_1} e^{-\frac{1}{2}a^2} da$$

$$= S_0 e^T N(d_1) \tag{12.18}$$

The area under the standard normal distribution curve from $-\infty$ to d represents the probability of the value of the standard normal variate z being less than or equal to any value; d is denoted by $N(d)$, as depicted in Fig. 12.3 and restated here:

$$P(z \leq d) = N(d) = \frac{1}{\sqrt{2\pi}} \int_{-\infty}^{d} e^{-\frac{z^2}{2}} dz$$

On similar lines we can find out the value of the second component of Eq. 12.11, i.e., $E(X; S_T \geq X) = E(X; z \geq -d_2)$

$$E(X; z \geq -d_2) = X \cdot \int_{-d_2}^{\infty} n(z)dz = X \cdot \int_{-\infty}^{d_2} n(z)dz = X \cdot N(d_2) \tag{12.19}$$

$N(d_2)$ represents the probability that z would be less than or equal to d_2, which is the same as stating that the stock price at time T, S_T, would exceed the exercise price X.

> Under risk-neutral valuation, the growth of a stock is taken to be equal to the risk-free return.

Substituting the values obtained in Eqs 12.18 and 12.19 in the value of the call given by Eqs 12.10 and 12.11, the value of a European call option on a non-dividend paying stock is as follows:

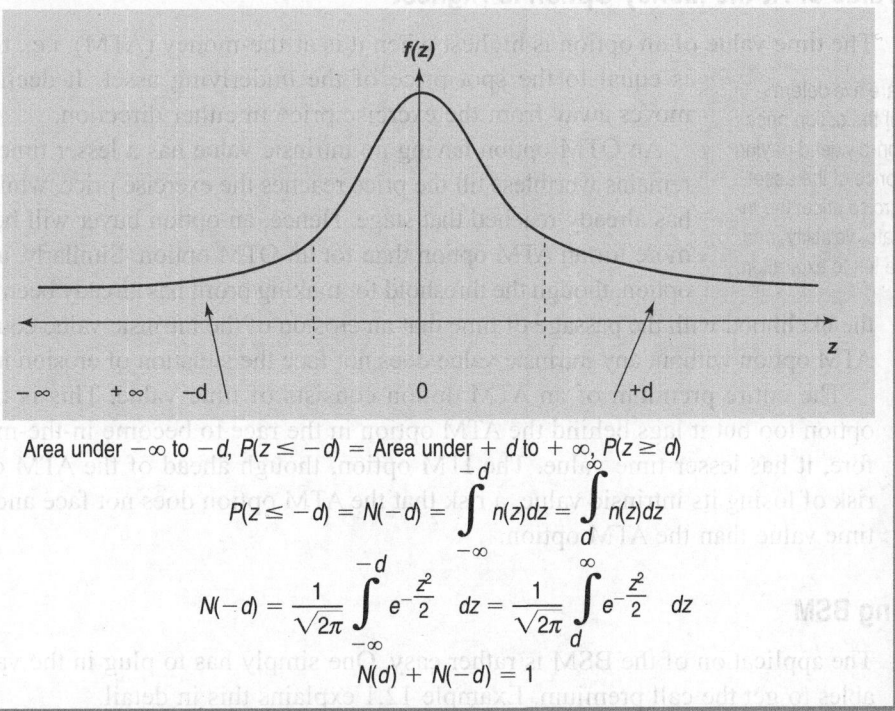

Fig. 12.3 Normal distribution: Area under curve

$$c_T = c_0 \cdot e^{rT} = S_0 \, e^{\mu T} . N(d_1) - X.N(d_2)$$

Under risk-neutral valuation, the growth rate of a stock, μ, would be equal to the risk-free rate, r. Putting $\mu = r$, we get the option value as per the BSM, as shown in Eq. 12.20.

$$c_0 = S_0.N(d_1) - X.e^{-rT}.N(d_2) \quad (12.20)$$

Black–Scholes Model for Option Price on Non-dividend Paying Stock

$$c = S.N(d_1) - X.e^{-rT}.N(d_2) \quad (12.21)$$
$$p = X.e^{-rT}.N(-d_2) - S.N(-d_1) \quad (12.22)$$

where $d_1 = \dfrac{\ln(S/X) + (r + \sigma^2/2)T}{\sigma \sqrt{T}}$; and $d_2 = \dfrac{\ln(S/X) + (r - \sigma^2/2)T}{\sigma \sqrt{T}}$ or $d_2 = d_1 - \sigma \sqrt{T}$

c = Call premium
p = Put premium
S = Spot price of the underlying asset
X = Exercise price
r = Risk-free interest rate (annualized) expressed as decimal

T = Time remaining for expiration of the option in years
σ = Annualized standard deviation of returns expressed as decimal
$N(d_1)$, $N(d_2)$ are cumulative normal distribution at d_1 and d_2, respectively
ln = Natural log

Time Value of At-the-Money Option is Highest

The time value of an option is highest when it is at-the-money (ATM), i.e., the exercise price is equal to the spot price of the underlying asset. It declines as the price moves away from the exercise price in either direction.

> There are five determinants of the option price for a non-dividend paying asset: price of the asset, the exercise price, the interest rate, volatility, and the time left to expiration.

An OTM option having no intrinsic value has a lesser time value because it remains worthless till the price reaches the exercise price, while an ATM option has already reached that stage. Hence, an option buyer will be prepared to pay more for an ATM option than for an OTM option. Similarly, in case of an ITM option, though the threshold for making profit has already been achieved, there is the likelihood with the passage of time that an erosion of the intrinsic value could take place. An ATM option without any intrinsic value does not face the situation of erosion in intrinsic value.

The entire premium of an ATM option consists of time value. This is true for an OTM option too but it lags behind the ATM option in the race to become in-the-money and, therefore, it has lesser time value. The ITM option, though ahead of the ATM option, faces the risk of losing its intrinsic value, a risk that the ATM option does not face and, hence, has less time value than the ATM option.

Applying BSM

The application of the BSM is rather easy. One simply has to plug in the values of the variables to get the call premium. Example 12.1 explains this in detail.

EXAMPLE 12.1 Applying BSM: Call option

Given the following information about a share:
Current market price: ₹50, annual volatility: 30%, risk-free interest rate: 10%.

1. Find out the value of a 3-m call option with an exercise price of (a) ₹40, (b) ₹50, and (c) ₹60.
2. What are the intrinsic and time values of the calls?

Solution
As per the BSM, the value of the call is given by
$$c = SN(d_1) - Xe^{-rT} N(d_2)$$
where $d_1 = \dfrac{\ln(S/X) + (r + \sigma^2/2)T}{\sigma\sqrt{T}}$; and $d_2 = \dfrac{\ln(S/X) + (r - \sigma^2/2)T}{\sigma\sqrt{T}}$ or $d_2 = d_1 - \sigma\sqrt{T}$

(a) *For an exercise price of ₹40*

First, we find the values of d_1 and d_2. All values used are annual and in decimal form. We have $S = 50$, $X = 40$, $r = 0.10$, $T = 0.25$, and $\sigma = 0.30$. These are plugged in the formula:
$$d_1 = \frac{\ln(50/40) + (0.10 + 0.30 \times 0.30/2) \times 0.25}{0.30 \times \sqrt{0.25}} = 1.7293$$
$$d_2 = d_1 - 0.30 \times \sqrt{0.25} = 1.7293 - 0.15 = 1.5793$$

From the normal distribution tables, or using the Excel function NORMSDIST(d), we find out the area under normal distribution for values less than d_1 and d_2.

We get $N(d_1) = 0.9581$ and $N(d_2) = 0.9429$

Inserting the values in the equation in the call premium c, we get:
$$c = S\,N(d_1) - Xe^{-rT} N(d_2) = 50 \times 0.9581 - 40\, e^{-0.1 \times 0.25} \times 0.9429$$
$$= 47.9050 - 39.0124 \times 0.9429 = ₹11.12$$

The intrinsic value of the call is ₹10 (50 − 40), and the remaining ₹1.12 represents the time value.

(b) *For an exercise price of ₹50*
$$d_1 = \frac{\ln(50/50) + (0.10 + 0.30 \times 0.30/2) \times 0.25}{0.30 \times \sqrt{0.25}} = 0.2417$$
$$d_2 = d_1 - 0.30 \times \sqrt{0.25} = 0.2417 - 0.15 = 0.0917$$

We get $N(d_1) = 0.5955$ and $N(d_2) = 0.5365$

Inserting the values in the equation in the call premium c, we get:
$$c = S\,N(d_1) - Xe^{-rT} N(d_2) = 50 \times 0.5955 - 50\, e^{-0.1 \times 0.25} \times 0.5365$$
$$= 29.7750 - 48.7655 \times 0.5365 = ₹3.61$$

The call is at-the-money, with zero intrinsic value, and the entire call premium of ₹3.61 is the time value.

(c) *For an exercise price of ₹60, we get*:
$$d_1 = -0.9738,\ d_2 = -1.1238,\ N(d_1) = 0.1651\ \text{and}\ N(d_2) = 0.1305$$
and call premium $c = ₹0.62$

Here, the call is out-of-money, and the entire premium represents the time value; the value attached with the likelihood of call becoming in-the-money before expiry.
The time value is maximum for an ATM call.

ASSUMPTIONS OF BSM

The following assumptions were made in the derivation of the BSM.

Prices are Log-normally Distributed The BSM assumes the behaviour of the spot price of the underlying asset to be random, which implies that the price is log-normally distributed. Log-normal distribution is similar to normal distribution with the difference that the random variable can take any positive or negative value under normal distribution, while it is restricted to positive values under log-normal distribution. The other property of log-normal distribution is that the natural log of the variable is normally distributed.

No Dividend till Expiration Date of Call Option The BSM assumes that no dividend is paid during the tenure of the option. In practice, firms declare dividend from time to time, and in an efficient market the option price falls by the amount of dividend when it becomes ex-dividend. The BSM will predict the same price for options on two firms that are identical in all respects, except that one of them pays some dividend before the expiry of the option. One way of overcoming the problem is to reduce the present value of the dividend from the spot price of the asset, using continuously compounding rates.

Applies to European-style Options The BSM applies for European options, which can be exercised only upon maturity. American options can be exercised at any point of time till the maturity date. One would imagine that the American option, which can be exercised at any time, should be more valuable than the European option, which offers exercise only at maturity. As stated earlier, it is always more prudent to sell the option rather than to exercise it. When one exercises an American call option well before maturity, one realizes only the intrinsic value, and foregoes the time value. The call will always be selling for more than its intrinsic value. By selling the call option, one realizes both the intrinsic value and the time value. Since it is always more prudent to sell a call rather than to exercise it, the BSM can be applied to American calls too without much problem. This is not true in the case of American puts. Further, it may be prudent to exercise the call very close to its maturity, sacrificing the time value remaining as protection against erosion in the intrinsic value.

> The BSM is applicable to European-style options only.

Other assumptions of BSM include (a) efficient markets, (b) no transaction costs, and (c) constant risk-free interest rates and (d) continuous trading.

INTERPRETING THE BSM

The log-normal distribution of price implies that the natural log is normally distributed, i.e., ln S is normally distributed. The mean and standard deviation of the natural log of the variable, i.e., of ln S, are given by

$$\text{Mean} = \ln S + (\mu - \sigma^2/2) \quad (12.23)$$
$$\text{Standard deviation} = \sigma \sqrt{T} \quad (12.24)$$

where S is the current price, μ is the expected return per annum and σ is the annual volatility of the price (μ is the annualized expected return in a short period of time).

Let us interpret the BSM for each of the terms that are included in the formula for determining the call price c:

$$c = SN(d_1) - Xe^{-rT} N(d_2)$$

where $d_1 = \dfrac{\ln(S/X) + (r + \sigma^2/2)T}{\sigma\sqrt{T}}$; and

$d_2 = \dfrac{\ln(S/X) + (r - \sigma^2/2)T}{\sigma\sqrt{T}}$ or $d_2 = d_1 - \sigma\sqrt{T}$

The first term $SN(d_1)$ can be said to be the cash inflow and the second term $Xe^{-rT} N(d_2)$ can be said to be the potential cash outflow of the exercise price.

The term $N(d_1)$ refers to the delta of the option, which represents the fraction of stock bought for each call written in a hedged portfolio. Hence, the first term is the value of the fraction of stock owned and is an asset.

The expression Xe^{-rT} reflects the present value of the exercise price discounted on a continuous basis. $N(d_2)$ can be interpreted as the probability of the call becoming in the money, i.e., the spot price exceeding the strike price. And it does entail cash outflow of X, the present value of which is Xe^{-rT}. The expected value of cash outflow is $Xe^{-rT} \times N(d_2)$.

The call price is the surplus of the asset owned, less any likely liability for the call written. Hence, the difference between the value of the stock position taken per call and the present value of the expected liability represents the call value at any point of time.

Put Pricing using BSM

The BSM can also be applied to the pricing of a put option. A put price as per BSM is given by

$$p = Xe^{-rT} N(-d_2) - SN(-d_1) \qquad (12.25)$$

where $d_1 = \dfrac{\ln(S/X) + (r + \sigma^2/2)T}{\sigma\sqrt{T}}$; and

$d_2 = \dfrac{\ln(S/X) + (r - \sigma^2/2)T}{\sigma\sqrt{T}}$ or $d_2 = d_1 - \sigma\sqrt{T}$

The formula is similar to that of the call price, with changed signs of X and S, as also with d_1 and d_2 being replaced by $-d_1$ and $-d_2$, respectively. We directly apply the BSM for determination of put prices. Please refer to Example 12.2.

MERTON MODEL FOR VALUING OPTIONS ON DIVIDEND PAYING STOCK

The BSM can be readily modified to work with dividend paying stocks. Robert Merton developed a simple extension of the BSM. Assuming a continuous compounded dividend of q, the BSM can be modified to obtaining the value of a call option on a dividend paying stock by (a) modifying the spot value by the present value of the dividend, and (b) modifying the growth $m = r + \sigma^2/2$ to $r - q + \sigma^2/2$. Adjusting the spot price with the dividend would result in the substitution of S with $S.e^{-qT}$. Similarly, the calculation of d_1 and d_2 would be adjusted to reflect the dividend, as stated in Eqs 12.27 and 12.28.

> With a little modification to the stock price, the BSM can be adapted for dividend paying stocks.

The rationale for such adjustment is that when a stock pays dividend, the price falls by the amount of dividend, because a stock that pays dividend should provide the same return as the one that pays no dividend. If a non-dividend paying stock grows by r, then a stock that pays dividend of q would grow by $r - q$, so that the total return stays the same at r.

EXAMPLE 12.2 Application of BSM: Put Premium

Given the following information about a share:
Current market price: ₹50, annual volatility: 30%, risk-free interest rate: 10%.

1. Find out the value of 3-m put options with exercise prices of (a) ₹40, (b) ₹50, and (c) ₹60.
2. What are the intrinsic and time values of these puts?

Solution
As per the BSM, the value of the put is given by:

$$p = Xe^{-rT} N(-d_2) - SN(-d_1)$$

where $d_1 = \dfrac{\ln(S/X) + (r + \sigma^2/2)T}{\sigma\sqrt{T}}$; and $d_2 = \dfrac{\ln(S/X) + (r - \sigma^2/2)T}{\sigma\sqrt{T}}$ or $d_2 = d_1 - \sigma\sqrt{T}$

(a) *For an exercise price of ₹40*
First, we find the values of d_1 and d_2. We have $S = 50$, $X = 40$, $r = 0.10$, $T = 0.25$, and $\sigma = 0.30$. These are plugged in the formula:

$$d_1 = \frac{\ln(50/40) + (0.10 + 0.30 \times 0.30/2) \times 0.25}{0.30 \times \sqrt{0.25}} = 1.7293$$

$$d_2 = d_1 - 0.30 \times \sqrt{0.25} = 1.7293 - 0.15 = 1.5793$$

From the normal distribution tables, or using the Excel function NORMSDIST(d), we find out the area under normal distribution for values less than $-d_1$ and $-d_2$.

We get $N(-d_1) = 0.0419$ and $N(-d_2) = 0.0571$

Inserting the values in the equation in the put premium, p

$$p = Xe^{-rT} N(-d_2) - S N(-d_1) = 40\, e^{-0.1 \times 0.25} \times 0.0571 - 50 \times 0.0419$$
$$= 2.2267 - 2.0950 = ₹0.13$$

The intrinsic value of the put is zero and the entire value of ₹0.13 represents the time value, the value attached with the chances that the put would turn ITM before expiry.

(b) *For an exercise price of ₹50*

$$d_1 = \frac{\ln(50/50) + (0.10 + 0.30 \times 0.30/2) \times 0.25}{0.30 \times \sqrt{0.25}} = 0.2417$$

$$d_2 = d_1 - 0.30 \times \sqrt{0.25} = 0.2417 - 0.15 = 0.0917$$

We get $N(-d_1) = 0.4045$ and $N(-d_2) = 0.4635$

Inserting the values in the equation in the put premium, p

$$p = Xe^{-rT} N(-d_2) - S N(-d_1) = 50\, e^{-0.1 \times 0.25} \times 0.4635 - 50 \times 0.4045$$
$$= 22.6028 - 20.2250 = ₹2.38$$

The put is ATM with zero intrinsic value. The premium of ₹2.38 belongs to the time value.

c) *For an exercise price of ₹60, we get*

$$d_1 = 0.9738,\ d_2 = 1.1238,\ N(-d_1) = 0.8349,\ \text{and } N(-d_2) = 0.8695$$
and put premium, $p = ₹9.14$

Here the put is in-the-money with an intrinsic value of ₹10. The present value of the exercise price is ₹58.52, and the minimum value of a European put option would be ₹8.52. The remaining premium of ₹0.62 represents the time value, the value attached with the likelihood of the put remaining in-the-money before expiry.
Notice that (a) the put can sell for less than its intrinsic value, and (b) the time value is highest for the ATM option.

> **Merton Model for Option Price on Dividend Paying Stock**
>
> $$c = Se^{-qT}.N(d_1) - X.e^{-rT}.N(d_2) \quad (12.26)$$
> $$p = X.e^{-rT}.N(-d_2) - Se^{-qT}.N(-d_1) \quad (12.27)$$
>
> where $d_1 = \dfrac{\ln(S/X) + (r - q + \sigma^2/2)T}{\sigma \sqrt{T}}$; and
>
> $d_2 = \dfrac{\ln(S/X) + (r - q - \sigma^2/2)T}{\sigma \sqrt{T}}$ or $d_2 = d_1 - \sigma \sqrt{T}$
>
> q = Dividend yield (continuous compounding basis)

In the computation of d_1 and d_2, the spot price S too would be replaced by Se^{-qt}. Since $\ln \dfrac{Se^{-qT}}{X} = \ln \dfrac{S}{X} - qT$, r would be replaced by $r - q$ in computing d_1 and d_2.

VALUING OPTIONS ON INDICES

> Stock indices are assumed to pay a continuous dividend. With changes in the spot price and the growth rate, the BSM applies to options on indices.

Options on indices are the same as options with dividend paying stocks. In the Indian stock market, options on indices are European in nature and as stated earlier, are cash settled on maturity. The lot size for option contracts is 50, and each point of Nifty is worth ₹1. For example, if on the last day of trading the clearing price of the index stood at 4150, a call option on Nifty with a strike of 4100 would be cash settled by payment of ₹2500 [(4150 − 4100) × 50] by the call writer to the call holder for each option contract.

The valuation of such an option would be the same as the valuation of an option on a dividend paying stock, where q would represent the average dividend yield on the index during the life of the option. The valuation of call and put options on an index is explained by way of Example 12.3.

VALUING OPTIONS ON CURRENCIES

Currency options are traded on exchanges, and are also available over the counter (OTC) all over the world. Options on currencies provide protection for receivables and payables against adverse movements of exchange rates, while retaining the upside potential. They are extremely useful for firms having assets and liabilities denominated in foreign currencies. Currency options remain very popular in the OTC market, where banks offer a variety of options for exporter and importer clients, as compared to exchange-traded options.

> The BSM applies to options on currencies with foreign risk-free interest rates, replacing the dividend yield in the valuation formula of options on indices.

Options on currencies are virtually the same as options on dividend paying stocks or options on indices. The valuation of options on currencies can be done by simply replacing the dividend yield on the index with the risk-free interest rate on the foreign currency, as given by Eqs 12.28 and 12.29. The spot price of the foreign currency must be expressed as a direct rate (number of units of domestic currency per unit of foreign currency, e.g., ₹45 per dollar in India).

EXAMPLE 12.3 Black–Scholes model for index options

The Nifty is currently at 4500. If the risk-free interest rate is 8% and the continuous dividend yield on Nifty is assumed at 3%, what would the value of a 3-m call option with an exercise of 4600 be? The volatility of the Nifty is placed at 25% p.a. One Nifty point is equal to ₹1.

Solution
As per the BSM, the value of the call on the index is given by

$$c = Se^{-qT} N(d_1) - Xe^{-rT} N(d_2)$$

where $d_1 = \dfrac{\ln(S/X) + (r - q + \sigma^2/2)T}{\sigma\sqrt{T}}$; and $d_2 = \dfrac{\ln(S/X) + (r - q - \sigma^2/2)T}{\sigma\sqrt{T}}$ or $d_2 = d_1 - \sigma\sqrt{T}$

Here, $S = 4500$, $X = 4600$, $r = 0.08$, $q = 0.03$, $Tt = 3/12 = 0.25$ years, and $\sigma = 0.25$, which can be used in the Black–Scholes–Merton formula for valuation of the call.

For an exercise value of index of 4600

First, we find the values of d_1 and d_2. All values used are annual and in decimal form. We have $S = 4500$, $X = 4600$, $r = 0.08$, $q = 0.03$, $T = 3$ months or 0.25 years, and $\sigma = 0.25$. These are plugged in the formula.

$$d_1 = \frac{\ln(4500/4600) + (0.08 - 0.03 + 0.25 \times 0.25/2) \times 0.25}{0.25 \times \sqrt{0.25}} = -0.0133$$

$$d_2 = d_1 - 0.25 \times \sqrt{0.25} = -0.1383$$

From the normal distribution tables, or using the Excel function NORMSDIST(d), we find out the area under normal distribution for values less than d_1 and d_2. We get

$$N(d_1) = 0.4947 \quad \text{and} \quad N(d_2) = 0.4450$$

Inserting the values in the call premium c,

$$c = Se^{-qT} N(d_1) - Xe^{-rT} N(d_2) = 4466.37 \times 0.4947 - 4600\, e^{-0.08 \times 0.25} \times 0.4450$$
$$= 2209.52 - 2006.47 = ₹203.05$$

Option Price on Foreign Currency

$$c = S.e^{-r_f T}.N(d_1) - X.e^{-rT}.N(d_2) \quad (12.28)$$
$$p = X.e^{-rT}.N(-d_2) - S.e^{-r_f T}.N(-d_1) \quad (12.29)$$

where $d_1 = \dfrac{\ln(S/X) + (r - r_f + \sigma^2/2)T}{\sigma\sqrt{T}}$; and

$d_2 = \dfrac{\ln(S/X) + (r - r_f - \sigma^2/2)T}{\sigma\sqrt{T}}$ or $d_2 = d_1 - \sigma\sqrt{T}$

r_f = Risk-free interest rate in foreign currency

Let us consider a 3-m ATM European call and a put on the euro with a spot price of ₹75 per euro. The risk-free interest rates in rupee and euro are 8% and 4%, respectively. The volatility of the exchange rate for the euro is 15%.

Here, $S = 75$, $X = 75$, $r = 0.08$, $r_f = 0.04$, $T = 3$ months (0.25 years), and $\sigma = 0.15$. Putting these values in Eqs 12.28 and 12.29 for valuing the call and the put, respectively, we get

$$d_1 = \frac{\ln(75/75) + (0.08 - 0.04 + 0.15 \times 0.15/2) \times 0.25}{0.15 \times \sqrt{0.25}} = 0.1708$$

$$d_2 = d_1 - 0.15 \times \sqrt{0.25} = 0.0958$$

$$N(d_1) = 0.5678 \quad N(d_2) = 0.5382 \quad N(-d_1) = 0.4322 \quad N(-d_2) = 0.4618$$

The call price, c = $S\,e^{-r_f T} N(d_1) - Xe^{-rT} N(d_2)$
= $75.00 \times e^{-0.04 \times 0.25} \times 0.5678 - 75\,e^{-0.08 \times 0.25} \times 0.5382$
= $74.25 \times 0.5678 - 73.51 \times 0.5382 = 42.16 - 39.17$
= ₹2.59

Put price, p = $Xe^{-rT} N(-d_2) - S\,e^{-r_f T} N(-d_1)$
= $75\,e^{-0.08 \times 0.25} \times 0.4618 - 75.00 \times e^{-0.04 \times 0.25} \times 0.4322$
= $73.51 \times 0.4618 - 74.25 \times 0.4322 = 33.99 - 32.09$
= ₹1.90

VALUING AMERICAN OPTIONS

We already know that for the same underlying asset and the same time to expiration, American options are like European options in all features except that the American options provide for an early exercise, as against exercise only at maturity in the case of European options. Is this flexibility of early exercise worth some extra value? If the extra value can be captured, then valuation of the American option would be a simple matter of adding this value to the price of the European option.

American Call vs European Call on Non-dividend Paying Asset

We have seen in Chapters 10 and 11 that for a non-dividend paying asset, it is never optimal to exercise a call option prior to its maturity because one gets only the intrinsic value of the option at the time of exercising and foregoes the time value attached. The entire value of a call option, i.e., the sum of the intrinsic value and the time value, would be captured in the selling price, and, hence, selling a call option is always a better proposition than exercising it. In the binomial model, this may be checked by comparing the exercise value with the market value at each node. Mathematically, the minimum value of a European call is

> For a non-dividend-paying asset, the feature of early exercise of call is worth nothing.

$$c \geq S - PV \text{ of } X \text{ or } S - Xe^{-rT}$$

Upon exercising the option, one gets the intrinsic value, i.e., $S - X$. As long as there is time remaining for maturity and the interest rates are not negative, the minimum price of a European call, c_{min}, would be larger than the intrinsic value, the value obtained by exercising an American call. Hence, the flexibility to exercise early in case of a call on a non-dividend paying asset has no extra value. Therefore, an American call should sell for no more than a European call for an underlying asset paying no dividend.

American Call on Dividend Paying Asset

In the case of a dividend paying stock, there may be a rationale to exercise early, because the amount of dividend the holder gets may be larger than the value of the call. We all know that immediately after a dividend (ex-dividend date), the stock price should fall by the amount of dividend. Therefore, the intrinsic value of the call would fall by the amount of dividend between the cum-dividend date and the ex-dividend date. Between these two dates, there would not be much loss of the time value of the call option. Hence, the dividend payout, even though causes some reduction in the intrinsic value, may far exceed the loss of time value, and prompt the holder of the call to exercise early.

As may be guessed, an early exercise is optimal just before the dividend payment date, and not at any other time. This would be applicable only in the case of an unknown dividend, where the call would be priced without adjusting for the dividend. However, if the dividend is known prior to the opening of the call position and the payment date falls before its maturity, the option pricing would be adjusted automatically for such anticipated and known dividend amount by replacing the asset price with the dividend-adjusted asset price, as was done in valuation using the Merton model.

Pseudo-pricing of American Call

First established by Fisher Black, the pseudo American call pricing model for a dividend-paying stock is based on the premise that it is optimal to exercise the call only just before the dividend payment date and not at any other point of time. Based on this, one may find call prices on each dividend date by using the BSM, suitably adjusting the stock price, the strike price, and the time to maturity. A stepwise approach is listed as follows:

> For a dividend paying asset, it may make sense to exercise a call just prior to dividend, and at no other time.

1. Modify the current stock price by subtracting the present values of all dividends until the expiration date of the option.
2. On each dividend date, subtract the present values of all the dividends remaining to be paid from the exercise price.
3. Consider each dividend date as a potential exercise date, and find the value of the option using the BSM with the asset prices as found in the first step in this list and the exercise price as found in the second step.
4. Compare the call prices computed and choose the one with the maximum value as the American call price.

We illustrate the procedure with the help of a numerical exercise. Assume that the current stock price is ₹100, and we need to value an American call with an exercise price of ₹100 expiring at the end of nine months from today. The stock is expected to pay dividends of ₹2.00, ₹2.50, and ₹3.00 at the end of two, five, and eight months from now, respectively. The volatility of the stock is 20% and the risk-free rate of return is 8%.

As per the pseudo-pricing, we treat the American call as a series of European calls maturing at the end of two, five, and eight months, i.e., the dividend paying dates, and nine months, i.e., the expiry date, assuming that the American call would be optimal to exercise only on these times and at no other time. Therefore, the American call, as a portfolio of a series of European calls, should command a premium equal to the maximum of the European calls.

> An American call on a dividend paying asset can be considered equivalent to a series of European calls on each dividend date.

Now we shall find out the values of four calls maturing at the end of two, five, eight, and nine months, making adjustments to the spot and exercise prices. The spot price as adjusted for the present values of the dividend would remain the same for all the four calls. The present value of all the dividends is:

$$= 2.00 \times e^{-0.08 \times 2/12} + 2.50 \times e^{-0.08 \times 5/12} + 3.00 \times e^{-0.08 \times 8/12}$$
$$= 1.9735 + 2.4180 + 2.8442 = ₹7.2357$$

Therefore, the adjusted stock price to be used in the BSM is $100 - 7.2357 = ₹92.7643$.

The calls maturing after two, five, eight, and nine months would have exercise prices X_2, X_5, X_8, and X_9, respectively. Each of them would be reduced by the present values of the remaining dividends just before the stock becomes ex-dividend. These are as follows:

$$X_9 = 100 - 0 = ₹100$$
$$X_8 = 100 - 3 = ₹97.00$$
$$X_5 = 100 - 2.50 - 3 \times e^{-.08 \times 3/12} = 100 - 2.50 - 2.9406 = ₹94.5594$$
$$X_2 = 100 - 2.00 - 2.50 \times e^{-.08 \times 3/12} - 3 \times e^{-.08 \times 6/12}$$
$$= 100 - 2 - 2.4505 - 2.8824 = ₹92.6671$$

Now the inputs for valuing all the four calls maturing at the end of two, five, eight, and nine months are known as required in the BSM. The spot price remains at ₹92.7634, with a standard deviation of 20% and a risk-free rate of 8% for all the four calls. The remaining inputs of exercise prices and times to maturity change. All figures relevant for the BSM are shown in Fig. 12.4.

For a standard deviation of 20% and a risk-free rate of 8%, the call prices for maturities of nine, eight, five, and two months are, respectively, ₹5.77, ₹6.42, ₹5.43, and ₹3.71. These are the prices derived for exercises just prior to dividend dates. An investor in the American

Figures in ₹

Time (months)	0	2	5	8	9 (Maturity)
Dividend		2.0000	2.5000	3.0000	
Total PV of dividend					
PV of dividend today	7.2357	1.9735	2.4180	2.8442	
PV of remaining dividends on dividend dates		2.8824	2.9406	3.0000	—
		2.4505	2.5000	—	
		2.0000	—		
Total PV of remaining dividends		7.3329	5.4406	3.0000	0.0000
Adjusted exercise price		92.6671	94.5594	97.0000	100.0000
Adjusted spot price				92.7634	
Call price today as per BSM		3.7113	5.4254	6.4218	5.7735
American call price = Max(call prices)		6.4218			

Standard deviation = 20% and risk-free rate = 8%

Fig. 12.4 Pseudo-American call pricing

EXAMPLE 12.4 Valuing an American call

A 12-m American call with an exercise price of ₹1100 is available on the stock of TCS Ltd. This stock is expected to pay quarterly dividends of ₹5.00, ₹6.00, ₹6.50, and ₹7.00 at the end of 1, 4, 7, and 10 months from now. The spot price of TCS is ₹1100. With a standard deviation of returns on TCS at 20% and a risk-free rate of 10%, find out the values of the inputs for valuing the 12-m American call on TCS.

Solution
To value a 12-m American call, we need to value five European calls maturing at 1, 4, 7, 10, and 12 months, with spot and exercise prices modified by the dividend amounts.

The price of the underlying asset, i.e., the stock of TCS, would remain the same for all the calls, and would be equal to the current stock price less the present values of all the dividends expected over the life of the option. The present value of the expected dividends are as follows:

$$= 5.00 \times e^{-0.1 \times 1/12} + 6.00 \times e^{-0.1 \times 4/12} + 6.50 \times e^{-0.1 \times 7/12} + 7.00 \times e^{-0.1 \times 10/12}$$
$$= 4.96 + 5.80 + 6.13 + 6.44 = ₹23.33$$

The spot price S that would be considered in all the calls would be

$$= 1100 - 23.33 = ₹1076.67$$

The exercise prices for the five calls would be arrived at by subtracting the present value of remaining dividends as on the date of respective dividend. These are as follows:

Call maturing at 12 months, X_{12} = ₹1100.00
Call maturing at 10 months, X_{10} = 1100 − 7.00 = ₹1093.00
Call maturing at 7 months, X_7 = 1100 − 7.00 × $e^{-0.1 \times 3/12}$ − 6.50
  = 1100 − 6.83 − 6.50 = ₹1086.67
Call maturing at 4 months, X_4 = 1100 − 7.00 × $e^{-0.1 \times 6/12}$ − 6.50 × $e^{-0.1 \times 3/12}$ − 6.00
  = 1100 − 6.66 − 6.34 − 6.00 = ₹1089.00
Call maturing at 1 month, X_1 = 1100 − 7.00 × $e^{-0.1 \times 9/12}$ − 6.50 × $e^{-0.1 \times 6/12}$
  − 6.00 × $e^{-0.1 \times 3/12}$ − 5.00
  = 1100 − 6.49 − 6.18 − 5.86 − 5.00 = ₹1076.47

Remaining inputs of standard deviation and risk-free rate would remain the same as given for valuing the 5 European options. The maximum value of these would be taken as price of an American option.

---

call can be assumed to be holding a series of four calls with four potential exercising opportunities available on any of the four cum-dividend dates. As is evident from the calculations shown in Fig. 12.4, it is optimal to exercise just prior to the third dividend payment, i.e., at the eighth month from now. Therefore, an American call would sell for ₹6.42.

In contrast, a 9-m European call with $S = 92.76$, $X = 100.00$, $T = 9$ months, $r = 8\%$, and $\sigma = 20\%$ would sell for ₹5.7624, as given by the BSM option pricing formula.

EXACT PRICING OF AMERICAN OPTION

An exact analytical solution for any American option is possible only for an asset that pays only a single dividend during the option period. This is known as the Roll, Geske, and Whaley formula for a dividend of D at time t before the expiry of the option at T. The valuation is dependent on some critical asset price S^* just prior to the dividend date. It is that price of the asset at which, on the dividend payment date, the intrinsic value is equal to the call value plus the dividend on that date. The exercise would be made only when the intrinsic value $S^* - X + D$ is greater than the call value at that time. The Roll, Geske, and Whaley formula for American call options on assets with single dividends is given in the box.

When several dividends are anticipated, it is generally believed that it would be optimal to exercise only on the last dividend date. Under that assumption, such options can also be treated as options with single dividends. Therefore, the Roll, Geske, and Whaley formula can be used by reducing the spot price by the present value of all the dividends except the last one.

Valuation of American Call for Single Dividend

$$c = (S - De^{-rt}).N(b_1) - (X - D)e^{-rT}.N(b_2)$$
$$+ (S - De^{-rt}).M\left(a_1, -b_1, -\sqrt{\frac{t}{T}}\right) - Xe^{-rT}.M\left(a_2, -b_2, -\sqrt{\frac{t}{T}}\right)$$

where
$$a_1 = \frac{\ln\left[\frac{S - De^{-rt}}{X}\right] + \left(r + \frac{\sigma^2}{2}\right)T}{\sigma\sqrt{T}}; \text{ and } a_2 = a_1 - \sigma\sqrt{T}$$

$$b_1 = \frac{\ln\left[\frac{S - De^{-rt}}{S^*}\right] + \left(r + \frac{\sigma^2}{2}\right)T}{\sigma\sqrt{T}}; \text{ and } b_2 = b_1 - \sigma\sqrt{T}$$

Roll, Geske, and Whaley Formula

- S = Price of underlying asset
- X = Exercise price
- S^* = Critical stock price at dividend payment
- D = Dividend amount at time t
- T = Time for expiration
- t = Time of dividend payment $< T$
- σ = Annualized standard deviation
- r = Risk-free rate of return
- $N(x)$ = Cumulative normal distribution function at x
- $M(a, b, r)$ = Value of cumulative bivariate normal distribution with first variable less than a and second variable less than b with correlation of r
- ln = Natural log

VOLATILTY

Option price calculation using the BSM formula requires inputs of stock price S, exercise price X, risk-free rate of return r, time to maturity T, and volatility of the prices of the stock σ.

Of these variables, X and T are those characteristics of the option that are defined. The stock price S is directly observable for traded assets. The remaining two variables, the risk-free rate and the volatility of the stock price need to be obtained. The risk-free rate r can be observed from debt markets from the yield on T–bills for a maturity matching the life of the option. At present, the life of the options is restricted to three months in India, for which T-bill returns are readily available. The last variable, i.e., the volatility of stock prices, is not directly observable from the traded information. It is required to be estimated. Normally, historical volatility of the stock prices is used as an input of standard deviation in the BSM of option valuation.

> Volatility in spot prices is a major driver of option premium. The more the volatility, the more valuable is the option, irrespective of it being a call or a put.

We reiterate that volatility of return over time interval T is proportional to the standard deviation of returns measured over a small interval multiplied by the square root of the number of time intervals. This means that if daily prices are observed for finding the standard deviation of daily returns σ_{daily}, then the annual volatility is equal to $\sigma_{daily} \times \sqrt{250}$ if we assume 250 to be the number of trading days in a year. Similarly, if weekly data for 52 weeks is used, then we can approximate the annual volatility as $\sigma_{weely} \times \sqrt{52}$.

> Volatility of the price of an underlying asset is the non-observed parameter in option price determination. It needs to be measured.

MEASURING HISTORICAL VOLATILITY

The BSM assumes log-normal distribution of returns on stocks. The volatility of returns may be derived from past price data. The past price data have to be converted into price relative (S_n/S_{n-1}) and the natural log of the price relative is taken. This natural log is deemed to have a normal distribution. The historical volatility can be calculated using EXCEL in the following manner.

1. Feed the price data (daily, weekly, or monthly) for a sufficient number of periods, n. The number of observations required for estimation of volatility is not easy to determine. As we increase the observations, the older data lose relevance, and if we reduce the number of observations, we compromise on accuracy. Data more than one year old cannot be relied upon.
2. Find out the relative return for a period by dividing the price of the period by that of the preceding period.
3. Find out the natural log of the relative return, X
4. Find out the mean of natural log returns and its variance as follows:

$$\text{Mean}, \overline{X} = \frac{\text{Sum of natural log returns}}{\text{No. of observations}, n}, \text{ and}$$

$$\text{Variance}, \sigma^2 = \sum_{1}^{n} \frac{(X - \overline{X})^2}{n - 1}$$

5. The standard deviation calculated for the period is not the same for annual returns. This needs to be converted into an annual measure as shown in Eq. 12.30.

$$\sigma_{annual} = \sigma_{period} * \sqrt{T} \qquad (12.30)$$

where T = number of periods per annum

We know that the variance, σ^2, is proportional to time.

The annual standard deviation from the weekly data will be equal to the calculated standard deviation $\times \sqrt{52}$. This is the volatility that needs to be used in the BSM formula.

> Volatility of the stock can be measured from the past price data. The measured volatility may be used as input for determining the option value.

One such calculation of historical volatility is shown in Table 12.2, where the weekly closing prices for 52 weeks are taken in column 2. The relative returns and their natural logs are shown in the next two columns. The mean is calculated by dividing the sum of the natural logs by 51, the number of observations. The weekly variance is calculated by dividing the sum of variance by $n - 1$, i.e., 50, and converted into annual variance using Eq. 12.30. The weekly standard deviation is 3.17%, which is equivalent to an annual

Table 12.2 Calculating historical volatility

Week No.	Observed price (₹)	Relative return	Natural log of relative return	Variance
1	510			
2	525	1.02941	0.02899	0.00084
3	530	1.00952	0.00948	0.00009
4	490	0.92453	−0.07847	0.00616
5	460	0.93878	−0.06318	0.00399
6	495	1.07609	0.07333	0.00538
7	495	1.00000	0.00000	0.00000
8	478	0.96566	−0.03495	0.00122
9	468	0.97908	−0.02114	0.00045
10	483	1.03205	0.03155	0.00100
11	496	1.02692	0.02656	0.00071
12	501	1.01008	0.01003	0.00010
13	515	1.02794	0.02756	0.00076
14	513	0.99612	−0.00389	0.00002
15	512	0.99805	−0.00195	0.00000
16	505	0.98633	−0.01377	0.00019
17	525	1.03960	0.03884	0.00151
18	530	1.00952	0.00948	0.00009
19	545	1.02830	0.02791	0.00078
20	536	0.98349	−0.01665	0.00028
21	533	0.99440	−0.00561	0.00003
22	541	1.01501	0.01490	0.00022
23	536	0.99076	−0.00929	0.00009
24	528	0.98507	−0.01504	0.00023
25	509	0.96402	−0.03665	0.00134
26	522	1.02554	0.02522	0.00064
27	516	0.98851	−0.01156	0.00013
28	519	1.00581	0.00580	0.00003
29	489	0.94220	−0.05954	0.00355
30	493	1.00818	0.00815	0.00007
31	496	1.00609	0.00607	0.00004
32	513	1.03427	0.03370	0.00114
33	515	1.00390	0.00389	0.00002
34	522	1.01359	0.01350	0.00018

(Contd)

Table 12.2 contd

Week No.	Observed price (₹)	Relative return	Natural log of relative return	Variance
35	534	1.02299	0.02273	0.00052
36	500	0.93633	−0.06579	0.00433
37	495	0.99000	−0.01005	0.00010
38	499	1.00808	0.00805	0.00006
39	490	0.98196	−0.01820	0.00033
40	521	1.06327	0.06134	0.00376
41	509	0.97697	−0.02330	0.00054
42	533	1.04715	0.04607	0.00212
43	538	1.00938	0.00934	0.00009
44	546	1.01487	0.01476	0.00022
45	524	0.95971	−0.04113	0.00169
46	520	0.99237	−0.00766	0.00006
47	495	0.95192	−0.04927	0.00243
48	505	1.02020	0.02000	0.00040
49	516	1.02178	0.02155	0.00046
50	511	0.99031	−0.00974	0.00009
51	532	1.04110	0.04027	0.00162
52	525	0.98684	−0.01325	0.00018
Sum			0.02899	0.05025
Mean			0.00057	
Variance (weekly)				0.00101
Standard deviation (weekly)				0.03170
Annual variance				0.05226
Annual standard deviation				0.22861

volatility of 22.86% (3.17 × 52). In case we use the daily prices, the data will provide daily volatility and in that case, the annual volatility will be calculated by multiplying the computed figure by 250, assuming 250 trading days in a year.

Volatility is dynamic. To produce realistic results, the calculation of volatility has to find a balance between the number of observations and the age of the observations. For accuracy and reliability required to produce a reasonable predictor of future volatility, we need to have a sufficiently large sample (say about 50) and recent data; both requirements are difficult to comply with simultaneously. If we increase the sample size, the data becomes old and loses relevance for future usage. If we believe only in relatively recent data, then the number of observations becomes limited. Therefore, more often than not, daily data for stock prices is used. At most, we can take only weekly closings, which would mean the sample data is not more than a year old. Data older than one year cannot be deemed as truly representative of future volatility, as volatility cannot be assumed to be constant for longer periods, especially if the sectors are evolving and dynamic, such as information technology or telecommunication. One may be more assured of reliability if the sectors are traditional, such as cement and steel.

Another way of overcoming the limitation in measurement of volatility from past data is to assign more weight to recent data and less weight to older data. This method, known as exponential smoothing, is normally followed by stock exchanges in calculating margin requirements for derivative traders. It is easier to apply this concept than calculating on a daily basis.

Adjusting Dividend While calculating the relative returns, adjustments for dividend also need to be made. We all know that in efficient markets, the price of a stock falls by the amount of dividend on the ex-dividend date. Hence, the returns on the ex-dividend date will stand modified to $(S_{n+1} + D)/S_n$. The data in Table 12.2 assumes a non-dividend paying stock. If the stock pays a dividend of ₹20 and becomes ex-dividend in week 36, then the relative return of 0.93633 (500/534) for week 36 will stand modified to 0.97378 (520/534). All other figures remain the same.

Actual vs Trading Days Another issue that needs attention is the number of periods to be used while converting the period volatility to annual volatility. The question is whether to use the actual elapsed time or the number of trading days. It is generally believed that volatility is caused by the flow of information, which does not depend on trading. In fact, trading depends upon information flow. In view of the continuous flow of information, it is argued that the actual number of days should be used for translation into annual volatility. However, it has been studied that though volatilities are higher in periods with intervening holidays, they are not proportionate with the lengths of time. Volatility is much higher when trading takes place. Hence, we use only the number of trading days to arrive at annual volatility.

IMPLIED VOLATILITY

The volatility used in the BSM is an unobservable statistic. Using historical volatility in the BSM formula for arriving at option prices may not match with the market prices prevailing for calls and puts. The reason for the divergence between the theoretical prices as per the BSM and the actual market prices may lie in the different estimates of volatility used by the market, which may not conform to the historical volatility used in the BSM formula.

To illustrate, we may calculate the price of a call option as per BSM as ₹29.36, with $S = 500$, $X = 500$, $T = 0.25$ years, and $r = 10\%$, using $\sigma = 23\%$ as measured using historical data. The actual market price happens to be ₹35.00. How do we explain this divergence in the prices? The only plausible explanation can lie in the different estimates of volatility used by the market and the BSM, as there exists no ambiguity about the other four variables, $S, X, T,$ and r, that affect the call price.

> Options when traded imply volatility in price, which may be different than the measured volatility based on historical data.

While the BSM used historical volatility in its calculation of the call premium, the market is more concerned with the future volatility of returns. As long as historical volatility truly represents future volatility, the actual prices would not deviate from the theoretical prices. Since the market price represents the collective wisdom of investors, we have to accept it as a better estimate of volatility, even though it does not agree with the theory. All theories must explain practice, else they become redundant. Assuming that the market price of a call is correct, and also that the BSM is valid, the actual call price must reflect a volatility that is implied in the BSM formula. Hence, given the four parameters of S, X, T, and r and the market-determined call price, we can solve the BSM equation for σ. This volatility, derived from the BSM, is implied in the call premium prevailing in the market, and makes the equation of the option price hold. Implied volatility is that σ which makes the BSM formula hold.

Estimating Implied Volatility

There is a repetitive iterative procedure to find implied volatility. It is to compute the price of the option using the BSM with assumed volatility till it matches the actual price of the option prevailing in the market. Unfortunately, there is no direct way to solve for σ using market-determined call prices.

> The volatility that matches the Black–Scholes price to the actual market price is called implied volatility.

Since a call premium is an increasing function of volatility, the price must rise with increasing volatility and reduce with decreasing volatility. Suppose the market price of a call is ₹35. We start the iterative process of matching the theoretical price to the actual price by changing the volatility. As a first guess, we use $\sigma = 23\%$, and find BSM value of the call. If the BSM value, say ₹33.00, is less than ₹35, we need to increase the σ, or else decrease it. If the BSM price is equal to the market price, then our estimate of volatility is correct. We continue this process till we achieve the desired accuracy in the volatility estimates.

As a first attempt, we increase the value of σ from 23% to 30% and calculate the call premium. Say, we get a value of ₹36. Since this value is greater than the market price, we may try the reduced number of 28% as the next approximation. Assume that this time the call premium comes to ₹34. Now we can do a linear extrapolation of the two figures of ₹34 and ₹36 for volatilities of 28% and 30% (₹1.00 per 1%). We conclude that the implied volatility at the call price of ₹35 is around 29%.

Does implied volatility mean that historical volatility is of no significance? Certainly not! Historical volatility provides insight into what has been the general level of risk with the stock prices. Implied volatility is something that is assigned by the market for the future. Though the future is not necessarily dependent upon the past, it is not independent of it either. One must find an explanation for divergence in the estimates of volatility. Historical volatility will provide a base for further study of causes of divergence.

Volatility Smiles It is not necessary that implied volatility as reflected in the call premium of one option is the same for all other calls, even though they are on the same underlying assets and have the same expiration, though with different exercise prices. Using two different calls with different strike prices will most likely provide different implied volatilities. The implied volatility of deep ITM and deep OTM options is expected to be larger than for ATM options. As the strike price moves away from the spot price, volatility is expected to rise. A sample plot of implied volatility with an increasing exercise

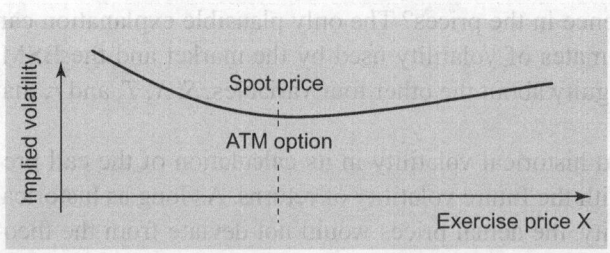

Fig. 12.5 Volatility smiles

price is shown in Fig. 12.5. It gets the name volatility smile from its shape, resembling a smile. It is suggested to use the weighted average of all such implied volatilities as a measure of total volatility of the stock. The weights of different strike prices are left to investors' discretion. There may be no fixed formula for the weights due to the varying characteristics of stocks. Alternatively, one can use the implied volatility of an ATM option, as it is regarded as a truer representative of price change.

SOLVED PROBLEMS

SP 12.1: Application of the BSM: Call premium

Assume a share is trading at ₹100. A dividend of ₹1.50 each is expected at the end of 3, 6, 9, and 10 months from now. The risk-free rate of interest is 8%, and the stock price has volatility of 25%. What is the value of (a) a call option with an exercise price of ₹110, with maturity of six months, and (b) a call option with an exercise price of ₹100, with maturity of 12 months?

Solution
As per the BSM, the value of the call is given by

$$c = SN(d_1) - Xe^{-rT} N(d_2)$$

where $d_1 = \dfrac{\ln(S/X) + (r + \sigma^2/2)T}{\sigma\sqrt{T}}$; and

$d_2 = \dfrac{\ln(S/X) + (r - \sigma^2/2)T}{\sigma\sqrt{T}}$ or $d_2 = d_1 - \sigma\sqrt{T}$

(a) For a 6-m call, there would be two dividends at the end of three and six months that are expected to be paid within the option period. The PV of these dividends is

$$= D_1 e^{-rt_1} + D_2 e^{-rt_2} = 1.50\, e^{-0.08 \times 0.25} + 1.50\, e^{-0.08 \times 0.50}$$
$$= 1.50 \times 0.9802 + 1.50 \times 0.9608$$
$$= 1.47 + 1.44 = ₹2.91$$

Under the BSM, the spot price would be reduced by the PV of the dividends. The variables in BSM would then be:

$S = 100 - 2.91 = 97.09$, $X = 110$, $T = 0.50$, $r = 0.08$, and $\sigma = 0.25$

$$d_1 = \dfrac{\ln(97.09/110) + (0.08 + 0.25 \times 0.25/2) \times 0.5}{0.25 \times \sqrt{0.5}} = -0.3916$$

$$d_2 = d_1 - 0.25 \times \sqrt{0.5} = -0.5683$$

$N(d_1) = 0.3477$ and $N(d_2) = 0.2849$

Inserting the values in the equation in the call premium c,

$$c = S\, N(d_1) - Xe^{-rT} N(d_2) = 97.09 \times 0.3477 - 110 e^{-0.08 \cdot 0.25} \times 0.2849 = 33.76 - 30.11 = ₹3.65$$

(b) For a 12-month call, there would be four dividends at the end of 3, 6, 9, and 12 months that are expected to be paid within the option period. The PV of these dividends is

$$= D_1 e^{-rt_1} + D_2 e^{-rt_2} + D_3 e^{-rt_3} + D_4 e^{-rt_4}$$
$$= 1.50\, e^{-0.08 \times 0.25} + 1.50\, e^{-0.08 \times 0.50} + 1.50\, e^{-0.08 \times 0.75} + 1.50\, e^{-0.08 \times 1.00}$$
$$= 1.50 \times 0.9802 + 1.50 \times 0.9608 + 1.50 \times 0.9418 + 1.50 \times 0.9231$$
$$= 1.47 + 1.44 + 1.41 + 1.38 = ₹5.70$$

Under the BSM, the spot price would be reduced by the PV of the dividends. The variables in BSM would then be:

$S = 100 - 5.70 = 94.30$, $X = 100$, $T = 1.00$, $r = 0.08$, and $\sigma = 0.25$

$$d_1 = \dfrac{\ln(94.30/100) + (0.08 + 0.25 \times 0.25/2) \times 1.0}{0.25 \times \sqrt{1.0}} = 0.2102$$

$$d_2 = d_1 - 0.25 \times \sqrt{1.0} = -0.0398$$

$N(d_1) = 0.5833$ and $N(d_2) = 0.4841$

Inserting the values in the equation in the call premium c,

$$c = S\,N(d_1) - Xe^{-rT} N(d_2) = 94.30 \times 0.5833 - 100\,e^{-0.08 \times 0.25} \times 0.4841 = 55.00 - 44.69 = ₹10.31$$

SP 12.2: Black–Scholes model for index options

The Nifty is currently at 4500. If the risk-free interest rate is 8% and the continuous dividend yield on Nifty is assumed at 3%, what would the value of a 3-m put option with an exercise of 4600 be? The volatility of the Nifty is placed at 25% p.a.

Solution
As per the BSM, the value of the put on the index is given by

$$p = Xe^{-rT} N(-d_2) - Se^{-qT} N(-d_1)$$

where
$$d_1 = \frac{\ln(S/X) + (r - q + \sigma^2/2)T}{\sigma\sqrt{T}}; \text{ and}$$

$$d_2 = \frac{\ln(S/X) + (r - q - \sigma^2/2)T}{\sigma\sqrt{T}} \quad \text{or} \quad d_2 = d_1 - \sigma\sqrt{T}$$

Here $S = 4500$, $X = 4600$, $r = 0.08$, $q = 0.03$, $T = 3/12 = 0.25$ years, and $\sigma = 0.25$, which can be used in the Black–Scholes–Merton formula for valuation of the call.

For an exercise value of 4600
First we find the values of d_1 and d_2. All values used are annual and in decimal form. We have $S = 4500$, $X = 4600$, $r = 0.08$, $q = 0.03$, $T = 3$ months or 0.25 years, and $\sigma = 0.25$. These are plugged in the formula as follows:

$$d_1 = \frac{\ln(4500/4600) + (0.08 - 0.03 + 0.25 \times 0.25/2) \times 0.25}{0.25 \times \sqrt{0.25}} = 0.2102$$

$$d_2 = d_1 - 0.25 \times \sqrt{0.25} = -0.1383$$

$N(-d_1) = 0.5053$ and $N(-d_2) = 0.5550$

Inserting the values in the equation in the put premium p

$$p = Xe^{-rT} N(-d_2) - S\,e^{-qT} N(-d_1) = 4600\,e^{-0.08 \times 0.25} \times 0.5550 - 4466.37 \times 0.5053 = 2502.45 - 2256.86 = ₹245.59$$

SP 12.3: Currency Option

The exchange rate for the US dollar in India is ₹49.00. The risk-free interest rate in India and the USA are 4% and 8%, respectively. The volatility of the exchange rate is 20%. What is the value of a 3-m call with an exercise price of ₹50.00?

Solution
Here $S = 49$, $X = 50$, $r = 0.04$, $r_f = 0.08$, $T = 3$ months (0.25 years), and $\sigma = 0.20$. Putting these values in Eq. 12.28 for valuing the call, we get

$$d_1 = \frac{\ln(49/50) + (0.04 - 0.08 + 0.20 \times 0.20/2) \times 0.25}{0.20 \times \sqrt{0.25}} = 0.2520$$

$$d_2 = d_1 - 0.20 \times \sqrt{0.25} = 0.3520$$

$N(d_1) = 0.4005$ and $N(d_2) = 0.3624$

Call price, $c = S\,e^{-r_f T} N(d_1) - Xe^{-rT} N(d_2)$
$= 49.00 \times e^{-0.08 \times 0.25} \times 0.4005 - 50\,e^{-0.04 \times 0.25} \times 0.3624$
$= 48.03 \times 0.4005 - 49.50 \times 0.3624 = 19.24 - 17.94$
$= ₹1.30$

SUMMARY

Determination of option premiums has been one of the most challenging areas. Various methodologies have been used. Two methods of valuation—the binomial model and the BSM—are discussed.

Six factors that impact the value of options are the spot value of the underlying asset, the exercise price of the option, the maturity of the option, volatility in price of the underlying asset, the risk-free interest rate, and the dividend. The price of a call increases and of a put decreases with an increase in the spot price. With an increase in the exercise price, the value of the put increases and that of the call decreases. With more time to maturity and increasing volatility, the value of the call as well as the put increases. An increased risk-free rate increases the value of the call and decreases the value of the put.

The BSM has been one of the landmarks in the history of financial management. The model applies to European-style options on non-dividend paying stocks. It assumes log-normal distribution of stock prices and uses extensive mathematics to provide an analytical solution. Valuations by the BSM are used by managers and industry analysts alike.

Merton modified the BSM formula for European options on stock that pay a dividend. This formula can be modified to apply to value options on indices by replacing the dividend by the yield on the index. Similarly, it can also be used, by substituting the dividend with the foreign risk-free interest rate, for valuing options on foreign currencies.

An American option is extremely difficult to value, as there are innumerable times where the holder has to make a choice between exercising or not exercising. For a non-dividend paying asset, it is already established that early exercise is worth nothing. However, for a dividend paying asset, it may be worth something. Pseudo-pricing of American options assumes that the optimal time to exercise can only be just prior to dividend payment, and prescribes a method based on this principle. An American call can be viewed as a portfolio of calls with exercises at each dividend payment date, and the value of the American call can be said to be the maximum of all the calls. An exact analytical solution is available for American options on dividend-paying stock that pay only a single dividend over their life spans.

Volatility in the price of the underlying asset is the key determinant of option prices. Of all the five parameters that affect option value, only this one parameter, volatility, is not observable. Using an analytical model requires input of a volatility value, which can be measured from past prices. However, option prices are observable and incorporate estimates of future volatility. The observed option price would imply volatility. Volatility that equates the value of an option by an analytical model to the actual price is called implied volatility.

KEY TERMS

Historical volatility The standard deviation of returns in the past.
Implied volatility The volatility at which the fair price of an option as determined by the BSM matches the actual market price.

Normal distribution A bell-shaped probability distribution that is completely defined by its mean and variance.

QUESTIONS

12.1 What are the determinants of option prices? How would a call price change with changes in (a) the spot price, (b) the exercise price, (c) volatility, and (d) the risk-free interest rate?

12.2 What are the assumptions of the BSM?

12.3 How does the BSM change to incorporate valuation of an option on (a) dividend paying stock, (b) indices, and (c) currencies?

12.4 Outline the assumptions under the pseudo American pricing method developed by Black.

12.5 How would you measure volatility of a stock? Describe the process.

12.6 What are the differences between historical volatility, future volatility, and implied volatility?

PROBLEMS

P 12.1 Value of call—the BSM
A stock is trading at ₹105.00. You are willing to write a call on the stock, exercisable at the end of three months, with a strike price of ₹110.00. If the risk-free rate of interest is 12% p.a. and the stock has exhibited volatility of 30% based on past data, what premium would you like to charge for writing the call?

P 12.2 Put value by the BSM—put–call parity
Refer to P 12.1. Find out the value of a put having the same parameters as the call. Confirm whether put–call parity holds.

P 12.3 Value options on indices with the BSM
Find the value of a 3-m call option on the Nifty with a strike of 4900, with the index trading at 4800. The volatility of the index is 10%, and the index provides a yield of 2%. The risk-free rate is 8% p.a.

P 12.4 Put options on indices and put–call parity
Find also the value of a put option based on the parameters given in P 12.3 using the BSM. Verify your result using put–call parity.

P 12.5 Black–Scholes valuation for options on currencies
The spot rate for the euro is ₹68.00. A call option with a strike of ₹69.00 expiring in three months is available. What would be the premium on the call option if the risk-free interest rate for the Indian rupee and the euro are 12% and 8%, respectively, and the volatility of the rupee–euro exchange rate is 20%? Find also the value of the put using the same parameters and establish put–call parity for an option on a currency.

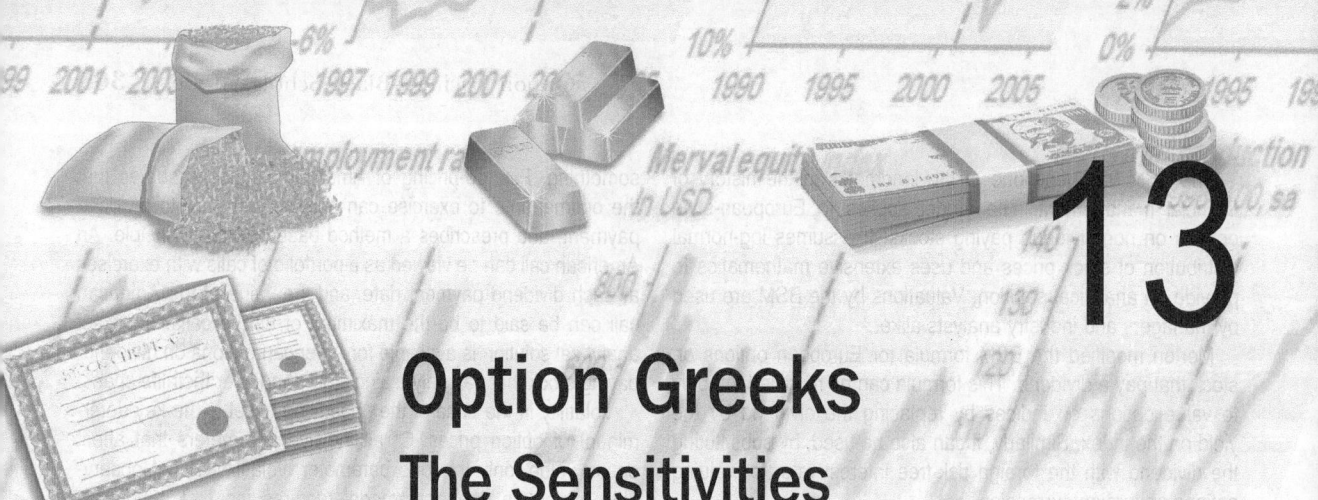

13

Option Greeks
The Sensitivities

INTRODUCTION

In the previous chapters, we have learnt that option value depends upon five parameters, namely, the spot value of the underlying asset S, the exercise price X, the time remaining for expiration T, the risk-free rate of return, and the volatility measured by standard deviation σ. Once the option has been traded, its value keeps changing with any change in each variable, except the exercise price. Those holding a portfolio of options, therefore, have to constantly monitor the prices with respect to each variable. It is easily understood that each determinant would have the some impact on an option's price.

In this chapter, we study the impact of change in each variable on option price. Variations in option value with respect to each determinant of price are denoted by Greek letters such as delta, gamma, theta, rho, and vega (an exception, as vega is not a Greek letter), and, hence, they are also referred to as *option Greeks*. Any change in the value of an option with respect to any variable is found by identifying the partial derivative[1] of the price equation with respect to the single determinant of price. Options Greeks for determinants of price are as follows:

> Option Greeks refer to the sensitivity of option prices with respect to the determinants of price.

Learning Objectives

After going through this chapter, readers should be familiar with

- the behaviour and sensitivity of option value with respect to each of its various determinants
- the computation of delta, theta, gamma, vega, and rho—the parameters of sensitivity of option value
- the importance of delta and delta hedging
- the study of gamma
- the meaning of delta neutrality and gamma neutrality, and how to achieve them simultaneously
- the concept of time decay

Greek letter	Variable/determinant of option price
Delta	Change in asset price
Theta	Time left for maturity
Gamma	Change of change in price
Rho	Change in the risk-free rate
Vega	Change in volatility

---
[1] Partial derivative is found by taking differentiation of the function, including many determinants, with respect to one determinant, assuming the rest of them constant.

DELTA AND DELTA HEDGING

While discussing the pricing of a call option under the equivalent portfolio approach, we defined the term *option delta*. The option delta represents the sensitivity of the option price to change in the price of the underlying asset.

The option delta, denoted by Δ (Greek letter delta) is defined as the first partial derivative of the price of the option with respect to changes in the spot price. It indicates the magnitude of change in the option value with the spot price of the underlying asset.

$$\Delta_c = \frac{\partial c}{\partial S} \qquad (13.1)$$

where ∂c = change in the value of the call option, and
∂S = change in the spot price of the underlying asset

The price of a European call option as per the Black Scholes model (BSM) for a non-dividend paying stock using the five determinants is given by

$$c = SN(d_1) - Xe^{-rT} N(d_2)$$

where d_1 and d_2 are defined as follows:

$$d_1 = \frac{\ln(S/X) + (r + \sigma^2/2)T}{\sigma\sqrt{T}}; \text{ and}$$

$$d_2 = \frac{\ln(S/X) + (r - \sigma^2/2)T}{\sigma\sqrt{T}} \quad \text{or} \quad d_2 = d_1 - \sigma\sqrt{T}$$

Computing Delta

Taking the first partial derivative of the call value with respect to the spot price S, we get the delta of the call option:

> A call delta is positive and less than 1, and a put delta is negative, but less than –1.

$$\Delta_c = \frac{\partial c}{\partial S} = N(d_1) \qquad (13.2)$$

Similarly, the value of the put is given by

$$p = Xe^{-rt} N(-d_2) - SN(-d_1)$$

and the delta of the put option is found by taking the partial derivative with respect to the price of the underlying asset S, given by

$$\Delta_p = \frac{\partial p}{\partial S} = -N(-d_1) = N(d_1) - 1 \qquad (13.3)$$

Alternatively, the delta of the put option can also be found by using put–call parity, which states that

$$c - p = S - Xe^{-rT}$$

The delta of stock is one, and the delta of bonds is zero, providing the relationship between the deltas of calls and puts as

$$\Delta_p = \Delta_c - 1 = N(d_1) - 1$$

Meaning of and Limits on Value of Delta

> Positive delta implies that any change would be in the same direction as that of the asset price. It is also referred to as the hedge ratio.

Remember from our discussions on call option pricing under the binomial approach that the delta denoted the number of shares one must have for each call written to have the same payoffs at the end of option period.

Since the value of $N(d_1)$ is between 0 and 1, the delta of a call would always be ≥ 0 and ≤ 1. For a stock trading at ₹500 with a standard deviation of 25% and a risk-free rate of 6%, the value of the delta for a 3-m call option with $X = 500$ is 0.5724. An option delta of 0.5724 means that if the value of the underlying asset changes by ₹1, the value of the option would change by ₹0.5724 in the same direction as that of the asset value.

Similarly, the delta of a put option is always between 0 and −1.00. The negative value of the delta for a put option indicates an inverse relationship of the put value with the price of the underlying asset. If the delta of the call is 0.55, the delta of the put on the same asset would be −0.45, and this would mean that an increase in the price of the underlying asset by ₹1 would cause the put value to decrease by ₹0.45.

From Eqs. 13.2 and 13.3, we can make out that the sum of the mod (absolute) values of delta for non-dividend paying European call and put options on the same underlying asset, with the same time to maturity, and the same strike price, equals one. For American options, the sum can exceed one, though marginally only.[2]

The delta is also referred to as the hedge ratio, as it indicates how many units of the underlying asset are required to replicate the returns on the option. The delta of a short position in an option would be the opposite of that for the long position. If a call option delta was 0.45, then the value of a long position on the call would increase by ₹0.45 and of a short position decrease by ₹0.45 with ₹1 increase in the price of the underlying asset. While a long position in a put has a negative delta (the price of the put falls with an increase in the spot price), it is positive for short positions.

Assumption of Linearity

The expected change in the value of a call option for a given change in the spot value is given by

> The option delta is the change in the price of an option with respect to a small change in the price of the asset. It is not valid for large changes.

$$\delta c = \Delta c \delta S \qquad (13.4)$$

The validity of Eq. 13.4 holds only for infinitesimally small changes in the price of the underlying asset. The value of the call option does not change linearly with the underlying. The assumption of linearity holds good only for a small range of changes in the value of the underlying asset, as depicted in Fig. 13.1. This implies that as the value of the asset undergoes more than a small change, the value of the delta too would change. The estimate of change in the value of the option based on the delta is at best an approximation. The extent of change in the value of the delta would depend upon the curvature of the option value with the spot price. The change in the delta with the change in the spot value is denoted by another Greek letter called gamma, discussed later.

---

[2] Rendleman Jr, Richard J., *Applied Derivatives - Options, Futures and Swaps,* Blackwell Publishers, 2002, p. 124.

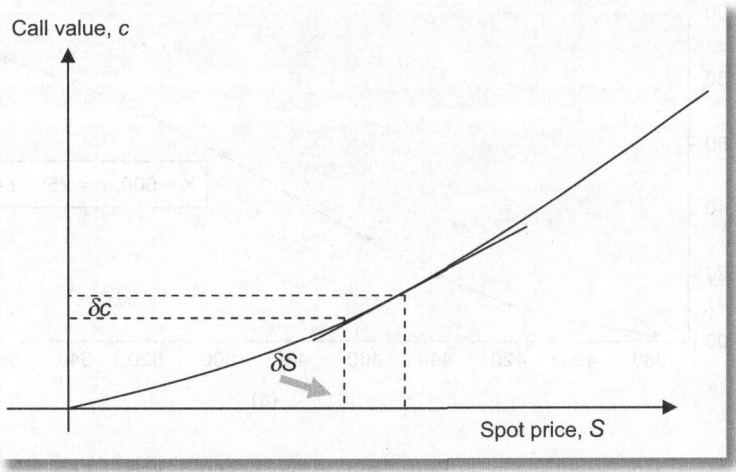

Fig. 13.1 Delta of call option

Behaviour of Delta

The delta of a call option depends upon the moneyness of the option.

> The option delta for an ATM option remains around 0.5.

For a deep out-of-the-money (OTM) call option, the delta would be close to zero, signifying that there would hardly be any change in the price with a change in the price of the underlying. When the call is deep OTM, the put would be deep in-the-money (ITM), and its delta is close to -1.00.

For a deep ITM call option, a change in the spot price of the asset would cause an equivalent change in the call option price. For a deep ITM call option, the value is primarily intrinsic, which increases by the same amount as the price of the underlying does. When a call is deep in-the-money, its delta is 1. At this price of the asset, the put is deep out-of-the-money, and its delta is almost zero.

For an at-the-money (ATM) call, the value of the delta is close to 0.5, meaning that the call value changes by about 50%, signifying that there is an approximately 50% chance of it becoming in-the-money before the expiry of the option. Under BSM, the likelihood of the option turning in-the-money at the time of expiry is given by $N(d_2)$ for the call and $N(-d_2)$ for the put, not by $N(d_1)$. Yet $N(d_1)$ can be taken as an approximate measure of such a probability, though it may be slightly overstated.[3]

The summary of the behaviour of the delta is as follows:

Moneyness of the call option	Value of delta
Deep out-of-the-money	close to zero
Deep in-the-money	one
At-the-money	close to 0.5

Similar observations can be made about the delta of the put option, which has values between 0 and -1.00. The deltas of the call and the put options are depicted in Figs 13.2(a) and (b), respectively, for different values of the asset price for an option with $X = 500$, $T =$

---

[3] Refer to page 170, *Derivatives - An Introduction* by Robert A. Strong, Thompson South Western.

370 Derivatives and Risk Management

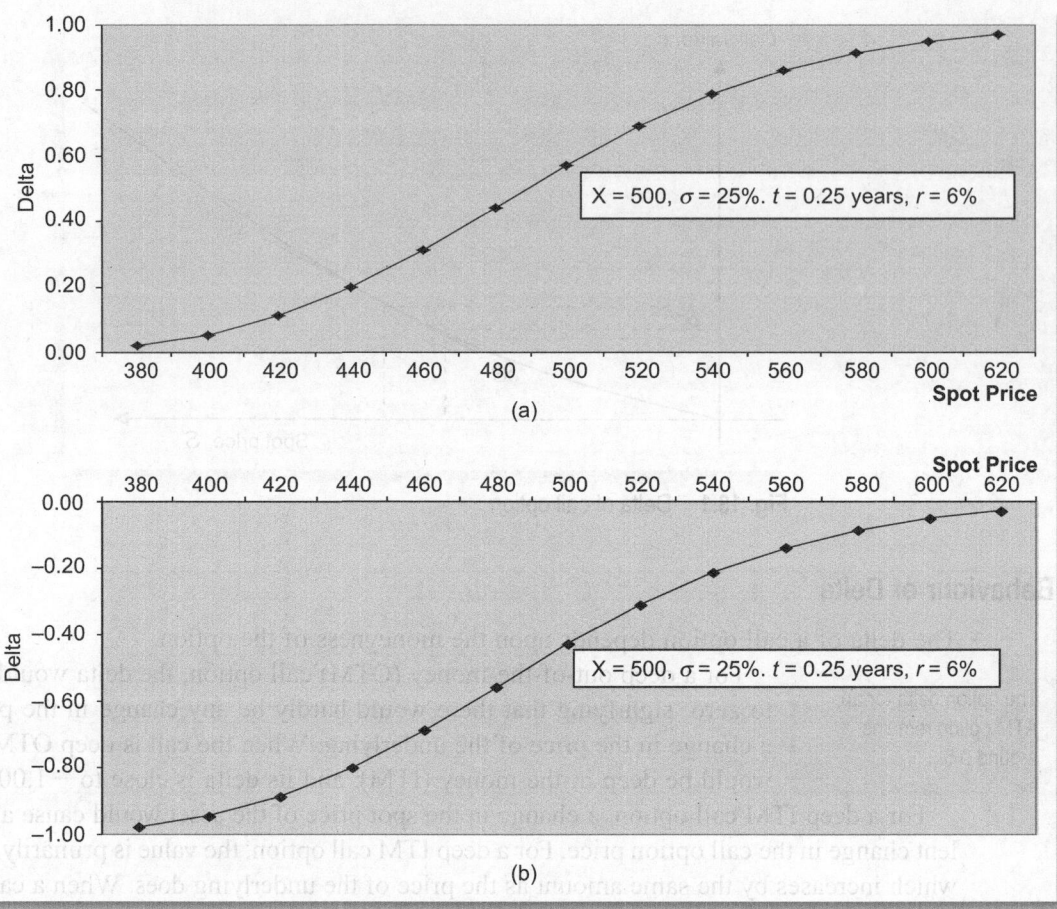

Fig. 13.2 Delta for non-dividend paying stock (a) Call option (b) Put option

3 months, $r = 6\%$, and $\sigma = 25\%$. Note that changes in the delta for the call and the put are similar, as reflected in the shape of the curve. They differ by a constant factor of 1.00, and, hence, the behaviour of the options delta for calls and puts essentially remains the same.

Delta and Time to Maturity

The value of the delta does not remain constant even if the value of the underlying asset does not change. The value of the delta also changes with time. Figure 13.3 shows the values of the delta for ITM, ATM, and OTM call options at $r = 6\%$ and $\sigma = 25\%$ from time $T = 3$ months till expiration.

For ITM calls, the value is slightly less than 1.00 initially and approaches 1.00 when it is close to expiration, representing a change in the option value equal to that of the spot. Close to maturity, the option behaves more like the asset itself. For ATM options, the value remains at around 0.5, indicating that there is as much chance of it turning in-the-money as is for it becoming out-of-the-money. With more time to expiration, investors tend to assign a greater chance for it to become in-the-money, but close to maturity, the uncertainty is

> The option delta falls to zero for OTM options when they are close to maturity. For ITM options, it approaches 1.

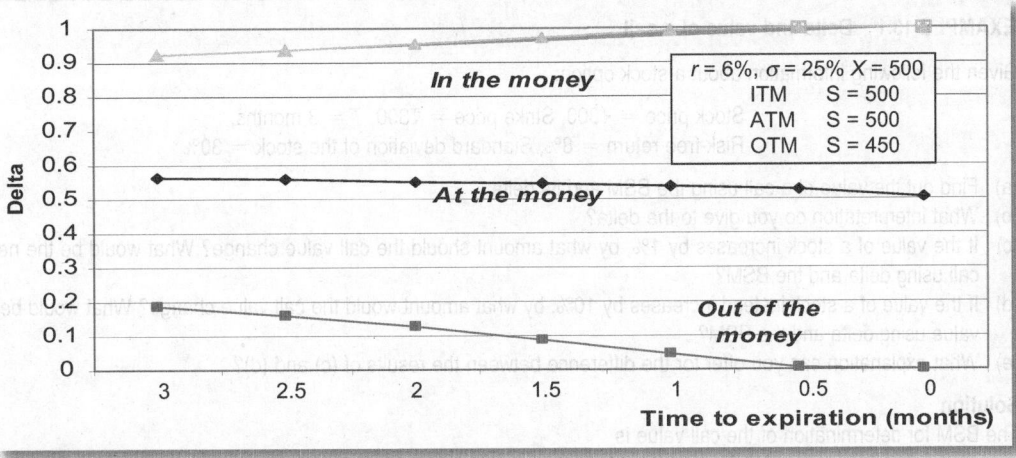

Fig. 13.3 Delta as function of time to expiration

somewhat heightened. For OTM options, the variations are not significant, as the entire value consists of time value. As maturity approaches, one can anticipate practically no change in the value of an OTM option, making its delta close to zero.

Additivity of Delta: Portfolio Delta

An extremely useful property of the delta is its additivity. Additivity implies that the delta of a portfolio is the weighted average of the securities comprising the portfolio. Mathematically, this is represented as

$$\Delta = w_1 \Delta_1 + w_2 \Delta_2 + w_3 \Delta_3 \ldots\ldots\ldots = \Sigma w_i \Delta_i \qquad (13.5)$$

> The delta of a portfolio of assets is the weighted sum of the deltas of the securities comprising it.

where w_n is the number of nth options and Δ_n is the delta of an option position on the same asset.

As an example, consider a short position of an ATM straddle[4] for 3 months on a stock with a spot price of ₹500, a standard deviation of 25%, and a risk-free return of 6%. The value of the straddle (one call and one put written at $X = 500$) and its delta would be as given in Table 13.1.

We can see that the writing of the straddle generates an income of ₹49.84. The delta of the call written is -0.5724, indicating that a one-rupee change in the spot price would cause the call price to go up by ₹0.57. Since the call has been written, the writer would face a loss of

Table 13.1 Value and delta of short straddle

Spot = ₹500, $T = 3$ months, $r = 6\%$, and $\sigma = 25\%$

Position	Value as per BSM	Delta
Short call at $X = 500$	₹28.64	-0.5724
Short put at $X = 500$	₹21.20	$+0.4276$
Income	₹49.84	
Portfolio delta		-0.1448

---

[4] A long (short) straddle is a combination of long (short) call and long (short) put on same asset, with same style and same time to maturity.

> **EXAMPLE 13.1   Delta and value of a call**
>
> Given the following information about a stock option:
>
> Stock price = ₹300, Strike price = ₹300, T = 3 months,
> Risk-free return = 8%, Standard deviation of the stock = 30%
>
> (a) Find out the value of a call using the BSM and its delta.
> (b) What interpretation do you give to the delta?
> (c) If the value of a stock increases by 1%, by what amount should the call value change? What would be the new value of a call using delta and the BSM?
> (d) If the value of a stock instead increases by 10%, by what amount would the call value change? What would be the new call value using delta and the BSM?
> (e) What explanation can you offer for the difference between the results of (c) and (d)?
>
> **Solution**
> The BSM for determination of the call value is
>
> $$c = SN(d_1) - Xe^{-rT} N(d_2)$$
>
> where $d_1 = \dfrac{\ln(S/X) + (r + \sigma^2/2)T}{\sigma\sqrt{T}}$; and $d_2 = \dfrac{\ln(S/X) + (r - \sigma^2/2)T}{\sigma\sqrt{T}}$ or $d_2 = d_1 - \sigma\sqrt{T}$
>
> (a) Putting the values in the BSM formula, we get
> $d_1 = 0.2083$, $d_2 = 0.0583$, $N(d_1) = 0.5825$, and $N(d_2) = 0.5233$
> And call value as ₹20.87, option delta = $N(d_1)$ = 0.5825
> (b) If the delta of a call is 0.5825, this implies that for a small change in the spot price, the value of the call would change by 58.25%.
> (c) If the value of the underlying asset increases by 1%, i.e., to ₹303
> The value of the call with a 1% increase in the spot value to ₹303 = delta × 3 = 0.5825 × 3 = ₹1.75
> Therefore, the new value of the call based on the delta = 20.87 + 1.75 = ₹22.62
> The value of the call as per the BSM = ₹22.67
> The error in the estimated value = ₹0.05 (understated by the delta)
> (d) If the value of the underlying asset increases by 10%, i.e., to ₹330
> The value of the call with a 1% increase in the spot value to ₹330 = delta × 30 = 0.5825 × 30 = ₹17.48
> Therefore, the new value of the call based on the delta = 20.87 + 17.48 = ₹38.35
> The value of the call as per the BSM is = ₹41.86
> The error in the estimated value = ₹3.51 (understated by the delta)
> (e) The error in the first case (1% increase) is far less than the error in the second case (10% increase). The error in estimate using the delta and the value by BSM is due to the assumption of linearity. The value of the call does not increase linearly with the spot price, which is assumed in calculations by the delta.

₹0.57. However, the put written would cause improvement in the position by ₹0.43, with a unit increase in the spot price. The delta of the short straddle would be −0.1448, using Eq. 13.5.

$$\text{Delta of the straddle} = \text{no. of calls} \times \text{delta of calls} + \text{no. of puts} \times \text{delta of puts} \quad (13.5)$$
$$= -1 \times 0.5724 + (-1) \times (-0.4276) = -0.1448$$

The negative delta of the short straddle signifies that with the spot price increasing by ₹1, the portfolio would deteriorate in value by about ₹0.14 (the value of the straddle would increase by ₹0.14). Table 13.2 examines the change in the position of a short straddle with a ₹1 change in the spot price.

Note that an increase in the spot price causes a rise in the value of the straddle, representing a deterioration on the short position. Further, note that the change in value of the straddle is not exactly equal but only approximately equal for the same increase or decrease in the value of the spot due to convexity.

Table 13.2 Change in the value of short straddle with change in spot price as per BSM

Position	Spot price = ₹501	Spot price = ₹499
Short call at X = 500	₹29.22	₹28.08
Short put at X = 500	₹20.77	₹21.63
New value of straddle	₹49.99	₹49.71
Old value of straddle	₹49.84	₹49.84
Deterioration in value	−₹0.15	+₹0.13

EXAMPLE 13.2 Portfolio Delta

Under the BSM, the value of $N(d_1)$ is 0.75. What would be the delta of portfolios consisting of a) 4 long positions in stock and 4 calls, b) 4 long positions of stock and 4 puts, and c) 4 long calls and 4 long puts? Which of the portfolios has least sensitivity to the changes in the stock price?

Solution
The delta of call option on the stock = $N(d_1)$ = 0.75
The delta of put option on the stock = $N(d_1) - 1 = -0.25$
Delta of a) 4 long positions each in stock and call   = 4 × 1.00 + 0.75 × 4 = 7.00
            b) 4 long positions each in stock and put   = 4 × 1.00 − 0.25 × 4 = 3.00
            c) 4 long positions each in call and put   = 4 × 0.75 − 0.25 × 4 = 2.00
The portfolio of four long calls and four long puts is having least delta and therefore would change least with the change in the price of the underlying asset.

Deltas of Other Derivatives

The delta as a concept tells us about the change in the value of an option with a change in the value of the underlying asset. Without any explanation, we can say that the delta of stock would be one. Similarly, the delta of a bond would be close to zero, as the value of the bond does not change with a change in the value of the stock.

The concept of delta can be extended to other derivatives such as forwards and futures contracts. The delta of a forward contract is the change in the value of the forward contract with a change in the value of the underlying asset. Assuming that the forward contract at $t = 0$ is for F_0, the delivery price, the value of the forward contract would change by as much as the change in the value of the underlying. Therefore, the delta of the forward contract is 1.00. It means that after having entered into a forward contract at F_0, one needs to take an equivalent opposite position in the underlying to neutralize the impact of changes in value.

Since the value of the futures is Se^{rT}, the delta of a futures contract is given by e^{rT}. Any change in the value of the spot (δS) would cause a change in the futures by $\delta S e^{rT}$. Therefore, a change in the spot value by ₹1 would cause the futures value to change by e^{rT}.

In case the stock pays dividend (continuously at the rate of q), then the deltas of a call and a put option on it stand modified to $e^{-qT} N(d_1)$ and $e^{-qT}[N(d_1) - 1]$, respectively. For a futures on a dividend paying stock, the delta is $e^{(r-q)T}$. Similarly, the delta for a forward contract on a stock paying dividend is e^{-qT}.

> A long position in stock has a delta of 1, while for a short position, the delta is −1.

Table 13.3 Delta for different assets

Asset	For non-dividend paying	For dividend paying @ q (continuously compounded)
Call on stock	$N(d_1)$	$e^{-qT} \times N(d_1)$
Put on stock	$N(d_1) - 1$	$e^{-qT} \times [N(d_1) - 1]$
Bond	0	0
Stock	1	e^{-qT}
Forward contract on stock	1	e^{-qT}
Futures contract on stock	e^{rT}	$e^{(r-q)T}$
Call option on foreign currency		$e^{-r_f T} \times N(d_1)$
Put option on foreign currency		$e^{-r_f T} \times [N(d_1) - 1]$
Call option on futures		$e^{-rT} \times N(d_1)$
Put option on futures		$e^{-rT} \times [N(d_1) - 1]$

For options on foreign currency, the dividend is the rate of return in foreign currency, r_f. It follows from interest rate parity, where the deliverable asset, the foreign currency, earns an income equal to the foreign interest rate.

The deltas of various instruments are tabulated in Table 13.3 for our understanding.

DELTA HEDGING

Options are bought to contain loss and yet retain profit potential. Further, options are sold to earn premiums under the expectation that the price of the stock would not change enough. Writing options is fraught with the risk of large potential losses for a small premium. A call option writer assumes significant risk with upward movements of the spot price and so does a put writer for downward movements in the price. The call seller hopes that the spot price does not exceed the strike price, and, therefore, expects to pocket the premium earned.

> The lower the delta, the lesser is the change in the value of the portfolio with changes in the prices of the underlying assets.

However, if the position taken is large, the option writer needs to cover for the portion of risk that exceeds the investor's profile.

Stop-loss Strategy One strategy of containing the potential losses from a call written is to acquire the asset the moment its price goes above the exercise price, X. In such a case, the asset would be ready for delivery on maturity/exercise. Since the asset is acquired at a price close to the strike price, the loss would be rather small. Here, a naked call writer converts to a covered call writer the moment the option turns in-the-money. However, the option writer may sell the underlying stock if the price comes below the strike price, to save on the cost of funds. The savings on the cost of funds would have to be weighed against (a) the transaction costs and (b) the loss incurred on a buying price higher than X and a selling price lower than X. The strategy of acquiring the asset when it just exceeds the exercise price and selling it when it just falls below the exercise price is referred to as the stop-loss strategy.

As an alternative to the stop-loss strategy, one can consider the strategy of not covering the position as long as the price remains less than X, buying the asset (cover the short position) the moment it crosses X, but not selling when the price falls below X. Therefore, once covered, one would always remain covered.

Delta Neutrality

More often than not, the stop-loss strategy is not preferred by large-volume traders in derivatives due to the loss that is made on each transaction of buying and selling of the asset, apart from the transaction costs. Instead, traders consider a delta-neutral position a better alternative.

Delta neutrality means that a small change in price of the underlying would have no impact on the value of the portfolio. In terms of Eq. 13.5, which states the delta of the portfolio to be the weighted sum of the deltas of the individual assets comprising the portfolio, delta neutrality can be achieved by making the portfolio delta equal to zero.

Consider the short straddle position in Table 13.1. The delta of the short straddle was computed as -0.1448. A long position of 0.1448 shares in the underlying stock (the long stock has a delta of 1.00) along with the short straddle would make the portfolio delta very close to zero. A change in the value of a portfolio consisting of one short straddle and a long position of 0.145 stocks is depicted in Table 13.4.

Table 13.4 Change in the portfolio value of short straddle and long stock, values as per BSM

Position	Spot price = ₹501	Spot price = ₹499
Short call at $X = 500$	₹29.22	₹28.08
Short put at $X = 500$	₹20.77	₹21.63
New value of straddle	₹49.99	₹49.71
Old value of straddle	₹49.84	₹49.84
Deterioration in value of straddle	−₹0.15	+₹0.13
Value of 0.145 stock	₹72.65	₹72.36
Old value of 0.145 stock	₹72.50	₹72.50
Change in long position of stock	₹0.15	−₹0.14
Net impact on portfolio	—*	—*

*Even when the delta of a portfolio is set exactly at zero, an equal increase/decrease in the spot price would not bring about an exact identical change due to non-linearity.

Traders having large positions in options prefer to hold portfolios that are delta neutral when the risk is presumed to exceed a particular level. With delta neutrality, they achieve immunization of their portfolios to small changes in spot prices.

For example, consider an investor who is long on the stock of Infosys, with 10,000 shares currently trading at ₹1250. In order to protect against a fall in value, the investor buys 10,000 put options with a strike of ₹1150, currently valued at ₹19.99, with a delta of −0.1915 as per the BSM (using $T = 6$ months, $r = 6\%$, and $\sigma = 20\%$). An initial outflow of ₹1,99,900 is required for availing the protection below a spot price of ₹1150; the investor decides to write 4-m calls with a strike of ₹1300, selling at ₹46.77 as per the BSM. The calls have a delta of 0.4567. Assume that the investor sells 4300 calls to generate ₹2,01,111. This results in a cash inflow of ₹1211. The portfolio would have a delta of 6121, as shown in Table 13.5 and the following paragraph.

> Delta neutrality means the delta of the portfolio is zero. Traders with large positions in derivatives strive to achieve it.

Table 13.5 Portfolio delta

Spot = ₹1,250, r = 6%, and σ = 20%

Position	Quantity	Value as per BSM	Delta
Short call at X = 1,300 T = 4 m	−4,300	₹46.77	+0.4567
Long put at X = 1,150 T = 6 m	10,000	₹19.99	−0.1915
Long stock	10,000	—	+1.0000
Portfolio delta			6121

The portfolio delta is given as follows:

$$10{,}000 \times 1.0000 + 10{,}000 \times (-0.1915) - 4300 \times 0.4567 = 6121$$

A portfolio delta of 6121 implies that if the spot value rises by ₹1, the portfolio would rise by ₹6121. Similarly, a fall of ₹1 in the stock of Infosys would cause a decline in the portfolio value of ₹6121. To make the portfolio insensitive to price changes in the underlying stock, we need to make the portfolio delta neutral, i.e., make the delta of the portfolio zero.

One possible way of achieving the objective is to go short on futures on Infosys. The delta of a futures contract is e^{rT}. With $r = 6\%$ and using a 6-m futures contract, the delta would be $e^{-.06 \times 0.5} = 1.03$. For delta neutrality, we need the futures position to have a delta of 6121. Therefore, the number of futures to be sold (a short position would have a negative delta) is 6121/1.03 = 5943, or, say, 6000.

Since deltas of derivatives change continuously with changes in factors that determine option premium, such as time to maturity, interest rates, or volatility, delta neutrality does not hold for long. A trader with substantial exposures needs to review the delta periodically. The periodicity of review would depend upon the risk appetite of the trader. A portfolio made delta neutral does not remain so after some time. To keep the portfolio delta neutral, one is required to adjust it frequently.

THETA

The theta is the sensitivity of the option value with respect to time. As we know, the value of the option consists of two components, i.e., the intrinsic value and the time value. The intrinsic value would be the value one gets if the option is exercised, while the time value represents the value attached to the option becoming more in-the-money before it expires. With all other determinants of the option value remaining constant, the time value diminishes as maturity approaches, and becomes zero on the day of maturity for call and put options. Mathematically, the time value of an option can be expressed as

> The theta represents time decay in the value of the option as it nears maturity.

$$\theta_c = -\frac{\partial c}{\partial t}, \text{ for a call}; \quad \theta_p = -\frac{\partial p}{\partial t}, \text{ for a put}$$

The negative sign indicates that with passage of time, time value decreases, since the time remaining for maturity is reduced. For a non-dividend paying stock, the thetas for calls and puts are given by

$$\Theta_c = -\frac{SN'(d_1)\sigma}{2\sqrt{T}} - rXe^{-rT}N(d_2) \qquad (13.6)$$

$$\Theta_p = -\frac{SN'(d_1)\sigma}{2\sqrt{T}} + rXe^{-rT}N(-d_2) \qquad (13.7)$$

where

$$N'(d) = \frac{1}{\sqrt{2\pi}}e^{-0.5d^2}$$

Computing Theta

Note that the value of the theta for a call would always be negative, signifying that time value decays with the passage of time. For a 3-m ATM call on a stock selling at ₹500 with a risk-free rate of 6% and a volatility of 25%, the call sells at ₹28.64, and the value of the theta is ₹64.49, shown as below:

$$\begin{aligned}\Theta_c &= -\frac{SN'(d_1)\sigma}{2\sqrt{T}} - rXe^{-rT}N(d_2) \\ &= -\frac{500 \times 0.3923 \times 0.25}{2\sqrt{0.25}} - 0.06 \times 492.55 \times 0.5229 \\ &= -49.04 - 15.45 = -₹64.49\end{aligned}$$

Meaning of Theta

It may seem strange that while the call sells at ₹28.64, time decay occurs at the rate of ₹64.49. Note that the value of the theta is annual, while the call has a maturity period of three months only. Since most options have a maturity of less than a year, and, further, since traders in options need to keep abreast of changes almost on a daily basis, it would make better sense to have the value of the theta expressed on a per day basis. Transforming the annual value of ₹64.49, the option would lose a value of ₹0.1767 every day (₹64.49/365).

Note that the entire value of the call of ₹28.64 represents only time value as for an ATM call the intrinsic value is zero. The decay of ₹0.1767 per day implies that the value of the option would turn to zero in about 162 days (₹28.65/0.1767). However, the option lasts only for three months or 91 days. Is the value of the theta as computed here reasonable? The value of the theta is true for the moment or the day. The next day, the value of the theta would change. It increases as time elapses, i.e., the fall in value is greater on a given day than what it was the preceding day.

Theta and Time

Call options lose time value at an increasing rate as maturity approaches, i.e., the value of the theta increases as the option nears maturity. The value of the theta for an option that stood at ₹64.49 at the start would increase to ₹137.03 when only 15 days are left to maturity. The increasing rate of time decay of a call option is demonstrated in Table 13.6, and is depicted in Fig. 13.4 for an ATM call.

For OTM and ITM calls, the decay is at an increasing rate as maturity approaches. For deep OTM calls, neither the time value nor the intrinsic value (which in any case is zero) plays any significant role. For an ITM call, the decay in the time value would be arrested once the traders realize that there is only a remote chance of its value declining. Then the intrinsic value becomes the major constituent of the value of the call.

Table 13.6 Increasing rate of time decay for call option

(−sign ignored)
Spot = ₹500, X = ₹500 r = 6%, and σ = 25%

Time to maturity, t	3.0 m	2.5 m	2.0 m	1.5 m	1.0 m	0.5 m
Theta (₹ p.a.)	64.49	69.30	75.80	85.29	101.20	137.03
Theta (₹ per day)	0.1767	0.1899	0.2077	0.2337	0.2773	0.3754

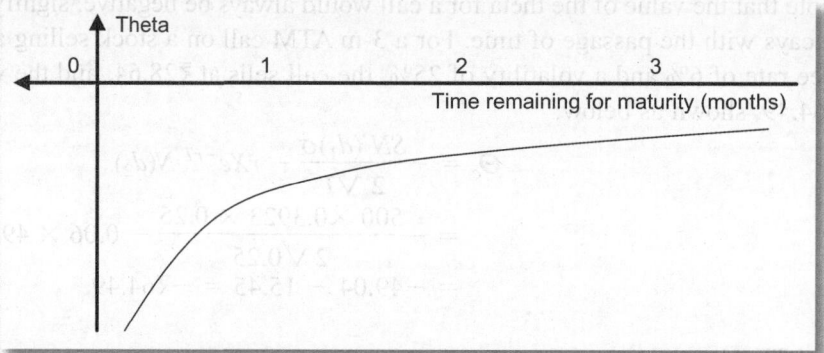

Fig. 13.4 Theta of ATM call with time

Theta for Put Option

> While theta of a call is always negative, there is a possibility of increasing the value of the put option as it approaches maturity.

The value of the theta for put options in most cases would be negative, but for deep ITM European put options, the theta may be positive. For deep ITM puts, the value would be approximately equal to the present value (PV) of X less the spot price, S, i.e., $Xe^{-rT} - S$. Assuming all else remains the same, and with time elapsing, the PV of the exercise would increase (as lesser time remains for maturity), and, hence, the value of the put would rise. At maturity, the value of the put would be the highest at $X - S$. In fact, the theta would be a balance between (a) the time value of the exercise price that causes an increase in the put price on one hand, and (b) a natural decline in value due to reduced volatility with the passage of time, on the other hand. From Eq. 13.7, we may say that the theta for a put would be positive as long as the following is true:

$$rXe^{-rT} N(-d_2) \geq \frac{SN'(d_1)\sigma}{2\sqrt{T}}$$

Portfolio Theta

> Like the portfolio delta, the theta too has an additive property. It is of little significance, as positions cannot be hedged with respect to time decay.

Like the delta, the portfolio theta too is the sum of the thetas of the options comprising the portfolio, weighted with the number of options. The value of the theta as such does not have much significance for the purpose of hedging, as one has no control over time. It remains a figure of interest for traders who want to know the amount by which the value of a portfolio would change as one day elapses, all else remaining constant, of course.

	No dividend yield	Continuous dividend paying at Q
Call, θ_c	$-\dfrac{SN'(d_1)\sigma}{2\sqrt{T}} - rXe^{-rT}N(d_2)$	$-\dfrac{SN'(d_1)\sigma}{2\sqrt{T}} - rXe^{-rT}N(d_2) + qSe^{-qT}N(d_1)$
Put, θ_p	$-\dfrac{SN'(d_1)\sigma}{2\sqrt{T}} + rXe^{-rT}N(-d_2)$	$-\dfrac{SN'(d_1)\sigma}{2\sqrt{T}} + rXe^{-rT}N(-d_2) - qSe^{-qT}N(-d_1)$

where $N'(d_1) = \dfrac{1}{\sqrt{2\pi}} e^{-0.5 d_1^2}$

EXAMPLE 13.3 Computing theta

At what rate will the value of ATM call and put options with six months to expiry decay for an asset selling at ₹40, with a volatility of 30%? The risk-free rate is 8%.

Solution

First we find the values of d_1 and d_2 for $S = 40$, $X = 40$, $T = 0.5$, $r = 8\%$, and $\sigma = 30\%$

$$d_1 = \frac{\ln(S/X) + (r + \sigma^2/2)T}{\sigma\sqrt{T}} = \frac{0 + (0.08 + 0.09/2)0.50}{0.30\sqrt{0.50}} = 0.2946$$

$$d_2 = d_1 - \sigma\sqrt{T} = 0.2946 - 0.3\sqrt{0.50} = 0.0825$$

The normal distribution values are given as under:

$N(d_1) = 0.6159 \quad N(d_2) = 0.5329 \quad N(-d_1) = 0.3841 \quad N(-d_2) = 0.4671$

We also get $N'(d_1) = \dfrac{1}{\sqrt{2\pi}} e^{-0.5 d_1^2} = 0.3819$

Call theta $= -\dfrac{SN'(d_1)\sigma}{2\sqrt{T}} - rXe^{-rT}N(d_2)$

$= -\dfrac{40 \times 0.3819 \times 0.30}{2 \times \sqrt{0.50}} - 0.08 \times 40e^{-0.08 \times 0.5} \times 0.5329$

$= -3.2407 - 1.6384 = -4.8791$

or $-₹0.0134$ per day

Put theta $= -\dfrac{SN'(d_1)\sigma}{2\sqrt{T}} + rXe^{-rT}N(-d_2)$

$= -\dfrac{40 \times 0.3819 \times 0.30}{2 \times \sqrt{0.50}} + 0.08 \times 40e^{-0.08 \times 0.5} \times 0.4671$

$= -3.2407 + 1.4361 = -1.8046$

or $-₹0.0049$ per day

The values of theta for a dividend paying asset for call and put options are given in the table above. These values are computed based on the BSM.

GAMMA AND GAMMA NEUTRALITY

From the point of view of utility to traders, the second-most important parameter of significance is the gamma of the option. The gamma (γ) is the rate of change of the delta of the option or of the portfolio of options.

> The gamma is the rate of change of the delta, and is a second partial derivative with respect to the spot price.

Mathematically, the delta is the first derivative of option value, and the gamma is the second derivative of option value with respect to the spot price. Alternatively, the gamma is the derivative of the delta with respect to price. We may define the gamma as:

$$\Gamma_c = \frac{\delta^2 c}{\delta S^2} \text{ or } \frac{\delta \Delta_c}{\delta S} \text{ for a call option, and } \Gamma_p = \frac{\delta^2 p}{\delta S^2} \text{ or } \frac{\delta \Delta_p}{\delta S} \text{ for a put option}$$

The rate of change of the delta would depend upon the curvature of the option value with respect to the spot value.

Since $\Delta_c = N(d_1)$ and $\Delta_p = N(d_1) - 1$, i.e., they differ only by a constant, the change of delta obtained by differentiation with respect to S for a call and a put would be identical. Therefore, the gamma of a call and a put would be the same. In terms of the BSM, the value of the gamma for calls and puts is given by

$$\Gamma = \frac{N'(d_1)}{S\sigma\sqrt{T}} \tag{13.8}$$

where $N'(d_1) = \frac{1}{\sqrt{2\pi}} e^{-0.5 d_1^2}$

Computing Gamma

An ATM call with spot = ₹500, X = ₹500, r = 6%, T = 3 months (0.25 years), and σ = 25% has a gamma of 0.0063.

> The gammas of a call and a put are equal and positive for the same value of X and the same t.

$$d_1 = \frac{\ln(S/X) + (r + 0.5\sigma^2)T}{\sqrt{T}}$$

$$= \frac{\ln(1) + (0.06 + 0.5 \times 0.25 \times 0.25) \times 0.25}{0.25\sqrt{0.25}} = 0.1825$$

$$N'(d_1) = \frac{1}{\sqrt{2\pi}} e^{-0.5 d_1^2} = \frac{1}{\sqrt{2\pi}} e^{-0.5 \times 0.1825^2} = 0.3923$$

Using Eq. 13.8, we get 0.0063 as the value of the gamma, as shown here:

$$\Gamma = \frac{N'(d_1)}{S\sigma\sqrt{T}} = \frac{0.3923}{500 \times 0.25 \times \sqrt{0.25}} = \frac{0.3923}{62.5} = 0.0063$$

The gamma of a put option with the same determinants would be the same as that of the call, i.e., 0.0063. The gammas of the stock and the forward contract are zero since their deltas are constant at 1.

Behaviour of Gamma with Spot Price and Time

The behaviour of the gamma with respect to the spot value is depicted in Fig. 13.5. The gamma of an ATM option is at the maximum. As an option turns in-the-money or out-of-the-money, the gamma tends to approach zero, signifying that for low and high spot values the curvature of the option value vanishes (refer to Fig. 13.1). The delta for such values of spot would approach 0 or 1. Though the plot of the gamma looks like a normal distribution, it is indeed not so. It appears to be normal because of the factor $N'(d_1)$ appearing in its value, but for higher values, its tail extends more than normal distribution because of the presence of the spot value, S, in the denominator in Eq. 13.8.

The behaviour of a gamma with respect to time is depicted in Fig. 13.6 for an ATM call option. For ITM and OTM options, the variability of the delta is rather low, and its study is rather unimportant. A look at Fig. 13.6 would reveal that changes in the gamma are extremely small for a considerable time, till it almost reaches maturity. The value of the gamma rises very rapidly when the option is close to maturity, even though the value of the delta remains in the vicinity of 0.5.

> The value of the gamma rises very rapidly as it approaches its maturity.

Option Greeks—The Sensitivities 381

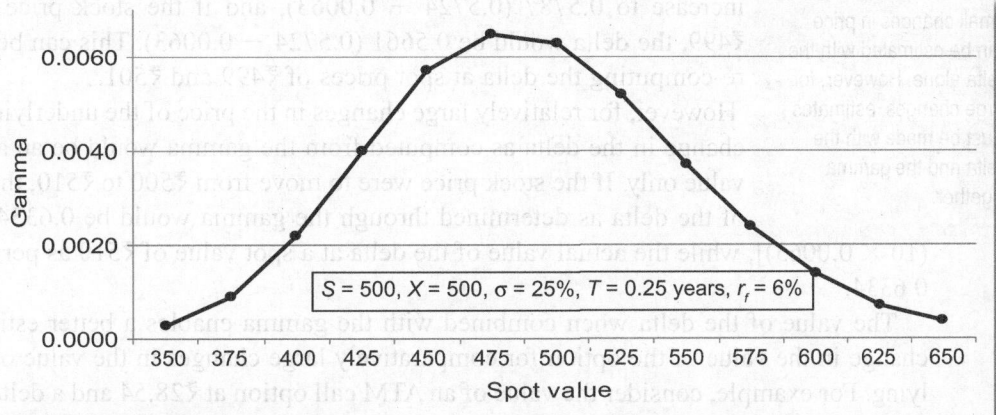

Fig. 13.5 Gamma with spot value

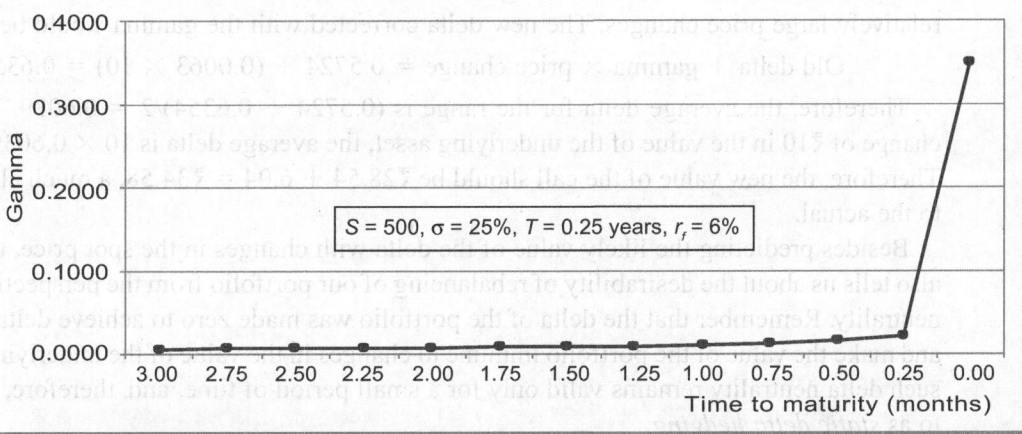

Fig. 13.6 Gamma with spot time

From Figs 13.5 and 13.6, one may conclude that the gamma is at its maximum for ATM options, when they are near maturity.

Meaning of Gamma

The gamma of an option tells the extent to which the value of the delta would change. It is a measure of the non-linearity of the option value. The more the value of the gamma, the more is the non-linearity. The value of the delta remains valid only for small changes in price under the assumption of linearity. In a way, the value of the gamma tells us the extent to which any change in price predicted by the delta could be relied upon.

> The gamma represents non-linearity, and helps in knowing the frequency of portfolio balancing. Higher value of gamma implies more frequent balancing.

In the example of straddle (refer Table 13.1), the value of the call option is ₹28.64, with a call delta of 0.5724. The value of the gamma is 0.0063, which means that the change in value of the delta for a unit change in the value of the underlying asset would be 0.0063. The value of the gamma implies that if the stock price moves from ₹500 to ₹501, the value of the delta would

> Small changes in price can be estimated with the delta alone. However, for large changes, estimates must be made with the delta and the gamma together.

increase to 0.5787 (0.5724 + 0.0063), and if the stock price declines to ₹499, the delta would be 0.5661 (0.5724 − 0.0063). This can be verified by re-computing the delta at spot prices of ₹499 and ₹501.

However, for relatively large changes in the price of the underlying asset, the change in the delta as computed from the gamma would be an approximate value only. If the stock price were to move from ₹500 to ₹510, the new value of the delta as determined through the gamma would be 0.6354 [0.5724 + (10 × 0.0063)], while the actual value of the delta at a spot value of ₹510 as per the BSM is 0.6334.

The value of the delta when combined with the gamma enables a better estimate of the change in the value of the option for comparatively large changes in the value of the underlying. For example, consider the value of an ATM call option at ₹28.54 and a delta of 0.5724. If the spot changes to ₹510, the expected value of the call would be ₹34.26 [28.54 + (0.5724 × 10)], as estimated from the delta. However, the theoretical value of the call as per the BSM at a spot of ₹510 is ₹34.64. The divergence is due to the fact that the delta is not constant for relatively large price changes. The new delta corrected with the gamma would be given by:

Old delta + gamma × price change = 0.5724 + (0.0063 × 10) = 0.6354

Therefore, the average delta for the range is (0.5724 + 0.6354)/2 = 0.6039. Now, for a change of ₹10 in the value of the underlying asset, the average delta is 10 × 0.6039 = ₹6.04. Therefore, the new value of the call should be ₹28.54 + 6.04 = ₹34.58, a much closer figure to the actual.

Besides predicting the likely value of the delta with changes in the spot price, the gamma also tells us about the desirability of rebalancing of our portfolio from the perspective of delta neutrality. Remember that the delta of the portfolio was made zero to achieve delta neutrality and make the value of the portfolio immune to changes in the value of the underlying. At best, such delta neutrality remains valid only for a small period of time, and, therefore, is referred to as *static delta hedging*.

If nothing else changes, the time to maturity would change. What is delta neutral today would not be so after some time. In fact, the deltas of the assets and portfolios change continuously. Though small changes in the delta may be ignored, the portfolio may require periodic adjustment to maintain delta neutrality if substantial time has elapsed or the value of the underlying has changed. How often the portfolio needs to be rebalanced with the passage of time and with changes in the value of the underlying is gauged by the gamma. Higher the value of the gamma, more often the portfolio needs rebalancing. Adjustment to the portfolio with the objective of keeping it delta neutral (or to peg it to a specific value of the delta) is called *dynamic hedging*.

Portfolio Gamma

Like the delta and the theta, the gamma too has an additive property. The gamma of a portfolio can be found by adding the gammas of the securities comprising it, weighted by the number of securities. For example, the gamma of a short straddle (as reproduced from Table 13.1) would be the sum of the gammas of one short call and one short put. Therefore, the gamma of the short straddle would be 0.0126. This is shown in Table 13.7.

Table 13.7 Value of delta and gamma of short straddle

Spot = ₹500, t = 3 months, r = 6%, and σ = 25%

Position	Value as per BSM	Delta	Gamma
Short call at X = 500	₹28.64	−0.5724	0.0063
Short put at X = 500	₹21.20	+0.4276	0.0063
Total	₹49.84		
Portfolio delta and gamma		−0.1448	0.0126

One can forecast the value of the delta if the price changes by ₹1. The new values of the delta of the portfolio would be 0.1448 + .0126 = 0.1574 when the price increases by ₹1, and 0.1448 − 0.0126 = 0.1322 when the price decreases by ₹1.

If the portfolio consists of i securities with numbers n_1, n_2, n_3 .... with gammas of $\Gamma_1, \Gamma_2, \Gamma_3$ ..., then the portfolio gamma Γ_p can be expressed as

$$\Gamma_p = n_1 \times \Gamma_1 + n_2 \times \Gamma_2 + n_3 \times \Gamma_3 \ldots\ldots\ldots n_i \times \Gamma_i \qquad (13.9)$$

Gamma Neutrality

It is often considered that once the applications of the delta are understood, the study of the gamma is futile. We understood the need for making the portfolio delta neutral to immunize it from changes in the spot value.

> Gamma neutrality means the portfolio gamma is equal to zero, which can be achieved through its additive property.

Though the stock can be used to achieve delta neutrality, it cannot be used to manage the gamma, which is zero. Inclusion or exclusion of the stock in the portfolio would have no impact on the gamma of the portfolio. In order to influence the gamma of the portfolio, only a position in derivatives can help. One of the ways to achieve delta and gamma neutrality simultaneously is to (a) first make a portfolio gamma neutral, then (b) compute the delta of the portfolio, and finally (c) take a position in stock to achieve delta neutrality.

Alternatively, we are required to take positions in at least three derivatives to achieve neutrality of the delta and the gamma simultaneously. Using two options, we may have delta neutrality but it would have some gamma. Adding another derivative security to get gamma neutrality would disturb the delta neutrality achieved earlier, because the new security would have its own Greeks. To make the portfolio delta and gamma neutral, we need to solve simultaneous equations. For example, consider three options with price, delta, and gamma, as given in Table 13.8.

Assume that an investor writes 100 puts with a strike of 550. The delta of the portfolio would be −79.10, and the gamma would be 0.54 for an income of ₹5206. The investor has identified

Table 13.8 Option values, deltas, and gammas of three select options

Spot = ₹500, T = 3 months, r = 6%, and σ = 25%

Option	Value as per BSM	Delta	Gamma
Put at X = 550	₹52.06	−0.7910	0.0054
Call at X = 500	₹28.64	0.5724	0.0063
Call at X = 550	₹10.25	0.2810	0.0054

Table 13.9 Values, deltas, and gammas of portfolio of three select options

Spot = ₹500, T = 3 monthes, r = 6%, and σ = 25%

Option	Individual assets			Portfolio			
	Value (₹)	Delta	Gamma	No.	Cash flow (₹)	Delta	Gamma
Put at X = 550	52.06	−0.7190	0.0054	−100	+5,206	71.90	−0.54
Call at X = 500	28.64	0.5724	0.0063	−409	+11,672	−234.11	−2.57
Call at X = 550	10.25	0.2810	0.0054	+577	−5,914	162.14	3.11
Total					+11,005	0.07	0

two calls with strikes of 500 and 550 to achieve delta and gamma neutrality. Assume that the number of options traded are n_1 and n_2, respectively, for the calls at strikes of 500 and 550. We need to solve the following equations simultaneously:

$0.2810\, n_1 + 0.5724\, n_2 + 71.90 = 0$ for delta neutrality

and $0.0054\, n_1 + 0.0063\, n_2 − 0.54 = 0$ for gamma neutrality

Solving these equations, we get $n_1 = 577.03$ (say, 577) and $n_2 = -408.88$ (say, 409). Now the portfolio would comprise (a) 100 puts short, with $X = 550$, (b) 577 calls long, with $X = 500$, and (c) 409 calls short, with $X = 550$. The income, delta, and gamma of this portfolio are computed in Table 13.9 demonstrating delta and gamma neutrality.

> The gamma of a stock is zero, and it is easier to achieve delta and gamma neutrality simultaneously with a position in stock, as compared to achieving it only through derivatives.

The value of gammas for call and put options for non-dividend paying and dividend-paying assets are tabulated in the table below:

	No dividend yield	Continuous dividend paying at q
Call gamma, Γ_c Put gamma, Γ_p	$\Gamma = \dfrac{N'(d_1)}{S\sigma\sqrt{T}}$	$\Gamma = \dfrac{N'(d_1)e^{-qT}}{S\sigma\sqrt{T}}$

EXAMPLE 13.4   Gamma: calculation, interpretation, and neutrality

Refer to the data given in Example 13.3.
(a) Find the gamma of a call and a put. If a trader has written 1000 puts on the stock, what would be the gamma of the position?
(b) What does this figure mean?
(c) How could he/she achieve gamma neutrality through calls on the same asset?

Solution
(a) Gamma of call = gamma of put =

$$\Gamma = \frac{N'(d_1)}{S\sigma\sqrt{T}} = \frac{0.3819}{40 \times 0.30 \times \sqrt{0.50}} = \frac{0.3819}{8.4853} = 0.0450$$

(b) For the 1000 puts written, the gamma would be = $-1000 \times 0.0450 = -₹45$.
This implies that if the value of the asset rises by ₹1 from ₹40 to ₹41, the value of delta of his/her position decreases by ₹45. Similarly, if the stock fell to ₹39, the value of delta of his/her position rises by ₹45. This is consistent with the option price, as the value of the put increases with the fall in asset price.
(c) To make the gamma of the position zero, the investor would have to buy an equal number of calls on the same asset with the same strike and maturity. The gamma of the long positioning call is equal to 0.0450, and 1000 calls bought would give a gamma of ₹45, annulling the gamma of the put position.

OTHER GREEKS

Vega

> The vega is the rate of change of value of an option with respect to changes in the volatility. It is the same for calls and puts.

Among the lesser known and lesser used parameters of option price sensitivity is the variability of option value with respect to the volatility of the underlying. It is denoted by vega, a non-Greek letter; those used to only Greek letters know it by the name of lambda or kappa.

The vega is the change of value of the option if the volatility changes. Note that in option pricing, volatility is not an observable statistic. Instead, it is implied in the option value.

$$\text{Vega}_c = \frac{\partial c}{\partial \sigma} \text{ for call;} \quad \text{Vega}_p = \frac{\partial p}{\partial \sigma} \text{ for put}$$

The vega is positive for both calls and puts. In fact, it is volatility that drives the prices of call and put options. Irrespective of the nature of option, an increased volatility means increased valuation of the option and vice versa. We know that only historical volatility can be measured, while the estimate of future volatility is implied in the option price. The vega is a measure of change in the value with any change in the implied volatility.

Vegas for calls and puts are equal. In terms of the BSM, the vega for a call and a put option on a non-dividend paying stock is given by

$$\text{Vega} = S\sqrt{T} N'(d_1) \tag{13.10}$$

For a 3-m ATM call option with a strike of ₹500 on a stock with $\sigma = 25\%$ and $r = 6\%$, the value of the vega is 0.9844, computed as follows:

$$d_1 = \frac{\ln(S/X) + (r + 0.5\sigma^2)T}{\sigma\sqrt{T}}$$

$$= \frac{\ln(1) + (0.06 + 0.5 \times 0.25 \times 0.25) \times 0.25}{0.25\sqrt{0.25}} = 0.1825$$

$$N'(d_1) = \frac{1}{\sqrt{2\pi}} e^{-0.5 d_1^2} = \frac{1}{\sqrt{2\pi}} e^{-0.5 \times 0.1825^2} = 0.3923$$

The computation of the vega using Eq. 13.10 is as follows:

$$\text{Vega} = 500 \times 0.3923 \times 0.25 = 98.07$$

The call value is ₹28.64. The value of the vega of 98.07 suggests that for a 1% increase or decrease in volatility (with σ changing by 1% or 0.01), the value of the option would change by 0.98 (98.07 × 0.01). As per the BSM, we find the value of the call with $\sigma = 24\%$ at ₹27.66 and with $\sigma = 26\%$ at ₹29.62.

The vega is at its maximum when the option is at-the-money. As the option becomes in-the-money or out-of-the-money, the value of the vega declines. For deep ITM and deep OTM options, the value of the vega approaches zero, suggesting the declining importance of volatility in determination of option values, as the spot price moves away from the exercise price. Figure 13.7 depicts the behaviour of the vega with respect to the spot price.

The pattern of the vega with the spot value looks extremely similar to normal distribution. It is because of the term $N'(d_1)$ in the computation. However, it gets modulated by multiplication by the spot price S.

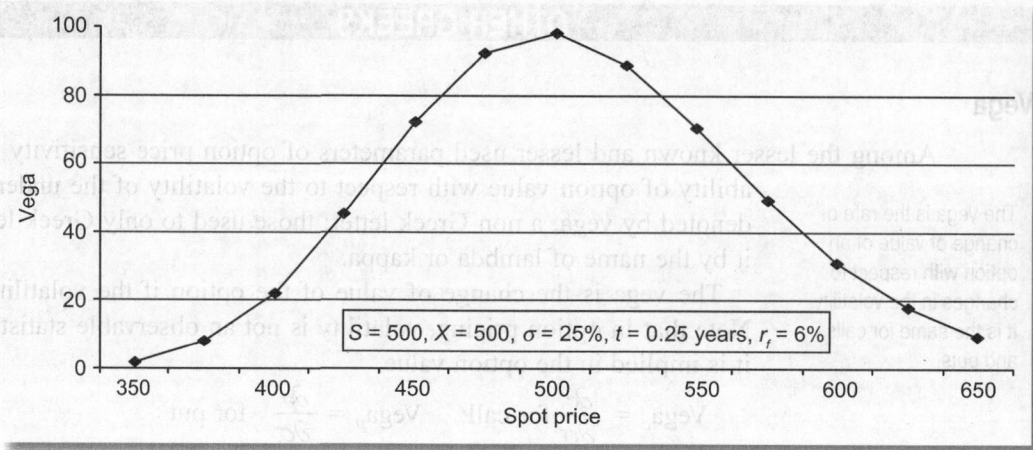

Fig. 13.7 Vega with price

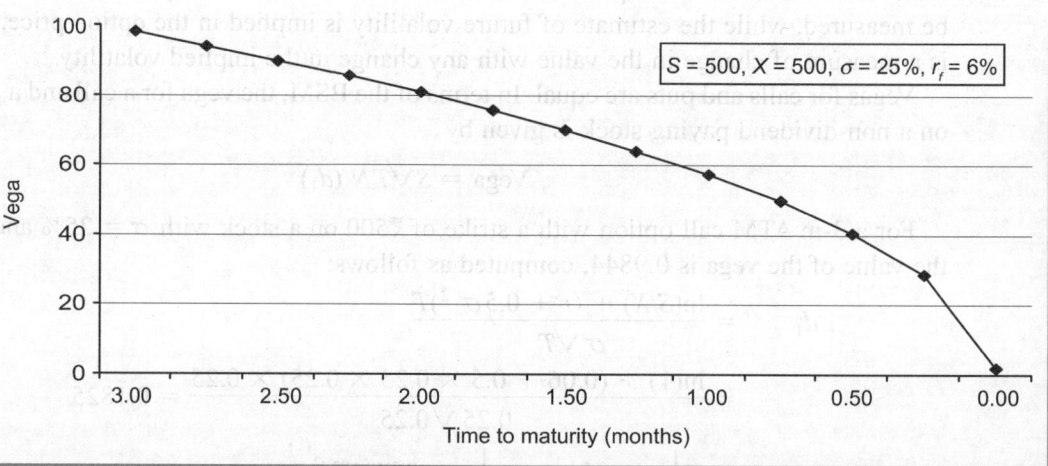

Fig. 13.8 Vega with time

With the passage of time, there is reduced scope for volatility to influence the price. Volatility is directly proportional to the time available. When an ATM option comes into existence, the importance of volatility is at the maximum, because maximum time is available for the values to change. At maturity, the value of the option must be determined purely by its intrinsic worth, as large fluctuations in the price (volatility concerns with changes in the price) are almost ruled out. The behaviour of the vega with the passage of time is depicted in Fig. 13.8.

The values of the vega for non-dividend paying and dividend paying assets are given below:

	No dividend yield	Continuous dividend paying at q
Call vega, = Put vega	$S\sqrt{T}\,N'(d_1)$	$Se^{-qT}\sqrt{T}\,N'(d_1)$

Rho

> The rho is the rate of change of the value of an option with respect to changes in the risk-free interest rate.

The last of the Greek letters that denote sensitivity of option price is the rho, ρ, which gives the rate of change of the option price with respect to a change in the risk-free interest rate. The rhos for call and put options are defined as follows:

$$\rho_c = \frac{\delta c}{\delta r} \text{ for call}; \quad \rho_p = \frac{\delta p}{\delta r} \text{ for put}$$

The rhos for call and put options for non-dividend paying stock are given by Eqs 13.11 and 13.12.

For a call option: $\quad \rho_c = TXe^{-rT} N(d_2)$ $\quad$ (13.11)
For a put option: $\quad \rho_p = -TXe^{-rT} N(-d_2)$ $\quad$ (13.12)

The value of the rho is positive for a call and negative for a put. With a rise in the interest rate, the present value of the exercise price would decrease, and therefore, the value of the call, being proportional to $(S - \text{PV of } X)$, would increase. The reverse would apply for the value of the put, which is proportional to $(\text{PV of } X - S)$. For dividend paying stock, the formula for the rho remains the same as in Eqs 13.11 and 13.12. However, the value of d_2, and, hence, $N(d_2)$ would change.

In terms of the BSM, $N(d_2)$ represents the probability that the option would be exercised. The value of the rho is the time-weighted present value of the exercise price multiplied by the probability of the option being exercised.

For options on currency, rho would stand modified by the foreign currency interest rates. If r_f denotes the risk-free rate abroad, then options on foreign currency would have the following rhos:

For a call option: $\quad \rho_c = TSe^{-r_f T} N(d_2)$
For a put option: $\quad \rho_p = -TSe^{-r_f T} N(-d_2)$

For ATM 3-m call and put options on an asset selling at ₹500 with a volatility of 25% and a risk-free rate of 6%, the value of the rhos are worked out as follows:

$$d_1 = \frac{\ln(S/X) + (r + 0.5\sigma^2)T}{\sqrt{T}}$$

$$= \frac{\ln(1) + (0.06 + 0.5 \times 0.25 \times 0.25) \times 0.25}{0.25\sqrt{0.25}} = 0.1825$$

$d_2 = d_1 - \sigma \sqrt{T} = 0.1825 - 0.25 \sqrt{0.25} = 0.0575$
and $\quad N(d_2) = 0.5229 \quad N(-d_2) = 0.4771$

Therefore, $\sigma_c = XTe^{-rT} N(d_2) = 500 \times 0.25 \times e^{-.06 \times 0.25} \times 0.5229$
$\quad = 125 \times 0.9811 \times 0.5229 = 64.39$

and $\quad \sigma_p = -XTe^{-rT} N(-d_2) = -500 \times 0.25 \times e^{-.06 \times 0.25} \times 0.4771$
$\quad = -125 \times 0.9811 \times 0.4771 = -58.75$

The meaning of rhos of 64.39 for a call and -58.75 for a put is that with a 1% increase in the risk-free rate, the call value would increase by approximately ₹0.6439 (0.01 × 64.39) and the put value would decrease by approximately ₹0.5875 (0.01 × 0.5875). The change in the value of the option would be rather low with a change in the interest rate when compared with the other determinants of option value.

Among the option Greeks, the rho has the least importance since changes in the risk-free interest rate are neither large enough to impact portfolio values substantially nor frequent enough to demand portfolio rebalancing. Only in cases of option portfolios with very large maturities can the rho be of some significance.

SOLVED PROBLEMS

SP 13.1: Delta for call and put

Find the values of the delta for ATM call and put options with 3 months to maturity. The volatility of the asset price is at 30% and the risk-free interest rate is 6% p.a.

Solution

For an ATM option, $S = X$ and $\ln(S/X) = 0$. The value of d_1 is 0.1750, shown as follows:

$$d_1 = \frac{\ln(S/X) + (r + \sigma^2/2)T}{\sigma\sqrt{T}} = \frac{0 + (0.06 + 0.09/2)0.25}{0.3\sqrt{0.25}} = 0.1750$$

Delta of call option = $N(d_1)$ = 0.5695
Delta of put option = $N(d_1) - 1 = -0.4305$

SP 13.2: Portfolio delta and neutrality

Under the BSM, the value of $N(d_1)$ is 0.75. If you have a long position of 120 shares, how can you make it insensitive to small changes in the prices of the asset using derivatives?

Solution

The delta of stock is 1.00
The delta of a call option on the stock = $N(d_1)$ = 0.75
The delta of a put option on the stock = $N(d_1) - 1 = -0.25$

The delta of a 120 long position in stock is 120, meaning that the value of the position would change by ₹120 if spot price changes by ₹1. In order to make the value insensitive to price, we need to have a portfolio delta equal to zero, which can be had from the delta of a derivative equal to −120. A short position in calls or a long position in puts would have negative delta, and can be used for neutralizing the delta of the long position in stock.

No. of calls to be short = 120/0.75 = 160 calls
No. of puts to be bought = 120/(−0.25) = 480 puts

Either of the positions would make the portfolio delta equal to zero.

SP 13.3: Gamma of call and put

Find the values of the gamma of a call and a put for the data of the stock in SP 13.1, assuming the value of the stock at ₹200.

Solution

For an ATM option $S = X$ and $\ln(S/X) = 0$. The value of d_1 is 0.1750, as shown here:

$$d_1 = \frac{\ln(S/X) + (r + \sigma^2/2)T}{\sigma\sqrt{T}} = \frac{0 + (0.06 + 0.09/2)0.25}{0.3\sqrt{0.25}} = 0.1750$$

$$N(d_1) = \frac{1}{\sqrt{2\pi}}e^{-0.5d_1^2} = \frac{1}{\sqrt{2\pi}}e^{-0.5 \times 0.1750^2} = 0.3928$$

$$\Gamma = \frac{N'(d_1)}{S\sigma\sqrt{T}} = \frac{0.3928}{200 \times 0.30 \times \sqrt{0.25}} = \frac{0.3928}{30} = 0.0131$$

Gamma of call option = gamma of put option = 0.0131

SP 13.4: All Greeks

An asset is trading at ₹40 with volatility of 30%. The risk-free rate is 8%.

(a) Find the values of call and put options with an exercise price of ₹40 and maturity of six months. Further, find the delta, gamma, theta, vega, and rho of the options.

(b) Repeat the exercise for call and put options with a strike price of ₹50 and maturity of six months.

Solution
For $S = ₹40$, $\sigma = 30\%$, $r = 8\%$, and $T = 0.5$ years

(a) For options with $X = 40$
We already have from Example 13.3
$N(d_1) = 0.6159 \quad N(d_2) = 0.5329 \quad N(-d_1) = 0.3841 \quad N(-d_2) = 0.4671$

We also get $N'(d_1) = \dfrac{1}{\sqrt{2\pi}} e^{-0.5 d_1^2} = 0.3819$

Value of call $= S N(d_1) - X e^{-rT} N(d_2)$
$= 40 \times 0.6159 - 40 \times 0.9608 \times 0.5329 = 24.6360 - 20.4802 \quad = 4.1558 \approx ₹4.16$

Value of put $= X e^{-rT} (N-d_2) - S N(-d_1)$
$= 40 \times 0.9608 \times 0.4671 - 40 \times 0.3841 = 17.9514 - 15.3640 \quad = 2.5874 \approx ₹2.59$

Delta of call $= 0.6159$ Delta of put $= -0.3841$
Gamma of call $=$ gamma of put $= 0.0450$ (Refer Example 13.4)
Theta of call $= -0.0134$/day
Theta of put $= -0.0049$/day (Refer Example 13.3)
Vega of call $=$ Vega of put $= S\sqrt{T} N'(d_1) = 40 \times \sqrt{0.5} \times 0.3819 = 10.8023$
Rho of call $= \sigma_c = TXe^{-rT} N(d_2) = 0.50 \times 40 \times 0.9608 \times 0.5329 = 10.2401$
Rho of put $= -TXe^{-rT} N(-d_2) = -0.50 \times 40 \times 0.9608 \times 0.4671 = -8.9757$

(b) Option with $X = 50$
$d_1 = \dfrac{\ln(S/X) + (r + \sigma^2/2)T}{\sigma \sqrt{T}} = \dfrac{\ln(40/50) + (0.08 + 0.09/2)0.50}{0.3\sqrt{0.50}} = -0.7573$

$d_2 = d_1 - \sigma\sqrt{T} = -0.7573 - 0.3\sqrt{0.50} = -0.9694$

$N(d_1) = 0.2244 \quad N(d_2) = 0.1662 \quad N(-d_1) = 0.7756 \quad N(-d_2) = 0.8338$

We also get $N'(d_1) = \dfrac{1}{\sqrt{2\pi}} e^{-0.5 d_1^2} = 0.2994$

Value of call $= S N(d_1) - X e^{-rT} N(d_2)$
$= 40 \times 0.2244 - 50 \times 0.9608 \times 0.1662 = 8.9760 - 7.9842 \quad = 0.9918 \approx ₹0.99$

Value of put $= X e^{-rT} (N - d_2) - S N(d_1)$
$= 50 \times 0.9608 \times 0.8338 - 40 \times 0.7756 = 40.0553 - 31.0240 \quad = 9.0313 \approx ₹9.03$

Delta of call $= N(d_1) = 0.2244$
Delta of put $= N(d_1) - 1 = 0.2244 - 1 = -0.7756$

Gamma of call and put $= \Gamma = \dfrac{N'(d_1)}{S\sigma\sqrt{T}} = \dfrac{0.2994}{40 \times 0.30 \times \sqrt{0.50}} = \dfrac{0.2994}{8.4853} = 0.0353$

Call theta $= -\dfrac{SN'(d_1)\sigma}{2\sqrt{T}} - rXe^{-rT} N(d_2) = -\dfrac{40 \times 0.2294 \times 0.30}{2 \times \sqrt{0.50}} - 0.08 \times 50 e^{-0.08 \times 0.5} \times 0.1662$
$= -2.5407 - 0.6387 = -3.1794$
or $-₹0.0087$/day

Put theta $= -\dfrac{SN'(d_1)\sigma}{2\sqrt{T}} + rXe^{-rT} N(-d_2) = -\dfrac{40 \times 0.2994 \times 0.30}{2 \times \sqrt{0.50}} + 0.08 \times 50 e^{-0.08 \times 0.5} \times 0.8338$
$= -3.2407 + 3.2044 = 0.6377$
or $+₹0.0018$ per day

Vega of call $=$ vega of put $= S\sqrt{T} N'(d_1) = 40 \times \sqrt{0.5} \times 0.2994 = 8.4691$
Rho of call $= TXe^{-rT} N(d_2) = 0.50 \times 50 \times 0.9608 \times 0.1662 = 3.9921$
Rho of put $= -TXe^{-rT} N(-d_2) = -0.50 \times 50 \times 0.9608 \times 0.8338 = -20.0277$

Values of all the four options are tabulated here:

The greeks $S = 40$, $r = 8\%$, $T = 0.5$, $\sigma = 30\%$

	For $X = 40$		For $X = 50$	
	Call	Put	Call	Put
Value (₹)	4.16	2.59	0.99	9.03
Delta (₹)	0.6159	−0.3841	0.2244	−0.7756
Gamma (₹)	0.0450	0.0450	0.0353	0.0353
Theta (₹/day)	−0.0134	−0.0049	−0.0087	0.0018
Vega	10.8023	10.8023	8.4691	8.4691
Rho	10.2401	−8.9757	3.9921	−20.0277

SP 13.5: Delta and gamma neutrality

Refer to the data of SP 13.4. If a trader starts with a short position of puts with $X = 50$, how would you make the portfolio delta and gamma neutral simultaneously?

Solution

Initial position: short 1000 puts with $X = 50$
Income = 1000 × 9.03 = ₹9030
Delta = −0.7756 × −1000 = 775.60
Gamma = 0.0350 × −1000 = −35.30

For gamma neutrality with call at $X = 40$:
Gamma of call = 0.0450
Long position of calls required to neutralize the gamma = 53.30/0.0450 = 785 calls

For delta neutrality with stock:
Delta of position of 1000 short puts with $X = 50$, and 785 long calls with $X = 40$
= −1000 × −0.7756 + 785 × 0.6159 = 775.6 + 483.5 = 1259.1 say ₹1260

To have delta neutrality, the trader should short 1260 shares.

SUMMARY

The value of an option does not remain constant even if the price of the underlying asset does not change. Though the primary determinant of the value of an option is the price of the underlying, there are other factors too that cause this to change. Once an option position is taken, the exercise price remains the same, while the rest of the parameters, such as spot price, time to maturity, volatility, and risk-free interest rate are dynamic.

The sensitivity of an option price with respect to each of the determinants except the exercise price is denoted by a Greek letter, and as such, option sensitivities are often referred to as option Greeks. The delta of an option is the change in the option value with a small change in the spot price. In terms of the BSM, the delta is given by $N(d_1)$ for a call and is positive, while for a put, it is $N(d_1) - 1$ and negative. A negative sign represents the inverse relationship of the option value with the price of the underlying asset. The value of a delta represents the number of stock required for each unit of option for a hedging. The value of the delta is close to 1 for deep ITM calls, close to zero for deep OTM calls, and around 0.5 for ATM calls.

One property of the delta is that it is additive in nature. The delta of a portfolio is equal to the delta of the individual securities comprising it, weighted by the number of securities. This helps in achieving delta neutrality, i.e., setting the delta of the portfolio equal to zero, implying immunity of the portfolio value to small changes in the price of the underlying asset.

The theta of the option is the change in the option value with the passage of time. The value of the call declines as it approaches maturity. However, this may not be true for put options. It is an important statistic in the context of options to know by what value the call would change each day. However, there is no hedging possible with respect to the theta of an option. The theta is normally expressed in terms of per day change in value.

The gamma is the rate of change of the delta. It is the second partial derivative of the option value with respect to spot prices. It is the same for call and put options, and is always positive. The desired value of delta that is achieved once does not remain the same. The portfolio needs to be re-balanced because the delta changes with time. How often a portfolio needs to be re-balanced is judged by the value of the gamma. The higher the value of gamma, the more frequent is the adjustments. Like the delta, the gamma too has an additive property.

For large positions, delta neutrality as well as gamma neutrality is desired. This can be achieved by combining at least three different derivatives. Since the gamma of a stock is zero, it is easier to achieve delta neutrality and gamma neutrality simultaneously by taking a position in the underlying asset itself.

The vega is a change in the value of the option with respect to changes in the volatility of the underlying asset. It is identical and positive for call and put options. Though said to be deriving the value of the derivative, the changes in volatility are not sudden. Therefore, a study of the vega is relatively unimportant. So is the case with the rho, which is the change in value of the option with respect to changes in the risk-free rate.

KEY TERMS

Delta The rate of change of the value of the option with respect to the spot price of the underlying asset.
Delta neutrality A portfolio whose delta is zero is called a delta-neutral portfolio. Its value remains the same for any small change in the price of the underlying asset.
Gamma The rate of change of the value of the delta of the option with respect to the spot price of the underlying asset.
Gamma neutrality A portfolio whose gamma is zero is called a gamma-neutral portfolio. The value of a delta remains constant for any small change in the price of the underlying asset for a gamma-neutral portfolio.
Rho The rate of change of the value of the option with respect to changes in the risk-free interest rate.
Theta The rate of change of the value of the option with respect to the time to maturity.
Vega The rate of change of the value of the option with respect to the volatility of the underlying asset.

QUESTIONS

13.1 What do you understand by the sensitivities of option prices? Describe all the parameters and their importance.
13.2 What do you understand by the delta of an option? Describe its behaviour with respect to the spot price and time to maturity. How is it measured for call and put options?
13.3 How do you find the delta of a portfolio? What are delta neutrality and delta hedging? Describe with the help of an example.
13.4 What do you understand by the term time decay of option?
13.5 What is the gamma of an option and why is its study important?
13.6 What is gamma neutrality? What major problem would you face in trying to achieve gamma neutrality?
13.7 How would you make a portfolio delta as well as gamma neutral? Illustrate with an example.
13.8 What do you understand by the vega and rho of an option?

PROBLEMS

P 13.1 Option value and delta
The value of a 3-m ATM European call option on an asset whose current price is ₹100 in terms of the BSM is expressed as follows:
Call value $c = 100 \times 0.5678 - 100 \times 0.9901 \times 0.5382$

(a) What is the expected change in the value of the call if the spot value goes up to ₹102?
(b) What is the expected change in the value of the put if the spot value moves to ₹105?

P 13.2 Delta of options
Find the value of the delta of ATM call and put options with three months to expire. The volatility of the underlying stock is 40% and the risk-free rate is 8%.

P 13.3 Gamma of call and put
For a spot price of ₹100, find the value of the gamma of the call and put option for the data given in P 13.2.

P 13.4 Delta neutrality
Refer to the data in P 13.2. If you are holding 10,000 shares, what would you do to make them delta-neutral using (a) only call options and (b) only put options?

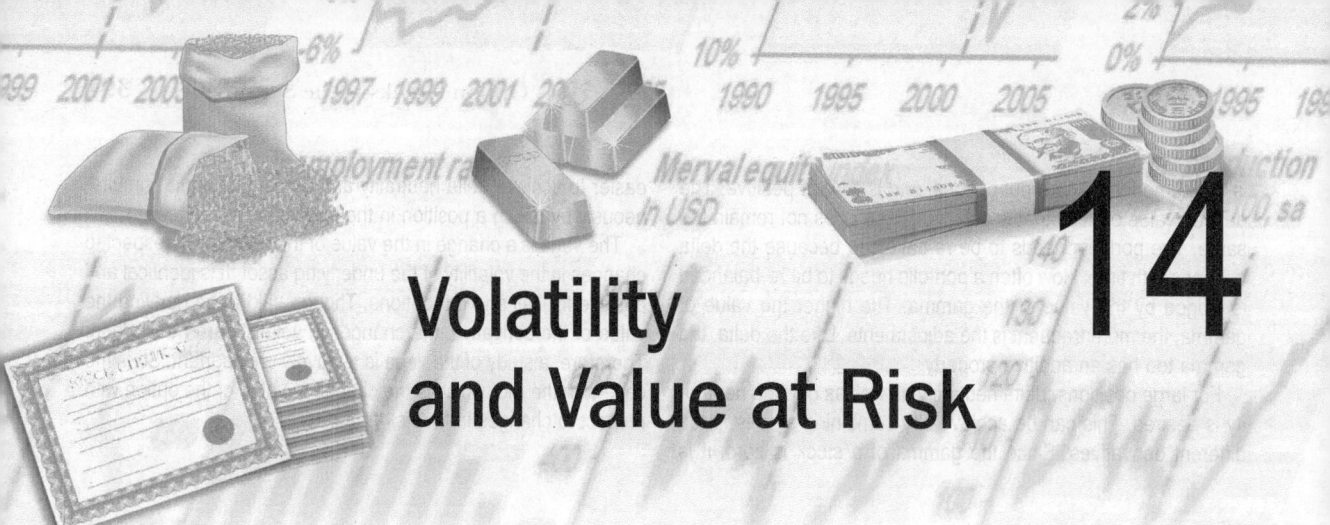

Volatility and Value at Risk

14

INTRODUCTION

Understanding risk and its management is becoming increasingly complex over time. The variables that can impact outcomes are becoming larger and larger in number as we progress increasingly from isolation to global integration and liberalization. In the olden times, the primary concern used to be the prices of commodities, which faced uncertainty due to weather conditions. As time progressed, investment and savings got channelized into a variety of instruments that exposed the returns to economic conditions, interest rates, and exchange rates. With the factors governing risk becoming larger, we made increasing use of derivatives. Risk manifestations developed from one factor to another. For managing price risk, we resorted to the use of derivatives. Societies prospered more and more, resulting in increased savings and investments. With horizons expanding, investment portfolios not only increased in terms of newer and newer products, they also expanded in terms of the number of risk factors that determined the values of these products, and, hence, of the investment. The expanding menu of investment products was accompanied by the derivatives to manage the risks on these products. Portfolios now consist of basic products and derivatives based on them. Portfolios became sensitive to changes in spot prices, interest rates, volatility, time remaining for expiry, etc. For better understanding and management of risk, we explored sophisticated risk measurement parameters such as Greek symbols in Chapter 13

> With globalization, liberalization, and newer investment products, risk factors have grown in number, making risk assessment and its management complex.

Learning Objectives

After going through this chapter, readers should be familiar with

- the meaning of volatility
- different ways of measuring volatility
- exponential smoothing and exponential weighted average method of computing volatility
- the basics of the GARCH approach
- the conveyed volatility index
- the meaning of value at risk (VaR) and its description
- methods for finding VaR
- the historical simulation approach
- the need for stress testing

MEASURES OF RISK

> There are different measures of risk for different investments and instruments. These predict changes in values based on given changes in the value of a critical determinant.

We have had several measures of risk, depending on the sensitivity of the instruments to various factors. Not all determinants affect value in the same manner; some affect it more and some are less important. Changes in value with respect to a dominant risk factor can be evaluated by one measure of risk. A list of measures of risk and their meanings is presented in Table 14.1.

Besides these measures, we also used techniques such as sensitivity analyses and scenario analyses in corporate finance to improve our understanding of the risk emanating from the large number of factors that are beyond our control.

Table 14.1 Different measures of risk and meanings

Measure	Meaning
Standard deviation, σ	A measure of risk of the changes in the returns of a stock or a portfolio, irrespective of whether the changes occur due to unsystematic or systematic factors
Duration/modified duration/ Macaulay's duration	A measure of risk with respect to the changes in the term structure of interest rates (yield curve) for a bond or a portfolio of bonds
Systematic risk, β	A measure of systematic risk (market risk) causing changes in the value of a well-diversified portfolio of stocks under the assumption that unsystematic risk has been diversified away
Degree of operating leverage	A measure of risk quantifying changes in the level of earnings due to the composition of cost structure in the firm
Degree of financial leverage	A measure of risk of changes to shareholders' returns due to changes in the capital structure of the firm; a measure of shareholders' returns due to increasing/decreasing levels of debt
Delta	A measure of risk of changes in the value of an option or a portfolio of options due to change(s) in the value of the underlying asset(s)
Theta	A measure of the risk of changes in the value of an option or a portfolio of options due to the passage of time
Gamma	A measure of the risk of changes in the value of an option or a portfolio of options due to changes in the value of the delta
Vega	A measure of the risk of changes in the value of an option or a portfolio of options due to changes in the volatility of the underlying asset
Rho	A measure of the risk of changes in the value of an option or a portfolio of options due to changes in the value of the risk-free rate of return

VOLATILITY

> With our inability to forecast the future, we rely on the historical past to peep into future events and hope that history repeats itself.

Volatility relates to changes in value arising from changes in market variables. The source of the change is usually new information that arrives continuously, causing changes in the overall market scenarios. Volatility is the key measure of risk to the value of assets—stocks, commodities, derivatives, etc. Volatility is said to be the key driver of the value of options. It is measured by standard deviation.

We also discussed implied volatility, which is reflected in the prices of options. Since the value of options is driven by expected volatility, it was reasonable to peep into the future through the prices of options. If options trade is healthy, it may be said to be a collective reflection of the value the market places on volatility. The use of implied volatility, however, is limited to valuing options that are not being traded heavily. Volatility estimates from deep in-the-money (ITM) and deep out-of-the-money (OTM) options cannot be relied upon, because intrinsic value comprises a major component of the price for ITM options, and the pricing of OTM options is too skewed for measuring volatility.

The standard way to measure volatility, probably arising out of our inability to look into the future without considering the past, is to rely on historical data and assume that what has been happening in the past would also happen in the future. Such an approach is appropriate in situations where the concern is the immediate future, or where the forecast period is small enough—for example, estimating probable losses over the next one day. As the time period extends further back, the relevance of the past to the forecast starts decreasing.

EXPONENTIAL WEIGHTED MOVING AVERAGE

When we measured volatility by historical data in Chapter 12, we assigned equal weights to each observation. For 100 daily returns (101 daily prices), we found the average and the standard deviation to arrive at the historical variability of returns and formed an opinion about the probable volatility of returns in the future. A more rational approach would be to assume that the recent past is more valuable than the distant past. Hence, recent variability in returns must get more prominence in our forecast for the future, i.e., what happened yesterday is more important than what happened 10 days back. Similarly, what happened 100 days back is less important than what happened 10 days back, and even less important than the events that happened one day back.

One way of assigning relative importance to past data based on its age is called the *exponential weighted moving average* (EWMA). Decreasing weights can be assigned to older data. If weights are exponentially decreasing with the age of the data, it is called *exponential smoothing*. The general form of assigning different weights to different observations (returns, r) is given by Eq. 14.1.

> The exponential moving average method to estimate volatility uses past data, with importance given in an exponentially decreasing manner as the data gets older.

$$\sigma_n^2 = \sum_{1}^{n-1} \alpha_i r_{n-1}^2 \qquad (14.1)$$

where α_i is the weight assigned to the observation i days ago. All α_i's are positive, and their sum must equal one. Where the weights α_i decrease exponentially, it becomes EWMA Model. The EWMA is called a moving average model because every day, the oldest observation in the data set is replaced by the latest one.

Translated in terms of variance, Eq. 14.1 for the variance of the nth day would become Eq. 14.2, given here:

$$\sigma_n^2 = \lambda \sigma_{n-1}^2 + (1 - \lambda) r_{n-1}^2 \qquad (14.2)$$

Here the variance for the day n is equal to the sum of (a) the variance for the previous day multiplied by its weight and (b) the square of the most recent return multiplied by its weight. The sum of the weights of the past variances and the most recent returns must equal 1. Specifically, if λ is the weight of the past variance, then the new variance would be given by Eq. 14.2.

We compute the variance progressively, i.e., by updating it with each observation, usually made once a day. This is often referred to as the *variance rate*. The biggest advantage of the EWMA is that one does not need to store all past values; only two values are required to find the volatility—the most recent volatility, σ, and the most recent return, r. Every day, we need to have the most recent estimate of volatility and return to arrive at the estimate of volatility for the next day. Volatility estimates based on historical values of volatility would require storage of all past data to the extent we consider them important for inclusion in our estimate.

If the daily volatility at the opening of Monday was estimated at 1.5%, and on Monday the stock registered a gain of 2%, then the estimate of volatility with $\lambda = 0.90$ for the next day, i.e., Tuesday, would be 1.5572%, which can be estimated by using Eq. 14.2, as shown here:

$$\sigma_n^2 = 0.90 \times 0.015^2 + 0.10 \times 0.02^2 = 0.0002025 + 0.00004 = 0.0002425$$
or $\sigma_n = 1.5572\%$

Looking at Eq. 14.2, one may believe that the values on the left hand side are positive, and, therefore, there would always be an increase in volatility from the past. However, this is not always true. A previous volatility at 1.5% means that under the random behaviour of stock prices, the expected return the next day is zero, with a standard deviation of 1.5%. If the actual returns are less than 1.5%, then there would be a reduction in volatility. If the returns are more than 1.5%, volatility would increase, and if the returns stay at 1.5%, the volatility for the next day remains unchanged. Assume that on Monday the return was not 2, but 1%. In this case, the estimate of volatility for Tuesday would be 1.46% as shown here, again using Eq. 14.2:

$$\sigma_n^2 = 0.90 \times 0.015^2 + 0.10 \times 0.01^2 = 0.0002025 + 0.00001 = 0.0002125$$
or $\sigma_n = 1.4577\%$

> The big advantage of the EWMA method is the low quantum of data that needs to be stored.

One parameter that requires managerial discretion in the EWMA model is the selection of the weight to be assigned to past volatility, λ,. A higher value of λ would give greater importance to the past and lesser importance to recent data. A decreasing value of λ would imply that the past is less important compared to recent changes. A low value of λ would make the estimates of volatility fluctuate more wildly with current returns and there would be less of a smoothing effect. We need to find the correct balance between the importance of past volatility and the most recent returns. The λ is, therefore, referred to as the smoothing constant.

RiskMetrics® (developed by J.P. Morgan) and its database, made public in 1994, used a value of $\lambda = 0.94$ after testing and confirming that this value provided the best results when measured in terms of estimated variance and actual variances. Therefore, the value of $\lambda = 0.94$ is the most widely used in the industry. The variance calculations for the purpose of determination of margins by the National Stock Exchange (NSE) in India also use the EWMA method with $\lambda = 0.94$. The physical significance of λ is that with each progressing day, the weight reduces by the factor of λ. If $\lambda = 0.94$, then the observation on a given day would have 6% (100 − 94%) weight for the next day. Therefore, λ is also referred to as the

Derivatives in Practice

Volatility and Risk Management

Margining system with EWMA and VaR

Standard deviation is the central component when it comes to managing risk. Exchanges all around the world assume default risk, and, therefore, seek to adequately protect themselves. A single default has the potential to cause an avalanche with catastrophic proportions. Stock exchanges in India (the NSE and the Bombay Stock Exchange, BSE) adopt three layers of margin—*initial margin* to cover for potential loss over one day, *marking-to-the-market margin* to settle daily profits or losses, and *extreme loss margin* to cover for situations not covered by the initial margin.

The initial margin is determined by using EWMA with $\lambda = 0.94$ as follows:

Calculate the log returns $R_n = \ln(P_n/P_{n-1})$ on a daily basis for one year.

Calculate the initial standard deviation of returns as $\sigma_0 = \sqrt{\sum_{1}^{250} \frac{(R - \overline{R})^2}{n}}$

After σ_0, obtain standard deviation for day 1 as $\sigma_1 = \sqrt{\lambda \sigma_0^2 + (1 - \lambda) R_1^2}$

This is calculated on a daily basis for each stock listed on the exchanges. For example, on a given day, if the previous volatility was 3.14% and the stock closed at ₹360 with the previous closing at ₹340, then the updated standard deviation would be

$$\sigma_1 = \sqrt{\lambda \sigma_0^2 + (1 - \lambda) R_1^2}$$
$$= \sqrt{0.94 \times 0.0314^2 + 0.06 \times 0.0588^2} = 0.0337 \equiv 3.37\%$$

The standard deviations for the two indices, i.e., Nifty for NSE, σ_{Nifty}, and SENSEX for BSE, σ_{SENSEX}, are calculated in the same fashion.

The initial margin is considered a function of (a) the stock volatility, characterized by its standard deviation and (b) its liquidity, characterized by the frequency of trade and impact cost. The margins for individual stocks are divided in three groups—Group I, Group II, and Group III—and the applicable initial margins are worked out as follows (σ is the standard deviation of the shares):

Groups	Definition	Margin
Group I	Traded on at least 80% of the days in the last six months, with an impact cost of less than 1%	$3.5 \times \sigma$, subject to a minimum of 7.5%
Group II	Traded on at least 80% of the days in the last six months, but with an impact cost of more than 1%	$\sqrt{3} \times 3$ (higher of σ_{Nifty} and σ_{SENSEX}) or $3.5 \times \sigma$, whichever is higher.
Group III	All others	$\sqrt{3} \times 5$ (higher of σ_{Nifty} and σ_{SENSEX})

The extreme loss margin for any security is 5% or 1.5 times the standard deviation of the daily logarithmic returns of the security price in the last six months, whichever is higher. This computation is done at the end of each month by taking the price data on a rolling basis for the past six months, and the resulting value is applicable for the next month.

Source: Based on information available at the website of NSE, www.nseindia.com, last accessed on 10 October 2012.

decay rate. There would be an exponential decrease in the value of any observation as time progresses, i.e., an observation of the previous day would have a weight of $6 \times 0.94 = 5.64\%$ and an observation for two days earlier would have a weight of 5.30% ($5.64\% \times 0.94$).

CORRELATION AND COVARIANCE

> The EWMA method can be extended to update correlations and covariances.

While dealing in multiple assets, not only is variance important but also the relationships among the assets gain prominence. In a portfolio of large assets, the risk is dominated more by covariance and not as much by variance, as has been demonstrated by Harry Markowitz. We can use a similar approach in the EWMA model for updating volatility and covariance between assets, and, hence, updating the coefficient of correlation that impacts covariance. Using

EXAMPLE 14.1 Revising volatility

The volatility of a stock A today is estimated to be 5%. If during the day the stock declines by 3%, what would your estimated volatility for tomorrow be under the EWMA method if the decay rate is assumed at 94%?

Solution
Using Eq. 14.2 of the EWMA for finding the revised volatility estimates, we have

$$\sigma_n^2 = \lambda\sigma_{n-1}^2 + (1-\lambda)r_{n-1}^2 = 0.94 \times 0.05^2 + 0.06 \times 0.03^2$$
$$= 0.00235 + 0.000054$$
$$= 0.002404$$

Or $\sigma_n = \sqrt{0.002404} = 0.0490 \equiv 4.90\%$

The volatility has declined from the previous day, because the return of the stock for the day (3%) was less than the previous estimate of volatility (5%).

---

a logic similar to that used for updating variance, the EWMA method for covariance is given by Eq. 14.3, replacing variance with covariance.

$$Cov(x, y)_n = \lambda Cov(x, y)_{n-1} + (1-\lambda)x_{n-1}y_{n-1} \quad (14.3)$$

where $Cov(x, y)_n$ is the new estimate of covariance, $Cov(x, y)_{n-1}$ is the most recent covariance available and x_{n-1} and y_{n-1} are the most recent returns of assets X and Y, respectively.

Assume that the correlation, ρ, between two assets X and Y is 0.7 today. The assets' volatilities are 2% and 6%, respectively. The covariance today between the two assets is, therefore, $\rho\sigma_x\sigma_y = 0.7 \times 0.02 \times 0.06 = 0.00084$.

If today, assets X and Y registered returns of 2% and 3%, respectively, then the respective volatility estimates for tomorrow would be (using Eq. 14.2 with $\lambda = 0.9$) as follows:

For X, $\sigma_n^2 = \lambda\sigma_{n-1}^2 + (1-\lambda)r_{n-1}^2 = 0.9 \times 0.0004 + 0.1 \times 0.0004 = 0.00040$

Therefore, the new volatility for X is $\sqrt{0.0004} = 0.02 \equiv 2\%$

For Y, $\sigma_n^2 = \lambda\sigma_{n-1}^2 + (1-\lambda)r_{n-1}^2 = 0.9 \times 0.0036 + 0.1 \times 0.0009 = 0.00333$

The new volatility for Y is $\sqrt{0.00333} = 0.0577 \equiv 5.77\%$

The revised estimate of covariance between X and Y using Eq. 14.3 is

$$Cov(x, y)_n = \lambda Cov(x, y)_{n-1} + (1-\lambda)x_{n-1}y_{n-1}$$
$$= 0.9 \times 0.00084 + 0.1 \times 0.02 \times 0.03 = 0.000816$$

Therefore, the new coefficient of correlation would be

$$Corr(x, y)_n = \frac{Cov(x, y)_n}{\sigma_{x_n}\sigma_{y_n}} = \frac{0.000816}{0.02 \times 0.0577} = 0.7071$$

GARCH (1, 1) MODEL

Volatility changes over a period of time. A volatility estimate made in the past does not continue to remain valid in the future. In 1982, Robert Engle measured the time-varying volatility of inflation rates in the UK. The model used by him was named *auto regressive conditional heteroskedasticity* (ARCH), which meant that the natural way to revise an estimate of variance is to average it out with the most recent observed variance. The model assumes

> **EXAMPLE 14.2 Revising covariance and correlation**
>
> Along with stock A as described in Example 14.1; consider another stock B, whose volatility estimate for today is 10%. Its correlation with stock A is estimated at 0.60. Stock B's return today is +5%.
>
> What is the new estimate of volatility for tomorrow under the EWMA method if the weight assigned to the past variance is 94% for stock B?
>
> What is the present covariance and new estimate of covariance for tomorrow after today's outcomes using the EWMA method, with the weight assigned to the existing covariance at 94%?
>
> **Solution**
> The present estimate of covariance between A and B, $Cov(A, B)_{n-1}$ is $0.60 \times 0.05 \times 0.10 = 0.003$.
>
> Using Eq. 14.2 of the EWMA for finding the revised volatility estimates for stock B, we have
>
> $$\sigma_n^2 = \lambda \sigma_{n-1}^2 + (1-\lambda)r_{n-1}^2 = 0.94 \times 0.1^2 + 0.06 \times 0.05^2$$
> $$= 0.0094 + 0.00015$$
> $$= 0.00955$$
> Or $\sigma_n = \sqrt{0.00955} = 0.0977 \equiv 9.77\%$
>
> The new estimate for covariance would be
>
> $$Cov(A, B)_n = \lambda Cov(A, B)_{n-1} + (1-\lambda)x_{n-1}y_{n-1}$$
> $$= 0.94 \times 0.003 + 0.06 \times -0.03 \times 0.05 = 0.00282 - 0.000090 = 0.00273$$
>
> The new estimate for the coefficient of correlation is
>
> $$Corr(A, B)_n = \frac{Cov(A, B)_n}{\sigma_{x_n}\sigma_{y_n}} = \frac{0.00273}{0.049 \times 0.0977} = 0.5703$$
>
> Correlation has reduced because of the opposite movement caused by stocks with A registering a loss of 3% and those with B showing a gain of 5%.

that volatility evolves over time slowly, as new observations are added. It depends upon the previous estimate and the most recent squared residual return, which is an unbiased estimate of variance. The method allows updating of the variance with the previous estimate, and an unbiased estimate of the new information is obtained.

The important difference between the ARCH and EWMA methods is that ARCH assumes that variance is mean reverting—it tends to get back to its long-term average. The weight given to the long-term average in the computation of variance would be the rate of reversion. The EWMA model is not a mean-reverting model. In practice, it is observed that variance tends to revert to a value that can be called a long-term average, and, therefore, the ARCH model is considered better than the EWMA.

> The exponential moving average is not mean-reverting. It is seen that volatility returns to the long-term average. The ARCH and GARCH approaches assume mean reversion, and hence, are preferred over the EWMA.

Another model, *generalised auto regressive conditional heteroskedasticity* (1,1) (GARCH, developed by Robert Engle and Bollerslev) states that variance comprises the following three components:

(a) Long-term average variance, V_L
(b) The variance in the immediate past, σ_{n-1}
(c) The return in the immediate past, r_{n-1}

Under GARCH (1, 1), variance at time *n* would be given by Eq.14.4.

$$\sigma_n^2 = aV_L + b\sigma_{n-1}^2 + cr_{n-1}^2 \qquad (14.4)$$

where a, b, and c are the non-negative weights assigned to the long-term average variance, recent volatility, and recent returns, respectively, and

$$a + b + c = 1$$

The model assumes that variance tends to revert to some mean value given by the long-term variance. The weight assigned to it, a, signifies the rate of reversion. The variance tends to be pulled back towards the long-term average. In case the value of a is negative, the variance would not be mean reverting but mean diverging. Under such a case it is better to use the EWMA model, which is a special case of the GARCH model. With $a = 0$, $b = \lambda$, and $c = 1 - \lambda$, the model reduces to the EWMA model.

The (1,1) signifies that variance estimates include one recent observation each of immediate variance and immediate returns. Similarly, (2,3) would mean that the variance includes two recent observations of variance, and three recent observations of returns. The most popular version used is GARCH (1,1). The GARCH model has been applied extensively for stock markets, interest rates, and exchange rates.

VOLATILITY INDEX

Volatility measurement from past data is needed to find the value of options. It is one extremely critical input that is not observable, but options values are heavily dependent on it. However, the prices of options are observable. The value of an option implies volatility. The higher the value of the option, the higher is the volatility. Assuming that the Black–Scholes Model (BSM) correctly assigns values, any divergence in the market value and the BSM value is attributable to the estimates of volatility. For correctly valuing an option, we need an estimate of volatility that holds good for the coming days till the expiry of the option. Hence, the market values of options that imply volatilities for the option period should be reflective of the future, not in isolation but in aggregation. The values of options are higher with higher expected volatilities and vice versa.

Based on these concepts, an estimate of future volatility on any asset can be derived from the values of the options traded on those assets. If the underlying is a stock, the option values would reflect its volatility as anticipated for the option period. If the underlying is an index, the volatility values would represent general sentiments about market volatilities anticipated in the immediate future, with a broader measure of risks in the future. Just as we treat inflation as a representative of economic performance, and a stock market index as reflective of the market's general sentiments, a volatility index (VIX) is used to represent the general perception of market volatility anticipated for the future. While inflation rates and stock indices measure performance based on current observations and have historical significance, the VIX is not a measure of past volatility but of future volatility and has prospective significance. It is because of this fact that option values hide future volatility within themselves.

> The volatility index is an attempt to forecast volatility over a fixed short-term period based on the prices of actively traded options.

Volatility measurement based on the prices of options was first introduced by the Chicago Board Options Exchange (CBOE) in 1993. It was a weighted measure of the implied volatility of eight S&P 100 at-the-money (ATM) put and call options. It was called the *Volatility Index* (VIX®). Ten years later, in 2003, CBOE changed the composition and methodology of the VIX for a more accurate and robust view of investors expectations on future market volatility in the following ways:

- The underlying asset was expanded to use options based on a broader index, the S&P 500 rather than the S&P 100. A broader index meant greater participation of investors.
- It included a wide range of strike prices rather than only ATM options to capture the whole volatility skew, rather than just the volatility implied by ATM options.
- It calculated volatility directly from index option prices, rather than using an algorithm that involved finding implied volatilities out of an option pricing model.

The CBOE also introduced products based on VIX, such as futures and options, in 2003.

The original VIX was constructed using the implied volatilities of eight different OEX® (ticker for American-style options at the CBOE, and XEO®, which represents European-style options) option series so that, at any given time, it represented the implied volatility of a hypothetical ATM OEX option with exactly 30 days to expiration.

The VIX measures the market expectation of near-term volatility conveyed by stock index option prices. VIX values of greater than 30 are generally associated with a large amount of volatility as a result of investor fear or uncertainty, while values below 20 generally correspond to less stressful or even complacent times in the markets.

The VIX is based on real-time option prices, which reflect investors consensus view of future expected stock market volatility. During periods of financial stress, which are often accompanied by steep market declines, option prices—and VIX—tend to rise. The greater the fear, the higher is the VIX level. As investors' fear subsides, option prices tend to decline, which in turn causes VIX to decline.

Most major exchanges, including those in India and Hong Kong, have adopted the VIX methodology of CBOE to find their own estimates of volatility. Volatility indices for Nifty in India and Hang Seng in Hong Kong are already using the same methodology, adapted to local conditions.

The methodology followed by NSE to arrive at the India VIX in a simplified version is presented in the box, which can be skipped without any loss of continuity.

COMPUTATION OF INDIA VIX*

The VIX in India, computed by the NSE, is arrived at using prices of the near-month series and the next-month series of OTM options on the NIFTY index to cover the next 30 days.

In computing the VIX, only OTM options are considered. When a call is in-the-money, the put is out-of-the-money, and vice versa. A chain of option series with different strikes is considered for computation of India VIX.

The India VIX gives the volatility estimates over the near term, which is assumed to be the next 30-day period. For a larger change in price, volatility is higher, and the VIX would have a higher value. For steady markets, the VIX would be lower. It is expressed as an annualized percentage based on the option prices, as option values are considered a function of anticipated volatility. Higher prices of options indicate more volatility and vice versa. The electronic order book for options at exchanges may be used as investors' perception of future volatility.

*Based on the India VIX methodology used by NSE

To arrive at volatility for the near term, the standard deviation of two time series of option prices are used—one for the near term and another for the next month. The volatility, σ, in terms of variance from the option prices is derived using Eq. 14.5:

$$\sigma^2 = \frac{2}{T} \sum \frac{\Delta X_i}{X_i^2} e^{rT} Q_i - \frac{1}{T}\left[\frac{F}{X_0} - 1\right]^2 \quad (14.5)$$

The meanings of various terms and methods for arriving at their values are given in the following paragraphs.

Forward Price, F

The forward price is the value of Nifty in the futures market. For the near month and the next month, the values of a futures contract would be different. We have assumed that the near-month futures trades at 5011 and the next-month futures trades at 5025.

Finding ATM Option, X_0

The ATM option is decided on the basis of Nifty futures prices. An ATM option is the immediate strike below the futures price. Say a near-month futures contract on the Nifty index is trading at 5011. Therefore, an ATM option (with a strike immediately below the futures price) is 5000. This would be the ATM strike for the next month's option.

Time to Expiry, T

A near-month option expires nine days from now. Therefore, the time to expiry, T, = 9/365 = 0.02466 years. The next month's option series expires 37 days from now, and, therefore, the time to expiry for the next-month series would be 37/365 = 0.10137 years.

Risk-free Rate, r

The risk-free rate is taken to be the NSE MIBOR rate for the term of expiry. It is taken here at 5%. Assuming a flat-term structure, the risk-free rate for the near month and the next month series of options, the risk-free rate remains the same, at 5%.

Option Values, Q_i

All options below and above the ATM strike that are traded are considered. Including the ATM strike, we have considered 11 strikes: five below the ATM strike and five above the ATM strike. The price of calls and put are as given in Table 14.1. However, the prices of only OTM options are relevant. Mid prices, the average of bid and ask values for call and put options are considered as appropriate values, Q_i. For ATM options, the appropriate value is the average of the mid of the call and the put.

Option Interval, ΔX

The option interval is the average of the immediately lower and the immediately upper strikes. Since options introduced are separated by 100 in the strikes, the value of the option interval is fixed at 100.

Table 14.1 Prices of calls and puts for near-month expiry

Strike price	Call prices			Put prices			Q_i	$\frac{\Delta X_i}{X_i^2} e^{rT} Q_i$
	Bid	Ask	Mid	Bid	Ask	Mid		
4,500				1.00	1.20	1.10	1.10	0.000005439
4,600				5.00	6.00	5.50	5.50	0.000026025
4,700	Ignored, being ITM options			12.00	13.00	12.50	12.50	0.000056656
4,800				33.00	35.00	34.00	34.00	0.000147751
4,900				41.00	42.00	41.50	41.50	0.000173058
5,000	50.00	52.00	51.00	45.00	46.00	45.50	48.25	0.000193238
5,100	40.00	41.00	40.50				40.50	0.000155901
5,200	30.00	32.00	31.00				31.00	0.000114786
5,300	20.00	21.00	20.50	Ignored, being ITM options			20.50	0.000073070
5,400	12.00	14.00	13.00				13.00	0.000044637
5,500	4.00	5.00	4.50				4.50	0.000014894
$\sum \frac{\Delta X_i}{X_i^2} e^{rT} Q_i$								0.001005456
$\frac{2}{T} \sum \frac{\Delta X_i}{X_i^2} e^{rT} Q_i$								0.081553640

Variances for the near-month option series and next month option series are shown in Tables 14.1 and 14.2, respectively.

$$\frac{1}{T}\left[\frac{F}{X_0} - 1\right]^2 = \frac{1}{0.02466}\left[\frac{5{,}011}{5{,}000} - 1\right]^2 = 0.000196289$$

$$\sigma_1^2 = \frac{2}{T}\sum \frac{\Delta X_i}{X_i^2} e^{rT} Q_i - \frac{1}{T}\left[\frac{F}{X_0} - 1\right]^2 = 0.081553640 - 0.000196289 = 0.081357351$$

Note that the last column in Table 14.1 implies the contribution of that option to the overall variance. For example, the put option with a strike of 4500 contributes 0.000005439 to the overall variance.

The variance estimate based on the prices of options expiring in the near month is 0.081357351, meaning a volatility of 0.2852 or 28.52%.

Proceeding in the same manner, we find the variance implied by option prices expiring next month in Table 14.2.

$$\frac{1}{T}\left[\frac{F}{X_0} - 1\right]^2 = \frac{1}{0.10137}\left[\frac{5{,}025}{5{,}000} - 1\right]^2 = 0.000246622$$

$$\sigma_2^2 = \frac{2}{T}\sum \frac{\Delta X_i}{X_i^2} e^{rT} Q_i - \frac{1}{T}\left[\frac{F}{X_0} - 1\right]^2 = 0.024335978 - 0.000246622 = 0.024089357$$

The variance estimate based on prices of options expiring next month is 0.024089357, meaning a volatility of 0.15852 or 15.52%. The difference in the expiry dates of near-month and next-month futures is taken as 28 days.

Table 14.2 Prices of calls and puts for next-month expiry

Strike price	Call prices			Put prices			Q_i	$\frac{\Delta X_i}{X_i^2} e^{rT} Q_i$
	Bid	Ask	Mid	Bid	Ask	Mid		
4,500				2.00	3.00	2.50	2.50	0.000012408
4,600				7.00	8.00	7.50	7.50	0.000035624
4,700	Ignored, being ITM options			13.00	14.00	13.50	13.50	0.000061424
4,800				38.00	40.00	39.00	39.00	0.000170131
4,900				48.00	50.00	49.00	49.00	0.000205119
5,000	60.00	63.00	61.50	65.00	68.00	66.50	64.00	0.000257301
5,100	55.00	56.00	55.50				55.50	0.000214464
5,200	34.00	35.00	34.50				34.50	0.000128237
5,300	22.00	23.00	22.50	Ignored, being ITM options			22.50	0.000080507
5,400	14.00	15.00	14.50				14.50	0.000049978
5,500	5.00	6.00	5.50				5.50	0.000018274
$\sum \frac{\Delta X_i}{X_i^2} e^{rT} Q_i$								0.001233467
$\frac{2}{T} \sum \frac{\Delta X_i}{X_i^2} e^{rT} Q_i$								0.024335978

The values of variance are interpolated to provide the volatility estimates for 30 days, as shown here:

$$\sigma^2 = \left[T_1 \sigma_1^2 \left[\frac{T_2 - 30}{T_2 - T_1} \right] + T_2 \sigma_2^2 \left[\frac{30 - T_1}{T_2 - T_1} \right] \right] \times \frac{365}{30}$$

$$\sigma^2 = \left[0.02466 \times 0.08136 \left[\frac{37 - 30}{28} \right] + 0.10137 \times 0.02409 \left[\frac{37 - 9}{28} \right] \right] \times \frac{365}{30}$$

$$\sigma^2 = [0.0005015 + 0.0018315] \times \frac{365}{30} = 0.02838$$

This gives σ as 0.1685, and the VIX is $100 \times \sigma = 16.85\%$.

The methodology explained here differs from the one adopted by the NSE in several ways. These differences are detailed here:

- The selection of a series of options stretches to all options being traded. We considered only eight options.
- Spreads between calls and puts exceeding 30% of the mid value are not considered appropriate. They are replaced by cubic spline fitting, and not by extrapolation of the prices of adjacent options, since option values do not change linearly. In our example, this has been ignored.
- Time to expiry is calculated with precision of minutes and not days as done here.

VALUE AT RISK

> VaR is a comprehensive measure or estimate that tells users if the loss on a portfolio over a specified period would not exceed it (VaR) with some specified confidence level.

While academicians and practitioners kept investigating risk measurement and management as products developed, the need was felt to have a rather simplified and yet comprehensive measure of risk. While different risks impact different securities, there is a need for tools that enable integrated views on the potential losses that can be made on a portfolio in a given period of time, for the purposes of examining the adequacy of capital and ensuring the preparedness of financial institutions to overcome crisis situations.

The value at risk (VaR) approach is one such tool, which has become popular recently. The credit for using VaR as a risk-measurement tool is attributed to Dennis Weatherstone, CEO of JP Morgan, who wanted a consolidated and comprehensive, yet simple and singular measure to understand what deterioration can take place in the value of a portfolio at the end of each trading day, i.e., what dollar amount could be lost over the next day to assess the risk the bank was exposed to. In a way, he sought an answer to the question "How much worse can things get?"

The portfolio of the bank would consist of a huge variety of investments, and each investment is sensitive to several macro-economic factors, though we tend to condense the risk into one or two important measures. A portfolio of stock is primarily exposed to market risk measured by its beta. A portfolio of fixed-income securities is exposed to changes in the interest rates. If the yields rise, the value of the portfolio falls. Similarly, holding stocks of various currencies is subject to the risk of changing foreign exchange rates. A loan portfolio is subject to credit risk. If the portfolio was global, the situations and risk parameters would become increasingly complex. For a financial institution such as a bank, the size of the portfolio is large, which adds to the complexity of risk management. In addition, if derivatives are also included in the portfolio, several other risk factors are added.

In case a portfolio consists of stocks, bonds, and currencies, the individual measures of risk such as duration of bonds, beta of the portfolio, standard deviation of stock, and option Greeks do not provide for a firm-wide comprehensive assessment of risk. These measures focus on one variable and the sensitivity of the value due to a single variable. A firm is exposed to several investments that are predominantly sensitive to one or two variables. While it is important to understand the implications of changes in the major variables on the value of a specific investment, it is perceived that since the variables are correlated, a change in any of the variables is capable of influencing other investments, and, hence, the total portfolio value. For example, the risk of change in the value of a portfolio of stocks is condensed in its beta, but changes in the interest rates (predominantly affecting the portfolio of bonds) also cause changes in the value of the portfolio of stocks, due to changes in market returns, even though the beta may remain unchanged.

A comprehensive measure of risk becomes extremely important for those who hold a variety of investments. One such situation is a firm in the financial sector that is exposed to a variety of risks—deriving from a credit portfolio subject to default risk; investments in government securities subject to interest rate risk; exposure to foreign currencies subject to exchange rate fluctuation risk; investment in stocks subject to market risk; and so on.

Features and Concerns of the Financial Sector

> Financial institutions and banks are different from industrial corporations with respect to high debt, lack of tangible assets, lack of control by depositors, and the possibility of a run on the banks.

The distinguishing features of banks and financial institutions as compared to any conventional industrial firm are (a) the high degree of leverage and (b) the absence of tangible and physical assets. Financial institutions operate in a highly leveraged environment; their depositors lend to them rather than subscribe to the capital, and, hence, these institutions are susceptible to failure. They need to be capitalized adequately to protect their lenders (depositors) by providing for potential losses. They should be able to absorb adverse situations with their own financial reserve strength and not by impinging upon the claims of depositors. Further, financial firms typically have very little fixed and tangible assets to back them in adverse situations or to provide a sense of security to their shareholders. Due to high leverage and lack of tangible assets in financial sectors, the position of shareholders of financial firms such as banks or insurance companies is extremely precarious. To create shareholder value, the measurement of risk and its management assume great significance. Shareholders of financial institutions/firms do not have much of an ability to diversify the credit or default risk they face from the operations of these institutions/firms.

The financial sector is also characterized by a *run on banks* in case of adverse scenarios. The banking sector and financial institutions remain fragile, and, hence, must handle risk with utmost care. One way of safeguarding the interest of shareholders as well as creditors (depositors) is to capitalize the bank adequately, so as to take care of potential losses in most situations. A comprehensive firm-wide measure of risk is required to manage it. One such measure is the VaR.

DEFINITION AND MEANING OF VaR

> VaR is defined in terms of absolute or percent value of loss that can take place over a period of N days with X% confidence level. X and N are parameters chosen by the user.

The value at risk is defined as the level of potential loss on a portfolio over a period of N days that it would not be exceeded with X% chance, called the confidence level. Typically, a period of one day is taken for computing VaR, and the confidence level is between 99% and 95%. For example, if 1-day VaR with a 95% confidence level is, say, ₹1 crore, it simply means that the bank/firm holding the portfolio would see a loss on the portfolio of less than ₹1 crore on 95 out of 100 days. For the remaining five days, the loss would exceed ₹1 crore. This loss would be on account of market risk, with other risks such as counterparty risk excluded.

The VaR can be expressed either as an absolute value or as a percentage of the value of the portfolio. It is dependent upon the time horizon (number of days) and the confidence level. All these parameters are user-defined.

VaR with Normal Distribution

To illustrate the concept of VaR, we take recourse to the all familiar bell-shaped curve of normal distribution. Assume that portfolio returns are normally distributed with a mean of

μ and a standard deviation of σ. In such a case, a 95% 1-day VaR would correspond to the area under the standard normal distribution curve at $100 - X = 5\%$ cumulative probability. This typically happens at $\mu \pm 1.65\sigma$.

Any portfolio that has a distribution of return as normal can be converted to an equivalent z-score for standard normal distribution by subtracting the mean and then dividing by the standard deviation. The z-score in standard normal distribution is given by $(x - \mu)/\sigma$. The 95% confidence interval happens at a z-score of 1.65 and the 99% confidence interval occurs at 2.33. Therefore, the VaR is given by

VaR with an $X\%$ confidence level
= Probability that loss does not exceed $(100 - 95)\%$
= $P(z \leq (100 - X))$

For example, consider a bank that owns stock of Reliance Industries Ltd, with an expected return of 10% and a standard deviation of 20%. The VaR with a 95% confidence would be $10 - (1.65 \times 20) = -23\%$ return. This is depicted in Fig. 14.1.

If the market value of the holding is ₹10 crore, then there is a 95% chance that any loss on the value would not exceed -23%, i.e., ₹2.30 crore over a period of one year. For the purpose of risk management for a bank, the implications of VaR may be either of the following.

(a) The VaR method provides a summary measure of the risk the bank is exposed to, and hence, serves as a comprehensive measurement of capital adequacy. Thus, for the bank, which likes to provide for 95% of possible situations, a capital cushion of ₹2.30 crore is required.

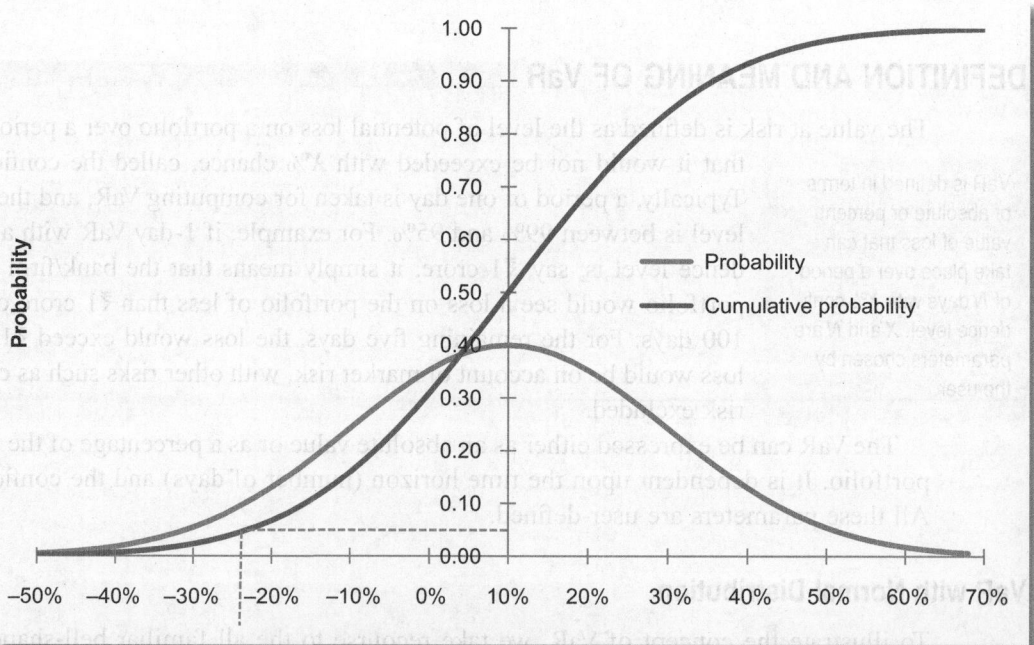

Fig. 14.1 Normal and cumulative normal distribution

(b) The VaR method can serve to arrive at a comprehensive figure that may limit the risk-weighted assets of financial institutions. If the bank is capitalized to a lesser extent, say ₹1.50 crore, and cannot capitalize to the desired level, then it must reduce its exposure to the stock of Reliance Industries Ltd to ₹6.52 crore (1.50/0.23). The sale proceeds of ₹3.48 crore may be invested in risk-free securities. (Remember, though, that these securities too would not really be free from risk, as they would predominantly carry interest rate risk.)

Risk and Time Risk compounds with time, but not linearly. If one holds a portfolio for longer than one year, say for two years, would the risk increase to twice as much? The risk, as measured by standard deviation, compounds with the square root of the period. Our illustration for explaining VaR was based on the annual distribution of returns on the stock of Reliance Industries. Typically, for the purpose of determining VaR, a period of one day is taken. Under the assumption of returns being independently and identically distributed normally, the following relationships prove handy in converting the risk measurement of the VaR for the period under consideration.

> The VaR is usually calculated for one day and then scaled for the time horizon; the confidence interval chosen is usually between 95% and 99%.

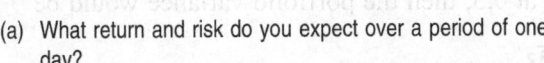

$$N\text{-day VaR} = 1\text{-day VaR} \times \sqrt{N}$$

or

$$1\text{-day VaR} = \text{Annual VaR}/\sqrt{N}$$

EXAMPLE 14.3 Return, risk, and VaR for a single asset

Assume that the stock of ITC has an annual expected return of 25%, with an annual volatility of 15%.

(a) What return and risk do you expect over a period of one day?
(b) What return and risk do you expect over a period of 10 days?
(c) What is the range of returns for one day and 10 days with 95% and 99% confidence?
(d) What percentage of value would you provide for losses over one day and 10 days for covering 95% and 99% outcomes?

Assume 250 days in a year.

Solution

(a) One day
   The 1-day return on ITC stock = 25/250 = 0.1%
   The 1-day standard deviation = 15/√250 = 0.95%
(b) 10 days
   The 10-day return on ITC stock = 25/25 = 1.00%
   The 10-day standard deviation = 15/√25 = 3.00% or (0.95√10)
(c) The range of return over one day
   With 95% confidence = 0.10 ± 1.65 × 0.95; −1.4675 to + 1.6675%
   With 99% confidence = 0.10 ± 2.33 × 0.95; −2.1135% to + 2.3125%
   Range of return over 10 days
   With 95% confidence = 1.00 ± 1.65 × 3.00; −3.95% to + 5.95%
   With 99% confidence = 1.00 ± 2.33 × 3.00; −5.99% to
+ 7.99%
(d) Value at risk
   1-day VaR with 95% confidence = 1.65 × 0.95 = 1.5675%
   1-day VaR with 99% confidence = 2.33 × 0.95 = 2.2135%
   10-day VaR with 95% confidence = 1.65 × 3.00 = 4.95%
   10-day VaR with 99% confidence = 2.33 × 3.00 = 6.99%

If the 95% VaR in this illustration was −23%, then, based on roughly 250 trading days, the 1-day VaR would be $-23/\sqrt{250} = -1.46\%$, i.e., ₹14.60 lakh, and the 2-week VaR with 10 trading days would be $-1.46 \times \sqrt{10} = -4.62\%$, i.e., ₹46.20 lakh. The daily returns would have a mean of $10/250 = 0.04\%$, and a standard deviation of $20/\sqrt{250} = 1.26\%$. With normal distribution, the returns would fluctuate between $0.04 + 1.65 \times 1.26 = 2.12\%$ and $0.04 - 1.65 \times 1.26 = -2.04\%$ on 95% (about 238 in number) of the days.

VaR is usually computed for a 10-day period. The normal way of arriving at this figure would be to compute the VaR based on 1-day returns and then find the 10-day VaR as the 1-day VaR $\times \sqrt{10}$.

Portfolio Effect on VaR

Under the portfolio approach, broadly classified as the parametric approach, calculation of the VaR for a portfolio would be based on the portfolio returns and risk, and would involve correlation coefficients among the stocks of the portfolio as additional inputs. Assume that a bank has a portfolio of Reliance and ITC shares with equal investment of ₹10 crore in each. Based on a 10-day period, the VaR with a 99% confidence on each of the stocks would be ₹163.10 lakh (refer to the table as follows).

Stock	Investment	Annual volatility	10-day volatility	99% 10-day VaR
Reliance	₹1000 lakh	20%	4%	9.32% = ₹93.20 lakh
ITC	₹1000 lakh	15%	3%	6.99% = ₹69.90 lakh

If the correlation of the two is estimated at 0.5, then the portfolio variance would be

$$\sigma^2 = f_1^2 \sigma_1^2 + f_2^2 \sigma_2^2 + 2\rho f_1 f_2 \sigma_1 \sigma_2$$
$$= 0.25 \times 400 + 0.25 \times 225 + 2 \times 0.5 \times 0.5 \times 0.5 \times 20 \times 15 = 231.25$$

The standard deviation of the portfolio is 15.21%, and the 10-day standard deviation would be 3.04%. For a 99% 10-day period, the VaR would be $2.33 \times 3.04 = 7.09\%$.

The VaR would be $7.09\% \times 2000 = ₹141.80$ lakh. The VaR stands reduced due to the portfolio effect.

In practice, loss in a portfolio may not be normally distributed. If so, the actual distribution of loss over a given period is computed and the probability distribution plotted. For a 95% VaR, the fifth-percentile loss gives the VaR. For example, if 100 observations are made and the portfolio loss or profit is tabulated, then the fifth worst loss would correspond to the 95% VaR. Similarly, for a confidence interval of 99%, the first percentile would give a 99% VaR.

DECISIONS IN VaR

There are two variables in computing VaR that managers have to keep in mind while making decisions:

- Selection of confidence level
- Selection of time period

Selection of Confidence Level

The confidence level specifies the frequency of occurrence of maximum loss. A 95% VaR implies that on 5 out of 100 days, the loss would exceed the VaR estimate. Similarly, a 99.9% VaR assumes that the loss would exceed the VaR estimate on 1 out of 1000 days, i.e., approximately once in three years.

Providing capital adequacy according to the VaR method would mean increased safety, with an increased confidence level of VaR. The larger the confidence level, the lower is the risk of facing capital inadequacy. A 99.9% VaR would be much higher than a VaR based on a 95% confidence interval. Not only is the provision of capital adequacy large but also it would be unrealistic, to have a confidence level as high as 99.9%. It is unrealistic because it is indeed difficult to verify the statistical accuracy of a confidence level that is over-cautious.

Confidence interval selection is based on normal distribution assumptions. It may be argued that bad events do take place more often than suggested by normal distribution. Further, when such events do occur, the magnitude of losses would be much higher because of the high degree of correlation amongst the variables that determine the returns. For example, political instability may cause a simultaneous crash of the bonds market, the stock market, and the exchange rate market. Under extremely adverse conditions, they tend to act together to the detriment of the value of portfolios. Under normal conditions, these markets may have a lower correlation with each other, or their relationship can be established through a model. The model breaks down under extremely adverse conditions.

It is observed that a confidence level of more than 95% tends to lose validity.

Selection of Time Horizon

The other important determinant of VaR is the time horizon. The usual calculation of VaR is based on the daily returns, and then an appropriate scaling factor is used for the number of days of safety required, depending upon the organisational needs. Under the assumption of normal distribution, the scaling factor is the square root of the time period.

A financial institution having a marketable portfolio can unwind its position in a short period of time and, hence, can use a lower time period. Corporates that do not have a trading portfolio may choose to opt for longer time horizons, such as a quarter. It may also be suggested that selection of the time horizon must be based on the liquidity of the assets. Different assets trade in different markets characterized by asset classes and geographies. For example, bonds in an emerging market may take longer to unwind than stocks held in a developed economy. However, more often than not, institutions do not differentiate between asset classes and markets, and, instead, apply the same scaling factor to the entire portfolio.

METHODS OF CALCULATING VaR

In any method for calculating the VaR, the two inputs required are

- the value of the portfolio; and
- the variability of the market, i.e., volatility.

Valuation

> The method of calculating VaR involves two steps—a valuation approach to value the portfolio and estimation of volatility of market factors.

The valuation of a portfolio is easy when the securities comprising the portfolio are traded. We then have market value and do not need to make any assumptions. For illiquid or non-traded assets in the portfolio, no market data are available. The approach used most often is *cash flow mapping*, where the cash flows attached with the instrument are broken down in the form of standard products whose valuation is available. For example, a bond that matures after 14 months can be represented as bonds with maturities of 3, 6, 12, and 18 months, whose valuations are readily available as they may be traded. For the projected value of the portfolio, we may either use past values and changes in them or may have some analytical model that establishes the value based on its determinants.

Estimation of Volatility

Changes in the value of a portfolio occur due to changes in market variables, referred to as volatility. To estimate volatility, we need (a) specific scenarios and (b) correlations among market variables. If the value depends upon multiple factors, then the change in value is a function of (a) volatility of each factor, (b) correlation among factors, and (c) sensitivity of value with respect to each factor.

Changes in value of the portfolio can be achieved through analytical models, where the relationship of the value with respect to market variables is established; for example, returns on a portfolio of stock are given by its beta, changes in the value of a portfolio of bonds are given by duration, and changes in the value of a portfolio of derivatives are given by the delta.

An analytical approach also requires correlations and variances as inputs; this is sometimes referred to as the *variance–covariance* approach. The advantages of such an approach, based on models, include (a) easier comprehension, (b) lesser data requirement, and (c) fast computing. Once a valuation model is developed, computations become easy. The disadvantage of the model building approach is that it ignores historical data that may defy the validity of the pricing model itself. Though the model is built on historical correlations and variances, they may not hold good in the future. Another disadvantage with such an approach is the non-linearity of payoffs in case of derivatives like options. Estimates based on the delta would be invalid under certain conditions, and full valuation methods such as the BSM, may be required to arrive at true changes in value. For instruments with linear payoffs, the model approach may work fine.

The second approach uses past data for computing VaR. Under simulation, we are not measuring changes in value; we are re-computing the values of the portfolio afresh, under different possible scenarios. The issue revolves around how to generate scenarios. There are two ways of doing it—historical and Monte Carlo simulations.

Under historical simulation, we assume that history can foretell the future. One has to decide how far back in history one goes to generate as many scenarios as possible. We treat each past day as one possible scenario and re-value the portfolio for the future, assuming no specific distribution for the scenarios except what is contained in the history. Under Monte Carlo simulation, the process remains the same as the historical one, except for the method of generating different scenarios. Unlike historical simulation, we create different scenarios based on defined stochastic processes, where we assume specific distributions.

HISTORICAL SIMULATION

As mentioned, one way of arriving at the VaR is based on historical data. The value of the portfolio is a function of several parameters. These are often broad economic variables such as the state of the stock markets, interest rates, exchange rate, inflation rates, and growth rates. Due to varying degrees of correlations of these variables, it is naïve to assume predictability based on model building.

> Historical simulation is based on the underlying assumption that historical changes contain possible scenarios of market variables, and can form the basis for future estimate.

One way of finding the potential impact of changing economic variables without establishing the exact cause–effect relationship is to examine how the portfolio behaved under different scenarios in the past. Based on the past, the likely change in the value of the portfolio the next day would give an idea of the potential loss that can be incurred over a period of one day. The underlying idea is that for the next day, the variables can change in any of the ways they changed in the past.

For computing VaR based on historical simulation, we need to undertake the following actions:

(a) Identify and select the variables that impact the value of the portfolio
(b) Take the actual past values of these variables, i, on a daily basis
(c) Compute the value of the portfolio for each previous day with the corresponding values of the identified variables
(d) Replicate the same changes in the values of the variables for the next day and develop as many scenarios as possible
(e) Re-compute the portfolio values to arrive at the scope of the loss for each of the scenarios
(f) Find out the fifth percentile worst loss or first percentile worst loss to arrive at the 95% or 99% 1-day VaR.

Thus, the VaR method does not presume any probability distribution while relying on the past data. Whatever be the patterns of past, they are translated into as many scenarios, and, hence, the user determines the number of possible scenarios.

Historical simulation is best explained by way of an example. Assume that today is 14 October and we need to determine the VaR for the next day, 15 October, for a portfolio aggregating ₹10,000 crore today that consists of

(a) a long position in foreign exchange worth ₹2000 crore, with a sensitivity of 1.00 for changes in the US dollar exchange rate
(b) a long position in a well-diversified stock portfolio worth ₹5000 crore, with a beta of 1.5
(c) a long position in short-term securities worth ₹3000 crore, with interest sensitivity (duration) of −0.6

The list of variables that can cause changes in the value of the portfolio is indeed large but for the purpose of illustration, the three variables chosen are (a) the US dollar exchange rate, (b) the value of the Nifty index, and (c) the yield on 91-day T-bills. We list the actual value of each of the variables over the previous 51 days so as to develop 50 scenarios. A set of hypothetical data from 1 August to 14 October is shown in Table 14.3. In practice, a sample of 50 historical values is too small, and a much larger sample is taken.

Table 14.3 Historical data for select variables for simulation for VaR calculation

Date	US dollar exchange rate, ₹/$	Nifty index	91-d T-bill yield, %	One day change in US dollar exchange rate, %	One day change in Nifty index, %	One day change in 91-d T-bill yield, %	Scenario
01 Aug	44.05	5517	8.35	—	—	—	
02 Aug	44.23	5457	8.33	0.41	−1.09	−0.24	1
03 Aug	44.38	5405	8.35	0.34	−0.95	0.24	2
04 Aug	44.42	5332	8.05	0.09	−1.35	−3.59	3
05 Aug	44.80	5211	8.34	0.86	−2.27	3.60	4
08 Aug	44.96	5119	8.21	0.36	−1.77	−1.56	5
09 Aug	45.17	5073	8.28	0.47	−0.90	0.85	6
10 Aug	45.21	5161	8.10	0.09	1.73	−2.17	7
11 Aug	45.27	5138	8.30	0.13	−0.45	2.47	8
12 Aug	45.37	5073	8.05	0.22	−1.27	−3.01	9
16 Aug	45.25	5036	8.20	−0.26	−0.73	1.86	10
17 Aug	45.37	5057	8.15	0.27	0.42	−0.61	11
18 Aug	45.61	4944	8.31	0.53	−2.23	1.96	12
19 Aug	45.95	4846	8.30	0.75	−1.98	−0.12	13
22 Aug	45.69	4899	8.24	−0.57	1.09	−0.72	14
23 Aug	45.77	4949	8.30	0.18	1.02	0.73	15
24 Aug	46.13	4889	8.29	0.79	−1.21	−0.12	16
25 Aug	46.05	4840	8.04	−0.17	−1.00	−3.02	17
26 Aug	45.87	4748	8.27	−0.39	−1.90	2.86	18
29 Aug	46.02	4920	8.32	0.33	3.62	0.60	19
30 Aug	45.90	5001	8.22	−0.26	1.65	−1.20	20
02 Sep	45.94	5040	8.31	0.09	0.78	1.09	21
05 Sep	46.13	5017	8.38	0.41	−0.46	0.84	22
06 Sep	46.02	5064	8.34	−0.24	0.94	−0.48	23
07 Sep	46.18	5125	8.30	0.35	1.20	−0.48	24
08 Sep	46.38	5153	8.77	0.43	0.55	5.66	25
09 Sep	46.97	5059	8.35	1.27	−1.82	−4.79	26
12 Sep	47.10	4947	8.17	0.28	−2.21	−2.16	27
13 Sep	47.81	4941	8.33	1.51	−0.12	1.96	28
14 Sep	47.84	5013	8.40	0.06	1.46	0.84	29
15 Sep	47.47	5076	8.20	−0.77	1.26	−2.38	30
16 Sep	47.79	5084	8.30	0.67	0.16	1.22	31

19 Sep	47.79	5032	8.35	0.00	−1.02	0.60	32
20 Sep	48.22	5140	8.32	0.90	2.15	−0.36	33
21 Sep	47.89	5133	8.42	−0.68	−0.14	1.20	34
22 Sep	48.82	4924	8.35	1.94	−4.07	−0.83	35
23 Sep	49.67	4868	8.25	1.74	−1.14	−1.20	36
26 Sep	49.62	4835	8.35	−0.10	−0.68	1.21	37
27 Sep	49.18	4971	8.29	−0.89	2.81	−0.72	38
28 Sep	48.91	4946	8.39	−0.55	−0.50	1.21	39
29 Sep	48.93	5015	8.26	0.04	1.40	−1.55	40
30 Sep	48.93	4943	8.34	0.00	−1.44	0.97	41
03 Oct	49.42	4850	8.27	1.00	−1.88	−0.84	42
04 Oct	49.23	4772	8.39	−0.38	−1.61	1.45	43
05 Oct	49.19	4751	8.33	−0.08	−0.44	−0.72	44
07 Oct	49.14	4888	8.26	−0.10	2.88	−0.84	45
10 Oct	49.07	4980	8.27	−0.14	1.88	0.12	46
11 Oct	49.03	4974	8.39	−0.08	−0.12	1.45	47
12 Oct	49.24	5099	8.40	0.43	2.51	0.12	48
13 Oct	49.02	5078	8.35	−0.45	−0.41	−0.60	49
14 Oct	49.07	5132	8.30	0.10	1.06	−0.60	50

Three variables, the US dollar exchange rate, the Nifty index, and 91-day T-bill yield, indicate a percentage change of +0.41, 1.09, and −0.24, respectively, from 1 August to 2 August. This gives Scenario 1. Similarly, 50 such scenarios can be obtained. For example, on 8 September (Scenario 25) the changes in the values of the exchange rate, the Nifty and T-bill yield are +0.43, +0.55, and +5.66%, respectively.

Percentage changes in the values of the variables are analysed, rather than the absolute values, for two reasons. The first is to eliminate the base effect, i.e., the general level of a selected variable may have changed during the sample period. For example, the US dollar exchange rate, which was at around ₹44.00 on 1 August is at ₹49.00 on 14 October. Secondly, the composition of the portfolio would change through addition or deletion of securities during the sample period.

> Historical data over a sufficient number of days back in history is analysed to know what level of VaR is adequate for a portfolio for a given period with a given confidence level.

These percent changes are viewed as possible scenarios for working on the current value of the portfolio. The value of the portfolio at the end of 14 October is ₹10,000 crore. It is assumed that any of the 50 scenarios that occurred during the sample period immediately preceding the current date, as detailed in Table 14.1, can occur on 15 October, the next trading day. The value of the portfolio is assumed to change in accordance with the sensitivity of the portfolio with respect to each of the variables selected. For example, changes in values of the variables under Scenario 20 are −0.26% in the US dollar exchange rate, +1.65% in the Nifty index, and −1.20% in 91-day T-bill yield. Therefore, the portfolio value would change as shown here:

Portfolio of foreign exchange = −0.26% × 1.0 × 2000 ₹ crore = −5.22
Portfolio of stocks = +1.65% × 1.5 × 5000 = +123.47
Portfolio of short-term securities = −1.20% × −0.6 × 3000 = +21.63
Total change in value of portfolio = +139.88

The 95% 1-day VaR is arrived at by looking at the value of the fifth-percentile worst scenario. For a sample of 50 observations, finding the 95% VaR would be difficult, as it corresponds to the worst 2.5 scenarios, but we may find the 98% 1-day VaR by choosing the second-percentile worst scenarios, i.e., the one worst scenario in a set of 50 observations. In a sample of 500 observations, the 99% VaR would be the last five worst scenarios and the 95% VaR would be the last 25 worst scenarios.

In the illustration we have just discussed, we may find the 98% VaR by observing the value of the worst scenario. This happens at **Scenario 35**, with a loss of ₹251.57 crore, as highlighted in Table 14.4.

Table 14.4 Scenarios based on past data for 15 October

One-day change in % for				Change in the value of the portfolio, ₹crore			
USD exchange rate, ₹/$	Nifty index	91-d T-bill yield, %	Scenario	Foreign exchange	Stocks	Short-term securities	Total
0.41	−1.09	−0.24	1	8.17	−81.56	4.31	−69.08
0.34	−0.95	0.24	2	6.78	−71.47	−4.32	−69.01
0.09	−.35	−3.59	3	1.80	−101.30	64.67	−34.83
0.86	−2.27	3.60	4	17.11	−170.20	−64.85	−217.94
0.36	−1.77	−1.56	5	7.14	−132.41	28.06	−97.21
0.47	−0.90	0.85	6	9.34	−67.40	−15.35	−73.41
0.09	1.73	−2.17	7	1.77	130.10	39.13	171.00
0.13	−0.45	2.47	8	2.65	−33.43	−44.44	−75.22
0.22	−1.27	−3.01	9	4.42	−94.88	54.22	−36.24
−0.26	−0.73	1.86	10	−5.29	−54.71	−33.54	−93.54
0.27	0.42	−0.61	11	5.30	31.28	10.98	47.56
0.53	−2.23	1.96	12	10.58	−167.59	−35.34	−192.35
0.75	−1.98	−0.12	13	14.91	−148.67	2.17	−131.59
−0.57	1.09	−0.72	14	−11.32	82.03	13.01	83.72
0.18	1.02	0.73	15	3.50	76.55	−13.11	66.94
0.79	−1.21	−0.12	16	15.73	−90.93	2.17	−73.03
−0.17	−1.00	−3.02	17	−3.47	−75.17	54.28	−24.36
−0.39	−1.90	2.86	18	−7.82	−142.56	−51.49	−201.87
0.33	3.62	0.60	19	6.54	271.70	−10.88	267.36
−0.26	1.65	−1.20	20	−5.22	123.47	21.63	139.88

0.09	0.78	1.09	21	1.74	58.49	−19.71	40.52
0.41	−0.46	0.84	22	8.27	−34.22	−15.16	−41.11
−0.24	0.94	−0.48	23	−4.77	70.26	8.59	74.08
0.35	1.20	−0.48	24	6.95	90.35	8.63	105.93
0.43	0.55	5.66	25	8.66	40.97	−101.93	−52.30
1.27	−1.82	−4.79	26	25.44	−136.82	86.20	−25.18
0.28	−2.21	−2.16	27	5.54	−166.04	38.80	−121.70
1.51	−0.12	1.96	28	30.15	−9.10	−35.25	−14.20
0.06	1.46	0.84	29	1.25	109.29	−15.13	95.41
−0.77	1.26	−2.38	30	−15.47	94.25	42.86	121.64
0.67	0.16	1.22	31	13.48	11.82	−21.95	3.35
0.00	−1.02	0.60	32	0.00	−76.71	−10.84	−87.55
0.90	2.15	−0.36	33	18.00	160.97	6.47	185.44
−0.68	−0.14	1.20	34	−13.69	−10.22	−21.63	−45.54
1.94	−4.07	−0.83	35	38.84	−305.38	14.97	−251.57
1.74	−1.14	−1.20	36	34.82	−85.30	21.56	−28.92
−0.10	−0.68	1.21	37	−2.01	−50.84	−21.82	−74.67
−0.89	2.81	−0.72	38	−17.73	210.96	12.93	206.16
−0.55	−0.50	1.21	39	−10.98	−37.72	−21.71	−70.41
0.04	1.40	−1.55	40	0.82	104.63	27.89	133.34
0.00	−1.44	0.97	41	0.00	−107.68	−17.43	−125.11
1.00	−1.88	−0.84	42	20.03	−141.11	15.11	−105.97
−0.38	−1.61	1.45	43	−7.69	−120.62	−26.12	−154.43
−0.08	−0.44	−0.72	44	−1.63	−33.01	12.87	−21.77
−0.10	2.88	−0.84	45	−2.03	216.27	15.13	229.37
−0.14	1.88	0.12	46	−2.85	141.17	−2.18	136.14
−0.08	−0.12	1.45	47	−1.63	−9.04	−26.12	−36.79
0.43	2.51	0.12	48	8.57	188.48	−2.15	194.90
−0.45	−0.41	−0.60	49	−8.94	−30.89	10.71	−29.12
0.10	1.06	−0.60	50	2.04	79.76	10.78	92.58

The advantage of historical simulation is that it requires very few modelling assumptions. In our illustration, we used the sensitivities of the portfolio values with respect to selected variables in the economy. It (historical simulation) is essentially driven by the actual distribution of loss, without necessarily assuming that the returns on the portfolio follow normal distribution.

The disadvantages of historical simulation may emanate from the theoretical arguments that economic fundamentals do change from one period to another, and, hence, the historical data that form the basis for finding the VaR may not be repeated in the future with an identical effect. Here, we have combined the analytical model with historical data for predicting the values of the portfolio while scenarios are built on the past data. With a purely historical approach, we must have historical values of the portfolio from the past. However, this would mean that the composition of the portfolio remains the same for the entire past period and the forthcoming period; this is a difficult proposition indeed.

MONTE CARLO SIMULATION

A similar exercise would be performed under the Monte Carlo approach, except that the distribution of the scenarios would be different. While no specific assumption about the probability distribution of market variables was used under the historical simulation, the Monte Carlo simulation provides for a distribution pattern that may be expected. The very purpose of estimating VaR is to provide for unlikely scenarios, and it is believed that normal distribution does not take care of such situations, because adverse events are *fat-tailed*, i.e., losses would be much larger than computed under normal distribution. Historical data would take care of such situations if the period under consideration includes the occurrence of such events. However, if historical data are devoid of such events, we need to incorporate these by choosing some skewed distribution pattern under the Monte Carlo approach.

> The Monte Carlo simulation is same as a historical simulation, except that expected probability distribution is generated by design, while historical simulation does not assume any specific probability distribution.

LIMITATIONS

Though VaR as a measure of risk may appear to be comprehensive, it really is not so. In calculating VaR using any of the approaches, it was assumed that future risk can be predicted from the historical distribution of returns. Further, it fails to deal with new asset classes such as exotics, for which neither pricing models nor historical price data are readily available.

> The VaR as a measure of risk has been criticized because of its inability to consider the view that under extremely adverse situations, variables tend to have strong correlations.

Under the analytical approach, we assumed normal distribution. It does not apply to abnormal situations such as crises that cannot be handled by normal distribution. Further, it cannot deal with non-linear payoffs.

Historical simulation assumes no historical fitting of portfolio values. Instead, it simply assumes historical distribution to be repeated in the future. If crises do not form a part of the data set, it also fails to give a true picture of possible losses. The approach overestimates the meaningfulness of historical data, and allocates same weight to every observation.

The Monte Carlo approach addresses fat-tailed problems by allowing a variety of distributional assumptions. However, volatility, correlation forecasts, and relationships are still based on historical observations.

STRESS TESTING

Besides calculating VaR based on normal or past distributions, it is necessary to take care of some extreme situations that seem to occur more often than one imagines. Under extreme situations, market variables tend to show unusually high correlations. Steep changes in yields on bonds in short periods of time and huge depreciation/appreciation of currencies happening simultaneously occur far more frequently than normal distribution would suggest.

Crises happen more often than any of the distribution patterns predict. Further, crises also do not exhibit any distribution pattern that can be studied to form the basis for future provisioning. The history of global crises suggests that they happen often. For example, in the period from 1990 till date, we have seen many such crises, such as the Gulf war, the Mexican debt crisis, the Asian currency crisis, the Russian rouble devaluation, the sub-prime crisis, and the Greek/Euro crisis. Further complexity is added by natural disasters such as tsunamis, earthquakes, floods, and droughts. Events like wars or political coups have similar threats. Natural disasters, wars, and coups do not have any pattern, and are not subject to statistical forecasting. All these events can cause systemic risk, where the inability of one to meet commitments leads to impairment for others in the system. As a result of this, losses may be of much larger magnitude than what VaR results may prescribe.

> Stress testing complements the VaR by analysing past positions during periods of crises that happened over the last 10–20 years.

VaR bands are dramatically exceeded in such situations, and therefore, it is imperative to take additional precautionary measures, apart from computing VaR. Many financial institutions carry out stress testing by examining the performance and adequacy of capital under extreme conditions in crises that occurred over the last 10 to 20 years. Stress testing combined with the VaR method would be a more comprehensive measure of risk.

SOLVED PROBLEMS

SP 14.1: Volatility measurement

At the beginning of the week on Monday, the annual volatility of an index was 24%. On Monday, Tuesday, and Wednesday, the index registered a return of 1.5%, −2.0%, and 0.5%, respectively. What estimates of volatility would you make for Tuesday, Wednesday, and Thursday, based on the EWMA approach with a decay factor of 0.90 and 256 trading days in a year?

Solution
With 256 days in a year and annual volatility of 24%, the daily volatility would be $24/\sqrt{256} = 1.5\%$.

The estimate of volatility for Tuesday, Wednesday, and Thursday would be found successively using revised estimates for each day, based on Eq. 14.1.

For Tuesday $\sigma_n^2 = \lambda \sigma_{n-1}^2 + (1-\lambda)r_{n-1}^2$ = $0.90 \times 0.015^2 + 0.10 \times 0.015^2$
= $0.90 \times 0.000225 + 0.1 \times 0.000225$ = 0.000225

Or $\sigma n = \sqrt{0.000225}$ = $0.015 \equiv 1.50\%$

For Wednesday $\sigma_n^2 = \lambda \sigma_{n-1}^2 + (1-\lambda)r_{n-1}^2$ = $0.90 \times 0.015^2 + 0.10 \times 0.02^2$
= $0.90 \times 0.000225 + 0.1 \times 0.0004$ = 0.0002425

Or $\sigma n = \sqrt{0.0002425}$ = $0.01557 \equiv 1.56\%$

For Thursday $\sigma_n^2 = \lambda \sigma_{n-1}^2 + (1-\lambda)r_{n-1}^2$ = $0.90 \times 0.0156^2 + 0.10 \times 0.005^2$
= $0.90 \times 0.00024336 + 0.1 \times 0.000025$ = 0.000221524

Or $\sigma n = \sqrt{0.000221524}$ = $0.01488 \equiv 1.49\%$

SP 14.2: Historical simulation
Under historical simulation for the last 100 days for a portfolio observation, the following table was created:

Profit (+)/loss (−) ₹ lakh	No. of times
More than −220	1
Between −180 and −200	4
Between −160 and −180	5
Between −100 and −160	14

Between −50 and −100	20
Between −50 and −0	10
Between +0 and +50	28
Between +50 and +80	7
Between +80 and +150	8
Between +150 and +200	3

What will be (a) the 1-day VaR with 99%, 95%, and 90% confidence levels and (b) the 10-day VaR with 99%, 95%, and 90% confidence levels?

Solution
For 99%, 95%, and 90%, we have to find the number of occasions (not exceeding 1, 5, and 10, respectively) out of 100 the VaR level would be the loss incurred.

Therefore, the VaR for

99% confidence	= loss occurred no more than 1 time out of 100	= ₹220 lakh
95% confidence	= loss occurred no more than 5 times out of 100	= ₹180 lakh
99% confidence	= loss occurred no more than 10 times out of 100	= ₹160 lakh

For a 10-day VaR the levels would be

99% confidence	$220 \times \sqrt{10}$	= ₹696.70 lakh
95% confidence	$180 \times \sqrt{10}$	= ₹569.21 lakh
90% confidence	$160 \times \sqrt{10}$	= ₹505.96 lakh

SUMMARY

The world is integrating, with increased liberalization policies adopted by different nations. This has made the world a global village. The factors governing risk have multiplied. Risk characterised by standard deviation as a universal measure has been condensed in different ways—beta, delta, gamma, etc. They measure changes in the value for a given change in the value of a determinant perceived to be the most important. In a global environment, such measurement of risk may not be comprehensive and true.

Recognizing the need to rely on past data, the EWMA attempts to forecast volatility on the basis of past trends, giving lesser and lesser importance to older data and emphasising more recent data. The weight of each past observation decreases exponentially in the new estimate of volatility. As per the EWMA, the updated volatility is a function of past volatility modulated by the latest returns. The advantage of the EWMA is that estimating volatility requires only two sets of data—a single comprehensive figure for volatility of the past and the latest returns; this is unlike the historical method, which needs storage of substantial past data. The EWMA approach can be extended to covariance too. Like variance, covariance would also be a function of past volatility contained in the single figure and the latest covariance.

It has been found that variance is mean reverting, i.e., it tries to come back to some long-term average. The ARCH/GARCH approach has been used to incorporate mean reversion. The EWMA, which does not recognize mean reversion, is a special case of GARCH.

The VIX is a new concept for foretelling general expectations about the market and is derived from option prices. While option prices are observable, volatility is not. Since option prices are dependent on future volatility, they can be used to derive future volatility. The VIX, developed by the CBOE is a method to arrive at the volatility that is widely accepted and adapted by stock exchanges worldwide. The NSE, too, is one such exchange, which uses the prices of OTM options to derive volatility estimates for the next 30 days.

The VaR measure is considered to be a comprehensive measure of risk for portfolios that consist of a variety of instruments spread across several nations. It gives an idea of what possible losses can be foreseen with the objective of providing for them for continued and healthy operations. Since losses get multiplied with time and the magnitude of loss depends upon probability distribution, the VaR becomes dependent upon two critical inputs to be decided by management—the level of protection required and the time horizon. A 99% 10-day VaR implies that over a period of 10 days, the loss exceeding the VaR is expected to occur only once out of 100 days. For this, we continue to assume normal distribution for returns on the portfolio.

Banks and financial institutions are more concerned about risk because of (a) high leverage, (b) absence of tangible securities, and (c) lack of control by the major suppliers of funds, i.e., the depositors.

Since a large number of factors influence portfolio value, the applicability of the model building approach for valuation is suspect. One possible way to arrive at expected losses is to do a scenario analysis. The usual practice is to find out the 1-day VaR and then scale up for the desired period. There are two ways of generating scenarios—historical or Monte Carlo. Under historical simulation, each of the past observations is treated as one scenario for the next day. Creating about 200–500 scenarios would provide a distribution pattern of portfolio values, and with the desired confidence levels, we can have a 1-day VaR. No specific distribution is assumed. We repeat the distribution pattern of the past. Under the Monte Carlo approach, we develop scenarios based on the probability distribution of the variables that we expect and re-compute the value of the portfolio.

Despite quite exhaustive data analysis, the VaR is found to be deficient in true measurement of risk, because it is observed that under extreme negative outlooks, the correlations amongst the determinants become very large and, therefore, capital adequacy based on the VaR may not suffice. To bolster the VaR, a few financial institutions have started stress testing, to see the actual performance over the last 10–20 years under extreme negative scenarios.

KEY TERMS

Decay factor The rate at which the importance of past data decreases.
Exponential smoothing A situation where the weight of past date decreases exponentially at each new observation.
GARCH It is an approach where volatility is assumed to revert to a long-term average.
Historical simulation A method of arriving at the VaR using past data as source, assuming history can foretell future events.
Monte Carlo simulation A method of arriving at the VaR by generating scenarios according to the expected pattern of market variables.

Standard deviation A measure of volatility as a percentage of deviation from average returns.
Stress testing An exercise conducted to establish how a portfolio/an organisation would withstand a crisis situation on the basis of analysis of crises that occurred over the last 10–20 years.
Value at risk A measure of risk that quantifies losses for a time horizon with a certain confidence level.
Volatility index An index that reflects on expected volatility in the short term.

QUESTIONS

14.1 What are the different measures of risk for different kinds of assets? Describe their importance and limitations in risk measurement.
14.2 What are the assumptions made in the exponential weighted average model for updating volatility?
14.3 How is the GARCH model different from the EWMA model?
14.4 What do you understand by VIX? Briefly describe how VIX is calculated in India.
14.5 Describe what you understand by VaR and its utility.
14.6 What are the different ways of measuring VaR?
14.7 Elaborate the steps of historical simulation involved in finding out the VaR and differentiate it from the Monte Carlo simulation.
14.8 What are the limitations of VaR?
14.9 Describe what you understand by stress testing.

PROBLEMS

P 14.1 Updating volatility
Stocks A and B have annual volatilities of 20% and 30%, respectively. You are updating volatility on a weekly basis. In the past week, the returns of stocks A and B were 3% and −2%, respectively. What is your revised estimate of annual volatility for the coming week using the EWMA method, with a 95% decay rate and 52 weeks per annum?

P 14.2 Updating correlation
If the coefficient of correlation between stocks A and B is 0.7 in P 14.1, what would the correlation between them for the coming week be?

P 14.3 Value at Risk
Assuming normal distribution applies, what would be your estimate of VaR for one month for a portfolio that has an annual mean return of 20% and an annual standard deviation of 10%, with confidence levels of (a) 95% and (b) 98%?

P 14.4 VaR and historical simulation
Consider the data given in SP 14.2. Find out the VaR with a 90% confidence level for (a) 1 day, (b) 1 month, and (c) 1 year.

15

Hedging with Options

INTRODUCTION

Options have an impressive and huge array of applications, certainly greater than most other derivatives. Some of these applications are unique to options. The extended applications of options emanate from their distinctive payoffs. While the obligations of counterparties are mutual and equal in other derivatives, options have a unique payoff that is unequal. While one party holds the option and has a right without an obligation, the other party is obligated to perform. This unequal payoff, also referred to as a *non-linear payoff*, makes possible several applications that are not feasible with other derivatives.

Though options can be used for hedging, speculating, and arbitrage, just the same way as other derivatives, the applications seem somewhat different due to uneven payoffs. We shall discuss the various applications of options under the following four heads:

> Due to the non-linear payoffs, there are many more applications available with options than with other derivatives.

Learning Objectives
After going through this chapter, readers should be familiar with
- the hedging applications of options
- the hedging of a long position with puts
- the hedging of a short position with calls
- the hedging of a long/short portfolio with index put/call options with
  - beta equal to 1; and
  - beta equal to a value other than 1
- the concept of hedging with currency options
- how to reduce hedging costs with options
- strategies of range forward, ratio range forward, and zero cost structures

- *Hedging strategies* to concentrate on how to use options to hedge against adverse price movements for a long or a short position in the underlying asset.
- *Income generation strategies* to focus on how to use options to enhance portfolio yields. This is possible because the writer of an option earns a premium.
- *Trading strategies* by highlighting different options to achieve the desired risk and return profiles, depending upon the perception of the market by the trader.
- *Synthesizing strategies*, demonstrating the power of options to create synthetic positions of other financial instruments. The replication of the payoff effectively means lesser investment without compromising returns enhancing the return on investment (RoI).

We discuss them one by one, covering hedging in this chapter and the remaining strategies in the next chapter.

Hedging may be defined as an action that protects against the effects of adverse events such as inflation, adverse price movement of stocks, and errant behaviour of foreign exchange. Due to their uneven payoffs, options provide hedging opportunities that are somewhat different from those provided by forwards and futures.

Options, like Contracts, are All-pervasive We all encounter options contracts in our everyday lives. These contracts often go unnoticed and are not given much thought or attention. For example, each one of us obtains insurance in some form or the other. Consider car insurance against theft or house insurance against fire. Each year, we pay an insurance premium to protect against the loss of the asset due to theft or fire. Insurance firms charge a premium and both the parties hope that the fire or theft will not take place. If it does, you will be able to recover the loss from the insurance firm. If the fire or theft does not take place, you and the insurance firm feel good. In any case, the premium paid to the insurance firm is foregone by you. It is the price for buying peace of mind.

> Options are all pervasive and we hardly recognize their presence in our day-to-day lives.

Look at the situation in another way: by taking out an insurance policy on an asset we own, we hedge against any loss in the value of that asset. If an asset gets stolen or damaged by fire, its value would reduce substantially, even to zero. In options terminology, buying an insurance policy is nothing but the equivalent of holding a put option that protects against any loss in the value of the asset owned. The insurance firm has in fact written a put. You exercise your option if the fire takes place, when the insurance firm is obligated to compensate you for the loss.

Is insurance different from options? Yes, indeed, because insurance covers against risk arising from an event, and one is required to prove that a loss, indeed, has occurred. Such is not the case with options as financial products. Insurance covers a different nature of risk, called event risk, while options cover price risk. Further, with options, one does not need to prove that a loss has, indeed, occurred.

As another example, consider the purchase of a real estate property. When buying a property, we normally enter into an 'agreement to buy/sell', which states the firm price of the property and provides for a token payment by the prospective buyer to the prospective seller at the time of the agreement. The balance is to be paid within an agreed time period. Before the expiry of the agreement, the prospective owner has the right to pay the balance and take delivery of the property in question. If the prospective buyer does not exercise this option within the stipulated time, the prospective seller is absolved of the obligation to deliver the property. This agreement to buy/sell closely resembles a call option that is a right to buy an asset at an agreed price within a stipulated time frame.

The call option is exercised if the price goes up but not when the price falls. Though most of us buy property with the intention of taking delivery, if the property is considered to be an investment, the agreement to sell can be viewed as a call option on the asset. The prospective buyer would exercise the option if the price of the property has gone up. Instead, if the price has fallen, the buyer would not seek delivery of the property, and would let the agreement to sell expire. In either case, the front-end payment made is forfeited, and belongs to the seller. Such an agreement to sell provides protection to the buyer and is a hedge against any rise in price of the property.

Depending upon the situation, people need protection against changes in price. Sometimes, a fall in value is damaging, as is the case when one buys an insurance policy. Here, one already owns an asset—called 'long on asset' in financial terminology—and needs protection against a fall in the value of the asset. At other times, a rise in value is adverse to the interests of the people concerned, as is the case in entering into an 'agreement to buy' for buying property, where one does not own the asset—called 'short on asset' in financial terminology—and needs protection against a rise in prices. Both the situations emphasize the need for hedging.

Financial Markets Provide Easier Comprehension of Options Examples from the financial market are most apt for explaining and comprehending the concept of hedging. Therefore, such examples are used here with the belief that similar processes can be adopted for protecting against adverse price movement for any other asset. When an investor takes a position in stock (either long or short), he/she faces the risk of losses when prices move in a direction opposite to the anticipated one. If one has purchased stock, he/she expects to gain from a rise in the price of the stock. If the price falls instead, he/she incurs a loss. Similarly, an investor who has taken a short position (a planned acquisition of an asset in the future is considered a 'short' position, till the asset is actually acquired) in stock expects to gain from a fall in the price. Instead, if the price rises, the investor faces a loss.

HEDGING WITH STOCK OPTIONS

The unique feature of hedging with options is that it protects one from possible losses that could arise from adverse movements in prices, while at the same time retaining the potential for gain from the favourable movement of prices. Returns from the favourable movement are reduced only marginally by the amount of premium paid to buy the option. In contrast, hedging with forwards or futures locks-in a price. Though protecting against loss, they also deny any gain from the possible favourable movements of the prices. In case of forwards and futures, protection is provided at the expense of foregoing potential gain.

> An option is an excellent instrument to hedge because it protects against adverse movements in prices while retaining the potential to gain.

We now consider hedging for long and short positions in an asset with options. The long position needs protection against falling prices, and the short position must be protected against rising prices.

Hedging Long Position in Stock with Put Option

An investor takes a long position in a stock or an asset in the hope that its price would rise. A long position carries risk if the price falls. If the purchase price of the asset was S_0 and the current price is S, the loss or profit is given by $S - S_0$. If $S > S_0$, the investor is happy. If $S < S_0$ the investor suffers a loss, and this is a situation that he/she needs to safeguard against.

When an investor is holding an asset, he/she has the potential to make an unlimited gain as well as an unlimited loss (limited to the buying price, since the price cannot fall below zero) depending upon the price of the asset at the end of the investment horizon. However, he/she needs protection against fall in value of the asset. When an investor buys a put option (giving him/her the right to sell at the exercise price) alongside the asset, it forms a portfolio, called *long on asset with a put*. A loss in a long position on an asset can be covered by exercise of the put, in the event of a fall in price below the exercise price. Therefore, it is called a *protective put*. The payoff on the protective put, which is shown in Fig. 15.1, emerges from combinations of the payoffs on a long position in the stock and the put option.

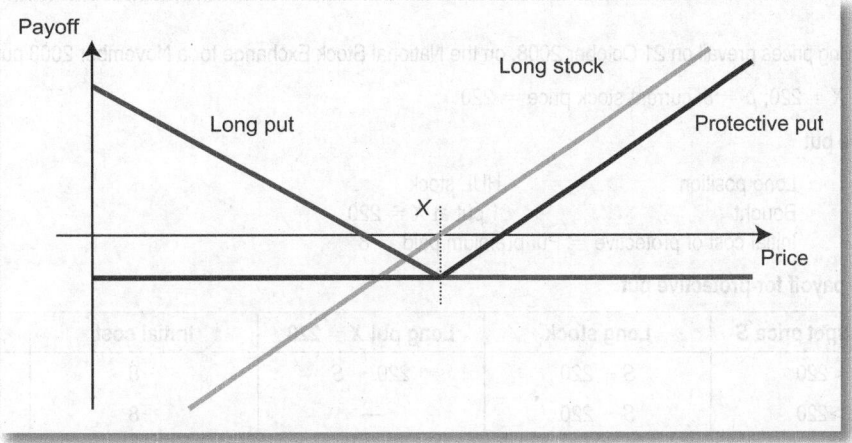

Fig. 15.1 Protective put

Note that loss in case of a fall in price is contained to the extent of the premium paid for the put. If the price falls below the exercise price, the investor exercises his/her right to sell, thereby providing protection against a fall in price below the exercise price. In case of a rise in price, the put is worthless, and, thus, not exercised. The long position in the asset gives a profit. However, the profit would stand reduced by the amount of premium paid while buying the put. When $S > S_0$, for a long position on the asset, the profit will be $S - S_0$, while for an asset with a put, the profit will be $S - S_0 - p$, where p is the put premium.

> A long position in an asset deteriorates with a fall in price. Protection against the expected loss is gained by buying a put. If prices move up, the long position continues to gain.

An example of a protective put with the stock of Hindustan Unilever Ltd. (HUL) as the underlying asset is shown in Exhibit 15.1, which contains the hedging strategy, a table for the payoff, and a graphical view of the combined position of the asset with a put option. If the investor does not buy the put—if he/she remains unhedged—his/her loss could be very large. Buying a put limits the losses to ₹8, and yet retains the profit potential, except for the premium paid on the put, as may be seen from the figure in Exhibit 15.1.

Hedging Short Position in Stock with Call Option

> A short position in an asset deteriorates with a rise in price. Protection against the expected loss is gained by buying a call. If prices go down, the short position continues to gain.

Now consider an opposite position, with no asset in possession. Many of us would wonder what protection one may need on an asset that is not yet owned. Of course, one has nothing to lose because one does not own the asset. However, we must see it in a different way—in terms of a plan to own the asset. Protection is required if one is intending to own the asset in the near future, possibly because one does not have funds to acquire the asset now. Such a position is considered a short position.

For a short position, a price fall is favourable but a price rise is unfavourable. If the price rises, then owning the asset becomes more expensive in the future. It is

EXHIBIT 15.1 Hedging long position—Protective put

Strategy (All figures in ₹)

- Long position on stock of Hindustan Unilever Ltd (HUL)
- To hedge against fall in price: Buy a put on the same asset for the period of hedge.

Example
The following prices prevail on 21 October 2008, on the National Stock Exchange for a November 2008 put option on HUL:

$X = 220$; $p = 8$; current stock price = 220

Protective put

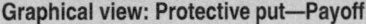

Long position	HUL stock
Bought	1 put at $X = 220$
Initial cost of protective	= Put premium paid = 8

Table for payoff for protective put

When spot price S	Long stock	Long put $X = 220$	Initial cost	TOTAL
<220	$S - 220$	$220 - S$	−8	−8
>220	$S - 220$	—	−8	$S - 228$

Graphical view: Protective put—Payoff

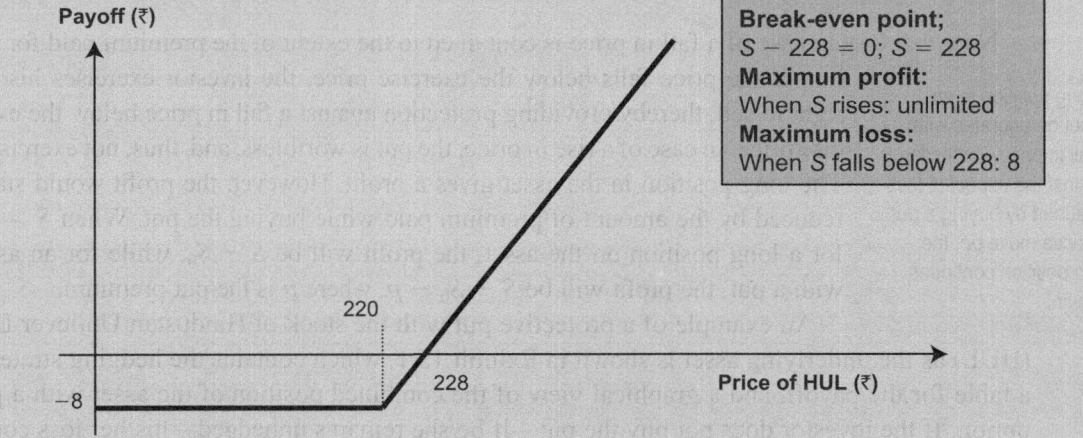

Break-even point;
$S - 228 = 0$; $S = 228$
Maximum profit:
When S rises: unlimited
Maximum loss:
When S falls below 228: 8

precisely here that protection is required. Alternatively, where short selling is allowed, an investor may short sell the asset, expecting a fall in price, and buy back later. In such a case, the investor carries a risk if the price rises subsequently.

If the current price of the asset is S_0 and the expected price is S, the loss or profit is given by $S - S_0$. If $S < S_0$, the investor gains because he/she executes the purchase at a lower price, otherwise he/she suffers a loss. To protect against losses due to a rise in the price, the investor buys an at-the-money (ATM) call option on the stock. If the price indeed rises, the investor can exercise the call owned and compensate for the losses incurred on the short position in stock. If the price falls, the investor lets the call expire. The payoff on the combined position of short stock and long call is shown in Fig. 15.2.

Note that any loss in case of a rise in price is contained to a maximum of the premium paid for the call c. In case of a fall in price, the profit from the stock stands reduced by the amount of the premium paid on the call. If the investor were short on the asset, the profit will

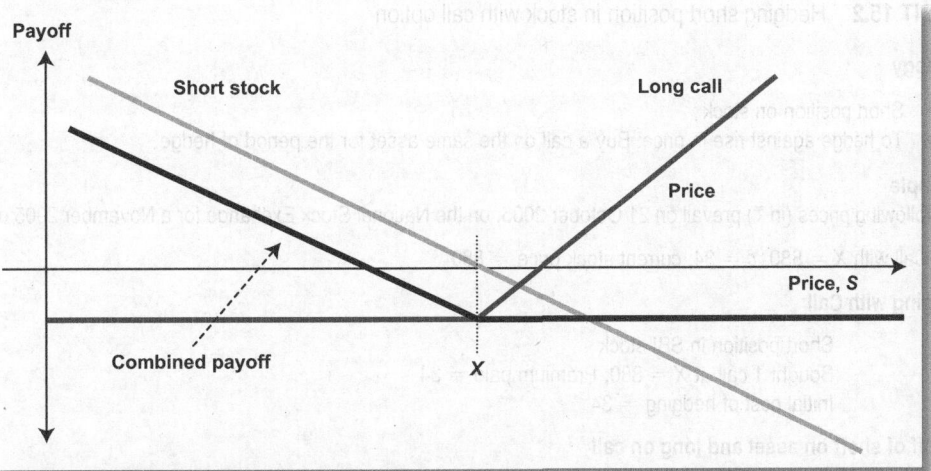

Fig. 15.2 Short on stock and long on call

be $S_0 - S$, but when combined with the call at $X = S_0$, the profit will be $S_0 - S - c$, where c is the call premium.

Buying a call option places a maximum limit on the purchase value, consisting of the strike price, X, plus the call premium, c. Consider, for example, an investor who has bought a call option at ₹5, with a strike of ₹100. In case the price remains less than ₹100, the investor allows the call option to lapse and acquires the asset at the market price. After adding the call premium, the cost would be $S + c$, or $S + 5$. If the price of the asset is more than ₹100, the investor exercises the call to acquire the asset from the call writer by paying ₹100. Add ₹5, the value of the premium paid earlier, and the maximum cost of the acquisition is thus pegged at $X + c$, i.e., ₹105. This is shown in Fig. 15.3.

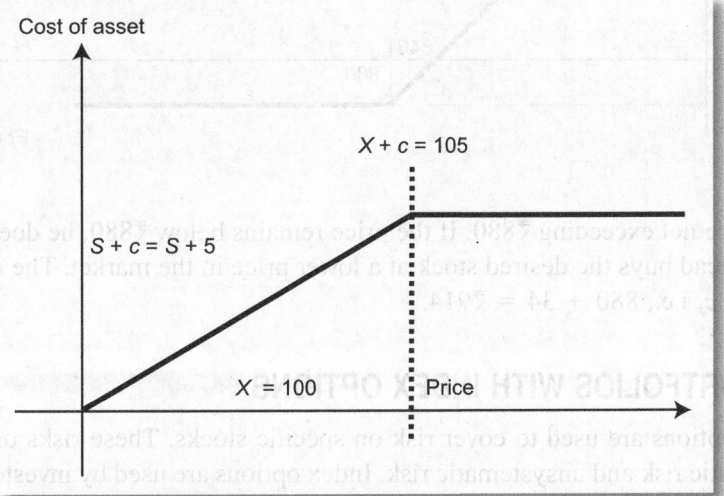

Fig. 15.3 Cost of acquiring on asset

Similar to a protective put, Exhibit 15.2 depicts the complete strategy for a short position in the stock of State Bank of India (SBI), trading at ₹880, with a call option on it with a strike of ₹880, selling at ₹34. With a call option, the investor is assured of getting the stock of SBI

EXHIBIT 15.2 Hedging short position in stock with call option

Strategy (All figures in ₹)

- Short position on stock
- To hedge against rise in price: Buy a call on the same asset for the period of hedge.

Example

The following prices (in ₹) prevail on 21 October 2005, on the National Stock Exchange for a November 2005 option on SBI:

Call with $X = 880$, $c = 34$; current stock price = 880

Hedging with Call

Short position in SBI stock
Bought 1 call at $X = 880$; Premium paid = 34
Initial cost of hedging = 34

Payoff of short on asset and long on call

Spot price S	Short stock	Long call $X = 880$	Initial cost	Total
$S < 880$	$880 - S$	—	-34	$846 - S$
$S > 880$	$880 - S$	$S - 880$	-34	-34

Graphical view: Short stock and long call payoff

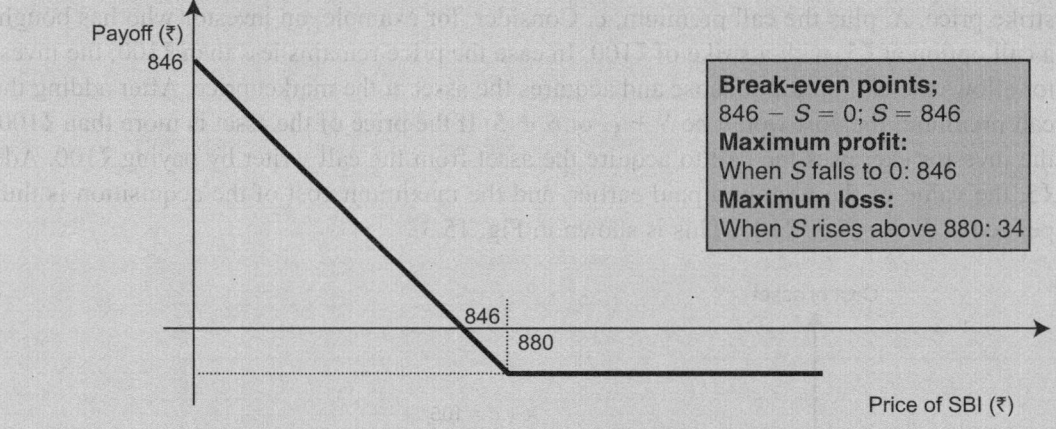

Break-even points;
$846 - S = 0$; $S = 846$
Maximum profit:
When S falls to 0: 846
Maximum loss:
When S rises above 880: 34

at a price not exceeding ₹880. If the price remains below ₹880, he does not exercise the call, and instead buys the desired stock at a lower price in the market. The maximum price would be $X + c$, i.e., $880 + 34 = ₹914$.

HEDGING PORTFOLIOS WITH INDEX OPTIONS

Stock options are used to cover risk on specific stocks. These risks on stock comprise both systematic risk and unsystematic risk. Index options are used by investors to cover systematic risk or market risk. In case of portfolios, unsystematic risk is diversified away, while market risk remains. Therefore, options on an index are best suited for large funds that already have minimized unsystematic risk by diversification. To protect against market risk, one can take a position in index options.

> Index options are mostly used by mutual funds to hedge against systematic risk.

Options on an index are cash settled, with the difference between the closing value of the index, S and the strike value, X, being paid if the option is in-the-money. For call options, it is Max($S - X$, 0), and for puts, it is Max($X - S$, 0).

Hedging Long Portfolio with Put on Index

We know that buying a put on an individual stock insures against price fall below a particular level. A long position in stock trading at ₹140, with a put on the same with a strike of, say, ₹120 would protect the value of the stock from falling below ₹120. Similarly, in case of a portfolio, protection against a general fall in the market can be had by buying a put on an index.

For example, consider an investor who has a portfolio with a current market value of ₹10 lakh. Assume that the beta of the portfolio is the same as that of the market, and the index is currently at 4000. With a beta of 1, the portfolio moves equivalently with the market. When the sentiments of the market are weak, and a general fall in equity prices is expected. The investor needs to protect the value of the portfolio for erosion in value by not more than 10%.

A simple way to protect against a likely fall of the market is to buy a put with a strike of 10% below the current level of the index, i.e., 3600. If the contract size is 50 indices with ₹1 as the value of one point, then the value that would be covered by one contract is 50 × 4000 = ₹2 lakh. The investor needs to buy five put contracts to cover the exposure. If the index falls by more than 10%, the shortfall in the portfolio would be compensated by the payoff on the put. The position of the investor at the expiry of the option period for two contrasting situations—a 20% fall and a 10% rise in the index—is presented here (ignoring the premium paid for buying the put).

> A long portfolio position can be protected against systematic risk by buying a put on an index.

Figures in ₹

Index	Put payoff	Portfolio value	Total value
S = 3200	Exercise put (3600 − 3200) × 50 × 5	8,00,000	9,00,000
S = 4400	Let put lapse 0	11,00,000	11,00,000

When Beta of Portfolio is Other than 1 The hedging value of a portfolio against a fall in price with index options involves three decisions: (a) the value of the exposure in the options, (b) the protection level desired, and (c) the strike price on the put option. In case of a portfolio with a beta equal to 1.00, all the three decisions were simple. The exposure in options was equal to the value of the portfolio. Protection desired for a fall of more than 10% fixed the strike price of the put option at 10% below the current value of the index. Normally, a well-diversified portfolio would have the same beta as the market.

However, portfolios may at times be either aggressive (beta > 1.0), aiming at higher than market returns under bullish sentiments, or defensive (beta < 1.0) aiming at less than market losses under bearish sentiments. In such cases, while hedging the value of the exposure in options, their strike prices need to be modified. Consider the same portfolio of ₹10 lakh but with a beta of 1.60, with a desired protection level of 10% over a period of one year. The current value of the index is 4000. Would buying a put of 3600 serve the purpose, as it did in the earlier case, when the beta of the portfolio was 1.00?

> When the beta of the portfolio is other than 1, the values of the put option and its strike need to be adjusted for the value of the beta.

The relationship between portfolio protection and market decline has to be viewed in the perspective of the capital asset pricing model (CAPM). As per CAPM, portfolio returns in excess of the risk-free rate would be beta times the index returns in excess of the risk-free rate, i.e.,

$$\text{Excess returns of portfolio} = \beta \times \text{excess returns on index}$$

If the risk-free rate is 8% and the dividend yields on the portfolio and the index are the same at 2%, then the strike price of the put to be bought is calculated as follows:

All values on p.a. basis

Acceptable level of decline in portfolio value, the capital loss	−10%
Dividend yield on portfolio	2%
Returns net of dividend yield	−8%
Returns on portfolio with respect to risk-free rate = −8% − 8%	−16%
Beta of the portfolio	1.60
Equivalent excess returns on the index = −16%/1.60	−10%
Return on the index with respect to the risk-free rate = −10% + 8%	−2%
Dividend yield on the index	2%
Capital loss on index = −2% − 2%	−4%
Therefore, the strike price of the put (percentage of the current index value) =	96%

Hence, in order to hedge against a fall beyond 10%, a strike price on the put option below 4% of the current index value is required, as compared to 10% below in the case where the beta of the portfolio was 1.00. Therefore, to hedge the portfolio of ₹10 lakh for a minimum value of ₹9 lakh (10% below), the hedger would buy

> To hedge a portfolio with beta > 1, a higher number of puts with higher strike prices needs to be bought.

(a) a number of puts equivalent to the beta × the portfolio value
   = 1.6 × 10,00,000/4000 = 400
(b) at a strike price of 4% below the current index level
   = 0.96 × 4000 = 3840

This implies that when the portfolio beta is more than 1, hedging would be costlier for two reasons: (a) the need to buy a higher number of puts, and (b) a higher strike price. We know that a put with a higher strike price costs more.

Now let us assume that the value of the portfolio falls by 15% to ₹8.50 lakh. Is the investor protected with a level of ₹9.00 lakh? If the portfolio has fallen by 15%, we find the value of the index and the payoff from the puts as follows:

Capital loss suffered		= −15%
Return after dividend yield	= −15% + 2%	= −13%
Return with reference to the risk-free rate	= −13% − 8%	= −21%
Return on the index with reference to the risk-free rate = −21%/1.6		= −13.13%
Return on the index	= −13.13% + 8%	= −5.13%
Capital return on the index after dividend yield	= −5.13 − 2%	= −7.13%
New value of the index	= (1 − 7.13%) × 4000	= 3715
Gain from the put	= (3840 − 3715) × 400	= ₹50,000
Value of the portfolio after the put	= 8,50,000 + 50,000	= ₹9,00,000

Note that in all these analyses, the period of hedging is taken as one year. In case the period is different, all returns would need to be modified for the contemplated period of hedge.

Hedging Short Portfolio with Call on Index

A short position on a portfolio needs to be protected against price rise. A plan to acquire a portfolio in the future is analogous to a short position in a portfolio. Any rise of the market in general would be disadvantageous to the prospective investor. This risk of price rise may be covered by buying a call option.

> A short position in a portfolio can be protected against systematic risk by buying a call on an index.

Consider an investor who needs to acquire a portfolio worth ₹10 lakh with a beta of 1.00. The index is currently at 4000. The investor needs to cap the cost of acquiring the portfolio at 110%, or ₹11 lakh. To do so, the investor needs to buy a call with a strike of 10% above the current level of the index, i.e., at 4400, worth ₹10 lakh. If the index rises by more than 10%, the shortfall in the portfolio would be compensated by the payoff of the call. Thus the cost would not exceed ₹11 lakh.

The position of the investor at the expiry of the option period for two assumed scenarios—a 10% fall and a 20% rise in the index—is presented here (ignoring the premium paid for buying the call):

Figures in ₹

Index	Call payoff	Portfolio value	Total cost
S = 4800	Exercise call (4800 − 4400) × 50 × 5	12,00,000	11,00,000
S = 3600	Let call lapse 0	9,00,000	9,00,000

When Beta of Portfolio is Other than 1 In case the proposed portfolio has a beta other than 1.00, the analysis for determining the strike price of the call and exposures to the derivative would have to be done on a similar basis as was done in case of hedging long portfolio with a put.

Assuming the beta of the proposed portfolio as 2.00, with a current index value of 4000, a risk-free rate at 8% and dividend yields on the portfolio and the index at 2% each, as before the calculation of the strike price of the call, the option for protection beyond 10% rise in the price is shown as follows:

All values on p.a. basis

Acceptable level of rise in the portfolio value	10%
Dividend yield on the portfolio	2%
Returns after dividend yield	12%
Returns on portfolio with respect to the risk-free rate = 12% − 8%	4%
The beta of the portfolio	2.00
Equivalent excess returns on the index = 4%/2	2%
Return on the index with respect to the risk-free rate = 2% + 8%	10%
Dividend yield on the index	2%
Capital loss on the index = 10% − 2%	8%
Therefore strike price of the call (% of current index value)	108%

> **EXAMPLE 15.1 Hedging long portfolio with put option on index**
>
> A mutual fund owns an aggressive portfolio of stocks with a beta of 1.15. Due to political uncertainty, the market is expected to decline in the near future, for six months, after which the political uncertainty is likely to end. The portfolio is worth ₹10 crore, and provides a dividend yield of 3%. The current level of the index is 5000, and yield on the index is 4%. The mutual fund needs to limit its losses to 10% for the next six months. Find out the value of a put option and its strike price for hedging capital losses not exceeding 10%. Assume a risk-free rate of return of 6%.
>
> **Solution**
> To find out what level of decline in the index would cause the portfolio to lose 10% of its value, we use the CAPM, incorporating the dividend yields on the portfolio and the index. The CAPM, with returns broken into capital gains and dividend yields, is given by
>
> $$R_p + D_p = R_f + \beta(R_m + D_m - R_f)$$
>
> where R_p and D_p represent capital gain and dividend yield on the portfolio, respectively, and R_m and D_m are capital gain and dividend yield on the index, respectively. R_f is the risk-free rate of return.
> Substituting the values of the expected decline of 10%, we solve for an equivalent percentage fall in the index.
>
> $$-10 + 1.5 = 3 + 1.15(R_m + 2 - 3) \text{ gives } R_m = -9\%$$
>
> A fall of 9% in the index would protect loss beyond 10% in the portfolio. The mutual fund must buy put options with a strike price of 9% below the market, i.e., 5000 × 9% = 450 points. The strike price of the put, therefore, should be 4550.
> The value of the put options must be 1.15 × the portfolio value = 1.15 × 10 = ₹11.5 crore.
> Assuming one rupee equals one index point, the number of puts bought = $\frac{11{,}50{,}00{,}000}{5000}$ = 23,000
> If the market falls by 10% to 4500 levels, then the return on the portfolio would be
>
> $$R_p + D_p = R_f + \beta(R_m + D_m - R_f) = -11.15\%$$
> $$R_p + 1.5 = 3 + 1.15(-10 + 2 - 3) \text{ gives } R_p$$
>
> Hence the portfolio would now be worth (1 − 0.115) × 10 = ₹8.885 crore.
> The payoff from each put would be 50(4550 − 4500), and the total payoff is 23,000 × 50 = ₹11.50 lakh.
> Hence, the portfolio would be insured at ₹9.00 crore, i.e., 10% less than the existing value, as desired in the hedge.

Hence, in order to hedge against a price rise beyond 10%, a call option above 8% of the current index value is required. Therefore, to hedge a portfolio worth ₹10 lakh today for a cost not to exceed ₹11 lakh (10% above the value) the prospective investor would buy

> To hedge a short position in a portfolio with beta > 1, a higher number of calls with lower strike prices is needed, increasing hedging costs.

(a) Number of calls = beta × portfolio value
    = 2.0 × 10,00,000/4000 = 500
(b) Strike price = 8% above the current index level
    = 1.08 × 4000 = 4320

This implies that when a short position has a beta in excess of 1, the investor needs to buy more calls with a lesser strike price than if the portfolio beta were 1.00. Again, such a hedge would be costlier because (a) more calls are bought, and (b) calls with lower strikes cost more.

Now let us check if it works. If the portfolio has risen by 20%, we find the index level, and hence, the payoff from the call as follows:

The additional cost for acquiring the portfolio		= 20%
Return after dividend yield	= 20% + 2%	= 22%
Return above the risk-free rate	= 22% − 8%	= 14%
Return on the index above the risk-free rate	= 14%/2	7%
Return on the index	= 7% + 8%	15%
Capital return on the index after dividend yield	= 15% − 2%	13%
New value of the index	= (1 + 13%) × 4000	4520
Gain from the call	= (4520 − 4320) × 200	₹1,00,000

Effective cost of the portfolio after the call = 12,00,000 − 1,00,000 = ₹11,00,000

EXAMPLE 15.2 Hedging short portfolio with call option on index

A mutual fund wants to acquire an aggressive portfolio of stocks worth ₹10 crore, with a beta of 1.5. The market is on the rise, and funds would be available only after six months. The current level of the index is 5000, and the yields on the index and the proposed portfolio are identical at 4%. The mutual fund needs to limit its losses to 5% for the next six months. Find out the value of a call option and its strike price for hedging against any rise in the value of the new portfolio by 5%. Assume a risk-free rate of return of 8%. All returns and yield are for a 6-m period. Examine the position of the mutual fund if the market rises by 10% in six months.

Solution
To find out what level of decline in the index would cause the portfolio to lose 5% of its value, we use CAPM, as given in Example 15.1.

$$R_p + D_p = R_f + \beta(R_m + D_m - R_f)$$

Substituting the values of the expected decline of 5%, we solve for the percentage fall in the index.

$5 + 2 = 4 + 1.5 (R_m + 2 - 4)$ gives $R_m = \quad +4\%$

A rise of 4% in the index would mean a loss of 5% in the portfolio. The mutual fund must buy call options with strike prices of 4% above the market, i.e., 5000 × 4% = 200 points. Therefore, the strike price of the call should be 5200.
The value of the call option must be 1.5 × the portfolio value = 1.5 × 10 = ₹15 crore.
Assuming one point as one rupee, the number of calls bought

= 15,00,00,000/5000 = 30,000

If the market rises by 10% to the 5500 level, then the capital loss on the portfolio would be 4% as below:

$R_p + D_p = R_f + \beta(R_m + D_m - R_f)$ \quad 14%
$R_p + 2 = 4 + 1.5 (10 + 2 - 4)$ gives $R_p =$

Hence the portfolio would now cost 1.14 × 10 = ₹11.4 crore.
The payoff from each call would be 300 (5500–5200) and total payoff is 30,000 × 300 = ₹0.90 crore.
After the payoff from the call, the portfolio would cost 11.40–0.90 = 10.50 crore, the maximum level, i.e., 5% above the current value afforded by the mutual fund.

HEDGING WITH CURRENCY OPTIONS

Exposures on a foreign currency can be hedged through options on that foreign currency. The underlying is the spot exchange rate of the foreign currency. We discuss hedging receivables and payables with options.

Hedging Foreign Currency Receivable with Put Option

> Receivables in a foreign currency can be protected against depreciation of that foreign currency by buying a put option.

Buying put option protects long position in assets. The concept of a protective put can be extended to foreign currency exposures. Exporters who sell their products on credit face exchange rate risk. Having invoiced in a foreign currency, the position of the exporter is equivalent to having a long position in a foreign currency equal to the amount of the account receivable in the foreign currency. The value of the asset would drop if the foreign currency depreciates. Like with stock, the position in the receivable too can be protected by buying put options with the strike price at which protection is desired. Foreign currency options are mostly available over-the-counter (OTC) with banks.

For example, assume that an exporter has sold goods worth US $10,000 with payment due in six months' time. The value of the dollar after six months is uncertain. The exporter has planned his profit by assuming that his dollar receivable would be paid to him at around ₹45 per dollar. Realizing more than ₹45 (the dollar appreciating) would be a pleasing situation, but anything less than ₹45 could seriously dent the target profit. The exporter can protect his/her position by buying a put with a strike price of ₹45, valid for six months, by paying a small premium of, say, ₹0.50 per dollar.

Should the exporter hedge his position with a put, the net realization would always be greater than ₹44.50 per dollar (the strike exchange rate − the premium). Should the rate happen to be less than ₹45, say ₹43.00, the exporter can exercise his/her put, resulting in a profit of ₹2.00 (45 − S). The exporter sells his/her dollars at ₹43.00 and is short of the target by ₹2.00. The shortfall is made good by exercising the put. The realized exchange rate with put under two different scenarios for the exchange rates at the time of actual receipt of foreign currency are as follows:

Figures in ₹

Spot price	Position of put	Put payoff	Asset value	Realized price
S < 45.00	Exercise put	45.00 − S − 0.50	S	44.50
S > 45.00	Let put lapse	−0.50	S	S − 0.50 (larger than 44.50)

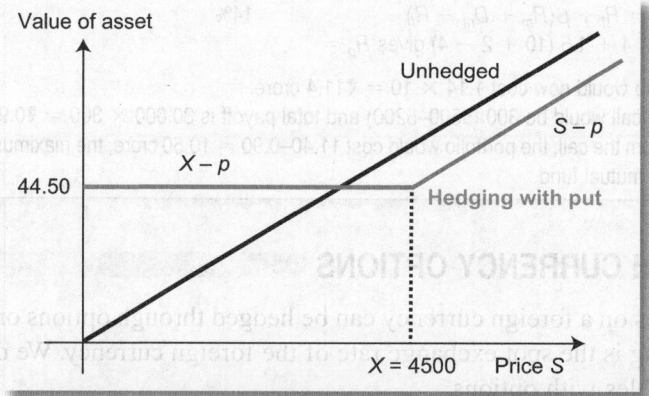

Fig. 15.4 Hedging receivable with put

As can be seen from this, hedging a receivable through a put not only protects the value to some minimum level, but also helps in retaining potential gain if the currency appreciates. At the time of realization, if the spot price were ₹48, then the exporter would end up getting ₹47.50 for each dollar. Hedging with a put provides a floor to the exporter, as depicted in Fig. 15.4. The exporter retains the potential to make gains in case of depreciation of the local currency by paying a small cost of ₹0.50, simultaneously protecting against downside losses.

Hedging Foreign Currency Payable with Call Option

> Payables in a foreign currency can be protected against appreciation of that foreign currency by buying a call option.

A call option provides an effective hedge for the exposures of importers who make payments in foreign currency on a deferred basis. Importers who buy their products on credit also face exchange rate risk. Having accepted the obligation to make a certain payment in a foreign currency, they fear appreciation of foreign currency. Their requirement of the foreign currency in future is analogous to a short position in the foreign currency. The value of the liability would rise as the foreign currency appreciates. Like a short position on stock, the payable can be protected by buying a call option with a strike price at the level at which protection is desired.

For example, assume that an importer has bought goods for US $10,000 for which he/she has committed payment in six months' time. The current exchange rate is ₹47.00/$. The value of the dollar after six months is uncertain. The importer has planned his/her profit by assuming that the dollar rate for his payable would not exceed ₹50. Paying more than ₹50 (the dollar appreciating) would be a disaster for the bottom line. The importer can protect his/her position by buying a call option with the strike price of ₹50, valid for six months, by paying a small premium of, say, ₹0.50/$.

If the importer hedges his/her position with a call, the maximum payment is capped at ₹50.50 (strike exchange rate + premium). Should the rate happen to be less than ₹50, say ₹48.00, the importer can buy the foreign currency at ₹48.00, limiting the overall cost to ₹48.50. However, if the rate happens to be in excess of ₹50, the importer exercises the call option to get dollars at ₹50, limiting the overall cost to ₹50.50. This is shown in the following table:

Figures in ₹

Spot price	Position of call	Call payoff	Payable value	Net price
$S < 50.00$	Let call lapse	−0.50	S	$S − 0.50$ (Less than 50.50)
$S > 50.00$	Exercise call	$S − 50.00 − 0.50$	S	50.50

Like a put works for a receivable, a call works for a payable. Hedging a payable with a call not only protects the cost but also helps in retaining the potential for gain if the foreign currency depreciates. At the time of realization, if the spot price is ₹48, then the importer would end up paying ₹48.50 for each dollar.

Hedging with a call provides a cap to the importer, as depicted in Fig. 15.5. The importer retains the potential to make gains in case of appreciation of the local currency by paying

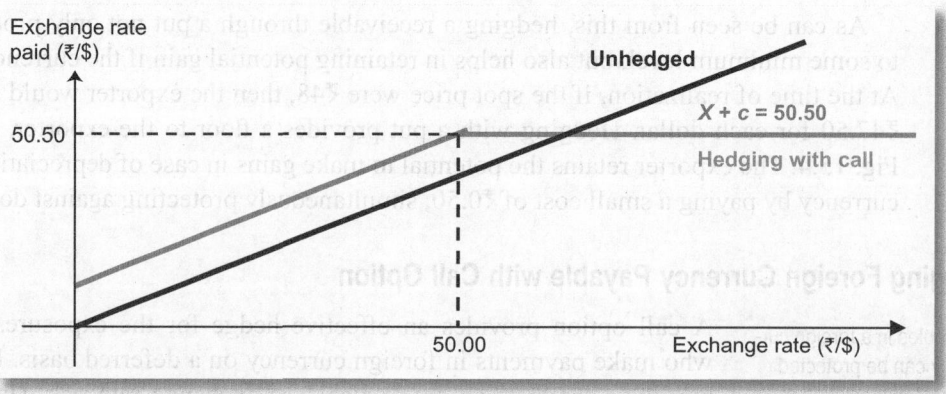

Fig. 15.5 Hedging payable with call

a small cost of ₹0.50. Of course, he/she protects himself/herself against losses arising from depreciation of the local currency.

Range Forward—Zero Cost Collar

We considered hedging of a long position by buying a put and a short position by buying a call. Both the strategies required an initial cost equal to the price of the option that must be paid upfront. While the put assured a minimum value of the underlying asset, the call ensured the maximum cost of a liability. Hedging through options involves a cost, as buying an option requires an upfront payment.

> To offset the cost of hedging with options, one may sell another option, earning a premium but sacrificing some gain, and assuming part of the risk.

The cost of options has always been a consideration for importers and exporters. Remember that the party who sells an option earns the premium. As a cost-saving strategy, one may consider buying one option while writing another, so that the initial outlay on the position is minimized. If the strike price of both the options is the same but notional is different, the position is called a *participating forward*. Where the strike prices of the options bought and options sold are different, the position is called a *range forward*. For example, to protect against a price fall (for a receivable), one may buy an out-of-the-money (OTM) put and write an in-the-money (ITM) call. Since the OTM option would be cheaper than the ITM option, the net initial position can be set up with zero cost by writing a smaller number of calls than the number of puts bought. The puts would provide protection against any price falls, while the call would not fully negate the advantages of price rises. Protection would not be available till the price falls below the strike of the put, which is OTM. However, some part of the risk would have to be borne by the investor (the current price and the strike price of the put).

In the range, given by the difference between the two strike prices of the options, the position of the hedger is not covered. For currency options, the following positions constitute a range forward for importers and exporters, as depicted in Fig. 15.6.

Exporters A range forward is created by buying a put with a lower strike price, X_1, and writing a call with a higher strike price, X_2. Buying a put is a right to sell, and writing a call

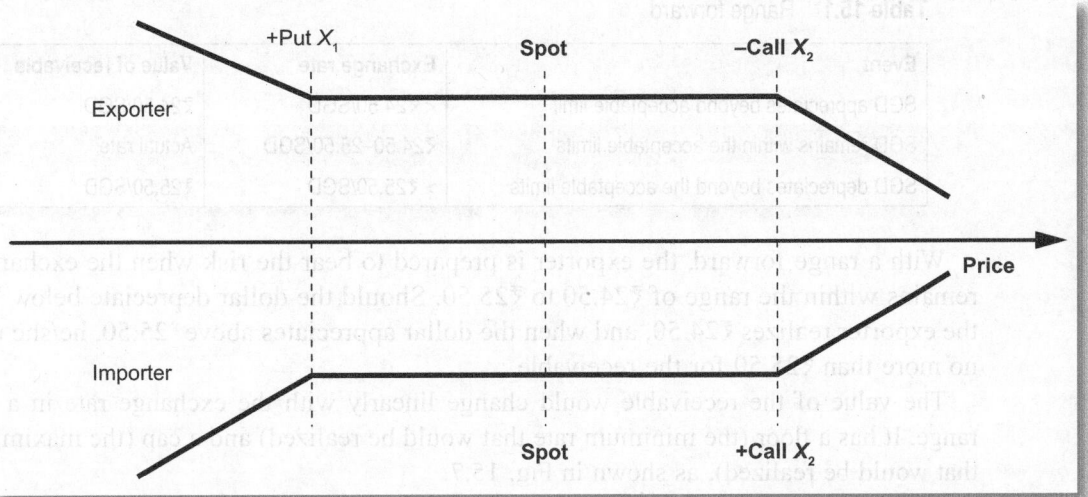

Fig. 15.6 Range forward—pay off

is an obligation to sell. Both positions are consistent as exporters sell foreign currency. They have a right at one price and an obligation at another. For a spot price below X_1, the put would provide protection; between X_1 and X_2, the market price prevails; and above X_2, the benefits of increased realization are foregone, as the obligation under the call written arises.

Importers A range forward is created by buying a call with a higher strike price, X_2, and writing a put with a lower strike price, X_1. Buying a call is a right to buy and writing a put is an obligation to buy. Both positions are consistent as importers buy foreign currency. They have a right at one price and an obligation at another. For a spot price above X_2, the call would provide protection; between X_1 and X_2, the market price prevails; and below X_1, the benefits of a lesser cost are foregone as the put becomes activated.

Depending upon the premiums of the call and the put, the range forward may be set up at zero cost by adjusting the strike prices of the options bought and sold. The range forward would have a cost of zero or close to zero. Does this mean that hedging can be done at no cost? Certainly not. The protection is available only after some losses are borne by the hedger and potential gains are sacrificed. The guaranteed price is more unfavourable under a zero cost option than it would be with a single option. Therefore, it is a compromise between the cost and the objective of hedging.

The payoffs on range forwards for exporters and importers are shown in Fig. 15.6. Long-term contracts involving cash flows in foreign currency involve range forwards in different fashions. This is done by incorporating clauses on payment terms based on exchange rates. Such clauses work like range forwards. However, financial markets provide risk sharing based on the buying of one option and the selling of another.

As a receivable-related example, consider an Indian exporter who has sent goods to Singapore invoiced in Singapore dollars (SGD). If the current spot rate is ₹25/SGD, the exporter may set a range forward by buying a put at the exchange rate of ₹24.50/dollar and selling a call at ₹25.50/dollar. The payoff on such a position is presented in Table 15.1.

> A range forward is a product based on options that helps reduce the cost of hedging.

Table 15.1 Range forward

Event	Exchange rate	Value of receivable
SGD appreciates beyond acceptable limit	< ₹24.50/SGD	₹24.50/SGD
SGD remains within the acceptable limits	₹24.50–25.50/SGD	Actual rate
SGD depreciates beyond the acceptable limits	> ₹25.50/SGD	₹25.50/SGD

With a range forward, the exporter is prepared to bear the risk when the exchange rate remains within the range of ₹24.50 to ₹25.50. Should the dollar depreciate below ₹24.50, the exporter realizes ₹24.50, and when the dollar appreciates above `25.50, he/she realizes no more than ₹25.50 for the receivable.

The value of the receivable would change linearly with the exchange rate in a limited range. It has a floor (the minimum rate that would be realized) and a cap (the maximum rate that would be realized), as shown in Fig. 15.7.

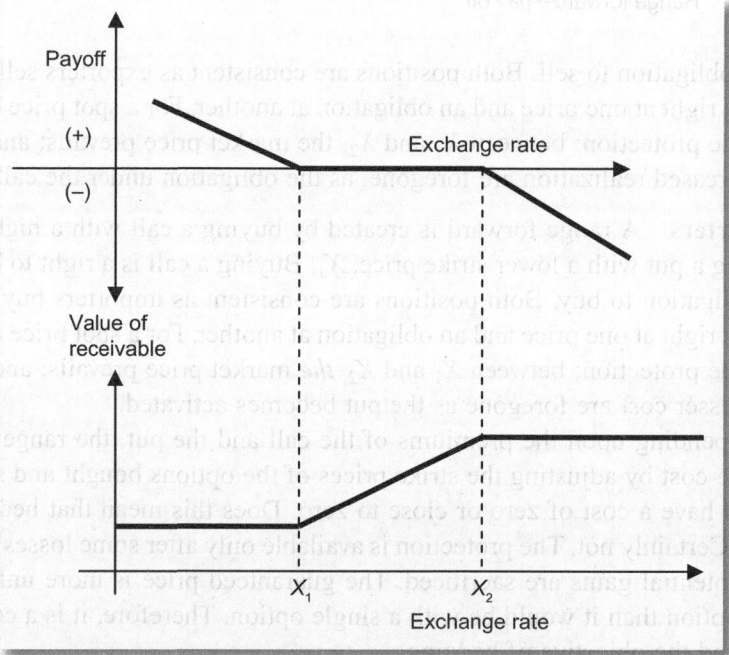

Fig. 15.7 Range forward

As we know, a forward contract has a cost. Further, the buyer of a forward contract foregoes the potential to make a profit in order to protect against losses. A range forward would be more economical as compared to a forward contract because the buyer of the range forward contract assumes some risk within an acceptable range.

Example 15.3 presents a comparison of hedging strategies with a forward, a put, and a range forward. In the range forward, the net cost of the hedging was brought down from ₹0.70 for the put option to ₹0.35 by writing a call at ₹47.00, thus foregoing any gain from an upside movement of the exchange rate beyond ₹47.00. In order to achieve a zero cost

EXAMPLE 15.3 Hedging strategies with options

Assume that an exporter is expecting to collect some receivables denominated in US dollars three months from now, and is worried about fluctuations in the foreign exchange markets. He/she wants to analyse hedging benefits available under various scenarios based on the following information.

The spot exchange rate is ₹45 per dollar and a 3-m forward contract is offered at ₹45.50 per dollar. Call and put options at various strike prices are also available. A put option with a strike price of ₹45.50/dollar sells at a premium of ₹0.70 and a call option with a strike price of ₹46.50 is selling at ₹0.35.

Tabulate the payoffs and value of receivables for the exporter for a given range of final exchange rates between ₹40.00 to ₹50.00 at the end of three months if the exporter

(a) decides to remain unhedged
(b) buys a forward contract at ₹45.50
(c) buys a put with a strike price of ₹45.
(d) buys a range forward with *at market* between ₹45.50 and 46.50

Further, plot the payoffs and values under the given scenarios.

Solution

If the exchange rate at the end is S_T, then the exporter is likely to reap the following payoffs and values:

(a) Under an unhedged position, the payoff would be $(45.00 - S_T)$, and the total value realized would be equal to the market rate, S_T.
(b) With a forward contract, the payoff would be (forward rate $- S_T$) and the total value realized would be equal to the forward rate, irrespective of the value of S_T.
(c) With a put option at a strike of X_p and a premium of p, the payoff would be $\text{Max}(X_p - S_T - p, -p)$ and the total value realized would be a minimum of ₹45.30 when S_T is below ₹46.00/dollar and $(S_T - 0.70)$ when the exchange rate is above ₹46.00/dollar.
(d) With range forward, a call with a strike price, $-X_c$, of 47.00 would be written earning a premium, c, of 0.35 with a put option at a strike of 46.00 and a premium of ₹0.70 paid. The net cash outflow would be ₹0.35. The payoff would be {Max$(X_p - S_T - p, -p)$ - Max$(S_T - X_c - c, -c)$} for exchange rates less than 46.00 and more than 47.00. In between the two, the realization would be $(ST - 0.35)$. The minimum would be ₹45.65 and the maximum would be ₹46.65.

The payoffs and values of realization are shown in the following table:

Payoffs and values under different scenarios (₹/$)

Exchange rate	Unhedged		Forward		With put		Range forward	
	Payoff	Value	Payoff	Value	Payoff	Value	Payoff	Value
40.00	−5.00	40.00	6.00	46.00	5.30	45.30	5.65	45.65
41.00	−4.00	41.00	5.00	46.00	4.30	45.30	4.65	45.65
42.00	−3.00	42.00	4.00	46.00	3.30	45.30	3.65	45.65
43.00	−2.00	43.00	3.00	46.00	2.30	45.30	2.65	45.65
44.00	−1.00	44.00	2.00	46.00	1.30	45.30	1.65	45.65
45.00	—	45.00	1.00	46.00	0.30	45.30	0.65	45.65
46.00	1.00	46.00	—	46.00	−0.70	45.30	−0.35	45.65
47.00	2.00	47.00	−1.00	46.00	−0.70	46.30	−0.35	46.65
48.00	3.00	48.00	−2.00	46.00	−0.70	47.30	−1.35	46.65
49.00	4.00	49.00	−3.00	46.00	−0.70	48.30	−2.35	46.65
50.00	5.00	50.00	−4.00	46.00	−0.70	49.30	−3.35	46.65

The payoffs and values of realization are depicted in the following figures:

Contd

Example 5.3 *contd*

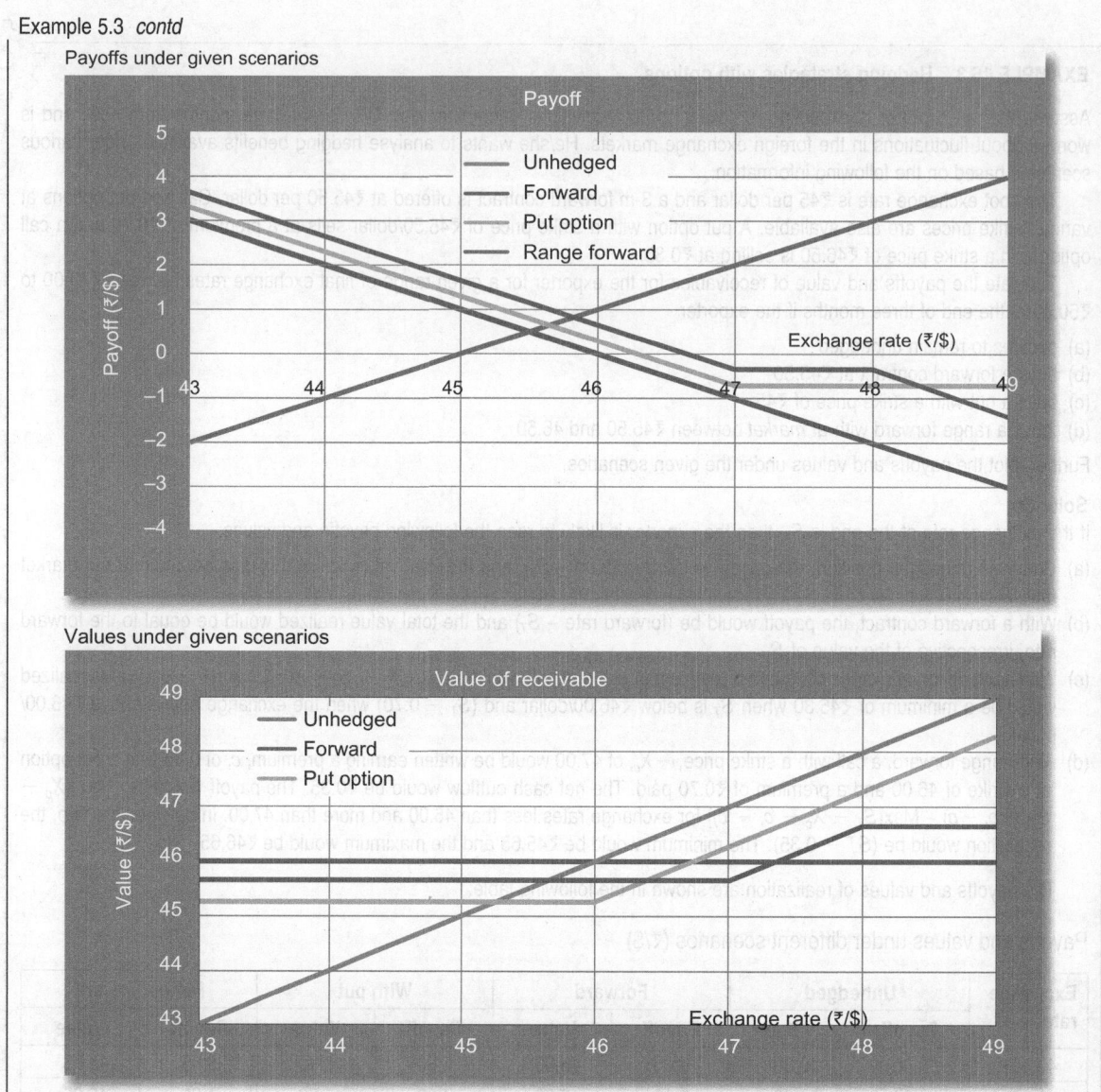

structure, one can consider writing two calls rather than one to compensate fully for the cost of the put option. In such a case, the ratio of calls written to puts bought would exceed 1. Such a combination for hedging is called a *ratio range forward*.

We now examine the position of a hedge with a ratio range forward, with the ratio of calls written to put bought at 2. The payoffs and the value of the receivable are presented in Table 15.2.

Notice that in the ratio range forward, once the exchange rate goes beyond ₹47.00/dollar, the receivable starts losing in value because the extra call written turns in-the-money and creates a liability for the writer. The payoffs are shown in Fig. 15.8 and the values of the receivable are depicted in Fig. 15.9.

Table 15.2 Forward, range forward, and ratio range forward

Exchange rate	Forward		Range forward		Ratio range forward	
	Payoff	Value	Payoff	Value	Payoff	Value
40.00	6.00	46.00	5.65	45.65	6.00	46.00
41.00	5.00	46.00	4.65	45.65	5.00	46.00
42.00	4.00	46.00	3.65	45.65	4.00	46.00
43.00	3.00	46.00	2.65	45.65	3.00	46.00
44.00	2.00	46.00	1.65	45.65	2.00	46.00
45.00	1.00	46.00	0.65	45.65	1.00	46.00
46.00	–	46.00	−0.35	45.65	–	46.00
47.00	−1.00	46.00	−0.35	46.65	0.00	47.00
48.00	−2.00	46.00	−1.35	46.65	−2.00	46.00
49.00	−3.00	46.00	−2.35	46.65	−4.00	45.00
50.00	−4.00	46.00	−3.35	46.65	−6.00	44.00

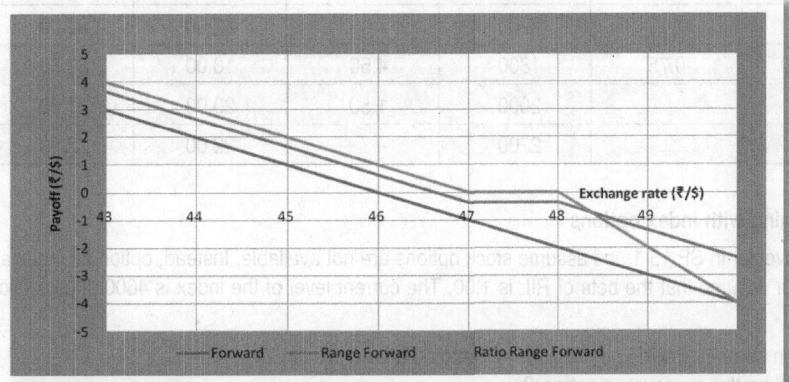

Fig. 15.8 Payoffs of forward, range forward, and ratio range forward

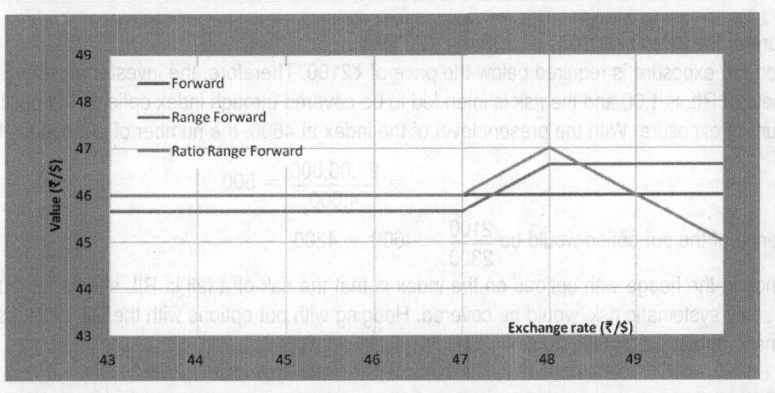

Fig. 15.9 Values–forward, range forward, and ratio range forward

SOLVED PROBLEMS

SP 15.1: Hedging with stock options

An investor is holding 1000 shares of Reliance Industries Ltd (RIL), currently trading at ₹2300. A put option on RIL with a strike of ₹2100 and maturity of one month is available at ₹50. What purpose would buying the put option serve? Analyse the position after one month for stock prices of ₹1800, ₹2000, and ₹2200 if the investor buys (a) 500 puts, (b) 1000 puts, and (c) 1500 puts.

Solution

Buying the put option would provide insurance to the value of the stock for prices below ₹2100. When the stock price falls below ₹2100, the holder can exercise the put option of selling the asset at ₹2100. This would happen if the position in the put option is the same as the position in the underlying stock. In case of overbooking or underbooking of the put, the hedge would not be perfect, as may be seen from the following table:

No.	Cost	Price ₹	Value of put	Value of stock	Total value	Net value
500	0.25	1800	1.50	18.00	19.50	19.25
		2000	0.50	20.00	20.50	20.25
		2200	–	22.00	22.00	21.75
1000	0.50	1800	3.00	18.00	21.00	20.50
		2000	1.00	20.00	21.00	20.50
		2200		22.00	22.00	21.50
1500	0.75	1800	4.50	18.00	22.50	21.75
		2000	1.50	20.00	21.50	20.75
		2200	–	22.00	22.00	21.25

SP 15.2: Hedging with index options

Consider the investor in SP 15-1 and assume stock options are not available. Instead, option on index are available for hedging the position. Further assume that the beta of RIL is 1.00. The current level of the index is 4600. If protection below the price of ₹2100 is desired, then

(a) What option strategy would you consider for hedging a long position?
(b) What would be the exposure in options?
(c) What would be the strike price of the options?
(d) How is this hedge different from the hedge taken in SP 15-2?

Solution

(a) The exposure of the investor is 1000 × 2300 = ₹23 lakh.
   Protection on the exposure is required below the price of ₹2100. Therefore, the investor must buy put options.
(b) Since the beta of RIL is 1.00 and the risk is intended to be covered through index options, the position in options must be equal to the amount of exposure. With the present level of the index at 4600, the number of put options to be bought

$$= \frac{23,00,000}{4,600} = 500$$

(c) The strike price of the put option would be $\frac{2100}{2300} \times 4600 = 4200$.

(d) The difference in the hedge with options on the index is that the risk of a fall in RIL shares attributable to a general fall in the market, i.e., only systematic risk, would be covered. Hedging with put options with the RIL stock as the underlying would cover both systematic and unsystematic risks.

SP15.3: Hedging long portfolio with put option on index

Consider Example 15-1 in the chapter. Assuming that the dividend yield and the index yield are the same at 3%, find out the new strike price of the put and the number of puts to be bought for protection below 10% of the current value of the portfolio. Examine the value of the portfolio if the market falls by 15%.

Solution
To find out what level of decline in the index would cause the portfolio to lose 10%, again using CAPM with segregated capital gains and dividend yields,

$$R_p + D_p = R_f + \beta(R_m + D_m - R_f)$$

Substituting the values of the expected decline of 5%, we solve for the percentage fall in the index.

$$-10 + 1.5 = 3 + 1.15(R_m + 1.5 - 3) \text{ gives } R_m = -8.5\%$$

A fall of 8.5% in the index would cause a loss of 10% in the portfolio. The mutual fund must buy put options with a strike price of 8.5% below the market, i.e., $5000 \times 8.5\% = 425$ points. The strike price of the puts, therefore, should be 4575.

The value of the put options must be 1.15 times the portfolio value $= 1.15 \times 10 = ₹11.5$ crore.

Assuming one put as one index, the number of puts bought

$$= 11{,}50{,}00{,}000/5000 = 23{,}000$$

If the market falls by 15% to the 4250 level, then the return on the portfolio would be

$$R_p + D_p = R_f + \beta(R_m + D_m - R_f)$$
$$R_p + 1.5 = 3 + 1.15(-15 + 1.5 - 3) \text{ gives } R_p = -17.475\%$$

Hence the portfolio would now be worth $(1 - 0.17475) \times 10 = 8.2525$ crore.
The payoff from each put would be $100(4575 - 4250)$ and total payoff is

$$23{,}000 \times 325 = ₹74.75 \text{ lakhs}$$

Hence, the portfolio would be insured at a level of ₹9.00 crore, i.e., 10% less than the existing value as desired in the hedge.

SP 15.4: Hedging with currency option

Opto Electronics Ltd has imported machinery worth €100,000 for which payment is due in six months' time. The exchange rate prevailing is ₹85/£. In six months, time, the pound is likely to appreciate to an estimated level of ₹90/£. A call option and a put option with a strike exchange rate of ₹87/£ are available at ₹1.50 and ₹3.00. What should Opto Electronics Ltd do to hedge its exposure in pounds? If it hedges, what would the maximum exchange rate it would pay to liquidate the liability be?

Solution
The firm is facing an appreciating foreign currency. To protect against the rise of the pound to as high a level as ₹90, the firm must buy call option with a strike of ₹87/pound at a price of ₹1.50. For exchange rates of ₹85 and ₹90 per pound, the combined position of the payable on the due date would be as follows:

Figures in ₹/€

Exchange rate	Call option	Call cash flow	Payable cash flow	Net rate
85.00	Let call lapse	−1.50	−85.00	86.50
90.00	Exercise call	+1.50	−90.00	88.50

The firm can exercise its call option to buy the currency at a strike of ₹87/pound. The total cost of the payable would then be limited to ₹88.50/pound, including the premium for buying the call option.

SP 15.5: Hedging with zero cost structures

Export Experts is an exporting firm that is very conscious of both the exchange rates it realizes on its receivables as well as the costs of hedging. The current spot rate is ₹50.50/dollar, and the firm believes that the rupee would be depreciating further. However, it decides to hedge by buying a put option with a strike of ₹50.50 at a cost of ₹0.70. In order to offset the cost, it also writes a call with a strike of ₹51.50, because it can afford to forego any gains beyond this level. Since it believes that the rupee would be depreciating only, and in order to recover its cost, it also writes a put option with a strike of ₹49.50, also selling at ₹0.35.

For a range of possible exchange rates at the end from ₹48.00 to ₹55.00, find out (a) the payoffs on all the three positions and (b) the value of the receivables. Further, depict the position graphically.

Solution

The spot exchange rate is ₹50.00/dollar. The exporter firm decides to buy a put with a strike of ₹50.50 at a premium of ₹0.70, assuring itself of a minimum exchange rate of ₹49.80 (50.50 − 0.70) if it does not engage in any other option. By writing a put at 49.50 and a call at 51.50, it has recovered the premium on the put in full. This would have an impact on the position of the receivable. This is shown in the following table.

Payoffs and values under zero cost structure

All figures in ₹

Exchange rate (₹/$)	Put bought		Put written		Call written		TOTAL	
	Payoff	Value	Payoff	Value	Payoff	Value	Payoff	Value
48.00	1.80	49.80	−1.15	46.85	0.35	48.35	1.00	49.00
48.50	1.30	49.80	−0.65	47.85	0.35	48.85	1.00	49.50
49.00	0.80	49.80	−0.15	48.85	0.35	49.35	1.00	50.00
49.50	0.30	49.80	0.35	49.85	0.35	49.85	1.00	50.50
50.00	−0.20	49.80	0.35	50.35	0.35	50.35	0.50	50.50
50.50	−0.70	49.80	0.35	50.85	0.35	50.85	0.00	50.50
51.00	−0.70	50.30	0.35	51.35	0.35	51.35	0.00	51.00
51.50	−0.70	50.80	0.35	51.85	0.35	51.85	0.00	51.50
52.00	−0.70	51.30	0.35	52.35	−0.15	51.85	−0.50	51.50
52.50	−0.70	51.80	0.35	52.85	−0.65	51.85	−1.00	51.50
53.00	−0.70	52.30	0.35	53.35	−1.15	51.85	−1.50	51.50

The payoffs per dollar of the three options with the total values of the receivable are shown in the following figures. It may be observed that for a range between ₹49.50 and ₹50.50, the realization is fixed at 50.50, and for a range between ₹50.50 and ₹51.50, the exporter capitalizes on depreciation. However, beyond ₹51.50, he/she foregoes the benefit, and the maximum realization is pegged at ₹51.50 for an exchange rate beyond ₹51.50. However, if the rupee starts appreciating beyond ₹49.50, contrary to expectations, the value of the realization starts falling.

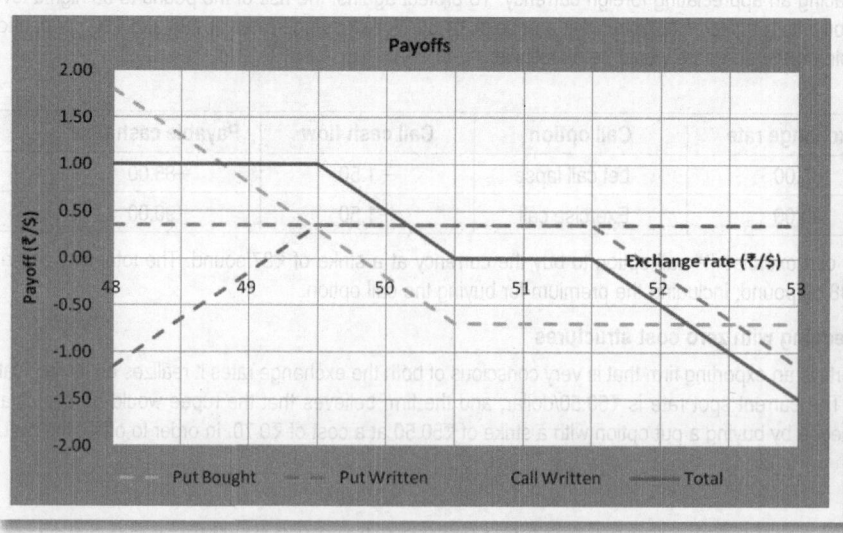

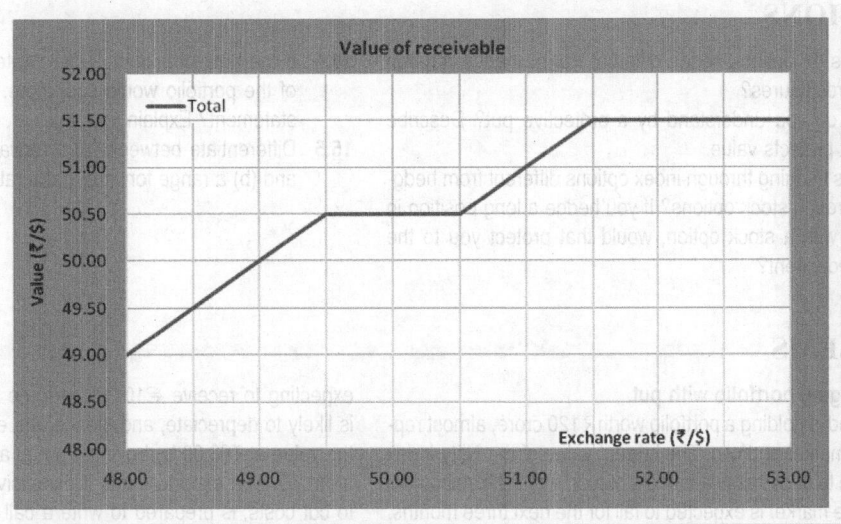

SUMMARY

Options, because of their unique non-linear payoffs, offer a broader range of applications than other derivatives. These applications can be categorized in four types—hedging, income generation, trading, and synthesizing.

Hedging with options is different from hedging with other derivative instruments in that options protect the downside but retain the upside potential for gain. Of course, this does not come free of cost. Exposures to stocks can be hedged with stock options. Market risks for a portfolio can be effectively managed with index options. Foreign currency exposures are managed by options on foreign currency. Long positions in stock, portfolio, or foreign currency are hedged through puts, while short positions are protected by buying calls.

A long position in stocks can be protected by buying a put at the strike level to which the stock holder can sustain loss. Similarly, a short position in stocks can be covered by buying a put. Hedging of a portfolio with index options requires selection of the appropriate strike price and the amount of exposure in the options. When the beta of the portfolio is 1 and the dividend yield is the same for the index and the portfolio, then determining the appropriate strike price of the option is rather easy. However, when the beta of the portfolio is not 1, or the portfolio yield is not the same as the index yield, or when both situations exist, then we have to apply CAPM to find the appropriate strike price of the option. The exposure in the options would simply be beta times the value of the portfolio.

Exporters hedge receivables by buying puts and importers hedge payables by buying calls. Since the cost of buying options is high sometimes, the exporters and importers strive to reduce the cost by writing some options that fetch a premium and thus help bring down the cost of hedging, while sacrificing some potential gains. The selection of strike prices of the options to be bought and to be sold is governed by the hedger's desired outcome as well as the risk profile acceptable to him/her. Many such structures, such as range forwards or ratio range forwards, are available to suit individual needs.

KEY TERMS

Beta The sensitivity of the value of a portfolio with respect to changes in the market.
Protective put A long position in an asset is protected against decline in value by buying a put.
Range forward A combination of options—one long and the other short—created with the objective of reducing cost and limiting the holder's market risk to a small range.
Ratio range forward Where the numbers of options bought and options written are not equal but in a certain ratio.

QUESTIONS

15.1 How is an options hedge different from a hedge through forwards/futures?

15.2 What do you understand by a protective put? Describe how it protects value.

15.3 How is hedging through index options different from hedging through stock options? If you hedge a long position in stock with a stock option, would that protect you to the desired extent?

15.4 If the beta of a portfolio is greater than 1, the insurance of the portfolio would cost more. Do you agree with this statement? Explain your answer.

15.5 Differentiate between (a) a forward and a range forward and (b) a range forward and a ratio range forward.

PROBLEMS

P 15.1 Hedging portfolio with put

A mutual fund is holding a portfolio worth ₹120 crore, almost replicating the market portfolio. The current value of the Nifty index is 4800. Due to uncertainty about the outcome of the forthcoming elections, the market is expected to fall for the next three months. The mutual fund needs protection against likely erosion in the value of the portfolio not exceeding 5%.

The yields on the portfolio and index are 4% and 3%, respectively, and the risk-free rate is 8%.

Find out the

(a) strike price of the put option
(b) number of contracts you would buy if each contract is for 50 indices and each index point is worth ₹1

P 15.2 Beta and hedging for long portfolio

What change in the hedging strategy would take place if the beta of the portfolio were 2.00, instead of 1.00?

P 15.3 Range forward and zero cost collar

The spot exchange rate for the euro is ₹64.00. An exporter is expecting to receive €10,000 in three months' time. The euro is likely to depreciate, and, hence, the exporter wants to lock-in the value at ₹63.00 by buying a put at a strike of ₹63.00, priced at ₹1.60. The exporter finds it expensive, and, hence, in order to cut costs, is prepared to write a call with a strike of ₹65.00, selling at ₹2.00, and forego any advantage if the spot rate goes beyond ₹65.00.

If the exporter wants to have no initial cost, how many calls should he/she write for every put bought? What would be the value of his/her receivables at spot exchange rates from ₹62.00 to ₹68.00?

If the exporter can write one call for every put bought, what would be the value of his/her receivables at spot exchange rates from ₹62.00 to ₹68.00?

Depict the value of the receivables for both the strategies. At what level of exchange rate does the first strategy become superior to the second strategy?

Options Trading Strategies

INTRODUCTION

We discussed hedging applications of options in Chapter 15. Like other derivatives, options too have speculative and arbitrage possibilities. In addition to these possibilities, options also offer unique applications that no other derivative do, because other derivatives have linear and unidirectional payoffs. Some of these applications unique to options are not feasible with other derivatives. The extended applications of options emanate from the non-linear payoff of options.

We have described various applications of options under the following four heads:

> Due to their non-linear payoff, there are many more applications available with options than with other derivatives.

- *Hedging strategies* concentrate on using options to hedge against the adverse price movement for a long or a short position in the underlying asset.
- *Income-generation strategies* focus on using options to enhance yields of the portfolios. This is possible because the writer of options earns a premium.
- *Trading strategies* highlight different options to achieve desired risk and return profiles, depending on the perception of the market by the trader.
- *Synthesizing strategies* demonstrate the power of options to create synthetic positions of other financial instruments. The replication of the payoff effectively means a lesser investment without compromising on returns, thus enhancing return on investment.

While hedging has already been discussed, we now describe the rest of the applications in this chapter. They are also referred to as trading strategies.

Learning Objectives

After going through this chapter, readers should be familiar with

- the various applications of options
- using options to enhance income
- trading in options to obtain desired returns and risk profiles, including combinations such as
  - straddle
  - strangle
  - spreads
- timing and methods for using different combinations of options
- synthesizing other financial assets using options

INCOME GENERATION WITH OPTIONS

Hedging strategies with options, as discussed earlier, entail some cost in the form of a premium to get the desired protection from the risks of fluctuating prices while retaining the upside potential. Options can also be used for enhancing income. We know writing or selling options entitles the seller to earn an option premium. Writing an option is done with the intention of pocketing the premium, hoping that the option would not turn in-the-money till expiry. However, under certain circumstances, options can be used as income-generating tools to enhance yields, without assuming significantly large risk.

> Options can be used as tools for enhancing income when prices are stagnant.

NAKED CALL AND COVERED CALL

Writing options is extremely tempting for investors (*read speculators*) for their potential to provide gains, though small in value, on zero investments. In fact, returns on investment can be made infinite by writing options. To earn premium, an investor may choose to write a call option hoping that the price will not exceed the exercise price. This would be done by an investor who is extremely bearish about market conditions. If the expectations come true, the call will not be in-the-money and it would not be exercised by the holder. The seller can pocket the premium. However, in case the price exceeds the exercise price, the option holder will exercise the call, and the seller will have to deliver the underlying asset by buying it at the current market price. Such a strategy is called naked call *writing*, i.e., writing a call on an asset not owned. Naked call writing is deemed to be an extremely speculative strategy in nature, since for a very small profit, i.e., the call premium, a call writer assumes the large, potentially unlimited risk of incurring losses, as shown in Fig. 16.1.

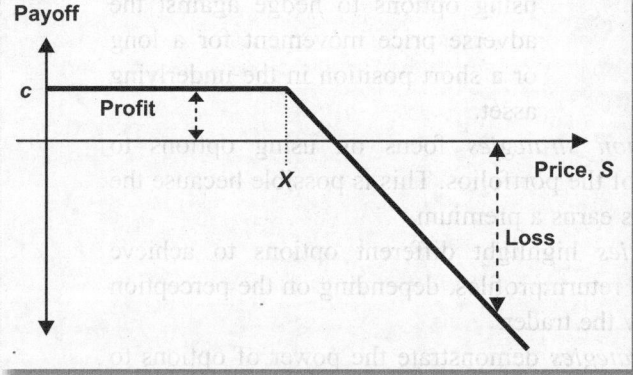

Fig. 16.1 Payoff—naked call writer

In contrast to naked call writing, the strategy behind *covered call writing* is to write a call on an asset already in possession. In case the writer of the call already owns the underlying asset, delivery can be made without going to the market to obtain the asset. This strategy can be fruitfully deployed to enhance income when markets are dormant. Since not much gain is foreseen on the asset owned in such market conditions, the holder of the asset may choose to write a call to earn a premium and enhance return. In the rather unlikely circumstances

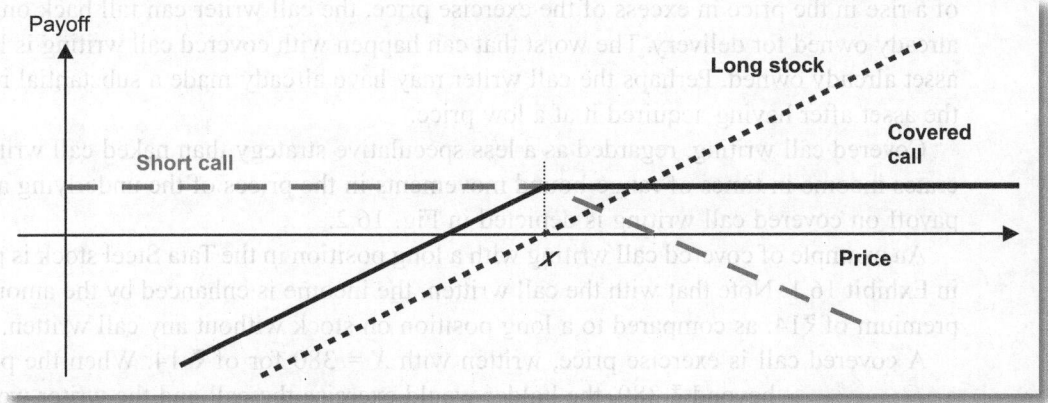

Fig. 16.2 Writing a covered call

EXHIBIT 16.1 Covered call writing

Strategy
- Long position on stock
- To generate income, write a call on the same asset for the hedging period

Example
The following prices prevail on 21 October 2005 on the National Stock Exchange (NSE) for November 05 calls on Tata Steel:

$$\text{Call with } X = 380 \quad c = 14$$

Covered call
Long position in Tata Steel stock
Sold one call at $X = 380$ Premium earned = 14
Initial income from the call = 14

Table for payoff on the covered call

(All figures in ₹)

When spot price S	Long stock	Short call $X = 380$	Initial cash flow	TOTAL
$S < 380$	$S - 380$	—	14	$S - 366$
$S > 380$	$S - 380$	$-(S - 380)$	14	14

Graphical view: Covered call payoff

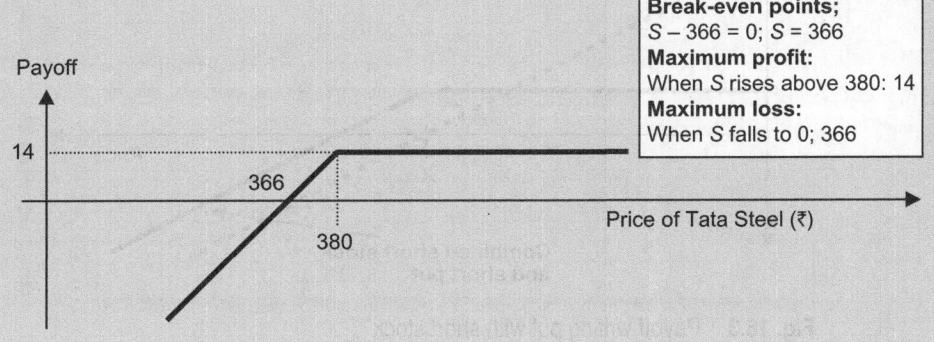

Break-even points:
$S - 366 = 0; S = 366$
Maximum profit:
When S rises above 380: 14
Maximum loss:
When S falls to 0; 366

of a rise in the price in excess of the exercise price, the call writer can fall back on the asset already owned for delivery. The worst that can happen with covered call writing is losing the asset already owned. Perhaps the call writer may have already made a substantial reward on the asset after having acquired it at a low price.

Covered call writing, regarded as a less speculative strategy than naked call writing, generates income in times of range-bound movements in the prices of the underlying asset. The payoff on covered call writing is depicted in Fig. 16.2.

An example of covered call writing with a long position in the Tata Steel stock is presented in Exhibit 16.1. Note that with the call written, the income is enhanced by the amount of the premium of ₹14, as compared to a long position on stock without any call written.

A covered call is exercise price, written with $X = 380$ for of ₹ 14. When the price goes beyond ₹ 380, the holder would exercise the call and the writer would meet his/her obligations without going to the market. If the price remains below ₹380—the expectation with which he/she chose to write the call—the call writer pockets ₹14 and continues to keep the asset.

> Writing a call with an asset in hand is called covered call writing. It enhances income when markets are not volatile.

Writing a call can be used repeatedly to earn frequent premiums, as long as the markets remain sluggish. Calls are not a hedge against falling prices while owning stock but provide a cushion in return to the extent of the premium earned on the calls. Hedging against a fall in price can be achieved by buying a put option on the asset.

WRITING PUT

The strategy of writing a covered call is used when no upside movement in the price is forecast. Similarly, one can write a put when no downside movement in the asset price is anticipated. When an investor is short on stock (and is contemplating buying some) and foresees no downside movement, he/she may decide to write a put to earn some return in the short term. Writing a put option, while short on the underlying, is analogous to writing a covered

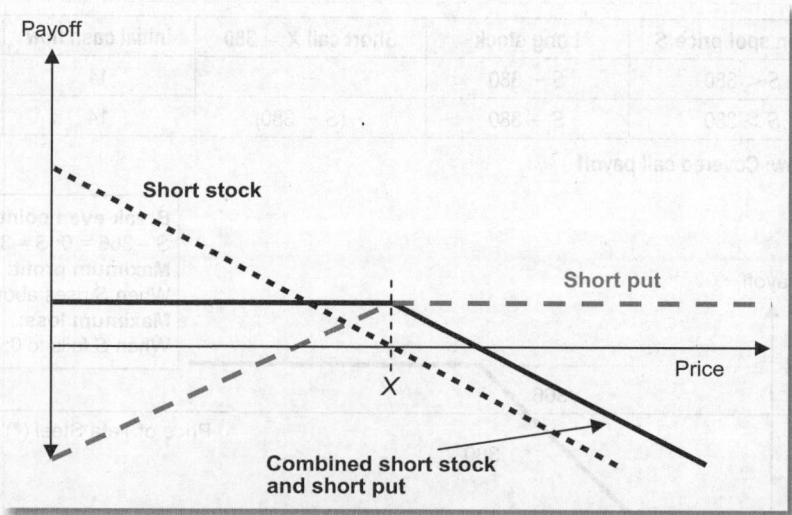

Fig. 16.3 Payoff writing put with short stock

call. Though the term covered call is prevalent, the term covered put does not exist in usage, though having cash equivalent to the exercise price amounts to possessing the underlying asset. If one writes a put, one must buy the stock when required by the put holder at the exercise price. The writer of the put gets the stock at the exercise price, which can be used to fulfil the position of short stock.

Despite its income-generating potential, writing a put is seldom used. It may be because short positions on stock are either not permitted or seldom taken by investors. The payoff on a combined position (short on stock and short on put), which is similar to writing a call, is depicted in Fig. 16.3.

Speculation with Single Option

Speculative strategies with options are rather simple—possibly as simple as with futures or forwards. When the market is bullish, buying futures now and selling them later is appropriate, while under bearish conditions, investors would sell futures first and buy them back later.

> As speculation, one buys a call when the market is bullish, and buys a put when the market is bearish.

Similar speculative positions are possible with options. When the market is bullish, buying a call option provides a gain of $S - X$ if the price exceeds the strike price, where S and X are the spot price at expiration/exercise and the strike price, respectively. Similarly, under bearish conditions, buying a put would provide a gain of $X - S$ if the spot price is less than the strike price of the put. Depending upon his/her opinion about future price movement, an investor can take up the speculative position of buying a call or a put.

Unlike speculation with forwards/futures, speculation with options costs money. Buying forwards and futures does not require any up front payment, and though there is a requirement for margins in futures. It is refundable and is only deposited as a form of security. On the contrary, taking a long position in options requires payment of premiums. Therefore, buying options as a speculative strategy must necessarily be done when the potential for gain is likely to exceed the premium paid. Much is dependent upon the confidence level of the investor in the direction of future movement.

Since volatility is a double-edged sword, a position in futures is more risky than a position in options. Therefore, the levels of volatility must be reasonable when taking speculative positions in futures. When volatility is high, it makes more sense to speculate with options due to their ability to limit losses on one side of volatility. There is a big difference between speculation with futures and speculation with options. Speculation with futures is without protection against adverse price movement, while options do provide this protection. The maximum possible loss is already paid up as an upfront premium. This is shown in Fig. 16.4.

Arbitrage with Options

Arbitrage opportunities with options, in the manner that we are familiar with in respect of futures, are not available. Processes such as cash-and-carry and reverse cash-and-carry arbitrage are not possible for implementation with options due to the absence of convergence of

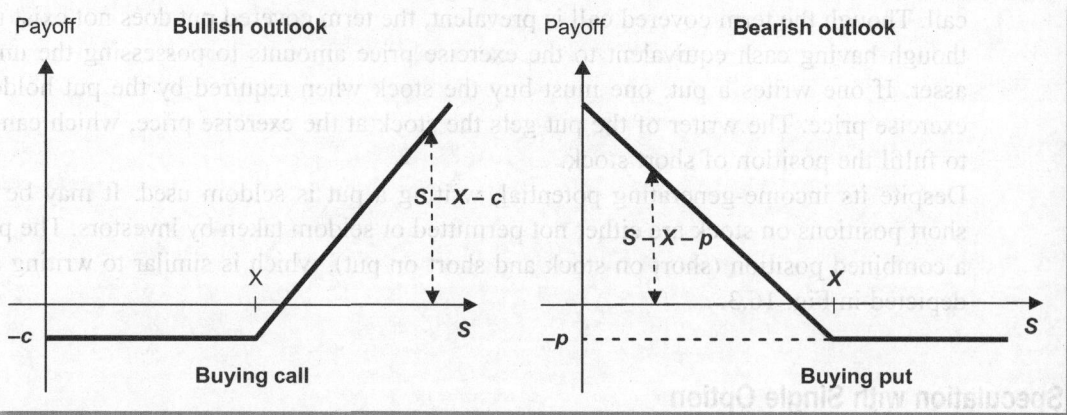

Fig. 16.4 Speculation with options

the kind that applies in the case of forwards or futures contracts. Options either expire worthless or are exercised at maturity depend upon price at maturity and exercise price.

However, arbitrage within options is possible. If two or more options are mispriced, arbitrage can be done by buying the underpriced option and selling the overpriced one. A few such strategies were discussed in Chapter 10.

OPTION TRADING STRATEGIES

> By combining options, a wide menu of risk and return profiles is available for investors to choose from.

A position on a single option provides uneven gains or losses with changes in the price of the underlying asset. A call option gives unlimited upside gain potential in exchange for a small premium, while a put option provides potential for large gains in falling markets in exchange for a small premium, as depicted in Fig. 16.4. Due to the non-symmetric profile of risks and returns, options can be used in various combinations that can generate a vast number of risk–return profiles. Investors can choose from hordes of risk–return profiles to match their individual risk appetite and return preferences.

These strategies are used for trading as well as for hedging purposes. If options are combined with the objective of risk containment, it is called hedging; when combined to take a specific or directional view on future prices and risks, it would become a speculation. The major distinction between hedge and speculation depends on whether the intention behind the position taken is to reduce risk or to assume risk. Unlike other derivative values, option values are dependent on many determinants, and the dimensions of risk can be with respect to any of these parameters. These parameters are maturity, volatility, nature of assets, type of options, exercise prices, option prices, etc., and form the basis on which many positions can be formed. With futures and forwards, only long and short positions are possible.

Combinations of options can be done on any one or more of these various parameters, such as,

- the different types of options (calls and puts)
- different exercise prices
- different ratios of calls and puts

- different expiration dates
- different underlying assets

The risk profile of a combination of options is an aggregation of the risk profiles of the individual options constituting the combination. Some of the most common and popular combinations (but certainly not exhaustive), are discussed here. Creativity is boundless, and, as such, there is no limit to the combinations of options that can be invented by investors, depending upon the risk–return profiles desired.

LONG AND SHORT STRADDLE

> A long straddle is formed by buying a call and a put on the same asset with the same maturity.

A straddle is a combination of simultaneous positions taken in call and put options on the same underlying asset with the same time to expiry. A long straddle constitutes a long call and a long put, and a short straddle comprises a short call and a short put. Both the call and the put have identical features. As both the options are bought, cash is needed to set up a long straddle. A short straddle would have cash inflow.

If the price remains equal to the exercise price, both the call and the put remain unexercised and the investor loses the premium. However, if the price moves away from the exercise price, either the call or the put becomes in-the-money, depending on the direction of the price movement. The long straddle starts recovering the cost incurred in setting up the position. The short straddle would start losing from drift on either side of the strike price.

> A long straddle is suitable when prices are volatile, while a short straddle is good when prices are range bound.

If the price goes higher than the exercise price, the call option becomes in-the-money, and if the price is below the exercise price, the put option is in-the-money. The payoff on a long straddle is depicted in Fig. 16.5 (a). A long straddle is a suitable strategy when one expects volatility in the prices of the underlying asset with no directional bias. An investor with a long straddle gains with price movements in either direction. It is suitable at times when a large movement in the price is forecast but the direction of the movement is unknown.

A short straddle is formed by simultaneously selling a call and a put on the same asset with the same strike price and the same expiry. It generates income as premiums on both the options, i.e., the call and the put written, are received. With any change in the price of the underlying asset, either the call or the put written becomes in-the-money. A movement

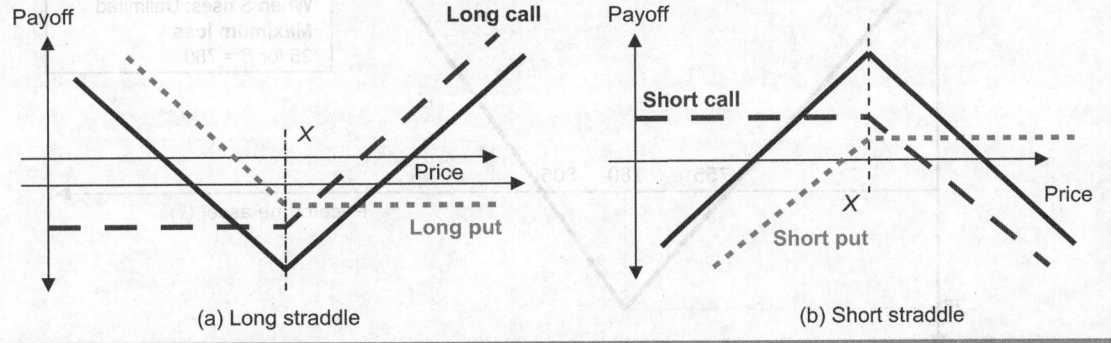

Fig. 16.5 Straddle (a) Long (b) Short

of the price away from the exercise price is detrimental to the interests of an investor with a short straddle. A short straddle position is suitable for an investor who foresees range-bound movement of the price around the exercise price, as can be seen from Fig. 16.5 (b).

Note that the combined position of a long and a short straddle results in zero payoff, confirming our earlier view that options are a zero-sum game.

An example of the long straddle is shown in Exhibit 16.2, where the investor has bought a call and a put, both with a strike price of ₹780 on the same underlying asset, Reliance stock, with the same expiry dates. In setting up this portfolio, the investor incurs a cost of ₹25, equal to the sum of the premiums on the call and the put. This would be the maximum

EXHIBIT 16.2 Long straddle

Strategy
- Buy a call for a strike price
- Buy a put for the same strike price on the same asset and with the same expiration

Example
The following prices prevail on 17 October 2005 on the NSE for October 05 options on Reliance:

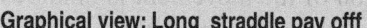

$X = 780$ $c = 15$; $p = 10$

Long straddle

Bought	1 call at $X = 780$	Premium paid = 15
Bought	1 put at $X = 780$	Premium paid = 10

Initial cost of the long straddle spread = 15 + 10 = 25

Table for payoff on the long straddle

(All figures in ₹)

When spot price S	+ Call $X = 780$	+ Put $X = 780$	Initial cash flow	TOTAL
$S < 780$	—	$780 - S$	-25	$755 - S$
$S > 780$	$S - 780$	—	-25	$S - 805$

Graphical view: Long straddle pay off

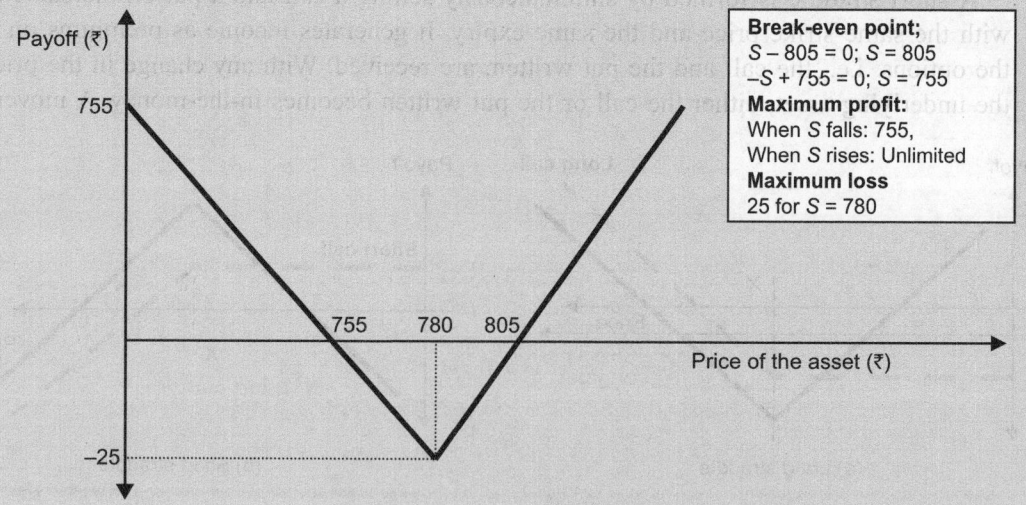

Break-even point;
$S - 805 = 0$; $S = 805$
$-S + 755 = 0$; $S = 755$
Maximum profit:
When S falls: 755,
When S rises: Unlimited
Maximum loss
25 for $S = 780$

loss. The investor breaks even with a price of ₹755 for Reliance stock, when the put comes in-the-money, and of ₹805, when the call becomes in-the-money. Thus, a long straddle ends up in profit with the price of the Reliance stock below ₹755 or above ₹805. Within the range of ₹755 to ₹805, there would be some losses, with peak losses at a price equal to the strike price of the two options, i.e., ₹780.

The payoff for the investor in a short straddle, called the writer of the straddle, would be exactly opposite to that of an investor in a long straddle. His/her peak profit would be ₹25 when the price of the Reliance share remains static at ₹780—the strike price of the options written. Such an investor would incur losses when the price of the Reliance share falls below ₹755 or goes above ₹805. However, the break-even would be the same as that of an investor with a long straddle.

A long straddle is not an appropriate strategy if the price stays within a tight trading range and does not break out sufficiently before the expiry of the options. The right time to set up a straddle would be just before the anticipated price breakout. Once the breakout has occurred, some small amount can be earned by selling the option that has now gone out-of-the-money.

Being a combination of independent call and put options, a long straddle may be created without an investor, with an equivalent short straddle. Call and put options may be bought from different persons to have a long straddle. The same principle applies to the creation of a short straddle, which may be created without a corresponding long straddle. However, few exchanges offer straddles as an independent and composite product.

LONG AND SHORT STRANGLE

> While a long straddle is chosen with ATM options, a long strangle is formed by buying a call at a higher strike price and a put at a lower strike.

A strangle is similar to a straddle, except that in a strangle the exercise prices of the call and put options bought/written are different. A straddle is usually created with ATM options. As there is no intrinsic worth, the entire premium consists of time value, which is the highest in case of ATM options. If we move away from ATM options towards OTM options, the cost of the set-up should be less, as OTM options would have no intrinsic value and less time value.

For a long strangle, the exercise price chosen for the put is less than the spot price, while the call option strike is chosen to be higher than the spot price. Hence, the strike of a put is lower than that of a call option. If the price remains within the two exercise prices, none of the options is exercised, and the premium paid on the options is lost. If the price goes above the strike of the call or goes below that of the put, a long strangle starts, paying off the cost initially and then resulting in a profit.

For a short strangle, the premiums earned by the investor is the profit if the price remains within the band of the two exercise prices. The payoff on the short strangle is opposite to that of the long strangle. The payoffs for long and short strangles are shown in Figs 16.6 (a) and (b), respectively.

Exhibit 16.3 provides a comprehensive view of a long strangle. Both the call and the put options are out-of-the-money when the long strangle is set up, as is indicated for the shares of Reliance, trading at ₹780. The strangle is created by buying a call at $X = 800$ and a put at $X = 760$. Within the price range of ₹760–800, both the call and put options are worthless.

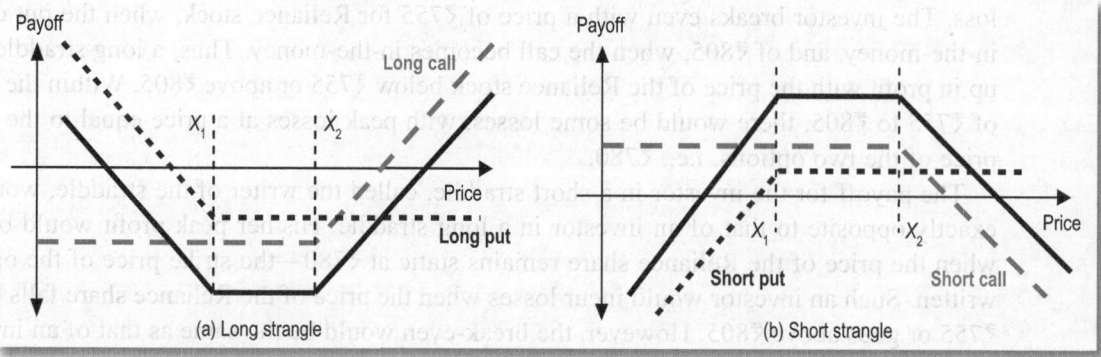

Figure 16.6 Payoff of strangle (a) Long strangle (b) Short strangle

EXHIBIT 16.3 Long strangle

Strategy
- Buy a call for a strike price that is preferably higher than that of the long straddle
- Buy a put for a strike price that is preferably lower than that of the straddle on the same asset and for the same expiration

Example
The following prices prevail on 17 October 2005 on the NSE for October 05 options on Reliance:

$X = 800\ c = 5$
$X = 760\ p = 5$

Long straddle

Bought	one call at $X = 800$	Premium paid = 5
Bought	one put at $X = 760$	Premium paid = 5
Initial cost of long strangle spread = 5 + 5 = 10		

Table for payoff on the long straddle

(All figures in ₹)

When spot price S	+ Call $X = 800$	+ Put $X = 760$	Initial cash flow	TOTAL
$S < 760$	–	$760 - S$	–10	$750 - S$
$760 < S < 800$	–	–	–10	–10
$S > 800$	$S - 800$	–	–10	$S - 810$

Graphical view: Long strangle-payoff

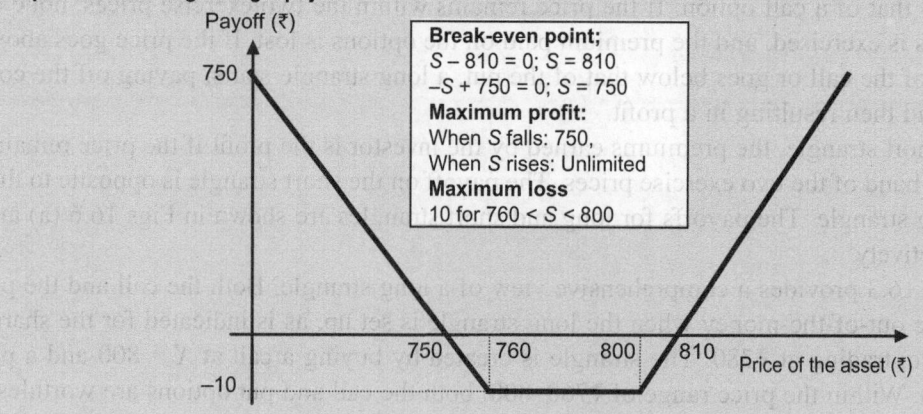

Break-even point;
$S - 810 = 0;\ S = 810$
$-S + 750 = 0;\ S = 750$
Maximum profit:
When S falls: 750,
When S rises: Unlimited
Maximum loss
10 for $760 < S < 800$

When the price goes below ₹760, the put becomes valuable and when the price is greater than ₹800, the call turns in-the-money.

Like the straddle, the strangle too becomes profitable with a large breakout of the price in either direction. However, the straddle starts paying earlier than the strangle. The strategy is fruitful under situations where volatility is expected to be high, with no directional bias. Some of these situations are described here, as follows:

- One situation arises when stocks are trading in the range with well-identified resistance and support levels, and when one does not know which of the two would be pierced. Breakouts are usually significant whenever they occur.
- Another situation favourable for creating a long strangle is at the time of a takeover attempt. Great uncertainty exists when takeover attempts are made. The situation is similar when some litigation reaches a point of decision specific to a particular firm. Depending upon the outcome of the event, prices move rather significantly.
- Yet another time to have a long strangle is when widespread uncertainty prevails at the time of a major or significant economic or political event, such as presentation of the budget, announcements of monetary and fiscal policies, and declaration of election results; these are events that cause large movements in market prices but with direction unknown.

On the contrary going short on a straddle or a strangle makes sense when the investor expects stability rather than volatility in prices.

Exhibit 16.3 shows the payoff on a long strangle with puts and calls at strike prices of ₹760 and ₹800, respectively, both selling at ₹5 each. The investor breaks even at prices of ₹750 and ₹810, and turns into profit with prices less than ₹750 and more than ₹810. This may be compared with the payoff on a straddle in Exhibit 16.2. A strangle costs lesser than a straddle, as a call with a higher exercise price and a put with a lower exercise price would cost less. With a lesser cost of strangle, an investor with a long position loses some of the likely gains from volatility, as compared to a long straddle position. An investor with a long strangle earns a lesser profit (a) over a broader range of prices, and (b) for every price as compared to the investor with a long straddle. This is a natural outcome, as a strangle costs less, thus providing lesser profit and a larger range for loss.

STRAPS AND STRIPS

In a long straddle or strangle, the payoffs from volatility are equal for equal price movements in either direction. This is due to the equal positions taken in call and put options in terms of the number of contracts.

The payoffs from changes in price can be made unequal by changing the ratio of the call and put options. For example, if the investor not only expects volatility in prices but also believes that the likelihood of prices going up is far more than the prices coming down, he/she can buy more than one call for every put bought. In the case of two calls for one put, the gains from an upside movement would double, as two calls will become in-the-money. The gains from an upside movement will be larger than the straddle, but will remain the same for a downside movement. This combination is known as a strap and is shown in Fig. 16.7.

Similarly in the opposite situation, where volatility is expected to be higher for a downside movement as compared to an upside movement, the investor can buy two puts and one call. When the price goes down, the two puts become in-the-money, and when the prices go up, only one call becomes in-the-money, making gains unequal for the same degree of rise or fall in the prices. This combination is known as a strip and its payoff is depicted in Fig. 16.8.

Strips and straps make sense in markets with high expected volatility, with some directional bias.

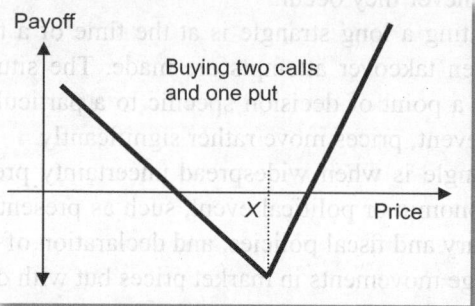

Fig. 16.7 Payoff of strap

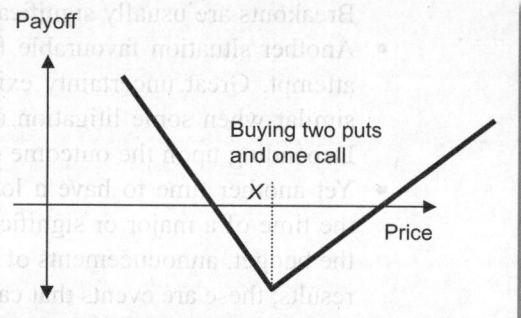

Fig. 16.8 Payoff of strip

BULL SPREAD

The combinations discussed so far were created using two different types of options on the same asset and the same expiration dates. Spreads are created with positions on the same type of options on the same underlying asset but with different exercise prices. Spreads can be created using either calls only or puts only. We discuss bull and bear spreads here.

> A bull spread is set up with the buying of a call with a lower strike and the selling of a call with a higher strike.

A bull spread is used by one who is moderately bullish about the market in the near future. One buys a call when a bullish but high premium for the call becomes a major consideration. When the prospects of a price rise are not as high, then one can reduce the investment in a single call by writing another call at a higher strike price. The call with the higher strike would sell for a lower value than the one bought, thereby offsetting only part of the cost. However, it would result in a better risk–reward ratio.

A call with a higher strike price trades at a lower premium than a call with a lower strike price. There will be net cash outflow while setting up a bull spread. A spread that results in cash outflow at the time of set-up is called a *debit spread*.

> A bull spread is used when one is moderately bullish about the market scenario.

If the market does not rise as expected and the price remains lower than both the strike prices, both calls would expire worthless. The loss will be limited to the difference between the premium paid and received on the call bought and written, respectively. If the spot price is higher than both the strike prices, both of the calls will be in-the-money, and the payoff shall be equal to the difference between the strike prices, less the cost of set-up. An illustration of a bull spread is shown in Exhibit 16.4.

EXHIBIT 16.4 Bull spread with calls

Strategy
- Buy a call for a strike price X_1
- Sell another call at the strike price $X_2 > X_1$ on the same asset and for the same expiration

Example
The following prices prevail on 17 October, 2005, on the NSE for October 05 options on the NIFTY:

$$X = 2500 \; c = 35, \; X = 2600 \; c = 7$$

Bull spread
Bought   one call at $X = 2500$ Premium paid = 35
Sold   one call at $X = 2600$ Premium received = 7
Initial cost of bull spread = 35 − 7 = 28

Table for payoff for bull spread

(All figures in ₹)

When spot price S	+Call X = 2,500	−Call X = 2,600	Initial cash flow	TOTAL
S < 2,500	−	−	−28	−28
2,500 < S < 2,600	S − 2,500	−	−28	S − 2,528
S > 2,600	S − 2,500	−(S − 2,600)	−28	72

Graphical view: Bull spread-payoff

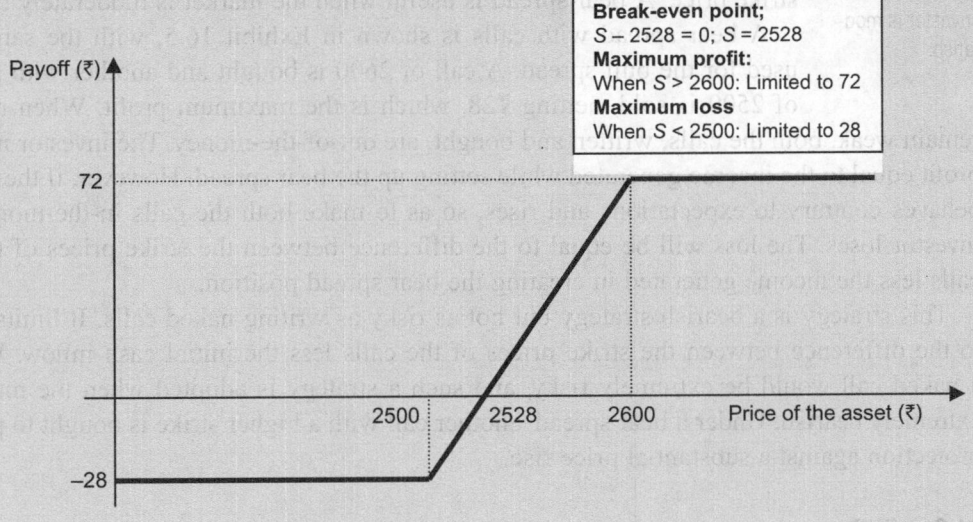

Break-even point;
S − 2528 = 0; S = 2528
Maximum profit:
When S > 2600: Limited to 72
Maximum loss
When S < 2500: Limited to 28

The maximum profit on a bull spread occurs when the price of the underlying asset is higher than the higher of the two call strike prices. The maximum profit is given by

$$\text{Profit} = (X_2 − X_1) − (c_1 − c_2)$$

where X_1 and X_2 are the two strike prices, and $X_2 > X_1$
c_1 and c_2 are the call premiums with strikes of X_1 and X_2 respectively

Adverting to the data in Exhibit 16.4, with the investor setting a bull spread by buying a call at a strike of 2500 and writing another at a strike of 2600, the investment stands reduced from ₹35 as compared to a single call to ₹28, which is the maximum loss. His/her profit would be pegged at ₹72 because beyond a strike of 2600, the call written offsets the gains on the call exercised at 2500.

An extremely bullish investor would create a bull spread with both the calls initially out-of-the-money. It would cost little, since both calls are out-of-the-money, with relatively lower chances of high payoff. This is termed as aggressive strategy. A rather less aggressive strategy will have one call in-the-money and the other out-of-the-money. The most conservative bull spread is created with both calls initially in-the-money.

A bull spread can be created using puts only—buying a put with a lower strike and selling a put with a higher strike. Such a spread would be a *credit spread* as it provides a cash inflow at the time of the set-up, because a put with a higher strike sells for more than one with a lower strike.

BEAR SPREAD

> A bear spread is set up with the buying of a call with a higher strike and the selling of a call with a lower strike. It is used when the investor is moderately bearish.

The opposite of a bull spread is a bear spread. An investor who believes that the market will be weak in the near future deploys a bear spread by buying a call with a higher strike price and simultaneously writing a call with a lower strike price. The set-up of a bear spread is likely to generate a positive cash flow, since a call written with a lower strike earns more than a call bought with a higher strike price. A bear spread is useful when the market is moderately bearish.

A bear spread with calls is shown in Exhibit 16.5, with the same data used for the bull spread. A call of 2600 is bought and another with a strike of 2500 is sold, netting ₹28, which is the maximum profit. When markets remain weak, both the calls, written and bought, are out-of-the-money. The investor makes a profit equal to the income generated while setting up the bear spread. However, if the market behaves contrary to expectations and rises, so as to make both the calls in-the-money, the investor loses. The loss will be equal to the difference between the strike prices of the two calls less the income generated in creating the bear spread position.

This strategy is a bearish strategy but not as risky as writing naked calls. It limits losses to the difference between the strike prices of the calls less the initial cash inflow. Writing a naked call would be extremely risky, and such a strategy is adopted when the market is extremely bearish. Under a bear spread, another call with a higher strike is bought to provide protection against a substantial price rise.

Debit and Credit Spreads

> A debit/credit bear spread is one that results in an initial cash outflow/inflow.

Both bull and bear spreads can also be created using just put options rather than calls. They would have almost the same payoff profiles as for calls. However, the difference may lie in whether a debit or a credit spread is being created. Whether the initial cash is an inflow or an outflow is an important consideration for investors. A debit spread would provide for losses initially and wait for the profit to accrue. A credit spread would book the profit initially, and then see if erosion takes place. However, the payoffs remain the same, and it is a matter of individual choice.

EXHIBIT 16.5 Bear spread with calls

Strategy

- Sell a call for a strike price X
- Buy another call at the strike price $X_2 > X_1$ on the same asset and for the same expiration

Example

The following prices prevail on 17 October 2005 on the NSE for October 05 options on the NIFTY:

$$X = 2500 \; c = 35, \; X = 2600 \; c = 7$$

Bear spread

Sold	one call at $X = 2500$	Premium received = 35
Bought	one call at $X = 2600$	Premium paid = 7

Initial cash flow of long bear spread = 35 − 7 = 28 (cash inflow)

Table for payoff on bear spread

(All figures in ₹)

When spot price S	−Call $X = 2{,}500$	+Call $X = 2{,}600$	Initial cash flow	TOTAL
$S < 2{,}500$	−	−	28	28
$2{,}500 < S < 2{,}600$	$-(S - 2{,}500)$	−	28	$-S + 2{,}528$
$S > 2{,}600$	$-(S - 2{,}500)$	$(S - 2{,}600)$	28	−72

Graphical view: Bear spread payoff

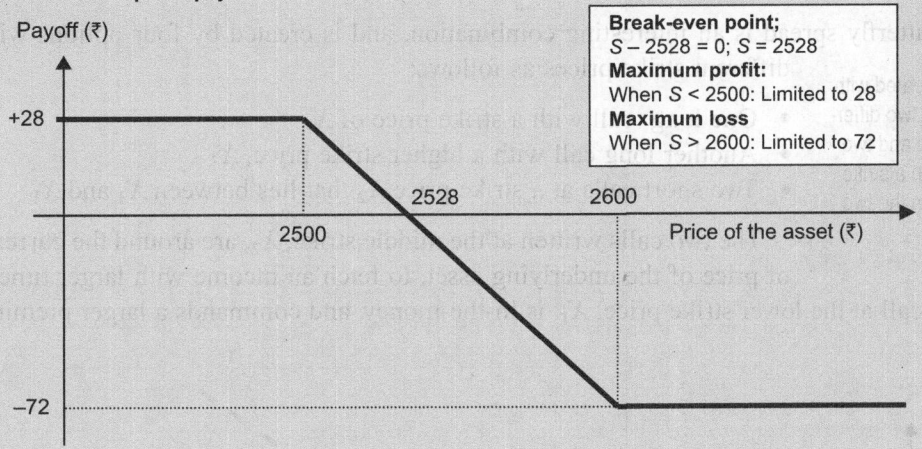

Break-even point;
$S - 2528 = 0; \; S = 2528$
Maximum profit:
When $S < 2500$: Limited to 28
Maximum loss
When $S > 2600$: Limited to 72

Bull and bear spreads with puts can be created as follows;

For a bull spread : Buy a put with exercise price X_1, and sell another put with exercise price $X_2 > X_1$

For a bear spread : Buy a put with exercise price X_2, and sell a put with exercise price $X_1 < X_2$

> Both bull and bear spreads can be created with puts alone or with calls alone.

Both bull and bear spreads limit the upside and downside potential, as compared to positions in a single option. Buying a call provides unlimited upside gain while protecting against downside loss. By writing another call at a higher strike price in a bull spread, one reclaims some of the premium paid on the first call, sacrificing upside potential. Similarly, writing a call implies unlimited downside loss while earning a premium. By buying another call at a higher strike price while creating a bear spread, the investor limits downside loss and sacrifices some income.

Risk–Reward Ratio

Investors trading in spreads are often concerned with the risk–reward ratio—a ratio that compares potential gains with potential losses. The examples considered for bull and bear spreads created with the same options highlight the difference between the two. Under the bull spread, the potential for gain was ₹72, with a risk of ₹28. The bear spread results in a potential gain of ₹28, with a risk of ₹72. The risk–reward ratio is of the order of approximately 3, favouring the bull spread. This ratio perhaps is compared with the likelihood of upside and downside movements. For non-investors in derivatives who are investors in underlying assets, an important clue about the potential directional movement may be provided. For example, it may be construed (though it may be wrong) from the risk–reward ratios of bull and bear spreads that the market is more likely to be bullish, since more investors would be choosing bull spreads than those opting for bear spreads. The contradictory interpretation would be that the market is heading for a bearish outlook because there may be too many bulls now.

BUTTERFLY SPREAD

A butterfly spread is an interesting combination, and is created by four options with three different strike prices as follows:

> A butterfly is created with one long call at two different strike prices and two calls written with a strike price in between the two bought.

- One long call with a strike price of X_1
- Another long call with a higher strike price, X_3
- Two short calls at a strike price X_2 that lies between X_3 and X_1

The two calls written at the middle strike, X_2, are around the current levels of price of the underlying asset, to fetch an income with larger time values. The call at the lower strike price, X_1, is in-the-money, and commands a larger premium. The

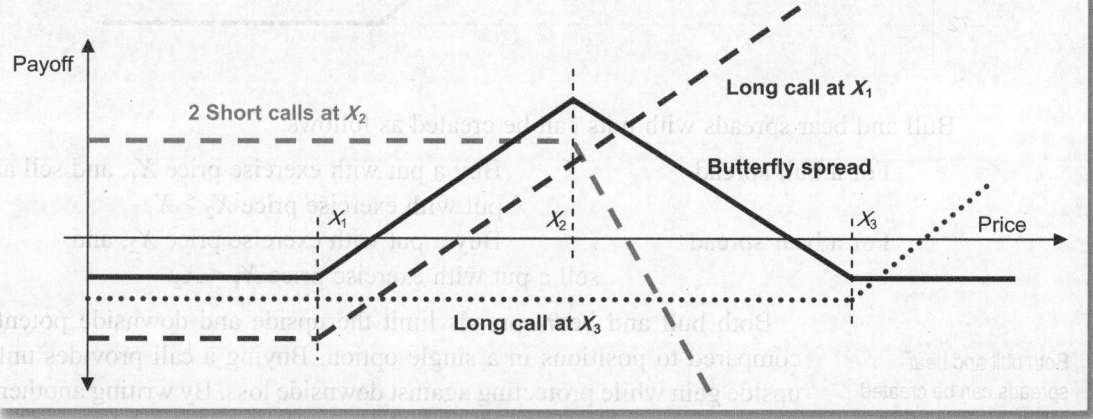

Fig. 16.9 Payoff of butterfly spread

EXHIBIT 16.6 Butterfly spread with calls

Strategy
- Buy two calls, with two different strike prices, X_1 and X_3; and
- Two short calls for a strike price X_2 in between the strike prices of the calls bought

Example
The following prices prevail on 24 June 2004 on the NSE for July call options on Infosys:

$X = 5100\ c = 425;\ X = 5200\ c = 350;\ X = 5300\ c = 280$

Butterfly spread

Bought	one call at X = 5100	Premium paid = 425
Sold	two calls at X = 5,200	Premium received = 700
Bought	one call at X = 5300	Premium paid = 280

Initial cash flow of long butterfly spread = $-425 + 2 \times 350 - 280 = -5$

Payoff for butterfly spread

(All figures in ₹)

When spot price S	+ Call X = 5,100	– 2 Calls X = 5,200	+ Call X = 5,300	Initial cash flow	TOTAL
$S < 5,100$	–	–	–	–5	–5
$5,100 < S < 5,200$	$S - 5,100$	–	–	–5	$S - 5,105$
$5,200 < S < 5,300$	$S - 5,100$	$-2(S - 5,200)$	–	–5	$-S + 5,295$
$S > 5,300$	$S - 5,100$	$-2(S - 5,200)$	$S - 5,300$	–5	–5

Graphical view: Butterfly spread-payoff

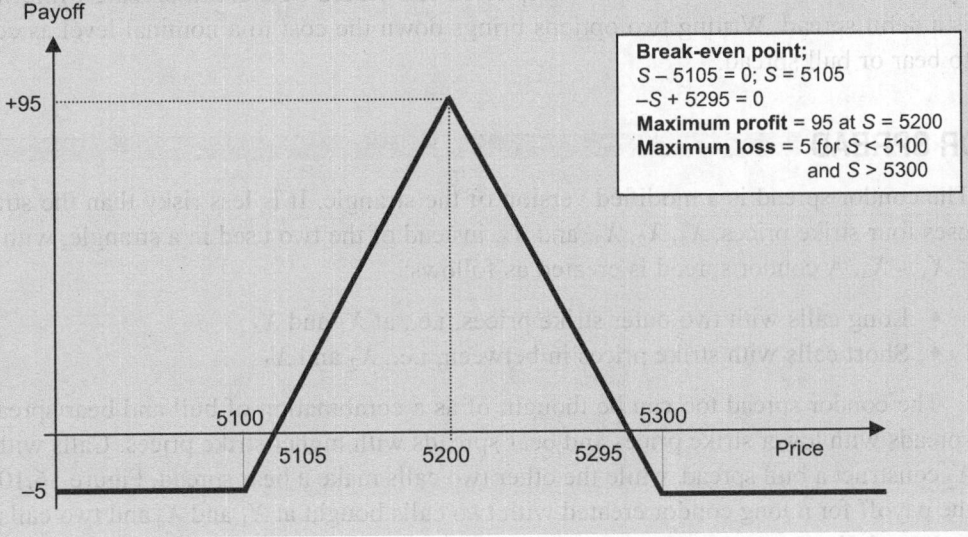

Break-even point;
$S - 5105 = 0;\ S = 5105$
$-S + 5295 = 0$
Maximum profit = 95 at S = 5200
Maximum loss = 5 for $S < 5100$ and $S > 5300$

other call, bought with a higher strike price, X_3, is out-of-the-money, and has a lower price. The nominal initial cost of creating a butterfly spread is one of its great attractions.

If the two calls that are bought have the strike prices as X_1 and X_3, the strike price of the two calls written at X_2 is normally chosen as the average of X_1 and X_3. If the price remains below X_1, all calls are worthless, and expire without exercise. The investor suffers a nominal loss, equivalent to the set-up cost. If the price exceeds X_3, all calls are in-the-money, and are exercised. The two calls bought compensate exactly for the liabilities of the two calls written, and the investor again ends up with a nominal loss equal to the set-up cost.

When the price is above X_1 but below X_2, only one call bought is in-the-money, and the investor starts making a profit. He/she has maximum profit when the price reaches X_2, beyond which both the calls written become in-the-money and get exercised. The investor starts losing out on the profit, as he/she pays on two calls and receives from one call. When the price reaches X_3, the second call bought also becomes in-the-money, matching the aggregate liabilities on the calls written. The payoff on the butterfly spread is depicted in Fig. 16.9.

The strategy generates a profit if the price stays close to the current levels around X_2 and results in modest losses with a large change in price in either direction.

An example of a butterfly spread is shown in Exhibit 16.6, with a nominal cost of ₹5, with potential to make a profit of ₹95 with two calls written at $X = 5200$, one call bought at $X = 5100$, and another call bought at $X = 5300$ in respect of the shares of Infosys. The risk–reward ratio is 5:95, a very attractive proposition that limits the losses to ₹5, with the potential to gain ₹95.

> A butterfly is an extremely tempting strategy that involves a low outlay with potential for a huge payoff.

A butterfly spread can also be created with put options by buying two separate puts at X_1 and X_3 and selling two puts at the same strike price of X_2. There also exist other combinations of calls and puts that may be used in constructing a butterfly spread.

The butterfly spread can be viewed as a combination of a bull spread immediately followed by a bear spread. Used with the call options, one would be a credit spread, while with puts is a debit spread. Writing two options brings down the cost to a nominal level as compared to bear or bull spread.

CONDOR SPREAD

The condor spread is a modified version of the strangle. It is less risky than the strangle. It uses four strike prices, X_1, X_2, X_3, and X_4, instead of the two used in a strangle, with $X_1 < X_2 < X_3 < X_4$. A condor spread is created as follows:

- Long calls with two outer strike prices, i.e., at X_1 and X_4
- Short calls with strike prices in between, i.e., X_2 and X_3

The condor spread too can be thought of as a combination of bull and bear spreads; bull spreads with lower strike prices and bear spreads with higher strike prices. Calls with X_1 and X_2 construct a bull spread, while the other two calls make a bear spread. Figure 16.10 depicts the payoff for a long condor created with two calls bought at X_1 and X_4 and two calls written at X_2 and X_3.

All calls are out-of-the-money for a price below X_1. Between X_1 and X_2, the call bought with the lower price is in-the-money, leading to gain. Between X_2 and X_3, the call written and the call bought cancel out, and the other sets of calls have not become in-the-money as yet. Between X_3 and X_4, the second call written is operational and the liability arises. For a price beyond X_4, all four calls are in-the-money, but the calls bought and the calls written cancel each other out.

Derivatives In Practice

Safe Spread

Brokers market 'Butterfly Spread' for assured returns

On 24 May 2012, rich investors were advised by their brokers to opt for a conservative options strategy involving four legs to make limited profits, as the market is expected to move in a range-bound, albeit indecisive, way in the near term.

Called a short butterfly spread, the strategy involves simultaneous selling of a put and a call option of the same strike price and using part of the money from this to buy a call and a put of different strikes, but with the same expiration. By buying two OTM options, the trader aims to hedge himself/herself in case the market breaches a forecast range.

In May 2012, most of the activity in options indicated that writers or option sellers expected 4,800 on the NIFTY to be a strong support and 5,000 a strong resistance. With a week left for the May series options to expire, brokers were advising clients to sell 4,800 strike (ATM) put and call options and to use part of the sale proceeds to purchase a 4,900 call and a 4,700 put.

The amount, or premium, received from selling the two 4,800 strike options stood at ₹150, while the combined purchase of a call and a put tailed an outflow of ₹65. The maximum profits accrue when the NIFTY May futures expire at around the middle strike price (4800). If the series expires at 4,800, the gain (excluding brokerage, etc.) will be ₹85 (150 – 65) as the OTM options expire worthless.

If NIFTY futures expire at 4,600, the gain will be ₹16 (₹66 profit from the OTM put purchased at ₹34 – 50, the payout for the ATM put sold). Similarly, if the NIFTY expires at 5,000, the gain will be ₹19. 'As we feel the market could move in a narrow range on either side, the butterfly spread is a good tool to make relatively risk-free returns', said Sahaj Agarwal, AVP (derivatives research), Kotak Securities.

'The butterfly spread is a safer way to make money in a range-bound and otherwise indecisive market', agreed Shashank Mehta, derivatives strategist, Shah Investor's Home.

Based on The Economic Times, 24 May 2012.

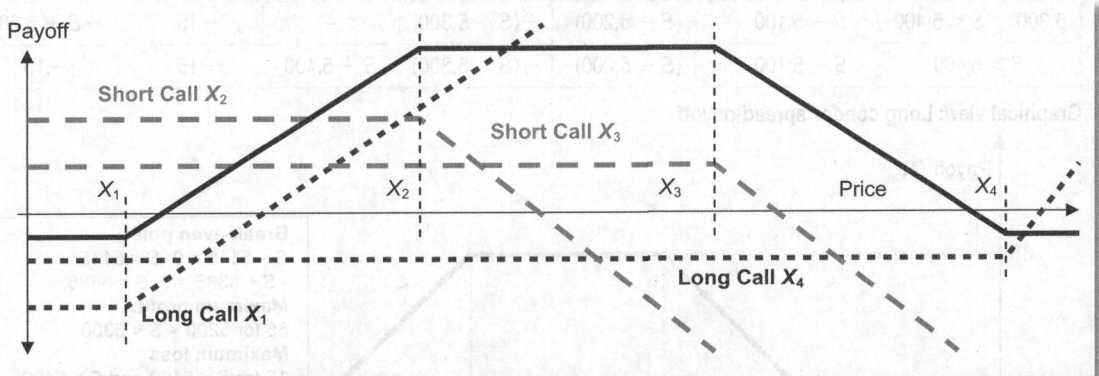

Fig. 16.10 Long Condor Payoff

An example of a condor is presented in Exhibit 16.7. Figure 16.10 and Exhibit 16.7 indicate that a long condor is a suitable strategy when the markets are expected to remain in a rather flat range. Under these circumstances, the condor gives the maximum profit. The risk–reward ratio is 15:85 for the condor spread depicted in Exhibit 16.7. As compared to a butterfly spread, the condor would have a larger range of prices that yield a profit. A butterfly spread, therefore, is useful when markets are expected to be within a very narrow range, while the condor affords a larger range of prices of the underlying asset. With a larger profit range, it costs more.

A condor, created with two long calls at two outer strike prices and two short calls with in-between strike prices, has an attractive risk–reward ratio.

EXHIBIT 16.7 Long condor spread with calls

Strategy
- Buy two calls, at two different strike prices of X_1 and X_4
- Short two calls at different strike prices in between the two strike prices of the calls bought on the same asset and with the same expiration.

Example
The following prices prevail on 24 June 2004 on the NSE for July call options on Infosys:

$$X = 5100\ c = 425;\ X = 5200\ c = 350;\ X = 5300\ c = 280;\ X = 5400\ c = 220$$

Long condor spread

Bought	one call at $X = 5100$	Premium paid = 425
Sold	one call at $X = 5200$	Premium received = 350
Sold	one call at $X = 5300$	Premium received = 280
Bought	one call at $X = 5400$	Premium paid = 220

The initial cost of the long condor spread = 425 − 350 − 280 + 220 = 15

TABLE: Payoff on the long condor spread

(All figures in ₹)

When spot price S	+Call $X = 5,100$	−Call $X = 5,200$	−Call $X = 5,300$	+Call $X = 5,400$	Initial cash flow	TOTAL
$S < 5,100$	−	−	−	−	−15	−15
$5,100 < S < 5,200$	$S − 5,100$	−	−	−	−15	$S − 5,115$
$5,200 < S < 5,300$	$S − 5,100$	$−(S − 5,200)$	−	−	−15	+85
$5,300 < S < 5,400$	$S − 5,100$	$−(S − 5,200)$	$−(S − 5,300)$	−	−15	$−S + 5,385$
$S > 5,400$	$S − 5,100$	$−(S − 5,200)$	$−(S − 5,300)$	$S − 5,400$	−15	−15

Graphical view: Long condor spread-payoff

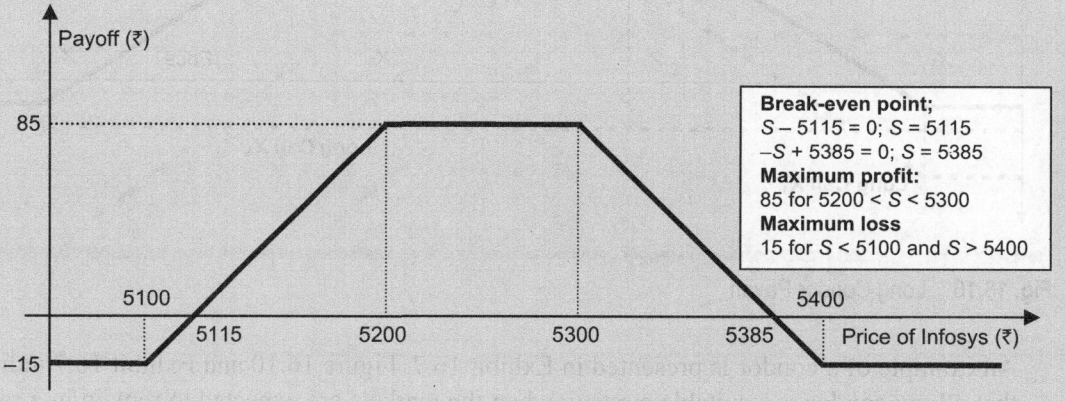

Break-even point;
$S − 5115 = 0;\ S = 5115$
$−S + 5385 = 0;\ S = 5385$
Maximum profit:
85 for $5200 < S < 5300$
Maximum loss
15 for $S < 5100$ and $S > 5400$

A condor can also be formed just with puts or from a combination of calls and puts. Refer to this chapter's *Derivatives in Practice*, where a butterfly was made from calls and puts. If an investor buys two puts with outer strike prices of X_1 and X_4 and writes two with strike prices in between at X_2 and X_3, he/she will have the same profile as one created with calls.

A condor can also be formed with a set of calls, long at X_1 followed by short at X_2, and a set of puts, short at X_3 and long at X_4.

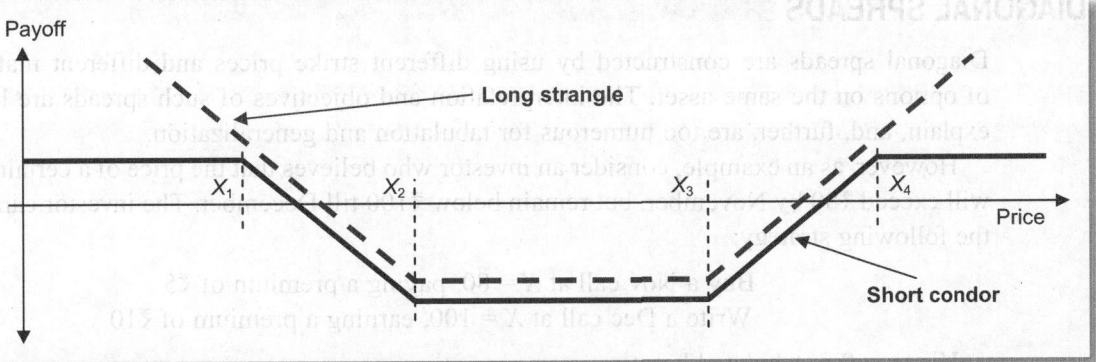

Fig. 16.11 Long strangle and short condor payoffs—Comparison

A long condor looks like a short strangle with extremes curtailed to the wings. Similarly, a short condor is similar to a long strangle. The difference, as illustrated in Fig. 16.11, lies in the risk characteristics of the two. The condor can be deemed to be a less risky version of the strangle. A long condor can also be seen as a butterfly spread with a flattened top. A strangle when chipped at the ends forms the condor. The condor costs less, and the compromise is on curtailing gains at extreme prices. A long condor can also be treated as a combination of a bull spread (the first half) and a bear spread (the second half). Investors are enabled to choose the exact risk profiles desired by them.

CALENDAR SPREADS

> Calendar spreads are created with options expiring at different times. They offer an opportunity to capitalize on temporary mispricings that are likely to be corrected over time.

Calendar spreads are formed by using options on the same asset with the same exercise price but with different expiration dates. An investor in a calendar spread is aiming to make a profit based on the time value of the options. With the passage of time, the values must correct to yield gains.

A bullish investor takes a position in a calendar spread on the premise that the price of the asset would not increase enough in the near term but would exceed a predetermined level in the longer term. Therefore, a bullish investor buys a distant call and writes a near call, expecting the distant call bought to be in-the-money at expiration, while reducing the cost by writing a near call. Only very experienced investors use such a strategy.

Similarly, a bearish investor may buy a near call but sell a distant call in the hope that the price would rise enough in the near term to make the near call in-the-money, but will fall thereafter, making the distant call out-of-the-money. The bearish calendar spread investor aims to make a profit at the time of set-up, as the distant call written provides a greater premium than the premium he/she has to pay for the near call.

We know that the value of an option consists of two parts, i.e., the intrinsic value and the time value. Unlike other spreads, calendar spreads play on the time value of options. With a larger time to maturity, the time value declines, but not fast enough. The time value declines more rapidly as maturity approaches. An investor in a calendar spread capitalizes by writing options whose time values decline more rapidly.

DIAGONAL SPREADS

Diagonal spreads are constructed by using different strike prices and different maturities of options on the same asset. The interpretation and objectives of such spreads are hard to explain, and, further, are too numerous for tabulation and generalization.

However, as an example, consider an investor who believes that the price of a certain stock will exceed ₹80 by November, but remain below ₹100 till December. The investor can adopt the following strategy:

Buy a Nov call at $X = 80$, paying a premium of ₹5
Write a Dec call at $X = 100$, earning a premium of ₹10

His payoff is tabulated here:

	Price < 80		80 < Price < 100		Price > 100	
	In Nov	In Dec	In Nov	In Dec	In Nov	In Dec
Sold Dec call at $X = 100$	–	–	–	–	$-(S - 100)$	$-(S - 100)$
Bought Nov call at $X = 80$	–	–	$S - 80$	–	$S - 80$	–
Initial income	5	5	5	5	5	5
Max profit	5	5	25	5	25	$-(S - 105)$

It is apparent that the investor rules out the possibility of a price in excess of ₹100 at the end of December, and, hence, the payoff is larger than the strategy of simply buying a November call at ₹80, which would give him a maximum of ₹15 as a profit. By writing another call at ₹100 for the distant future, the investor earns an extra premium of ₹10, and at the same time has an option to square up the Dec call at any time, in case his/her forecast about the future price appears to be failing.

Spreads on Different Assets

Very rarely do investors construct spreads on different underlying assets. Options on different underlying assets provide an opportunity to investors to capitalize on the relative valuation of the two or more assets in question. Investors have a tendency to value assets in comparative terms, and any divergence may create an opportunity to make some gains. For example, rather than concentrating on the absolute values of Infosys and Wipro, investors may watch the relative valuation of the two. If an investor feels that as an aberration, Infosys is overpriced compared to Wipro and that the situation will correct itself with time, he/she may choose to sell a call option on Infosys and buy a call option on Wipro. With time, as the relative valuation corrects, the investor squares up by buying a call option on Infosys and selling a call option on Wipro, negating the earlier position. The major advantage of such a strategy would be the reduced cost. Buying one call and selling another on different assets brings down the initial cost.

When asset prices are related, spreads on different assets can be used profitably. Investors believe that there is large correlation between the prices of gold and silver, and, therefore,

> A spread on different assets is used when the derivative pricing is inconsistent with the relative pricing of two assets.

may like to benefit from their judgment about the price of silver given the price of gold, or vice versa.

BOX SPREAD

Though options are thought to be risky in nature, their combinations can be remarkably stable. Different options can be combined to obtain a risk-free position. We used this in the valuation of options by forming a risk-free portfolio comprising the underlying and options on it. From derivatives alone can such risk-free positions be created. One such position, called the box spread, is depicted in Exhibit 16.8.

> One can create a riskless position using derivatives.

EXHIBIT 16.8 Box spread

Strategy
- Buy a call and sell a put with the same strike price
- Once again, buy a call and sell a put with the same strike price, but higher than that of the first set of a call and a put, on the same asset and with the same

Example
The following prices prevail on 17 October 2005 on the NSE for October 05 options on Hindustan Unilever:

$$X = 170\ c = 7;\ X = 185\ c = 1.45;\ X = 170\ p = 1.30;\ X = 185\ p = 11.55$$

Box spread

Bought	one call at $X = 170$	Premium paid = 7.00
Sold	one call at $X = 185$	Premium received = 2.05
Sold	one put at $X = 170$	Premium received = 1.95
Bought	one put at $X = 185$	Premium paid = 11.55

Initial cost of box spread = 7.00 − 2.05 − 1.95 + 11.55 = 14.55

Table for payoff on the box spread

When spot price S	+Call $X = 170$	−Call $X = 185$	−Put $X = 170$	+Put $X = 185$	Initial cash flow*	Total payoff of options
$S < 170$	–	–	$-(170 - S)$	$(185 - S)$	−14.55	15
$170 < S < 185$	$S - 170$	–	–	$(185 - S)$	−14.55	15
$S > 185$	$S - 170$	$-(S - 185)$	–	–	−14.55	15

*Must represent discounted value of the payoff (Difference of strike prices)

Graphical view: Box spread payoff

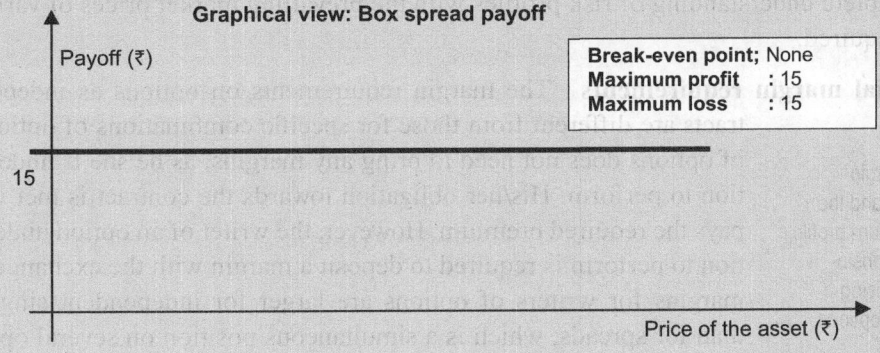

Break-even point: None
Maximum profit : 15
Maximum loss : 15

A box spread is created by two sets of a call and a put, with each set at different strike prices. Specifically, a box spread can be created by,

- going long on a call and short on a put at the same strike price
- going short on another call and long on another put, again at the same strike price, though different from that in the first case.

This combination results in a certain fixed profit equal to the difference between the two strike prices. This may be used for arbitrage in the pricing of different options as follows:

Cost of box spread > discounted value of the box spread; go short on the box spread
Cost of box spread < discounted value of the box spread; go long on the box spread

A box spread can also be thought of as a synthetic bond providing a certain value equal to the difference in strike prices over the remaining life of the options. In the example in Exhibit 16.8. the box spread is like a bond with a maturity value of ₹15.

The cost will determine the returns, which must be comparable with those prevailing in the bonds market. This would keep the derivatives market and the bonds market in balance. If the return on the box spread is higher, investments would flow in the derivatives market from bonds, increasing the prices, reducing the returns on derivatives, and decreasing bond prices to increase returns in the bonds market. In the opposite scenario, the reverse would happen. The existence of such a risk-free position out of derivatives alone makes their pricing accurate, in tandem, and consistent with the capital markets dealing in fixed income securities.

FACTORS AFFECTING SPREADS

While trading on independent and single options is rather easy, creating a spread requires deep thinking and understanding before assuming a position. Though, in general, spreads are safer, their construction needs prior evaluation in terms of the following factors:

Initial cost of spread Dealing in spreads means trading in multiple options involving long and short positions. While a short position implies a cash inflow, the long position means a cash outflow, resulting in an income or a cost at the time of set-up. An investor has to determine the additional parameter of the initial income or cost in setting up the spread. Further, since a similar risk profile is obtainable in several ways from either puts or calls, one has to find a way to create a spread at minimum cost or with maximum income. A complete understanding of risk profiles with the prevailing market prices of various options is required.

Initial margin requirements The margin requirements on options as independent contracts are different from those for specific combinations of options. A buyer of options does not need to bring any margins, as he/she is under no obligation to perform. His/her obligation towards the contract is met when he/she pays the required premium. However, the writer of an option under an obligation to perform is required to deposit a margin with the exchange. Normally, margins for writers of options are larger for independent single contracts than for spreads, which is a simultaneous position on several options.

> Initial cost, margin requirements, and the desired risk return profile are the main considerations in devising spreads using options.

Risk profile and selection of exercise prices An additional parameter in the construction of spread is the exact risk profile that needs to be generated, which in turn involves selection of a particular set of exercise prices out of the many that are available. The liquidity of distant options and those that are deep in-the-money or deep out-of-the-money is poor compared to near options and ATM options. Therefore, pricing may be non-competitive for distant and deep ITM/OTM options. This restricts the choices for spread trading. It is suggested to create a spread with frequently traded options to obtain competitive pricing and necessary liquidity, as one may need to unwind (not necessarily) the original spread before the expiration of the options. It is possible that at around the expiration time, the spread may become illiquid and difficult to unwind.

SYNTHESIZING INSTRUMENTS AND POSITIONS

We have seen that options can be combined to form a large array of risk and return profiles. Options can also be combined to synthesize basic instruments such as risky positions on stocks and riskless positions on bonds. One can synthesize these basic instruments, as discussed now.

SYNTHETIC LONG POSITION IN STOCK

When an investor is bullish, he/she goes long on the asset now and hopes to sell it later at an increased price to make a gain. A long position in stock can be synthesized with options. For example, consider a stock with the current price of ₹100. The stock also has call and put options, and for a strike price of ₹100, they are selling for ₹10 and ₹6, respectively.

> Options can be combined to synthesize various positions in stock, multiplying gains as well as losses.

Consider the two alternatives: (a) buy stock at ₹100 and (b) buy a call and write a put, both at $X = 100$. Let us now compare the initial investment and the payoffs under rising and falling price scenarios for the stock:

	Initial cash flow	Payoff	
		Price > 100 say ₹120	Price < 100 say ₹80
Buy stock	−100	$S − 100 = +20$	$S − 100 = −20$
Portfolio of call and put: Call bought Put written	−10 +6	$S − 100 − 4 = +16$ Worthless	Worthless $−(100 − S) − 4 = −24$
Total portfolio	4	+16	−24

It is evident that while the payoff on a long position in stock is similar to that on a portfolio of calls bought and puts written at the current market prices, the investment in the portfolio of calls and puts is far less at ₹4, as compared to the investment in the long position in stock of ₹100. A portfolio of long calls and short puts with the same exercise price and maturity synthesizes the long position in the stock, the underlying asset, at a price equal to the strike prices of the options, as the payoffs are identical. This portfolio provides great leverage and enhances returns as well as losses several times (in this case, 25 times).

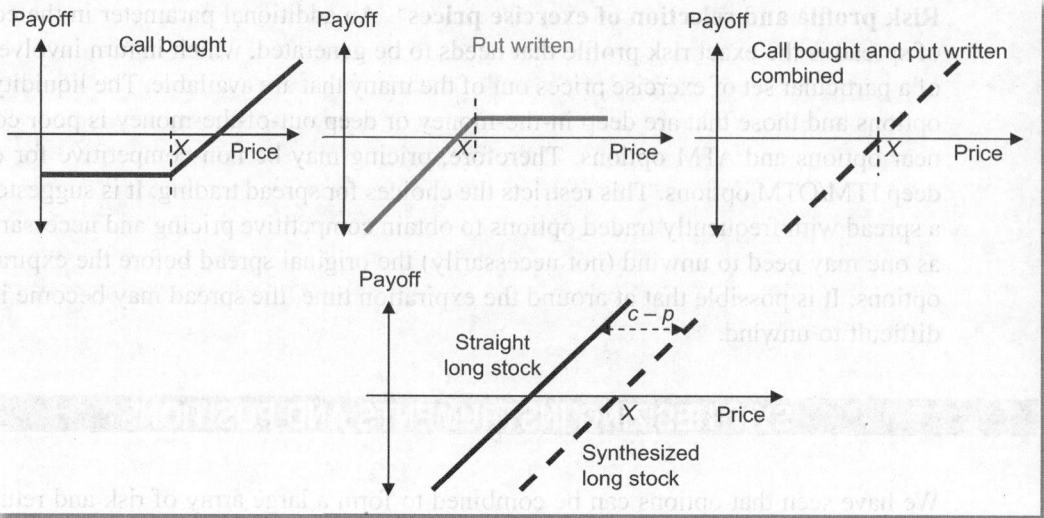

Fig. 16.12 Synthetic long position and straight long position (mimicking stock)

A synthetic long position with a put written and a call bought with a straight long position is depicted in Fig. 16.12. Synthetic position in stock with options is also called as *mimicking* stock.

The payoff on a synthetic long position created with a call and a put is less than on a straight long position by the amount of the cost of setting up the synthetic long position. The synthetic long position would cease to exist upon expiry of the options. If the investor wants to continue with the synthetic position, it can be recreated with a fresh set of options that come into existence upon expiry of the first set of options.

SYNTHETIC SHORT POSITION IN STOCK

When an investor is bearish, he/she sells the asset short now and hopes to buy it later at a decreased price to make a gain. This is called a short position. A short position in stock can also be synthesized with options. To synthesize a short position in a stock with the current price of ₹100, we write a call and buy a put at strike prices of ₹100. Again, assume that the call and the put are selling for ₹10 and ₹6, respectively.

Consider the two alternatives: (a) sell the stock short at ₹100, and (b) write a call and buy a put, both at $X = 100$. Let us now compare the initial investment and the payoffs under rising and falling price scenarios for the stock:

	Initial Investment	Payoff	
		Price > 100 say ₹120	Price < 100 say ₹80
Sell stock short	+100	$100 - S = -20$	$100 - S = +20$
Portfolio of call and put:			
Call written	+10	$-(S - 100) + 4 = -16$	Worthless
Put bought	−6	Worthless	$(100 - S) + 4 = +24$
Total	+ 4	−16	+24

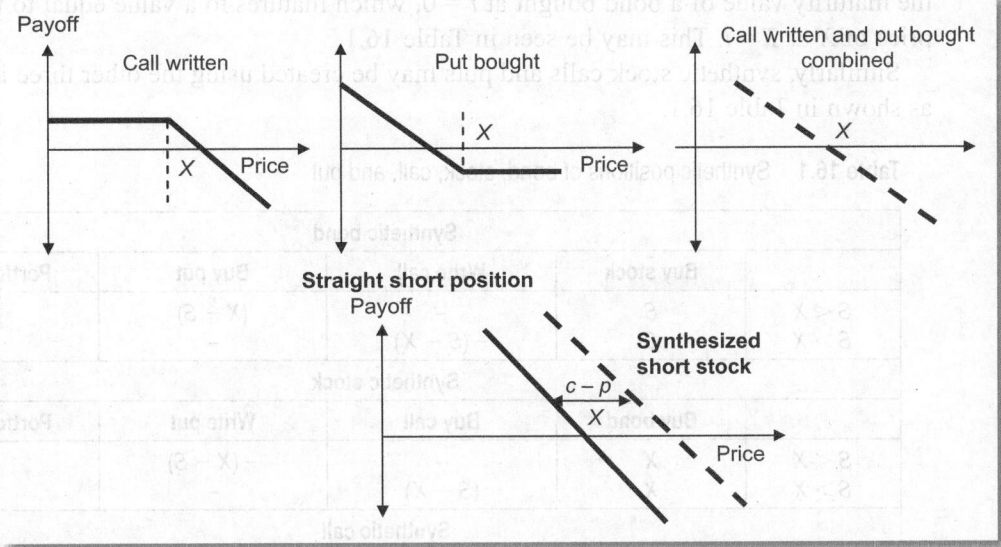

Fig. 16.13 Synthetic short position and straight short position (mimicking stock)

It is evident that the payoff on a short position in stock is similar to that on a portfolio of a call written and a put bought at the current market prices. This would result in a cash inflow, since the call is priced higher than the put for the same asset, the same exercise price, and the same expiry. A portfolio of a short call and a long put with the same exercise price and maturity synthesizes the short position in stock, the underlying asset, at a price equal to the strike prices of the options, as the payoffs are identical, as depicted in Fig. 16.13. The position can be continued if the portfolio is reconstructed upon expiry of the options.

OTHER SYNTHETIC POSITIONS

Recall the put–call parity. It is depicted in Fig. 16.14 in an explanatory form. Put–call parity establishes a relationship among four assets, i.e., the call option, the put option, the stock, and the bond. It implies that if put–call parity holds, then any instrument can be synthesized using the other three.

> Put–call parity relates four instruments—call put, stock, and bond. Using any three of these instrument, the fourth can be synthesized

For example, consider a portfolio of a long stock, a short call, and a long put. Options are available at strike price X and mature after time T. At maturity, assuming a stock price of S, the value of the portfolio would be X, irrespective of the price of the stock. This value of the portfolio is the same as

$$S_0 - c + p = Xe^{-rt}$$

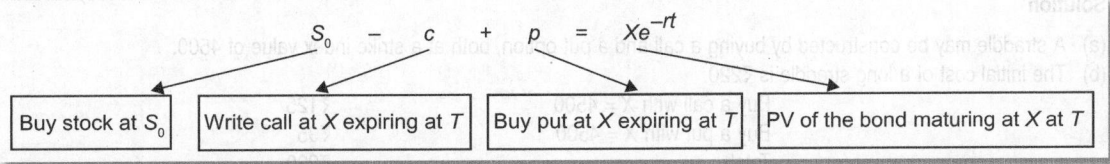

Fig. 16.14 Put–call parity—synthetic positions

the maturity value of a bond bought at $t = 0$, which matures to a value equal to the exercise price of X at $T = t$. This may be seen in Table 16.1.

Similarly, synthetic stock calls and puts may be created using the other three instruments, as shown in Table 16.1.

Table 16.1 Synthetic positions of bond, stock, call, and put

	Synthetic bond			
	Buy stock	Write call	Buy put	Portfolio value
$S < X$	S	–	$(X - S)$	X
$S > X$	S	$-(S - X)$	–	X
	Synthetic stock			
	Buy bond	Buy call	Write put	Portfolio value
$S < X$	X	–	$-(X - S)$	S
$S > X$	X	$(S - X)$	–	S
	Synthetic call			
	Sell bond	Buy put	Buy stock	Portfolio value
$S < X$	$-X$	$-(S - X)$	S	0
$S > X$	$-X$	–	S	$S - X$
	Synthetic put			
	Buy bond	Buy call	Sell stock	Portfolio value
$S < X$	X	–	$-S$	$X - S$
$S > X$	X	$(S - X)$	$-S$	0

SOLVED PROBLEMS

SP 16.1: Constructing a long straddle

At the NSE, the following were the prices of 1-m call and put options on its index NIFTY on 15 June, 2009, when the NIFTY was at 4500.

Exercise price	Call option	Put option
4,450	165	75
4,500	125	95
4,550	100	125

(a) How would you construct a straddle at the index value of 4500?
(b) Find out its cost, payoff, break-even point, and maximum loss.
(c) What would be the profit/loss if after one month the index value were (a) 4100, and (b) 5000?

Solution

(a) A straddle may be constructed by buying a call and a put option, both at a strike index value of 4500.
(b) The initial cost of a long straddle is ₹220.

Buy a call with X = 4500	₹125
Buy a put with X = 4500	₹95
Total	₹220

The payoff would be

Spot price at maturity	Long call X = 4500	Long put X = 4500	Initial cash flow (₹)	Total (₹)
S < 4,500	–	4,500 – S	–220	4,280 – S
S > 4,500	S – 4,500	–	–220	S – 4,720

Break-even points: 4280 – S = 0 gives S = 4280 S – 4720 = 0 gives S = 4720
Maximum loss   at S = 4500   Loss = Initial cost = ₹220
(c) Profit at   S = 4100   :   4280 – S = 4280 – 4100 = ₹180
            S = 5000   :   S – 4720 = 5000 – 4720 = ₹280

SP 16.2: Constructing a short strangle

From the data of SP 16.1, how would you construct a short strangle with 4500 as the central point?
(a) Find out its cost, payoff, and break-even point.
(b) At what levels would the position result in maximum profit?
(c) What is the profit at a level of (a) 4100 and (b) 5000?
(d) Depict the payoff diagram with all important parameters marked.

Solution
A short strangle can be created by selling a call at a higher strike price and selling a put at a lower strike price than the central point. Hence, we sell a call at a higher strike of 4550 and sell a put at a lower strike of 4450 for a short strangle.

(a) Initial inflow short strangle
    Sell a call with X = 4550   ₹100
    Sell a put with X = 4450   ₹75
    Total   ₹175

The payoff would be

Spot price at maturity	Short call X = 4,550	Short put X = 4,450	Initial cash flow (₹)	Total (₹)
S < 4,450	–	–(4,450 – S)	175	S – 4,275
4,450 < S < 4,550	–	–	175	175
S > 4,550	–(S – 4,550)	–	175	4,725 – S

Break-even point: 4725 – S = 0 gives S = 4725   S – 4275 = 0 gives S = 4275
(b) Maximum profit: S Between 4450 and 4550   Profit = Initial cash flow = ₹175
(c) Profit at   S = 4100   S – 4275 = 4100 – 4275 = –₹175
            S = 5000   4725 – S = 4725 – 5000 = –₹275
(d) The short strangle would look as follows:

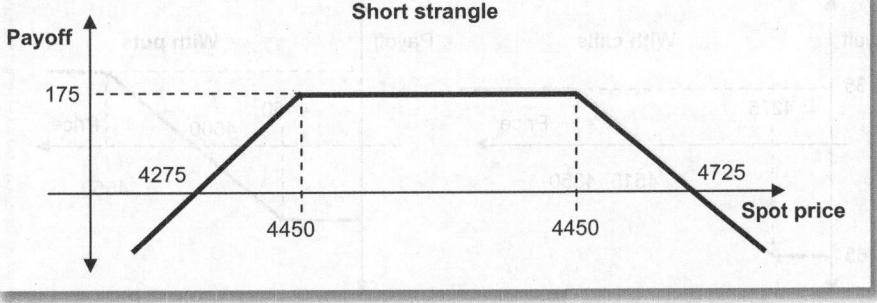

SP 16.3: Constructing bull spreads

Use the data from problem SP 16.1 to do the following:
(a) Construct a bull spread using call options and find out its cost, payoff, and break-even point.
(b) Construct a bull spread using put options and find out its cost, payoff, and break-even point.
(c) Depict the bull spreads of a) and b) with different levels of the index at maturity, indicating all relevant points of break-even, maximum, and minimum levels of profit/loss.

Solution
(a) A bull spread with calls can be created by buying a call at a lower strike price and selling a call at a higher strike price. Hence, we buy a call at a lower strike of 4450 and sell a call at a higher strike of 4550.
The initial cash flow of the bull spread with calls would be

Buy a call with $X = 4450$	– ₹165
Sell a call with $X = 4550$	+ ₹100
Total	– ₹65

The payoff would be

Spot price at maturity	Long call $X = 4,450$	Short call $X = 4,550$	Initial cash flow (₹)	Total (₹)
$S < 4,450$	–	–	–65	–65
$4,450 < S < 4,550$	$S - 4,450$	–	–65	$S - 4,515$
$S > 4,550$	$S - 4,450$	$-(S - 4,550)$	–65	35

Break-even point: $S - 4515 = 0$ gives $S = 4515$

The maximum loss would be ₹65 for an index below 4450 and the maximum profit would be ₹35 for an index above 4550.

(b) A bull spread with puts can be created by buying a put at a lower strike price and selling a put at a higher strike price. Hence, we buy a put at a lower strike of 4450 and sell a put at a higher strike of 4550.
The initial cash flow of the bull spread with puts would be

Buy a put with $X = 4450$	– ₹75
Sell a put with $X = 4550$	+ ₹125
Total	+ ₹50

The payoff would be

Spot price at maturity	Long put $X = 4,450$	Short put $X = 4,550$	Initial cash flow (₹)	Total (₹)
$S < 4,450$	$4,450 - S$	$-(4,550 - S)$	50	–50
$4,450 < S < 4,550$	–	$-(4,550 - S)$	50	$S - 4,500$
$S > 4,550$	–	–	50	50

Break-even point: $S - 4500 = 0$ $S = 4500$

Maximum loss would be ₹50 for index below 4450 and maximum profit would be ₹50 for index above 4550.

(c) A bull spread using calls and puts is depicted here:

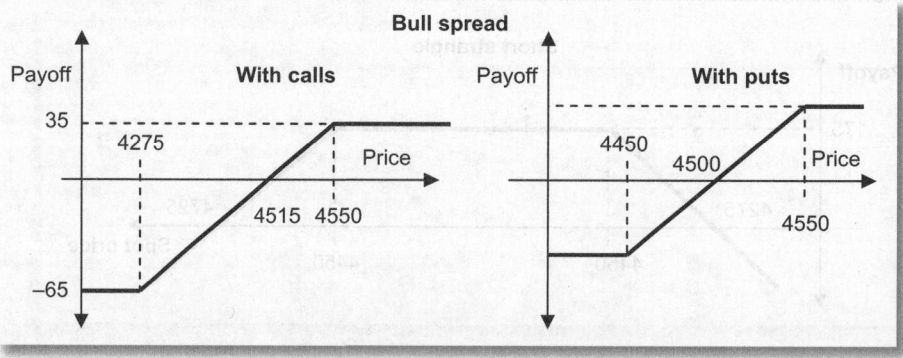

SP 16.4: Constructing bear spreads

Use the data from problem SP 16.1 to do the following.

(a) Construct a bear spread using call options and find out its cost, payoff, and break-even point.
(b) Construct a bear spread using put options and find out its cost, payoff, and break-even point.
(c) Depict the bear spreads of a) and b) with different levels of the index at maturity, indicating all relevant points of break-even, maximum, and minimum levels of profit/loss.

Solution

(a) A bear spread with calls can be created by selling a call at a lower strike price and buying a call at a higher strike price. Hence, we sell call at a lower strike of 4450 and buy a call at a higher strike of 4550.
The initial cash flow of the bear spread with calls would be

Sell a call with $X = 4450$	+ ₹165
Buy a call with $X = 4550$	– ₹100
Total	+ ₹65

The payoff would be

Spot price at maturity	Short call $X = 4,450$	Long call $X = 4,550$	Initial cash flow (₹)	Total (₹)
$S < 4,450$	–	–	65	65
$4,450 < S < 4,550$	$-(S - 4,450)$	–	65	$4,515 - S$
$S > 4,550$	$-(S - 4,450)$	$(S - 4,550)$	65	-35

Break-even point: $4515 - S = 0$ $S = 4515$

The maximum profit would be ₹65 for an index below 4450 and the maximum loss would be ₹35 for an index above 4550.

(b) A bear spread with puts can be created by selling a put at a lower strike price and buying a put at a higher strike price. Hence, we sell a put at lower strike of 4450 and buy a put at a higher strike of 4550.
The initial cash flow of the bear spread with puts would be

Sell a put with $X = 4450$	+ ₹75
Buy a put with $X = 4550$	– ₹125
Total	– ₹50

The payoff would be

Spot price at maturity	Short put $X = 4,450$	Long put $X = 4,550$	Initial cash flow (₹)	Total (₹)
$S < 4,450$	$-(4,450 - S)$	$(4,550 - S)$	-50	50
$4,450 < S < 4,550$	–	$(4,550 - S)$	-50	$4,500 - S$
$S > 4,550$	–	–	-50	-50

Break-even point: $4500 - S = 0$ $S = 4500$

The maximum profit would be ₹50 for an index below 4450 and the maximum loss would be ₹50 for an index above 4550.

(c) A bear spread using calls and puts is depicted here:

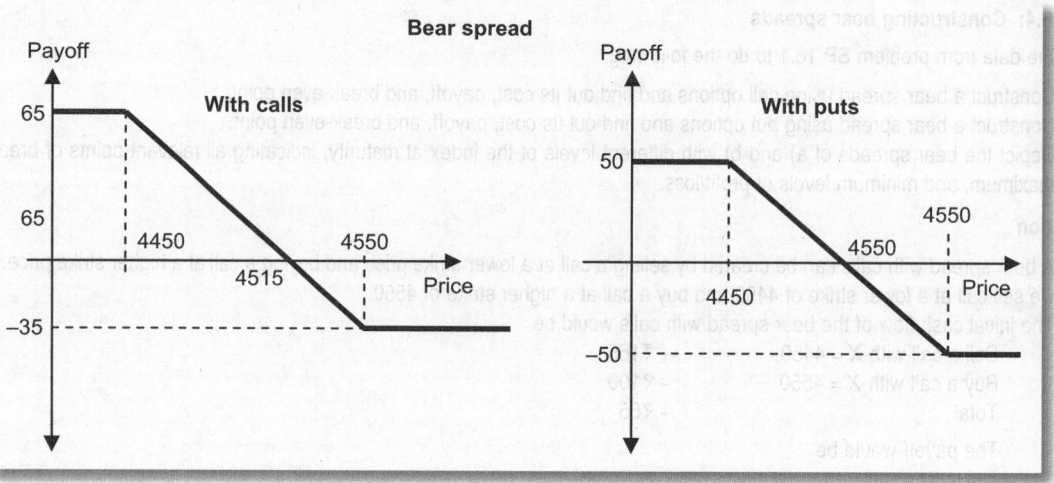

SP 16.5: Mimicking stock

A stock is currently selling for ₹100. ATM calls and puts on the stock with a maturity of three months are selling for ₹3 and ₹2, respectively.

(a) What would the payoff of a long position on the stock be? Depict the long position.
(b) How can you replicate the payoff of a long position in the stock using call and put options?
(c) What is the difference in payoffs between a) and b)?

Solution

(a) The long position on the stock would have a payoff of $S - 100$ where S is the stock price at the end of the investment period. If it is more than ₹100, the position would end up in a profit. For a spot price less than ₹100, there would be a loss. If it remains the same, the position gives neither a profit nor a loss. This is depicted as folloes:

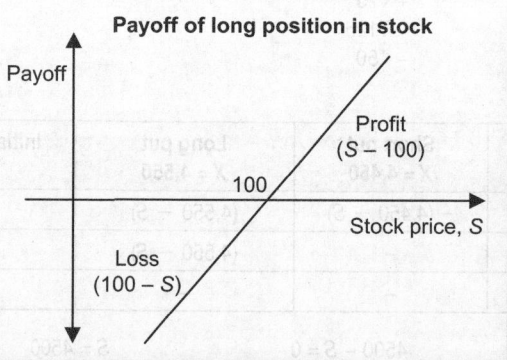

(b) The long position on the stock can be mimicked with a long call and a short put, both with ATM. The initial cost of such a position would be the premium paid for buying the call less the premium earned by selling the put. With ₹1 as the initial cost (3 – 2), the payoff on the position would be as follows:

Spot price	Short put $X = 100$	Long call $X = 100$	Initial cost	Total payoff
$S < 100$	$-(100 - S)$	–	-1	$S - 101$
$S > 100$	–	$S - 100$	-1	$S - 101$

This is the same as a long position in stock, as depicted here:

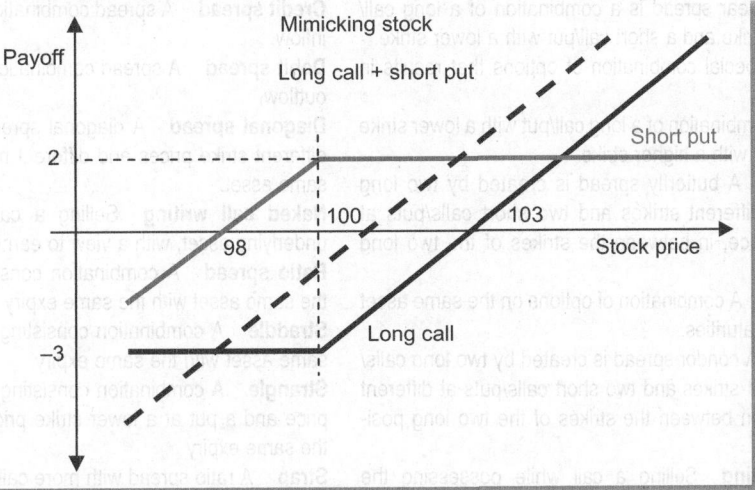

(c) The difference would be the initial cost. While taking a long position would entail an investment of ₹100, the same payoff can be obtained at a much lesser cost (₹1 in this case).

SUMMARY

Options, because of their unique non-linear payoffs, offer a much wider range of applications than other derivatives. These applications can broadly be categorized in four groups—hedging, income generation, trading, and synthesizing.

Since writing options results in earnings, premium investors also use options to enhance yields on their portfolios. Without an asset in hand, option writing can be used for pure speculative gains. Speculation with options can be done otherwise also, by buying a call when the market is bullish and buying a put when the market is bearish. Speculation with options is at a cost, but is safer than other derivatives, as options cap the extent of losses to the premium paid.

There is a huge array of risk return profiles that can be created with options. Among the most popular of them are straddles, strangles, and spreads. A long straddle is created by buying a call and a put at the same strike and the same maturity on the same asset. It is extremely appropriate to have a long straddle when volatility is expected but with direction unknown. A strangle is the same as a straddle but the strike prices of the options are different. It costs less to create a strangle than to create a straddle. Accordingly, the profit making range is smaller than with a straddle. Ratio spreads can be used when an investor believes somewhat more in either a rise or a fall in price.

A bull spread is created when the investor is moderately bullish. If confidently bullish, he/she can buy a call. When he/she is moderately bullish, the investor can sell a call at a higher strike price to reduce cost and sacrifice gains. A bull spread can also be created with put options. When the written option is priced higher than the bought option, the spread may result in an initial cash inflow. It is referred to as credit spread, in contrast with debit spread, which involves an initial cash outflow. Similarly, a bear spread is created by selling a call with a higher strike and buying a call with a lower strike, and is constructed when the investor is moderately bearish.

There are other combinations, such as butterfly and condor, which involve more than two options. Similarly, a risk-less position too can be constructed from options alone, referred to as a box spread. Spreads can be created on the basis of time; these are known as calendar spreads. When options on the same asset but with different expiries are combined, it is called a calendar spread. Using different assets, different maturities, and different strike prices, there are numerous combinations possible, and it remains a challenge to obtain the desired characteristics.

Options can be used to synthesize various positions, such as stocks and bonds. Put–call parity helps in identifying what instruments can be synthesized, and how they can be synthesized. Put–call parity relates four instruments—call, put, stock, and bond. With three of them, the fourth may be synthesized.

KEY TERMS

Bear spread A bear spread is a combination of a long call/put with a higher strike and a short call/put with a lower strike.

Box spread A special combination of options that results in risk-less payoff.

Bull spread A combination of a long call/put with a lower strike and a short call/put with a higher strike.

Butterfly spread A butterfly spread is created by two long calls/puts at two different strikes and two short calls/puts at the same strike price, in between the strikes of the two long positions.

Calendar Spread A combination of options on the same asset but with different maturities.

Condor spread A condor spread is created by two long calls/puts at two different strikes and two short calls/puts at different strike prices, both in between the strikes of the two long positions.

Covered call writing Selling a call while possessing the underlying asset, with a view to earning a premium, but with delivery of the asset in hand.

Credit spread A spread combination that results in initial cash inflow.

Debit spread A spread combination that results in initial cash outflow.

Diagonal spread A diagonal spread is constructed by using different strike prices and different maturities of options on the same asset.

Naked call writing Selling a call without possessing the underlying asset, with a view to earning a premium.

Ratio spread A combination consisting of calls and puts on the same asset with the same expiry but in different proportions.

Straddle A combination consisting of a call and a put on the same asset with the same expiry.

Strangle A combination consisting of a call at a higher strike price and a put at a lower strike price on the same asset with the same expiry.

Strap A ratio spread with more calls than puts.

Strip A ratio spread with more puts than calls.

QUESTIONS

16.1 What is a straddle and when is it appropriate to use it?

16.2 Compare a strangle with a straddle, with suitable examples.

16.3 How would you construct a bull spread with put options?

16.4 Differentiate between debit spread and credit spread.

16.5 What is a box spread? Explain with a suitable example

16.6 How would you synthesize a put option with a call, a stock, and a bond?

PROBLEMS

P 16.1 Butterfly spread with calls

An investor has the following portfolio of call options on the same asset and with the same expiration dates:

  Long one call at a strike price of ₹95, at a premium of ₹5
  Short two calls at a strike price of ₹100, at a premium of ₹7
  Long one call at a strike price of ₹105, at a premium of ₹10

Graphically depict the payoff and find the following:

(a) The price of the asset yielding maximum profit, and the extent of profit.

(b) The price of the asset yieling maximum loss, and the extent of loss.

(c) The price of the asset yielding no profit or loss.

P 16.2 Short straddle

Currently, the value of Nifty is 4500, and ATM call and put options with three months to maturity are selling for ₹120 and ₹60, respectively. If an investor believes that the market is going to remain range bound for the coming three months, how can he/she benefit from the options being traded in the market? What maximum profit can be made and what losses are possible?

P 16.3 Ratio spread

Refer to the data in P 16.2. Another investor believes that the market would be volatile, with a downward bias. He/she wants to have twice as much gain from the downside movement as compared to an upside movement. What strategy do you suggest for him/her? Find out the maximum loss and the range in which the investor would be making loss. Further, find the payoff for the ending index values of 4150 and 4450.

P 16.4 Mimicking bond from stocks and derivatives

A stock is currently trading at ₹1000, and ATM call and put options with three months maturity are trading at ₹75 and ₹50, respectively. If the stock markets and derivative markets are pricing products competitively, what best estimates can you make for the risk-free rate of return?

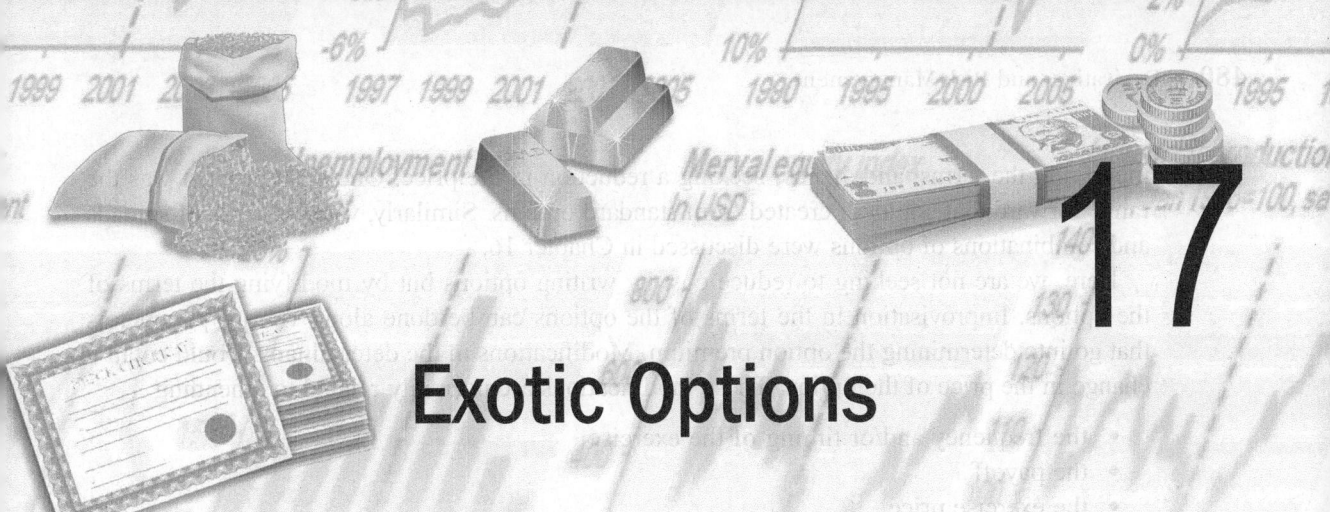

Exotic Options

INTRODUCTION

Exchange-traded options are plain vanilla products with routine features, as described in earlier chapters. The prices of these options are generally available, as they are regularly traded. Apart from regular exchange-traded options, which are conventional in nature, there is a large variety of tailor-made over-the-counter (OTC) products, normally referred to as exotics. The valuation of such options is complex, as the Black-Scholes Model (BSM) works only for standardized options that are normally exchange-traded. There have been substantial efforts to find analytical solutions to these options with the BSM as a base.

The reasons and motivations for deviating from the conventional features of options are many. Where standard products traded on exchanges do not meet specific requirements of users, some modifications in the features of the derivatives may be sought. A major reason for seeking modification of the features is to meet the specific requirements of traders and hedgers. Some of these requirements were discussed in options trading, where desired risk–return profiles were obtained by combining standard exchange-traded options.

One universal motivation that causes improvisation in the features of options is reduction in the cost of hedging. For option buyers, the premium payable has always been a matter of concern, and they are constantly looking for ways and means of reducing the cost of the options by (a) sacrificing some of the potential gains, (b) eliminating highly improbable scenarios that are included in the calculation of the premium, or (c) both. Where an option buyer considers that the premium payable includes an extremely unlikely scenario, he/she would like to exclude such a scenario by

> One primary reason for the popularity of exotic options is the reduction in premium for the buyer.

Learning Objectives

After going through this chapter, readers should be familiar with

- changing the terms of an option to suit specific needs
- the forward start option, its valuation, and its use
- the binary option and its valuation
- the chooser option and its valuation
- the shout option and its working
- the exchange option and its valuation
- the gap option and its valuation
- the pay-later option and its valuation
- compound options
- barrier options, their types, and their valuation by the binomial method
- Asian options and their valuation by the binomial method
- lookback options and their valuation by the binomial approach

modifying the terms, and, hence, seeking a reduction in the price. One such product was the range forward that could be created from standard options. Similarly, various kinds of spreads and combinations of options were discussed in Chapter 16.

Here, we are not seeking to reduce cost by writing options but by modifying the terms of the options. Improvisation in the terms of the options can be done along various parameters that go into determining the option premium. Modifications in the determinants would entail a change in the price of the option. These modifications are normally related to amending

- the frequency and/or timing of the exercise
- the payoff
- the exercise price

We know that the value of the option is a function of five parameters for a non-dividend paying underlying—the spot price, the exercise price, the time to expiry, the risk-free rate, and volatility. Most exotic options play around modification of the manner of exercise, the frequency of exercise, the behaviour of the spot, shortening or extending of the time to expiry, adjustment of the exercise price, and so on. There is hardly any role played by the risk-free rate and volatility that can be altered as per business requirements, as they are broad exogenous variables beyond the control of the parties to an options contract. For the purpose of this chapter, we shall denote the price of the option as a function of the spot, S, the exercise price, X, and the time to expiry, T. These parameters are subject to negotiations between the buyer and the seller of the option. For convenience, the value of a call option is denoted by $c(S, X, T)$ and that of a put option as $p(S, X, T)$, as function of S, X, and T.

Though the range can be tremendous, we discuss some of the exotics in this chapter.

FORWARD START OPTION

> In a forward start option the right is conferred now, but commences some time in the future.

Conventional options confer a right at the inception of the option to exercise on or before the maturity. If one wants to acquire the right to exercise the option not at its inception but at a later date one has to wait for the appropriate time to arrive. Such a situation is most common for firms that want to confer the right to acquire shares of the firms only after employees have served the firm for some minimum time. These are commonly called employee stock options. The firms would like to confer the right to buy shares now, but exercise can take place only after the employees have served for a minimum period of time. Such options are vested now, but start at some future date/time, t, and expire at T; these options are called *forward start options*.

Valuation

To value a forward start option, we use the property of homogeneity of option pricing. The implication of homogeneity in pricing is that a forward option starting after one month and ending after four months should have the same value as an option starting today, with an expiry of three months. It is the time remaining for expiry that determines the value of the option, and not when that time commences. Of course, the value changes not because it depends upon when the right commences but because the spot value changes. If the forward commencement time is t with a spot at S_t and the time remaining for maturity is $T - t$, then the value of the call would be denoted as $c_t(S_t, X, T - t)$. This value should be no different from the value of the call today that matures at $T - t$, rather than at T, $c_0(S_0, X, T - t)$. From homogeneity, we may say that

$$c_t(S_t, X, T - t) = c_0(S_0, X, T - t) \tag{17.1}$$

Again, using risk neutrality, the value of a forward start option at time $t = 0$ with a forward time of t, and maturing at T, F_t is

$$F_t = e^{-rt} \times c_t(S_t, X, T - t) = e^{-rt} \times c_0(S_0, X, T - t) \tag{17.2}$$

For easier comprehension, the valuation of a forward start option is depicted in Fig. 17.1.

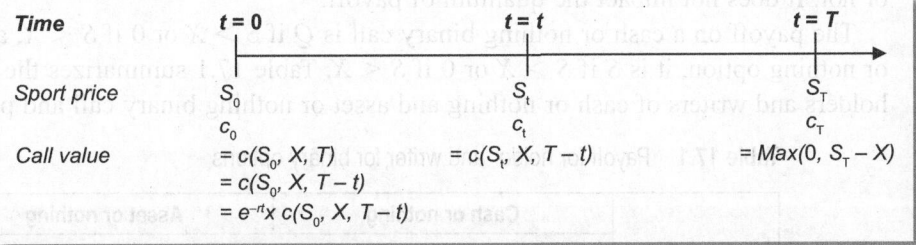

Fig. 17.1 Forward start call option

Applications

Employee stock options are like forward start options in that they start at some time in the future.

Consider, for example, a firm making an offer to a senior executive where part of his/her remuneration is in the form of stock options. With a current stock price of ₹100, the executive is offered an option to acquire the firm's stock at a strike price of ₹110 (i.e., 10% higher than the current stock price) at the end of two years. However, to ensure his/her commitment towards the firm, the executive would have to work for at least 12 months (one year). Remember, the right is being conferred now but would commence only after 12 months. Assuming a risk-free rate of return at 8% and volatility of the stock at 25%, the value of the call option as per the BSM, without the condition about working for at least 12 months, is

$$c_0(S_0, X, T) = c_0(100, 110, 2) = ₹16.95$$

However, if the option cannot be exercised before 12 months, the value of the option at the end of 12 months would be $c_1(S_1, 110, 1)$, where S_1 is the spot price at the end of 12 months (one year). From Eq. 17.1, this must be equal to $c_0(100, 110, 1)$. As per the BSM, the value is ₹9.27. Therefore, the value of a forward start option today with a start period of 12 months and expiry 12 months thereafter, using Eq. 17.2, is

$$e^{-rt} \times c_0(100, 110, 1) = e^{-0.08 \times 1} \times 9.27 = 0.9231 \times 9.27 = ₹8.56$$

BINARY OR DIGITAL OPTION

> A binary option has two discrete payoffs; Q or nothing for a price above or below X. Alternatively, it could be the asset or nothing.

The binary option, also called the digital option, has a payoff that has only two possible values. Conventional options have numerous payoffs, depending upon the value of the asset at expiry. In a binary option, only two payoffs are possible—a fixed cash amount or nothing, depending upon the price of the underlying and the exercise price. For a binary call option, the payoff for the holder would be a fixed sum, Q (rather than $S - X$, as in a conventional call option), if the spot, S, exceeds the exercise price, X; otherwise, it is nothing. Such an option is called a cash or nothing option. Alternatively, the payoff can be the asset or nothing, where the call holder would get the value of the asset, S, if the spot exceeds X. The payoff on the option does not reflect the exercise price. In case of a call, there would be no payment of the exercise price to arrive at the payoff, and in case of a put, no payment would be made by the writer. The exercise price merely determines whether the payoff exists or not. It does not impact the quantum of payoff.

The payoff on a cash or nothing binary call is Q if $S > X$ or 0 if $S < X$, and for an asset or nothing option, it is S if $S > X$ or 0 if $S < X$. Table 17.1 summarizes the payoffs for the holders and writers of cash or nothing and asset or nothing binary call and put options.

Table 17.1 Payoff for holder and writer for binary options

State	Cash or nothing		Asset or nothing	
	Call option			
	Holder	Writer	Holder	Writer
$S > X$	Q	$-Q$	S	$-S$
$S < X$	–	–	–	–
	Put option			
$S > X$	–	–	–	–
$S < X$	Q	$-Q$	S	$-S$

Applications

> Binary option valuation is often used in deciding the collective reward of employees.

Binary options are very popular and widely used, perhaps without many users actually realizing that they are doing so. The options obviate the need for complex computations. The settlement of these options is extremely simple. They may have practical use in the design of incentive schemes for collectively rewarding employees. As a motivation tool, firms reward all employees equally if the performance of the stock exceeds a certain level of expectation. For example, a manufacturing organization may announce a reward of a bonus equal to one month's salary if the production achieves a certain target level. It is a cash or nothing call option, where the payoff is fixed at one month's salary or nothing, and is independent of the extent by which the target is exceeded. Similar incentive schemes are formulated by marketing departments that reward sales employees or members of distribution channels with fixed amounts upon achieving a pre-set sales target. Further, most bets are win-or-lose situations and are, by nature, cash or nothing options.

An asset or nothing option is a situation where one is ready to part with the asset if the value achieves a certain level. For example, if one is ready to offer a share of ITC Ltd should its price cross ₹200 at the end of six months, he is writing an asset or nothing call with an exercise price of ₹200 and time to expiry of six months. For doing so, he is entitled to a premium to be paid by the buyer of such an option. Note that the buyer of the binary option only pays the premium and not the exercise price for acquiring the asset, provided the value of the share exceeds ₹200 at the end of six months.

Valuation

The valuation of a binary option is surprisingly easy. Under the BSM, we know that the probability of a spot exceeding the exercise price is given by $N(d_2)$. Under the risk-neutral method,

The value of a binary call option $= e^{-rT}$ (payoff $\times$ probability of $S > X$)
For a fixed payoff of ₹1, the value is $= e^{-rT} \times 1 \times N(d_2)$

For a cash or nothing call with a fixed payoff of Q, the value would be

$$= e^{-rT} \times Q \times N(d_2) \qquad (17.3)$$

Using put–call parity, the value of a binary cash or nothing put option that is paying Q at maturity is

$$= e^{-rT} \cdot Q \cdot N(-d_2) \qquad (17.4)$$

> The computation of payoff on a binary option is extremely simple.

The value of a cash or nothing binary option is given by the second term in the BSM, with a payoff equal to the exercise price. Since normal distribution is symmetrical, the sum of $N(d)$ and $N(-d)$ is always equal to 1.00. Therefore, having a cash or nothing call and a cash or nothing put with same features would always result in a payoff equal to the discounted value of the fixed cash, irrespective of the value of the underlying at expiration. Mathematically,

Cash or Nothing call + Cash or Nothing put $= e^{-rT} \times Q \times N(d_2) + e^{-rT} \cdot Q \cdot N(-d_2)$
$= e^{-rT} \times Q$

Similarly, for *asset or nothing* binary options, the value is given by the first term of the BSM. Using the properties described earlier, the values of asset or nothing options are given by Eqs 17.5 (a) and (b).

For a call option: $\qquad S_0 \times N(d_1) \qquad$ (17.5)(a)
For a put option: $\qquad S_0 \times N(-d_1) \qquad$ (17.5)(b)

Like cash or nothing options, a position in asset or nothing calls and asset or nothing puts with identical terms would always be equal to the value of the underlying asset.

Asset or Nothing call + Asset or Nothing put $= S_0 \times N(d_1) + S_0 \times N(-d_1)$
$= S_0$

For a continuous dividend of q on the stock, S_0 becomes $S_0 e^{-qT}$.

From the payoffs on binary options, we may say that a regular European call is equal to a long position in an *asset or nothing call* and a short position in a *cash or nothing call*, with the cash payoff equal to the exercise price. This helps in valuing asset or nothing options.

Long Asset or Nothing call + Short Cash or Nothing call = European call

Therefor,
Asset or Nothing call = $S_0 N(d_1)$
Similarly, Asset or Nothing put = $S_0 N(-d_1)$.

A look at Fig. 17.2 (a) and (b) would reveal that short cash or nothing and long asset or nothing call is same as payoff of standard European call.

The payoffs for a binary call option (*cash or nothing* and *asset or nothing*) and a binary put option (*cash or nothing* and *asset or nothing*) are depicted in Figs 17.2 and 17.3, respectively. Note that long positions in cash or nothing calls and cash or nothing puts would always equal the fixed payoff at maturity, as can be obtained by adding Figs 17.2(a) and 17.3(a). Similarly, a position in a call and a put for an asset or nothing option is equal to a position in the asset itself, as may be obtained by adding Figs 17.2(b) and 17.3(b).

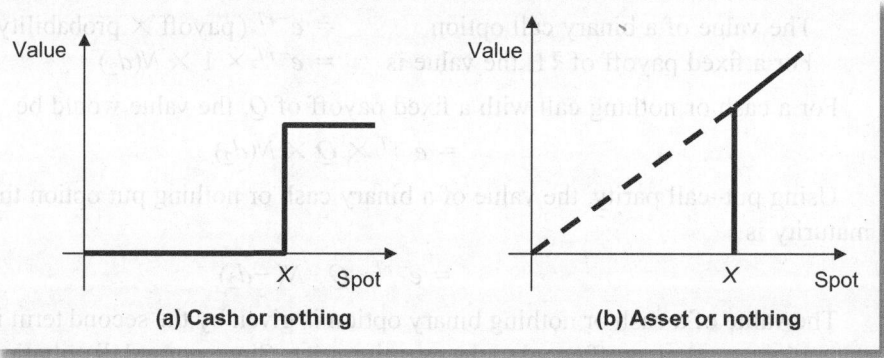

Fig. 17.2 Binary call option

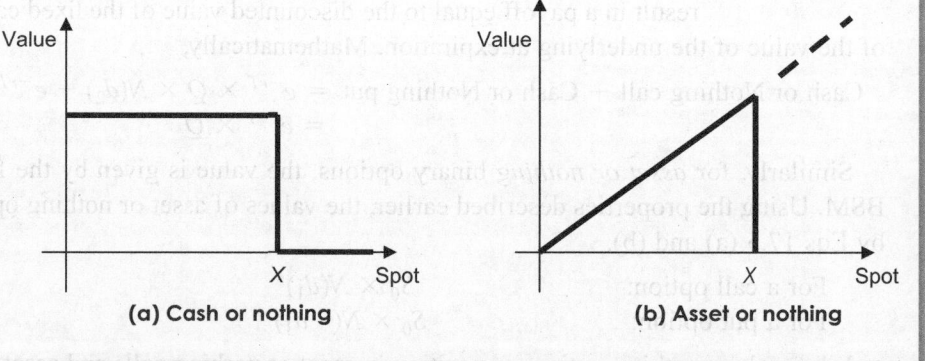

Fig. 17.3 Binary put option

CHOOSER OPTION

A chooser option is an option that gives the right to the holder at time t to have either a call or put option, with an exercise price X and time to maturity T, where $T > t$. The holder has time till t to decide whether he/she would like to have a call or a put for the remaining period, $T - t$. Since this option allows flexibility to choose between a call and a put, it is also called an *as you like it* option.

> A chooser option provides flexibility to the holder to choose between the call or the put at its maturity.

A chooser option provides time for uncertainty to settle in the mind of the investor. In situations where an investor is uncertain about the future behavior of the price of an underlying asset but believes that the directional uncertainty will resolve in times to follow, a chooser comes as a handy choice. For example, if certain events such as the presentation of a fiscal budget, an announcement about election results, etc., make directional forecast difficult prior to option expiry, this may distract investors, leading them to defer trading in options till the time of uncertainty passes. Taking positions after the event has occurred would be a compromise on the potential profits as calls or puts may rise in value. An ideal product would be one that allows holding both calls and puts till the time of the event, and, thereafter, holding either of them, depending upon the outcome of the event that guides the directional movement of the price of the underlying asset.

With a straddle or a strangle strategy, the risk of the directional volatility of the price is neutralized with simultaneous positions in call and put options. A call gives a payoff in case of a price rise, while a put becomes in-the-money on a decline in the price, thus providing protection against movements in either direction.

Valuation

A chooser option is like a straddle but should be relatively less expensive. A straddle comprises simultaneous positions of an at-the-money (ATM) call and an ATM put. With either option turning into money, a straddle yields a decent payoff if the underlying moves sufficiently in either direction. However, to take advantage, one would be required to have both the call and the put with expiry at T. Therefore, with a straddle, one is required to pay an option premium equivalent to the time period $2 \times T$. Instead, a chooser option is like holding both a call and a put till $t < T$ and, thereafter, holding either a call or a put for the remaining time, $T - t$. Therefore, for a chooser option expiring at t, the investor at best can pay for two options (a call and a put) for time t and either a call or a put for $T - t$. The cost of such a chooser option cannot exceed that of a straddle. Hence, the cost of the straddle places an upper bound to the price of the chooser.

The valuation of a chooser option at time t would depend upon the value of the call and the put at time t. The holder would make a choice in favour of the greater of the two. Therefore,

$$\text{Value of a chooser at time, } t = Max\,(c_t, p_t) \qquad (17.6)$$

where c_t, p_t are the values of the call and the put, respectively, at time t.

The value of the call and the put at time t would be dependent upon the price of the underlying asset at t, the exercise price X and the time remaining, $T - t$, represented as $c(S_t, X, T - t)$ and $p(S_t, X, T - t)$, respectively.

Using put–call parity for the value of the put at t, we have $p_t = c_t + X e^{-r(T-t)} - S_t$
Substituting the value of the put in Eq. 17.6 at time t, we get

$$\text{Value of chooser at } t = Max\,(c_t, p_t) = Max\,(c_t, c_t + X e^{-r(T-t)} - S_t)$$

Adding and subtracting c_t, we get

$$\begin{aligned}\text{Payoff of chooser} &= Max\,(c_t, p_t) \\ &= c_t + Max\,(0, X e^{-r(T-t)} - S_t)\end{aligned} \qquad (17.7)$$

> Valuation of the chooser option is based on the expected payoff of the call and the put. The larger of the two would determine the value.

The payoff on the chooser at time t is the sum of the value of the call and the put. The first term in Eq. 17.7, c_t, is the value of the call at time t. It is a function of the price of the underlying, S_t, the exercise price, X, and the time remaining for maturity, $T - t$. The value today would be equal to the value of the call with the spot price, S_0, the exercise price, X, and the time remaining for maturity, T.

$$c_t(S_t, X, T - t) \equiv c(S_0, X, T)$$

The second term in Eq. 17.7 is the value of the put option maturing at time t with an exercise price of $X e^{-r(T - t)}$. Its value today would be $p(S_0, X e^{-r(T - t)}, t)$. Therefore, the value of the chooser option today would be

$$\text{Value of chooser} = c(S_0, X, T) + p(S_0, X e^{-r(T - t)}, t) \quad (17.8)$$

One way of interpreting the value of the chooser is that it must comprise the value of the straddle (value of the call and value of the put) till the time of choosing, and, thereafter, for the remaining period, it must be the value of either the call or the put, whichever is higher. For ATM options, the call value is higher than the put value. Stated another way, the value of the chooser is the sum of (a) the value of the call for the entire period, and (b) the value of the put for the period till the choice is made.

For example, consider an underlying asset trading at ₹100. The buyer of the option wants a chooser with an exercise price of ₹100 for a period of four months with a right to choose between a call and a put, to be exercised at $t = 1$ month. The value of the chooser would be equal to the sum of (a) the value of the call maturing in four months, with $X = 100$, and (b) the value of the put maturing after one month with an exercise price equal to three months' discounted value of ₹100, assuming a risk-free rate of 8% ($100 \times e^{-0.08 \times 3/12} = ₹98.02$). Therefore,

$$\text{Value of the chooser} = c(100, 100, 4/12) + p(100, e^{-0.08 \times (4 - 1)/12} 100, 1/12)$$

The value of a call with spot and exercise prices of ₹100 each, time to maturity of four months, a risk-free rate of 8%, and volatility of 25% would have $d_1 = 0.2569$, $d_2 = 0.1126$, $N(d_1) = 0.6014$, and $N(d_2) = 0.5448$. This gives a call value of ₹7.09. A put with same features would cost ₹4.46. Hence a 4-month straddle would be at ₹11.55 (7.09 + 4.46).

The second component of the chooser option would be a put with maturity of one month, with an exercise price of 98.02. Such a put would cost ₹1.72. Hence, the chooser would cost ₹8.81 (7.09 + 1.72).

The reduction in value as compared to straddle is mainly due to the fact that while with a straddle chooser, we pay a premium for eight months (four months each for the call and the put) while with a chooser, we pay a premium for five months, comprising two months for holding both the call and the put till the chooser expires and then three months for the call. Another small reduction comes from the reduced strike price of the put.

SHOUT OPTION

> A shout option enables the holder to assure a minimum payoff by permitting booking of the intrinsic value at the time of the shout.

A shout option is an option where the holder has the option of 'shouting' at any time t before maturity, so as to ensure a minimum payoff of $S_t - X$. At the end of the option period, the holder of the shout option gets the higher of (a) the intrinsic value at the time of the shout or (b) the payoff at maturity. Such an option provides flexibility to the holder, whereby he/she feels that the payoff at the time of the shout would be more than the payoff at maturity. The payoff of the shout option is given by Eq. 17.9.

$$\text{Payoff of shout option} = Max\ (0, S_t - X, S_T - X) \tag{17.9}$$

Note that if the call option holder does not shout till maturity, it becomes a regular European call.

Valuation

Normally the value at the time of the shout would have a positive intrinsic value, i.e., $(S_t - X) > 0$. Therefore, the term zero in Eq. 17.9 is redundant, and the payoff on the shout option at maturity,

$$c_T = Max\ (S_t - X, S_T - X)$$
$$= S_t - X + Max\ (0, S_T - S_t)$$

Therefore, the value of the shout at time t is

$$= e^{-r(T-t)} \times (S_t - X)$$
+ the value of the call at t with a strike of S_t and time to maturity of $T - t$

$$\text{Value of the shout at } t = e^{-r(T-t)} \times (S_t - X) + c_t(S_t, S_t, T - t) \tag{17.10}$$

This may be priced using the binomial method, in just the way American options are valued. While valuing an American option, starting backwards from the terminal value, we compare the payoffs from the succeeding nodes based on risk-neutral probabilities with the value upon exercise. At each node, we retain the more favourable value of the two. Similarly, while valuing a shout option, we compare the risk-neutral value at each node with the payoff given by Eq. 17.10, and retain the most favourable value. The process can be reiterated till the last node at $t = 0$, proceeding backwards. Another valuation method can be based on the Monte Carlo simulation.

EXCHANGE OPTION

An exchange option may be defined as the right to exchange one risky asset for another. One asset is already owned and the other asset is acquired by surrender of the owned asset. Typically in mergers and acquisition markets, an acquiring firm offers its shares in exchange for some shares in the target firm. This is like an option to exchange shares of one firm for those of another with both the assets being risky, albeit with different volatilities.

> An exchange option is an option to exchange one risky asset for another risky asset, such as one share for another share.

For example, consider Firm A, whose shares trade at ₹100; this firm is acquiring Firm B, whose shares trade at ₹48. Firm A offers one of its own shares for two of B's. This situation can be considered as an exchange option held by the shareholders of Firm B, enabling them to acquire shares in Firm A. This is equal to having a call option (a right to have the shares of Firm A) with an exercise price, X, of ₹96 (exchange ratio × current market price of Firm B, the target firm), because the shareholders of Firm B surrender two of their shares to obtain one share in Firm A. The value surrendered is equivalent to paying the exercise price for acquiring one share in Firm A, the underlying asset with a current selling price, S, of ₹100. Note that not all merger situations qualify to be exact exchange call options. Since the shares of Firm B are extinguished completely by its delisting consequent to the merger, it is not a call option in the true sense, as the shareholders of the target firm have a right but are also under an obligation to surrender their shares. If the target firm is allowed to exist even after the offer is made, the situation resembles a call option.

Applications

Margrabe, who first published a paper on exchange options in 1978, discussed four specific applications of exchange options—manager's incentive fee, margin account, standby arrangements, and exchange offers. The valuation of an exchange offer is discussed in the following paragraphs.

Valuation

The valuation of an exchange option could be based on the BSM formula for call option pricing. Assuming no dividend by either firm till the acquisition is complete, the parameters for valuation that need modifications are (a) volatility, σ, (b) the risk-free rate of return, r, and (c) the time to maturity, T. The volatility that needs to be used is the volatility of the underlying asset after acquisition. This would be dependent upon the volatilities of Firm A and Firm B, i.e., σ_A and σ_B, respectively, and their correlation coefficient, ρ. The new volatility of the surviving firm, A, is now equivalent to the volatility of a long position in the shares of Firm A and a short position in Firm B. Hence, the relevant volatility that must be considered would be given by:

$$\sigma^2 = \sigma^2_A + \sigma^2_B - 2\rho\,\sigma_A\,\sigma_B \qquad (17.11)$$

The risk-free rate to be used must be essentially on a net basis, i.e., the saving of the interest on the exercise price net of the interest earned on the underlying asset. It is analogous to buying an option on a foreign currency, where the exercise price is reduced by the interest rate on the domestic currency, while the asset price is adjusted for the interest earned on the foreign currency, the underlying asset. Here, since the exercise is done by surrender of one set of shares for another, the two interest rates are the same, and, hence, the risk-free rate is zero on a net basis.

EXHIBIT 17.1 Exchange option price on non-dividend paying stocks

$$c = S.N(d_1) - X.N(d_2) \qquad (17.12)$$

where $d_1 = \dfrac{\ln(S/X) + \sigma^2 T/2}{\sigma\sqrt{T}}$; and

$d_2 = \dfrac{\ln(S/X) - \sigma^2 T/2}{\sigma\sqrt{T}}$ or $d_2 = d_1 - \sigma\sqrt{T}$

S = stock price of acquiring firm; X = exercise price exchange ratio x market price of target
T = time remaining for expiration of the option in years; σ = annualized standard deviation as decimal and is given by

$$\sigma^2 = \sigma^2_A + \sigma^2_B - 2\rho\,\sigma_A\,\sigma_B$$

$N(d_1)$ and $N(d_2)$ are cumulative normal distribution functions at d_1 and d_2, respectively
ln = natural log

EXAMPLE 17.1 Exchange option

Assume that Firm A, whose shares trade at ₹100, is willing to offer its shares to the shareholders of Firm B, whose shares trade at ₹48. Firm A is willing to exchange one of its own shares for two of Firm B. The volatility of the shares of Firms A and B are 30% and 20%, respectively, with a coefficient of correlation of 0.50. The exchange can be exercised within three months from today. What is the value of exchange for the shareholders of Firm B?

Solution
Here, the underlying asset is the share of Firm A with the current value, S = ₹100. The shareholders of Firm B could exercise by surrendering two of their own shares, providing an exercise price, X, of ₹96 (48 × 2). The volatility of the underlying asset would not be equal to 30%, but would stand modified by the influence of the shares of Firm B. The effective volatility would be σ, given by Eq. 17.11.

$$\sigma^2 = 30^2 + 20^2 - 2 \times 0.5 \times 30 \times 20 = 700 \text{ or } \sigma = 26.46\%$$

With $r = 0$ and $T = 0.25$ years, we have $d_1 = 0.3747$ $d_2 = 0.2424$ $N(d_1) = 0.6461$ and $N(d_2) = 0.5958$

The value of the exchange option, call value

$$c = 100 \times 0.6461 - 96 \times 0.5958 = 64.61 - 57.20 = ₹7.41$$

The time remaining for the option can be considered to be equal to the time difference between the announcement date and its completion of exchange of shares.

With this information, the exchange option can be valued by Eq. 17.12, by making suitable substitutions in d_1 and d_2.

GAP OPTION

Normally, payoffs on options are non-linear, with discontinuity in the payoffs at the exercise prices. Gap options are options where payoffs are non-linear, and also have gaps in the payoffs at the exercise prices. The payoffs of a gap call option and a gap put option are given in Table 17.3 and depicted in Fig. 17.4. A look at Fig. 17.4 would justify the name given to the option.

It may seem that gap options are similar to regular options with X replaced by another figure, G, but there are two critical differences. As can be seen from Table 17.3, payoff for regular options is a function of the exercise price, but for gap options, it is determined by another variable, G. However, the exercise price continues to determine whether the option is exercised or not. Further, the buyer of regular options exercises only when it is ITM; otherwise, he/she lets it expire. A gap option may or may not be ITM when exercised. It would depend upon the value of G.

> A gap option is similar to a regular option except that the quantum of payoff is decided independent of the exercise price.

Table 17.3 Payoffs on gap options at maturity

Asset price at maturity	Gap call option	Gap put option
When $S_T < X$	0	$G - S_T$
When $S_T \geq X$	$S_T - G$	0

where S_T = Asset price at maturity T, X = Exercise price, G = Gap

Applications

The strategy of using a gap option achieves a balance between a reduction in the cost of hedging with options and a sacrifice of the potential gains in case G is fixed higher than X for call option. If $G < X$, the potential gain is enhanced, with a commensurate increase in the cost of the option. For put option the situation is reverse. Therefore, what value of G would be fixed is predominantly a function of extra costs and extra gains depending upon the likely behaviour of the asset price. Figure 17.4 clearly compares the payoffs on regular options and on gap options.

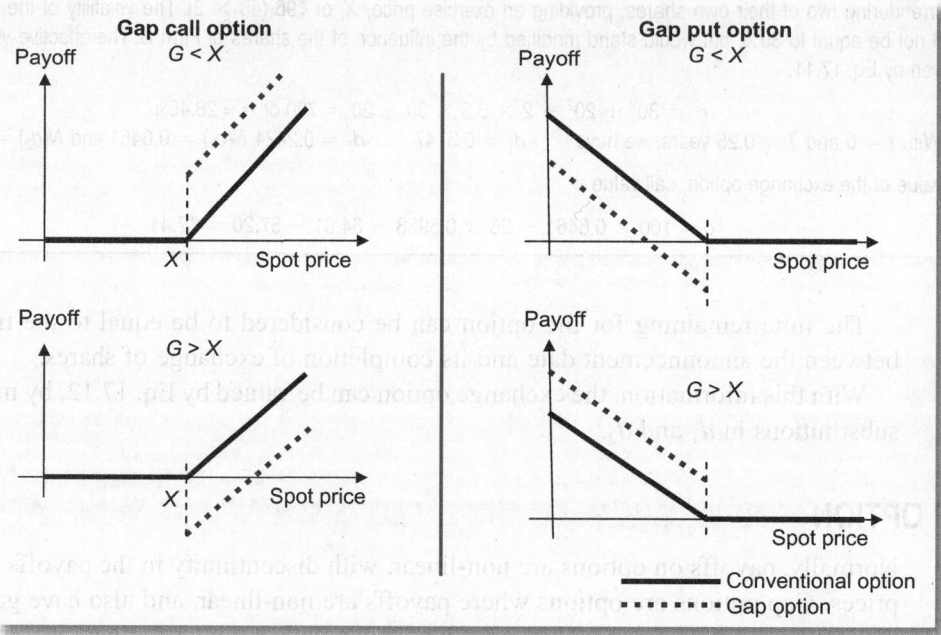

Fig. 17.4 Payoff of gap options at maturity

Valuation

Valuation of gap options is rather easy. The payoff on a gap call option at maturity, T, is given by

$$c_T(gap) = \begin{cases} S_T - G & \text{when } S_T > X \\ 0 & \text{when } S_T \leq X \end{cases}$$

or

$$\begin{cases} S_T - X + X - G & \text{when } S_T > X \\ 0 & \text{when } S_T \leq X \\ 1 \end{cases}$$

or

$$\begin{cases} S_T - X & \text{when } S_T > X \\ 0 & \text{when } S_T \leq X \end{cases} + X - G \times \begin{cases} 1 \text{ when } S_T > X \\ 0 \text{ when } S_T > X \end{cases}$$

= Payoff on a regular call at maturity with exercise price, X + Payoff on a cash or nothing binary call at maturity with a fixed amount, $X - G$

Therefore, the value of a gap call at maturity is the same as the value of a regular call and a cash or nothing option with $X - G$ as the payoff, $c(CON)$. The value of the gap call option before maturity should be the sum of the values of the regular call and the cash or nothing call, and can be written as[1]

$$c(gap) = c + (X - G) \times c(CON) \qquad (17.13)$$

> A gap option is a combination of a regular option and a binary option. For hedging, it is a sacrifice of the payoff for saving the premium.

A similar logic would prove that the value of a gap put option is the sum of the values of a regular put and a cash or nothing put with $G - X$.

$$p_T(gap) = \begin{cases} G - S_T & \text{when } S_T < X \\ 0 & \text{when } S_T \geq X \end{cases}$$

or

$$\begin{cases} X - S_T + G - X & \text{when } S_T < X \\ 0 & \text{when } S_T \geq X \end{cases}$$

or

$$\begin{cases} X - S_T & \text{when } S_T < X \\ 0 & \text{when } S_T \geq X \end{cases} + G - X \times \begin{cases} 1 & \text{when } S_T > X \\ 0 & \text{when } S_T \geq X \end{cases}$$

= Payoff on a regular put at maturity with exercise price, X + Payoff on a cash or nothing binary put at maturity with a fixed amount, $G - X$

$$p(gap) = p + (G - X) \times p(CON) \qquad (17.14)$$

The valuation of gap options can also be arrived at by using the BSM with some modifications. The payoffs on a regular call and a gap call are decided by the exercise price and the gap, respectively. However, the rules regarding exercising the options remain the same in both the cases. Therefore, the payoffs on the options in terms of the exercise price need to be replaced from X to G for gap options, as if the exercise price is not X but G. Incorporating

EXHIBIT 17.2 Valuation of gap call and put options

$$c(gap) = c + (X - G) \times c(CON)$$
$$c = Se^{-qT} \cdot N(d_1) - Xe^{-rT} \cdot N(d_2) \quad \text{and} \quad c(CON) = e^{-rT} \times N(d_2)$$

$$p(gap) = p + (G - X) \times p(CON)$$
$$p = Xe^{-rT} \cdot N(-d_2) - Se^{-qT} \cdot N(-d_1) \quad \text{and} \quad p(CON) = e^{-rT} \times N(-d_2)$$

where

$$d_1 = \frac{\ln(S/X) + (r - q + \sigma^2/2)T}{\sigma\sqrt{T}}; \text{ and}$$

$$d_2 = \frac{\ln(S/X) - (r - q + \sigma^2/2)T}{\sigma\sqrt{T}} \quad \text{or } d_2 = d_1 - \sigma\sqrt{T}$$

S = Price of underlying asset
T = Time remaining for expiration
r = Risk-free rate of return
$N(x)$ = Cumulative normal distribution function at x
X = Exercise price
σ = Annualized standard deviation
q = Dividend yield on the asset
G = Gap
$\ln$ = Natural log

---

[1] Wherever the value of the difference between G and X is negative, it can be deemed to have written an option.

> **EXAMPLE 17.2 Gap option call**
>
> Assume that an importing firm has a payment of US $10,000 to make at the end of six months from now. The spot price is ₹50/$. The volatility of the dollar exchange rate is estimated to be 20%, and the risk-free rates in the Indian rupee and the US dollar are 10% and 5%, respectively.
>
> (a) What would the maximum cost for the firm be if it decides to hedge with a regular call with a strike of ₹51.00?
> (b) If the firm is willing to sacrifice ₹1 from its likely gains by hedging with a gap option, what would its maximum cost be?
> (c) Under what circumstance would the strategy of a gap call prove better than hedging with a regular call?
>
> **Solution**
> (a) If the importer hedges with regular a call with a strike price of ₹51.00, the cost of the call option would be given by the Merton model.
>
> $$c = Se^{-qT} \cdot N(d_1) - Xe^{-rT} \cdot N(d_2)$$
>
> With $S = 50$, $X = 51$, $r = 10\%$, $q = 5\%$, $T = 0.5$ years, and $\sigma = 20\%$, the values of the intermediate parameters are
>
> $d_1 = 0.1075$, $d_2 = -0.0339$, $N(d_1) = 0.5428$ $N(d_2) = 0.4865$
>
> And the value of the call $= 48.7655 \times 0.5428 - 48.5127 \times 0.4865$
> $= 26.4699 - 23.6014 = ₹2.8685/\$$.
>
> By taking a regular call, the importer ensures that the maximum cost would be frozen at $X + c$, i.e., ₹51.00 + ₹2.8685 = ₹53.8685/$.
>
> (b) If the importer decides to sacrifice up to ₹1.00 by fixing the gap, G, at ₹52, the value of the call would be reduced by the value of the binary call with the value $X - G$ being negative. The value of the binary call would be $(X - G) \times e^{-rt} \times N(d_2) = -1.00 \times 0.9512 \times 0.4865 = -₹0.4628$.
> Therefore, the cost of the gap call is ₹2.4064. The importer's maximum cost would be $G + c$, i.e., ₹52.00 + ₹2.4064 = ₹54.4064 per dollar.
> (c) Gap call would reduce the cost by ₹0.4628/dollar. The strategy with gap call would be beneficial if rupee appreciates rather than depreciating.

the change in the payoffs, the value of gap options as modified under the BSM would be as follows:

$$c(gap) = Se^{-qT} \cdot N(d_1) - Ge^{-rt} \cdot N(d_2)$$
$$p(gap) = Ge^{-rT} \cdot N(-d_2) - Se^{-qT} \cdot N(-d_1)$$

PAY-LATER OPTION

As the name signifies, pay-later options allow the payment of the premium on the option later rather than upfront, while initiating a position as in a regular option. For pay-later options, the premium is adjusted in the payoffs. The payoffs on pay-later call and put options for the holder are given in Table 17.4.

Table 17.4 Payoffs on pay-later options at maturity

Asset price at maturity	Pay-later call option	Pay-later put option
When $S_T < X$	0	$X - A_p - S_T$
When $S_T \geq X$	$S_T - X - A_c$	0

Where S_T = Asset price at maturity T, X = Exercise price, A_c and A_p are premiums of the call and the put

Exotic Options   **493**

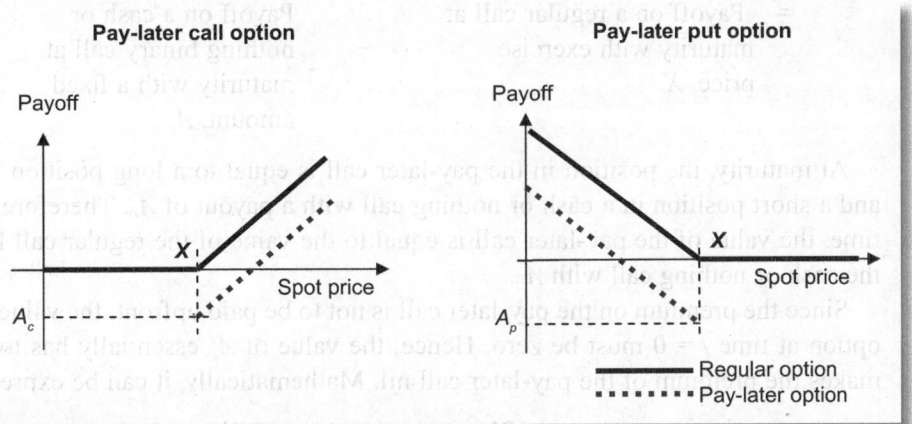

Fig. 17.5 Payoff on pay-later options at maturity

The payoffs on the pay-later call and the put options are depicted in Fig. 17.5. A look at the figure would suggest that the payoffs on the pay-later options look just the same as those for the gap options when G more than X. They are strikingly similar. However, there is an important difference. The premium in the case of the pay-later option is not payable at maturity; the liability arises only if the option ends up ITM. No premium is payable if the option is out-of-the-money (OTM). Under the gap option the premium is payable upfront.

Applications

As no premium is payable upfront, the pay-later option enables hedging at zero cost. A pay-later option becomes useful when a large one-way movement in the asset price is foreseen. The pay-later call would be useful to importers when the local currency is expected to depreciate substantially. If that happens, the importer does not mind paying the premium, but does not want to pay it upfront. If a foreign currency of interest is expected to depreciate substantially, an exporter could hedge against unfavourable movements through purchase of a pay-later put option with no initial cost. If the expected forecast comes true, the hedger does not mind sharing part of payoff with the writer of the option. If the forecast does not come true, the hedger has no liability to pay.

Valuation

The valuation of pay-later options can be done on similar lines as the valuation of gap options. However, unlike gap options, where the gap value, G, is a choice of the buyer, with pay-later options, the amount of decrease/increase in the payoff is decided by the seller of the option. The valuation of pay-later options is stated here:

$$c_T(PL) = \begin{cases} S_T - X - A_c & \text{when } S_T > X \\ 0 & \text{when } S_T \leq X \end{cases}$$

or

$$\begin{cases} S_T - X & \text{when } S_T > X \\ 0 & \text{when } S_T \leq X \end{cases} - A_c \times \begin{cases} 1 \text{ when } S_T > X \\ 0 \text{ when } S_T > X \end{cases}$$

	Payoff on a regular call at maturity with exercise price, X	−	Payoff on a cash or nothing binary call at maturity with a fixed amount, A_c

At maturity, the position in the pay-later call is equal to a long position in a regular call and a short position in a cash or nothing call with a payout of A_c. Therefore, at any point of time, the value of the pay-later call is equal to the value of the regular call less the value of the cash or nothing call with A_c.

Since the premium on the pay-later call is not to be paid upfront, the value of the pay-later option at time $t = 0$ must be zero. Hence, the value of A_c essentially has to be a value that makes the premium of the pay-later call nil. Mathematically, it can be expressed as follows:

$$c_0(PL) = c_0 - A_c \times c_0(CON) = 0 \qquad (17.15)$$

or

$$A_c = \frac{C_0}{C_0(CON)} = \frac{C_0}{e^{-rT} N(d_2)} \qquad (17.16)$$

For comparison, consider the data in Example 13.2 on a gap call option on the US dollar exchange rate with $S = 50$, $X = 51$, $r = 10\%$, $q = 5\%$, $T = 0.5$ years, and $\sigma = 20\%$. The values of the intermediate parameters were

$$d_1 = 0.1075, \quad d_2 = -0.0339, \quad N(d_1) = 0.5428 \quad N(d_2) = 0.4865$$

The value of the regular call was found as ₹2.8685/dollar. If this premium is not to be paid by opting to go for a pay-later option, the value of A_c would be fixed by dividing the call price by the value of the cash or nothing call, i.e., $e^{-rT} \cdot N(d_2)$. This comes to ₹0.4628. Hence, the value of A_c is 2.8685/0.4628 = ₹6.1982. For these values, if the ending exchange rate finishes at ₹54/dollar, the pay-later call would have to be exercised with the payoff as $S - T - A_c$ = 54.00 − 51.00 − 6.20 = −₹3.20/dollar. The payoff would not be positive till the spot exchange rate on maturity closes above ₹57.20. Hence, the pay-later option makes sense only when the direction is almost certain and substantial movement is also foreseen. Until this happens, it may not be worthwhile to go for a pay-later option just to avoid the upfront premium, as it may land up costing the holder dearly at the end of the hedging period.

> Pay-later options are deceptively attractive for cost saving, but are really very expensive. They may have to be exercised even when not ITM at expiry.

On similar lines, we may value a pay-later put option as shown here:

$$p_T(PL) = \begin{cases} X - A_p - S_T & \text{when } S_T < X \\ 0 & \text{when } S_T \geq X \end{cases}$$

or

$$\begin{cases} X - S_T & \text{when } S_T < X \\ 0 & \text{when } S_T \geq X \end{cases} - A_p \times \begin{cases} 1 & \text{when } S_T < X \\ 0 & \text{when } S_T \geq X \end{cases}$$

	Payoff on a regular put at maturity with exercise price, X	−	Payoff on a cash or nothing binary put at maturity with a fixed amount, A_p

EXAMPLE 17.3 Pay-later put option

Assume that an exporting firm has a receivable of US $10,000 at the end of six months from now. The spot exchange rate is ₹50/dollar. Volatility is estimated to be 20%, and the risk-free rates in the Indian rupee and the US dollar are 10 and 5%, respectively.

(a) What would the minimum exchange realized by the firm be if it decides to hedge with a regular put option with a strike of ₹51.00?
(b) If the firm is not willing to pay a premium upfront, then what would the equivalent pay-later put option be?

Solution
(a) If the exporter hedges with a regular put option with a strike price of ₹51.00, the cost of the put option would be given by the Merton model.

$$p = Xe^{-rT} \cdot N(-d_2) - Se^{-qT} \cdot N(-d_1)$$

With $S = 50$, $X = 51$, $r = 10\%$, $q = 5\%$, $T = 0.5$ years and $\sigma = 20\%$, the values of the intermediate parameters would be

$d_1 = 0.1075$, $d_2 = -0.0339$, $N(-d_1) = 0.4572$, $N(-d_2) = 0.5135$

and the value of the put would be
$= 48.5127 \times 0.5135 - 48.7655 \times 0.4572$
$= 24.9113 - 22.2956 = ₹2.6157$ per $.

By taking a regular put, the exporter ensures the minimum realization of $X - p$, i.e., $51.00 - 2.6157 = ₹48.3843$ per dollar.

(b) If the exporter is not willing to pay the premium upfront, he/she would need to buy a pay-later put option with a gap of A_p, arrived at by dividing the regular put price by the value of the cash or nothing put. The value of the cash or nothing put is $p = 0.4884$. The value of A_p would be $2.6157/0.4884 = 5.3557$.

EXHIBIT 17.4 Valuation of pay-later call and put options

$$c(PL) = c - A_c \times c(CON)$$
$$c = Se^{-qT} \cdot N(d_1) - Xe^{-rT} \cdot N(d_2) \quad \text{and} \quad c(CON) = e^{-rT} xN(d_2)$$
$$p(PL) = p - A_p xp(CON)$$
$$p = Xe^{-rT} \cdot N(-d_2) - Se^{-qT} \cdot N(-d_1) \quad \text{and} \quad p(CON) = e^{-rT} \times N(-d_2)$$

where
$$d_1 = \frac{\ln(S/X) + (r - q + \sigma^2/2)T}{\sigma\sqrt{T}}; \quad \text{and}$$
$$d_2 = \frac{\ln(S/X) + (r - q + \sigma^2/2)T}{\sigma\sqrt{T}} \quad \text{or} \quad d_2 = d_1 - \sigma\sqrt{T}$$

S = Price of underlying asset
A_c, A_p = Ratio of prices of regular and cash or nothing option while initiating
T = Time remaining for expiration
r = Risk-free rate of return
$N(x)$ = Cumulative normal distribution function at x

X = Exercise price
σ = Annualized standard deviation
q = Dividend yield on the asset
ln = Natural log

Just as we determined the premium adjustment in case of a pay-later call, the premium for a pay-later put would be adjusted as follows:

$$p_0(PL) = p_0 - A_p \times p_0(CON) = 0 \quad (17.17)$$

or
$$Ap = \frac{p_0}{p_0(CON)} = \frac{p_0}{e^{-rT} N(-d_2)} \quad (17.18)$$

COMPOUND OPTIONS

A compound option is an option on an option, and is ideal for covering contingent exposures.

A compound option is an option on an option. The underlying in the regular option is an asset that is conventionally a stock, a commodity, an index, a foreign currency, an interest rate instrument, etc. In a compound option, the underlying asset is another option that gives a right to buy or sell the underlying asset. In a compound option, there would be two options with two different maturities, t and T, and two different exercise prices, x and X. There can be four types of compound options that are described for a stock.

Call on Call A compound option of a call on a call would comprise of two calls, one maturing earlier at t and the other later at T. When the first call expires at t, it gives a right to the holder to acquire another call by paying the exercise price of the first call, x. On expiry of the second call at T, the holder gets a right to buy the underlying asset, say a stock, by paying its exercise price, X.

Put on Call A compound option of a put on a call would comprise of one put maturing earlier at t and one call maturing later at T. When the put expires at t, it gives a right to the holder to sell a call by receiving the exercise price, x. On expiry of the call at T, the holder gets a right to buy the underlying asset, say a stock, by paying its exercise price, X.

Put on Put A compound option of a put on a put would comprise of two puts, one maturing earlier at t and the other later at T. When the first put expires at t, it gives a right to the holder to sell another put by receiving the exercise price of the first put, x. On expiry of the second put at T, the holder gets a right to sell the underlying asset, say a stock, by receiving its exercise price, X.

Call on Put A compound option of a call on a put would comprise of one call maturing earlier at t and one put maturing later at T. When the call expires at t, it gives a right to the holder to buy a put by paying the exercise price, x. On expiry of the put at T, the holder gets a right to sell the underlying asset, say a stock, by receiving its exercise price, X.

Applications

Compound options are ideal to cover contingent exposures where forwards do not serve hedging purposes. Consider the situation of a supply contract for equipment, where a firm has quoted a price in a foreign currency, say euro. Whether the bid is successful or not would be known after three months. If the firm bags the order, it would take another three months to supply and realize payment. The firm expects the euro to depreciate. The firm faces many alternatives to hedge against the depreciating euro:

- One alternative with the firm is to book a 6-m forward contract to sell euro. That could prove disastrous if the firm does not succeed in getting the order. A forward contract is a binding commitment, and, therefore, the firm would have to honour the commitment, irrespective of whether it succeeds in getting the order or not.
- Another alternative would be to buy a plain vanilla put option for six months. Though not obligatory in nature, the put option would be expensive in terms of the premium.

- Further, it does not allow for the possibility of failing in the tender, as the premium of put is paid in any case.
- As a third alternative, the firm can buy a compound option. It would be a call on a put with the call at the end of three months, giving it a right to sell euro in six months. If successful, the firm exercises the call to have the put option to sell euro in six months, otherwise it allows the call to lapse. An additional decision with the firm in this case would be to fix the exercise price of the call, the first option.

On similar lines, an importer uncertain about procurement being contingent on some event and apprehending an appreciation in the foreign currency he/she is dealing in may like to have a call on a call that gives a right to buy the foreign currency at the expiry of the first call. It may be a more preferable alternative than a forward buy contract or a plain vanilla call.

A put on a call and a put on a put would be appropriate in situations where one wants to sell either a call or a put, respectively, not now but later. At maturity, a compound option with the put as the first option would give a right to sell a call (for a put on a call) or sell a put (for a put on a put). All situations that warrant selling of an option on a deferred basis are suitable for compound options with a put as the first option.

Valuation

The valuation of a compound option is dependent upon the value of the second option at the expiry of the first option. In the case of a compound option of call on a call, the holder would exercise it on maturity only if the value of the second call exceeds the exercise price of the first call. Similarly, for a compound option of a put on a call, the holder would exercise the put on its maturity only if the value of second option, i.e., the call, is less than the strike of the first option.

The decision to exercise the first option or let it expire is dependent on the payoff at the expiry of the first option, which in turn is decided by the strike price of the first option and the value of the second option at that time.

Consider a call on a call. At the expiry of the first call at t, one would like to exercise it only when the value of the second call (the underlying asset in this case) at that time, c_t, is greater than the exercise price of the first call, x. The payoff is positive. If the value of the second call is less than the exercise price of the first, the compound option would not be exercised. Similarly, a compound option of a put on the call is exercised only when the value of the subsequent call, c_t, is less than the strike price of the first put, x. The payoffs on the four compound options at the expiry of the first are summarized in Table 17.5.

Table 17.5 Payoff on a compound option at maturity of first option, t

At maturity of first option, t	Call on a Call	Put on a Call	Call on a Put	Put on a Put
Exercise when	$c_t - x > 0$	$x - c_t > 0$	$p_t - x > 0$	$x - p_t > 0$
Do not exercise	$c_t - x < 0$	$x - c_t < 0$	$p_t - x < 0$	$x - p_t < 0$

where x = exercise price of the first option,
c_t and p_t = Value of the second call/put option at the expiry of the first option at time, t

The value of the second option at the expiry of the first would be governed by not just the risk-free rate of return and volatility but also the (a) asset price at t, S_t, (b) exercise price of the second option, X, and (c) time remaining for maturity, $T - t$. With a given and known X and $T - t$ that are determined initially, the asset price at the time t becomes crucial in the exercise of the option. The option holder is indifferent to exercising if the value of the second option is exactly equal to the exercise price of the first. We define S^* as that asset price that equates the value of the option equal to the exercise price of the first, i.e.,

For a call: $c_t = c_t(S^*, X, T - t) = x$
For a put: $p_t = p_t(S^*, X, T - t) = x$

An analytical solution to European compound options can be found in terms of the bivariate normal distribution denoted by $M(a, b, \rho)$, which represents the bivariate cumulative probability of the first variable less than or equal to a and the second variable less than or equal to b, with ρ as the coefficient of correlation between the two. Analytical solutions to the valuation of the four compound options are given in Exhibit 17.5 known as Roll, Geske and Whaley formula.

EXHIBIT 17.5 Valuation of compound options

Call on call $\quad Cc = S e^{-qT} \cdot M\left(a_1, b_1, \sqrt{\dfrac{t}{T}}\right) - X \cdot e^{-rT} \cdot M\left(a_2, b_2, \sqrt{\dfrac{t}{T}}\right) - x \cdot e^{-rT} \cdot N(a_2)$

Put on call $\quad Pc = X \cdot e^{-rT} \cdot M\left(-a_2, b_2, -\sqrt{\dfrac{t}{T}}\right) - S \cdot e^{-qT} \cdot M\left(-a_1, b_1, -\sqrt{\dfrac{t}{T}}\right) - x \cdot e^{-rT} \cdot N(-a_2)$

Call on put $\quad Cp = X \cdot e^{-rT} \cdot M\left(-a_2, -b_2, \sqrt{\dfrac{t}{T}}\right) - S \cdot e^{-qT} \cdot M\left(-a_1, -b_1, \sqrt{\dfrac{t}{T}}\right) - x \cdot e^{-rT} \cdot N(-a_2)$

Put on put $\quad Pp = S \cdot e^{-qT} \cdot M\left(a_1, -b_1, -\sqrt{\dfrac{t}{T}}\right) - X \cdot e^{-rT} \cdot M\left(a_2, -b_2, -\sqrt{\dfrac{t}{T}}\right) - x \cdot e^{-rT} \cdot N(-a_2)$

where $\quad a_1 = \dfrac{\ln\left[\dfrac{S}{S^*}\right] + \left(r - q + \dfrac{\sigma^2}{2}\right)t}{\sigma\sqrt{t}}$ and $a_2 = a_1 - \sigma\sqrt{t}$

$b_1 = \dfrac{\ln\left[\dfrac{S}{X}\right] + \left(r - q + \dfrac{\sigma^2}{2}\right)T}{\sigma\sqrt{T}}$ and $b_2 = b_1 - \sigma\sqrt{T}$

S = Price of stock now
x = Exercise price of first option
X = Exercise price of second option
σ = Annualized standard deviation
q = Continuous dividend on asset underlying the second option
$M(a, b, \rho)$ = Value of cumulative bivariate normal distribution with first variable less than a and second variable less than b with correlation of ρ

S^* = Critical stock price at expiry of first option at time t
t = Time of expiration of first option $t < T$
T = Time for expiration of second option
r = Risk-free rate of return
$\ln$ = Natural log
$N(x)$ = Cumulative normal distribution function at x

*Roll, Geske, and Whaley Formulae

BARRIER OPTIONS

> Barrier options are amongst the most popular options, as they reduce the cost of hedging.

Among the most popular and most traded exotic options are barrier options because they are cheaper than standard options. Barrier options either come to life or expire at a specific level, called the barrier price. Plain vanilla options have one reference price, i.e., the strike price X, to which the spot is compared when determining the payoff. For barrier options, there is another reference, the barrier B, which determines if the option is alive or dead. However, when alive, it is like a standard option. The reference point that determines whether the option is alive or dead is called the barrier. Barrier options are also known as path-dependent options, as the value of these options depends not only upon the value of the underlying asset at maturity but also on whether the value touched the barrier during the period of the option.

Barrier options can be either *knock-in or knock-out*. Knock-in options come to life only when the barrier is touched, otherwise they remain worthless. Knock-out options are those that may be currently alive but become worthless if the spot touches the barrier. The up or down direction towards the barrier gives rise to two more possibilities for knock-in or knock-out options. Whenever alive, these barrier options behave like plain vanilla options.

A knock-in option comes to life if the spot touches the barrier, and, thereafter, becomes a plain vanilla option. It can be *up-and-in*, meaning that if the spot goes above the barrier, it becomes alive. Similarly, *down-and-in* options would be alive if the spot goes below the barrier.

Knock-out options remain standard options till they expire upon the spot touching the barrier. They too can be *up-and-out* or *down-and-out*. The spot price going above the barrier makes the option worthless for *up-and-out*. Similarly, a *down-and-out* option expires when the spot goes below the barrier. Remember, once out the option is always dead. If during the life of the option the barrier is never touched, then the knock-out option would always remain alive, while the knock-in option would never come to life.

For example, consider a call option with ₹110 as the strike and ₹120 as the barrier on an asset trading at ₹100. An *up-and-in* option would be an option that remains dead till the spot touches the barrier of ₹120. Once the price goes above the barrier, the option comes to life. It remains alive irrespective of the subsequent price levels. The payoff would be decided as in the case of a plain vanilla call option. Similarly, if the barrier were ₹90, a *down-and-in* option would remain dead till the spot is above ₹90 and become alive when the spot goes below ₹90. The four types of barrier call options are described in Table 17.6. There would be another set of four matching combinations of barrier options involving puts.

Barrier Options are Less Expensive Since barrier options are not expected to remain alive for the entire life of the option, they are less expensive than plain vanilla options. A bullish trader would buy a call option with a strike 10% higher than the current spot and pay the entire premium. However, bullish sentiments may turn negative if the spot falls by more than 10%. Therefore, he/she may buy a down-and-out option and save some cost.

> Barrier options cost less than regular options because they remain alive only for a part of the option period, depending upon the path the final values take.

Some of the barrier options exhibit abrupt behaviour in prices because they gain or lose value without warning. For example, an *up-and-in* call with the spot at ₹100, the exercise at ₹110, and the barrier at ₹120 suddenly becomes valuable when the price starts approaching the barrier of ₹120. If

Table 17.6 Barrier call options

Assumed spot = ₹100

Type	Exercise price, X	Barrier price, B	Description	Features
Knock-in options				
Up and In	110	120	The option comes to life only when S goes above the barrier of ₹120; otherwise, it is worthless.	The call option suddenly gains an intrinsic worth of ₹10 the moment it comes to life.
Down and In	110	90	The option comes to life only when S goes below ₹90; otherwise, it is worthless.	A call option gets activated only when the spot falls to the barrier of ₹90. Thereafter, it behaves like a regular option.
Knock-out options				
Up and Out	110	120	The option is valuable as long as S does not touch ₹120. It expires when S goes above ₹120.	The call option, gaining in value with any rise in price, suddenly loses the entire intrinsic worth of ₹10 upon touching the barrier.
Down and Out	110	90	If S goes below ₹90, the option becomes worthless.	The call option becomes OTM prior to the spot touching the barrier. The value consists only of time value. The time value becomes zero upon the spot touching the barrier.

the spot value remains between ₹110 and ₹120, the option does not become alive, despite being in-the-money. Naturally, there is loss of value in some price ranges and, hence, this option would cost less than a vanilla option.

Similarly, an up-and-out call with the spot at ₹100, the strike at ₹110, and the barrier at ₹130 would become in-the-money after the price crosses ₹110, but would lose its worth (of at least ₹20) when the spot crosses ₹130. It would start falling in value as the asset price approaches the barrier. This too would cost less than a vanilla option, as it is worthless beyond a spot price of ₹130.

Valuation

The valuation of a barrier option needs a high level of mathematical understanding, which is beyond the scope of the book. Besides, barrier options can be valued in many ways: by the analytical method, by the numerical method, and by simulation.

We may use the binomial method to value barrier options much in the same way as we do for valuing American options. At each node, we may examine if the barrier comes into action. If it does, we eliminate the node and continue to evaluate the nodes that are alive.

Let us examine the application of the binomial method to value a barrier option that not only illustrates the decision-making process, but also shows how a barrier option is cheaper than a regular option. Assume a stock trades at ₹100. We value a call with an exercise price of ₹85 and an expiry of 12 months with a barrier at ₹90. It is a down-and-out call, implying that if the stock price falls to ₹90 or below at any time before maturity, the call option becomes worthless.

We shall use three-stage binomial tree with each binomial period of four months for call expiring after 1 year. This tree is depicted in Fig. 17.6, with a risk-free rate of 3% per period, and up and down movements of 10% each.

Exotic Options **501**

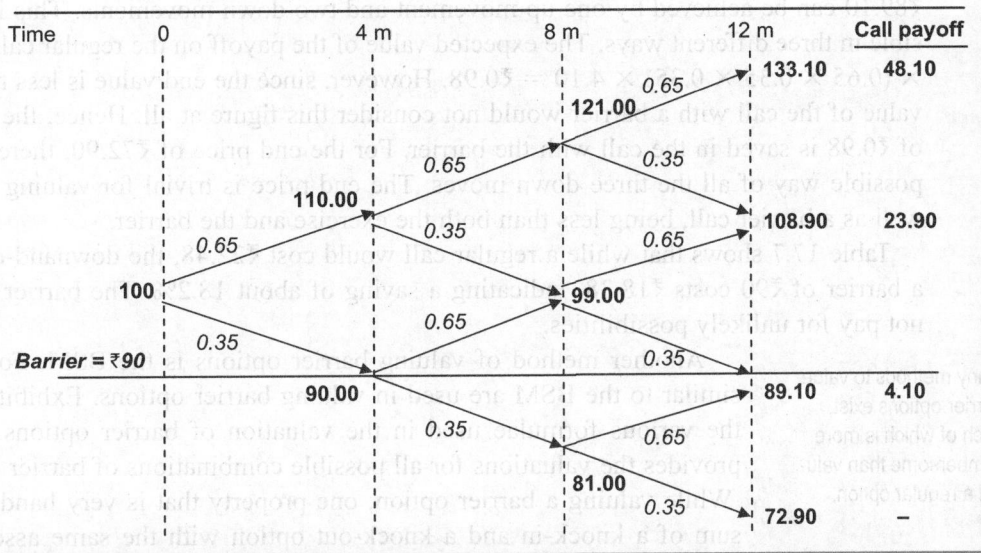

Fig. 17.6 Binary tree for barrier option pricing

The risk-neutral probabilities for up and down movements are 0.65 and 0.35, respectively. As shown in the binomial tree, there are four possible terminal values of the stock. The payoff on a regular call with $X = 85$ would be as follows:

End price	Call payoff
₹133.10	₹48.10
₹108.90	₹23.90
₹89.10	₹4.10
₹72.90	—

The values of a regular call and a down-and-out call with a barrier of ₹90 are condensed in Table 17.7, with irrelevant paths (where the stock has touched or gone below the barrier of ₹90) for the barrier option struck out.

There are eight possible paths in the tree. Whenever the stock price is less than ₹90, the option expires and its value becomes zero.

The end price of ₹133.10 is achieved by all the three up movements with the probability of each at 0.65. With a call payoff of ₹48.10, the expected value of a regular call would be $(0.65 \times 0.65 \times 0.65) \times 48.10 = ₹13.21$. Since the path to reach the value never crosses the barrier, it is also included in the pricing of the barrier option.

The end price of ₹108.90 can be achieved by two up movements and one down movement. This is possible in three different ways. The expected value of the payoff on the regular call would be $3 \times (0.65 \times 0.65 \times 0.35) \times 23.90 = ₹10.61$. However, of the three possible paths to reach the value of ₹108.90, one (down–up–up) path on three branches of the binomial tree would cross the barrier, and, hence, is eliminated from computation of the call price with a barrier. This would reduce the value to ₹7.07 for the call with the barrier.

Similarly, we may value nodes with end prices of ₹89.10 and ₹72.90. The end price of ₹89.10 can be achieved by one up movement and two down movements. This is again possible in three different ways. The expected value of the payoff on the regular call would be 3 × (0.65 × 0.35 × 0.35) × 4.10 = ₹0.98. However, since the end value is less than ₹90, the value of the call with a barrier would not consider this figure at all. Hence, the entire value of ₹0.98 is saved in the call with the barrier. For the end price of ₹72.90, there is only one possible way of all the three down moves. The end price is trivial for valuing a regular as well as a barrier call, being less than both the exercise and the barrier.

Table 17.7 shows that while a regular call would cost ₹22.48, the downand-out call with a barrier of ₹90 costs ₹18.38, indicating a saving of about 18.2%. The barrier option does not pay for unlikely possibilities.

> Many methods to value barrier options exist, each of which is more cumbersome than valuing a regular option.

Another method of valuing barrier options is the BSM. Four formulae similar to the BSM are used in valuing barrier options. Exhibit 17.6[2] gives the various formulae used in the valuation of barrier options. Table 17.8 provides the valuations for all possible combinations of barrier options.

While valuing a barrier option, one property that is very handy is that the sum of a knock-in and a knock-out option with the same asset, the same exercise, and the same barrier are nothing but equal to a European option.

$$\text{Knock-in option} + \text{knock-out option} = \text{European option} \tag{17.19}$$

Table 17.7 Binomial valuation of barrier option

Call payoff (₹)	Path			Probabilities			Call value at $T = 12$ m	
				Strike = 85	Barrier = 90		Nature = down-and-out	
	4	8	12				Standard	Barrier
48.10	u	u	u	0.65	0.65	0.65	13.21	13.21
23.90	u	d	u	0.65	0.35	0.65	10.61	7.07
	u	u	d	0.65	0.65	0.35		
	d	u	u	0.35	0.65	0.65		
4.10	u	d	d	0.65	0.35	0.35	0.98	–
	d	u	d	0.35	0.65	0.35		
	d	d	u	0.35	0.35	0.65		
0.00	d	d	d	0.35	0.35	0.35	–	–
Call value at $T = 12$ m							24.80	20.28
Call value today = discounted at							22.70	18.56
Saving with barrier option 3 % per period								18.24%

---

[2]Adapted from Peter James, *Option Theory*, John Wiley and Sons, England, 2003, pp. 180, 181; and Desmond Higham, *An Introduction to Financial Option Valuation*, Cambridge University Press, 2004, p. 190.

Exotic Options

EXHIBIT 17.6 Important formulae for valuing barrier options

$$B: \quad S \cdot N(d_1) - X \cdot e^{-rT} \cdot N(d_2)$$

$$E: \quad S \cdot N(e_1) - X \cdot e^{-rT} \cdot N(e_2)$$

$$F: \quad \left(\frac{B}{S}\right)^{\frac{2r}{\sigma^2}+1} \cdot S \cdot N(f_2) - \left(\frac{B}{S}\right)^{\frac{2r}{\sigma^2}-1} \cdot X \cdot e^{-rt} \cdot N(f_1)$$

$$G: \quad \left(\frac{B}{S}\right)^{\frac{2r}{\sigma^2}+1} \cdot S \cdot N(g_2) - \left(\frac{B}{S}\right)^{\frac{2r}{\sigma^2}-1} \cdot X \cdot e^{-rt} \cdot N(g_1)$$

Where

$$d_1 = \frac{\ln(S/X) + (r + \sigma^2/2)T}{\sigma\sqrt{T}}; \quad d_2 = \frac{\ln(S/X) + (r - \sigma^2/2)T}{\sigma\sqrt{T}} \quad \text{or} \quad d_2 = d_1 - \sigma\sqrt{T}$$

$$e_1 = \frac{\ln(S/B) + (r + \sigma^2/2)T}{\sigma\sqrt{T}}; \quad e_2 = \frac{\ln(S/B) + (r - \sigma^2/2)T}{\sigma\sqrt{T}} \quad \text{or} \quad e_2 = e_1 - \sigma\sqrt{T}$$

$$f_1 = \frac{\ln(S/B) - (r - \sigma^2/2)T}{\sigma\sqrt{T}}; \quad f_2 = \frac{\ln(S/B) - (r + \sigma^2/2)T}{\sigma\sqrt{T}} \quad \text{or} \quad f_2 = f_1 - \sigma\sqrt{T}$$

$$g_1 = \frac{\ln(S/B^2) - (r - \sigma^2/2)T}{\sigma\sqrt{T}}; \quad g_2 = \frac{\ln(SX/B^2) - (r + \sigma^2/2)T}{\sigma\sqrt{T}} \quad \text{or} \quad g_2 = g_1 - \sigma\sqrt{T}$$

Table 17.8 Valuation of barrier options

Call			Put	
Type	Barrier conditions	Valuation*	Type	Barrier conditions
Knock-in options				
Down-and-In	$X < B$	$B - E + F$	Up-and-In	$X > B$
Down-and-In	$X > B$	G	Up-and-In	$X < B$
Up-and-In	$X < B$	$E + F - G$	Down-and-In	$X > B$
Up and In	$X > B$	B	Down-and-In	$X < B$
Knock-out options				
Down-and-out	$X < B$	$E - F$	Up-and-out	$X > B$
Down-and-out	$X > B$	$B - G$	Up-and-out	$X < B$
Up-and-out	$X < B$	$B - E - F + G$	Down-and out	$X > B$
Up-and-out	$X > B$	0	Down-and out	$X < B$

*Refers to expressions given in Exhibit 17.6

Consider the holder of knock-in and knock-out call options with a spot of ₹100, an exercise of ₹110, and a barrier of ₹90. At the time of creating the position, the knock-in option is in-the-money but dead. The down-and-out call is alive. If the spot remains above the barrier of ₹90, the original position continues till maturity. If the spot falls below the barrier of ₹90, the knockout call option expires, but the knock-in call becomes alive. Therefore, one of the options would always be alive and thus, the combination of a knock-in with same barrier and strike prices and a knock-out is equal to a plain vanilla option.

The application of Eq. 17.19 may be verified in the values of the knock-in and knock-out options given in Table 17.8. They would add up to B, the BSM value of a European call.

ASIAN OPTIONS

Asian options have a payoff that is not entirely determined by the price of the underlying asset at maturity but is based on the average price during the life of the option. These options are also called average options. Like barriers, they are also path dependent, as their values also depend upon the path the asset values take during the option periods. The payoff on an average option is given by Eq. 17.20.

> Asian options provide payoff depending upon the average over option period, and suit business needs.

$$\text{For a call} \quad \text{Max}(0, S_a - X)$$
$$\text{For a put} \quad \text{Max}(0, X - S_a) \quad (17.20)$$

where S_a is the average of the spot prices during the option period.

Another kind of Asian option is the average strike option, where the strike price is based on the average. The payoff on an average strike option is based on the final price, S_T, and the average price during the period, as given by Eq. 17.21.

$$\text{For a call} \quad \text{Max}(0, S_T - S_a)$$
$$\text{For a put} \quad \text{Max}(0, S_a - S_T) \quad (17.21)$$

where S_a is the average of the spot price during the option period and S_T is the price at maturity of the option.

Average strike options ensure that the final price during the period matches the average during the period.

Applications

Asian options are very popular because of:

> Asian options are popular because they provide hedging based on averages rather than end values.

- the practice of judging performance for a given period based on the average during the period;
- the averages present a fairer view, as they are more difficult to manipulate than end-of-the-period prices; and
- being cheaper than plain vanilla options because averages have less volatility than end-of-the-period prices.

Due to these reasons, hedging based on average rather than end-of-the-period values makes more sense in terms of fairness of comparison and cost effectiveness.

Asian options are more common in foreign currency transactions, where exporters and importers are more interested in the average exchange rate during a given period than in one single value at the end of the period. The underlying for determining the payoff is the average. An exporter would like to buy a put option whose payoff is determined by the average over a quarter, rather than the end-of-the-quarter value. Similarly, an importer would buy a call option with the average over the quarter to compare the actual cost over the period. Investments in the equity market and financial assets also follow a common strategy of averaging for purposes of smoothing the investment value. For those who want to avoid extreme views on the prices of assets, Asian options have tremendous appeal, irrespective of the exposure in any underlying asset.

Average options are cheaper than regular options. For example, consider, as an alternative to an average option, the buying of 13 weekly options covering the quarter. The payoff in the case of 13 weekly options would be better than the one quarterly average option. The logic is simple. Of the 13 weekly options, some of the options would expire worthless when the price is not favourable. In the case of put options for exporters, the spot rate could be higher than the strike during some of the weeks. These spot values are not counted. In case of an average option, none of the values would be ignored, as they are used in calculating the average. All the values would be included in the average, and, hence, the payoff would be smaller than the series of independent equivalent options. Further, the average itself is a smoothing phenomenon and has less volatility. We know that option prices are driven by the volatility of the underlying asset. This makes average options cheaper than vanilla options based on end-values.

> Asian options are cheaper because averages include all values, and have less volatility than spot values.

Valuation

The question of averaging has two dimensions:

- How often will price samples be taken? The options can be daily, weekly, or monthly.
- Which average would be considered? The choices are arithmetic or geometric.

The valuation of Asian options presents problems due to the fact that while the distribution of stock prices is known to be log-normal, the probability distribution of the average is unknown. Most average options are based on the arithmetic average. This poses great problem in valuation because the probability distribution of the arithmetic average is not known, and, therefore, an analytical solution such as the BSM is not possible. However, it is possible to have an analytical solution for Asian options that is based on geometric averages, because geometric averages would have the same probability distribution as prices.

Arithmetic Average, $A_a = (S_0 + S_1 + S_2 \ldots\ldots S_N)^{1/(N+1)}$

$$= \frac{1}{N+1} \sum_{0}^{N} S_n \quad (17.22)$$

Geometric Average, $A_g = (S_0 \times S_1 \times S_2 \ldots\ldots S_n)^{1/(N+1)}$

Natural log of geometric average, A_G

$$= \ln \frac{A_g}{S_0} = \frac{1}{N+1} \sum_{0}^{N} \ln S_n \quad (17.23)$$

From Eq. 17.23, it is clear that the geometric average, being the sum of the log-normal of the spot values, is normally distributed because the log of the stock prices is normally distributed. Such an inference is not possible for the arithmetic average.

The valuation of average options based on the geometric average is possible on the lines of the BSM with the parameters of drift and volatility changing. The expected value of the geometric average is given by:

$$E(A_g) = \frac{1}{N+1} \sum_{0}^{N} E(r_1 + r_2 + r_3 \ldots\ldots r_n) = \frac{1}{N+1} \sum_{0}^{N} n \cdot E(r) \text{ with } E(r) = m\partial t$$

$$= \frac{1}{N+1} m \, \partial t \sum_{0}^{N} = \frac{1}{N+1} m \, t \frac{N(N+1)}{2}$$

$$= m \, \partial t \frac{N}{2} = \frac{mT}{2} \qquad (17.24)$$

Similarly, the variance of the geometric mean is stated as

$$Var(A_g) = \frac{1}{(N+1)^2} \sum_{0}^{N} Var(r_1 + r_2 + r_3 \ldots\ldots r_n)$$

$$= \frac{1}{(N+1)^2} \sum_{0}^{N} n^2 \cdot VarE(r) \text{ with } VarE(r) = \sigma^2 \partial t$$

$$= \frac{1}{(N+1)^2} \sigma^2 \, \partial t \sum_{0}^{N} n^2 = \frac{1}{(N+1)^2} \sigma^2 \, \partial t \frac{N(N+1)(2N+1)}{6}$$

$$= \sigma^2 \, \partial t \frac{N(2N+1)}{3(2N+2)} = \sigma^2 T \frac{(2N+1)}{3(2N+2)}$$

$$= \frac{\sigma^2 T}{3} \text{ (For large N)} \qquad (17.25)$$

From Eqs 17.24 and 17.25, we may state that

- the expected growth of the average, m_g, would be half of the growth of the underlying spot, m; and
- the variance of the average, σ_g^2, can be approximated to one third of the variance of the underlying, σ^2.

With these modifications, we may now apply the BSM for valuing the geometric average options. Under the BSM, the growth, $m = r - q - \sigma^2/2$, would stand modified to $m_g = m/2 = \frac{1}{2}(r - q - \sigma^2/2)$ and $\sigma_g = \sigma/\sqrt{3}$, with dividend yield changing to $q_g = \frac{1}{2}(r + q + \sigma^2/2)$. The value of the call with geometric average is given by Eq. 17.18.

$$c_g = S.e^{-q_g T} \cdot N(d_1) - X.e^{-rT} \cdot N(d_2) \qquad (17.26)$$

where $d_1 = \dfrac{\ln(S/X) + \frac{1}{2}(r - q + \sigma^2/6)T}{\sigma\sqrt{T/3}}$; and

$d_2 = \dfrac{\ln(S/X) + \frac{1}{2}(r - q + \sigma^2/6)T}{\sigma\sqrt{T/3}}$ or $d_2 = d_1 - \sigma\sqrt{T/3}$

> The valuation of Asian options is extremely difficult because the average is not log-normally distributed, for which an analytical model like the BSM applies

The value of the average options as given by Eq. 17.26 applies to the geometric average. In practice, average options are based on the arithmetic average. Since the arithmetic average and the geometric average are fairly close, the normal approach is to apply a correction factor to the value of the geometric average option. One such approach is to calculate the first moment and the second moment of the average in the risk-neutral world, which are given as M_1 and M_2, respectively (with $a = r - q$), as follows:

$$M_1 = \frac{e^{aT} - 1}{aT} S$$

$$M_2 = \frac{2e^{(2a + \sigma^2)T} \cdot S^2}{(a + \sigma^2)(2a + \sigma^2)T^2} + \frac{2S^2}{aT^2}\left(\frac{1}{2a + \sigma^2} - \frac{e^{aT}}{a + \sigma^2}\right)$$

Assuming the average as a log-normal distribution, the value of the call can be calculated by using Black's model (for future options) by substituting the forward price, F_0, and standard deviation, σ, by the following[3]:

$$F_0 = M_1$$
$$\sigma^2 = \frac{1}{T} \ln \frac{M_2}{M_1^2}$$

Using the binomial model for valuing Asian options Like with the valuation of barrier options, the binomial method may be used for valuing options based on averages. Being path dependent, the interim values become important and are aptly considered in binomial trees. Consider an ATM Asian call option based on the average for a stock trading at ₹100. Let us attempt the valuation of a call option using a three-stage binomial tree. Assume the risk-free rate at 2% per period and the up and down movements at 10% in each period. The risk-neutral probability of the up and down movements would be 0.60 and 0.40, respectively.

While valuing a regular call option, we need to find only the end values in the binomial tree and then determine the payoff on the option with the given strike price. The values in the intermediate periods have no significance. While valuing an option based on averages, there is little to do with end values. It is because the payoff is not dependent upon the end value alone, but also on the path taken to reach the end value. The path decides the average, and, hence, the payoff. The end value is only one of the values used in calculation of the average.

There are four end values and eight possible paths, as depicted in the binomial tree in Fig. 17.7. The valuation of average options by a binomial tree is more complex because for this kind of valuation, all eight paths need to be evaluated separately. This is because the average under each path would be different, even though multiple or many paths lead to the same end value. For binomial valuation of regular options, all paths that lead to the same end value may be combined.

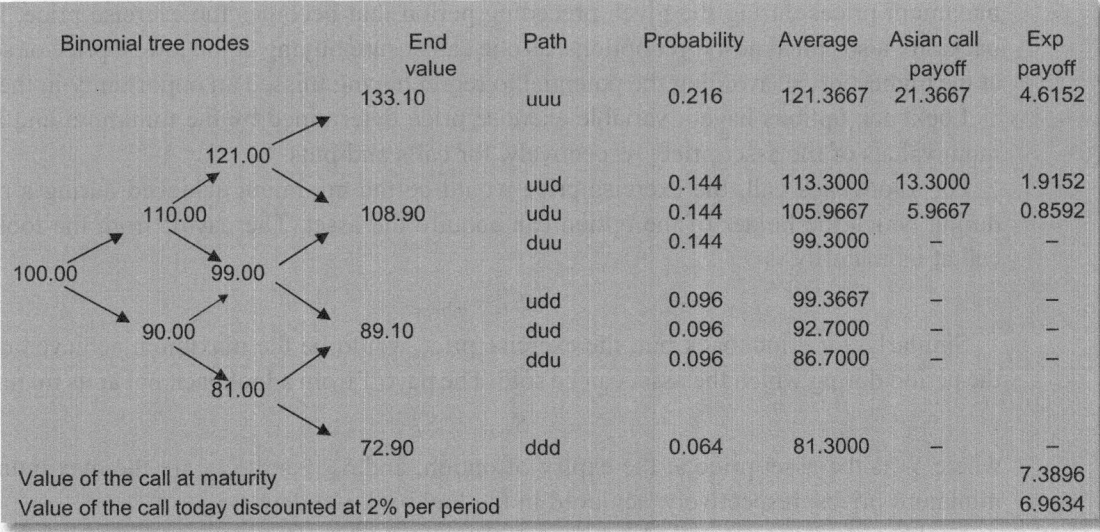

Fig. 17.7 Binomial valuation of Asian call

---
[3]Hull, John C., *Options, Futures, and Other Derivatives*, 7th Ed, Pearson Education, 2009, p. 557.

Consider two in-between values of the tree. They can be achieved by three paths each. For a regular call, the payoff would be the same for these middle nodes. However, for an Asian option, there would be three different payoffs at each of the middle nodes because the average in each path would be different. The average is calculated on the path taken for three prices in three periods. The payoff is Max(Average − X, 0), which is multiplied by the respective probabilities to get the expected payoff. This is discounted at the risk-free rate of 2% per period to get the value of the Asian call option today.

All calculations are shown in Fig. 17.7.

We may check if an Asian option costs less than a regular call. The value of the regular call may be computed by discounting the expected payoff at the risk-free rate. The payoff at the four final nodes would be ₹33.10, ₹8.90, ₹0.00, and ₹0.00, respectively, with a strike price of ₹100.00.

The value of the expected payoff at the end = 33.10 × 0.216 + 8.90 × 0.432
$$= 7.1496 + 3.8448 = ₹10.9944$$

Therefore, the value of the call at $t = 0 = 10.9944/1.02^3 = ₹10.3602 \approx ₹10.36$ (rounded off)

A call based on the average is cheaper than a regular call due to the reduced payoff and reduced volatility.

LOOKBACK OPTIONS

Lookback options are options that allow the holder to exercise them to (a) buy the asset at the minimum price over a given past period, for a call, and (b) sell the asset at the maximum of the prices for a given past period, for a put. The holder is allowed to look back at the price data for a period and determine the exercise price. The distinctive feature of the lookback option is that it would not remain unexercised, as there would always be some minimum and maximum prices during the given preceding period that becomes the exercise price. Lookbacks are also called no-regret options, as one can ensure buying at the lowest price or selling at the highest price, avoiding the potential to regret having missed an opportunity in the past.

Lookback options have a variable exercise price determined by the minimum and maximum values of the asset price, respectively, for calls and puts.

For a lookback call, the exercise price would be the minimum achieved during a period during which the holder of the option can acquire the asset. The payoff from the lookback call at its maturity is

$$S_T - S_{min}$$

Similarly, for a lookback put, the exercise price would be the maximum achieved during the period during which the asset can be sold. The payoff from a lookback put at its maturity is

$$S_{max} - S_T$$

where S_T is the asset price at the expiry of option, and S_{max} and S_{min} are the maximum and minimum prices, respectively, achieved in the lookback window.

Lookback options are path dependent as the payoff is dependent upon the prices achieved in the past rather than on the ending values alone.

Applications

Lookback options are very attractive for investors because of their potential to provide large payoffs. Usually, investment in mutual fund is made by vesting equivalent units at the current net asset value (NAV). The units are redeemed at the NAV prevailing at the time of exit. The NAV changes as the prices of stocks change. The product may be modified and made attractive for investors by incorporating a feature that enables subscribers to look back at the NAVs during the investment horizon for the purpose of redemption. For example, a mutual fund may offer a product where it undertakes to redeem units from subscribers at the maximum NAV achieved during a pre-specified period. It is kind of lookback put option where subscribers hold a right to redeem their investments at a highest NAV.

Valuation

In most cases, the payoff from a lookback option would be positive and substantial. It can at worst be zero. This would happen only when the minimum or maximum happens at the expiry of the option period. The lookback option, therefore, would not expire worthless and would necessarily be exercised. Hence, the cost of lookback options would be prohibitively high as compared to their counterpart plain vanilla options.

The lookback option can be valued using the binomial approach with risk neutrality, in the similar manner as that used for Asian options.

The payoff on the lookback call at maturity is $S_T - S_{min}$. For a lookback call with maturity at T, the value at its inception would be the discounted value of its expected payoff. Mathematically, this is expressed as

$$c(LB) = e^{-rT} \times E(S_T - S_{min})$$
$$= e^{-rT} E(S_T) - e^{-rT} E(S_{min})$$

For risk neutrality, the stock must grow at the risk-free rate. Therefore, $E(S_T) = e^{rt} \cdot S_0$. The value of the call now is

$$c(LB) = S_0 - e^{-rT} E(S_{min}) \qquad (17.27)$$

The payoff of the lookback put at maturity is $S_{max} - S_T$. For a lookback put with maturity at T, the value at its inception would be the discounted value of its expected payoff. Mathematically, this is expressed as

$$p(LB) = e^{-rT} \times E(S_{max} - S_T)$$
$$= e^{-rT} E(S_{max}) - e^{-rT} E(S_T)$$

For risk neutrality the stock must grow at the risk-free rate. Therefore, $E(S_T) = e^{rt} \cdot S_0$. The value of the put now is

$$p(LB) = e^{-rT} E(S_{max}) - S_0 \qquad (17.28)$$

A simple illustration would demonstrate the applicability of the binomial approach. Assuming that the current price of an asset is ₹100, which can change by ±10%. With a risk-free return of 3% per period, the probability of an up move is (1.03 − 0.9)/(1.1 − 0.9) = 0.65 or 65% and the probability of a down move is 1 − 0.65 = 0.35 or 35% under the binomial approach. A two-stage binomial tree is depicted in Fig. 17.8.

510 Derivatives and Risk Management

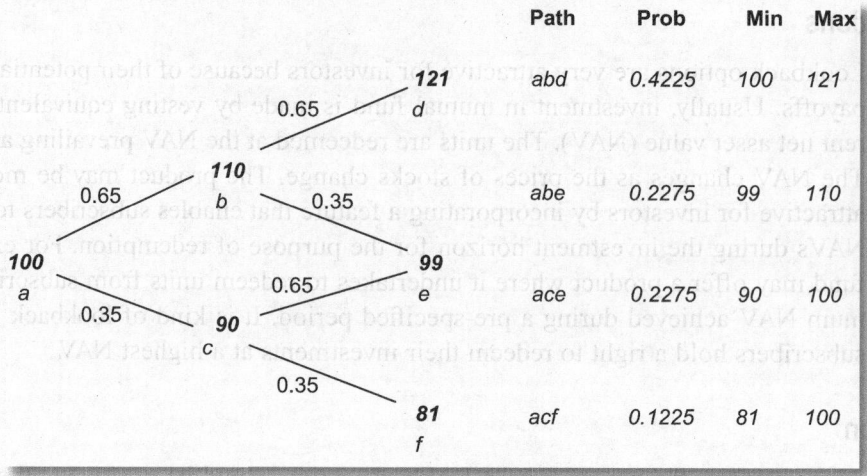

Fig. 17.8 Binomial tree for valuation of lookback options

The expected minimum price $E(S_{min})$ would be

$$E(S_{min}) = 100 \times 0.4225 + 99 \times 0.2275 + 90 \times 0.2275 + 81 \times 0.1225$$
$$= ₹95.1700$$

The present value of the expected minimum price is $95.1700/1.03^2 = 89.71$. Hence, the value of the lookback call is

$$c(LB) = S_0 - e^{-rT} E(S_{min}) = 100.00 - 89.71 = ₹10.29$$

The expected maximum price $E(S_{max})$ would be

$$E(S_{max}) = 121 \times 0.4225 + 110 \times 0.2275 + 100 \times 0.2275 + 100 \times 0.1225$$
$$= ₹111.1475$$

The present value of the expected minimum price is $111.1475/1.03^2 = 104.77$. Hence the value of a lookback put is

$$p(LB) = e^{-rT} E(S_{max}) - S_0 = 104.77 - 100.00 = ₹4.77$$

Lookback options are more expensive than vanilla options. The values of plain vanilla call and put options with an exercise price of ₹100 are worked out as ₹8.36 and ₹2.62, respectively, in the following table.

Table 17.9 Valuing regular call and put

Node	Probability	Call option		Put option	
		Payoff	Value	Payoff	Value
d	0.4225	21.00	8.8725	–	–
e	0.4550	–	–	1.00	0.4550
f	0.1225	–	–	19.00	2.3275
Expected payoff at maturity, ₹			8.8725		2.7825
Value of the option today, ₹			8.36		2.62

EXAMPLE 17.4 Lookback options

An investor observes that a stock has been trading in a narrow range between ₹90 and ₹100, but is likely to break out of the resistance at ₹100 soon. The investor regrets having missed a buying opportunity at ₹90. Assuming volatility at 30%, a dividend yield at 5%, and a risk-free rate at 10%, compare the values of a plain vanilla call and a lookback call with expiry of six months from now.

Solution

With $S = ₹100$, $S_{min} = ₹90$, $r = 10\%$, $q = 5\%$, $T = 0.5$ years, and $\sigma = 30\%$, the values of the intermediate parameters would be

$a_1 = 0.7209$	$N(a_1) = 0.7645$	$N(-a_1) = 0.2355$
$a_2 = 0.5088$	$N(a_2) = 0.6946$	$N(-a_2) = 0.3054$
$a_3 = 0.4851$	$N(a_3) = 0.6862$	$N(-a_3) = 0.3138$
$b_1 = 0.4375$	$N(b_1) = 0.6691$	$N(-b_1) = 0.3309$
$b_2 = 0.2254$	$N(b_2) = 0.5892$	$N(-b_2) = 0.4108$
$b_3 = 0.6733$	$N(b_3) = 0.7496$	$N(-b_3) = 0.2504$
$Y1 = 0.0117$		$e^{Y1} = 1.0118$
$Y2 = 0.0106$		$e^{Y2} = 1.0107$

The value of the lookback call using the formula given in the Exhibit 17.7 comes to ₹18.89.

For the same parameters of $S = ₹100$, $X = ₹90$, $r = 10\%$, $q = 5\%$, $T = 0.5$ years, and $\sigma = 30\%$, the values of the intermediate parameters for the plain vanilla option would be

$$d_1 = -0.2254, \quad d_2 = -0.4375, \quad N(d_1) = 0.4108, \quad N(d_2) = 0.3309$$

And the value of the call is ₹12.55 as per the Merton model.

In contrast, the lookback call costs ₹18.89, approximately 50% more than the plain vanilla call.

EXHIBIT 17.7 Valuation of lookback options#

$$c(LB) = S.e^{-qT}.N(a_1) - S.e^{-qT}\frac{\sigma^2}{2(r-q)}.N(a_1) - S_{min}.e^{-rT}\left[N(a_2) - \frac{\sigma^2}{2(r-q)}e^{Y1}.N(-a_3)\right]$$

$$p(LB) = -S.e^{-qT}.N(b_2) + S.e^{-qT}\frac{\sigma^2}{2(r-q)}.N(-b_2) + S_{max}.e^{-rT}\left[N(b_1) - \frac{\sigma^2}{2(r-q)}e^{Y2}.N(-b_3)\right]$$

where

$$a_1 = \frac{\ln\left[\frac{S}{S_{min}}\right] + \left(r - q + \frac{\sigma^2}{2}\right)T}{\sigma\sqrt{t}} \qquad b_1 = \frac{\ln\left[\frac{S_{max}}{S}\right] + \left(-r + q + \frac{\sigma^2}{2}\right)T}{\sigma\sqrt{T}}$$

$$a_2 = a_1 - \sigma\sqrt{T} \qquad b_2 = b_1 - \sigma\sqrt{T}$$

$$a_3 = \frac{\ln\left[\frac{S}{S_{min}}\right] + \left(-r - q + \frac{\sigma^2}{2}\right)T}{\sigma\sqrt{T}} \qquad b_3 = \frac{\ln\left[\frac{S_{max}}{S}\right] + \left(r - q + \frac{\sigma^2}{2}\right)T}{\sigma\sqrt{T}}$$

$$Y_1 = \frac{\ln\left[\frac{S}{S_{min}}\right] \times 2\left(r - q + \frac{\sigma^2}{2}\right)T}{\sigma^2} \qquad Y_3 = \frac{\ln\left[\frac{S_{max}}{S}\right] \times 2\left(r - q - \frac{\sigma^2}{2}\right)}{\sigma^2}$$

S = Price of stock now
S_{min} = Minimum stock price before initiating lookback option
S_{max} = Maximum stock price before initiating lookback option
T = Time for expiration of option
σ = Annualized standard deviation

r = Risk-free rate of return
q = Continuous dividend on asset
$N(x)$ = Cumulative normal distribution function at x
ln = Natural log

Goldman, Sosin, and Gatto Formula

Analytical solutions for pricing of lookbacks are provided in the box for continuously observed values of the underlying asset.

Bermudan Option The Bermudan option allows exercise at several predetermined times rather than at any time, as is the case with American option, or only at maturity, as is the case with European option.

Basket Option A basket option is an option whose payoff depends upon several assets rather than a single asset. These are normally several stocks, indices, or foreign currencies.

SOLVED PROBLEMS

SP 17.1: Forward start option

The CEO of a firm has promised the board a 50% increase in performance in three years, as measured by the firm's stock price. The board of directors of the firm has offered a stock option plan to the CEO whereby he can acquire shares in the firm at 110% of the current price at the end of three years. However, they have placed the condition that the option would start only after one year from today. Assume that the current stock price is ₹100, the risk-free rate is 8%, and volatility is 25%. What is the value of this option to the CEO?

Solution

The value of the option at the commencement of the forward period depends upon the price of the stock at the end of one year, S_1, the exercise price of ₹110, and the period of two years remaining thereafter. This is equal to the value of the option today with time to maturity of $(3 - 1) = 2$ years. Using the BSM, the value of the call, c(100, 110, 2), is ₹16.95. Discounting the value at the commencement of the exercise arrived at ₹16.95, the value of the call starting one year forward is $0.9231 \times 16.95 = ₹15.64$.

If the CEO were offered the stock options commencing now, the value of the call, c(100,110, 3), is ₹23.60.

SP 17.2: Valuing the barrier option

Refer to Fig. 17.7, showing a binomial tree used for valuing a down-and-out barrier call option with a strike of ₹85 and a barrier of ₹90. Use the same tree for valuing an up-and-out call option with a strike of ₹100 and a barrier of ₹120.

Solution

The up and out option means that any time the price goes above the barrier of ₹120, the call option becomes worthless. The current price is ₹100. For the three-stage binomial tree with a risk-free rate of 3% per period and an up and down movement of 10%, there would be four end prices with eight possible routes.

The four end prices are ₹133.10, ₹108.90, ₹89.10, and ₹72.90. With a call strike of ₹100, there would be a positive payoff only at the two upper prices. The value of a regular call would be

End price (₹)	Call payoff (₹)	Probability	Expected payoff (₹)
133.10	33.10	$0.65 \times 0.65 \times 0.65$	9.09
108.90	8.90	$0.65 \times 0.65 \times 0.35 \times 3$	3.95
Total expected payoff at maturity			13.04
Value of the regular call at $t = 0$ ($13.04/1.03^3$)			11.93

For valuation of the up and out barrier call, the node with end price of ₹133.10 becomes worthless, as the price is above the barrier. There is only one price, ₹108.90, which is above the strike and below the barrier. The end price of ₹108.90 can be achieved by the following three paths, each with a probability of $0.65 \times 0.65 \times 0.35$.

$100 \rightarrow\rightarrow 110 \rightarrow\rightarrow 121 \rightarrow\rightarrow 108.90$ The barrier is crossed

$100 \rightarrow\rightarrow 90 \rightarrow\rightarrow 99 \rightarrow\rightarrow 108.90$

$100 \rightarrow\rightarrow 110 \rightarrow\rightarrow 99 \rightarrow\rightarrow 108.90$

Therefore, the value of the call would be the payoff times the probability = $8.90 \times 0.65 \times 0.65 \times 0.35 \times 2 = ₹2.63$. The discounted value of the call at the risk-free rate of 3% per period is $2.63/1.03^3 = ₹2.41$.

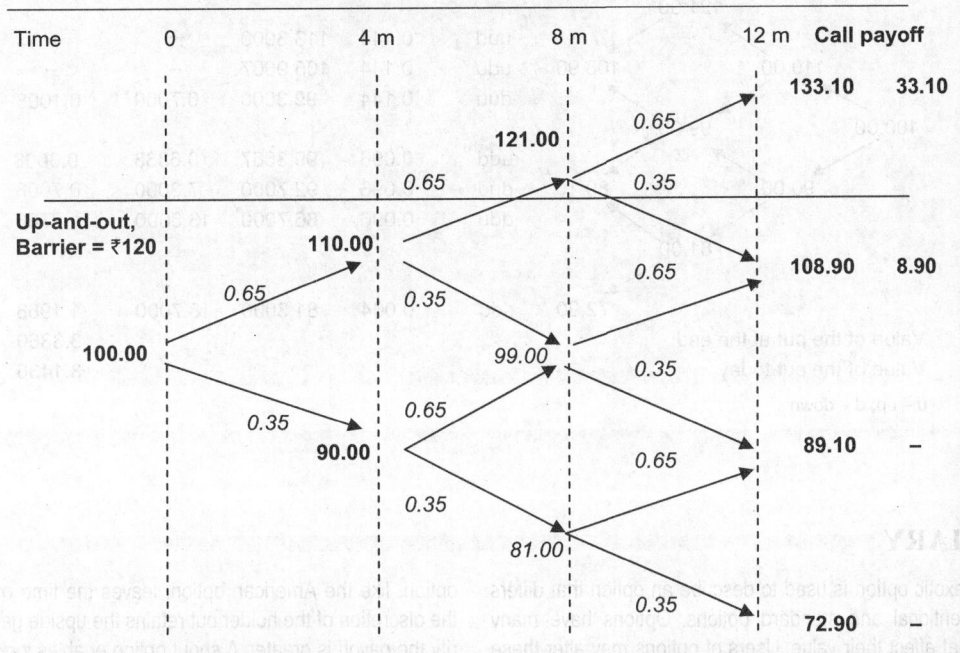

Binary tree for barrier option pricing for SP 17.2
Value of underlying asset with 10% up and 10% down movement
Exercise price of call ₹ = 100, Barrier price ₹ = 120. Up and out
Risk-free rate = 3% per period

SP 17.3: Binomial valuation of Asian put option

Consider the data in Fig. 17.4 for valuing an Asian call with a strike of ₹100. Use the same data for valuing an Asian put option with a strike of ₹100. Further, find the value of a regular put option with a strike of ₹100 and compare the values of the regular and the Asian put options.

Solution
For an option with a risk-free rate of 2% and up and down movement of 10% each, the risk-neutral probabilities of the up and down movements would be 60% and 40%, respectively. It would lead to four end values, but also eight paths that would have different averages for the purpose of valuation of the average option. These are shown in the following table, together with the respective probabilities. The average is calculated at three different points of time.

With a strike price of ₹100, the expected payoff and its value at the maturity of the put option are shown for each branch. The value of the Asian put option works out to ₹3.14.

The value of the regular put option would be independent of the path the end values take. The value of the regular put is calculated as follows:

End price (₹)	Put payoff (₹)	Probability	Expected payoff (₹)
133.10	–	–	–
108.90	–	–	–
89.10	10.90	$0.60 \times 0.40 \times 0.40 \times 3$	3.1392
72.90	27.10	$0.40 \times 0.40 \times 0.40$	1.7344
Total expected payoff at maturity			4.8736
Value of the regular call at $t = 0$ discounted at 2% per period			4.5925

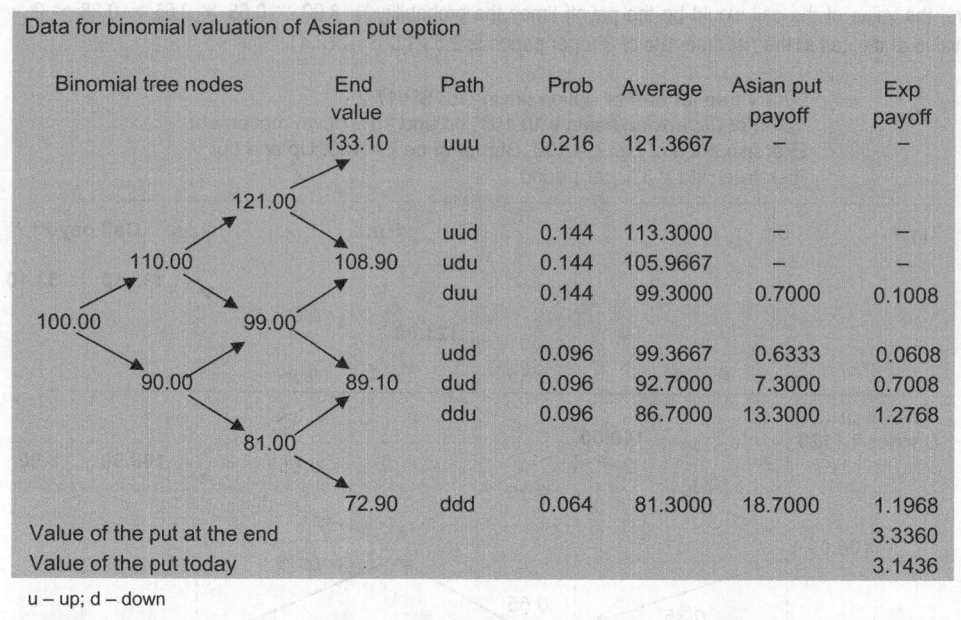

SUMMARY

The term exotic option is used to describe an option that differs from conventional and standard options. Options have many features that affect their value. Users of options may alter these features to accommodate their specific needs. The terms of the options are changed with respect to the type of option, the exercise price, the frequency and time of exercise, the path for determination of the payoff, the commencement date, etc.

Innovations in changing the terms and conditions of the option are primarily motivated by (a) the specific needs of the users and (b) the reduced cost of these products. Some people may believe that since the terms of exotic options are not standard, they would cost more. On the contrary, most exotic options are cheaper because while a standard option charges a premium for all possible situations, the exotic option rules out some of them. That is one of the reasons for its popularity.

Forward start options start at some time in the future. Starting later means reducing the life of the option, and, hence, the premium. They are used mainly in the employee stock option schemes aimed at motivating employees. Another simple option is the binary or digital option, which is characterized by two discrete levels of payoff. It pays a fixed sum or nothing (called a cash or nothing option) or the underlying asset or nothing (called an asset or nothing option). The payoff is easier to comprehend, and, hence, so is the valuation. Another interesting exotic option is the chooser option, which permits the holder to have another option at maturity—which can be either a call or a put. A shout option, like the American option, leaves the time of exercise to the discretion of the holder but retains the upside gain if at maturity the payoff is greater. A shout option enables locking-in of the intrinsic value of the option at any time during its life.

An exchange option is one where one asset is exchanged for another. Mergers and acquisitions are instances where the shares of the acquired firm are exchanged for the shares of the acquiring firm. A gap option, as the name implies, has a payoff that depicts a gap on exercise. The gap is governed by a figure different from the strike price, though the strike price continues to decide the exercise. A pay-later option is one where the premium is payable only at its expiry, when it is exercised. A compound option is an option on another option. The exercise of the first option gives another option to the holder.

Barrier options are unique in several ways. Besides the strike price, they have another price called the barrier, which is used to determine whether the option is dead or alive. The payoff on the option is not only dependent on the price at maturity but also on the path it took in reaching that price. If the option becomes alive on reaching the barrier, it is called a knock-in option, and if it becomes dead, it is called a knock-out option. If the price goes above the barrier and the option becomes alive only then, it is called an up and in option, and if it becomes dead, it is an up and out option. Similarly, a down and in option becomes alive if the price goes below the barrier, and a down and out option is dead if the price goes below the barrier. Valuation of these options is complex because of an extra element, the barrier price. Under all circumstances, these options are cheaper than regular options because they have situations that do not keep them alive for part of the life of the options.

Another type of path-dependent options is the Asian option, whose payoff is based on the average price during the period rather than on the price at expiry. It is a better way of hedging, as most business performances are compared against the average. It makes Asian options extremely popular. Apart from representing business needs better, Asian options are also cheaper than regular options for two reasons. First, for options on average, the payoff is smaller than for regular options, as while calculating the average, all prices during the period are included, while for regular options, calculations exclude the prices that make them out-of-the-money. Second, the volatility of options based on averages would be less than that of options based on single prices, because the average smoothens out variations. The valuation of average options is extremely difficult, because the arithmetical average does not follow any known probability distribution.

Lookback options also are path dependent, as they provide an opportunity to the holder to buy (lookback call) the asset at the minimum price or sell (lookback put) the asset at the maximum price observed in the past.

There are a large number of other exotics that are also available. They are OTC products, essentially leaving the terms and conditions to be decided upon by the two parties involved.

KEY TERMS

Asian option An option whose payoff depends upon the average for the period of the option rather than the terminal value of the asset price.

Asset or nothing binary option An option that pays either the asset or nothing at maturity.

Barrier option An option whose value depends not only on the spot and exercise prices but also on another price called the barrier.

Binary option or digital option Options that have only two states of payoff.

Cash or nothing binary option An option that pays a fixed amount of cash or nothing at the maturity.

Chooser option A chooser option grants the holder the right to choose between the call and the put at maturity.

Compound option An option on another option where exercise of the first option gives another option to the holder.

Down-and-in option An option that comes to life only when the price of the underlying asset goes below a pre-specified level, called the barrier price.

Down-and-out option An option that becomes dead when the price of the underlying asset goes below a pre-specified level, called the barrier price.

Exchange option An option where one asset is exchanged for another.

Forward start option An option on which the commencement date starts some time in the future, and not now.

Gap option A gap option has a payoff that is governed by a figure different from the strike price, though the strike price continues to decide the exercise.

Lookback option A lookback option provides an opportunity to buy the asset at the minimum price or sell the asset at the maximum price observed in the past.

Pay-later option A option is one where the premium is payable only at its expiry, and only when it is exercised.

Shout option A shout option provides flexibility to the holder to book the minimum of the intrinsic values or the final value at the end of the option period.

Up-and-in option An option that comes to life only when the price of the underlying asset goes above a pre-specified level, called the barrier price.

Up-and-out option An option that becomes dead when the price of the underlying asset goes above a pre-specified level, called the barrier price.

QUESTIONS

17.1 What are exotic options and why are they popular?

17.2 What is a forward start option? What could its possible usages be?

17.3 How does advancing the commencement of a forward start option affect its price?
Describe how you would value such an option maturing at T but starting at t?

17.4 Describe the payoff on cash or nothing binary call and put options. How are they different from asset or nothing binary options?

17.5 What is a chooser option and how would you value it?

17.6 A shout option allows the holder to lock in the minimum value that he/she thinks is the maximum. Elaborate on the statement.

17.7 What difficulties are faced in valuing shout options?

17.8 Describe barrier options and distinguish between knock-in and knock-out options.

17.9 When do you think you would use (a) up and out barrier options, and (b) down and in barrier options? Illustrate with suitable examples.

17.10 What are Asian options? Why are they popular and what are the difficulties faced in valuing them?

PROBLEMS

P 17.1 Forward start option
Executives in the top management of an IT firm have been offered a total of one lakh stock options with an exercise price 20% higher than the current stock price of ₹120. The options would come into operation one year from now and would remain valid for another three years. The value of the stock options has to be reflected in the financial statements of the company as employee compensation. If the volatility of the stock is 20% and the risk-free rate is 8%, what is the amount that would be charged in the financial statement for the options so granted?

P 17.2 Binary option
A firm has announced that every middle-level manager would get a bonus of one month's salary if the performance of the company exceeds the expectations of its stockholders. The current stock price is ₹1000, and for entitlement to the bonus, the stock price at the end of the year must be ₹1200 or more. The volatility of the stock is placed at 20% and the risk-free rate is 8%. Find out the value of the option for an executive whose monthly salary is ₹10,000.

P 17.3 Asset or nothing binary option
What would the value of the option in P 17.2 be if the firm decided to give five shares instead of a fixed amount of bonus? Which of the two schemes, i.e., the fixed amount or the shares, would you choose?

P 17.4 Chooser option
The current price of a stock is ₹120. An investor is uncertain about the likely movement of the stock price but expects lot of volatility. He/she wants to choose in one month's time from now whether to buy an ATM call or put with a maturity of three months thereafter. The volatility of the stock is 30%, while the risk-free rate is 8% per annum. What price would you charge for allowing the investor to choose a call or a put after one month?

P 17.5 Valuing the Asian option
The spot value of a stock is ₹200. It can either go up by 20% or fall by 20% over a period of four months. Using the 3-stage binomial model with a risk-free rate of 2.50% per period, what would the value of a 12-m call option that pays off the excess of the average over the strike of ₹200 be? Include the initial price in computing the average. Further, value a standard call with a strike of ₹200.

P 17.6 Valuing the barrier option
Refer to the data in P 17.5. Find out the value of a 12-m down-and-In put option with a strike of ₹55 and a barrier of ₹45. Further, calculate the value of a 12-m standard put option with a strike of ₹55.

Interest Rate Options

INTRODUCTION

In this chfapter, we shall discuss some derivatives on interest rates—options on interest rates and options on bonds whose value is primarily dependent upon their interest rates. These derivatives are more complex to value than other options as the behaviour of their interest rates is more difficult tounderstand. The main products that are dependent on interest rates are bonds and swaps. Besides options with interest rates as direct underlying assets, we can have options on products such as bonds and swaps whose values are primarily dependent on interest rates, and, hence, can serve the purpose of hedging against interest rate fluctuations.

As usual, we need to highlight that forward contracts on interest rates, i.e.,the forward rate agreements (FRAs) discussed earlier are obligatory in nature. We also discussed interest rate futures in earlier chapter. Commitments under FRAs as well as interest rate futures are binding, irrespective of the outcome at maturity. Options on interest rates would provide a right without creating an obligation, just as options on any other assets do. In this chapter, we discuss interest rate options and options on bonds.

Learning Objectives

After going through this chapter, readers should be familiar with

- the description of interest rate options such as cap, floor, and collar
- hedging interest rate risk with cap, floor, and collar
- an introduction to Black's model for valuing options on interest rates
- managing interest rate risk through interest rate options
- options on bonds and the way to value these options
- valuing options on bonds using Black's model

INTEREST RATE OPTIONS

We examined the management of interest rate risk through interest rate swaps and interest rate futures. A swap is an instrument to transform a fixed rate liability/asset into a floating rate liability/asset, and vice versa. A borrower who has issued a floating rate bond can convert the interest rate liability to a fixed rate liability by entering into a swap when the

> Interest rate options work in the same manner as options on other assets. They cover the risks of changing interest rates.

interst rates start rising. Futures could be used to lock in the prevailing interest rate implied in treasury bills (T-bills) or treasury bonds. Under the FRA, one could lock-in interest rates for borrowings and deposits in advance, and thus, manage the interest rate risk. All these hedging instruments implied a cost in terms of sacrifice of potential gain from favourable changes in the interest rates.

In this section, we discuss another tool for managing interest rate risk, i.e., options. We can have options based on interest rates like we have options based on any other financial instrument as the underlying asset. Options that have interest rates as the underlying asset are referred to as *interest rate options*. They are called *caps*, *floors*, and *collars*. Unlike swaps and FRAs, options on interest rates are not firm commitments but are onlyrights for which a price has to be paid upfront. Options on interest rates are over-the-counter (OTC) products. Further, many bonds have these options embedded in the product itself.

CAP

> A cap is a series of call options exercised at those times that provide a payoff equal to the difference between the actual rate and the cap rate when the actual rate exceeds the strike.

Consider, for example, a borrowing firm that has issued bonds with semi-annual coupons determined on the basis of Mumbai Interbank Offer Rate (MIBOR). Assume that the firm pays interest to subscribers to the bond at each 6-m interval on the basis of the MIBOR that prevailed at the beginning of the period (coupons on floating rates are decided one period in advance). If MIBOR goes up, the liability of the firm too goes up. Can anything be done to contain the rising cost of debt?

To manage interest rate risk, one usual way is to issue a callable bond. The flexibility of making the bond callable is available only once, i.e., at the time of issue, and depends upon the interest rate scenario forecast made then. Further, it is usually once in a lifetime, before maturity, that the bond may be called. As the tenure of the bond increases, forecasting the future interest rate scenario becomes increasingly complex and difficult. One may issue a bond of 10 years with a right to call back at ₹110 between three and five years, at ₹105 between six and eight years, and at ₹102 anytime thereafter. Subscribers to such a bond can be considered to be holders of the bond with a call written, having conferred a right to the issuer to call back the bond. The issuer is short on the bond but long on the call.

Managing interest rate risk by issuing a callable bond does not offer flexibility and is based on perceptions at the time of the issue of the bond. Swaps, FRAs, and interest rate futures provide flexibility but forego profitable opportunities.

A cap is a call option on interest rates that gives a right without obligation to the holder to exercise the call and provides for flexibility as well as profitable opportunities. With a cap on interest rates, when the interest rate exceeds the strike interest rate, the holder exercises; otherwise, he/she lets the call expire. The cash flow under a call option is based on a notional principal, just as is the case with FRAs and swaps.

Hedging with Cap

Managing interest rate risk with a call provision is indeed difficult due to our limited ability to forecast interest rate scenarios for the distant future. Further, one needs to offer higher yields for callable bonds than for plain bonds. Therefore, callable bonds would trade at a lower price than comparable non-callable bonds. This implies a higher cost of borrowing for the firm issuing the callable bonds. As stated in the section titled 'Cap', fixing of the call price can only be done once, and, therefore, interest rate risk management does not remain flexible.

Alternatively, the borrowing firm can enter into another independent contract where the counterparty, normally a bank, undertake to compensate if the interest rate goes beyond a pre-specified level, called the strike. Rather than buying a call option from the subscriber to the callable bond, the interest rate option can be bought from another party at any time the issuing firm chooses.

Let us consider a firm that had issued a floating rate bond that has five years remaining for maturity, with semi-annual interest payments. Assume that the next 10 values of MIBOR will be as given in column 2 of Table 18.1. The firm would pay interest as per MIBOR. To limit its outflow, the firm may buy a cap from a bank with a strike of 7.60%. Under this cap, the firm would have a payoff of Max $(M - 7.60\%, 0) \times ½ \times$ notional principal. In case the MIBOR exceeds 7.60%, the firm would get the excess over 7.60% from the bank, and hence, limit the interest outgo to 7.60%.

> To contain the cost of borrowing, a firm buys a cap as a hedge against rising interest rates.

Table 18.1 Interest with and without cap

Time (months)	MIBOR %	Floating, rate interest %	Interest with cap %
0	7.00		
6	7.25	7.00	7.00
12	8.00	7.25	7.25
18	7.50	8.00	7.60
24	8.50	7.50	7.50
30	7.60	8.50	7.60
36	7.80	7.60	7.60
42	8.20	7.80	7.60
48	8.50	8.20	7.60
54	7.80	8.50	7.60
60	–	7.80	7.60

Payoff on Cap A cap is a series of European call options, called caplets, on interest rate. The buyer of a cap receives the payoff from the cap writer at each exercise date for a specified number of periods on a notional sum. It is an OTC product that is bought by a floating rate payer to protect against rising interest rates.

Based on the data in Table 18.1, the cost of borrowing to the firm is depicted in Fig. 18.1, where the firm limits the maximum outflow to 7.60%, the strike rate of the cap. The payoff from the cap at each exercise date, called a *caplet,* is like the payoff from a call option with the interest rate as underlying, as depicted in Fig. 18.2.

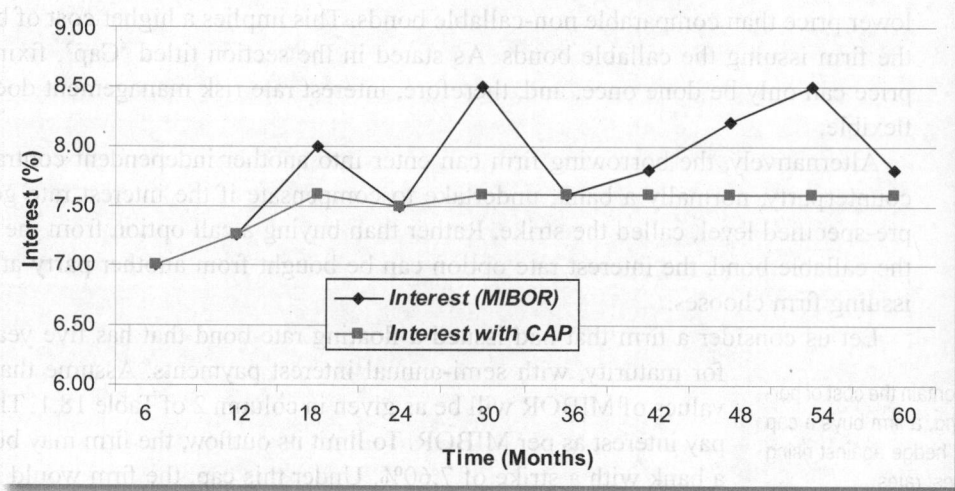

Fig. 18.1 Interest under Cap

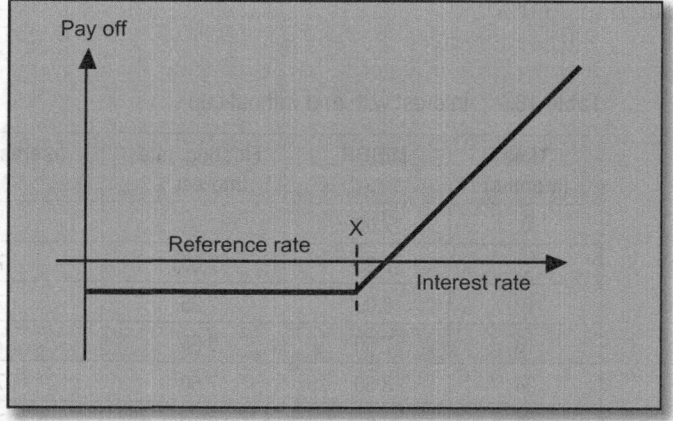

Fig. 18.2 Payoff of caplet at maturity

The payoff on the cap on each exercise date would depend upon (a) the reference rate, M, (b) the cap rate, X, (c) the notional loan amount, L, and (d) the number of times per year interest, m, is paid. The payoff on each exercise date is given by Eq. 18.1.

$$\frac{L}{m} \times Max\,(M - X,\,0) \qquad (18.1)$$

Like the FRA and the swap, the cap is an independent product, and it is immaterial whether an actual floating rate interest payment liability exists or not.

> A cap is a series of call options, called caplets, which pays the excess of the interest cost determined now, but paid one period later.

How Cap Works Let us assume that a firm has three years remaining on a floating rate borrowing based on MIBOR. Today ($t = 0$), it has observed a rate of MIBOR, M_0. It perceives a rising trend in MIBOR and, therefore, would like to contain the cost of borrowing to X. Let the amount of borrowing be L; it pays coupons semi-annually. The MIBOR observed today determines the next coupon payment due six months later.

To hedge against the rising interest rate, the firm can buy a cap with a cap rate of X. The first payoff on the cap would be decided after six months, when the coupon obligation would be known, but actual payment would be made at the end of 12 months. Thus, the cap would consist of a maximum of five payoffs, and the obligations of the cap writer would be determined at the end of 30 months, while the cash flow obligations would terminate at the end of 36 months from now. This is depicted in Fig. 18.3. Cash flows are crystallized one period in advance and paid on the due date.

Instant, n	0	1	2	3	4	5	6
Time in months	0	6	12	18	24	30	36
Observed MIBOR	M_0	M_1	M_2	M_3	M_4	M_5	
Interest flow		I_1	I_2	I_3	I_4	I_5	I_6
Cash flow from cap	—		CF_1	CF_2	CF_3	CF_4	CF_5

M_n is the observed 6-m MIBOR at time instant n
Cash flow from Cap, CF_n (at $t = n + 1$) = $L/2 \times \text{Max}(M_n - X, 0)$; X is the cap rate

Fig. 18.3 Determination of obligations and cash flows under cap

Valuation of Cap

In order to value a cap, we need to value each caplet separately as a call option and aggregate them to determine the premium that would be paid by the buyer of the cap. In interest rate options, the underlying asset is the interest rate at maturity. Interest rate derivatives are more complex than derivatives on stocks, indices, commodities, or foreign exchange because of the more complex behaviour of interest rates. Further, in the valuation model, we need to discount the cash flows, and for an interest rate derivative, the underlying asset is the interest rate itself.

The commonly used model for valuing interest rate options has been the binomial model. However, it is fairly complex. We turn our attention to the analytical model called Black's model. The Black–Scholes model (BSM), applicable for non-dividend paying stock, was extended to fit valuations of other options, such as those on indices and foreign currencies. It has also been extended for use in valuing interest rate options.

Under the assumption of deterministic interest rates, we can adopt a variation of the BSM to value interest rate options. In interest rate options, the underlying asset is the value of the interest rate at the expiration of the option period. The estimate of the interest rate today at the expiration of the option period would be the forward rate, i.e., the interest rate expected today to be applicable after 30 days if the option expiry is 30 days. Therefore, the underlying asset in an interest rate option becomes the forward interest rate. This rate can be derived by using the current term structure.

For using a valuation approach based on the BSM, we need the continuous compounding rate. This can be obtained from the term structure of the interest rates. If the 30-day MIBOR is 5% and the 120-day MIBOR is 5.2%[1], then the continuous compounding 30-day forward rate for 90-day investments is 5.28%.

---
[1]MIBOR follows the 30/360 convention.

$$\ln\left[\frac{1 + 0.052 \frac{120}{360}}{1 + 0.050 \frac{30}{360}}\right] \times \frac{365}{90} = 0.0528 \equiv 5.28\%$$

Each caplet may be valued using Black's model, given as Eq. 18.2, also known as the *standard market model*.

Value of caplet $= \frac{L}{m} \times c$

$$c = e^{-r(T + 1/m)}[F_0 \cdot N(d_1) - X.N(d_2)] \qquad (18.2)$$

Where L = notional amount of cap,
m = Nos of payments every year,
(2 for semi-annual and 4 for quarterly)

where

$$d_1 = \frac{\ln(F_0/X) + \sigma^2 T/2}{\sigma \sqrt{T}}, \text{ and}$$

$$d_2 = \frac{\ln(F_0/X) - \sigma^2 T/2}{\sigma \sqrt{T}} = d_1 - \sigma \sqrt{T}$$

Here, F_0 is the forward interest rate, σ is the volatility of the forward rate, X is the cap rate, T is the expiry of the caplet, and m is the number of annual payments ($m = 2$ in our case). Notice that the value of c is the same as in Black's model for finding the value of options on futures, except for the discounting period. While for options on futures, discounting is done up to the maturity of the option (refer to Chapter 19), and in the case of options on interest rates, the time span for discounting is extended by one period $(T + 1/m)$ due to the delayed payment under each caplet.[2]

> A cap can be valued as the sum of some caplets, each of which in turn may be valued using Black's model.

To find the values of the input for Black's model, we need the term structure for the interest rates, which provides (a) the implied forward rates F for all caplets at time $t = 0$, and (b) the price of zeros (the rate of discount) for all periods. For illustration, consider the data in Table 18.2, which gives the term structure for three years at half-yearly intervals, the discount rates applicable, and the forward interest rates implied in the term structure.

To keep the exercise computationally simple, we have used discrete compounding rather than continuous compounding to find the forward rates from the zeros.

Table 18.2 Term structure for finding zeros and forward rate

Time	1	2	3	4	5	6
Time in months	6	12	18	24	30	36
Term structure (%)	3.0000	3.4000	4.0000	4.7000	5.4000	6.2000
Price of zeros	0.98522	0.96685	0.94232	0.91127	0.87528	0.83262
Forward rate for next 6 months (%)	3.000	3.8008	5.2053	6.8144	8.2240	10.2470

---

[2] The discount rate to be used here could be split into two periods: the risk-free rate for the period over which the option is valid, and the forward rate for the period from maturity of the option to payment under the caplet.

Let us value a caplet with a cap of 4.8% for a coupon payment determined 12 months from now, and paid six months thereafter. To value this caplet, the inputs to the Black's model would be as follows:

- The forward rate F is the likely value of the 6-m MIBOR at the end of one year. This is the investment rate beginning 12 months from now for an investment ending 18 months from now.
- The volatility of the forward rate is assumed to be 20%.
- The time of maturity of the option, T, is 12 months.
- The discount rate required is for 18 months, as the cash flow would take place then. This would be the same as the price of a zero maturing 18 months from now.
- The cap rate, X, is 4.80%.

The forward interest rate implied by the term structure is found by equating the direct investment for period n with the rollover of investment by first investing for $n-1$ periods and again investing the matured amount for an additional period. We can find the 6-m forward rate at the end of one year by equating the (a) 18-m direct investment, and (b) the 12-m investment, and rolling over the matured amount at the forward rate for the next six months. Mathematically, for the given term structure, we may find the 6-m forward rate at the end of one year as follows:

$$\left(1 + \frac{0.034}{2}\right)^2 \times \left(1 + \frac{F}{2}\right) = \left(1 + \frac{0.04}{2}\right)^3$$

This gives the 6-m forward rate at the end of one year as 5.2053%. Similarly, all other forward rates may be found. The forward rates are calculated in the last row of Table 18.2.

> Among the basic inputs for Black's model for valuing a cap would be the term structure, to forecast the forward rate, and the price of zeros.

The term structure at half yearly intervals directly gives the value of the zeros as

$$\text{Price of zero maturing at } t = T, \quad P = \frac{1}{\left(1 + \frac{r}{2}\right)^{2T}} \quad (18.3)$$

where T is time in years and r is annual yield.

For the caplet, the cash flow is due 18 months from now but its value is determined 12 months from now. The price of a zero maturing after 18 months is $=1/1.02^3 = 0.94232$.

Using Eq. 18.2, the value of the caplet may be found as ₹0.0001213, which is equivalent to ₹12.13 per lakh of the notional amount. Using, $F = 5.2053\%$, as found in Table 18.2, and $X = 4.80$, as shown here:

$$c = 0.9423 \,[25.2053 N(d_1) - 4.8000 \cdot N(d_2)]$$
$$= 0.9423 \,[25.2053 \times 0.0551.48000 \times 0.0426] = ₹0.0001213$$

For convenience, the value is expressed as ₹12.13 per lakh. On a semi-annual basis, the price of the caplet would be ₹6.065 per lakh of the notional amount.

Likewise, each caplet can be valued. The values of all the caplets are found in Table 18.3. Five caplets constitute the value of the cap. For a notional principal of ₹1 crore, the value of the cap is ₹5,02,105.

The model described here for valuing interest rate options is generally adopted by traders, despite its limitations. The assumption of constant volatility for interest rates is likely to be

Table 18.3 Input for Black's model finding cap value

Time	1	2	3	4	5	6
Forward rate, F_0(%)	3.8008	5.2053	6.8144	8.2240	10.2470	–
Cap rate, X(%)	4.80	4.80	4.80	4.80	4.80	–
Time to expiration, T (months)	6	12	18	24	30	36
Variance of forward rate, σ	0.04	0.04	0.04	0.04	0.04	0.04
d_1		−1.5797	0.5053	1.5531	2.0451	2.5563
d_2		−1.7212	0.3053	1.3081	1.7623	2.2401
$N(d_1)$		0.0571	0.6933	0.9398	0.9796	0.9947
$N(d_2)$		0.0426	0.6199	0.9046	0.961	0.9875
$F_n \times N(d_1)$		0.00217	0.03609	0.06404	0.08056	0.10193
$X \times N(d_2)$		0.00204	0.02976	0.04342	0.04613	0.04740
Discount factor (zero for $n+1$)		0.96685	0.94232	0.91127	0.87528	0.83262
Call value ₹ per lakh of notional		12.13	596.80	1,879.17	3,013.99	4,540.02
Notional principal amount(₹lakh)				100		
Caplet value (₹)		606	29,840	93,958	1,50,699	2,27,001
Cap price						₹5,02,105

more untrue than for stocks. Since the values of bonds today and at maturity are known with certainty, there is no volatility now and at maturity. In between now and maturity, volatility increases first and then declines. Here, we have assumed a constant figure for σ for valuing each of the caplets.

FLOOR

A floor is a series of put options on interest rates, just as a cap is a series of call options. As a cap protects against rising interest rates, a floor protects against falling interest rates. It is used by investing firms deriving income from floating rate instruments. As long as the interest rates are increasing, they are beneficial for the investing firms. However, the firms may need protection when the interest rates are falling.

> A floor is used by investing companies to protect against the income going below a certain minimum level.

Payoff of Floor As stated in the preceding paragraph, a *floor* is a series of put options on interest rates. Each option exercisable on its maturity, based on an interest rate, is called a *floorlet*. The payoff on a floorlet would be Max $(X − M, 0)$, where X is the floor rate and M is the floating rate on the maturity of the floorlet. When the interest falls below X, the investing firm receives M from its investment and $X − M$ from the floorlet, ensuring a minimum aggregate return of X. On each exercise date, the payoff would be determined, and a guaranteed return, as fixed by the floor value, can be achieved for the desired tenure.

The payoff on a floorlet is depicted in Fig. 18.4, which is similar to a put holder with an interest rate as underlying. Like the cap, the floor is also independent of the investment contract. Since the investment and the position in floors can be with different parties, it is not necessary that the underlying investment asset must exist to have a position on a floor option.

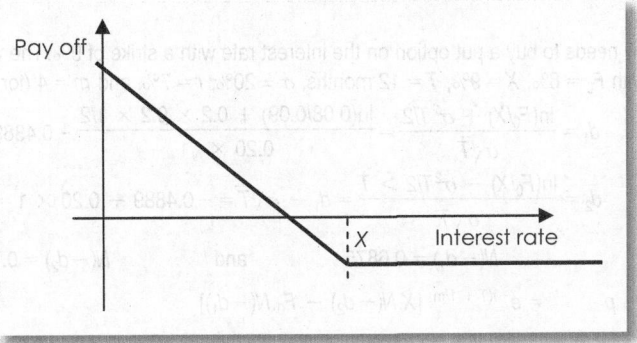

Fig. 18.4 Payoff of floorlet at maturity

Valuation of Floor

The valuation of a floor is the same as that of a cap. To find the value of a floor, each of the floorlets must be valued using Black's model for put pricing. The value of each floorlet would be $L/m \times p$, where p is as per Eq. 18.4.

> Like the cap, the floor, too, is a series of put options exercised at different times, when the actual rate falls below the strike.

$$p = e^{-r(t + 1/m)} [X.N(-d_2) - F_0.N(-d_1)] \quad (18.4)$$

where

$$d_1 = \frac{\ln(F_0/X) + \sigma^2 T/2}{\sigma\sqrt{T}}, \text{ and}$$

$$d_2 = \frac{\ln(F_0/X) - \sigma^2 T/2}{\sigma\sqrt{T}} = d_1 - \sigma\sqrt{T}$$

Relationship between Cap and Floor A relationship exists between the values of cap and floor. Each caplet is like a call option and each floorlet is like a put option. Buying a cap and selling a floor with the same strike is like entering into a swap with a fixed rate equal to the strike rate. For example, consider buying a cap and selling a floor, both at a strike of 10%. It always results in a cash inflow of I, the floating rate, and a cash outflow of 10%, the strike. This is identical with the cash flows of a swap to receive a floating rate and pay a fixed rate, as shown here:

> The value of the cap and the value of the floor would represent the value of the swap.

	Cash flow	Interest in %	
	Sold floor	Bought cap	Total
When $M < 10$	$-(10-M)$	–	$M - 10$
When $M > 10$	–	$(M-10)$	$M - 10$

Therefore, we may say

Value of cap − value of floor = value of swap

EXAMPLE 18.1 Value of floorlet

What would the price of an option that has to commence after 12 months be for an investing company that wants to protect the interest rate of 9% on its investments? The interest rate expected after 12 months is 8%. The interest rates have shown a volatility of 20%. The seller of the option would pay his/her liability after three months when it arises. The risk-free rate for all maturities up to two years is a flat 7%. Find the value per lakh of the investment amount.

Solution
The investing company needs to buy a put option on the interest rate with a strike of 9%. The value of the put on the interest rate is given by Eq.18.4, with $F_0 = 8\%$, $X = 9\%$, $T = 12$ months, $\sigma = 20\%$, $r = 7\%$, and $m = 4$ (for three months' deferred payment).

$$d_1 = \frac{\ln(F_0/X) + \sigma^2 T/2}{\sigma\sqrt{T}} = \frac{\ln(0.08/0.09) + 0.2 \times 0.2 \times 1/2}{0.20 \times \sqrt{1}} = -0.4889 \text{ and}$$

$$d_2 = \frac{\ln(F_0/X) - \sigma^2 T/2 > T}{\sigma\sqrt{T}} = d_1 - \sigma\sqrt{T} = -0.4889 - 0.20 \times 1 = 0.6889$$

$$N(-d_1) = 0.6875 \quad \text{and} \quad N(-d_2) = 0.7546$$

$$p = e^{-r(T + 1/m)}[X \cdot N(-d_2) - F_0 \cdot N(-d_1)]$$

$$= e^{-0.07 \times 1.25}[0.09 \times 0.7546 - 0.08 \times 0.6875] \times 1,00,000/.$$

$$= ₹295.80$$

COLLAR

> A collar is a combination of one option bought and another sold to contain the cost of hedging.

A *collar* is a combination of a cap and a floor. A borrowing firm desirous of containing the cost of borrowing may choose to buy a cap. The buying of a cap provides protection from rising interest costs while retaining the benefit of falling interest rates. The holder lets the caplet expire unexercised if the floating rate is less than the cap rate. Like any other option, buying a cap would involve payment of a premium upfront.

Similarly, a firm, having invested in floating rate instruments, seeks protection by buying a floor where the downside risk is covered while retaining the potential gain from any upside movement of the interest rates. This, too, costs money upfront.

Like any option, the payoffs on caps and floors for the seller (writer) would be opposite to those for the holder. The writer of a cap or a floor earns the premium paid by the holder. As a strategy of cost cutting, just as we use range forwards for foreign exchange risks, a borrowing firm may buy a cap and simultaneously sell a floor to earn some premium. This offsets the cost of the cap either completely or partially. The cap rate and the floor rate may be adjusted in such a way that the premium on the cap equals the premium on the floor for achieving zero cost. Buying a cap and writing a floor or buying a floor and writing a cap is called a collar. The premiums on the cap and the floor depend upon the strike rate chosen. Choosing the appropriate strikes for the cap and the floor may result in a collar with zero cost. Such a collar is referred to as a *zero-cost collar*.

To attain zero cost, a borrowing firm buys a cap and sells a floor. In such a collar, the borrowing firm would give up some of the gains that could accrue on any downside movement of the interest rate. Hedging with a cap, a floor, and a collar is depicted in Figs 18.5 and 18.6.

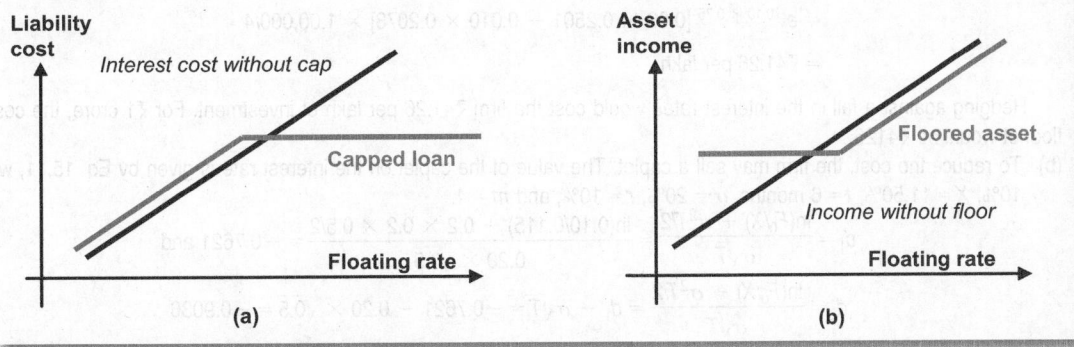

Fig. 18.5 Hedging (a) With cap (b) With floor

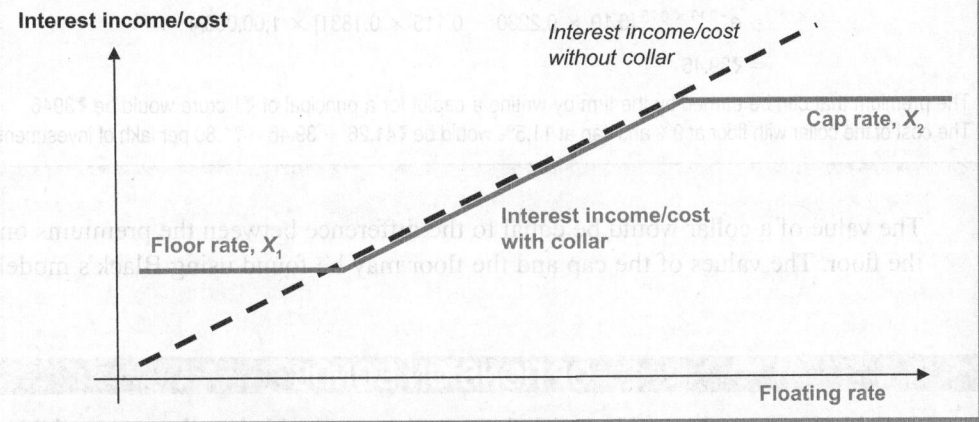

Fig. 18.6 Interest rate collar

EXAMPLE 18.2 Valuing interest rate collar

An investing firm would have ₹1 crore to invest after six months. It is expected that the interest rate would be 10% after six months. The firm wants to lock-in a minimum return of 9%.

(a) What can it do to safeguard against loss of income due to a fall in the interest rate?
(b) If the firm is willing to sacrifice gains beyond 11.5%, can it reduce the cost of hedging?

Solution

(a) The investing company needs to buy a put option on the interest rate with a strike of 9% to lock-in a minimum return. The value of the put on the interest rate is given by Eq.18.4, with $F_0 = 10\%$, $X = 9\%$, $T = 6$ months, $\sigma = 20\%$, $r = 10\%$, and $m = 4$ (for three months' deferred payment).

$$d_1 = \frac{\ln(F_0/X) + \sigma^2 T/2}{\sigma \sqrt{T}} = \frac{\ln(0.10/0.09) + 0.2 \times 0.2 \times 0.5/2}{0.20 \times \sqrt{0.5}} = 0.8157 \text{ and}$$

$$d_2 = \frac{\ln(F_0/X) - \sigma^2 T/2}{\sigma \sqrt{T}} = d_1 - \sigma\sqrt{T} = 0.8157 - 0.20 \times \sqrt{0.5} = 0.6743$$

$$N(-d_1) = 0.2073 \quad \text{and} \quad N(-d_2) = 0.2501$$

$$p = e^{-r(t + 1/m)} [x.N(-d_2) - F_0.N(-d_1)]$$

$$= e^{-0.10 \times 0.75} [0.09 \times 0.2501 - 0.010 \times 0.2073] \times 1{,}00{,}000/4$$
$$= ₹41.26 \text{ per lakh}$$

Hedging against a fall in the interest rates would cost the firm ₹41.26 per lakh of investment. For ₹1 crore, the cost of the floorlet would be ₹4126.

(b) To reduce the cost, the firm may sell a caplet. The value of the caplet on the interest rate is given by Eq. 15.11, with $F_0 = 10\%$, $X = 11.50\%$, $t = 6$ months, $\sigma = 20\%$, $r = 10\%$, and $m = 4$.

$$d_1 = \frac{\ln(F_0/X) + \sigma^2 T/2}{\sigma\sqrt{T}} = \frac{\ln(0.10/0.115) + 0.2 \times 0.2 \times 0.5/2}{0.20 \times \sqrt{0.5}} = -0.7621 \text{ and}$$

$$d_2 = \frac{\ln(F_0/X) - \sigma^2 T/2}{\sigma\sqrt{T}} = d_1 - \sigma\sqrt{T} = -0.7621 - 0.20 \times \sqrt{0.5} = -0.9036$$

$$N(d_1) = 0.2230 \quad \text{and} \quad N(d_2) = 0.1831$$

$$c = e^{-r(t + 1/m)} [F_0 \cdot N(d_1) - X \cdot N(d_2)]$$
$$= e^{-0.10 \times 0.75} [0.10 \times 0.2230 - 0.115 \times 0.1831] \times 1{,}00{,}000/4$$
$$= ₹39.46$$

The premium that can be earned by the firm by writing a caplet for a principal of ₹1 crore would be ₹3946. The cost of the collar with floor at 9% and cap at 11.5% would be ₹41.26 − 39.46 = ₹1.80 per lakh of investment, or ₹180 only.

The value of a collar would be equal to the difference between the premiums on the cap and the floor. The values of the cap and the floor may be found using Black's model.

OPTIONS ON BONDS

Callable bonds and puttable bonds have options embedded in them. A callable bond is one that gives the issuer the right to buy back the bond at a pre-designated price. Thus, the holder of the bond is a combination of a long position on the bond and a short position on a call option on the bond. Similarly, puttable bonds give a right to the holder of the bond to seek early redemption of the bond from the issuer at a designated price. Therefore, the holder of a puttable bond is equivalent to a long position on the bond and a long put thereon. As stated earlier, these embedded features are one-time tools for managing interest rate risk.

A portfolio of bonds can be hedged by buying a put with a strike price equal to the level of protection desired. If a fund owns a portfolio of bonds valued at ₹120 crore and needs to protect the value at the level of ₹100 crore, the fund needs to buy a put option with a strike of ₹100 crore. The put on the bonds would entitle the fund to sell the portfolio at ₹100 crore in case the value of this portfolio falls below ₹100 crore. Note that there exists an inverse relationship between the interest rate and the bond price. A protective put would be required not for falling interest rates but for interest rates that are likely to rise, resulting in a fall in the value of the bond.

> A portfolio of bonds can be hedged by buying a protective put on the bonds.

Valuation of Options on Bonds

European options on bonds can be valued using Black's model in the same way as for pricing caps and floors. Forward interest rates were used as the underlying assets in valuing caps and floors. For valuing options on bonds, we replace the forward interest rates with the forward prices of the bond, F_B. As usual, T is the time to maturity of the option and σ is the volatility of the bond prices.[3] The value of a call and a put option on the bonds can be computed with Eqs 18.5 and 18.6, respectively.

$$c = e^{-rT}[F_B N(d_1) - X N(d_2)] \qquad (18.5)$$

$$p = e^{-rT}[X N(-d_2) - F_B N(-d_1)] \qquad (18.6)$$

$$d_1 = \frac{\ln(F_B/X) + \sigma^2 T/2}{\sigma \sqrt{T}}, \text{ and}$$

$$d_2 = \frac{\ln(F_B/X) - \sigma^2 T/2}{\sigma \sqrt{T}} = d_1 - \sigma \sqrt{T}$$

The forward price of the bond, F_B, can be computed by using the cost of carry model for finding the futures price. For non-dividend paying stock, the futures or forward price is given by the spot value plus the cost of carry for the forward period. For a dividend paying stock, the present value (PV) of the dividend during the forward period needs to be subtracted from the spot value before adding the cost of carry. Bonds are akin to dividend paying stocks in terms of forward pricing. Bonds carry periodic coupons that are equivalent to dividend. Therefore, the forward price of the bond, F_B, is

> The forward price of a bond is the current price less the present value of the coupons payable in the forward period, compounded through the forward period.

F_B = current price − PV of coupons in the option period)(1+ the cost of carry)
    = $(B_0 - I_0) \times e^{rt}$

where I_0 is the present value of the coupons till the expiry of the option and r is the risk-free rate for the period of option maturity. The volatility of the forward price is assumed to be constant over the option period.

As an example, consider a call option for three years at a strike of ₹120 on a bond with a face value of ₹100, with semi-annual coupons at 12%. The current price of the bond is ₹145. The volatility of the price can be taken as 10%. The term structure as reflected in the price of zeros up to 36 months, is as given below:

Time (months)	6	12	18	24	30	36
Yields (%)	5.00	5.20	5.50	6.80	6.00	6.50

To find the value of the call option on the bond, we first need to find the forward price of the bond at the expiry of the option period, i.e., 36 months. This would be equal to the current market price less the present value of the coupons with the cost of carry for 36 months. With the given term structure, the present values of the six coupons that would be paid before the option's expiry are calculated in Table 18.5 with the amount of coupons discounted at the corresponding yields given by the zeros, as shown in Table 18.4:

> Options on bonds can be valued using Black's model for pricing options on futures.

---

[3] Volatilities quoted are yield volatilities and not price volatilities. A quoted volatility can be converted to a price volatility using the concept of duration and formula: *Price volatility* = $D \times y_0 \times$ *yield volatility*, where D is the modified duration and y_0 is the initial forward yield.

Table 18.4 Finding forward price

	Amount (₹)	Time (months)	Yield (%)	PV (₹)
Coupon 1	6	6	5.00	5.85
Coupon 2	6	12	5.20	5.70
Coupon 3	6	18	5.50	5.52
Coupon 4	6	24	5.80	5.34
Coupon 5	6	30	6.00	5.16
Coupon 6	6	36	6.50	4.94
PV of coupons in the option period				32.52
Value of the bond				145.00
Forward price of the bond at cost of carry of 6.50%			6.50	136.70

The present value of the coupons is ₹32.52 and the forward price of the bond works out to ₹136.70 as follows:

The forward price of the bond, $F_B = (145.00 - 32.52) \times e^{0.0650 \times 3} = ₹136.70$.

The values of the determinants of a three-year call on bonds under Black's model are

$F_B = 136.70$, $\quad X = 120$, $\quad T = 3$ years,
$r = 6.50\%$, $\quad$ and $\quad \sigma = 10\%$.

Inserting these values, we get

$d_1 = 0.8390 \quad\quad N(d_1) = 0.7993$
$d_2 = 0.6658 \quad\quad N(d_2) = 0.7472$

EXAMPLE 18.3 Valuing put option on bonds

A 10-year bond is trading at ₹120, and pays coupons of 10% with face value ₹100 on a semi-annual basis. The next coupon payment is due exactly after six months. The interest rate up to one year is a flat 8%. What is the value of a put option on the bond with a strike of ₹100 and maturity of one year? The volatility of bond prices is 10%.

Solution
The present value of the coupon payments would be

$$5 \times e^{-0.08 \times 0.5} + 5 \times e^{-0.08 \times 1} = 4.80 + 4.62 = ₹9.42$$

The forward price of the bond, $F_B = (120.00 - 9.42) \times e^{0.08 \times 1} = ₹119.79$
In Black's model, $F_B = 119.79$, $X = 100$, $T = 1$, and $\sigma = 0.10$

$$d_1 = \frac{\ln(F_B/X) + \sigma^2 T/2}{\sigma\sqrt{T}} = \frac{\ln(119.79/100) + 0.1 \times 0.1 \times 1/2}{0.1\sqrt{1}} = 1.8557 \text{ and}$$

$$d_2 = \frac{\ln(F_B/X) - \sigma^2 T/2}{\sigma\sqrt{T}} = d_1 - \sigma\sqrt{T} = 1.8557 - 0.1\sqrt{1} = 1.7557$$

$N(-d_1) = 0.0317 \quad$ and $\quad N(-d_2) = 0.0396$

Put value = $e^{-rt}\{X \times N(d_2) - F_B \times N(-d_1)\}$

$= 0.9048 (3.9600 - 3.7974)$

$= ₹0.15$

$$\text{Call value} = e^{-rT}\{F_B \times N(d_1) - X \times N(d_2)\}$$
$$= e^{-0.065 \times 3}\{136.70 \times 0.7993 - 120.00 \times 0.7472\}$$
$$= 0.8228\,(109.2660 - 89.6640)$$
$$= ₹16.13$$

For a put on the same bond with the same strike, the values are

$$N(-d_1) = 0.2007 \text{ and } N(-d_2) = 0.2525$$
$$\text{Put value} = e^{-rT}\{X \times N(-d_2) - F_B \times N(-d_1)\}$$
$$= e^{-0.065 \times 3}\{120.00 \times 0.2525 - 136.70 \times 0.2007\}$$
$$= 0.8228\,(30.3360 - 27.4361)$$
$$= ₹2.39$$

SOLVED PROBLEMS

SP 18.1: Value of caplet
Find the value of the caplet for the data in Example 18.1.

Solution
The value of the caplet on the interest rate is given by Eq.18.1, with $F_0 = 8\%$, $X = 9\%$, $T = 12$ months, $\sigma = 20\%$, $r = 7\%$, and $m = 4$ (for three months' deferred payment).

$$d_1 = \frac{\ln(F_0/X) + \sigma^2 T/2}{\sigma\sqrt{T}} = \frac{\ln(0.08/0.09) + 0.2 \times 0.2 \times 1/2}{0.20 \times \sqrt{1}} = -0.4889 \text{ and}$$

$$d_2 = \frac{\ln(F_0/X) - \sigma^2 T/2}{\sigma\sqrt{T}} = d_1 - \sigma\sqrt{T} = -0.4889 - 0.20 \times 1 = -0.6889$$

$$N(-d_1) = 0.3125 \quad \text{and} \quad N(d_2) = 0.2454$$

$$c = e^{-r(T + 1/m)}[F_0 \cdot N(d_1) - X \cdot N(d_2)]$$
$$= e^{-0.07 \times 1.25}[0.08 \times 0.3125 - 0.09 \times 0.2454] \times 1{,}00{,}000/4$$
$$= ₹64.29$$

SP 18.2: Valuing put option on bonds
Refer to Example 18.3. What would the price of the put be if the exercise price is changed to ₹120?

Solution
The present value of the coupon payments and the forward price of the bond would stay the same, and would be

$$5 \times e^{-0.08 \times 0.5} + 5 \times e^{-0.08 \times 1} = 4.80 + 4.62 = ₹9.42$$

The forward price of the bond, $F_B = (120.00 - 9.42) \times e^{0.08 \times 1} = ₹119.79$

In Black's model, $F_B = 119.79$, $X = 120$, $T = 1$, and $\sigma = 0.10$

$$d_1 = \frac{\ln(F_B/X) + \sigma^2 T/2}{\sigma\sqrt{T}} = \frac{\ln(119.79/120) + 0.1 \times 0.1 \times 1/2}{0.1\sqrt{1}} = 0.0325 \text{ and}$$

$$d_2 = \frac{\ln(F_B/X) - \sigma^2 T/2}{\sigma\sqrt{T}} = d_1 - \sigma\sqrt{T} = 0.0325 - 0.1\sqrt{1} = -0.0675$$

$$N(-d_1) = 0.4870 \quad \text{and} \quad N(-d_2) = 0.5269$$

$$\text{Put value} = e^{-rT}\{X \times N(-d_2) - F_B \times N(-d_1)\}$$
$$= e^{-0.08 \times 1}\{120.00 \times 0.5269 - 119.79 \times 0.4870\}$$
$$= 0.9048\,(63.2280 - 58.3377)$$
$$= ₹4.42$$

SUMMARY

Interest rate risk is of primary concern to banks and financial institutions, whose income and expenses are extremely sensitive to the interest rate scenario. Firms are also affected if they have significant borrowing or income from investments. Options on interest rate provide an excellent means of hedging against falling or rising interest rates. Long-term exposures to interest rate risk can be managed by caps, floors, and collars.

A cap is a series of call options called caplets, each of which has a common strike called cap rate. A caplet is exercised at predetermined intervals of time. It is used to cover against rising interest rate. Similarly, a floor is a series of put options, called floorlets, with the same strike, and is exercised at different intervals of time. Each of the caplets or floorlets may be valued with Black's model for calls and puts on futures, respectively. The basic determinants of caplet or floorlet valuation would be the term structure of interest rate to find the forward price and the prices of zeros, besides the normal inputs for valuing option such as strike, volatility, and time to maturity. Since hedging costs money, the strategy to reduce the cost of buying options is to write another option at a different strike rate so that the front-end cost of buying an option is offset either completely or partially. This combination of buying one option and selling another option is called a collar.

Options on long-term bonds cover the risk of fluctuating interest rates on a portfolio of bonds. One needs to buy a put option on the bonds to protect against a fall in the value of the portfolio due to rising interest rates. These options on bonds can be valued using Black's model, where the forward price of the bond would be dependent upon the price of the bond less the present value of coupons that would be paid before the expiry of the option on the bond. Another caution that is worth mentioning is that the volatility that must be used in Black's formula is for bond prices, which are not available. The available volatilities are on yields that need to be converted to price volatility using the concept of duration.

KEY TERMS

Cap A cap is a series of call options called caplets, each exercisable at successive intervals of time, to provide payoff to the excess of the actual rate over the agreed (strike) rate.

Caplet A call option on interest rates that constitutes one strip of a cap and pays the excess of the actual interest rate over the strike rate.

Collar A combination of a call and a put, one bought and the other sold, to contain the cost of hedging. Options sold fetch premium offset the cost of options bought.

Floor A floor is a series of put options called floorlets, each exercisable at successive intervals of time, to provide payoff to the excess of the agreed (strike) rate over the actual rate.

Floorlet A put option on interest rates that constitutes one strip of a floor and pays the excess of the strike rate over the actual interest rate.

Option on bond An option that entitles the holder to buy or sell the underlying bond at a specified price within or at any time before maturity of the option.

QUESTIONS

18.1 What is a cap and how is it used for hedging interest rate risks?
18.2 What is a collar and why do investors use it?
18.3 Describe a caplet and a floorlet. How is each valued?
18.4 What are options on bonds and how to value them?

PROBLEMS

P 18.1 Valuing interest rate options
A firm intends to cap its interest payment liability at 14%, to be determined six months in advance for two semi-annual instalments of interest falling due after 12 and 18 months, respectively, for a principal amount of ₹100 crore. The forward interest rates for 6-m maturity as reflected in the term structure for six and 12 months are 13% and 13.5%, respectively. The volatility of the forward interest rates is placed at 10%. The risk-free rates for 12 and 18 months are 12 and 12.5%, respectively. All rates are continuously compounded. What is the value of the cap the firm would pay for a notional principal of ₹100 crore?

P 18.2 Option on bonds
The current price of a bond having 12 years to maturity is ₹130. It pays annual coupons on the face value of ₹100 at 12%. Assuming that a coupon has just been paid, find out the value of a 2-year call option on the bond with the strike price of ₹120 if the risk-free rate is 8% and the volatility of the bond price too is 8%.

P 18.3 Put option on bonds
From the data in Problem 18.2, find the value of a 2-year put option. Further, find the value of the put using put–call parity.

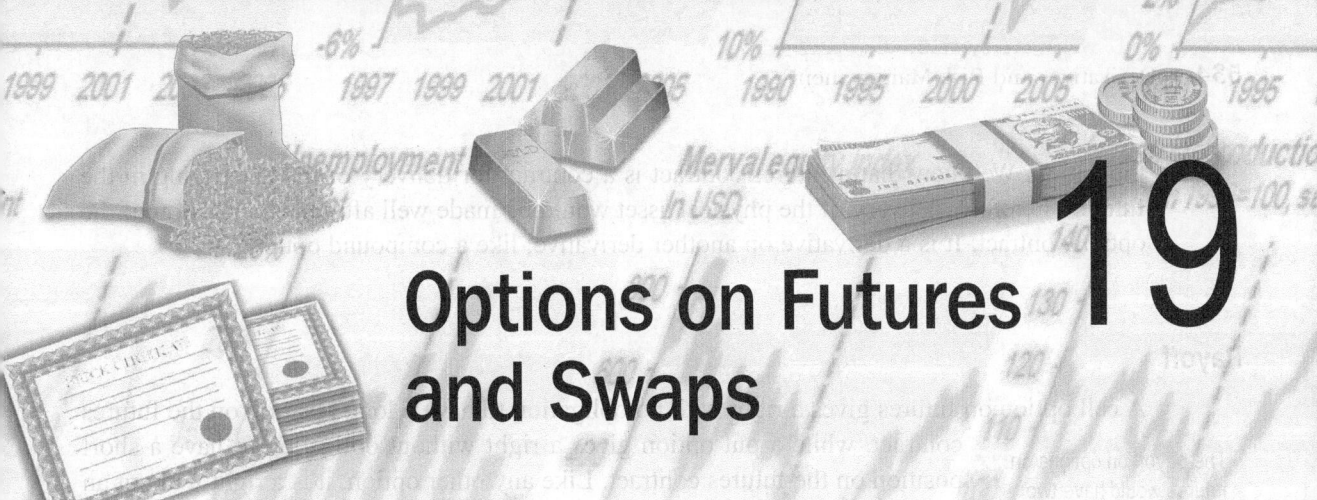

Options on Futures and Swaps 19

INTRODUCTION

In this chapter, we shall discuss some advanced options. These include derivatives on derivatives, such as options on futures and options on swaps. These products are rather recent developments and allow traders to take positions not on the underlying but on the derivatives on the underlying. Traders have started to deal in options on futures on commodities rather than option on commodities themselves, because they are not interested in delivery. They prefer to take a view on price changes.

FUTURES OPTIONS

Options on futures are traded on many exchanges. These are a relatively recent development as they came into existence as late as 1982 and became popular only after 1987. Currently, no such contracts are traded in India.

Since futures are essentially exchange-traded contracts, options on futures are exchange-traded too.

Options on futures are mostly American options that can be exercised any time by asking for delivery of the underlying asset, i.e., a futures contract.

Options on spot give a right without obligation to buy or sell the underlying assets. In case of options on futures, the underlying asset is a futures contract. When an option gives a right to buy or sell a futures contract without an obligation, it is known as an option on futures or a futures option.

> Options on futures give the holder the right to have a long or a short position in a futures contract.

Learning Objectives

After going through this chapter, readers should be familiar with

- Black's model for valuing options on futures contracts
- the differences between the binomial model for derivatives on spot assets and for futures on the assets
- swaptions, their uses, and their valuation using Black's model

When an option, a derivative, is exercised, it is settled either by cash or by delivery of the asset. An option on futures is concluded upon taking a position in the futures contract on the maturity of the option. We know that a futures contract is a contract for delivery of the underlying in the future. Therefore, delivery of the physical asset would be made well after the conclusion of the option contract. It is a derivative on another derivative, like a compound option.

Payoff

> The payoff on options on futures would have two components: (a) the intrinsic value in cash, and (b) a long position (for a call) or a short position (for a put) in the futures contract.

A call option on futures gives a right with no obligation to have a long position on the futures contract, while a put option gives a right without obligation to have a short position on the futures contract. Like any other option, it is a right without an obligation. The value of this option would depend upon the value of the futures contract, which in turn depends upon the value of the underlying in the spot market. The payoff on options on futures would consist of two components:

- A cash amount equal to the difference between the last settlement price of the futures contract and the exercise price of the option
- A long or short position on the underlying futures contract

As an example, consider a call option on futures on the Nifty, the index of the National Stock Exchange (NSE). The spot value of Nifty is 3540, and a futures contract expiring two months later in November is trading at 3610. The last settlement price of the November futures on the previous day was 3600. The strike price of the call option on November futures on Nifty is 3570. If the holder of the call exercises the option, then

- one gets cash equal to its intrinsic worth
  = Max (last settlement price − exercise price, 0)
  = Max (3600 − 3570, 0) = ₹30, and
- a long position on the November Nifty futures contract.

The holder may continue with the long position in futures. However, if the holder wants to square off the long position immediately, he/she would do so at the current price of the futures, i.e., ₹3610. Thus he/she gains ₹10 (3610 − 3600). Therefore, the aggregate payoff would be ₹40, i.e., the difference between the current futures price and the exercise price (3610 − 3570). If one futures contract consists of 50 indices, the call on futures has a value of 50 × 40 = ₹2000. This is the intrinsic worth of the call option on Nifty futures.

The writer of the call futures option would pay ₹30 and obtain a short position on the November Nifty futures.

Similarly, we can explain the put option on futures. If an investor holds a put option on the November Nifty futures with a strike price of ₹3640, with the last settlement done at 3600, and decides to exercise, the investor gets

- cash equal to its intrinsic worth
  = Max (exercise price − last settlement price, 0)
  = Max (3640 − 3600, 0) = ₹40, plus
- a short position on the November Nifty futures contract.

As a holder of a short position, the investor may continue or square off immediately. If he/she decides to square off, he/she loses ₹10 (3610 − 3600). Therefore his/her payoff would be ₹30, i.e., the difference between the exercise price and the current price (3640 − 3610). If one futures contract consists of 50 indices, the put on futures is worth 50 × 30 = ₹1500.

The writer of the put futures option would pay ₹40 and obtain a long position on the November Nifty futures.

Therefore, the payoffs on options on futures would be

$$\text{For a call option on futures:} \quad \text{Max}(0, F - X) \quad (19.1)$$
$$\text{For a put option on futures:} \quad \text{Max}(0, X - F) \quad (19.2)$$

where F is the current futures price (i.e., at the time of exercising the option) and X is the exercise price of the option.

An options contract on futures must have a maturity prior to that of the futures contract, the underlying asset in this case. If the futures contract matures on the same date as the option, then by the phenomenon of convergence of the futures price to the spot, the futures price would be the same as the spot price. The option on futures would then be the same as an option on the underlying spot. Hence, options on futures are American style and have the same maturity as that of the underlying futures contract. Options on futures are referred to using the time at which the underlying futures expires. If a futures contract on index expires on 25 May, it is called a May futures contract. Then an option on this index futures would also be called a *May option*.

Need for Options on Futures

> Options on futures are becoming increasingly popular because of the ready visibility of the prices of futures as compared to those of spots, and the uneven payoff of options.

Why should one trade in options on futures rather than in options on underlying assets? We may like to recall the properties of futures and options to understand this. It may be realized from the examples in the previous section on payoffs, that options on futures would in most circumstances be cash settled, because a futures position is almost always settled in cash by entering into an opposite contract. Therefore, an option on futures makes sense to traders, who are not really interested in the possession or dispossession of the final underlying asset.

If this be the case, one can take a futures position. However, a futures position would expose the trader to downside risk too. A long position on futures would gain with a price rise and lose when the price of the underlying falls. In order to have protection on the downside, one may prefer an option contract to a futures contract. A futures contract provides leverage but exposes the holder to the downside, while the option contract safeguards against the downside. Thus, options on futures serve the purpose of providing leverage as well as protection from the downside.

Another reason that options on futures are becoming increasingly popular is the instant availability of futures prices. If one needs to take a position in crude oil, knowing the spot price would be the first prerequisite. It is easier to know the price of futures on crude oil than the spot price of oil. Hence, rather than trading an option contract on oil, it becomes easier to trade an option on oil futures, especially when the futures and the options on futures are being traded at the same platform or exchange.

Since both derivatives are on the same exchange, trading in two derivatives becomes easier than trading that involves an interaction with the spot market. With options on futures, the futures serve as a better and more convenient proxy for the spot, as futures prices are available instantly and are transparent.

Put–Call Parity for Options on Futures

We know the relationship between call and put prices for an underlying asset that was derived by constructing a portfolio of long stock, long put, and short call that created a synthetic bond. We now examine a similar position using futures, puts, and calls. Let the futures price be F_0, with the call and put prices denoted as $c(S_0, X, T)$ and $p(S_0, X, T)$, respectively, where S_0 is the current spot price, X is the exercise price of the options, and T is the time to maturity. All the derivatives expire at the same time T. We now see the maturity value of the portfolio consisting of long futures, long puts, and short calls. With the final asset price S_T, the payoff on the portfolio is shown in Table 19.1.

Table 19.1 Put–call parity for futures (forwards)

Portfolio	Current value	$S_T \leq X$	$S_T > X$
Long futures	–	$S_T - F_0$	$S_T - F_0$
Long put	$p(S_0, X, T)$	$X - S_T$	0
Short call	$-c(S_0, X, T)$	0	$-(S_T - X)$
Total	$p(S_0, X, T) - c(S_0, X, T)$	$X - F_0$	$X - F_0$

The portfolio matures without any uncertainty to a fixed value—the strike price less the current futures price $(X - F_0)$—irrespective of the asset price. A certain outcome must yield no more than the risk-free rate of return, r, for the period, T. Therefore, at $t = 0$,

$$p(S_0, X, T) - c(S_0, X, T) = \frac{X - F_0}{1 + r} \quad (19.3)$$

Equation 19.3 can also be obtained from Eq. 10.8 or 10.9 by substitution of $S = F_0/(1 + r)$. This is shown in Eq. 19.14 in terms of the Black Scholes Model (BSM).

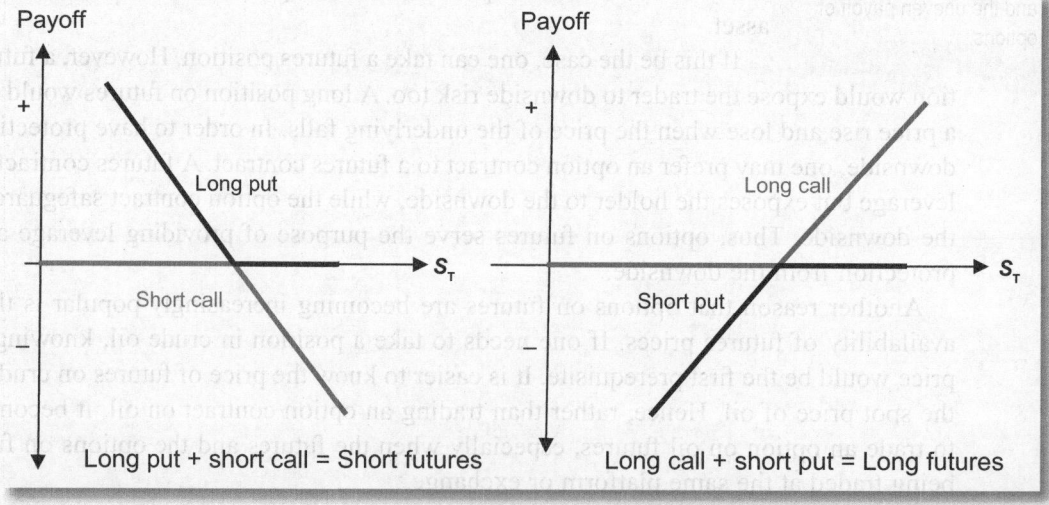

Fig. 19.1 Put, call, and futures

> **EXAMPLE 19.1 Put, call, and futures**
>
> Assume that today's spot price for the Nifty index is ₹5000. A June futures on the Nifty expiring 45 days from now is trading at ₹5075. June call and June put options on futures with strike prices of ₹5,100 for expiry on the same day as the futures are trading at ₹5 and ₹35, respectively. If the risk-free rate of interest is 1.5% for 45 days, find out the following:
>
> (a) What is the price of the synthetic futures created by a bond, a call, and a put?
> (b) Is there an arbitrage opportunity?
> (c) If yes, how would you execute the arbitrage?
>
> **Solution**
> (a) As per Eq. 19.3, using simplified notations, the futures price should be $F = X - (1 + r)(p - c) = 5100 - (1.015) \times (35 - 5) = ₹5069.55$
> (b) The actual futures price is ₹5075, which as per put–call parity for options on futures is overpriced, suggesting that an arbitrage profit of ₹5.45 can be made.
> (c) To execute the arbitrage, one would go short on the futures, and create a synthetic futures by (a) buying a bond that matures to ₹5,100 after 45 days, (b) buying a call, and (c) going short on the put. The bond is selling for 5100/1.015 = 5024.63, the call would cost 5.00, and the put would give 35.00 with the total cost of the portfolio at ₹4,994.63, which can be borrowed at 1.5% for 45 days. The long futures and the portfolio would match at maturity. The payable on the borrowing would be 1.015 × 4994.63 = ₹5099.55 and the receivable against the short futures would be ₹5075, yielding a profit of ₹5.45.

From Eq. 19.3, we may say that a long position on a put with a short call is equal to a short futures contract, and a short put and a long call make a long futures contract, as they have identical payoffs. These positions, ignoring the option premiums, are depicted in Fig. 19.1. The position in the call and the put can be used to create a synthetic futures contract.

Binomial Model for Pricing Futures Options

Let us consider some of the differences between options on the spot and option on futures with the help of a binomial tree. Recall that under risk neutrality, we set up a hedged portfolio of Δ long stock and one short call at a cost of $\Delta S_0 - c$. With the up and down movement of the stock at uS_0 and dS_0, and respective call payoffs of c_u and c_d, the hedged portfolio would have the same value, irrespective of any price change. Equating the portfolio at the upper and the lower nodes would give the value of delta as

> Since a position in futures is without investment as compared to a position in the spot, no growth of the futures price can be presumed in valuing options on futures.

$$\Delta = \frac{C_u - C_d}{S_0(u - d)} \qquad (19.4)$$

As the payoff on the portfolio at maturity is certain, it would yield nothing greater than the risk-free rate. Therefore, the payoff at maturity discounted at the risk-free rate should be equal to the cost of the portfolio.

Discounted value of the portfolio at the up move: $(\Delta u S_0 - c_u)e^{-rT} = \Delta S_0 - c$
Discounted value of the portfolio at the down move: $(\Delta d S_0 - c_d)e^{-rT} = \Delta S_0 - c$

Putting the value of Δ would give

Value of the call, $c = e^{-rT}[pc_u + (1-p)c_d] \qquad (19.5)$

where
$$p = \frac{e^{rT} - d}{u - d} \qquad (19.6)$$

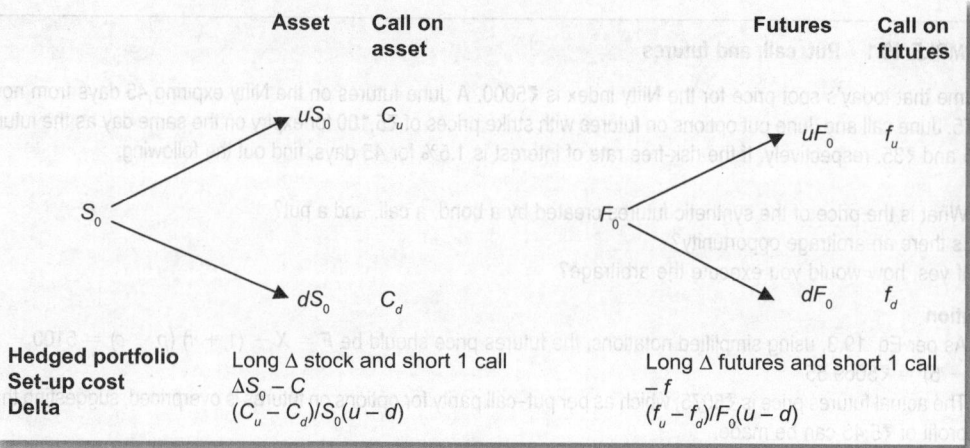

Fig. 19.2 Binomial tree for option on spot and futures

We adopt the same approach for valuing the call option on futures. Consider the current futures price of F_0. The futures does not require an initial outlay for the hedged portfolio of long Δ futures, and a short call would be set up at $-f$, where f is the value of the call on futures.

With up and down movements of u and d of the futures, the value of the futures at expiry of the call option would be uF_0 and dF_0, respectively. If the respective values of the call on futures at the up and down movements are f_u and f_d, then the value of the delta would be

$$\Delta = \frac{f_u - f_d}{F_0(u-d)} \quad (19.7)$$

In this case too, payoff at maturity would be certain and, thus, it would provide a return equal to the risk-free rate, and, therefore, we may find the value of the call on futures.

Discounted value of the portfolio at the up move: $(\Delta uF_0 - f_u)e^{-rT} = -f$
Discounted value of portfolio at the down move: $(\Delta dF_0 - f_d)e^{-rT} = -f$

With Δ as calculated in Eq. 19.7, the call on futures would be

Value of the call on futures, $f = e^{-rT}[pf_u + (1-p)f_d] \quad (19.8)$

$$\text{where } p = \frac{1-d}{u-d} \quad (19.9)$$

The comparative position of the call on stock and the call on futures under the binomial approach is depicted in Fig. 19.2.

The risk-neutral probability, p, in case of the call on futures suggests that the futures price does not grow as does the stock price at the risk-free rate. It is consistent with the notion that if there is no initial investment, as is the case with a position on futures, the return would have to be zero under risk neutrality.

Further, the futures price itself represents the expected value of the spot at the expiry of the futures.

Valuation of Futures Options—Black's Model

The valuation of an option on futures can be done by what is referred to as Fisher Black's model. It is on the same lines as BSM for dividend paying stock or for indices, where the dividend q is set equal to the risk-free rate. Setting $q = r$ makes the growth equal to zero. The value of the call and put options on futures is stated in Eqs 19.10 and 19.11.

> The Black-Scholes model for valuation can be applied to value options on futures by assuming zero growth or by setting $q = r$.

$$c = e^{-rT}[F_0 \cdot N(d_1) - X \cdot N(d_2)] \quad (19.10)$$
$$p = e^{-rT}[X \cdot N(-d_2) - F_0 \cdot N(-d_1)] \quad (19.11)$$

Note that the valuation of option on futures is same as that for the BSM with simple substitution of S_0 by the equivalent futures price of $F_0 \times e^{-rT}$. The computation of d_1 and

---

EXAMPLE 19.2 Binomial valuation of call on futures

The spot value of gold is ₹14,000 per 10 g. A futures contract on gold for delivery one month later is selling for ₹14,150. What is the price of a call on gold spot and gold futures expiring in one month with a strike price of ₹14,250? Assume a risk-free interest rate of 1% per month, a price movement of ±10%, and the last settlement price of the futures as ₹14,150.

(a) Draw a single-stage binomial tree.
(b) What would the payoff on the call on futures be if the holder exercises the option?

Solution
(a) With a risk-free interest rate of 1% per month and an up and down movement of 10% each, the risk-neutral probability of an up movement, using Eqs 19.6 and 19.9, is

For a call option on spot gold $p = (e^{rT} - d)/(u - d) = (1.01005 - 0.9)/0.2 = 0.55025$
For a call option on futures $p = (1 - d)/(u - d) = 0.1/0.2 = 0.50$

Binomial tree for option on spot and futures on gold

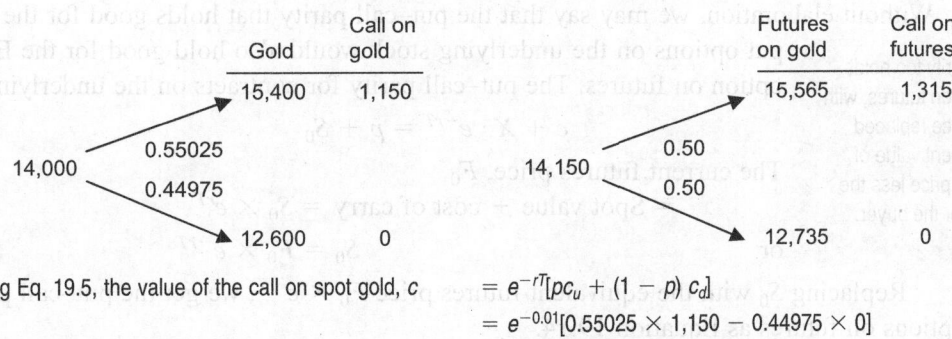

Using Eq. 19.5, the value of the call on spot gold, c
$= e^{-rT}[pc_u + (1 - p) c_d]$
$= e^{-0.01}[0.55025 \times 1,150 - 0.44975 \times 0]$
$= 0.99005 \times 632.79 = ₹626.49$

Using Eq. 19.8, the value of the call on futures, f
$= e^{-rT}[pf_u + (1 - p) f_d]$
$= e^{-0.01}[0.5 \times 1315 - 0.5 \times 0]$
$= 0.99005 \times 657.50 = ₹650.96$

(b) If the holder of the call wants to exercise his/her option, he/she would get
  (i) cash of $(14,500 - 14,250) = ₹250$; and
  (ii) a long position on the futures contract on gold.

> **EXAMPLE 19.3 Value call on index futures**
>
> The Nifty index is trading at 4500. A 3-m Nifty futures contract is at 4600. The volatility of the futures contract is 25%. What is the value of a 1-m call option on a 3-m futures contract with a strike of 4600 if the risk-free rate is 12% p.a.?
>
> **Solution**
> The value of the call option on the futures is given by Black's model
>
> $$c = e^{-rt}[F_0 \cdot N(d_1) - X \cdot N(d_2)]$$
>
> The values are $F_0 = 4600$, $X = 4600$, $r = 12\%$, $T = 1$ month, and $\sigma = 25\%$
>
> $$d_1 = \frac{\ln(F_0/X) + \sigma^2 T/2}{\sigma\sqrt{T}} = \frac{\ln(1) + 0.25 \times 0.25 \times 1/24}{0.25\,\sigma\sqrt{1/12}} = 0.0361 \text{ and}$$
>
> $$d_2 = \frac{\ln(F_0/X)\,\sigma^2 T/2}{\sigma\sqrt{T}} = d_1 - d_1 - \sigma\sqrt{T} = 0.0361 - 0.25\sqrt{1/12} = -0.361$$
>
> $N(d_1) = 0.5144$ and $N(d_2) = 0.4856$
>
> Value of the call = $e^{-0.12 \times 1/12}[4{,}600 \times 0.5144 - 4{,}600 \times 0.4856]$ = ₹131.36
> Value of one contract = 50×131.36 = ₹6568

d_2, too, would stand modified. The computation of d_1 and d_2 includes the drift of r. For the futures, the drift can be stated to be equal to zero. The drift on the stock that pays a dividend of q is equal to $r - q$. The futures is equivalent to the stock with the dividend yield equal to r. Therefore, the net drift for the futures would be zero. The modified values of d_1 and d_2 for valuing options on futures are shown in Eqs 19.12 and 19.13.

$$d_1 = \frac{\ln(F_0/X) + \sigma^2 T/2}{\sigma\sqrt{T}}, \qquad (19.12)$$

and

$$d_2 = \frac{\ln(F_0/X) - \sigma^2 T/2}{\sigma\sqrt{T}} = d_1 - \sigma\sqrt{T} \qquad (19.13)$$

> *Put–call parity too holds for options on futures, with the spot price replaced by the present value of the futures price less the premium for the buyer.*

Without elaboration, we may say that the put–call parity that holds good for the call and put options on the underlying stock would also hold good for the European option on futures. The put–call parity for contracts on the underlying is

$$c + X \cdot e^{-rT} = p + S_0$$

The current futures price, F_0

= Spot value + cost of carry = $S_0 \times e^{rT}$

or

$$S_0 = F_0 \times e^{-rT}$$

Replacing S_0 with the equivalent futures price $F_0 \times e^{-rT}$, we get the put–call parity for options on futures as Equation 19.14.

$$c + X e^{-rT} = p + F_0 e^{-rT} \qquad (19.14)$$

OPTION ON SWAPS—SWAPTIONS

Swap options are options on swaps. They are also called swaptions. Options on swaps give the holder the right, but no obligation, to enter into a swap contract at some time in the future on payment of a premium.

> *A swaption gives the right to the holder to enter into a swap at the expiry of the option.*

The underlying swap can be fixed payer–floating receiver (called payer's swaption) or floating payer–fixed receiver (receiver's swaption). The strike rate in a swaption is the interest rate that would be applicable for the fixed leg of the underlying swap. For a payer's swaption, the holder would pay a fixed interest rate for receiving the floating rate, and for a receiver's swaption, the holder receives a fixed rate and pays a floating rate. A payer's swaption would be entered by one who expects interest rates to go up and a receiver's swaption would be chosen by one who expects interest rates in the future to come down.

The exercise can be American style or European style. Upon exercise, the underlying swap contract is entered into. However, swaptions can be cash settled too. The rules of exercise of swaptions are as follows:

Rate on expiry	Payer's swaption	Receiver's swaption
When interest > strike	Exercise	Do not exercise
interest < strike	Do not exercise	Exercise

Forward Swap and Swaption

Let us examine a payer's swaption with a 3-year swap as underlying, with a strike rate of 10%. The swaption matures in two years, at which time the holder gets a right, but no obligation, to enter into the underlying swap by paying a fixed rate at 10% for receiving a floating rate.

Such an option would be useful for a firm that (a) pays a floating interest rate on its borrowing, (b) anticipates a rise in the interest rates in the future, and (c) believes that the swap, if entered into after two years, would have a swap rate greater than 10%, the strike rate in the swaption. This situation can be effectively covered by entering a forward swap with two years as the forward period and three years as the swap period. However, with a forward swap, it would be obligatory on the firm to enter into the swap at 10%, which would be disadvantageous if the market rate for the swap happens to be lower than 10%. With a swaption, it is not obligatory to enter the underlying swap. If the swap rate happens to be less than 10%, the firm would enter the swap on the market rate rather than exercise the swaption.

Similarly, one can demonstrate that for a receiver's swaption, the underlying swap would require paying a floating rate for receiving a fixed rate specified in the strike of the swaption. This would be exercised when the swap rate on the expiry of the swaption is less than the strike rate. It would be applicable for a firm expecting to enter into a swap to convert either an existing liability from a fixed rate to a floating rate, or an existing asset from a floating rate to a fixed rate.

Payoff on Swaption

> The payoff on a swaption is the difference between the swap rate and the strike rate at the end of the option period.

The payoff on a swaption may be viewed in terms of the differential between the swap rate, S_w, and the strike rate of the swaption, X. Assume that a European payer's swaption with two years to expiry has a strike rate of 10% for an underlying 3-year swap with semi-annual payments. At the end of two years, the holder of the swaption would compare the swap rate, S_w, with the strike rate. The payoff in terms of percentage would be Max($S_w - X$, 0).

Assume that the swap rate on the expiry of the swaption happens to be 11.90%. Therefore, the gain from exercising the swaption would be (11.90 − 11.00) = 1.90%, or 0.95% of the notional principal amount on each semi-annual payment. Assuming a notional principal of ₹100 lakh, the saving on each semi-annual payment would be 0.95% × 100 = ₹0.95 lakh.

To know the aggregate payoff on the swaption, we need to value each semi-annual payment in present value terms. Assume that the term structure observed at the expiry of the swaption is as follows:

Time (months)	6	12	18	24	30	36
Yields (%)	10.50	10.80	11.20	11.50	11.70	12.00

From the term structure, one can find the value of the zero, which is the correct discount factor for cash flows occurring at that point of time. Table 19.2 provides the amount of saving the holder of swaption would make by exercising the swaption. It comes to ₹4.7087 lakh for the notional principal of ₹100 lakh.

Table 19.2 Payoff from swaption

Time (months)	6	12	18	24	30	36
Yields (%)	10.50	10.80	11.20	11.50	11.70	12.00
Price of zeros	0.9501	0.9002	0.8492	0.7996	0.7526	0.7050
Amount saved (₹ lakh)	0.9500	0.9500	0.9500	0.9500	0.9500	0.9500
Present value (₹ lakh)	0.9026	0.8552	0.8067	0.7596	0.7149	0.6697
Payoff from swaption (₹ lakh)	4.7087					

The payoff of ₹4.7087 lakh, signifying the saving from entering into the underlying swap, also implies that if a cash settlement of the swaption is made, then the holder of the swaption should receive ₹4.7087 lakh. In that case, it is immaterial whether the underlying swap is actually entered into or not.

Swaptions and Options on Bond

From the payoff on the swaption shown in Table 19.2, it can be stated that swaptions are like options on a bond. A payer's swaption is like a put option on a bond with a face value of ₹1 and a coupon at the strike price of the swaption, X. The value of such a bond is $Z_N - X \times$ (Sum of zeros till maturity of bond), where Z_N is the value of the zeros for the period till maturity of the bond. From Chapter 18, we know that a put option on a bond with the exercise price, X, equal to a face value of ₹1 with a coupon of X, would have the following payoff:

Payoff on put option on a bond = Max(1 − value of bond, 0)

The payoff on the payer's swaption is Max($S_w - X$, 0), where S_w is the swap rate. The swap rate discussed in Chapter 8 is calculated by Eq. 8.6. In terms of our notations here, it is as given by Eq. 19.15.

$$\text{Swap rate} = \frac{1 - \text{last discount factor}}{\text{Sum of all discount factors}} = \frac{1 - Z_N}{\sum_{1}^{N} Z_i} \quad (19.15)$$

The payoff on the payer's swaption represented in terms of zeros is given in Eq. 19.16:

$$\text{Payer swaption payoff} = \text{Max}\left[\frac{1 - Z_N}{\sum_1^N Z_i} - X, 0\right]$$

$$= \text{Max}\left[(1 - Z_n) - X\sum_1^N Z_i, 0\right]$$

$$= \text{Max}\left[\left(1 - \left(Z_n + X\sum_1^N Z_i\right)\right), 0\right]$$

$$= \text{Max}(1 - \text{value of bond}, 0) \quad (19.16)$$

The payer's swaption payoff is the same as the payoff on a put option on a bond. On similar lines, the value of a receiver's swaption can be shown to be equal to a call option on a bond with a face value of 1 and a coupon at the strike price of the swaption. Therefore,

- A payer's swaption is equal to a put option with an exercise price of ₹1 on a bond with a face value of ₹1 and a coupon rate equal to the strike of the swaption.
- A receiver's swaption is equal to a call option with an exercise price of ₹1 on a bond with a face value of ₹1 and a coupon rate equal to the strike of the swaption.

Valuation of Swaptions

A swaption can be valued using Black's model by assuming that the swap rate of the underlying swap has log-normal distribution. We may value the payer's swaption, where the holder has the right to pay a fixed rate, X, the strike rate of the swaption, for receiving a floating rate.

> The payoff on a swaption is like an interest rate caplet or floorlet repeated at each payment.

Payer swaption value,

$$c = L.A.[F_s \cdot N(d_1) - X \cdot N(d_2)] \quad (19.17)$$

Receiver swaption value,

$$p = L.A.[X \cdot N(-d_2) - F_s \cdot N(-d_1)] \quad (19.18)$$

where

$$A = \frac{1}{m}\sum_1^N Z_i;\ d_1 = \frac{\ln(F_s/X) + \sigma^2 T/2}{\sigma\sqrt{T}},\ \text{and}\ d_2 = \frac{\ln(F_s/X) - \sigma^2 T/2}{\sigma\sqrt{T}} = d_1 - \sigma\sqrt{T}$$

Z_i = Value of zeros (discount factor for i^{th} cash flow),
X = Strike interest rate of swaption
m = Number of payments in a year
L = Notional principal
T = Life of swaption, when the underlying swap starts
F_s = Forward price of underlying swap
σ = Volatility of forward swap price

Note the difference in valuation of a swaption from that of an interest rate option or an option on a bond. The value of a swaption includes a discount factor, A. In the valuation of an interest rate option, the cash flow is discounted using the discount rate applicable to the respective cash flows of the option. Each caplet is discounted at the applicable rate (the value of zero) at the time of the cash flow. In a caplet, there is only one cash flow, but a swap involves repeated cash flows at each scheduled date. Therefore, the discount factor becomes an annuity, A, because a swaption is a repeated payoff on the swap rate.

We now value a swaption with following parameters:

Strike interest rate, X	: 6.50%
Time to expiry, T	: 2 years
Underlying swap	: 3-year swap commencing two years from now, with the right to pay a fixed rate on a semi-annual basis
Volatility of swap rate, σ	: 20%

The only unknown parameter under Black's model for valuing a swaption is the forward swap rate, F_s, which is arrived at using the term structure or the values of zeros, and is described in the paragraphs that follow.

> Swaptions can be valued using Black's formula with the forward swap rate derived from the term structure.

Calculating Forward Swap Rate The swap rate is the fixed rate of interest that would be paid/received in exchange for a floating rate of interest. The determination of the swap rate is discussed in the valuation of swaps in Chapter 8. Swap rates are derived from zero rates that are available for the period till the cash flows are committed in the swap.

$$\text{Swap Rate} = m \times \frac{1 - \text{Discount factor for last cash flow}}{\text{Sum of all discount factors}} = m \times \frac{1 - Z_N}{\sum_{1}^{N} Z_i} \quad (19.19)$$

where Z_i = Value of zero (discount factor for i^{th} cash flow)
N = Number of swap cash flows
m = Number of cash flows in a year

Table 19.3 demonstrates the calculation of the swap rate for a five-year swap with semi-annual and annual cash flows for a given term structure (yields for the corresponding

Table 19.3 Finding swap rate

Cash flow	Time (months)	Yield (%)	Discount factor	
			Semi-annual	Annual
1	6	5.00	0.9756	
2	12	5.50	0.9479	0.9479
3	18	6.00	0.9174	
4	24	6.30	0.8881	0.8881
5	30	6.50	0.8602	
6	36	6.80	0.8306	0.8306
7	42	7.00	0.8032	
8	48	7.20	0.7764	0.7764
9	54	7.40	0.7502	
10	60	7.60	0.7246	0.7246
Sum of all discount factors			8.4742	4.1676
Swap rate			6.50%	6.61%

periods). The discount factors mentioned are also referred to as values of zeros. The swap rate is 6.50% for semi-annual payments and 6.61% for annual payments.

$$\text{For semi-annual, swap rate} = 2 \times \frac{1 - 0.7246}{8.4742} = 0.0650 \text{ or } 6.50\%$$

$$\text{For annual, swap rate} = \frac{1 - 0.7246}{4.1676} = 0.06615 \text{ or } 6.61\%$$

To find the forward swap rate for a swap starting two years from now for the next three years with semi-annual fixed rate payments, we need to find the forward discount factors and the forward swap rate using Eq. 19.19. The forward discount factors are obtained directly from the values of the zeros. The forward discount factor is arrived at by dividing the discount factor in the semi-annual period by 0.8881 (the last discount factor prior to the commencement of the forward swap), as shown here:

Forward discount factor for the first payment = 0.8602/0.8881 = 0.9686
Forward discount factor for second payment = 0.8306/0.8881 = 0.9352

....
....

Forward discount factor for sixth payment = 0.7246/0.8881 = 0.8159

The forward swap rate may be found using Eq. 19.19.
It is shown to be 6.89% in Table 19.4.

Table 19.4 Finding forward swap rate 2-year forward for 3-year swap

Cash flow	Time (months)	Yield (%)	Discount factor	
			Semi-annual	Annual
1	6	5.00	0.9756	
2	12	5.50	0.9479	
3	18	6.00	0.9174	
4	24	6.30	0.8881	
5	30	6.50	0.8602	0.9686
6	36	6.80	0.8306	0.9352
7	42	7.00	0.8032	0.9044
8	48	7.20	0.7764	0.8742
9	54	7.40	0.7502	0.8447
10	60	7.60	0.7246	0.8159
Sum of all discount factors				5.3431
Forward swap rate (2 year forward, 3 year swap)				6.89%

Value of Swaption The inputs for Black's model for valuing swaptions are: the forward swap rate, F_s, 6.89%, $X = 6.50\%$, $m = 2$, $T = 2$ years, and $\sigma = 20\%$. For an assumed notional principal, $L = ₹100$, we get

$$d_1 = 0.3472, \quad d_2 = 0.0644,$$
$$N(d_1) = 0.6358, \quad N(d_2) = 0.5257 \text{ and } A = 2.6716$$

The value of the payer's swaption is ₹2.5744.
For the same underlying, the receiver's swaption would have

$-d_1 = -0.3472$, $-d_2 = 0.0644$,
$N(-d_1) = 0.3642$, $N(-d_2) = 0.4743$ and $A = 2.6716$

The value of the receiving swaption is ₹1.5324.

EXAMPLE 19.4 Valuing swaption

ABC Ltd has a floating rate liability for the next six years. It expects interest rates to rise in the future, and, therefore, may have to enter into a swap for receiving a floating rate and paying a fixed rate. A 1-year swaption is available with a strike of 10.50% for paying a fixed rate and receiving a floating rate for five years thereafter. The term structure for the next six years is

Year	1	2	3	4	5	6
Interest, %	9.50	9.75	10.00	10.25	10.50	11.00

If the volatility of the forward swap rate is 20%, what price is appropriate for the firm to pay for the payer's swaption? Assume an annual payment for the notional principal of ₹100 under the swap.

Term structure			
Year	Rate	Zeros	1-year Forward zeros
1	9.50%	0.91324	
2	9.75%	0.83022	0.9091
3	10.00%	0.75131	0.8227
4	10.25%	0.67684	0.7411
5	10.50%	0.60700	0.6647
6	11.00%	0.53464	0.5854
Sum		4.31325	3.7230
Swap rate $t = 0$		10.789%	
Forward swap rate $t = 1$			11.136%

The swap rate is found by using Eq. 19.15. The forward swap rate works out to 11.136%. The value of the payer's swaption is given by Eq. 19.17. We have $F_s = 11.135\%$, $X = 10.50\%$, $m = 1$, $T = 1$ year, and $\sigma = 20\%$.

$$A = \frac{1}{m}\sum_1^N Z_i = 3.7230$$

$$d_1 = \frac{\ln(F_s/X) + \sigma^2 T/2}{\sigma\sqrt{T}} = \frac{\ln(11.135/10.5) + 0.2 \times 0.2 \times 1/2}{0.2\sqrt{1}} = 0.3937 \text{ and}$$

$$d_2 = d_1 - \sigma\sqrt{T} = 0.3937 - 0.2\sqrt{1} = 0.1937$$
$$N(d_1) = 0.6531 \quad \text{and} \quad N(d_2) = 0.5768$$

Payer swaption value, c = $L.A.[F_s.N(d_1) - X.N(d_2)]$
= $100 \times 3.7230[0.1135 \times 0.6531 - 0.1050 \times 0.5768]$
= ₹4.53

SOLVED PROBLEMS

SP 19.1: Binomial pricing of put on futures

Refer to Example 19.2. What would the values of a put option on spot gold and a futures contract on gold be, with the same strike of ₹14,250 and one month to expiry? Assume a risk-free interest rate of 1% per month. Draw a single-stage binomial tree.

What would the payoff on a put on the futures be if the holder exercises the option?

Solution

With a risk-free interest rate of 1% per month and up and down movements of 10% each, the risk-neutral probability of up movement, using Eqs 19.6 and 19.9, is:

For a put option on spot gold = $(e^{rt} - d)/(u - d) = (1.0105 - 0.9)/0.2 = 0.55025$
For a put option on futures = $(1 - d)/(u - d) = 0.1/0.2 = 0.50$

Using Eq. 19.5 modified for a put (replacing p for c), the value of the call on spot gold,

$$p = e^{-rt}[pp_u + (1 - p) p_d]$$
$$= e^{-0.01}[0.55025 \times 0 - 0.44975 \times 1650]$$
$$= .99005 \times 805.50 = ₹797.48.$$

Binomial tree for option on spot and futures on gold

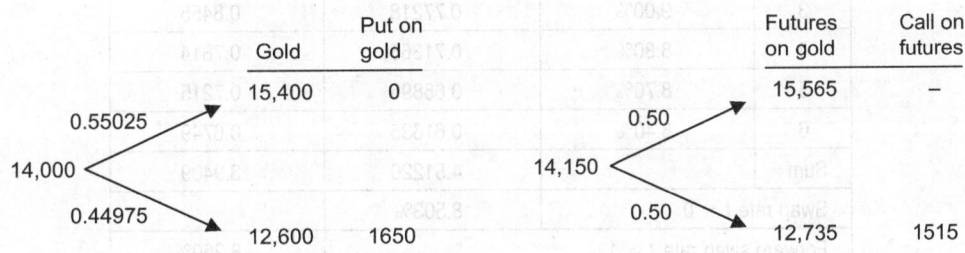

Using Eq. 19.8, the value of the put on futures, $f = e^{-rt}[pf_u + (1 - p) f_d]$
$$= e^{-0.01}[0.5 \times 0 + 0.5 \times 1515]$$
$$= 0.99005 \times 757.50 = ₹749.96$$

The value of the call in Example 19.2 was derived at ₹ 650.96. Using put–call parity as given by Eq. 19.3, the value of the put would be

$$p = c + Xe^{-rt} \times F_0 e^{-rt}$$
$$= 650.96 + 0.99005 \times 14,250 - 0.99005 \times 14,150$$
$$= 0.99005 \times 757.50 = ₹749.96$$

SP 19.2: Value put on index futures

Use the date in Example 19.3 and find the value of a put option on Nifty of the same parameters as those of the call.

Solution

The value of the put option on futures as given by Black's model is

$$p = e^{-rt}[XN(-d_2) - F_0 \times N(-d_1)]$$

The values are $F_0 = 4600$, $X = 4600$, $r = 12\%$, $T = 1$ month, and $\sigma = 25\%$

$$d_1 = \frac{\ln(F_0/X) + \sigma^2 T/2}{\sigma \sqrt{T}} = \frac{\ln(1) + 0.25 \times 0.25 \times 1/24}{0.25 \sqrt{1/12}} = 0.0361 \text{ and}$$

$$d_2 = \frac{\ln(F_0/X) - \sigma^2 T/2}{\sigma \sqrt{T}} = d_1 - \sigma\sqrt{T} = 0.0361 - 0.25\sqrt{1/12} = -0.361$$

$$N(-d_1) = 0.4846 \quad \text{and} \quad N(-d_2) = 0.5144$$

Value of the put = $e^{-0.12 \times 1/12}[4600 \times 0.5144 - 4600 \times 0.4856] = ₹ 131.36$
Value of one contract = $50 \times 131.36 = ₹ 6568$

SP 19.3: Valuing swaption

XYZ Ltd has a fixed rate liability for the next six years. It expects interest rates to fall in the future, and, therefore, may have to enter into a swap for receiving a fixed rate and paying a floating rate. A one-year swaption is available with a strike of 9.00% for receiving a fixed rate and paying a floating rate for five years thereafter. The term structure for the next six years is as follows:

Year	1	2	3	4	5	6
Interest, %	9.50	9.25	9.00	8.80	10.50	8.70	8.40

If the volatility of the forward swap rate is 20%, what price would be appropriate for the firm to pay for a receiver's swaption? Assume annual payments under the swap for a principal sum of ₹100.

Solution

We need to find out the likely swap rate after a year. According to the term structure, the present swap rate must be 8.50% (see the following table). With an upward sloping term structure, the one-year forward swap rate works out to 8.25%, as shown here:

Term structure			
Year	Rate	Zeros	Forward zeros
1	9.50%	0.91324	
2	9.25%	0.83783	0.9174
3	9.00%	0.77218	0.8455
4	8.80%	0.71365	0.7814
5	8.70%	0.65895	0.7215
6	8.40%	0.61635	0.6749
Sum		4.51220	3.9409
Swap rate $t = 0$		8.503%	
Forward swap rate $t = 1$			8.250%

The swap rate is calculated by using Eq. 19.15. The forward swap rate works out to 8.25%. The value of the receiver's swaption is given by Eq. 19.17. We have $F_s = 8.25\%$, $X = 9.00\%$, $m = 1$, $T = 1$ year, and $\sigma = 20\%$.

$$A = \frac{1}{m}\sum_{1}^{N} Z_i = 3.9409$$

$$d_1 = \frac{\ln(F_s/X) + \sigma^2 T/2}{\sigma\sqrt{T}} = \frac{\ln(8.25/9.00) + 0.2 \times 0.2 \times 1/2}{0.2\sqrt{1}} = -0.3354 \text{ and}$$

$$d_2 = d_1 - \sigma\sqrt{T} = 0.3937 - 0.2\sqrt{1} = -0.5354$$

$N(-d_1) = 0.6313$ and $N(-d_2) = 0.7038$

Receiver Swaption Value, p = $L.A.[X.N(-d_2) - F_s.N(-d_1)]$
= $100 \times 3.9409[0.90 \times 0.7038 - 0.0825 \times 0.6313]$
= ₹ 4.44

SUMMARY

A futures option, or option on futures, gives the right to the holder of the option to have a long or a short position in the futures contract upon exercise or on expiry of the option. A call option on futures upon exercise provides cash equal to the intrinsic value of the option and a long position on the underlying futures contract. Similarly, a put option on futures provides cash equal to the intrinsic worth plus a short position on the futures contract.

Futures options have gained popularity because they combine the advantages of both options and futures. While an option protects the holder from downside risk, it retains the upside potential gain. A future obviates delivery by rendering flexibility to enter into an offsetting contract.

The valuation of options on futures can be done in a manner similar to that used for options on the spot by assuming a dividend yield equal to the risk-free rate, implying zero growth of the futures price in the risk-neutral world. Black's model incorporates such a modification and can be used for valuing options on futures contracts.

A swaption is an option on swaps. It gives the holder the right to enter into a swap at the end of the option period. Under a payer's swaption, the holder pays a fixed rate and receives a floating rate, and under a receiver's swaption, floating rate payments are made in exchange for receiving fixed rate payments. The holder of a swaption compares the strike rate of the option with the swap rate at the end of the option period. Under a payer's swaption, the holder would like to pay the lesser of the strike or the swap rate. Hence, if the swap rate is higher, the holder exercises the option. For a receiver's swaption, the reverse is true.

Swaptions provide a hedge for entities that are likely to enter into a swap in the future. The objective can be achieved by a forward swap too. However, it would be obligatory to enter the swap at the end of the forward period, while with a swaption, it is an option. The payoff under swaptions is like that for an interest rate option. With an interest rate option, payment under each caplet or floorlet would be different, while under a swaption, the same payoff would result on each date, till the swap period is over.

Swaptions can be valued with Black's formula for options on futures. The forward swap rate can be obtained from the term structure of interest rates. The remaining determinants can be fixed between the buyer and the seller of the swaption.

KEY TERMS

Forward swap A swap that commences at a future date with a swap rate fixed now.
Futures option An option that gives the right to the holder to have a long or a short position on a futures contract.
Payer's swaption Under a payer's swaption, the holder pays a fixed rate for receiving a floating rate.

Receiver's swaption Under a receiver's swaption, the holder pays a floating rate in exchange for receiving a fixed rate.
Swaption An option that gives a right to the holder to enter into a swap at a future date.

QUESTIONS

19.1 Describe Black's model for valuing options on futures.
19.2 Why are options on futures popular despite options on spot being available?
19.3 How is a binomial model for valuing futures options different from the one for valuing options on spot?
19.4 Differentiate between (a) a forward swap and swaption and (b) a payer's and receiver's swaption.

PROBLEMS

P 19.1 Payoff—options on index futures
What is the payoff on call and put options on Nifty futures with a strike price of ₹ 4800? The last settlement price for Nifty futures was ₹ 4775, and, currently, it is trading at ₹ 4820. Would the options be exercised?

P 19.2 Valuation—options on index futures
Nifty futures with three months to maturity is currently trading at ₹ 4700. What would be the value of a 2-m call option on Nifty futures with an exercise price of ₹ 4650? The risk-free rate is 8% and the volatility of the futures price is 20%.

P 19.3 Black's model for put on futures
Refer to the data in P 19-2. Find the value of a put option on Nifty futures with the same strike and time to maturity as the call option. Further, compute the put price using put–call parity.

P 19.4 Swaptions—payoff
Determine the payoff on a receiver's swaption with a strike of 11% and a payer's swaption with a strike of 10.50%, with a three-year semi-annual swap as underlying, when the following term structure was observed at the end of the option period.

Period (months)	6	12	18	24	30	36
Yield (%)	9.00	9.50	9.90	10.20	10.50	10.70

Credit Risk, Securitization, and Credit Derivatives

20

INTRODUCTION

This chapter deals with another dimension of risk that, of late, has become extremely important—credit risk. It is also referred to as a *default risk*, and its understanding, measurement, and management have been gaining prominence, as it gives rise to systemic risk. Systemic risk relates to the impairment of the ability of an organization to honour its commitments due to the failure of others. Since financial markets and institutions are integrated and are mutually dependent to a great degree, adversity faced by one institution has the potential to be transmitted to the others in the system. If adversity affects several sectors or large parts of the financial system, it culminates in a global crisis.

> Understanding credit risk is crucial because it threatens to lead to systemic risk and cause a financial crisis.

Under such circumstances, it is not as important to understand what causes systemic risk as it is to manage it. The roots of default may lie in market factors such as interest rates, commodity prices, or exchange rates, which manifest into credit risk, or may emerge from wrong policies and structural decisions within an organization, such as an inordinate amount of leverage. In the context of derivatives, default risk becomes more important due to the high degree of leverage used. Derivative exposures also escape getting recorded in the financial statements, making exposures invisible, and thus avoid scrutiny by regulators and those who might be affected by these highly leveraged transactions. Most of the exposures in derivatives are contingent in nature and get crystallized only upon the happening of some event or the maturity of the derivatives.

We deal with credit risk first, before discussing the derivatives used for managing it.

Learning Objectives

After going through this chapter, readers should be familiar with

- credit risk and credit risk measurement
- assessment of probability of default, default rates, and default losses
- finding credit value at risk
- credit default swaps and how they work
- valuation of credit default swaps using the Merton model
- total return swaps and how they work
- the process of securitization and its benefits
- how securitization creates credit derivatives
- credit-linked notes
- collateralized debt obligations
- synthetic collateralized debt obligations

CREDIT RISK

Credit risk is the risk that the counterparty in a transaction would not honour or pay the obligations undertaken by it. In financial circles, terms such as non-performing assets (NPAs) are in common use; the NPA ratio with total credit often serves as an important indicator of the quality of business and the creditworthiness of borrowers. It is also taken as a measure of the effectiveness of due-diligence and post-credit supervision.

All organizations in business are exposed to credit risk. A firm supplying goods or services on credit to its customers always faces the possibility of the customers not paying their full amounts on the due dates. However, their core area lies in making profit through the supply of goods and services, and credit is generated only out of business necessity. Business organizations largely take market risk and not credit risk. Credit risk primarily affects those who are mainly in the business of providing credit and generating profit out of assuming credit risk, such as banks and financial institutions.

> Credit risk is the risk of default by the counterparty to a loan transaction, and is different from market risk.

Credit risk, as distinct from market risk, is concerned with default by counterparties in loan transactions. There are ways of assessing market risk, but the same principles used in measuring market risk cannot be applied to measure credit risk, as borrowers do not pay in excess of what they owe. A trading portfolio may pay more than expected if the going is good, while a loan portfolio never pays in excess of the interest promised and the principal due. Therefore, returns from debt cannot be regarded as having a normal distribution. Further, a debt is not traded as much as equity and is rather illiquid. A significant part of debt is mobilized over the counter (OTC), as financial institutions and banks make loans that are never traded, and, hence, there are no market prices available for loans and debt.

All individuals, firms, financial institutions, and governments can default on their commitments. Credit risk arises out of some credit event, and, therefore, credit risk measurement is a complex process. It is a function of (a) the probability of default, (b) the loss once the default has occurred, i.e., loss given default (LGD), or (c) its opposite, the recovery rate.

One of the key determinants of credit risk is the rating. The ratings of bonds and firms are based on the probability of default. The price of a bond is dependent upon the expected yield, its maturity, and the default risk associated with rated bonds. Since treasury bonds are presumed to be free from default risk, the yields on them would purely reflect on the expected returns of the investors for the given maturity. If a bond trades with higher yields, then the differential from the yield on treasury bonds can be attributed to default associated with the issuer.

PROBABILITY OF DEFAULT

The first step to comprehend credit risk is the understanding of the probability of default. The prices of bonds may throw some light on the probability of default.

The value of a bond issued by a firm when compared with the value of a corresponding treasury bond must reflect the expected losses from the bond issued by the firm. For ease of computation and understanding, let us deal with zero coupon bonds, called *zeros*. Assume that a one-year zero coupon bond issued by ABC is trading at a yield of 6.30%, while one-year treasury zeros are trading at a yield of 6%. To what factor do we associate the difference in yield between the treasury zero and the corporate bond? Given that all other features are identical, the difference in yields of 0.30% must reflect on the ability/inability of ABC to redeem the bond in a timely fashion. Therefore, the difference in yield from a risk-free bond is on account of the default risk associated with the firm ABC.

What does the difference in value represent? It must represent the present value of the loss expected due to a default in the period. The value of the one-year treasury zero coupon bond at 6% yield is $100 \times e^{-0.06 \times 1} = ₹94.1765$, and the value of the one-year zeros issued by ABC at 6.30% is $100 \times e^{-0.063 \times 1} = ₹93.8943$. The difference in the values of the two, i.e., ₹0.2821, must be the present value of the loss expected due to default by ABC in one year. As the percentage of the value of the risk-free zeros, this corresponds to a probability of default of 0.2996% (0.2821/94.1765) in one year.

> The probability of default is factored into the prices of bonds. The difference in price with a risk-free bond represents the present value of the expected losses from any default.

Similarly, if five-year treasury zeros trade at 7.50% and zero coupon bonds issued by ABC are trading at 8.10%, the values would be ₹68.7289 and ₹66.6977, respectively. The difference in value of ₹2.0312 represents the expected loss due to a default by ABC over a period of five years, which is equivalent to a cumulative probability of 2.9954% (2.0312/68.7289), expressed as a percentage of the value of the five-year risk-free zero.

The yields and values of zeros issued by the treasury and firm ABC are presented in Table 20.1, for a period of 10 years. The difference in values represents the present value of the expected loss till the end of the period. The difference as a percentage of the risk-free zero is the cumulative probability of default till the end of the period.

From the values of the bonds, it may be said that the probability that ABC would default by the end of the third year is 1.4889%. The difference in the cumulative probabilities of the two periods represents the probability of default during the intervening periods. The probability

Table 20.1 Finding probability of default

Maturity	Risk-free zeros		Zero coupon bonds of ABC		Difference in value, ₹	Cumulative probability of default, % of risk-free zeros	Probability of default in the year, % of risk-free zeros
Years	Yield, %	Value, ₹	Yield, %	Value, ₹			
1	6.00	94.1765	6.30	93.8943	0.2822	0.2997	0.2997
2	6.20	88.3380	6.60	87.6341	0.7039	0.7968	0.4971
3	6.50	82.2835	7.00	81.0584	1.2251	1.4889	0.6921
4	6.90	75.8813	7.50	74.0818	1.7995	2.3715	0.8826
5	7.50	68.7289	8.10	66.6977	2.0312	2.9554	0.5839
6	7.80	62.6254	8.50	60.0496	2.5758	4.1130	1.1576
7	7.85	57.7238	8.65	54.5801	3.1437	5.4461	1.3331
8	7.90	53.1528	8.80	49.4603	3.6925	6.9470	1.5009
9	8.00	48.6752	9.00	44.4858	4.1894	8.6068	1.6598
10	8.20	44.0432	9.30	39.4554	4.5878	10.4166	1.8098

EXAMPLE 20.1 Expected loss and probability of default

Refer to the data presented in Table 20-1 and answer the following:
(a) What is the present value of the loss expected due to default by ABC by the end of year 6?
(b) What is the probability that ABC would default in the next six years?
(c) What is the probability of default by ABC in year 5?
(d) What is the probability of default between the third and the seventh years?

Solution
(a) The present value of the loss expected in the next six years due to default by ABC is the difference between the prices of the six-year risk-free zeros and the six-year zeros by ABC, i.e., ₹2.5758 (₹62.6254 − ₹60.0496)
(b) The cumulative probability that ABC would default in the next six years is 4.1130%.
(c) The probability that ABC would default in the fifth year is the difference between the cumulative probabilities of defaults in the fifth and the fourth year, i.e., 0.5839% (2.9554 − 2.3715).
(d) The probability of default between the third and the seventh years is the difference between the cumulative probabilities of default at the end of the seventh and the third year, i.e., 3.9272% (5.4461 − 1.4889).

of default between 1 to 5 years is 2.9554 − 0.2997 = 2.6557%. The last column of Table 20.1 is the probability of default in the year.

The data presented in Table 20.1 are valid only if we assume that in case of default, the value of ABC's bonds would be zero, i.e., the recovery rate is nil, and the loss is the entire value of the bonds.

With some recovery rate (R) associated, the probabilities of the default and expected losses would undergo a change. This may be seen from the following formulation.

Let r and r^* be the yields on the risky and the risk-free zero coupon bonds, respectively, for identical maturity periods, T, and identical face values of ₹1.00. The values of the bonds would be as follows:

$$\text{Risky bond:} \quad 1.00\, e^{-rT}$$
$$\text{Risk-free bond:} \quad 1.00\, e^{-r^*T}$$

If the probability of default before period T is P_T and the risky bond has a value of R in the case of default, then the expected value of the risky bond at maturity is

$$P_T \times R + (1 - P_T) \times 1.00$$

> Under risk neutrality, the present value of losses can be converted into the probability of default.

In the risk-neutral world, we can discount the expected value at maturity at the risk-free rate to arrive at the present value of the bond. Therefore,

$$\text{Present value of the bond} = [P_T \times R + (1 - P_T) \times 1.00] \times e^{-r^*T}$$

The risk-neutral value must be equal to the present value of the bond. Hence,

$$\{P_T \times R + (1 - P_T) \times 1.00\} \times e^{-r^*T} = 1.00\, e^{-rT}$$

Solving for P_T, we get

$$P_T = \frac{1 - e^{-(r - r^*)T}}{1 - R} \tag{20.1}$$

With recovery rate $R = 0$, Eq. 20.1 reduces to Eq. 20.2.

$$P_T = 1 - e^{-(r - r^*)T} \tag{20.2}$$

> **EXAMPLE 20.2 Probability of default and recovery rate**
>
> Using the data in Table 20-1 and Eqs 20.1 and 20.2, find out the following:
>
> (a) The probability of default by firm ABC in five years (i) with no recovery, and (ii) with recovery of 50% in the case of default.
> (b) The probability of default by firm ABC in 10 years (i) with no recovery, and (ii) with recovery of 30% in case of default.
>
> **Solution**
>
> (a) The probability of default is governed by the spread in yields over five years. The spread in the yields of the risk-free and risky bonds is 8.1 − 7.5 = 0.6%. Therefore, using Eq. 20.2, the probability of default with no recovery is
> $$P_T = 1 - e^{-(r-r^*)T} = 1 - e^{-0.006 \times 5}$$
> $$= 1 - 0.970446 = 0.029554 = 2.9554\%$$
> The probability of default with expected recovery of 50% using Eq. 20.1 would be.
> $$P_T = 2.9554/(1 - 0.5) = 5.9108\%$$
> (b) Similarly, the probability of default in ten years is governed by the spread in yields over 10 years. The spread in the yields of the risk-free and risky bonds is 9.3 − 8.2 = 1.1%. Therefore, using Eq. 20.2, the probability of default with no recovery is
> $$P_T = 1 - e^{-(r-r^*)T} = 1 - e^{-0.011 \times 10}$$
> $$= 1 - 0.895834 = 0.104166 = 10.4166\%$$
> The probability of default with expected recovery of 50% using Eq. 20.1 would be
> $$P_T = 10.4166/(1 - 0.3) = 14.8806\%$$

From Eq. 20.2, we may infer that the probability of default is a function of the spread in yields of the risky and the risk-free bonds, i.e., $(r - r^*)$, and not so much of the actual absolute yields. Refer to Example 20.2.

The outcome in Example 20.2 is subject to some misleading interpretation. We observe that the probability of default increased with an increased recovery rate. It is truly not so. With an increasing recovery rate, the probability of default must decline. In the example, we get increased probability of default with increased recovery rate because we assumed that the price of the bond of ABC remains the same. With an increased recovery rate, the value of the bond must increase, indicating a decreasing spread with the risk-free rate. Despite the increased recovery, if the bond continues to sell for the same price, it implies that the probability associated with default has indeed increased. For better understanding, refer to Solved Problem SP 20.1 at the end of this chapter.

Recovery Rates

Recovery rate is the estimate of the face value that bondholders expect to receive after a credit event such as bankruptcy, or restructuring. It is expressed as a percentage of the face value. Generally, recovery rates are difficult to obtain. The recovery rate is dependent on several factors. The most important of them are (a) the nature of priority of any claims over the cash flows of the firm, and (b) the level/kind of security available. Secured debt would have higher recovery rates in case of default due to the charge over the assets of the firm, and, hence, would provide lesser returns commensurate with lesser risk.

The preceding section provided an overview of credit risk measurement. We made extremely simplified assumptions such as (a) availability of the prices of zero coupon bonds, which is rarely the case, as bonds issued by firms are not large in numbers, and most corporate bonds are coupon bearing; (b) default occurs only at the end of periods, whereas in practice defaults can take place at any time; (c) estimates of recovery in the case of default are known; again, a difficult condition to fulfil due to the extended and complicated legal procedures of liquidation and the resultant deterioration in the value of the assets over the intervening period of time between the default and the actual recovery, impacting the claims and recovery rates.

Default Rates

One of the ways to assess default rates is to rely on some historical data on defaults. Rating agencies monitoring firms over long periods of time collect data on defaults, upgrades, and downgrades periodically, which can prove to be an invaluable source in the understanding of credit risk. Figures 20.1 and 20.2 provide the default rates of Indian firms and the historical patterns, respectively, as compiled by CRISIL in their recent default study of 2011.

One-, Two-, and Three-year CDRs, between 1988 and 2011				
Rating	Issuer-months	One-year	Two-year	Three-year
CRISIL AAA	11846	0.00%	0.00%	0.00%
CRISIL AA	24368	0.04%	0.40%	1.09%
CRISIL A	25694	0.82%	3.52%	7.66%
CRISIL BBB	29366	1.89%	5.34%	12.27%
CRISIL BB	22685	5.80%	12.52%	24.58%
CRISIL B	11489	8.25%	17.89%	37.90%
Total	127798			

Fig. 20.1 Trends in default rates

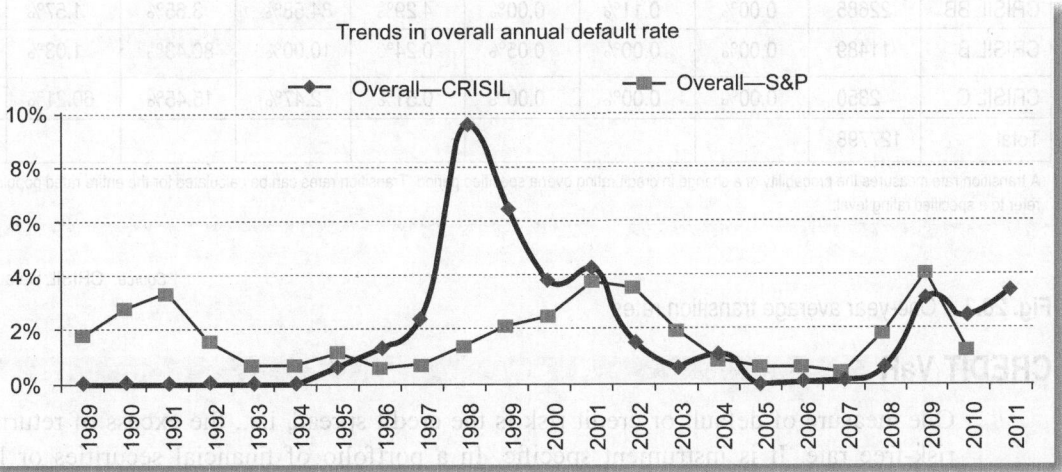

Fig. 20.2 Trends in default rates

> Historical data about recovery rates and default rates can be used to arrive at the potential loss due to default.

The data have been compiled over a long period of time, and, therefore, can be presumed to have incorporated all possible adverse market scenarios. They cover a span of three years and a large number of firms. For example, CRISIL A rated firms have defaulted to the extent of 0.82, 3.52, and 7.66% in a period of one, two, and three years, respectively. These figures can serve as unbiased benchmarks for predicting the likelihood of default by firms in the future, as the size of data and period of coverage are sufficiently large. These historical default rates render objectivity to unbiased default rates. They should serve as a better estimate than a subjective prediction of likelihood of default.

Transition Rates

Similarly, transition rates relate to the probability of the migration of firms from one rating to another. In assessing credit risk, not only a default but also a downgrade of rating is a credit event that throws light on the credit risk. Here again, the period of coverage and the size of data are sufficiently large to serve as reasonable estimates for the probability of upgrade or downgrade to another rating. The transition matrix depicted in Figure 20.3 provides transition probabilities over a period of one year, the usual horizon for assessing credit risk and estimation of capital adequacy.

> Historical data about transition rates can be used to determine the probability of changes in rating, including default.

One-year average transition rates: between 1988 and 2011									
Rating	Issuer-months	CRISIL AAA	CRISIL AA	CRISIL A	CRISIL BBB	CRISIL BB	CRISIL B	CRISIL C	CRISIL D
CRISIL AAA	11846	96.79%	3.21%	0.00%	0.00%	0.00%	0.00%	0.00%	0.00%
CRISIL AA	24368	1.77%	91.87%	5.27%	0.72%	0.26%	0.05%	0.03%	0.04%
CRISIL A	25694	0.00%	4.00%	85.71%	6.02%	2.84%	0.20%	0.41%	0.82%
CRISIL BBB	29366	0.00%	0.15%	3.95%	85.78%	6.69%	0.89%	0.65%	1.89%
CRISIL BB	22685	0.00%	0.11%	0.00%	4.29%	84.58%	3.65%	1.57%	5.80%
CRISIL B	11489	0.00%	0.00%	0.05%	0.24%	10.00%	80.43%	1.03%	8.25%
CRISIL C	2350	0.00%	0.00%	0.00%	0.51%	2.47%	15.45%	60.21%	21.36%
Total	127798								

A transition rate measures the probability of a change in credit rating over a specified period. Transition rates can be calculated for the entire rated population, or can refer to a specified rating level.

Source: CRISIL Default Study 2011

Fig. 20.3 One-year average transition rates

CREDIT VaR

One measure of default or credit risk is the credit spread, i.e., the excess of return over the risk-free rate. It is instrument specific. In a portfolio of financial securities or loans, the concern for financial institutions is to examine their ability to meet the risk of default by providing for a given level of losses through capital adequacy.

One measure is the credit VaR, i.e., the value of the loss associated with a portfolio of credit instruments/loans. It is similar to the VaR discussed earlier in Chapter 14. It reflects the losses over a given period of time for a portfolio of loans or bonds with a certain level of confidence desired. The losses are not taken into consideration when the bond defaults, but any deterioration in the value of the loan/bond too is considered while finding the credit VaR.

The rating of loan/bond determines its value and the profit or loss from its current value. However, the rating of instruments or firms takes place after the event causing deterioration has taken place. There seems to be no way other than to rely on the historical data about migration of ratings of a firm over the risk horizon. The usual period of consideration in computing credit VaR is one year, rather than the few days used for a portfolio of investment assets.

Credit risk is concerned with the deterioration of the quality of assets over time. Surveillance by rating agencies is done to monitor upgrades and downgrades of firms. *Credit migration* analyses the probability of moving from one credit rating to another, including default within a time, usually a year. This may be used as one of the inputs for the determination of VaR for a credit portfolio.

The credit migration approach computes the forward distribution of values that an asset can take over one year, where changes are related to credit migration alone. Since credit risk can have its source in market risk, we must also capture market risk while assessing credit risk. It must be noted that the cause is irrelevant, but the fact that a downgrade has taken place is relevant.

> Credit VaR is a comprehensive measure of credit risk that helps plan capital adequacy to absorb potential losses.

The best way to highlight the determination of credit VaR is by way of an example. For the purpose of illustration, we find the credit VaR on a single asset or a bond with a maturity of five years and an annual coupon of 15%, redeemable at par value of ₹100; the asset is presently rated as *CRISIL A*.

Transition Matrix The transition matrix serves the purpose of assessing the probability of moving from one credit rating to another, including default. Based on the historical data in the transition matrix shown in Fig. 20.3, the probabilities of a CRISIL A-rated bond moving to another rating or remaining in the same rating over the next one year is as follows:

%	AAA	AA	A	BBB	BB	B	C	D
A	–	4.00	85.71	6.02	2.84	0.20	0.41	0.82

The table shows that an *A*-rated bond has an 85.71% chance of remaining in the same rating after a year; it has a 4% chance of being upgraded to *AA*, and no chance of being upgraded two notches above to *AAA*. Similarly, it has a chance of 6.02% of being downgraded to *BBB*.

Forward Rates After knowing the probabilities for upgrades and downgrades, we need to know the likely values of the bond after the end of the horizon of the VaR period, i.e., one year. The values are required for different grades of ratings after one year.

How do we know what value the bond would have one year from now? The present yield curve helps to forecast future yields. The values of forward yields may be derived, and are called forward rates, as implied in the prices of zeros today. This is dependent upon the rating of the instrument. We use the forward zero curve to find the forward value of the bond under various rating scenarios. Assume that the forward rates for various graded instruments are as given in Table 20.2.

Table 20.2 Forward interest rates for bonds with different ratings

%	1-year	2-year	3-year	4-year
AAA	3.60	4.27	4.73	5.12
AA	3.65	4.22	4.78	5.17
A	3.72	4.32	4.93	5.32
BBB	4.10	4.67	5.25	5.63
BB	5.55	6.02	6.78	7.27
B	6.05	7.02	8.03	8.52
CCC	15.05	15.02	14.03	13.52

Revalue Bond From the forward rates, we find the value of the bond as seen today. It would depend upon the likely rating after one year. Assuming that the rating of the bond remains the same at A, the value of the bond after one year would be arrived at by discounting the remaining cash flows at the appropriate discount rates from Table 20.2. The forward value of the bond, if it stays in the same rating of A, comes to ₹149.70, as given in Table 20.3.

Table 20.3 One-year forward value of a bond rated A

Year	1	2	3	4	5
Cash flow, ₹	15.00	15.00	15.00	15.00	115.00
Discount rate for a rated bond, %		3.72	4.32	4.93	5.32
Present Value, ₹	15.0000	14.4620	13.7834	12.9835	93.4662
Forward value of bond after 1 year, ₹					149.70

However, if the rating undergoes a change during the year, the value of the bond too would change. We can arrive at this value today using forward rates applicable to the rating as discount rates on the cash flows of the bond. Using the forward rates given in Table 20.2 for the respective ratings, we can find the value of the bond upon migration in the same manner as done in Table 20.3. The values of the bond with different ratings are shown in Table 20.4.

Table 20.4 Forward value of bond with different ratings ₹

New rating	Present values of cash flows at forward fates					Value of bond
	1	2	3	4	5	
AAA	15.0000	14.4788	13.7966	13.0580	94.1795	**150.51**
AA	15.0000	14.4718	13.8099	13.0394	94.0005	**150.32**
A	15.0000	14.4620	13.7834	12.9835	93.4662	**149.70**
BBB	15.0000	14.4092	13.6914	12.8654	92.3738	**148.34**
BB	15.0000	14.2113	13.3449	12.3203	86.8530	**141.73**
B	15.0000	14.1443	13.0967	11.8976	82.9199	**137.06**
C	15.0000	13.0378	11.3382	10.1166	69.2482	**118.74**
Default	Assumed recovery at 54% of face value					**54.00**

The value of the bond is most difficult to work out in case of a default, as no discount rates can be visualized and recovery varies from case to case. Estimating market value is almost impossible, as there is no market for such assets. The recovery rate is dependent upon (a) the seniority of the claim and (b) the security available. It becomes increasingly difficult to assess recovery as time elapses, as the process of recovery is prolonged and stretched. Again, one would rely on past data to get an idea of the recovery in case of default. Based on recoveries made in the past, one can estimate the present recovery. Historical data serve as another input here. For illustration, it is assumed that in case of default, a recovery of 54% of the face value can be made.

> Transition matrices, forward rates, and recovery rates are crucial inputs to find the credit VaR.

With the value of the asset computed and the probabilities of ratings known, we may compute the expected value and standard deviation of the bond value to get an idea of the credit risk involved. The expected value is ₹148.48 and the standard deviation is ₹8.93, as shown in Table 20.5.

Table 20.5 Mean and variance of bond value

New rating	Value, ₹	Probability %	Expected value, ₹	Variance
AAA	150.51	0.00	0	0
AA	150.32	4.00	6.0128	0.1355
A	149.70	85.71	128.3079	1.2765
BBB	148.34	6.02	8.9301	0.0012
BB	141.73	2.84	4.0251	1.2938
B	137.06	0.20	0.2741	0.2608
CCC	118.74	0.41	0.4868	3.6262
Default	54.00	0.82		
Expected value, ₹				148.4796
Variance				79.7905
Standard deviation, ₹				8.93

Table 20.6 Computing credit value at risk

Probability, %	Cumulative probability, %	Value, ₹	Deviation from expected value, ₹
0.00	0.00	150.51	2.03
4.00	4.00	150.32	1.84
85.71	89.71	149.70	1.22
6.02	95.73	148.34	−0.14
2.84	98.57	141.73	−6.75
0.20	98.77	137.06	−11.42
0.41	99.18	118.74	−29.74
0.82	100.00	54.00	−94.48

One-year 99.18% confidence credit VaR = ₹29.74

We can now get the credit VaR for the confidence level desired by computing the deviation from the expected value. For example, if we need a 99% confidence level, then the expected loss that does not exceed 1% of time would provide the required figure. A 99.18% one-year credit VaR is found to be ₹29.74, as shown in Table 20.6

CREDIT DERIVATIVES

> A credit derivative is an instrument whose value is dependent upon the credit risk of the underlying asset.

The latest forms of derivatives that have surfaced and have gained prominence are credit derivatives. They are devised to cover the risks that are inherent in credit. Credit is the essence of modern society, as it enables increased consumption over and above what the current income can provide. Thus, with a growing economy, credit essentially has to grow. Banks perform the function of moving funds from those with surplus capital to those wanting capital. In the discharge of this function, banks create exposures to their operations. These exposures contain market risks (predominantly, interest rate risk) and default risk. Default risk is referred to as credit risk. Similarly, firms too borrow from the capital market by issuing debt instruments called bonds, and investors hold these bonds in anticipation of good return. Besides market risk, these investors are exposed also to the credit risk inasmuch as the promised payment of coupons and/or principal may not fructify as per the terms and conditions agreed upon.

Credit derivatives largely remain products confined to the banking sector, which has exposures to various kinds of loans, and, therefore, faces the inherent risk of default or rapid deterioration in value of these loans. Banks advance these loans to earn a reasonable rate of return. The reward for assuming credit risk is built-in loan pricing. Credit derivatives are instruments that provide a hedge against credit risk by segregating the risk premium for credit risk from the overall pricing. Credit derivatives are also used by large mutual funds, as they may have made a sizable proportion of their investments in corporate bonds.

Actual default may take place directly or be preceded by some events that signify a gloomy future. The events that signify a default could be downgrading of the firms and the bonds issued by them, bankruptcy, etc. The banks face the risk of default on these loans or receivables. The defaults may be a result of delinquency, losses, failing economies, adverse movement of interest rates and exchange rates, etc. At times, such risks may become exceedingly high for the banks, and they may feel the need to transfer such risks to those willing to take them in exchange for returns commensurate with the risks.

Credit derivatives came into existence around 1993–1994. As the volumes grow, these credit derivatives allow participants to increase trade on financial instruments such as loans to enterprises or the value of firms based on their credit risks. However, credit derivatives remain OTC products, where the specific needs of participants may be matched in the contract, which derives its value on the basis of the credit-based value of the underlying exposures.

CREDIT DERIVATIVE

> Credit derivatives are instruments intended to cover credit risk for a fee.

We may broadly define a credit derivative as an asset whose returns are determined by its credit risk, as assessed by the credit rating or any other such indicator. The definition of a credit derivative is not easy to find. The reason would lie in the fact that there could hardly be any other instrument whose value depends exclusively on its credibility. One definition is that *credit derivative is a class of financial instruments, the value of which is derived from an underlying market value driven by the credit risk of private or government entities other than the counterparties to the credit derivative transaction itself.*[1]

We know that the value of financial instruments depends upon several factors. For example, corporate bonds issued by two different firms do not provide the same yield even if all the conditions and cash flows of the bonds are identical. These yields are expected to compensate the investor for the various kinds of risk he/she takes. The yields on different bonds can be viewed as rewards for investment in the risk-free asset and as rewards for taking up credit risk. The difference in the yields of any two bonds is attributable to the difference in the risk profiles of the firms issuing those bonds. Yield in excess of the risk-free rate of return is the reward for taking up credit risk on the bond or on the entity that has issued the bond. Credit risk primarily refers to the possibility that the bond would not pay its promised cash flow. A credit derivative would then be an instrument that would derive its value from the spread of the yield over and above the risk-free rate, rather than from the absolute yield on the instrument.

Normally, credit risk is embedded in the returns. We need to segregate the returns attributable to credit risk from the returns on investment and those bearing other risks. Credit derivatives perform the function of separation and isolation of credit risk, facilitating trading with the purpose of (a) replicating, (b) transferring, and (c) hedging credit risk. Credit becomes a separate dimension, where any reward predominantly is a function of credit risk alone.

When an investor acquires an asset, he/she takes up all the risk associated with the asset, including its credit risk. With credit derivatives, it is feasible to acquire the credit risk without acquiring the asset. This requires replication and transfer of the credit risk. This enables hedging against the credit risk. For a firm assuming a risk, credit derivatives offer many advantages, such as gaining exposure without (a) originating the asset, (b) locking-in funds, and (c) requiring any kind of credit administration and supervision infrastructure.

> Credit derivatives permit gaining exposure without (a) origination, (b) funding, and (c) necessary credit administration infrastructure.

Types of Credit Risks

The risk that is covered by the credit derivative instrument is the default risk, offering credit-related returns. Banks advancing loans to firms face this risk on the asset side of their balance sheets. All assets are not equally prone to default; some are more prone and some are less prone. The sub-prime crisis in 2008 is an example of default on the loans made by various borrowers, where a certain class of borrowers failed to honour the committed repayments.

Likewise, firms also borrow by issuing instruments in the shape of bonds, whereby they commit to pay a coupon value as well as the initial investment on the due dates to the investors. The cash flows of the firm may deteriorate, causing a default on committed payments. The default would normally be preceded by a progressive decline in the market values of the instruments.

Credit Risk from Rating All popular instruments of debt are normally subjected to periodic evaluation by independent agencies, called rating firms, with regard to the safety of

---

[1] Das, Satyajit, *Credit Derivatives, CDOs, and Structured Credit Products*, Wiley Finance, 3rd Edition, John Wiley & Sons (Asia) Pte Ltd, 2005.

investments. The assessment is generally made in terms of the repayment obligations of a firm relative to its cash-generating capacity. With time, the cash-generating capacity of the firm is subject to change. A deteriorating cash flow of the firm results in the downgrading of the debt instruments or the firm itself. This type of downgrading is normally referred to as a *credit event*. A credit derivative instrument may cover such credit events. Similarly, bankruptcy is another such credit event that could govern the payoff of credit derivative instruments.

The return on debt instruments is supposed to cover the risk of default as well as the downgrade. With each downgrade, the market value of the debt instrument declines. Since low-rated bonds offer substantially higher returns, investment in such assets is a lucrative proposition because if the investment is upgraded the returns would become phenomenal. However, when the risk in the instruments exceeds the risk appetite, the investor may like to prevent excess losses and look for transfer of the risk. Such a transfer could be achieved with a tailor-made derivative product whose payoff is dependent upon the specified credit events actually coming to pass.

Credit Risk from Illiquidity Unlike corporate bonds, bank loans are not traded and are subject to credit rating. The risk of default is normally covered in the appraisal process of the bank when they decide the pricing of the loan. Since a loan is reviewed periodically, it is analogous to the rating review and an increase in the interest rate is analogous to a downgrade of the loan. However, due to the availability of collateral, the credit risk in bank loans can be considered to be less in intensity than that associated with bonds issued by firms.

> Credit derivatives enable passing the credit risk of an asset to a third party.

Market Risk and Credit Risk Credit risk in the case of corporate bonds or bank loans is somewhat different from the risk faced by investors in stocks or bonds that are traded in larger volumes on a daily basis. Returns on such assets are normally distributed, whereas returns on credit seem to have larger tails than what they would have if the returns were normally distributed.[2] The downside tail in the returns represents a larger probability of a downside risk.

CREDIT DEFAULT SWAPS

There are broadly two kinds of credit derivatives—funded and unfunded. In an unfunded credit derivative, the returns are commensurate with credit risk, which is replicated without acquiring the risky asset. In a funded derivative, there would be part or whole funding of the asset bearing credit risk.

An unfunded credit derivative permits an investor to replicate the returns of a financial instrument, a portfolio of assets, or an entity, without directly engaging in the underlying transaction of advancing a loan or making an investment in bonds. Under a credit derivative transaction, the loan or the investment in the portfolio of risky assets continues to remain with the original investor, while the credit risk stands transferred to another party. It is pertinent to add here that to engage in the trade of credit derivatives, it is not necessary that either party has a

---

[2] Anson, Mark J. P., Frank J. Fibozzi, Moorad Choudhry, and Ren-Raw Chen, *Credit Derivatives—Instruments, Applications, and Pricing* by, John Wiley & Sons, Inc., 2004, p. 15.

credit risk exposure, in the same manner that one need not hold the asset while buying a put option. One can trade a put or a call option with or without a position on the underlying asset. Probably a credit default swap (CDS) is the only instrument whose payoff is purely governed by events signifying the credit risk. It is the most popular credit derivative. CDS is an OTC product contracted between two counterparties—one, called the *protection buyer*, needing protection against default on an asset or an entity (referred to as the *reference asset* or *entity*) and the counterparty, called the *protection seller*, who provides protection for a specified period against the happening of a specified credit event in exchange for receiving a periodic premium. The pricing of the loan includes the market risk premium as well as the credit risk premium. Can the credit risk be segregated and traded? Credit default swaps achieve precisely this. Figure 20.4 depicts a plain vanilla CDS.

> The CDS is an arrangement where a protection buyer pays a periodic premium for compensation of the potential loss from default.

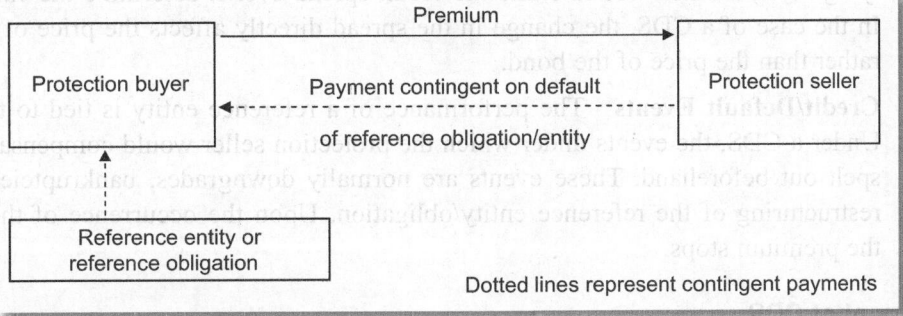

Fig. 20.4 Credit default swap

For example, a bank may have advanced a loan to a corporate entity or may be holding the bonds of a company, called the *reference entity or reference obligation*. The loan may be defaulted, or the bond may deteriorate in value. The bank, the protection buyer, may require protection/ insurance against credit risk. The protection seller undertakes to compensate the protection buyer in the event of the happening of a particular event (called the *credit event*). It is a de facto insurance for the protection buyer against deterioration in the value of the asset. The protection buyer passes the credit risk to the protection seller for a fee.

Besides the protection buyer and the protection seller, there is a third party involved in the CDS, called the reference entity. The reference entity may be a corporate availing a loan, whose quality is monitored regularly; when its ability to pay back the obligation is jeopardized, the protection seller pays off the protection buyer.

Cash Flows of CDS

A CDS is depicted in Fig. 20.4. Note that while the protection buyer pays a regular premium, the protection seller makes payment only upon the happening of specific credit events. The protection payment is typically made in arrears. The premium payment is quoted as a percentage, on per annum basis, of the notional principal. For example, if the payment is 240 bps, it implies a payment of 60 bps every quarter. If fee payments are in arrears, there would be an accrual payment at the time of the default event. For example, in a CDS involving annual payment, if default takes place after three years and four months, then the protection buyer would have to pay for the four months (after having paid three annual instalments till then) on a pro-rata basis.

If no event related to a default occurs during the contract period, no cash flow accrues to the protection buyer. The liability of the protection seller is contingent. It is a kind of option to swap the credit asset if there is a default. The option can be exercised only when a default occurs, unlike options on financial assets.

> The obligations of a protection seller are contingent upon the defined default events actually coming to pass.

Even though the payoff on a CDS is asymmetric and resembles that of options, it is called a swap for the reason that the payoff does not conform to the characteristics of that on an option. It resembles the swap to a larger degree. In a swap, one party pays at a fixed rate while receiving a floating rate. The option premium depends upon the price of the underlying asset. A CDS has an asymmetric payoff, but its price performance is more like a swap than an option. When a risky bond is the underlying asset, the risk-free rate and the credit spread over it determine the value of the bond. In the case of a CDS, the change in the spread directly affects the price of the transaction, rather than the price of the bond.

Credit/Default Events The performance of a reference entity is tied to the credit event. Under a CDS, the events under which the protection seller would compensate the buyer are spelt out beforehand. These events are normally downgrades, bankruptcies, mergers, and restructuring of the reference entity/obligation. Upon the occurrence of the default event, the premium stops.

Settlement of CDS

A CDS concludes on its scheduled termination date or on the happening of the credit event, whichever is earlier. If the period of swap ends without a credit event happening, there is no payment from the protection seller to the protection buyer. The premium too ceases to exist. However, if the credit event occurs, then settlement can take place either in the cash mode or in the physical mode.

Cash Settlement Under the cash settlement mode, the protection payment is settled in cash. The value is the difference between the nominal value of the reference obligation and its market value at the time of the credit event. The market value of the reference obligation when the credit event happens is extremely difficult to ascertain. Normally, an agent, called a *calculation agent,* is appointed to calculate the value. Since the value of the asset at the time of default is likely to be extremely volatile, irrespective of the method of valuation, one may appoint several independent and impartial agents. When the credit event occurs, the asset may be subjected to extraordinary changes in value, making fair assessment of value difficult. Usually, a cooling-off period (the time between the credit event and the actual valuation date, usually about three months) is provided to allow for aberrations in valuation to settle down and for a rational price of the asset to emerge. A swap that fixes the amount in case of default irrespective of the assessment of actual loss is called a *binary swap.*

> Under a cash settlement the asset remains with the protection buyer, with any loss compensated by the protection seller.

Under cash settlement, the underlying asset remains with the protection buyer. The protection seller pays the difference between the face value and the value of the deliverable asset, as determined by a calculation agent.

Derivatives in Practice

Credit Events

Greek swap deal classified as 'Credit Event'

On 9 March 2012, the finance ministers of 17 Eurozone member nations released the second bailout package of €35 billion to debt-ridden Greece after the Greek government achieved a landmark deal with its private creditors on a swap that implied a more than 50% reduction in its debt to them of €107 billion.

The Greek government successfully entered a pact with its lenders, who subscribed to government bonds to write down 53% of their claims in nominal terms and 74% in real terms by exchanging their bonds with new ones with (a) lesser value, (b) longer maturity, and (c) lower interest rates. The Eurozone was highly appreciative of the participation by banks, insurance companies, and other private investors in restructuring Greek debt. Since Greece fulfilled the conditions laid down by the troika—the IMF, the ECB, and the European Commission—it became eligible for receiving a second bailout package of €130 billion. Remember that the Greece bond exchange is a package deal with three parts. For every old bond tendered, the holder gets (a) a new Greek bond, (b) new EFSF (European Finance Stability Fund) bonds, and (c) new warrants linked to the GDP of Greece.

By 8 March 2012, the last date for exchange of debts, bondholders tendered Greek-law bonds worth €152 billion (about 86% of the total) and other foreign law bonds worth €20 billion (about 69%). This enabled the Greek government to activate a collective action clause (CAC) to achieve full participation, whereby those who did not participate in the debt swap deal would be forced to tender their old debt instruments for the new ones.

Greece is activating its CACs, and, thus, there will be a credit event for the purposes of its CDSs—as there should be. If one sold protection on Greek bonds, then he will end up having to pay out roughly 75 cents on the dollar. However, given where the CDSs have been trading of late, one has almost certainly put up that much money in margins already. So there was nothing unexpected here, and there will not be any nasty surprises on the CDS front.

Due to the activation of the CAC, the International Swaps and Derivatives Association (ISDA) classified the debt swap deal as a 'credit event', triggering insurance payments likely to run into billions of dollars. Losses on the bonds would have to be paid out under CDSs. The payment of CDSs is likely to destabilize the financial institutions who sold the credit protection. Recall that in the past, after 2008 financial crisis, the insurance giant American Insurance Group had to be bailed out by the US government after it could not meet obligations under CDSs on mortgage debts in the US property markets.

Source: Reuters, Business *Standard*, and *Business Line*.

Physical Settlement Under the physical settlement mode, the protection buyer delivers the asset to the seller in exchange for the nominal value of the swap. In case the CDS has been entered into with respect to a firm (a reference entity) rather than a specific instrument (a reference obligation) and in the event physical settlement has been agreed upon, the contracts would specify the deliverables. If the value of the CDS is a notional ₹10 crore, then the protection buyer would deliver acceptable assets with a face value of ₹10 crore and receive cash from the protection seller.

> Under a physical settlement, the asset is delivered to the protection seller at face value.

Physical settlement obviates the need for determining the market value of the reference obligation but forces another decision. The protection buyer would have to determine the cheapest-to-deliver instruments if the CDS is on a reference entity. The deliverable instruments must meet the requirement of seniority and maturity. This situation is similar to that of futures contracts on T-bonds, where the seller has the option to decide which bonds to deliver.

Under physical settlement, the asset goes into the hands of the protection seller, who stands to gain in case the value of the asset increases subsequent to the credit event.

Exhibit 20.1 depicts the standard CDS structure, the associated cash flows and the modes of settlement.

EXHIBIT 20.1 A credit default swap and its cash flows

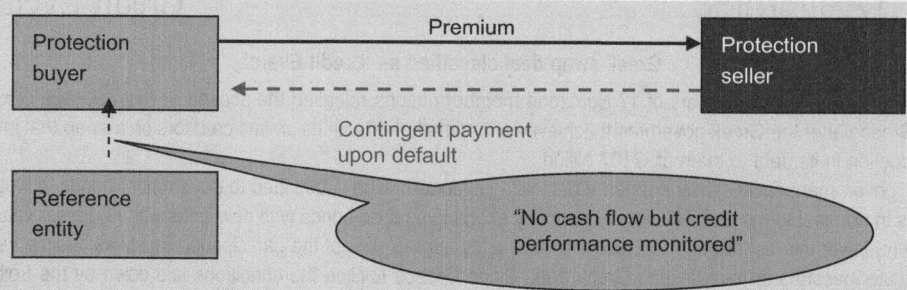

CDS structure
Semi-annual payments of 50 bps for a notional principal of ₹1000 for a period of three years

Time in months	CDS cash flow			
	No default		Default at the end of 2 years	
	Payment by protection buyer	Payment by protection seller	Payment by protection buyer	Payment by protection seller
6	5	—	5	—
12	5	—	5	—
18	5	—	5	—
24	5	—	5	600
30	5	—	Assumed cash settlement	
36	5	—		
TOTAL	30	—		

Cash settlement
The protection seller and the protection buyer appoint a calculation agent to value the asset. The protection seller pays the difference between the notional and the market" value at the time of the credit default event. If the market value is ₹400, the protection payment of ₹600 is made.

Physical settlement
The protection buyer delivers the asset and receives ₹1000. The protection seller acquires the asset and may sell it at its market value.

Variants of CDS

As the CDS is an OTC product, the terms and conditions of the swap are mutually decided upon by the contracting parties. Besides the standard CDS just discussed, there are many variants available. Some of these are as follows:

Digital CDS Under a CDS cash settlement, the assessment of market value is indeed difficult to make. This leads to uncertainty over the payoff in case of default. In a digital CDS, the value of the payoff is fixed, eliminating the need for calculating the market value of the asset under a default situation.

Basket CDS The standard CDS depicted in Exhibit 20.1 was for a single asset. Where the protection buyer is looking for protection on a portfolio (holding several bonds or covering exposure on them), the reference entities would be many. Such a CDS is called a basket CDS, where the protection payment is made in the event of any of the reference entities defaulting. The CDS terminates upon the first default. A portfolio of loans or bonds is viewed as a bundle of credit risk. This portfolio carries the risk that some of the loans would be defaulted upon, or there is deterioration in value, as signified by a rating downgrade. The banks or investors in the bonds may bundle them in different tranches, representing different classes of credit risk. Such a product would be a basket credit derivative.

Portfolio CDS A basket CDS comes to an end with the first default. Under a portfolio CDS, many assets are covered but the CDS continues even after the first default. A portfolio CDS covers a pre-specified sum and till the total represented by all defaults matches this amount, the CDS continues to be valid.

Applications of CDS

CDS can be viewed in many ways. Some of the uses of CDS are mentioned here.

CDS and Insurance The payment made by the protection seller in case a default event occurs is called the protection payment. This is similar to an insurance contract. The difference between an insurance contract and a CDS is that under the former, a loss that can be ascertained must actually have been incurred, and compensation is paid only to the extent of that loss, whereas under a CDS, the mere happening of the credit event is a sufficient cause for the protection payment to be made; the actual suffering of a loss is immaterial.

> Under CDS, the happening of an event is sufficient reason for a claim, unlike insurance, where the loss needs to be proved.

CDS and Financial Guarantee Credit derivatives allow hedging with a third party, without the reference obligation performing any role in the transaction. This enables the creditor to transfer the credit risk without letting the debtor know of it. This is a major difference between a CDS and a financial guarantee, as the former is bilateral, while the latter is normally trilateral.

Income Generation for Protection Seller While the protection buyer has insured himself against any default, the protection seller in a CDS has a synthetic position on the reference obligation, say a bond. It has, in effect, created a position on the reference asset or entity without actually owning it. The protection seller has not funded the asset or loan, and yet receives a return in the form of a premium that is determined on the basis of the credit performance. With respect to default, the protection seller has synthesized the reference asset. Should there be no default, the protection seller pockets the premium. The motivation for a protection seller is yield enhancement without increase in financial exposure, similar to of the motivation for an option writer. Even if a default occurs, the protection seller would acquire the asset (in case of physical settlement), and hopes to gain in the future from an improved position of the defaulted asset.

Risk-free Position for Protection Buyer The CDS enables a risk-free position for the protection buyer. Assume an investor has a portfolio of corporate bonds providing, say, 200 bps over risk-free bonds. By entering a CDS to protect against default, the investor may make 200 bps as protection payment. Post the CDS, the investor would earn a risk-free return. By entering into the CDS, the investor obviated the need for changing his portfolio. He also gets protection for the desired time. For example, if the portfolio matures in seven years and doubts about the default are limited up to three years, then the investor can enter a CDS for three years. Here, the investor would earn risk-free returns for three years and get normal expected returns for the remaining period.

Diversification of Risk for Buyer and Seller Another interesting application of the CDS is that it helps achieve diversification. Assume a situation involving two counterparties that are banks, each involved in specialized financing. One bank does agricultural loans, and the other concentrates on the automobile sector. Bank A, which advances farm loans, faces default risk emanating primarily from weather conditions. Bank B, which concentrates on auto loans, faces default risk that primarily emanates from economic conditions. Both the banks can trade their risks by entering into two independent CDSs: (a) Bank A pays a premium to Bank B for defaults on farm loans and (b) bank B pays a premium to Bank A for default of auto loans. Thus, with the differential of the premium for the two defaults, both banks can diversify their credit risks in both the agricultural and the automobile sectors, without either having to resort to the costly proposition of actual lending in the other's sector. Besides funds, the lending to specific sectors requires specialized domain knowledge, acquiring which is doubtful and time consuming. The synthetic positions of both the banks created by way of CDSs help achieve safe and rather instantaneous diversification of credit risk at little cost. Both the banks get the benefits of each other's expertise in their respective specific fields.

> The CDS can also serve as a diversification tool by providing returns and exposure to different sectors.

VALUATION OF CREDIT DEFAULT SWAP—MERTON MODEL

One of the most popular methods to price credit risk is the Merton model. It is a model to value debt with the option pricing model developed by Black and Scholes. It is considered a structural model, where a firm is replicated in the economic structure. It assumes that a firm defaults when the value of the firm drops to a certain level, called the default value. For the Merton model, it is necessary to value the assets and for that reason, it is also referred to as the asset value model.

> The valuation of a CDS can be done on the basis of the option pricing theory, using the BSM.

The underlying idea behind Merton's model for default on debt by firms is that a firm defaults if the value of its assets falls below the value of its debt. The first step in the process is the valuation of its assets and liabilities. For ease of comprehension and expression, we divide the balance sheet into three elements—equity and debt on one side and assets on the other side. Both equity and debt holders have claims on the asset of the firms, though the nature of their claims are significantly different.

From accounting, we know that the value of assets and liabilities must be equal for a balance sheet to balance. However, Merton speaks of economic values and not asset values. The book value needs to be replaced by economic/market values. For a traded firm, the value of its equity is easy to obtain. When traded, the value of debt can also be obtained. However,

Derivatives in Practice

Credit Default Swaps

What do CDS rates mean?

Credit default swap rates are good proxies to understand risk perception and investor appetite for the underlying asset, called reference entity in CDS parlance.

On 4 October 2011 Moody's downgraded the state-owned State Bank of India (SBI), the largest Indian bank, from C− to D+ due to (a) increased concerns about its mounting proportions of NPAs in its lending portfolio, and (b) inadequacy of Tier I capital. The ratings of its competitors from the private sector, such as HDFC Bank, ICICI Bank, and Axis Bank remained unchanged. In the April–June quarter of 2011, the bank had a Tier I capital adequacy ratio of 7.60%, which was lower than the other top local lenders such as ICICI Bank Ltd, HDFC Bank Ltd, and Axis Bank Ltd.

As per Moody's, a rating of D implies "modest intrinsic financial strength, potentially requiring some outside support at times", while a C rating denotes "adequate intrinsic financial strength".

Global investors seem to have shared Moody's concerns about SBI. This is indicated by the rise in CDS rates for investments in SBI paper. SBI's five-year CDS rate rose 91% since August 2011. CDS rates for SBI paper widened from 189 basis points in early August 2011 to 363 basis points on 4 October 2011, as per Bloomberg.

These rates seem to indicate that SBI would have to face a higher cost of borrowing for future funding plans. Interestingly, the CDS rates on ICICI Bank have also doubled from 238 basis points to 468 basis points during the same period.

In line with the increasing CDS rates, Moody's downgraded the outlook on India's banking sector to 'negative' from 'stable' on 9 November 2011.

Source: Based on a report in the *Business Line*, 5 October 2011.

the assets of the firm, such as land and building, plant and machinery, loans, creditors, and debtors are never traded, and it is impossible to find the true economic value of the firm's assets in the market place.

The principle of the claims of equity and debt holders is that any deterioration in the value of assets is first absorbed by the equity holders. The equity holders are owners of the residual. Till such time the drop in value is less than the value of equity, the claim of debt holders does not get affected. In this context, Merton views debt and equity as options, discussed in a subsequent chapter.

> Under the option pricing model, equity can be viewed as a call option, while debt is seen as a combination of a bond and a short put.

If the value of the equity is E, the face value of debt is D, and the value of assets is A, then the equity has a payoff of Max $(0, A - D)$ which is a call option with a strike price of D. The debt has a payoff of Min (A, D). This does not correspond to the payoff on any standard option. However, it is a combination of a bond that pays the face value of the debt at maturity and a short put with an exercise price of D. It may be seen as below:

	Long bond	Short put	Total	
$A < D$	D	$-(D - A)$	A	(Min(A, D))
$A > D$	D	$-$	D	

The payoffs on the equity and debt of a firm are depicted in Fig. 20.5. The values of the call and the put would be given by the Black–Scholes Model (BSM) for a non-dividend paying stock, as described in Eqs 12.25 and 12.26, reproduced here for convenience.

Let us now value debt under the Merton model under the simplified circumstances of a firm. Let us assume the following values:

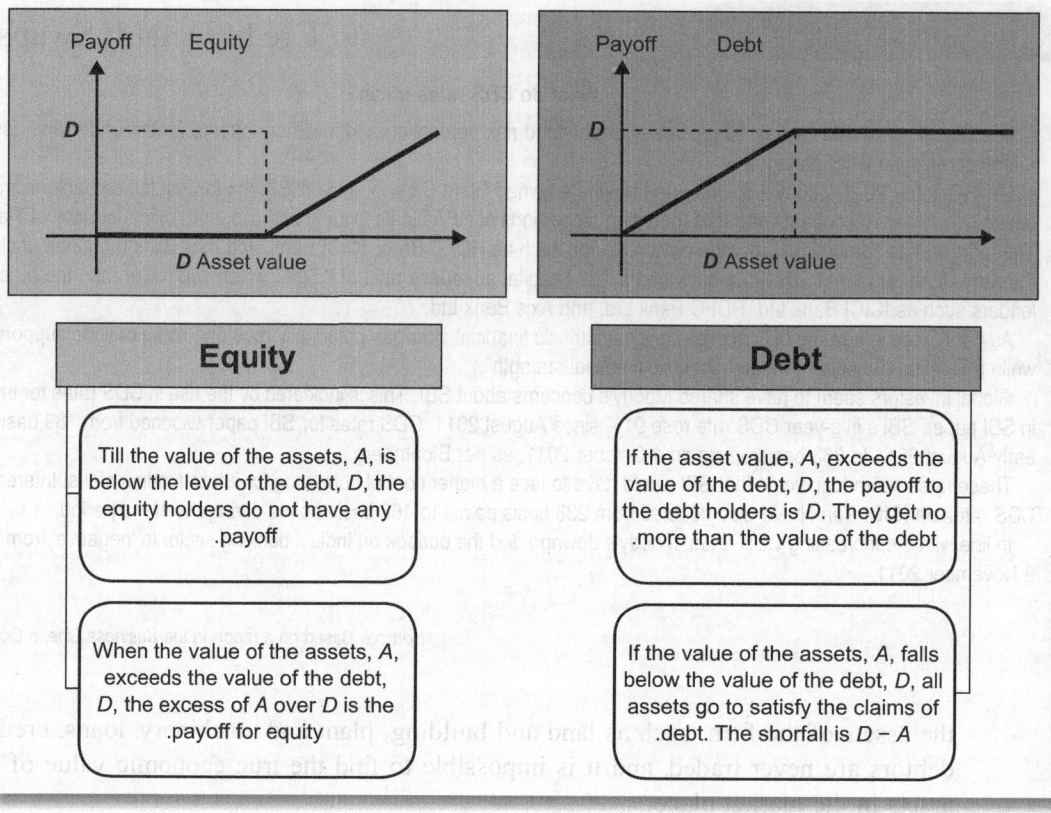

Fig. 20.5 Debt and equity as options

Value of assets, A = ₹100
Face value of debt, D = ₹60
Volatility of asset price = 20%
Time to maturity, T = 5 years
Risk-free rate, r = 5%

In the context of the BSM, the spot price, S, is the value of the assets, A, while the exercise price, X, is the value of the debt, D. Volatility would be equal to the asset prices, with a time to maturity of five years and a risk-free rate of 5%.

The value of the firm's equity, considered as a call option with a strike price of ₹60 and an asset price of ₹100, would be computed by Eq. 12.25. The intermediate values are as follows:

Equity and debt that are considered as options can be valued for the option prices by using the BSM.

d_1	1.9249	$N(d_1)$	0.9729	$N(-d_1)$	0.0271
d_2	1.4777	$N(d_2)$	0.9303	$N(-d_2)$	0.0697

and the value of equity $= A \cdot N(d_1) - D \cdot e^{-rT} \cdot N(d_2)$
$= 100 \times 0.9729 - 46.73 \times 0.9303$
$= 97.29 - 43.47 = ₹53.82$

With equity valued as a call option, the remaining value of the firm belongs to debt holders. Therefore, the value of the debt is

$$\text{Value of debt} = 100.00 - 53.82 = ₹46.18$$

Alternatively, the value of the debt is a long position on a bond with a maturity value of D after five years with a short position on the put. The value of the put as per the BSM—as shown in Eq. 12.26—is:

The value of the put $= X \cdot e^{-rT} \cdot N(-d_2) - A \cdot N(-d_1)$
$= 46.73 \times 0.0697 - 100 \times 0.0271$
$= 3.26 - 2.71 = ₹0.55$

The value of the risk-free bond $= D\, e^{-rT} = ₹46.73$

The value of the debt $=$ The value of the risk-free bond $-$ the value of the put
$= 46.73 - 0.55 = ₹46.18$ (the same as was found using the call)

Credit Spread Once the value of the debt is established, we can find the credit spread (the difference between the yield on the bond and the risk-free rate). The yield on debt, r, is given by

$$60.00 = 46.18 \times e^{-5 \times r}$$

Solving for r, we get $r = 5.236\%$.

Hence, the credit spread of the yield over the risk-free rate $= 5.236\% - 5.000\%$
$= 0.236\% = 23.6$ bps.

Thus, the price of the credit risk of the bond is 23.6 bps. The larger the spread, the more the likelihood that the firm would default.

Probability of Default under Merton Model Though we calculated the credit spread with the Merton model, we still do not know what the probability of default is. Though we cannot get an exact figure, we can have a reasonable estimate of the probability of default. If we assume a risk-neutral world, i.e., a world where the investor earns sums equal to the risk-free rate—a concept used repeatedly in the valuation of derivatives—we can have a fair idea of the probability of default.

Recall that while explaining the interpretation of terms in the BSM, it was stated that the probability of the asset price exceeding the exercise price was given by $N(d_2)$. If the asset price is the value of the firm and the exercise price is the face value of the debt (as is the case in the Merton model), then default would take place if the asset price is less than the strike price, $X = D$. Hence, we have the probability of the value of the firm being less that of the strike; the face value of the debt would be $1 - N(d_2)$, which is also equal to $N(-d_2)$.

> The probability of default on a debt under option prices is given by $N(-d_2)$, which can be derived with values of the equity and debt.

With risk neutrality, the probability of default under Merton's model is given by $1 - N(d_2) = N(-d_2)$. In the present case, this value is 0.0697 (6.97%) over a period of five years.

CDS Premium Under a CDS, there are two legs of payment—the premium payments, which are made as long as no default occurs, and the protection payment, which is made when a default occurs. At the time of entering the CDS, the expected present value of these payments must be equal. Since the present value factor is common on both sides of the payments, there is no need to discount the cash flows of the CDS payments.

If the probability of default over five years is $N(-d_2)$, then it can easily be converted into an equivalent probability over a year, or for any other period like a quarter or half an year, given that the probability each year remains constant. If the probability of default in each year for the next five years is constant, q, then the probabilities of 'default' and 'no default' over the period of the next five years are as follows:

$$\text{Probability of no default} = (1-q)^5$$
$$\text{Probability of default} = 1-(1-q)^5$$

The value of $N(-d_2)$ can be converted into an equivalent constant annual probability of default by following Eq. 20.3.

$$N(-d_2) = 1 - (1-q)^5 = 0.0697 \tag{20.3}$$

Solving Eq. 20.3, we get $q = 1.4346\%$.

The protection buyer makes a fixed premium payment, s, for each period.

With the probabilities of default taken as q and of no default as $(1-q)$, the expected values of the cash flows of the premium and protection values can be found. The expected value of the premium at the end of the nth period (payment in arrears) would be

Expected value of premium
$$= \text{Premium} \times \text{Probability of no default} = s \times (1-q)^n$$

The protection payment depends on the notional principal and the recovery rate, R. The notional principal is assumed to be the face value of the debt/bond, D. The expected value for the nth period would be:

The expected value of protection payment
$$= D(1-R) \times \text{Probability of default} = D(1-R) \times q(1-q)^{n-1}$$

For a period of five years, these values are shown in Table 20.7.

Table 20.7 Cash flow under CDS

Year	Probability of default	Probability of no default	Expected value of premium payment	Expected value of protection payment
1	q	$(1-q)$	$s \times (1-q)$	$D(1-R) \times q$
2	$q(1-q)$	$(1-q)^2$	$s \times (1-q)^2$	$D(1-R) \times q(1-q)$
3	$q(1-q)^2$	$(1-q)^3$	$s \times (1-q)^3$	$D(1-R) \times q(1-q)^2$
4	$q(1-q)^3$	$(1-q)^4$	$s \times (1-q)^4$	$D(1-R) \times q(1-q)^3$
5	$q(1-q)^4$	$(1-q)^5$	$s \times (1-q)^5$	$D(1-R) \times q(1-q)^4$

The probability of default can be used to find the credit spread, which is a measure of default, and is used in pricing credit derivatives.

Equation 20.4 would give the amount of premium for a CDS in case the premium is paid in arrears, i.e., after the end of the period. Note that there is no need to discount the expected cash flows, as they are already measured in present value terms.

$$\sum_{1}^{n} s \times (1-q)^t = \sum_{1}^{n} D \times (1-R) \times q(1-q)^t \tag{20.4}$$

Using the methodology just described, we find the amount of premium in Table 20.8 for the firm with the face value of debt of ₹60 and the probability of default over five years 6.97% as follows:

$$\text{The probability of default, } [1 - N(d_2)] = N(-d_2) = 0.0697$$
$$\text{Annual probability of default, } q = 1.4346\%$$
$$\text{where } N(-d_2) = 1 - (1 - q)^n$$
$$\text{Protection payment} = \text{Face value} = 1$$
$$\text{Recovery rate, } R = 40\%$$

Table 20.8 Pricing CDS

Year	Probability of default	Probability of no default	Expected value of premium payment	Expected value of protection payment
1	1.4346%	98.5654%	0.9857	0.008607
2	1.4140%	97.1514%	0.9715	0.008484
3	1.3937%	95.7577%	0.9576	0.008362
4	1.3737%	94.3840%	0.9438	0.008242
5	1.3540%	93.0300%	0.9303	0.008124
Sum			4.7889	0.041820
Premium per 100				0.873272
				87.33 bps

TOTAL RETURN SWAP

A total return swap (TRS) is an arrangement where one party pays a total return on a reference asset, say, a bond, in exchange for a floating rate of return plus a spread, as depicted in Fig. 20.6.

The total returns on the reference asset would include the periodic coupon payments, as well as the gains and losses on the reference asset for the period of swap. For example, if the coupon rate is 10% payable semi-annually and the swap has been entered for a period of five years for London Interbank Offer Rate (LIBOR) + 50 bps on a notional principal of $10 million, then every six months, the payer would pay 5% (the semi-annual coupon) in

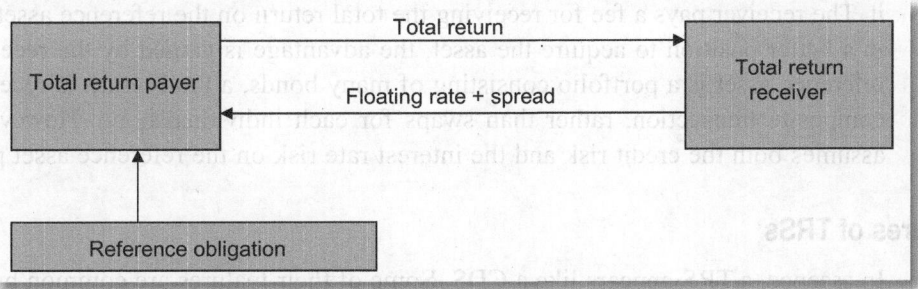

Fig. 20.6 Total return swap

exchange for receiving LIBOR (decided one period prior, as in the case of interest rate swaps) + 50 bps. At the end of the swap, the capital gains/losses on the value of the reference asset would be exchanged. If there is a gain, it shall be paid by the payer, and if there is a loss, it would be compensated for by the receiver. However, if there is a default prior to the expiry of the bond, the swap is terminated with the difference between the notional amount and the market value of the reference asset. We can describe the cash flows of the TRS as follows:

On each coupon date	The payer pays the coupon value and receives the floating rate plus the spread. The payer passes the regular return in the form of the coupon. Capital gains/losses can be paid/received either at each payment date or at the conclusion of the swap period.
On conclusion of the swap	The payer pays capital gain on the value of the asset to the receiver. If there is a loss, the receiver pays the difference. This compensates for capital gain/loss on the reference asset by finding the difference in the market values at the inception and the conclusion of the swap.
If there is a default during the swap period	The swap is terminated with the receiver being compensated for the loss on the reference asset due to the default by the receiver.

From the viewpoint of the payer, the TRS can be taken as a fully hedged position, except for the counterparty risk taken on the receiver. If the reference asset—a corporate bond—is acquired, the payer would get all the benefits of ownership, which are passed to the receiver, resulting in a neutral position on the asset. The acquisition of the asset can be deemed to be financed at the floating LIBOR rate, which the payer gets from the receiver in a TRS. A TRS thus provides the spread over (say 50 bps) the floating rate as a reward for the payer, as depicted in Fig. 20.7. The spread over the floating rate is compensation to the payer for assuming the counterparty risk.

> Under a TRS, the swap coupon as well as capital appreciation are passed to the receiver, who also assumes the credit risk on the asset.

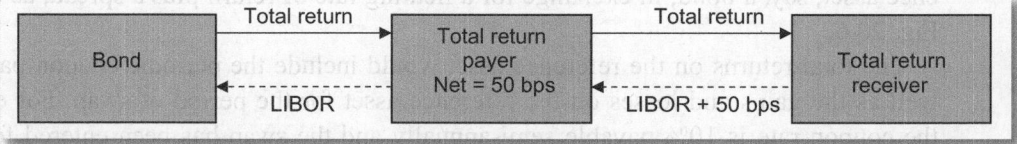

Fig. 20.7 Total return swap—payer's position

To the receiver, the TRS provides the total return on the reference asset without owning it. The receiver pays a fee for receiving the total return on the reference asset. If the payer is in a better position to acquire the asset, the advantage is gained by the receiver. Where the reference asset is a portfolio consisting of many bonds, a total return is received in a single composite transaction, rather than swaps for each individual bond. However, the receiver assumes both the credit risk and the interest rate risk on the reference asset/portfolio.

Features of TRSs

In essence, a TRS appears like a CDS. Some of their features are common but some are different. The following are some of the common features:

- Under a TRS, the reference asset is usually a widely quoted and traded bond.
- The amount in the transaction is a notional principal, and, as such, no funds are provided to acquire the asset, as would be the case with a CDS.
- The financing for acquiring the asset is provided with assumed funding at the floating LIBOR rate.
- The notional amount reduces in line with the amortization of the underlying bond. The usual term for a TRS is relatively less, typically between six months and one year.
- Like a CDS, it would terminate on the happening of a credit event.
- All payments are calculated on a notional principal.
- A TRS is normally cash-settled. In case of appreciation of the price of the bond, the total return receiver receives the price difference. In case of depreciation, the total return receiver pays the difference. As an option, changes in the price can be exchanged periodically rather than on maturity.
- In the case of physical settlement, the total return payer would deliver the asset to the receiver. The payer would receive a cash payment equal to the notional principal (adjusted for any amortization) from the receiver. Physical settlement is more practical where it is difficult to get the price of the asset (illiquid asset, defaulted asset).

> A TRS is similar to a CDS except that the TRS embeds default risk, while the CDS has only default risk.

Total Return Swaps vs Swaps and CDS

If we compare the TRS with the plain vanilla interest rate swap, we find two critical differences, as follows:

- Under a conventional interest rate swap, there is a fixed rate payment in exchange for a floating rate payment. Fixed rate payments are analogous to the fixed coupon payments. There is no compensation for any gain/loss on the value of the asset.
- A default on the reference asset has no implication on the cash flows of the conventional interest rate swap. It continues as a contract whether or not there has been a default on the underlying asset. The default risk is passed by the return payer, if he/she owns the bond/asset, to the return receiver.

The TRS can be compared with the CDS too. The TRS provides a superior protection for the 'payer' in comparison to the protection a CDS provides for the 'protection buyer'. In a CDS, there is no compensation for any decline in the value of the reference asset. It only covers the default risk. In a TRS, the receiver would compensate for any loss on the value of the reference asset, apart from the default risk. The TRS thus covers the interest rate risk as well as the default risk of the reference asset. Thus, a TRS can be deemed to be a combination of an interest rate swap and a CDS.

The motivation to enter into a TRS lies in having exposure to an asset in respect of both market risk and default risk. The advantage for the receiver is getting returns on the asset without acquiring it. Only the financing cost is paid on a floating basis. For the receiver, it also obviates the requirement of credit administration associated with due diligence and supervision. Hence, the transaction is off balance sheet. Further, to the total return payer, it is not necessary to acquire the asset, if he/she so chooses. If the total return payer decides to acquire it, he/she also has leverage available to do so. Finally, the consent of the issuer is not

> A CDS covers only default risk and an interest rate swap covers interest rate risk only. A TRS covers both.

required if the total return payer and the receiver opt to exchange the cash flow for a floating rate and a total return.

SECURITIZATION

When banks hold assets to cover loans or receivables, they not only take the risk on the returns but also expose themselves to the risk of default. These assets may become non-performing. Further, these loans essentially are non-transferable and lack liquidity. Therefore, the holder of these loans may convert such non-tradable assets into tradable ones by a process called securitization and then market them as packaged products to others who chase higher returns, and, in the process, also assume the risk of credit, i.e., the risk of default. Securitization forms the backbone of funded credit derivative transactions. However, securitization is not essential to credit derivatives.

Securitization is a process of converting rather illiquid cash flows into freely tradable assets that are transferable by endorsement and delivery. It is a financial innovation where a lender finds a way of augmenting financial resources for furthering business and, at the same time, for improving liquidity and the free market price determination of the value of such illiquid claims. Of late, securitization as an innovation in modern finance has been stretched too far, and possibly has eclipsed the honest purpose that it came into being for initially.

> Securitization is a process of converting illiquid, non-transferable assets into tradable assets whose value is market determined.

Generally speaking, a lender financing property (more popularly called *mortgages*) collects the instalments covering the principal and interest from the owners of the property over a long period of time. While there is one large lump sum paid at the initiation of the loan, causing drainage of financial resources, the recovery of funds is made in small bunches from a large number of borrowers. To put it in simple words, a firm in the business of granting housing loans with the repayment stretching to, say, 20 years, would end up exhausting its initial 100% corpus only to recover 5% each year over a period of 20 years. Apart from suffering from liquidity problems and constrained financial resources, the lender bears the credit risk of repayment by the borrowers. Further, these receivables are also not tradable.

To overcome these problems, the lender bundles the loan instalments, i.e., the financial claims into an instrument that is sold to third-party investors at a price. The price is paid by these new investors to the original lender. Now, the new investors are entitled to receive the instalments that provide them the required returns. This process enables transfer of the returns from the original lender to the new investors.

If these instalments are backed by mortgages, the process is called mortgage-based securitization (MBS), and in case of loan repayment instalments on any other asset, such as vehicles, it is referred to as asset-based securitization (ABS). Such a process (a) enables the augmenting of resources for the original lender, (b) provides liquidity, and (c) allows market determination of the pricing of the instruments, leading to free pricing in case these securities were listed. The securitization is done without the original borrowers knowing that the instalments are now actually going to a third party that did not participate in the original loan transaction.

> Securitization started with mortgage loans, where instruments were issued to investors with loan repayments providing the returns.

Mortgage-based securitization is said to have had its origin in the 1980s, when government-sponsored agencies in the USA pooled relatively safe and homogeneous loans and repackaged them into some securities, i.e., the bonds known as *pass through certificates* that were sold to investors. The instalments on the loans were designated to service the investors. However, the certificates were guaranteed by the government-sponsored agencies against default. Investors subscribed to these bonds by parting with the initial price in return for the claims on the cash flows that were to be received from the mortgages. With these known cash flows, the returns for the investors were fixed. Thus, they assumed the interest rate risk, and the value of the bonds would now change in accordance with changes in the interest rate scenario.

Securitization could be with recourse or without recourse. In securitization with recourse, the original lender who created the MBS guarantees the cash flows to the investors, thereby retaining the risk of default. In a non-recourse structure, the risk of default is passed on from the original lenders to the new investors. Hence, both interest rate risk and credit risk are borne by the new investors in securitized papers.

Figure 20.8 depicts the structures and various participants in securitization. The originator, the lender in the first place to the borrowers, floats a special purpose vehicle (SPV) with the intention of making the loan instalments tradable and liquid. The homogeneity of the receivables is established. The originators sell the claims on the receivables. Pooling of cash flow is done, and the rating agency divides the pool of receivable into various grades (tranches) such as A, B, and C or Senior, Mezzanine, and Junior, setting different grades of priorities

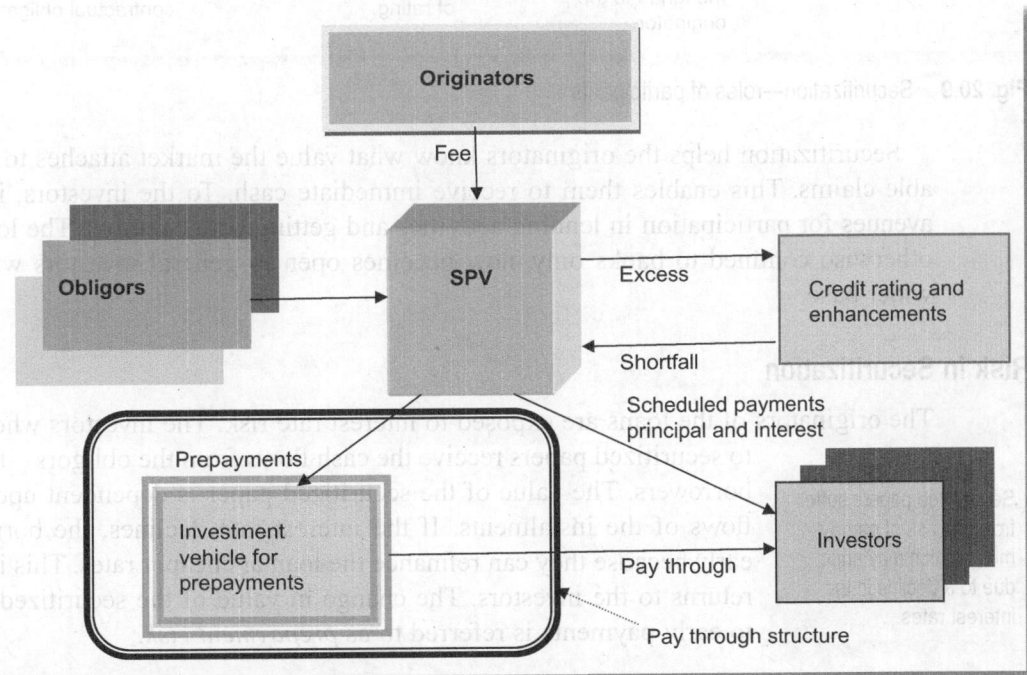

Fig. 20.8 Securitization structures—pass through and pay through

of claims on the cash flows. Cash flows from the asset service the investors in the tranches in the order of the seniority of the claims. Junior grade claims carry a higher return, with more risk. The cash flows of the receivables first service the senior grade and then go on to the lower grades.

Investors subscribe to the graded paper depending upon their risk–return profile. The junior-most tranche is the first that bears losses or shortfalls in the cash flow; hence, it is also referred to as equity tranche. Normally, a junior tranche is not sold to investors for commercial and moral reasons. Instead, it is kept by the issuers themselves to indicate that they are not passing on junk to the investors, and, thus, would themselves be the first sufferers in case of default. The process of securitization is highlighted in Fig. 20.9.

Originator	SPV	Rating agency	Investors
• A bank grants loans to its customers, on which instalments are repaid over a period of time. • The bank becomes an *originator* and floats an SPV to generate additional resources and pledge receivables of loan instalments.	• The SPV receives a fee for bundling the receivables into various categories, depending upon the past performance of loans from the original borrowers, called the *obligors*. • The SPV establishes the expected cash flows, and based on return expectations, advances the funds to the originator.	• Rating agencies look at the quality of receivables and obligors. • Depending upon the rating, they divide the receivables into various tiers, setting priority of claims for the subscribers, called investors. • The cash flows would service the cash flow commitments in the order of rating.	• Investors, depending upon their risk appetite, subscribe to the appropriate paper for their desired return and risk profile. • The issuer of the certificates receives the subscription. • The SPV passes through the receivables in accordance with the contractual obligations.

Fig. 20.9 Securitization—roles of participants

Securitization helps the originators know what value the market attaches to the receivable claims. This enables them to receive immediate cash. To the investors, it opens up avenues for participation in lending activities and getting better returns. The loan market, otherwise confined to banks only, now becomes open to general investors with a much wider base.

Risk in Securitization

The originators of the loans are exposed to interest rate risk. The investors who subscribe to securitized papers receive the cash flows from the obligors—the original borrowers. The value of the securitized paper is dependent upon the cash flows of the instalments. If the interest rate declines, the borrowers pay early because they can refinance the loan at cheaper rates. This impacts the returns to the investors. The change in value of the securitized paper due to early payments is referred to as *prepayment risk*.

> Securitized papers suffer from the risk of prepayment, which may arise due to a decline in the interest rates.

STRUCTURED CREDIT DERIVATIVES

In the section of Credit Derivatives, we discussed CDS and TRS, which were non-funded credit derivatives. In' this section we discuss more credit derivatives which are structured and funded inst.

CREDIT-LINKED NOTES

In a CDS, there is no cash flow from the protection seller to the protection buyer at the inception of the swap. A deal like the CDS is said to be non-funded or unfunded. With no investment, an unfunded derivative instrument synthesizes a position on an instrument. However, depending upon specific needs, the contract can be converted into a funded product, where the protection seller may make a full or partial upfront payment to the protection buyer at the inception of the contract to enable the purchase of the reference obligation. This is usually achieved by the issue of a note by the protection buyer, which is bought by the protection seller. Such an instrument is called a credit-linked note (CLN).

In a CLN, the position of the protection seller who buys the note is referred to as the investor, while that of the protection buyer who issues a note is referred to as the issuer. The payout on the note issued would bear some resemblance to the performance of the reference asset, such as an investment grade bond. The market value of the note is linked to the performance of the underlying asset. Initially issued at par, the final payment would depend upon the happening of any credit events. Thus, a CLN becomes a funding instrument, like a bond, and provides protection against default or a credit event, like a CDS.

A CLN may be defined as a hybrid instrument that offers investors a synthetic credit exposure to a specified *reference entity*. The CLN is a combination of fixed income security and an embedded credit derivative. The CLNs are designed to capture the returns of a bond or its portfolio. The funding given to the issuer replicates a direct exposure to a bond/loan, and is a refinance compounding the credit risk. The investor would be exposed to dual credit risk—one on the reference entity and the other on the note issuer.

> A CLN is a funded product that augments the resources of the issuer and also transfers the credit risk.

Credit exposure can be gained through a variety of methods like a CDS, a credit spread swap, a TRS, or as a repackaged note where the issuer passes on the risk of the underlying credit to the note holder in exchange for an enhanced return. For example, a note may provide for its principal repayment to be reduced below par in the event a reference obligation is defaulted upon[3].

The motivation behind funding a derivative is to enhance the resources of the issuer for furtherance of his/her business, apart from using it as a hedge against the credit risk faced by the issuer. The motivation for the investor is to enhance yield, as CLNs offer attractive returns.

---

[3]Anson, Mark J.P., Frank J. Fibozzi, Moorad Choudhry, Ren-Raw Chen, *Credit Derivatives—Instruments, Applications, and Pricing*, John Wiley & Sons, Inc., 2004, p. 120

The CLN is, therefore, a structured product where the coupon/interest payment and principal are linked to the performance of a reference obligation or reference entity. It is a funded CDS. It becomes an on-balance sheet product in contrast to the CDS, which is an off-balance sheet product. For example, consider a bank involved in the issue of credit cards, housing loans, and automobile finance. All these loans are payable periodically and bear the risk of default. The bank may pool certain class of assets and issue a note for a specified maturity that may be bought by an investor at face value. The bank gets funds by issuing the note. The payout on the note would depend upon the performance of the assets on which the note is issued. For example, the payment at maturity may be 80% of the par value if any default within the specified period exceeds a certain proportion of the value of the assets, based on which the credit note was initially issued. Alternatively, the issuer could have securitized the loans and issued separate instruments to augment his/her resources; to hedge against credit risk, he/she could have entered into a CDS. The CLN, as a composite instrument, would help to achieve these twin objectives. The cash flows of CLNs are shown in Fig. 20.10.

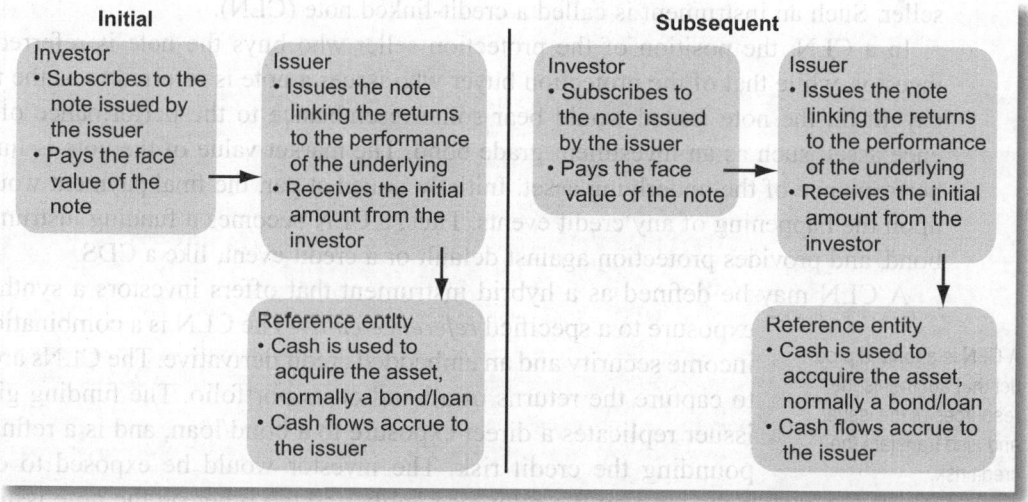

Fig. 20.10 Credit-linked note—cash flows, initial and subsequent

The investor in the CLN may derive yield in two forms—the regular return and the capital gains. The investor would subscribe to the CLN as it would offer a larger regular return in the form of a higher coupon than that on a plain bond from the same issuer. For example, if an investment grade entity can mobilize at 200 bps above the risk-free rate, the CLN may have to offer a coupon of, say, 400 bps above the risk-free rate. This regular coupon payment is expected to cover the return on the investment and the premium for the credit risk. Besides a regular coupon, the investor can benefit from capital gains too if the CLN is issued below par and redeemed at par at maturity.

Regular coupon payment can be variable and made proportional to credit performance. For example, the coupon payment value may increase with any downgrading of the underlying reference asset.

These returns would be realized only if the specified credit events do not occur. At the end of the contracted period, and if no specified credit event has occurred, the original investment, the par value, must be paid by the issuer (protection buyer) to the investor (protection seller). However, if any credit event occurs during the tenure of the CLN, then settlement at the expiry is done at less than par value, transferring the losses to the protection seller (investor).

COLLATERALIZED DEBT OBLIGATIONS

Collateralized debt obligations (CDOs), first introduced in 1988, are essentially structured finance products that package risk in different classes, called tranches, as described in the section on securitization in this chapter.

Securitization forms the backbone of CDOs. Illiquid and non-transferable debt obligations are converted into a tradable form through securitization, having claims on the debts. It is a repackaging of the debt obligations that have collateral securities in the form of underlying assets financed by the loans. The underlying pool of assets can be a portfolio of bonds or a portfolio of loans. The former is called a *collateralized bond obligation* (CBO) and the latter is called a collateralized loan obligation (CLO). If the underlying pool of assets is mortgaged, it is called a *collateralized mortgage obligation* (CMO).

Once securitized, the cash flows accrue to the holders of these instruments. The securitized instruments are categorized according to the risk and returns, called tranches. Each tranche would have a different priority over the cash flows received from the debt obligations. Each tranche is sold to investors interested in yield enhancement (while assuming commensurate risk). Each tranche has a different risk–return profile, dependent upon the credit performance of the underlying pool of assets.

> Collateralized debt obligations have categories of credit risk, and investors choose the risk–return profile.

Figure 20.11 depicts a typical CDO. Assume that a bank, called the originator, has a pool of loans, say, for housing, issued to its customers, from whom regular cash flows are expected. These cash flows are not uniform

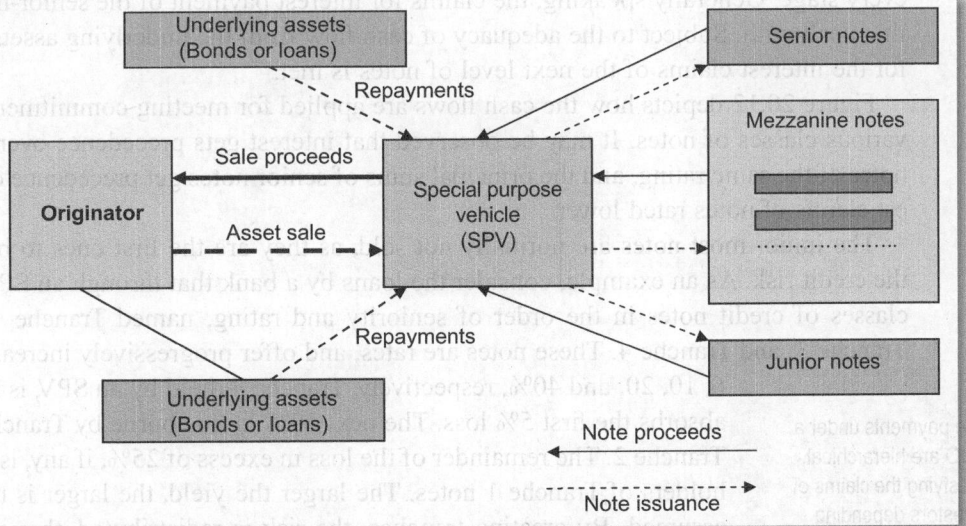

Fig. 20.11 Typical CDO

because some of the customers may not be making timely payments, while some are making pre-payments. The originator, for reasons discussed later, may decide to sell the pool of assets (the underlying) to an SPV, who makes a payment to the originator and assumes the ownership of the assets that entitles him/her to receive the periodic cash flows generated from the underlying assets. This is referred to as securitization of the loans by the originator.

In the subsequent stage, the SPV may grade the cash flows into different categories of risks and issues notes with varying levels of entitlement to receive the cash flows from the underlying. These notes, with varying returns, are sold to various investors. This transaction is analogous to a CLN. However, here the underlying asset serves as collateral for these notes, as they are serviced from the cash flows of the underlying assets.

The notes issued by the SPV do not bear the same claim on the cash flows from the underlying. The notes are categorized on the basis of those who are entitled to have prior claims on the cash flows. The notes that are serviced first are the senior most. Only after satisfying the obligations to the senior-most notes are the claims of the next level, the mezzanine, met. There may be several layers of mezzanine notes. After the claims of the mezzanine notes are settled, the junior-most notes are satisfied. Hence the junior-most notes become most risky. Since the underlying are subject to credit risk, the junior-most notes are the first ones to suffer the initial part of the loss of cash flows from the underlying. They behave more like equity and are normally subscribed by the originators themselves to show that they are the first sufferers of any default and to absorb loss due to non-payment of the debt obligations. This helps in marketing the remaining tranches by creating confidence in investors that bad loans are not being sold off to them.

The notes issued by the SPV are normally rated by rating agencies, with the senior-most notes accorded the highest rating. The junior-most notes are generally not rated, and they behave more like equity, having the last claim on the cash flows. For determination of the order of servicing the different categories of notes, the adequacy of the cash flows from the underlying assets needs to be ascertained, and, therefore, coverage tests are conducted at every stage. Generally speaking, the claims for interest payment of the senior-most notes are first dealt with. Subject to the adequacy of cash flow from the underlying assets, the liability for the interest claims of the next level of notes is met.

Figure 20.12 depicts how the cash flows are applied for meeting commitments toward the various classes of notes. It may be observed that interest gets precedence over principal for notes of the same rating, and the principal sums of senior notes get precedence over the interest claims of notes rated lower.

The junior-most notes are normally not sold, as they are the first ones to be affected by the credit risk. As an example, consider the loans by a bank that through an SPV issues four classes of credit notes in the order of seniority and rating, named Tranche 1, Tranche 2, Tranche 3, and Tranche 4. These notes are rates, and offer progressively increasing yields of 6, 10, 20, and 40%, respectively. Tranche 4, held by an SPV, is not rated, and absorbs the first 5% loss. The next 10% loss is borne by Tranche 3 and then Tranche 2. The remainder of the loss in excess of 25%, if any, is passed to the holders of Tranche 1 notes. The larger the yield, the larger is the credit risk assumed. By creating tranches, the risk is redistributed, though the risk on the underlying does not change merely because tranches have been created.

> The payments under a CDO are hierarchical, satisfying the claims of investors depending upon their seniority.

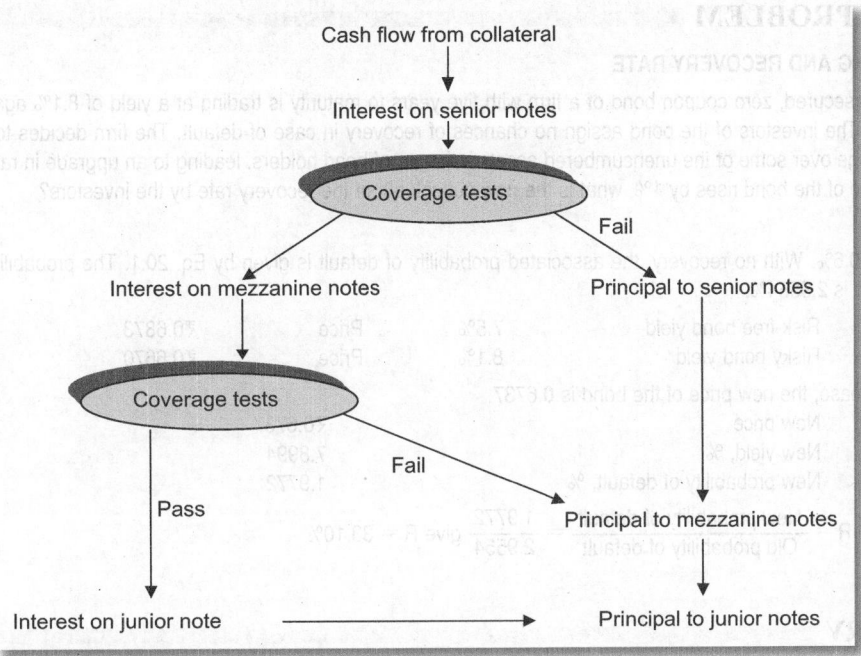

Fig. 20.12 Priority of cash flow under CDO

A major benefit of a CDO is that it enables the originators to transfer risky debt off their balance sheets, improve their debt–equity ratios, and raise additional resources for furthering their businesses.

Synthetic CDO The underlying debt obligations decide the nature of CDOs. The structure described in the last section is referred to as a cash CDO. Where the underlying asset is a credit derivative, such as a CDS, the CDO would be called a synthetic CDO. It repackages the credit derivatives rather than the debt obligations.

Normally, a protection seller in a CDS becomes the issuer in a synthetic CDO. The issuer takes up the credit risk exposure on a portfolio of CDSs under which credit risk has been assumed on a portfolio of reference assets or entities. These are converted into tranches of different risk–return profiles for onward sale to different investors. Since the protection seller in a CDS would have only nominal cash inflows by way of premium, he/she would have to acquire fresh assets to support the CDO programme. This achieves twin objectives—first, these assets can serve as collateral, and, second, they provide the required cash flows to service cash flow obligations undertaken in CDOs.

The investors agree to provide funding if losses take place, in return for some premium. This would be a pure synthetic, i.e., an unfunded CDO. A prudent investor in an unfunded CDO would make provisions for payment by investing funds in safe securities, because when several simultaneous defaults take place, there would be many investors wanting cash that may not be available. As a variant, we may have a fully or partially funded CDO, where some initial payment is made by the investors to the issuer.

> Synthetic CDOs have another derivative, i.e., the CDS, as the underlying asset.

SOLVED PROBLEM

SP 20.1 RATING AND RECOVERY RATE

Suppose an unsecured, zero coupon bond of a firm with five years to maturity is trading at a yield of 8.1% against treasury zeros yielding 7.5%. The investors of the bond assign no chances of recovery in case of default. The firm decides to create security by creating a charge over some of the unencumbered assets in favour of bond holders, leading to an upgrade in rating by rating agencies. If the price of the bond rises by 1%, what is the new outlook about the recovery rate by the investors?

Solution

The spread is 0.6%. With no recovery, the associated probability of default is given by Eq. 20.1. The probability of default over a five-year period is 2.9554%.

Risk-free bond yield	7.5%	Price	₹0.6873
Risky bond yield	8.1%	Price	₹0.6670

With a 1% increase, the new price of the bond is 0.6737.

New price	₹0.6737
New yield, %	7.8994
New probability of default, %	1.9772

$$1 - R = \frac{\text{New probability of default}}{\text{Old probability of default}} = \frac{1.9772}{2.9554} \text{ give } R = 33.10\%$$

SUMMARY

Credit risk is the risk of default faced by a lender that his/her borrower would not pay on time, for whatever reason. Credit risk is different from market risk or the risk of a portfolio of traded assets, which may provide lower or higher returns than expected. On the contrary, a loan transaction never pays more than what is promised under the loan agreement. The assessment of credit risk is not easy, as it cannot be said to follow a distribution on which models are available.

Some idea of default can be had from the return the asset of a firm provides in excess of the risk-free yield. The difference in the price of the bond with respect to risk-free bonds represents the present value of the expected losses. The expected losses can be used to oblation the probability of default and the difference in yields serves as an input for pricing credit derivative products. The transition rate indicates the chances of migration of the rating of a debt instrument over a given period of time.

One measure of credit risk for financial institutions holding a portfolio of financial instruments is credit VaR. It is similar to VaR, which gives the potential loss over a chosen period with a chosen confidence level. It serves as a benchmark for capital adequacy and for assessing loss-absorbing capacity.

A CDS is an arrangement or instrument designed to exclusively cover the default risk of an asset, referred to as reference obligation, or a firm called the reference entity. The premium payable by the protection seeker, called the protection buyer, would be proportional to the excess return one gets over and above the risk-free rate. In return for periodic payment, the protection buyer covers the risk of default on the reference asset or reference entity.

Should any of the specified default events actually take place, the CDS terminates. If it is cash-settled, the protection buyer gets the difference between the notional value and the market value, as determined by a calculation agent. Under physical settlement, the instrument is delivered to the protection seller for payment of the notional value.

Other than covering default risk, a CDS has many applications, as it is a synthetic exposure on the reference asset.

A TRS is another instrument where the returns on an asset are exchanged for receiving a floating rate. One party, called the total return payer, pays regular coupons as well as the capital appreciation to another party, called the total return receiver. The TRS is different from the interest rate swap and the CDS, as the TRS covers two risks—the interest rate risk and the default risk. Interest rate swaps provide hedge against interest rate risks and are not concerned with default. A CDS covers only default risk. The TRS covers both for the payer in exchange for receiving a floating return plus a spread.

Securitization is essential for certain credit derivatives. Securitization is a process of transforming illiquid non-transferable loans into freely tradable marketable securities with features of ready transferability. It forms the backbone of credit derivatives such as CLNs and CDOs.

The CLN is a funded instrument that covers credit risk and also provides funds to the issuer through a note issued on the reference entity/obligation. The issuer pays the regular coupon based on the credit performance of the reference obligations. These coupons could be variable. Thus, the investor in the note absorbs the credit risk. The note is terminated upon occurrence of the default event, with losses absorbed by the investor. If no credit event occurs, the funded amount is paid back to the investor.

The CDO is a way of segregating the risks of a pool of assets into different classes, with each class having different claims on the cash flows from the pool of assets. These claims, providing different returns, are satisfied on the basis of adequacy of cash flows determined periodically, with junior-most claims absorbing the shortfall in the cash flows.

KEY TERMS

Calculation agent   An agent who determines the market value of an asset after a default event has occurred.

Collateralized debt obligation   Under collateralized debt obligation, a pool of assets is categorized under different risk classes with varying returns and priorities, set to be subscribed by different classes of investors, with the cash flow from the underlying asset serving as collateral.

Credit default swap   A CDS is an arrangement between two parties where one party compensates the other for losses due to default on the occurrence of defined events, in return for receiving a premium at periodic intervals.

Credit event   A credit event is an event that triggers default on a loan and payment from the protection seller to the protection buyer.

Credit-linked note   A funded instrument where the investor pays for a note issued on the reference entity and agrees for a return based on the credit performance.

Credit risk   The risk of a default by the borrower in a loan transaction.

Credit VaR   The expected loss that can occur due to default on a given portfolio over a period of time and with a given confidence level.

Probability of default   The probability of default relates to the chances that a debtor would not pay interest and/or the principal on the due dates.

Protection buyer   A protection buyer seeks protection against default by a reference entity or an asset owned by paying a premium.

Protection seller   A protection seller, in exchange for receiving a periodic premium, compensates against loss due to default on an asset upon the happening of some default event.

Recovery rate   The proportion of debt that can be claimed once a default has occurred.

Reference entity   An entity on whose credit performance protection is sought under a CDS.

Securitization   A process of converting illiquid and non-transferable cash flows into tradable and marketable securities with values determined by market conditions.

Synthetic CDO   The CDO where the underlying asset is a basket of CDSs.

Total return payer   The total return payer pays the total returns on an asset by way of regular coupons and end-of-the-period capital gains or losses, and receives a floating rate plus the spread.

Total return receiver   The total return receiver gets regular coupons as well as capital gains and pays on a floating basis, assuming the credit risk as well as the interest rate risk.

Total Return swap   An arrangement where one party pays total returns on an asset for receiving a floating rate plus a spread.

Transition rate   The probability that a debt instrument may undergo a change of its rating over a given period of time.

QUESTIONS

20.1 Describe what credit risk is, and how it is different from market risk.
20.2 What are CDSs? Illustrate with a diagram, indicating the roles of the swap and cash flow participants.
20.3 Describe the Merton model for finding credit risk using option pricing.
20.4 What do you understand by credit VaR?
20.5 What is a transition matrix?
20.6 How is a TRS different from an interest rate swap and a CDS?
20.7 Explain the process of securitization, its benefits and risks.
20.8 Describe a CLN.
20.9 Illustrate a CDO with a diagram.

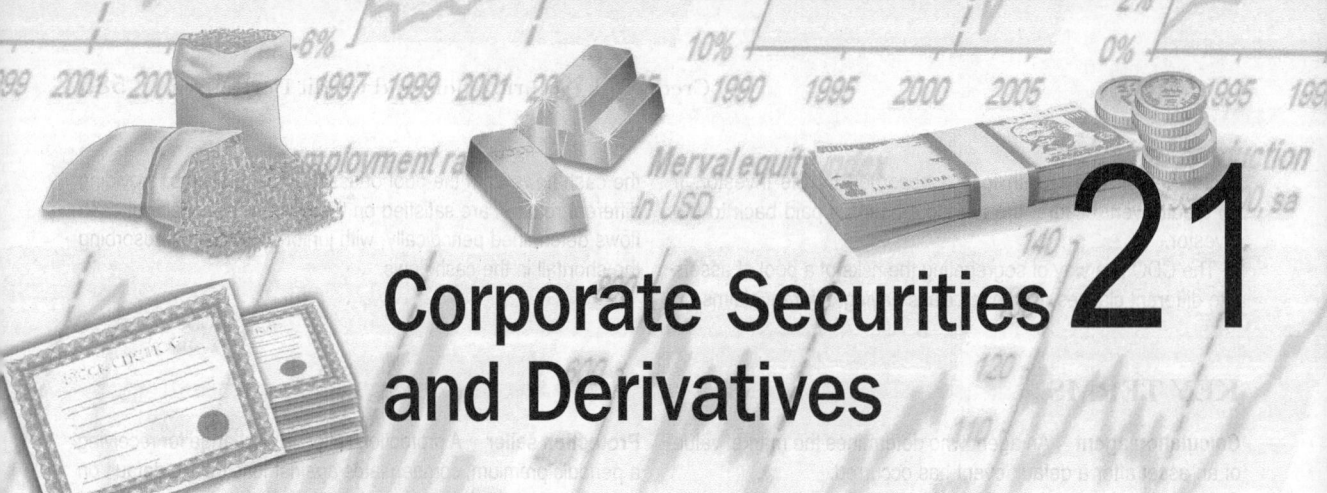

Corporate Securities and Derivatives

21

INTRODUCTION

Firms raise funds by issuing different kinds of securities that are claims against their cash flows. The market prices of these securities govern the values of the derivatives on them. Corporate securities that act as underlying assets for derivatives can in fact be viewed as derivatives themselves. Managers in corporate finance may not be very familiar with the terminology or functioning of derivatives, but they do have the ingenuity to come out with innovative products to raise resources, by including features that are practically identical or similar to derivatives. These securities often have embedded derivatives in them.

These embedded derivatives in corporate securities are invented due to the felt need of investors for inclusion of features that make instruments more attractive for them. For example, firms issue callable bonds rather than straight bonds to contain the cost of capital. Such bonds have call options embedded. The purpose of this chapter is to provide an exposition on corporate securities visualized in terms of derivatives. If corporate securities can be seen as derivatives, it would not only enhance our understanding of these securities but may also prove helpful in their pricing. The ad-hoc approach used by naive managers in valuing them can be replaced by a technically more sound approach using option pricing models. Interpretation of corporate securities as derivatives would enhance our understanding of not only corporate securities but also derivatives.

We have all heard of the popular versions of corporate securities issued by firms, such as common stock, debt, preference shares, warrants, convertible bonds, and callable bonds. These

> Corporate securities often have derivatives embedded in them, more because of the felt need of investors and as a strategy to attract them, rather than as a deliberate attempt to include these derivatives.

> **Learning Objectives**
> After going through this chapter, readers should be familiar with
> - corporate securities' resemblance to combinations of options
> - equity's resemblance to a call option on the firm
> - debt as a combination of options
> - the application of put–call parity for corporate securities
> - warrants
> - the valuation of warrants
> - the differences between the value of a warrant and that of a regular call

instruments have been in use for a long time and are evolving continuously. They came into existence much before derivatives. Although it is quite natural for one to think of the value of derivatives as driven by their underlying assets, it is rather strange to see these securities used as derivatives. A cursory look at the terms and conditions stipulated in these instruments would reveal that they actually embed a derivative or a combination, and we may use the principles of valuation of derivatives in the pricing of such instruments.

EQUITY SHARES—COMMON STOCK

The most common method for raising capital is issuing common stock/equity shares. Investors in the shares of a firm, called shareholders, have a right to manage the assets of the firm. To maintain the continuity of the firm's capital, these shares are transferable. If a shareholder decides not to exercise his/her right or ownership, he/she has another alternative: to sell his/her shares. If the shares are listed and traded, the objective of selling can be achieved rather easily.

Ownership of Residual However, a shareholder's right to manage the assets of the firm is not unambiguous. In terms of the priority of claims, the shareholder occupies the last place. Therefore, the shareholder is often said to be the owner of the residual, i.e., the leftover remaining after the claims of all others who precede the shareholders have been settled. In fact, shareholders come last in the list. As long as shareholders satisfy the claims of all others, the right to manage remains with them. Any failure to meet the claims of others, such as creditors, workers, lenders, and the government jeopardizes the right of the shareholders to manage.

> The common stock of a firm can be considered as a call option, with the maturity value of debt as the exercise price.

The total value of a firm is given by the sum total of the value of its debts and the value of its equity. Since debt holders have priority of claims over shareholders, the value that can be derived by shareholders is only the remainder after the claims of the debt holders have been satisfied. In an efficient market, the residual nature of the claim would be recognized in the market value of the equity. In an all-equity firm, the entire value rests with the shareholders. At worst, the value of the equity can be zero; it cannot be negative.

The total value of the firm, V, is the sum of the value of its equity, E, and the value of its debts, D, i.e., $V = E + D$. The value of all claims is supposed to represent the total value of the assets of the firm. The market value of the equity is supposed to reflect the residual of assets that belong to the shareholders.

Limited Liability Another feature of equity is limited liability, i.e., the maximum loss that can be incurred by any shareholder is the price he/she paid to acquire his/her equity. In any case, the price paid to acquire equity has no significance for future decision making, since it is a sunk cost. At best, it can be a consideration before acquiring equity. It is like paying a premium to buy an option that loses its significance thereafter for any further decisions, though its recovery remains a consideration. For example, the decision to buy a call or a put option for hedging may be influenced by the option's price, but after the option is acquired, the price paid becomes immaterial for exercising it, except for the psychological satisfaction or dissatisfaction at the end of the option period of having ended up with a profit or a loss. At worst, the payoff of equity is zero.

> Shareholders' rights to manage the assets of a firm with limited liability can be exercised only after satisfying all prior claims.

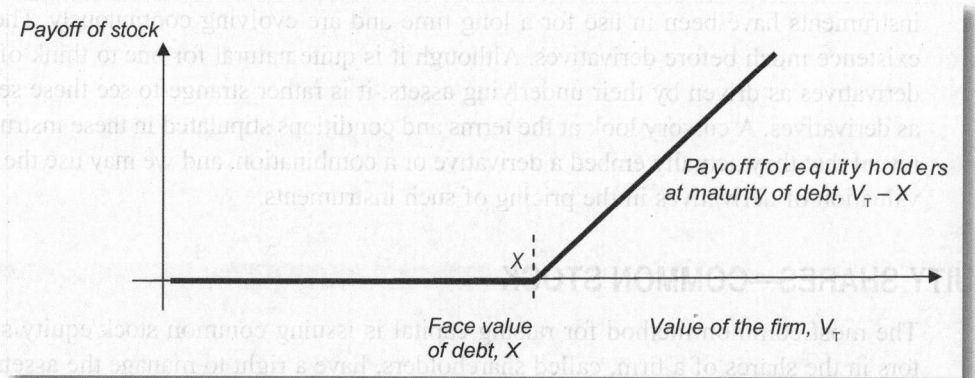

Fig. 21.1 Common equity as call option

Equity as Call Option When a firm has debts, the value for the shareholder is the excess of the value of the firm over the value of the debt. Debt claims cannot exceed their maturity values. More often than not, the maturity value is the same as the face value. If the total value, V_T, of the firm is less than the maturity value of its debt, the shareholder gets nothing. If the maturity value of the debt is X, then the payoff for the shareholders at maturity, S_T, of the debt is

$$S_T = \text{Max }(0, V_T - X) \qquad (21.1)$$

The payoff for shareholders, as given by Eq. 21.1, is identical to that of a call option. Hence, common stock is regarded as a call option with an exercise price equal to the maturity value of the debt of the firm, as shown in Fig 21.1. The value of shareholding today, S_0, is the difference between the current value of the firm, V_0, and the current value of its debt, $D = Xe^{-rT}$, i.e.,

$$S_0 \geq V_0 - Xe^{-rT} \qquad (21.2)$$

Agency Cost of Debt

Exponents of corporate finance often mention the agency cost of debt as a conflict between debt holders and equity holders. From the payoff for holders of equity as a call option, it can be surmised that the value of the equity can be increased by increasing the risk. Risk can be increased by increasing leverage. Therefore, shareholders, being at the helm of decision making, work towards increasing the payoff, tempted to avail of more and more debt. There may be a tendency to increase debt to an inordinately high level. If the risk pans out, the shareholders gain, while the debt holders get no more than the promised return. In case the risk fails to pan out, debt holders lose more than the shareholders, who have limited liabilities. Therefore, while approving additional debt beyond a limit, lenders often impose restrictive covenants that limit the freedom of shareholders to take major policy decisions.

Equity as Put Option From this perspective, shareholding can be viewed in terms of put option. The position of shareholders can be described as ownership of the firm with prior obligation to pay the maturity value to debt holders. Since shareholders can default on this

Derivatives in Practice: Takeover and Options

Essar puts Vodafone on call

Hutchinson Essar Ltd, a joint venture between Hutchinson Telecom International, the Cayman Islands, (HUTCH) and Essar Group of India (ESSAR), held licences to operate cellular services in 23 circles in India since 1994. HUTCH held 67% of the equity, with the balance of 33% held by ESSAR.

In 2007, after operating for more than a decade, HUTCH decided to exit by selling its stake to Vodafone NV, Netherlands, (VODAFONE) globally the largest telecom firm. VODAFONE was desirous of operating in India. In an offshore all-cash deal between the two, VODAFONE acquired HUTCH's 67% holding in the Indian venture for US $11.1 billion. The Indian venture was rechristened Vodafone Essar Ltd.

ESSAR's 33% holding was split in two tranches—10.97% (a third) held by ESSAR Telecom Holding Pvt. Ltd, a firm incorporated in India and 22.03% (two thirds) held by ESSAR Communication (Mauritius) Ltd, a foreign entity registered in the tax haven of Mauritius. At the time of acquisition by VODAFONE, the Indian stakeholder ESSAR did not deem it fit to exit at the pro-rata value of US $5.6 billion, but instead chose to have a put option (a right to sell) for its entire 33% equity for a total of US $5 billion, to be exercised by May 2011. The agreement gave ESSAR the right to be on the board of the firm, together with veto power, because of its retained 33% holding. The shareholder agreement also provided for part sale of the equity, but at a mutually decided price and not by proration of US $5 billion. Since the venture was not listed in any of the stock exchanges in India, the part sale would be done on the basis of valuation to be done by an independent agency.

By March end, i.e., two months prior to the option window closing, ESSAR decided to exercise its put option in respect of its two-third holding. VODAFONE contended that such an exercise of the put option by ESSAR gave a call option (right to buy) for the remaining one third too. A part sale would raise the question of valuation, and, hence, a two-third put option for ESSAR without a corresponding call option for VODAFONE was against the shareholders' agreement. ESSAR repudiated the claim of a call option for one third by VODAFONE, and contended that the exercise of the put for a two-third stake was in order.

According to ESSAR, the two tranches could not be valued by the same yardstick, as the two-third share was held by an offshore firm, while the one-third share was owned by an Indian entity, falling under a separate jurisdiction. What perplexed people the most was the valuation of the two-third stake held by the offshore entity at US $3.8 billion, and of the one-third stake owned by the Indian entity at US $1.2 billion. The 50% premium for valuation of the foreign holding over that of the Indian holding was mired in regulatory controversy, as the Indian valuation for an unlisted firm could only be done on a free cash flow basis by a competent and independent agency, and was subject to regulatory approval. VODAFONE and ESSAR appointed the likes of Standard Chartered Bank, Goldman Sachs, and UBS to conduct the valuation. Since the telecom sector had fared badly since 2007, experts feared that the entire 33% stake could not be valued at more than US $3.00 billion in 2011, as against what was considered to be about US $5 billion in 2007. Under the circumstances, would the regulatory authorities in India accept valuation of the Indian stake at less than what was being paid for the stake held overseas? If the valuation of the offshore two-third stake was considered fair, then the value of the one-third Indian stake would be higher by about US $700 million, taking it to US $1.9 billion instead of US $1.2 billion.

Mired in controversies, claims, and counterclaims, the issue of the put option value forcing the call valuation continued till July 2011. The issue was put to rest by VODAFONE and ESSAR by both agreeing to exercise their call and put respectively, and entering into an agreement to pay US $5.46 billion, comprising[1]

- a net payment of US $3.32 billion for the two-third stake, after withholding tax of US $0.88 billion;
- a payment of US $1.26 billion for the remaining one-third stake. This payment will be made by 15 February 2012; and
- the expectation that 1.35%[2] of the shares will be transferred to an Indian investor to ensure VODAFONE's continued compliance with Indian foreign direct investment rules.

Consequently, both VODAFONE and ESSAR agreed that all outstanding claims between them were terminated, and that all future claims were renounced. The parties also agreed to cooperate fully in seeking all regulatory approvals necessary for the completion of these transactions. ESSAR relinquished all of its board seats in VODAFONE.

The settlement marks the end of a four-year partnership between VODAFONE and ESSAR in India.

[1] *Source:* www.vodafone.com, accessed on 6 March 2012.
[2] To make a minimum holding of 26% by Indians, as per the foreign direct investment policy of the telecom sector in India. Of the original VODAFONE's stake of 67%, about 24.6% was held by entities deemed resident Indians. The foreign holding, i.e., VODAFONE's holding, could not exceed 74%.

obligation if the cash flows are not adequate to cover the maturity value of the debts, they would have to hand over the assets, i.e., the firm, to the debt holder. Therefore, the shareholders have a put option with an exercise price equal to the maturity value of the debts. This put option is implicitly written by the debt holders.

DEBT AS OPTIONS

> The position of the debt holders in the firm is equal to having (a) a long position on bonds with a maturity value equal to the debt, and (b) a short position on puts with a strike equal to the value of the debt.

Debt has the feature that it cannot provide returns in excess of what has been promised. If the value of a firm exceeds the value of its debts, the debt holders get their face values and no more. In case the value of the firm is less than the maturity value of the debts, the holders get only as much as possible given the value of the firm. Hence, the payoff to the debt holders is capped at the face value of their respective debts (refer to Fig. 21.2c).

This can be seen as a long position on a bond maturing at X and a short position on a put with an exercise price of X. The put is written by the debt holders to the shareholders. If the value of the firm is less than the face value of the debts, the shareholders exercise their puts and to that extent, the debt

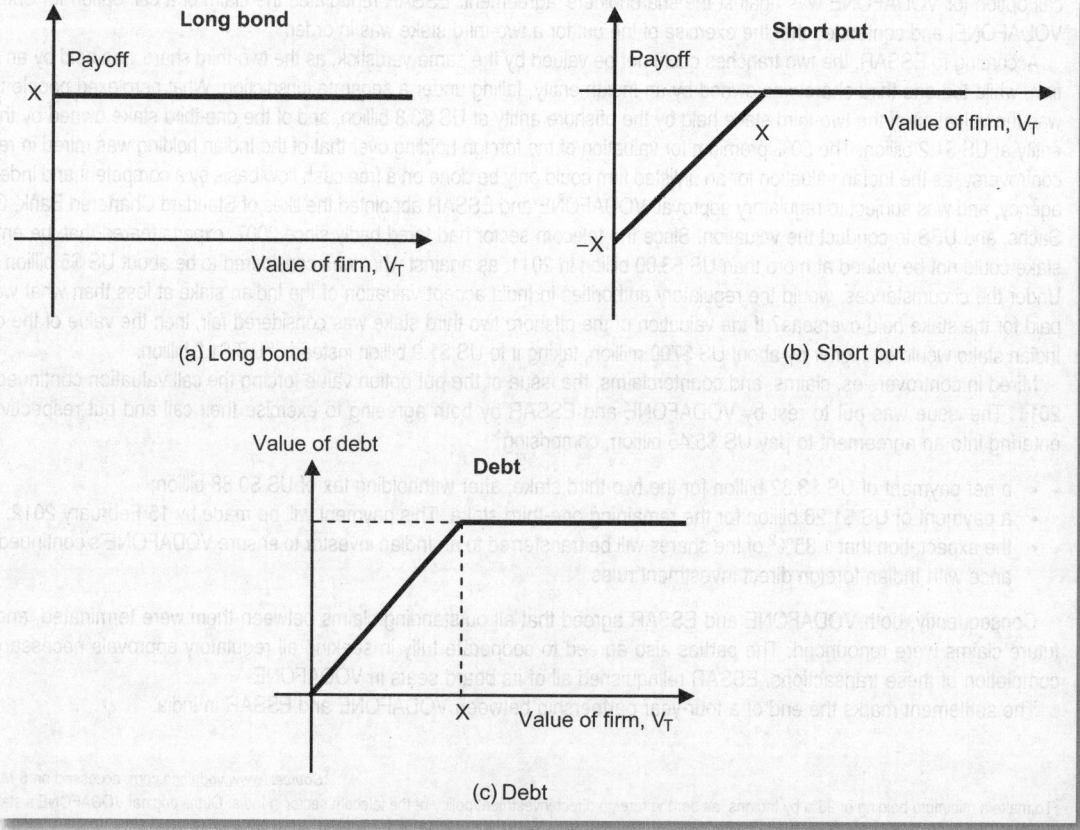

Fig. 21.2 Debt as options (a) Bond and value of firm value of firm (b) Put and value of firm (c) Debt and value of firm

holders lose a part of the value of the long bond that they hold. The position of the debt holders is depicted in Fig. 21.2, and the payoff is tabulated in Table 21.1.

Table 21.1 Payoff to debt holders

	$V_T \leq X$	$V_T > X$
Short put	$-(X - V_T)$	—
Long bond	X	X
Total	V_T	X

In this context, shareholders can be viewed as holding a combination of

- a long position on the firm;
- a short position on bond with the maturity value of the debt; and
- a long position on put, with a strike price equal to the maturity value of the debt.

Earlier, we said that equity can be viewed as a call option. The above combination is no different from a call option, as put–call parity would imply. Under put–call parity, a call can be synthesized with a long stock, a long put, and a short bond. This can easily be verified by the put–call parity discussed in Chapter 10, reproduced here for convenience.

Put–call parity;
$$\text{Stock} + \text{put} = \text{bond} + \text{call}$$
For shareholders, equity is a call option. Re-arranging put–call parity, we get;
$$\text{Call} = \text{stock} + \text{put} - \text{bond}$$

Yet another way of looking at the position of debt holders is through the value of the firm. The value of the firm at maturity is the sum of the maturity values of the debts and the value of equity. This implies

$$X = V_T - S_T, \text{ or}$$
$$= V_T - \text{Max}(0, V_T - X)$$

This is equal to a long position on the entire value of the firm, with a short position on a call option and a strike equal to the face value of the debt.

Subordinated Debt

Debts have different levels of seniority in terms of their claims on the cash flows of a firm. Senior debt has claims that take priority over anyone else. Figure 21.2 depicts the payoff for only one category of debt holders. Firms normally have several types of creditors who have different priorities over one another. We now analyse the changes in the claims of equity holders and debt holders if there is another category called subordinated debt, with claims superior to the equity holders but inferior to the holders of senior debt.

The position of shareholders remains unaffected because any debt has prior claim over them. However, the strike price of the call would now include the total value of all the debts, senior and subordinated. The payoff for any senior debt with face value X_1, too, remains unchanged, because to them subordinate debt is like an equity holder. Subordinated debt is sandwiched between senior debt and the shareholders. The payoff for subordinated debt would appear similar to the payoff for senior debt, with two modifications. First, the claim would start later than that of senior debt, shifting the strike price to the right. Till the senior debt is paid off fully (maturity value X_1), the claims of subordinated debt do not start. Second, the payoff would be smaller than for senior debt. This is depicted in Fig. 21.3 for subordinated debt with an amount equal to $X_2 - X_1$, the total debt being X_2.

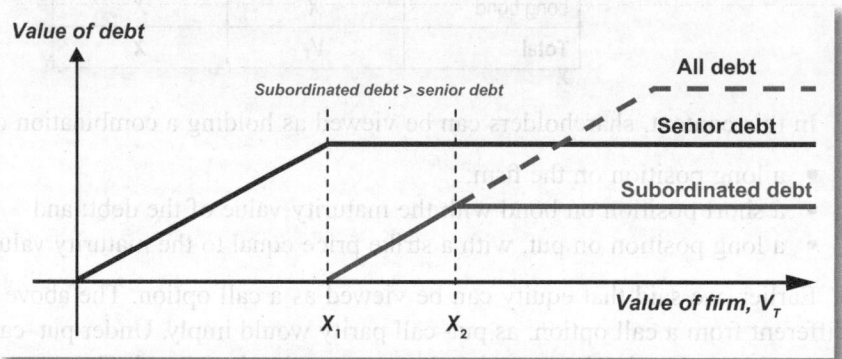

Fig. 21.3 Value of subordinated debt

CALLABLE AND PUTTABLE BONDS

Firms issuing bonds make commitments to the subscribers of the bonds, which are generally not amendable. The commitments, in terms of coupon rates and tenure, are decided at the time of issue with other terms contained in the indenture. These terms and conditions cannot be altered without the consent of the bond holders. Therefore, an indenture is issued after a lot of deliberation.

> Callable bonds are issued by firms to gain protection from falling yields after the issue of debts.

We know that there is an inverse relationship between price and yield. The higher the yield, the lower is the price, and vice versa. The coupon offered becomes the cost of debt for the issuing firm. A commitment to pay the coupon lasts for a longer time horizon. In a dynamic world, the situation may become adverse to the firm if the interest rate declines after the issue of debt. For example, a firm may have issued a 15-year debt at an attractive 10% coupon that is consistent with the current expectations of investors. However, after five years, the economic scenario might change to lower interest rates. This would adversely affect the competitive position of the issuer, as other competing firms would be able to raise debt at much cheaper rates.

A convenient way to overcome the problem of falling yields is to build in a clause in the indenture to call back the bond from the holders at a price that corresponds to the lowest yield at which the issuer feels it necessary to cut down the cost of debt. Such bonds are called callable bonds. The price at which the issuer can call back the bond is known as the call price. As the yield falls, the bond price moves up. It would happen in the case of all bonds. For a callable bond, though, the rise in price would be capped at the call price, as shown in Fig. 21.4. Up to a certain fall in the yield, callable and non-callable bonds would move almost the same way. For a callable bond, the price would not rise above the call price because investors know that the bond would be called back by the issuer.

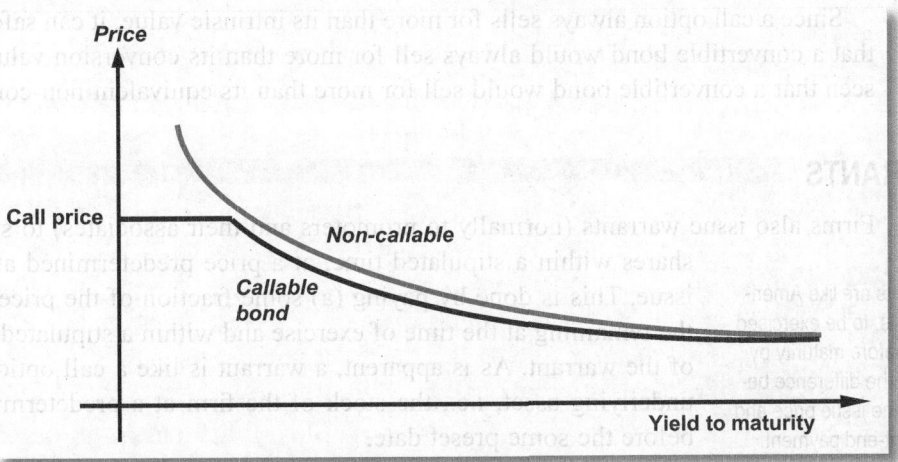

Fig. 21.4 Callable and non-callable bonds—price and YTM

In terms of the option, the holder of a callable bond is equivalent to a long position in a non-callable bond, with a call sold to the issuer at a strike equal to the call price. When the yield falls to a level corresponding to the call price, the issuer would exercise the call option by paying the call price to acquire the underlying security, i.e., the bond. By a similar logic, the issuer can be deemed as long on a call with a short position on a non-callable bond.

As issuer, a firm would protect against falling yields by inserting a callable feature. It may also like to safeguard the interest of its subscribers by offering them an opportunity to sell the bond back. A bond with such a feature is called a *puttable bond*. The holders of such bonds would like to exercise the put option when prices fall. In terms of options, the holder of a puttable bond is equivalent to a long position in a non-puttable bond and a long position in a put with a strike equal to the put price.

CONVERTIBLE BONDS

While callable bonds are issued by firms to protect themselves from falling yields, convertible bonds are issued to induce the subscribers to draw on the charm of equity. The intention of the issuer is to bring down the coupon rate by offering conversion of part (or the whole) of the debt into more lucrative equity. The number of shares converted upon extinguishing the bond is called the conversion ratio. The conversion ratio multiplied by the share price would give the conversion value. For example, consider a bond with a face value of ₹100, with a maturity of five years and coupons of 8%. At the end of two years, the bond offers an option to convert ₹60 into two shares of the firm. The bond would have a conversion ratio of 2 and a conversion value of ₹60, assuming a stock price of ₹30. This bond may be seen as combination of:

- a non-convertible bond of ₹100 maturing after two years
- a non-convertible bond of ₹40 maturing after five years
- a call option to get two shares at an exercise price of ₹60 (₹30 per share)

Since a call option always sells for more than its intrinsic value, it can safely be concluded that a convertible bond would always sell for more than its conversion value. It can also be seen that a convertible bond would sell for more than its equivalent non-convertible bond.

WARRANTS

Firms also issue warrants (normally to promoters and their associates) to subscribe to their shares within a stipulated time, at a price predetermined at the time of the issue. This is done by paying (a) some fraction of the price upfront and (b) the remaining at the time of exercise and within a stipulated time, the expiry of the warrant. As is apparent, a warrant is like a call option to acquire the underlying asset, i.e., the stock of the firm at a predetermined price on or before the some preset date.

> Warrants are like American calls, to be exercised on or before maturity by paying the difference between the issue price and the front-end payment.

However, there are some critical differences between a call and a warrant. While exercising a warrant, there is a new issue of capital, which does not happen in the case of a regular call. A call is written or bought with the same number of shares outstanding. Besides, warrants are issued for longer maturities than those usually available for traded options. Since warrants are issued by a firm, the value enhances by the amount of the exercise value, and the firm issues the required number of additional shares exercised under the warrants.

When one exercises a warrant, the number of shares increase. The capital structure in terms of the ownership of the firm undergoes a change. Equity increases if warrants are exercised. In order to keep the capital structure unchanged in terms of the debt–equity ratio, the issuance of warrants is often accompanied by the issuance of bonds. The bonds and warrants are detachable. They can be traded independent of each other.

Due to the enhanced capital, there is dilution in the payoff on the warrant, as compared to the payoff on a call. Consider the payoffs in two situations of 25 calls sold and 25 warrants issued with identical expiry and exercise prices of ₹ 100. Assume that there are 100 shares outstanding. The payoffs under alternative scenarios for calls and warrants would be as given in Table 21.2.

Table 21.2 Dilution effect of warrants

	Call	Warrant
(a) Price of share before exercise, ₹	150	150
(b) No. of new shares issued	–	25
(c) Total no. of shares after exercise	100	125
(d) Exercise value accruing to firm (25 × 100) ₹	–	2500
(e) Value of firm after exercise (a × c), ₹	15,000	17,500
(f) Share price after exercise, ₹	150	140
(g) Exercise price, ₹	100	100
(h) Payoff, ₹	50	40

Derivatives in Practice

Unwarranted Warrants

Call option in warrants

A warrant is a security, entitling its holder to convert it into equity shares at a fixed price within a stipulated date. The current law governing the issuance of warrants in India is that,

- they can be issued only at the current market price, as governed by a formula;
- the maximum period allowed would not be more than 18 months from the date of issue;
- 25% of the price would be paid upfront, to be adjusted against the exercise, i.e., only the remaining 75% is required to be paid; and
- if not exercised, there is no refund of the money paid upfront.

Promoters of firms issue warrants to themselves, invariably increasing their own stakes in their firms. The motives for issuing warrants include improving the debt–equity ratio, better control, avoidance of takeover threats, and raising resources for expansion.

Besides these features, warrants are also supposed to have significant information content, as they reflect on the minimum intrinsic value of the firm as perceived by its management. For shareholders, the conversion price of a warrant is supposed to be a floor because of the general belief that promoters would allocate shares to themselves at a price that is favourable to them at the time of conversion of the warrants.

However, in a large number of cases, this has not come true. The promoters of JSW Steel, the second largest steel producer in India with a capacity of 10 million tonnes, did not exercise their 1.75 crore warrants, allotted in June 2010 at a price of ₹ 1210 per share and due for conversion in December 2011, because the share price had fallen more than 50% since the allotment of the warrants. As a result, they had to surrender 25% of the initial deposit of ₹ 529 crore to the firm. Similarly, another firm, Pantaloon Retail, having allotted themselves 1 crore warrants at ₹ 400, also due for conversion in December 2011, surrendered the initial deposit of ₹ 100 crore, i.e., 25% of the conversion price when the share was trading in the vicinity of ₹ 150 against the conversion price of ₹ 400.

This trend is not new. In April 2009, several companies, such as Raymond, Bombay Dyeing, Aditya Birla Nuvo, Usha Martin, and Jindal Saw also surrendered warrants due to sharp falls in prices from the dates of allotment of the warrants to the dates of conversion. However, the losses in 2009 were much less because at that time, warrants could be allotted by paying only 10% of the conversion price. These incidunets reflect holders not exercising the call option because asset-price falls better exercise price.

Source: Based on information in the *Economic Times* and the *Business Standard* of April 2009 and December 2011

If the value of the firm is V with n shares outstanding prior to the exercise of the calls/warrants, then for m calls/warrants issued with exercise price X, the payoffs under calls and warrants are given by

For Call; $$\text{Payoff per call} = \frac{V}{n} - X \qquad (21.3)$$

For Warrants; $$\text{Payoff per warrant} = \frac{V + X.m}{n + m} - X \qquad (21.4)$$

Since the payoff on the warrants is different from the payoff on the calls due to the issue of additional shares, the value of one warrant would be less than the value of one normal traded call. The payoff on the warrant can be expressed in terms of the payoff on a traded call, as shown in Eq. 21.5.

$$\text{Payoff per warrant} = \frac{n}{n + m}\left(\frac{V}{n} - X\right) \qquad (21.3)$$

> Warrants imply issue of fresh stock, while regular calls are traded on already existing stocks. Therefore, the value of a warrant is less than the value of a regular call.

$$\text{Value of warrant} = \frac{n}{n + m} \times \text{Value of traded call} \qquad (21.5)$$

Equation 21.5 enables us to value the warrant using the Black-Scholes option pricing model. First, we find the value of a regularly traded call using the given X, T, r, and σ, and then simply multiply it by the ratio of the number of shares before and the number of shares after the exercise of the warrants.

SOLVED PROBLEMS

SP 21.1: Value of warrant

The promoters of a listed firm, ABC Ltd, have issued warrants to themselves equivalent to 10% of the present capital, exercisable at a price of ₹ 200 per share within one year from the date of issue. The current price of the share is ₹ 240. Regular calls on the stock with a strike price of ₹ 200 and an expiry of one year are trading at ₹ 66. A potential investor has offered to purchase the warrants from the promoters at ₹ 62. Should the promoters sell the warrants to the investor?

Solution:

The exercise of the warrants would increase the capital of the firm by 10%. Even though the regular call is trading at a premium of ₹ 66, the value of the warrants is not as much due to the issue of fresh capital. The value of the warrant, as given by Eq. 21.5, is ₹ 60.

Value of warrant = 100/110 × 66 = ₹ 60.

Since the investor offers more, the promoters should consider his/her proposal favourably.

SUMMARY

Firms issue various kinds of securities to raise capital. The form of capital issued by these securities provides different kinds of rights to the holders on the cash flows of the firms. The basic forms of capital are equity and debt. While debt has a fixed claim on the cash flow, equity owners have a claim on the residual.

The securities issued by firms can be viewed as combination of options. The value of a firm can be seen in two ways—one on the liability side and the other on the asset side. The value of the firm should be equal to the value of the assets. If the value of the firm is less than the claims of the debt holders, equity holders do not get anything. The excess of value over the value of debt belongs to the shareholders. Hence, a shareholder's position is considered as a call with a strike price equal to the value of the debt at maturity.

A debt holder gets no more than the face value of the debt provided the value of the firm is in excess of it. If the value is less than the debt, the holder loses. This is equivalent to a long position on a bond with a maturity value equal to the face value of the debt and a short position on a put.

The position of the equity holder can also be analysed in terms of put–call parity as a combination of a long position on the firm, a short position on bonds with a maturity value of debt, and a long position on puts with a strike price equal to the maturity value of the debt.

Callable bonds are issued by firms to gain protection from falling yields after the issue of debt. The position of bond holders is equivalent to (a) a long position on a non-callable bond and (b) a short position on calls with a strike equal to the call price.

Warrants are like American calls, to be exercised on or before maturity by paying the difference between the issue price and the front-end payment. Warrants imply issue of fresh stock, while regular calls are traded on already existing stocks. Therefore, the value of warrants is less than the value of regular calls.

KEY TERMS

Callable bond A debt issued with a right to the issuer to call back after some time at a pre-specified price.
Puttable bond A puttable bond gives the right to the subscriber to sell back the bond to the issuer at a pre-specified price some time after the issue of the bond.

Warrants Instruments that give the right to their holders to subscribe to the stock of the firm at a pre determined price within some time upon initial part payment, with remaining payable at the time of exercise.

QUESTIONS

21.1 How does the derivative perspective help in understanding corporate securities?
21.2 Can you describe the equity of a firm in the terminology of options, apart from it being considered a call option?
21.3 Debt holders are only holding bonds of the firm. Do you agree?
21.4 How are warrants different from calls? Does a warrant have the same value as a regularly traded call?

Real Options

22

INTRODUCTION

Strategic decisions are not as straightforward as routine capital budgeting decisions. Firms and managers usually have various options in terms of investing in real assets. The standard capital budgeting problem is solved by discounting cash flows (DCFs) at an appropriate discount rate to arrive at the net present value (NPV). Traditional capital budgeting approaches assume no action once the project is accepted or rejected on the basis of DCFs. The implied assumption is that nothing can be altered once the decision is taken and all is left to chance.

In real life situations, the problems are not as clearly defined as is assumed in capital budgeting exercises. There remain substantial ambiguities about the timing of investments, the gain or loss of competitive advantage as time elapses, and the strategic position of the firm in the competitive world. All of these factors vary with time. Such strategic decisions often relate to expenditure in research and development, where the outcome of the efforts as well as of the cash flows is totally unknown. In fact, a firm has the option of whether to invest or not, and, if yes, when to escalate the capital investment. If the initial outcome is not on expected lines, the firm has to decide whether or not to abandon the effort.

Standard techniques assume that all managerial actions are absent once the cash flow estimates are prepared. Capital budgeting decisions are not passive and static. Instead, they are subject to managerial actions with several options as time progresses. For example, after having implemented a project, managers have options to reduce capacity utilization or undertake intensive advertising campaigns if volumes are not picking up. On the contrary, if

> Routine capital budgeting exercises involving discounting of cash flows to find the net present value is flawed, because the value so derived ignores the managerial actions that are available later.

Learning Objectives

After going through this chapter, readers should be familiar with

- the meaning of real options
- the difference between financial options and real options
- the three important real options faced in the corporate world, namely,
    - the option to delay
    - the option to expand
    - the option to abandon
- the valuation of real options by the discounted cash flow (DCF) method
- the limitations of the application of DCF valuation to real options
- application of the binomial model to value real options
- application of the Black Scholes Model to value real options
- reconciliation of different real option values obtained from different methods

the product finds more than expected acceptance, the managers have options such as increasing production, raising prices, and developing more product variants. The list of available future courses of actions is endless. Each situation is different, and throws up several possible actions. In fact, each capital budgeting decision is a complex set of options.

Discounted cash flow-based techniques assume that once an action has been taken, the possibility of changes in the cash flows due to managerial action does not exist. This holds good for financial assets like stocks and bonds; once this type of asset is purchased, the investor does not have any control over the cash flows attributable to it. In the case of real assets, though, significant managerial leeway is always available to influence the cash flows of the project, sometimes substantially and sometimes only marginally.

KINDS OF REAL OPTIONS

As distinct from financial options, options on real assets are referred to as *real options*. Firms and managers usually have three different kinds of options on projects, as follows:

- The option to delay the project
- The option to expand the project
- The option to abandon the project

Option to Delay

The option to delay a project, also referred to as the option to wait, refers to timing decisions regarding commencement of the project. Managers have several choices as to the right time to start a project. Conflicts arise, for example, from the toss-up between the benefits of capitalizing on early bird advantages on the one hand and taking a greater risk by starting immediately on the other hand. Firms may face a choice between starting right away and starting a year later. They are mutually exclusive projects. Delaying a project may mean leaving the field open to competitors and foregoing the early bird advantage, which means capitalizing on the market share acquired in the nascent stage. The option to delay is a valuable one where there is some kind of exclusivity about the venture or where the entry barriers are substantial. It is a meaningless option if competitors can start the same project right then or soon.

> The three basic real options are the option to delay, the option to expand, and the option to abandon. There are other options, too, that allow managerial flexibility for adjusting prices, volumes, shutting and re-opening, etc.

In a strategic sense, no project is acceptable merely because it has a positive NPV now. It is possible to have a greater NPV if the project is delayed. This may happen due to the greater certainty of cash flows, reductions in discount rates, expanding markets due to increased awareness, etc., all of which go to increase the NPV. Similarly, no project can be permanently rejected merely because it has a negative NPV then. It may turn positive later due to reasons such as greater demand, higher prices, lack of competition, reduced capital cost, etc.

Option to Expand

The option to expand emanates from a firm's exploration of new markets and new products. Capacity expansion to meet increased demand also provides options regarding the size of the project. The size of the project has a direct effect on the value of the investment in fixed assets and working capital. This is also referred to as the growth option. A firm also has the option of starting a pilot project; depending upon the outcome of the pilot project, it may decide to go in for a full-fledged investment later. Normally the data available for starting of a pilot project are rather uncertain and inadequate. The pilot project may be having a negative NPV, and, therefore, may be rejected. Yet, firms do start a pilot project to gain experience. It also provides a competitive edge to the firm and the possibility of expansion at a later stage. Pilot projects provide an option to grow, and, hence, have value that must be considered before a decision is made.

Option to Abandon

The option to abandon is the option to discontinue operations before the useful life of the project is over. Normally, cash flows are projected for the entire useful life of the project and rarely do we account for the possibility of making an early exit. Having undertaken a project that shows a promising future, the expected cash flows of the project may not fructify. Under such situations, the firm always has the option of abandoning the project and realizing its salvage value available, as doing so may be more beneficial than continuing the business and wasting good money over a bad decision.

> The options available add value to projects that is not captured in standard capital budgeting exercises.

These embedded options in strategic capital investment add value to the project. This value must be considered while evaluating capital budgeting. The value of these options sometimes makes a negative NPV of the project worthy of a favourable consideration. The strategic value of these options is significant and should not be ignored, as they create future opportunities for the firm that can be exploited at the right time. Firms that recognize such values tend to outperform their competition.

The identification and valuation of options is a tricky proposition, since business scenarios are complex. Several options may be built into a single business situation, and several real options may run concurrently. For example, assume that an infrastructure development firm is considering construction of a road, connecting two towns, which reduces the distance and time of travel. However, the level of traffic between the towns is low, and toll charges are subject to a ceiling prescribed by the government. These factors give the project a negative NPV. However, this project may have multiple options embedded in it simultaneously. The project may offer the options of expanding in scope (from a single lane to double lane), abandoning it (handing it over to the government at a predetermined price after a few years), or delaying (deferring it till more traffic is generated or the toll ceiling gets revised upwards). All of these flexibilities will add value to the project. More importantly, they can turn a project with negative NPV into one with a positive NPV.

> Real options are strategic in nature, and are difficult to value in a well-defined mathematical model or framework.

DIFFERENCES BETWEEN FINANCIAL AND REAL OPTIONS[1]

The principles used in valuing financial options can be extended to value real options. Before we attempt valuation of real options on the basis of tools used for valuing financial options,

---

[1] For a more elaborate discussion refer to *Corporate Finance – Theory & Practice* by Aswath Damodaran, John Wiley & Sons Inc.

let us consider the distinguishing features that will help to explain the distortions that may show up in the results.

Real Assets are Not Traded

> Real options can be valued on the basis of models applicable for options on financial assets. However, real options are significantly different from financial options, and hence, limit the applicability of valuation models.

The principles used in option pricing theories assume a set-up of equivalent portfolios and risk neutrality. A call option can be replicated by borrowing at the risk-free rate and owning the underlying asset. This replication has the same payoff as that of a call option, and, hence, the two must trade at the same price to prevent arbitrage. This implies that both the call option and the replicated portfolio are widely traded assets. Such an assumption in the case of real assets is far from reality as the underlying assets, which are the cash flows of the project itself, do not have many buyers and sellers, and, as such, are not easily tradable. Valuing real options as if they are financial options demands great care in reaching conclusions.

Variance of Real Options is Difficult to Estimate

Another difficulty with real options is the estimate of volatility of their cash flows. It is extremely difficult to obtain the variance of projects though techniques such as simulation and scenario analysis exist. In the case of financial assets, it is far easier to obtain the estimate of variance because historical price data are available. Option pricing for financial assets assumes that the variance remains constant over the life of the option. Since financial assets are short term, the assumption seems valid. For real options, this assumption cannot hold, as most real options are long term in nature. Even if the variance of the project may be obtainable, it cannot be regarded as constant over the life of the option.

Exercise of Real Options is Time Consuming

The exercise of real options is a time-consuming process, unlike the exercise of financial options, which takes place rather instantaneously. The exercise of a call option on a stock can be done the moment the stock price exceeds the exercise price, and, otherwise, whenever the investor desires. In contrast, the exercise of real options, such as setting up additional capacity, will require substantial time. This gestation period means a substantial delay from the time the decision to exercise is made to the time the exercise is implemented. The benefits of the exercise of the option accrue much later, once the decision to exercise is made and implemented. Effectively, it means that the option period is less than what it may appear to be.

Terms of Exercise of Real Options are Not Clearly Defined

Further, the terms of exercise of financial options are well defined. In the case of real options, the right to exercise is ambiguous. Further, the actual exercise of a real option is doubtful and usually gets deferred because of human behaviour patterns. The exercise of financial options requires only economic and financial considerations, while the exercise of real options involves subjectivity and managerial prudence. The data required to value real options and the considerations to exercise them are not as well defined as in the case of options on financial assets.

Real Options

Though valuing real options is complex, we attempt to value some simple looking real options to provide insights to the valuation process in this chapter.

OPTION TO DELAY—TIMING DECISION

> An option to delay is the flexibility of timing of implementing a project.

Some high-technology firms engaged in developmental work often face an uncertain situation regarding timing of the investment. When the product is in the preliminary stage, doubts over its commercial viability or its success are rather high. Under such situations, the firm may prefer to wait, since uncertainty reduces as time elapses. Making an investment earlier than warranted exposes the firm to a greater risk, which can be reduced significantly if the firm waits a while to achieve clarity in future scenarios.

The apprehensions of the firm about whether to invest now or later may emanate from any of a number of reasons. Normally, the demand situation is fluid for new products, or the products are not fully developed and require some refinements. An unrefined product may not receive an enthusiastic response from customers. The firm may have to make an extra effort to launch a more refined product later. At the same time, if the product is not launched now, the firm may be apprehensive about losing business to its competitors, who may take greater initiatives and show more entrepreneurship. The firm may not want to lose the advantages normally associated with an early bird presence in the market. Under such circumstances, the option to delay the investment is ruled out, since competitors would introduce the product anyway.

However, in some circumstances where the firm has exclusivity by way of a right or a patent, the option to delay the implementation or timing of the investment is somewhat a matter of choice that is less subject to pressure.

Evaluating Timing Decision with DCF

> Merely because the NPV of a project is positive, it is not necessary that it must be implemented now. By deferring the project, one may get a higher NPV.

One way to value an option to wait is the standard DCF analysis. In the nascent stage, there is a lot of uncertainty about cash flows. In terms of financial management, this uncertainty and ambiguity is reflected in the negative NPV at present, calling for its rejection. Strategically, though, the managers are not inclined to do so. The dilemma arises due to the negative NPV of the project. The DCF technique uses the decision criteria now or never. If the NPV is negative, we do not consider the project. However, the future potential may be large enough to more than offset the present negative NPV of the project.

Under such situations, another alternative emerges, i.e., to wait until the uncertainty about the project reduces to an acceptable level. In terms of the DCF valuation, we expect the NPV of the project to improve and turn positive either due to improved cash flows or due to reduction in the discount rates.

The rule: The standard technique in capital budgeting to evaluate the timing issue is to find out the NPVs of different timing options and choose the one that has the maximum NPV.

Let us consider a simple example to illustrate the decision-making process.

Assume that a software firm SOFTBANK has developed a new banking product and is uncertain about its demand potential. SOFTBANK expects the life of the product to be four years, and its launch will cost ₹100 lakh today. SOFTBANK knows that there is no competitor presently for the product developed. If the firm faces a good demand for its product, the annual cash inflows are expected to be ₹50 lakh. However, if the demand is not good, the annual cash flows will reduce to ₹30 lakh. The managers at SOFTBANK estimate equal likelihoods of the 'good' and 'not so good' demand scenarios. The expected annual cash flow would be ₹40 lakh (0.50 × 50 + 0.50 × 30). With a 12% discount rate considered appropriate for the cash flow risk, the expected NPV of the project if launched now is ₹21.49 lakh.

$$NPV = \frac{40}{1.12} + \frac{40}{1.12^2} + \frac{40}{1.12^3} + \frac{40}{1.12^4} - 10 = ₹21.49 \text{ lakh}$$

With a positive NPV, the project must be implemented now. However, some managers of SOFTBANK feel that it is worthwhile to wait for another year before launching the product, as the preferences of the customers will be better known next year. The cost of launching the product a year later will be no different from what it is now. The decision to implement a year later will depend upon the demand scenario prevailing then. If the demand remains good, SOFTBANK must go ahead with the launch. Otherwise, it must drop it altogether (this would be the option to abandon).

This situation can be considered as a choice between two mutually exclusive options, with the decision to be based on the rule of the higher NPV.

> The option to delay a project (a) helps in reducing the uncertainties of cash flows, and (b) provides for learning. Therefore, it adds value to the project.

Option I: Launch now
Option II: Launch a year later

Options I and II are mutually exclusive, as selection of one precludes the other. As a first step, we compute the NPV of the project for immediate launch. If we considered the NPV of option I, which is positive, we would have gone ahead with immediate implementation, forgoing option II. We cannot let option II lapse unless an immediate launch proves a better choice. To know which of them is better, we need to compare the NPVs of both the options. The expected NPVs of options I and II are computed in Table 22.1.

Note that the present values that need to be compared must coincide in time. The investment of ₹100 lakh in Option II in Year 1 is equivalent to ₹89.29 lakh as on this day (Year 0). The expected NPV of option I is ₹21.49 lakh, and that of option II is ₹23.16 lakh. Since the expected NPV of option II is greater, the product must be launched a year later. The value of the option to wait for one year, therefore, is the difference between the two NPVs, i.e., ₹1.67 lakh. We have assumed the following here:

> A higher NPV of the project when delayed indicates that the option to wait is valuable.

- The firm implements the project if the demand scenario is 'good' in Year 1.
- The firm abandons the project if the demand scenario is 'not so good' in Year 1.
- The initial outlay and the cash flows for the next four years remain the same.
- The discount rate too remains the same at 12%.

While the first two assumptions seem valid, the latter two may be challenged. The annual cash flows for the life of the project may turn out to be more or less than ₹50 lakh. If the

Table 22.1 Option to delay for SOFTBANK ₹ lakh

	Option I: Launch now							
							Discount rate 12%	
	Year					NPV	Probability p	p × NPV
Good	0	1	2	3	4			
Cash flow	(100.00)	50.00	50.00	50.00	50.00			
PV	(100.00)	44.64	39.86	35.59	31.78	51.87	0.50	25.93
Not good								
Cash flow	(100.00)	30.00	30.00	30.00	30.00			
PV	(100.00)	26.79	23.92	21.35	19.07	(8.88)	0.50	(4.44)
						Expected NPV		21.49
	Option II: Launch a year later							
							Discount rate 12%	
	Year					NPV	Probability p	p × NPV
Good	1	2	3	4	5			
Cash flow	(100.00)	50.00	50.00	50.00	50.00			
PV at year 0	(89.29)	39.86	35.59	31.78	28.37	46.31	0.50	23.16
Not good								
Cash flow	–	–	–	–	–			
PV	–	–	–	–	–	–	0.50	–
						Expected NPV		23.16

competition catches on, the likely cash flows may reduce; if the demand proves better than expected, they may increase.

Likewise, if other options of different timings for the investment are available, they may be analysed utilizing the DCF technique and comparing the expected NPVs to choose the option with the largest NPV. Based on the calculation of the NPVs for SOFTBANK for both the options, it is worthwhile to wait for the launch, as the NPV for the delay option is higher.

Valuing Option to Delay with Binomial Model

Since there are only two possibilities, the situation of the timing option for SOFTBANK is tailor made to apply the binomial model of option pricing. The situation for SOFTBANK is displayed in Fig. 22.1. The present value in case the demand is high is ₹170.09 lakh, being the present value of the annual cash flows of ₹50 lakh at $t = 1$ year discounted at 12%. Similarly the present value of the cash inflows in case the demand is not so good is ₹102.05 lakh, with annual cash flows of ₹30 lakh.

The firm has the option to delay the launch by one year, implying that it implements the project with an exercise price of ₹100 lakh. In case the demand is good, the firm implements

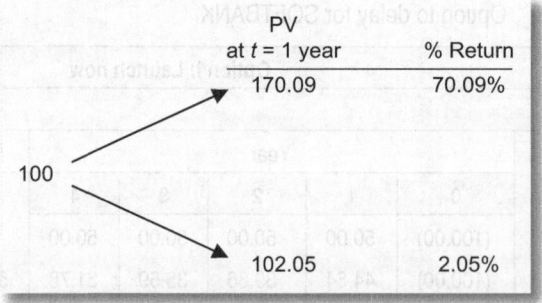

Fig. 22.1 Option to wait: Binary option pricing

> The binomial method for valuation of financial options can be applied to value real options, too.

the project and the payoff is ₹70.09 lakh after a year. In case the demand is not so good the payoff on the call option is at ₹2.09 lakh.

We adopt the risk-neutral method to value the call option. Assuming that the risk-neutral probability of high demand is p, the expected payoff of the two branches must yield a return equal to the risk-free rate of 9%. Then

$$p \times 7009\% + (1 - p) \times (-2.09\%) = 9\%$$
$$p = 10.21\%$$

With a probability of 10.21%, the value of the call at the end of option periods computed at ₹15.26 lakh.

Value of the call today = $(0.1021 \times 70.09 + 0.8979 \times 205)/1.09$ = ₹8.30 lakh

Option pricing through the binomial model suggests that the option to wait is worth ₹8.30 lakh, as against the NPV of the project at ₹21.49 lakh if implemented today. Therefore, SOFTBANK must implement the project now. It is not worth waiting for another year.

Discounted Cash Flow and Binomial Option Valuation

> Due to the presence of options, the risk profiles of cash flows change in each scenario, and therefore, the standard DCF analysis is not suitable. No single rate of discount can capture the risks of cash flows.

Here, we face a contradiction in the outcomes derived from DCF valuation and the binomial model. Which of them is correct? It is hard to belie the DCF approach, because it has been used so successfully in financial decision making. However, we must point out the deficiencies of the DCF analysis when the situation involves options. In the DCF approach, we made two vital assumptions—the first was regarding the probability of the demand being good at 50%, and the second was regarding the discount rate of 12%. The probability assigned to the demand being good was subjective, and each individual would assign a different value depending upon his/her perception. The NPV, therefore, would be different for different persons. In contrast, option valuation by the binomial method is independent of individuals' expectations and perceptions. It is defined for the risk-neutral world.

Second, we assumed a discount rate of 12% for all situations. While valuing an option, there are contingent situations, which change the risk of the cash flows. Here, the option to wait includes a decision not to implement the project if in the first year the demand faced is not so good. The risk faced in such a situation would be zero. There cannot be a single discount rate that captures all the situations and corresponding risks. We have to necessarily use different rates for discounting the cash flows for different situations. The validity of using a single discount rate is questionable. The valuation of the option, however, is independent of individual preferences for probabilities and the discount rates.

Under the risk-neutral assumption in binomial option pricing, we need neither the probabilities of different demand scenarios nor the discount rates. With the binary model taking contingent situations into account, the use of the DCF method is inappropriate.

Option valuation is dependent upon the current price of the underlying asset. The current price is assumed to contain the probability estimates. The risk-neutral method implies the probability of facing an upside demand of ₹50 lakh per annum of 10.21% as against the assumed figures of 50% in the DCF method. The other determinant of the option price is the risk. The risk is supposed to be contained in the estimates of volatility. This also means that the implied volatility in the binary model[2] is 53.11%, as against 28.00% in the DCF method, calculated later in this chapter.

Using Black-Scholes Model for Investment Timing

The binomial model takes care of two possible future values of the underlying asset. We can also use the Black-Scholes option-pricing model (BSM) to value the option to wait, which provides further insight to the analysis, as it allows all possible values and continuous compounding. The BSM developed for pricing financial options can be used to value real options too, though with certain limitations, as stated in the earlier part of this chapter.

Of the five inputs of BSM, the three inputs X, T, and r are available readily. The exercise price, X, is ₹100 lakh. The time to expiry of this option is one year. The risk-free rate can be obtained from the yield on the government securities. Let us assume this at 9%.

The underlying asset on the option is the cash flow of the delayed project. The expected present value of the cash inflows of only the project (not the expected NPV, which is the intrinsic value of the option) will be equivalent to the spot price, S. The spot price of the underlying asset values can be arrived at as follows:

Present value of inflows—the spot price							₹ lakh
						Discount rate 12%	
	Year				PV	Probability p	p × PV
	1	2	3	4	5			
Cash flow	–	50.00	50.00	50.00	50.00			
PV	–	39.86	35.59	31.78	28.37	135.60	0.50	67.80
Cash flow	–	30.00	30.00	30.00	30.00			
PV	–	23.92	21.35	19.07	17.02	81.36	0.50	40.68
					Present value at t = 0		108.48

The last input required is the variance of the returns. We need to compute the variance of the expected returns on the option to delay at the time the option expires, i.e., after one year. The value of the underlying asset at expiration is as follows:

---

[2] The volatility implied in the binary option pricing is given by $(1 + u) = e^{\sigma/\sqrt{t}}$

Present value of inflows at expiry of the option

Discount rate 12%

	Year				PV	Probability (p)	p × PV
	1	2	3	4			
Cash flow	50.00	50.00	50.00	50.00			
PV	44.64	39.86	35.59	31.78	151.87	0.50	75.93
Cash flow	30.00	30.00	30.00	30.00			
PV	26.79	23.92	21.35	19.07	91.12	0.50	45.56
			Present value at t = 1				121.49

> One standard model of valuing options is the Black Scholes option pricing formula, developed for valuing options on financial assets.

Note that the expected value of the asset at the time of expiration is 12% higher than the values at the beginning of the option period, as the cash flows are discounted at a weighted average cost of capital (WACC) of 12%.

Calculating variance of option

	Expected Price at t = 1	Spot price	% Return	Probability	p × Return	p × dev2
Good	151.87	108.48	40%	0.50	0.20	0.0392
Not good	91.12	108.48	–16%	0.50	(0.08)	0.0392
			Expected return		12%	
			Variance			0.0784
			Standard deviation			28.00%

The variance of the call option is 0.0784, equivalent to a standard deviation of 0.28 (28.00%). Now all the inputs for valuing the option are available for using the BSM, applicable for valuing financial options.

The BSM for valuing call options is reproduced as Eq. 22.1.

$$c = SN(d_1) - Xe^{-rT} N(d_2)$$

where $d_1 = \dfrac{\ln(S/X) + (r + \sigma^2/2)T}{\sigma\sqrt{T}}$; and (22.1)

$d_2 = \dfrac{\ln(S/X) + (r + \sigma^2/2)T}{\sigma\sqrt{T}}$; or $d_2 = d_1 - \sigma\sqrt{T}$

The values of the input are

Spot price, S	₹108.48 lakh
Exercise price, X	₹100.00 lakh
Time to expiry, T	1 year
Interest rate, r	9%
Standard deviation, σ	28%

Inserting these values in Eq. 22.1, we find the value of the call option to be ₹21.67 lakh.

It may be observed that the NPV of the option is just about the same if implemented today (₹21.49 lakh). The option pricing method recommends implementation now. The NPV of the delayed project is computed as ₹23.16 lakh using the DCF method. It recommends delaying implementation by a year. How do we reconcile the contradiction?

The answer possibly lies in the assumptions of option pricing not holding good. The standard deviation of the project is computed with a limited number of scenarios, and, hence, may not be reflecting the variability truly. Options derive their values from volatility. The larger the variance, the greater is the value of the option. The implied volatility of the cash flow appears to be higher than what is assumed in the option pricing model. However, our failure to accurately project the variance of the cash flows in real world situations should not be treated as a deterrent to use of the model. Instead, we must strive for a better estimate of volatility.

OPTION TO EXPAND

> The option to expand relates to the ability of firms to improve their cash flows subsequent to implementation by increasing the price, increasing the volumes, and improving the quality of products.

Many strategic situations demand investment in the initial stages despite a negative NPV because such an investment provides the firm with an opportunity to make a further investment that is profitable enough to compensate for the loss incurred in the first investment. Firms cannot let go such investment opportunities, simply because they lose a more profitable business opportunity that arises subsequently, as a consequence to the initial investment. We shall examine how to value such opportunities to expand the business that is basically embedded in the first investment.

Consider a firm called GrowMotors, developing an electric car that requires no fossil fuel and works on batteries and solar energy. The initial cost of a project for developing the pilot model is estimated at ₹200 crore. The product is new, and offers considerable advantages over normal petrol-driven cars. However, the selling price is relatively high, and the new car suffers from the drawback of low speed. Since the product is high priced and cannot achieve a speed of more than 50 kmph, its consumer acceptability is doubtful. Based on estimates for the next three years, the cash flows are projected evenly at ₹75 crore annually (assumed for simplicity). The project has a negative NPV of ₹13.49 crore, as can be seen in Table 22.2, and, therefore, is not worthy of consideration. The discount rate used is 10%, being the risk-adjusted WACC considered appropriate for the risky electric car venture.

Table 22.2 GrowMotors—launch of electric car—Phase I

(₹crore)	Discount rate 10%			
	Year			
	0	1	2	3
Cash flow	(200.00)	75.00	75.00	75.00
Present value	(200.00)	68.18	61.98	56.35
			NPV	(13.49)

However, this project has an option to grow embedded in it. GrowMotors is engaged in continuous and sustained developmental work. It expects to remove the deficiencies of the car over the next three years. Let this be called Phase II. It could commence in the third year. It would cost another ₹600 crore to launch the improved model in terms of the present value at Year 3. This is clearly a call option with an exercise price of ₹600 crore that is available only when Phase I is implemented, and arises only when the present investment of ₹200 crore is made. Depending upon the experiences gained in the initial launch period, the decision to introduce Phase II will be made. At present, however, management expects either of the following two scenarios:

- There is a 60% probability of facing a good demand with a cash flow of the present value of ₹1000 crore, providing an NPV of ₹400 crore in Year 3.
- There is a 40% probability of facing a poor demand with a cash flow of the present value of ₹300 crore, providing an NPV of –₹300 crore in Year 3.

This is depicted in Fig. 22.2.

Conventionally evaluated, the expected NPV at Year 3 of the commercial model is

$$0.60 \times 400 + 0.40 \times -300 = ₹120 \text{ crore}$$

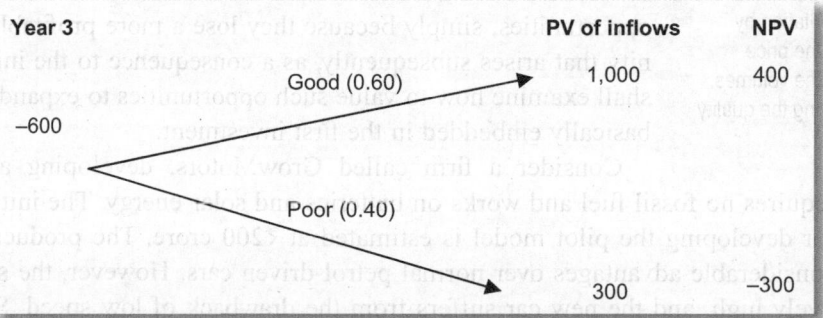

Fig. 22.2 Option to expand—Growmotors—Phase II

DCF Valuation

The commercial model in Phase II, as a stand-alone project, has a positive NPV as on today. Note that Phase II has considerable uncertainty. However, this is a contingent project, which cannot be pursued without the pilot project of Phase I. At the end of Year 3, the option to expand will be exercised, depending upon the demand scenario. If the demand is poor, the investment (exercise of the option) will not be made, and if the demand happens to be good, the investment will be made. In such a case, the NPV of the project for expansion would be

$$0.60 \times 400 + 0.40 \times 0 = ₹240 \text{ crore}$$

Therefore, the NPV of the electric car project with the option to launch Phase II will be a positive ₹126.32 crore, as shown in Table 22.3 and Fig. 22.3.

Notice that under the DCF approach, we have used a risk-free rate of 5% for discounting the initial investment of ₹600 crore because of its certainty. The rest of the figures that carry operational risk are discounted at a WACC of 10%. If we go by the standard capital budgeting

Table 22.3 GrowMotors—launch of electric car Phase I and Phase II

Discount rate 10%

Present value with high demand		Expand			
Cash flow	0	1	2	3	PV at T = 0
Phase I	(200.00)				(200.00)
Investment	(200.00)				
Inflows		75.00	75.00	75.00	186.51
Phase II					
Investment	–	–	–	–600	(518.30)*
Inflows				1,000	751.31
Net present value with high demand					219.53
Present value with low demand		Do not expand			
Phase I	–				–
Investment	(200.00)				(200.00)
Inflows		75.00	75.00	75.00	186.51
Phase II					
Investment	–	–	–	–	–
Inflows	–	–	–	–	–
Net present value with low demand					(13.49)

*Being certain discounted at 5%

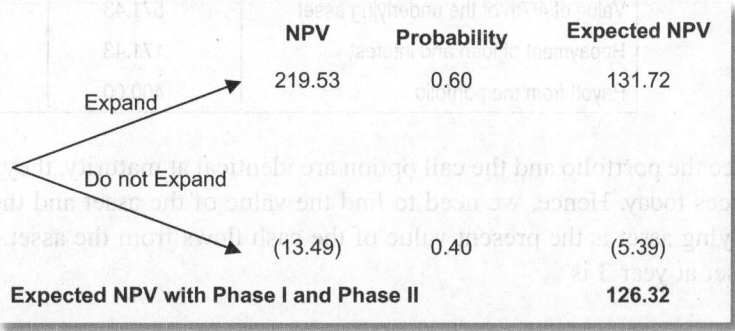

Fig. 22.3 NPV GrowMotors—with phase I and phase II (₹ crore)

process in evaluating the pilot Phase I as a standalone project, we would end up rejecting it. With the option to expand, though, the project becomes viable.

In the appraisal of Phase I, we did not consider the value of the option to expand. We need to value this option, which is a call option with an exercise price of ₹600 crore, with time to expiry of three years.

Valuing Option to Expand with Binomial Method

We shall consider the value of the option to expand using the binomial method, as there are only two possible demand scenario outcomes. The payoff on the call option at expiry is

Figures in ₹ crore

Demand scenario	Good	Poor
Value of the underlying asset	1,000	300
Exercise price	600	600
Payoff from the call option	400	0

This time, we value the call option with the equivalent portfolio approach. The equivalent portfolio can be constructed by owning some fraction of the asset and borrowing in such a way as to give the same payoff as that of the call option. The delta of the call option is given by

Delta = Spread of payoff of call/spread of value of underlying asset
= (400 − 0)/(1000 − 300) = 400/700 = 4/7

Therefore, we shall buy 4/7 of the underlying asset and borrow in a manner that makes the payoff equal to the payoff on the call option. The amount of borrowing that will equal the cash flow of the call option to expand on the expiration date would be ₹171.43, which is the difference between the value of the asset and the payoff on the call (4/7 × value of asset − payoff on the call option = 571.43 − 171.43 or 171.43 − 0). The value of the portfolio of 4/7 of the asset and the borrowing on the expiry of the option period of three years is identical to that of the call option, as depicted here:

Figures in ₹ crore

Demand scenario	Good	Poor
Value of the asset on expiry	1,000.00	300.00
Value of 4/7th of the underlying asset	571.43	171.43
Repayment of loan and interest	171.43	171.43
Payoff from the portfolio	400.00	0.00

Since the portfolio and the call option are identical at maturity, they must command identical prices today. Hence, we need to find the value of the asset and the loan today. Here, the underlying asset is the present value of the cash flows from the asset. The expected value of the asset at year 3 is

Figures in ₹ crore

Demand scenario	PV of cash flows	Probability	p × cash flow
Good	1,000	0.60	600
Poor	300	0.40	120
Expected value			720

The current value of the underlying asset can be computed by discounting the year 3 value at a WACC of 10%. The current value of the underlying asset is $720/1.10^3$ = ₹540.95 crore, and the value of the 4/7 portion is ₹309.11 crore. The borrowing will be done at a risk-free rate of 5%, and the present value of borrowing is $171.43/1.05^3$ = ₹148.09 crore. We arrive at the value of the call by setting it equal to the current value of the equivalent portfolio. Therefore, the value of the call is

= Value of 4/7 share − present value of borrowing
= 309.11 − 171.43/1.05³ = 309.11 − 148.09 = ₹161.02 crore

Value of Phase I of the electric car project

= NPV of Phase I + value of the embedded call option
= −13.49 + 161.02 = ₹147.53 crore.

Valuing Option to Expand using BSM

Amongst the five inputs required to find the value of the call, we already have four: the exercise price, X, at ₹600 crore; the risk-free rate, r, at 5%; the time to expiry, T, of three years; and the spot price of the underlying asset, S, at ₹540.95 crore (The expected value of ₹720 crore at $t = 3$ years discounted at 10%). The remaining input, the standard deviation of the underlying asset, σ, is calculated in Table 22.4.

Table 22.4 Calculation of standard deviation of returns

Value of the asset at $t = 3$	Return relative	Annual returns (%)	Prob	Expected value	Variance
540.95	1000	1.85	22.73	0.60	13.64	158.01
540.95	300	0.55	(17.84)	0.40	−7.14	237.02
Expected return (%)					6.50	
Variance						395.03
Standard deviation (%)						19.88

With all the inputs known, GrowMotors' option to expand can be valued using the BSM with the following values:

Exercise price, X	₹600.00 crore
Spot price, S	₹540.95 crore
Standard deviation, σ	19.88%
Annual interest, r_f	5.00%
Time for expiration, t	3.00 years

Inserting the input values in the BSM, we get the value of the call as

$$c = N(d_1) \times S - N(d_2) \times \text{PV of } X$$
$$c = 0.6205 \times 540.95 - 0.4851 \times 516.42 = ₹85.16 \text{ crore}$$

The value of the call option is ₹85.16 crore.

Note that the delta of the option under the binomial method and the BSM is 0.5714 and 0.6205, respectively, which is one source of variation in the value of the call. The other source of variation between the values of the call derived by the binomial method and the BSM is rooted in the volatility calculated by the two models.

OPTION TO ABANDON

> An option to abandon relates to a situation where a firm can take a decision to exit some activity to reduce or avoid cash losses.

All projects are subject to constant review by the managers of the firm, taking into consideration the latest happenings and the future potential. One of the possible scenarios relates to discontinuation of the project under circumstances where the managers face adverse conditions that no longer generate the expected cash flows. In such conditions, the managers may estimate that the project will be better off if its assets are disposed off, rather than put to continued use. Such a right to abandon or make an exit is valuable, as it may release financial resources for exploring new, more profitable business avenues, or may simply help contain the future losses that may arise as a result of continuation of the project. Such an option is analogous to a put option where the holder has the option to sell at a predetermined price within a predetermined time period.

Consider the example of Ganga Toll Bridge Company (GANGA), which is contemplating participating in a tender to build a bridge across a river. The tender stipulates the maximum toll fee that can be charged. The terms and conditions of the tender also specify that the bridge must be made toll free after 25 years. The cost of building the bridge is ₹10 crore.

Based on the present level and future estimates of traffic, GANGA has estimated that it would be able to generate a cash flow of ₹1 crore evenly for the next 25 years. The present value of the cash inflows of ₹1 crore for next 25 years at a WACC of 12% works out to ₹7.843 crore, and the NPV is a negative ₹2.157 crore.

NPV = PV of annuity of ₹1.00 crore for 25 years at 12% − ₹10 crore
    = 7.843 − 10.000 = −₹2.157 crore

Since the project has a negative NPV, GANGA is not keen on pursuing it.

GANGA rejects the proposal, but the tender authorities then offer the following additional information:

- The local government is also planning to develop an amusement park and a township on the other side of the river, which are likely to enhance the traffic on the bridge. The estimated time to complete the development is five years.
- In view of its developmental objective, the local government has also offered to buy back the bridge at the end of five years at ₹6 crore from GANGA, if it finds the bridge non-remunerative at that time.

DCF Valuation

Under the revised scenario, GANGA faces the following situation:

- It implements the project now and expects cash flows of ₹1 crore for the next five years, when it would be time to take another decision.
- At the end of five years, GANGA faces two possible traffic scenarios:
  - If traffic volume is high, it gives an annual cash flow of ₹2.50 crore for 20 years, which if valued at 12% has a present value of ₹18.674 crore. GANGA continues the project. The chances of such a situation coming to be are estimated at 60%.

- If traffic volume is low (for which the chances would be 40%), it gives an annual cash flow of ₹0.50 crore for 20 years, which if valued at 12%, has a present value of ₹3.735 crore. GANGA abandons the project and realizes ₹6.00 crore from the government, because the asset is worth less than the put option.

The new scenario is presented in Fig. 22.4.

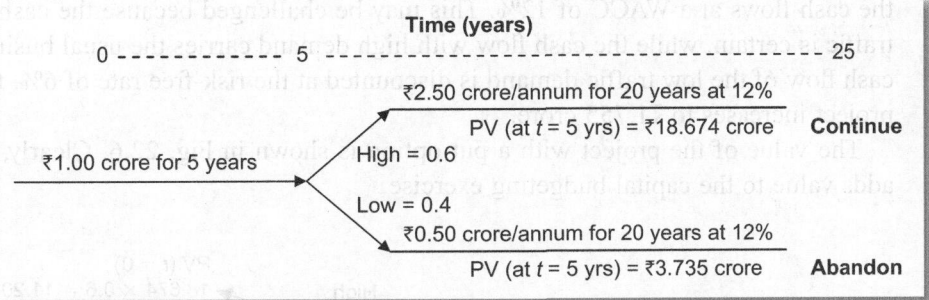

Fig. 22.4 Option to abandon: Ganga toll bridge

DCF Valuation without the Put Option

Without the additional new information, the NPV of the project was negative at ₹2.16 crore. With the changed scenario of traffic from year 6 onwards, we revalue the project assuming (a) annual cash flows of ₹1 crore for the first five years, and (b) the expected value of two possible traffic scenarios—high traffic and low traffic—with probabilities of 0.6 and 0.4, respectively, for the next 20 years. All the cash flows are discounted at 12%, considered appropriate for the risk associated with the project. The expected value of the cash flows at $t = 5$ years is ₹12.698 crore.

This is further discounted at 12% for five years to give a present value of ₹7.205 crore. We add the present value of the cash flows of ₹1 crore for five years to provide an NPV of ₹0.81 crore. This makes the project marginally acceptable, even without the exercise of the put option. This is depicted in Fig. 22.5.

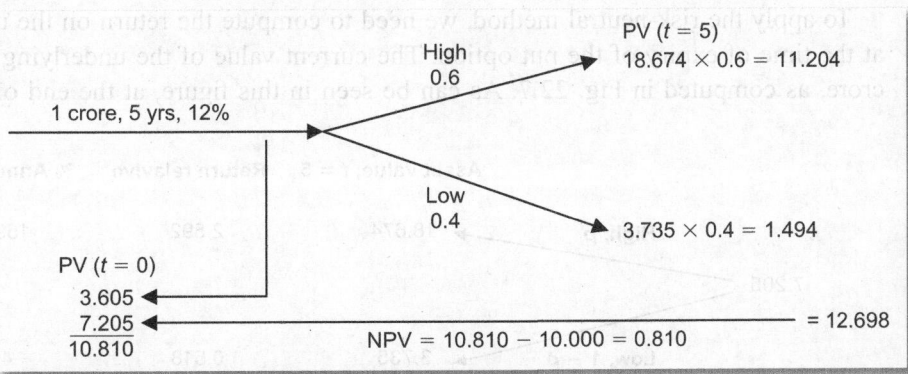

Fig. 22.5 Expected value and NPV without put option (₹ crore)

DCF Valuation with Option to Abandon

The offer of the local government is a put option for GANGA, with an exercise price of ₹6 crore and time to expiry of five years. At the end of five years, GANGA can exercise the option depending upon the situation at that time. This changes the cash flow for the low traffic scenario from ₹3.735 crore to ₹6 crore because GANGA exercises the option to abandon the project. This would enhance the value of the project. Here again, we have discounted all the cash flows at a WACC of 12%. This may be challenged because the cash flow with low traffic is certain, while the cash flow with high demand carries the usual business risk. If the cash flow of the low traffic demand is discounted at the risk-free rate of 6%, the NPV of the project increases to ₹1.755 crore.

The value of the project with a put option is shown in Fig. 22.6. Clearly, the put option adds value to the capital budgeting exercise.

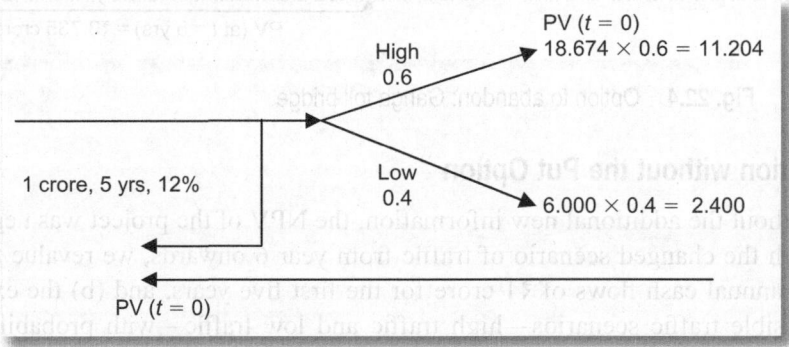

Fig. 22.6 Expected value and NPV with put option   (₹crore)

Valuing Put Option with Binomial Method

Since GANGA faces only two possible traffic situations, we may use the binomial method to value the put option. The underlying asset is the present value of the cash flows of the bridge that are likely from the sixth year onwards. Note that the cash flows of the first five years do not form part of the underlying asset.

To apply the risk-neutral method, we need to compute the return on the underlying asset at the time of expiry of the put option. The current value of the underlying asset is ₹7.205 crore, as computed in Fig. 22.7. As can be seen in this figure, at the end of five years, the

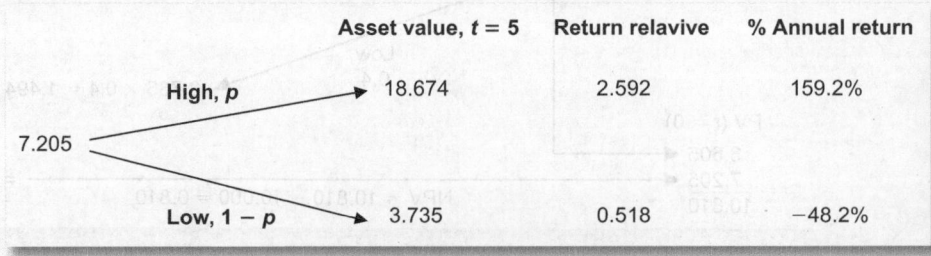

Fig. 22.7 Risk-neutral valuation of put option—Ganga toll bridge   (₹crore)

asset has a value of ₹18.674 crore with high traffic, providing a return of 159.2%, and ₹3.735 crore with low traffic, providing a return of −48.2% over five years.

Assuming risk neutrality with probability of the high traffic as p, we must have

$$\{(1.06)^5 - 1\} = p \times 159.2\% + (1 - p) \times (-48.2\%)$$

Solving this equation for p, we get the implied probability as 39.55%.

$$p = \frac{33.82 + 48.20}{159.20 + 48.20} = \frac{82.02}{204.40} = 39.55\%.$$

The value of the put at maturity of the option p would be the expected value of the payoff on the put option with the implied probabilities of high and low traffic. Therefore,

Value of the put at expiry

$= p \times$ payoff with high traffic $+ (1 - p) \times$ payoff with low traffic
$= 0.3955 \times 0 + 0.6045 \times 2.265 = ₹1.369$ crore

The current price of the put would be the present value of the put at expiry discounted at the risk-free rate of 6%. Therefore, the value of the put option is ₹1.023 crore.

The value of the put today $= 1.369/1.06^5 = ₹1.023$ crore

Value of Put with BSM

Amongst the five inputs required to find the value of the put, we already have four: the exercise price, X, at ₹6.00 crore; the risk-free rate, r, at 6%; the time to expiry, T, of five years; and the spot price of the underlying asset, S, at ₹7.205 crore. The remaining input, the standard deviation of the underlying asset, σ, can be found from the variability of the returns on the underlying asset. The return when the traffic scenario is high is 159.5%, which is equal to an annualized return of 20.98%. Similarly, the annualized return when the traffic scenario is low is −12.33%. The scenario relating to the expected returns on an annualized basis is depicted in Fig. 22.8.

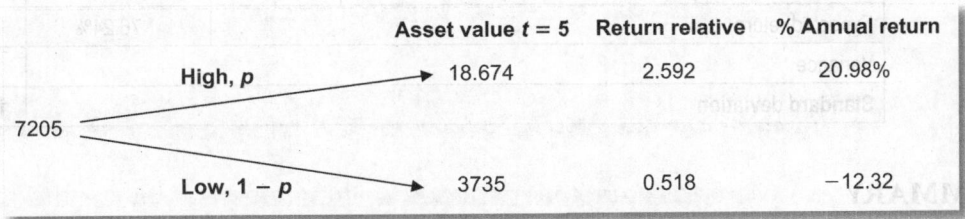

Fig. 22.8 Percentage return for BSM valuation of put option—GANGA toll bridge (₹crore)

The calculation of standard deviation of the annualized returns on the underlying asset is shown in Table 22.5. It is 16.31%.

Now we may compute the value of the put option using the BSM.
With these inputs we find

$d_1 = -1.5067$ and $N(-d_1) = 0.0659$
$d_2 = -01.1420$ and $N(-d_2) = 0.1267$

Table 22.5 Standard deviation of returns on underlying asset

	Annual cash flow (₹crore)	Annual return (%)	Probability	Expected return (%)	Variance
High traffic	2.50	20.98	0.60	12.59	0.010645
Low traffic	0.50	−12.32	0.40	−4.93	0.015968
Expected return				7.66%	
Variance					0.026613
Standard deviation					16.31%

Inserting the input values in the BSM, we get the value of the put as ₹0.089 crore.

The option to sell back the bridge to the government is valuable, as can be seen from visualizing what happens after the fifth year. The put option works as insurance for GANGA in the event that the demand keeps low due to non-development of the amusement park and the new township. GANGA can also use this valuation to renegotiate the buyback price to upwards of ₹6 crore to accept the project.

The difference in the valuation of the put with the binomial model and the BSM is due to the difference in the volatility used. In the BSM, the annual volatility is taken as 16.31%. For a five-year period, this volatility is equivalent to $\sigma \sqrt{t} = 16.31\sqrt{5} = 36.49\%$. As against this, the volatility in the binomial method for the five-year period is 101.60%, as shown in Table 22.6. This is equivalent to an annual standard deviation of $\sigma/\sqrt{t} = 101.66/\sqrt{5} = 45.43\%$. Using the value of σ as 45.43%, we get a put value of ₹1.108 crore.

Table 22.6 Standard deviation of returns on underlying asset under binomial method

	Annual cash flow (₹ crore)	Annual return (%)	Probability	Expected return (%)	Variance
High traffic	2.50	159.20	0.60	95.92	0.412942
Low traffic	0.50	−48.20	0.40	−19.28	0.619412
Expected return				76.24%	
Variance					1.032354
Standard deviation					101.60%

SUMMARY

Capital budgeting decisions are strategic in nature, where management has the flexibility to make decisions subsequent to implementation of a project. These decisions have an implication on the cash flows of the project. These cash flows, once projected, are assumed constant over the life of the project. Decisions can be made on the basis of these static cash flows. The standard capital budgeting exercise ignores the strategic value of these decisions.

The flexibility of management and its ability to change the cash flows of a project subsequently is referred to as an option on real assets. We are familiar with options on financial assets. Options on real assets are normally of three types—the option to delay, the option to expand, and the option to abandon.

The option to delay refers to decisions regarding timing of the implementation of a project. An option to expand is the flexibility to increase production, increase prices, or add product lines to enhance the cash flows of the project later, depending upon the experiences gained in the initial phases. It is like a call option that has an exercise price equal to the cost of the additional investment required at a later date. The option to abandon refers to the flexibility of management to exit a project after having implemented it and realize the salvage value. It is the equivalent of a put option that is exercised when the cash flows of the project fail to meet expectations, with the exercise price equal to the salvage value.

A standard capital budgeting analysis on the basis of DCFs treats the situation as now or never. If the NPV of the project is positive, we implement the project; otherwise, we drop it. The real options approach suggests that there exists the possibility of increasing value by deferring implementation. It is like a call option, because there is no compulsion to implementing the project earlier or later. The option to delay can be valued in many ways. The DCF approach compares the NPVs of different options by changing the timing of implementation. Since an option to implement now and an option to implement later are two mutually exclusive projects, we choose the implementation timing that provides the largest NPV.

Many real options situations are apt for valuation using the binomial method. The advantages of the binomial method over the decision tree using DCFs are the elimination of the requirements for knowing (a) the probabilities of the various scenarios and (b) the discount rate. The current price of the asset and its volatility are assumed to contain the expected value. The estimates of probabilities for the likely future price are extremely subjective. The process of valuation of an option by the binomial method is independent of an individual's risk preferences. While this remains true for financial assets, which are traded, it may not be applied to real assets, because they are not traded. This makes the price of options independent of individual choice. It is a risk-neutral valuation.

The valuation of real options on the basis of the model developed for options on financial assets suffers from the limitations imposed by (a) the non-tradability of real options, (b) the fact that option exercise is not instantaneous, (c) the problem of estimating the volatility of the cash flows, and (d) the inability to clearly define the option.

KEY TERMS

Option to abandon It is a decision to exit a project and realize the salvage value in case the cash flows happen to be lesser than expected. It is equivalent to a put option.

Option to delay An option to delay allows the decision on when to implement a project to rest with management. It is also referred to as an option to wait for a timing decision.

Option to expand An option to expand refers to the flexibility to start a project at a lower scale and then expand it as time progresses and uncertainties get resolved.

Real option Options on real assets as distinct from financial assets.

QUESTIONS

22.1 What are real options and how do they add value to capital budgeting proposals?

22.2 What are the different kinds of real options? Define all of them.

22.3 What are the differences between real options and financial options?

22.4 Why do you think that DCF analysis is not an appropriate tool for evaluating capital budgeting proposals involving real options?

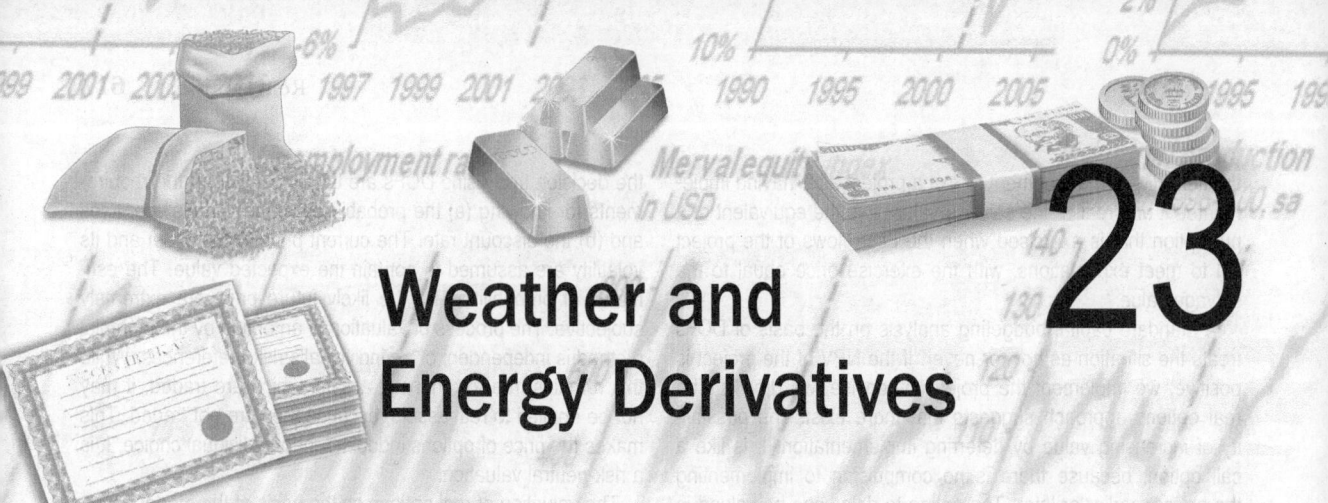

23
Weather and Energy Derivatives

INTRODUCTION

In this chapter, we will discuss some of the unusual underlying assets on which derivatives have been developed. The most recent innovation in the derivative market is that of derivatives on weather and energy. They are briefly described in this chapter, along with some insights on hedging with such derivatives.

Learning Objectives

After going through this chapter, readers should be familiar with
- weather derivatives
- carbon credits and its trading
- energy derivatives
- how weather derivatives are different from others

WEATHER DERIVATIVES

All of us are familiar with the vagaries of weather. Though the weather is not as unpredictable as stock prices, the havoc it can cause is far more damaging than a stock market meltdown. Like derivatives can effectively manage the risk of stock prices, there can be derivatives whose payoff would depend upon weather conditions. While extreme conditions of weather, such as floods and droughts, may be the subject matter of insurance, as they deal with large losses with small probabilities, derivatives can effectively deal with the risk of small losses with large probabilities.

In India, timely rain is one important factor that not only affects the day-to-day life of the masses but also causes a lot of concern to industries, primarily those that are dependent upon agricultural products. Industries such as sugar, fertilizers, breweries, and food processing have a direct relationship with weather conditions. Adverse weather also affects the tourism industry. Besides, general economic conditions and purchasing power are crucially dependent upon timely rain, which governs rural demand patterns. It is believed that industries such as consumer durables, automobiles, and consumer products are also affected. Further, winter fog in the

> Weather derivatives are aimed at providing a hedge against business losses due to weather conditions.

northern parts of India affects the aviation industry. Likewise, cold waves during winter or heat waves during summer cause dips in tourism and adversely affect the hospitality industry. In some way or the other, life is dependent on the weather. Some things are extremely susceptible to weather, while some others are less so.

While large changes in the weather are predictable, small changes are not. For example, in India, we do not expect freezing temperatures in the summers or sweaty heat during the winters. However, small changes in temperatures are always unpredictable, and more often than not, any attempted predictions become a laughing stock. When we talk of weather derivatives, it is the damage of risk or potential loss due to small changes that we are trying to cover. With the increased usage of technology and the availability of past data, weather has become measurable and quantifiable in respect of heat or cold, rainfall, humidity, etc.

Derivatives were invented and designed for assets that we can own. Therefore, we feel the need to cover any risk that may arise in relation to those assets. Weather, though it cannot be owned, is a source of risk to many businesses, predominantly agriculture. Through derivatives, we can manage the risk of several industries whose performance is weather dependent, especially when it is measurable.

Temperature

In Western countries, including the USA, weather extremities are related to temperature conditions rather than rain. Though weather-related contracts would remain specific to the parties concerned, the scope exists for exchange-traded products to have greater liquidity. Started as an over-the-counter (OTC) product, temperature was conceived as a tradable commodity by Chicago Mercantile Exchange (CME) in September 1999, when it introduced weather derivatives based on temperature, trade in weather futures, and options on weather futures.

The contracts of CME are based on heating degree day (HDD) or cooling degree day (CDD), which effectively states that heating or cooling energy requirements are directly related to the deviations from a base temperature taken at 65°F (18.33 °C). For European cities, the reference is 18°C.

The HDD is defined as Max $(0, 65 - A)$ and the CDD as Max $(0, A - 65)$, where A is the average temperature for the day for a specific location.

If the average temperature of a location is, say, 85°F (mean of the highest of 95°F and the lowest of 75°F) then the values of HDD and CDD would be 0 and 20, respectively. This implies that the day has been hotter than normal, and, hence, energy requirement is for cooling. Similarly, if the average temperature is 55°F, the day would be cooler than normal, and energy is consumed for heating homes. The measurement of average temperature at a given location has to be transparent, prompt, and free from ambiguities. The CME offers temperature-related futures and options for about 42 locations[1] in the USA and other parts of the world such as Europe, Japan, Canada, and Australia.

> In the USA, derivatives based on the temperatures at various locations are in place to serve the hedging needs of energy-producing firms.

The payoff on a contract can be decided by taking the cumulative HDD or CDD for a specific period, and attaching a monetary value to each degree. Most derivatives are based on accumulated HDD or CDD over a month or a season. A greater value for CDD means hotter days and greater requirements

---

[1] www.cmegroup.com, accessed on 14 May 2009.

for cooling. Similarly, higher HDD values mean lower temperatures, and, hence, a greater need for heating. This becomes directly relevant to energy-producing firms.

Derivative Products on Temperature

Most contracts on weather are call or put options on the cumulative HDD or CDD. Assume that HDDs have aggregated to 750 for a month. Now for a call option on CDD with a strike of 700 and each degree worth US $1000, the payoff would be 1000 × Max (0, Cum HDD − 700) = 50 × 1000 = $50,000, hopefully compensating the energy producer with the cost required to produce extra electricity for air conditioning. Cum HDD is the number of cumulative HDDs in a specified period per month. Of course, the buyer of the option would have to pay a premium for having this potential payoff. Similarly, a put option on an HDD would have a payoff 1000 × Max (0, 700 − Cum HDD).

Options with a CDD can be similarly stated.

Normally, the payoff on calls and puts on an HDD or a CDD is capped at a certain level. If in the example of a HDD in this section, the cap was fixed at US $30,000, the holder of the call would not get $50,000, but only $30,000.

The other product based on weather is the swap. It is a combination of a long call and a short put. Swaps are contracts where two parties agree to exchange the risks. This will produce a more stable cash flow when weather conditions are volatile. In simple terms, one party agrees to pay the other if the contracted index settles above a certain level, while the other agrees to pay if the index settles below that level. Swaps have no premium, but provide protection from adverse weather in return for giving up some of the upside of favourable weather.

Pricing Weather Derivatives

Though trading in weather derivatives has started, there is no robust model that can value a derivative on weather. In the absence of any such model, some experts are using the Black-Scholes Model (BSM) to value weather derivatives.

It is clearly a compromise because the non-applicability of BSM for weather derivatives is well known. The assumptions of normal distribution and random walk of the prices of the asset do not hold good for weather. Temperature seems to follow a pattern, and cannot have any value for the same time of the year at a particular location, unlike stock prices, which can vary wildly. Further, weather is a mean reverting phenomenon, as it is observed that temperature tends to revert to the average in two or three days, whereas under a random walk, no mean reversion is assumed.

One solution to value weather derivatives may lie in performing the Monte Carlo simulation, incorporating the probability distribution and mean reversion in the process of generation of random numbers.

Derivatives on Rain The weather element that affects life the most in India is rain, rather than temperature, and, therefore, derivatives based on the quantum of rain at different geographical locations may have a larger market and greater appeal for all those wanting to hedge against an excess or a shortfall of rain. Some banks in India have already made a beginning in terms of providing weather-based derivative products. In 2005, the NCDEX in India, for

> Like derivatives based on temperature, derivatives based on rainfall, too, can be developed that would better suit the hedging needs in India.

information purpose only, defined a *rain day* as a 24-hour period during which precipitation was in excess of a reference of 20 mm and an index for Mumbai cumulating the number of rain days between June 1 and September 30. This is probably a preparatory exercise before the launch of exchange-traded derivative products on weather in India. The users could be agriculturalists and the food processing industry. A brief on rain indexes is presented as follows.

Derivatives In Practice — Weather Derivatives

Rainfall Indices

The rainfall indexes RAINDEXMUM, RAINDEXIDR, and RAINDEXJAI record rainfall at Mumbai (Colaba), Indore, and Jaipur, respectively. They are designed in such a way that they also consider the normal historical rainfall in Mumbai, Indore, and Jaipur, respectively. All historical and current data have been taken from the Indian Meteorological Department (IMD).

These indexes are computed on the basis of historical annual cumulative rainfall, and are adjusted for the net surplus or deficit of actual cumulative rainfall on a given day. The adjustment factor takes into account the impact of historical and actual rainfall during the period. The normal index values for Mumbai, Indore, and Jaipur are 1950, 950, and 350, respectively. A cap is adopted on the maximum daily rainfall to reduce the impact on the index at times of unprecedented rainfall on a single day (e.g., 26 July 2005). The rainfall index values are posted on a daily basis on the index websites during the monsoon season (June to October) every year.

Source: www.mcxindia.com, accessed on 14 May 2009.

EMISSION TRADING

Concerned with the increasing environmental hazard due to rapid industrialization causing long-term climate changes disturbing the ecological balance, an effort was made to regulate the dangerous emissions of gases. Industries such as steel, power, cement, fertilizer, metals, and so on, emit hazardous gases that have long-term adverse implications on climate changes.

United Nations Framework Convention on Climate Change (UNFCCC) with the objective of stabilizing the concentration of greenhouse gases (GHGs) placed obligations on industrialized nations to reduce emissions of four gases, i.e., carbon dioxide, methane, nitrous oxide, and sulphur hexafluoride, collectively referred as *greenhouse gases,* and two more gases, i.e., hydrofluorocarbons and perfluorocarbons. These gases trap infra-red energy and induce climate changes.

The treaty referred as Kyoto Protocol signed in Kyoto, Japan, set emission reduction targets for 37 industrialized nations to reduce emission levels by 5.2% (later revised to 4.2% due to withdrawal of USA) from the base year of 1990 in a period from 2008 to 2012. These emission reduction levels were translated in terms of carbon dioxide equivalent (CO_2e). Under the second phase conducted at Doha, nations have agreed to bring down emissions in another eight years commencing 1 January 2013 to 31 December 2020 by 18% from the base level emissions of 1990.

In order to meet the objectives of the protocol, the nations were mandated to follow policies and adopt measures for the reduction of GHGs in their respective countries. These emissions were measured as Assigned Amount Units (AAUs). In addition, they are required to increase the absorption of these gases and utilize all mechanisms available. A national authority is appointed to take inventory of GHGs and also decide which projects are fit for accreditation for earning credits.

The interesting feature of the protocol was that it provided for three flexible mechanisms within the industrialized nations and other developing nations to trade in the emission levels with the objective of reducing cost and contain emission of GHGs according to the protocol. These mechanisms were a) Joint Implementation (JI), b) Clean Development Mechanism (CDM), and c) International Emission Trading (IET).

Joint implementation allows one developed country with high emissions to help set up projects in another developed country with low emissions. Clean development mechanisms provides for a developed country to sponsor a GHG reduction project in a developing country that has low emission levels and get credit for reduction of GHG emissions. The benefit to the developing nations is that it receives desired capital investment. International emission trading allows a nation with low emissions to sell its surplus AAUs to the nation that has high AAUs.

These three mechanisms place a financial cost on reduction of emissions and allow for purchasing of emission reduction credits by deficit nations from other surplus nations through a financial exchange. The JI and CDM are credit generation tools for emission reduction while IET allows exchanging shortfall and excess to strike a balance among nations.

MCX India contract on carbon credit	
Symbol	CFI
Description	CFIMMMYY
Contracts available for trading	
December 08 contract	1 January to 15 December of the contract year
December 09 contract	1 January to 15 December of the contract year
December 10 contract	1 January to 15 December of the contract year
December 11 contract	1 January to 15 December of the contract year
December 12 contract	1 January to 15 December of the contract year
Trading	
Trading period	Mondays through Saturdays
Trading unit	200 tonnes of carbon credits (carbon emission allowances)
Quotation/base value	₹ per tonne
Maximum order size	10,000 tonnes
Tick size (minimum price movement)	50 paise per tonne
Initial margin	6%
Delivery	
Delivery unit	200 tonnes of carbon credits (carbon emission allowances)
Quality specifications	Carbon credits (CO_2 emission allowance). Each CO_2 emission allowance being an entitlement to emit one tonne of CO_2 equivalent gases.

Source: www.mcxindia.com, accessed on 14 May 2009.

The rationale for providing the flexible mechanisms in the KP was to enable industrialized countries to reduce the cost of reducing emissions. With financial values assigned by the trading mechanism, it is expected that nations would strive for reduction of emissions realizing the cost implications determined by market forces. Such an approach is expected to reduce the aggregate cost of reducing emissions. This is also expected to create incentives for producers and consumers to significantly invest in low GHG products, technologies, and processes.

Emission reductions projects are given credit in the form of *carbon credit,* called Certified Emission Reductions (CERs). Under CDM, projects could be registered in the first phase ending 2012 to earn carbon credits. The CDM was expected to produce substantial COe in emission reductions. Most of these reductions are through renewable energy, energy efficiency, and fuel switching. China and India are expected to be leading producers of CERs.

With trading among the industrialized nations, some were deficit and some were surplus. Major surplus countries are Latvia, Estonia, Czech Republic, and Poland.

The trading was to be done in the form of carbon credit. A carbon credit is a generic term for any tradable certificate or permit representing the right to emit one tonne of carbon dioxide or the mass of another GHG with a CO_2e, equivalent to one tonne of carbon dioxide. The trading of carbon credit can be done at an exchange or over the counter.

Climate exchanges have been established to provide a spot market in allowances, as well as futures and options market to help discover a market price and maintain liquidity. Currently there are five exchanges trading in carbon allowances

Carbon trading is expected to be one of the largest markets. As the use of energy grows, the demand for CERs would rise substantially with time. Firms needing to buy these credits would increase while those generating would decrease. With great mismatch of demand and supply, the prices are expected to move up. High price of carbon credit is expected to induce behavioural changes in production and consumption of energy substituting high emission fuels such as coal and oil with low emission fuels such as natural gas and nuclear energy. High price would also motivate invention of energy-saving devices.

Carbon credits create a market for reducing GHG emissions by giving a monetary value to the cost of polluting the air. Emissions become an internal cost of doing business and are visible on the financial statements. For example, consider a project that emits 10,000 tonnes of GHG emissions in a year. Due to commitments made to reduce emission, the government limits the emissions to say 8000 tonnes per year. Here, the firm is now required to reduce emissions to the prescribed level by investing in environmental-friendly technology or buying carbon credits from open markets. The decision to buy or to invest in technology would now be compared financially because the cost of buying carbon credit would be known. The seller of carbon credit would receive cash flows to reduce cost of production. The price may be more likely to be perceived as fair by those paying it while the sellers would have more control over their own costs.

Carbon emissions trading has been steadily increasing in recent years. According to the World Bank's Carbon Finance Unit, 374 million metric tonnes of CO_2e were exchanged through projects in 2005, a 240% increase relative to 2004 (110 mt CO_2e), which was itself a 41% increase relative to 2003 (78 mt CO_2e). In terms of dollars, the World Bank has estimated that the size of the carbon credit market was 11 billion USD in 2005, 30 billion USD in 2006, and 64 billion in 2007. In 2008, Barclays Capital predicted that the new carbon credit market would be worth $70 billion worldwide that year.

Distinctive Features of Weather Derivatives

The following distinct features of weather derivatives must be noted:

- From their name, it appears that weather derivatives provide insurance against adverse weather conditions. However, there are some vital differences between weather deriva-

> Weather derivatives are not insurance products. They are non-deliverable, free from manipulation, and do not require complex valuation models.

tives and insurance. While insurance would take care of extremities in weather, compensation for small changes in weather conditions is not possible. There does not seem to be a way to compensate for the 'loss of business or profit' due to adverse weather conditions. Further, in case of insurance, loss due to adverse weather conditions would have to be proved before any compensation is awarded. In the case of weather derivatives, proof of having incurred a loss is not required.

- Weather derivatives would be contracts where the underlying is non-deliverable. One can neither buy nor sell rain, snow, or temperature. Therefore, contracts on weather are necessarily cash-settled. Hedging can only be done by initiating a position and then having an offsetting contract, unlike hedging in other commodities and products, where derivatives can be combined with positions in the underlying assets to have an effective hedge.
- The weather is a natural phenomenon and is not subject to manipulation by anyone. Weather risk is also unique to a location. It cannot be controlled and despite great advances in meteorological sciences, it still cannot be predicted precisely and consistently.
- The pricing of weather derivatives, fortunately, does not require complex mathematics or any analytical formulation such as the BSM. Weather can be priced based on historical data and the forecast. One can use past data on temperature or rain to find a probability distribution that can be used to determine derivative payoffs.

ENERGY DERIVATIVES

We consume energy in various forms, such as fossil fuel for transportation; electricity for lighting houses and factories producing industrial goods, and temperature control; and gas for cooking and running turbines. The maximum energy is produced from fossil fuel, coal, and the sun.

The market for energy derivatives can trace its roots back to 1983, when crude oil futures were first traded on the New York Mercantile Exchange (NYMEX). Since then, oil and other energy market derivatives have also been traded on the Tokyo Commodities Exchange (TOCOM), the Energy Market Exchange (EMEX), and the newly opened Dubai Mercantile Exchange.

Like other derivative products, energy derivatives can be used as a form of insurance to protect against the often-volatile changes in energy prices.

Energy derivatives are chiefly traded through two different financial instruments—swaps and futures.

An energy swap is a transaction that trades on the prices two parties pay for an energy commodity. For example, a company purchasing oil at a variable rate can participate in a swap so that it can purchase oil at a fixed rate for a certain amount of time. In a swap transaction, there is no transfer of oil, only a transfer of the prices paid for oil. In contrast, a futures contract is an agreement for one part to deliver or receive the energy commodity at a certain price for a specified period of time.

Hedgers are usually large energy providers or purchasers who use energy derivatives to protect themselves from the volatile nature of energy prices. An energy producer, for example, would use energy futures to guarantee a selling price of energy so that it would be protected from a sudden drop in prices and, thus, from a decrease in profits. Large consumers of energy, such as transportation service companies and city and state governments, use energy futures to lock-in a low price of energy so that they are not subject to the risk of rising energy costs.

The airline industry is a huge hedge player in the energy derivatives market. Each year, airlines compete to purchase energy futures contracts in an attempt to lessen their fuel costs, which often take up more than 20% of their annual budgets.

The other part of the energy derivative market is composed of speculators—entities who do not produce or purchase energy but simply make investments by betting on the price of energy. Energy speculators have made a significantly higher number of trades than energy hedgers—that is, more trading of energy derivatives was concerned with essentially betting on the price of energy than with protection from volatile price changes.

Products covered by energy derivatives include crude oil, heating oil, natural gas, electricity, jet fuel, and kerosene.

Crude Oil

Crude oil has become a commodity that impacts economies the world over in ways that possibly no other commodity does. With rising consumption and shrinking supply of this natural resource, oil has become the most sought after commodity in the world. It will remain so until alternative sources of energy are developed.

Crude oil price risk was perceived as more serious in the 1970s, when the need to manage the price risk emanating from changes in crude oil prices gathered momentum and products to manage crude oil price risk were developed.

India is among the 10 largest consumers of crude oil in the world, and almost 70–75% of the requirements are met by imports. Thus, India faces relatively very large risk from changing crude oil prices. Volatility in the prices is much high, and so is the risk. Further, since the prices of end products from crude oil are still administered in India, price fluctuations in the international crude oil markets cannot be transferred to consumers readily. Crude oil also happens to be a major revenue earner commodity by way of customs duty and cess for the Government of India, constraining the developmental public expenditure. On a broader scale, therefore, crude oil prices impact the economy in much larger ways than most of us would imagine. Unlike most commodities and financial assets, the crude oil industry is dominated by the actions of a cartel, namely, the Organization of the Petroleum Exporting Countries (OPEC), whose actions and decisions with respect to production and supply hugely impact crude oil prices worldwide.

MCX India contract on crude oil	
Symbol	CRUIDEOIL
Description	CRUIDEOILMMMYY
Contracts available for trading	
January contract	20 July of the previous year to 19 January of the contract year
February contract	20 August of the previous year to 21 February of the contract year
March contract	21 September of the previous year to 21 March of the contract year
April contract	20 October of the previous year to 18 April of the contract year
May contract	19 November of the previous year to 19 May of the contract year
June contract	18 December of the previous year to 20 June of the contract year

MCX India contract on crude oil	
July contract	20 January to 19 July of the contract year
August contract	22 February to 19 August of the contract year
September contract	22 March to 19 September of the contract year
October contract	19 April to 19 October of the contract year
November contract	20 May to 17 November of the contract year
December contract	21 June to 19 December of the contract year
Trading	
Trading period	Mondays through Saturdays
Trading unit	100 barrels
Quotation/base value	₹ per barrel
Maximum order size	10,000 barrels
Tick size (minimum price movement)	₹1
Initial margin	5%
Delivery	
Delivery unit	50,000 barrels with ±2% tolerance unit
Quality specifications	Light sweet crude oil conforming to the following quality specification is deliverable: Sulphur 0.42% by weight or loss API gravity: between 37–42 degrees

Source: www.mcxindia.com, accessed on 17 September 2012.

> The world is critically dependent on energy that is limited and non-renewable. Derivatives on crude oil are traded worldwide.

The Multi-commodity Exchange (MCX) in India has futures contracts on crude oil, Brent crude oil, and air turbine fuel, thus providing opportunities for hedging to crude oil users such as refineries, airlines, crude oil exploration firms, and other petro-based industries. Contracts on crude oil are among the most traded at the MCX. Since crude oil is traded globally, the international price and the local price must be the same when quoted in the same currency. International prices are quoted in terms of US dollar per barrel and contracts at the MCX are denominated in Indian rupees. Hedgers must understand the movements of crude oil prices as well as exchange rates. However, there is no need to consider exchange rate risk separately.

Electricity

The electricity market in India is characterized by government regulation. With increased deregulation, the need for hedging against electricity production and revenue would surely mount. The MCX has weekly as well as monthly contracts with electricity as the underlying. The contract size is 1 MW × 24 hours with prices quoted in terms of ₹per MWH and a tick size of ₹1. Contract duration is eight weeks, and eight weekly contracts are available at any point of time. The delivery unit is MWH × 24 h × calendar days in the week. The contract is for even delivery of 1 MWH of electricity.

Natural Gas

Another important natural source of energy is natural gas. Futures contracts on natural gas came into being in 1990. NYMEX launched option contracts on natural gas in October 1992. Subsequently, Canada and the United Kingdom have also launched derivative contracts on natural gas. The growth of derivative contracts in gas has been phenomenal.

Natural gas in various forms such as liquefied (LNG), compressed (CNG), and piped (PNG) natural gas has a vast amount of uses and users. Natural gas is used as feedstock in the fertilizer industry, petrochemicals, automobile fuels, domestic cooking, solvents, and chemicals. Besides the fertilizer industry, users include the transportation industry and electricity producers, apart from domestic consumers. As the economy grows, there will be more and more consumption of natural gas, as it is environment friendly.

The MCX has introduced futures contracts in India with contract sizes of 500 mmBtu and delivery in multiples of 10,000 mmBtu. The price quotation is in terms of rupees per mmBtu, with a tick size of ₹0.10.

Energy price behaviour is characterized by mean reversion and truncated distribution with seasonality in both prices and volatility. Products have been developed with payoff based on energy prices. These products include energy commodity-linked bonds and treasury notes where the coupons are decided on the basis of energy prices.

SUMMARY

A recent development in the derivatives market is the introduction of weather derivatives aimed at covering risks emanating from the weather. This should not be construed to indicate that extreme weather conditions can be hedged with these derivatives. Extreme losses due to unforeseen and extreme weather conditions remain in the domain of insurance. The derivatives already in use in the USA are aimed at covering energy losses due to hot or cold weather conditions. These derivatives are cash-settled, and are based on the temperature conditions during a period. In India, efforts are on to introduce derivatives based on rainfall. Carbon credits are already being traded in India. For pricing weather derivatives, complex models such as the BSM are not required.

Energy derivatives such as those on crude oil, electricity, and natural gas, also have gained popularity because of the overdependence of the world economy on very limited and non-renewable sources of energy. There are derivatives on varieties of crude oil, electricity, and natural gas being traded all over the world.

KEY TERMS

CDD Cooling degree days, defined as Max(0, A – 65).

HDD Heating degree days, defined as Max(0, 65 – A).

QUESTIONS

23.1 Describe weather derivatives on temperatures.
23.2 Why do you think that derivatives on temperatures are not useful in India?
23.3 What problems do you see in pricing of weather derivatives using standard valuation methods?
23.4 How are weather derivatives different from derivatives on other underlying assets?

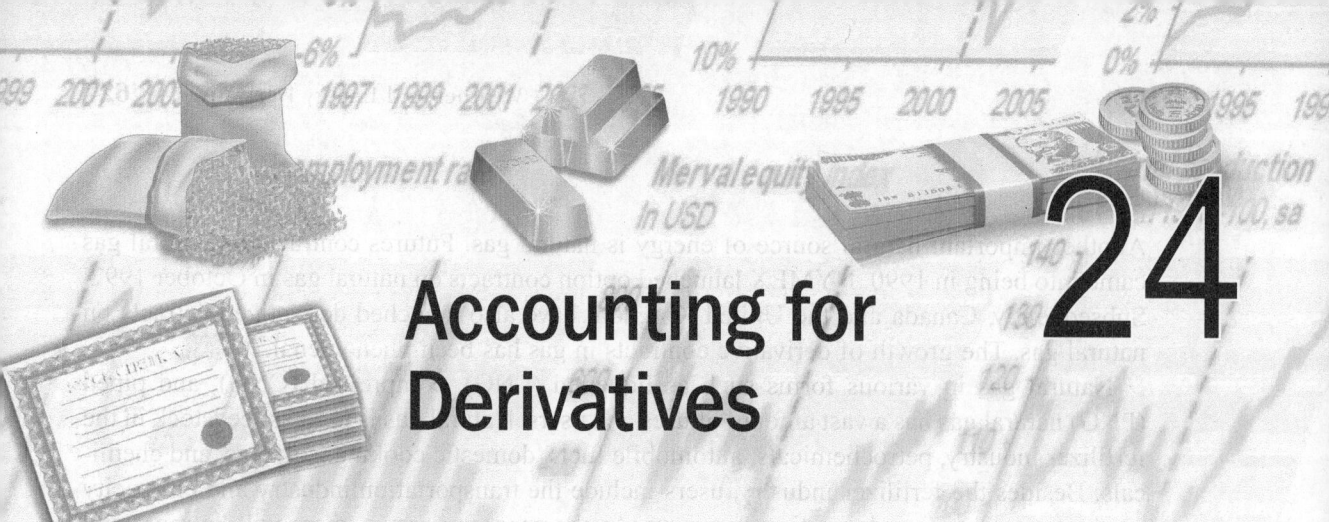

Accounting for Derivatives

24

INTRODUCTION

For several reasons, accounting for derivatives has always been a complex issue. The definition and financial implication of derivatives are difficult to comprehend from the accounting perspective. One prominent reason has been that positions in derivatives involve no/nominal cash outlay, as compared to the outlay required in the acquisition of the underlying financial assets or creation of liabilities. A second reason is that derivative contracts are contingent in nature, and more often than not, are settled in cash. The cash inflows or outflows occur on a net basis, when the original position is squared up.

> Accounting for derivatives is complex because they require no/very little initial investment, and obligations under derivatives are contingent in nature.

Accounting for any transaction is done only when financial implications of the contract materialize fully. Just like no accounting entries are passed when a firm only anticipates a big order, there is no recognition at the inception of a derivative contract when there is no cash flow. Futuristic positions cannot be recorded and accounted for beforehand. Accounting has the convention of recording transactions only after they have occurred. A position in derivatives may have zero cost or no initial cash flow, and, therefore, goes unrecorded. When an actual cash flow takes place upon settlement, the obligations are over. However, at the same time, non-reporting of the financial obligations assumed by initiating positions in derivatives would not represent the true picture of the financial commitments an organization makes. Due to the natural leverage in derivatives, a seemingly small commitment has massive and extremely disproportionate financial implications. The accounting perspective has to be transformed to record firm commitments that have not yet crystallized.

Learning Objectives

After going through this chapter, readers should be familiar with

- the differences of derivatives from other financial instruments in terms of accounting
- fair value and fair value accounting
- the measurement of fair value
- hedged items, hedging instruments, and hedging relationships
- hedge accounting
- differences in hedge accounting as compared to other accounting practices
- fair value hedges and cash flow hedges
- the difference between a fair value hedge and a cash flow hedge
- accounting for derivatives in different circumstances

Recording transactions only after they have occurred implies that the value shown is based on historical cost. After recording the asset or liability, if the value changes, the asset or liability remains stated at the original historical value. The value of the derivative changes as the value of the underlying changes. While the underlying remains stated at one value, the derivative position as a hedge would lead to an accounting anomaly. Stating the underlying at its historical value and the derivative at its market value would be conceptually inconsistent. Changes in the value of the derivative would not be accompanied by changes in the value of the underlying. It would not reflect the true nature of hedging. Therefore, accounting for derivatives demands radical changes in accounting approaches.

These extremely complicated and basic issues of accounting for derivatives have been addressed by the *Accounting Standard AS 30* (*Financial Instruments: Recognition and Measurement*) issued by the Institute of Chartered Accountants of India. Internationally, accounting for derivatives is prominently governed by the IAS 39 (Financial Instruments: Recognition and Measurement) issued by the International Accounting Standard Board, and the FAS 133 (Accounting for Derivatives and Hedging Activities) issued by the Financial Accounting Standards Board. There is no material difference between the AS 30 and the IAS 39. Each of these standards is too massive for comprehension and yet there were lacunae and complexities that have surfaced subsequently. These complexities have possibly arisen due to the attempts by issuing bodies to generalize rather than treat each derivative separately. A simplified discussion of the AS 30 follows.

> Conventional accounting is based on historical cost, while derivatives need to be recorded at fair value. The AS 30 prescribes accounting for derivatives on the lines of international practices.

ACCOUNTING DEFINITION OF DERIVATIVES

The AS 30 and all other international standards governing accounting for derivatives define derivatives in a generic way; there is no instrument-specific definition. Since newer and newer instruments are evolving in the field of derivatives, the generic definition is expected to take care of the long-term future and obviate the need for revision from time to time.

As per the AS 30, a derivative is a financial instrument with the following three characteristics:

- Its value changes with the interest rate, the price of the instrument, the foreign exchange rate, the index, its credit rating, etc.
- It requires no/very little net initial investment.
- It is settled at a future date.

> As per AS 30, a derivative is a financial instrument that changes is value based on the underlying, requires no/marginal investment and is settled at a future date. The term derivative excludes bank guarantees and insurance contracts.

The definition of derivatives involves (a) risk, (b) futurity, (c) origination, and (d) investment. Insurance and bank guarantees do have risk and futurity but their originations are based on past events, and, therefore, are excluded.

The IAS 39 has a similar definition for derivatives. Embedded derivatives are defined separately. An example of an embedded derivative would be a callable bond. Some part of the values or cash flows of the instrument behaves in the same manner as that of derivatives. Due to the difference in the method of recording, the derivative needs to be separated from the host instrument; otherwise, it leads to an accounting anomaly. To enable recording the host instrument at its historical cost and the embedded derivative at its fair value, the derivative needs to be separated from the host contract. Segregation of the derivative and the host contract is extremely complex, and no amount of explanation is enough to resolve the issue. Seemingly simple terms of business contract such as the pricing of long-term contracts based on exchange rates could be seen as embedding options. To simplify, several conditions are laid down for segregating the embedded derivative from the host contract.

TYPES OF FINANCIAL INSTRUMENTS

In order to identify what principles must be followed for recording assets and liabilities, the AS 30, like other international accounting standards, classifies financial instruments into four broad categories. We are already aware that cash or a promise to pay or receive cash represents the basis of recognizing, measuring, and recording financial assets and liabilities. Besides financial assets, there are non-financial assets that do not give rise to cash transactions, such as warranties and prepaid expenses in the financial statements. The AS 30 classifies financial instruments in the following four categories:

> The AS 30 has four categories for financial instruments: (a) financial instruments at fair value through profit and loss, (b) held to maturity investments, (c) loans and advances, and (d) available-for-sale.

- A financial asset or liability at fair value through profit or loss
- Held-to-maturity (HTM) investments
- Loans and receivables
- Available-for-sale

Financial assets or liabilities at fair value (FaFV) *through profit and loss* are instruments that are

- held for trading; and
- initially recognized at their fair values.

All financial derivatives, unless held for hedging purposes, would fall in this class. Almost all positions in derivatives are essentially short term in nature, and are held with the motive of making speculative profit. All instruments held for trading must be recorded at fair value.

> FaFV instruments are recorded at fair value, and gains/losses are routed to the profit and loss account upon re-measurement. HTM investments are held till maturity, and mostly are not subject to hedging.

The *HTM investments* are non-derivative financial assets with fixed and determinable payments at fixed maturities. Further, there must be a clearly demonstrated intention and ability to hold the investment till maturity. Items that are classified as FaFV, loans and receivables, and available-for-sale are excluded. The firm must demonstrate that it has the intentions of holding the asset till maturity. Naturally, equity cannot be classified as HTM as it has no fixed payment or term to maturity.

Loans and receivables are non-derivative financial assets and liabilities with fixed or determinable payments that are not quoted in an active market, other than those classified as HTM, FaFV etc. This definition is intended to include accounts receivable and accounts payable.

Available-for-sale financial instruments are those non-derivative financial assets that are not classified in any of the first three categories. These assets are, therefore, a residual category.

This classification is meant for disclosure requirements as well as to gain knowledge of the values at which such instruments would be recorded in financial statements upon acquisition, and how subsequent gains/losses would be treated in financial statements. Table 24.1 summarizes the treatment to be accorded to measurement in the balance sheet and treatment of gains/losses as provided for in the AS 30.

> Derivatives are recorded at fair value and would be MTM. Changes in fair value would be routed through the profit and loss account. When the derivative is used in a hedge, the MTM changes would be clubbed with those of the hedged item.

With specific reference to derivatives, the classification can be made in two ways—those held for trading and those designated as hedging instruments. The accounting with respect to derivatives held for trading would be

- to recognize the initial position at cost, with the transaction cost expensed out; and
- re-measure the fair value at each reporting date, recognize the gains or losses in the profit and loss account, and record the difference from the initial fair value recorded as a liability or an asset in the balance sheet.

Derivatives designated as hedging instruments would be subject to hedge accounting.

Table 24.1 Recognition of financial instruments and gains/losses

Financial assets and liabilities	Initial measurement	Treatment of gains/losses
FaFV	Fair value on date of acquisition	Profit and loss account
Short-term receivables and payables	Invoice amount	–
Other financial assets and liabilities	Fair value ± transaction cost	
HTM investments	Amortized cost	
Derivatives designated as hedge instrument	Hedge accounting	
Available-for-sale	Fair value	Reserves; to be transferred to the profit and loss account on derecognition
Unquoted equity investment	At cost	Profit and loss account

FAIR VALUE

Derivatives are financial instruments whose value can be determined accurately by the observed prices that are quoted in exchanges or over the counter (OTC) in domestic and international markets, and, thus, the practice is to value derivative instruments at their fair values rather than at their historical costs. Easy entry and exit at market prices makes accounting possible at fair values, and historical costs lose relevance.

> The fair value is the amount at which the asset could be exchanged between knowledgeable and willing parties. It excludes forced and distress sale situations.

Hitherto, Indian accounting standards prescribed the historical cost as the basis for recording transactions, including those of financial instruments. Short-term investments are stated at cost or market value, whichever is lesser, whereas long-term investments are recorded at cost. With the introduction of the AS 30, fair value accounting has gained acceptance, and become consistent with international practices.

Fair value is defined as be the amount for which an asset could be exchanged or a liability settled between knowledgeable and willing parties in an arm's length transaction.

Measurement of Fair Value

Fair value is determined on the basis of continuing operations, and eliminates prices in forced transactions, involuntary liquidations, and distress sales. The following are possible methods for measurement of fair value.

When Active Market Exists When an active market for the instrument and hedged item exists, the quoted prices form the basis of fair value. The quoted prices that can be used are:

> The fair value must be market determined or based on valuation techniques/models, making maximum use of market-determined inputs.

- the bid price for an asset held or a liability to be issued;
- the ask price for an asset to be acquired or a liability to be held;
- the mid price for an asset and a liability with offsetting risk, and then apply bid or ask price for the net position; and
- the most recent prices with suitable adjustments when the bid and ask prices are not available.

When No Active Market Exists When no active market exists or the quoted price is not available, then valuation techniques need to be used. The valuation principle includes:

- the use of the most recent arm's length price between knowledgeable and willing parties, if it is available;
- the fair value of another instrument that is substantially the same as the instrument in question;
- a discounted cash flow (DCF) analysis; and
- option pricing models.

The valuation technique or model must (a) use the maximum inputs from the market, (b) reasonably reflect the risk–return factors just as the market would, and (c) be applied consistently.

The following are some of the useful rules for establishing fair value:

- While arriving at the discount rate, the time value of money is needed for determining the risk-free rate. It must be derived from the observed prices of government bonds and the yield curves for different time horizons. Market-based rates such as LIBOR or MIBOR are not regarded as risk-free rates, because they incorporate credit risk. If these rates are used, the adjustment for the benchmark rate and the hedging instrument/item must be made for the credit risk.
- Credit risk premiums must be based on observable market prices of traded instruments of a similar risk class.
- Foreign currency, commodity, and equity prices must be used as they are quoted in the respective markets.
- Volatility measurement must be based on observed historical data, or the volatility implied in the price.
- Prepayment and surrender risks must be gauged from historical data.

HEDGE ACCOUNTING

A position in derivatives can either be speculative or constitute a hedge. When it is part of a hedge, the intention of the hedger is to protect against any unfavourable movement in the value of the asset or liability by having an offsetting position in derivatives, implying that any profit/loss on the asset or liability is compensated fully or substantially by loss/profit on the derivative position. Therefore, when used as a hedge, the profit or loss needs to be assessed on an aggregate basis, rather than separately on the asset/liability and the derivative position.

When the position is accounted for in an isolated manner, the principle of conservatism of 'providing for unrealized loss and not recognising the unrealized gain' causes a distorted view of the financial positions and makes profits volatile. Though this could be classified as a correct representation, it is not a fair view of profit till the position in the derivative is closed.

For example, consider that a firm invests ₹20 lakh in the shares of another company (10,000 shares at ₹200) on 28 February. To protect against any decline in the value of his/her investment, the investor takes a short position on index futures expiring on 25 April, worth ₹20 lakh (assuming a beta of 1.00) at an index value of 5000 involving 400 indices. The financial position of the investing firm on the date of acquisition would be:

> Hedge accounting treats the combined position of the hedged item and the hedging instruments rather than either in isolation. This requires that both the hedged item and the hedging instruments are represented at fair value and are MTM.

Equity	20,00,000	Investment	20,00,000

On 31 March, the day of reporting, the investment, and the futures position thereon must be re-assessed. Assume that the value of the shares fell to ₹180 (a decline of 10%) while the index came down to 4600 (a fall of 8%). How would the investing firm present its financial position on 31 March?

If the position on index futures is deemed squared up (marked-to-market—MTM), it would entail a gain of ₹1,60,000 (400 × 400), which is unrealized, and under conservative reporting or prudence, would not be recognized. However, an unrealized loss of ₹2,00,000 (10,000 shares × ₹20) on the investment, again on prudence, would be recorded.

Equity	20,00,000	Investment	18,00,000
Loss	(2,00,000)		

Instead, if the markets moved up, a loss on the futures would be recorded, while a gain on the investment asset would go unrecorded with prudent accounting. This also follows the accounting principle that investments must be recorded at cost or market price, whichever is less. Hence, any gain in financial assets would not be recognized. Note that both gains and losses are unrealized. In either case, recognizing losses but not profits is a fallacious view.

Instead, the fair view would be to understand that the position in futures was taken to hedge and make value of the asset stable. When a comprehensive view is taken, there is an unrealized loss of ₹40,000 (a loss of ₹2,00,000 on the value of the asset less a gain on the futures position of ₹1,60,000). If so, the true financial position on 31 March would be as follows:

Equity	20,00,000	Investment	18,00,000
Loss	(40,000)	Receivable from the futures	1,60,000

If the investor had squared up on 31 March, the receivable would translate into cash from the exchange.

This was an example where the asset already existed in the books. The issue becomes far more complex if the asset/liability does not exist but a hedging position is taken on the basis of forecast cash flows. Consider, for example, an exporter aiming at exports worth ₹120 lakh, evenly spaced over 12 months, to be denominated in euros. Anticipating depreciation of the euro, the exporter sells 12-m forward contracts worth ₹10 lakh at ₹60/euro (assuming the same forward rate for all the 12 contracts, for simplicity). After two months when the performance needs to be recorded, there would be 10 forward contracts worth ₹100 lakh still outstanding. These would have to be valued for loss or gain as per the exchange rate prevailing then. If the euro had instead appreciated by 10%, there would be a loss of ₹10 lakh (10% of ₹100 lakh) that needs to be accounted for, making the results volatile, because there is no receivable existing in the books that would have a value higher by the same amount, annulling the loss in the derivative position. The purpose of the forward contracts was the exactly opposite, i.e., rendering stability to the cash flows and profits.

Hedge accounting relates to the combined effect of changes in the values of the asset/liability that is being hedged and of the derivative instrument used for such purpose against the risk of adverse movement of market variables such as interest rate, price, credit rating, and prepayment. This necessitates valuation of the asset or liability as well as of the hedging instrument at fair value. Therefore, concepts of historical cost and accounting based on past transactions need to be changed.

TYPES OF HEDGES

Recognizing the need for a comprehensive view on the hedged position, the rules for hedge accounting are laid down. The AS 30 classifies hedges into three types:

> There are basically two types of hedges—the fair value hedges that protect the fair value of the recorded asset, and the cash flow hedge to protect the cash flow from a forecast transaction. Foreign currency exposures may be hedged by either of the two.

- Fair value hedge
- Cash flow hedge
- Net investment in foreign operations

However, from the perspective of accounting, there are basically only two different types of hedges, i.e., the fair value hedge and the cash flow hedge.

Fair Value Hedge A fair value hedge is intended to protect the fair value. The values of assets and liabilities are subject to change due to changing economic and market conditions. A fair value hedge is aimed at protecting the fair values of the recognized assets/liabilities. Apart from recorded assets and liabilities, the AS 30 also permits hedging of unrecognized firm commitments (such as pending supply against a firm order).

Cash Flow Hedge A cash flow hedge is used for protection against variability in the anticipated cash flows that are subject to a particular risk associated with a recognized asset/liability or a possible forecast transaction. Obviously, such variability could affect the profit/loss. An example befitting a cash flow hedge could be a repayment of debt on a variable interest rate that can be covered with a swap for paying a fixed rate in exchange for receiving a floating rate.

From the definitions of the fair value hedge and the cash flow hedge, it is clear that an account payable or an account receivable in foreign currency could be classified as either of the two.

The third type of hedge, i.e., net investment in foreign operations, is equivalent to a cash flow hedge from the accounting perspective.

STEPS FOR HEDGE ACCOUNTING

In order to prevent misuse and arbitrariness in hedge accounting, there are prerequisites that need to be established before exposures in assets/liabilities and positions in derivatives become eligible for hedge accounting. The various requirements and steps that need to be followed are as follows:

> For hedge accounting, the basic requirements include (a) identification of the hedged item, (b) a hedging instrument, and (c) a relationship between the two, demonstrating offsetting effects against a particular risk.

- Identification of the asset, liability, or firm commitment, referred to as the *hedged item,* that needs to be hedged
- Identification of the risk parameters that cause changes in the fair value and/or cash flow
- Identification of the derivative instrument intended to offset the changes in fair value or cash flow of the hedged item against risk parameters, referred to as the *hedging instrument*
- Establishment of a relationship between the hedged item and the hedging instrument, called the *hedging relationship*
- Determination of the criterion for measuring the effectiveness of the hedge (applicable for a cash flow hedge only), i.e., the extent to which the hedging instrument has been able to offset the changes in the fair value or cash flow of the hedged item

Hedged Item

The first question that arises in hedging is: What is the asset or liability that is being hedged? An asset or liability that is exposed to the risk of changes in its fair value or its cash flows, including a highly probable forecast transaction, can be designated as a hedged item. The hedged item may not be an individual item; instead, it can be a group of assets or liabilities permitting the adoption of a portfolio approach.

The AS 30 categorizes the following as possible hedged items:

> Recognized financial assets and liabilities and highly probable forecast transactions can be categorized as hedged items. However, assets and liabilities cannot be netted.

- Recognized assets or liabilities
- Unrecognized firm commitments

For those items that are eligible for hedging, the relevant risk factors must be identified, and changes in the fair value or cash flows caused by such identified factors are to be included in the hedge accounting. Any excluded portion of the asset cannot form a part of the hedge accounting, and such excluded portions must be accounted for separately in the profit and loss account.

Held-to-maturity investments cannot be a qualifying hedge item with respect to interest rate risks or prepayment risks, because designating an investment as HTM implies the

> An HTM investment cannot be classified as a hedged item for covering interest rates or prepayment risks.

intention to hold it till maturity without regard to changes in the fair value or the cash flow all through. Therefore, the interest rate risk is presumed to be absorbed while designating an item as HTM. However, an HTM investment can be qualified as a hedged item with respect to the risk from changes in foreign exchange rates and credit risks.

Normally, only transactions with external parties are covered in hedged items. Hedge accounting for transactions within the group can be considered only for hedged items in a stand-alone financial statement, not those in the consolidated financial statement. However, foreign currency transactions within the group (payables and receivables) may qualify as hedged items even if they are in consolidated financial statements, if they can result in gains/losses that are not fully offset upon consolidation.

Hedging Instrument

The next issue in the determination of a hedge is the identification of the derivative that is planned for hedging the exposure. This is referred to as the hedging instrument in the AS 30. The standard does not confine hedging instruments only to derivative products. Even a non-derivative may be designated as a hedging instrument for hedging foreign currency risks.

As long as the relationship demonstrates an offsetting effect, it can be classified as a hedging instrument. A designated derivative or a designated non-derivative financial asset/liability whose fair value or cash flows are expected to offset changes in the fair value of the cash flow of the hedged item can be termed as a hedging instrument.

> Writing options is contrary to the hedging principle because of the significantly larger risk for a small premium. As such, an option written cannot be a hedging instrument unless as a means of offsetting the premium paid for a long position.

However, the AS 30 specifically precludes short positions in options (writing options) from being classified as hedging instruments. Since writing options results in a small inflow of premium with potentially disproportionate losses, they cannot constitute effective hedges. Thus, written options do not qualify as hedging instruments unless the hedging is done to offset the price of the option bought, including the one that is embedded (writing a call to hedge a callable liability). Buying options entails little cost but has the potential to provide substantially large gains. Therefore, options bought qualify as hedging instruments.

Part of exposure in derivative instruments that can be attributed to hedging can be classified as 'hedging instrument' while the remainder could be treated as speculative and is subject to normal accounting. For example, one may book a forward contract of US $20 million against an exposure of US $10 million and designate 50% of the amount of the forward contract as a hedging instrument.

Similarly, more than one instrument may be designated as a hedging instrument. A combination of derivatives (or their proportions) may also be designated as hedging instruments, because risks arising from one derivative may be offset by another derivative. Several derivatives may be combined and jointly designated as a hedging instrument.

However, a derivative combination that involves a written option such as an interest rate collar cannot be classified as a hedging instrument if it is a *net written option* providing an option premium. Any written option or a net written option does not qualify to be designated as a hedging instrument.

The factors that affect the value of derivatives are co-dependent. Therefore, a hedging relationship is designated in its entirety, except (a) when separating the intrinsic and time values of an option and designating only the intrinsic value, while excluding the time value, as part of the hedge relationship, and (b) separating the interest element and the spot price of the forward contract. The intrinsic value of an option and the premium on a forward contract are measured separately.

Self-owned equity cannot be designated as a hedging instrument. An investment in an unquoted equity instrument and a derivative thereon that needs to be settled by delivery of the unquoted instrument cannot be designated as a hedging instrument.

Hedging Relationship

> Hedging relationships and hedge effectiveness have to be established at the inception of a hedge, and need to be documented to safeguard against the discretionary misuse of hedge accounting.

A hedging relationship between the hedged item and the hedging instrument needs to be established for accounting treatment. A prior designation of the hedging instrument, the hedged item, and their relationship is essential to eliminate subjective interpretation of the hedging.

According to AS 30, all the following conditions must be satisfied:

- At inception, a formal designation of the hedged item and the hedging instrument must be made, and documentation stating the objective, the hedging strategy, the transaction, etc., must be prepared.
- It must be established that the hedge is expected to be highly effective in offsetting changes in the value of the hedged item and the hedging instrument. Hedging effectiveness is determined on the basis of the ability of the hedging instrument and the hedged item to offset each other's gains and losses.
- *Hedging effectiveness:* A hedge is regarded as highly effective only if both the following conditions are met:

> A hedge is called effective if changes in the values of the hedged item and the hedging instruments are within 80% to 125% of each other.

  - At inception and later, the hedge is expected to offset changes in fair value or cash flow for the period of the hedge. The hedge ratio may be adjusted based on past statistical data.
  - The actual result of the hedge is within 80% to 125%, i.e., the offsetting changes must result in a loss no greater than 80% on the hedged item/hedging instrument with a gain of 100% on the hedging instrument/hedged item.
- For a cash flow hedge, a forecast transaction must be prepared.
- A reliable measurement of the effectiveness and determination of changes in the cash flows or fair value must be specified.
- The hedge must be assessed on an ongoing basis for the hedge period.

Once the designations of the hedged item and the hedging instrument and their relationship are completed, the nature of hedge must be ascertained.

Accounting for fair value hedges differs from accounting for cash flow hedges, as tabulated in Table 24.2. While a fair value hedge recognizes the combined effect of changes in the fair values of the hedged item and the hedging instrument through the profit and loss account, the cash flow hedge does so through a designated reserve equity account.

Table 24.2 Hedge accounting

	Fair value hedge	Cash flow hedge
Hedging instrument	Gain/loss on re-measuring the instrument at a fair value must be recognized in the profit and loss statement	The portion of effective hedge must be recognized directly in an appropriate equity account (hedging reserve account) and the remaining in the profit and loss account
Hedged item	Gain or loss should adjust the carrying amount and be recognized in the profit and loss statement	

In the case of a cash flow hedge, there is the additional dimension of effectiveness of the hedge. We all know that a perfect correlation between the hedged item and the hedging instrument does not exist, meaning that the gains or losses in one would not be completely offset by the losses or gains in the other. Therefore, while the intentions of the hedge would be to achieve such perfect offsetting, the actual position when the hedge is lifted would be somewhat different.

For a cash flow hedge, the appropriate hedging account associated with the hedged item must be adjusted to the lesser of the following:

- Cumulative gain/loss on the hedged instrument
- Cumulative change in fair value of the expected future cash flows on the hedged item

> The fair value routes the combined change in the fair value of the hedged item and the hedging instruments through the income statement, while the cash flow hedge routes it to the equity account.

Any remaining amount is to be adjusted in the profit and loss account.

ACCOUNTING FOR DERIVATIVES

If there is a hedging relationship between the hedged instrument and the hedged item, then accounting for gain or loss on both the hedging instrument and the hedged item must follow hedge accounting. An example each for a stand-alone derivative, a fair value hedge, and a cash flow hedge follows.

Derivative Held for Trading

Assume that in January, an oil company is expecting a rise in the prices of crude oil. Futures on crude oil are quoted on the exchange. Let the crude oil futures price for a July contract be ₹3000 per barrel, with a contract size of 100 barrels.

Expecting a rise in oil prices, the firm goes long on the July futures on crude oil at ₹3000 for one contract of 100 barrels. Let us examine the accounting for such a position at inception, at some intervening reporting date when the position in the derivative is outstanding and at the expiry/closing of the derivative position.

> Derivatives held for trading are MTM at each reporting interval, and unrealized gains or losses are presented in the income statement.

On Initiation of Long Position No accounting entries are passed, assuming no margin and no transaction cost. Transaction cost may be expensed out and margin money would create a receivable in the margin account, with an equivalent decline in the cash position. The fair value of the derivative position is the cost of acquiring the position.

On Reporting Date Let 31 March be the reporting date. As per the AS 30, the futures must be marked to market. The fair value would be recalculated and shown in the balance sheet, and any profit or loss would be recognized in the income statement. Assume that the closing price of crude oil futures on 31 March is ₹3200.

Marking to market would lead to a gain of ₹20,000 for one contract of 100 barrels, i.e., 100 × (3200 − 3000). This amount would be due from the exchange. This would be recorded as follows:

Dr	Derivative account	200 × 100	20,000
Cr	Profit and loss account	200 × 100	20,000

On Closing of Position The firm must close out its long position in the oil futures prior to the expiry of the contract. Assume that the futures price has declined to ₹3100 when the firm sells the contract to nullify the original position.

Since the derivative was marked to market on 31 March at ₹3200, there would be a loss of ₹100. In fact, the firm made a profit of ₹10,000 on the futures position, having bought them at ₹3000 and sold them at ₹3100. Since a profit of ₹20,000 was already recognized in the preceding reporting period, the current period would have to recognize a loss of ₹10,000. This brings the total gain to ₹10,000.

The firm would receive the net profit of ₹10,000 from the exchange, book a loss of ₹10,000 and derecognize the asset with the following accounting entries:

Dr	Profit and loss account	100 × 100	10,000
Dr	Bank	100 × 100	10,000
Cr	Derivative Account	200 × 100	20,000

Derivative as Fair Value Hedge

Now let us examine how hedge accounting would be carried out if the position in futures were taken for the purpose of a hedge. Consider the following situation:

- In January, an inventory of 100 barrels of crude oil exists with the firm. The current value is ₹2,90,000 at a spot price of ₹2900 per barrel.
- The inventory is expected to be sold in July.
- Prices are expected to fall by July.
- A July futures in crude oil is trading at ₹3000 per barrel.
- The firm sells a July futures contract at ₹3000 to hedge against any fall in the oil price by July.
- The inventory of oil is designated as the hedged item and the futures contract is designated as the hedging instrument.

- Since the value of the inventory is being protected with a short position in the futures contract, it qualifies for hedge accounting, and is a fair value hedge.

On Initiation of Short Position No entries would be passed for assuming a short position in oil futures. The margin and transaction cost are ignored. Any transaction cost may be expensed out and the margin money would create a receivable in the margin account, with an equivalent decline in the cash position. The fair value of the derivative position is the cost of acquiring the position.

On Intervening Reporting Date On 31 March, the fair value would be re-assessed and shown in the balance sheet, and any profit or loss would be recognized in the income statement. The oil inventory is being hedged, and, therefore, it needs to be recorded at fair value. Assume that the futures contract trades at ₹3200, while the spot price of oil is ₹3050.

There would be a loss of ₹20,000 on the derivative, which is MTM, and a gain of ₹15,000 on the asset, whose fair value in the book of accounts has gone from the initial spot price of ₹2900 to the present spot price of ₹3050. In aggregate, the loss would be ₹5000, as can be seen from the following entries:

Dr	Profit and loss account	200 × 100	20,000
	Cr Derivative account	200 × 100	20,000
Dr	Inventory account	150 × 100	15,000
	Cr Profit and loss account	150 × 100	15,000

The fair value of the inventory would rise by the difference between the spot price of oil on the day of initiating the hedge and that on the reporting date, i.e., ₹150 per barrel. Note that the value of the inventory would not change if historical cost valuation was followed. Under hedge accounting, the asset too would have to be recorded at fair value. The position in the derivative too would be marked to market on the reporting date. The short position when marked to market would show a loss of ₹20,000, being the difference in the present futures price from that on the date of inception of the hedge.

The net impact of such accounting would be recognition of the MTM loss of ₹5000, comprising an increase in the liability of ₹20,000 and an increase in the value of the asset of ₹15,000. Now, the derivative position stands at ₹3200 per barrel and inventory valuation is ₹3050 per barrel.

On the Day of Square-up or Disposal of Inventory The hedge would be lifted in case the position in the futures is squared up (no hedging instrument would exist), or when the inventory is disposed off (no hedging item would exist). Assuming a futures price of ₹3180 and a spot price of ₹3150 when the futures is squared up (with the inventory still existing), the following accounting entries would result:

Dr	Derivative account	200 × 100	20,000
Dr	Inventory account	100 × 100	10,000
	Cr Profit and loss account	120 × 100	12,000
	Cr Bank	180 × 100	18,000

The fair value of the inventory would rise by another ₹10,000 because of an increase in the valuation rate from ₹3050 to ₹3150. The liability on account of the futures position would be extinguished with payment to the exchange of ₹18,000, being the difference between the sold position at the rate of ₹3000 and the bought position at ₹3180 per barrel for 100 barrels. There would be a profit of ₹12,000.

With hedge accounting, the position of the oil inventory and the oil futures would be split into two reporting periods. The overall impact would remain the same, as highlighted in Table 24.3.

Table 24.3 Impact of fair value hedge   *Figures in ₹*

Hedged item /instrument	Aggregate	In the current accounting year	In the previous accounting year
On inventory of oil	25,000 100 × (3,150 − 2,900)	10,000 100 × (3,150 − 3,050)	15,000 100 × (3,050 − 2,900)
On futures position	−18,000 100 × (3,180 − 3,000)	2000 100 × (3,200 − 3,180)	−20,000 100 × (3,200 − 3,000)
TOTAL	7,000	12,000	−5,000

Derivative as Cash Flow Hedge

To see how a cash flow hedge works and is accounted for, let us consider the following situation:

- In January, the firm estimates that 100 barrels of crude oil would be required in July. At current prices, the value would be ₹2,90,000, with a spot price of ₹2900 per barrel.
- The inventory is expected to be purchased in July. Prices in July are expected to be more than ₹2900.
- A July futures contract for crude oil is trading at ₹3000 per barrel.
- The firm buys a July futures contract at ₹3000 to hedge against any fall in the oil price by July, and locks-in a price of ₹3000.
- The inventory of oil is designated as the hedged item and the futures contract is designated as the hedging instrument.
- Since the future cash flow for acquisition of the asset (inventory) is being protected with a position in a futures contract, it qualifies for hedge accounting, and is a cash flow hedge.

On Initiation of Long Position Upon initiation of a long position in futures again, no entries would be passed, assuming no margin and no transaction cost. Any transaction cost may be expensed out, and the margin money would create a receivable in the margin account, with an equivalent decline in the cash position. The fair value of the derivative position is the cost of acquiring the position.

On Intervening Reporting Date On 31 March, the fair value would be reassessed and shown in the balance sheet, and any profit or loss would be recognized in the income statement. Assume that the futures price is ₹3200 and the spot price has risen to ₹3050. The following entries would result on 31 March:

Dr	Derivative account	200 × 100	20,000
	Cr Hedging reserve account	200 × 100	20,000

There is no asset that is being hedged, and, therefore, there would be no accounting for the prospective asset. It is a future transaction only that is being hedged. Only a long position on the futures contract when marked to market would show a receivable and increase in reserve of ₹20,000, each being the difference between the futures prices on the date of inception of the hedge and on the date of reporting. Note that any change in the fair value is routed through the equity account in a cash flow hedge and not through the profit and loss account.

On the Day of Square-up or Acquisition of Inventory The hedge would be lifted in case the position in the futures is squared up (no hedging instrument would exist) or when the inventory is acquired (no hedging item would exist). In case further protection of the inventory is felt necessary, a fair value hedge can be initiated afresh. Assuming a futures price of ₹3180 and a spot price of ₹3150 when the futures is squared up and the inventory acquired, the following accounting entries would result:

For extinguishing the asset created by the derivative position, by receipt of cash:

Dr	Hedging reserve account	200 × 100	2,000
Dr	Bank	180 × 100	18,000
	Cr Derivative account	200 × 100	20,000

Here, the hedging reserve account is debited rather than the income statement, since the hedge is determined to be effective. The change in value of the hedging instrument is ₹18,000 and the change in value of the forecast transaction is ₹15,000 (the difference between the expected price of ₹3000 and the actual price of ₹3150 for 100 barrels), which is within 80% of one and 125% of the other. Had this not been true, the excess amount would have been debited to the profit and loss account.

For acquiring inventory (the forecast transaction) by actual flow of cash:

Dr	Inventory	3,150 × 100	3,15,000
	Cr Bank	3,150 × 100	3,15,000

For valuing inventory at the hedged amount by actual flow of cash:

Dr	Hedging reserve account	18,000	3,15,000
	Cr Inventory	18,000	3,15,000

The value of the inventory upon acquisition would be ₹2,97,000. If the hedge were perfect, the value would have been ₹3,00,000. The difference has occurred due to the basis risk inherent in futures.

The hedging reserve account is adjusted to the lesser of the following absolute amounts:
- The cumulative gain/loss on the hedging instrument from the inception of the hedge
- The cumulative change in present value of the forecast cash flow on the hedged item

The liability on account of the futures position would be extinguished with payment to the exchange of ₹18,000, which is the difference between the sold position at a rate of ₹3000 and the bought position at ₹3180 per barrel for 100 barrels.

CONCLUSION

The AS 30 has ushered in a new era in accounting. It is an attempt to reconcile the accounting process to the conceptual approach of finance. The accounting standard has far reaching implications, and would require several modifications in the accounting standards issued in the past. They relate to the rules for recognizing assets and liabilities in the books of accounts, their measurement, and the treatment of profit and loss on transactions relating to financial assets and liabilities. It may warrant significant changes in accounting practices, so much so that some parts of the accounting standard may have to be re-written. It involves changes to old practices that are firmly rooted in traditional accounting concepts.

Besides causing a rethink of past accounting practices, the AS 30 in itself (as well as IAS 39 and FAS 33) is too complex and leaves many holes. For example, can barrier options form a hedging instrument? A knock-in option for which a premium has been paid has not become alive because the barrier has not been touched. Similarly, a knock-out option may expire upon reaching the barrier, and the hedge becomes ineffective. All the issues starting from the definition of assets, the designations of hedging instruments and hedged items, the establishment of a hedge relationship, and the measurement of hedge effectiveness leave sufficient scope for ambiguities, convenience of interpretation, and use of discretion.

SUMMARY

Accounting for derivatives is not as simple as for other routine business transactions of sale, purchase, and expense. Derivative contracts are different in nature because they require no/marginal cash flows, and commitments are large and contingent in nature because more often than not the contracts are cash settled. Accounting recognizes transactions that have already occurred, and does not recognize forecast transactions. The AS 30, issued by the Institute of Chartered Accountants of India, which has come into vogue, prescribes accounting treatment for derivatives. Its prescriptions are on the same lines as the international practices contained in IAS 39 and FAS 133.

The AS 30 defines derivatives on the basis of futurity, origination, and investment. It also categorizes financial instruments in four classes—FaFV, HTM investments, loans and advances, and those available for sale. This classification is done for prescribing the values at which financial instruments would be recorded, and for how profits and losses would be accounted for. Further, it facilitates decisions on what can be hedged and what cannot. The FaFV are recorded at fair value and gains/losses on revaluation are routed through the profit and loss account. The HTM investments are intended to be held till maturity. Loans and advances have fixed and determinable cash flows that are not quoted, such as payables and receivables, and are recorded at invoice value. All remaining assets are classified as available for sale.

Derivatives would be recorded at fair value, and the accounting treatment for gains/losses would depend upon whether they are held for trading or are used for hedging. The fair value is the amount that an asset or liability would be exchanged for between knowledgeable and willing parties. In either case (trading or hedging), they would be marked to market on each reporting date. If held for trading, MTM gains/losses would be recognized in the profit and loss account. If they form part of a hedge, then the MTM item would be clubbed with the hedged item.

When an active market exists, the measurement of fair value is easy. In the absence of active markets, alternative methods of arm's length price, discounted cash flow techniques, or other valuation models may be used. Even in these measurements, the most reliance must be placed on inputs that are market determined.

Hedge accounting is central to the AS 30. It is concerned with presenting cumulative changes in the fair values of hedging instruments, derivatives, and hedged items. Hedge accounting would depend upon the type of hedge. There are two types of hedge—the fair value hedge and the cash flow hedge. Foreign currency exposures are classified and can be treated as either of the two. Under a fair value hedge, the changes in the fair values of derivatives and hedged instruments are cumulated and routed through the profit and loss account. Under a cash flow hedge, the cumulated changes in the fair value are adjusted in an equity account to the extent of the effective portion, while the ineffective portion is charged to the revenue account.

The basic prerequisites to qualify for hedge accounting are very onerous and involve establishing a hedging relationship between the item being hedged and the hedging instrument being used. There are rules regarding what instruments can be designated as hedging instruments and what can be hedged items. Further, in the case of a cash flow hedge, the measurement of effectiveness of the hedge too has to be documented.

The HTM investment cannot be categorized as hedged items for interest rates or prepayment risks. A writing option or a net written position cannot be a hedging instrument because the writing option assumes an extremely risky position for earning a small premium. A long position in options is a hedging instrument. A combination of derivatives can be designated as a hedging instrument because the risk in one derivative may be annulled by another. A hedging relationship and hedging effectiveness have to be demonstrated at the inception of the hedge.

A fair value hedge takes a comprehensive view of gains and losses on the designated hedged item and hedging instrument, both of which are recorded at fair value and market to market. The net position of gains and losses in fair value is charged to the profit and loss account. For a cash flow hedge, the changes in the cash flow have to be segregated into two—the effective portion and remaining ineffective portion. The effective portion is accounted for in the equity account, while the ineffective portion is charged to the profit and loss account.

KEY TERMS

Cash flow hedge A hedge that protects against changes in the cash flows attributable to a particular risk of a recognized asset/liability or a highly probable forecast transaction.

Derivative A derivative is a financial instrument
- whose value changes with the interest rate, the price of the financial instrument, the foreign exchange rate, the index, its credit rating, etc.;
- that requires no/very little net initial investment; and
- that is settled at a future date.

Fair value The amount at which an asset could be exchanged or a liability settled between knowledgeable, willing parties in an arm's length transaction.

Fair value hedge A hedge that protects against changes in the fair value that are attributable to a particular risk.

Financial instrument at fair value through profit and loss Instruments that are held for trading and initially recognized at their fair values.

Hedge accounting Hedge accounting permits clubbing of gains/losses of fair values or cash flows of hedged items and designated hedge instruments.

Held for trading Financial instruments that are held for the purpose of making speculative profits through changes in the values of these instruments.

Held-to-maturity Investment It is a non-derivative financial asset with fixed and determinable payments at fixed maturity.

Net written option A combination of options at inception involving a sold position, in such a way that it results in a cash inflow.

QUESTIONS

24.1 What is the definition of derivatives as per the AS 30, and why do you think they have been defined in a generic way?
24.2 What do you understand by hedge accounting?
24.3 Describe a fair value hedge and a cash flow hedge.
24.4 What is the basic difference between a fair value hedge and a cash flow hedge?
24.5 What do you understand by (a) a hedged item, (b) a hedging instrument, and (c) a hedging relationship?
24.6 What is the reason that a short position in option cannot be designated as a hedging instrument?
24.7 Illustrate with an example how you would account for a derivative when it is used as (a) a speculation product, (b) a fair value hedge, and (c) a cash flow hedge.
24.8 What radical changes in the AS 30 have been made with regard to the recognition of financial assets and liabilities in the balance sheet and the treatment of gains/losses in values?

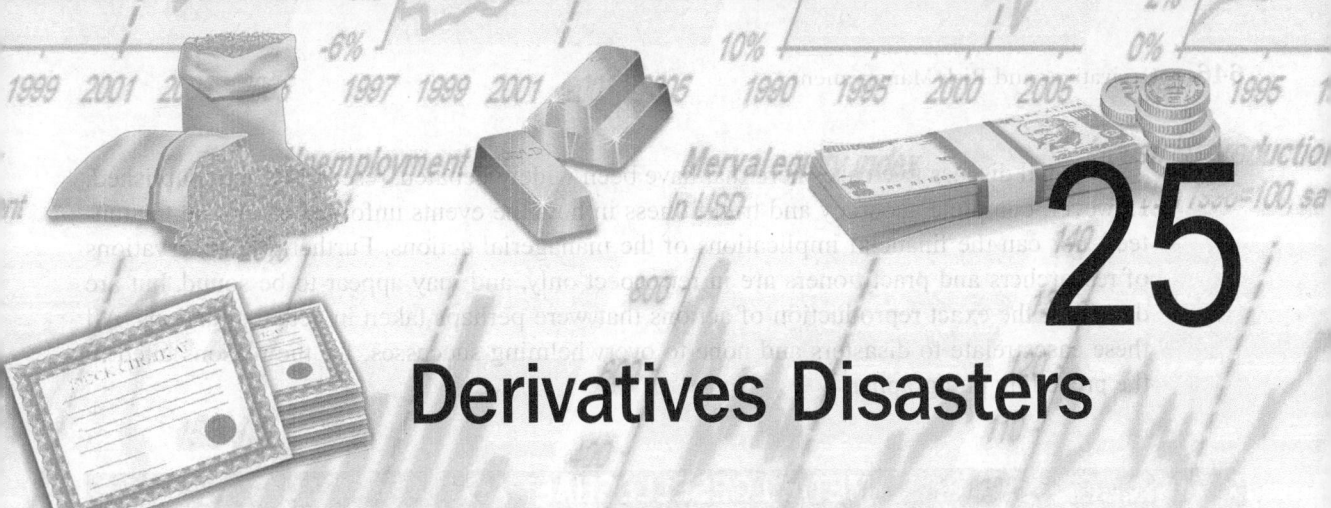

25

Derivatives Disasters

INTRODUCTION

In this chapter, we look at some of the most publicized cases involving huge losses in derivative transactions. These cases help to understand the complex nature of the subject. Transactions in derivatives do not become a matter of common knowledge or come into the public domain, partly because of the tendency of people to not disclose actual positions when they are fraught with risk and partly because of the fact that they avoid conventional accounting. Cash transactions, even when they are not disclosed publicly, come to light when financial statements are prepared, presented, and made public.

Success stories in derivative trading do not come into the limelight because of the confidentiality maintained. Of late, there has been increasing concern about the proportion of 'other income' in the profits of various firms. This income is suspected to be emanating from derivative trading, albeit in the name of hedging. However, they do not make headlines. On the contrary, when firms make huge losses that seemingly are not related to their core activities, they make headlines for the wrong reasons.

Though there are many instances of huge losses in derivative trading in history, the actual processes leading to these losses are rarely disclosed. People often wonder how such huge losses suddenly come to light one single day, and why such losses never got reported as they were accumulating. This phenomenon is due to the basic nature of derivatives, where exposures only remain notional and liabilities remain contingent. Only when the contingent liabilities get crystallized do they become topics of public debate and scrutiny. Since notional transactions remain under wraps, very little becomes known about the actual processes behind such mishaps. It is left to analysts, who use their wild imagination to speculate on these processes.

Learning Outcomes

- how derivative transactions remain unreported
- why controls and reporting of derivative transactions are important
- how supervisors ignore day-to-day actions of subordinates that could be threatening

We shall discuss five cases here that have been widely debated, researched, and published. However, complete accuracy and truthfulness in how the events unfolded cannot be guaranteed, nor can the financial implications of the managerial actions. Further, the observations of researchers and practitioners are in retrospect only, and may appear to be sound, but are devoid of the exact reproduction of actions that were perhaps taken in actual situations. All these cases relate to disasters and none to overwhelming successes, for the reasons cited in the preceding paragraphs.

METALLGESELLSCHAFT AG
An Intelligent Hedging Programme That Went Awry

Metallgesellschaft AG, (MG), a German conglomerate is owned largely by Deutsche Bank AG, Dresdner Bank AG, Daimler-Benz, Allianz, and the Kuwait Investment Authority. It was amongst the largest corporations in Germany in 1993. Founded in 1883, MG had 58,000 employees and 251 subsidiaries across the world. Its businesses were related to mining, metal, and energy.

In 1993 and early 1994, MG incurred losses of $1.3 billion on futures trading equal to about 50% of its capital at that time. It was saved by a bailout package of $1.9 billion raised by a consortium of banks that were its house banks. Only the massive rescue operation of this large banking consortium kept MG from bankruptcy.

Metallgesellschaft Refining and Marketing Inc. (MGRM) was a US subsidiary of MG in charge of refining and marketing petroleum products in the USA. MGRM's expanded venture into the derivatives world began in 1991 with the hiring of Mr Arthur Benson from Louis Dreyfus Energy.

In December 1993, MG was effectively bankrupt after huge losses in the oil business that was conducted in MGRM, its New York-based subsidiary.

THE CONTRACT

The roots of the crises lay in the marketing strategy of MGRM.

In 1992, MGRM began implementing an aggressive marketing programme in which it offered long-term price guarantees on deliveries of gasoline, heating oil, and diesel fuels for up to five or ten years to its customers, both wholesalers and retailers. The same price was offered without considering the time value of the credit. The scheme had two novel contracts —a 'firm-fixed' programme, under which a customer agreed to take monthly deliveries of fixed quantities at fixed prices, and a 'firm-flexible' contract that did specify a fixed price and the total volume of future deliveries and also gave the customer some flexibility in setting delivery schedules.

Under the firm-flexible system, a customer could request 20% of its contracted volume for any one year with a 45-day notice. By September 1993, MGRM had committed to sell forward the equivalent of over 150 million barrels of oil for delivery at fixed prices, with most contracts for terms of 10 years. These contracts also contained an 'option' that enabled the counterparties to terminate the contracts early if the front month futures contract of the

New York Mercantile Exchange (NYMEX) was greater than the fixed price at which MGRM was selling the oil products. If the buyer exercised this option, MGRM would be required to pay in cash one half of the difference between the futures price and the fixed price multiplied by the total volume remaining to be delivered under the contract. Under the firm-flexible contract, the compensation was 100% of the price difference.

The MGRM provided its customers with a means that enabled them to shift or eliminate some of their oil price risks. These contracts initially proved to be very successful since they guaranteed a price over the spot price, and the sales of MGRM tripled.

HEDGING PROGRAMME

With a short position in the forward contracts, MG was exposed to the risk of rising prices of oil. If prices rose, MG would incur a loss on the forward deliveries committed under the contracts.

The short position is offset by a long position in futures. MGRM's hedge strategy to manage the spot price risk was to use the front-end month futures contracts of NYMEX. Since the liquidity of distant futures contracts is poor, MGRM chose to cover the risk by taking a long position in stacks of short-dated futures and then rolling them for the next stack of futures. This would be done repeatedly. Such a strategy is referred to as a *stack-and-roll* hedging strategy.

Covering for the entire deliverable quantity in the future, the rollover would stand reduced by the deliveries already made. Each rollover for a month would be lessened by the amount of deliveries already made during the month.

The MGRM also entered into over-the-counter (OTC) energy swap agreements to receive floating and pay fixed energy prices. According to the NYMEX, MGRM held futures positions on the equivalent of 55 million barrels of oil in different oil products such as gasoline, crude oil, and heating oil. The futures contracts MGRM used to hedge were those on unleaded gasoline and the No. 2 heating oil. Of the total commitment of about 160 million barrels (assuming that MGRM hedged fully), their swap positions may have accounted for as much as 110 million barrels to completely hedge their commitments under the forward contracts.

MGRM's hedges adequately transferred its market risk. When oil prices dropped, they lost money on their hedge positions but the value of their forward contracts increased. If oil prices increased, they would gain on the futures and compensate for losses in the forward delivery-based contracts.

PROBLEMS

What appeared to be safe and sound promotional programmes bolstered by a seemingly foolproof hedging strategy, had many deficiencies. We address them one by one as they surfaced over time:

Size of the Exposure

The sheer size of the positions both in forward and futures contracts created an enormous amount of risk. The assumption of economies of scale was mistaken. According to an estimate, this position was the equivalent of 85 days' worth of the entire oil output of Kuwait. If oil prices were to drop, MGRM would lose money on their hedge positions and would receive huge margin calls on their enormous futures positions. The positions of MGRM in futures included about 55,000 contracts, against a daily market volume of 15,000–30,000 contracts. To liquidate its futures positions completely, MGRM would require anywhere between 30 and 45 days. The liquidation of the huge number of positions in itself would have been a big problem, in case such a need did arise. In essence, MGRM was a market maker rather than a small market participant, and failed to recognize that its impact cost would be too high and would defy the normal behaviour of prices.

Hedge Ratio and Mismatch of Positions and Timings

The MGRM employed a naive hedge ratio of 1:1 without concern for deliveries under its forward contracts. Against a future supply of 150–160 million barrels spread over a period of 10 years, monthly deliveries were of the order of 1.2–1.3 million barrels. This entailed a mismatched maturity and quantity structure.

Under futures, hedge price risk gets replaced by a much smaller basis risk. The basis risk is the difference between the price of the instrument and the price of the underlying asset being hedged. Hedgers in the futures market are said to be 'speculators on basis'. In terms of aggregate delivery, the sizes in the forwards and the futures did match, but considered from the viewpoint of monthly delivery schedules, the positions in futures were 120 times the forward positions. Thus, MGRM was exposed to an excessive quantum of basis risk (about 120 times its physical positions). Therefore, variations in the value of the short-dated futures positions were not compensated by equal and opposite variations in the value of the long-dated delivery contracts because of the one-for-one hedges entailed. One barrel of oil for delivery in one month is simply not equal in present value to one barrel of oil for delivery in 10 years, and the values of two obligations of different dates do not move in lock step.

Marked-to-market and Cash Flow Mismatch

Another problem MGRM encountered was the timing of cash flows required to maintain the hedge. Over the entire life of the hedge, these cash flows would have balanced out. Due to the mismatch of delivery positions in the forward and the futures, the profit/loss in the futures would be 120 times the loss/profit in the forwards, even though they tended to cancel out over the entire period of 10 years. MG's problem was the lack of the necessary funds needed, to maintain their position in futures that are marked-to-market (MTM) in case oil prices dropped. If prices increased, the futures would have a positive cash flow for MG that would far exceed the losses in the forwards. However, if prices declined, the negative cash flow would be massive, and would far outweigh the gains in the forwards.

Given the fact that this risk management strategy did play a key role in acquiring business pursuant to their corporate objectives, the management should have obtained a complete understanding of the strategy. The MGRM followed a textbook hedging strategy that was not properly understood by its supervisory board and house banks. The MGRM placed the entire hedge in short-dated delivery months rather than spreading this amount over many, longer-dated delivery months, because the call options were tied to front-month futures contracts at the NYMEX. Studies have demonstrated the effectiveness of using stacked hedging. MGRM's strategy was sound from an economic standpoint.

A rolling stack of short-dated futures initially increases the variance of the cash flows. This occurs because movements in the price of oil within a month create losses or gains for the entire stack of contracts. These losses or gains must be settled by the end of the month, while compensations for gains or losses on deliveries are realized only gradually over the remaining part of the 10–year tenure of the delivery contract. When cash flows matter, the rolling stack may be worse than no hedge at all. It was the realized losses through MTM against the unrealized gains in forwards that caused a massive fund outflow that was beyond the means of MG.

From Backwardation to Contango

Oil prices decreased and futures went in contango because the Organization of the Petroleum Exporting Countries (OPEC) had problems in holding its quota. Oil prices started falling and fell about 33% in 1993. In the particular case of crude oil, the backwardation can be considered the market's judgement that OPEC's cartel pricing was unsustainable over the long run, and prices would someday collapse. As OPEC managers became deadlocked on reaching production quotas in late 1993, the spot price tumbled in accordance with the expectations reflected in the inverted market, and oil markets moved from backwardation to a strong carry.

In the oil futures market, the spot price is normally greater than the futures price due to convenience yield. When this occurs, the market is said to be in backwardation. When futures markets are in backwardation, the rolling over of a long hedge would result in cash inflow. The rollover of a long position into a new contract would come at a lesser value than the contract just settled. However, if the market is in contango, the rollover would result in a cash outflow. The issue of contango compounded MG's crisis. Since MGRM was long on futures with its *stack-and-roll* strategy, the contango market created rollover losses that were indeed unrecoverable. The MGRM entered into 'stacked' futures positions in the front-month contracts and then rolled its position forward at the expiration of each contract.

In the contango market, the spot price decreased more than the futures prices. As long as the market stayed in contango, MGRM continued to lose on the rollover. The contango market compounded MGRM's problem, but their real problem was created by their inability to handle the cash flow problems created by the drop in oil prices, in conjunction with the huge volume of futures contracts that they entered into.

The fall in price meant losses in the long futures position, while the market turning from backwardation to contango meant losses on the rollovers. It was the fall in price that caused the cash flow crisis, and the contango markets compounded it. If the market had stayed in normal backwardation, MGRM would actually have picked up a gain on the rollover of their hedge positions. MGRM's rollover gains turned into rollover losses. The rollover loss that resulted from the contango market was the only real economic loss suffered by MGRM. By this, we mean that the rollover loss was unrecoverable and was not offset by another position.

The rollover risk that the oil market might go into contango should have been factored into the price of the call options within MGRM's forward fixed-rate contracts. The contango market simply meant that the market was at full carry. The contango market did not make their hedge a bad hedge. It simply compounded their cash flow crunch.

US and German Accounting Methodologies

Accounting also created some problems for MG, which was a German firm, and MGRM, which was incorporated in the USA. They were governed by different sets of accounting rules and practices. German accounting standards compounded MG's problems, while US accounting permitted hedge accounting. German standards followed the rules of *lower of cost or market* (LCM) accounting. In the USA, MGRM met the requirements of a hedge and used permitted hedge accounting, under which forwards and futures positions could be combined. Therefore, in the USA, MGRM actually showed the net position of its short forwards and its long futures. It could be a minor loss or a minor profit because of netting. Their hedge losses were deferred because they could offset the gains of their forward fixed rate positions. Using LCM in Germany, MG was required to book its current losses but could not recognize gains on their fixed-rate forward positions until they were realized. Since German accounting standards did not allow for the netting of positions, MG's income statement in Germany presented a dismal picture and bleak outlook. As such, their credit rating came under scrutiny, and the financial community speculated on the demise of MG.

This drastically changed the market arena for MGRM. Their swap counterparties required additional capital to maintain their swap positions. On the contrary, NYMEX imposed super-margin requirements on MGRM, more than doubling their performance bond requirement. This further constrained the cash position. MG would have to either meet its MTM requirements through an additional drain on its financial resources or liquidate its futures positions. If hedge accounting were acceptable in Germany, MGRM's positions would not have alarmed the market place, and they might have been able to reduce their positions in the OTC market without getting their eyeballs pulled out.

The timing of margin calls could not have been worse. MG in Germany was passing through a bad phase in business, and was forced to sell some assets and reduce manpower to meet its liquidity crisis. As it is, the company planned to skip any dividend issue too. Without adequate funding in case of immediate margin calls, this seemingly sound strategy becomes reckless.

In view of the huge cash drain on account of MTM, MG had no option but to lift the futures hedge. Now the forward position was unhedged, and was prone to the risk of price rise. Unfortunately this is precisely what happened. All the ground lost in 1993 was made up for in the next year. Had MGRM continued with the futures hedge, it would have paid back the cash flows lost in MTM. To make things worse, it was now its turn to lose on the forward contracts.

The MGRM accounted for such a great percentage of the total open interest on the NYMEX that liquidation of their position was problematic. MGRM's hedge adequately transferred its market risk. When oil prices dropped, they lost money on their hedge positions but the value of their forward contracts increased. The MGRM exposed itself to funding risk by entering into these positions. In that sense, they were speculating. They were speculating by entering into medium-term fixed-rate forward positions totaling approximately 160 million barrels of oil. The sheer size of this position created an enormous amount of risk.

THE OUTCOME

MG's losses in the futures and swaps markets have raised questions about whether MG was really hedging or speculating. The hedging strategy of MG has been widely debated. On the one hand, it is repeatedly argued that the 1:1 hedge strategy of MGRM was a basically sound strategy. On the other hand, Edwards and Canter, Mello and Parsons, and Ross argue that a 1:1 hedge strategy was significantly oversized, given MGRM's underlying oil business.

When news of MG's losses began to leak to the public, it was rumoured that the company had speculated, betting that oil prices would rise. If it was hedging, as initially reported in the press, it would be indifferent to changes in the prices. The MGRM was not indifferent to the direction of oil price movements because it was engaged in an indirect hedge of its forward positions. The enormous losses it incurred did not result from its naked futures positions, in which MGRM gambled that the price of oil would rise. The position was more complex than that. MGRM's futures and swaps positions were hedges of the medium-term fixed-rate oil products they had sold forward. The hedge scenarios were as follows: if oil prices dropped, the hedge lost money and the fixed-rate positions increased in value. If oil prices rose, the hedge gains offset the fixed-rate position losses. A hedge is supposed to transfer market risk, not increase it. If this were a hedge, as we have proposed, we must answer the question: how did MG lose over $1 billion?

While a financial crisis of MG's magnitude is rare, the nature of their losses is becoming more frequent in the financial marketplace. Are derivatives the cause of these unexpected losses that seem to commonly blindside companies? Every few weeks, we hear about a new company that lost money either speculating in the derivatives market or lacking an understanding of a hedge position they entered into. As the derivatives markets continue to grow, we will continue to hear of losses.

MG's disaster in the oil markets should be seen as a reminder to the corporate community to understand the nature of positions in the financial markets and to understand the ramifications of market movements on financial positions.

At the same time, it should not be seen as a warning sign to corporate CFO's to stay away from the derivatives markets. These markets provide tremendous value to their users. The swaps and futures markets provided MGRM with an opportunity to transfer its market risk. It successfully did this, but failed, however, to accurately estimate the funding risk of its hedge position.

Critics assert that MGRM's strategy exposed it to three significant and related risks: rollover risk, funding risk, and credit risk, because of the maturity mismatch between the hedge and the delivery contracts and other features. It was exposed to rollover risk because of uncertainty about whether it would sustain gains or losses when rolling its derivative positions forward. It was exposed to funding risk because of the MTM conventions that applied to its short-dated derivative positions. It was exposed to credit risk because its forward delivery counterparties might default on their long-dated obligations to purchase oil at fixed prices. If energy prices fell, this risk is expected to increase because of the increase in the difference between contractual prices and prevailing spot prices. To minimize the credit risk, MGRM limited the annual volume supplied under a contract to no more than 20% of the customer's needs, and included in the contracts a cash-out option. It could, however, be a factor in MGRM's ability to raise funds against the collateral of these contracts.

By January, the firm was close to declaring bankruptcy and its future was unclear. The MG eventually negotiated a $1.9 billion bailout from its bankers in tandem with a plan to shed assets such as its auto parts manufacturing business, its tin mining operations, its recently acquired heating equipment, and others. The price of MG shares fell by half between November 1993 and February 1994 as a consequence. The MGRM exposed itself to funding risk by entering into these positions.

BARINGS PLC
The Earthquake That Crumbled the Old Strong Edifice

Another highly publicized case of derivatives-linked losses relates to Barings PLC, largely due to a single person named Nick Leeson, who unmindfully carried on with unauthorized loss-making trades in derivatives and succeeded in fooling the bank's management by ingenious accounting methods to convert those losses into profits.

Barings PLC was one of the oldest merchant banks in Great Britain. Founded in 1762, the bank had a long and distinguished history. Barings had helped a fledgling USA arrange the financing for the Louisiana Purchase in 1803. It had also helped Britain finance the Napoleonic Wars, a feat that prompted the British government to bestow five noble titles on the Baring family. Despite not being in the list of largest banks, with equity of only £440 million, it was an extremely respected and reputed bank that enjoyed the patronage of an elite clientele, including the royal family of England.

Barings had long enjoyed a reputation as a conservatively run institution. However, that reputation was shattered on 24 February 1995, when Peter Baring, the bank's chairman, contacted the Bank of England to explain that a trader in the firm's Singapore futures subsidiary had lost huge sums of money speculating on NIKKEI 225 stock index futures and options. In the days that followed, investigators found that the bank's total losses exceeded US $1 billion, a sum large enough to bankrupt the institution.[1]

Barings had almost failed once before in 1890, after losing millions in loans to Argentina, but it was rescued then by a consortium led by the Bank of England. A similar effort was mounted in February 1995 but the attempt failed when no immediate buyer could be found, and the Bank of England refused to assume liability for Barings' losses. On the evening of Sunday, 26 February 1995, the Bank of England took action to place Barings in administration, a legal proceeding resembling the Chapter 11 bankruptcy-court proceedings in the USA. The crisis brought about by Barings' insolvency ended just over one week later when a large Dutch financial conglomerate, the Internationale Nederlanden Groep (ING), assumed the assets and liabilities of the failed merchant bank for a token sum of £1.

Dual Role

In 1992, Barings sent Nicholas Leeson, a clerk from its London office, to manage the back-office accounting and settlement operations at its Singapore futures subsidiary, Baring

---
[1] Anatoli Kuprianov Federal, Derivatives Debacles; Case Studies of Large Losses in Derivatives Markets by Reserve Bank of Richmond *Economic Quarterly* Volume 81/4 Fall 1995.

Futures (Singapore) (BFS). Soon, Leeson passed Singapore International Monetary Exchange (SIMEX) examinations that made him eligible to trade on the floor of the exchange. Leeson was made the general manager and head trader of BFS.

Nick Leeson now had a dual role to discharge—one as the in-charge of settlement operations; reporting to Gordon Bowser and Mike Killian, Head Global Futures and Options sales in London, and the other as floor manager on SIMEX, reporting to the Singapore office to its Managing Director, and Simon Jones, Director Finance. This dual reporting led to disinterest in his superiors in exercising supervisory control over the activities of Nick Leeson.

Though supposed to trade NIKKEI 225 futures on behalf of Barings' clients on SIMEX, he was also allowed to conduct proprietary trades for Barings. The NIKKEI 225 futures contract is a bundle of stocks that are equal in proportion to the stocks that make up the Tokyo Stock Exchange's NIKKEI 225 stock average. The value of futures is derived from the NIKKEI 225 average.

Switching

The NIKKEI 225 was traded on SIMEX and the Osaka Stock Exchange (OSE). At times, price discrepancies existed on the two exchanges, and in order to take advantage, Barings would allow arbitrage transactions that were hedged. If the NIKKEI 225 futures traded at a higher price at the OSE than at the SIMEX, the arbitrage transaction would comprise selling NIKKEI 225 at the OSE and buying it at the SIMEX. When the prices corrected, Barings would unwind its positions in the two exchanges. This strategy, referred to as *switching,* gave assured but limited profit. Barings had been using the conservative approach in line with its tradition of undertaking hedged transactions only on its own account.

Nick Leeson was allowed to avail of arbitrage opportunities on NIKKEI futures listed in Tokyo, the OSE, and the SIMEX. The strategy of *switching* was to hedge a position in one exchange with an opposite position in another in respect of all proprietary positions to contain risk. Unhedged trades were allowed for Leeson to the very limited extent of the following levels:

1. 200 NIKKEI futures contracts
2. 100 Japanese bond contracts
3. 500 euroyen futures contracts

Unauthorised Trading and Misrepresenting Accounts

Leeson, however, embarked upon a much riskier trading strategy. Rather than remaining confined to *switching,* as Barings' management had permitted, he began placing bets on the direction of price movements on the Tokyo stock exchange. From the beginning itself, the bets proved wrong, and Leeson started making losses.

On 3 July 1992, an account with the number 88888 was created as an error account. Leeson asked his technical computer personnel to modify the software so that trades, prices, and positions were not reported to the London office, and only margin balances were reported. Having worked in London, Leeson knew that only the trade and prices of positions were downloaded in the internal reporting system of Barings, and margin balances were ignored by the London office.

The London office had allotted code 99002 as the account for the Singapore trades, but Leeson kept on trading in 88888. For cross trades, i.e., buy and sell transactions from the same firms, the London office allotted account 92000 (Barings Securities [Japan] Govt Bond Arbitrage account); account 98007 (Barings Securities [London] Govt Bond Arbitrage account); account 98008 (euroyen arbitrage) to satisfy the requirement of the SIMEX. Leeson would ask the staff to break down transactions in many lots and record them in the Barings accounts at prices higher than those he had paid on SIMEX, hence showing profits. Gains in these three accounts also resulted in losses that were buried in 88888.

Leeson ignored hedging/switching tactics, and went long on both the OSE and the SIMEX. By doing so, he was exposed to twice the risk he would have faced in being hedged if the markets fell.

The Trap of Losses

By the end of 1992, i.e., just a few months after he began trading, Leeson had accumulated a hidden loss of £2 million. He used his position in the back office to hide the losses. In September 1992, he debited money from a Barings receivables account at Citibank and credited it to 88888 to hide the trading losses in that account. The loss figure remained unchanged until October 1993, when his losses again began to rise sharply. He lost another £21 million in 1993 and £185 million in 1994. The cumulative losses at the end of 1994 stood at £208 million.

However, his reported trading profits were spectacular. The bank's senior management regarded him as a star performer. In fact, the loss of £208 million was slightly larger than the £205 million profit reported by the Barings Group as a whole, before accounting for taxes and for £102 million in scheduled bonuses.

Sometime in 1994, Leeson began selling large numbers of option straddles, a strategy that involved the simultaneous sale of calls and puts on the NIKKEI 225. The seller of an option straddle earns a profit only when the markets remain range bound, which Leeson thought would be so. The NIKKEI 225 had been trading in a very narrow range in the past. He was perhaps motivated to write options to earn some money to meet his large losses, as also the margin calls for the MTM losses on the futures position. Once Leeson lost, he kept doubling down to extricate himself from the situation. He did not hedge because to cover up the losses, he had to follow the first in first out (FIFO) principle in account 88888.

The Straddle

By 1 January 1995, Leeson was short on 37,925 NIKKEI calls and on 32,967 NIKKEI puts. He also held a long position of just over 1000 contracts in NIKKEI stock index futures, which would gain in value if the stock market were to rise. He sold straddles on the NIKKEI, hoping for range bound movements between 19,000 and 19,500. With a double long position in futures in the OSE and the SIMEX and the straddles, he was hoping that if the NIKKEI remained flat, he would pocket the straddle premium. If the index increased, the futures would give profits. He was already down £ 208 million by the end of 1994. It seemed to him to be the only way to recover. The only risk was if the NIKKEI moved down, when the futures and the straddles would both lose.

Kobe Earthquake

That was precisely what happened. Disaster struck on 17 January, when news of a violent earthquake in Kobe, Japan, sent the Japanese stock market into a tailspin. The NIKKEI went down to 18,950, making puts in-the-money. Over the next five days, the NIKKEI index fell over 1500 points, and Leeson's options positions sustained a loss of £68 million. The long futures positions lost, as did the put options. After the Kobe earthquake, Leeson believed the NIKKEI had over-reacted and was undervalued. Hence, he went additionally long on 10,814 NIKKEI futures contracts on 20 January to break even or even to make profits. On 20 January at the OSE, the NIKKEI lost 220 points and at the SIMEX, it lost 195. If Leeson were short on the SIMEX and long on the OSE, the loss would have been only 25 points. If it were the other way round, there would have been a profit of 25 points. With long positions in both the exchanges, however, the loss was 415 points.

This strategy seemed to work for a short time. By 6 February, the Japanese stock market had recovered by over 1000 points, making it possible for Leeson to recoup most of the losses resulting from the market's reaction to the earthquake. However, within days, the market began falling again, and Leeson's losses began to multiply. The NIKKEI went below 18,000 in mid-February 1995. He also placed a side bet on Japanese interest rates, selling Japanese government bond (JGB) futures by the thousands in the expectation of rising interest rates and falling bond prices. Market risk got coupled with event risk: the Kobe earthquake sent the NIKKEI down. It also increased volatility in the equity markets. The increase in volatility increased option prices.

He could not have squared up on the short straddles too. Even if he wanted to hedge, he could not do so. If he used official accounts, he had to establish huge positions. He could not hedge in 88888 because of the FIFO rule applied. One hedging strategy would be to liquidate all NIKKEI long and JGB and euroyen short. In that case, the unrealized loss would turn to realized loss.

The Exposure

Leeson did not believe that prices would crash further. He continued to increase his exposure as the market kept falling. By 23 February, Leeson had bought over 61,000 NIKKEI futures contracts, representing 49% of the total open interest in the March 1995 NIKKEI futures contracts, and 24% of the open interest in the June contracts. His position in JGB futures totalled up to just over 26,000 contracts sold, representing 88% of the open interest in the June 1995 contracts. Leeson also took on positions in euroyen futures. He began 1995 with long positions in euroyen contracts (a bet that Japanese interest rates would fall), but then switched to selling the contracts. By 23 February, he had accumulated a short position in euroyen futures, equivalent to 5% of the open interest in the June 1995 contracts and 1% of the open interest in both the September and December contracts.

Funding MTM Losses

The question that now arises is: with the futures showing MTM losses, how were the margin calls made good? Leeson was able to meet margin calls in Singapore because he convinced the London office to provide him easy access to funds, in view of the purported difficulties in raising money from Japanese banks in Singapore. The London office thought that though there were losses at the SIMEX, they were covered by the profits in the OSE, because they always believed that Leeson was doing *switching*. Possibly, given the compulsions of meeting margins coupled with the observation that the NIKKEI was range bound, Leeson decided to write straddles. Till February 1995, Nick Leeson was able to receive funds from London without being questioned about his ability to meet margin calls.

The Outcome

Barings faced massive margin calls as Leeson's losses mounted. While these margin calls raised eyebrows at the bank's London and Tokyo offices, they did not prompt an immediate inquiry into Leeson's activities. It was not until 6 February that the Barings group's treasurer, Tony Hawes, flew to Singapore to investigate irregularities in the accounts at BFS. Under the impression that liabilities in the SIMEX were matched by corresponding assets at the OSE, he assured the SIMEX that there would be no problem in meeting the huge liabilities. Only later was it learnt that Leeson had stand-alone positions, and no *switching* was done.

On 24–25 February, Leeson left Singapore with his wife and faxed his resignation to the Barings London office from a hotel in Kuala Lumpur, stating, in part, 'My sincere apologies for the predicament I have left you in. It was neither my intention nor aim for this to happen'. Leeson was later detained by authorities at the airport in Frankfort, Germany, and was extradited to Singapore the following November. In Singapore, Leeson pleaded guilty to charges of fraud, and was sentenced to a 6 1/2-year prison term.

The payment to be made to the SIMEX was $835 million (Barings had a capital of $615 million) led to bankruptcy. Accounts could not be reconciled, and it was discovered later that Leeson had lost astronomical sums of money.

Peter Baring, the bank's chairman, was forced to call the Bank of England to ask for assistance when he learnt of the bank's difficulties. Most of the cost of the Barings debacle was borne by its shareholders and by ING, the financial institution that bought Barings. Barings was a privately held firm; most of its equity was held by the Baring Foundation, a charity registered in the United Kingdom. Although ING was able to buy the failed merchant bank for a token amount of £1, it had to pay £660 million to recapitalize the firm. The SIMEX subsequently reported that the funds Barings had on deposit with the exchange were sufficient to meet the costs incurred in liquidating its positions. It is not known whether the OSE suffered any losses as a result of the Barings collapse.

Analysis

Several studies have been made analysing the causes of the debacle. Almost all of them converge with the opinion that lack of supervision largely contributed to the debacle at one of the world's oldest and most respected banks. Dual control created ambiguity in supervision between the London headquarters and the subsidiary in Singapore, a situation that Leeson seems to have taken great advantage of. Normally, the functions of trading and settlements are kept separate within an organization, as the head of settlements is expected to provide independent verification of the records of trading activity. However, Leeson was never relieved of his authority over the subsidiary's back-office operations when his responsibilities were expanded to include trading.

After Barings failed, however, investigators found that Leeson's reported profits had been fictitious from the start. His duties included the supervision of both trading and settlement activities for the Singapore subsidiary, and, therefore, Leeson was able to manufacture fictitious reports concerning his trading activities.

Some observers have also remarked that at the SIMEX and the OSE, which were fierce competitors, there were relaxations such as the position limits granted to Barings, the largest customer. Though exemptions on margins are granted on hedged positions and to esteemed customers, there was no effort by the SIMEX to crosscheck the offsetting positions with its rival exchange.

LONG TERM CAPITAL MANAGEMENT
The Risk Management Models That Crashed

Long Term Capital Management (LTCM) was a Connecticut-based hedge fund founded by John Meriwether—erstwhile Salomon Brothers executive—that started operations in 1994. Meriwether believed in strong analytics and academicians, and put together a management team that included Robert Merton and Myron Scholes, the Nobel laureate of the famous Black–Scholes Model (BSM), and David Mullins, who as vice chairman of the US Federal Reserve had helped to write the famous Brady report, which had investigated the 1987 stock market crash.

HEDGE FUNDS

Hedge funds are investment vehicles for wealthy investors that are largely unregulated, since they do not mobilize funds from the public like other financial institutions, pension funds, and mutual funds. Their investors are presumed to be sophisticated enough not to require the same protection as an average investor needs.

Hedge funds can invest in anything that is legal, with no limits on the amount of risk. The fees charged are high, and the managers of a successful fund are very well paid. However, the principals normally invest a substantial amount of their own wealth in their fund to align incentives, on the premise that the managers' incentives are better aligned when the fund managers are investors, too.

The first hedge fund was set up in 1949 by Alfred Winslow Jones. He used a strategy of selling short stocks that he considered to be overvalued and using the proceeds to buy stocks that he thought were cheap. A portfolio constructed in this manner would not be adversely affected by broad market movements, because losses on one side would be offset by profits on the other. In this way, the portfolio would be protected or hedged, hence the name 'hedge fund'.

Hedge funds operate without much publicity till they deliver noteworthy performance, good or bad. The only time they are in the news is when a large fund is involved in something dramatic, such as the case under study.

Another feature of hedge funds is the extraordinary leverage they have, and their extensive use of derivatives. The leverage multiplies gains as well as losses. In general, any investment restrictions are self-imposed. Hedge fund returns do not always move exactly the same way as those of the market as a whole, and this feature can be attractive to investors seeking additional diversification. Hedge funds also provide benefits to the financial system. Hedge funds are in the business of taking risk, and they can absorb the risks that other market participants wish to shed. Paradoxically, the very features of hedge funds that are beneficial to the system can be dangerous if taken to excess, to the extent that the stability of an entire financial system is threatened, leading to systemic risk due to the huge positions taken.

GROWTH OF LTCM

The stellar reputations of the firm's principals made it much easier for LTCM to raise money than if it was just another hedge fund. The LTCM was able to obtain cash from quasi-governmental agencies, and even the central bank of Italy invested US $250 million. LTCM had the target of raising US $2.5 billion in initial capital. The firm was able to raise US $1.25 billion, which was an unprecedented corpus in a new hedge fund.

Hedge fund charges are based on performance incentives as well as fees on asset size. As against the performance-based benchmark of 20% of the profit, LTCM's incentive was 25%, with an annual fee of 2% of the asset size, as against the industry norm of 1%.

The LTCM promised annual returns in excess of 30% to its investors, after adjusting for incentives and fees. For the first three years of its operations, the fund lived up to this promise. Its returns, net of fees and management charges, were around 40% for the two years 1995 and 1996, and slightly less than 20% in 1997.

THE STRATEGY

Hedge funds do not have any restrictions on the way they operate. They can adopt any profit-making strategy on offer in the market place. The key issues are risk appetite and the size of operations. They take advantage of global economic developments, capitalizing on event-driven opportunities like mergers and acquisitions, reorganization, and bankruptcies, and engage in *relative value trading*. The LTCM initially was focussed on this kind of trading.

Relative value trading is basically identifying temporary price discrepancies and exploiting these opportunities to make profits. If two bonds were mispriced relative to each other, the fund would buy the cheaper one and sell the dearer one until the prices came back into line with one another. Bonds necessarily have to converge to face value at their maturity. The initial strategy of LTCM typically involved the buying and selling of two US T-bonds with very similar maturities, whose prices were slightly out of line, and holding them till their prices fell in line. The fund bought the cheaper bond and sold the same amount of the dearer bond. This is called *convergence trade*. Under relative value trade, there is no guarantee that the prices would converge but there is strong expectation that the difference would shrink. The LTCM did active relative value trading on bonds—taking long positions on undervalued bonds and short positions on overvalued bonds of the same maturities but different issue dates. They must sell at the same yield, but do not. Based on the convergence of prices brought about by taking offsetting positions in two related products, the strategy worked well in 1995, providing a 43% return; in 1996, it yielded 41%.

The LTCM used its models and trading expertise to take calculated risks that were very profitable in the fund's first few years. It was able to identify and exploit even small price discrepancies between bonds of differing maturities or of different types. For example, if LTCM noticed that the spread between the yields on corporate bonds and T-bonds was higher than the historical spread, it would buy the corporate bonds and sell T-bonds in the hope that the spread would return to its normal and historical level. If that happened, LTCM would make money, but if the spread persisted, or if it widened, then the trade would lose money.

Due to its highly leveraged position, the fund made very profitable trades on Japanese convertible bonds, junk bonds, interest rate swaps, and Italian bonds. It was also able to exploit a spread between French bonds and German bonds that seemed unsustainable. The reason LTCM focused on bonds was that very robust models on interest rates are available.

Successful strategies are susceptible to imitation. By the end of 1996, the opportunities for profitable trades in this area were diminishing. This was partly because of competition from other institutions. By 1997, other firms started following LTCM, reducing opportunities for LTCM in the bonds markets. The LTCM struggled to get a mere 17% return in 1997.

Digression from Practice and Beyond Frontiers

The lack of opportunities due to imitation forced LTCM to expand its activities in order to achieve higher returns. The firm moved from bonds to riskier equity avenues. They also expanded to markets beyond the USA, including emerging markets, while continuing to employ the relative value trading concept.

From Bonds to Equity

The LTCM set up a trade of this type based on the shares of two oil companies—Shell Transport (listed in London) and Royal Dutch Petroleum (listed on the Amsterdam exchange)—on the assumption that the prices would converge. This was risk arbitrage. The idea of *paired share trade* involved finding a stock that is listed on two exchanges whose value represents roughly the same claim on the firm's assets. The prices of the pair should be equal, but for institutional reasons, price discrepancies can open up and persist. Royal Dutch Petroleum and Shell Transport derived their income from the same asset, which they jointly owned. Historically, the shares of the English company traded below those of the Dutch company. According to LTCM, the spread would contract as European markets became more integrated; and the firm proceeded to go long on Shell and short on Royal Dutch Petroleum, with a position of at least a billion dollars in each stock. This was a riskier strategy than some of the earlier bond plays because the convergence of the stock prices was less assured. The sheer size of the trade meant that LTCM's positions in these two stocks could not be unwound quickly at current market prices.

Directional Trade and Derivatives

The LTCM also engaged in *directional trades,* where it would take a position based on its view of the future. For example, when the value of index stock options increased, reflecting a higher degree of uncertainty about the future than normal, LTCM took up positions in index options. The portfolio of LTCM expanded to bonds and derivatives in developed nations such as Canada, France, Germany, Italy, Japan, and the UK. The fund also invested in equities and corporate bonds, as well as in emerging markets. It made extensive use of both exchange-traded and OTC derivatives, because this afforded a cheap way to gain exposure to different markets and increase leverage. In particular, it took significant positions in equity index futures and interest rate futures in a number of countries. It was also extremely active in the OTC derivatives markets, and had a very large portfolio of swaps with a number of different counterparties.

Speculation of Corporate Activities

The LTCM also entered a riskier arena by speculating in mergers and acquisitions outcomes. This involved buying stocks of companies that were potential takeover targets and profiting from the price rise that would occur when the takeover was announced. This trade is a form of *risk arbitrage* that requires considerable research to be profitable, as so many imponderables are involved. One such trade involved the stocks of a communication company based in Chicago, called Tellabs, which had planned to acquire another telecommunications company called Ciena Corporation. This trade was information sensitive. The LTCM took a position worth US $300 million in Ciena's stock. The acquisition was announced on 3 June 1998 but was unexpectedly withdrawn on 21 August 1998. This caused Ciena's stock price to drop by 45% and LTCM lost about US $50 million.

Volatility Trades

Another of LTCM's strategies was to take positions based on volatility. As is well known, high volatility means high option prices. Based on the BSM, LTCM worked out implied volatilities. It took the view that when the implied volatility in the market reached 20%, it would eventually revert to more normal levels of 13–15%, under the assumption of mean reversion, and when that happened, the option prices would fall. In 1997, LTCM began to sell five-year options on the S&P 500 Index, expecting to buy the options back at a lower price when volatility returned to normal levels. This was LTCM's plan but implied volatility remained high throughout 1998, which resulted in the firm losing money.

EVENTS

There were a number of events that occurred around the same time that failed to live up to the theories and principles applied by LTCM.

Asian Financial Crisis

The Asian crisis also affected global equity markets, culminating in a severe fall in October 1997. Investors became more frightened, and the levels of implied volatility in equities increased. Seeing an opportunity to make money, LTCM began to take on large option positions based on the assumption that the implied volatility levels would fall. The bets on volatility went awry.

Russian Default and Brazil's Devaluation

On 17 August 1998, Russia declared a moratorium on its domestic dollar debt, and this triggered a flight to US government debt, which meant that the price of US bonds rose. LTCM was long on Russian debt, to the extent of about 8% of its portfolio, and it was also short on US bonds. The hedge fund lost money on both these positions. On 21 August, LTCM lost US $553 million. Many of the hedge funds' trades were losing heavily at this time, and the counterparties on the other side of these transactions were requiring cash payments from LTCM to protect their own interests. The devaluations saw funds withdraw from these markets in search of safer markets. Prices in more stable markets increased, while they fell in emerging markets, once again causing divergence to increase.

Salomon Brothers' Withdrawal

The risk arbitrage group at Salomon, Meriwether's former group, had been using some of the same types of strategies as LTCM, and was also facing the same sorts of difficulties. In 1998, Salomon's risk arbitrage group began to scale back its operations and decrease its leverage. In June 1998, the Travelers Group, which had acquired Salomon in 1997, made a decision to close down its risk arbitrage operations. In September, Travelers reported that Salomon lost US $360 million in July and August because of the 'extreme volatility' in global markets. The swap positions that Salomon and other firms were unwinding this time were similar to those held by LTCM, and so, as these trades came to the market, they put downward pressure on market prices.

There were a number of factors that led to the collapse of the LTCM fund in 1998. LTCM's financial position was very sensitive to market movements because of its highly leveraged positions.

FAILURE OF RISK MODELS

The strategy of LTCM was heavily dependent upon models of determining arbitrage opportunities and risk management. They believed that money management was a quantifiable science rather than an art. Initially, success prompted increased and more sophisticated modelling.

Volatility

In 1998, the bets on volatility were based on market volatility and the assumption that it would decline back to its historical average level. By mid-September 1998, equity volatility was up to 33%, with each point increase costing the fund $40 million. Against a normal volatility of 1% per day, it became 9%.

Correlations

The LTCM also assumed low correlation in market variables across the globe. However, all factors became strongly correlated in 1998. Their portfolio consisting of Danish mortgages, US T-bonds, Russian bonds, US stocks, mortgage bonds, Latin American bonds, UK bonds, and US swaps was assumed to be highly diversified, with low correlation coefficients. On

17 August 1998, Russia defaulted on bonds; the interest rate surged to 200%. On 21 August 1998, the Dow fell 280 points; in US swap deals, the spread rose to 20 points (200 bps) and mortgage rates climbed.

Normal Distribution

The LTCM relied too heavily on the bell-shaped normal distribution. As per normal distribution, bad events are remote, but they happened several times in August 1998. When a firm has to sell in a market without buyers, prices run to the extremes, beyond the bell curve.

Value at Risk

For LTCM, a 95% 1-m VaR was $448 million. With $4.7 billion as capital, it was more than adequately covered for an assumed volatility of 20%. Risk was thought to be within manageable limits. LTCM's objective was to have volatility not exceeding 20%. Till April 1998, volatility measured below 11.5%. The LTCM used VaR based on historical data. It studied various markets in various countries. When the relationship diverged, it placed bets that the relationship would return to historical levels. The market factors became correlated with the Russian default, capital outflows from Brazil, the inability to unwind positions, etc. It made the VaR look irrelevant to risk measurement and management. As per the VaR, LTCM was not likely to lose more than $40 million on any given day. In August 1998, it lost $500 million in a day. It lost the same amount in September, and kept losing day after day.

Liquidity

The LTCM assumed that market risk remains the same, irrespective of the leverage used by a firm. This is true if liquidity is good. However, when the trader becomes a market maker, liquidity is not guaranteed. The LTCM possibly ignored the fact that it was not a small part of the market but formed a substantial chunk of it. It assumed that its positions could be squared up if the risk exceeded the target level. This did not happen, and LTCM could not liquidate due to its huge positions.

Leverage

At the end of 1997, LTCM had assets on its balance sheet worth $130 billion, with its equity at $4.7 billion, providing a leverage of 28:1. Besides these, it had off-balance sheet exposures in derivatives of a notional value of $1.4 trillion (including $500 billion in futures and $750 billion in OTC derivatives). From the perspective of leverage, both on and off the balance sheet, LTCM matched larger investment houses such as Goldman Sachs (34:1 and 3.41 trillion), Lehman Brothers (28:1 and 2.4 trillion), Merrill Lynch (30:1 and 3.47 trillion), and Morgan Stanley (22:1 and 2.86 trillion)[2].

LTCM's increased leverage was partly due to the high reputation of its management team. In OTC and swap deals with non-banking firms, the practice is to insist on collateral at the time of initiating contracts. This practice was diluted by bankers in Wall Street due to the high

---

[2]Gallati, Reto R., *Risk Management and Capital Adequacy,* McGraw Hill, 2003, p. 470.

reputation of the principals of LTCM, thus providing them with infinite leverage. Partly, the increased leverage also resulted from the decision of LTCM to return $2.7 billion (182%) as dividend to its investors in 1997 to gain market reputation and credentials, showing little concern for leverage. The capital came down suddenly from $4.67 billion in the beginning of 1998 to $2.9 billion. Now, the leverage was 55 times, apart from the exposures in derivatives. An investment of $1 in 1994 grew to $4 at the end of 1997, but shrank to 50 cents by mid-1998.

Convergence

One of the fundamental strategies was relative value trading, based on the convergence or reduction of divergence of value over a period of time for similar assets. In August 1998, the situation changed when Russia defaulted on its debts and devalued the rouble. Devaluation of the rouble caused a global margin call. The currencies and values of bonds declined simultaneously and sharply.

In July 1998, Salomon Brothers decided to disband its bond arbitrage unit. Interest rate spread, on the US T-bills and bonds increased. The LTCM counted on the spread closing on low-liquid and high-liquid treasuries. Salomon was selling positions that increased divergence rather than convergence. The LTCM assumed that divergence between swap rates and T-bonds would narrow. Every five basis points were equal to $2.8 million. For five such adverse jumps, the loss could only be $5 \times 2.8 =$ US $14 million. It was not so. On 21 September, the fund lost $553 million.

As per the LTCM models, it was a once in a lifetime occurrence. The LTCM lost 15% of its capital, while according to the model they were not supposed to lose more than $35 million on a single day. It was more than 10 times the daily volatility. By the month end, LTCM lost 15% of its capital. The spread between corporate and government debt securities also increased. The Russian crisis forced investors to invest in more liquid US treasuries, increasing divergence further.

The convergence theory of LTCM was not working. The LTCM lost 44% of its capital in August alone (52% for the year). It put itself into the position that it could fail before convergence happened. It needed more collateral to cover for margin calls, which was unavailable.

Non-convergence is due to a variety of reasons such as restrictions on free trade or a minor difference in the characteristics of seemingly identical assets. The differential in price may persist for a longer time than one would expect.

For example, we find that in India, Tata Motors have voting and non-voting shares, with the latter providing extra dividend. The price differential between the two (apparently on account of the control of the firm) persists at 40%, despite the fact that both values are driven by the same cash flow. The same was the case with Nestle's registered and bearer shares in Switzerland for a long time, before they became one in 1988.

THE OUTCOME

During the last week of August, the firm's partners tried in vain to raise the US $1.5 billion in additional capital needed to keep the fund afloat. This proved to be impossible and by mid-September, a collapse was inevitable. The excessive leverage and market-maker position of LTCM posed the hazard of systemic risk. Defaults by LTCM could lead to a chain of defaults in the financial system, and could lead to the collapse of others. Fourteen leading banks decided to invest US $3.65 billion and obtain a 90% stake in LTCM. The margin calls for LTCM was answered by a bail-out package.

The fall of LTCM was highly publicized, and it was subsequently analysed in a number of reports. The near collapse of the huge hedge fund renewed fears about the vulnerability of the entire financial system to systemic risk. Questions were raised concerning the role of hedge funds in the economy and the extent to which the trading practices of LTCM contributed to the crisis. In the aftermath of the fall, questions were raised about the risk management practices of not only LTCM but also the institutions that had lent it so much money.

SUMITOMO
The Perils of Price Manipulation

Sumitomo was a large Japanese bank with specific interests in copper trading. They had $50 billion worth of assets globally and controlled about 8% of the world's copper supplies and markets. With more than 200 years of experience and expertise in metals, they bought and sold roughly 8,00,000 tonnes of copper every year around the world, selling primarily in Southeast Asia. The key person handling the global purchases was Yasuo Hamanaka.

With its dominance in the copper market, the actions of Sumitomo were important clues for traders in copper. With huge positions in copper, the prices could not remain aloof to Sumitomo's actions.

Overconfidence of Leader

Due to the small size of the global copper market as compared to other metals and the significant proportions held by Sumitomo, Yasuo Hamanaka believed that he could influence, if not control, the prices of copper. This very belief of his caused a loss of about US $2.6 billion to Sumitomo in June 1996, when Hamanaka miscalculated and ruled out the possibility of copper prices falling; he made an all-out attempt to cause the prices to go up.

The strategy of Yasuo Hamanaka was to corner all the copper stored in the warehouses of the London Metal Exchange (LME). He would create long positions in physical copper, pay for them, and hoard the copper at the warehouses of the LME. Large positions in copper were thought to be genuine requirements of Sumitomo in view of their huge trading interests in the past.

Concentration of Authority

With an increasing physical copper inventory, supplies were drying up, causing an upward pressure on copper prices. Yasuo Hamanaka operated with reputed banks and trading houses of the calibre of Merrill Lynch, JP Morgan, Chase Manhattan, etc. He was given a power of attorney by the management of Sumitomo to trade, which in turn he passed on to the broking houses. The banks and trading houses conducted trades in copper with the world and all markets knowing that the operations were acting on behalf of Sumitomo. All these operations were neither checked nor monitored at the apex level.

Due to the confidence that he could drive the prices up, Hamanaka started writing put options to earn a premium. With prices going up, the puts would not be exercised and the premium would be pocketed. As long as prices remained up and rising, writing puts would remain a profit-making strategy.

The freedom given to Hamanaka possibly developed an attitude of carelessness, even though Hamanaka could not make a profit every time. Trading in physical copper and futures caused losses too. To hide losses, he prepared duplicate sets of accounts, which showed profits to the management.

THE OUTCOME

In December 1995, copper prices rose close to $2800 per tonne on the LME, when events started happening rapidly. Suspecting a price manipulation in copper, the US Commodity Futures Trading Commission (CFTC) and Britain's Securities and Investments Board (SIB) asked Sumitomo to cooperate. The prices remained in the band of $2500 to 2600 till about mid-April 1996. Then they shot up to $2800 again by May 1996.

Sumitomo discovered Hamanaka's actions, and he was relegated to a junior position. The positions in physical copper held by Sumitomo were substantially out of proportion to its business needs. Apart from the physical positions, Sumitomo also had significant long positions in copper futures. These large positions in physical copper and futures were considered to be speculative and motivated by profit, through artificial manipulation of the price of copper. The market suspected something amiss, and investors started off-loading their long positions, hoping that Sumitomo would do the same. Prices fell abruptly by about 15% in four days and by the third week of June, copper was ruling close to US $1800 per tonne at the LME.

Hamanaka's folly was that he could not accept that even the most successful market manipulator must face unfavourable situations. Rather than selling copper in the downward market, he thought he could still drive the prices up. He kept picking short sales in order to raise the prices. He thought that he could still do it in the falling markets. Hamanaka failed to minimize the downside risk of the falling copper prices. With huge physical long positions, Sumitomo was extremely vulnerable to declining prices. He also financed his long positions through credit lines and prepayment of swaps with major banks.

Sumitomo was able to unwind some of its positions at a huge loss, and suffered a penalty of US $150 million for being guilty of price manipulation. The total estimated loss was to the order of US $2.6 billion. Hamanaka was fired, arrested, and jailed.

PROCTER AND GAMBLE
The Gamble That Didn't Pay Off

Another classic case of derivatives being put to misuse is that of Procter and Gamble (P&G). Procter and Gamble entered an exotic swap deal with Bankers Trust in November 1993 for a period of five years, with semi-annual exchange of cash flows, wherein Bankers Trust paid a fixed 5.30 % and P&G paid the 30-day commercial paper rate less 75 bps plus a spread.

The spread was the differential between the prices of five-year treasury notes and a specified 30-year T-bond. This is often referred to as a '5/30' swap. Procter and Gamble hoped that the spread would be zero, and it would lock-in a financing rate of 75 bps less than the commercial paper rate. The swap, therefore, would transform the fixed rate obligations of 5.30% into floating rate obligations, as they expected the interest rates to remain low.

Procter and Gamble entered into another swap deal with Bankers Trust, linked to the exchange rates of the Deutsche mark. Both parties paid each other based on German interest rates. Procter and Gamble hoped that swap rates in the Deutsche mark would remain within the 4.05–6.10% band, when they would receive higher coupons. Both the swap deals were bets that the US interest rate as well as the German interest rate would not rise.

The bets went wrong and barely six months after the swaps, P&G disclosed a loss of US $157 million. The cost of borrowing went as high as 1400 bps above the commercial paper rate. When P&G wanted to unwind the position, they had to depend upon the pricing of Bankers Trust based on their proprietary model.

Procter and Gamble sued Bankers Trust, who argued that P&G had sufficient knowledge of derivatives in view of their successful experience of hedging with derivatives, and that P&G fully understood the complex nature of the swap deals they had entered into. Procter and Gamble alleged that they were misled by the advisers, i.e., Bankers Trust. Ultimately, even though optimistic of a favourable outcome to the legal case, Bankers Trust chose to settle the dispute with P&G by paying US $80 million in May-June 1996.

LEARNINGS FROM THE CASES

The cases described in this chapter offer many points of learning. Some of these are not unique to management. They simply reinforce the validity of the fundamental principles that are applicable to any discipline of management. These principles also apply to derivatives, which are no exception. Some of these points of learning are specific to the area of derivatives in view of their special characteristics. These are highlighted in this section.

Markets are Supreme

Many investors, not only in derivatives but in all forms of markets, seem to believe that they know the market too well. They assume that they have been in the markets long enough to have seen several up and down cycles, and, therefore, can predict the market moves. Experience in the market is a good thing to have, but to believe that it imparts a complete understanding is bad. This presumption leads to rising stakes, and that proves detrimental to the investor when the market behaves unfavourably. It must be said that the markets have the capacity to surprise one and all. Markets do not care for reputation (Barings), size (Sumitomo), needs (MG), or superlative knowledge (LTCM).

Models Do Not Work Always

We have seen several models of pricing and theoretically strong arguments for arbitrage. These models do make some simple underlying assumptions, which are sometimes forgotten or overlooked. These assumptions place limitations on the applicability of models. One of the limitations that practically every model faces is the normal conditions in the markets. Howsoever robust a model is, it tends to fail when the markets are abnormal. The episode of LTCM is a case in point. When abnormality in the market persists for some time, defying all logic, several assumptions fall flat. This is an important realization for all researchers, academicians, and practitioners alike.

Complacency and Lack of Supervision

Another important lesson to be learned from the cases highlighted in this chapter is the importance of supervision in all business activities. In the case of derivatives, supervision assumes much greater significance due to two additional facts that are generally not present in other business situations. One, derivative transactions involve much greater value than suggested by the cash outlay. For taking a futures position, one has to put in the margins only. For forwards, there is no cash flow and for options, there may be an inflow if one has written them. Little do we know of about the mammoth exposure in the value underwritten. Two, derivatives escape accounting treatment for a long time till they are settled; the profit and loss becomes known only at maturity. By then, all control over the situation has been lost. Since there in no accounting, derivative transactions escape scrutiny by auditors, supervisors, and management.

The leveraged nature of derivatives and the absence of accounting demand that an organization develops adequate and extra control mechanisms outside the routine accounting-based controls. This may be by way of special detailed reports that must be analysed comprehensively. Organizations do have several reports, but the tendency is to give them only a cursory look.

Star Status

The lack of supervision is also partly due to the fact that we are all prone to hero worship. An individual who has delivered is seen as a star performer. This dilutes the supervision and also discourages people from pointing out shortcomings, if any. We see this happening time and again. Nick Leeson's contribution to the profits made him a star at Barings. Furthermore, he was too important for SIMEX. People with star status not only get heard by all but also get what they desire, even if it means bending of the rules. Special treatment makes the star increasingly important and, possibly, unmanageable and uncontrollable. Star status helps in hiding some crucial actions that have the potential for causing huge damage. Similarly, Robert Citron operated Orange County, California (case not discussed), solely on the basis of his past reputation, resulting in a $1.6 billion loss to one of the richest counties in the USA. Similarly, Yasuo Hamanaka was too important to be questioned till events reached massive negative proportions.

Organizations tend to relax controls and grant greater discretionary powers to such people. This was the case with Yasuo Hamanaka in Sumitomo, when he was granted extraordinary power to execute deals; in turn, he transferred this power to the brokerage firms. As long as discretion is used pragmatically, the situation remains healthy. However, when discretion is misused, it results in extremely embarrassing situations for the organization.

How else can one justify the overlooking of the high levels of funding requested by Leeson? Barings provided Leeson with huge sums to meet margin calls without questioning him. Leeson purportedly asked for margins on account of customers' positions. This was acceded and accepted without any verification, and with the full knowledge that the SIMEX prohibits funding of customers by brokerage houses. Leeson was a star performer, and his contributions to the overall profit were never scrutinized to ascertain if he really was engaged in a conservative switching strategy.

Concentration of Power and Responsibilities

One of the reasons attributed to the Barings and Sumitomo cases is operational risk. In both the cases, there was organizational failure to detect malafide activities or the overstepping of designated authority levels. Segregation of operations and controls is a fundamental principle of management. In the case of Barings, the operations and settlement activities were entrusted to the same person, permitting Leeson to hide his losses for a long time. In the case of Sumitomo, Hamanaka was entrusted with absolute power to deal, without any requirement for approvals. He operated with complete freedom. In the case of derivatives, such concessions are obtained on the pretext of fast-changing scenarios and the need for immediate action on the spot, without the delays that are an unavoidable part of sanction and approval procedures.

Complexity of Long Term and Short Term

The cases of MG and P&G tend to highlight the time perspective. Derivatives are essentially sets of instruments whose pricing is governed by short-term changes. Whether they were the appropriate instruments for hedging on a long-term basis remains a debatable point. Metallgesellschaft attempted to hedge long-term risks spanning 10 years of forward contracts with its futures position, while P&G attempted to play on the differential between 5-year and 30-year yields. This seems to be a case of drilling a hole with a needle. Derivatives are characterized by their nature in terms of (a) their short-term lives, (b) their tactical aspects, (c) their economical aspects, and (d) their reversibility, as highlighted in Chapter 1. If one needs to hedge for the long term, other strategic tools in marketing and production functions are available. Perhaps, firms are motivated to hedge with financial products because such hedges are perceived to be cheap. However, they become expensive if the markets behave in directions that are opposite to the anticipated directions, as the MG and P&G cases highlight.

Systemic Risk

Speculators provide the all-important function of providing liquidity that helps in price discovery on a continuous basis. Speculators are driven by leverage. Since markets are dominated by speculators who deploy massive leverage to magnify gains, it becomes extremely important for regulators to monitor developments. In cash or physical markets, control over leverage is automatic, since commitments have to be met in cash, borrowed or otherwise. Thus, one can take speculative positions depending upon the borrowing capacity available. Derivatives by themselves are instruments of leverage, and comprise a market that works only on promises. Therefore, exposure in derivatives is always in terms of notional amounts.

This poses great risk to entire systems as one default tends to trigger a chain of defaults, causing entire markets to collapse. The fear of failure gives rise to the loss of confidence in market mechanisms, and, therefore, it becomes a primary concern for society, regulators, and other participants. The need to act and bail out in the public interest is paramount, lest people lose faith in the markets. The fear of systemic failure was the reason for the massive bailout of LTCM. Systemic failure was also a concern for the SIMEX in the case of Barings. The exposure of MG too was considered huge enough to cause a systemic failure. Time and again, the International Monetary Fund (IMF) has considered bail-out plans for nations. Mexico and Thailand in the past and more recently, Greece, Ireland, etc., are cases in point. Though the IMF has been criticized for 'privatising profit and socialising losses', these attempts were made to avoid systemic failures.

Need vs Greed

Almost all transactions in derivatives are initially motivated by the need for hedging. When they become successful, the participants get encouraged. Due to the leverage effect, the derivatives have another side too. They hold tremendous potential to magnify losses as well as gains. In case an initial transaction fails to deliver the expected outcome, one tends to blame it on adverse market conditions and wrong forecasts. Expecting that adversity does not last long and forecasts do not go consistently wrong, there is a tendency to make up for earlier losses by doubling the stakes in the next venture. It is like a gambler on a losing streak; he keeps doubling the stakes in each round, hoping for good times to appear and for recovery of past losses in a single stroke. At such a juncture, it becomes difficult to determine whether the actions are motivated by need or by greed. Perhaps this was one bit of the psychology that dominated the thinking of Nick Leeson, when in order to recover losses he kept boosting the stakes. The times never favoured him, and the result was a doubling of losses, rather than a recovery of the past losses. Perhaps for Nick Leeson in Barings and Yasuo Hamanaka in Sumitomo, when the need morphed into greed may never be known.

Absence of Legal Framework

Legal risk poses special problems for the derivatives markets. Though the legal systems are fairly well developed for cash-based contracts, the innovations in derivatives, especially those that are OTC, present many novel ideas that are not foreseen by legal systems; hence, there is an absence of legal remedies. The novelty of many derivatives makes them susceptible to legal risk because of the uncertainty that exists over the applicability of existing laws and regulations to such contracts.

Index

3-m MIBOR 159
3-m Mumbai Interbank Offer Rate 159

A
Accounting standard AS 30 629
Add-on yield 195
Agency cost of debt 588
 debt as options 590
American call 356, 357
 valuation 357
 valuing 356
American options 284
 valuing call 310, 311
 valuing put 530, 531, 614
Arbitrageurs 10
Arch 397
As you like it options 484
AS 30 630
Asian financial crisis 660
Asian options 504
 applications 504
 binomial valuation 507, 513, 514, 539
Asian options 504, 513
 applications 504
 binomial model 507
 binomial valuation 513
 valuation 505
Ask rate 118
Asset allocation 109
Asset-based securitization 576
Assignment 269, 277
At-the-money option 346
Average option 504

B
Back-to-back/parallel loans 216, 231
Backward induction 309
Badla 87, 88
Barings plc 652
Barrier option 499–504, 512, 515
 binomial tree 507
 valuation 500, 505, 509
 valuing the 512
Basis risk 68–73

hedging 70
Basis swap 228
Basis 68
 convergence 68
Basket CDS 567
Basket option 512
Bear spread 458–460, 467, 475, 476
 calls 459
 with calls 476
 with puts 476
Bermudan option 512
Beta 102, 103
Bid rate 118
Binary options 482, 483
 application 482
 call 482
 payoff for 482
 put 482
 valuation 483
Binomial method 332
Binomial model 298, 307–312, 325, 327, 331, 332
 American call 314
 call on futures 534
 call pricing 331, 332
 currency options 326
 equivalent portfolio approach 306, 334
 European call 312
 European put 315
 index options 325
 multi-period/stage 309, 322, 324
 put pricing 307, 309
 valuing call 311
 valuing a call 324
Binomial option pricing model 299
Binomial pricing model 304
 payoff 304
Black's model 522, 525, 539
Black–Scholes model 336, 346, 352, 605
 assumptions of 348
 call pricing 354–355
 currency option 351, 431
 index futures 540, 547
 index options 352, 364

interpretation of 571
interpreting 348
put premium 350
put pricing 349
Black–Scholes option pricing model 339
Bombay Cotton Exchange 16, 55
Bombay Stock Exchange/BSE 86, 205, 396
Bond equivalent yield 182
Bond price 205, 208–209
 and duration 208
 and modified duration 207, 209
 duration 209
Bootstrapping 162
Borrower's FRA 167, 168
Box spread 467–468
Brazil's devaluation 661
Broken date 123
BSM 347, 363
 call 347, 363
 currency option 364
 index options 364
Bull spread 456–458, 474, 478
 calls 457
Business risk 3
Butterfly spread 460–463
 calls 461
 payoff of 460

C
Calendar spread 77, 79, 107, 465
 arbitrage 661
Call on call 496
Call on put 496
Call option 259–261, 264, 279, 280, 305
 lower bound 281
 moneyness 264
 payoff 260, 261, 263, 279
 premium 260, 305
 value 281, 305
Callable bonds 592
 non-callable bonds 593
 price and YTM 593
Cap 518–524, 527
 cash flows 521

hedging with 518, 527
payoff 519
valuation of 521
Caplet 519, 520, 531
value 531
Carbon credit 553, 622
Cash flow hedge 634, 635, 638, 641, 642
Cash flow mapping 410
Cash flows 574
Cash-and-carry arbitrage 41–43, 53, 190, 193
Cash-and-carry 70
CDO 583
  cash flow 583
  synthetic 583
CDS premium 571
CDS 564, 572
  applications of 567
  cash flow 572
  cash flows 566
  credit event 565
  financial guarantee 567
  insurance 567
  settlement 566
  settlement of 564
  variants 566
Central limit theorem 342
Certified emission reductions/CERs 623
Cheapest-to-deliver bond 204, 205
Chicago Board of Trade/CBOT 15, 55, 199
Chicago Mercantile Exchange/CME 16, 109, 139, 181, 619
Chooser option 484–486
  valuation 485
Clearing 92
Close-out 32
Clean price 198, 200
Collar 518, 526–528
  valuing 527
Collateralized bond obligation/CBO 581
Collateralized debt obligations/CDO 581–583
Collateralized loan obligation/CLO 581
Collateralized mortgage obligation/CMO 581
Commodity futures 50, 191
  arbitrage 191
  benefits of 56

calendar spread 81
cost of credit 59
financial futures 59
government's revenue 58
hedging 62
national economy 58
pricing 61
speculation 78, 81
spread strategies 79
subsidies 58
volatility 56
Commodity futures 50, 53, 55, 56, 59–61
  benefits of 56
  calendar spread 77, 107
  financial futures 54
  hedging with 62
  pricing of 60
  speculation with 78
Commodity swap 251
  valuation of 251
Commodity swaps 250
Common stock 587
Compound option 496–498
  applications 496
  payoff 497
  valuation 497, 498
Condor spread 462–465
Condor 463, 465
  payoff 463
Consumption assets 43
Contango 48, 649
Continuous compounding rate 162
Continuous compounding 312
Contract size 90
Contract value 90
Convenience yield 44
Convergence 53, 663, 664
Conversion factor 201–203, 212, 214
  invoice price 212
Convertible bonds 593
Converting asset/liability from one currency to another 234
Cooling degree day 619
Correlation 396, 398
Correlations 661
Cost of carry model 59, 145
  IRP 145
Counterparty risk 26, 28, 54, 219, 244, 256
Covariance 396, 398
Covered call 446, 478

Crack spread 77
Credit default swap/CDS 568
  mean 569
  Merton model 568
  valuation 568
Credit default swaps 562–569
  and financial guarantee 567
  and insurance 567
  applications 562
  cash flows 563
  credit/default events 564
  settlement of 564
Credit derivative 550, 560
Credit-linked notes 579–581
Credit quality spread 227
Credit risk 551, 561, 562
  market risk 562
  rating 561
  types 561
Credit spreads 458, 571
Credit value at risk 559
  computing 559
Credit VaR 556
Credit-linked note 580
  cash flows 580
CRISIL 555
Cross hedge 67, 72–74
Currency futures 50, 139–143, 145, 146, 148, 149, 152, 153
  arbitrage 148, 149, 152
  contract specifications 140
  fair value 145
  hedging 146
  pricing 143–146
  settlement 168
  speculation with 149, 152
  trading 141
Currency option 284, 285, 294, 441
  hedging with 431–439
  lower bounds 284, 285
  payoff 299
Currency swap 228–237, 246, 248, 250, 254
  converting asset/liability from one currency to another 232, 234
  cost of funds 232
  exchange rate risk 233
  features of 236
  fixed-to-fixed 236
  fixed-to-floating 236
  floating-to-floating 237
  hedging against exchange rate risk 231

Index

reducing cost of funds   232, 254
series of forward contracts   248
value   250
value of   246
valuing   246

D

Day traders   88
Debit spread   456
Debit spreads   458
Debt   590
  as options   590
  value of firm   590
Default events   564
Default rates   555
Default risk   180, 550
Degree of financial leverage   393
Degree of operating leverage   393
Delivery logic
  compulsory   34
  option of buyer   34
  option of seller   34
Delivery notice period   60
Delta hedging   367, 374, 382
Delta   366–375, 388, 393
  additivity of   371
  and gamma neutrality   379
  and time to maturity   370
  behaviour of   369
  call   388
  call option   367
  computing   367
  limits on value   368
  meaning of   368
  neutrality   375
  put   388
  put option   367
  value of the call   372
Deltas   373
  derivative as   640
  other derivatives   373
Derivatives   4, 5, 9, 566
  accounting definition of   630
  accounting for   539
  classification of   1
  criticism   21
  diversification   6
  evolution of   15–19
  functions of   19
  insurance   7
  misuses   21
  participants in   13
  products   9

strategic risk management   8
types of   9
Diagonal spreads   466, 467
Digital CDS   566
Digital option   482
  valuation   483
Directional trade   659
Discount on T-bills   181
Discount   150
Down-and-in option   499, 515
Down-and-out option   499, 515
Down-and-out   499
Due date rate (DDR)   34
Duration   207, 208
  bond price   208
Duration/modified duration/
  Macaulay's duration   393
Duration-based hedging   209
Dynamic hedging   382

E

Electricity derivatives   627
Emission trading   621
Energy derivatives   10, 618,
  624–627
  contract on crude oil   625
  crude oil   625
  electricity   626
  natural gas   627
Entity   563
Equity shares   587
Equity swaps   251, 252
  valuation   252
Equivalent portfolio approach   306
Eurodollar futures   194–197
  borrower's hedge   197
  hedging with   196
  investor's hedge   211
  pricing of   196
Eurodollars   194, 195
European options   265
European put   315
  valuing   315
Event risk   8
Evolution   136
Exchange option   487, 488
  applications   488
  valuation   488
Exchange rate risk   4
Exchange-traded derivatives   11
Exchange-traded options   265
Exchange-traded   11, 12, 264
Expectancy theory   49

Expectation hypothesis   49
Exponential smoothing   394
Exponential weighted moving
  average   394

F

Fair value hedge   634, 635, 638, 639
Fair value   631–633
  features of   574
  measurement   632
Features   136
Financial assets or liabilities at fair
  value   630
Financial derivatives   16
Financial futures   50
  commodity futures   59
Floor   524–527
  payoff   524
  valuation of   525
Floorlet   524–526
Foreign exchange markets   118
Foreign exchange rates   118–119,
  121
  arbitrage   121
  condition for arbitrage   122
  condition for no arbitrage   122
Foreign exchange risk   117
Forward and futures contracts   40
Forward contract   5, 25–27, 44, 45,
  86, 128, 133
  arbitrage with   133
  cancellation   26
  features of   26, 136
  hedging   128–132
  motive for   25
  offsetting   27
  on stocks   86–88
  pricing   38, 39
  settlement of   27
  speculation with   133
  value of   44, 45
Forward contracts   86, 123, 128,
  133
  hedging receivables   128
Forward discount   119, 120
Forward exchange rate   144
  determination   144
Forward hedge   132
  cost of   132
Forward interest rates   169, 171,
  173, 558
  determining   173, 176
  term structure   177

Forward interest rates 172, 176
  determining 172, 176
Forward premium 119, 120, 150
Forward premium/discount 199,
  120, 150, 153
Forward price
  obligation to 26
Forward rate agreement 166
Forward rate agreements/
  FRAs 158, 165, 241, 517
  arbitrage with 175
  hedging with 184
  settlement of 179
Forward rate 119, 151
  bounds 151
Forward rates 134, 557
  bounds 135
  determining 134
Forward start option 480, 512
  applications 481
  valuation 480
Forward rolling of the hedge 73
Forward start option 480, 512
  application 481
  valuation 483
Forward swap rate 544
Forward swap 544
Forward transaction 123
Forward/futures contract 36, 39
Forward–forward swap 125
Forwards hedging 151
  receivables 151
Forwards 9, 143
Forwards/futures 271
  options 271
FRA 167, 175, 176
  arbitrage 175
  borrower's 167
  hedging 172
  Indian practices 170
  investor's 168, 176
  pricing 169
  settlement 169
  speculation 175
Futures contract 28–36, 195, 199
  and forward 47
  comparison 38
  convergence 46
  eurodollars 195
  indices 88
  individual stocks 88
  pricing 38

specification of 30
T-bills 181
T-bonds 199
Futures exchange 29
Futures market 78
Futures options 533, 539
  binomial model 537
  binomial valuation 539
  Black's model 539
  payoff 534
  put–call parity 536
  value 540
  valuation of 539
Futures price 33, 39
  and expected spot price 47
  expectancy theory 49
  upper bound 44
Futures pricing 49
Futures style options 269
Futures 9, 10, 23, 46, 113
  arbitrage 113
  forward 33, 46
  on consumption asset 62
  on investment asset 61
  spread strategies 76, 79
  types of 49
  yield enhancement 106
Futures/forward position 272, 273
  payoffs 272, 273
Futures/forwards 273
  options 273
Futures: yield enhancement 106
  arbitrage 106

G
Gamma neutrality 379
Gamma 366, 379–384, 388, 393
  behaviour 380
  calculation 384
  call 388
  call option 387
  computing 380
  interpretation 384
  meaning of 381
  neutrality 383, 384
  portfolio 382
  put 388
  put option 387
  spot price 380
  time 380
Gap option 489, 492
  applications 490

call 490, 492
payoffs 489
put 490
valuation 490
Garch (1, 1) model 397

H
Heating degree day 619
Hedge accounting 633, 634, 636,
  639
  steps for 636
  types of hedges 634
Hedge funds 657
Hedge ratio 71–74, 83, 84, 97,
  207, 648
  conversion factor 201
Hedge 72, 100
  forward rolling 72
  market risk 100
Hedged item 635, 636, 638
Hedgers 13
Hedging effectiveness 637, 638
Hedging for 73
  gross profit 77
Hedging instrument 635–638
Hedging payable 129
Hedging payables 131
Hedging relationship 635, 637–645
Hedging with futures 97
Hedging 3, 62, 73, 76, 173, 174,
  185, 188, 211, 422, 423, 427,
  429–433, 441
  against falling interest rates 174
  against falling yield 185
  against rising interest 172, 188
  against rising interest rates 172
  basis risk 70
  call on index 429
  call option 423
  call option on 431
  currency option 441
  exchange rate risk 231, 233
  falling interest rates 174
  falling yields 185
  for gross profit margin 76
  foreign currency payable 432
  foreign currency receivable 432
  gross profit margin 76
  long position in stock 115, 422
  payable with call option 433
  portfolio 97, 99, 100
  put on index 427

put option 422
put option on index 430, 441
receivable with put option 432
rising interest 188
rising interest rates 173
volume 73
with futures 65, 96
with index futures 96
with index options 426, 440
with T-bills 181, 187, 211, 214
Held-to-maturity/HTM 630
investments 636, 645
Historical simulation 411
Historical volatility 358–385

I
Imperfect hedge 66
Implied repo rate 190–194, 201
Implied volatility 361–365
estimating 362
Index future
specifications 90
Index futures 85, 86, 93, 95
applications 95
fair price of 93, 94
hedging 95
hedging with 96
price 93
pricing 92
specifications 90
Index options 325
India VIX 400
computation 400
Initial margin 37, 47, 78, 112
Interbank transactions 158
Inter-commodity spreads 77, 79
Interest rate futures 50, 178, 179, 186, 188, 192, 193, 205, 206
arbitrage 192
borrowing 188
cash-and-carry arbitrage 193
contract specifications 206
hedging 186, 206
in India 205
on T-bills 179
specifications 199
Interest rate options 517
Interest rate parity 137, 153
Interest rate risk 4, 165, 180
Interest rate swap 4, 165, 180, 216–223, 226, 247, 254, 255
cost of funds 224
features 217

reduce funding 226
reducing cost of funds 254
value of 247, 248, 255
Interest rate swaps 220, 223, 227, 238
applications 220
fixed-to-floating 227
in India 223
reducing cost of funds 223
valuing 238
Interest rates 156
desirable features 156
Inter-market spreads 80
International Swaps and Derivatives
Association (ISDA) 565
In-the-money 263
Intrinsic value 277–279
Inverted market 46
Investment assets 43
Investor's FRA 168, 176
Invoice price 186, 192, 204

K
Kansas City Board of Trade 50, 86
Knock-in option 499, 500, 503
Knock-out option 499, 500, 503
Kyoto Protocol 621

L
Leveraging 20
LIBID 158
LIFFE 195, 200, 204
Log-normal distribution 340
London Inter Bank Offer Rate/
LIBOR 11, 158, 166, 179, 195–197, 574
Long butterfly spread 461
Long condor spread 464
Long hedge 64, 97, 112, 146, 185, 187
importer 146
Long hedge 65, 83, 422
Long position 276
synthetic 469
Long positions 62
Long put 273
Long-term capital management 657
Lookback options 508, 510, 511
applications 509
binomial 510
valuation 509–511
Loss given default 551

M
Margin call 37, 54
Margin requirements 36
Margining system 92
Market risk 98–100
Marking-to-market 36, 37, 39, 40, 112
Maturity date 259
MCX-SX 139–142
Merton model 349, 357, 568, 571
Metallgesellschaftag 646
MIBID 158, 160
Mimicking stock 470, 476, 477
Minimum margin 37
Minimum support price 58
Modified duration 207
Moneyness of options 264
Monte Carlo simulation 416, 328
limitations 416
Mortgage-based securitization 576
Mortgages 576
Mumbai Inter Bank Offer Rate/
MIBOR 11, 158–160, 217, 218, 221–228

N
Naked call 446
National Multi-commodity Exchange
of India/NMCE 16, 30, 37
National Stock Exchange/NSE 15, 17, 38, 86, 139, 158, 223
Nifty 51, 85–91
Non-deliverable forward/NDF 135–137, 151
and interest rate parity 137
features of 136
settlement 137, 151
Normal backwardation
hypothesis 48
Normal distribution 340, 342, 345, 662

O
Odd date 123
Offsetting 32
Oil derivatives 625
Open interest and
volume 36
Open interest 35
Open position trading 79
Optimal hedge ratio 209
duration based 209
Optimum hedge ratio 71

676 Index

Option delta 307, 334, 367
  behaviour 369
  call value 372
  computing 367
  meaning 368
  portfolio delta 371
  short straddle 371
  time to maturity 370
  value 368
Option forwards 127, 129
Option on bonds 530–532
  valuing 530, 531
Option on swaps—swaptions 540
  forward swap 541
  payoff 541
Option premium/pricing 260, 295
  arbitrage 281
  boundary conditions 280
  lower bound 282–285
Option price 337
  factors affecting 337
Option pricing 279, 285
  arbitrage 285
  boundary conditions 279
Option to abandon 599, 612
  binomial method 614
  BSM 615
  DCF valuation 612, 614
Option to delay 598, 601, 603
  binomial model 603
Option to expand 598, 607, 609, 611
  binomial method 609
  BSM 611
  DCF valuation 608
Option 268, 272, 294, 449
  arbitrage 449
  currency 272
  speculation
Options on bonds 528
Options on currencies 351
Options on futures 533–540
  binomial model 537
  need 535
  payoff 541
Options on indices 351, 365
Options on stock indices 286
Options valuing 351
  currencies 351
  dividend paying stock 319
  indices 351

Options 9, 10–23, 259, 263, 264, 266, 269, 271, 273, 274, 287, 292, 294, 295, 449
  American 264
  arbitrage with 105, 106, 133, 148, 149, 175, 287, 292, 294, 295
  binomial valuation 502
  European 264
  futures/forwards 271–273
  insurance 274
  margins in 269, 270
  moneyness 274
  moneyness of 263
  quotations 266–269, 288
  settlement 267, 268
  terminology 259, 260
  trading 267, 268
  types of 264, 265
Out-of-the-money options 264
Out-of-the-money 263
Outright forward 125
Overnight swap 223
Over-the-counter 11, 264

P
Par-yield 198
Pass through certificates 577
Pass through 577
Pay-later call option 493
  call 493
Pay-later call 495
  valuation 495
Pay-later option 492
  applications 493
  payoffs 492
  valuation 493
Pay-later 495
  put 495
Pay through 577
Payer swaption 543
Perfect hedge 66
Plain vanilla interest rate swap 220
Plain vanilla swap 217
Points-in-points/PIPs 126
Portfolio balancing 101, 103
Portfolio beta 101, 102, 428, 430
Portfolio CDS 567
Portfolio delta 371, 373
Portfolio gamma 382
Portfolio theta 378

Position trading 79
Premium style options 269
Premium 259
Prepayment risk 578
Price discovery 19, 56, 57
Price quotation 31
Price risk 3
Price 92, 194
Pricing forward contract 52
Pricing futures
  investment asset 61
Pricing T-bonds 198
Probability of default 551–554, 571
  expected loss 553
  finding 552
  Merton model 571
  recovery rate 554
Procter and Gamble 665
Protection buyer 563, 568, 585
Protection seller 563, 567, 585
Protective put 423, 424, 443
Pseudo-pricing of American call 354
Put–call parity 288, 289, 291–295, 471
  American options 292, 293
  currency options 293, 294
  dividend paying stock 293, 319
  synthetic positions 471
Put on call 496
Put on put 496
Put option 10, 259–262, 277, 281, 282, 294
  payoff 262–264, 294
  lower bound 283
  value of 282
Put
  pay-later option 493
Puttable bonds 592, 593

R
Rain derivatives 620
Range forward 435, 436
  pay off 435
Range forward—zero cost collar 434
Real options 598
  kinds 598
Receiver swaption 548
Recombining symmetrical 311

Recovery rate 551, 584
Recovery rates 554
Reference asset 563
Reference entity 579
Repo rate 156, 190
Reverse cash-and-carry
    arbitrage 42, 51, 52, 54, 190
Reverse cash-and-carry 51, 70
Reverse repo rates 156
Rho 366, 387, 391, 393
Risk diversification 23
Risk neutral valuation 303, 325, 333, 334
Risk of the portfolio 103
Risk transfer 23
Risk
    diffusing the risk 2
    diversification of risk 2
    non-financial risks 3
    transferring 3
Risk-neutral valuation 303, 325
Risk-neutral valuations 333
    call 333
    put 333
Risk–reward ratio 460
Russian default 661

S
SCRA 17, 19, 86
Securitization 576, 578
    participants 578
    risk in 578
SENSEX 51, 85–87, 90
Settlement and delivery 32
Settlement 91, 123
Short hedge 63, 65, 80, 83, 95, 98, 147, 188
    exporter 147
Short positions 62
Shout option 486
    valuation 487
Speculators 14, 123
Spot price 24
Spot rate 79, 119
Spot rates 123
Spot 123
Spread trading 79
Stack-and-roll strategy 649
Standard deviation 393
Standard market model 522
Stock futures 50, 95, 114

fair price 95
pricing 92
specifications 90
Stock index futures 86, 90, 104, 105
    arbitrage with 105
    speculation with 104, 133, 149
Stock index option
    lower bounds 285
Stock options 270, 271, 422
    and dividend 270, 285, 297
    and stock splits 270, 271
    bonus shares 270
    hedging with 470, 422, 431
Stock/index futures 90, 110, 111
Stop-loss strategy 374
Straddle 451–453, 472, 654
    long 451, 452, 472
    payoff on a long 451
    short 451
Strangle 453, 454, 465, 473, 478
    long 453, 454
    payoff 454
    short 453, 473
Strap 456
    payoff 456
Straps 455
Strike date/maturity date 260
Strike price 259, 260, 266
Strips 455
Sumitomo 664
Swap dealer 218
    counterparty risk 219
Swap dealer/bank 218
    need for 218
Swap for 217
    cash flow 217
Swap points 126
Swap quotes 242
Swap rate 244
Swap transaction 124, 153
Swap/Swaps 9, 10, 23, 124, 125, 153, 215, 216, 222, 237
    and forward contract 133
    applications of 220
    as pair of bonds 238, 244
    as series of forward
        contracts 240, 243, 248
    counterparty risk 244, 256
    exchange rate risk 23, 233
    features of 217

floating-to-fixed 228
hedging strategies 222
hedging with 222
pricing 242
rationale 225
term structure 245, 246
the comparative advantage 225
valuation of 237
transforming nature of
    assets 220, 221
Swap–comparative advantage 225
Swaption/Swaptions 540–547
    binomial 547
    options on bond 542
    payoff of 524
    value 547
    value of 545
    valuing 546, 548, 603, 609
    valuation 543
Switching 653
Synthetic long stock 469
Synthetic short stock 470
Systematic risk 6, 99, 114, 393
Systemic risk 550, 668

T
T-bill futures 182, 185, 189, 190, 192–194, 211
    arbitrage 190, 193, 194
    price quotation 182
    pricing of 192
    hedging 187, 211
    hedging strategy 189
    implied repo rate 194
    price 194
    speculation 189
T-bills futurs contract
    specifications 184
T-bills 181, 183, 185
    futures contract 181
    futures contract in India 183
    pricing of 181
    yield on 185
T-bond futures 200, 210, 212
    hedging 210, 212
    pricing 200
Term structure of interest
    rates 160, 161, 171
Theta 366, 376–378, 393
    computing 377
    portfolio 378

time   377
Tick size   32, 54, 91
Time spreads   80
Time value   277–279
Total return payer   573, 576, 585
Total return receiver   573–575, 585
Total return swap   573, 575
   CDS   575
   swaps   575
Tracking errors   108
Transfer of risk   20
Transition matrix   557
Transition rates   556
Treasury bills   180
Treasury bond futures   197–204
Treasury bonds   198
   pricing of   200
Treasury rates   157
Treasury zero rates   161
TRSs   574
   features of   574

U
Ultabadla   88
Unsystematic risk   6, 99, 114
Up-and-in option   499, 515
Up-and-out option   515

V
Value at risk   404, 408, 409, 662
   calculating   409
   confidence level   408
   limitations   416
Valuing options   319
VaR   405, 408
   definition and meaning   405
   normal distribution   405
   portfolio effect   408
Variance–covariance   410
Vega   366, 385, 393
Volatility index   399
Volatility smiles   362
Volatility trades   660
Volatility   21, 56, 357, 358, 393, 410, 661
   estimation   410
   historical   358
   measuring   358

W
Warehousing   219, 229
Warrants   594, 595

call option   595
dilution effect   594
payoff   595
value of   595
Weather derivatives   11, 618, 620, 621
   features   623
   pricing   620
   rainfall   621
   temperature   619, 620
World Bank–IBM currency swap   228

Y
Yield curve by bootstrapping   164
Yield curve   160
Yield curve, also term structure of interest rates   160
Yield on T-bills   185
Yield-to-maturity/YTM   244

Z
Zero cost collar   434, 444, 526
Zero rates   162